FAIRHURST, MORANO-FOADI AND NELLER'S LAW OF THE EUROPEAN UNION

Pearson

At Pearson, we have a simple mission: to help people make more of their lives through learning.

We combine innovative learning technology with trusted content and educational expertise to provide engaging and effective learning experiences that serve people wherever and whenever they are learning.

From classroom to boardroom, our curriculum materials, digital learning tools and testing programmes help to educate millions of people worldwide – more than any other private enterprise.

Every day our work helps learning flourish, and wherever learning flourishes, so do people.

To learn more, please visit us at **www.pearson.com/uk**

FOUNDATIONS SERIES

FAIRHURST, MORANO-FOADI AND NELLER'S LAW OF THE EUROPEAN UNION

Sonia Morano-Foadi
Jen Neller

Thirteenth Edition

Harlow, England • London • New York • Boston • San Francisco • Toronto • Sydney • Dubai • Singapore • Hong Kong
Tokyo • Seoul • Taipei • New Delhi • Cape Town • São Paulo • Mexico City • Madrid • Amsterdam • Munich • Paris • Milan

PEARSON EDUCATION LIMITED
KAO Two
KAO Park
Harlow CM17 9SR
United Kingdom
Tel: +44 (0)1279 623623
Web: www.pearson.com/uk

First published 1996 (print)
Second edition published under The Financial Times/Pitman Publishing imprint 1999 (print)
Further editions published 2002, 2003, 2006, 2007, 2010 (print)
Further editions published 2012, 2014, 2016, 2018 (print and electronic)
Thirteenth edition published 2020 (print and electronic)

© Pearson Professional Limited 1996 (print)
© Pearson Education Limited 1999, 2002, 2003, 2006, 2007, 2010 (print)
© Pearson Education Limited 2012, 2014, 2016, 2018, 2020 (print and electronic)

The rights of Sonia Morano-Foadi and Jen Neller to be identified as authors of this work have been asserted by them in accordance with the Copyright, Designs and Patents Act 1988.

The print publication is protected by copyright. Prior to any prohibited reproduction, storage in a retrieval system, distribution or transmission in any form or by any means, electronic, mechanical, recording or otherwise, permission should be obtained from the publisher or, where applicable, a licence permitting restricted copying in the United Kingdom should be obtained from the Copyright Licensing Agency Ltd, Barnard's Inn, 86 Fetter Lane, London EC4A 1EN.

The ePublication is protected by copyright and must not be copied, reproduced, transferred, distributed, leased, licensed or publicly performed or used in any way except as specifically permitted in writing by the publishers, as allowed under the terms and conditions under which it was purchased, or as strictly permitted by applicable copyright law. Any unauthorised distribution or use of this text may be a direct infringement of the authors' and the publisher's rights and those responsible may be liable in law accordingly.

All trademarks used herein are the property of their respective owners. The use of any trademark in this text does not vest in the author or publisher any trademark ownership rights in such trademarks, nor does the use of such trademarks imply any affiliation with or endorsement of this book by such owners.

Contains public sector information licensed under the Open Government Licence (OGL) v3.0.
http://www.nationalarchives.gov.uk/doc/open-government-licence/version/3/

Contains Parliamentary information licensed under the Open Parliament Licence (OPL) v3.0.
http://www.parliament.uk/site-information/copyright/open-parliament-licence/

Pearson Education is not responsible for the content of third-party internet sites.

ISBN: 978-1-292-29885-6 (print)
978-1-292-29883-2 (PDF)
978-1-292-29884-9 (ePub)

British Library Cataloguing-in-Publication Data
A catalogue record for the print edition is available from the British Library

Library of Congress Cataloging-in-Publication Data
Names: Morano-Foadi, Sonia, author. | Neller, Jen, author.
Title: Fairhurst, Morano-Foadi, and Neller's Law of the European Union / Sonia Morano Foadi, Jen Neller.
Other titles: Law of the European Union
Description: Thirteenth edition. | Harlow, England ; New York : Pearson, 2020.
Identifiers: LCCN 2019058664 | ISBN 9781292298856 (paperback) | ISBN 9781292298832 (ebk) | ISBN 9781292298849 (epub)
Subjects: LCSH: Law--European Union countries.
Classification: LCC KJE947 .F342 2020 | DDC 341.242/2—dc23
LC record available at https://lccn.loc.gov/2019058664

10 9 8 7 6 5 4 3 2 1
24 23 22 21 20

Cover: Novikov Aleksey/Shutterstock
Cover designed by Michelle Morgan At The POP Ltd.

Print edition typeset in 9.5 pt/12 pt ITC Galliard Pro by SPi Global
Printed in Slovakia by Neografia

NOTE THAT ANY PAGE CROSS REFERENCES REFER TO THE PRINT EDITION

Brief contents

Preface for educators	xiii
Preface for students	xv
Acknowledgements	xviii
Table of cases before the Court of Justice of the European Union (numerical)	xx
Table of cases before the Court of Justice of the European Union (alphabetical)	xxxiv
Table of cases before the European Court of Human Rights	xlviii
Table of cases before national courts	xlix
Table of European Union Decisions	l
Table of European Union Treaties	li
Table of other Treaties, etc.	lvi
Table of European Union Regulations	lvii
Table of European Union Directives	lviii
Rules of Procedure of the Institutions of the European Union	lxi
Table of Statutes	lxii
Table of Statutory Instruments	lxiii
List of abbreviations	lxiv
Equivalences	lxvi

Part 1 Constitutional and administrative law of the European Union — 2

1	An introduction to the European Union	4
2	Institutions of the European Union	52
3	Sources of European Union law (including general principles of law and fundamental rights)	106
4	Competence and supremacy of the Union	156
5	Judicial methodology and preliminary rulings of the Court of Justice	182
6	Review of the legality of Union acts	206
7	Infringement proceedings against Member States	244
8	Direct effect, indirect effect and state liability	272

Part 2 Substantive areas of EU law — 318

9	European Union citizenship and free movement rights	320
10	Free movement of workers	380
11	Freedom of establishment and the free movement of services	432
12	Free movement of goods	508

Glossary	590
Further reading	606
Index	622

Contents

Preface for educators	xiii
Preface for students	xv
Acknowledgements	xviii
Table of cases before the Court of Justice of the European Union (numerical)	xx
Table of cases before the Court of Justice of the European Union (alphabetical)	xxxiv
Table of cases before the European Court of Human Rights	xlviii
Table of cases before national courts	xlix
Table of European Union Decisions	l
Table of European Union Treaties	li
Table of other Treaties, etc.	lvi
Table of European Union Regulations	lvii
Table of European Union Directives	lviii
Rules of Procedure of the Institutions of the European Union	lxi
Table of Statutes	lxii
Table of Statutory Instruments	lxiii
List of abbreviations	lxiv
Equivalences	lxvi

Part 1 Constitutional and administrative law of the European Union — 2

1 An introduction to the European Union — 4

Learning objectives		5
1.1	The European Union today	6
	1.1.1 Values and objectives	6
	1.1.2 Institutions	8
	1.1.3 Union membership	10
	1.1.4 EU law	13
	1.1.5 Economic aspects of the Union	15
	1.1.6 The EU in the world	17
1.2	History of the European Communities and the EU	18
	1.2.1 Lessons from the World Wars	18
	1.2.2 The European Coal and Steel Community – 23 July 1952	19
	1.2.3 The European Economic Community and Euratom – 1 July 1958	21
	1.2.4 Enlargement – 1973–86	22
	1.2.5 The Single European Act – 1 July 1987	23
	1.2.6 The Treaty on European Union – 1 November 1993	25
	1.2.7 Enlargement – 1 January 1995	29
	1.2.8 The Treaty of Amsterdam – 1 May 1999	29
	1.2.9 The Treaty of Nice – 1 February 2003	31
	1.2.10 Enlargement – 2004–07	33

	1.2.11 The Treaty of Lisbon – 1 December 2009	34
	1.2.12 The Treaty on Stability, Coordination and Governance – 1 January 2013	34
	1.2.13 Enlargement – 1 July 2013	34
1.3	The Treaty of Lisbon	34
	1.3.1 The failed Constitutional Treaty	35
	1.3.2 Ratification of the ToL	35
	1.3.3 Changes introduced by the ToL	37
1.4	Future of the European Union	44
	1.4.1 Future enlargements	44
	1.4.2 Future contractions	45
	1.4.3 Future directions for the Union	47
Chapter summary		49

2 Institutions of the European Union — 52

Learning objectives		53
2.1	Introduction to the institutions	54
2.2	The European Council	56
	2.2.1 The function of the European Council	56
	2.2.2 Composition of the European Council	57
	2.2.3 Working procedures of the European Council	58
2.3	The Commission	58
	2.3.1 The functions of the Commission	59
	2.3.2 Composition of the Commission	61
	2.3.3 Working procedures of the Commission	67
2.4	The Council	69
	2.4.1 The functions of the Council	69
	2.4.2 Composition of the Council	70
	2.4.3 Working procedures of the Council	72
2.5	The High Representative of the Union for Foreign Affairs and Security Policy	75
	2.5.1 The Role of the High Representative	75
	2.5.2 The appointment of the High Representative	76
2.6	The European Parliament	76
	2.6.1 The functions of the European Parliament	76
	2.6.2 Composition of the Parliament	78
	2.6.3 Working procedures and conduct of the Parliament	82
2.7	Court of Justice of the European Union	86
	2.7.1 The Court of Justice	87
	2.7.2 The General Court	93
	2.7.3 Specialised courts	94
2.8	Other institutions	95
	2.8.1 Court of Auditors	95
	2.8.2 The European Central Bank	95
	2.8.3 The European Investment Bank	96
	2.8.4 The European Economic and Social Committee (EESC)	96
	2.8.5 The Committee of the Regions	97
	2.8.6 Agencies	98
2.9	Democratic accountability and transparency	98
	2.9.1 Democratic accountability	99
	2.9.2 Transparency	99
Chapter summary		103

3 Sources of European Union law (including general principles of law and fundamental rights) — 106

Learning objectives — 107
3.1 Introduction to the sources of EU law — 108
3.2 The EU Treaties — 109
    3.2.1 Origins of the Treaties — 109
    3.2.2 Role of the Treaties — 110
    3.2.3 Scope of the Treaties — 111
    3.2.4 Negotiating and amending the Treaties — 113
3.3 General principles (including fundamental rights) — 116
    3.3.1 Administrative procedural principles — 116
    3.3.2 Fundamental rights — 120
3.4 Secondary legislation – regulations, directives and decisions — 137
    3.4.1 Regulations — 138
    3.4.2 Directives — 138
    3.4.3 Decisions — 139
    3.4.4 Procedures for adopting legislative acts — 139
    3.4.5 Legal validity and grounds for annulment of legal acts — 146
3.5 Decisions of the Court of Justice of the European Union — 147
3.6 Soft law — 147
    3.6.1 Recommendations and opinions — 148
3.7 International sources of law — 148
    3.7.1 International treaties negotiated by the Union — 148
    3.7.2 International treaties negotiated by EU Member States — 151
Chapter summary — 153

4 Competence and supremacy of the Union — 156

Learning objectives — 157
4.1 Introduction — 158
4.2 Competence of the Union — 159
    4.2.1 The conferral of competence — 159
    4.2.2 Types of competence — 160
    4.2.3 Competence to adopt secondary legislation — 164
    4.2.4 The principles of subsidiarity and proportionality — 167
4.3 The supremacy of EU law — 169
    4.3.1 Recognition of the supremacy of EU law — 169
    4.3.2 Challenges to the supremacy of EU law — 170
4.4 The incorporation and extrication of Union powers in the UK — 176
    4.4.1 The European Communities Act 1972 — 176
    4.4.2 Division of competences in Brexit negotiations — 178
Chapter summary — 180

5 Judicial methodology and preliminary rulings of the Court of Justice — 182

Learning objectives — 183
5.1 Introduction — 184
5.2 Judicial methods of interpretation — 184
    5.2.1 Precedent — 185
    5.2.2 Literal interpretation — 186

	5.2.3	Historical interpretation	186
	5.2.4	Contextual interpretation	187
	5.2.5	Teleological interpretation	187
5.3	Preliminary Rulings under Article 267		189
	5.3.1	The jurisdiction of the Court of Justice to interpret Union law	189
	5.3.2	Discretion or obligation to refer	191
	5.3.3	Questions on the interpretation or validity of Union law	194
	5.3.4	Questions that are necessary to enable a national court to give a judgment	196
	5.3.5	Courts against whose decisions there is no judicial remedy under national law	201
5.4	Special forms of procedure		203
	5.4.1	Simplified procedure	203
	5.4.2	Accelerated (or expedited) procedure	204
	5.4.3	Urgent preliminary ruling procedure	204
Chapter summary			205

6 Review of the legality of Union acts — 206

Learning objectives — 207
- 6.1 Introduction — 208
- 6.2 Review of legality of Union acts under Article 263 TFEU — 209
  - 6.2.1 Grounds for judicial review — 210
  - 6.2.2 Reviewable acts — 214
  - 6.2.3 *Locus standi* (legal standing) — 217
  - 6.2.4 Time limits for applications — 232
  - 6.2.5 Consequences of annulment — 234
- 6.3 Other procedures — 234
  - 6.3.1 Challenging a failure to act under Article 265 TFEU — 234
  - 6.3.2 Indirect challenges to a Union act — 236
- 6.4 Damages for unlawful Union acts under Article 340 TFEU — 238
  - 6.4.1 Scope of liability — 239
  - 6.4.2 Liability for a lawful act — 241
  - 6.4.3 Remedies — 242

Chapter summary — 243

7 Infringement proceedings against Member States — 244

Learning objectives — 245
- 7.1 Introduction — 246
  - 7.1.1 The obligation on Member States — 246
  - 7.1.2 Actions by the Commission under Article 258 TFEU — 247
  - 7.1.3 Actions by another Member State under Article 259 TFEU — 248
- 7.2 The stages of Article 258 TFEU proceedings — 249
  - 7.2.1 The administrative stage — 250
  - 7.2.2 The reasoned opinion — 251
  - 7.2.3 The judicial stage — 252
- 7.3 Pecuniary penalties — 254
  - 7.3.1 Calculation of payments — 255
  - 7.3.2 Collection of payments — 260
  - 7.3.3 Article 260(3) TFEU — 263

	7.4 Interim measures	263
	7.4.1 Interim measures ordered by the Court of Justice	264
	7.4.2 Interim measures ordered by a national Court	266
	7.5 Measures under Article 7 TEU	266
	7.5.1 Rule of law in Poland	268
	7.5.2 Rule of law in Hungary	269
	Chapter summary	270

8 Direct effect, indirect effect and state liability — 272

	Learning objectives	273
	8.1 Introduction	274
	8.2 Direct effect	275
	8.2.1 The principle of direct effect	275
	8.2.2 The scope of direct effect	276
	8.2.3 Direct effect of directives	281
	8.3 Indirect effect	293
	8.3.1 The principle of indirect effect	293
	8.3.2 Limitations to the principle of indirect effect	297
	8.4 State liability	299
	8.4.1 State liability arising from unimplemented directives	299
	8.4.2 State liability arising from incorrect implementation	300
	8.4.3 Unimplemented directives revisited	303
	8.4.4 State liability arising from acts of the executive and the judiciary	304
	8.5 The enforcement of EU law in the UK courts	309
	8.5.1 Direct effect of EU law in the UK	309
	8.5.2 Indirect effect of EU law in the UK	314
	Chapter summary	317

Part 2 Substantive areas of EU law — 318

9 European Union citizenship and free movement rights — 320

	Learning objectives	321
	9.1 Introduction to the free movement of persons	322
	9.1.1 Free movement of persons and non-discrimination	322
	9.1.2 EU citizenship	324
	9.1.3 Directive 2004/38	325
	9.2 Free movement and EU citizenship	325
	9.2.1 Scope	325
	9.2.2 Rights of entry and residence	336
	9.3 Free movement rights of family members of EU citizens	342
	9.3.1 Scope	342
	9.3.2 Rights of entry and residence	349
	9.3.3 Rights of family members in the event of death, departure or divorce	351
	9.3.4 Rights to equal treatment	357
	9.4 Expulsion and restrictions on free movement rights	358
	9.4.1 General protection from expulsion	358
	9.4.2 Expulsion on grounds of public policy, public security or public health	358

	9.5 Social benefits	363
	9.5.1 Equal treatment regardless of nationality	363
	9.5.2 Rights of economically inactive EU citizens to social benefits	365
	9.5.3 Rights of EU students to social benefits	368
	9.6 The Schengen *acquis* and its integration into the European Union	372
	9.6.1 Development of the Schengen area	372
	9.6.2 Participation in the Schengen *acquis*	373
	9.6.3 Measures adopted by Schengen group members	375
	9.6.4 The Schengen Information System (SIS)	376
	9.6.5 Temporary reintroduction of border controls	376
	9.7 Free movement rights after Brexit	377
	Chapter summary	378
10	**Free movement of workers**	**380**
	Learning objectives	381
	10.1 Introduction to the free movement of workers	382
	10.1.1 Primary legislation	382
	10.1.2 Secondary legislation	384
	10.2 Scope of the term 'worker'	385
	10.2.1 Definition of a Union worker	385
	10.2.2 Retention of worker status after cessation of employment	390
	10.3 Rights of workers	393
	10.3.1 Rights to free movement	393
	10.3.2 Equal treatment in employment	397
	10.3.3 Equal access to social advantages	404
	10.3.4 Social security coordination	407
	10.4 Work-seekers	409
	10.4.1 Rights to free movement	410
	10.4.2 Rights to social benefits	412
	10.5 Family members of workers	418
	10.5.1 Definition of a family member	418
	10.5.2 Rights to free movement of family members	419
	10.5.3 Rights to social benefits for family members	422
	Chapter summary	430
11	**Freedom of establishment and the free movement of services**	**432**
	Learning objectives	433
	11.1 Introduction	434
	11.1.1 Primary legislation	435
	11.1.2 Secondary legislation	436
	11.2 Scope of establishment and services	438
	11.2.1 Establishment	438
	11.2.2 Services	439
	11.2.3 The 'official authority' exception	443
	11.3 Rights of service providers and their employees	444
	11.3.1 Rights to establishment and to provide services	444
	11.3.2 Rights of entry and residence	450
	11.3.3 Rights of posted workers	453
	11.3.4 Permissible restrictions on the rights of providers	458

	11.4	Recipients of services	476
		11.4.1 Rights of recipients under the Treaties	476
		11.4.2 Rights of recipients to residence	477
		11.4.3 Rights of recipients under Directive 2006/123	478
		11.4.4 Rights of recipients to social advantages	479
		11.4.5 Permissible restrictions on the rights of recipients	481
	11.5	Recognition of professional qualifications	486
		11.5.1 Treaty provisions	486
		11.5.2 Directive 2005/36: the recognition of professional qualifications	492
		11.5.3 Non-EU qualifications	499
		11.5.4 The internal situation	503
	Chapter summary		505

12 Free movement of goods   508

Learning objectives   509

12.1 Introduction to the free movement of goods   510
    12.1.1 Primary legislation   511

12.2 Customs duties and charges having equivalent effect (Arts 28–30 TFEU)   513
    12.2.1 The customs union   513
    12.2.2 Scope of the term 'goods'   514
    12.2.3 Duties and charges having equivalent effect (CEEs)   516
    12.2.4 Charges for the provision of a service   519
    12.2.5 Customs duty or internal taxation?   523

12.3 Internal taxation (Art 110 TFEU)   524
    12.3.1 Similar products (Art 110(1) TFEU)   526
    12.3.2 Indirect protection (Art 110(2) TFEU)   530

12.4 Quantitative restrictions and measures having equivalent effect (Arts 34 and 35 TFEU)   535
    12.4.1 Quantitative restrictions   535
    12.4.2 Measures having equivalent effect to quantitative restrictions (MEEs)   539
    12.4.3 Distinctly applicable MEEs   541
    12.4.4 Indistinctly applicable MEEs: dual-burden rules   545
    12.4.5 Indistinctly applicable MEEs: equal-burden rules   554
    12.4.6 Quantitative restrictions and MEEs on exports (Art 35 TFEU)   560

12.5 Permissible quantitative restrictions and MEEs   561
    12.5.1 Justifications under Article 36 TFEU   561
    12.5.2 The Cassis rule of reason defences for indistinctly applicable measures   572
    12.5.3 Derogations from harmonising legislation (Art 114 TFEU)   583

12.6 Free movement of goods after Brexit   584
    12.6.1 Models of EU trade arrangements with non-EU countries   585
    12.6.2 Northern Ireland and the Good Friday Agreement   586

Chapter summary   587

Glossary   590
Further reading   606
Index   622

Preface for educators

Dear educator,

We are excited to present the thirteenth edition of *Law of the European Union*. This is the second time we have updated this popular textbook, which was originally authored by Professor John Fairhurst, and we have continued to pursue an accessible but thorough approach throughout. We have worked to build on and improve the innovative features that we introduced in the last edition, including the addition of new **reflection boxes** to provide further consideration of interesting or difficult issues. Other features that facilitate accessibility and easy navigation of the material include: a brief **glossary** at the beginning of each chapter; **learning objectives** that correspond with chapter headings; the division of **case boxes** into 'facts', 'ruling' and 'significance'; **diagrams** to illustrate procedures or conditionality; and **chapter summaries**.

This edition is now also available as an ebook, which includes deep links to legal materials and self-assessment questions.

The book is divided into two main parts. Part 1 (chapters 1–8) covers the constitutional and administrative law of the European Union. Part 2 then delves into the substantive law of the European Union, with chapters 9–12 examining EU citizenship and the free movement of workers, services and goods.

For Chapter 1, we begin with an overview of the European Union as it currently exists, before then setting out the story of its creation and development. The rationale here is that students will be better able to understand the significance of the history of the Union if they first understand what it is a history of. Brexit is considered both in the opening 'current' section, where information on membership of the Union includes the procedures set out in the Treaties for both accession and withdrawal, and in the final section of the chapter, which considers the future of the Union. All information on Brexit is correct as of 1 February 2020.

Chapter 2 then sets out the institutions of the EU, with information provided on their functions, composition and working procedures in turn, and with new material added on comitology and EU agencies. This provides students with a firm understanding of the actors that variously produce and are bound by the sources of EU law, which are examined in Chapter 3. This chapter includes information on the legislative procedures for enacting sources of EU law and fundamental rights. The last section of Chapter 3, which covers agreements made between the Union external entities, also includes brief mentions of Brexit in relation to withdrawal agreements and association agreements.

Chapter 4 then moves deeper into questions regarding the nature of EU law with an examination of the competences and supremacy of the Union. This chapter includes questions relating to the division of competences in the Brexit negotiations.

Chapters 5, 6 and 7 are focused on the functions of the Court of Justice of the European Union. These are preliminary rulings, judicial review of the validity of EU law and infringement proceedings against Member States, respectively. Chapter 5 also includes a section on the judicial methodology of the Court of Justice. New material has been added to Chapter 6 to further clarify the scope of a regulatory act under Article 263 TFEU. A new section has been added to Chapter 7 providing information and analysis on Article 7 TEU (concerning enforcement of respect for Union values), which was first invoked against Poland in 2017 and Hungary in 2018.

Chapter 8 concludes Part 1 of the book with analysis of the principles of direct effect, indirect effect and state liability. While the history of the direct effect of EU law in the UK has been retained, brief comments are now also included on the future effect of EU law in the UK.

Part 2 on substantive areas of EU law begins with Chapter 9 on EU citizenship. This chapter now includes discussion of the controversial *Tjebbes* ruling of March 2019 on the withdrawal of EU citizenship. A new section has been added outlining freedom of movement after Brexit. Chapter 10 then examines the free movement of workers and includes a section on post-Brexit possibilities in this area. Chapter 11 on the free movement of services and the right to establishment includes analysis of new updates to the Posted Workers Directive. In Chapter 12 on the free movement of goods, we now take a less cautious approach to the Court of Justice's abandonment of the *Keck* formula in favour of the market access test. Again, a new section has been added to the end of the chapter to discuss the free movement of goods after Brexit.

For the most part, we have endeavoured to state the law as at 1 January 2020. However, information on Brexit has been updated so that it is correct as of 1 February 2020. This means that the UK is not counted as a current Member State of the European Union and it is assumed that the transition period will cease on 31 December 2020. Updates to the book are available online at go.pearson.com/uk/legalupdates.

We sincerely hope that this book will assist you in the delivery of your EU law module and that it will prove helpful to your students. We would be delighted to hear any feedback that could assist us with future editions.

Warmest regards,
Sonia Morano-Foadi and Jen Neller

Preface for students

Dear student,

Welcome to the thirteenth edition of *Law of the European Union*. We are delighted that this book has found its way into your hands. Before you get stuck in, we would like to take a moment to explain a few things about EU law and about this book that we think you might find helpful.

Brexit

At the time of writing, the UK is not a member of the European Union. This edition has been written **after** 'exit day' (31 January 2020), but **before** the transition period is due to end (31 December 2020). This means that the UK is not counted as a Member State of the European Union throughout this print edition, but that the future relationship between the UK and the EU has not yet been established. Therefore, while this book includes as much information on Brexit as possible, it is inevitable that further developments will have occurred between finalising this text and the time that you are reading it. Sections on Brexit have been written with this in mind and updates to the book are available at go.pearson.com/uk/legalupdates.

It is worth noting that 'Brexit' is a vague term. The phrase 'after Brexit' has been used variously in the media to refer to after the 2016 referendum, after the triggering of Article 50 TEU in March 2017, after 'exit day' on 31 January 2020 or after the end of the Brexit transition period on 31 December 2020. What is meant by 'after Brexit' therefore depends on the context and whether it is the political, institutional or legal situation that is being referred to.

Why study EU law?

If the UK is leaving the EU, then why should UK students continue to study EU law? While each law school or department is likely to have different ideas about this, we suggest three broad reasons.

1. EU law has had a **profound effect on UK** law that will not be erased by Brexit. The UK was a member of the EU for 47 years. Throughout the whole of that time, the UK Parliament enacted reams of legislation in order to transpose particular requirements of EU law into domestic legislation. Furthermore, UK policies, court judgments and practices across a wide range of policy areas have been required to conform to EU law. EU law is thus deeply embedded within UK law and practice and forms a core chapter within UK legal history, the impact of which will be relevant for decades to come.

2. With respect to the Brexit process and the future of UK law, an understanding of EU law has rarely ever been **in such high demand.** While it is initially expected that, for the most part, all EU law that has an effect in the UK will be automatically transposed into UK legislation, there will be some degree of opportunity, sooner or later, for such legislation to be reassessed. In areas of law that have been heavily affected by EU legislation, such as workers' rights and product standards, there is the potential for significant changes to be up for negotiation. UK lawyers who understand the impact of the EU legacy will be best

placed to help reshape UK law. Additionally, regardless of whether Brexit is 'hard' or 'soft', any kind of future engagement with the European Single Market will require knowledge of this entity and its rules.

3   From a constitutional perspective, the European Union is a **unique legal entity.** There is no other international system that compares to it. Although other regional organisations have sought to emulate its successes, they have yet to establish the means of producing effective and enforceable controls and genuine integration to the extent that the EU has achieved. The study of EU law is thus the study of regional politics, international diplomacy and the constant negotiation of interests at all levels. The EU may therefore be deemed to be of considerable intellectual interest regardless of the UK's relationship with it.

A couple of things you should know about EU law
As it is a unique legal entity, there are a couple of things that it would be helpful to note before your module begins. Attention to these details early on could give you a head start and help you to avoid common mistakes and confusion further down the line.

First, it is important to note the difference between the **Court of Justice of the European Union** (CJEU or sometimes ECJ) and the **European Court of Human Rights** (ECtHR). The former is an institution of the European Union, which sits in Luxembourg and rules on cases pertaining to EU law. The latter is an institution of the Council of Europe, which sits in Strasbourg and rules on cases pertaining to the European Convention on Human Rights (ECHR). The two courts are often confused with each other, especially when vague references are made in the media to 'the European Court', but it is important to understand that the Council of Europe is an entirely separate organisation to the European Union.

Secondly, it will be helpful to be aware that **the Treaties** of the European Union have been renamed and renumbered several times throughout the history of the EU. Since 2009, the primary Treaties have been called the **Treaty on European Union** (TEU) and the **Treaty on the Functioning of the European Union** (TFEU). It is from these two Treaties that all the powers of the EU institutions are derived. Prior to 2009, the TFEU was known as the Treaty on the European Communities (EC Treaty) and before that it was the Treaty on the European Economic Communities (EEC Treaty). The TEU has never been renamed, but both treaties have been renumbered. This means that the articles within them have moved around. For example, the article on the free movement of workers is currently Article 45 TFEU, but it was previously Article 39 EC Treaty, and before that it was Article 48 EEC Treaty. Don't panic – you will not need to remember all of these outdated article numbers! However, if you are reading older cases, books or journal articles, you should be aware that the Treaty articles that they refer to may now have a different number. The link provided on page lxvi directs you to a table where you can see equivalent pre- and post-2009 article numbers.

About this book
This book is divided into two main sections: Part 1 on the constitutional and administrative law of the EU (Chapters 1–8) and Part 2 on substantive EU law (Chapters 9–12). There are a number of useful features included within each chapter that we would like to draw to your attention.

Each chapter begins with a list of **objectives,** which are designed to help you to navigate the chapter and to keep track of your progress. The objectives are followed by **key terms and concepts**, which provide you with a head start on understanding some of the specific terminology of the topic and which can be referred back to as required. Then, at the end of each chapter, we have provided a brief **summary**, enabling you to rapidly revise the main points of the chapter and to identify any gaps in your knowledge. At the end of the book you can find a list of references and **further reading**, which sets out books and journal articles that you may find helpful for expanding your understanding of the complexities, controversies and uncertainties of the topic.

Within the main body of the chapters you will find **legislative excerpts**, which provide the exact wording of relevant legislation, **case boxes**, which set out the facts, ruling and significance of important cases, and **reflection boxes**, which draw attention to key issues. Where cases or issues are also mentioned elsewhere in the book, **cross-references** are provided in the margins. These features are designed to help you to navigate the law with relative ease and to help you to draw connections between the different topics. A variety of **diagrams** have also been provided throughout the book to complement the main text and reinforce your understanding of the topic. However, it should be noted that your greatest asset, as with all modules, will be the notes that you take. The features in this book are designed to support, but never to replace, your own notes and revision materials.

We sincerely hope that this book will help you to ace your EU law module and we would be delighted to hear any feedback that could assist us with future editions.

Best of luck and warmest regards,
Sonia Morano-Foadi and Jen Neller

Acknowledgements

The authors would like to thank Victoria Tubb of Pearson Education for providing us with the opportunity to work on this book and for supporting us throughout the process. We would also like to thank Akanksha Marwah, Vinay Agnihotri and Jennifer Mair for their work in bringing this book to completion. It has been a pleasure to work with you all.

Special thanks are due to Dr Alina Tryfonidou, Dr Oxana Golynker and Professor Stephen Wetherill for their valuable comments on previous draft chapters of this book.

Sonia Morano-Foadi would like to thank her husband James, her daughters Sophie and Nadine, her parents, zia Nella e zio Vincenzo, and her brother for their constant love and support. Sonia dedicates the book to all of them.

Jen Neller would like to thank Professor Leslie J Moran for his patience and encouragement during the interlude in her PhD studies that this book represents. Her work is dedicated to David Neller for always believing in her.

Publisher's acknowledgements

13 European Union: Article 50 Treaty on European Union © European Union: Withdrawal of a Member State from the EU, 2016 © European Union; **41 European Union:** Article 12 Treaty on European Union © European Union; **170 European Court of Justice:** *Costa* v *ENEL* (Case 64/4); **185 Weekly Law Reports:** English Court of Appeal, in *Bulmer* v *Bollinger* [1974] 3 WLR 202; **192 European Court of Justice:** *Broekmeulen* v *Huisarts Registratie Commissie* (Case 246/80); **209 European Union:** Article 263 Treaty on the Functioning of the European Union © European Union; **240 European Court of Justice:** *Bergaderm and Goupil* v *Commission* (Case C-352/98P); **254 European Union:** Article 260 Treaty on the Functioning of the European Union © European Union; **257 European Court of Justice:** *Commission* v *Greece* (Case C-387/97); **309–310 European Court of Justice:** *Macarthys Ltd* v *Smith* [1979] ICR 785 and [1981] QB 180; **313 European Court of Justice:** *Schiemann LJ National Union of Teachers and Others* v *The Governing Body of St Mary's Church of England (Aided) Junior School and Others* [1997] IRLR 242; **314 European Court of Justice:** Lord Templeman in *Foster* v *British Gas Plc* (No 2) [1991] 2 AC 306; **314 European Court of Justice:** *Duke* v *Reliance Systems Ltd* [1988] AC 618; **315 House of Commons:** *Litster* v *Forth Dry Dock* [1989] 2 WLR 634 © Parliamentary Copyright; **324 European Union:** Article 20(1) Treaty on the Functioning of the European Union © European Union; **327–328 European Court of Justice:** *Rottmann* v *Bayern* (Case C-135/08); **334–335 European Court of Justice:** *Toufik Lounes* v *Secretary of State for the Home Department* (Case C-165/16); **354 European Court of Justice:** *Diatta* v *Land Berlin* (Case 267/83); **387 European Court of Justice:** *Levin* v *Staatssecretaris van Justitie* (Case 53/81); **410 European Court of Justice:** *R* v *Immigration Appeal Tribunal, ex parte Antonissen* (Case C-292/89); **414 European Court of Justice:** *Brian Francis Collins* v *Secretary of State for Work and Pensions* (Case C-138/02); **420 European Court of Justice:** *Kaba* v *Secretary of State for the Home Department* (Case C-356/98); **424 European**

Court of Justice: *Baumbast and R* v *Secretary of State for the Home Department* (Case C-413/99); **445–446, 458–459 European Court of Justice:** *Van Binsbergen* v *Bestuur van de Bedrijfsvereninging voor de Metaalnijverheid* (Case 33/74); **468 European Court of Justice:** *Qestore di Verona* v *Zenatti* (Case C-67/98); **475–476 European Court of Justice:** *Harmsen* v *Burgemeester van Amsterdam* (Case C-341/14); **477 European Court of Justice:** *Luisi and Carbone* v *Ministero del Tesoro* (Joined Cases 286/82 and 26/83); **489 European Court of Justice:** *UNECTEF* v *Heylens* (Case 222/86); **490–491 European Court of Justice:** *Vlassopoulou* v*Ministerium für Justiz*, Bundes- *und Europaangelegenheiten Baden-Württemberg* (Case C-340/89); **501–502 European Court of Justice:** *Hocsman* v *Ministre de l'Emploi et de la Solidarité* (Case C-238/98); **517 European Court of Justice:** *Commission* v *Italy* (Case 24/68); **529 European Court of Justice:** *Commission* v *Greece* (Case C-132/88); **549 European Court of Justice:** *Commission* v *France* (Case 21/84); **555 European Court of Justice:** Keck and Mithouard (Joined Cases C-267 and 268/91); **568 European Court of Justice:** *Commission* v *Germany* (Case 178/84); **571 European Court of Justice:** *Centrafarm* v *Winthrop BV* (Case 15/74); **576–577 European Court of Justice:** Judgment of the Court of 16 December 1980 – Criminal proceedings against Anton Adriaan Fietje (Case 27/80); **579 European Court of Justice:** *Commission* v *Austria* (Case C-320/03); **583 European Union:** Article 114 Treaty on the Functioning of the European Union © European Union.

Table of cases before the Court of Justice of the European Union (numerical)

6/54 *Netherlands* v *High Authority* [1954–56] ECR 103 212

6/56, 7/56, 3/57 to 7/57 *Algera and Others* v *Common Assembly* [1957–58] ECR 139 243

7/61 *Commission* v *Italy* [1961] ECR 317, [1962] CMLR 39 252

2/62, 3/62 *Commission* v *Luxembourg and Belgium (Joined Cases)* [1962] ECR 855 187, 516–517

24/62 *Commission* v *Germany (Re Brennwein)* [1963] ECR 63, [1963] CMLR 347 252

25/62 *Plaumann & Co* v *Commission* [1963] ECR 95, [1964] CMLR 29 223–227, 231, 237, 243

26/62 *Van Gend en Loos* v *Nederlandse Administratie der Belastingen* [1963] ECR 1, [1963] CMLR 182 169, 275–279, 292, 294, 512, 593, 597, 605

28/62–30/62 *Da Costa en Schaake NV, Jacob Meijer NV, Hoechst-Holland NV* v *Nederlandse Belastingadministratie* [1963] ECR 31, [1963] CMLR 224 198

12/63 *Schlieker née Diepenbruck)* v *High Authority of the ECSC* [1963] ECR 85, [1963] CMLR 281 87

75/63 *Hoekstra (née Unger)* v *Bestuur der Bedrijfsvereniging voor Detailhandel en Ambachten* [1964] ECR 177, [1964] CMLR 319 385

106/63, 107/63 *Alfred Toepfer and Getreide-Import Gesellschaft* v *Commission* [1965] ECR 405 224–225

6/64 *Flaminio Costa* v *Ente Nazionale per l'Energia Elettrica (ENEL)* [1964] ECR 585, [1964] CMLR 425 14–15, 49, 171, 176, 180, 184, 201

56/64, 58/64 *Consten and Grundig GmbH* v *Commission (joined cases)* [1966] ECR 299, [1966] CMLR 418 569

32/65 *Italy* v *Commission* [1966] ECR 389, [1969] CMLR 39 236

57/65 *Alfons Lütticke (Firma) GmbH* v *Hauptzollamt Sarrelouis* [1966] ECR 205 512, 525, 527

24/67 *Parke, Davis and Co* v *Probel, Reese, Beintema-Interpharm and Centrafarm* [1968] EU:C:1968:11 569

27/67 *Fink-Frucht GmbH* v *Hauptzollamt Munchen-Landsbergerstrasse* [1968] ECR 223, [1968] CMLR 445 535

7/68 *Commission* v *Italy (Re Export Tax on Art Treasures No 1) (Italian Art Case)* [1968] ECR 423, [1969] CMLR 1 514, 515, 518

24/68 *Commission* v *Italy* [1969] ECR 193, [1971] CMLR 611 518, 520

2, 3/69 *Sociaal Fonds voor de Diamantarbeiders* v *SA Ch. Brachfeld & Sons* [1969] ECR 211, [1969] CMLR 335 518

4/69 *Alfons Lütticke GmbH* v *Commission* [1969] ECR 325 239

7/69 *Commission* v *Italy* [1970] ECR 111, [1970] CMLR 97 252–253

14/69 *Markus* v *Hauptzollamt Hamburg-Jonas* [1969] ECR 349 186

29/69 *Stauder* v *City of Ulm* [1969] ECR 419, [1969] CMLR 112 120

31/69 *Commission* v *Italy* [1970] ECR 25 251

77/69 *Commission* v *Belgium* [1969] ECR 237, [1974] 1 CMLR 203 253–254

9/70 *Grad (Franz)* v *Finanzamt Traunstein* [1970] ECR 975 280–283

11/70 *Internationale Handelsgesellschaft GmbH* [1970] ECR 1125, [1972] CMLR 255 117, 121, 171–173, 180

15/70 *Chevally* v *Commission* [1970] ECR 975 236

22/70 *Commission* v *Council* [1970] ECR 263, [1971] CMLR 335 186, 214

41/70–44/70 *International Fruit Company BV* v *Commission* [1975] ECR 1393 221, 225

5/71 *Zückerfabrik Schöppenstedt* v *Council* [1971] ECR 975 239

7/71 *Commission* v *France* [1971] ECR 1003, [1972] CMLR 453 250, 252

43/71 *Politi SAS* v *Italian Ministry of Finance* [1971] EU:C:1971:122 280

51/71–54/71 *International Fruit Company* v *Produktschap voor Grotenten en Fruit (No. 2)* [1971] ECR 1107 541

21/72–24/72 *International Fruit Co NV* v *Produktschap voor Groenren en Fruit (No. 3)* [1972] ECR 1219, [1975] 2 CMLR 1 149

29/72 *Marimex SpA* v *Italian Finance Administration* [1972] ECR 1309, [1973] CMLR 486 523

48/72 *Brasserie de Haecht SA* v *Wilkin (No. 2)* [1973] ECR 77, [1973] CMLR 287 279

76/72 Michel S v Fonds national de reclassement social des handicaps [1973] ECR 457 **405**
77/72 Capolongo v Azienda Agricola [1973] ECR 611, [1974] 1 CMLR 230 **523**
2/73 Geddo (Riseria Luigi) v Ente Nazionale Risi [1973] ECR 865, [1974] 1 CMLR 13 **535–536, 602**
4/73 J Nold KG v Commission [1974] ECR 491, [1974] 2 CMLR 338 **121, 131**
34/73 Fratelli Variola SpA v Amministrazione Italiana delle Finanze [1973] ECR 981 **280**
152/73 Sotgiu v Deutsche Bundespost [1974] ECR 153 **401, 403**
167/73 Commission v France (Re French Merchant Seamen) [1974] ECR 359, [1974] CMLR 216 **251, 254, 323, 397**
175/73 Union Syndicale v Council [1974] ECR 917, [1975] 1 CMLR 131 **130**
2/74 Reyners v Belgian State [1974] ECR 631, [1974] 2 CMLR 305 **278, 439, 443–446, 487**
8/74 Procureur du Roi v Dassonville [1974] ECR 837, [1974] 2 CMLR 436 **540, 541, 542, 546, 548, 559, 560, 587, 599**
9/74 Casagrande v Landeshauptstadt München [1974] ECR 773, [1974] 2 CMLR 423 **423**
12/74 Commission v Germany [1975] ECR 181, [1975] 1 CMLR 340 **543**
15/74, 16/74 Centrafarm BV v Adriaan de Peiper Winthrop BV (Sterling Drug Case) [1974] ECR 1147, [1974] 2 CMLR 480 **570–571**
33/74 Van Binsbergen v Bestuur van de Bedrijfsvereniging voor de Metaalnijverheid [1974] ECR 1299, [1975] 1 CMLR 298 **440, 445–446, 458–459**
36/74 Walrave and Koch v Association Union Cycliste Internationale [1974] ECR 1405, [1975] 1 CMLR 320 **279**
41/74 Van Duyn v Home Office [1974] ECR 1337, [1975] 1 CMLR 1, [1975] Ch 358, [1975] 3 All ER 190 **251, 283–284, 359**
94/74 IGAV v ENCC [1975] ECR 699, [1976] 2 CMLR 37 **523**
166/73 Rheinmühlen-Düsseldorf ('Rheinmühlen I') [1974] ECLI:EU:C:1974:3 **191**
4/75 Rewe-Zentralfinanz v Landwirtschaft-skammer [1975] ECR 843, [1977] 1 All ER 599 **541**
5/75 Deuka [1975] ECR 759 **118**
7/75 Mr and Mrs F v Belgian State [1975] ECR 679, [1975] 2 CMLR **382**
32/75 Fiorinin (née Cristini) v SNCF [1975] ECR 1085, [1976] 1 CMLR 573 **405, 423**
36/75 Rutili v Ministère de l'Intérieur [1975] ECR 1219, [1975] 1 CMLR 573 **130, 400**
43/75 Defrenne v SABENA (No. 2) [1976] ECR 455, [1976] 2 CMLR 98 **279, 281**
45/75 Rewe-Zentrale des Lebensmittel-Grosshandels Gmbh v Hauptzollamt Emmerich [1976] ECR 181 **526**
48/75 Procureur du Roi v Royer [1976] ECR 497, [1976] 2 CMLR 619 **188, 410**

87/75 87~75 Bresciani (Conceria Daniele) v Amministrazione Italiana delle Finanze [1976] ECR 129, [1976] 2 CMLR 62 v Amministrazione Italiana delle Finanze [1976] ECR 129, [1976] 2 CMLR 62 **521**
104/75 Officier van Justitie v De Peijper [1976] ECR 613, [1976] 2 CMLR 271 **566**
105/75 Giuffrida v Council [1976] ECR 1395 **212**
113/75 Frecasseti v Amministrazione delle Finanze dello Stato [1976] ECR 983 **195**
127/75 Bobie Getränkvertrieb v Hauptzollamt Aachen-Nord [1976] ECR 1079 **527**
169/73 Compagnie Continentale v Council [1975] ECLI:EU:1975:13 **118, 599**
1/76 Opinion of the Court of 26 April 1977 [1977] ECR 741 **163**
5/77 Tedeschi v Denkavit Commerciale srl [1977] ECR 1555 **561–562**
13/76 Donà v Mantero [1976] ECR 1333 **279, 393**
46/76 Bauhuis v Netherlands [1977] ECR 5 **521, 522**
53/76 Procureur de la République Besancon v Bouhelier [1977] ECR 197, [1977] 1 CMLR 436 **560**
63/76 Inzirillo v Caisse d'Allocations Familiales de l'Arondissement de Lyon [1976] ECR 2057, [1978] 3 CMLR 596 **422**
64/76 Dumortier Frères v Council [1976] ECR 3091, [1982] ECR 1733 **243**
71/76 Thieffry v Conseil de l'Ordre des Avocats à la Cour de Paris [1977] ECR 765, [1977] 2 CMLR 373 **279, 487–488, 489, 501, 506**
77/76 Fratelli Cucchi v Avez SpA [1977] ECR 987 **523**
78/76 Steinike und Weinlig [1977] ECR 595 **519, 587**
89/76 Commission v Netherlands (plant inspections) [1977] ECR 1355 **521, 522, 587**
107/76 Hoffman La Roche v Centrafarm [1977] ECR 597, [1977] 2 CMLR 334 **191**
7/78 R v Thompson [1978] 1 CMLR 47, [1980] QB 229, [1980] 2 All ER 102 **564**
11/77 Patrick v Ministre des Affaires Culturelles [1977] ECR 1199 **488, 489**
30/77 R v Bouchereau [1977] ECR 1999, [1977] 2 CMLR 800 **359, 484**
61/77R Commission v Ireland [1977] ECR 937, [1977] ECR 1411 **264**
70/77 Simmenthal v Amministrazione delle Finanze dello Stato [1978] 3 CMLR 670 **197**
82/77 Openbaar Ministerie of the Netherlands v Van Tiggele [1978] ECR 25, [1978] 2 CMLR 528 **550**
83/77 HNL v Council and Commission [1978] ECR 1209, [1978] 3 CMLR 566 **239**
87/77, 130/77, 22/83, 9/84, 10/84 Salerno and Others v Commission and Council (Joined Cases) [1985] ECR 2523 **237**
106/77 Amministrazione delle Finanze dello Stato v Simmenthal SpA [1978] ECR 629 **173–174, 180**
148/77 Hansen Jun & O. C. Balle GmbH & Co. v Hauptzollamt Flensburg [1978] ECR 1787, [1979] 1 CMLR 604 **526, 530**

92/78 *Simmenthal* [1979] ECR 777 237
115/78 *Knoors* v *Secretary of State for Economic Affairs* [1979] ECR 399, [1979] 2 CMLR 357 504
120/78 *Rewe-Zentrale AG* v *Bundesmonopolverwaltung für Branntwein (Cassis de Dijon)* [1979] ECR 649, [1979] 3 CMLR 494 545–546, 552, 554, 555, 556, 572–573, 574, 578, 581, 599, 602
128/78 *Commission* v *United Kingdom (Re Tachographs)* [1979] ECR 419, [1979] 2 CMLR 45 254
136/78 *Ministère Public* v *Auer* [1979] ECR 437, [1070] 2 CMLR 373 504
141/78 *France* v *United Kingdom* [1979] ECR 2923, [1980] 1 CMLR 6 248
148/78 *Pubblico Ministero* v *Ratti* [1979] ECR 1629, [1980] 1 CMLR 96 292
153/78 *Commission* v *Germany* [1979] ECR 2555 566
168/78 *Commission* v *France (Re French Taxation of Spirit)* [1980] ECR 347, [1981] 2 CMLR 631 525, 526, 533–534
170/78 *Commission* v *United Kingdom (Re Excise Duties on Wines) (No. 2)* [1983] ECR 2263, [1983] 3 CMLR 512 531–532, 575
171/78 *Commission* v *Denmark* [1980] ECR 447, [1981] 2 CMLR 688 525
207/78 *Ministère Public* v *Even and ONPTS* [1979] ECR 2019, [1980] 2 CMLR 71 405–406
232/78 *Commission* v *France (Re Sheepmeat)* [1979] ECR 2729, [1980] 1 CMLR 418 264
237/78 *Caisse Régionale d'Assurance Maldie de Lille* v *Palermo* [1979] ECR 2645, [1980] 2 CMLR 31 364
15/79 *PB Groenveld BV* v *Produktschap voor Vee en Vlees* [1979] ECR 3409, [1981] 1 CMLR 207 560
33/79 *Kuhner* v *Commission* [1980] ECR 1671 119
34/79 *R* v *Henn and Darby* [1979] ECR 3795, [1980] 1 CMLR 246, [1981] AC 850, [1980] 2 All ER 166 536, 562–563
37/79 *Marty SA* v *Estée Lauder SA* [1980] ECR 2481, [1981] 2 CMLR 143 279
44/79 *Hauer* v *Land Rheinland-Pflaz* [1979] ECR 3727, [1980] 3 CMLR 42 131
55/79 *Commission* v *Ireland* [1980] ECR 481, [1980] 1 CMLR 734 527
129/79 *Macarthys Ltd* v *Smith* [1980] ECR 1275, [1980] 2 CMLR 205, [1979] ICR 785 309–310, 317
138/79 *Roquette Frères* v *Council* [1980] ECR 3333 144–145, 211
140/79 *Chemial Farmaceutici* v *DAF SpA* [1981] ECR 1 529–530, 534
149/79 *Commission* v *Belgium (Re Public Employees)* [1980] ECR 3881, [1981] 2 CMLR 413 401–402, 443
155/79 *Australia Mining & Smelting Ltd* v *Commission* [1982] ECR 1575, [1982] 2 CMLR 264 135
157/79 *R* v *Pieck* [1980] ECR 2171, [1980] 3 CMLR 220, [1981] QB 571, [1981] 3 All ER 46 323

788/79 *Italian State* v *Gilli and Andres* [1980] ECR 2071, [1981] 1 CMLR 146 573
789/79, 790/79 *Calpak SpA and Societa Emiliana Lavorazione Frutta SpA* v *Commission* [1980] ECR 1649 226
27/80 *Fietje* [1980] ECR 3839, [1981] 3 CMLR 722 576–577
36/80 *Irish Creamery Milk Suppliers Association* v *Ireland* [1981] ECR 735, [1981] 2 CMLR 455 197
58/80 *Dansk Supermarket A/S* v *A/S Imerco* [1981] ECR 181 279
66/80 *International Chemical Corporation* [1981] ECR 1191 198–199
113/80 *Commission* v *Ireland (Re Restrictions on Importation of Souvenirs)* [1981] ECR 1625, [1982] 1 CMLR 706 543–544, 562
155/80 *Oebel* [1981] ECR 1993, [1983] 1 CMLR 390 554
193/80 *Commission* v *Italy* [1981] ECR 3019 575
244/80 *Foglia* v *Novello (No. 2)* [1981] ECR 3045, [1982] 1 CMLR 585 197–198
246/80 *Broekmeulen* v *Huisarts Registratie Commissie* [1981] ECR 2311 195
272/80 *Frans-Nederlandse* [1981] ECR 3277, [1982] 2 CMLR 497 566
279/80 *Criminal Proceedings against Webb* [1981] ECR 3305, [1982] 1 CMLR 719 449
8/81 *Becker* v *Finanzamt Münster-Innenstadt* [1982] ECR 53, [1982] 1 CMLR 499 284
14/81 *Alpha Steel* v *Commission* [1982] ECR 749 135
53/81 *Levin* v *Staatssecretaris van Justitie* [1982] ECR 1035, [1982] 2 CMLR 454 385, 387–388, 430, 596
60/81 *IBM* v *Commission* [1981] ECR 2639, [1981] 3 CMLR 635 214
70/81 *Kloppenburg* [1984] ECR 1075 118, 599
102/81 *Nordsee Deutsche Hochsee fischerei GmbH* v *Reederei Mond Hochsee fischerei AG* [1982] ECR 1095 191–192
104/81 *Kupferberg (Hauptzollamt) & Cie KG* [1982] ECR 3461, [1983] 1 CMLR 1 151
115/81, 116/81 *Adoui and Cornuaille* v *Belgian State* [1982] ECR 1165, [1982] 3 CMLR 631 359, 360, 485, 486, 563–564
124/81 *Commission* v *United Kingdom (Re UHT Milk)* [1983] ECR 203, [1983] 2 CMLR 1 566
246/81 *Lord Bethell* v *Commission* [1982] ECR 2277, [1982] 3 CMLR 300 236
249/81 *Commission* v *Ireland (Re 'Buy Irish' Campaign)* [1982] ECR 4005, [1983] 2 CMLR 104 537–538, 542, 581, 587
261/81 *Walter Rau Lebensmittelwerke* v *De Smedt PvbA* [1982] ECR 3961, [1983] 2 CMLR 496 546–547, 575
283/81 *CILFIT* v *Ministry of Health* [1982] ECR 3415 196, 198, 200
11/82 *Piraiki-Patraiki, A E and Others* v *Commission* [1985] ECR 207 221–222, 225–226

35/82, 36/82 *Morson and Jhanjan* v *Netherlands* [1982] ECR 3723, [1983] 2 CMLR 221 330, 385–386, 418, 430

74/82 *Commission* v *Ireland* [1984] ECR 317 252

94/82 *De Kikvorsch Groothandel-Import-Export BV* [1983] ECR 497, [1984] 2 CMLR 323 575

132/82 *Commission* v *Belgium (Re Customs Warehouses)* [1983] ECR 1649, [1983] 3 CMLR 600 519–520

166/82 *Commission* v *Italy* [1984] ECR 459, [1985] 2 CMLR 615 254

174/82 *Officier van Justitie* v *Sandoz BV* [1983] ECR 2445, [1984] 3 CMLR 43 562, 567, 568

222/82 *Apple and Pear Development Council* v *K J Lewis Ltd* [1983] ECR 4083 538, 543, 581, 587

237/82 *Jongeneel Kaas BV* v *Netherlands* [1984] ECR 483 561

271/82 *Auer* v *Ministère Public* [1983] ECR 2727, [1985] 1 CMLR 123 504

314/82 *Commission* v *Belgium* [1984] ECR 1543, [1985] 3 CMLR 134 522

13/83 *European Parliament* v *Council (Re Transport Policy)* [1985] ECR 1513, [1986] 1 CMLR 138 234, 235, 236

14/83 *Von Colson and Kamann* v *Land Nordrhein-Westfalen* [1984] ECR 1891 294–295, 298

72/83 *Campus Oil Ltd* v *Minister for Industry and Energy* [1984] ECR 2727, [1984] 3 CMLR 344 545, 564–565

79/83 *Harz* v *Deutsche Tradax* [1984] ECR 1921 295, 298, 317

207/83 *Commission* v *United Kingdom (Re Origin Marking of Retail Goods)* [1985] ECR 1202, [1985] 2 CMLR 259 547–548

222/83 *Municipality of Differdange and Others* v *Commission* [1984] ECR 2889 221

231/83 *Cullet* [1985] ECR 305 564

267/83 *Diatta* v *Land Berlin* [1985] ECR 567, [1986] 2 CMLR 164 354, 355

286/82, 26/83 *Luisi and Carbone* v *Ministero del Tesoro* [1984] ECR 377, [1985] CMLR 5226/83, [1989] ECR 2445 441, 477, 480, 506

293/83 *Gravier* v *City of Liège* [1985] ECR 593, [1985] 3 CMLR 1 426, 480

294/83 *Parti Ecologiste ('Les Verts')* v *European Parliament* [1986] ECLI:EU:1986:166 215

29/84 *Commission* v *Germany (Re Nursing Directives)* [1985] ECR 1661, [1986] 2 CMLR 579 254, 282, 323, 397

60/84, 61/84 *Cinéthèque SA* v *Fédération Nationale des Cinémas Français* [1985] ECR 2605, [1986] 1 CMLR 365 536–537, 554, 580

106/84 *Commission* v *Denmark* [1986] ECR 833 526

112/84 *Humblot* v *Directeur des Services Fiscaux* [1985] ECR 1367, 1986 2 CMLR 363 527–528, 529, 534

122/84 *Scrivner and Cole* v *Centre Public d'Aide Sociale de Chastre* [1985] ECR 1027, [1987] 3 CMLR 638 404–405, 413

137/84 *Ministère Public* v *Mutsch* [1985] ECR 2681, [1986] 1 CMLR 648 405

152/84 *Marshall* v *Southampton & South West Hampshire Area Health Authority* [1986] ECR 723, [1986] 1 CMLR 688 286, 287–289, 292, 293, 299, 308, 310, 311, 314, 597

175/84 *Krohn & Co Import-Export GmbH KG* v *Commission* [1987] ECR 97, [1987] 1 CMLR 745 243

178/84 *Commission* v *Germany ('German Bier')* [1987] ECR 1227, [1988] 1 CMLR 780 567–568, 574–575, 577

197/84 *Steinhauser* v *City of Biarritz* [1985] ECR 1819, [1986] 1 CMLR 53 436

216/84 *Commission* v *France* [1988] ECR 793 566

222/84 *Johnston* v *Chief Constable of the Royal Ulster Constabulary (RUC)* [1986] ECR 1651 122, 135, 247

243/84 *John Walker* v *Ministeriet for Skatter of Afgifter* [1986] ECR 875, [1987] 2 CMLR 275 534, 535

59/85 *Netherlands* v *Reed* [1986] ECR 1283, [1987] 2 CMLR 448 422

66/85 *Lawrie-Blum* v *Land Baden-Württemberg* [1986] ECR 2121, [1987] 3 CMLR 389 386, 388, 402–403, 430

121/85 *Conegate Ltd* v *Customs and Excise Commissioners* [1986] ECR 1007, [1987] QB 254, [1986] 2 All ER 688 563

131/85 *Gül* v *Regierungspräsident Düsseldorf* [1986] ECR 1573, [1987] 1 CMLR 501 357, 398

139/85 *Kempf* v *Staatssecretaris van Justitie* [1986] ECR 1741, [1987] 1 CMLR 764 388, 430

152/85 *Misset* v *Council* [1987] ECR 223 233

154/85 *Commission* v *Italy* [1987] ECR 2717 541

168/85 *Commission* v *Italy (Re Freedom of Establishment)* [1986] ECR 2495, [1988] 1 CMLR 580 446

184/85 *Commission* v *Italy (similar fruit)* [1987] ECR 4157 526–527, 532

186/85 *Commission* v *Belgium* [1987] ECR 2029 252

193/85 *Co-Frutta Srl* v *Amministrazione delle Finanze dello Stato* [1987] ECR 2085 526

196/85 *Commission* v *France* [1987] ECR 1597, [1988] 2 CMLR 851 530

239/85 *Commission* v *Belgium* [1986] ECR 3645 282

281/85, 283/85–285/85, 287/85 *Germany, France, Netherlands, Denmark and the United Kingdom* v *Commission* [1987] ECR 3203, [1988] 1 CMLR 11 162–163

314/85 *Firma Foto-Frost* v *Hauptzollamt Lubeck-Ost* [1987] ECR 4199 191, 196

316/85 *Centre Public d'Aide Sociale de Courcelles* v *Lebon* [1987] ECR 2811, [1989] CMLR 337 343–345, 406, 407, 410, 412, 414, 422–423, 426

325/85 *Bond van Adverteerders* [1987] ECR 5041 441

356/85 *Commission* v *Belgium* [1987] ECR 3299 533

433/85 *Feldain* v *Services Fiscaux du Departement du Haut-Rhin* [1987] ECR 3521 528

1/86 *Commission* v *Belgium* [1987] ECR 2797, [1989] 1 CMLR 474 253, 300

14/86 *Pretore di Saló* [1987] ECR 2545 298, 317
24/86 *Blaizot* v *University of Liège* [1988] ECR 379, [1989] 1 CMLR 57 406, 426
34/86 *Council* v *Parliament* [1986] ECLI:EU:1986:291 215
39/86 *Lair* v *University of Hannover* [1988] ECR 3161, [1989] 3 CMLR 545 391, 406, 426, 480
45/86 *Commission* v *Council (Generalised Tariff Preferences)* [1987] ECR 1493, [1988] 2 CMLR 131 211
63/86 *Commission* v *Italy (Re Housing Aid)* [1988] ECR 29, [1989] 2 CMLR 601 479
68/86 *United Kingdom* v *Council of the European Communities* [1988] ECR 855 75
80/86 *Officier van Justitie* v *Kolpinghuis Nijmegen BV* [1987] ECR 3969, [1989] 2 CMLR 18 118, 299
118/86 *Openbaar Ministerie* v *Nertsvoederfabriek Nederland BV* [1987] ECR 3883, [1989] 2 CMLR 436 561
120/86 *Mulder* v *Minister van Landbouw en Visserij* [1988] ECR 2321, [1989] 2 CMLR 1 118–119
197/86 *Brown* v *Secretary of State for Scotland* [1988] ECR 3205, [1988] 3 CMLR 403 406–407, 426
222/86 *UNECTEF* v *Heylens and Others* [1987] ECR 4097, [1989] 1 CMLR 901 120, 600
240/86 *Greece* v *Commission* [1998] ECR 1835 250
249/86 *Commission* v *Germany (Re Housing of Migrant Workers)* [1989] ECR 1263, [1990] 3 CMLR 540 429–430
263/86 *Belgium* v *Humbel* [1989] ECR 393, [1989] 1 CMLR 393 441, 478, 480, 506
286/86 *Ministère Public* v *Deserbais* [1988] ECR 4907, [1989] 1 CMLR 576 575, 576
298/86 *Commission* v *Belgium* [1988] ECR 4343 252
302/86 *Commission* v *Denmark ('Drink Containers')* [1988] ECR 4607 578
18/87 *Commission* v *Germany (animal inspections)* [1988] ECR 5427 521, 522–523, 587
45/87 *Commission* v *Ireland (Re Dundalk Water Supply)* [1988] ECR 4929, [1989] 1 CMLR 225 548–549
46/87 *Hoechst AG* v *Commission* [1989] ECR 2859, [1991] 4 CMLR 410 135
70/87 *Fediol* v *Commission* [1989] ECR 1781, [1991] 2 CMLR 489 149
81/87 *R* v *HM Treasury, ex parte Daily Mail and General Trust plc* [1988] ECR 5483 471–472
186/87 *Cowan* v *Le Trésor Public* [1986] ECR 195, [1990] 2 CMLR 613 477, 479–480, 484, 506
196/87 *Steymann* v *Staatssecretaris van Justitie* [1988] ECR 6159, [1989] 1 CMLR 449 389, 430
240/87 *Deville* v *Administration des Impôts* [1988] ECR 3513, [1989] 3 CMLR 611 528
266/87, 267/87 *R* v *Royal Pharmaceutical Society of Great Britain, ex parte API* [1989] ECR 1295, [1989] 2 CMLR 751 538
339/87 *Commission* v *Netherlands (Re Protection of Wild Birds)* [1990] ECR I-851, [1993] 2 CMLR 360 254
341/87 *EMI Electrola GmbH* v *Patricia* [1989] ECR 79, [1989] 2 CMLR 413 571–572
344/87 *Bettray* v *Staatssecretaris van Justitie* [1989] ECR 1621, [1991] 1 CMLR 459 389, 407
379/87 *Groener* v *Minister for Education* [1989] ECR 3967, [1990] 1 CMLR 401 400
C-2/88 *Imm Zwartveld* [1990] ECR I-3365 87
C-5/88 *Wachauf (Hubert)* v *Bundesamt Ehrnährung und Forstwirtschaft* [1989] ECR 2609, [1991] 1 CMLR 328 121–122, 131
C-21/88 *Du Pont de Nemours Italiana SpA* v *Unità sanitaria locale N° 2 di Carrara* [1990] ECLI:EU:C:1990:121 544–545
C-25/88 *Wurmser* [1989] ECR 1105, [1991] 1 CMLR 173 562
C-33/88 *Allué & Coonan* v *Università degli Studi di Venezia* [1989] ECR 1591, [1991] 1 CMLR 283 398, 403
C-54/88, 91/88, 14/89 *Nino, Prandini & Goti, Pierini* [1990] ECR I-3537, [1992] 1 CMLR 383 504
C-64/88 *Commission* v *France* [1991] ECR I-2727 258–260
C-70/88 *Parliament* v *Council (Chernobyl)* [1991] ECR I-2041, [1992] 1 CMLR 91 188
C-103/88 *Costanzo (Fratelli)* v *Comune di Milano* [1989] ECR 1839, [1990] 3 CMLR 239 188 247, 287
C-132/88 *Commission* v *Greece (Greek car tax)* [1990] ECR I-1567 528–529, 530
C-143/88 *Zückerfabrik Süderdithmarschen* v *Hauptzollampt Itzehoe* [1991] ECR I-415, [1993] 3 CMLR 1 266
C-145/88 *Torfaen Borough Council* v *B & Q plc (Sunday Trading Case)* [1989] ECR 3851, [1990] 1 CMLR 337 554, 580
C-170/88 *Ford España* v *Spain* [1989] ECR 2305 520
C-175/88 *Biehl* [1990] ECR I-1779, [1990] 3 CMLR 143 406
C-177/88 *Dekker* v *Stichting Vormingscentrum voor Jonge Volwassen (VJV-Centrum) Plus* [1990] ECR I-3941 132
C-213/88 and C-39/89 *Luxembourg* v *European Parliament* [1991] ECLI:EU:C:1991:449 215
C-262/88 *Barber* v *Guardian Royal Exchange Assurance Group* [1990] ECR I-1889, [1990] 2 CMLR 513 284
C-322/88 *Grimaldi* v *Fonds des Maladies Professionelles* [1989] ECR 4407, [1991] ECR 4402 148, 195, 296
C-23/89 *Quietlynn Ltd* v *Southend-on-Sea Borough Council* [1990] ECR I-3059, [1990] 3 CMLR 55 554
C-106/89 *Marleasing SA* v *La Commercial Internacional de Alimentacion SA* [1990] ECR I-4135, [1992] 1 CMLR 305 295–298, 314–317, 597, 598
C-113/89 *Rush Portuguesa Lda* v *Office National d'Immigration* [1990] ECR 1417, [1991] 2 CMLR 818 149
C-188/89 *Foster* v *British Gas* [1990] ECR I-3313, [1990] 2 CMLR 833 287–290, 292, 310–313, 317, 605
C-192/89 *SZ Service* v *Staatsecretaris van Justitie* [1990] ECR I-3461, [1992] 2 CMLR 57 247

C-213/89 *R v Secretary of State for Transport, ex parte Factortame (No. 2)* [1990] ECR I-2433, [1991] 1 AC 603, [1990] 3 CMLR 375, HL 188, 266, 303–305, 436, 597

C-221/89 *R v Secretary of State for Transport, ex parte Factortame (No. 1)* [1991] ECR I-3905, [1991] 3 CMLR 601 310, 438–439

C-231/89 *Gmurzynska-Bscher* [1990] ECR I-4003 173 190, 196

C-235/89 *Commission v Italy* [1992] ECR I-777, [1992] 2 CMLR 709 570

C-246/89R *Commission v United Kingdom (Re Nationality of Fishermen)* [1989] ECR 3125, [1989] 3 CMLR 601 264

C-260/89 *Elleneki Radiophonia Tileorasi (ERT)* [1991] ECR I-2925, [1994] 4 CMLR 540 121, 129

C-292/89 *R v Immigration Appeal Tribunal, ex parte Antonissen* [1991] ECR I-745, [1991] 2 CMLR 373 202, 410–411

C-297/88, C-197/89 *Dzodzi v Belgium* [1990] ECR I-3763 87

C-300/89 *Commission v Council (Re Titanium Dioxide Waste)* [1991] ECR I-2867, [1993] 3 CMLR 359 165, 210

C-306/89 *Commission v Greece* [1991] ECR I-5863, [1994] 1 CMLR 803 443

C-309/89 *Codorniu SA v Council* [1994] ECR I-853 226–227

C-340/89 *Vlassopoulou v Ministerium für Justiz, Bundes- und Europaangelegenheiten Baden- Württemberg* [1991] ECR I-2357, [1992] 1 CMLR 625 489–491, 500, 501, 506

C-357/89 *Raulin v Netherlands Ministry for Education and Science* [1992] ECR I-1027, [1994] 1 CMLR 227 388, 391, 406, 426

T-138/89 *NBV v Commission* [1992] ECRII-2181 220

C-2/90 *Commission v Belgium* [1992] ECR I-4431 516

C-6/90, C-9/90 *Francovich and Bonifaci v Republic of Italy* [1991] ECR I-5357, [1993] 2 CMLR 66 284–286, 299–301, 303, 304, 308, 317, 597, 604

C-18/90 *Kziber (Bahia) v ONEM* [1991] ECR I-199 [1991] ECR I-199 151

C-30/90 *Commission v United Kingdom* [1992] ECR I-829, [1992] 2 CMLR 709 570

C-56/90 *Commission v United Kingdom (Bathing Water Directive)* [1994] 1 CMLR 769 254

C-65/90 *European Parliament v Council* [1992] ECR I-4953 145

C-159/90 *Society for the Protection of the Unborn Child Ireland Ltd (SPUC) v Grogan* [1991] ECR I-4685, [1991] 3 CMLR 849 129, 441–442, 562

C-181/90 *Consorgan Lda v Commission* [1992] ECR I-3557 211

C-190/90 *Commission v Netherlands* [1992] ECR I-3300 254

C-195/90R *Commission v Germany* [1994] ECR I-3141 264–265

C-213/90 *Association de Soutien aux Travailleurs Immigrés* [1991] ECR I-3207, [1993] 3 CMLR 621 130, 400

C-282/90 *Vreugdenhil BV v Commission* [1992] ECR I-1937 243

C-284/90 *Council v European Parliament* [1992] ECLI:EU:C:1992:154 215

C-295/90 *European Parliament v Council* [1992] ECR I-5299, [1992] 3 CMLR 281 165, 210, 234

C-320–322/90 *Telemarsicabruzzo SpA v Circostel and Others* [1993] ECR I-393 197

C-355/90 *Commission v Spain, Judgment of 2 August 1993* [1993] ECR I-4221 254

C-369/90 *Micheletti and Others* [1992] ECR I-4239 327

C-370/90 *R v Immigration Appeal Tribunal and Surinder Singh, ex parte Secretary of State for the Home Department* [1992] All ER 798, [1992] ECR I-4265, [1992] 3 CMLR 358 332, 333, 336, 395, 421–422, 504

T-113/89 *Nefarma v Commission* [1990] ECR II-797 215

C-1/91 Opinion on Draft Agreement between EEC and EFTA [1991] ECR I-6079 110, 111

C-4/91 *Bleis v Ministère de l'Education Nationale* [1991] ECR I-5627, [1994] 1 CMLR 793 403

C-13, 113/91 *Debus v Ministère Public* [1992] ECR I-3617 577

C-45/91 *Commission v Hellenic Republic* [1992] ECR I-2509 254, 256–258

C-104/91 *Colegio Oficial de Agentes de la Propriedad Inmobiliara v Aguirre, Newman and Others* [1992] ECR I-3003 491

C-105/91 *Commission v Greece* [1992] ECR I-5871 254

C-156/91 *Hansa Fleisch Ernst Mundt* [1992] ECR I-5567 281

C-165/91 *Van Munster v Rijksdienst voor Pensioenen* [1994] ECR I-4661 408

C-181, 248/91 *Parliament v Council and Commission (Re Aid to Bangladesh)* [1993] ECR I-3685, [1994] 3 CMLR 317 216

C-188/91 *Deutsche Shell AG v Hauptzollamt Hamburg* [1993] ECR I-363 195, 196

C-267/91, C-268/91 *Keck and Mithouard* (joined cases) [1993] ECR I-6097, [1995] 1 CMLR 101 186, 555–559, 580, 581, 588

C-271/91 *Marshall v Southampton and South-West Hampshire Area Health Authority (No. 2)* [1993] ECR I-4367, [1993] 3 CMLR 293, [1993] 4 All ER 586 293

C-272/91 *Commission v Italy* [1994] ECR I-1409 443

C-327/91 *France v Commission* [1994] ECR I-2533, [1995] 4 CMLR 621 166

C-330/91 *R v IRC, ex parte Commerzbank* [1993] ECLI:EU:C:303 472

C-10/92 *Balocchi v Ministero delle Finanze dello Stato* [1993] ECR I-5105, [1995] 1 CMLR 486 197

C-91/92 *Paola Faccini Dori v Recreb SRL* [1994] ECR I-3325 287, 308

C-92/92 *Collins* v *Imtrat Handelsgesellschaft GmbH* [1993] ECR I-5145 570

C-127/92 *Enderby* v *Frenchay Health Authority and Secretary of State for Health* [1993] ECR I-5535 132

C-137/92 *P Commission* v *BASF AG & Others* [1994] ECR I-2555 67, 234

C-188/92 *TWD Textilwerke Deggendorf* v *Germany* [1994] ECR I-833 237–238

C-235/92 *Montecatini SpA* v *the Commission* [1999] ECR I-4539 135

C-275/92 *HM Customs and Excise Commissioners* v *Schindler* [1994] ECR I-1039, [1995] 1 CMLR 4 442–443, 515, 562

C-292/92 *Hunermund* [1993] ECR I-6787 556

C-319/92 *Haim* v *Kassenzahnarztliche Vereinigung Nordrhein* [1994] ECR I-425, [1994] 2 CMLR 169 490, 491, 500–501, 506

C-332/92 *Eurico Italia Srl* v *Ente Nazionale Risi* [1994] ECR I-711, [1994] 2 CMLR 580 197

C-334/92 *Wagner Miret* v *Fondo de Garantía Salarial* [1993] ECR I-6911 297–298, 308, 317

C-350/92 *Spain* v *Council* [1995] ECR I-1985 570

C-351/92 *Graff* v *Hauptzollamt Köln-Rheinau* [1994] ECR I-3361 132

C-375/92 *Commission* v *Spain* [1994] ECR I-923, [1994] CMLR 500 250

C-382/92, C-383/92 *Commission* v *United Kingdom* [1994] ECR I-2435 251

C-388/92 *European Parliament* v *Council* [1994] ECR I-2067 211, 234

C-394/92 *Municipality of Almelo and Others* v *Energiebedvijf NV* [1994] ECR I-1477 193–194

C-401/92, C-402/92 *Criminal Proceedings against Tankstation, 'T Heukske vof and JBE Boermans* [1994] ECR I-2199 556

C-404/92 *X* v *Commission* [1994] ECR I-4737 128

C-422/92 *Commission* v *Germany* [1995] ECR I-1097 252

T-74/92 *Ladbroke Racing (Deutschland) GmbH* v *Commission* [1995] ECR II-115 235

T-96/92 *Comité Central d'Enterprise de la Société Générale des Grandes Sources and Others* v *Commission and Comité Central d'Enterprise de la Société Anonyme Vittel and Others* v *Commission* [1995] ECR II-1213 222

C-32/93 *Webb* v *EMO Air Cargo (UK) Ltd* [1994] ECR I-3567 132, 316

C-37/93 *Commission* v *Belgium* [1993] ECR I-6295 251, 397, 403

C-39/93P *SFEI and Others* v *Commission* [1994] ECR I-2681 216, 234

C-43/93 *Van der Elst* v *OMI* [1994] ECR I-3803 453

C-45/93 *Commission* v *Spain* [1994] ECR I-911 480

C-46/93, C-48/93 *Brasserie du Pêcheur SA* v *Germany* [1996] ECR I-1029 240, 300–305, 317, 597, 604

C-47/93 *Commission* v *Belgium (Re University Fees)* [1994] ECR I-1593 480

C-48/93 *R* v *Secretary of State for Transport, ex parte Factortame Ltd and Others* [1996] ECR I-1029 300–301, 597, 604

C-58/93 *Yousfi* v *Belgium* [1994] ECR I-353 151

C-69/93, C-258/93 *Punto Casa SpA and Promozioni Polivalenti Venete Soc coop arl* v *Sindacos del Comunes di Capena and Torri di Quartesolo (Joined Cases)* [1994] ECR I-2355 556

C-154/93 *Tawil-Albertini* v *Ministre des Affaires Sociales* [1994] ECR I-451 499–501, 503

C-156/93 *Parliament* v *Commission* [1995] ECR I-2019 212, 214

C-279/93 *Finanzamt Köln-Altstadt* v *Schumacker* [1995] ECR I-225 406, 478

C-279/93 *Schumacher* [1995] ECR I-225 406, 478

C-280/93 *Commission* v *Germany (Re Banana Market)* [1994] ECR I-4873 130, 131

C-293/93 *Neeltje* v *Houtwipper* [1994] ECR I-4249 577

C-316/93 *Vaneetveld* v *SA Le Foyer* [1994] ECR I-763, [1994] 2 CMLR 852 293

C-320/93 *Lucien Ortscheit GmbH* v *Eurim-Pharm GmbH* [1994] ECR I-5243 561, 569

C-323/93 *Société Civile Agricole du Centre d'Insémination de la Crespelle* v *Coopérative d'Elevage de la Mayenne* [1994] ECR I-5077 539

C-358/93, C-416/93 *Aldo Bordessa, Mellado and Maestre (Criminal Proceedings)* [1995] ECR I-361 12

C-367/93, C-377/93 *FG Roders BV ea* v *Inspecteur der Inverrechten en Accijnzen* [1999] ECR I-2229 533

C-384/93 *Alpine Investments BV* v *Minister van Financiën* [1995] ECR I-1141 441, 443

C-392/93 *R* v *HM Treasury, ex parte British Telecommunications plc* [1996] All ER (EC) 411 302

C-399/92, C-409/92, C-425/92; C-34/93, C-50/93, C-78/93 *Helmig and Others* v *Stadt Lengerich* [1994] ECR I-5727 190

C-412/93 *Leclerc-Siplec* [1995] ECR I-179 556

C-415/93 *Union Royale Belge des Sociétés de Football/Association ASBL* v *Bosman* [1995] ECR I-4921 393–394, 460

C-417/93 *European Parliament* v *Council* [1995] ECR I-1185 145

C-422-424/93 *Teres Zabala Erasun and Others* v *Instituto Nacional de Empleo* [1995] 1 CMLR 861 198

C-465/93 *Atlanta Fruchthandelgesellschaft GmbH* v *Bundesamt für Ernährung und Forstwirtschaft* [1995] ECR I-3799 266

T-3/93 *Air France* v *Commission* [1995] ECLI:EU:T:45 215

T-10/93 *A* v *Commission* [1994] ECR II-179 121

T-432/93, T-434/93 *Socurte Lda and Others* v *Commission* [1995] ECR II-45 211

T-466/93, T-469/93, T-473/93, T-477/93 *O'Dwyer and Others* v *Council* [1996] 2 CMLR 148 118

T-489/93 *Unifruit Hellas* v *Commission* [1994] ECR II-1201 239

T-514/93 *Cobrecaf SA* v *Commission* [1995] ECR II-621 233

1/94 Opinion [1995] ECR I-2363 247

C-5/94 *R v Ministry of Agriculture, Fisheries and Food, ex parte Hedley Lomas (Ireland) Ltd* [1996] ECR I-2553, [1996] All ER (EC) 493 **240, 304–306, 317**

C-13/94 *P v S and Cornwall County Council* [1996] ECR I-2143 **132**

C-16/94 *Édouard Dubois & Fils SA and Général Cargo Services SA v Garonor Exploitation SA* [1995] ECR I-2421 **512**

C-55/94 *Gebhard (Reinhard) v Consiglio dell'Ordine degli Avvocati e Procuratori di Milano* [1995] ECR I-4165 **439, 459–460, 505, 506**

C-84/94 *United Kingdom v Council of the European Union (Working Time Directive)* [1996] ECR I-5755 **244–245**

C-87/94 *Commission v Belgium* [1994] ECR I-1395 **265–266**

C-90/94 *Haahr Petroleum Ltd v Abenra Havn* [1998] 1 CMLR 771 **524**

C-113/94 *Jacquier v Directeur Général des Impôts* [1995] ECR I-4203 **528**

C-157/94 *Commission v Netherlands* [1997] ECR I-5699 **537**

C-170/94R *Commission v Greece* [1995] ECR I-1819 **265**

C-178/94, C-179/94, C-188-190/94 *Dillenkofer and Others v Federal Republic of Germany* [1996] ECR I-4845, [1996] 3 CMLR 469 **240, 303, 306**

C-194/94 *CIA Security International v Signalson and Securitel* [1996] ECR I-2001 **291, 292**

C-209/94 *P Buralux SA v Council* [1996] ECR I-615 **227**

C-334/94 *Commission v France* [1996] ECR I-1307 **251**

T-85/94 *Eugénio Branco Lda v Commission* [1995] ECR II-45 **211**

C-7/95 *John Deere Ltd v Commission* [1998] ECR I-3111 **88**

C-18/95 *Terhoeve v Inspecteur van de Belastingdienst Particulieren/Ondernemingen Buitenland* [1999] ECR I-345 **396**

C-53/95 *Inasti* [1996] ECR I-703 **439**

C-122/95 *Germany v Council* [1998] ECR I-973 **233**

C-168/95 *Arcaro* [1997] ECR I-4705 **299**

C-171/95 *Tetik v Land Berlin* [1997] ECR I-329 **391**

C-189/95 *Harry Franzen* [1997] ECR I-5909, [1998] 1 CMLR 1231 **539**

C-265/95 *Commission v France ('Angry Farmers')* [1997] ECR I-6959 **541–542, 551, 564, 580, 582**

C-299/95 *Kremzow v Austria* [1997] ECR I-2629 **122**

C-337/95 *Parfums Christian Dior BV v Evora BV* [1997] ECR I-6013 **201, 203**

C-344/95 *Commission v Belgium* [1997] ECR I-1035 **411, 430**

C-345/95 *France v European Parliament* [1997] ECR I-5215 **83**

C-368/95 *Vereinigte Familiapresse Zeitungsverlags und Vertriebs GmbH v Heinrich Bauer Verlag* [1997] ECR I-3689 **556–557**

C-388/95 *Belgium v Spain* [2000] ECR I-3123, [2002] 1 CMLR 755 **248**

T-174/95 *Svenska Journalist-forbundet v Council of European Union* [1998] ECR I-2289, [1998] 3 CMLR 645 **217**

C-1/96 *R v Ministry of Agriculture, Fisheries and Food, ex parte Compassion in World Farming Ltd* [1998] ECR I-1251, [1998] 2 CMLR 661 **561**

C-15/96 *Schöning-Kougebetopoulou v Freie und Hansestadt Hamburg* [1998] ECR I-47, [1998] 1 CMLR 931 **397**

C-62/96 *Commission v Greece* [1997] ECR I-6725 **477**

C-64, 65/96 *Land Nordrhein-Westfalen v Uecker; Jacquei v Land Nordrhein-Westfalen* [1997] ECR I-3171 **326, 386**

C-69–79/96 *Garofalo and Others v Ministero della Sanità and Others* [1998] 1 CMLR 1087 **194**

C-85/96 *Martinez Sala v Freistaat Bayern* [1998] ECLI:EU:C:1998:217 **326, 364**

C-114/96 *Kieffer (Rene) and Romain Thill* [1997] ECR I-3629 **12**

C-118/96 *Safir v Skattemyndigheten i Dalarnas Lan* [1998] ECR I-1897 **443**

C-129/96 *Inter-Environnement Wallonie ASBL* [1997] ECR I-7411 **285**

C-253–258/96 *Kampelmann v Landschaftsverband Westfalen-Lippe and Others* [1997] ECR I-6907 **285, 289, 290**

C-264/96 *ICI* [1998] ECR I-4695 **439**

C-348/96 *Donatella Calfa* [1999] ECR I-11 **483–484**

C-350/96 *Clean Car Autoservice GmbH v Landeshauptmann von Wien* [1998] ECR I-2521, [1998] 2 CMLR 637 **383, 478**

C-369/96, C-376/96 *Arblade (Jean-Claude) Arblade & Fils SARL; Bernard Leloup, Serge Leloup, Sofrage SARL* [1999] ECR I-8453 **449**

C-386/96 *P Dreyfus v Commission* [1998] ECR I-2309 **221**

C-111/97 *Evobus Austria v Niederosterreichischer* [1998] ECR I-5411 **298**

C-226/97 *Lemmens* [1998] ECR I-3711 **299**

C-234/97 *Bobadilla (Fernandez de) v Museo Nacional del Prado and Others* [1999] ECR I-4773 **501, 504**

C-340/97 *Omer Nazli and Others v Stadt Nurnburg* [2000] ECR I-957 **135**

C-378/97 *Wijsenbeek* [1999] ECR I-6207 **322**

C-387/97 *Commission v Hellenic Republic* [2000] ECR I-5047 **135, 270**

C-421/97 *Yves Tarantik v Direction des Services Fiscaux de Seine-et-Marne* [1999] ECR I-3633 **528**

C-17/98 *Emesa Sugar (Free Zone) NV v Aruba* [2000] ECR I-665 **92**

C-67/98 *Questore di Verona v Diego Zenatti* [1999] ECR I-7289 **467–469**

C-97/98 *Jägerskiöld (Peter) v Torolf Gustafsson* [1999] ECR I-7319 **440, 514–516**

C-224/98 *D'Hoop (Marie-Nathalie) v Office national de l'emploi* [2002] 3 CMLR 12 **414**

C-238/98 *Hocsman (Hugo Fernando) v Ministre de l'Emploi et de la Solidarité* [2000] ECR I-6623 **501–503**

C-281/98 *Angonese* [2000] ECR I-4139 400
C-352/98P *Bergaderm and Goupil* v *Commission* [2000] ECR I-5291 240, 243
C-356/98 *Kaba* v *Secretary of State for the Home Department* [2000] ECR I-2623 420–421
C-376/98 *Germany* v *Parliament and Council 'Tobacco advertising I'* [2000] ECR I-8419 4–5
C-377/98 *Netherlands* v *European Parliament and Council of the European Union* [2001] ECR I-7079 126, 127
C-405/98 *Konsumentombudsmannen (KO)* v *Gourmet International Products AB (GIP)* [2001] ECR I-1795 466–467, 557
C-443/98 *Unilever Italia SpA* v *Central Food SpA* [2000] ECR I-7535 291, 292
T-166/98 *Cantina sociale di Dolianova and Others* v *Commission* [2004] ECR II-3991 241
C-43/99 *Ghislain Leclerc, Alina Deaconescu* v *Caisse Nationale des Prestations Familiales* [2000] ECR I-4265 409
C-157/99 *Geraets-Smits* v *Stichting Ziekenfonds and Peerbooms* v *Stichting CZ Groep Zorgverzekeringen* [2001] ECR I-5473 441, 481, 482
C-184/99 *Grzelczyk* v *Centre Public d'aide sociale d'Ottignies-Louvain-la-Neuve* [2001] ECR I-6193 326, 367–369, 407
C-234/99 *Nygård* [2002] ECR I-3657 524
C-387/99 *Commission* v *Germany* [2004] ECR I-3751 577
C-413/99 *Baumbast and R* v *Secretary of State for the Home Department* [2002] ECR I-7091 338–339, 369, 424, 425
C-414/99–C-416/99 *Zino Davidoff SA* v *A & G Imports Ltd and Levi Strauss & Co. and Others* v *Tesco Stores Ltd and Others (joined Cases)* [2001] ECR I-8691 131
C-439/99 *Commission* v *Italy* [2002] ECR I-305 252
C-516/99 *Schmid (Walter)* [2002] ECR I-4573 130, 193
T-222-99, T-327-99 & T-329-99 *Jean Claude Martinez et al.* v *Parliament* [1999] ECR II-3397, [2001] ECR II-2823 82
T-326/99 *Olivieri* v *Commission and European Agency for the Evaluation of Medicinal Products OJ* [2003] ECR II-6053 219
0T-151/00 *Laboratoire du Bain* v *Council and Commission* [2005] ECR II-23 241–242
C-1/00 *Commission* v *France* [2001] ECR I-9989 249, 264
C-12/00 *Commission* v *Spain* [2003] ECR I-459 575
C-14/00 *Commission* v *Italy* [2003] ECR I-513 575
C-17/00 *De Coster* v *Collège des Bourgmestres et Échevins de Watermael-Boitsfort* [2001] ECR I-9445 193
C-24/00 *Commission* v *France* [2004] ECR I-1277 577
C-31/00 *Conseil National de l'Ordre des Architectes* v *Nicholas Dreesen* [2002] ECR I-663 11
C-50/00P *Unión de Pequeños Agricultores* v *Council of the European Union* (supported by the Commission) [2002] ECR I-6677 208, 227–228, 231, 232

C-60/00 *Carpenter (Mary)* v *Secretary of State for the Home Department* [2002] ECR I-6279 128, 441, 452, 506
C-99/00 *Lyckeskog, Kenny Roland* [2002] ECR I-4839 202, 203
C-112/00 *Schmidberger* v *Austria* [2003] ECR I-5659 130, 551–552, 582
C-150/00 *Commission* v *Austria* [2004] ECR I-3887 577
C-318/00 *Bacardi-Martini and Cellier des Dauphins* [2003] ECR I-905 197–198
C-416/00 *Morellato* [2003] ECR I-9343 556
C-453/00 *Kühne & Heitz* [2004] ECR I-837 199
C-466/00 *Kaba* v *Secretary of State for the Home Department* [2003] ECR I-2219 421
T-69/00 *FIAMM and FIAMM Technologies* v *Council and Commission* [2006] 2 CMLR 9 241–242
T-147/00 *Laboratoires Servier* v *Commission* [2003] ECR II-85 166
T-228/00, T-229/00, T-242/00, T-243/00, T-245/00 to T-248/00, T-250/00, T-252/00, T-256/00 to T-259/00, T-267/00, T-268/00, T-271/00, T-275/00, T-276/00, T-281/00, T-287/00 & T-296/00 *Gruppo Ormeggiatori del porto di Venezia and Others* v *Commission* [2005] ECR II-787 220
T-269/00 *Sagar* v *Commission* [2005] unreported 220
T-288/00 *Gardena Hotels and Comitato Venezia Vuole Vivere* v *Commission* [2005] unreported 220
T-301/00 *Groupe Fremaux and Palais Royal* v *Council and Commission* [2005] ECR II-25 241–242
T-320/00 *CD Cartondruck* v *Council and Commission* [2005] unreported 241–242
T-353/00 *Le Pen* v *Parliament* [1992] ECLI:EU:T:1992:154 215
T-383/00 *Beamglow* v *Parliament and Others; and Fedon & Figli and Others* v *Council and Commission* [2006] 2 CMLR 10 241–242
C-56/01 *Inizan* – not reported (judgment delivered 23 Oct 2003) 482
C-87/1 *X* (unreported) 439
C-95/01 *Greenham* v *ABEL* [2004] ECR I-1333 577
C-101/01 *Bodil Lindqvist* [2003] ECR I-12971 128
C-109/01 *Akrich* [2003] ECR I-9607 350, 351
C-110/01 *Tennah-Durez* [2003] ECR I-6239 502–503, 505
C-131/01 *Commission* v *Italy* [2003] ECR I-1659 440
C-224/01 *Köbler* [2003] ECR I-10239 305–307, 317, 398, 399
C-243/01 *Gambelli* [2003] ECRI-1303 469
C-285/01 *Burbaud* [2003] 3 CMLR 21 493
C-313/01 *Morgenbesser* [2004] 1 CMLR 24 491
C-322/01 *Deutscher Apothekerverband eV* v *0800 DocMorris NV and Jacques Waterval* [2003] ECR I-14887 558, 577
C-388/01 *Commission* v *Italy* [2003] ECR I-721 480
C-397/01 to 403/01 *Pfeiffer and Others* (Joined Cases) [2004] ECR I-8835 296, 297, 298

TABLE OF CASES BEFORE THE COURT OF JUSTICE OF THE EUROPEAN UNION (NUMERICAL)   XXIX

C-405/01 *Colegio de Oficiales de la Marina Mercante Española* – not reported (judgment delivered 30 Sep 2003) **403–404**

C-413/01 *Ninni-Orasche* [2004] 1 CMLR 19 **388, 391**

C-422/01 *Skandia and Ramstedt* [2004] 1 CMLR 4 **554**

C-463/01 *Commission v Germany* [2004] ECR I-11705 **579**

T-64/01, T-65/01 *Afrikanische Frucht-Compagnie and Internationale Fruchtimport Gesellschaft Weichert & Co v Commission* [2004] ECR II-521 **241**

T-88/01 *Sniace v Commission* [2005] ECR II-1165 **220**

T-167/01 *Schmitz-Gotha Fahrzeugwerke v Commission* [2003] ECR II-1875 **218–219**

T-177/01 *Jégo-Quéré et Cie SA v Commission* [2002] ECR II-2365 **227**

T-377, T-379, T-380/00; T-260, T-272/01 *Philip Morris International and Others v Commission* [2003] ECR II-1 **216**

C-36/02 *OMEGA* [2004] ECR I-9609 **126, 482–483, 582**

C-47/02 *Anker and Others* [2004] 2 CMLR 35 **403–404, 430**

C-138/02 *Collins* [2004] ECR I-2703 **412, 413–415, 416, 418**

C-140/03 *Commission v Greece* [2005] ECR I-3177 **439**

C-153/02 *Neri (Valentina) v European School of Economics (ESE Insight World Education System Ltd)* [2003] ECR I-13555 **503, 505**

C-157/02 *Rieser Internationale Transporte GmbH v Autobahnen und Schnellstraßen-Finanzierungs-AG (Asfinag)* [2004] ECR I-1477 **289, 290**

C-171/02 *Commission v Portugal* [2004] ECR I-5645 **434, 440**

C-200/02 *Zhu and Chen* [2004] ECR I-9925 **330, 338, 345–348, 379**

C-201/02 *Wells v Secretary of State for Transport, Local Government and the Regions* [2004] ECR I-723 **293**

C-262/02 *Commission v France* [2004] ECR I-6569 **467**

C-304/02 *Commission v France* [2005] ECR I-6263 **258–260**

C-309/02 *Radlberger Getränke and S. Spitz* [2004] ECR I-11763 **579**

C-341/02 *Commission v Germany* [2005] ECR I-2733 **455–456**

C-386/02 *Baldinger* [2004] ECR I-8411 **405**

C-400/02 *Merida* [2004] ECR I-8471 **399**

C-456/02 *Trojani v CPAS* [2004] ECR I-7573 **389, 390**

T-17/02 *Olsen v Commission (under appeal, Case C-320/05P)* [2005] ECR II-2031 **232–233**

T-28/02 *First Data v Commission* [2006] 4 CMLR 4 **220**

T-139/02 *Instituto N. Avgerinopoulou and Others v Commission* [2004] ECR II-875 **217**

T-341/02 *Regione Siciliana v Commission* (under appeal, Case C-417/04P) [2004] unreported **222**

C-152/03 *Ritter-Coulais v Finanzamt Germersheim* [2006] AU ER (EC) 613 **399–400**

C-173/03 *Traghetti del Mediterraneo SpA v Italy* [2006] not reported **306–307**

C-208/03P *Le Pen v Parliament* [2005] ECR I-6051 **215**

C-209/03 *Bidar* [2005] ECR I-2119 **369–371**

C-275/03 *Commission v Portugal* (unreported) **216–217**

C-320/03 *Commission v Austria ('Austrian Lorries')* [2005] ECR I-9871 **579–581**

C-380/03 *Germany v Parliament and Council 'Tobacco advertising II'* [2006] ECR I-11573 **166–167**

C-419/03 *Commission v France* (unreported) (unreported) **262, 263**

C-446/03 *Marks & Spencer* [2005] ECR I-10837 **472–473**

T-29/03 *Comunidad Autónoma de Andalucía v Commission* [2004] ECR II-2923 **217**

T-218/03–T-240/03 *Boyle and Others v Commission* [2006] ECR II-1699 **226**

T-279/03 *Galileo v Commission* [2006] ECR II-1291 **242**

C-119/04 *Commission v Italy* [2006] ECR I-6885 **259**

C-144/04 *Mangold v Helm* [2005] ECR I-9981 **174, 175, 285**

C-145/04 *Spain v United Kingdom* [2006] ECR I-7917, [2007] 1 CMLR 87 **248**

C-177/04 *Commission v France* [2006] AU ER (D) 221 (Mar) **259**

C-244/04 *Commission v Germany* [2006] ECR I-885 **453**

C-258/04 *Ioannidis* [2005] ECR I-8275 **415**

C-290/04 *FKP Scorpio Konzertproduktionen GmbH v Finanzamt Hamburg-Eimsbuttel* [2007] 1 CMLR 937 **473**

C-372/04 *R (on the application of Yvonne Watts) v Bedford Primary Care Trust and the Secretary of State for Health* [2006] 3 CMLR 5 **482**

C-417/04 *Regione Siciliana v Commission* [2006] All ER (D) 11 (May) **217–218**

C-432/04 *Commission v Edith Cresson* (2006), unreported **64–65**

T-13/04 *Bonde and Others v Parliament and Council* [2005] unreported **222**

T-40/04 *Bonino (Emma) and Others v Parliament and Council* [2005] ECR II-2685 **223**

T-485/04 *COBB v Commission* (2005) (unreported) **232**

C-1/05 *Jia v Migrationsverket* [2007] ECR I-1 **343–344**

C-39/05 and C-52/05 *Sweden and Turco v Council* [2009] QB 269 **102**

C-77/05 and C-137/05 *United Kingdom v Council* [2007] All ER (D) 268 (Dec) **374–375**

C-110/05 *Commission v Italy (Trailers)* [2009] ECR I-519 **558, 559, 581, 588**

C-142/05 *Mickelsson and Roos* [2009] ECR I-4273 **558**

C-274/05 *Commission v Greece* [2008] ECR I-7969 **494**

C-291/05 *Minister voor Vreemdelingenzaken en Integratie v RNG Eind* [2007] ECR I-10719 **327, 332, 333**

C-320/05 *Olsen v Commission* [2007] ECR I-131 **231–232**

C-341/05 *Laval un Partneri Ltd v Svenska Byggnadsarbetareförbundet and Others* [2008] All ER (EC) 166 **446, 456–458**

C-411/05 *Félix Palacios de la Villa* v *Cortefiel Servicios SA* [2007] ECR I-8531 174
C-464/05 *Geurts* v *Belgische Staat* [2007] ECR I-9325 439
Case C-438/05 *International Transport Workers' Federation and The Finnish Seamen's Union* (*Viking Line ABP*) [2007] ECLI:EU:C:772 446, 551, 552
C-11/06 and C-12/06 *Morgan* v *Bezirksregierung Köln and Iris Butcher* v *Landrat des Kreises Düren* [2008] All ER (EC) 851 371–372
C-80/06 *Carp Snc di L Moleri e* v *Corsi* v *Ecorad Srl* [2007] ECR I-4473 281
C-221/06 *Stadtgemeinde Frohnleiten and Gemeindebetriebe Frohnleiten GmbH* v *Bundesminister für Landund Forstwirtschaft, Umwelt und Wasserwirtschaft* [2007] ECR I-9643 515–516
C-265/06 *Commission* v *Portugal* [2008] ECR I-2245 558
C-303/06 *Coleman* (*S*) v *Attridge Law and Steve Law* [2008] ECR I-5603 126, 132
C-311/06 *Consiglio degli Ingegneri* v *Minisero della Giustizia, Marco Cavallera* [2009] All ER (D) 255 (Jan) 495, 500
C-319/06 *Commission* v *Luxembourg* [2008] ECR I-4324 461
C-351/06 *Commission* v *Italy* (unreported) 463
T-139/06 *France* v *Commission* [2011] ECR II-7315 260–261
C-42/07 *Liga Portuguesa de Futebol Profissional and Bwin International Ltd* v *Departamento de Jogos da Santa Casa da Misericórdia de Lisboa* [2009] ECR I-7633 469
C-121/07 *Commission* v *France* [2008] ECR I-9159 262
C-158/07 *Förster* v *Hoofddirectie van de Informatie Beheer Group* [2009] All ER (EC) 399 370
C-171/07, C-172/07 *Commission* v *Italy* (*Apothekerkammer des Saarlandes and Others and Helga Neumann-Seiwert* v *Saarland and Ministerium für Justiz, Gesundheit und Soziales* [2009] ECR 0000 463–464
C-205/07 *Gysbrechts and Santurel Inter BVBA* [2008] ECR I-9947 560
C-316/07, C-358/07 to C-360/07, C-409/07 and C-410/07 *Markus Stoss and Others* v *Wetteraukreis and Kulpa Automatenservice Asperg GmbH and Others* v *Land Baden-Württemberg* [2010] ECR I-8069 469
C-369/07 *Greece* v *Commission* [2009] ECR 5073 259
C-531/07 *Fachverband der Buch-und Medienwirtschaft* v *LIBRO Handelsgesellschaft mbH* [2009] 2009 I-03717 559
C-555/07 *Kücükdeveci* v *Swedex GmbH & Co. KG* [2010] ECR I-365 132, 174–175
C-570/07 and C-571/07 *Pérez* (*José Manuel*) *and María del Pilar Chao Gómez* v *Consejería de Salud y Servicios Sanitarios, Principado de Asturias* [201] ECR I-4629 464–465
C-22/08, C-23/08 *Vatsouras and Koupatantze* v *Arbeitsgemeinschaft (ARGE) Nürnberg* [2009] ECR I-4585 415, 417

C-28/08P *Bavarian Lager Co Ltd* v *Commission* [2010] ECR I-6055, [2011] All ER (EC) 1007 101
C-28/09 *Commission* v *Austria* ('*Austrian Lorries II*') [2010] EU:C:2010:770 580
C-34/09 *Zambrano* (*Ruiz*) v *Office national de l'emploi* [2011] ECR I-1177 327, 331, 346–348, 379
C-46/08 *Carmen Media Group Ltd* v *Land Schleswig-Holstein and Others* [2010] ECR I-8149 469–470
C-64/08 *Criminal proceedings against Engelmann* [2010] ECR I-8129 470–471
C-92/09, C-93/09 *Volker und Markus Schecke and Eifert* (Joined Cases) [2010] ECR I-11063 128
C-127/08 *Metock and Others* v *Minister for Justice, Equality and Law Reform* [2009] All ER (EC) 40 350–351
C-135/08 *Rottmann* v *Bayern* [2010] ECR I-1449 327–330, 346
C-195/08 *Inga Rinau* (*PPU*) [2008] ECR I-5271 205
C-195/08 PPU *Inga Rinau* [2008] 203
C-203/08 and C-258/08 *Sporting Exchange* v *Minister van Justitie and Ladbrokes Betting & Gaming and Ladbrokes International* v *Stichting de Nationale Sporttotalisator* [2010] ECR I-4695 469
C-212/08 *Zeturf Ltd* v *Premier Ministre* [2011] ECR I-5633 469
C-310/08 *London Borough of Harrow* v *Ibrahim* [2010] ECR I-1065 425–426
C-317/08 to C-320/08 *Alassini and Others* (Joined Cases) [2010] ECR I-2213 135
C-325/08 *Olympique Lyonnais SASP* v *Olivier Bernard and Newcastle United FC* [2010] ECR I-2177 394–395, 460
C-403/08, C-429/08 *Football Association Premier League and Others* v *QC Leisure and Others; Karen Murphy* v *Media Protection Services Ltd* [2011] ECR I-9083 474
C-447/08, C-448/08 *Criminal proceedings against Otto Sjöberg and Anders Gerdin* [2010] ECR I-6921 469
C-480/08 *Teixeira* v *London Borough of Lambeth* [2010] ECR I-1107 425–426
C-506/08P *Sweden* v *MyTravel and Commission* [2011] ECR I-6237, [2012] All ER (EC) 968 101
C-512/08 *Commission* v *France* [2010] ECR I-8833 481
C-108/09 *Ker-Optika bt* v *ÁNTSZ Dél-dunántúli Regionális Intézete* [2010] ECR I-12213 558
C-118/09 *Koller* [2010] ECR I-13627 496
C-119/09 *Société fiduciaire nationale d'expertise comptable* v *Ministre du Budget, des Comptes publics et de la Fonction publique* [2011] ECR I-2551 479
C-137/09 *Josemans* v *Burgemeester van Maastricht* [2010] ECR I-5433 485–486
C-162/09 *Lassal* [2010] ECR I-9217 340
C-236/09 *Association belge des Consommateurs Test-Achats ASBL and Others* v *Conseil des ministres* [2011] ECR I-773 132
C-255/09 *Commission* v *Portugal* [2011] ECR I-547 481
C-345/09 *van Delft and Others* [2010] ECR I-9879 385

C-347/09 *Criminal proceedings against Jochen Dickinger and Franz Ömer* [2011] ECR I-8185 470
C-407/09 *Greece v Commission* [2011] ECR I-2467 259
C-424/09 *Toki v Ipourgos Ethnikis Pedias kai Thriskevmaton* [2011] ECR I-2587 496
C-434/09 *McCarthy* [2011] ECR I-3375 331, 333, 334, 335, 347, 348
C-542/09 *Commission v Netherlands* [2012] 3 CMLR 643, ECJ 427–428, 429
T-33/09 *Portugal v Commission* [2011] ECR II-1429 261
C-34/10 *Brüstle (Oliver) v Greenpeace e.V* [2011] ECR I-9821 126
C-72/10 and C-77/10 *Marcello Costa and Ugo Cifone* (not yet reported) 468–469
C-163/10 *Aldo Patriciello (Criminal proceedings against)* [2011] ECR I-7565, [2012] 1 CMLR 274 84, 86
C-211/10 *PPU Doris Povse v Mauro Alpago* [2010] ECR I-6673 133
C-282/10 *Dominguez (Maribel) v Centre Informatique du Centre Ouest Atlantique, Préfet de la région Centre* [2012] 2 CMLR 437, [2012] IRLR 321, ECJ 275, 317
C-347/10 *Salemink v Raad van bestuur van het Uitvoeringsinstituut Werknemersverzekeringen* [2011] EUECJ C-347/10 390
C-357/10 to C-359/10 *Duomo Gpa Srl and Others v Comune di Baranzate and Others* [2012] 3 CMLR 205 473–474
C-364/10 *Hungary v Slovakia (supported by European Commission, intervening)* [2013] All ER (EC) 666, [2013] 1 CMLR 651 248
C-379/10 *Commission v Italy* [2011] ECR I-180 307
C-416-10 *Križan v Slovenská inšpekcia životného prostredia* [2013] ECLI:EU:C:2013 191
C-610/10 *Commission v Spain* [2012] EUECJ C-610/10 (06 September 2012 259
C-617/10 *Åklagaren v Åkerberg Fransson* [2013] 2 CMLR 1273, [2013] STC 1905 125–126, 135
T-18/10 *Inuit Tapiriit Kanatami and Others v Parliament and Council (appealed C – 583/11 P)* [2011] ECR II-5599 228–229, 230
T-262/10 *Microban International Ltd and Microban (Europe) Ltd v Commission* [2011] ECR II-7697 228
C-4/11 *Bundesrepublik Deutschland v Kaveh Puid* [2013] EU:C:2013:740 127
C-5/11 *Donner, Re* [2012] All ER (D) 65 (Jul) 570
C-31/11 *Scheunemann* [2012] EU:C:2012:481 439
C-35/11 *Test Claimants in the FII Group Litigation v Commissioners of Inland Revenue and The Commissioners for Her Majesty's Revenue and Customs* [2013] 1 CMLR 1365, [2012] All ER (D) 229 (Nov) 473
C-40/11 *Iida v Stadt Ulm* [2013] 2 WLR 788, [2013] 1 CMLR 1289, ECJ 347, 355
C-171/11 *Fra.bo SpA v Deutsche Vereinigung des Gas - und Wasserfaches eV (DVGW)* [2012] EU:C:2012:453 550–551, 552, 587

C-176/11 *HIT and HIT LARIX v Bundesminister für Finanzen* [2012] EUECJ C-176/11 470
C-186/11 and C-209/11 *Stanleybet International Ltd and Others v Ypourgos Oikonomias kai Oikonomikon and Others* [2013] 2 CMLR 672, [2013] All ER (D) 216 (Jan) 470
C-256/11 *Dereci and Others v Bundesministerium für Inneres* [2011] EU:C:2011:734 347
C-279/11 *Commission v Ireland* [2012] All ER (D) 223 (Dec) 259
C-292/11P *Commission v Portugal* [2014] EU:C:2014:3 261
C-312/11 *Commission v Italy* [2013] EU:C:2013:446 134
C-374/11 *Commission v Ireland* [2012] All ER (D) 248 (Dec) 259
C-385/11 *Elbal Moreno v Instituto Nacional de la Seguridad Social* [2012] EU:C:2012:746 132
C-399/11 *Melloni v Ministerio Fiscal* [2013] EU:C:2013:107 135
C-523/11, C-585/11 *Prinz v Region Hannover and Seeberger v Studentenwerk Heidelberg* [2013] All ER (D) 73 (Nov), ECJ 372
C-539/11 *Ottica New Line di Accardi Vincenzo v Comune di Campobello di Mazara* [2013] EU:C:2013:591 465–466
C-575/11 *Nasiopoulos v Ipourgos Igias kai Pronoias* [2014] 1 CMLR 133, [2013] All ER (D) 252 (Jul) 491–492, 497
C-583/11 *P Inuit Tapiriit Kanatami and Others v European Parliament and Council* [2013] EU:C:2013:625 232, 237
T-346/11 and T-347/11 *Bruno Gollnisch v Parliament* [2011] EUECJ T-346/11 (30 September 2011) 85–86
C-20/12 *Giersch and others v Luxembourg* [2014] 1 CMLR 11, [2013] All ER (D) 179 (Sep), ECJ 428–429
C-86/12 *Alokpa, Moudoulou and Moudoulou v Ministre du Travail, de l'Emploi et de l'Immigration* [2013] EU:C:2013:645 347
C-87/12 *Ymerga v Ministre du Travail, de l'Emploi et de l'Immigration* [2013] EU:C:2013:291 344
C-131/12 *Google Spain v AEPD and Mario Costeja Gonzalez* [2014] EU:C:2014:317 128
C-140/12 *Pensionsversicherungsanstalt v Brey* [2013] EU:C:2013:565 358, 365, 367, 369, 417
C-199/12 *Minister voor Immigratie en Asiel* [2013] EU:C:2013:720 131
C-204/12 to C-208/12 *Essent Belgium NV v Vlaamse Reguleringsinstantie voor de Elektriciteits- en Gasmarkt (Joined Cases)* [2014] EU:C:2014:2192 569
C-245/12 Commission *v* Poland (Action brought on 16 May 2012) 263
C-274/12 P *Telefónica v Commission* [2013] ECLI:EU:C:2013:852 229

C-293/12, C-594/12 *Digital Rights Ireland and Seitlinger and Others* (Joined Cases) [2014] EU:C:2014:238 128

C-367/12 *Sokoll-Seebacher* [2014] EU:C:2014:68 447–448, 474

C-378/12 *Onuekwere* v *Secretary of State for the Home Department* [2014] EU:C:2014:13 340–342, 361

C-400/12 *Secretary of State for the Home Department* v *G* [2014] EU:C:2014:9 341, 360–361

C-423/12 *Reyes* v *Migrationsverket* [2014] EU:C:2014:16 344–345, 422

C-456/12, C-457/12 *O, B, S and G* v *Minister voor Immigratie, Integratie en Asiel* [2014] EU:C:2014:135 332–336, 348, 378, 396

C-483/12 *Pelckmans Turnhout NV* v *Walter Van Gastel Balen NV and Others* [2014] EU:C:2014:304 556

C-507/12 *Saint Prix (Jessy)* v *Secretary of State for Work and Pensions* [2014] EU:C:2014:2007 392

C-522/12 *Isbir* v *DB Services GmbH* [2013] EU:C:2013:711 456

C-544/12 *Commission* v *Poland (Action brought on 27 November 2012)* 263

C-573/12 *Ålands Vindkraft AB* v *Energimyndigheten* [2014] EU:C:2014:2037 569

E-15/12 *Wahl (Request for an Advisory Opinion from EFTA Court)* [2014] OJ C 118, 25.4.2013, p. 36–36 359–360

T-562/12 *Dalli* v *Commission* [2015] EU:T:2015:270 65

C-2/13 Opinion on the compatibility of the draft accession agreement (ECHR) with the EU Treaties ECJ 18 December 2014 [2014] EU:C:2014:48 42, 90, 122

C-39/13 to C-41/13 *SCA Group Holding* (Joined cases) [2014] EU:C:2014:1758 439

C-148/13 to C-150/13 *Staatssecretaris van Veiligheid en Justitie* [2014] EU:C:2014:2406 124–125

C-202/13 *McCarthy (Sean Ambrose) and Others* v *Secretary of State for the Home Department* [2014] EU:C:2014:2450 349

C-316/13 *Fenoll* v *APEI* [2015] EU:C:2015:200 390

C-320/13 *Commission* v *Poland* [2014] EU:C:2014:2441 263

C-333/13 *Dano (Elisabeta), Florin Dano* v *Jobcenter Leipzig* [2014] EU:C:2014:2358 366–369, 417

C-456~13 *P T & L Sugars and Sidul Açúcares* v *Commission* [2015] ECLI:EU:2015:284 229, 230

C-593/13 *Rina Services and Others* [2015] EU:C:2015:399 461

T-115/13 *Dennekamp* v *Parliament* [2015] EU:T:2015:497 102–103

C-62/14 *Gauweiler* [2015] EU:C:2015:400 172

C-67/14 *Jobcenter Berlin Neukölln* v *Nazifa, Sonita, Valentina and Valentino Alimanovic* [2015] EU:C:2015:597 367, 368, 415–417, 418

C-72/14, C-197/14 *X & Van Dijk* (Joined Cases) [2015] EU:C:2015:564 200–201

C-105/14 *Taricco and Others* – Taricco I [2015] EU:C:2015:555 118, 135, 173

C-160/14 *Ferreira da Silva and others* [2015] EU:C:2015:565 194, 201

C-165/14 *Rendón Marín* v *Administración del Estado* [2016] EU:C:2016:675 348

C-168/14 *Grupo Itevelesa SL and Others* v *OCA Inspección Técnica de Vehículos SA and Generalidad de Cataluña* [2015] EU:C:2015:685 474–475

C-198/14 *Visnapuu* v *Kihlakunnansyyttäjä (Helsinki) and Suomen valtio* [2015] ECLI:EU:C:2015:751 559

C-218/14 *Kuldip Singh and Others* v *Minister for Justice and Equality* [2015] EU:C:2015:476 338, 356, 357

C-293/14 *Hiebler* v *Schlagbauer* [2015] EU:C:2015:843 443

C-299/14 *Garcia-Nieto and others* [2016] EU:C:2016 417, 418

C-304/14 *Secretary of State for the Home Department* v *CS* [2016] EU:C:2016:674 348

C-333/14 *Scotch Whisky Association and Others* v *Advocate General for Scotland* [2015] EU:C:2015:845 558–559, 581, 588

C-341/14 *Harmsen* v *Burgemeester van Amsterdam (Request for a preliminary ruling)* [2014] OJ C 339, 29.9.2014, p. 9–10 475–476

C-358/14 *Poland* v *Parliament and Council* [2016] EU:C:2016:323 167

C-458/14, C-67/15 *Promoimpresa srl and Mario Melis and Others* (Joined Cases) [2016] EU:C:2016:558 449

C-477/14 *Pillbox 38(UK) Limited* v *Secretary of State for Health* [2016] EU:C:2016:324 167

C-547/14 *Philip Morris Brands SARL and Others* v *Secretary of State for Health* [2016] EU:C:2016:325 167

C-613/14 *James Elliott Construction Limited* v *Irish Asphalt Limited* [2016] EU:C:2016:821 551, 553

C-115/15 *Secretary of State for the Home Department* v *NA* [2016] EU:C:2016:487 346, 356–357

C-133/15 *Chavez-Vilchez and Others* [2017] EU:C:2017:354 348, 379

C-221/15 *Colruyt* [2016] ECLI:EU:C:704 559

C-413/15 *Farrell* v *Whitty* [2017] EU:C:2017:745 290–293, 313, 552

Opinion 2/15 Opinion on FTA between EU and Singapore [2017] EU:C:2017:376 179

T-600~15 *PAN Europe* v *Commission* [2016] ECLI:EU:T:2016:601 222

C-31/16 *Visser Vastgoed Beleggingen BV* v *Raad van de gemeente Appingedam* (unreported) 447, 448

C-165/16 *Lounes* [2017] EU:C:2017:862 334–335

C-426/16 *Liga van Moskeeën en Islamitische Organisaties Provincie Antwerpen VZW and Others* v *Vlaams Gewest* [2016] 129

C-42/17 *MAS and MB* – Taricco II [2017] EU:C:2017:936 118, 135, 173

C-221/17 *Tjebbes (M.G.) and Others* v *Minister van Buitenlandse Zaken* [2019] ECLI:EU:C:2019:189 328–331, 368

C-322/17 *Bogatu* v *Minister for Social Protection* [2019] ECLI:EU:C:2019:102 367

C-483/17 *Tarola (Neculai)* v *Minister for Social Protection* [2019] ECLI:EU:C:2019:309 **392**
C-591/17 *Austria* v *Germany* [2019] ECLI:EU:C:2019:504 **248**
C-713/17 *Ayubi* v *Bezirkshauptmannschaft Linz-Land* [2018] ECLI:EU:C:2018:929 **364**
C-129~18 *SM* v *Entry Clearance Officer* [2019] ECLI:EU:C:2019:248 **343**
C-161/18 *Villar Láiz* v *Instituto Nacional de la Seguridad Social* **132**
C-410/18 *Aubriet* [2019] ECLI:EU:C:2019:582 **429**
C-457/18 *Slovenia* v *Croatia* [2020] ECLI:EU:C:2020:65 **248**

C-621/18 *Wightman and Others* [2018] EU:C **13**
C-673/16 *Coman and Others* v *Inspectoratul General pentru Imigrāri* [2018] ECLI:EU:C:2018:385 **132, 343, 418**
C-93/17 *Cresco Investigation* v *Achatizi* [2019] ECLI:EU:C:2019:43 **132**
C-161/18 *Villar Láiz* v *Instituto Nacional de la Seguridad Social* [2019] ECLI:EU: C:2019:382 **132**
C-619/18 *Commission* v *Poland* [2019] ECLI:EU:C:2019:615 **269**
Rosengren (Klas) and Others v *Riksåklagaren* [2007] ECR I-4071 **536**

Table of cases before the Court of Justice of the European Union (alphabetical)

115/81, 116/81 *Adoui and Cornuaille* v *Belgian State* [1982] ECR 1165, [1982] 3 CMLR 631 359, 360, 485, 486, 563–564

T-64/01, T-65/01 *Afrikanische Frucht-Compagnie and Internationale Fruchtimport Gesellschaft Weichert & Co* v *Commission* [2004] ECR II-521 241

T-3/93 *Air France* v *Commission* [1995] ECLI:EU:T:45 215

C-617/10 *Åklagaren* v *Åkerberg Fransson* [2013] 2 CMLR 1273, [2013] STC 1905 125–126, 135

C-109/01 *Akrich* [2003] ECR I-9607 350, 351

C-573/12 *Ålands Vindkraft AB* v *Energimyndigheten* [2014] EU:C:2014:2037 569

C-317/08 to C-320/08 *Alassini and Others* (Joined Cases) [2010] ECR I-2213 135

C-358/93, C-416/93 *Aldo Bordessa, Mellado and Maestre* (Criminal Proceedings) [1995] ECR I-361 12

C-163/10 Aldo Patriciello (Criminal proceedings against) [2011] ECR I-7565, [2012] 1 CMLR 274 84, 86

57/65 *Alfons Lütticke (Firma) GmbH* v *Hauptzollamt Sarrelouis* [1966] ECR 205 512, 525, 527

4/69 *Alfons Lütticke GmbH* v *Commission* [1969] ECR 325 239

106/63, 107/63 *Alfred Toepfer and Getreide-Import Gesellschaft* v *Commission* [1965] ECR 405 224–225

6/56, 7/56, 3/57 to 7/57 *Algera and Others* v *Common Assembly* [1957–58] ECR 139 243

C-33/88 *Allué & Coonan* v *Università degli Studi di Venezia* [1989] ECR 1591, [1991] 1 CMLR 283 398, 403

C-86/12 *Alokpa, Moudoulou and Moudoulou* v *Ministre du Travail, de l'Emploi et de l'Immigration* [2013] EU:C:2013:645 347

14/81 *Alpha Steel* v *Commission* [1982] ECR 749 135

C-384/93 *Alpine Investments BV* v *Minister van Financiën* [1995] ECR I-1141 441, 443

106/77 *Amministrazione delle Finanze dello Stato* v *Simmenthal SpA* [1978] ECR 629 173–174, 180

C-281/98 *Angonese* [2000] ECR I-4139 400

C-47/02 *Anker and Others* [2004] 2 CMLR 35 403–404, 430

222/82 *Apple and Pear Development Council* v *K J Lewis Ltd* [1983] ECR 4083 538, 543, 581, 587

C-369/96 *Arblade (Jean-Claude), Arblade & Fils SARL; Bernard Leloup, Serge Leloup, Sofrage SARL* [1999] ECR I-8453 449

C-168/95 *Arcaro* [1997] ECR I-4705 299

C-236/09 *Association belge des Consommateurs Test-Achats ASBL and Others* v *Conseil des ministres* [2011] ECR I-773 132

C-213/90 *Association de Soutien aux Traveilleurs Immigrés* [1991] ECR I-3207, [1993] 3 CMLR 621 130, 400

C-465/93 *Atlanta Fruchthandelgesellschaft GmbH* v *Bundesamt für Ernährung und Forstwirtschaft* [1995] ECR I-3799 266

C-410/18 *Aubriet* [2019] ECLI:EU:C:2019:582 429

271/82 *Auer* v *Ministère Public* [1983] ECR 2727, [1985] 1 CMLR 123 504

155/79 *Australia Mining & Smelting Ltd* v *Commission* [1982] ECR 1575, [1982] 2 CMLR 264 135

C-591/17 *Austria* v *Germany* [2019] ECLI:EU:C:2019:504 248

T-10/93 *A* v *Commission* [1994] ECR II-179 121

C-713/17 *Ayubi* v *Bezirkshauptmannschaft Linz-Land* [2018] ECLI:EU:C:2018:929 364

C-318/00 *Bacardi-Martini and Cellier des Dauphins* [2003] ECR I-905 197–198

C-386/02 *Baldinger* [2004] ECR I-8411 405

C-10/92 *Balocchi* v *Ministero delle Finanze dello Stato* [1993] ECR I-5105, [1995] 1 CMLR 486 197

C-262/88 *Barber* v *Guardian Royal Exchange Assurance Group* [1990] ECR I-1889, [1990] 2 CMLR 513 284

46/76 *Bauhuis* v *Netherlands* [1977] ECR 5 521, 522

C-413/99 *Baumbast and R* v *Secretary of State for the Home Department* [2002] ECR I-7091 338–339, 369, 424, 425, 426

C-28/08P *Bavarian Lager Co Ltd* v *Commission* [2010] ECR I-6055, [2011] All ER (EC) 1007 101, 128

T-383/00 *Beamglow* v *Parliament and Others; and Fedon & Figli and Others* v *Council and Commission* [2006] 2 CMLR 10 240–242

8/81 *Becker* v *Finanzamt Münster-Innenstadt* [1982] ECR 53, [1982] 1 CMLR 499 284

263/86 *Belgium* v *Humbel* [1989] ECR 393, [1989] 1 CMLR 393 441, 478, 480, 506

C-388/95 *Belgium* v *Spain* [2000] ECR I-3123, [2002] 1 CMLR 755 **248**

C-352/98P *Bergaderm and Goupil* v *Commission* [2000] ECR I-5291 **240–241, 243**

344/87 *Bettray* v *Staatssecretaris van Justitie* [1989] ECR 1621, [1991] 1 CMLR 459 **389, 407**

C-209/03 *Bidar* [2005] ECR I-2119 **369–371**

C-175/88 *Biehl* [1990] ECR I-1779, [1990] 3 CMLR 143 **406**

24/86 *Blaizot* v *University of Liège* [1988] ECR 379, [1989] 1 CMLR 57 **406, 426**

C-570/07 and C-571/07 *Blanco Pérez (José Manuel) and María del Pilar Chao Gómez* v *Consejería de Salud y Servicios Sanitarios, Principado de Asturias* [201] ECR I-4629 **464–465**

C-4/91 *Bleis* v *Ministère de l'Education Nationale* [1991] ECR I-5627, [1994] 1 CMLR 793 **403**

C-234/97 *Bobadilla (Fernandez de)* v *Museo Nacional del Prado and Others* [1999] ECR I-4773 **491, 501, 504**

127/75 *Bobie Getränkvertrieb* v *Hauptzollamt Aachen-Nord* [1976] ECR 1079 **527**

C-101/01 *Bodil Lindqvist* [2003] ECR I-12971 **128**

C-322/17 *Bogatu* v *Minister for Social Protection* [2019] ECLI:EU:C:2019:102 **367**

T-13/04 *Bonde and Others* v *Parliament and Council* [2005] unreported **222**

325/85 *Bond van Adverteerders* [1987] ECR 5041 **441**

T-40/04 *Bonino (Emma) and Others* v *Parliament and Council* [2005] ECR II-2685 **223**

T-218/03–T-240/03 *Boyle and Others* v *Commission* [2006] ECR II-1699 **226**

48/72 *Brasserie de Haecht SA* v *Wilkin (No. 2)* [1973] ECR 77, [1973] CMLR 287 **279**

C-46/93, C-48/93 *Brasserie du Pêcheur SA* v *Germany* [1996] ECR I-1029 **240, 300–305, 317, 597, 604**

87/75 *Bresciani (Conceria Daniele)* v *Amministrazione Italiana delle Finanze* [1976] ECR 129, [1976] 2 CMLR 62 **521**

246/80 *Broekmeulen* v *Huisarts Registratie Commissie* [1981] ECR 2311 **195**

197/86 *Brown* v *Secretary of State for Scotland* [1988] ECR 3205, [1988] 3 CMLR 403 **406–407, 426**

T-346/11 and T-347/11 *Bruno Gollnisch* v *Parliament* [2011] EUECJ T-346/11 (30 September 2011) **85–86**

C-34/10 *Brüstle (Oliver)* v *Greenpeace e.V* [2011] ECR I-9821 **126**

C-4/11 *Bundesrepublik Deutschland* v *Kaveh Puid* [2013] EU:C:2013:740 **127**

C-285/01 *Burbaud* [2003] 3 CMLR 21 **493**

237/78 *Caisse Régionale d'Assurance Maldie de Lille* v *Palermo* [1979] ECR 2645, [1980] 2 CMLR 31 **364**

C-348/96 *Calfa (Donatella)* [1999] ECR I-11 **483–484**

789/79, 790/79 *Calpak SpA and Societa Emiliana Lavorazione Frutta SpA* v *Commission* [1980] ECR 1649 **226**

72/83 *Campus Oil Ltd* v *Minister for Industry and Energy* [1984] ECR 2727, [1984] 3 CMLR 344 **545, 564–565**

T-166/98 *Cantina sociale di Dolianova and Others* v *Commission* [2004] ECR II-3991 **241**

77/72 *Capolongo* v *Azienda Agricola* [1973] ECR 611, [1974] 1 CMLR 230 **523**

C-46/08 *Carmen Media Group Ltd* v *Land Schleswig-Holstein and Others* [2010] ECR I-8149 **469–470**

C-60/00 *Carpenter (Mary)* v *Secretary of State for the Home Department* [2002] ECR I-6279 **128, 441, 452, 506**

C-80/06 *Carp Snc di L Moleri e* v *Corsi* v *Ecorad Srl* [2007] ECR I-4473 **281**

9/74 *Casagrande* v *Landesshauptstadt München* [1974] ECR 773, [1974] 2 CMLR 423 **423**

120/78 *Cassis case. See* **120/78 *Rewe-Zentrale AG* v *Bundesmonopolverwaltung für Branntwein (Cassis de Dijon)***

T-320/00 *CD Cartondruck* v *Council and Commission* [2005] unreported **241–242**

15/74, 16/74 *Centrafarm BV* v *Adriaan de Peiper Winthrop BV (Sterling Drug Case)* [1974] ECR 1147, [1974] 2 CMLR 480 **570–571**

316/85 *Centre Public d'Aide Sociale de Courcelles* v *Lebon* [1987] ECR 2811, [1989] CMLR 337 **343–345, 406, 407, 410, 412, 414, 422–423, 426**

C-133/15 *Chavez-Vilchez and Others* [2017] EU:C:2017:354 **348, 379**

140/79 *Chemial Farmaceutici* v *DAF SpA* [1981] ECR 1 **529–530, 534**

15/70 *Chevally* v *Commission* [1970] ECR 975 **236**

C-194/94 *CIA Security International* v *Signalson and Securitel* [1996] ECR I-2001 **291, 292**

283/81 *CILFIT* v *Ministry of Health* [1982] ECR 3415 **196, 198, 200**

60/84, 61/84 *Cinéthèque SA* v *Fédération Nationale des Cinémas Français* [1985] ECR 2605, [1986] 1 CMLR 365 **536–537, 554, 580**

C-350/96 *Clean Car Autoservice GmbH* v *Landeshauptmann von Wien* [1998] ECR I-2521, [1998] 2 CMLR 637 **383, 478**

T-485/04 *COBB* v *Commission* (2005) (unreported) **232**

T-514/93 *Cobrecaf SA* v *Commission* [1995] ECR II-621 **233**

C-309/89 *Codorniu SA* v *Council* [1994] ECR I-853 **226–227**

193/85 *Co-Frutta Srl* v *Amministrazione delle Finanze dello Stato* [1987] ECR 2085 **526**

C-405/01 *Colegio de Oficiales de la Marina Mercante Española* – not reported (judgment delivered 30 Sep 2003) **403–404**

C-104/91 *Colegio Oficial de Agentes de la Propriedad Inmobiliara* v *Aguirre, Newman and Others* [1992] ECR I-3003 **491**

C-303/06 *Coleman (S)* v *Attridge Law and Steve Law* [2008] ECR I-5603 **126, 132**

C-138/02 *Collins* [2004] ECR I-2703 **412, 413–415, 416, 418**

C-92/92 *Collins* v *Imtrat Handelsgesellschaft GmbH* [1993] ECR I-5145 570
C-221/15 *Colruyt* [2016] ECLI:EU:C:704 559
C-673/16 *Coman and Others* v *Inspectoratul General pentru Imigrări* [2018] ECLI:EU:C:2018:385 132, 343, 418
T-96/92 *Comité Central d'Enterprise de la Société Générale des Grandes Sources and Others* v *Commission and Comité Central d'Enterprise de la Société Anonyme Vittel and Others* v *Commission* [1995] ECR II-1213 222
C-320/03 *Commission* v *Austria ('Austrian Lorries')* [2005] ECR I-9871 579–581
C-28/09 *Commission* v *Austria ('Austrian Lorries II')* [2010] EU:C:2010:770 580
C-150/00 *Commission* v *Austria* [2004] ECR I-3887 577
C-137/92 *Commission* v *BASF AG & Others* [1994] ECR I-2555 67, 234
132/82 *Commission* v *Belgium (Re Customs Warehouses)* [1983] ECR 1649, [1983] 3 CMLR 600 519–520
149/79 *Commission* v *Belgium (Re Public Employees)* [1980] ECR 3881, [1981] 2 CMLR 413 401–402, 443
C-47/93 *Commission* v *Belgium (Re University Fees)* [1994] ECR I-1593 480
77/69 *Commission* v *Belgium* [1969] ECR 237, [1974] 1 CMLR 203 253–254
314/82 *Commission* v *Belgium* [1984] ECR 1543, [1985] 3 CMLR 134 522
239/85 *Commission* v *Belgium* [1986] ECR 3645 282
186/85 *Commission* v *Belgium* [1987] ECR 2029 252
1/86 *Commission* v *Belgium* [1987] ECR 2797, [1989] 1 CMLR 474 253, 300
356/85 *Commission* v *Belgium* [1987] ECR 3299 533
298/86 *Commission* v *Belgium* [1988] ECR 4343 252
C-2/90 *Commission* v *Belgium* [1992] ECR I-4431 516
C-37/93 *Commission* v *Belgium* [1993] ECR I-6295 251, 397, 403, 430
C-87/94 R *Commission* v *Belgium* [1994] ECR I-1395 265–266
C-344/95 *Commission* v *Belgium* [1997] ECR I-1035 411
45/86 *Commission* v *Council (Generalised Tariff Preferences)* [1987] ECR 1493, [1988] 2 CMLR 131 211
C-300/89 *Commission* v *Council (Re Titanium Dioxide Waste)* [1991] ECR I-2867, [1993] 3 CMLR 359 165
22/70 *Commission* v *Council* [1970] ECR 263, [1971] CMLR 335 186, 214
171/78 *Commission* v *Denmark* [1980] ECR 447, [1981] 2 CMLR 688 525
106/84 *Commission* v *Denmark* [1986] ECR 833 526
302/86 *Commission* v *Denmark* [1988] ECR 4607 578
C-432/04 *Commission* v *Edith Cresson* (2006) unreported 64–65
C-265/95 *Commission* v *France ('Angry Farmers')* [1997] ECR I-6959 541–542, 551, 564, 580, 582
167/73 *Commission* v *France (Re French Merchant Seamen)* [1974] ECR 359, [1974] CMLR 216 251, 254, 323, 397

168/78 *Commission* v *France (Re French Taxation of Spirit)* [1980] ECR 347, [1981] 2 CMLR 631 525, 526, 533–534
232/78 *Commission* v *France (Re Sheepmeat)* [1979] ECR 2729, [1980] 1 CMLR 418 264
C-419/03 *Commission* v *France* (unreported) 262, 263
7/71 *Commission* v *France* [1971] ECR 1003, [1972] CMLR 453 250, 252
196/85 *Commission* v *France* [1987] ECR 1597, [1988] 2 CMLR 851 530
216/84 *Commission* v *France* [1988] ECR 793 566
C-64/88 *Commission* v *France* [1991] ECR I-2727 258–260
C-334/94 *Commission* v *France* [1996] ECR I-1307 251
C-1/00 *Commission* v *France* [2001] ECR I-9989 249, 264
C-24/00 *Commission* v *France* [2004] ECR I-1277 577
C-262/02 *Commission* v *France* [2004] ECR I-6569 467
C-304/02 *Commission* v *France* [2005] ECR I-6263 258–260
C-177/04 *Commission* v *France* [2006] AU ER (D) 221 (Mar) 259
C-121/07 *Commission* v *France* [2008] ECR I-9159 262–263
C-512/08 *Commission* v *France* [2010] ECR I-8833 481
18/87 *Commission* v *Germany (animal inspections)* [1988] ECR 5427 521, 522–523, 587
178/84 *Commission* v *Germany ('German Bier')* [1987] ECR 1227, [1988] 1 CMLR 780 567–568, 574–575, 577
C-280/93 *Commission* v *Germany (Re Banana Market)* [1994] ECR I-4873 130, 131, 212
24/62 *Commission* v *Germany (Re Brennwein)* [1963] ECR 63, [1963] CMLR 347 252
249/86 *Commission* v *Germany (Re Housing of Migrant Workers)* [1989] ECR 1263, [1990] 3 CMLR 540 429–430
29/84 *Commission* v *Germany (Re Nursing Directives)* [1985] ECR 1661, [1986] 2 CMLR 579 254, 282, 323, 397
12/74 *Commission* v *Germany* [1975] ECR 181, [1975] 1 CMLR 340 543
153/78 *Commission* v *Germany* [1979] ECR 2555 566
C-195/90 *Commission* v *Germany* [1994] ECR I-3141 264–265
C-422/92 *Commission* v *Germany* [1995] ECR I-1097 252
C-387/99 *Commission* v *Germany* [2004] ECR I-3751 577
C-463/01 *Commission* v *Germany* [2004] ECR I-11705 579
C-341/02 *Commission* v *Germany* [2005] ECR I-2733 455–456
C-244/04 *Commission* v *Germany* [2006] ECR I-885 453
C-132/88 *Commission* v *Greece (Greek car tax)* [1990] ECR I-1567 528–529, 530
C-306/89 *Commission* v *Greece* [1991] ECR I-5863, [1994] 1 CMLR 803 443
C-105/91 *Commission* v *Greece* [1992] ECR I-5871 254

TABLE OF CASES BEFORE THE COURT OF JUSTICE OF THE EUROPEAN UNION (ALPHABETICAL)

C-170/94R *Commission* v *Greece* [1995] ECR I-1819 **265**
C-62/96 *Commission* v *Greece* [1997] ECR I-6725 **477**
C-140/03 *Commission* v *Greece* [2005] ECR I-3177 **439**
C-274/05 *Commission* v *Greece* [2008] ECR I-7969 **494**
C-45/91 *Commission* v *Hellenic Republic* [1992] ECR I-2509 **254, 257**
C-387/97 *Commission* v *Hellenic Republic* [2000] ECR I-5047 **135, 256–258, 270**
249/81 *Commission* v *Ireland (Re 'Buy Irish' Campaign)* [1982] ECR 4005, [1983] 2 CMLR 104 **537–538, 542, 581, 587**
45/87 *Commission* v *Ireland (Re Dundalk Water Supply)* [1988] ECR 4929, [1989] 1 CMLR 225 **548–549**
113/80 *Commission* v *Ireland (Re Restrictions on Importation of Souvenirs)* [1981] ECR 1625, [1982] 1 CMLR 706 **543–544, 562**
61/77R Commission *v* Ireland [1977] ECR 937, [1977] ECR 1411 **264**
55/79 *Commission* v *Ireland* [1980] ECR 481, [1980] 1 CMLR 734 **527**
74/82 *Commission* v *Ireland* [1984] ECR 317 **252**
C-279/11 *Commission* v *Ireland* [2012] All ER (D) 223 (Dec) **259**
C-374/11 *Commission* v *Ireland* [2012] All ER (D) 248 (Dec) **259**
C-171/07, C-172/07 *Commission* v *Italy (Apothekerkammer des Saarlandes and Others and Helga Neumann- Seiwert* v *Saarland and Ministerium für Justiz, Gesundheit und Soziales* [2009] ECR 0000 **463–464**
7/68 *Commission* v *Italy (Re Export Tax on Art Treasures No 1) (Italian Art Case)* [1968] ECR 423, [1969] CMLR 1 **514, 515, 518**
168/85 *Commission* v *Italy (Re Freedom of Establishment)* [1986] ECR 2495, [1988] 1 CMLR 580 **446**
63/86 *Commission* v *Italy (Re Housing Aid)* [1988] ECR 29, [1989] 2 CMLR 601 **479**
184/85 *Commission* v *Italy (similar fruit)* [1987] ECR 4157 **526–527, 532**
C-110/05 *Commission* v *Italy (Trailers)* [2009] ECR I-519 **558, 559, 581, 588**
C-351/06 *Commission* v *Italy* (unreported) **463**
7/61 *Commission* v *Italy* [1961] ECR 317, [1962] CMLR 39 **252**
24/68 *Commission* v *Italy* [1969] ECR 193, [1971] CMLR 611 **518, 520**
31/69 *Commission* v *Italy* [1970] ECR 25 **251**
7/69 *Commission* v *Italy* [1970] ECR 111, [1970] CMLR 97 **252–253**
193/80 *Commission* v *Italy* [1981] ECR 3019 **575**
166/82 *Commission* v *Italy* [1984] ECR 459, [1985] 2 CMLR 615 **254**
154/85 *Commission* v *Italy* [1987] ECR 2717 **541**
C-235/89 *Commission* v *Italy* [1992] ECR I-777, [1992] 2 CMLR 709 **570**
C-272/91 *Commission* v *Italy* [1994] ECR I-1409 **443**
C-439/99 *Commission* v *Italy* [2002] ECR I-305 **252**
C-14/00 *Commission* v *Italy* [2003] ECR I-513 **575**
C-388/01 *Commission* v *Italy* [2003] ECR I-721 **480**
C-131/01 *Commission* v *Italy* [2003] ECR I-1659 **440**
C-119/04 *Commission* v *Italy* [2006] ECR I-6885 **259, 262**
C-379/10 *Commission* v *Italy* [2011] ECR I-180 **307**
C-312/11 *Commission* v *Italy* [2013] EU:C:2013:446 **134**
C-319/06 *Commission* v *Luxembourg* [2008] ECR I-4324 **461**
2/62, 3/62 *Commission* v *Luxembourg and Belgium (Joined Cases)* [1962] ECR 855 **187, 516–517**
89/76 *Commission* v *Netherlands (plant inspections)* [1977] ECR 1355 **521, 522, 587**
339/87 *Commission* v *Netherlands (Re Protection of Wild Birds)* [1990] ECR I-851, [1993] 2 CMLR 360 **254**
C-190/90 *Commission* v *Netherlands* [1992] ECR I-3300 **254**
C-157/94 *Commission* v *Netherlands* [1997] ECR I-5699 **537**
C-542/09 *Commission* v *Netherlands* [2012] 3 CMLR 643, ECJ **427–428, 429**
C-245/12 Commission *v* Poland (Action brought on 16 May 2012) **263**
C-544/12 Commission v Poland (Action brought on 27 November 2012) **263**
C-320/13 *Commission* v *Poland* [2014] EU:C:2014:2441 **263**
C-619/18 *Commission* v *Poland* [2019] ECLI:EU:C:2019:615 **269**
C-275/03 *Commission* v *Portugal* (unreported) **261**
C-171/02 *Commission* v *Portugal* [2004] ECR I-5645 **434, 440**
70/06 *Commission* v *Portugal* [2008] ECLI:EU:C:2008:3 **261**
C-265/06 *Commission* v *Portugal* [2008] ECR I-2245 **558**
C-255/09 *Commission* v *Portugal* [2011] ECR I-547 **481**
C-292/11P *Commission* v *Portugal* [2014] EU:C:2014:3 **261–262**
C-355/90 *Commission* v *Spain, Judgment of 2 August 1993* [1993] ECR I-4221 **254**
C-45/93 *Commission* v *Spain* [1994] ECR I-911 **480**
C-375/92 *Commission* v *Spain* [1994] ECR I-923, [1994] CMLR 500 **250**
C-12/00 *Commission* v *Spain* [2003] ECR I-459 **575**
C-610/10 *Commission* v *Spain* [2012] EUECJ C-610/10 (06 September 2012 **259**
C-56/90 *Commission* v *United Kingdom (Bathing Water Directive)* [1994] 1 CMLR 769 **254**
170/78 *Commission* v *United Kingdom (Re Excise Duties on Wines) (No. 2)* [1983] ECR 2263, [1983] 3 CMLR 512 **531–532, 575**
C-246/89R *Commission* v *United Kingdom (Re Nationality of Fishermen)* [1989] ECR 3125, [1989] 3 CMLR 601 **264**
207/83 *Commission* v *United Kingdom (Re Origin Marking of Retail Goods)* [1985] ECR 1202, [1985] 2 CMLR 259 **547–548**
128/78 *Commission* v *United Kingdom (Re Tachographs)* [1979] ECR 419, [1979] 2 CMLR 45 **254**

124/81 *Commission v United Kingdom (Re UHT Milk)* [1983] ECR 203, [1983] 2 CMLR 1 566
C-30/90 *Commission v United Kingdom* [1992] ECR I-829, [1992] 2 CMLR 709 570
C-382/92, C-383/92 *Commission v United Kingdom* [1994] ECR I-2435 251
169/73 *Compagnie Continentale v Council* [1975] ECLI:EU:1975:13 118, 599
T-29/03 *Comunidad Autónoma de Andalucía v Commission* [2004] ECR II-2923 217
121/85 *Conegate Ltd v Customs and Excise Commissioners* [1986] ECR 1007, [1987] QB 254, [1986] 2 All ER 688 563
C-31/00 *Conseil National de l'Ordre des Architectes v Nicholas Dreesen* [2002] ECR I-663 11
C-311/06 *Consiglio degli Ingegneri v Minisero della Giustizia, Marco Cavallera* [2009] All ER (D) 255 (Jan) 495, 500–501
C-181/90 *Consorgan Lda v Commission* [1992] ECR I-3557 211
56/64, 58/64 *Consten and Grundig GmbH v Commission (joined cases)* [1966] ECR 299, [1966] CMLR 418 569
C-103/88 *Costanzo (Fratelli) v Comune di Milano* [1989] ECR 1839, [1990] 3 CMLR 239 188 247, 287
34/86 *Council v Parliament* [1986] ECLI:EU:1986:291 215
186/87 *Cowan v Le Trésor Public* [1986] ECR 195, [1990] 2 CMLR 613 477, 479–480, 484, 506
C-93/17 *Cresco Investigation v Achatizi* [2019] ECLI:EU:C:2019:43 132
C-64/08 *Criminal proceedings against Engelmann* [2010] ECR I-8129 470–471
C-347/09 *Criminal proceedings against Jochen Dickinger and Franz Ömer* [2011] ECR I-8185 470
C-447/08, C-448/08 *Criminal proceedings against Otto Sjöberg and Anders Gerdin* [2010] ECR I-6921 469
C-401/92, C-402/92 *Criminal Proceedings against Tankstation, 'T Heukske vof and JBE Boermans* [1994] ECR I-2199 556
279/80 *Criminal Proceedings against Webb* [1981] ECR 3305, [1982] 1 CMLR 719 449
231/83 *Cullet* [1985] ECR 305 564
28/62–30/62 *Da Costa en Schaake NV, Jacob Meijer NV, Hoechst-Holland NV v Nederlandse Belastingadministratie* [1963] ECR 31, [1963] CMLR 224 198
T-562/12 *Dalli v Commission* [2015] EU:T:2015:270 65
C-333/13 *Dano (Elisabeta), Florin Dano v Jobcenter Leipzig* [2014] EU:C:2014:2358 366–369, 417
58/80 *Dansk Supermarket A/S v A/S Imerco* [1981] ECR 181 279
8/74 *Dassonville. See Procureur du Roi v Dassonville*
C-13, 113/91 *Debus v Ministère Public* [1992] ECR I-3617 577
C-17/00 *De Coster v Collège des Bourgmestres et Échevins de Watermael-Boitsfort* [2001] ECR I-9445 193
43/75 *Defrenne v SABENA (No. 2)* [1976] ECR 455, [1976] 2 CMLR 98 279, 281

94/82 *De Kikvorsch Groothandel-Import-Export BV* [1983] ECR 497, [1984] 2 CMLR 323 575
C-177/88 *Dekker v Stichting Vormingscentrum voor Jonge Volwassen (VJV-Centrum) Plus* [1990] ECR I-3941 132
T-115/13 *Dennekamp v Parliament* [2015] EU:T:2015:497 102–103
C-256/11 *Dereci and Others v Bundesministerium für Inneres* [2011] EU:C:2011:734 347
5/75 *Deuka* [1975] ECR 759 118
C-322/01 *Deutscher Apothekerverband eV v 0800 Doc-Morris NV and Jacques Waterval* [2003] ECR I-14887 558, 577
C-188/91 *Deutsche Shell AG v Hauptzollamt Hamburg* [1993] ECR I-363 195, 196
240/87 *Deville v Administration des Impôts* [1988] ECR 3513, [1989] 3 CMLR 611 528
C-224/98 *D'Hoop (Marie-Nathalie) v Office national de l'emploi* [2002] 3 CMLR 12 414
267/83 *Diatta v Land Berlin* [1985] ECR 567, [1986] 2 CMLR 164 354, 355
C-293/12, C-594/12 *Digital Rights Ireland and Seitlinger and Others (Joined Cases)* [2014] EU:C:2014:238 128
C-178/94, C-179/94, C-188-190/94 *Dillenkofer and Others v Federal Republic of Germany* [1996] ECR I-4845, [1996] 3 CMLR 469 240, 303, 306
C-282/10 *Dominguez (Maribel) v Centre Informatique du Centre Ouest Atlantique, Préfet de la région Centre* [2012] 2 CMLR 437, [2012] IRLR 321, ECJ 275, 317
13/76 *Donà v Mantero* [1976] ECR 1333 279, 393
C-5/11 *Donner, Re* [2012] All ER (D) 65 (Jul) 570
C-386/96 P *Dreyfus v Commission* [1998] ECR I-2309 221
64/76 *Dumortier Frères v Council* [1976] ECR 3091, [1982] ECR 1733 243
C-357/10 to C-359/10 *Duomo Gpa Srl and Others v Comune di Baranzate and Others* [2012] 3 CMLR 205 473–474
C-21/88 *Du Pont de Nemours Italiana SpA v Unità sanitaria locale Nº 2 di Carrara* [1990] ECLI:EU:C:1990:121 544–545
C-297/88, C-197/89 *Dzodzi v Belgium* [1990] ECR I-3763 87
C-16/94 *Édouard Dubois & Fils SA and Général Cargo Services SA v Garonor Exploitation SA* [1995] ECR I-2421 512
C-385/11 *Elbal Moreno v Instituto Nacional de la Seguridad Social* [2012] EU:C:2012:746 132
C-260/89 *Elleneki Radiophonia Tileorasi (ERT)* [1991] ECR I-2925, [1994] 4 CMLR 540 121, 129
C-17/98 *Emesa Sugar (Free Zone) NV v Aruba* [2000] ECR I-665 92
341/87 *EMI Electrola GmbH v Patricia* [1989] ECR 79, [1989] 2 CMLR 413 571–572
C-127/92 *Enderby v Frenchay Health Authority and Secretary of State for Health* [1993] ECR I-5535 132

C-204/12 to C-208/12 *Essent Belgium NV* v *Vlaamse Reguleringsinstantie voor de Elektriciteits- en Gasmarkt (Joined Cases)* [2014] EU:C:2014:2192 569

T-85/94 *Eugénio Branco Lda* v *Commission* [1995] ECR II-45 211

C-332/92 *Eurico Italia Srl* v *Ente Nazionale Risi* [1994] ECR I-711, [1994] 2 CMLR 580 197

13/83 *European Parliament* v *Council (Re Transport Policy)* [1985] ECR 1513, [1986] 1 CMLR 138 234, 235, 236

C-65/90 *European Parliament* v *Council* [1992] ECR I-4953 145

C-295/90 *European Parliament* v *Council* [1992] ECR I-5299, [1992] 3 CMLR 281 165, 210, 234

C-388/92 *European Parliament* v *Council* [1994] ECR I-2067 211, 234

C-417/93 *European Parliament* v *Council* [1995] ECR I-1185 145

C-111/97 *Evobus Austria* v *Niederosterreichischer* [1998] ECR I-5411 298

C-531/07 *Fachverband der Buch-und Medienwirtschaft* v *LIBRO Handelsgesellschaft mbH* [2009] 2009 I-03717 559

C-413/15 *Farrell* v *Whitty* [2017] EU:C:2017:745 290–293, 313, 552

70/87 *Fediol* v *Commission* [1989] ECR 1781, [1991] 2 CMLR 489 149

433/85 *Feldain* v *Services Fiscaux du Departement du Haut-Rhin* [1987] ECR 3521 528

C-411/05 *Félix Palacios de la Villa* v *Cortefiel Servicios SA* [2007] ECR I-8531 174

C-316/13 *Fenoll* v *APEI* [2015] EU:C:2015:200 390

C-160/14 *Ferreira da Silva and others* [2015] EU:C:2015:565 194, 201

C-367/93, C-377/93 *FG Roders BV ea* v *Inspecteur der Inverrechten en Accijnzen* [1999] ECR I-2229 533

T-69/00 *FIAMM and FIAMM Technologies* v *Council and Commission* [2006] 2 CMLR 9 241–242

27/80 *Fietje* [1980] ECR 3839, [1981] 3 CMLR 722 576–577

C-279/93 *Finanzamt Köln-Altstadt* v *Schumacker* [1995] ECR I-225 406, 478

27/67 *Fink-Frucht GmbH* v *Hauptzollamt Munchen-Landsbergerstrasse* [1968] ECR 223, [1968] CMLR 445 535

32/75 *Fiorinin (née Cristini)* v *SNCF* [1975] ECR 1085, [1976] 1 CMLR 573 405, 423

314/85 *Firma Foto-Frost* v *Hauptzollamt Lubeck-Ost* [1987] ECR 4199 191, 196

T-28/02 *First Data* v *Commission* [2006] 4 CMLR 4 220

C-290/04 *FKP Scorpio Konzertproduktionen GmbH* v *Finanzamt Hamburg-Eimsbuttel* [2007] 1 CMLR 937 473

6/64 *Flaminio Costa* v *Ente Nazionale per l'Energia Elettrica (ENEL)* [1964] ECR 585, [1964] CMLR 425 14–15, 49, 171, 176, 180, 184, 201

244/80 *Foglia* v *Novello (No. 2)* [1981] ECR 3045, [1982] 1 CMLR 585 197–198

C-403/08, C-429/08 *Football Association Premier League and Others* v *QC Leisure and Others; Karen Murphy* v *Media Protection Services Ltd* [2011] ECR I-9083 474–476

C-170/88 *Ford España* v *Spain* [1989] ECR 2305 520

C-158/07 *Förster* v *Hoofddirectie van de Informatie Beheer Group* [2009] All ER (EC) 399 370

C-188/89 *Foster* v *British Gas* [1990] ECR I-3313, [1990] 2 CMLR 833 287–290, 292, 310–313, 317, 605

C-171/11 *Fra.bo SpA* v *Deutsche Vereinigung des Gas - und Wasserfaches eV (DVGW)* [2012] EU:C:2012:453 550–551, 552, 587

C-327/91 *France* v *Commission* [1994] ECR I-2533, [1995] 4 CMLR 621 166

T-139/06 *France* v *Commission* [2011] ECR II-7315 260–261

C-345/95 *France* v *European Parliament* [1997] ECR I-5215 83

141/78 *France* v *United Kingdom* [1979] ECR 2923, [1980] 1 CMLR 6 248

C-6/90, C-9/90 *Francovich and Bonifaci* v *Republic of Italy* [1991] ECR I-5357, [1993] 2 CMLR 66 284–286, 299–301, 303, 304, 308, 317, 597, 604

272/80 *Frans-Nederlandse* [1981] ECR 3277, [1982] 2 CMLR 497 566

77/76 *Fratelli Cucchi* v *Avez SpA* [1977] ECR 987 523

34/73 *Fratelli Variola SpA* v *Amministrazione Italiana delle Finanze* [1973] ECR 981 280

113/75 *Frecasseti* v *Amministrazione delle Finanze dello Stato* [1976] ECR 983 195

T-279/03 *Galileo* v *Commission* [2006] ECR II-1291 242

C-243/01 *Gambelli* [2003] ECRI-1303 469

C-299/14 *Garcia-Nieto and others* [2016] EU:C:2016 417, 418

T-288/00 *Gardena Hotels and Comitato Venezia Vuole Vivere* v *Commission* [2005] unreported 220

C-69–79/96 *Garofalo and Others* v *Ministero della Sanità and Others* [1998] 1 CMLR 1087 194

C-62/14 *Gauweiler* [2015] EU:C:2015:400 172

C-55/94 *Gebhard (Reinhard)* v *Consiglio dell'Ordine degli Avvocati e Procuratori di Milano* [1995] ECR I-4165 439, 459–460, 505, 506

2/73 *Geddo (Riseria Luigi)* v *Ente Nazionale Risi* [1973] ECR 865, [1974] 1 CMLR 13 535–536, 602

C-157/99 *Geraets-Smits* v *Stichting Ziekenfonds and Peerbooms* v *Stichting CZ Groep Zorgverzekeringen* [2001] ECR I-5473 441, 481, 482

281/85, 283/85–285/85, 287/85 *Germany, France, Netherlands, Denmark and the United Kingdom* v *Commission* [1987] ECR 3203, [1988] 1 CMLR 11 162–163

C-122/95 *Germany* v *Council* [1998] ECR I-973 233

C-376/98 *Germany* v *Parliament and Council 'Tobacco advertising I'* [2000] ECR I-8419 4–5

C-380/03 *Germany* v *Parliament and Council 'Tobacco advertising II'* [2006] ECR I-11573 166–167

C-464/05 *Geurts* v *Belgische Staat* [2007] ECR I-9325 439

C-43/99 *Ghislain Leclerc, Alina Deaconescu* v *Caisse Nationale des Prestations Familiales* [2000] ECR I-4265 409

C-20/12 *Giersch and others* v *Luxembourg* [2014] 1 CMLR 11, [2013] All ER (D) 179 (Sep), ECJ 428–429

105/75 *Giuffrida* v *Council* [1976] ECR 1395 212

C-231/89 *Gmurzynska-Bscher* [1990] ECR I-4003 173 190, 196

C-131/12 *Google Spain* v *AEPD and Mario Costeja Gonzalez* [2014] EU:C:2014:317 128

9/70 *Grad (Franz)* v *Finanzamt Traunstein* [1970] ECR 975 280–283, 317

C-351/92 *Graff* v *Hauptzollamt Köln-Rheinau* [1994] ECR I-3361 132

293/83 *Gravier* v *City of Liège* [1985] ECR 593, [1985] 3 CMLR 1 426, 480

240/86 *Greece* v *Commission* [1998] ECR 1835 250

C-369/07 *Greece* v *Commission* [2009] ECR 5073 259

C-407/09 *Greece* v *Commission* [2011] ECR I-2467 259

C-95/01 *Greenham* v *ABEL* [2004] ECR I-1333 577

C-322/88 *Grimaldi* v *Fonds des Maladies Professionelles* [1989] ECR 4407, [1991] ECR 4402 148, 195, 296

379/87 *Groener* v *Minister for Education* [1989] ECR 3967, [1990] 1 CMLR 401 400

T-301/00 *Groupe Fremaux and Palais Royal* v *Council and Commission* [2005] ECR II-25 241–242

T-228/00, T-229/00, T-242/00, T-243/00, T-245/00 to T-248/00, T-250/00, T-252/00, T-256/00 to T-259/00, T-267/00, T-268/00, T-271/00, T-275/00, T-276/00, T-281/00, T-287/00 & T-296/00 *Gruppo Ormeggiatori del porto di Venezia and Others* v *Commission* [2005] ECR II-787 220

C-168/14 *Grupo Itevelesa SL and Others* v *OCA Inspección Técnica de Vehículos SA and Generalidad de Cataluña* [2015] EU:C:2015:685 474–475

C-184/99 *Grzelczyk* v *Centre Public d'aide sociale d'Ottignies-Louvain-la-Neuve* [2001] ECR I-6193 326, 367, 368–369, 407

131/85 *Gül* v *Regierungspräsident Düsseldorf* [1986] ECR 1573, [1987] 1 CMLR 501 357, 398

C-205/07 *Gysbrechts and Santurel Inter BVBA* [2008] ECR I-9947 560

C-90/94 *Haahr Petroleum Ltd* v *Abenra Havn* [1998] 1 CMLR 771 524

C-319/92 *Haim* v *Kassenzahnarztliche Vereinigung Nordrhein* [1994] ECR I-425, [1994] 2 CMLR 169 490, 491, 500–501, 506

C-156/91 *Hansa Fleisch Ernst Mundt* [1992] ECR I-5567 281

148/77 *Hansen Jun & O. C. Balle GmbH & Co.* v *Hauptzollamt Flensburg* [1978] ECR 1787, [1979] 1 CMLR 604 526, 530

C-341/14 *Harmsen* v *Burgemeester van Amsterdam (Request for a preliminary ruling)* [2014] OJ C 339, 29.9.2014, p. 9–10 475–476

C-189/95 *Harry Franzen* [1997] ECR I-5909, [1998] 1 CMLR 1231 539

79/83 *Harz* v *Deutsche Tradax* [1984] ECR 1921 295, 298, 317

44/79 *Hauer* v *Land Rheinland-Pflaz* [1979] ECR 3727, [1980] 3 CMLR 42 131

104/81 *Hauptzollamt Kupferberg & Cie KG* [1982] ECR 3461, [1983] 1 CMLR 1 151

C-399/92, C-409/92, C-425/92; C-34/93, C-50/93, C-78/93 *Helmig and Others* v *Stadt Lengerich* [1994] ECR I-5727 190

C-293/14 *Hiebler* v *Schlagbauer* [2015] EU:C:2015:843 443

C-176/11 *HIT and HIT LARIX* v *Bundesminister für Finanzen* [2012] EUECJ C-176/11 470

C-275/92 *HM Customs and Excise Commissioners* v *Schindler* [1994] ECR I-1039, [1995] 1 CMLR 4 442–443, 515, 562

83/77 *HNL* v *Council and Commission* [1978] ECR 1209, [1978] 3 CMLR 566 239

C-238/98 *Hocsman (Hugo Fernando)* v *Ministre de l'Emploi et de la Solidarité* [2000] ECR I-6623 501–503

46/87 *Hoechst AG* v *Commission* [1989] ECR 2859, [1991] 4 CMLR 410 135

75/63 *Hoekstra (née Unger)* v *Bestuur der Bedrijfsvereniging voor Detailhandel en Ambachten* [1964] ECR 177, [1964] CMLR 319 385

107/76 *Hoffmann La Roche* v *Centrafarm* [1977] ECR 597, [1977] 2 CMLR 334 191

112/84 *Humblot* v *Directeur des Services Fiscaux* [1985] ECR 1367, 1986 2 CMLR 363 527–528, 529, 534

C-292/92 *Hunermund* [1993] ECR I-6787 556

C-364/10 *Hungary* v *Slovakia (supported by European Commission, intervening)* [2013] All ER (EC) 666, [2013] 1 CMLR 651 248

60/81 *IBM* v *Commission* [1981] ECR 2639, [1981] 3 CMLR 635 214

C-264/96 *ICI* [1998] ECR I-4695 439

94/74 *IGAV* v *ENCC* [1975] ECR 699, [1976] 2 CMLR 37 523

C-40/11 *Iida* v *Stadt Ulm* [2013] 2 WLR 788, [2013] 1 CMLR 1289, ECJ 347, 355

C-2/88 *Imm Zwartveld* [1990] ECR I-3365 87

C-53/95 *Inasti* [1996] ECR I-703 439

C-195/08 PPU *Inga Rinau* [2008] ECR I-5271 205

C-56/01 *Inizan* – not reported (judgment delivered 23 Oct 2003) 482

T-139/02 *Institouto N. Avgerinopoulou and Others* v *Commission* [2004] ECR II-875 217, 222

C-129/96 *Inter-Environnement Wallonie ASBL* [1997] ECR I-7411 285

66/80 *International Chemical Corporation* [1981] ECR 1191 198–199

11/70 *Internationale Handelsgesellschaft GmbH* [1970] ECR 1125, [1972] CMLR 255 117, 121, 171–173

41/70–44/70 *International Fruit Company BV* v *Commission* [1975] ECR 1393 221, 225

51/71–54/71 *International Fruit Company* v *Produktschap voor Grotenten en Fruit (No. 2)* [1971] ECR 1107 541

21/72–24/72 *International Fruit Co NV* v *Produktschap voor Groenren en Fruit (No. 3)* [1972] ECR 1219, [1975] 2 CMLR 1 149

Case C-438/05 *International Transport Workers' Federation and The Finnish Seamen's Union (Viking Line ABP)* [2007] ECLI:EU:C:772 446, 551, 552

T-18/10 *Inuit Tapiriit Kanatami and Others* v *Parliament and Council (appealed C – 583/11 P)* [2011] ECR II-5599 228–229

63/76 *Inzirillo* v *Caisse d'Allocations Familiales de l'Arondissement de Lyon* [1976] ECR 2057, [1978] 3 CMLR 596 422

C-258/04 *Ioannidis* [2005] ECR I-8275 415

36/80 *Irish Creamery Milk Suppliers Association* v *Ireland* [1981] ECR 735, [1981] 2 CMLR 455 197

C-522/12 *Isbir* v *DB Services GmbH* [2013] EU:C:2013:711 456

788/79 *Italian State* v *Gilli and Andres* [1980] ECR 2071, [1981] 1 CMLR 146 573

32/65 *Italy* v *Commission* [1966] ECR 389, [1969] CMLR 39 236

C-113/94 *Jacquier* v *Directeur Général des Impôts* [1995] ECR I-4203 528

C-97/98 *Jägerskiöld (Peter)* v *Torolf Gustafsson* [1999] ECR I-7319 440, 514–516

C-613/14 *James Elliott Construction Limited* v *Irish Asphalt Limited* [2016] EU:C:2016:821 551, 553

T-222/99, T-327/99 & T-329/99 *Jean Claude Martinez et al.* v *Parliament* [1999] ECR II-3397, [2001] ECR II-2823 82

T-177/01 *Jégo-Quéré et Cie SA* v *Commission* [2002] ECR II-2365 227

C-1/05 *Jia* v *Migrationsverket* [2007] ECR I-1 343–344

C-67/14 *Jobcenter Berlin Neukölln* v *Nazifa, Sonita, Valentina and Valentino Alimanovic* [2015] EU:C:2015:597 367, 368, 415–417, 418

C-7/95 *John Deere Ltd* v *Commission* [1998] ECR I-3111 88

222/84 *Johnston* v *Chief Constable of the Royal Ulster Constabulary (RUC)* [1986] ECR 1651 122, 135, 247

243/84 *John Walker* v *Ministeriet for Skatter of Afgifter* [1986] ECR 875, [1987] 2 CMLR 275 534, 535

237/82 *Jongeneel Kaas BV* v *Netherlands* [1984] ECR 483 561

C-137/09 *Josemans* v *Burgemeester van Maastricht* [2010] ECR I-5433 485–486

C-356/98 *Kaba* v *Secretary of State for the Home Department* [2000] ECR I-2623 420–421

C-466/00 *Kaba* v *Secretary of State for the Home Department* [2003] ECR I-2219 421

C-253–258/96 *Kampelmann* v *Landschaftsverband Westfalen-Lippe and Others* [1997] ECR I-6907 285, 289, 290

C-267/91, C-268/91 *Keck and Mithouard* (joined cases) [1993] ECR I-6097, [1995] 1 CMLR 101 186, 555–559, 580, 581, 588

139/85 *Kempf* v *Staatssecretaris van Justitie* [1986] ECR 1741, [1987] 1 CMLR 764 388, 430

C-108/09 *Ker-Optika bt* v *ÁNTSZ Dél-dunántúli Regionális Intézete* [2010] ECR I-12213 558

C-114/96 *Kieffer (Rene) and Romain Thill* [1997] ECR I-3629 12

70/81 *Kloppenburg* [1984] ECR 1075 118, 599

115/78 *Knoors* v *Secretary of State for Economic Affairs* [1979] ECR 399, [1979] 2 CMLR 357 504

C-224/01 *Köbler* [2003] ECR I-10239 305–307, 317, 398, 399

C-118/09 *Koller* [2010] ECR I-13627 496

C-405/98 *Konsumentombudsmannen (KO)* v *Gourmet International Products AB (GIP)* [2001] ECR I-1795 466–467, 557

C-299/95 *Kremzow* v *Austria* [1997] ECR I-2629 122

C-416/10 *Križan* v *Slovenská inšpekcia životného prostredia* [2013] ECLI:EU:C:2013 191

175/84 *Krohn & Co Import-Export GmbH KG* v *Commission* [1987] ECR 97, [1987] 1 CMLR 745 243

C-555/07 *Kücükdeveci* v *Swedex GmbH & Co. KG* [2010] ECR I-365 132, 174–175

C-453/00 *Kühne & Heitz* [2004] ECR I-837 199

33/79 *Kuhner* v *Commission* [1980] ECR 1671 119

C-218/14 *Kuldip Singh and Others* v *Minister for Justice and Equality* [2015] EU:C:2015:476 338, 356, 357

C-18/90 *Kziber (Bahia)* v *ONEM* [1991] ECR I-199 151

T-151/00 *Laboratoire du Bain* v *Council and Commission* [2005] ECR II-23 241–242

T-147/00 *Laboratoires Servier* v *Commission* [2003] ECR II-85 166

T-74/92 *Ladbroke Racing (Deutschland) GmbH* v *Commission* [1995] ECR II-115 235

39/86 *Lair* v *University of Hannover* [1988] ECR 3161, [1989] 3 CMLR 545 391, 406, 426, 480

C-64, 65/96 *Land Nordrhein-Westfalen* v *Uecker; Jacquei* v *Land Nordrhein-Westfalen* [1997] ECR I-3171 326

C-162/09 *Lassal* [2010] ECR I-9217 340

C-341/05 *Laval un Partneri Ltd* v *Svenska Byggnadsarbetareförbundet and Others* [2008] All ER (EC) 166 446, 456–458

66/85 *Lawrie-Blum* v *Land Baden-Württemberg* [1986] ECR 2121, [1987] 3 CMLR 389 386, 388, 402–403, 430

C-412/93 *Leclerc-Siplec* [1995] ECR I-179 556

C-226/97 *Lemmens* [1998] ECR I-3711 299

T-353/00 *Le Pen* v *Parliament* [1992] ECLI:EU:T:1992:154 215

C-208/03P *Le Pen* v *Parliament* [2005] ECR I-6051 215

53/81 *Levin* v *Staatssecretaris van Justitie* [1982] ECR 1035, [1982] 2 CMLR 454 385, 387–388, 430, 596

C-42/07 *Liga Portuguesa de Futebol Profissional and Bwin International Ltd* v *Departamento de Jogos da Santa Casa da Misericórdia de Lisboa* [2009] ECR I-7633 469

C-426/16 *Liga van Moskeeën en Islamitische Organisaties Provincie Antwerpen VZW and Others* v *Vlaams Gewest* [2016] 129

C-310/08 *London Borough of Harrow* v *Ibrahim* [2010] ECR I-1065 425–426

246/81 *Lord Bethell* v *Commission* [1982] ECR 2277, [1982] 3 CMLR 300 236

C-165/16 *Lounes* [2017] EU:C:2017:862 334–335

C-320/93 *Lucien Ortscheit GmbH* v *Eurim-Pharm GmbH* [1994] ECR I-5243 561, 569

286/82, 26/83 *Luisi and Carbone* v *Ministero del Tesoro* [1984] ECR 377, [1985] CMLR 5226/83, [1989] ECR 2445 441, 477, 480, 506

C-213/88 and C-39/89 *Luxembourg* v *European Parliament* [1991] ECLI:EU:C:1991:449 215

C-99/00 *Lyckeskog, Kenny Roland* [2002] ECR I-4839 202, 203

129/79 *Macarthys Ltd* v *Smith* [1980] ECR 1275, [1980] 2 CMLR 205, [1979] ICR 785 309–310, 317

C-144/04 *Mangold* v *Helm* [2005] ECR I-9981 174, 175, 285

C-72/10 and C-77/10 *Marcello Costa and Ugo Cifone* (not yet reported) 468–469

29/72 *Marimex SpA* v *Italian Finance Administration* [1972] ECR 1309, [1973] CMLR 486 523

C-446/03 *Marks & Spencer* [2005] ECR I-10837 472–473

C-316/07, C-358/07 to C-360/07, C-409/07 and C-410/07 *Markus Stoss and Others* v *Wetteraukreis and Kulpa Automatenservice Asperg GmbH and Others* v *Land Baden-Württemberg* [2010] ECR I-8069 469

14/69 *Markus* v *Hauptzollamt Hamburg-Jonas* [1969] ECR 349 186

C-106/89 *Marleasing SA* v *La Commercial Internacional de Alimentacion SA* [1990] ECR I-4135, [1992] 1 CMLR 305 295–298, 314–317, 597, 598

152/84 *Marshall* v *Southampton & South West Hampshire Area Health Authority* [1986] ECR 723, [1986] 1 CMLR 688 286, 287–289, 292, 293, 299, 308, 310, 311, 314, 317, 597

C-271/91 *Marshall* v *Southampton and South-West Hampshire Area Health Authority (No. 2)* [1993] ECR I-4367, [1993] 3 CMLR 293, [1993] 4 All ER 586 293

85/96 *Martinez Sala* v *Freistaat Bayern* [1998] ECLI:EU:C:1998:217 326, 364

37/79 *Marty SA* v *Estée Lauder SA* [1980] ECR 2481, [1981] 2 CMLR 143 279

C-42/17 *MAS and MB* – Taricco II [2017] EU:C:2017:936 118, 135, 173

C-202/13 *McCarthy (Sean Ambrose) and Others* v *Secretary of State for the Home Department* [2014] EU:C:2014:2450 349

C-434/09 *McCarthy* [2011] ECR I-3375 331, 333, 334, 335, 347, 348

C-399/11 *Melloni* v *Ministerio Fiscal* [2013] EU:C:2013:107 135

C-400/02 *Merida* [2004] ECR I-8471 399

C-127/08 *Metock and Others* v *Minister for Justice, Equality and Law Reform* [2009] All ER (EC) 40 350–351

C-369/90 *Micheletti and Others* [1992] ECR I-4239 327

76/72 *Michel S* v *Fonds national de reclassement social des handicaps* [1973] ECR 457 405

C-142/05 *Mickelsson and Roos* [2009] ECR I-4273 558

T-262/10 *Microban International Ltd and Microban (Europe) Ltd* v *Commission* [2011] ECR II-7697 228

136/78 *Ministère Public* v *Auer* [1979] ECR 437, [1070] 2 CMLR 373 504

286/86 *Ministère Public* v *Deserbais* [1988] ECR 4907, [1989] 1 CMLR 576 575, 576

207/78 *Ministère Public* v *Even and ONPTS* [1979] ECR 2019, [1980] 2 CMLR 71 405–406

137/84 *Ministère Public* v *Mutsch* [1985] ECR 2681, [1986] 1 CMLR 648 405

C-199/12 *Minister voor Immigratie en Asiel* [2013] EU:C:2013:720 131

C-291/05 *Minister voor Vreemdelingenzaken en Integratie* v *RNG Eind* [2007] ECR I-10719 327, 332, 333

152/85 *Misset* v *Council* [1987] ECR 223 233

C-235/92 P *Montecatini SpA* v *the Commission* [1999] ECR I-4539 135

C-416/00 *Morellato* [2003] ECR I-9343 556

C-11/06 and C-12/06 *Morgan* v *Bezirksregierung Köln and Iris Butcher* v *Landrat des Kreises Düren* [2008] All ER (EC) 851 371–372

C-313/01 *Morgenbesser* [2004] 1 CMLR 24 491

35/82, 36/82 *Morson and Jhanjan* v *Netherlands* [1982] ECR 3723, [1983] 2 CMLR 221 330, 385–386, 418, 430

7/75 *Mr and Mrs F* v *Belgian State* [1975] ECR 679, [1975] 2 CMLR 382

120/86 *Mulder* v *Minister van Landbouw en Visserij* [1988] ECR 2321, [1989] 2 CMLR 1 118–119

C-394/92 *Municipality of Almelo and Others* v *Energiebedvijf NV* [1994] ECR I-1477 193–194

222/83 *Municipality of Differdange and Others* v *Commission* [1984] ECR 2889 22

C-575/11 *Nasiopoulos* v *Ipourgos Igias kai Pronoias* [2014] 1 CMLR 133, [2013] All ER (D) 252 (Jul) 491–492, 497

T-138/89 *NBV* v *Commission* [1992] ECRII-2181 220

C-293/93 *Neeltje* v *Houtwipper* [1994] ECR I-4249 577

T-113/89 *Nefarma* v *Commission* [1990] ECR II-797 215

C-153/02 *Neri (Valentina)* v *European School of Economics (ESE Insight World Education System Ltd)* [2003] ECR I-13555 503, 505

C-377/98 *Netherlands* v *European Parliament and Council of the European Union* [2001] ECR I-7079 126, 127

6/54 *Netherlands* v *High Authority* [1954–56] ECR 103 212

59/85 *Netherlands* v *Reed* [1986] ECR 1283, [1987] 2 CMLR 448 422

C-413/01 *Ninni-Orasche* [2004] 1 CMLR 19 **388, 391**

C-54/88, 91/88, 14/89 *Nino, Prandini & Goti, Pierini* [1990] ECR I-3537, [1992] 1 CMLR 383 **504**

4/73 *Nold KG* v *Commission* [1974] ECR 491, [1974] 2 CMLR 338 **121, 131**

102/81 *Nordsee Deutsche Hochsee fischerei GmbH* v *Reederei Mond Hochsee fischerei AG* [1982] ECR 1095 **191–192**

C-234/99 *Nygård* [2002] ECR I-3657 **524**

C-456/12, C-457/12 *O, B, S and G* v *Minister voor Immigratie, Integratie en Asiel* [2014] EU:C:2014:135 **332–336, 348, 378, 396**

T-466/93, T-469/93, T-473/93, T-477/93 *O'Dwyer and Others* v *Council* [1996] 2 CMLR 148 **118**

155/80 *Oebel* [1981] ECR 1993, [1983] 1 CMLR 390 **554**

104/75 *Officier van Justitie* v *De Peijper* [1976] ECR 613, [1976] 2 CMLR 271 **566**

80/86 *Officier van Justitie* v *Kolpinghuis Nijmegen BV* [1987] ECR 3969, [1989] 2 CMLR 18 **118, 299**

174/82 *Officier van Justitie* v *Sandoz BV* [1983] ECR 2445, [1984] 3 CMLR 43 **562, 567, 568**

T-326/99 *Olivieri* v *Commission and European Agency for the Evaluation of Medicinal Products OJ* [2003] ECR II-6053 **219**

T-17/02 *Olsen* v *Commission (under appeal, Case C-320/05P)* [2005] ECR II-2031 **232–233**

C-320/05 *Olsen* v *Commission* [2007] ECR I-131 **231–232**

C-325/08 *Olympique Lyonnais SASP* v *Olivier Bernard and Newcastle United FC* [2010] ECR I-2177 **394–395**

C-36/02 *OMEGA* [2004] ECR I-9609 **126, 482–483, 582**

C-340/97 *Omer Nazli and Others* v *Stadt Nurnburg* [2000] ECR I-957 **135**

C-378/12 *Onuekwere* v *Secretary of State for the Home Department* [2014] EU:C:2014:13 **340–342, 361**

82/77 *Openbaar Ministerie of the Netherlands* v *Van Tiggele* [1978] ECR 25, [1978] 2 CMLR 528 **550**

118/86 *Openbaar Ministerie* v *Nertsvoederfabriek Nederland BV* [1987] ECR 3883, [1989] 2 CMLR 436 **561**

1/94 Opinion of the Court of 15 Nov 1994 [1995] ECR I-2363 **247**

1/76 Opinion of the Court of 26 April 1977 [1977] ECR 741 **163**

C-1/91 Opinion on Draft Agreement between EEC and EFTA [1991] ECR I-6079 **110, 111**

Opinion 2/15 Opinion on FTA between EU and Singapore [2017] EU:C:2017:376 **179**

C-2/13 Opinion on the compatibility of the draft accession agreement (ECHR) with the EU Treaties ECJ 18 December 2014 [2014] EU:C:2014:48 **42, 90, 122**

C-539/11 *Ottica New Line di Accardi Vincenzo* v *Comune di Campobello di Mazara* [2013] EU:C:2013:591 **465–466**

C-13/94 *P./ S. and Cornwall County Council* [1996] ECR I-2143 **132**

T-600/15 *PAN Europe* v *Commission* [2016] ECLI:EU:T:2016:601 **222**

C-91/92 *Paola Faccini Dori* v *Recreb SRL* [1994] ECR I-3325 **287, 308**

C-337/95 *Parfums Christian Dior BV* v *Evora BV* [1997] ECR I-6013 **201, 203**

24/67 *Parke, Davis and Co* v *Probel, Reese, Beintema-Interpharm and Centrafarm* [1968] EU:C:1968:11 **569**

C-156/93 *Parliament* v *Commission* [1995] ECR I-2019 **212, 214**

C-70/88 *Parliament* v *Council (Chernobyl)* [1991] ECR I-2041, [1992] 1 CMLR 91 **188**

C-181, 248/91 *Parliament* v *Council and Commission (Re Aid to Bangladesh)* [1993] ECR I-3685, [1994] 3 CMLR 317 **216**

294/83 *Parti Ecologiste ('Les Verts')* v *European Parliament* [1986] ECLI:EU:1986:166 **215**

11/77 *Patrick* v *Ministre des Affaires Culturelles* [1977] ECR 1199 **488, 489**

15/79 *PB Groenveld BV* v *Produktschap voor Vee en Vlees* [1979] ECR 3409, [1981] 1 CMLR 207 **560**

C-209/94 *P Buralux SA* v *Council* [1996] ECR I-615 **227**

C-483/12 *Pelckmans Turnhout NV* v *Walter Van Gastel Balen NV and Others* [2014] EU:C:2014:304 **556**

C-140/12 *Pensionsversicherungsanstalt* v *Brey* [2013] EU:C:2013:565 **358, 365, 367, 369, 416, 417**

C-397/01 to 403/01 *Pfeiffer and Others* (Joined Cases) [2004] ECR I-8835 **296, 297, 298**

C-547/14 *Philip Morris Brands SARL and Others* v *Secretary of State for Health* [2016] EU:C:2016:325 **167**

T-377, T-379, T-380/00; T-260, T-272/01 *Philip Morris International and Others* v *Commission* [2003] ECR II-1 **216**

C-477/14 *Pillbox 38(UK) Limited* v *Secretary of State for Health* [2016] EU:C:2016:324 **167**

C-583/11 *P Inuit Tapiriit Kanatami and Others* v *European Parliament and Council* [2013] EU:C:2013:625 **232, 237**

11/82 *Piraiki-Patraiki, A E and Others* v *Commission* [1985] ECR 207 **221–222, 225–226**

25/62 *Plaumann & Co* v *Commission* [1963] ECR 95, [1964] CMLR 29 **223–228, 231, 237, 243**

C-358/14 *Poland* v *Parliament and Council* [2016] EU:C:2016:323 **167**

43/71 *Politi SAS* v *Italian Ministry of Finance* [1971] EU:C:1971:122 **280**

T-33/09 *Portugal* v *Commission* [2011] ECR II-1429 **261**

C-211/10 *Povse (Doris)* v *Mauro Alpago* [2010] ECR I-6673 **133**

14/86 *Pretore di Saló* [1987] ECR 2545 **298, 317**

C-523/11, C-585/11 *Prinz* v *Region Hannover and Seeberger* v *Studentenwerk Heidelberg* [2013] All ER (D) 73 (Nov), ECJ **372**

53/76 *Procureur de la République Besancon* v *Bouhelier* [1977] ECR 197, [1977] 1 CMLR 436 **460, 560**

8/74 *Procureur du Roi* v *Dassonville* [1974] ECR 837, [1974] 2 CMLR 436 540, 541, 542, 546, 548, 559, 560, 587, 599

48/75 *Procureur du Roi* v *Royer* [1976] ECR 497, [1976] 2 CMLR 619 188, 410

C-458/14, C-67/15 *Promoimpresa srl and Mario Melis and Others* (Joined Cases) [2016] EU:C:2016:558 449

148/78 *Pubblico Ministero* v *Ratti* [1979] ECR 1629, [1980] 1 CMLR 96 292

C-69/93, C-258/93 *Punto Casa SpA and Promozioni Polivalenti Venete Soc coop arl* v *Sindacos del Comunes di Capena and Torri di Quartesolo* (Joined Cases) [1994] ECR I-2355 556

C-67/98 *Questore di Verona* v *Diego Zenatti* [1999] ECR I-7289 467–469

C-23/89 *Quietlynn Ltd* v *Southend-on-Sea Borough Council* [1990] ECR I-3059, [1990] 3 CMLR 55 554

C-372/04 *R (on the application of Yvonne Watts)* v *Bedford Primary Care Trust and the Secretary of State for Health* [2006] 3 CMLR 5 482

C-309/02 *Radlberger Getränke and S. Spitz* [2004] ECR I-11763 579

C-357/89 *Raulin* v *Netherlands Ministry for Education and Science* [1992] ECR I-1027, [1994] 1 CMLR 227 388, 391, 406, 426

T-341/02 *Regione Siciliana* v *Commission* (under appeal, Case C-417/04P) [2004] unreported 222

C-417/04 *Regione Siciliana* v *Commission* [2006] All ER (D) 11 (May) 217–218

C-165/14 *Rendón Marín* v *Administración del Estado* [2016] EU:C:2016:675 348

120/78 *Rewe-Zentrale AG* v *Bundesmonopolverwaltung für Branntwein (Cassis de Dijon)* [1979] ECR 649, [1979] 3 CMLR 494 545–546, 552, 554, 555, 556, 572–573, 574, 578, 581, 588, 599, 602

45/75 *Rewe-Zentrale des Lebensmittel-Grosshandels Gmbh* v *Hauptzollamt Emmerich* [1976] ECR 181 526

4/75 *Rewe-Zentralfinanz* v *Landwirtschaft-skammer* [1975] ECR 843, [1977] 1 All ER 599 541

C-423/12 *Reyes* v *Migrationsverket* [2014] EU:C:2014:16 344–345, 422

2/74 *Reyners* v *Belgian State* [1974] ECR 631, [1974] 2 CMLR 305 278, 317, 439, 443–446, 487

166/73 *Rheinmühlen-Düsseldorf* ('*Rheinmühlen* I') [1974] ECLI:EU:C:1974:3 181

C-157/02 *Rieser Internationale Transporte GmbH* v *Autobahnen und Schnellstraßen-Finanzierungs-AG (Asfinag)* [2004] ECR I-1477 289, 290

C-593/13 *Rina Services and Others* [2015] EU:C:2015:399 461

C-152/03 *Ritter-Coulais* v *Finanzamt Germersheim* [2006] All ER (EC) 613 399–400

138/79 *Roquette Frères* v *Council* [1980] ECR 3333 144–145, 211

C-170/04 *Rosengren (Klas) and Others* v *Riksåklagaren* [2007] ECR I-4071 536

C-135/08 *Rottmann* v *Bayern* [2010] ECR I-1449 327–330, 346

C-113/89 *Rush Portuguesa Lda* v *Office National d'Immigration* [1990] ECR 1417, [1991] 2 CMLR 818 149

36/75 *Rutili* v *Ministère de l'Intérieur* [1975] ECR 1219, [1975] 1 CMLR 573 130, 400

30/77 *R* v *Bouchereau* [1977] ECR 1999, [1977] 2 CMLR 800 359, 484

34/79 *R* v *Henn and Darby* [1979] ECR 3795, [1980] 1 CMLR 246, [1981] AC 850, [1980] 2 All ER 166 536, 562–563

C-392/93 *R* v *HM Treasury, ex parte British Telecommunications plc* [1996] All ER (EC) 411 302

81/87 *R* v *HM Treasury, ex parte Daily Mail and General Trust plc* [1988] ECR 5483 471–472

C-292/89 *R* v *Immigration Appeal Tribunal, ex parte Antonissen* [1991] ECR I-745, [1991] 2 CMLR 373 202, 410–411

C-370/90 *R* v *Immigration Appeal Tribunal and Surinder Singh, ex parte Secretary of State for the Home Department* [1992] All ER 798, [1992] ECR I-4265, [1992] 3 CMLR 358 332, 333, 336, 378, 395, 421–422, 504

C-330/91 *R* v *IRC, ex parte Commerzbank* [1993] ECLI:EU:C:303 472

C-1/96 *R* v *Ministry of Agriculture, Fisheries and Food, ex parte Compassion in World Farming Ltd* [1998] ECR I-1251, [1998] 2 CMLR 661 561

C-5/94 *R* v *Ministry of Agriculture, Fisheries and Food, ex parte Hedley Lomas (Ireland) Ltd* [1996] ECR I-2553, [1996] All ER (EC) 493 240, 304–306, 317

157/79 *R* v *Pieck* [1980] ECR 2171, [1980] 3 CMLR 220, [1981] QB 571, [1981] 3 All ER 46 323

266/87, 267/87 *R* v *Royal Pharmaceutical Society of Great Britain, ex parte API* [1989] ECR 1295, [1989] 2 CMLR 751 538

C-48/93 *R* v *Secretary of State for Transport, ex parte Factortame Ltd and Others* [1996] ECR I-1029 300–301, 597, 604

C-221/89 *R* v *Secretary of State for Transport, ex parte Factortame (No. 1)* [1991] ECR I-3905, [1991] 3 CMLR 601 310, 438–439

C-213/89 *R* v *Secretary of State for Transport, ex parte Factortame (No. 2)* [1990] ECR I-2433, [1991] 1 AC 603, [1990] 3 CMLR 375, HL 188, 266, 303–305, 436

7/78 *R* v *Thompson* [1978] 1 CMLR 47, [1980] QB 229, [1980] 2 All ER 102 564

C-118/96 *Safir* v *Skattemyndigheten i Dalarnas Lan* [1998] ECR I-1897 443

T-269/00 *Sagar* v *Commission* [2005] unreported 220

C-507/12 *Saint Prix (Jessy)* v *Secretary of State for Work and Pensions* [2014] EU:C:2014:2007 392

C-347/10 *Salemink* v *Raad van bestuur van het Uitvoeringsinstituut Werknemersverzekeringen* [2011] EUECJ C-347/10 390

87/77, 130/77, 22/83, 9/84, 10/84 *Salerno and Others* v *Commission and Council (Joined Cases)* [1985] ECR 2523 237

C-39/13 to C-41/13 *SCA Group Holding* (Joined cases) [2014] EU:C:2014:1758 439

C-31/11 *Scheunemann* [2012] EU:C:2012:481 439

12/63 *Schlieker (née Diepenbruck* v *High Authority* [1963] ECR 85, [1963] CMLR 281 87

C-516/99 *Schmid (Walter)* [2002] ECR I-4573 130, 193

C-112/00 *Schmidberger* v *Austria* [2003] ECR I-5659 130, 551–552, 582

T-167/01 *Schmitz-Gotha Fahrzeugwerke* v *Commission* [2003] ECR II-1875 218–219

C-15/96 *Schöning-Kougebetopoulou* v *Freie und Hansestadt Hamburg* [1998] ECR I-47, [1998] 1 CMLR 931 397

C-279/93 *Schumacher* [1995] ECR I-225 406, 478

C-333/14 *Scotch Whisky Association and Others* v *Advocate General for Scotland* [2015] EU:C:2015:845 558–559, 581, 588

122/84 *Scrivner and Cole* v *Centre Public d'Aide Sociale de Chastre* [1985] ECR 1027, [1987] 3 CMLR 638 404–405, 413

C-304/14 *Secretary of State for the Home Department* v *CS* [2016] EU:C:2016:674 348

C-400/12 *Secretary of State for the Home Department* v *G* [2014] EU:C:2014:9 341, 360–361

C-115/15 *Secretary of State for the Home Department* v *NA* [2016] EU:C:2016:487 346, 356–357

C-39/93P *SFEI and Others* v *Commission* [1994] ECR I-2681 216, 234

92/78 Simmenthal [1979] ECR 777 237

70/77 *Simmenthal* v *Amministrazione delle Finanze dello Stato* [1978] 3 CMLR 670 197

C-422/01 *Skandia and Ramstedt* [2004] 1 CMLR 4 554

C-457/18 *Slovenia* v *Croatia* [2020] ECLI:EU:C:2020:65 248

C-129/18 *SM* v *Entry Clearance Officer* [2019] ECLI:EU:C:2019:248 343

T-88/01 *Sniace* v *Commission* [2005] ECR II-1165 220

2, 3/69 *Sociaal Fonds voor de Diamantarbeiders* v *SA Ch. Brachfeld & Sons* [1969] ECR 211, [1969] CMLR 335 518

C-323/93 *Société Civile Agricole du Centre d'Insémination de la Crespelle* v *Coopérative d'Elevage de la Mayenne* [1994] ECR I-5077 539

C-119/09 *Société fiduciaire nationale d'expertise comptable* v *Ministre du Budget, des Comptes publics et de la Fonction publique* [2011] ECR I-2551 479

C-159/90 *Society for the Protection of the Unborn Child Ireland Ltd (SPUC)* v *Grogan* [1991] ECR I-4685, [1991] 3 CMLR 849 129, 441–442, 562

T-432/93, T-434/93 *Socurte Lda and Others* v *Commission* [1995] ECR II-45 211

C-367/12 *Sokoll-Seebacher* [2014] EU:C:2014:68 447–448, 474

152/73 *Sotgiu* v *Deutsche Bundespost* [1974] ECR 153 401, 403

C-350/92 *Spain* v *Council* [1995] ECR I-1985 570

C-145/04 *Spain* v *United Kingdom* [2006] ECR I-7917, [2007] 1 CMLR 87 248

C-203/08 and C-258/08 *Sporting Exchange* v *Minister van Justitie and Ladbrokes Betting & Gaming and Ladbrokes International* v *Stichting de Nationale Sporttotalisator* [2010] ECR I-4695 469

C-148/13 to C-150/13 *Staatssecretaris van Veiligheid en Justitie* [2014] EU:C:2014:2406 124–125

C-221/06 *Stadtgemeinde Frohnleiten and Gemeindebetriebe Frohnleiten GmbH* v *Bundesminister für Landund Forstwirtschaft, Umwelt und Wasserwirtschaft* [2007] ECR I-9643 515–516

C-186/11 and C-209/11 *Stanleybet International Ltd and Others* v *Ypourgos Oikonomias kai Oikonomikon and Others* [2013] 2 CMLR 672, [2013] All ER (D) 216 (Jan) 470

29/69 *Stauder* v *City of Ulm* [1969] ECR 419, [1969] CMLR 112 120

197/84 *Steinhauser* v *City of Biarritz* [1985] ECR 1819, [1986] 1 CMLR 53 436

78/76 *Steinike und Weinlig* [1977] ECR 595 519, 587

196/87 *Steymann* v *Staatssecretaris van Justitie* [1988] ECR 6159, [1989] 1 CMLR 449 389, 430

T-174/95 *Svenska Journalist-forbundet* v *Council of European Union* [1998] ECR I-2289, [1998] 3 CMLR 645 217

C-39/05 and C-52/05 *Sweden and Turco* v *Council* [2009] QB 269 102

C-506/08P *Sweden* v *MyTravel and Commission* [2011] ECR I-6237, [2012] All ER (EC) 968 101

C-192/89 *SZ Service* v *Staatsecretaris van Justitie* [1990] ECR I-3461, [1992] 2 CMLR 57 247

C-456/13 P *T & L Sugars and Sidul Açúcares* v *Commission* [2015] ECLI:EU:2015:284 229–232

C-105/14 *Taricco and Others* – Taricco I [2015] EU:C:2015:555 118, 135, 173

C-483/17 *Tarola (Neculai)* v *Minister for Social Protection* [2019] ECLI:EU:C:2019:309 392

C-154/93 *Tawil-Albertini* v *Ministre des Affaires Sociales* [1994] ECR I-451 499–501, 503

5/77 *Tedeschi* v *Denkavit Commerciale srl* [1977] ECR 1555 561–562

C-480/08 *Teixeira* v *London Borough of Lambeth* [2010] ECR I-1107 425–426

C-274/12 P *Telefónica* v *Commission* [2013] ECLI:EU:C:2013:852 229

C-320–322/90 *Telemarsicabruzzo SpA* v *Circostel and Others* [1993] ECR I-393 197

C-110/01 *Tennah-Durez* [2003] ECR I-6239 502–503, 505

C-422-424/93 *Teres Zabala Erasun and Others* v *Instituto Nacional de Empleo* [1995] 1 CMLR 861 198

C-18/95 *Terhoeve* v *Inspecteur van de Belastingdienst Particulieren/Ondernemingen Buitenland* [1999] ECR I-345 396

C-35/11 *Test Claimants in the FII Group Litigation* v *Commissioners of Inland Revenue and The Commissioners*

for Her Majesty's Revenue and Customs [2013] 1 CMLR 1365, [2012] All ER (D) 229 (Nov) 473
C-171/95 Tetik v Land Berlin [1997] ECR I-329 391
71/76 Thieffry v Conseil de l'Ordre des Avocats à la Cour de Paris [1977] ECR 765, [1977] 2 CMLR 373 279, 487–488, 489, 501, 506
221/17 Tjebbes (M.G.) and Others v Minister van Buitenlandse Zaken [2019] ECLI:EU:C:2019:189 328–331, 368
C-424/09 Toki v Ipourgos Ethnikis Pedias kai Thriskevmaton [2011] ECR I-2587 496
C-145/88 Torfaen Borough Council v B & Q plc (Sunday Trading Case) [1989] ECR 3851, [1990] 1 CMLR 337 554, 580
C-173/03 Traghetti del Mediterraneo SpA v Italy [2006] not reported 306–307
C-456/02 Trojani v CPAS [2004] ECR I-7573 389, 390
C-188/92 TWD Textilwerke Deggendorf v Germany [1994] ECR I-833 237–238
222/86 UNECTEF v Heylens and Others [1987] ECR 4097, [1989] 1 CMLR 901 120, 600
T-489/93 Unifruit Hellas v Commission [1994] ECR II-1201 239
C-443/98 Unilever Italia SpA v Central Food SpA [2000] ECR I-7535 291, 292
C-50/00P Unión de Pequeños Agricultores v Council of the European Union (supported by the Commission) [2002] ECR I-6677 208, 227–228, 231, 232
C-415/93 Union Royale Belge des Sociétés de Football/ Association ASBL v Bosman [1995] ECR I-4921 393–394, 460
175/73 Union Syndicale v Council [1974] ECR 917, [1975] 1 CMLR 131 130
C-77/05 and C-137/05 United Kingdom v Council [2007] All ER (D) 268 (Dec) 374–375
68/86 United Kingdom v Council of the European Communities [1988] ECR 855 75
C-84/94 United Kingdom v Council of the European Union (Working Time Directive) [1996] ECR I-5755 244–245
33/74 Van Binsbergen v Bestuur van de Bedrijfsvereniging voor de Metaalnijverheid [1974] ECR 1299, [1975] 1 CMLR 298 440, 445–446, 458–459
C-345/09 van Delft and Others [2010] ECR I-9879 385
C-43/93 Van der Elst v OMI [1994] ECR I-3803 453
41/74 Van Duyn v Home Office [1974] ECR 1337, [1975] 1 CMLR 1, [1975] Ch 358, [1975] 3 All ER 190 251, 283–284, 317, 359
C-316/93 Vaneetveld v SA Le Foyer [1994] ECR I-763, [1994] 2 CMLR 852 293
26/62 Van Gend en Loos v Nederlandse Administratie der Belastingen [1963] ECR 1, [1963] CMLR 182 60, 169, 275–279, 292, 294, 317, 512, 593, 597, 605
C-165/91 Van Munster v Rijksdienst voor Pensioenen [1994] ECR I-4661 408

C-22/08, C-23/08 Vatsouras and Koupatantze v Arbeitsgemeinschaft (ARGE) Nürnberg [2009] ECR I-4585 415, 416, 417
C-368/95 Vereinigte Familiapresse Zeitungsverlags und Vertriebs GmbH v Heinrich Bauer Verlag [1997] ECR I-3689 556–557
C-161/18 Villar Láiz v Instituto Nacional de la Seguridad Social [2019] ECLI:EU: C:2019:382 132
C-198/14 Visnapuu v Kihlakunnansyyttäjä (Helsinki) and Suomen valtio [2015] ECLI:EU:C:2015:751 559
C-31/16 Visser Vastgoed Beleggingen BV v Raad van de gemeente Appingedam (unreported) 447, 448
C-340/89 Vlassopoulou v Ministerium für Justiz, Bundes- und Europaangelegenheiten Baden-Württemberg [1991] ECR I-2357, [1992] 1 CMLR 625 489–491, 500, 501, 506
C-92/09, C-93/09 Volker und Markus Schecke and Eifert (Joined Cases) [2010] ECR I-11063 128
14/83 Von Colson and Kamann v Land Nordrhein-Westfalen [1984] ECR 1891 294–295, 298, 317
C-282/90 Vreugdenhil BV v Commission [1992] ECR I-1937 243
C-5/88 Wachauf (Hubert) v Bundesamt Ehrnährung und Forstwirtschaft [1989] ECR 2609, [1991] 1 CMLR 328 121–122, 131
C-334/92 Wagner Miret v Fondo de Garantía Salarial [1993] ECR I-6911 297–298, 308, 317
E-15/12 Wahl (Request for an Advisory Opinion from EFTA Court) [2014] OJ C 118, 25.4.2013, p. 36–36 359–360
36/74 Walrave and Koch v Association Union Cycliste Internationale [1974] ECR 1405, [1975] 1 CMLR 320 279
261/81 Walter Rau Lebensmittelwerke v De Smedt PvbA [1982] ECR 3961, [1983] 2 CMLR 496 546–547, 575
C-32/93 Webb v EMO Air Cargo (UK) Ltd [1994] ECR I-3567 316
C-201/02 Wells v Secretary of State for Transport, Local Government and the Regions [2004] ECR I-723 293
C-621/18 Wightman and Others [2018] 13
C-378/97 Wijsenbeek [1999] ECR I-6207 322
C-25/88 Wurmser [1989] ECR 1105, [1991] 1 CMLR 173 562
C-87/1 X (unreported) 439
C-72/14, C-197/14 X & Van Dijk (Joined Cases) [2015] EU:C:2015:564 200–201
C-404/92 X v Commission [1994] ECR I-4737 128
C-87/12 Ymerga v Ministre du Travail, de l'Emploi et de l'Immigration [2013] EU:C:2013:291 344
C-58/93 Yousfi v Belgium [1994] ECR I-353 151
C-421/97 Yves Tarantik v Direction des Services Fiscaux de Seine-et-Marne [1999] ECR I-3633 528
C-34/09 Zambrano (Ruiz) v Office national de l'emploi v Office national de l'emploi [2011] ECR I-1177 327, 331, 346–348, 379

C-212/08 *Zeturf Ltd* v *Premier Ministre* [2011] ECR I-5633 469

C-200/02 *Zhu and Chen* [2004] ECR I-9925 330, 338, 345–348, 379

C-414/99–C-416/99 *Zino Davidoff SA* v *A & G Imports Ltd and Levi Strauss & Co. and Others* v *Tesco Stores Ltd and Others (Joined Cases)* [2001] ECR I-8691 131

5/71 *Zückerfabrik Schöppenstedt* v *Council* [1971] ECR 975 239

C-143/88 *Zückerfabrik Süderdithmarschen* v *Hauptzollampt Itzehoe* [1991] ECR I-415, [1993] 3 CMLR 1 266

Table of cases before the European Court of Human Rights

Open Door Counselling and Dublin Well Women and Others v *Ireland* (App Nos 14234/88 and 14235/88) 129

Table of cases before national courts

Germany
German Constitutional Court on the compatibility of the OMT programme with German constitutional law (Judgment of 21 June 2016, 2 BvR 2728/13 205
German Constitutional Court on the compatibility of the ToL with German Basic Law (Judgment of 20 June 2009, 2 BvE 2/08 172
Solange I (Judgment of May 29, 1974, 37 BVerfGE 271) 121, 172
Solange II (Judgment of Oct. 22, 1986, 73 BVerfGE 339) 121, 172

United Kingdom
Ahmad v *Secretary of Statte for the Home Department* [2014] EWCA Civ 988 339
Blackburn v *Attorney-General* [1971] 1 WLR 1037, [1971] All ER 1380 309
Bourgoin v *Ministry of Agriculture, Fisheries and Food (MAFF)* [1985] 3 All ER 385 [1986] QB 716 566
Bulmer v *Bollinger* [1974] 3 WLR 202 185
Doughty v *Rolls Royce plc* [1992] CMLR 1045; [1987] IRLR 447 311–312
Duke v *GEC Reliance* [1988] 2 WLR 359 314–315
Ellen Street Estates v *Minister of Health* [1934] 1 KB 590 176
Equal Opportunities Commission v *Secretary of State for Employment* [1994] 1 All ER 910 313
Factortame Ltd v *Secretary of State for Transport* [1989] 2 All ER 692 310
Foster v *British Gas* (No. 2) [1991] 2 AC 306 288, 314
Griffin and Others v *South West Water Services Lt*d [1995] IRLR 15 312
Holiday in Italy, Re [1975] 1 CMLR 184 202
Litster v *Forth Dry Doc*k [1989] 2 WLR 634 315
Lubberson v *Secretary of State for the Home Department* [1984] 3 CMLR 77 391
Macarthys Ltd v *Smith* [1981] QB 180, [1979] 1 WLR 1189, [1979] ICR 785 309–310
National Union of Teachers and Others v *The Governing Body of St Mary's Church of England (Aided) Junior School and Others* [1997] IRLR 242; [1995] ICR 317 312–314
Ridge v *Baldwin* [1964] AC 40 119
R v *Ministry of Agriculture and Fisheries, ex parte Hamble Fisheries* [1995] 2 All ER 714 119
R v *Secretary of State for Exiting the European Unio*n [2017] UKSC 5 178
R v *Secretary of State for Foreign and Commonwealth Office, ex parte Rees-Mogg* [1993] 3 CMLR 101 QBD 309
R v *Secretary of State for the Home Department, ex parte Flynn* [1995] 3 CMLR 397 322
R v *Secretary of State for Transport, ex parte Factortame* [1991] 1 AC 603, HL referred from [1990] 2 AC 85, HL 310
R v *Secretary of State for Transport, ex parte Factortame and Others (No. 5)* [1999] 3 WLR 1062 302
*Vauxhall Estates Lt*d v *Liverpool Corporation* [1932] 1 KB 733 176
Webb v *EMO Air Cargo (UK) Ltd* [1993] IRLR 27, [1993] 1 WLR 49, HL, reversing [1992] IRLR 116, CA, affirming [1990] IRLR 124, EAT 316
Webb v *EMO Air Cargo (UK) Ltd* (appeal dismissed) [1990] IRLR 124 (EAT); [1992] IRLR 116 (CA) 316
Webb v *EMO Air Cargo (UK) Ltd (No. 2)* [1995] IRLR 647 315–316

Table of European Union Decisions

Decision 76/787/ECSC 215
Decision 85/381 162–163
Decision 94/90 (OJ 1996 L 247/45) 99
Decision 2006/35/EC 44
Decision 2006/57/EC 45
Decision 2006/659/EC 260
Decision 2008/615/JHA 152
Decision 2008/616/JHA 152
Decision 2008/913 (Framework) 131
Decision 2011/119/EU 152
Decision 2016/1316 71
Decision 2018/994 215

Table of European Union Treaties

Constitution of the European Union 2004 (Constitutional Treaty) (Signed in Rome on 29 October 2004 (OJ 2004 C 310/1) 34, 35
EC Treaty (Post TEU, Pre Amsterdam) 38, 49
  Art 2 26
  Art 3 26
  Art 5 26
  Art 7 596
  Art 12 251, 370, 397, 480
  Art 13 30
  Art 16 518
  Art 17 26, 328
  Art 34 304
  Art 39 251
  Art 54(2) 487
  Art 57 487, 488, 501
  Art 57(1) 487
  Art 59 445, 446, 458, 459, 477
  Art 60 445, 446
  Arts 98–124 26
  Art 100 213
  Art 100a 165, 166
  Art 118a 213, 214
  Art 118a(2) 213
  Art 121(4) 28
  Art 171(2) 256, 257
  Art 173 214, 215, 237
  Art 178 239
  Art 184 237
  Art 215 239, 240
  Art 235 213
  Art 311 27–28
EC Treaty (Post Amsterdam)
  Art 2 30
  Art 3 30
  Art 3(2) 30
  Art 5 487
  Art 9 516, 517, 596
  Art 11 31
  Art 12 187, 516, 517
  Art 13 517
  Art 14 598
  Art 16 517
  Art 17 371
  Art 18 75, 346, 370, 371, 389
  Art 18(1) 338, 339, 345, 389
Art 23 591
Art 23(1) 511
Art 23(2) 513
Art 24 513
Art 25 511, 591
Art 28 536, 551, 579
Art 29 512, 579
Art 30 512, 542
Art 39 188, 389, 400, 403
Art 39(2) 414, 415
Art 39(4) 403
Art 42 590
Art 43 389, 434, 472, 501, 505
Art 46 485
Art 48 472
Art 49 193, 197, 389, 434, 452, 457, 482, 483
Art 50 457
Art 55 443
Arts 61–69 30
Art 70 236
Art 71 236
Art 81 235
Art 82 216, 235, 306
Art 90 512, 516, 525
Art 90(2) 592
Art 181a 33
Art 190(2) 79
Art 205(1) 72
Art 207 71
Art 210 162
Art 211 148
Art 213 64
Art 213(2) 64
Art 214 62
Art 219 65
Art 222 590
Art 225 93
Art 225a 94
Art 228 166
Art 228(2) 255, 258
Art 230 188, 210, 214, 215, 216, 217, 218, 232, 233
Art 230(1) 188
Art 234 193, 202, 442, 452, 501
Art 249 214, 590
Art 251 139, 591
Art 252 592
Art 255 100
Art 257 96
Art 263 591
Art 272 77
Art 272(8) 77
Art 288 238
Art 308 140
ECSC Treaty 1951 (Treaty of Paris) (Expired 23 July 2002) 20, 23
EEC Treaty 1957 (Treaty of Rome) 23, 25, 38, 49, 109–110, 169, 170, 594, 595–596, 605
  Preamble 21
  Art 2 387
  Art 3 21, 387
  Art 5 295, 300
  Art 7 310
  Art 8a 24
  Art 9 187, 514, 519
  Arts 9–13 524
  Art 12 187, 275, 276, 519
  Art 13 519
  Art 16 514, 518, 519
  Art 30 300, 301, 442, 537, 538, 540, 543–545, 547–550, 555, 557, 567, 573, 574, 584
  Art 34 560
  Art 36 304, 522, 562, 563, 567, 568
  Art 43 310
  Art 48 283, 387, 394, 402
  Art 48(1)–(3) 401
  Art 48(2) 398
  Art 48(4) 401
  Art 52 277, 300, 301, 444, 487, 488
  Art 54 444, 488
  Art 59 453
  Art 60 453, 458, 459, 477
  Art 63 444, 446
  Art 66 446
  Art 67 477
  Art 68 477
  Art 74 265
  Art 75 265
  Art 75(1) 161, 162
  Art 76 265

TABLE OF EUROPEAN UNION TREATIES

Art 90 525
Arts 92–93 518, 538
Art 95 166, 253, 265, 524, 525, 527, 528, 532–534
Art 95(2) 531
Art 97 239
Art 100 562
Art 106 477
Art 118 162, 163
Art 119 278, 309, 310
Art 169 253, 256, 514
Art 175 239
Art 177 192, 198–199, 278, 279, 283, 301, 453
Art 189 280, 283, 286, 294, 300
Art 189(3) 296
Art 210 162
Merger Treaty 1965 22, 110
 Art 4 71
Second Budgetary Treaty 1975 95
Single European Act 1986 23–25, 38, 49, 56, 110, 159, 510
 Preamble 23
Treaty Establishing the European Atomic Energy Community (Euratom) 1957 (now EA) 21, 23
Treaty establishing the European Stability Mechanism 2012 152
Treaty of Accession to the European Communities 1972 (Denmark, Ireland, UK) 23
Treaty of Accession to the European Communities 1981 (Greece) 23
Treaty of Accession to the European Communities 1986 (Spain, Portugal) 23
Treaty of Accession to the European Communities 1995 (Austria, Finland, Sweden) 29
Treaty of Accession to the European Communities 2004 (Cyprus (South), Czech Republic, Estonia, Hungary, Latvia, Lithuania, Malta, Poland, Slovakia, Slovenia) 33
Treaty of Accession to the European Communities 2007 (Bulgaria, Romania) 33–34
Treaty of Accession to the European Communities 2011 (Croatia) 34, 37, 124
 Art 19(1) 79
 Art 20 72
Treaty of Amsterdam 1997 29–31, 38, 49, 57, 110, 153, 267, 605
 Pt 1
 Arts 1–5 29
 Pt 2
 Arts 6–11 29
 Pt 3
 Arts 12–15 29
Treaty of Lisbon 2008 (Reform Treaty) 34–43, 56, 79, 110, 113, 124, 153, 177, 592, 595, 596, 605
 Preamble 38
 Art 1 38
 Art 2 38
 Arts 3–7 38
 Art 5(1) 38
 Declaration 17 on primacy of Treaties and EU law 169
Treaty of Nice 2000 31–33, 38, 42, 43, 49, 57, 110, 605
Treaty of Rome 1957 *see* EEC Treaty 1957 (Treaty of Rome)
Treaty on European Union 1992 (Maastricht Treaty) TEU
 Title I 26, 111
 Art A 26, 601
 Arts A–F 25
 Art B 27
 Art F(1) 267
 Art F(2) 27, 122
 Title II 25, 40, 111
 Art G 25, 26
 Title III 111
 Art H 25
 Title IV 111
 Art I 25
 Title V 111
 Art J 26
 Arts J.1–J.11 25
 Art J.3, para 2 27
 Title VI 111
 Art K 26
 Arts K.1–K.9 25
 Title VII
 Art K.4(3) 27
 Art L 27
 Arts L–S 25
 Preamble 111
Treaty on European Union 1992 (Maastricht Treaty) (as re-numbered by Art 5 Treaty of Lisbon) TEU 25–28, 110
 Title I
 Art 1 37, 38, 97, 110, 368, 594, 595, 596, 601, 605
 Art 2 6, 38, 39, 49, 116, 126, 131, 266, 267, 268
 Art 3 7, 39, 49, 188, 367, 510
 Art 3(3) 131, 133, 578
 Art 3(4) 16
 Arts 3–7 38
 Art 4(3) 246–247, 250, 251, 293–294, 295, 300, 310, 487, 542, 596
 Art 5 26
 Art 5(1) 117, 159, 180, 604
 Art 5(2) 14, 140, 153, 159, 180
 Art 5(3) 14, 117, 167, 180, 604
 Art 5(4) 14, 117, 167, 180
 Art 6 120, 121, 369
 Art 6(1) 36, 42, 116, 123, 153
 Art 6(2) 30, 42, 122, 595
 Art 6(3) 30, 116, 117, 153, 595
 Art 7 245, 246, 266–269
 Art 7(1) 247, 268, 269, 270
 Art 7(2) 247, 268, 269
 Art 7(3) 116, 247, 268, 270
 Title II
 Art 9 40, 132, 324, 378
 Art 10 40
 Art 10(4) 81
 Art 11 40
 Art 11(4) 41
 Art 12 41, 369
 Title III 25
 Art 13 209
 Art 13(1) 8, 39, 54, 95–97, 184, 592, 594, 595, 596
 Art 13(2) 54, 87
 Art 13(4) 54, 96, 97
 Arts 13–19 8, 39, 55
 Art 14 76
 Art 14(1) 9, 76
 Art 14(2) 9, 39, 79
 Art 14(3) 78–79
 Art 15 56
 Art 15(1) 8, 56, 595
 Art 15(2) 57
 Art 15(3) 57
 Art 15(4) 8, 58
 Art 15(5) 8, 57
 Art 15(6) 8, 9, 57, 58
 Art 16 69
 Art 16(1) 69
 Art 16(2) 9, 70
 Art 16(3) 10, 72, 144, 603
 Art 16(4) 10, 73–74, 602
 Art 16(6) 9, 10, 70
 Art 16(7) 71
 Art 16(8) 72, 99, 101
 Art 16(9) 10, 71
 Art 17 58, 369

Art 17(1) 59, 148, 247
Art 17(2) 9, 14, 59
Art 17(3) 62, 63, 65
Art 17(5) 62
Art 17(6) 65
Art 17(7) 62, 63, 76, 78
Art 17(8) 65, 78
Art 18 132, 310, 323
Art 18(1) 76
Art 18(2) 63, 75, 76
Art 18(3) 10, 70, 75
Art 18(4) 75, 76
Art 19 86, 132
Art 19(1) 10, 87, 93, 116–117, 147, 268
Art 19(2) 10, 88, 94
Title IV 25, 111
Art 20 43, 48
Art 20(2) 43
Title V 25, 111
Chapter 1 111
Art 21 17
Art 22(1) 56
Chapter 2 111
Section 1 14, 18, 76, 115, 216
Treaty on European Union 1992 (Maastricht Treaty) (as re-numbered by Art 12 Treaty of Amsterdam) (now EU)
Art 2 29
Art 3 30
Art 6 30
Art 6(1) 29, 32
Art 6(2) 30
Art 7 29, 32
Art 8 369
Art 20 31, 32
Art 25 32
Art 29 31
Art 31 31
Arts 43–45 31, 32
Art 43(c) 31
Art 46 30
Treaty on European Union 1992 (Maastricht Treaty) (as re-numbered by Art 5 Treaty of Lisbon) TEU
Title V
Chapter 2
Section 1 32
Section 2 14
Title VI 25
Art 47 17, 148, 154, 162
Art 48 113, 115, 596
Art 48(1)–(4) 114
Art 48(6) 114
Art 48(7) 115

Art 49 12, 13, 74, 77
Art 50 45–46, 57, 149, 178
Art 50(2) 13, 46, 149, 178, 605
Art 50(3) 13
Art 50(5) 47
Art 51 113
Treaty on European Union Protocol 2 (Application of the principles of subsidiarity and proportionality) 14, 117, 142, 180, 604
Art 4 168
Art 5 168
Art 7 168
Art 8 98, 168
Treaty on European Union Protocol 3 (on the Statute of the Court of Justice of the European Union) 86–87
Art 2 89
Art 4 89
Art 9 89
Art 16 89, 90
Art 17 90
Art 20 90, 204
Art 21 91
Art 23 91
Art 23a 204
Art 45 233
Art 48 94
Art 50 94
Art 51 94, 602
Treaty on European Union Protocol 6 on Location of Seats of the Institutions 83
Treaty on European Union Protocol 7 (Privileges and Immunities of the European Union)
Art 8 85, 86
Art 9 85, 86
Art 17 84
Treaty on European Union Protocol 19 (Schengen)
Art 1 373
Art 5 373, 374
Treaty on European Union Protocol 22
Art 4 373
Treaty on European Union Protocol 30
Art 1 36–37, 42, 124
Treaty on European Union Protocol 36 on Transitional Provisions
Art 2 79
Art 3(3) 72–73
Treaty on Stability, Coordination and Governance in the Economic and Monetary Union (1 April 2014) 34, 152

Treaty on the Functioning of the European Union (EC Treaty Post Lisbon) TFEU 108, 109, 169, 170
Preamble 112
Part One (Arts 1–24)
Title I (Arts 2–6) 112
Art 1(2) 38
Art 2(3) 161
Art 2(4) 161
Art 3 14, 160, 180
Art 4 14, 160, 180
Art 6 14, 161, 180
Title II (Arts 7–17) 112
Art 8 132
Art 10 132
Art 15 100, 102
Art 15(3) 100, 101, 129
Part Two (Arts 18–25) 112
Art 18 25, 279, 322, 363, 364, 366, 369, 370, 378, 379, 397, 400, 406, 416, 436, 444, 477, 479, 480
Art 19 400–401
Art 20 26, 322, 326, 328, 329, 331, 346, 347, 355, 371
Art 20(1) 324, 326
Art 20(2) 324, 366
Arts 20–25 324
Art 21 135, 322, 324–325, 329, 331, 335, 338, 345, 346, 355, 370, 371, 378, 389
Art 21(1) 325, 333–335, 338, 339, 366, 376
Art 24 40–41
Part Three (Arts 26–197)
Title I (Arts 26–27) 112
Art 26 24, 164
Art 26(2) 322, 323, 510, 598
Title II (Arts 28–37) 112, 525–526
Art 28 186, 187, 511, 514, 516, 517, 518, 519, 523, 587, 591, 592
Art 28(1) 511, 513
Art 28(2) 513, 526
Arts 28–30 513–525
Arts 28–37 526
Art 29 513, 535, 587
Art 30 186, 187, 275, 276, 511–514, 516–525, 535, 540, 587, 591, 592
Art 31 146
Art 34 279, 300, 301, 442, 512, 535–561, 564, 567, 569, 570, 572–576, 578, 579, 580, 581, 582, 587, 588, 593, 597, 599, 602

Arts 34–36 511–513, 536–537, 538
Art 35 279, 304, 512, 560–561, 587, 593, 597, 599, 602
Art 36 304, 509, 512, 522, 536, 542, 552, 554, 558, 559, 561–572, 573, 577, 578, 579, 581, 583, 584, 588
Art 37 539, 604
Title III (Arts 38–44)
Art 40(3) 60
Title IV (Arts 45–66)
Art 45 186, 188, 279, 283, 382–383, 384, 385, 386, 387, 389, 393, 394, 399, 400, 402, 403, 409, 410, 427
Art 45(1)–(3) 401
Art 45(2) 397, 398, 404, 414, 415, 430
Art 45(3) 396, 400, 430, 461, 563
Art 45(3)(d) 391
Art 45(4) 398, 401–404, 430, 443
Arts 45–48 323, 408
Art 46 25, 383
Arts 46–48 383
Art 47 383
Art 48 41, 227, 383, 385, 408, 590
Art 49 41, 277, 279, 300, 301, 310, 389, 434, 435, 436, 439, 444, 446, 460, 465, 469, 472, 474, 487–490, 501, 503–506, 552
Arts 49–54 323
Art 50 12–13, 25, 279, 444, 488
Art 50(1) 487
Art 51 443, 474
Art 52 461, 462, 481, 483, 484, 485, 506
Art 53 487, 488, 501
Art 53(1) 486–487, 492, 506
Art 54 435, 439, 472
Art 56 193, 197, 389, 434, 435, 440, 444–446, 452, 453, 457–459, 467, 469, 473, 476, 477, 478, 480, 481, 482, 483, 484, 506, 515, 537
Arts 56–62 323
Art 57 435, 436, 441, 444–446, 453, 457–459, 477, 478, 480
Art 59 444, 446
Art 61 436
Art 62 446, 462

Art 63 537
Art 64(3) 144
Title V (Arts 67–89)
Art 67 32
Arts 67–81 30
Art 70 41
Art 81 (Chapter 3) 115
Art 82 32
Arts 82–86 (Chapter 4) 55, 216
Art 83 32
Art 85 32, 41
Art 86(1) 144
Arts 87–89 (Chapter 5) 216
Art 88 41
Title VI (Arts 90–100)
Art 90 236, 265
Art 91 236
Art 91(1) 161, 162
Art 92 265
Title VII (Arts 101–118) 524–535
Art 101 60, 235, 279, 538–539
Art 102 60, 186, 216, 235, 279, 306, 538–539
Art 105(1) 235
Art 105(2) 139
Art 106(3) 145
Art 107(1) 604
Arts 107–108 538
Art 109 139
Art 110 253, 265, 511, 512, 515, 516, 523–535, 587
Art 110(1) 525–535
Art 110(2) 525, 527, 530–535, 592
Art 113 239, 511, 524
Art 114 25, 67, 164, 165, 166, 167, 552, 553, 583–584, 588
Art 114(1) 164
Art 114(3) 164
Art 114(4) 583
Art 115 139, 552, 562
Art 118 572
Title VIII (Arts 119–144)
Arts 119–144 26
Art 121(2) 99
Art 122 213
Art 123 477
Art 126(11) 99
Art 136(3) 152
Title IX (Arts 145–150)
Art 148(2) 595
Title X (Arts 151–161)
Art 153 116, 162, 213
Art 157 132, 278, 279, 309
Title XI (Arts 162–164)
Art 162 60
Art 163 60

Title XII (Arts 165–166) 112
Title XIII (Art 167) 112
Art 167(5) 591
Title XIV (Art 168) 112
Title XIX (Arts 179–190) 112
Title XV (Art 169) 112
Title XVI (Arts 170–172) 112
Title XVII (Art 173) 112
Title XVIII (Arts 174–178) 112
Art 176 60
Art 177 60
Title XX (Arts 191–193) 112
Art 192 116
Title XXI (Art 194) 112
Title XXII (Art 195) 112
Title XXIII (Art 196) 112
Title XXIV (Art 197) 112
Part Four (Arts 198–204) 112
Part Five (Arts 205–222) 112
Title I (Art 205) 112
Title II (Arts 206–207) 112
Art 20 369
Art 207(3) 61
Title III (Arts 208–214)
Art 212 33
Art 213 33
Title IV (Art 215) 112
Title V (Arts 216–219) 112
Art 216 17
Art 217 17, 150
Art 218 61, 247
Art 218(2) 148
Art 218(3) 13, 46, 148, 178
Title VI (Arts 220–221)
Art 220(1) 61
Art 220(2) 61
Title VII (Art 222) 112
Part Six (Arts 223–334) 8, 55, 76, 113
Title I (Arts 223–309) 8, 39, 55
Chapter 1 (Arts 223–287) 9–10, 13, 55, 56, 58, 60, 64, 65, 66, 67, 69, 70, 71, 74, 77, 78, 81, 82, 83, 86, 87, 88, 89, 90, 93, 94–95, 96, 113, 125, 141, 146, 165, 173, 184, 188, 189–196, 198–205, 208, 209–238, 239, 243, 245–258, 261, 262–265, 266, 269, 270, 274, 275, 276, 278, 282, 283, 301, 310, 405, 406, 423, 442, 445, 452, 453, 468, 474, 484, 488, 501, 514, 517, 527, 531, 536, 537, 540, 547, 548, 550, 555, 571, 577, 590, 597

Chapter 2 (Arts 288–299) 14, 55, 137–139, 140, 142, 143, 144, 145, 146, 148, 153, 154, 188, 211, 212, 214, 229, 241, 252, 279–280, 281–283, 286, 290, 294, 296, 300, 590, 591, 593, 598, 599, 600, 602, 603
Chapter 3 (Arts 300–307) 55, 96–97, 98, 591, 595
Chapter 4 (Arts 308–309) 96, 596
Title II (Arts 310–325)
Art 312 (Chapter 2) 115
Art 313 77
Art 314(4) 77–78
Art 314(4)(c) 78
Art 314(5) 78
Art 314(8) 78
Chapter 6 (Art 325) 118, 173
Title III (Arts 326–334) 31, 32, 43, 48
Art 329(1) 43
Art 329(2) 43
Art 333 116
Part Seven (Arts 335–358) 113
Art 340 88, 93, 207, 208, 238–243
Art 345 570
Art 352 74, 140, 163, 164, 168
Art 352(1) 13–14, 140, 163, 164
Art 352(3) 164
Art 352(4) 164, 213

Table of other Treaties, etc.

Association Agreement (EU-Turkey) 585
Benelux Agreement 1948 201, 590
Charter of Fundamental Rights of the European Union 2000 (Amended 12 December 2007) 36, 42–43, 108, 151, 212, 230, 328
  Title IV 37
  Art 1 126
  Art 2 127
  Art 3 127
  Art 4 127
  Art 5 127
  Art 7 128
  Art 8 128
  Art 9 128
  Art 10 129
  Art 11 129
  Art 12 130
  Art 14 130
  Art 15 130
  Art 17 131
  Art 18 131
  Art 20 132
  Art 21 132, 174
  Art 23 133
  Art 24 133
  Art 25 134
  Art 26 134
  Art 28 130
  Art 31 130
  Art 32 133
  Art 33(2) 128
  Art 34 134
  Art 35 134
  Art 37 134
  Art 38 134
  Art 42 129
  Art 45 135
  Art 47 135
  Art 48 135
  Art 49 135, 173
  Art 50 125, 135
Community Charter of Fundamental Social Rights of Workers 1989 (Strasbourg Summit December 1989) 130

Comprehensive Economic Trade Agreement (EU-Canada) 585–586
Dublin II Regulation (2003) 375
Dublin III Regulation (2013) 375
EC/Morocco Cooperation Agreement 151
EEC/Portugal Association Agreement
  Art 21 151
European Convention on Human Rights and Fundamental Freedoms (ECHR) 1950 153, 212, 582, 595
  Art 1 127
  Art 2 127
  Art 3 127
  Art 4 125, 127, 136
  Art 5 127, 136
  Art 6 122, 136
  Art 7 173
  Art 8 128, 430
  Art 9 129
  Art 10 129
  Art 11 130
  Art 12 128
  Art 13 122, 136
  Art 14 133
European Parliament Act concerning the election of the representatives of the Assembly by direct universal suffrage 1976
  Art 12(2) 215
Free Trade Agreement (EU and Singapore), 2013 179
General Agreement on Tariffs and Trade (GATT) 149
Interinstitutional Agreement on Better Law-Making of April 2016 145
  para 25 211
International Covenant on Civil and Political Rights
  Art 24(3) 327
International Plant Protection Convention 1951 522
Ioannina Declaration March 1994 74, 598

Law of Administrative Procedure of the EU 117
Paris Agreement 1954 19
Prüm Convention 152
Schengen acquis (1985, 1990, 1995) 151
Schengen Agreement 1985 and Convention 1990 151, 376, 602–603
Schengen Borders Code (2016) 379
  Art 25 377
  Art 29 376, 377
Schengen I – Schengen Agreement between the Governments of the States of the Benelux Economic Union, the Federal Republic of Germany and the French Republic on the gradual abolition of checks at their common borders 1985 *see* Schengen Agreement 1985 and Convention 1990
Schengen II – Convention for the Implementation of the Schengen Agreement of 14 June 1985 between the Governments of the States of the Benelux Economic Union, the Federal Republic of Germany and the French Republic on the gradual abolition of checks at their common borders (CISA) 1990 *see* Schengen Agreement 1985 and Convention 1990
Treaty of Versailles 1919 18
UN Convention on Access to Information, Public Participation in Decision-making and Access to Justice in Environmental Matters (Aarhus Convention) 232
UN Convention on the Nationality of Married Women 1957 327
UN Convention on the Reduction of Statelessness 1961 327
UN Convention relating to the Status of Stateless Persons 1954 327
Universal Declaration of Human Rights
  Art 15 327

Table of European Union Regulations

1612/68/EEC 369, 393, 398, 407, 410, 412, 413, 422
  Arts 1–4 397
  Art 3(1) 400
  Art 7 409
  Art 7(1) 398
  Art 7(2) 404, 405, 406, 409, 414, 420, 421, 422, 423, 427
  Art 7(3) 406
  Art 10 354, 412, 430
  Art 10(1) 354, 422
  Art 10(3) 429, 430
  Art 11 354
  Art 12 423, 424, 425, 426
1251/70/EEC 391
1408/71/EEC 364, 393, 408, 410
574/72/EEC 408
563/76/EEC 198
2950/83/EEC
  Art 6(1) 211
2045/89 227
2454/92/EC 212
404/93/EC 241
659/99/EC 233
1073/99/EC
  Art 9 217
45/2001/EC 101, 102
539/2001 349, 353
1049/2001/EC 129

Art 4 100, 101, 102
Art 4(1)(b) 101
Art 4(3) 100
Art 4(4) 100
Art 4(5) 100
1/2003/EC 236
2004/2003 222, 223
833/2004/EC
  Art 20(2) 481
  Art 20(1) 481
883/2004/EC 280, 363, 366–367, 384, 393, 408, 410, 506
  Art 4 364, 366, 408, 415, 418, 430
  Art 20(2) 481
  Art 70 415, 418
2007/2004/EC 374
2252/2004/EC 374
635/2006/EC 391
987/2009/EC 384, 408
988/2009/EC 364, 408
1007/2009 228
182/2011 68, 69
211/2011/EC
  Art 2(1) 41
  Art 7(2) 41
492/2011/EC 280, 349, 363, 369, 382, 384, 393, 397–400, 406, 407, 409, 410, 413, 422, 423

Preamble 382, 397
Arts 1–4 397
Arts 1–10 384, 393, 400
Art 1 397, 431
Art 3 397, 400, 431
Art 3(1) 400
Art 4 397, 400, 431
Art 5 397
Art 6 397, 400
Art 7 430
Art 7(1) 398
Art 7(2) 406, 407, 414, 420, 421, 422, 423, 426, 427, 431
Art 7(3) 406, 423, 426
Art 7(4) 398
Art 9 430
Art 10 343, 423, 424, 425, 426
465/2012 384
1224/2012 384
2016/589 384
2016/679 128
2016/1104 131
2017/458 376
2017/458/EU 376
2019/115 134
2019/1149 384

Table of European Union Directives

64/221/EEC 251, 477
   Art 3 484
   Art 3(1) 283
68/71/EEC 295
68/360 391, 413, 414
70/50/EEC
   Art 2 539
   Art 2(3) 539
   Art 3 540, 545
71/305/EEC 548
72/148/EEC 450
73/148/EEC 478
   Art 1(1)(d) 344
   Art 1(b) 477–478
74/557/EEC 304
75/362/EEC 192
75/442/EEC
   Art 4 256
   Art 6 256
76/160/EEC 254
76/207/EEC 286, 288, 294, 295, 311, 313
76/768/EEC 240
77/187/EEC 251, 312, 315
77/249/EEC 437, 450, 459
77/452/EEC 437
78/319/EEC
   Art 5 256, 257
   Art 12 256
78/686/EEC 437, 500
78/687/EEC 437
78/1026/EEC 437
78/1027/EEC 437
79/112/EEC 576
80/154/EEC 437
80/155/EEC 437
80/987/EEC 284, 285, 297, 299
83/189/EEC 291
   Art 8 291
   Art 9 291
85/384/EEC 437
85/432/EEC 437
85/433/EEC 437
85/577/EEC 287
88/361/EEC 515
89/48/EEC 437, 492, 494, 495, 504

90/314/EEC 303
90/364/EEC 339, 346, 370
   Art 1(1) 338, 345
90/531/EEC 265, 302
91/583/EEC
   Art 2(2)(c) 285
92/43/EEC 134
92/51/EEC 437, 492, 504
92/129 EC 312
93/16/EC 437, 503
93/104/EC 212–214, 274, 275
   Art 4 213
   Art 5 213
   Art 6 213
   Art 7 213
94/33/EC 133
96/71/EC 438, 453, 457, 458, 506
   Art 3 455, 484
   Art 3(1) 454
   Art 3(7) 454
98/5/EC 437, 450
98/43/EC 165
99/41/EC 492
2000/43/EC 131, 400
2000/78/EC 131, 175, 400–401
2001/29/EC 572
2001/118/EC 262
2002/58/EC 128
2003/9/EC 131
2003/33/EC
   Art 3 166
   Art 4 166
   Art 5 166
   Art 8 166
2003/86/EC 128
2003/109/EC 355
2004/38/EC 109, 120, 283, 322, 325, 346, 350, 384, 385, 393, 406, 410–411, 425, 430, 452, 506
   Art 2(2) 342, 343, 344, 352, 354, 379, 412, 419
   Art 2(2)(a) 422
   Art 2(2)(b) 422
   Art 2(2)(c) 344, 345, 412, 422
   Art 2(2)(d) 344

   Art 2(3) 356
   Art 3(1) 330, 331, 334, 335, 346, 378
   Art 3(2) 343, 349, 419, 420
   Art 3(2)(a) 343, 352
   Art 4 336
   Art 4(1) 336
   Art 4(2) 336
   Art 5 336
   Art 5(1) 336, 349, 353
   Art 5(2) 349, 353, 419
   Art 5(4) 336
   Art 5(5) 336, 358, 419
   Art 6 325, 337, 349, 378, 412, 438, 478
   Art 6(1) 337, 349, 411, 417, 419, 451
   Art 6(2) 349, 419
   Art 7 333, 336, 349–350, 354, 451
   Art 7(1) 337, 338, 349, 366, 367, 379, 391, 418, 438, 478
   Art 7(1)(a) 337, 339, 351, 352, 353, 438, 451
   Art 7(1)(b) 338, 339, 351, 352, 353, 365, 366, 368
   Art 7(1)(c) 339, 351, 352, 353, 368, 392
   Art 7(1)(d) 349, 351, 352, 353, 419
   Art 7(2) 349, 356
   Art 7(3) 337, 391, 392, 417, 426, 451
   Art 7(3)(a) 392
   Art 7(3)(c) 416
   Art 7(4) 343
   Art 8 349, 353
   Art 8(1) 339
   Art 8(2) 339
   Art 8(3) 339
   Art 8(4) 338, 365
   Art 8(5) 349, 419
   Art 9 349, 353
   Art 9(2) 349, 419
   Art 10(2) 349, 419
   Art 10(3) 354

Art 11(1) 349, 419
Art 11(2) 349–350, 420
Art 12 351, 355, 357, 358, 379, 421, 451
Art 12(1) 352, 353, 421
Art 12(2) 352, 353
Art 12(3) 352, 424
Art 13 351, 355–356, 357, 358, 379, 421, 451
Art 13(1) 352, 353
Art 13(2) 352, 353, 356, 357
Art 13(2)(a) 352, 356, 357
Art 13(2)(b) 352
Art 13(2)(c) 353, 356–357
Art 13(2)(d) 353
Art 14(1) 337, 412, 416
Art 14(2) 358
Art 14(3) 337, 358
Art 14(4) 337, 358, 396, 413, 451
Art 14(4)(b) 364, 411, 413, 416, 417, 418
Art 15(2) 358
Art 16 367, 370, 421, 451, 478
Art 16(1) 340, 366, 379, 396, 421, 451
Art 16(2) 340, 421, 451
Art 16(3) 340
Art 16(4) 341, 451
Art 17 341, 351, 391, 396, 421, 451
Art 17(4) 423
Art 19(1) 340
Art 20(1) 351
Art 20(2) 351
Art 20(3) 341, 451
Art 21 340, 396, 421, 451
Art 22 341
Art 23 345, 354, 357, 422
Art 24 366
Art 24(1) 364, 366, 367, 478
Art 24(2) 364, 366, 367, 368, 411, 413, 415, 416, 417, 418, 426, 480–481
Art 25(1) 342
Art 25(2) 342
Art 26 342
Art 27 359, 401, 461, 484
Art 27(1) 358, 379
Art 27(2) 358, 359, 379
Art 27(3) 358
Art 27(4) 359
Arts 27–29 362
Art 28 362
Art 28(1) 360
Art 28(2) 360
Art 28(3) 360, 362

Art 28(3)(a) 361
Art 29 361
Art 29(1) 361
Art 29(2) 361
Art 29(3) 362
Art 30(1) 362
Art 30(2) 362
Art 30(3) 362
Art 31 362
Art 32(1) 362
Art 32(2) 362
Art 33(1) 363
Art 33(2) 363
Recital 15 352
2004/81/EC 127
2004/83/EC 131
2004/113/EC 131
2005/36/EC 437–438, 450, 486, 492–499, 500, 502, 504, 506
Title I 433
Arts 1–4 492–493
Art 1 492
Art 2(1) 437, 493
Art 3(1)(a) 493
Art 3(2) 493
Arts 4a–4c 499
Art 4f 497, 499
Title II
Arts 5–9 493
Art 5(1) 493
Art 5(2) 493
Art 5(3) 493
Art 6 493
Art 7(1) 493
Art 7(2) 493
Art 7(3) 493
Art 7(4) 493
Art 8 493
Art 9 493
Title III 493, 494–498
Chapter 1, Arts 10–15 492
Art 10 494
Art 11 494, 497
Art 12 494
Art 13(1) 496, 497
Art 13(2) 496
Art 13(3) 496
Art 14(1) 496, 497
Art 14(2) 496, 497
Art 14(3) 496
Art 15(1) 496
Art 15(2) 496
Chapter II, Arts 16–20 492, 494, 497–498
Art 16 497
Art 17 498

Art 18 498
Art 19 498
Chapter III, Arts 21–49 492, 493, 494
Art 21 498
Art 22 498
Art 23 498
Arts 24–49 498
Art 49a 499
Art 49b 499
Chapter IV
Art 50 498
Art 51(1) 498
Art 51(2) 498
Art 51(3) 498
Art 52(1) 498
Art 52(2) 498
Title IV
Art 53 498, 499
Art 54 498
Art 55 498
Art 55a 499
Title V 498–499
Art 56 499
Art 56a 499
Art 57 499
Art 58 499
Art 59 499
Title VI
Art 61 496
Art 62 437, 492
Annex I 493
Annex IV
List I 497, 498
List II 497, 498
List III 497, 498
Annex V 498
Annex VI 498
Annex VII 498
2005/85/EC 131
2006/54/EC 131, 294, 314, 316, 401
2006/123/EC 433, 436–437, 446–450, 465, 476, 506
Chapters I–VIII 478–479
Art 2(2)(d) 474
Art 4 438
Art 4(8) 460, 475
Chapter II 448
Art 5(1) 448
Art 6(1) 448
Art 7(3) 448
Art 8 448
Chapter III 498
Art 9 448, 449
Art 10 449
Art 10(2)(c) 475

Art 10(3) 449
Art 11(1) 449
Art 12 449
Art 13 449
Art 14 449, 461
Art 15(2) 449
Art 15(3) 449
Art 16(1) 449, 461
Art 16(2) 449
Art 16(3) 449, 461
Art 17 497
Art 18 497
Art 19 478, 497
Art 20 478
Art 21 478
Art 22 479
Art 23 479
Art 24 479
Arts 24–49 498
Art 25 479
Art 26 479
Art 27 479
Recital 7 446
Recital 30 447
Recital 40 460
2009/28/EC 569
2011/83/EC 134, 476, 479
2011/92/EC 134
2013/55/EC 437, 492, 497, 499
2014/40/EC 167
2014/54/EC 384, 393
   Art 3 400
   Art 4 400
   Art 6 400
2015/2436/EC
   Art 15 571
2016/343/EC 135
2016/680/EC 128
2016/1919/EC 135
2018/957/EU 456, 457
2019/790 131

Rules of Procedure of the Institutions of the European Union

Rules of Procedure of the European Court of Justice (OJ 1991 L 176/7) (1 November 2012 and 18 June 2013 amendment) 94
- Art 8(4) 89
- Art 10 89
- Art 15(1) 89
- Art 27(1) 89
- Art 36 87
- Art 53(4) 93
- Art 59(1) 91
- Art 60 91
- Art 61 91
- Art 62 91
- Art 64(1) 91
- Art 64(2) 91
- Art 76(2) 91
- Art 82(1) 92
- Art 99 203
- Art 105(1) 204
- Art 105(2) 204
- Art 107 204
- Art 123 91
- Art 124 91
- Art 133(1) 93
- Art 160(3) 264

Rules of Procedure of the European Economic and Social Committee (EESC)
- Title II 97

Rules of Procedure of the European Parliament (Amendment of 30 November 2009)
- rule 29(1) 82
- rule 29(4) 82
- rule 32(1) 82
- rule 226(5) 82

Rules of Procedure of the European Parliament 13 December 2016 102

Rules of Procedure of the European Parliament January 2017
- rule 29(1) 82
- rule 32(1) 82
- rule 32(2) 81
- rule 129 78
- rule 168(2) 83
- rule 168(3) 83
- rule 177 83

Rules of Procedure of the European Parliament January 2019
- rule 32(1) 82
- rule 32(2) 81

Table of Statutes

Aliens Employment Act 1955 404
Basic Law (Germany) 171, 483
Beer Duty Act 1952 (Biersteuergesetz)(Germany)
    s 9 568
Code du Travail Maritime (France) 251
Commodities Act (Warenwet) (Netherlands) 576
Customs Consolidation Act 1876 536
Education Reform Act 1988
    s 46 313
Equal Pay Act 1970 309
European Communities Act 1972
    23, 46–47, 138, 310, 316
    s 2(1) 176, 177, 309, 310
    s 2(4) 176, 177, 309, 310
    s 3(1) 177, 185
European Parliamentary Elections Act 1999 79
European Union (Amendment) Act 2008 177
European Union (Amendment) Act 2011
    Part I, s 18 177
European Union (Notification of Withdrawal) Act 2017 178
European Union (Withdrawal) Act 2018 46, 138, 147, 180, 316
    s 5(2) 178
    s 5(4) 124
European Union (Withdrawal Agreement) Act 2019 23, 46
Foodstuffs Act 1974 (Germany) 567
Gas Act 1972 288
Human Rights Act 1998 123
Importation of Milk Act 1983 566
Income and Corporation Taxes Act 1988 472
Law No 31/2008 (Portugal) 261
Law No 67/2007 (Portugal) 261
Merchant Shipping Act 1988 310
Sex Discrimination Act 1975 288, 314
    s 5(3) 316
Social Code (SGB II), Germany 366
Trade Union and Labour Relations Act 1978 313
Unfair Competition Act 1992 (Austria) 556

Table of Statutory Instruments

European Communities (Employment in the Civil Service) Order 1991, SI 1991/1221 **404**

European Communities (Employment in the Civil Service) Order 2007, SI 2007/617 **404**

European Communities (Lawyer's Practice) Regulations 2000, SI 2000/1119 **450**

European Communities (Recognition of Professional Qualifications) Regulations 2015 **499**

European Communities (Services of Lawyers) Order 1978 **450**

Immigration (European Economic Area) Regulations 2006, SI 2006/1003 **334**
  reg 9 **335**

Immigration Rules 1994, 23 May 1994 **420**

Provision of Services Regulations 2009 **437**

Transfer of Undertakings (Protection of Employment) Regulations 1981 **251, 315**

Working Time Regulations 1998, SI 1988/1833 **274**

List of abbreviations

AFSJ	Area of Freedom, Security and Justice
AG	Advocate General
All ER	All England Law Reports
BGC	British Gas Corporation
CE	Compulsory Expenditure
CEE	Charge having an equivalent effect to a customs duty
CETA	Comprehensive Economic Trade Agreement
CTA	Common Travel Area
CFI	Court of First Instance
CFSP	Common Foreign and Security Policy
CJHA	Cooperation in Justice and Home Affairs
CLJ	Cambridge Law Journal
CML Rev	Common Market Law Review
COREPER	Committee of Permanent Representatives (*Comité des Représentants Permanents*)
DG	Directorate General
DSB	Dispute Settlement Board of the World Trade Organization (WTO)
EBL Rev	European Business Law Review
EC	European Community
ECB	European Central Bank
ECHR	European Convention on Human Rights
ECJ	European Court of Justice
ECLR	European Competition Law Review
ECL Rev	European Constitutional Law Review
ECR	European Court Reports
ECSC	European Coal and Steel Community
ECtHR	European Court of Human Rights
ECU	European Currency Unit
EEA	European Economic Area
EEC	European Economic Community
EESC	European Economic and Social Committee
EFTA	European Free Trade Association
EIB	European Investment Bank
EJML	European Journal of Migration and Law
ELJ	European Law Journal
EL Rev	European Law Review
EMU	Economic and Monetary Union
EP	European Parliament
EPL	European Public Law
ESCB	European System of Central Banks
EU	European Union

Euratom	European Atomic Energy Community
EUSS	European Union Settlement Scheme
FAO	Food and Agriculture Organisation of the United Nations
FTA	Free Trade Agreement
FYRM	Former Yugoslav Republic of Macedonia
GATT	General Agreement on Tariffs and Trade
GmbH	Gesellschaft mit beschränkter Haftung (Plc)
Harv Int LJ	Harvard International Law Journal
ICLQ	International and Comparative Law Quarterly
ICR	Industrial Cases Reports
IGC	Intergovernmental Conference
IRLR	Industrial Relations Law Reports
JCMS	Journal of Common Market Studies
JHA	Justice and Home Affairs
JSWFL	Journal of Social Welfare and Family Law
LQR	Law Quarterly Review
MAFF	Ministry of Agriculture, Fisheries and Food
MEE	Measure having Equivalent Effect to quantitative restrictions
MEP	Member of the European Parliament
MEQR	Measure having Equivalent Effect to Quantitative Restrictions
MLR	Modern Law Review
NATO	North Atlantic Treaty Organization
NCE	Non-Compulsory Expenditure
OECD	Organisation for Economic Cooperation and Development
OJ	Official Journal of the European Union
OLAF	European Anti-Fraud Office (Office Européen de Lutte Anti-Fraude)
QB	Queen's Bench
QMV	Qualified Majority Voting
QR	Quantitative Restriction
SEA	Single European Act
SI	Statutory Instrument
SIRENE	Supplementary Information Request at the National Entry
SIS	Schengen Information System
SPUC	Society for the Protection of the Unborn Child
TEU	Treaty on European Union
TFEU	Treaty on the Functioning of the European Union
ToA	Treaty of Amsterdam
ToL	Treaty of Lisbon
ToM	Treaty of Maastricht
ToN	Treaty of Nice
WHO	World Health Organization
WLR	Weekly Law Reports
WTO	World Trade Organization
YEL	Yearbook of European Law

Equivalences

For tables of equivalences as referred to in Article 5 of the Treaty of Lisbon, please refer to the document at the following web address: https://eur-lex.europa.eu/resource.html?uri=cellar:2bf140bf-a3f8-4ab2-b506-fd71826e6da6.0023.02/DOC_6&format=PDF

(© European Union, http://eur-lex.europa.eu/, 1998-2015)

Part 1
Constitutional and administrative law of the European Union

1 An introduction to the European Union

2 Institutions of the European Union

3 Sources of European Union law

4 Competence and supremacy of the Union

5 Judicial methodology and preliminary rulings of the Court of Justice

6 Review of the legality of Union acts

7 Infringement proceedings against Member States

8 Direct effect, indirect effect and state liability

Chapter 1
An introduction to the European Union

Learning objectives

At the end of this chapter you should understand:

1 The basic features of the Union and Union law as it exists today.

2 How the Union came to take its current form, including how and why the European Communities were established, their aims and objectives and their successes and challenges.

3 The changes brought by the Treaty of Lisbon.

4 Ways in which the Union might develop in the future.

Key terms and concepts

Familiarity with the following terms will be helpful for understanding this chapter.

Accession – the process by which new Member States join the Union

Competence – the authority to govern in a particular policy area

Conferral – the principle that the Union only has the power to act where such competence has been bestowed upon it (conferred) by the Member States

Enlargement – the addition of new Member States to the Union

Legal autonomy – the independence of a legal system such that it is not legally bound by any other system, except where it has expressly agreed to be

Ratification – formal consent to a treaty at the national level

1.1 The European Union today

Objective 1

▶ Updates are available at www.pearsoned.co.uk/legalupdates

This chapter aims to introduce some of the main concepts and features that define the Union and Union law as it currently exists. An overview of the history of the Union and the trajectories of its development is then provided, followed by some reflections on how the Union may develop in the future.

The EU comprises a network of institutions that seek to coordinate specific areas of governance between the 27 countries that are currently members (known as Member States). The scope of the Union – i.e. the composition and **competences** of its institutions, the procedures of their operation and their relationships with the Member States – is determined by the **Treaty on the Functioning of the European Union (TFEU)** and the **Treaty on European Union (TEU)**. The provisions of the Treaties have been developed by secondary legislation (directives and regulations), policy documents and the case law of the Court of Justice of the European Union. These features of the Union are all explained in greater depth in the subsequent chapters of Part 1 of this book.

The EU aims to engender political and economic cooperation between countries in Europe. To this end, the Union promotes **four freedoms**: the free movement of people, goods, services and capital. These are considered in Part 2, with the exception of free movement of capital, which is not covered in this book.

1.1.1 Values and objectives

The values that all Union activities are to be guided by are set out in **Article 2 TEU**. The text of Article 2 is as follows:

> The Union is founded on the values of respect for **human dignity**, **freedom**, **democracy**, **equality**, the **rule of law** and respect for **human rights**, including the rights of persons belonging to minorities. These values are common to the Member States in a society in which **pluralism**, **non-discrimination**, **tolerance**, **justice**, **solidarity** and **equality** between women and men prevail.

1.1 THE EUROPEAN UNION TODAY

> See section 7.5 for information on the use of Article 7 TEU to enforce adherence to the values set out in Article 2 TEU

Article 3 TEU then sets out the broad objectives of the Union; objectives which include not only economic policies but also social and political policies. The text of Article 3 is as follows:

1. The Union's aim is to promote **peace**, its **values** and the **well-being** of its peoples.
2. The Union shall offer its citizens an **area of freedom, security and justice** without internal frontiers, in which the **free movement of persons** is ensured in conjunction with appropriate measures with respect to external border controls, asylum, immigration and the prevention and combating of crime.
3. The Union shall establish an **internal market**. It shall work for the **sustainable development** of Europe based on balanced economic growth and price stability, a highly competitive social market economy, aiming at **full employment** and **social progress**, and a high level of protection and improvement of the quality of **the environment**. It shall promote **scientific and technological advance**.

   It shall combat social exclusion and discrimination, and shall promote **social justice** and protection, **equality** between women and men, **solidarity** between generations and protection of the **rights of the child**.

   It shall promote economic, social and territorial **cohesion**, and **solidarity** among Member States.

   It shall respect its rich cultural and linguistic **diversity**, and shall ensure that Europe's **cultural heritage** is safeguarded and enhanced.
4. The Union shall establish an **economic and monetary union** whose currency is the euro.
5. In its relations with the wider world, the Union shall uphold and promote its values and interests and contribute to the protection of its citizens. It shall contribute to **peace**, **security**, the **sustainable development** of the Earth, **solidarity** and **mutual respect** among peoples, **free and fair trade**, **eradication of poverty** and the protection of **human rights**, in particular the **rights of the child**, as well as to the strict observance and the development of **international law**, including respect for the principles of the United Nations Charter.
6. The Union shall pursue its objectives by appropriate means commensurate with the competences which are conferred upon it in the Treaties.

In recognition of the Union's primary foundational objective – to secure peace throughout Europe – the Union was awarded the Nobel Peace Prize on 12 October 2012 for its contribution to the advancement of peace and reconciliation, democracy and human rights in Europe. The President of the European Council and the President of the European Commission issued the following joint statement:

> It is a tremendous honour for the European Union to be awarded the 2012 Nobel Peace Prize. This Prize is the strongest possible recognition of the deep political motives behind our Union: the unique effort by ever more European states to overcome war and divisions and to jointly shape a continent of peace and prosperity. It is a Prize not just for the project and the institutions embodying a common interest, but for the 500 million citizens living in our Union.

1.1.2 Institutions

Article 13(1) TEU provides that the Union shall have an:

> institutional framework which shall aim to promote its values, advance its objectives, serve its interests, those of its citizens and those of the Member States, and ensure the consistency, effectiveness and continuity of its policies and actions.

The following seven Union institutions are recognised by Article 13(1) TEU:

- The European Parliament
- The European Council
- The Council
- The European Commission (herein after referred to as the 'Commission')
- The Court of Justice of the European Union
- The European Central Bank
- The Court of Auditors.

Articles 13–19 TEU clarify the role of the Union institutions. **Part Six of Title I**, **TFEU** then contains the detailed provisions governing the institutions. Together, these provisions constitute the Union's institutional framework. Each of these EU institutions must act within the powers granted to them by the EU Treaties. If any institution exceeds its powers as defined within the Treaties, any resultant act can be struck down as being *ultra vires*, i.e. in excess of its powers.

A very brief overview of the five most important of the Union institutions is now provided. In an attempt to more clearly delineate the institutions, they are considered here in a different order to that in which they are listed in Article 13(1) TEU. We begin with the European Council, which sets the agendas of the Union; then we outline the three decision-making institutions (the European Commission, the European Parliament and the Council); then finally the Court of Justice is briefly considered. Chapter 2 provides far greater detail on these institutions, along with the others that are listed in Article 13(1) TEU.

The European Council

The European Council (not to be confused with the Council) is composed of the **Heads of State and Government of the Member States**, the President of the European Commission and the High Representative for Foreign Affairs and Security Policy. The European Council normally meets in quarterly summits to establish the impetus for the Union's development and define its political directions and priorities. It does not exercise a legislative function (Art 15(1) TEU). The general rule regarding the adoption of decisions is consensus, except where the Treaties provide otherwise (Art 15(4) TEU).

The President of the European Council is required to 'ensure the external representation of the Union on issues concerning its common foreign and security policy, without prejudice to the powers of the High Representative of the Union for Foreign Affairs and Security Policy' (Art 15(6) TEU). The President is elected by a qualified majority of the European Council's members for a term of two-and-a-half years, which may be extended to a second term (Arts 15(5) and 15(6) TEU). The former Prime Minister of Poland, Donald Tusk, was elected to the post for the period from 1 December 2014 to 31 May 2017 and then re-elected for the period from 1 June 2017 to 30 November 2019. The President is not allowed to hold a national office at the same time as holding the Presidency (Art 15(6) TEU) and Tusk therefore had to relinquish his role as Prime Minister of Poland. From 1 December 2019 until 31 May 2022, the President of the European Council is the former President of Belgium, Charles Michel.

The European Commission

The Commission is an independent executive body that can be thought of as the main engine of the EU. The Commission is the only institution that has the **power to propose legislation** except when the Treaties provide otherwise (Art 17(2) TEU). It also plays a role in the **enforcement** of legislation, manages EU budgets and implements the decisions of the European Parliament and the Council. Furthermore, the Commission has a political function, as it represents the EU in international organisations and forums.

The Commission is composed of a Commissioner from each Member State. Prospective Commissioners are suggested by their countries and nominated by the President-elect of the Commission. They must be approved by the Parliament and are then appointed by the European Council. The President of the Commission is elected by the European Parliament on a proposal from the European Council (Art 14(1) TEU). Ursula von der Leyen became the first female President of the Commission on 1 November 2019.

The European Parliament

> The composition of the Parliament before and after Brexit is considered further in section 2.6.2

The European Parliament **debates, amends and passes EU laws** (together with the Council). The Parliament also decides on international agreements and **enlargements** of the Union and exercises supervisory and budgetary functions (Art 14(1) TEU).

Before Brexit, the Parliament was composed of 751 Members of European Parliament (MEPs) (Art 14(2) TEU), who were directly elected by the population of their Member State. After Brexit, 46 of the UK's 73 seats will be left vacant, reducing the total number of MEPs to **705**. The remaining 27 seats will be distributed among 14 Member States that are currently slightly underrepresented. The allocation of MEP seats to each Member State is determined according to 'degressive proportionality' (Art 14(2) TEU). Degressive proportionality in this context means that MEPs from more populous Member States represent more people than those from less populated Member States, so that smaller Member States are afforded a louder voice than if uniform ratios of representation were applied. No Member State will have fewer than 6 nor more than 96 MEPs (Art 14(2) TEU). The President of the European Parliament represents the Parliament to the other Union institutions. The presidency has been held by Italian politician David Sassoli since July 2019.

The Council

The Council (also known as the Council of the European Union, previously known as the Council of Ministers) **negotiates and adopts EU laws** (together with the Parliament). The Council also coordinates the policies of Member States, develops the Union's foreign and security policies and concludes international agreements.

The Council is composed of **ministerial representatives** from each of the Member States (Art 16(2) TEU). However, there is no fixed composition of the Council; **Article 16(6) TEU** instead provides for the Council to meet in different configurations according to the area of policy that is being discussed. These configurations and their presidencies are determined by the European Council (Art 236 TFEU), except for the Foreign Affairs Council (Art 236

TFEU). Article 16(6) TEU specifically provides for the creation of the Foreign Affairs Council, which is presided over by the High Representative of the Union for Foreign Affairs and Security Policy (Art 18(3) TEU). Additionally, the General Affairs Council, which is another configuration specifically mentioned in Article 16(6) TEU, ensures 'consistency in the work of the different Council configurations' (Art 16(6) TEU). All configurations other than the Foreign Affairs Council are presided over by one of the Council's Member State representatives, on the basis of a system of equal rotation (Art 16(9) TEU).

Depending upon the specific Treaty provision at issue, **qualified majority** is the general rule for the adoption of decisions within the Council (Art 16(3) TEU). Since 1 November 2014, a qualified majority requires two thresholds to be achieved before a measure can be adopted:

(i) the support of at least 55 per cent of the members of the Council, i.e. the support of at least 15 Member State representatives; and

(ii) the support of Member States comprising at least 65 per cent of the population of the EU (Art 16(4) TEU).

In addition, a blocking minority must include at least four Member States, failing which the qualified majority will be achieved. This provision prevents three or fewer of the more populous Member States from being able to block a proposal. A requirement of unanimity remains in areas of direct taxation, social security, foreign policy and common security policy. See Chapter 4 for further detail on the decision-making requirements and procedures.

The Court of Justice of the European Union

The Court of Justice of the European Union (CJEU) **interprets and enforces EU law** to ensure that it is applied correctly and consistently across the Union. Regarding interpretation, Member State courts may call upon the CJEU to clarify an aspect of EU law through what is known as the **preliminary rulings** procedure (Art 267 TFEU) (see Chapter 5). The CJEU also considers requests brought by Member State governments or one of the decision-making institutions for Union acts to be annulled on the grounds that they are incompatible with the Treaties or fundamental rights (Art 263 TFEU) (see Chapter 6). Regarding enforcement, the CJEU determines whether Union law has been infringed by a Member State in cases that are brought by either the European Commission or another Member State (Art 258 and Art 259 TFEU) (see Chapter 7). The CJEU also presides over cases against EU institutions, which may be brought by individuals, companies or other organisations.

The CJEU is composed of two courts, the **Court of Justice** and the **General Court** (Art 19(1) TEU). The latter rules on actions brought against Union institutions, while the Court of Justice produces preliminary rulings and deals with all other cases. The decisions of the General Court may be appealed to the Court of Justice on points of law only. The Court of Justice consists of a Judge from each Member State and eleven Advocates General (Art 19(2) TEU). On 1 September 2019, the number of Judges in the General Court increased to two Judges from each Member State in response to a rising workload.

1.1.3 Union membership

The EU has **27 Member States** at the time of writing. In the order in which they joined the Union, these are:

1958: Belgium, France, Germany, Italy, Luxembourg, Netherlands

1973: Denmark, Ireland (the UK also joined in 1973, but left in 2020)

1981: Greece

1986: Portugal, Spain

1995: Austria, Sweden, Finland

2004: Cyprus, Czech Republic, Estonia, Hungary, Latvia, Lithuania, Malta, Poland, Slovakia, Slovenia

2007: Bulgaria, Romania

2013: Croatia

There are currently five candidate countries seeking to join the EU. These are Albania, Republic of North Macedonia, Montenegro, Serbia and Turkey. The latter three of these countries have commenced negotiations but are not likely to accede in the near future. Following approval from the Commission and the European Parliament, accession negotiations with Albania and Republic of North Macedonia were due to commence in October 2019. However, the European Council failed to unanimously agree to this progress, as required, at their October 2019 summit. Iceland applied for membership in July 2009 during the global financial crisis and commenced **accession** negotiations in June 2010, but subsequently withdrew from negotiations in May 2013. Additionally, Bosnia and Herzegovina and Kosovo have the status of 'potential candidates', which means that it has been agreed that they can become candidate countries when they are ready. The status of these countries facilitates cooperation with and assistance from the EU towards greater stability and development. Member States, candidate countries and potential candidate countries are shown in **Map 1.1**.

▶ See section 1.4.1 for further detail on the progress of candidate countries towards accession

Map 1.1 Member States, candidate countries and 'potential candidates'

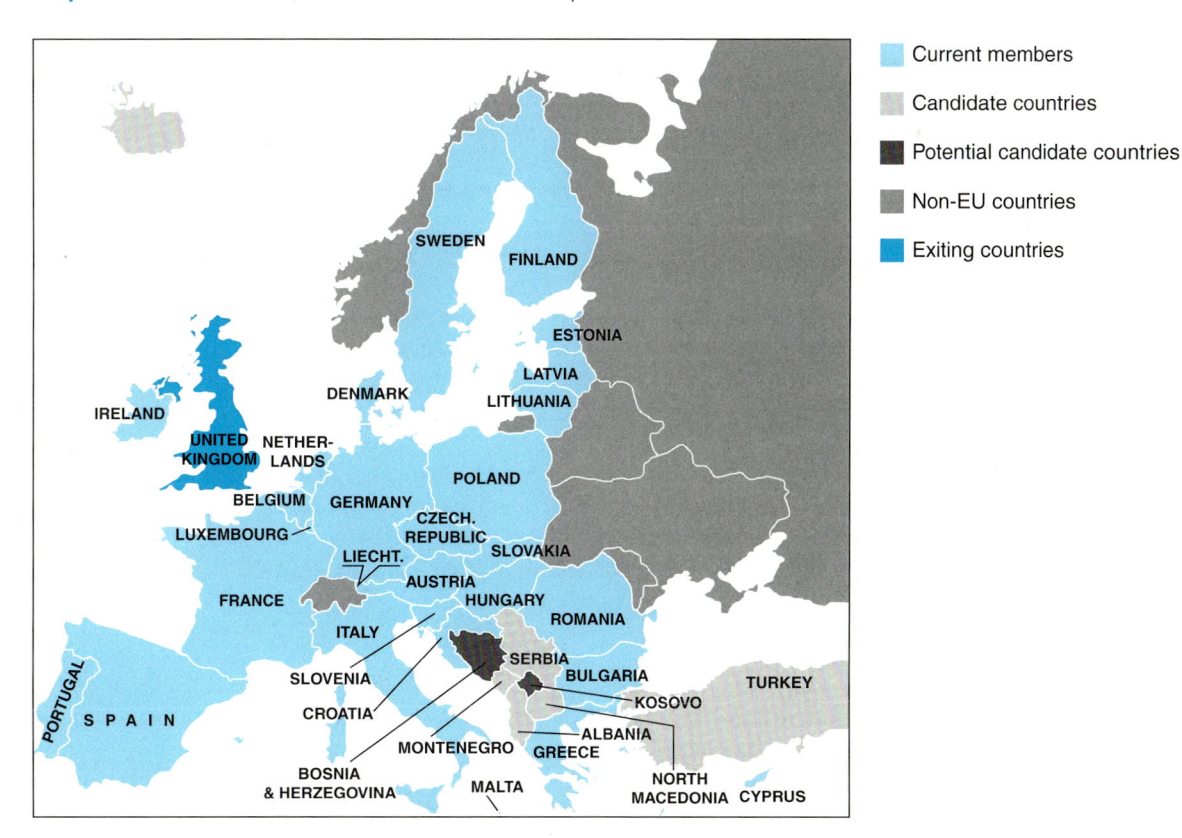

Accession criteria

Article 49 TEU sets out the conditions of eligibility and the procedure for accession to the Union. Any European State 'which respects the values referred to in Article 2 and is committed to promoting them' can apply to become a member of the Union.

In 1993, the European Council met at Copenhagen and established further conditions of eligibility for accession, after agreeing to open membership to Central and Eastern European countries. These are known as the **Copenhagen criteria** and require the following from a prospective member:

- stability of institutions guaranteeing democracy, the rule of law, human rights and respect for and protection of minorities;
- the existence of a functioning market economy as well as the capacity to cope with competitive pressure and market forces within the Union;
- the ability to take on the obligations of membership including adherence to the aims of political, economic and monetary union.

Accession process

A country wishing to join the EU must first have their application accepted unanimously by the Council. The Council decides after consulting the Commission and after obtaining the consent of the European Parliament. The Parliament consents if a majority of its members support the application.

Once the Council has accepted a country's application, it becomes an official **candidate** for membership of the EU and **accession negotiations** can begin. Negotiations are undertaken between ministers and ambassadors of the Member State governments and those of the candidate country. The negotiations cover 35 different policy areas, which are referred to as **chapters**. First, the candidate country undergoes a process of screening, which entails a detailed assessment of the current situation in the country. For most policy areas, the EU will then set benchmarks that the candidate country will need to achieve before negotiations in that chapter can be closed. Negotiations therefore remain open for as long as it takes the candidate country to undertake the required reforms and to align with EU legislation. The Commission monitors the progress of the candidate country, but the closure of a chapter requires every Member State to be satisfied that the candidate country has progressed sufficiently in the relevant area. The negotiation process can only be concluded once all chapters have been closed. Parallel to accession negotiations, the Union will engage with the candidate state in an intensive political and cultural **dialogue** with the aim of enhancing mutual understanding.

After the negotiations, an **accession treaty** is drafted. This treaty contains the details of any transitional arrangements and sets the date on which the candidate country will accede. An accession treaty must be supported by the Commission, the Council and the European Parliament, and must be signed and ratified by all Member States and the candidate country, according to each country's constitutional requirements.

Exit process

Article 50 TEU sets out the procedure for a Member State's voluntary withdrawal from the Union. The full text of Article 50 is as follows:

1. Any Member State may decide to withdraw from the Union in accordance with its own constitutional requirements.

2. A Member State which decides to withdraw shall notify the European Council of its intention. In the light of the guidelines provided by the European Council, the Union shall negotiate and conclude an agreement with that State, setting out the arrangements for its withdrawal, taking account of the framework for its future relationship with the Union. That agreement shall be negotiated in accordance with Article 218(3) of the Treaty on the Functioning of the European Union. It shall be concluded on behalf of the Union by the Council, acting by a qualified majority, after obtaining the consent of the European Parliament.

3. The Treaties shall cease to apply to the State in question from the date of entry into force of the withdrawal agreement or, failing that, two years after the notification referred to in paragraph 2, unless the European Council, in agreement with the Member State concerned, unanimously decides to extend this period.

4. For the purposes of paragraphs 2 and 3, the member of the European Council or of the Council representing the withdrawing Member State shall not participate in the discussions of the European Council or Council or in decisions concerning it.

    A qualified majority shall be defined in accordance with Article 238(3)(b) of the Treaty on the Functioning of the European Union.

5. If a State which has withdrawn from the Union asks to rejoin, its request shall be subject to the procedure referred to in Article 49.

Article 218(3) TFEU, which is to be applied to exit negotiations, reads as follows:

> The Commission . . . shall submit recommendations to the Council, which shall adopt a decision authorising the opening of negotiations and, depending on the subject of the agreement envisaged, nominating the Union negotiator or the head of the Union's negotiating team.

▶ See section 1.4.2 for further detail on Brexit and section 3.7.1 for an overview of the procedure for negotiating a withdrawal agreement

Following a negative referendum result on continued membership of the Union, the UK notified the Council of its intention to leave the EU in accordance with Article 50(2) TEU on 29 March 2017. In *Wightman and Others* (C-621/18), the Court of Justice ruled that the UK would be free to unilaterally revoke this at any point prior to withdrawal. In accordance with Article 50(2) TEU and Article 218(3) TFEU, withdrawal negotiations between UK and EU representatives began on 19 June 2017. Multiple extensions to the negotiating period were then agreed under Article 50(3). The UK formally exited the Union on 31 January 2020, but then entered into transition period. EU law continues to apply to the UK during this transition period, which is expected at the time of writing to terminate on 31 December 2020.

1.1.4 EU law

Legislative procedures and competence

Article 352(1) TFEU provides the Union with a general legislative power:

> If action by the Union should prove necessary . . . to attain one of the objectives set out in the Treaties, and the Treaties have not provided the necessary powers, the Council . . . shall adopt the appropriate measures.

The power of legislative initiative rests with the Commission, 'except where the Treaties provide otherwise' (Art 17(2) TEU). **Article 289 TFEU** provides that a legislative act can be adopted by the **'ordinary legislative procedure'** or a **'special legislative procedure'**. The ordinary legislative procedure applies in the vast majority of cases. Further information on legislative procedures can be found in Chapter 3.

The institutions of the EU may only act in the areas in which they are granted the competence to do so by the treaties. This is known as the principle of **conferral** and is established by **Article 5(2) TEU** as follows:

> Under the principle of conferral, the Union shall act only within the limits of the competences conferred upon it by the Member States in the Treaties to attain the objectives set out therein. Competences not conferred upon the Union in the Treaties remain with the Member States.

> See section 3.3.1 for further information on the principles of subsidiarity and proportionality

The scope of the Union is also limited by the principle of **subsidiarity** (Art 5(3) TEU), which determines that the Union can only act in the pursuit of an objective that cannot be sufficiently achieved by a Member State acting alone, and the principle of **proportionality** (Art 5(4) TEU), which determines that the Union may not take any action beyond that which is necessary to achieve the objectives of the treaties. **Protocol No. 2**, which is annexed to the TEU and TFEU, concerns the application of these two principles.

The EU has three levels of competence. In areas where the Union has **exclusive competence**, Member States have transferred all capacity to enact legislation to the Union (Art 3 TFEU). In areas of **shared competence**, both the EU and its Member States can enact legislation, but Members States may only do so where the Union has not (Art 4 TFEU). However, the Union's activities in areas of shared competence are restricted by the principle of subsidiarity. Finally, in areas of **supporting competence**, the Union can support, coordinate or supplement the actions of Member States at a European level (Art 6 TFEU). Further information on the competences of the Union in all of the areas mentioned above can be found in Chapter 4.

There are two particular areas of competence that warrant further mention here: the **area of freedom, security and justice** (AFSJ) and the **common foreign and security policy** (CFSP). The establishment of the AFSJ is one of the aims of the Union that is set out in Article 3 TEU. It refers to issues arising from the free movement of people, such as immigration, asylum, trafficking, cooperation in criminal justice and terrorism. The CFSP, on the other hand, refers to the external relations of the Union (other than in the area of trade) (Art 24(1) TEU). The CFSP encompasses several bodies, including the European Defence Agency and the Foreign Affairs Council, which is a configuration of the Council and is presided over by the High Representative for Foreign Affairs and Security Policy. The common security and defence policy is an integral part of the CFSP (Art 42(1) TEU).

The 'special character' of EU law

The law of the Union was established as autonomous – i.e. as being an independent legal system – in the case of ***Costa* v *ENEL*** (Case 64/4), where the Court of Justice stated that

> See section 4.3 for further detail on the principle of supremacy

the Community (now the Union) has 'its own legal capacity and capacity of representation on the international plane and, more particularly, real powers stemming from a limitation of sovereignty or a transfer of powers from the states to the community'. As a consequence of this, the Court determined that Union law 'could not because of its special and original nature, be overridden by domestic legal provisions'. This position of Union law as authoritative over national law is known as the **supremacy** of EU law.

Union law is described as having a 'special character' due to the unique composition and powers of the Union. As De Búrca and Weiler (2011, p. 3) state, the EU is 'a political and legal entity which has long defied easy categorization in the language of constitutional law or of international organizations'. While the Treaties of the Union do not formally comprise a supranational constitution (such a formal EU constitution was drafted in 2005 but never ratified), the Union possesses many constitutional characteristics, such as fully established procedures for creating law, a binding charter of fundamental rights and a supreme court.

Additionally, the supremacy of EU law has led the EU to be compared to a federation or a confederation (depending on whether more power is perceived to be held by the EU or its Member States respectively). However, neither term fully reflects the unique composition and division of powers between the Union institutions and its Member States.

1.1.5 Economic aspects of the Union

The European Economic Area

As stated in Article 3(3) TEU, the establishment of an internal market is one of the core objectives of the Union. However, the European Economic Area (EEA), throughout which the internal market operates, extends beyond the 27 Member States of the EU to also include three out of the four European Free Trade Association (EFTA) states. EFTA is composed of Iceland, Lichtenstein, Norway and Switzerland, the former three of which are also member of the EEA **(see Map 1.2)**. The EEA gives the three EFTA states access to the markets of the Union for their goods, persons, services and capital. Equally, the same facilities are granted by EFTA states in their territories to Member States of the EU. In the EEA, all the economic rules of the EU apply, although the Member States of EFTA are not represented in any of the EU institutions and do not participate in the EU's decision-making process. Four bodies coordinate the functioning of the EEA:

- The EEA Council
- Joint Committee
- Joint Parliamentary Committee
- Consultative Committee.

Additionally, the EFTA states have monitoring and judiciary institutions in parallel with the Union. Thus, while compliance with Union law in the Union Member States is monitored by the Commission, compliance with EEA law in the relevant EFTA states is monitored by the **EFTA Surveillance Authority**; and while cases concerning Union law are brought before the Court of Justice, cases concerning EEA law in the relevant EFTA states are brought before the **EFTA Court**. The UK was a founding member of EFTA, but left the association when it joined the EU. At the time of writing, the UK government does not intend for the UK to remain a part of the EEA or to rejoin EFTA after it has ceased to be a Member State of the Union. Thus, while Map 1.2 shows the UK as an 'EU non-euro zone' country, it is expected that, after the withdrawal transition period has expired on 31 December 2020, the UK will simply become a 'non-EU country'.

Map 1.2 EU and EFTA countries

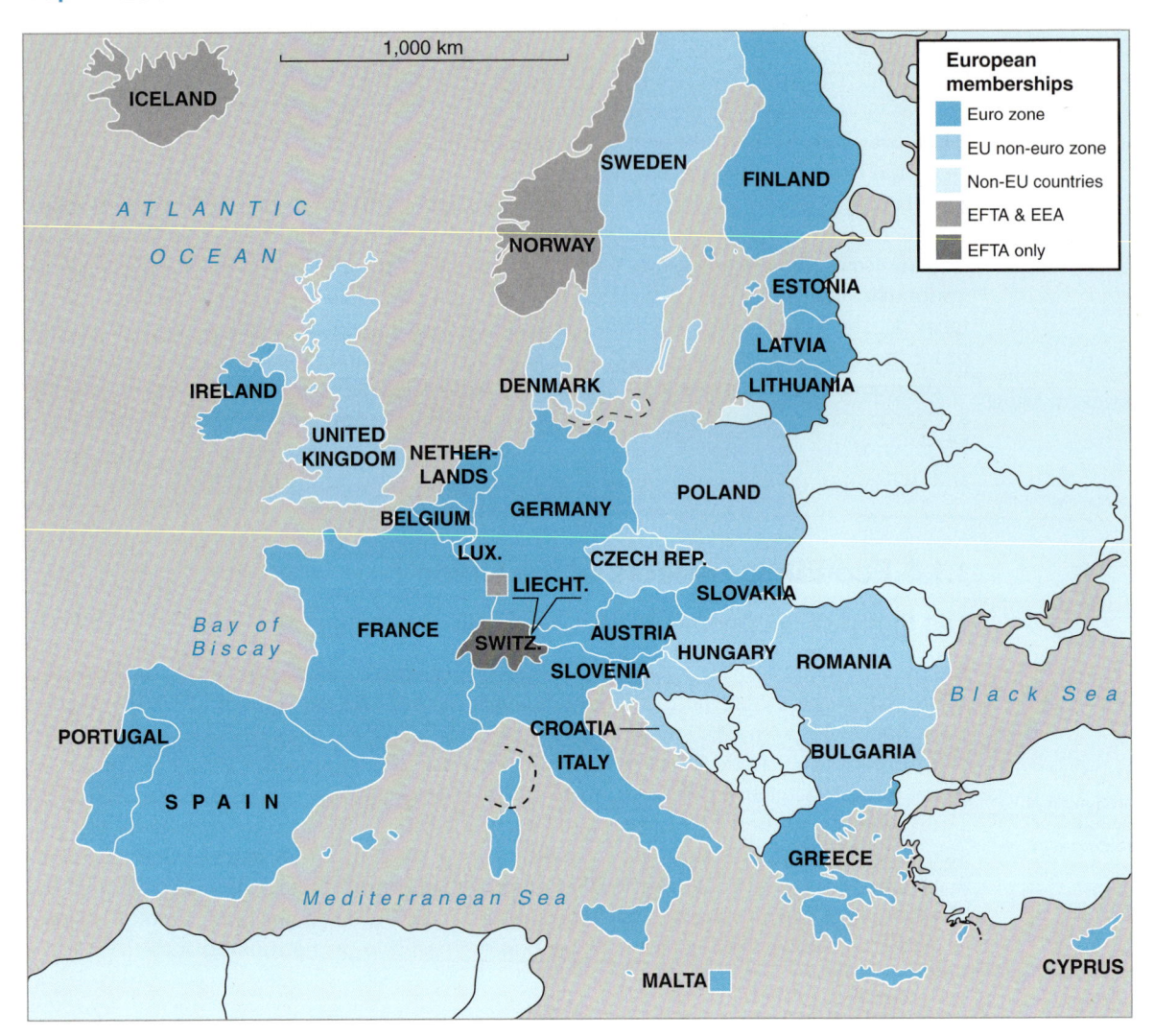

The Eurozone

Pursuant to **Article 3(4) TEU**, which states that 'The Union shall establish an economic and monetary union whose currency is the euro', 19 countries currently use the **euro**. The euro came into effect in 2002, but not all of the current Eurozone countries adopted the common currency at that time.

Other Member States, aside from the UK and Denmark which have opted out, are obliged to adopt the euro once they meet the criteria for doing so.

The Eurozone facilitates the internal market by eliminating fluctuating exchange rates and costs, which makes trade across borders easier and more predictable. The euro therefore produces greater economic stability, growth and global power than could be achieved with separate national currencies. It also encourages travel and shopping across borders, which

Figure 1.1 The growth of the Eurozone

Original euro countries	Joined the euro						
1999	2001	2007	2008	2009	2011	2014	2015
Austria, Belgium, Finland, France, Germany, Ireland, Italy, Luxembourg, Netherlands, Portugal, Spain	Greece	Slovenia	Cyprus, Malta	Slovakia	Estonia	Latvia	Lithuania
							Total = 19 euro countries

contributes to the free movement of people and goods. **Figure 1.1** lists the Eurozone countries in the order in which they joined.

The **monetary policy** of the Eurozone is administered by the **European Central Bank** (ECB), which is governed by a president and a board of the heads of national central banks. The primary aim of the ECB is to maintain price stability within the Eurozone. Its functions and procedures are set out in the Statute of the European Central Bank.

1.1.6 The EU in the world

Article 47 TEU states that 'The Union shall have legal personality'. This enables the Union to enter into international treaties and agreements on the behalf of the Member States. This capacity is expanded upon in **Articles 216 and 217 TFEU**, which expressly establish that the Union has the competence to enter into international agreements with other countries and international organisations. This can have the effect of placing extra obligations on Members States, but can also bring extra benefits derived from the greater negotiating power of the Union compared to that of an individual Member State. **Article 21 TEU** sets out the objectives of the Union's international relations and the principles that the Union should abide by in its external action.

▶ See section 3.7 on international sources of EU law

The Union interacts most closely with international organisations with which it shares the same goals and values. Some of the most influential of these include:

The Council of Europe (CoE)

All 27 EU Member States are also members of the Council of Europe, which has 47 Member States in total (including the UK). The EU has interacted with the Council of Europe since its inception and the two bodies have engaged in joint programmes since 1992. In 2007, a **Memorandum of Understanding** was signed by the EU and the Council of Europe, formalising their future cooperation along lines of complementarity and coherence. The Court of Justice has also developed a close relationship with the **European Court of Human Rights**, which is the Council of Europe's specialised court that presides over the **European Convention on Human Rights**.

▶ The European Convention on Human Rights is discussed in further detail in section 3.3.2

The World Trade Organization (WTO)

As the Union has exclusive competence in governing the EU Customs Union, it represents the Member States in the WTO. The Union supports the work of the WTO on multilateral rule-making, trade liberalisation and sustainable development.

The United Nations (UN)

In addition to the full individual membership of its 27 Member States, the Union has held **'enhanced observer'** status at the UN since 2011. This means that it can speak among representatives of major groups, submit proposals and amendments and circulate documents. Moreover, internal Union meetings are held to develop a common stance and to coordinate Member State votes on issues before the UN. **Article 34 TEU** requires Member States that are members of the UN Security Council to 'defend the positions and the interests of the Union'.

> **Reflection:** Is the European Union a global superpower?
>
> During the Cold War, the US and the USSR were described as the world's two competing superpowers, with each possessing the military strength to dominate – or destroy – the rest of the world, were it not for the other. Since the end of the Cold War and the collapse of the USSR, the US has become the dominant force in global affairs, albeit not without competition from countries such as Russia and China, nor indeed heavy recent criticism of its international credibility. It has been argued, however, that the EU might also qualify as a superpower, not due to any military credentials, but rather due to the global reach of its economic prowess and political influence. Factors such as the relatively high quality of life and technological advance of the EU have also led to it being described as a successful modern-day empire, which will be further enhanced by future expansion. For others, however, the Union's lack of military power and political disunity – as exacerbated by the Eurozone economic crisis – mean that it is unlikely to ever become a superpower. Indeed the answer to the question comes down to not only how a superpower is defined in the contemporary world, but also whether it is believed that the Union is destined to grow stronger and more influential or to fracture and decline.

1.2 History of the European Communities and the EU

Objective 2

The current EU is the result of over 60 years of political ambitions, challenges and compromises. Some understanding of these developments is important for understanding the Union as it is today – and especially the context in which influential judgments of the Court of Justice were passed. The historical overview provided here covers the main treaties that have shaped the Union, the machinations of the relevant institutions and its enlargement as new Member States have joined. Detailed discussion of the Treaty of Lisbon (ToL), which entered into force in 2009 and established the current Union structure, is reserved for the next section of this chapter (section 1.3).

1.2.1 Lessons from the World Wars

The European Communities came into existence in the aftermath of the Second World War, but the impetus for their creation, to a large extent, came from a desire not to repeat the mistakes made by the victorious powers after the First World War. The Treaty of Versailles of 1919 recognised the new nation-states of Central and Eastern Europe that had emerged following the collapse of the Austro–Hungarian and Ottoman empires. It also imposed heavy reparations on Germany, which the new Weimar Republic was unable to pay. The hyperinflation that followed, and the crash of 1929, wiped out the savings of the large German middle class and pushed unemployment in Germany to more than 40 per cent of the labour force (Hobsbawm,

1994). The instability that this created led directly to the rise of the Nazi Party and the outbreak of the Second World War. It also gravely affected the economies of the other Western European powers. The UK, France and Italy, the victors of the First World War who were the architects of Versailles, suffered almost as much as the vanquished from its consequences. Attempts at protecting national economies by tariff barriers were largely unsuccessful and did little more than maintain the economies of Western Europe in a state of stagnation until they were lifted by preparations for another world war. The experience of the inter-war years made clear beyond doubt that it was no longer possible for the states of Western Europe, including states like the UK and France which still had large colonial markets, to operate their national economies without regard to the effect on their immediate neighbours.

Another important lesson of the First World War and its aftermath was learned from the failure of resultant defence treaties and the new League of Nations to avert war. The French, above all, grasped the importance of binding Germany's coal and steel industry, the sinews of its war machine, into a new political and economic alliance. At the same time, fear of the apparently expansionist Soviet Union that now occupied the whole of Eastern and Central Europe, including the former East Germany, impelled the democratic states of Western Europe and North America to come together in 1949 to form the North Atlantic Treaty Organization (NATO). The former West Germany did not join NATO until October 1954 (The Paris Agreements). The USA, instead of withdrawing from Europe as it had in 1919, was a founding member of NATO, the new defence organisation, and played a major part in European rehabilitation and reconstruction. Millions of dollars were poured into the former West Germany in grants and loans under the Marshall Plan, and it started on a rapid economic recovery. Other European states were also assisted under the Plan.

The recognition of the reality and, indeed, the need for mutual interdependence by Western European states, created a receptive atmosphere for resurgent ideas about European political unity. These were expressed with force and vision by Winston Churchill (the former UK Prime Minister) at Zurich in September 1946, when he proposed a 'sovereign remedy' to European tensions. He proposed the creation of 'a European family, or as much of it as we can', which would be provided with 'a structure under which it can dwell in peace, in safety and in freedom. We must build a kind of United States of Europe.' Although he did not envisage the UK becoming a member of this 'European family', he stated that the first step in its creation should be based on a partnership between France and Germany. This would have required an imaginative leap by the French, who had been the victims of three wars of aggression by Germany and who were only just beginning to recover from German occupation. The idea of a European federation based on a Franco–German partnership was, however, taken up with enthusiasm by two French politicians, Jean Monnet and Robert Schumann, the former with responsibility for French economic planning and the latter as foreign minister. The first step in the construction of the new European order was the creation of the European Coal and Steel Community.

1.2.2 The European Coal and Steel Community – 23 July 1952

On 9 May 1950, less than four years after Churchill made his Zurich speech, Robert Schumann (the former French Foreign Minister) stated that a united Europe was essential for the maintenance of world peace. He further stated that a European alliance was essential and that would require the century-old opposition between France and Germany to be eliminated. He proposed that the first stage on this road to European integration would require the whole of France and Germany's coal and steel production to be placed under one authority.

His proposal provided that other countries within Europe could become members of the organisation which would be created.

France, Germany, Italy and the Benelux countries (Belgium, the Netherlands and Luxembourg) accepted the proposal and negotiations started immediately. The negotiations progressed rapidly and less than one year later, on 18 April 1951, the **Treaty Establishing the European Coal and Steel Community (ECSC)** was signed by these six countries in Paris. Because it was signed in Paris it is often referred to as the **Treaty of Paris**. **Ratification** of the Treaty (i.e. approval) by the six states was a mere formality.

Following ratification, the Treaty entered into force on 23 July 1952, thus establishing the ECSC. This Treaty had a 50-year lifespan and this Community therefore came to an end on 23 July 2002. By this point it had become one of the three Communities which were collectively referred to as the European Communities; this is discussed further below.

It is stated above that European integration was necessary to ensure world peace. So how did the ECSC further this aim? Coal and steel were, in the 1950s, essential components in the production of arms and munitions. Thus, by depriving France and Germany of their independence in the production of these commodities, it was widely believed that future conflicts between France and Germany would be avoided. However, the Preamble to the Treaty made it quite clear that the long-term aims of the participants went a great deal further than the control of the production of coal and steel. The Treaty recognised that 'Europe can be built only through practical achievements which will first of all create solidarity, and through the establishment of common bases for economic solidarity'. The participants were 'resolved to substitute for age-old rivalries the merging of their essential interests; to create, by establishing an economic community, the basis for a deeper and broader community among peoples long divided by bloody conflicts' (Preamble).

There was little UK enthusiasm for involvement and successive UK governments (including the then Conservative administration under the Premiership of Winston Churchill) were prepared to support only the loosest association with their continental neighbours. These fell far short of the aspirations of the six founding states and, for two decades, the UK remained on the sidelines of Community developments.

The ECSC Treaty created five institutions:

- an executive, called the High Authority;
- a Consultative Committee attached to the High Authority;
- a Special Council of Ministers;
- an Assembly;
- a Court of Justice.

The most striking thing about this new Community was the fact that it had legal personality. The High Authority was responsible for policy relating to the coal and steel industries in the Member States and had the power to make decisions directly affecting the economic agents in each country without regard to the wishes of the governments of those states. Investment in the coal and steel industries was influenced by the High Authority, though not subject to much control. Powers were reserved to regulate prices and production, but only if there were crises of shortage or over-production. There was also a social dimension to this Community: policies were to be framed for training, housing and redeployment. Competition was, at the same time, stimulated by rules on price transparency, as well as anti-trust laws which were modelled on those of the United States. These decisions were enforceable against the Member States in the new Court of Justice.

1.2.3 The European Economic Community and Euratom – 1 July 1958

Three of the founding states of the ECSC (Belgium, the Netherlands and Luxembourg) had already formed themselves into the **Benelux customs union**. From 1 January 1948, customs barriers were removed between Belgium, the Netherlands and Luxembourg, and a common customs tariff was agreed between them in relation to the outside world. The effect of this was that goods could freely pass between the three countries, with minimal formalities. In 1954 they also authorised the free flow of capital, which meant the freedom of investment and unrestricted transfer of currency between the three countries, and in 1956 they introduced the free movement of labour. The internal trade of these countries increased by 50 per cent between 1948 and 1956, making this mini common market profitable to all three countries involved. Its success whetted the appetites of neighbouring states and led to pressure to expand this experiment on a European scale.

This pressure created the political climate for a much more ambitious project. On 25 March 1957, the **Treaty Establishing the European Economic Community (EEC Treaty)** was signed in Rome by the six founding states of the ECSC, the aim being to establish a European Economic Community (EEC) in goods, persons, services and capital among these six states. The common market established by the EEC Treaty (often referred to as the Treaty of Rome) was, at the time, the biggest free trade area in the world. At the same time, the **Treaty Establishing the European Atomic Energy Community (Euratom)** was signed, providing for cooperation in the use of atomic energy. The UK participated in the initial negotiations for both Treaties but withdrew because it feared a loss of national sovereignty and damage to its favourable trading links with the Commonwealth – concerns which have never been fully resolved. The EEC and Euratom Treaties came into force on 1 July 1958, following their ratification by the six states. This resulted in the existence of three Communities: the EEC, the ECSC and Euratom, which were collectively referred to as **the European Communities**. As stated above, the ECSC came to an end on 23 July 2002, and therefore from that date 'the European Communities' referred only to the EEC (by then known as the EC) and Euratom.

The preamble to the EEC Treaty set out the objectives of the founding states:

> . . . to lay the foundations of an **ever closer union** among the peoples of Europe . . . to ensure the **economic and social progress** of their countries by common action to eliminate the barriers which divide Europe . . . [to secure] the constant improvement of the **living and working conditions** of their peoples . . . [and] to strengthen the unity of their economies and to ensure their **harmonious development** by reducing differences existing between various regions . . . [and] by means of a **common commercial policy**, to [secure] the progressive abolition of restrictions on international trade.

The common market, which was created by the EEC Treaty, covered the whole economic field except those areas falling within the scope of the ECSC or Euratom. As initially formulated, **Article 3 EEC Treaty** vested the Community with the power to pursue, *inter alia*, the following activities:

- the elimination, as between Member States, of customs duties and of quantitative restrictions on the import and export of goods, and of all other measures having equivalent effect;

- the establishment of a common customs tariff and a common commercial policy towards third countries (i.e. countries not within the Community);
- the abolition, as between Member States, of obstacles to the free movement of persons, services and capital;
- the adoption of a common agricultural policy;
- the adoption of a common transport policy;
- the creation of a Community competition policy;
- the approximation of the laws of the Member States to the extent required for the proper functioning of the common market;
- the association of overseas countries and territories in order to increase trade and promote economic development.

Article 3 empowered the Community (through its institutions) to pursue these economic activities and thus to create economic conditions similar to those in the market of a single state i.e. similar to the position in the UK where there is free movement of goods, persons, services and capital between England, Scotland, Wales and Northern Ireland. These objectives reflected what had already largely been achieved in the Benelux states.

The main institutions of the EEC – the Commission, the Council of Ministers (now the Council), the Assembly (now the European Parliament) and the Court of Justice – were modelled on those of the ECSC and the Community had a similar legal structure.

In contrast, the object of Euratom was to develop nuclear energy, distribute it within the Community and sell the surplus to the outside world. For political reasons originally associated with France's nuclear weapons programme and, subsequently, as a result of widespread doubts about the safety and viability of nuclear power, Euratom never developed as originally envisaged. Euratom has, however, remained an important focus for research and the promotion of nuclear safety.

Merger of the institutions

Immediately after the EEC and Euratom Treaties were signed, agreement was reached to have only one Parliamentary Assembly and one Court of Justice for the ECSC, EEC and Euratom. For some time after the new Treaties came into effect, however, there remained separate Councils of Ministers and separate executive bodies – a High Authority in the case of the ECSC and a Commission each for the EEC and Euratom.

On 8 April 1965, the simplification of the institutional structure of the Communities was completed by the signature of a **Merger Treaty**, the result of which was that there was thereafter one Council, one European Commission, one European Court of Justice and one Assembly (now the European Parliament) for all three Communities.

1.2.4 Enlargement – 1973–86

UK, Denmark and Ireland – 1 July 1973

The UK's response to the creation of the EEC in 1958 was to propose a much looser 'free trade area'. This proposal was not welcomed by the Community, but in 1959 it resulted in the creation of a rival organisation, the **European Free Trade Association (EFTA)**, comprising Austria, Denmark, Norway, Portugal, Sweden, Switzerland and the United Kingdom.

> See section 1.1.5 for the current status of EFTA

Although trade increased between these states, EFTA lacked the structure and coherence of the EEC and its members' economies grew only modestly by comparison.

By 1961, the UK government realised that it could have benefited significantly from joining the European Communities and, in that year, the Conservative Macmillan government applied for membership. After prolonged negotiations, the application, which needed the unanimous agreement of the Member States, was vetoed by the French President, General de Gaulle. The French were reluctant to accept the UK's membership because it was feared the UK would attempt to retain preferences for Commonwealth trade and also because the UK government was felt to be too close, politically, to the USA. France was afraid that the special relationship between the UK and the USA would obstruct French efforts to create a European defence community, free from US dominance. A further UK membership attempt was made by the Labour government of Harold Wilson in 1967, but this was again vetoed by the French. In 1970, a third application was made by Edward Heath's Conservative government and on this occasion the application was successful. The **Treaty of Accession** was signed on 22 January 1972 and the UK, together with Denmark and Ireland, became members of the European Communities on 1 January 1973. Norway, which had participated in the accession negotiations, did not join, as a result of an adverse national referendum.

The Treaty of Accession bound the new Member States to accept the three Treaties (ECSC, EEC and Euratom) and to accept the existing rules of the Communities. The UK Parliament, after a debate that split both the Conservative and Labour parties, enacted the **European Communities Act 1972**, which was intended to give both present and future Community law effect in the UK. Divisions within the Labour Party about membership of the European Communities led the Labour government to promise a national referendum in their manifesto for the October 1974 general election. This was held in 1975 and resulted in the endorsement of continuing membership by a majority of almost 2:1.

Greece – 1 January 1981

Greece became a member of the European Communities on 1 January 1981, increasing the number of Member States to 10.

Portugal and Spain – 1 January 1986

Portugal and Spain became members of the European Communities on 1 January 1986, increasing the number of Member States to 12.

1.2.5 The Single European Act – 1 July 1987

The Single European Act (SEA) is a Treaty that was concluded between the Member States, the purpose of which was to amend the three founding Treaties of the Communities (ECSC, EEC and Euratom). It was signed in Luxembourg in February 1986 and entered into force on 1 July 1987.

The main provisions of the SEA will now be considered.

A European Union?

The Preamble to the SEA set out a commitment to transform relations between the Member States into a European Union; a Union which would operate way beyond the solely economic sphere. Political cooperation between the Member States was considered to be of paramount importance to the creation of this European Union.

The SEA separated provisions relating to political cooperation from those relating to economic integration. Those provisions relating to economic integration were implemented by amending the founding EEC Treaty. However, in relation to political cooperation, those provisions were implemented outside the existing Treaty. It was provided that the representatives of the Member States (i.e. Prime Minister/President and Foreign Secretary) should meet regularly for the purpose of drawing up common political objectives through a body referred to as the **European Council**.

Therefore, at the economic level, policies were implemented through the structure of the EEC (having its own special methods of decision-making and enforcement), whereas political policies were developed outside this structure, through cooperation between the Member States; an intergovernmental arrangement which did not bind the Member States unless *all* the Member States were in agreement.

➤ See section 2.2 on the European Council

Amendments to the EEC Treaty

Completing the internal market and new policy objectives

The Treaties came into force during the 1950s when concerns about war in Western Europe and mass unemployment were high. However, by the mid-1970s and early 1980s, these concerns had largely given way to pressure for greater consumer protection and protections at work. There were also growing anxieties about the degradation of the natural environment. The response to these new concerns was initially tackled at national level, rather than Community level, which resulted in a whole range of different national standards for both goods and industrial production that seriously threatened the growth of a genuine common market in goods and services. The development of a multiplicity of national standards was accompanied by a slowing down of the economies of all the Member States following the explosion of oil prices in 1973. Implementing the recommendations of the Commission's White Paper, *Completing the Internal Market* (1985), the SEA attempted to tackle this problem on two fronts. First, it extended the competence of the EEC to enable it to legislate for the whole area of the Community on the following:

- environmental matters;
- economic and social cohesion, including health and safety;
- consumer protection;
- academic, professional and vocational qualifications;
- public procurement (i.e. competition for public contracts);
- Value Added Tax (i.e. VAT, which is a tax levied internally on goods and services);
- excise duties and frontier controls;
- research and technological development.

Secondly, the SEA set a target for the creation of a new internal market by 1 January 1993. This would be achieved through the removal of all the remaining legal, technical and physical obstacles to the free movement of goods, persons, services and capital. This objective was set out in the former Article 8a EEC Treaty (added by the SEA, now Art 26 TFEU), where the internal market was described as 'an area without internal frontiers in which the free movement of goods, persons, services and capital is ensured'.

Increasing the European Parliament's legislative powers

Until 1979, members of the European Assembly were nominated by their national parliaments. The first direct elections to the newly named European Parliament took place in June 1979 and the effect was that the Parliament became the only directly elected Community institution. It had, at the time, only a consultative status in the legislative process. It was often said that the European Commission proposed legislation and the Council of Ministers disposed of it (i.e. adopted it). This situation generated pressure on the Member States to address the 'democratic deficit' in the Communities' decision-making process. The SEA added a new '**cooperation procedure**' to the EEC Treaty, giving the Parliament a more important role in the legislative process in four areas:

- prohibition of discrimination on the grounds of nationality (now Art 18 TFEU);
- the achievement of the free movement of workers (now Art 46 TFEU);
- promotion of the right of establishment (now Art 50 TFEU);
- measures for implementation of the internal market (now Art 114 TFEU).

This new legislative procedure required the Council of Ministers to cooperate with the European Parliament. For the first time, the Parliament would have a real input into the legislative process by being able to propose amendments. In addition to Parliamentary input, legislative measures in these four areas could be adopted by the Council by 'qualified majority' rather than unanimity, thus preventing a Member State from blocking developments. The current legislative process is considered in detail in Chapter 3.

1.2.6 The Treaty on European Union – 1 November 1993

The next step in the constitutional development of the EU was the adoption of the Treaty on European Union (TEU), which is also known as the **Treaty of Maastricht**. The TEU was signed on 7 February 1992 and came into force on 1 November 1993 once it had been ratified by the Member States.

The TEU consisted of the following seven titles:

- Title I: Common provisions (Arts A to F)
- Title II: Provisions amending the EEC Treaty (Art G)
- Title III: Provisions amending the ECSC Treaty (Art H)
- Title IV: Provisions amending the Euratom Treaty (Art I)
- Title V: Provisions on a Common Foreign and Security Policy (Arts J.1 to J.11)
- Title VI: Provisions on Cooperation in Justice and Home Affairs (Arts K.1 to K.9)
- Title VII: Final Provisions (Arts L to S).

Titles II, III and IV of the TEU simply amended the three founding Treaties (as previously amended by the SEA). Titles V and VI introduced two new 'pillars', and subsequently a whole new structure, to what was now to be collectively called the European Union. The Treaty of Maastricht also introduced a number of protocols, which were attached to the amended EEC Treaty.

These developments will now be discussed in greater detail.

Amendments to the EEC Treaty (which became the EC Treaty)

Articles 2 and 3 EC Treaty, as amended by the TEU, extended the tasks and activities of the European Community beyond those with a purely economic base to now encompass political and social goals. Article 2, for example, provided that the Community's tasks included the promotion of 'a high level of employment and of social protection, the raising of the standard of living and quality of life, and economic and social cohesion and solidarity'.

Reflecting this development, the TEU changed the title of the Treaty establishing the European Economic Community (EEC Treaty) to the European Community Treaty (EC Treaty). From 1 November 1993 until 1 December 2009, the EEC Treaty was known as the EC Treaty (on 1 December 2009, the Treaty of Lisbon (ToL) renamed the EC Treaty the Treaty on the Functioning of the European Union (TFEU), see below).

The EC Treaty is the most important of the three founding Treaties. Amendments made to the EC Treaty by Article G (i.e. Title II) TEU were as follows:

- creation of a **citizenship** of the European Union (Art 17 EC Treaty, now Art 20 TFEU);
- **common economic and monetary policy**, with a timetable for the implementation of a common currency (Arts 98–124 EC Treaty, now Arts 119–144 TFEU);
- adoption of the principle of **subsidiarity** (Art 5 EC Treaty, now Art 5 TEU);
- amendment of the **decision-making process** – extension of qualified majority voting for the adoption of Council Acts into new policy areas and further powers given to the European Parliament;
- introduction of **new areas** of tasks and activities (the former Arts 2 and 3 EC Treaty were amended; now, in substance, Art 3 TEU).

The European Union

Title I of the TEU did not amend the EC Treaty, but simply set out the basic aims and principles of the EU.

Three pillars of the EU

Article A TEU provided for the establishment of a European Union:

> The Union shall be founded on the European Communities, supplemented by the policies and forms of cooperation established by this Treaty.

It followed from this that the EU was to be composed of three pillars:

- The European Communities – EC, ECSC, Euratom
- Common Foreign and Security Policy (CFSP) – Title V (Art J)
- Cooperation in Justice and Home Affairs (JHA) – Title VI (Art K).

Although intergovernmental in nature, and thus falling outside the formal Community structure, the second and third pillars of the Union did have a connection in that some of the Community institutions (in particular the Council of Ministers) played a part in their policy development.

As its name suggests, the second pillar (Common Foreign and Security Policy) provided for joint foreign and security (i.e. defence) action by the Member States. This action would be taken by the Council acting unanimously. However, there was scope for the Council to provide that certain decisions could be adopted by a qualified majority vote (Art J.3, para 2 TEU). There was minimal involvement of the European Parliament and the Commission in the process. Article L TEU excluded the Court of Justice from ruling on these provisions.

The third pillar (Cooperation in Justice and Home Affairs) provided for cooperation in policy areas such as asylum, immigration, 'third country' (i.e. non-EU) nationals, international crime (e.g. drug trafficking) and various forms of judicial cooperation. Action would again be taken by the Council of Ministers acting unanimously, with very limited provision for qualified majority voting (Art K.4, para 3 TEU). Once again there was little involvement of the European Parliament and the Commission and Article L TEU also excluded the Court of Justice from ruling on these provisions.

Objectives of the EU

Article B TEU set out the objectives of the Union, some of which mirrored those contained in the EC Treaty. The objectives established by Article B include:

- to **promote economic and social progress** which is balanced and sustainable, in particular through the creation of an area without internal frontiers, through the strengthening of economic and social cohesion and through the establishment of economic and monetary union, ultimately including a single currency in accordance with the provisions of this Treaty;
- to assert its identity on the international scene, in particular through the implementation of a **common foreign and security policy** including the eventual framing of a common defence policy, which might in time lead to a common defence;
- to strengthen the protection of the rights and interests of the nationals of its Member States through the introduction of a **citizenship of the Union**;
- to develop close cooperation on **justice and home affairs**.

Protection of human rights

Article F(2) TEU provided that the Union would respect fundamental rights 'as guaranteed by the European Convention for the Protection of Human Rights and Fundamental Freedoms . . . as general principles of Community law'.

However, Article L TEU provided that all the common provisions of Title I (which included Art F(2) TEU) were not justiciable by the European Court of Justice, i.e. the Court did not have the power to rule on their application or validity. Despite this, it was possible that the Court of Justice would take the common provisions into account, including Article F(2), when interpreting the Treaties. This is considered further below and in Chapter 3.

Protocols

Annexed to the EC Treaty, as amended by the TEU, were a number of protocols. Protocols formed part of the Treaty by virtue of Article 311 EC Treaty, which provided that:

> The protocols annexed to this Treaty by common accord of the Member States shall form an integral part thereof.

Two highly controversial protocols provided for the UK to opt out of certain Community policy areas which the UK government of the day found unacceptable. These were (i) social policy; and (ii) economic and monetary union.

Protocol on social policy

All Member States, except the UK, supported an amendment to the EC Treaty for greater Community competence to legislate in the area of social policy (e.g. employee protection rights). Margaret Thatcher was the UK Prime Minister at the time and her government objected to this proposal and would not compromise its position. Therefore, the UK agreed to a protocol which would enable all other Member States to have recourse to the Community institutions and Treaty procedures when adopting acts and decisions in the area of social policy not otherwise covered by the Treaties. The Agreement on Social Policy was annexed to the protocol.

Following the election of a Labour government in the UK on 1 May 1997, it was announced that the UK would no longer retain its opt-out and would take the necessary steps to be bound by the Agreement on Social Policy. This was put into effect by the Treaty of Amsterdam, which incorporated an amended version of the Agreement into the EC Treaty (see below).

Protocol on economic and monetary union: UK and Denmark

Under the SEA, economic and monetary policy, including working towards a single European currency, was introduced outside of the formal structures of the Communities and was to be dealt with on an intergovernmental basis. However, the TEU amended the EC Treaty to provide for this policy area (including a timetable for the introduction of a single European currency) to be dealt with under the formal structure of the Communities, thus making it more difficult for a recalcitrant Member State to block policy developments. The UK was not ready to sign up to full economic and monetary union. This protocol therefore provided the UK with an opt-out; the UK would not be:

> . . . obliged or committed to move to the third stage of Economic and Monetary Union without a separate decision to do so by its Government and Parliament.

This protocol is often referred to as the UK's opt-out from the single currency, but it is more akin to an 'opt-in'. Denmark has a similar opt-out, provided for by the 'Protocol on certain provisions relating to Denmark'. Denmark rejected entry to the single currency in a referendum held on 28 September 2000, by a 53 per cent to 46 per cent majority. Sweden negotiated a similar opt-out to the UK and Denmark when it became a member of the EU on 1 January 1995 (see below). Sweden rejected entry to the single currency in a referendum held on 14 September 2003.

The third and final stage on the road to economic and monetary union required the Member States to decide which of them had met the criteria laid down in the Treaty for the forming of a common currency. Article 121(4) EC Treaty at the time stipulated that the third stage would start on 1 January 1999 at the latest. All 12 Member States were found to have satisfied the criteria, except Greece. However, Greece was subsequently adjudged to have satisfied the economic criteria and joined the original qualifying states.

1.2.7 Enlargement – 1 January 1995

Three of the remaining EFTA members – **Finland**, **Austria** and **Sweden** – joined the EU on 1 January 1995, increasing the number of Member States to 15. Norway, having once more successfully negotiated terms for entry, again failed to join after a second adverse national referendum.

1.2.8 The Treaty of Amsterdam – 1 May 1999

The Treaty of Amsterdam (ToA) was agreed by the Member States in June 1997 and was formally signed by the Member States on 2 October 1997. This Treaty was concluded on behalf of the UK by the Labour government elected to office on 1 May 1997, under the Premiership of Tony Blair. The Treaty came into force on 1 May 1999 once it had been ratified by the then 15 Member States.

It was anticipated that the ToA would take the first major steps towards restructuring the institutions of the EU. This was widely seen as essential if the institutions, which had originally been set up for a European Community of six states, were to continue functioning effectively in an enlarged European Union. In the event, the Treaty achieved little in the way of institutional reform. A limit was set on the number of MEPs in the European Parliament, the powers of the President of the Commission were made more specific and administrative support for the Council of Ministers was strengthened. The difficult decisions which further enlargement would inevitably bring were postponed.

The most obvious changes brought about by the ToA were the renumbering of the provisions of the TEU and the EC Treaty, although the wording of these provisions remained identical in most cases. The Treaty of Amsterdam is divided into three parts:

- Part One (Arts 1–5) contains substantive amendments to, *inter alia*, the TEU and the EC Treaty.
- Part Two (Arts 6–11) contains provisions to simplify, *inter alia*, the TEU and the EC Treaty, including the deletion of lapsed provisions.
- Part Three (Arts 12–15) contains general and final provisions, including provisions to renumber articles of the TEU and the EC Treaty.

Some of the main changes that were brought by the ToA will now be outlined.

Further expansion beyond economic objectives

The ToA broadened the objectives of the EU, moving it further away from the narrow economic base of its early years. There were specific commitments to a number of important non-economic goals, with much more emphasis placed on the rights and duties of EU citizenship and the EU's commitment to human and civil rights. In particular, Article 6(1) of the new TEU (now Art 2 TEU) provided that:

> The Union is founded on the principles of liberty, democracy, respect for human rights and fundamental freedoms, and the rule of law, principles which are upheld by the Member States.

Respect for these principles was made an explicit condition of application for membership. Correspondingly, under a new Article 7 TEU, the rights of Member States could be suspended if the Council of Ministers determined that a Member State was in 'serious and persistent breach' of the principles established in Article 6 TEU.

Article 6(2) TEU (since renumbered Art 6(3) TEU by the Treaty of Lisbon) provided that:

> The Union shall respect fundamental rights as guaranteed by the European Convention for the Protection of Human Rights and Fundamental Freedoms . . . as general principles of Community law.

Moreover, Article 46 of the new TEU established that Article 6(2) would be justiciable by the Court of Justice, meaning that the Court could now explicitly take the Convention into account when interpreting and applying EU law.

Article 2 EC Treaty was amended to include new tasks, including:

- the promotion of equality between men and women;
- a high level of protection and improvement of the quality of the environment;
- the promotion of a high degree of competitiveness;
- economic development which must be 'sustainable' as well as 'balanced and harmonious'.

Article 3 EC Treaty listed the activities of the Community which could be undertaken in order to achieve the tasks set out in Article 2. Additionally, a new Article 3(2) EC Treaty provided that:

> In all the activities referred to in this Article, the Community shall aim to eliminate inequalities, and to promote equality, between men and women.

Following the entry into force of the Lisbon Treaty, Articles 2 and 3 EC Treaty were repealed and replaced, in substance, by Article 3 TEU.

Article 13 EC Treaty (now Art 19 TFEU) provided a new non-discriminatory provision which conferred legislative competence on the Community to combat discrimination based on sex, racial or ethnic origin, religion or belief, disability, age or sexual orientation. Additionally, one year after the Treaty of Amsterdam entered into force, the **Charter of Fundamental Rights** of the European Union was adopted. At this time, the Charter only had the status of a political declaration, but it is nevertheless indicative of increasing attention to human rights and non-economic policies during this time.

▶ The Charter of Fundamental Rights is discussed in more detail in section 3.3.2

Adjustments to the three pillars

The ToA reformulated the three-pillar structure of the Union, which had previously been as follows:

- First pillar: the European Communities (the EC, ECSC and Euratom)
- Second pillar: Common Foreign and Security Policy (CFSP)
- Third pillar: Cooperation in Justice and Home Affairs (JHA).

The ToA amended this structure by incorporating part of the third pillar into the EC Treaty and thus into the first pillar (Arts 61–69 EC Treaty (now Arts 67–81 TFEU)). The third pillar, which no longer included visas, asylum, immigration and other policies relating to

> See Figure 1.3 on page 39

the free movement of persons, was subsequently renamed 'Police and Judicial Cooperation in Criminal Matters'.

Under the TEU as it was signed in Maastricht, only the first pillar used legally binding decision-making structures (see Chapter 3). Decisions made under the other two pillars were taken 'intergovernmentally' (i.e. politically) and they could not be enforced or challenged in the Court of Justice. The sharpness of this division between legally binding decisions and the political decision-making process began to blur a little under the ToA. Decisions in what remained of the third pillar had limited input from the European Parliament and involvement by the Court of Justice was negligible. Decision-making in relation to the second pillar (CFSP) remained intergovernmental, outside the formal, legally binding Community decision-making structure. However, important changes were made to the decision-making structure of the Communities (the first pillar), giving the European Parliament greater powers to amend and block legislative proposals.

The new 'Police and Judicial Cooperation in Criminal Matters' third pillar stated the Union's objective as being able to 'provide citizens with a high level of safety within an area of freedom, security and justice' (Art 29 TEU) and to develop 'common action' among the Member States in the field of police and judicial cooperation and preventing and combating racism and xenophobia. The new Article 29 TEU stipulated that this would be achieved by:

> Preventing and combating crime, organised or otherwise, in particular terrorism, trafficking in persons and offences against children, illicit drug trafficking and illicit arms trafficking, corruption and fraud . . .

Closer cooperation

The ToA inserted a new title of 'Closer cooperation' into the TEU, which contained three articles (Arts 43–45, now Art 20 TEU). These provisions enabled Member States to establish closer cooperation between themselves with the use of the institutions, procedures and mechanisms of the TEU and EC Treaty. However, Article 43(c) TEU provided that these provisions could only be used as a 'last resort where the objectives of the . . . Treaties could not be attained by applying the relevant procedures laid down therein'.

These provisions allowed flexibility in the future development of the European Communities and the EU, recognising the right of Member States to 'opt out' from new policy initiatives not otherwise covered by the Treaties. This formalised the situation whereby the UK had opted out of the Social Policy Agreement and single European currency, for example (however, the newly elected Labour government ended the UK's opt out of the Social Policy Agreement at Amsterdam).

Article 11 EC Treaty (now Art 20 TEU and Arts 326–334 TFEU) presented a similar framework for intergovernmental cooperation.

1.2.9 The Treaty of Nice – 1 February 2003

The Treaty of Nice (ToN) was agreed by the Member States in December 2000. It was formally signed by the Member States on 26 February 2001 but it could only enter into force once it had been ratified by all the Member States. In a referendum during June 2001, the Irish electorate, by a majority of 54 per cent to 46 per cent, refused to ratify the Treaty. The other 14 Member States had already, or subsequently, ratified it. Ireland held a second referendum during October 2002, and this time there was a positive vote in favour of ratification (63 per cent to 37 per cent). Having been ratified by the then 15 Member States, the Treaty came into force on 1 February 2003.

Below is an overview of the main amendments which the ToN made to the TEU and the EC Treaty.

Institutional reform

The main reason for the ToN was to reform the institutions, by amending the founding Treaties, in preparation for EU enlargement up to a potential 27 Member States.

Some legal bases for the adoption of secondary Community instruments (see Chapter 3), which originally required a unanimous vote by the Council of Ministers in order to be adopted, were amended to provide for their adoption by a qualified majority. For example, the ToN amended Article 7 TEU to provide that the suspension of a Member State's Treaty rights on the grounds of a 'serious and persistent' breach of Article 6(1) principles could be imposed if the Council of Ministers voted in favour by a four-fifths majority of its membership. Prior to the ToN it had required a unanimous vote by the Council.

In addition, the role of the European Parliament was enhanced within selected policy areas.

Security and defence

Article 25 TEU (now Art 38 TEU) provided for the monitoring of the international situation within the areas covered by the second pillar (Common Foreign and Security Policy) and the development of associated policies. In a meeting of the European Council, immediately prior to the meeting at which the ToN was agreed, a policy for the establishment of a European rapid reaction force was adopted. This 60,000-strong force would be used primarily for peace-keeping and emergency missions within the region.

Eurojust

Articles 29 and 31 TEU (now Arts 67, 82, 83 and 85 TFEU) were amended to provide that in the application of the third pillar (Police and Judicial Cooperation in Criminal Matters) there would be cooperation with, *inter alia*, the European Judicial Cooperation Unit (Eurojust). A declaration specified that Eurojust would comprise national prosecutors and magistrates (or police officers of equivalent competence) who were detached from each Member State.

Enhanced cooperation

Articles 43–45 TEU (now Art 20 TEU and Arts 326–334 TFEU) were substantially amended to better enable a minimum of eight Member States to establish closer cooperation between themselves and to use the institutions, procedures and mechanisms of the TEU and EC Treaty to do so. Similar to the existing provisions, the amended provisions provided that closer cooperation could be undertaken only if it was 'aimed at furthering the objectives of the Union and the Community, at protecting and serving its interests'. This new provision also required that 'enhanced cooperation may be engaged in only as a last resort, when it has been established within the Council that the objectives of such cooperation cannot be attained within a reasonable period by applying the relevant provisions of the Treaties'.

New policies

A limited number of new policies were introduced and some of the existing policies were refined. One new policy related to economic, financial and technical cooperation with non-EU countries following the insertion of a new Article 181a EC Treaty (now Arts 212–213 TFEU). It was stated that this new policy would 'contribute to the general objective of developing and consolidating democracy and the rule of law, and to that of respecting human rights and fundamental freedoms'.

1.2.10 Enlargement – 2004–07

A10 countries – 1 May 2004

On 1 May 2004, membership of the EU increased to 25 with the admission of ten new Member States, which are sometimes referred to as the A10 countries. These countries are:

- Cyprus (South)
- Czech Republic
- Estonia
- Hungary
- Latvia
- Lithuania
- Malta
- Poland
- Slovakia
- Slovenia.

The ten new Member States did not join the euro on 1 May 2004. They only became eligible to do so once they achieved a high degree of sustainable economic convergence with the euro area. They needed to fulfil the same convergence criteria which were applied to the existing euro area members, namely a high degree of price stability, sustainable government finances (in terms of both public deficit and public debt levels), a stable exchange rate and convergence in long-term interest rates. The levels of convergence required for membership are assessed by the Council of Ministers (now the Council) on a proposal from the Commission and on the basis of convergence reports by the Commission and the ECB. These reports are produced at least every two years or on the request of a Member State seeking to join the euro.

On 11 July 2006, the Council adopted a decision allowing Slovenia to join the euro area on 1 January 2007. Slovenia became the first of the ten new Member States to join. Slovenia was followed by Cyprus and Malta who joined on 1 January 2008, Slovakia on 1 January 2009, Estonia on 1 January 2011, Latvia on 1 January 2015 and Lithuania on 1 January 2015. Nineteen Member States have now joined the euro. The UK, Denmark and Sweden continue to exercise their opt-out from the single European currency (see above).

Bulgaria and Romania – 1 January 2007

On 25 April 2005, the then 25 Member States, together with Bulgaria and Romania, signed an Accession Treaty (OJ 2005 L 157/1) paving the way for Bulgaria and Romania's membership of the EU. Bulgaria and Romania became Member States on 1 January 2007, raising the number of Member States to 27.

Bulgaria and Romania have not yet joined the euro. As with the A10 countries, which joined the EU on 1 May 2004, they are only eligible to join the euro once they have achieved a high degree of sustainable economic convergence with the euro area.

1.2.11 The Treaty of Lisbon – 1 December 2009

The Treaty of Lisbon (ToL) made significant amendments to the founding treaties, including changing the name of the Treaty establishing the Economic Community (EC Treaty) to the Treaty on the Functioning of the European Union (TFEU) and renumbering the articles of both the Treaties. To enable a fuller explanation of the scope and significance of these changes and to reflect its contemporary relevance, the ToL is considered in its own section (section 1.3) outside of this timeline.

1.2.12 The Treaty on Stability, Coordination and Governance – 1 January 2013

In response to the Eurozone's sovereign debt crisis, the EU concluded the Treaty on Stability, Coordination and Governance (TSCG) with the aim of tightening fiscal discipline in the Eurozone and deepening economic integration. This new treaty constitutes an intergovernmental agreement outside of the EU legal framework. This is because the UK vetoed its incorporation within the existing EU Treaties (i.e. the TEU and the TFEU). It is unclear how Union institutions such as the European Commission and the Court of Justice can be used to enforce what is, essentially, an international agreement among sovereign states.

The text of the treaty was finalised on 30 January 2012 and signed by 25 of the then 27 Member States (excluding the UK and the Czech Republic) on 2 March 2012. To come into force, the treaty required ratification by 12 of the 17 Eurozone members, which was achieved on 21 December 2012. The treaty came into force on 1 January 2013 and was ratified by the last of the 25 signatories on 1 April 2014.

1.2.13 Enlargement – 1 July 2013

At the end of 2011, after the entry into force of the ToL (see below), all the Member States, together with **Croatia**, signed an Accession Treaty paving the way for Croatia's membership of the EU. This enabled Croatia to become an EU Member State on 1 July 2013, raising the number of Member States from 27 to 28.

1.3 The Treaty of Lisbon

Objective 3

This section of the chapter deals separately with the Treaty of Lisbon (ToL), which was signed on 13 December 2007 and entered into force on 1 December 2009, reflecting the significant changes that it brought and its importance as the most recent Union-wide treaty. First, however, it is necessary to consider how the ToL was negotiated in the wake of a failed attempt to establish a Constitutional Treaty of the European Union.

1.3.1 The failed Constitutional Treaty

At a meeting of the European Council in Laeken, Belgium on 14 and 15 December 2001, a declaration on the 'Future of the Union' was adopted. This declaration provided for the establishment of a Convention on the Future of Europe, where a broad spectrum of representatives would discuss four topics in detail: the division of powers, the simplification of the treaties, the role of the national parliaments and the status of the Charter of Fundamental Rights.

The Convention formed the basis of an Intergovernmental Conference (IGC) during 2004, which resulted in the text of a Constitutional Treaty being agreed at the meeting of the European Council on 18 June 2004. The **Treaty establishing a Constitution for Europe** was formally signed in Rome on 29 October 2004. This Constitutional Treaty, if it had come into force, would have replaced the TEU and the EC Treaty.

The Constitutional Treaty could only come into force once it had been ratified by all the then 25 Member States. The ratification process in an individual Member State depends upon its own national constitutional requirements, with some Member States constitutionally required to hold a referendum before being able to ratify the Treaty. On 29 May 2005, France held a referendum; 54.68 per cent rejected the Treaty. A few days later, on 1 June 2005, the Netherlands held a referendum; 61.7 per cent rejected the Treaty. Despite the Treaty having been rejected by two Member States it was not yet officially abandoned.

Although the UK's constitution did not require a referendum to be held before the Treaty could be ratified, the UK Prime Minister at the time, Tony Blair, stated that he would hold a referendum. After the negative French and Dutch referenda, however, the UK stated that it was suspending the ratification process (i.e. no referendum would be held). Other Member States – the Czech Republic, Denmark, Ireland and Portugal – postponed their scheduled referenda, while Poland and Sweden also put the ratification process on hold.

At a meeting of the European Council on 16–17 June 2005, the Heads of State and Government agreed to come back to the issue of ratification in the first half of 2006 in order to conduct an overall assessment of the national debates and to agree on how to proceed. This was launched as part of a 'period of reflection'. At its meeting on 15–16 June 2006, the European Council stated that the 'period of reflection' had been useful in enabling the EU to assess the concerns and worries expressed in the course of the ratification process and that further work was needed before decisions on the future of the Constitutional Treaty could be taken. This was an implicit admission that the Constitutional Treaty would not come into force in its current form.

At a European Summit held in Brussels on 21–23 June 2007, the proposed European Constitution was formally abandoned. It was decided to proceed with a new Reform Treaty, which would amend the TEU and the EC Treaty rather than replace them. This became the ToL.

1.3.2 Ratification of the ToL

The Reform Treaty, titled the Treaty of Lisbon (ToL), was signed by the representatives of the then 27 Member States on 13 December 2007 in Lisbon, Portugal. The ToL could only come into force once it had been ratified by each of the then 27 Member States (the ToL was signed and entered into force before Croatia became a Member State). Although it had been anticipated that the ToL would come into force on 1 January 2009, ratification problems caused the entry into force to be delayed until 1 December 2009.

Ratification by Ireland

The ratification process varies from Member State to Member State. Ireland was the only Member State constitutionally required to hold a referendum before being able to ratify the ToL. On 12 June 2008, Ireland held a referendum and 53.4 per cent rejected the Treaty.

Following Ireland's rejection of the ToL, the question to be answered was whether this would confine the ToL to the history books along with the Constitutional Treaty, or whether the EU would negotiate a compromise to enable Ireland to ask the Irish people to approve the ToL in a second referendum. At a meeting of the European Council, which concluded on 19 June 2008, it was decided to continue with the ratification process. Ireland was required to bring proposals forward to the December 2008 meeting of the European Council to enable it to ratify the Treaty. The ToL could not be amended without requiring all Member States to start the ratification process again. At the meeting of the European Council, which concluded on 12 December 2008, a compromise was reached whereby Ireland would agree to hold a second referendum.

The compromise with Ireland provided that all Member States would retain their Commissioner (under the original treaty, the number of Commissioners would have been reduced from 1 November 2014). Ireland also received guarantees on, for example, respect for the country's neutrality, and an acknowledgement that it had control over its own policies relating to direct taxation and abortion.

Ireland held a second referendum on 2 October 2009: 67.13 per cent voted in favour of the Treaty. The Irish President (Mary McAleese) gave final approval to the Treaty on 16 October 2009.

Ratification by Poland and the Czech Republic

Ratification had been delayed in the Czech Republic while a legal challenge was pursued through the Czech courts. On 26 November 2008, the Czech Republic's highest court ruled that the ToL was consistent with the country's constitution, clearing the way for the Czech Parliament to approve the Treaty. However, the Czech Republic's President (Václav Klaus) refused to give final approval until the outcome of the second Irish referendum was known. The Polish President (Lech Kaczyński) likewise refused to give final approval. Following the positive referendum vote in Ireland, Kaczyński approved the Treaty on 10 October 2009.

The position in the Czech Republic was more problematic. Although the ToL had been approved by both houses of the Czech Parliament, Klaus continued to withhold his approval. He raised concerns about the implications for the Czech Republic of **Article 6(1) TEU**, which, as amended by the ToL, provides that the Union shall 'recognise the rights, freedoms and principles set out in the Charter of Fundamental Rights of the European Union'. The UK and Poland had already sought assurances that the Charter would not be indirectly incorporated into their national law. Subsequently, Article 1 of Protocol No. 30 (which is annexed to the TEU and TFEU) provides as follows:

> 1 The Charter does not extend the ability of the Court of Justice of the European Union, or any court or tribunal of Poland or of the United Kingdom, to find that the laws, regulations or administrative provisions, practices or action of Poland or of the United Kingdom are

inconsistent with the fundamental rights, freedoms and principles that it [i.e. the Charter] reaffirms.

2 In particular, and for the avoidance of doubt, nothing in Title IV of the Charter creates justiciable rights applicable to Poland or the United Kingdom except in so far as Poland or the United Kingdom has provided for such rights in its national law.

The European Council sought to secure the Czech Republic President's signature to the Treaty at its meeting held in Brussels on 29–30 October 2009. It was agreed that at the time of the conclusion of the next Accession Treaty a new Protocol would be added to both the TEU and TFEU to provide that Protocol No. 30 (which applies to the UK and Poland) also applied to the Czech Republic. This was sufficient to secure the support of the President of the Czech Republic. However, by the conclusion of the next Accession Treaty in 2011, which concerned the accession of Croatia to the Union, there was no longer sufficient support for opting out of the Charter within the Czech Republic and the additional protocol thus never materialised.

A further complication arose following a second legal challenge on the compatibility of the Treaty with the Czech Constitution. The Czech Constitutional Court dismissed the application on 3 November 2009 and later the same day the Czech Republic President gave final approval to the ToL.

Having now been ratified by all the Member States, the ToL came into force on 1 December 2009.

1.3.3 Changes introduced by the ToL

Many of the changes which would have been implemented by the proposed Constitutional Treaty were replicated by the ToL. Some of the main changes introduced by the ToL are set out below.

Whereas the proposed Constitutional Treaty would have replaced the TEU and EC Treaty, the ToL retained and amended both of these Treaties, although the EC Treaty was renamed the **Treaty on the Functioning of the European Union (TFEU)**. The Union has replaced and succeeded the Community and the TEU and the TFEU constitute 'the Treaties' on which the Union is founded (Art 1 TEU). The following terms are therefore no longer used: European Community; European Communities; or Community law. Reference is made solely to the European Union (or the Union) and EU law (or Union law).

The articles within both the TEU and the TFEU have been renumbered as part of a simplification exercise. As stated above, the ToA also renumbered the provisions of the TEU and the EC Treaty when it came into force on 1 May 1999. Care must therefore be taken when referring to EU case law, legislation and documents, to ensure that the old numbering (i.e. pre-ToA and pre-ToL) is distinguished from the numbering used post-ToA and post-ToL. **Figure 1.2** provides an overview of how the TFEU and the TEU have changed since their inception. Subsequent chapters of this book are based on the post-ToL Treaty numbers but, where relevant, previous article numbers are provided in brackets.

Figure 1.2 The evolution of the Treaties

Year of entry into force and city (Treaty of . . .)	Evolution of the TFEU	Evolution of the TEU
1958, Rome	Introduced the treaty establishing the **European Economic Community** (EEC Treaty)	
1987, Luxembourg	Amended the EEC Treaty, also known as the **Single European Act**	
1993, Maastricht	Renumbered and renamed the EEC Treaty as the **Treaty establishing the European Community** (EC Treaty)	Introduced the **Treaty on European Union** (TEU)
1999, Amsterdam	Amended and renumbered the EC Treaty	Amended and renumbered the TEU
2003, Nice	Amended the EC Treaty to accommodate enlargement	Amended the TEU to accommodate enlargement
2009, Lisbon	Renumbered and renamed the TEC as the **Treaty on the Functioning of the European Union** (TFEU)	Amended and renumbered the TEU

The ToL is divided into three parts

- Article 1 amends the TEU
- Article 2 amends the EC Treaty and renames it the Treaty on the Functioning of the European Union (TFEU)
- Articles 3–7 contain the final provisions (e.g. Art 5(1) ToL concerns the renumbering of the Treaties).

The ToL introduced several significant changes 'with a view to enhancing the efficiency and democratic legitimacy of the Union and to improving the coherence of its action' (Preamble, ToL). Some of the main changes are set out below. Reference is made to the relevant Treaty provisions, as amended and renumbered by the ToL. The TEU and TFEU are collectively referred to as 'the Treaties' (Art 1 TEU and Art 1(2) TFEU).

The EU: merger of the three pillars

The construction of the EU (and its three pillars), as discussed above, was both complex and cumbersome. The ToL has therefore established a single EU, which has replaced and succeeded the European Community (Art 1 TEU). The three pillars have been merged, although special procedures have been maintained in the fields of foreign policy, security

Figure 1.3 The structural history of the European Union

Year of entry into force and city		European Communities (1958–2009)			
1952, Paris		European Coal and Steel Community	← Three pillars of the European Union (1993–2009) →		
1958, Rome (EEC Treaty)	Euratom		European Economic Community		
1987, Luxembourg (SEA)				European Political Cooperation	
1993, Maastricht (TEU)				Common Foreign and Security Policy	Justice and Home Affairs
1999, Amsterdam					Police and Judicial Cooperation in Criminal Matters
2003, Nice					
2009, Lisbon			European Union		

and defence. Reference is no longer made to the three pillars of the EU, nor to the European Communities. **Figure 1.3** illustrates this structural development.

Objectives and values

The Union's objectives, set out in Article 3 TEU, are much more succinct than the combined objectives in the former Article 3 EC Treaty (in respect of the European Community) and the former Article 2 TEU (in respect of the EU). Article 3 TEU has now, in substance, replaced both of these provisions. The aims listed in Article 3 place peace, values and the area of freedom, security and justice before the establishment of an internal market, suggesting that the Union is no longer primarily economic in nature. Article 2 TEU now establishes the values that the Union is founded on, including 'respect for human dignity, freedom, democracy, equality, the rule of law and respect for human rights'.

> See section 1.1.1 for the text of Articles 2 and 3 TEU

The institutional framework

> See section 1.1.2 for an overview of the roles and composition of the current institutions. See Chapter 2 for further detail

Articles 13–19 TEU clarify the role of the Union institutions. Part Six, Title I TFEU contains the detailed provisions governing the institutions. Some of the main changes to the institutions include:

- the formal recognition of the European Council as a Union institution (Art 13(1) TEU);
- the introduction of degressive proportionality as a means of distributing seats in the European Parliament between Member States (Art 14(2) TEU);
- renaming the Court of First Instance as the General Court;
- broadening the competence of the Court of Justice, especially in the area of freedom, security and justice.

These changes are considered in more detail in Chapter 2.

Democratic principles

Several provisions in the Lisbon treaty aimed to address the criticism of a 'democratic deficit' within the Union. Specifically, Title II of the TEU sets out a number of democratic principles that regulate how the Union functions and operates. Given their importance they are set out in full here.

Article 9 TEU sets out the principle of **equality**:

> In all its activities, the Union shall observe the principle of the equality of its citizens, who shall receive equal attention from its institutions, bodies, offices and agencies . . .

Article 10 TEU establishes the principle of **representative democracy**:

> 1. The functioning of the Union shall be founded on representative democracy.
> 2. Citizens are directly represented at Union level in the European Parliament.
>   Member States are represented in the European Council by their Heads of State or Government and in the Council by their governments, themselves democratically accountable either to their national Parliaments, or to their citizens.
> 3. Every citizen shall have the right to participate in the democratic life of the Union. Decisions shall be taken as openly and as closely as possible to the citizen.
> 4. Political parties at European level contribute to forming European political awareness and to expressing the will of citizens of the Union.

Article 11 TEU provides an **enhanced consultative role** for citizens and representative associations, including a 'citizens' petition for action':

> 1. The institutions shall, by appropriate means, give citizens and representative associations the opportunity to make known and publicly exchange their views in all areas of Union action.
> 2. The institutions shall maintain an open, transparent and regular dialogue with representative associations and civil society.
> 3. The European Commission shall carry out broad consultations with parties concerned in order to ensure that the Union's actions are coherent and transparent.
> 4. Not less than one million citizens who are nationals of a significant number of Member States may take the initiative of inviting the European Commission, within the framework of its powers, to submit any appropriate proposal on matters where citizens consider that a legal act of the Union is required for the purpose of implementing the Treaties.
>
>   The procedures and conditions required for such a citizens' initiative shall be determined in accordance with the first paragraph of Article 24 of the Treaty on the Functioning of the European Union.

Article 24 TFEU provides that a Regulation will be adopted to set out the procedures and conditions of the **European Citizens' Initiative** (ECI). **Regulation 211/2011** on the Citizens' Initiative was subsequently adopted on 16 February 2011 and became applicable from 1 April 2012. **Article 11(4) TEU** sets out the quantity of EU citizens who are needed to take the initiative: 'not less than one million citizens who are nationals of a significant number of Member States'. This has been made more specific in Regulation 211/2011. **Article 2(1) of Regulation 211/2011** provides that an ECI requires at least one million eligible signatories coming from a minimum of one-quarter of the EU Member States (i.e. at least seven Member States). In addition, **Article 7(2)** of Regulation 211/2011 requires that in at least one-quarter of the Member States, signatories will comprise at least the minimum number of citizens set out in Annex I. This minimum number of citizens per Member State corresponds to the number of MEPs for the specific Member State, multiplied by 750. So, for example, for the 2014–2019 parliamentary term, Estonia had six MEPs and therefore to comply with this requirement the minimum number of signatories from within Estonia is 4,500 (i.e. 6 × 750).

Article 12 TEU provides national parliaments with an enhanced and explicit role in the functioning of the Union:

> National Parliaments contribute actively to the good functioning of the Union:
>
> (a) through being informed by the institutions of the Union and having draft legislative acts of the Union forwarded to them in accordance with the Protocol on the role of national Parliaments in the European Union;
>
> (b) by seeing to it that the principle of subsidiarity is respected in accordance with the procedures provided for in the Protocol on the application of the principles of subsidiarity and proportionality;
>
> (c) by taking part, within the framework of the area of freedom, security and justice, in the evaluation mechanisms for the implementation of the Union policies in that area, in accordance with Article 70 of the Treaty on the Functioning of the European Union, and through being involved in the political monitoring of Europol and the evaluation of Eurojust's activities in accordance with Articles 88 and 85 of that Treaty;
>
> (d) by taking part in the revision procedures of the Treaties, in accordance with Article 48 of this Treaty;
>
> (e) by being notified of applications for accession to the Union, in accordance with Article 49 of this Treaty;
>
> (f) by taking part in the inter-parliamentary cooperation between national Parliaments and with the European Parliament, in accordance with the Protocol on the role of national Parliaments in the European Union.

Charter of Fundamental Rights of the European Union

▶ See section 3.3.2 for more detail on the contents of the Charter

The Charter of Fundamental Rights of the European Union was signed by the then 15 Member States during December 2000 at a meeting of the European Council in France. The Charter combines in a single text the civil, political, economic, social and societal rights which had previously been laid down in a variety of UN, European and national sources.

Originally, the Charter was not legally binding. A Declaration annexed to the Treaty of Nice provided that an Intergovernmental Conference would be held in 2004 to consider, *inter alia*, the status of the Charter. This conference resulted in the adoption of the proposed Constitutional Treaty and subsequently the adoption of the ToL.

The Charter, which was amended on 12 December 2007, is given legal status by the ToL. **Article 6(1) TEU** now provides that the Union shall 'recognise the rights, freedoms and principles set out in the Charter of Fundamental Rights of the European Union'. The Charter has therefore become an integral part of EU law, setting out the fundamental rights which every EU citizen can benefit from. However, the Charter does not extend the field of application of Union law beyond the powers of the Union nor establish any new powers or tasks for the Union; it only applies within the existing scope of EU law.

As noted above (section 1.3.2), the UK, Poland and the Czech Republic sought reassurance that the Charter would not be indirectly incorporated into their national law. This reassurance took the form of **Article 1 of Protocol No. 30** (which is annexed to the TEU and TFEU). See above section on 'Ratification' for further information on Protocol No. 30.

The European Convention on Human Rights and Fundamental Freedoms (ECHR)

> See section 3.3.2 for detail on the contents of the ECHR

The European Convention on Human Rights and Fundamental Freedoms (ECHR) was drafted in 1950 under the auspices of the Council of Europe, an international organisation originally composed of 21 Western European states, and now composed of 47 states. The ECHR is intended to uphold common political traditions of individual civil liberties and the rule of law. All the Member States of the EU are contracting parties to the ECHR.

The Court of Justice, like national courts, takes account of the ECHR when interpreting and applying Union law. Although the ECHR was recognised by the TEU as forming part of the **general principles** of EU law, the Union can *only* apply the ECHR to the execution and interpretation of EU law. While this remains the case post-ToL, **Article 6(2) TEU** now also provides that the Union will accede to the ECHR. Once the Union accedes to the ECHR, EU law will have to be interpreted and applied in accordance with the ECHR, not simply as a 'general principle'. However, it should be noted that Article 6(2) TEU provides that 'such accession shall not affect the Union's competences as defined in the Treaties'. This means that accession to the ECHR will not extend the Union's powers and tasks. Application of the ECHR by the Union will therefore continue to be limited to those areas which come within its competence. Following accession to the ECHR, it will be possible for a decision of the Court of Justice to be contested by taking the case to the European Court of Human Rights in Strasbourg and claiming that the Court of Justice has failed to uphold a provision of the ECHR.

Official ECHR accession talks started between the EU and the Council of Europe on 7 July 2010 and a draft agreement was concluded in April 2013. An opinion of the EU Court of Justice was then sought on the compatibility of the draft agreement with the EU treaties. Opinion 2/13 was delivered by the Court of Justice on 18 December 2014 and, because of problems it identified, the Court concluded that the draft agreement was not compatible with Union law. If the issues identified by the Court of Justice can be satisfactorily resolved through amendments to the draft agreement, the European Council must adopt a decision to authorise the signing of the accession agreement, acting unanimously.

All Member States would then have to complete their internal procedure to ratify the agreement. The Union would then ratify the agreement and the Committee of Ministers of the Council of Europe would have to adopt it. It would then have to be ratified (i.e. approved) by all 47 contracting parties to the ECHR (including the individual EU Member States) in accordance with their respective constitutional requirements. The path of the Union's accession to the ECHR will therefore be long and complex, with no successful outcome guaranteed.

> **Reflection:** Distinguishing between the two European courts
>
> It is important to distinguish the international structure created by the ECHR from the quite separate supranational institutions of the EU. The media often talks loosely about taking a case 'to Europe' without identifying whether the case is a human rights matter involving the ECHR to be dealt with by the European Court of Human Rights in Strasbourg, or a matter of Union law to be referred to the Court of Justice of the European Union in Luxembourg. Decisions made by the European Court of Human Rights (ECtHR) are not legally binding on national courts, although they will be taken into account by these courts. Such decisions may result in compensation being awarded against a state in favour of a victim of human rights abuses, but as they are not binding on the state they could (in theory) be ignored. Decisions of the Court of Justice (CJ), on the other hand, are legally binding on national courts. While the Court of Justice has ruled on many cases involving human rights issues, it also presides over the other areas of Union competence, unlike the Strasbourg Court which is exclusively focused on the human rights enshrined in the ECHR.

Enhanced cooperation

The ToL incorporated 'enhanced cooperation', which had first been introduced under the Treaty of Nice, into both the TEU and TFEU. **Article 20 TEU** provides for a system of enhanced cooperation, under which Member States may use the Treaties and institutions of the Union to further the aims of the Union, but without necessitating the involvement and agreement of all Member States. Enhanced cooperation only applies to the Union's non-exclusive competences (i.e. areas of shared or supporting competence. See Chapter 4). The detailed provisions for this system are set out within Articles 326–334 TFEU.

> ► See section 4.2.2 for an explanation of the Union's shared competencies

Under the ToL, enhanced cooperation requires the involvement of at least nine Member States (Art 20(2) TEU). Authorisation to proceed with enhanced cooperation requires a proposal from the Commission, the consent of the European Parliament and an affirmative decision by the Council acting by a qualified majority (Art 329(1) TFEU). With regard to the common foreign and security policy, authorisation to proceed may only be granted by a decision of the Council acting unanimously, after obtaining the opinion of: (i) the High Representative of the Union for Foreign Affairs and Security Policy; and (ii) the Commission. In this case, the European Parliament is merely informed (Art 329(2) TFEU). In both cases, the Council's decision to authorise enhanced cooperation may only be adopted 'as a last resort when it has established that the objectives of such cooperation cannot be obtained within a reasonable period by the Union as a whole' (Art 20(2) TEU).

1.4 Future of the European Union

Objective 4

The future of the EU will continue to be shaped by the political impetus for and challenges to the project from within the Member States and the capacity of the Union institutions to negotiate, innovate and implement solutions. This section begins by outlining possible additions and subtractions to the membership of the Union before briefly outlining some of the possible directions in which the Union could develop.

1.4.1 Future enlargements

▶ See section 1.1.3 on the accession criteria and the process of accession

As mentioned above (see Section 1.1.3), there are currently five candidate countries seeking to join the Union. These are Albania, Republic of North Macedonia, Montenegro, Serbia and Turkey. Additionally, Bosnia and Herzegovina and Kosovo have the status of 'potential candidates', which means that it has been agreed that they can become candidate countries when they are ready. The status of these countries facilitates cooperation with and assistance from the EU towards greater stability and development.

Every autumn, the Commission adopts a set of documents explaining EU policy on accepting new members, setting out the objectives and prospects for the coming year and assessing the progress made over past year by each country concerned. The Enlargement Strategy and Progress Reports for each candidate country and potential candidate country are available from the European Commission's website.

While the Commission's support of further enlargement is clear, tension currently exists within the European Council between Member States that are in favour of enlargement and those that are more reluctant. In particular, support for enlargement may be politically risky for the leaders of Member States where there are prominent popular concerns about immigration and the effects of widening the geographic scope of the free movement of persons.

Turkey

Turkey applied for EU membership as long ago as 14 April 1987, but its passage towards accession has not been smooth. Turkey was granted the status of a candidate country in 1999, accession negotiations opened on 3 October 2005 and an **Accession Partnership** was concluded on 23 January 2006 (Council Decision 2006/35/EC). The objective of the Partnership is to set out:

- priority areas that Turkey needs to address in preparation for accession;
- financial assistance guidelines for the implementation of these priority areas.

The accession negotiations were halted in June 2006 because of a trade dispute between Turkey and Southern Cyprus. The negotiations subsequently resumed in March 2007 but on 8 December 2009 the Commission decided to progress slowly with negotiations as Turkey was still refusing to open its ports and airports to Southern Cyprus.

As of June 2016, 16 out of the 35 chapters for negotiations have been opened, of which one – 'science and research' – has provisionally been closed. In June 2018, the General Affairs Council (which is a configuration of the Council – see section 2.4.2) concluded that negotiations with Turkey were effectively frozen. No further chapters could be opened or closed as a result of deterioration in the country's rule of law, fundamental rights protections and judiciary. In its 2019 progress report, the Commission remained highly critical of the Turkish government's response to an attempted coup in July 2016, which has included widespread dismissal of public employees, sweeping arrests and detentions and deteriorating judicial independence and freedom of expression.

The Republic of North Macedonia

The Republic of North Macedonia (known as the Former Yugoslav Republic of Macedonia prior to February 2019) applied for EU membership on 22 March 2004 and was granted candidate status by the European Council on 17 December 2005. A European Partnership (the precursor to an Accession Partnership) was concluded between the EU and North Macedonia on 30 January 2006 (Council Decision 2006/57/EC). North Macedonia has made strong progress, leading the Commission to recommend the opening of accession negotiations. In June 2019, disagreement between EU Member States about the prospect of further enlarging the EU caused a decision on opening negotiations to be delayed until the European Council summit in October 2019. At this summit, the President of France, Emmanuel Macron, led objections to the commencement of negotiations, arguing that North Macedonia had not made sufficient progress. The failure of the European Council to decide in favour of North Macedonia (and Albania), in contravention of the Commission's finding that the relevant criteria were satisfied, was described as a 'mistake' by both Jean-Claude Junker and Donald Tusk, the presidents of the Commission and the European Council at the time.

Montenegro

Montenegro applied for EU membership on 15 December 2008, was granted candidate status in December 2010 and accession negotiations were opened on 29 June 2012. At the time of the Commission's 2019 progress report, 32 negotiating chapters have been opened, of which three have been provisionally closed.

Serbia

Serbia was granted the status of a candidate country in 2012 and accession negotiations commenced on 21 January 2014. Serbia has made strong progress towards meeting the accession criteria across a number of areas. Sixteen negotiating chapters has been opened at the time of the Commission's 2019 progress report, two of which have been provisionally closed.

Albania

Albania was granted candidate status in June 2014. The government has initiated EU-related reforms and was found by the Commission to have made sufficient progress in May 2019. Along with North Macedonia, a decision on the opening of accession negotiations was expected in June 2019, but was delayed until October 2019, when the required agreement of the European Council was not attained. Albania faced wider opposition to its progress towards accession than North Macedonia, with the Netherlands and Denmark supporting France's objections.

1.4.2 Future contractions

With Brexit, **Article 50 TEU** has been invoked for the first time and the UK became the first country to leave the Union on 31 January 2020. At the time of writing, much is unknown about how the transition period will pan out and what the consequences will be for both the Union and the UK. For this reason alone, it is unlikely that other Member States will seriously examine the prospect of leaving the Union until the consequences of Brexit have materialised, although Euro-sceptic political parties across the Union will be paying close attention.

Brexit

On 23 June 2016, the UK population voted in a non-binding referendum to leave the EU. Nine months later, on 29 March 2017, the new Prime Minister of the UK, Theresa May, notified the Council of the country's intention to leave the Union in accordance with Article 50(2) TEU. On 27 July 2016, Jean-Claude Junker, the President of the European Commission, appointed French politician Michel Barnier to the position of Chief Negotiator for Brexit, in accordance with Article 218(3) TFEU.

The European Council met on 29 April 2017, where the 27 other Member States agreed upon the **European Council (Art 50) guidelines for Brexit negotiations**. These negotiating guidelines established three priorities for the EU:

1 securing the rights of EU nationals residing in the UK;
2 agreeing the settlement of the UK's financial commitments to the EU;
3 ensuring that the border between the Republic of Ireland and Northern Ireland remains peaceful.

▶ See section 1.1.3 for the text of Article 50 TEU
▶ See section 4.4.1 on the European Communities Act
▶ Updates are available at www.pearsoned.co.uk/legalupdates

An exit agreement should also include details of the UK's future relationship with the EU, trade arrangements and any transitional measures. Negotiations between the EU and UK officially commenced in June 2017. The UK government published a Withdrawal Agreement in November 2018, which was approved by the EU. However, the Withdrawal Agreement was then brought before the UK Parliament on three separate occasions and was rejected each time. This impasse led to the resignation of Prime Minister Theresa May. Her successor, Boris Johnson, amended the Withdrawal Agreement but was still unable to gain the necessary approval of the UK parliament, in which his government did not hold a majority of seats. A general election on 12 December 2019 returned a parliamentary majority for Johnson's Conservative Party. Subsequently, Johnson's **European Union (Withdrawal Agreement) Act** was passed by the House of Commons on 20 December 2019 and was granted royal assent (i.e. became law) on 23 January 2020. The Act had the effect of terminating UK's membership of the Union on 31 January 2020 ('exit day'). However, the extent to which this was the day on which the UK 'exited' the Union is blurred by the provision in the Act for a transition period. During this transition period, which is to last until the end of 2020, the EU Treaties will continue to apply to UK. The Treaties will therefore not have ceased to apply to the UK as per Article 50(3) TEU. Additionally, the European Union (Withdrawal Agreement) Act 2020 leaves many matters related to the relationship between the UK and the Union to be decided during the transition period. This makes it unclear at the time of writing what that relationship will look like, with many commentators fearing that the transition period will expire before trade arrangements can be agreed – a so-called 'no deal' scenario.

Under Article 50 TEU, the period for negotiating Brexit was initiallly due to expire on 29 March 2019. However, the UK used Article 50(3) to successfully extended this period, first until 30 June 2019, then until 31 October 2019 and then until 31 January 2019. Domestic arrangements in relation to Brexit are set out in the **European Union (Withdrawal) Act 2018**. Under this Act, the European Communities Act 1972 was repealed on 'exit day' and all directly applicable Union legislation in force at the time was transposed into UK law as 'retained EU law'.

Article 50(5) leaves open the possibility that the UK could rejoin the Union in the future, provided that it meets the accession criteria, as with any other prospective member.

The possibility of Grexit from the Eurozone

Following the global credit crunch in 2008, Greece experienced severe economic problems which resulted in the country taking loans from the International Monetary Fund (IMF) and the European Central Bank (ECB). During June 2015, Greece defaulted on repayments of its loan to the IMF. The IMF and the ECB refused to lend Greece any additional funds until Greece implemented further 'austerity reforms' to reduce its debt. The Greek government, which had been elected to office in January 2015 on an anti-austerity platform, called a referendum to enable the Greek people to vote on whether or not to accept the new austerity reforms proposed by the IMF and the ECB. The referendum, which was held on 5 July 2015, resulted in the Greeks rejecting the new austerity reforms. Greece subsequently entered into new agreements with the IMF and the ECB which prevented it from having to withdraw from the euro, but which also required further austerity measures despite the referendum result.

Economically, things have started to improve for Greece. In 2017, the national recession ended and the economy slowly began to grow. In August 2018, Greece successfully completed the series of bailouts (emergency loans) which began in 2010. While debt, bureaucracy, unemployment, poverty and a steady influx of refugees continue to pose major challenges, the financial crisis – and with it the risk of Grexit appears – to be passing.

1.4.3 Future directions for the Union

In March 2017, the Commission published a white paper detailing five scenarios that could be pursued to shape the future of the Union. These options sought to move away from the simple dichotomy of 'more Europe' or 'less Europe' to explore some of the more nuanced ways in which the 27 Member States could move forward as a Union. The possibilities put forward in the white paper are:

- **Carrying on:** the Union persists with its current objectives, decision-making procedures and reform agenda.
- **Nothing but the common market:** the Union focuses its activities on the common market, while less energy is directed into other policy domains. New areas of cooperation would mostly be agreed by Member States bilaterally.
- **Those who want more do more:** where the Union as a whole fails to agree, Member States can form coalitions to deepen their cooperation in specific areas, with the possibility that other Member States may join later.
- **Doing less more efficiently:** where the Union agrees on certain priorities, greater attention and resources are focused on achieving progress in those specific areas.
- **Doing much more together:** more power, resources and decision-making is shared within the Union, with cooperation between the Member States enhanced across policy areas.

The white paper can be accessed on the Commission's website.

In June 2019, a new Strategic Agenda 2019-2024 was drawn for the Union. The Agenda provides the overall framework and direction for the work of the institutions in the next five years. It focuses on four main priorities of protecting citizens and freedoms, developing a strong and vibrant economic base, building a climate-neutral, green, fair and social Europe and promoting European interests and values on the global stage. Arguably this new Agenda move behind the idea of 'more' or 'less' Europe and re-focus the attention on values, which are at the heart of citizens.

Whether Member States will seek greater or more restrained cooperation across all or some of the Union's policy areas will depend on many factors, including national political and economic factors and the outcomes and consequences of Brexit. However, as achieving consensus is likely to continue to be a challenge, the option of a 'two-speed Europe', where Member States are individually able to opt for more or less cooperation, will now be considered further.

A two-speed Europe

The idea of a 'two-speed Europe' was much canvassed before the Amsterdam Intergovernmental Conference, at which the ToA was adopted. The concept of a 'two-speed Europe' meant that the states which were keen to embrace closer political and economic cooperation would be free to do so, while the other more reluctant states could follow at their own pace. To some extent, this had already happened in relation to economic and monetary union, with the UK, Denmark and Sweden negotiating opt-outs (see above). Now, the system of enhanced cooperation under Article 20 TEU and Articles 326–334 TFEU provides a legal framework for greater harmonisation among only those Member States who opt to be involved in specific initiatives.

> See section 1.3.2 for further information on enhanced cooperation

While opt-outs and enhanced cooperation enable the Union to progress despite the objections of one or a few obstinate Member States, it is unlikely that the Commission will generally favour non-uniform processes of development. There are two main reasons for this. First, an EU in which there are different rules for the varied periphery areas and the uniform core areas will be extremely difficult to operate in practice. The Commission would not be in favour of having different bodies of rules operating in different parts of the Union. Second, any further development of an 'inner core' of Member States which is moving towards greater integration will tend to exacerbate the already serious drift of commerce and industry towards the geographical centre of Western Europe. If Germany is in the 'inner core', because its economy is usually strong and it enjoys the largest market of all the Member States, businesses may tend to look for locations in states which are in the inner core rather than in states on the periphery. Measures facilitating a two-speed Europe may therefore inhibit the integration of Member State markets in practice, and are therefore likely to be resisted by the Commission. However, Bruno de Witte (2018) argues that the difficulty of attaining the agreement of so many Member States on politically sensitive matters means that 'differentiated integration' in the form of opt-outs, opt-ins and enhanced cooperation is likely to remain a feature of EU development.

CHAPTER SUMMARY

The EU today

- The scope of the Union is established by the **Treaty on European Union (TEU)** and the **Treaty on the Functioning of the European Union (TFEU)**.
- The Union aims to achieve certain objectives (**Art 3 TEU**) and is guided by certain values (**Art 2 TEU**).
- The Union is a unique, **autonomous legal order** (*Costa* v *ENEL*).
- The Union has **27 Member States**, since the departure of the UK on 31 January 2020.
- In order to join the Union, a state must meet the **Copenhagen criteria** and undergo comprehensive **accession negotiations**.
- The **European Economic Area (EEA)** includes all EU Member States as well as three of the four European Free Trade Association states – **Iceland**, **Lichtenstein** and **Norway**.
- The economic and monetary union (the **Eurozone**) is composed of 19 EU Member States that use the euro as their currency.

The history of the European Communities

- **1952**: the **European Coal and Steel Community** was created by six Member States, with aims of engendering economic growth and lasting peace between France and Germany.
- **1958**: the **Treaty of Rome** established the **European Economic Community (EEC)** and **Euratom**.
- **1973–86**: the EEC expanded to 12 Member States, including the UK in 1973.
- **1987**: the **Single European Act** amended the EEC and began to broaden the agenda beyond the economic sphere.
- **1993**: the **Treaty of Maastricht** introduced the **Treaty on European Union** and renamed the EEC Treaty the **Treaty on the European Communities (EC Treaty)**. It also established the 'three pillar' structure of the Union and created EU citizenship.
- **1999**: the **Treaty of Amsterdam** renumbered the provisions of the **EC Treaty** and the **TEU** and further grounded the Union on principles and rights.
- **2003**: the **Treaty of Nice** reformed the EU institutions in preparation for the expansion of the Union and introduced the enhanced cooperation mechanism.

The Treaty of Lisbon (ToL) (2009)

- The **ToL** was created after a failed attempt at a **Constitutional Treaty**.
- It **abolished the 'three pillar' structure** and replaced all references to 'the Communities' with 'the Union'.

- It renamed the Court of First Instance the **General Court** and broadened the jurisdiction of the Court of Justice.
- It provided for greater representative and participatory **democratic input** into the Union.
- It enhanced the status of the **Charter of Fundamental Rights** and the European Convention on Human Rights.

Future directions for the Union

- There are five **candidate countries** at various stages of **accession negotiations**.
- The UK is is expected to withdraw from the Union in 2020.

Chapter 2
Institutions of the European Union

Learning objectives

At the end of this chapter you should understand:

1 The provisions in the Treaties pertaining to the institutions of the Union.

2 The functions, composition and working procedures of the European Council.

3 The functions, composition and working procedures of the Commission.

4 The functions, composition and working procedures of the Council.

5 The role of the High Representative of the Union for Foreign Affairs and Security Policy.

6 The functions, composition and working procedures of the European Parliament.

7 The jurisdictions and compositions of the Court of Justice and the General Court.

8 The roles of other institutions, including the Court of Auditors, the European Central Bank, the European Economic and Social Committee, the Committee of the Regions and EU agencies.

9 Measures taken to enhance democratic accountability and transparency across the Union institutions.

Key terms and concepts

Familiarity with the following terms will be helpful for understanding this chapter:

Comitology – law-making procedures in the EU which involve committees composed of civil servants of the Member States

COREPER – the Committee of Permanent Representatives of the Council

Double-majority – a type of qualified majority where two types of majority thresholds must be met in order for a measure to be adopted

Plenary meeting – a meeting that all members of the institution attend

Qualified majority – a requirement to reach a certain voting threshold that is greater than a simple majority

Quorum – a minimum threshold for persons present or votes cast in order for proceedings to be valid

Simple majority – a voting threshold of more than half of the total votes

2.1 Introduction to the institutions

Objective 1

Article 13(1) TEU provides that:

> The Union shall have an institutional framework which shall aim to promote its values, advance its objectives, serve its interests, those of its citizens and those of the Member States, and ensure the consistency, effectiveness and continuity of its policies and actions.

The following seven institutions are recognised as institutions of the Union by **Article 13(1) TEU**:

1. The European Parliament
2. The European Council
3. The Council
4. The European Commission (to be referred to as the 'Commission')
5. The Court of Justice of the European Union
6. The European Central Bank
7. The Court of Auditors.

Each institution has a defined role: (i) in the decision-making and law-making processes; (ii) in relation to adjudication; and/or (iii) in the audit of the Union's accounts. **Article 13(2) TEU** further provides that each institution 'shall act within the limits of the powers conferred on it by the Treaties'. Each institution can, in other words, only act if and in so far as it has been expressly authorised to do so by the Union Treaties (see Chapter 4). The Court of Justice has been quite strict in limiting the activities of the other institutions to their specified functions, although at times it has been more liberal when interpreting the powers of the European Parliament.

Two additional bodies are expressly mentioned in **Article 13(4) TEU**: the **European Economic and Social Committee** and the **Committee of the Regions**. These committees are mentioned separately as they only have an advisory function in the decision-making process. The institutions and the committees are shown in Figure 2.1.

The institutions do not fit easily into categories such as legislature, executive and judiciary. Although the Union performs legislative, executive and judicial functions, there is no formal 'separation of powers' doctrine built into the Union's constitution. Furthermore, the competence of each institution has not remained static; amendments to the founding Treaties have generally resulted in changes to the balance of power between these Union institutions. For example, the introduction of direct elections in 1979 and subsequent amendments to the EU Treaties (by the SEA, ToM, ToA, ToN and ToL) have transformed the European Parliament from a mere debating chamber with limited supervisory powers to a much more powerful institution. This shifting of the balance of powers among the institutions will be explored throughout this chapter.

Articles 13–19 TEU clarify the current roles of the Union institutions. **Title I of Part Six, TFEU** contains the detailed provisions governing the institutions, as laid out below:

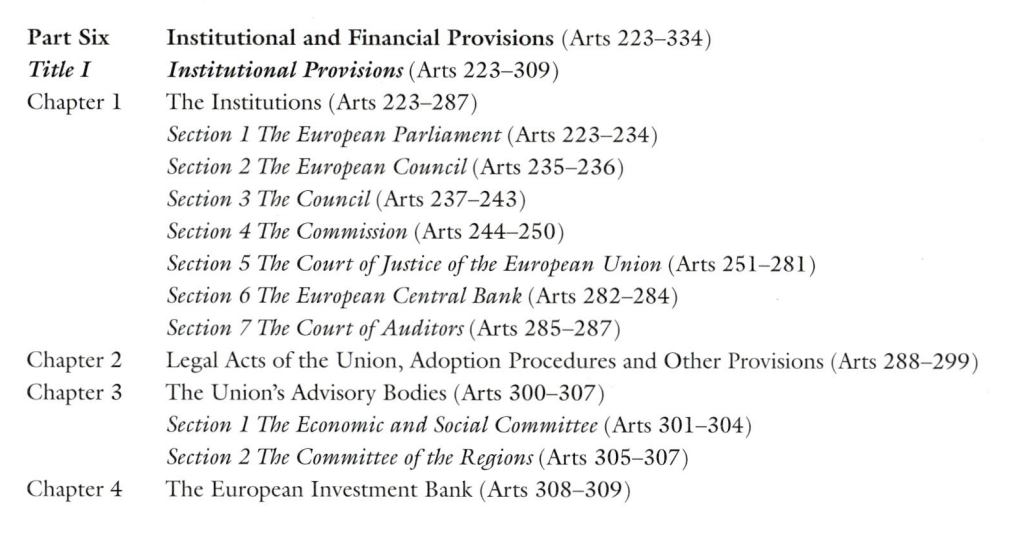

Part Six	**Institutional and Financial Provisions** (Arts 223–334)
Title I	*Institutional Provisions* (Arts 223–309)
Chapter 1	The Institutions (Arts 223–287)
	Section 1 The European Parliament (Arts 223–234)
	Section 2 The European Council (Arts 235–236)
	Section 3 The Council (Arts 237–243)
	Section 4 The Commission (Arts 244–250)
	Section 5 The Court of Justice of the European Union (Arts 251–281)
	Section 6 The European Central Bank (Arts 282–284)
	Section 7 The Court of Auditors (Arts 285–287)
Chapter 2	Legal Acts of the Union, Adoption Procedures and Other Provisions (Arts 288–299)
Chapter 3	The Union's Advisory Bodies (Arts 300–307)
	Section 1 The Economic and Social Committee (Arts 301–304)
	Section 2 The Committee of the Regions (Arts 305–307)
Chapter 4	The European Investment Bank (Arts 308–309)

Figure 2.1 The institutions of the European Union

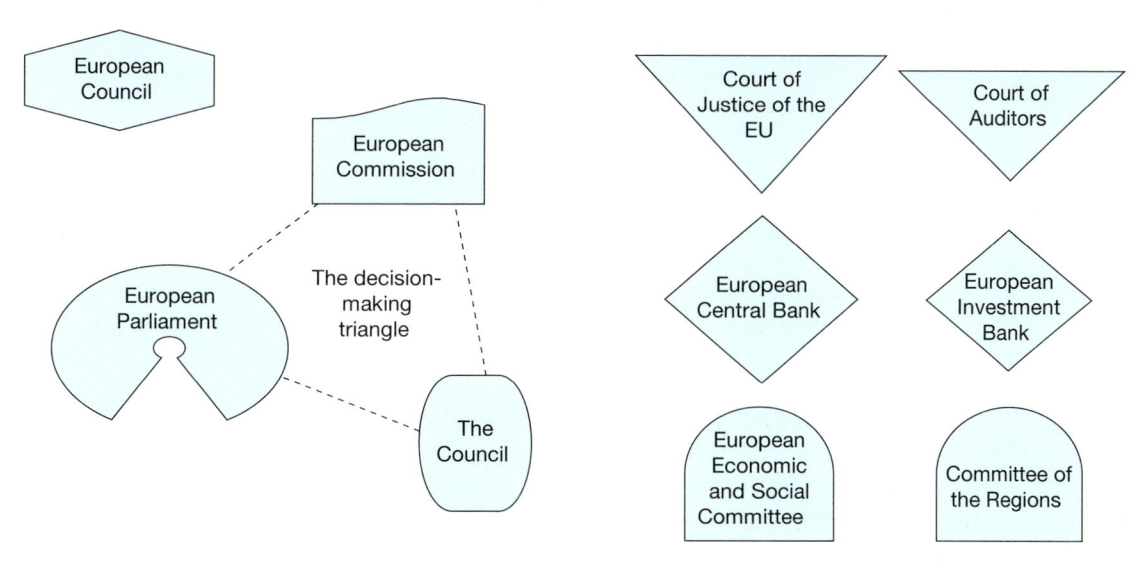

Each of the above institutions will be considered in this chapter. However, with the aim of more clearly delineating the roles of the institutions, they will be examined in a different order to that in which they are listed in the Treaties.

This chapter looks first at the **European Council**, which sets the agendas of the Union. Then the three main decision-making institutions (the **European Commission**, the **European Parliament** and the **Council**) are considered, followed by the **Court of Justice of the European Union**. The more specialised institutions of the **Court of Auditors**, the **European Central Bank** and the **European Investment Bank** follow, before the advisory bodies of the **European Economic and Social Committee** and the **Committee of the Regions**. Lastly, agencies of the EU are briefly considered. In the final section of this chapter, some attention is paid to the governance of the institutions and the drive towards greater democratic accountability and transparency that has been instrumental to recent institutional developments.

2.2 The European Council

> **Objective 2**

The provisions of the EU Treaties which govern the European Council are **Article 15 TEU** and **Articles 235–236 TFEU**. The European Council's website can be accessed at:

> www.consilium.europa.eu

The European Council was created as an informal forum following a meeting of the heads of state and government in Paris in 1974. It received recognition in the Single European Act in 1987, was granted a formal status in 1992 and was finally recognised as an official Union institution in the Treaty of Lisbon in 2009.

> ➤ See section 1.1.6 for information on the Council of Europe

The European Council should not be confused with the Council of the European Union (the Council, see below) or the Council of Europe, which is not an EU organisation.

2.2.1 The function of the European Council

Article 15(1) TEU establishes that:

> The European Council shall provide the Union with the necessary impetus for its development and shall define the general political directions and priorities thereof. It shall not exercise legislative functions.

Accordingly, the European Council is essentially a political forum in which the Member States' heads of state or government, together with its President and the President of the Commission, determine the political agenda for the Union. General programmes that are outlined at meetings of the European Council are taken up and fleshed out by the Commission and may, in some cases, form the background to a whole raft of legislation or more detailed policy in such areas as the internal market and monetary policy. It is also at European Council meetings that discussions will take place on matters relating to the common foreign and security policy and other areas of the Union's external action (**Art 22(1) TEU**).

The subject matter of European Council meetings depends on a number of different factors and will be influenced, to some extent, by the political issues which currently preoccupy the majority of the heads of state or government. These issues might involve, for example, a foreign policy crisis, a run on the national currencies in the financial markets or a major environmental disaster. To illustrate this point, meetings in 2014 included discussions on the situation in Ukraine, and migration featured heavily in meetings in 2015 and 2016. Other items will appear regularly on the European Council's agenda, such as the general economic situation, the level of unemployment and a review of the development of the internal market.

> The European Council guidelines for Brexit negotiations are briefly outlined in section 1.4.2

On 29 April 2017, a Special European Council was held to establish the Union's position regarding the UK's decision to withdraw from the Union. The result of the meeting was the adoption of the **European Council (Art 50) guidelines for Brexit negotiations**. These guidelines establish a framework for the Brexit negotiations, including the positions and principles that are to be prioritised by the Union.

Major initiatives have started life in the European Council and have then been brought forward and developed by the Commission, such as those leading to the adoption of the Social Charter at the Strasbourg Summit in 1989 and the programmes that ultimately resulted in the signing of the TEU in 1992, the ToA in 1997, the ToN in 2000 and the ToL in 2007. The European Council has proved valuable for ensuring that Commission proposals are actually approved: once they have been accepted by the European Council they are much more likely to be accepted by the Council of Ministers because they will, in principle at least, have been accepted by the heads of state or government of which the European Council is comprised (see below).

2.2.2 Composition of the European Council

> See section 2.5 on the High Representative of the Union for Foreign Affairs and Security Policy

Article 15(2) TEU establishes the composition of the European Council:

> The European Council shall consist of the Heads of State or Government of the Member States, together with its President and the President of the Commission. The High Representative of the Union for Foreign Affairs and Security Policy shall take part in its work.

The heads of state or government of the EU Member States may also be assisted at meetings of the European Council by one of their ministers (normally their foreign minister (Art 15(3) TFEU)).

The president of the European Council

Since the Treaty of Lisbon, the European Council has been led by a President with specific powers. The President is elected by a **qualified majority** of the European Council's members for a term of two-and-a-half years, renewable once (Art 15(5) and (6) TEU). The former Prime Minister of Belgium, Herman Van Rompuy, was elected to the post on 20 November 2009 and was subsequently elected for a second term which ended on 30 November 2014. The former Prime Minister of Poland, Donald Tusk, was elected and then re-elected to the post and served from 1 December 2014 to 30 November 2019. The President is not allowed to hold a national office at the same time as holding the Presidency (Art 15(6) TEU) and therefore Donald Tusk had to relinquish his role as Prime Minister of Poland. The current President is Charles Michel, former Prime Minister of Belgium, who will serve from 1 December 2019 until 31 May 2022. During this time, he will also be the President of the Euro Summit, which is a meeting of the heads of state or government of those Member States that are in the Eurozone.

> See section 1.1.5 on the Eurozone

Article 15(6) TEU provides that the President of the European Council:

> (a) shall chair it and drive it forward;
> (b) shall ensure the preparation and continuity of the work of the European Council in cooperation with the President of the Commission, and on the basis of the work of the General Affairs Council;
> (c) shall endeavour to facilitate cohesion and consensus within the European Council;
> (d) shall present a report to the European Parliament after each of the meetings of the European Council.

Additionally, Article 15(6) TEU states that the President of the European Council shall:

> ensure the external representation of the Union on issues concerning its common foreign and security policy, without prejudice to the powers of the High Representative of the Union for Foreign Affairs and Security Policy.

2.2.3 Working procedures of the European Council

The European Council meets at least twice a year. These meetings are often referred to as European Summits.

Article 15(4) TEU provides that the general rule regarding the adoption of decisions by the European Council is **consensus**, except where the Treaties provide otherwise. Alternative decision-making procedures are stipulated in **Articles 235 and 236 TFEU**. For example, Article 235(3) TFEU provides that the European Council shall act by a **simple majority** with regard to procedural questions and for the adoption of its Rules of Procedure. When a vote is taken, any member of the European Council can act on behalf of one other member (Art 235(1) TFEU). Abstention by members present at the meeting, or who are represented by another member, does not prevent the European Council from adopting an act which requires unanimity (Art 235(1) TFEU).

Article 235 TFEU also provides that 'Where the European Council decides by vote, its President and the President of the Commission shall not take part in the vote'.

2.3 The Commission

Objective 3

The provisions of the EU Treaties which govern the Commission are **Article 17 TEU** and **Articles 244–250 TFEU**. The Commission's website can be accessed at:

http://ec.europa.eu

2.3.1 The functions of the Commission

The role of the Commission is set out in **Article 17(1) TEU**:

> The Commission shall **promote the general interest of the Union** and take appropriate initiatives to that end. It shall ensure the application of the Treaties, and measures adopted by the institutions pursuant to them. It shall oversee the application of Union law under the control of the Court of Justice of the European Union. It shall execute the budget and manage programmes. It shall exercise coordinating, executive and management functions, as laid down in the Treaties. With the exception of the common foreign and security policy, and other cases provided for in the Treaties, it shall ensure the Union's external representation. It shall initiate the Union's annual and multiannual programming with a view to achieving interinstitutional agreements.

Essentially, the Commission's function is: to act as the executive of the Union and to see that Union policy is carried out; to formulate new policy and to draft legislation to give it effect; to police observance of Union rules (whether primary, in the form of Treaty provisions, or secondary, in the form of regulations, directives and decisions); and, to a lesser extent, to act as a legislative body in its own right. This latter function is largely related to the making (and enforcement) of detailed rules for the implementation of the Common Agricultural Policy.

Initiation of new legislation and policies

Article 17(2) TEU explicitly states that:

> Union legislative acts may only be adopted on the basis of a Commission proposal, except where the Treaties provide otherwise. Other acts shall be adopted on the basis of a Commission proposal where the Treaties so provide.

Although the Commission is often described as the Union's executive, that description does not do justice to its major policy-making role. In recent years, the Commission has adopted an annual *Work Programme* as a part of this process. The Work Programme for 2019 was published on 23 October 2018 (COM (2018) 800 final) and it provides a useful indication of the Commission's priorities. The current Work Programme and related documents are available on the Commission's website.

Most Commissioners see themselves as having quite a free hand in devising and promoting new policies. Unlike national politicians, they have no political platform to which they must adhere. They simply need to follow the very broad objectives established by the EU Treaties and, increasingly, by the European Council (see above). Commissioners also need to promote a good working relationship with the European Parliament, although there will be few issues which will unite the Parliament sufficiently to prompt them to remove the Commission *en bloc* (see below).

'Guardian of the Treaties'

The expression 'Guardian of the Treaties' is used to describe the Commission's role both as the keeper of the 'soul' of the Union, maintaining its course towards its declared aims of political and economic unity, and the more mundane, but equally important, role of ensuring that EU law is effectively implemented and obeyed. This role is discharged both through political contact and, if need be, by the initiation of proceedings against Member States under **Article 258 TFEU**.

The Commission is empowered by Article 258 TFEU to bring an action against a Member State which is acting in breach of Union law. This is a very important provision and is considered in greater detail in Chapter 7. The Commission will first of all ask the defaulting Member State for its own observations on the default. If the matter cannot be settled, the Commission will deliver a reasoned opinion. This will set out why the Commission considers the Member State to be in breach of Union law and what the Member State must do to remedy the situation. If the Member State still fails to act, the Commission may bring proceedings against the Member State before the Court of Justice. The action will be listed as *Commission* v [*Member State*].

The Commission has another important policing and regulating function in relation to **Articles 101 and 102 TFEU**. The preservation of a genuine internal market within the Union of goods, services and capital is dependent not just on the collaboration of governments in removing both visible and invisible barriers, but also on the exercise, by the Union, of substantial powers to prevent large private and state undertakings using **restrictive agreements** and other abuses of their dominant market position, to exclude Union-produced goods and services from domestic markets.

Allocation of EU funding

Every year, the Commission submits a **draft EU budget**, which reflects the Union's priorities for the forthcoming year. For the 2019 budget, for example, the top two priorities were job creation and youth opportunities, and migration. The draft is then subject to amendment by both the Council and the European Parliament before it is agreed.

The Commission is also the holder of Union funds and administers four special funds:

- **The European Social Fund,** which is primarily concerned with expanding vocational training for workers in order to promote employment and occupational mobility (Arts 162 and 163 TFEU).
- **The Cohesion Fund,** which was established in 1993 to provide financial support for projects in the fields of environment and trans-European networks in the area of transport infrastructure (Art 177 TFEU). It was created as part of a process of transferring resources from some of the Union's wealthier states to those with less-developed economies. The four countries which initially benefited from the Cohesion Fund – those with Gross National Products (GNP) *per capita* at 90 per cent or less of the Union average – were Greece, Ireland, Portugal and Spain. Most of Member States that have joined since 2004 now also qualify for the fund.
- **The European Agricultural Guidance and Guarantee Fund,** which was set up to assist with the restructuring of national agricultural economies (Art 40(3) TFEU).
- **The European Regional Development Fund,** which is intended to help to redress the main regional imbalances in the Union through participation in the development of regions which are lagging behind economically (Art 176 TFEU).

International representation

The Commission also has an important external role, representing the Union in negotiations with other groups of states and trading organisations. This is specifically recognised by **Article 207(3) TFEU**, which provides that:

> Where agreements with one or more third countries [i.e. non-EU countries] or international organisations need to be negotiated and concluded, Article 218 shall apply, subject to the special provisions of this Article.
>
> The Commission shall make recommendations to the Council, which shall authorise it to open the necessary negotiations. The Council and the Commission shall be responsible for ensuring that the agreements negotiated are compatible with the internal Union policies and rules.
>
> The Commission shall conduct these negotiations in consultation with a special committee appointed by the Council to assist the Commission in its task and within the framework of such directives as the Council may issue to it. The Commission shall report regularly to the special committee and to the European Parliament on the progress of negotiations.

Under Article 207(3) TFEU, and subject to the procedure set out within Article 218 TFEU, the Commission is empowered, subject to the necessary Council approval, to negotiate world trade agreements.

The Commission (through the High Representative of the Union for Foreign Affairs and Security Policy) represents the Union at a number of important international organisations. Article 220(2) TFEU provides that the High Representative and the Commission shall be instructed to implement **Article 220(1) TFEU**, which provides that:

> The Union shall establish all appropriate forms of cooperation with the organs of the United Nations and its specialised agencies, the Council of Europe, the Organisation for Security and Cooperation in Europe and the Organisation for Economic Cooperation and Development.
>
> The Union shall also maintain such relations as are appropriate with other international organisations.

2.3.2 Composition of the Commission

The Commission is composed of one Commissioner from each Member State, including the President. Each Commissioner is assigned particular areas of responsibility, known as portfolios, by the President. Additionally, there are approximately 32,000 staff employed by the Commission.

This section covers five aspects of the composition of the Commission: the number of Commissioners, the appointment of Commissioners, the termination of office, the role of the President and the structural organisation of the Commission.

The number of Commissioners

The number of Commissioners has not always aligned with the number of EU Member States; the allocation of Commissioners among the Member States has been negotiated and renegotiated as the Union has enlarged. **Article 17(5) TEU** provides that:

> As from 1 November 2014, the Commission shall consist of a number of members, including its President and the High Representative of the Union for Foreign Affairs and Security Policy, corresponding to two thirds of the number of Member States, unless the European Council, acting unanimously, decides to alter this number.

Article 17(5) goes on to specify that the Commissioners shall be nationals of the Member States, chosen on the basis of a system of 'strictly equal rotation between the Member States, reflecting the demographic and geographical range of all the Member States'.

However, as discussed in Chapter 1, in order to satisfy the concerns of Ireland and to pave the way for the second Irish referendum on the ratification of the ToL, the European Council agreed that it would make the decision to revert to the established (pre-Brexit) composition of 28 Commissioners. As stipulated in Article 17(5) TEU, this required a unanimous decision by the European Council. Subsequently, the Commission continues to consist of **one national from each Member State**. Currently, after Brexit, the number of Commissioners is 27.

The appointment of Commissioners

Article 17(7) TEU (previously Art 214 EC Treaty) provides for the appointment of the President and the other members.

The European Council acting by a qualified majority proposes to the European Parliament a candidate for President of the Commission. The European Council's proposal will be made 'taking into account the elections to the European Parliament and after having held the appropriate consultations' (Art 17(7) TEU). The President is elected by the European Parliament by a majority of its component members. If this majority is not forthcoming, then the European Council, again acting by a qualified majority, shall within one month propose a new candidate who shall be elected by the European Parliament following the same procedure (Art 17(7) TEU). The current Commission President is Ursula von der Leyen. She is the first woman to hold the post and will be in office from 1 November 2019 until 31 October 2024. The previous Presidents include Jean-Claude Junker (2014–2019) José Manuel Barroso (2004–2014), Romano Prodi (1999–2004), Jacques Santer (1995–1999) and Jacques Delors (1985–1995).

The President is then involved in the appointment of the individual Commissioners: 'The Council, by common accord with the President-elect, shall adopt the list of the other persons whom it proposes for appointment as members of the Commission' (Art 17(7) TEU). The potential Commissioners who are proposed by the Council and the President of the Commission are first suggested to them by the Member States. **Article 17(3) TEU** states that:

> The members of the Commission shall be chosen on the ground of their general competence and European commitment from persons whose independence is beyond doubt.

Article 17(7) TEU then provides that the President, the High Representative and the other members of the Commission shall be subject *as a body* to a vote of consent by the European Parliament. On the basis of this consent the Commission shall be appointed by the European Council, acting by a qualified majority (see below). The members are appointed for a renewable period of five years (Art 17(3) TEU).

It should be noted that the power of the European Parliament to veto the appointment of the Commission is only a power to block the appointment of the Commission as a body; it cannot block the appointment of an individual member (although it can block the President's appointment). However, the Parliament may be able to negotiate a redistribution of portfolios to ensure that a member of which it disapproves does not have responsibility for a high-profile portfolio. The Parliament may threaten to veto the appointment of the whole Commission if its request is not met.

> **Reflection:** Controversial Commissioners
>
> The period of office of the 2004–2009 Commission started on 22 November 2004. This was three weeks later than planned due to political problems which surfaced during the appointments process. During the European Parliamentary approval process, the Parliament opposed the appointment of Rocco Buttiglione (from Italy) because of his views on homosexuality and marriage. As stated above, the European Parliament cannot block the appointment of an individual member; it can only vote to block the appointment of the Commission as a whole. The Parliament felt so strongly about Buttiglione's appointment that it became clear they would vote against the appointment of the proposed Commissioners *en bloc*. At this stage, the Commission-elect was withdrawn. Franco Frattini (from Italy) took the place of Rocco Buttiglione. The President-elect also requested the replacement of Latvia's Ingridia Udre because of her views on EU taxation. He also reshuffled two portfolios. Following these changes, on 18 November 2004 the European Parliament approved the new appointments by 449 votes to 149, with 82 abstentions.
>
> These events demonstrate the influence that the Parliament can exert over the appointment of the Commission, despite not being able to block the appointment of individual Commissioners, and therefore shows the balance of power between democratically-elected and appointed officials.

The independence and integrity of Commissioners

Article 17(3) TEU codifies the principle that the Commission will be independent and will act with integrity, by providing that:

> ... The members of the Commission shall be chosen on the ground of their general competence and European commitment from persons whose independence is beyond doubt.
>
> In carrying out its responsibilities, the Commission shall be completely independent. Without prejudice to Article 18(2), the members of the Commission shall neither seek nor take instructions from any Government or other institution, body, office or entity. They shall refrain from any action incompatible with their duties or the performance of their tasks.

This principle of independence and integrity is further amplified by **Article 245 TFEU** (previously Art 213(2) EC Treaty), which provides that:

> The Members of the Commission shall refrain from any action incompatible with their duties. Member States shall respect their independence and **shall not to seek to influence them** in the performance of their tasks.
>
> The Members of the Commission **may not, during their term of office, engage in any other occupation**, whether gainful or not. When entering upon their duties they shall give a solemn undertaking that, both during and after their term of office, they will **respect the obligations** arising therefrom and in particular their duty to **behave with integrity and discretion** as regards the acceptance, after they have ceased to hold office, of certain appointments or benefits. In the event of any breach of these obligations, the Court of Justice may, on application by the Council acting by a simple majority or the Commission, rule that the Member concerned be, according to the circumstances, either compulsorily retired in accordance with Article 247 or deprived of his right to a pension or other benefits in its stead.

It is thereby provided that the Commission shall act in the general interests of the Union. The Commission members are not representatives of the Member States of their nationality.

The following case, decided by the Court of Justice in 2006, concerns the issue of whether or not a former Commissioner had breached the former Article 213(2) EC Treaty (now Art 245 TFEU), in failing to respect the obligations arising from her office as Commissioner:

Commission v Edith Cresson (Case C-432/04)

Facts:

When Edith Cresson entered office as a European Commissioner on 24 January 1995, she sought to appoint a dental surgeon named Berthelot as a 'personal adviser'. Cresson was advised that Berthelot could not be appointed as a member of a Commissioner's Cabinet because he was 66 years old and because her Cabinet was already fully staffed as far as personal advisers were concerned. Cresson requested the administration to consider how it might be possible to appoint Berthelot, who was then engaged as a visiting scientist from September 1995 until the end of February 1997. Despite this appointment as a scientist, Berthelot worked exclusively as a personal adviser to Cresson.

Berthelot's contract was then renewed for a period of one year, expiring at the end of February 1998, bringing his appointment as a visiting scientist to a total period of two-and-a-half years. The rules, however, specify a maximum duration of 24 months.

In January 2003, the Commission sent Cresson a statement of complaints against her concerning Berthelot's appointment. After hearing Cresson, the Commission brought an action before the Court of Justice based on the former Article 213 EC Treaty (now Art 245 TFEU).

Ruling:

The former Article 213 EC Treaty required members of the Commission to respect the obligations arising from their office. The Court stated that this should be understood as including all of the duties which arose from the office of member of the Commission and not only the duties of integrity and discretion that are expressly mentioned in the Article. Thus, the Court stated that it is 'the duty of Members of the Commission to ensure that the general interest of the Community takes precedence at all times, not only over national interests, but also over personal interests' (para 71). However, the Court stated that a digression of certain gravity is required for a breach of the former Article 213(2) EC Treaty (now Art 245 TFEU) to be committed.

> The Court went on to hold that Cresson had acted in breach of the obligations arising from her office, as Berthelot's appointment constituted a circumvention of the rules on appointing members of a Cabinet and visiting scientists. Furthermore, Cresson was found to be responsible for the breach since Berthelot's appointment took place at her express request after she had been informed that she could not recruit Berthelot to her Cabinet.
>
> **Significance:**
>
> This was the first instance in which the Court of Justice ruled that a Commissioner had breached their duties whilst in office. It was therefore significant for demonstrating that Commissioners will be held to account for malfeasance. Additionally, the ruling determined that such a lengthy period between the alleged misconduct and the initiation of administrative proceedings did not vitiate the case.

Termination of office

Termination may occur by:

- expiry of the five-year period of office (Art 17(3) TEU);
- death (Art 246 TFEU);
- voluntary resignation (Art 246 TFEU) – see *Dalli* v *Commission* (Case T-562/12);
- compulsory resignation pursuant to **Article 17(6) TEU**: 'A member of the Commission shall resign if the President so requests' – see *Dalli* v *Commission* (Case T-562/12);
- compulsory retirement pursuant to **Article 247 TFEU**: 'If any member of the Commission no longer fulfils the conditions required for the performance of his duties or if he is guilty of serious misconduct, the Court of Justice may, on application by the Council acting by a simple majority or the Commission, compulsorily retire him'; or
- compulsory *collective* resignation where the European Parliament passes a vote of no confidence pursuant to **Article 17(8) TEU** and **Article 234 TFEU**. Such a vote requires a two-thirds majority of the votes cast which must represent a majority of the total membership of the European Parliament. On 15 March 1999, the dominant socialist bloc of MEPs withdrew support for the President (Jacques Santer) and his 19 Commissioners following a damning report by an external fraud inquiry that charged them with losing political control over the Brussels executive. Their immediate resignation was demanded and this was forthcoming. If they had not resigned, a vote of no confidence would have been carried and the President and Commissioners would have been legally required to resign.

Article 246 TFEU sets out the procedures which apply when a Commissioner's term of office comes to an end through death, resignation or compulsory retirement.

Role of the President

The ToA inserted a new paragraph into the former Article 219 EC Treaty providing that the 'Commission shall work under the political guidance of its President'. The President was therefore conferred authority to lead the Commission. The political role of the President of the Commission has been further reinforced by the ToL. **Article 17(6) TEU**, as amended by the ToL, provides that the President shall:

- lay down guidelines within which the Commission is to work;
- decide on the internal organisation of the Commission, ensuring it acts consistently, efficiently and as a collegiate body;

- appoint Vice-Presidents, other than the High Representative (see below), from among the members of the Commission;
- have the power to request the resignation of an individual Commissioner or the High Representative.

Article 248 TFEU empowers the President of the Commission to allocate areas of responsibility to individual members of the Commission and to reshuffle such allocations during the Commission's term of office. Article 248 TFEU further provides that 'The Members of the Commission shall carry out the duties devolved upon them by the President under his authority'.

It will depend upon the President as to how influential and powerful they are. The former President Jacques Delors was a very influential and powerful leader, who contributed greatly to the shaping of the Union. It was said that under Jacques Delors during the 1980s, 'the office became a key focus of power, not just in the Commission, but in Europe as a whole. He gave the Commission a purpose and taught it to respond to his will' (Grant, 1994). Under a weak President, it becomes a fragmented bureaucracy, as demonstrated during Jacques Santer's period of office, which culminated in his resignation on 15 March 1999.

Organisational structure

Each Commissioner is responsible for one or more policy areas (portfolios), which will be allocated by the President (Art 248 TFEU). Each Commissioner will be assisted by a small Cabinet of officials (similar to UK civil servants) whom they personally appoint. The Cabinet is headed by a Chef de Cabinet, who will liaise closely with the Commissioner.

The Commission itself is divided into a number of departments referred to as Directorates-General (DGs) and each DG is headed by a Director General who is individually responsible to the relevant member of the Commission. Each DG is further divided

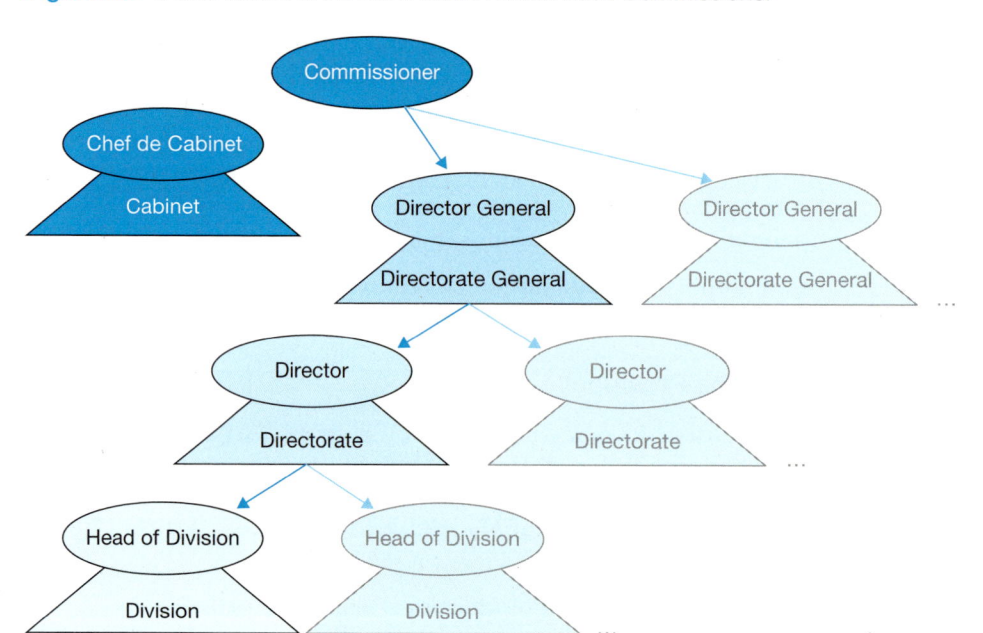

Figure 2.2 The structure of the Commission under each Commissioner

into a number of Directorates (usually between four and six), each headed by a Director. The Director is individually responsible to the relevant DG. Each Directorate is further sub-divided into a number of Divisions, with each headed by a Head of Division who is individually responsible to the relevant Director (see Figure 2.2).

Each DG used to be referred to by a number (e.g. DGI External Economic Affairs; DGV Employment, Industrial Relations and Social Affairs). However, in 1999 it was decided to label each DG with a clear name, in what was largely a symbolic change designed to facilitate understanding by outsiders. It was also announced that the number of DGs would be reduced from 42 to 36, which has since decreased further to 31.

2.3.3 Working procedures of the Commission

The Commission acts as a collegiate body. This means that each Commissioner must be consulted on a proposal and decisions are taken collectively. Once taken, such decisions bind the Commissioners.

Article 250 TFEU stipulates that Decisions by the Commission on whether or not to adopt a proposal are taken by a **simple majority** of its members. Although the appropriate Director General will initiate a proposal, the Commission as a body has no power to delegate approval of the details of that proposal to an individual Commissioner. The Court of Justice made the position clear in the case of *Commission* v *BASF and Others* (Case C-137/92), where it stated:

> The functioning of the Commission is governed by the principle of collegiate responsibility . . . The principle of collegiate responsibility . . . [is] based on the equal participation of the Commissioners in the adoption of decisions, from which it follow[s] in particular that decisions should be the subject of collective deliberation and that all the members of the college of Commissioners should bear collective responsibility on the political level for all decisions adopted. [paras 62 and 63]

Although the Commissioners are bound to act as a collegiate body on behalf of the Union rather than for the states from which they originate, it would be unrealistic to expect them to divest themselves of all political contacts with their national governments. Indeed, it would not be helpful to the Union for them to do so. They frequently use such contacts within the governments and civil services of Member States to promote Union policies and to sound out the extent of support new legislation might secure in the European Parliament and the Council. Tensions do arise, however, when they appear to be too set on promoting the policies of their own states.

The role of the Commission as the primary proposer of legislative acts has often been summarised by the *maxim* 'the Commission proposes and the Council disposes'. However, when considering the decision-making process, this no longer accurately reflects the position, partly because of the increasingly important role of the European Council and partly because of the much-enhanced role of the European Parliament (see below).

DGs, assisted by a large number of specialist advisory committees drawn from the appropriate industrial, commercial and other sectors in the Member States, take an active part in drafting new provisions. This process has been particularly visible in the measures proposed to harmonise product standards, consumer safety measures and health and safety at work measures in the internal market under Article 114 TFEU.

Policy initiation takes place at many levels within the Commission. Senior Commission officials who have moved from civil service posts within their Member States are often surprised by the extent to which they are able to bring forward their own policy initiatives. As there is no equivalent of a governmental cabinet with a political programme, either at Council or Commission level, there is much greater scope for even middle-ranking officials to bring forward proposals for the implementation of the Work Programme.

In its role of overseeing the implementation of EU law through the adoption of **delegated acts** and **implementing acts**, the Commission applies a system of consultation known as **comitology**. This involves the consultation of standing committees comprised of experts from the Member States. The procedures for such consultations are set out in **Regulation 182/2011**, laying down the rules and general principles concerning mechanisms for control by Member States of the Commission's exercise of implementing powers (the Comitology Regulation). As suggested by the title of this regulation, comitology enables the Member States to be involved in the implementation of Union legislation and is thus designed to enhance the democratic legitimacy and acceptance by the Member States of the resulting implementing acts. In February 2017, the Commission proposed amendments to the Comitology Regulation with the aims of enhancing the transparency and accountability of the procedure and providing for further political guidance where pertinent. This proposal is part of a broader attention to the principle of transparency, which is examined further in section 2.9 of this chapter.

▶ See section 3.4.4 on delegated acts and implementing acts

Reflection: Comitology

Up until 2006, comitology powers were distributed between the Council and the Commission: the Commission proposed and implemented regulations, while the Council approved or blocked them. Reforms in 2006 incorporated the Parliament into the division of powers. They also grouped implementing measures into two clear categories:

– **comitology** *stricto sensu*, covering the most technical, administrative or individual measures;
– **quasi-legislative measures**, amending or supplementing non-essential elements of laws adopted by the Parliament and Council, and which are sent to the Parliament and the Council for approval.

In February 2011, 15 months after the entry into force of the ToL, **Regulation 182/2011** was adopted. Daniel Guéguen (2017), a Professor of Comitology at the College of Europe, describes this Regulation as modifying a system that worked well and turning it into one which works badly. While nothing changed for comitology *strictu sensu*, the new procedure for quasi-legislative measures was composed of two levels: an **examination committee** at first instance and a complex and *ad hoc* **appeal committee**. In either committee, a **qualified majority** must be secured in order to block or approve a Commission proposal. Securing such a majority is difficult because 'the timeframes are tight and the decision is often more political than technical' (Guéguen, 2017). The political nature of such decisions is problematic given that the distinction between the technical and the political is 'an essential element in legitimising comitology, its boundaries (the issues covered by it) and the way comitology works (the parties ultimately involved in it)' (Robert, 2019).

If Member State representatives fail to attain a qualified majority in committee, this is referred to as a **'no opinion scenario'**, and the initiative is returned to the Commission. Thus, the

> Commission now finds itself having to take sole responsibility for decisions on a range of politically controversial subjects, such as in the areas of genetically modified organisms (GMOs) and plant protection products. Subsequently, the Commission is trying to reform comitology procedures once again to reduce the risk of no opinion scenarios and thereby improve the democratic legitimacy of delegated and implementing acts. The proposal to amend Regulation 182/2011 is based on four measures:
>
> 1. Making public the voting positions of Member States in the appeal committee.
> 2. Discounting abstentions in the calculation of qualified majorities in order to push Member States to declare whether they are for or against any given policy.
> 3. Creating a higher-level variant of the appeal committee involving national ministers.
> 4. Referring matters to the Council for a non-binding advisory opinion.
>
> However, the proposed amendments have stalled. Guéguen has subsequently argued that the EU should prioritise strengthening the credibility of and trust in its agencies, to enable the Commission to rely on this source of expertise when it needs to make a technical decision. This would not attend, though, to the democratic legitimising function of comitology, which is especially important for politically sensitive technical decisions.

▶ See section 2.8.6 on EU agencies

2.4 The Council

Objective 4

The provisions of the EU Treaties which govern the Council are **Article 16 TEU** and **Articles 237–243 TFEU**. The Council's website can be accessed at:

www.consilium.europa.eu

The Treaties now refer to the Council, but some commentators still refer to the Council of Ministers, as it was previously known, due to its being composed of Member State politicians.

2.4.1 The functions of the Council

The function of the Council is set out in **Article 16(1) TEU** in very broad terms:

> The Council shall, jointly with the European Parliament, exercise legislative and budgetary functions. It shall carry out policy-making and coordinating functions as laid down in the Treaties.

Decision-making remains the central role of the Council; the different methods of decision-making are considered in detail below. Despite the increasingly important role of the European Parliament, particularly following amendments made to the Treaties by the ToL, in the overwhelming majority of cases the Council is the place where **final decisions** will be made.

While the Commission promotes the interests of the Union, the Council primarily represents the **national interests** of the Member States.

2.4.2 Composition of the Council

The Council consists of a representative of each Member State at ministerial level 'who may commit the government of the Member State in question and cast its vote' (Art 16(2) TEU). The Council is therefore made up of politicians from the Member States who are authorised to bind the Member State they represent.

Configurations

There are **no fixed members** of the Council and membership will vary according to the matter under discussion. **Article 16(6) TEU** provides for the Council to meet in different configurations. These configurations are determined by the European Council acting by a qualified majority (Art 236 TFEU). In total, the Council meets in ten configurations:

- Agriculture and fisheries
- Competitiveness
- Economic and financial affairs
- Education, youth, culture and sport
- Employment, social policy, health and consumer affairs
- Environment
- Foreign affairs
- General affairs
- Justice and home affairs
- Transport, telecommunications and energy.

Article 16(6) TEU mentions two specific configurations:

> The **General Affairs Council** shall ensure consistency in the work of the different Council configurations. It shall prepare and ensure the follow-up to meetings of the European Council, in liaison with the President of the European Council and the Commission.
> The **Foreign Affairs Council** shall elaborate the Union's external action on the basis of strategic guidelines laid down by the European Council and ensure that the Union's action is consistent.

▶ The High Representative of the Union for Foreign Affairs and Security Policy is considered in section 2.5

The General Affairs Council is therefore notable for its special coordinating role. **Article 18(3) TEU** then stipulates that the Foreign Affairs Council is to be presided over by the High Representative of the Union for Foreign Affairs and Security Policy.

Although Member States are normally represented in the Council by the senior minister from the relevant governmental department, this may not always be possible and there are occasions when Council meetings are composed of ministers of different levels of seniority.

President of the Council

The office of President of the Council is held in turn by each Member State for a period of six months in the order decided by the Council acting unanimously. The handover of the chair of the Council of the EU takes place from each rotating Presidency to the next one on

1 January and 1 July each year. Following a Council Decision of 26 July 2016, the order of rotating presidencies was determined up until 2030.

Each rotating Presidency ensures the smooth functioning of the Council, represents the EU in international conferences, organises meetings and sets the agenda for the Council, **COREPER** (see below) and other Council preparatory bodies. The Presidency also promotes policy decisions, acting as a broker with the aim of reaching consensus among the Member States in a way that supports the interests of the Union.

In order to achieve coherence and effectiveness as the Council works towards implementing the Union's objectives, it was decided in 2007 to establish a group of presiding countries. In particular, three consecutive Presidencies (the so-called 'Trio' presidency) coordinate their objectives for an 18-month period and prepare a common programme which presents these objectives. The Presidency has the opportunity to formulate, in cooperation with Union institutions, the decisions taken by the Council on the basis of the dossiers that are inherited by previous Presidencies, as well as the forthcoming proposals. However, the Presidency can focus on certain key issues, which may define the identity of the Presidency.

Team presidencies

The ToL, which came into force on 1 December 2009, introduced the concept of team presidencies for the Council configurations. All configurations, other than the Foreign Affairs Council, are presided over by one of the Council's Member State representatives, on the basis of a system of equal rotation (Art 16(9) TEU). The European Council, acting by a qualified majority, determines the Presidency of each configuration, other than that of the Foreign Affairs Council (Art 236 TFEU).

The President of a particular configuration is responsible for preparing the agenda for Council meetings. This means that holding the presidency provides an opportunity for Member States to ensure that issues that are important to them are placed at the top of the agenda.

COREPER

COREPER, which is the French acronym for the **Committee of Permanent Representatives**, plays an important role in providing continuity during the inevitable absences of relevant ministers from the Council. The Committee consists of senior national officials who are permanently located in Brussels. The Committee was originally established by Article 4 of the Merger Treaty in 1965, but it was formally integrated into the Union's decision-making structure by the former Article 207 EC Treaty (now Art 16(7) TEU and Art 240(1) TFEU). **Article 16(7) TEU** now provides that:

> A Committee of Permanent Representatives of the Governments of the Member States shall be responsible for preparing the work of the Council.

Additionally, **Article 240(1) TFEU** provides that:

> A committee consisting of the Permanent Representatives of the Governments of the Member States shall be responsible for preparing the work of the Council and for carrying out the tasks assigned to it by the latter. The Committee may adopt procedural decisions in cases provided for in the Council's Rules of Procedure.

The Committee operates on two levels: COREPER I, which consists of the ambassadors from the Member States who are seconded to the Union in Brussels, and COREPER II, which is staffed by the ambassadors' deputies. The primary task of COREPER is to prepare items for discussion at Council meetings and it will be assisted in this by a wide range of specialist advisory committees. If the text of a policy statement or legislation can be agreed before the meeting, it will be tabled in Part A of the Council agenda, where it will normally be adopted without further discussion. More difficult, controversial items, on which agreement has not been possible, will appear in Part B of the agenda. In these cases, the issue may, subject to the appropriate legal base, have to be decided by a qualified majority vote. Now that Article 16(8) TEU requires the Council to meet in public when it deliberates and votes on a draft legislative act, each Council meeting is divided into two parts, dealing respectively with deliberations on Union legislative acts and non-legislative activities.

2.4.3 Working procedures of the Council

The Treaties provide for three voting methods in the Council:

- simple majority;
- qualified majority;
- unanimity.

Prior to the ToL, the former Article 205(1) EC Treaty provided that simple majority voting was to be used unless otherwise provided in the Treaty. However, the Treaty almost invariably provided for some other system. Following the ToL, qualified majority has become the general rule for the adoption of decisions within the Council, as **Article 16(3) TEU** states that 'The Council shall act by a qualified majority except where the Treaties provide otherwise'. The three voting methods are now outlined.

Simple majority

Under the 'simple majority' voting system, one vote either for or against is allocated to each Member State and the decision is made in favour of the option that receives the most votes. It is largely used for the establishment of sub-committees of the Council and for procedural matters.

Qualified majority

Before 31 October 2014

Prior to 31 October 2014, qualified majority voting (QMV) was a system of voting which was weighted according to the population size of the Member State. **Article 3(3) of Protocol No. 36** (which is annexed to the TEU and the TFEU and which was amended by Article 20 of the Accession Treaty for Croatia), provided that for acts of the European Council and of the Council requiring a qualified majority, members' votes would be weighted as follows in numerical order (Table 2.1).

Article 3(3) of Protocol No. 36 further provided that in order for an act to be adopted by qualified majority, two thresholds had to be satisfied: (i) at least 260 votes had to be cast in favour; and (ii) a majority of Member States had to vote in favour of a Commission proposal, or two-thirds of Member States had to vote otherwise.

Table 2.1 QMV Member State vote allocation up until 31 October 2014 (numerical)

Member State	QMV allocation	Member State	QMV allocation
France	29	Sweden	10
Germany	29	Croatia	7
Italy	29	Denmark	7
UK	29	Finland	7
Poland	27	Ireland	7
Spain	27	Lithuania	7
Romania	14	Slovakia	7
Netherlands	13	Cyprus	4
Belgium	12	Estonia	4
Czech Republic	12	Latvia	4
Greece	12	Luxembourg	4
Hungary	12	Slovenia	4
Portugal	12	Malta	3
Austria	10		
Bulgaria	10	**Total**	**352**

Article 3(3), Protocol No. 36, further provided that:

> A member of the European Council or the Council may request that, where an act is adopted by the European Council or the Council by a qualified majority, a check is made to ensure that the Member States comprising the qualified majority represent at least 62% of the total population of the Union. If that proves not to be the case, the act shall not be adopted.

From 1 November 2014

On 1 November 2014, the formula for determining a qualified majority changed to one based on the '**double-majority**' principle. Votes are no longer weighted; all Member States now cast one vote each. However, the population size of a Member State is taken into account and may influence the outcome of a vote.

Article 16(4) TEU requires two thresholds to be achieved before a measure can be adopted:

(i) the support of at least **55 per cent of the members** of the Council, comprising at least 15 of them; and

(ii) the support of Member States comprising at least **65 per cent of the population** of the Union.

In addition, the qualified majority will be considered to have been achieved if fewer than four Member States vote against a measure. This provision will prevent three or fewer of the more populous Member States from being able to block a proposal.

Article 238(2) TFEU provides a derogation from Article 16(4) TEU where the Council does not act on a proposal from either the Commission or the High Representative of the Union for Foreign Affairs and Security Policy. In this instance, the first threshold is increased, requiring the support of at least 72 per cent of the Member States.

Article 238(3) TFEU sets out the qualified majority formula where not all Member States participate in the voting (e.g. where they are using the enhanced cooperation procedure (see below)).

A decision adopted by the Council incorporates a revised **'Ioannina' compromise**. This decision enables a small number of Member States, which is close to a blocking minority, to demonstrate their opposition to a proposed measure. **From 1 April 2017**, a decision can be delayed if opposition is expressed by:

(i) 55 per cent of the population of the Union; or
(ii) at least 55 per cent of the number of Member States, necessary to constitute a blocking minority under Article 16(4) TEU or 238(2) TFEU).

Unanimity

Unanimity is reserved for the most important decisions or those for which Member States are least prepared to pool their national sovereignty. Although this effectively gives Member States a veto, that veto must be exercised for a measure to be blocked; abstention by Members present or represented does not prevent the adoption of an act which requires unanimity (Art 238(4) TFEU). Unanimity is, for example, required for the admission of new Member States (Art 49 TEU) and for approval of any other matter within the competence of the Union for which the Treaty does not provide a legal base (Art 352 TFEU).

The Luxembourg Accords

The Luxembourg Accords (also referred to as the Luxembourg Compromise) were the result of an impasse between France and the other Member States in relation to farm prices in 1965. The decision had to be determined, under the Treaty, by the Council acting by a qualified majority. The French insisted on the right to secure a unanimous decision in cases such as this, where a vital national interest was at stake. The other Member States could not agree. France then remained absent from all but technical meetings of the Council for seven months and important decision-making in the Union virtually drew to a halt. The Accords were negotiated in a reconvened meeting of the Council in January 1966. The three points that emerged from this meeting, as far as voting procedures were concerned, were as follows:

1 Where, in the case of decisions which may be taken by majority vote on a proposal of the Commission, very important interests of one or more partners are at stake, the members of the Council will endeavour, within a reasonable time, to reach solutions which can be adopted by all the members of the Council while respecting their mutual interests and those of the Union.

2 With regard to the preceding paragraph, the French delegation considers that where very important interests are at stake the discussion must be continued until unanimous agreement is reached.

3 The six delegates note that there is a divergence of views on what should be done in the event of a failure to reach complete agreement.

The six delegations concluded by observing that the divergence noted in point 3 did not prevent the Union's work from being resumed in accordance with the normal procedure.

There are a number of things to be said about the Accords. In the first place, the title 'Accord' is inappropriate. There was, in fact, no agreement, only an agreement to disagree. Secondly, the Accords have no standing in law. In so far as it purports to amend the voting procedure laid down by the Treaty in certain circumstances, it cannot be effective. Changes to the text and substance of the EU Treaties have to be carried out in the appropriate form, after consultation with the European Parliament and the Commission. This was not done in the case of the Accords. The Commission has never accepted that the Accords have any validity and has disassociated itself from them (Commission 1982, p. 8). Pierre Pescatore, a former judge of the Court of Justice, has described the Accords as 'a mere press release, without the least force of law' (Pescatore, 1987, p. 13). The Court of Justice has stated (but not in the context of the Accords) that 'the rules regarding the manner in which the Community [i.e. Union] institutions arrive at their decisions [i.e. by a qualified majority vote or by unanimity] are laid down in the Treaty and are not at the disposal of the Member States or of the institutions themselves' (***United Kingdom* v *Council*** (Case 68/86)). There is no *general* right to veto proposed legislation. What there has been is a willingness, in some cases where Member States appear to be in difficulties in relation to a domestic political situation, to refrain from pressing to a qualified majority vote where the Treaties authorise it.

The Accords have undoubtedly encouraged Member States to reach a compromise wherever possible. However, the formal invocation of the Accords has been rare and has not always achieved the desired result. In 1982, for example, when the UK sought to block the adoption of an agricultural price package in order to put pressure on the other Member States to agree to a reduction of the UK's contributions, its purported 'veto' was ignored and a vote was taken. However, in 1985, Germany invoked the Accords to forestall an increase in cereal prices and was successful. It is significant that no Member State which has been overridden, following an appeal to the Accords, has ever taken the decision to the Court of Justice. Recent changes to the Treaties have tended to increase the use of QMV and reduce the use of unanimity. Due to the blocking mechanisms that are incorporated within QMV, it is therefore likely that appeals to vital national interests under the Accords will become even rarer than at present.

2.5 The High Representative of the Union for Foreign Affairs and Security Policy

Objective 5

Article 18 TEU provides for the appointment of the High Representative of the Union for Foreign Affairs and Security Policy. Although clearly not one of the EU institutions, this is an appropriate point to consider the High Representative.

2.5.1 The Role of the High Representative

The High Representative:

- conducts the Union's common foreign and security policy (Art 18(2) TEU);
- chairs the Foreign Affairs Council (Art 18(3) TEU);
- serves as one of the Vice-Presidents of the Commission (Art 18(4) TEU).

In this 'two-hatted' role (Commission–Council), the High Representative ensures the consistency of the Union's external action as a whole (Art 18(4)). The High Representative conducts the Union's common foreign and security policy, and common security and defence policy, contributing to policy development in these areas (Art 18(2) TEU). The High Representative is aided by a European External Action Service (Art 27(3) TEU), which consists of officials from relevant departments of the Council's General Secretariat and the Commission, as well as staff seconded from Member States' national diplomatic services (Art 27(3) TEU).

2.5.2 The appointment of the High Representative

The High Representative is appointed by the European Council, acting by a qualified majority, with the agreement of the President of the Commission (Art 18(1) TEU). Josep Borrell, the former Spanish foreign minister, was appointed High Representative of the Union for Foreign Affairs and Security Policy from 1 November 2019, with the agreement of Ursula von der Leyen, the newly elected President of the Commission.

As a Vice-President of the Commission, the High Representative is subject to a collective vote of approval by the European Parliament (Art 17(7) TEU) and, possibly, a vote of censure.

2.6 The European Parliament

Objective 6

The provisions of the EU Treaties governing the European Parliament are **Article 14 TEU** and **Articles 223–234 TFEU**. The European Parliament's website can be accessed at:

www.europarl.europa.eu

2.6.1 The functions of the European Parliament

The EEC Treaty, as it was originally enacted in 1957, included provision for 'an Assembly' whose task was to 'exercise the advisory and supervisory powers' conferred upon it. The Assembly is now called the European Parliament and the words 'advisory and supervisory' have disappeared. In 1979, the Parliament became a directly elected body.

Article 14(1) TEU now states that:

> The European Parliament shall, jointly with the Council, exercise legislative and budgetary functions. It shall exercise functions of political control and consultation as laid down in the Treaties. It shall elect the President of the Commission.

The Parliament represents the **interests of citizens** of the Union.

However, the name 'Parliament' is somewhat misleading. It shares a number of important features with national parliaments and has considerable influence, but it falls short of being a genuine, sovereign parliament as the term is understood in the UK. The principal difference is that it lacks the power both to initiate legislation and to impose taxes. Its powers have increased, however, following the changes to decision-making procedures made by the SEA, TEU, ToA, ToN and ToL. The rationale for the increase in the Parliament's powers has been to counter the argument that the Union was insufficiently democratic due to the lack of real powers invested in its only directly elected body. These increased powers are discussed below and in Chapter 3.

There are three main powers exercised by the Parliament:

- participation in the legislative processes of the Union;
- acting as the budgetary authority;
- supervision of the Commission.

The European Parliament can request that the Commission submit a proposal for legislation (Art 225 TFEU, see below) and must approve the admission of new Member States (Art 49 TEU).

In addition, Parliament has the power to set up a temporary **Committee of Inquiry** to 'investigate . . . alleged contraventions or maladministration in the implementation of Union law' (Art 226 TFEU) and to appoint a **Parliamentary Ombudsman** to investigate complaints about any of the other Union institutions, except the Court of Justice of the European Union acting in its judicial role (Art 228 TFEU). Emily O'Reilly is the current European Ombudsman. The Ombudsman can investigate complaints against the Union institutions of maladministration, which includes such matters as unfairness, discrimination, abuse of power, lack or refusal of information or unnecessary delay. The Ombudsman's website can be accessed at:

www.ombudsman.europa.eu

Alongside these formal powers, the Parliament takes an active part in the political life of the Union, commissioning reports and passing resolutions on social and political issues, human rights, defence and foreign policy and many other matters. It can, however, do little more than express a view on the issues about which a majority of MEPs are concerned.

The main powers of the Parliament pertaining to the budget and the supervision of the Commission will now be outlined, while the Parliament's legislative functions are explained in Chapter 3.

The budget

In relation to the budget, the Parliament has an important function, which it shares with the Council. The Union's budget is drafted by the Commission and placed before the Council and the European Parliament before 1 September each year. This is necessary because the Union's financial year runs from 1 January to 31 December (Art 313 TFEU). The budget is divided into two parts: compulsory expenditure (CE) and non-compulsory expenditure (NCE). CE relates to those items where the expenditure is required by the EU Treaties, primarily the Common Agricultural Policy, which usually absorbs around 50 per cent of the total budget. NCE covers such items as social and regional policy, research and aid to non-EU countries.

Prior to the ToL, Parliament had wide powers to amend NCE items, but only limited powers to modify CE items under the former Article 272 EC Treaty. Parliament could, however, acting by a majority of its members, representing a two-thirds majority of the votes actually cast, reject the whole of the draft budget and ask for a new draft to be submitted (former Art 272(8) EC Treaty).

Following amendments made by the ToL, the European Parliament's role in the budgetary process has been enhanced. **Article 314(4) TFEU** provides that the European Parliament may amend any part of the draft budget, irrespective of whether the item concerns CE or NCE. The Parliament adopts amendments by a simple majority of its component members (Art 314(4)(c) TFEU). If this occurs, a meeting of the Conciliation Committee is convened, comprising members of the Council and the European Parliament. The aim of this Committee is to seek agreement between the members on a joint text (Art 314(5) TFEU). Ultimately, if a joint text cannot be agreed, the Commission is required to submit a new draft budget (Art 314(8) TFEU).

Supervision of the Commission

There is close and continuous contact between the Commissioners and the European Parliament. Although Commissioners are not members of the Parliament, they frequently take part in debates where legislation is under discussion and they will often attend the specialist committees of the Parliament to deal with detailed points arising from Commission proposals. Commissioners have the right to attend the European Parliament and to be heard (Art 230 TFEU).

Under **Article 230 TFEU**, Commissioners have a duty to respond, orally or in writing, to questions put to them by the European Parliament or its members. Since 1974, this has become formalised into a Westminster-type Question Time which is held at each part-session (Rule 129, Rules of Procedure, January 2017). Outside these part-sessions, there are regular exchanges between the Commission, the various Parliamentary Committees and individual MEPs.

Parliament has the right to dismiss the Commission *en bloc* under **Article 17(8) TEU** and **Article 234 TFEU**. Although it has never done so, it effectively forced Jacques Santer's Commission from office when Parliament threatened to use its censuring powers, as discussed above. The Commission accepted defeat and resigned, rather than face the humiliation of a certain defeat.

The powers of the Parliament have been reinforced by the requirement that a new Commission is subject to a vote of consent by the Parliament (Art 17(7) TEU). As discussed above, the effectiveness of this provision was demonstrated in the Parliament's scrutiny of the 2004–2009 Commission. The Parliament opposed the appointment of Rocco Buttiglione (from Italy), who was subsequently replaced by Franco Frattini and the President-elect requested the replacement of Latvia's Ingridia Udre and reshuffled two portfolios.

As previously discussed, the Commission's Work Programme is put together and implemented in close conjunction with Parliament and there is a considerable coincidence of interest between the Commission and Parliament in developing Union-wide policies.

2.6.2 Composition of the Parliament

Originally, the European Parliament's members were nominated by the national parliaments, but now it is the only **directly elected** institution in the Union. **Article 14(3) TEU** states that:

> The members of the European Parliament shall be elected for a term of five years by direct universal suffrage in a free and secret ballot.

Members of the European Parliament (MEPs) are elected on different variants of proportional representation and are elected for a term of five years (Art 14(3) TEU). Prior to the June 1999 election, UK MEPs were elected by the first-past-the-post system, as is used for general elections (except in Northern Ireland where MEPs had previously been elected by a system of proportional representation). The UK Labour Party, which was elected to government following a landslide general election victory on 1 May 1997, had stated in its manifesto that: 'We have long supported a proportional voting system for election to the European Parliament'. The European Parliamentary Elections Act 1999 was duly enacted and was in force in time for the June 1999 MEP elections. The Act divided the UK into electoral regions, with MEPs being elected by a regional list system. The electorate votes either for *a registered party* (e.g. Labour, Conservatives, etc. – i.e. a closed party list system) or *an individual candidate* who stands as an independent. The first seat is allocated to the party or individual candidate with the greatest number of votes. The second and subsequent seats are allocated in the same way, but the number of votes given to a party to which one or more seats have already been allocated is divided by the number of seats allocated plus one.

Northern Ireland uses a different system, which is the same as that used for elections to the Northern Ireland Assembly.

2009–2014 European Parliamentary term

If the Treaty of Lisbon (ToL) had come into force prior to the European Parliament elections in June 2009, the EU Treaties would have been amended to enable a decision to be made, prior to these elections, which would have specified the total number of MEPs and the allocation of seats to each Member State.

Because the ToL was not in force when the June 2009 elections to the European Parliament took place, the total number of MEPs was restricted to 736, distributed in accordance with the former Article 190(2) EC Treaty. However, at its December 2008 meeting, the European Council adopted a declaration as follows:

> In the event that the Treaty of Lisbon enters into force after the European elections of June 2009, transitional measures will be adopted as soon as possible, in accordance with the necessary legal procedures, in order to increase, until the end of the 2009–2014 legislative period, in conformity with the numbers provided for in the framework of the IGC which approved the Treaty of Lisbon, the number of MEPs of twelve Member States for which the number of MEPs was set to increase. Therefore, the total number of MEPs will rise from 736 to 754 until the end of the 2009–2014 legislative period. The objective is that this modification should enter into force, if possible, during the year 2010.

Once the ToL came into force, a decision was made to increase the number of MEPs from 736 to 754. The additional 18 MEPs were elected for the remainder of the 2009–2014 parliamentary term. Article 19(1) of Croatia's Accession Treaty provided for an additional 12 MEPs from Croatia, bringing the total number to 766 from 1 July 2013. This increase was expressly stipulated to be 'By way of derogation from Article 2 of the Protocol on transitional provisions … and by way of derogation from the maximum number of seats provided for in … Article 14(2) of the TEU'.

2014–2019 European Parliamentary term

The elections for the 2014–2019 European Parliamentary term were held during June 2014. The number of MEPs was reduced from 766 to 751, to comply with **Article 14(2) TEU**.

2019–2024 European Parliamentary term

Current MEPs were elected in May 2019. This election saw over 50 per cent of adult citizens turn out to vote for the first time since 1994.

The allocation of seats to each Member State for the 2019–2024 European Parliamentary term is the same as for the previous term. A decision of the Council adopted in June 2018 established that, after Brexit, 46 of the UK's 73 seats would be left vacant, reducing the total number of MEPs to 705. These seats will become available to new Member States if there are accessions in the future. The remaining 27 seats will be distributed among 14 Member States that are currently slightly underrepresented, as set out in Table 2.2).

Table 2.2 Allocation of seats to each Member State for the 2019–2024 European Parliamentary term (numerical)

Member State	MEPs (pre-Brexit)	Post-Brexit change	Member State	MEPs (pre-Brexit)	Post-Brexit change
Germany	96	0	Bulgaria	17	0
France	74	+5	Denmark	13	+1
Italy	73	+3	Finland	13	+1
UK	73	−73	Slovakia	13	+1
Spain	54	+5	Croatia	11	+1
Poland	51	+1	Ireland	11	+2
Romania	32	+1	Lithuania	11	0
Netherlands	26	+3	Latvia	8	0
Belgium	21	0	Slovenia	8	0
Czech Republic	21	0	Cyprus	6	0
Greece	21	0	Estonia	6	+1
Hungary	21	0	Luxembourg	6	0
Portugal	21	0	Malta	6	0
Sweden	20	+1			
Austria	18	+1	**Total**	**751**	**705**

Political groups

MEPs stand as members of national political parties, but sit within broad political groups rather than national affiliations in the European Parliament. The representation of the political groups in the European Parliament as of July 2019 is set out in Table 2.3. The number of seats held by each political group after Brexit will depend on the affiliation of the 27 new MEPs.

Table 2.3 European Parliament political groups as of July 2019 (pre-Brexit)

Political Party	Number of seats
European People's Party	182
Socialists and Democrats (includes UK Labour Party MEPs)	153
Renew Europe	108
Greens/European Free Alliance	75
Identity and Democracy	73
European Conservatives and Reformists (includes UK Conservative MEPs)	62
Europe of Freedom and Direct Democracy Group	43
European United Left/Nordic Green Left	41
Others (unattached and vacant seats) plus the President	14
Total	**751**

Article 10(4) TEU states that 'Political parties at European level contribute to forming European political awareness and to expressing the political will of citizens of the Union'. Political activity in the European Parliament largely takes place through the groups. **Article 224 TFEU** provides that the European Parliament and the Council shall lay down the regulations governing political parties at European level and in particular the rules regarding their funding.

Rule 32(2) of the **Rules of Procedure** of the European Parliament (January 2019 version) governs the formation of political parties within the Parliament:

> A political group shall consist of Members elected in at least one-quarter of the Member States. The minimum number of Members required to form a political group shall be 25.

There are a number of reasons why groups have developed. Primarily they are formed to provide mutual ideological support and identification. In addition, there are organisational benefits, including funds for administrative and research purposes which are better deployed in support of groups than for individuals. There are also advantages in the conduct of Parliamentary business that stem from group status, as the Parliament arranges much of its business around the groups. Although non-attached members are not formally excluded, and indeed are guaranteed many rights under the Rules of Procedure, they can, in practice, be disadvantaged in the distribution of committee chairmanships or in the preparation of the agendas for plenary sessions (i.e. meetings of the full Parliament).

A section of the Parliament's website is set aside for the political groups, each of which publishes a plethora of information. The website for the political groups can be accessed at:

www.europarl.europa.eu/aboutparliament

In 1999, 29 formerly unattached MEPs sought to form a group (and therefore receive the financial and organisational benefits bestowed upon groups). The MEPs informed the President of the European Parliament (as required under Rule 29(4) of the Rules of Procedure (now Rule 32(1))) of the formation of their group: the Technical Group of Independent Members – Mixed Group. The 'rules of constitution' for this new group declared that:

> ... the individual signatory members affirm their total independence of one another. And hence: freedom to vote independently both in committee and plenary session; each member shall refrain from speaking on behalf of the Members of the group as a whole; the purpose of meetings of the group shall be to allocate speaking time and to settle any administrative and financial matters concerning the group; and the Bureau of the group shall be made up of the representatives of the individual members.

At the time, Rule 29(1) (now Rule 32(1)) provided that 'members may form themselves into groups according to their political affinities'. Having been through various Parliamentary procedures, on 13 September 1999 the Parliament determined that Rule 29(1) should be interpreted such that 'the formation of a group which openly rejects any political character and all political affiliation between its Members is not acceptable within the meaning of this Rule'. Given the new group's constitution, which guaranteed its members total independence, the Parliament resolved to dissolve the group. Members of the group issued proceedings before the Court of First Instance (now the General Court) contesting these decisions, but the Court dismissed the applications. (*Jean Claude Martinez, Charles De Gaulle, Front National, Emma Bonino, Marco Pannella, Marco Cappato, Gianfranco Dell'Alba, Benedetto Della Vedova, Olivier Dupuis, Maurizio Turco, Lista Emma Bonino* v *European Parliament* (Joined Cases T-222, 327 and 329/99)).

This case provided that political groups within Parliament must share some common ideological platform and must work together within Parliament. If that is not the case then Parliament can refuse to recognise the group and thus prevent it from being provided with the financial and organisational benefits bestowed upon groups. In the above case it did seem quite clear that the group members shared very little in common, were not prepared to work together within the Parliament and were simply forming the group so that they could take advantage of the benefits. Rule 226(5) of the Rules of Procedure provides that 'Uncontested interpretations and interpretations adopted by Parliament shall be appended in italic print as explanatory notes to the appropriate Rule or Rules'. Rule 32(1) now includes the following explanatory note:

> Parliament need not normally evaluate the political affinity of members of a group. In forming a group together under this Rule, the Members concerned accept by definition that they have political affinity. Only when this is denied by the Members concerned is it necessary for Parliament to evaluate whether the group has been constituted in accordance with the Rules.

2.6.3 Working procedures and conduct of the Parliament

Voting procedures

Except as otherwise provided in the Treaties, the European Parliament acts by a majority of the votes cast (Art 231 TFEU). This is sometimes referred to as a **simple majority**, as abstentions by MEPs within the chamber and MEPs not present are not taken into account. However, some Treaty articles provide for something more than an absolute majority of the votes cast. For example, Article 225 TFEU provides that 'The European Parliament may, acting by a majority of its component members … '. At the time of writing there are 751 MEPs and therefore a minimum of 376 votes are required regardless of how many votes are cast. After Brexit, there will be 705 MEPs, so a minimum of 353 votes will be required. Article 234 TFEU (concerning a censure motion against the Commission) requires a 'two-thirds majority of the votes cast, representing a majority of the component Members of the European Parliament'. The second limb of this is similar to that under Article 225 TFEU, in that there have to be at least 376 votes in favour before Brexit or 353 votes after Brexit. However, the first limb provides an additional hurdle to overcome: those votes must amount to at least two-thirds of the total votes cast.

A **quorum** exists when one third of the MEPs are present in the Chamber (Rule 168(2), Rules of Procedure, January 2017): based on 751 MEPs, at least 251 MEPs must be present in the Chamber. After Brexit, the quorum requires at least 235 MEPs to be present. However, all votes are valid whatever the number of voters unless the President of the Parliament, acting on a request made by at least 40 MEPs, ascertains that, at the moment of voting, the quorum is not present. In that case, the vote is placed on the agenda of the next sitting (Rule 168(3), Rules of Procedure). The right to vote is a personal right and MEPs are required to cast their votes individually and in person (Rule 177). Although members of the European Council, the Council and the Commission have the right to attend debates of the European Parliament and to participate in the discussion, they have no right to vote (Art 230 TFEU).

Plenary meetings

The Parliament holds plenary sessions (i.e. all MEPs congregating together in one chamber) in Strasbourg, committee meetings in Brussels and is serviced by staff located in Luxembourg. A new building was erected in Brussels for full Parliamentary sessions but the European Council meeting in Edinburgh in December 1992 confirmed that the Parliament would remain in Strasbourg. A new Parliament building was opened in Strasbourg in December 1999 to ensure that the chamber could accommodate all the MEPs; enlargement of Union membership and the resultant increase in the number of MEPs, meant that the previous chamber was too small. A decision by the Parliament to increase the number of plenary sessions held in Brussels was struck down by the Court of Justice in October 1997 (***France* v *European Parliament*** (Case C-345/95)). MEPs and officials will continue to live a highly peripatetic existence, largely because the Parliament is a major employer and the Member States cannot agree on a single, permanent site for it. Indeed, Protocol No. 6, which is annexed to the Treaties, confirms the split location for the Parliament:

> The European Parliament shall have its seat in Strasbourg where the 12 periods of monthly plenary sessions, including the budget session, shall be held. The periods of additional plenary sessions shall be held in Brussels. The Committees of the European Parliament shall meet in Brussels. The General Secretariat of the European Parliament and its departments shall remain in Luxembourg.

With the exception of August, the Parliament sits for one week in each month in Strasbourg. It occasionally sits for additional periods to discuss special items, such as the budget. Between the monthly part-sessions, two weeks are set aside for meetings of the Parliamentary committees and one week for meetings of the political groups.

Full details of the Parliamentary agenda and post-session reports are available on the Parliament's website at:

www.europarl.europa.eu/plenary

Committee meetings

The Parliament has a large range of specialist committees. Some are permanent, while others are *ad hoc* (i.e. set up to consider a particular matter). The committees cover such matters as Internal Market and Consumer Protection; Economic and Monetary Affairs; Employment and Social Affairs; Transport and Tourism; Budgets; and Foreign Affairs.

Much of Parliament's legislative groundwork will be conducted in committee. When Parliament receives a request from the Council or Commission for an opinion, approval or assent, the request will be sent to the relevant committee for a report to be prepared for full debate and vote in the chamber. The committee will appoint a member to be responsible for preparing the report. This person is called the '**Rapporteur**'. The Rapporteur will lead the debate when the report of the committee comes before the full Parliament (i.e. when the Parliament sits in plenary session in Strasbourg).

The committees follow legislative and policy matters in detail and, as they usually meet *in camera* (i.e. the public are excluded from their meetings unless invited to attend by the Chairperson), they are given confidential information, both by Commission officials and by the independent experts and representatives of pressure groups who appear before them.

Protocol on the Privileges and Immunities of the European Union

MEPs enjoy protection under the Protocol on the Privileges and Immunities of the European Union. In particular, Article 8 of the Protocol provides that MEPs may not be subject to any form of inquiry, detention or legal proceedings in respect of opinions expressed or votes cast by them in the performance of their duties. However, Article 17 of the Protocol states that privileges and immunities 'shall be accorded to officials and other servants of the Union solely in the interests of the Union'. A Union institution is therefore required to waive the immunity of an official **unless** to do so would be contrary to the interests of the Union.

When legal proceedings are brought against an MEP on account of opinions they have expressed or votes they have cast, it falls within the exclusive jurisdiction of the national court hearing the case to take account of this immunity.

The question of the scope of an MEP's immunity was raised in the following case:

Aldo Patriciello (Case C-163/10)

Facts:

Criminal proceedings were brought before the Tribunale di Isernia (Italian District Court) against Mr Patriciello, an MEP. He was charged with making false accusations against a public official in the performance of their duties. It was alleged that, in the course of an altercation in a public car park, he wrongfully accused a police officer of falsifying evidence relating to car parking offences. In 2009, acting on Patriciello's request, the European Parliament decided to defend the MEP's immunity.

> The Italian court referred the case to the Court of Justice to enable the Court to define the relevant tests for determining when an MEP's statement constitutes 'an opinion expressed in the performance of his parliamentary duties' and may, on that ground, be subject to immunity.
>
> **Ruling:**
> The Court of Justice noted that the immunity granted to MEPs is intended to protect their freedom of expression and their independence. It is therefore a bar to political proceedings. It follows that if the substantive conditions for recognition of immunity have been met, immunity may not be waived by the European Parliament and the national court is bound to dismiss the action brought against the MEP concerned.
>
> The Court then made it clear that although parliamentary immunity essentially covers statements made within the precincts of the European Parliament, **it is not impossible that a statement made beyond those precincts may also amount to an opinion expressed in the performance of parliamentary duties**. Whether or not it is such an opinion must therefore be determined having regard to its character and content, not to the place where it was made. On the basis of those findings, the Court stated that **in order to enjoy immunity, an opinion must be connected with parliamentary duties**. Furthermore, immunity may be granted only if the connection between the opinion and the exercise of parliamentary duties is **direct and obvious**. It was for the Italian court to determine whether such a link was obvious in this particular case.
>
> The Court stated, however, that having regard to the descriptions of the circumstances and the content of the allegations made by Patriciello, the statements in question appeared to be far removed from his duties as an MEP. In the circumstances they were hardly capable of presenting a direct link to a general interest of concern to citizens.
>
> Moreover, the Court noted that **the European Parliament's decision to defend immunity was no more than an opinion without any binding effect on national courts**. If, having regard to the interpretation provided by the Court of Justice, the national court decided not to follow the opinion of the European Parliament, EU law does not place the national court under any particular obligation as regards the reasons given for its decision.
>
> **Significance:**
> This case negotiated the delicate balance between protecting freedom of expression and democratic integrity on the one hand and protecting the right to remedy in the event of damaging expressions on the other. To do this, the Court limited the scope of application of MEP immunity to the expression of opinions in **direct and obvious connection** with the performance of parliamentary duties.

Article 9 of the Protocol further provides that during sessions of the European Parliament, MEPs enjoy, *inter alia*, in the territory of their State, the immunities accorded to members of their national parliament. This is a matter of MEPs' privilege, which may be lifted in certain cases by the European Parliament. The following case concerned the application of Articles 8 and 9 of the Protocol:

> ### *Bruno Gollnisch* v *Parliament* (Joint cases T-346/11 and T-347/11)
>
> **Facts:**
> Bruno Gollnisch was an MEP and was also President of the Front National group of the Rhône-Alpes (France) regional council. On 3 October 2008, that group issued a press release. Following a complaint from the International League against Racism and Anti-Semitism (LICRA), the French authorities opened a judicial inquiry on 22 January 2009 for incitement to racial hatred.

The European Parliament subsequently received a request from Gollnisch to **defend** his immunity under the Protocol and a request from the French authorities to **waive** Gollnisch's parliamentary immunity so that they could pursue the investigation of the complaint. On 10 May 2011, the European Parliament adopted two decisions: (i) not to defend Gollnisch's immunity; and (ii) to waive his immunity. Gollnisch brought an action before the General Court seeking annulment of those two decisions and for compensation for the non-material damage he claimed to have suffered.

Ruling:

Regarding Gollnisch's request for defence of his immunity, the General Court clarified that the defence of immunity only covered a case where there had been no request for the waiver of an MEP's immunity.

Regarding the Parliament's decision to waive Gollnisch's immunity, the General Court referred to the Court of Justice's ruling in *Patriciello* (Case C-163/10), whereby an MEP's opinion was only covered by immunity if there was a direct and obvious link between the opinion expressed and the performance of the parliamentary duties. The General Court noted that the statement set out in the press release directly concerned the duties carried out by the applicant acting in his capacity as regional councillor and President of the Front National group. Consequently, **there was no link between the statement allegedly made by Gollnisch and his duties as MEP**. The Parliament could not therefore be criticised, having regard to the circumstances of the present case and to France's application, for having lifted the immunity of Gollnisch under Article 8 of the Protocol so as to allow the French authorities to pursue their investigation.

In the same way, the General Court held that Gollnisch was not protected by Article 9 of the Protocol, as the immunities afforded by his own Member State for the protection of national members of parliament only applied to opinions expressed in the performance of their official duties. The press release did not fall into this category.

The General Court then considered Gollnisch's assertion that the Parliament had failed to adhere to its own 'jurisprudence' on immunity and had therefore acted inconsistently. In relation to the principles established by the Parliament's past decisions, the Court held that the Parliament considered correctly that the judicial investigation initiated in France had not been brought with the intention of causing damage to his political activity as a MEP. In addition, the proceedings did not concern either historical matters or acts carried out during an electoral campaign and, further, there was no evidence to show that the manifest purpose of the proceedings was to make an example out of him.

The obligation for the Parliament to examine, with care and impartiality, all the pertinent elements of the present case had been met. Consequently, the General Court dismissed the applications and the subsidiary application for compensation.

Significance:

This case affirmed the capacity of the European Parliament to waive the immunity of an MEP who faces prosecution for the expression of an opinion that is not directly and obviously connected to the performance of their parliamentary duties. In particular, it clarified the careful considerations that the European Parliament must undertake in ensuring that the freedom of expression of MEP's is adequately protected.

2.7 Court of Justice of the European Union

> Objective 7

The Court of Justice of the European Union plays a pivotal role in the Union. The provisions of the EU Treaties governing the Court of Justice of the European Union are **Article 19 TEU** and **Articles 251–281 TFEU**, as well as the Protocol No. 3 on the **Statute of the**

Court of Justice of the European Union, which is appended to the Treaties. This new Statute came into effect when the ToL came into force on 1 December 2009. A consolidated version of the Statute was published on 1 July 2013, the full text of which is available on the Court's website:

https://curia.europa.eu/jcms/jcms/j_6/en/

While some of the legal principles which govern the way the Union functions are found in the Treaties or the legislative acts made under it, others are to be found in the case law of the Court.
Article 19(1) TEU states that:

> The Court of Justice of the European Union shall include the Court of Justice, the General Court and specialised courts. It shall ensure that in the interpretation and application of the Treaties the law is observed.

In addition, to the Treaties, the Statute and general principles, the Court of Justice and the General Court are each governed by their own **Rules of Procedure**.

Besides the general function of ensuring that Union law is observed, the Court of Justice and the General Court have a number of other tasks. As the Courts, like the other Union institutions, can act only within the limits of their powers, they have jurisdiction only if jurisdiction has been expressly conferred upon them (Art 13(2) TEU, see Chapter 4). This means that the Courts cannot hear cases that do not expressly fall within their jurisdiction. It has, for example, been held that judicial protection cannot be afforded to private individuals who might otherwise be deprived of all legal redress at both national and Union level, since there is no express provision authorising the Union Courts to do so (*Schlieker* v *HA* (Case 12/63). However, the Court of Justice has shown some flexibility in ruling on cases which it might, hitherto, have refused to adjudicate (*Imm Zwartveld* (Case 2/88); *Dzodzi* v *Belgium* (Case C-297/88)).

The Court of Justice of the European Union is permanently in session in Luxembourg and vacations are fixed according to the workload. A case may be conducted in any one of the Union's 23 official languages, or Irish, which is not an official language (Art 36, Rules). The Court itself will use French as its working language. This is despite a majority of citizens of the Member States now speaking English rather than French. French was chosen as the working language of the Court when the first Community (the ECSC, which expired on 23 July 2002) was created by the six founding Member States, at which time French was the official language of three of them (France, Belgium and Luxembourg).

The Court of Justice, the General Court and the provision for specialised courts will now be examined in turn.

▶ See 'Reflection: Distinguishing between the two European courts' in section 1.3.3 (page 43)

2.7.1 The Court of Justice

Jurisdiction of the Court of Justice

The main areas of jurisdiction of the Court of Justice are as follows:

- to give preliminary rulings under Article 267 TFEU at the request of a national court or tribunal;

- to establish whether or not a Member State has failed to fulfil an obligation under the Treaty. Actions for this purpose may be brought by the Commission under Article 258 TFEU, or by a Member State under Article 259 TFEU;
- to exercise unlimited jurisdiction with regard to penalties in actions brought by the Commission under Articles 260(2) and 261 TFEU;
- to review the legality of an act, or of a failure to act, of the Union institutions, at the request of Member States, the European Parliament, the Council or the Commission;
- to grant compensation for damage caused by Union institutions in actions brought by Member States, and natural and legal persons under Articles 268 and 340 TFEU.

Each of these functions is considered in depth in Chapters 5, 6 and 7.

The Court of Justice also has the jurisdiction to act as a Court of Appeal from the General Court under Article 256(1) TFEU. Such appeals may only be made on a point of law; the Court of Justice has ruled that, in hearing appeals from the General Court, it has no jurisdiction to review the facts established by the General Court (*John Deere Ltd* v *Commission* (Case C-7/95)).

Composition of the Court of Justice

Judges and Advocates General

Article 19(2) TEU provides that the Court of Justice will consist of one judge from each Member State, who will be assisted by Advocates General. An Advocate General is an independent adviser to the Court. The title 'Advocate' is something of a misnomer, because the Advocate General represents no one and does not present a case on anyone's behalf. Although not a judge, the Advocate General enjoys equal status with the judges. Each case is assigned one Judge-Rapporteur and one Advocate General.

Article 252 TFEU prescribes the role of the Advocate General as being:

> . . . to make, in open court, reasoned submissions on cases which, in accordance with the Statute of the Court of Justice of the European Union, require his involvement.

Article 252 TFEU provides for 8 Advocates General and also provides for this number to be increased by the Council acting unanimously, at the request of the Court of Justice. Subsequent to such a request, the number of Advocate Generals was increased to 9 in July 2013 and then to 11 in October 2015. France, Germany, Italy, Poland and Spain each have a permanent Advocate General and a rotation system is applied for the remaining Advocates General. There continue to be 11 Advocates General after Brexit.

Article 253 TFEU provides that both judges and Advocates General:

> . . . shall be chosen from persons whose independence is beyond doubt and who possess the qualifications required for appointment to the highest judicial offices in their respective countries or who are jurisconsults of recognised competence.

The requirements for these appointments are therefore not intended to be confined to those who have made a career in the courts and are destined for, or already sit, on the bench in their Member State. Article 253 TFEU also provides that judges and Advocates General are appointed by common accord of the governments of the Member States 'after consultation of the panel provided for in Article 255'. This panel comprises seven persons chosen from among former members of the Court of Justice and the General Court, members of national supreme courts and lawyers of recognised competence, one of whom is proposed by the European Parliament (Art 255 TFEU). The purpose of the panel is to give an opinion on the candidates' suitability to perform their duties.

A new judge is required to take an oath to perform their duties impartially and conscientiously and to preserve the secrecy of the deliberations of the Court. They also sign a solemn declaration to behave with integrity and discretion in relation to the acceptance of benefits after they have left office (Arts 2 and 4, Statute of the Court of Justice). Judges may not hold any political or administrative office (Art 4 Statute). They may not follow any other occupation, paid or unpaid, during their period of office unless exemption is exceptionally granted by the Council acting by a simple majority (Art 4 Statute).

Article 253 TFEU provides for the appointments to be for a renewable six-year term. Appointment and reappointment of the judges and Advocates General is staggered: 'Every three years there shall be a partial replacement of the Judges ... in accordance with the conditions laid down in the Statute of the Court of Justice of the European Union'. Article 9 of the Statute provides that: 'When, every three years, the Judges are partially replaced, fourteen judges shall be replaced.'

President

Article 254 TFEU provides for the election by the judges of a **President** for a term of three years, which may be renewed. The President directs the judicial business and administration of the Court. Thus, they preside at hearings of the full court, fix and extend time limits for lodging pleadings, documents, etc. and usually deal with interlocutory applications (i.e. applications within the course of the proceedings, prior to the full hearing). As stated above, the appointments panel will act 'on the initiative of the President' (Art 255 TFEU).

Article 15(1) of the Rules of Procedure provides for the President to designate a **Judge-Rapporteur** to each case before the Court. The function of the Judge-Rapporteur is to manage the case throughout its progression through the Court's system. The Judge-Rapporteur is responsible for drafting the final judgment.

Article 8(4) of the Rules of Procedure provides for the election of a **Vice-President**, whose responsibilities are set out in Article 10 of the Rules of Procedure.

Chambers

Article 251 TFEU provides as follows:

> The Court of Justice shall sit in chambers or in a Grand Chamber, in accordance with the rules laid down for that purpose in the Statute of the Court of Justice of the European Union. When provided for in the Statute, the Court of Justice may also sit as a full court.

Article 16 of the Statute provides that the Court shall form **chambers of three or five judges**. The **Grand Chamber** consists of 15 judges and will be presided over by the President of the Court (Art 27(1), Rules). The Grand Chamber shall sit whenever a Member State or

Union institution that is a party to the proceedings so requests. After hearing the Advocate General, the Court may decide to refer the case to the full Court, if it considers the case to be of exceptional importance. The majority of cases brought before the Court of Justice are heard by a five-judge chamber.

Article 16 of the Statute provides that the Court shall sit as a **full Court** where cases are brought to it pursuant to:

- Article 228(2) TFEU – dismissal of the Ombudsman;
- Article 245(2) TFEU – compulsory retirement of a Commission member;
- Article 247 TFEU – compulsory retirement of a Commission member; or
- Article 286(6) TFEU – compulsory retirement of a member of the Court of Auditors.

Additionally, matters of exceptional importance have been brought before the full court, such as when the Court of Justice produced Opinion 2/13 on the accession of the Union to the European Convention on Human Rights.

Article 17 of the Statute provides that decisions of the Court shall be valid only when an odd number of its members are sitting in the deliberations. It further provides that decisions are only valid in chambers consisting of three or five judges if they are taken by at least three judges, those of the Grand Chamber are valid only if at least 11 judges are sitting, and those of the full Court are valid only if at least 17 judges are sitting.

Working procedures of the Court of Justice

The Court's process is essentially inquisitorial. Unlike an English adversarial process, the procedure of the Court, after the initiation of the case by one or more of the parties, is Court-led. The Court can request the parties to provide documents and statements; witnesses are heard at the instigation of the Court. Their evidence is part of the investigation by the Judge-Rapporteur and not, as in an English case, part of the oral hearing. The procedure in a direct action (as opposed to a reference under Article 267 TFEU, which is considered in Chapter 5) generally has the following stages:

1. written proceedings;
2. preliminary report;
3. measures of organisation and measures of inquiry;
4. oral hearing;
5. Advocate General's opinion;
6. judgment.

These stages are now considered in further detail.

Written proceedings

Article 20 of the Statute provides that:

> The written procedure shall consist of the communication to the parties and to the institutions of the Communities [i.e. Union] whose decisions are in dispute, of applications, statements of case, defences and observations, and of replies, if any, as well as of all papers and documents in support or of certified copies of them.

Direct actions are initiated by the applicant filing an application (this is known as a 'pleading') at the Court's registry in accordance with Article 21 of the Statute. At this stage, the case may be assigned to a chamber or Grand Chamber and a Judge-Rapporteur and Advocate General will be appointed. Articles 123 and 124 of the Rules require the Registrar to serve the application on the defendant and any Union institution affected, following which the defendant has two months within which to lodge his defence, if any (this is also known as a 'pleading').

After the close of pleadings, the defendant can argue separately that the application is not admissible, e.g. they may argue that the proceedings were not issued within any relevant time-limit. The Court may hear such an application at this stage and, if successful, the action will be struck out. Alternatively, the Court may decide to hear the argument as to admissibility at the hearing of the main application.

Preliminary report

When the written part of the procedure is concluded, the President will fix a date for the Judge-Rapporteur to present a preliminary report to the general meeting of the Court (Art 59(1), Rules). This preliminary report will contain advice on whether measures of organisation of procedure or measures of inquiry should be undertaken. The report will also contain advice on the formation of the Court to which the case should be referred (Article 60, Rules) and whether or not to forego the Advocate General's Opinion.

Since 2004, where the procedure in a case does not require an oral hearing in accordance with the Rules of Procedure, a report of the Judge-Rapporteur is no longer produced.

Measures of organisation and measures of inquiry

With regard to measures of organisation, Article 61 of the Rules provides that the Court may invite the parties (or other interested persons referred to in Art 23 of the Statute) to answer certain questions in writing or to answer the questions at the actual hearing. Article 62 of the Rules provides that the Judge-Rapporteur or the Advocate General may request the parties (or other interested persons referred to in Art 23 of the Statute) to submit information relating to the facts, documents or other particulars. They may also submit questions to be addressed at the hearing.

With regard to measures of inquiry, if the Court decides a measure of inquiry is necessary, it will, after hearing the Advocate General, prescribe the measures of inquiry that it considers appropriate by means of an order setting out the facts to be proved (Art 64(1), Rules). Article 64(2) of the Rules provides that the following measures of inquiry may be adopted:

- the personal appearance of the parties;
- a request for information and production of documents;
- oral testimony;
- the commissioning of an expert's report;
- an inspection of the place or thing in question.

Oral hearing

Article 76(2) of the Rules provides that the Court may decide not to hold an oral hearing if it considers it has sufficient information to give a ruling. This will enable the Court to give rulings within a shorter period of time.

The oral proceedings are brief compared to those in an English court in a contested action. They consist of the addresses by counsel for the parties followed by the Opinion of the Advocate General (see below). Addresses by counsel tend to be quite brief. They are expected to have lodged a copy of their submission before the hearing and will normally use their address to emphasise their strongest arguments and to attack the weakest points in those of their opponents. The judges will quite frequently challenge points made, but the cut and thrust of forensic debate is somewhat blunted by the need for instant translation by interpreters as the argument proceeds.

Advocate General's Opinion

Article 82(1) of the Rules provides that if an oral hearing takes place and the Court has not decided to forego the Opinion of the Advocate General, the Advocate General's Opinion shall be delivered after the close of the hearing. If there is no oral hearing, the Advocate General's Opinion will be delivered in open court at some future date.

The recommendation in the Opinion is not binding on the Court, or on the parties, and the Court is free to follow it or not, as it chooses. However, in spite of their non-binding nature, the Opinions of Advocates General normally deal thoroughly with every aspect of the case, and will generally be much longer and more wide-ranging than the judgment of the Court. Such Opinions therefore carry considerable weight on account of the very high standard of legal analysis they contain and they are frequently cited in the Court, as well as in legal writing, as persuasive sources of authority. In the vast majority of cases, judgments of the Court will follow the Opinion.

The Court has held that it is not open to the parties to submit written observations in response to the Advocate General's Opinion (*Emesa Sugar (Free Zone) NV* v *Aruba* (Case C-17/98)). Immediately after delivery of the Opinion the Court goes into deliberation.

Judgment

Articles 86 to 92 of the Rules govern the procedural aspects associated with the delivery of a judgment. Judgment is always reserved by the Court, i.e. it goes into **secret deliberation** and will deliver its judgment in open court at some future date. This is necessary because a **single judgment** is delivered. The deliberation may be lengthy, taking weeks or months to conclude.

A draft judgment will be prepared by the Judge-Rapporteur. This draft will form the basis of the deliberation. It may be necessary to go through the judgment sentence by sentence, voting on individual sentences. The votes of the judges are taken in ascending order of seniority; this is to ensure that the younger judges do not merely follow their seniors. The judgment may be short on reasons, or it may include differing (maybe conflicting) reasons, in order to obtain the necessary majority (see above).

The deliberation will be conducted in French and the judgment will be drafted in French and then translated into the language of the hearing, which is the authentic version of the judgment.

The formal ruling of the judgment (the 'operative part') is published in the Official Journal. Prior to May 2004, the whole of the judgment together with the Advocate General's Opinion would be published in the official European Court Reports (ECR). The reports are published in each of the official languages.

During early 2004 the Court of Justice reviewed its methods of work, in order to make them more efficient and to counteract the expanding average length of proceedings. Given that not all the judgments it delivers are equally significant from the point of view of the development of Union law, the Court decided to adopt a policy of **selective publication** of its decisions in the ECR. In an initial stage, as regards direct actions and appeals, judgments are no longer published in the Reports if the case is decided by a chamber of three or five judges and without an Opinion of the Advocate General. It will, however, be open to the chamber giving judgment to decide to publish such a decision in whole or in part in exceptional circumstances. Texts of the decisions not published in the Reports are accessible in electronic form in the language or languages available. Judgments and Opinions of Advocates General are now available from the Court's website.

The Court decided not to extend the practice of selective publication to references for a preliminary ruling in view of their importance for the interpretation and uniform application of Union law in all the Member States (see Chapter 5).

Expedited hearing

Article 53(4) of the Rules provides that a case may be dealt with under an expedited procedure. Originally, the expedited procedure had only been available in a reference for a preliminary ruling pursuant to Article 267 TFEU. With regard to a direct action, Article 133(1) of the Rules provides as follows:

> At the request of the applicant or the defendant, the President of the Court may, where the nature of the case requires that it be dealt with within a short time, after hearing the other party, the Judge-Rapporteur and the Advocate General, decide that a case is to be determined pursuant to an expedited procedure derogating from the provisions of these Rules.

The expedited procedure provides for truncated written and oral procedures to enable the court to deliver its judgment in a shorter period of time.

2.7.2 The General Court

To cope with the great increase in the work of the Court of Justice, the SEA provided for the creation of a **Court of First Instance** (CFI) to be attached to the Court of Justice (former Art 225 EC Treaty). When the ToL came into force on 1 December 2009, the CFI was renamed the **General Court** (Art 19(1) TEU).

Jurisdiction of the General Court

Article 256 TFEU sets out the jurisdiction of the General Court. Article 256(1) TFEU provides the General Court with jurisdiction in the following categories of case:

- Article 263 TFEU – acts of the Union institutions;
- Article 265 TFEU – failures of the Union institutions to act;
- Article 268 TFEU – compensation for damage pursuant to the second and third paragraphs of Article 340 TFEU;
- Article 270 TFEU – staff cases;
- Article 272 TFEU – pursuant to an arbitration clause contained in a contract concluded by or on behalf of the Union.

Article 256(1) TFEU excludes from the above categories those cases assigned to a specialised court (see below) and also those reserved to the Court of Justice within the Statute. Article 51 of the Statute reserves to the Court of Justice certain types of case brought by a Member State pursuant to Articles 263 and 265 TFEU. Article 256(1) further provides that the Statute may expand the General Court's jurisdiction to other categories of case.

Article 256(2) TFEU provides a limited right of appeal from decisions of the specialised courts. Article 256(3) TFEU provides for the General Court to have jurisdiction, in specific areas laid down by the Statute, to hear and determine questions referred for a preliminary ruling pursuant to Article 267 TFEU. However, the Statute has not made provision for the General Court to have jurisdiction to hear Art 267 TFEU cases.

Composition of the General Court

As with the Court of Justice, **Article 19(2) TEU** provides that the General Court shall include one judge from each Member State. Article 254 TFEU provides for the exact number of judges of the General Court to be determined by the Statute. Prior to 2015, the Statute provided that the General Court consisted of 28 judges. **Article 48 of the Statute** now provides that the General Court shall consist of:

(a) 40 Judges as from 25 December 2015;

(b) 47 Judges as from 1 September 2016;

(c) two Judges per Member State as from 1 September 2019.

This expansion was agreed to deal with the General Court's increasing case load and the consequent delays in dealing with cases. After 31 January 2020, there are 54 Judges.

Article 254 TFEU requires members of the General Court to 'possess the ability required for appointment to high judicial office'. This is the same requirement as that for membership of the Court of Justice.

Article 19(2) TEU provides that judges of the General Court will be appointed by common accord of the governments of the Member States for six years. Article 254 TFEU further provides that they shall be appointed by common accord 'after consultation of the panel provided for in Article 255'. This is identical to the appointment of Judges and Advocates General to the Court of Justice under Article 253 TFEU. The panel under Article 255 TFEU comprises seven persons chosen from among former members of the Court of Justice and the General Court, members of national supreme courts and lawyers of recognised competence, one of whom is proposed by the European Parliament. The purpose of the panel is to provide an opinion on the candidates' suitability to perform the duties.

Article 50 of the Statute provides that the General Court may sit in **chambers** of three or five judges. The Rules of Procedure can determine when the General Court may sit in plenary session or even be constituted by a single judge. As with the Court of Justice, a Grand Chamber can be established.

2.7.3 Specialised courts

Article 257 TFEU empowers the European Parliament and the Council to establish 'specialised courts' – this is a renaming of the former judicial panels which were established by the Council, acting unanimously, under the former Article 225a EC Treaty.

Decisions of a specialised court are subject to a right of appeal on points of law (and in certain circumstances matters of fact) to the General Court (Art 257 TFEU). Article 256(2)

TFEU provides that the Court of Justice may exceptionally review a decision of the General Court (where the General Court has acted as a court of appeal from a specialised court) if there is a serious risk of the unity or consistency of Union law being affected. The members of the specialised courts are appointed by the Council, acting unanimously (Art 257 TFEU).

The only specialised court to have been established so far was the European Union Civil Service Tribunal, which operated between 2005 and 2016. The Tribunal was formed due to the special nature of this field of litigation and in anticipation of an increased workload for the General Court resulting from the application of new Staff Regulations. Initially created as a judicial panel, the Tribunal became a specialised court with the entry into force of the ToL and was then dissolved in 2016 as part of reforms to the judicial architecture of the Union. Upon dissolution, its competences were transferred back to the General Court.

2.8 Other institutions

> **Objective 8**

While the European Council, the Commission, the Council, the Parliament and the Court of Justice of the European Union are the primary institutions that shape the Union and Union law, other institutions also play important roles in the regulation and functioning of the Union. This section considers the **Court of Auditors**, the **European Central Bank**, the **European Investment Bank**, the **European Economic and Social Committee**, the **Committee of the Regions** and **Agencies**.

2.8.1 Court of Auditors

The Court of Auditors was established by an amendment to the Treaties in 1975 (second Budgetary Treaty 1975). It is not, strictly speaking, a court, but more an audit commission. It is responsible for the external audit of the general budget of the Union. The internal audit is the responsibility of the Financial Controller of each institution.

The Court partly came into being due to the desire of some of the newer Member States to establish more effective audit arrangements and partly due to the desire of the European Parliament to have greater power in the financial affairs of the Union. An independent audit body is seen by the European Parliament as an important part of establishing greater financial control. It had, initially, the status of a separate body but, since the TEU came into effect in 1993, it has been classed as one of the Union institutions (Art 13(1) TEU).

The Court consists of one full-time member from each Member State (Art 285 TFEU). The Council, after consulting the European Parliament, adopts the list of members drawn up in accordance with proposals made by each Member State (Art 286(2) TFEU). Article 286(1) stipulates that the members shall be chosen from 'among persons who belong or have belonged in their respective States to external audit bodies or who are especially qualified for this office. Their independence must be beyond doubt'. The Court of Auditors' website can be accessed at:

www.eca.europa.eu

2.8.2 The European Central Bank

Article 13(1) TEU recognises the **European Central Bank** (ECB) as one of the Union institutions. The ECB was initially set up as part of the progression towards economic and monetary union. The ECB has legal personality and can enact legislation, impose fines, submit opinions and be consulted within its field of operation (Arts 282–284 TFEU).

The ECB works with the national banks of the Member States to form the **European System of Central Banks** (ESCB). The main purpose of the ESCB is to maintain price stability. Additionally, the ECB works with the national banks of the Member States whose currency is the euro to form the **Eurosystem**, through which they conduct the monetary policy of the Union (Art 282 TFEU).

The ECB's website can be accessed at:

www.ecb.europa.eu

2.8.3 The European Investment Bank

The European Investment Bank (EIB) is not recognised as a Union institution by Article 13(1) TEU, but it is granted legal personality by Article 308 TFEU. The purpose of the EIB is then defined in **Article 309 TFEU**:

> The task of the European Investment Bank shall be to contribute, by having recourse to the capital market and utilising its own resources, to the balanced and steady development of the internal market in the interest of the Union.

The EIB operates on a non-profit basis to provide loans and guarantees to projects that aim to develop less-developed regions, facilitate the functioning of the internal market or that are in common interest to several Member States (Art 309 TFEU). The EIB's website can be accessed at:

www.eib.org

2.8.4 The European Economic and Social Committee (EESC)

The European Economic and Social Committee was established by the former Article 257 EC Treaty to assist the Council and the Commission in an advisory capacity. The Committee's website can be accessed at:

www.eesc.europa.eu

Function of the EESC

The EESC is not recognised by Article 13(1) TEU as one of the Union institutions. However, **Article 13(4) TEU** states that:

> The European Parliament, the Council and the Commission shall be assisted by an Economic and Social Committee and a Committee of the Regions acting in an advisory capacity.

Article 304 TFEU provides that the EESC must be consulted by the European Parliament, the Council or the Commission where the Treaties so provide; in other cases consultation is at the discretion of those institutions. When the Committee is consulted, it responds by submitting an opinion to the relevant institutions (Art 304 TFEU). These institutions can, if they wish, impose a deadline for the submission of an opinion, but this must not be less than one month (Art 304 TFEU). Failure by the EESC to deliver an opinion cannot prevent the institutions from progressing with the relevant measures. The Committee also has the right to submit opinions on its own initiative where it considers such action appropriate (Art 304 TFEU). Opinions of the EESC are prepared by a section designated by the Chairperson and then discussed and adopted at plenary sessions of the full Committee held during the last seven days of the month (Title II, EESC's Rules of Procedure). Although the Committee's opinions are not legally binding, the expertise of the Committee's membership does mean that they carry considerable weight with the institutions. Where the Treaties require consultation with the EESC, failure to do so could lead to the annulment of a measure by the Court of Justice of the European Union on the basis of failure to meet an essential procedural requirement (see Chapter 6).

Composition of the EESC

Since the ToL, **Article 300(2) TFEU** provides that the Committee shall consist of 'representatives of organisations of employers, of the employed, and of other parties representative of civil society, notably in socio-economic, civic, professional and cultural areas'. The Council adopts the list of members drawn up in accordance with proposals made by each Member State. Before adopting the list, the Council has to consult with the Commission and it may additionally obtain the opinion of European bodies which are representative of the various economic and social sectors and of civil society to which the Union's activities are of concern (Art 302 TFEU).

Members are appointed for a period of five years and they may be reappointed (Art 302 TFEU). Seats are allocated according to the relative population of each Member State. Article 301 TFEU provides that the number of members of the EESC shall not exceed 350.

Members of the Committee shall not be bound by any mandatory instructions and they shall be 'completely independent in the performance of their duties, in the Union's general interest' (Art 300(4) TFEU).

2.8.5 The Committee of the Regions

The Committee of the Regions, like the EESC, is not recognised by Article 13(1) TEU as one of the Union institutions but is mentioned in Art 13(4) TEU, as cited above. It was intended to represent a move towards more region-orientated decision-making and to create 'an ever closer union among the peoples of Europe', as required by **Article 1 TEU**. The Committee's website can be accessed at:

> http://cor.europa.eu

Function of the Committee

Prior to the ToL, the Committee's basic role was comparable to the EESC, its principal role being to deliver opinions on legislation when consulted by the European Parliament, the Council or the Commission. It issues opinions on its own initiative in appropriate cases (Art 307 TFEU). The Committee's members are not bound by mandatory instructions and members are completely independent in the performance of their duties 'in the Union's general interest' (Art 300(4) TFEU).

Following the entry into force of the ToL on 1 December 2009, the Committee has been given the power to challenge legislative proposals it considers to be in breach of the principle of subsidiarity. This power is established by **Article 8, Protocol No. 2** which is attached to the Treaties. It only applies if the legal base for a legislative proposal requires consultation with the Committee. The President of the Committee of the Regions, or the Committee's member who is responsible for drawing up the draft opinion, may propose that an action be brought before the Court of Justice. This proposal will be considered by the full Committee, which will decide on the proposal by a majority of the votes cast. If such a decision is adopted, the action shall be brought before the Court of Justice by the President on behalf of the Committee.

► See section 3.3.1 on the principle of subsidiarity

Composition of the Committee

Members are appointed for a period of five years and they may be reappointed (Art 302 TFEU). Seats are allocated according to the relative population of each Member State. **Article 305 TFEU** provides that the number of members of the Committee of the Regions shall, like the EESC, not exceed 350.

The members were previously representatives of regional and representative bodies in the Member States. Since the entry into force of the ToN, the Committee shall consist of 'representatives of regional and local bodies who either hold a regional or local authority electoral mandate or are politically accountable to an elected assembly' (Art 300 TFEU). Members therefore need to have an **electoral mandate** to represent citizens at a local level. No member of the Committee shall at the same time be a Member of the European Parliament (Art 305 TFEU).

2.8.6 Agencies

EU agencies are independent legal entities, distinct from the main Union institutions, which are created by secondary legislation to perform specific tasks. There are two main types of agency. **Decentralised agencies** are established for an indefinite period of time and are situated throughout the Union. They contribute to the implementation of EU policies within a particular policy area and develop relevant technical and specialist expertise. Examples include the European Environment Agency, the European Food Safety Authority and the European Border and Coastguard Authority (known as FRONTEX). **Executive agencies** are established by the Commission for a limited period of time to manage specific tasks, often in Brussels. For example, the Research Executive Agency was established to assist the Commission in achieving specific objectives related to research and technological development in the EU. In addition to decentralised and executive agencies, Euratom agencies have also been established to support the aims of the European Atomic Energy Community.

► See section 1.2.3 on Euratom

By dealing with the technical detail and everyday implementation of EU policy, agencies free up the main Union institutions to concentrate on policy-making and broader agendas. In the case of *Meroni* (Case 9/56), it was established that only 'clearly defined executive powers' can be transferred to agencies.

2.9 Democratic accountability and transparency

Objective 9

In the final section of this chapter, efforts that have been made to improve the governance of the Union institutions are considered, particularly with regards to democratic accountability and transparency. These two issues are closely linked – democratic processes can be undermined by a lack of access to relevant information – and can therefore be seen as part of a broad trend to make the operations of the Union more accessible and accountable to its citizens.

2.9.1 Democratic accountability

The Union has been described as having 'a double democratic mandate through a Parliament representing EU citizens and a Council representing the elected governments of the Member States' (Commission 2001). Yet a common criticism of the Union has been that it lacks direct democratic accountability to its citizens. This argument reflects the limited powers of the European Parliament, which is the only institution where citizens directly elect the members that represent them at the Union level.

The role of Parliament in the legislative process has been strengthened following amendments to the EU Treaties by the SEA, TEU, ToA, ToN and ToL. In particular, the ToA introduced the co-decision procedure, which placed the Parliament on an equal footing with the Council in the legislative process. This procedure, which now applies in the vast majority of cases, was renamed as the **ordinary legislative procedure** by the ToL. As explained in Chapter 3, the ordinary legislative procedure empowers the Parliament to put forward amendments to a legislative proposal and ultimately to block the Council from adopting it.

> The ordinary legislative procedure is considered in full in section 3.4.4

In most other, less common, legislative decisions the Parliament has, at least, the right to be consulted. Under some Treaty provisions there is no right of consultation at all, although Commission and Council practice is, nonetheless, to seek the Parliament's views. In other cases, especially in relation to decisions in the field of economic and monetary policy, the Parliament has no more than the right to be informed of the decision reached by the Council (Art 121(2) TFEU and Art 126(11) TFEU). Even where Parliament's opinion must be sought, there remains considerable scope for the Council to reject its view, provided that it has been properly considered. It has widely been felt that these limitations are inappropriate for the only democratically elected institution in the Union.

> See section 1.3.3 for further information on the democratic deficit

Additionally, it can also be argued that a 'democratic deficit' remains in relation to Parliament's inability to dismiss individual Commissioners and to hold members of the Council to account. Although Council documents are now available after meetings and Council deliberations on legislative acts are now open to the public (Art 16(8) TEU), other meetings of the Council generally take place in more or less complete secrecy. There is considerable support, largely among MEPs, for a Minister from the Council to be required to attend the Parliamentary debate and to report back to the Parliament at the conclusion of the ministerial meeting. However, prior to Brexit the UK government remained firmly opposed to these proposals on the grounds that they would have further undermined the powers of the UK Parliament to which national ministers are, in the last resort, solely accountable.

2.9.2 Transparency

Attitudes towards openness and transparency have changed rapidly within all the Union institutions. In accordance with the wish expressed at several European Council meetings, the Commission adopted a decision on public access to Commission documents in February 1994. This implemented a joint code of conduct between the Commission and the Council. The general principle was that the public should have the widest possible access to documents held by these two institutions, subject to public or private interests being protected (Commission Decision 94/90 of 8 February 1994 on public access to Commission documents).

The Treaty of Amsterdam amended the EC Treaty to include a new Article 255 (now Art 15 TFEU), which provided for access to documents of the Union institutions.

Article 15(3) TFEU now provides as follows:

> Any citizen of the Union, and any natural or legal person residing or having its registered office in a Member State, shall have a **right of access to documents of the Union institutions**, bodies, offices and agencies, whatever their medium, subject to the principles and the conditions to be defined in accordance with this paragraph.
>
> General principles and limits on grounds of public or private interest governing this right of access to documents shall be determined by the European Parliament and the Council, by means of regulations, acting in accordance with the ordinary legislative procedure.

Pursuant to the former Article 255 EC Treaty (now Art 15 TFEU), **Regulation 1049/2001** was adopted by the Council. This Regulation replaced Decision 94/90 with effect from 3 December 2001. Refusal to grant access must be based on one of the exceptions provided for in the Regulation and must be justified on the basis that disclosure of the document would be harmful. Article 4 of the Regulation sets out the exceptions, including:

1. The institutions shall refuse access to a document where disclosure would undermine the protection of:
   (a) the public interest, as regards:
   - public security
   - defence and military matters
   - international relations
   - the financial, monetary or economic policy of the Community or a Member State

   (b) privacy and the integrity of the individual, in particular in accordance with Community legislation regarding the protection of personal data.

2. The institutions shall refuse access to a document where disclosure would undermine the protection of:
   - commercial interests of a natural or legal person, including intellectual property
   - court proceedings and legal advice
   - the purpose of inspections, investigations and audits unless there is an overriding public interest in disclosure.

Article 4(3) of the Regulation also provides an exception if the disclosure of the document would seriously undermine the decision-making process of the institution. **Article 4(4)** provides that an institution which is requested to disclose a document originating from a third party has to consult the third party with a view to assessing whether one of the exceptions provided for by the Regulation is applicable, unless it is clear that the document is or is not to be disclosed. **Article 4(5)** provides that a Member State may request the institution not to disclose a document originating from that Member State without its prior agreement.

Transparency in the Commission

A number of measures have been taken to open up the work of the Commission to public scrutiny, as a means of enabling citizens to take part in the debate on the future of the Union in an informed way. This includes the publication of information on the **comitology** network of committees and the frequent use of **Green Papers** and **White Papers**. Green Papers are communications published by the Commission on a specific policy area. Primarily they are documents addressed to interested parties, organisations and individuals, who are invited to participate in a process of consultation and debate. In some cases they provide an impetus for subsequent legislation. White Papers, which often follow a Green Paper, are documents containing proposals for Union action in a specific area. While Green Papers set out a range of ideas presented for public discussion and debate, White Papers contain an official set of proposals in specific policy areas and are used as vehicles for their development. These documents can be accessed from the 'Documents and Publications' section of the Europa website.

> Comitology is discussed in section 2.3.3

There is a significant body of case law involving the Commission where the scope of the right to access documents, as established in **Article 15(3) TFEU** and in light of the derogations provided for in **Article 4 of Regulation 1049/2001**, is developed. For example, in *Sweden* v *Mytravel and Commission* (Case C-506/08) the Court of Justice established that the right to access the documents of Union institutions should be granted a wide application, ruling that:

> it is ... precisely openness in this regard that contributes to conferring greater legitimacy on the institutions in the eyes of European citizens and increasing their confidence in them by allowing divergences between various points of view to be openly debated.

Correspondingly, derogations from this right, as set out in Article 4 of Regulation 1049/2001 should be interpreted narrowly and applied restrictively. When denying a request for documents, a Union institution must therefore explain precisely why the disclosure of particular documents would be harmful, rather than merely citing one or more of the Article 4 exceptions to the right of access.

The case of *Bavarian Lager Co Ltd* v *Commission* (Case C-28/08) illustrated the balance that Union institutions must strike between transparency, as required by **Article 4(1)(b) of Regulation 1049/2001**, and the protection of personal data, as required by **Regulation 45/2001**. In particular, the case established that the right to access documents of the Union institutions does not override the rule established in Regulation 45/2001 that personal data may only be transferred to third parties once the entity requesting the data has established the need for its disclosure and if the disclosure will not harm the legitimate interests of the individual concerned.

Transparency of the Council

Discussions in the Council have previously been held in secret. However, in order to meet the requirement of transparency, **Article 16(8) TEU** now provides that the Council will meet in public when it deliberates and votes on a draft legislative act.

As stated above, **Article 15 TFEU** confers a right of access to all Council documents, which has been implemented by **Regulation 1049/2001**. Refusal to grant access must be based on one of the exceptions provided for in Article 4 of the Regulation and must be justified on the ground that disclosure of the document would be harmful. In *Sweden and Turco* v *Council* (Joined Cases C-39/05 and C-52/05), as with the cases on Regulation 1049/2001 concerning the Commission (see above), the Court of Justice determined that a wide scope is to be granted to the right to access documents of the Union institutions and a narrow interpretation is to be given to exceptions to that right. The harm that forms the basis of a refusal to release documents must be reasonably foreseeable and specified in detail by the relevant institution.

Transparency of the Parliament

On 13 December 2016, the Parliament adopted changes to its Rules of Procedure with the aim of enhancing the transparency and efficiency of the institution. The changes require MEPs to make more frequent and detailed declarations of their financial interests and bans MEPs from taking paid lobbying jobs whilst in office. Additionally, the rules provide for greater scrutiny by the Parliament of Commissioners' potential conflicts of interest, both at the beginning of their term and at any point when there are significant changes to a Commissioner's portfolios or interests.

Regarding **Regulation 1049/2001**, the Court of Justice issued the following ruling in 2016, which concerned the tension between the right to access Parliament documents and the right of MEPs to privacy of personal data:

Dennekamp v *Parliament* (Case T-115/13)

Facts:

Gert-Jan Dennekamp applied to the European Parliament for access to the names of MEPs who benefited from a new additional pension scheme with the aim of exposing any potential conflicts of interest. The Parliament issued a decision that refused Dennekamp's application on the grounds that disclosure of the information would risk undermining the protection of MEPs privacy and integrity in contravention of Regulation 45/2001 on the protection of personal data. Dennekamp then brought an action to the General Court to have the Parliament's decision annulled.

Ruling:

The Court first considered the extent to which the private interests of MEPs would be at risk from the disclosure of the data, stating that:

> As regards MEPs' interests, a distinction should be made between those falling into the public sphere, which must be subject to a lesser degree of protection when being weighed against an interest that would favour the transfer of personal data, and those forming part of the private sphere, which must be protected.

The Court considered that, because MEPs are public figures, because the pension scheme concerned the use of Parliamentary funds and because MEPs' voting behaviour is part of their public activities, the interests of MEPs in question fell into the public rather than the private sphere and should therefore be subject to a lesser degree of protection.

Then, in examining the whether Dennekamp had sufficiently established the necessity of access to the data concerned, the Court stated that:

> bringing to light potential conflicts of interest of MEPs, which is the aim of the transfer of data requested, ensures better scrutiny of the actions of MEPs and of the functioning of an EU institution which represents the peoples of the Member States, and improves the transparency of its actions.

However, in order to achieve the purpose of assessing conflicts of interest, it was only necessary to grant access to the names of the MEPs who had voted on the pension scheme, rather than all MEPs who were in the scheme. The General Court therefore partially annulled the decision of the Parliament to refuse disclosure of the data requested.

Significance:

This case demonstrates the potential for public interests in access to data to outweigh the interests of public figures whom the data concerns. In particular, it places a strong emphasis on the role of transparency in the functioning of the Union.

CHAPTER SUMMARY

Summary of the function, composition and procedures of the main institutions:

Institution	Function	Composition	Procedures
European Council (Art 15 TEU; Arts 235–236 TFEU)	**Political** Establishes the impetus and direction of the Union.	**Heads of State or Government of the Member States**, a President and the President of the Commission.	Meets at least twice a year. Decisions adopted by **consensus**, except for where the Treaties provide otherwise.
European Commission (Art 17 TEU; Arts 244–250 TFEU)	**Executive** Proposes legislation and draft budget. Oversees the application and implementation of Union law ('Guardian of the Treaties'). Initiates and manages programmes. External representation. Represents **interests of the Union**.	**One Commissioner for each Member State**, including a President and the High Representative of the Union for Foreign Affairs and Security Policy. Commission staff are divided into Directorates General, Directorates and Divisions.	Decisions made by a **simple majority**. **Comitology** procedures for the adoption of implementing acts (see Chapter 3).
The Council (Art 16 TEU; Arts 237–243 TFEU)	**Legislative/executive** Legislative and budgetary functions. Makes final decisions. Represents **national interests** of the Member States.	**No fixed members**, but rather **governmental ministers** from each Member State who are responsible for the particular policy area under discussion. Ten **configurations**. Six month rotating presidency.	Voting by **qualified majority** in most instances. This requires 55 per cent of Member States and 65 per cent of the population. **Simple majority** for procedural decisions. **Unanimity** for the most important decisions.
European Parliament (Art 14 TEU; Arts 223–234 TFEU)	**Legislative** Legislative and budgetary functions. Supervision of the Commission. Represents **interests of citizens**.	751 **directly elected members**, including the President, before Brexit. 705 members after Brexit. Seats allocated between Member States according to the principle of **degressive proportionality**.	**Plenary** and **Committee** meetings. Voting by **simple majority** of votes cast in most instances.

Court of Justice of the EU (Art 19 TEU; Arts 251–281 TFEU)	**Judicial** Enforces and interprets EU law. (See Chapters 5, 6 and 7.)	**Court of Justice**: 1 Judge per Member State and 11 Advocates General. **General Court**: 2 Judges per Member State Specialised courts	**Court of Justice:** Non-binding **Opinion** presented by an Advocate General. Private deliberations to produce **single decisions**.
Other institutions:			
Court of Auditors	Audits the general budget. (Arts 285–286 TFEU)	European Economic and Social Committee	Advises the main decision-making institutions. Composed of civil society representatives. (Arts 300–304 TFEU)
European Central Bank	Conducts the monetary policy of the Union. (Arts 282–284 TFEU)	Committee of the Regions	Advises the main decision-making institutions. Composed of regional representatives with an electoral mandate from each Member State. (Arts 300 and 305–307 TFEU)
European Investment Bank	Provides loans and guarantees for projects benefiting the Union. (Arts 308–309 TFEU)	Agencies	Independent bodies producing technical expertise or charged with implementing Union policies

Democratic accountability and transparency

- Powers of the Parliament have been strengthened to address the **'democratic deficit'**, including an equal role with the Council in what is now the **ordinary legislative procedure**.
- **Article 15(3) TFEU** provides for access to Union institution documents.
- **Article 4 of Regulation 1049/2001** provides legitimate justifications for refusing access to documents.
- The tension between the **right to access documents** and **rights to data protection** has been examined in case law (e.g. *Bavarian Lager Co Ltd* v *Commission* and *Dennekamp* v *Parliament*).

Chapter 3
Sources of European Union law (including general principles of law and fundamental rights)

Learning objectives

At the end of this chapter you should understand:

1 The hierarchy of the sources of EU law.

2 The status and scope of the primary Treaties (the Treaty on European Union (TEU) and the Treaty on the Functioning of the European Union (TFEU)) and how they are adopted and amended.

3 The status and scope of the general principles of EU law, including fundamental rights.

4 The differences between directives, regulations and decisions, the procedures for their adoption and the conditions they must meet in order to be legally valid.

5 The role of case law in the EU legal system.

6 The significance of 'soft law'.

7 The influence of international sources of law, including the European Convention on Human Rights, international treaties negotiated by the Union and intergovernmental treaties made between Member States.

Key terms and concepts

Directive – a secondary act of Union law that requires Member States to achieve certain outcomes

Directly applicable – describes an act of Union law that becomes valid law within the legal systems of Member States without them having to take any further action

Legal base – the provision in primary legislation (the EU Treaties) that authorises the adoption of an act of secondary legislation (sometimes also referred to as legal basis)

Official Journal – the official publication of the Union, in which the Treaties often specify that legal acts must be published

Passerelle clauses – clauses within the Treaties that allow for derogations from particular procedures, provided that certain conditions are met

Qualified majority – a requirement to reach a certain voting threshold that is greater than a simple majority

Regulation – a secondary act of Union law that is directly applicable within the legal systems of Member States

Simple majority – a voting threshold of more than half of the total votes

Soft law – acts that may influence legal decisions, but which are not legally binding

3.1 Introduction to the sources of EU law

Objective 1

This chapter divides the sources of EU law into six categories. These categories can be arranged into a hierarchy that indicates the status of each source of law (see Figure 3.1).

In Union law, the greatest legal weight is given to the **Treaty on the Functioning of the European Union (TFEU)** and the **Treaty on European Union (TEU)**. These Treaties then empower the EU institutions to enact **secondary legislation**, which must not only be mandated by a provision in the Treaties, but must also comply with all of the principles contained within the primary sources. Indeed, the legal validity of the secondary sources is dependent upon their compliance with the primary sources. The **case law** of the Court of Justice of the European Union is then placed lower in the hierarchy as it seeks to clarify how the rules that are established in primary and secondary law should be interpreted and applied in particular circumstances. **Recommendations** and **opinions** are then placed towards the bottom of the hierarchy to reflect the fact that they are not legally binding and are therefore classified as '**soft law**'. Finally, the Union is bound by the **international treaties** to which it is a party and may refer to any other treaties that its Member States have entered into. However, these external treaties may only be entered into by the Union and by the Member States so long as doing so does not infringe any laws of the Union.

It should be noted that the placement of the **general principles** at the top of the hierarchy, alongside the Treaties, is a little controversial; there is no consensus among academics and experts as to the exact status and contents of the general principles. Additionally, the hierarchy depicted in Figure. 3.1 may be helpful for gaining an overview of the status of different sources of EU law, but it is an over-simplification of the relationship between these sources. For example, the ECHR is an international source of Union law that has been expressly elevated to the level of primary legislation, first through the case law of the Court of Justice and then, since the Treaty of Maastricht, explicitly through the Treaties as a source of general principles of EU law. Or, as another example, many of the general principles of EU law, including those which are now codified in the Charter of Fundamental Rights of the EU,

Figure 3.1 Hierarchy of EU law

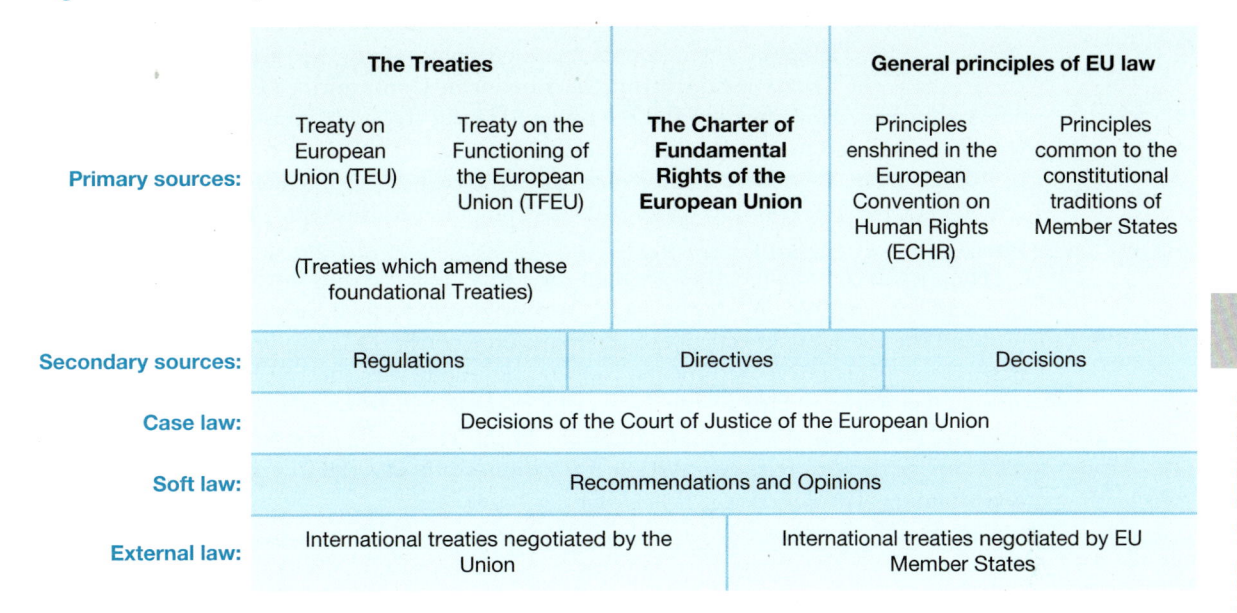

	The Treaties			General principles of EU law	
Primary sources:	Treaty on European Union (TEU)	Treaty on the Functioning of the European Union (TFEU)	The Charter of Fundamental Rights of the European Union	Principles enshrined in the European Convention on Human Rights (ECHR)	Principles common to the constitutional traditions of Member States
	(Treaties which amend these foundational Treaties)				
Secondary sources:	Regulations		Directives		Decisions
Case law:	Decisions of the Court of Justice of the European Union				
Soft law:	Recommendations and Opinions				
External law:	International treaties negotiated by the Union			International treaties negotiated by EU Member States	

were initially granted such status by the rulings of the Court of Justice. Thus, particular principles may move up the hierarchy over time.

The hierarchy of sources depicted above reflects the **deductive method** that characterises Union law. A deductive method is one where a general rule is taken as a starting point, from which more particular rules and applications are then derived, or deduced. This is in contrast to an **inductive method**, whereby specific instances are examined to determine more general rules. EU law can be viewed as both deductive, insofar as Union legislation establishes general rules that may then be further refined through lower order legislation or case law, and inductive in so far as the Court of Justice of the European Union may establish specific rules in relation to particular cases that later become codified in legislation of general application. For example, the primary Treaties established the principle of free movement for workers, the details of which were then determined in a series of cases by the Court of Justice. Several of these developments were then codified in the Citizen's Rights **Directive** (see Chapter 10). Thus, EU law develops deductively from legislative initiative and inductively from judicial interpretation.

3.2 The EU Treaties

Objective 2

The foundational EU Treaties as amended are:

- the Treaty on European Union (TEU);
- the Treaty on the Functioning of the European Union (TFEU).

3.2.1 Origins of the Treaties

The TFEU began life as the **Treaty establishing the European Economic Community** (EEC Treaty) in 1958. This Treaty, also known as the Treaty of Rome, set out the original aims of establishing a customs union, a single market and some initial common policies between the six founding Member States. The EEC Treaty was first amended in 1978 by the Single European Act and was then amended more substantially by the Treaty of Maastricht in 1993. Here, the amendments included renumbering the articles and renaming the treaty as the **Treaty establishing the European Community** (TEC, or EC Treaty). The treaty was again amended and renumbered by the Treaty of Amsterdam in 1999, and was then amended to accommodate the enlargement of the Union by the Treaty of Nice in 2003. Finally – or at least most recently – the treaty was amended, renumbered and renamed by the Treaty of Lisbon in 2009, whereupon it became the **TFEU** that is in force today.

The TEU is considerably younger than the TFEU, as it was only introduced by the Treaty of Maastricht in 1993. While the TFEU was originally focused on the economic community and the technical aspects of the economic project, the TEU was broadly introduced to engender stronger intergovernmental cooperation. Along with the TFEU, the TEU was also amended and renumbered by the Treaty of Amsterdam in 1999, amended by the Treaty of Nice in 2003 and amended and renumbered by the Treaty of Lisbon in 2009; however, the TEU has never been renamed. **Article 1 TEU** now provides that the TEU and the TFEU constitute the Treaties on which the Union is founded.

> See section 1.3.3 for a summary table on the evolution of the TFEU and the TEU (Figure 1.2, page 38)

Treaties which amend the original EU Treaties are themselves a source of EU law. Within this category are the Merger Treaties, the Single European Act (SEA), the Treaty of Maastricht (ToM), the Treaty of Amsterdam (ToA), the Treaty of Nice (ToN) and the Treaty of Lisbon (ToL).

Prior to the ToL it was common to refer to the European Community in addition to the European Union. However, the ToL amended the TEU to provide that the Union replaces and succeeds the Community (Art 1 TEU). Throughout the Treaties, the word 'Community' has been replaced with the word 'Union'. The following terms are therefore no longer used: European *Community*; European *Communities*; and *Community* law. Reference is made solely to the European *Union* (or the *Union*) and European *Union* law (or *Union* law).

As the articles of the TFEU and the TEU have been renumbered with the aim of simplifying the amended legislation, care must be taken when referring to EU case law, legislation and documents to ensure that the old numbering is distinguished from the numbering used post-ToL. In order to identify the correct article that is being referred to, it may be necessary to look up the contemporary version of the relevant Treaty. Furthermore, it should be considered that an article may have been amended as well as renumbered during a revision of the Treaties. Subsequent chapters of this book are based on the post-ToL Treaty numbers but, where case excerpts refer to pre-ToL article numbers, references are provided to the corresponding post-ToL numbers.

3.2.2 Role of the Treaties

The TEU and the TFEU form the 'constitution' of the EU and are therefore an important source of Union law. Although they do not purport to create the constitution of a federal state, in some respects they do have that effect. The Court of Justice interpreted the TFEU in this way in its Opinion 1/91 on the Draft Agreement between the EEC and EFTA. Here, the Court stated that:

> The EEC Treaty [now the TFEU], albeit concluded in the form of an international agreement, nonetheless constitutes the constitutional charter of a Community [i.e. Union] based on the

rule of law. As the Court of Justice has consistently held, the Community [i.e. Union] Treaties established a new legal order for the benefit of which the States had limited their sovereign rights, in ever wider fields, and the subjects of which comprised not only the Member States but also their nationals.

Although they fulfil many of the functions of a constitution for the Union, the EU Treaties still fall far short of creating a federal state. Even though EU law prevails in Member States (see Chapter 4), the Union depends on national courts and enforcement agencies to implement it. The EU Treaties most closely resemble a constitution in the way in which they define the competence of the Union itself, each of its constituent parts and, to a lesser extent, the rights of its citizens. Although the Treaties do not contain a complete catalogue of citizens' rights, they do confer a number of rights (see Chapter 9) which can be enforced directly in the national courts. Ultimately, the Court of Justice acts as guarantor of those rights and has, in fact, quite consciously used the doctrine of 'direct enforcement' (also referred to as 'direct effect') to empower citizens in their own courts and, if need be, against their own governments. A whole range of TFEU provisions have been held to create directly enforceable rights. This principle of direct effect is considered in detail in Chapter 8.

3.2.3 Scope of the Treaties

As the Court of Justice stated in **Opinion 1/91** (see above): '... the Community [i.e. Union] Treaties established a new legal order for the benefit of which the States had limited their sovereign rights, in ever wider fields'. The reference to 'ever wider fields' in Opinion 1/91 refers, in part, to the limited nature of the Union's competences, as the Union institutions can act only in those policy areas and to the extent that the Member States have expressly mandated them to in the Treaties. It also recognises the fact that each time the Treaties have been amended, the powers of the Union have been enhanced through, for example, the inclusion of more policy areas. The competences and characteristics of EU law are examined in depth in Chapter 4, but in order to understand the extent of the Union's legal competences it is essential to be familiar with the contents of the TEU and the TFEU. A useful starting point is to consider the indexes to both Treaties. The full text of both Treaties, as amended, is available from the Eur-Lex website:

> https://eur-lex.europa.eu/homepage.html

Index to the TEU

The index to the TEU, as amended, is as follows:

Preamble		
Title I	Common Provisions	
Title II	Provisions on Democratic Principles	
Title III	Provisions on the Institutions	
Title IV	Provisions on Enhanced Cooperation	
Title V	General Provisions on the Union's External Action and Specific Provisions on the Common Foreign and Security Policy	
	Chapter 1	*General provisions on the Union's external action*
	Chapter 2	*Specific provisions on the common foreign and security policy*
Title VI	Final Provisions	

Index to the TFEU

The index to the TFEU, as amended, is as follows:

Preamble

Part One	Principles	
	Title I	*Categories and areas of Union competence*
	Title II	*Provisions having general application*
Part Two	Non-discrimination and Citizenship of the Union	
Part Three	Union Policies and Internal Actions	
	Title I	*The internal market*
	Title II	*Free movement of goods*
	Title III	*Agriculture and fisheries*
	Title IV	*Free movement of persons, services and capital*
	Title V	*Area of freedom, security and justice*
	Title VI	*Transport*
	Title VII	*Common rules on competition, taxation and approximation of laws*
	Title VIII	*Economic and monetary policy*
	Title IX	*Employment*
	Title X	*Social policy*
	Title XI	*The European social fund*
	Title XII	*Education, vocational training, youth and sport*
	Title XIII	*Culture*
	Title XIV	*Public health*
	Title XV	*Consumer protection*
	Title XVI	*Trans-European Networks*
	Title XVII	*Industry*
	Title XVIII	*Economic, social and territorial cohesion*
	Title XIX	*Research and technological development and space*
	Title XX	*Environment*
	Title XXI	*Energy*
	Title XXII	*Tourism*
	Title XXIII	*Civil protection*
	Title XXIV	*Administrative cooperation*
Part Four	Association of overseas countries and territories	
Part Five	External action by the Union	
	Title I	*General provisions on the Union's external action*
	Title II	*Common commercial policy*
	Title III	*Cooperation with third countries and humanitarian aid*
	Title IV	*Restrictive measures*
	Title V	*International agreements*
	Title VI	*The Union's relations with international organisations and third countries and Union delegations*
	Title VII	*Solidarity clause*

Part Six	Institutional and financial provisions	
	Title I	*Institutional provisions*
	Title II	*Financial provisions*
	Title III	*Enhanced cooperation*
Part Seven	**General and Final Provisions**	

In many instances, the TFEU provides a framework of broad policies, which are to be supplemented by further measures to be adopted by certain Union institutions. Often, such measures take the form of secondary legislation, the different types of which are considered later in this chapter. The institutions and their decision-making procedures are considered in detail in Chapter 2.

Protocols, annexes and declarations

Both the TEU and TFEU are followed by a number of protocols, annexes and declarations. Protocols and annexes are given legal effect within the Union system by **Article 51 TEU**, which provides that:

> The Protocols and Annexes to the Treaties shall form an integral part thereof.

Declarations may be legally effective within the Union legal system if they are adopted by the Council (which most are). Declarations that are not adopted by the Council are more akin to international agreements and do not form part of the Union legal system.

3.2.4 Negotiating and amending the Treaties

Negotiating a new treaty or amending the existing Treaties takes several years, as the changes must be agreed to by the relevant Union institutions and all of the Member States. The Treaties may be amended by one of three procedures, the details of which are set out in **Article 48 TEU**:

- The **ordinary revision procedure** is used in most instances. This is the most thorough procedure, but also the only procedure by which the Treaties can be amended to grant new competences to the Union.
- A **simplified revision procedure** can be used to amend areas of the TFEU relating to Union policies and internal actions.
- **Passerelle clauses** enable legislative procedure to be simplified under certain conditions.

➤ See section 1.3 on the negotiation of the Treaty of Lisbon

The ordinary revision procedure was developed during the negotiation of the Constitutional Treaty – a process which began in 2000 – to include a new convention stage. Innovatively, the convention provided for a phase of debate that was open to all stakeholders. While the negotiation of the Constitutional Treaty was ultimately unsuccessful, the same revision procedure, including the convention stage, was used to successfully negotiate the Treaty of Lisbon.

The three types of revision procedure are now examined in detail.

Ordinary revision procedure

The ordinary revision procedure is set out in paragraphs 1 to 4 of **Article 48 TEU**. The ordinary revision procedure is followed in most instances where the Treaties are amended, including the Treaty of Lisbon.

The stages of the ordinary revision procedure are shown in Figure 3.2.

If each stage is successful, amendments to the Treaties will then enter into force; if agreement is not reached at any of the stages, the amendments will fail. For example, the Treaty establishing a Constitution for Europe, which would have replaced the Treaties, was agreed upon and finalised at an intergovernmental conference in 2004, but negative referenda in France and the Netherlands caused the ratification stage to stall and led to its demise (see section 1.3.1).

With the consent of the European Parliament, the Council may decide by a **simple majority** to skip the convention stage if the amendments are not considered to be sufficiently consequential to warrant it.

Simplified revision procedure

The ToL introduced the simplified revision procedure in **Article 48(6) TEU**, by which amendments may be made to Part Three of the TFEU. Such amendments may therefore affect Union policies and internal actions, but may not confer new powers upon the Union.

The stages of the simplified revision procedure are shown in Figure 3.3.

The simplified revision procedure essentially enables proposals to be submitted directly to the European Council and skips the convention and intergovernmental conference stages of the ordinary procedure. It does, however, require a unanimous vote rather than a simple majority from the European Council. As with the ordinary revision procedure, all stages of

Figure 3.2 The ordinary revision procedure

A Member State, the Commission or the European Parliament **submits proposals to the Council** for the amendment of the Treaties. The Council submits the proposals to the European Council and the national parliaments are notified.

↓

After consulting the European Parliament and the Commission, the **European Council approves** the proposals by a **simple majority.**

↓

The President of the European Council convenes a **convention** composed of representatives from the Member States, the European Parliament and the Commission. The Convention undertakes **preparatory work** on the proposed amendments.

↓

An **intergovernmental conference** is held, at which representatives from each Member State discuss the work produced by the convention and **finalise the amendments.**

↓

All **Member States ratify** the agreed upon amendments according to their respective constitutional requirements.

Figure 3.3 The simplified revision procedure

> A Member State, the Commission or the European Parliament **submits proposals to the European Council** for the amendment of all or part of Part Three of the TFEU.

> After consulting the European Parliament and the Commission, and the European Central Bank if the monetary area is to be affected, the **European Council approves** the proposals **unanimously**.

> Each Member state **ratifies** the decision of the European Council according to their respective constitutional requirements.

the simplified revision procedure must be successful in order for the proposed amendments to enter into force.

Passerelle clauses

Passerelle clauses enable a less burdensome legislative procedure to be followed in specific instances, provided that certain conditions are met. A passerelle clause is therefore not so much a means of formally revising the Treaties as it is a means of derogating from certain provisions of the Treaties. The ToL introduced a general passerelle clause in **Article 48(7) TEU**, which provides for the following:

> (i) Where the Treaties require the Council to act unanimously, the European Council may adopt a decision authorising the Council to act by **qualified majority**, excluding decisions with military implications or in the area of defence.
>
> (ii) Where the TFEU requires the Council to follow a special legislative procedure, the European Council may adopt a decision authorising the Council to follow the ordinary legislative procedure.

In both instances, the change to legislative procedure may be applied in a particular instance or to all instances within a particular policy area. The European Council must act unanimously and must acquire the consent of the European Parliament. This means that all of the Member States must agree to the change. Furthermore, national parliaments, which must be notified, can prevent the adoption of a European Council decision under Article 48(7) by expressing their objection within six months.

In addition to Article 48 TEU, there are six passerelle clauses written into the areas of the Treaties to which they apply. The particular requirements of the specific passerelle clauses are not the same as those in Article 48, but are specified within the clauses themselves. For example, national parliaments are not granted a veto in five of the clauses and their use may be authorised by the Council rather than the European Council. The six specific passerelle clauses are found in the areas of:

- multiannual financial framework (Art 312 TFEU);
- Common Foreign and Security Policy (Art 31 TEU);
- judicial cooperation concerning family law (Art 81 TFEU);

- reinforced cooperation in areas governed by unanimity or by a special legislative procedure (Art 333 TFEU);
- social affairs (Art 153 TFEU);
- environmental matters (Art 192 TFEU).

3.3 General principles (including fundamental rights)

Objective 3

In interpreting primary and secondary Union legislation, the Court of Justice of the European Union has developed a number of general principles of law, some based on laws of the constitutions of the Member States, some based on principles of international law and some derived from the European Convention on Human Rights (ECHR). There is no exhaustive list of the general principles within EU legislation, nor any academic consensus as to exactly what should and should not be included in such a list. However, several principles are now listed in the Treaties. For example, **Article 2 TEU** states that:

> The Union is founded on the values of respect for human dignity, freedom, democracy, equality, the rule of law and respect for human rights, including the rights of persons belonging to minorities. These values are common to the Member States in a society in which pluralism, non-discrimination, tolerance, justice, solidarity and equality between men and women prevail.

The importance of these principles is emphasised, not only by their position at the beginning of the TEU, but also by the powers conferred on the Council by Article 7(3) TEU to suspend, *inter alia*, the voting rights of any Member State found to be in breach of them (although Art 7(3) has never been invoked and has been criticised for relying on the willingness of Member States to take action against each other). Furthermore, any secondary legislation that is found to contravene one of the general principles can be declared invalid by the Court of Justice of the EU (see section 3.4.5).

Additionally, **Article 6(1) TEU**, as amended by the ToL, provides that the Union shall recognise the rights, freedoms and principles set out in the **Charter of Fundamental Rights of the European Union** (the Charter), which shall have the same legal value as the EU Treaties. **Article 6(3) TEU** further provides that fundamental rights 'as guaranteed by the European Convention for the Protection of Human Rights and Fundamental Freedoms and as they result from the constitutional traditions common to the Member States, shall constitute general principles of the Union's law'.

The development and application of these general principles of Union law are considered further below. This is divided into two main sections: (i) administrative procedural principles and (ii) fundamental rights principles. This division is made for ease of discussion here; in practice there is considerable overlap, with administrative procedural principles often being codified within human rights instruments.

3.3.1 Administrative procedural principles

Although the jurisdiction of the Court of Justice of the European Union is limited by Article 19(1) TEU to the interpretation of the Treaties, this is to be done in such a way as to ensure that 'the law is observed'. This has widely been interpreted to mean not only the law established by the Treaties but 'any rule of law relating to the Treaty's application' (Pescatore, 1970).

In January 2013 and June 2016, the European Parliament adopted resolutions that recommended that the Commission consider adopting a **regulation** on Law of Administrative Procedure of the EU, which would codify the principles of good administration. Attached to the latter resolution was a proposal for a regulation for an open, efficient and independent EU administration. The Commission responded that they were not convinced of the need for such a regulation and suggested that the costs might outweigh the benefits. This section therefore considers some of the administrative procedural principles that have been embraced by the Court of Justice of the European Union when interpreting and applying Union law, but which have not been consolidated in any single comprehensive document.

Subsidiarity

Subsidiarity is the principle that the Union may only act when the objectives in question cannot be better or equally well achieved by action at the national level. The principle of subsidiarity is provided for in **Article 5(3) TEU** and **Protocol No. 2,** which is annexed to the Treaties. It is discussed in depth in Chapter 4.

Proportionality

Proportionality is a general principle imported from German law and is often invoked to determine whether an item of subordinate legislation or an action purported to be taken under Union law goes beyond what is necessary to achieve the declared, lawful objectives. The principle holds that 'the individual should not have his freedom of action limited beyond the degree necessary for the public interest' (*Internationale Handelsgesellschaft* (Case 11/70)).

Article 5(1) TEU specifically provides that the use of EU competences is governed by the principle of proportionality. **Article 5(4) TEU** further provides that 'Under the principle of proportionality the content and form of Union action shall not exceed what is necessary to achieve the objectives of the Treaties'. **Protocol No. 2,** which is annexed to the TEU and the TFEU, concerns the application of the principles of subsidiarity and proportionality. Article 5(4) TEU specifically provides that the EU institutions shall apply the principle of proportionality as laid down in the Protocol. Consequently, the Court of Justice will rule that actions taken by the Union institutions are invalid if the principle of proportionality has not been upheld (see Chapter 6).

The principle of proportionality is applied in many of the cases that are discussed in the following chapters of this book, as it is applicable to the actions of Member States as well as the Union institutions (and also individuals and private undertakings under certain conditions – see Chapter 8). Where Member States are permitted to derogate from a certain Treaty obligation on certain grounds, derogating measures will only be found lawful by the Court of Justice if they are proportionate to those grounds. In other words, a derogating measure must go no further than is necessary to protect a certain interest or to pursue a certain objective that is recognised as legitimate under EU law. A failure to adhere to the principle of proportionality in such cases will lead to the Court of Justice ruling that the Member State in question is in breach of EU law.

Legal certainty and non-retroactivity

Legal certainty and **non-retroactivity** are general principles of law familiar to all the legal systems of the Member States. In its broadest sense, it means that 'Community [i.e. Union] legislation must be unequivocal and its application must be predictable for those who are subject to it' (***Kloppenburg*** (Case 70/81), para 11). In ***Kolpinghuis Nijmegen*** (Case 80/86), the Court of Justice stated that the national court's obligation to interpret domestic law to comply with Union law was 'limited by the general principles of law which form part of Community [i.e. Union] law, and in particular, the principles of legal certainty and non-retroactivity' (para 13). This means, for example, that the principle of the **indirect effect** of directives does not apply in relation to national provisions with criminal sanctions, because the need for legal certainty requires that the effect of national criminal law should be absolutely clear to those subject to it.

> The principle of indirect effect is explained in detail in section 8.3

The principle of legal certainty was thrown into the spotlight by the contentious case of ***Taricco and Others*** (Case C-105/14 – **Taricco I**), for which the Court of Justice was widely criticised for seeming to prioritise the implementation of Article 325 TFEU on countering fraud over the principle of legal certainty. However, when the issue was referred to the Court of Justice for a second time (***MAS and MB*** (*Case* C-42/17 – **Taricco II**)), the Court took the opportunity to reverse its position and reaffirm that fiscal objectives must be balanced by fundamental rights, including the rights of individuals to legal certainty and non-retroactivity.

> The Taricco cases are also considered in section 4.3.2 (page 173)

Legitimate expectation

Legitimate expectation is based on the concept that 'trust in the Community's [i.e. Union's] legal order must be respected' (Opinion of Advocate General Trabucchi in ***Deuka*** (Case 5/75)). Under this principle, 'assurances relied on in good faith should be honoured' (Opinion of Advocate General Trabucchi in ***Compagnie Continentale*** v ***Council*** (Case 169/73)). The principle of legitimate expectation is illustrated in the following case:

Mulder (Case 120/86)

Facts:

In order to stabilise milk production, Union rules required dairy farmers to enter into a five-year non-marketing agreement, in exchange for which they would receive a premium. In 1984, the Union introduced a system of milk quotas, under which milk producers would have to pay a levy on milk produced in excess of their quota in any one year. Those who had entered into the non-marketing agreement for 1983 were not allowed any quota, because there was no provision in the regulations for them to do so. Having suspended production for the non-marketing period, they were effectively excluded from subsequent milk production. A farmer excluded in this way challenged the validity of the regulations.

Ruling:

The Court of Justice held that:

> ... where such a producer, as in the present case, has been encouraged by a Community [i.e. Union] measure to suspend marketing for a limited period in the general interest and against payment of a premium, he may legitimately expect not to be subject, upon the expiry of his undertaking, to restrictions which specifically affect him because he has availed himself of the possibilities offered by the Community [i.e. Union] provisions.

Significance:

This case demonstrates the Court's recognition that persons must feel that their engagements with the Union have been honoured in good faith and that they have not been tricked or betrayed by the Union.

The principle of legitimate expectation seeks to ensure a fair process, although it cannot fetter the Union's freedom of action. This balance between expectation and freedom is not always easy to strike, and was discussed in an English court by Sedley J in the following case, which also illustrates the close connections between legitimate expectation and legal certainty:

R v Ministry of Agriculture and Fisheries, ex parte Hamble Fisheries [1995] 2 ALL ER 714

Facts:
The court was required to determine whether the legitimate expectation of the holders of fishing licences had been infringed when the Ministry introduced a more restrictive fishing licensing policy to protect the remaining fish stocks allocated to the UK under the Union's quota system.

Ruling:
Sedley J stated that:

> The principle of legal certainty and the protection of legitimate expectation are fundamental to European Community [i.e. Union] law. Yet these principles are merely general maxims derived from the notion that the Community [i.e. Union] is based on the rule of law and can be applied to individual cases only if expressed in enforceable rules. Moreover, in most instances there are other principles which run counter to legal certainty and the protection of legitimate expectations; here the right balance will need to be struck. For instance, in the field of Community [i.e. Union] legislation the need for changes in the law can conflict with the expectation of those affected by such a change that the previous legal situation will remain in force …

The court ruled that legitimate expectation had not been infringed in this instance.

Significance:
The principle of legitimate expectation cannot be used to argue that laws and regulations should not be changed solely on the basis that a complainant expected that they would stay the same.

The CFI (now the General Court) has held that operators in the Union's agricultural markets cannot have a legitimate expectation that an existing situation will prevail as the Union's intervention in these markets involves constant adjustments to meet changes in the economic situation (*O'Dwyer and Others* v *Council* (Joined Cases T-466, 469, 473 and 477/93)).

Natural justice

Natural justice is a concept derived from English administrative law, but closely linked to the concept of 'due process' in the United States. It is sometimes used by the Court of Justice to mean no more than 'fairness' and is not always distinguishable from 'equity'. In the English administrative law sense, it implies two underlying principles: (i) the right to an unbiased hearing; and (ii) the right to be heard before the making of a potentially adverse decision affecting the person concerned (see, for example, *Ridge* v *Baldwin* [1964] AC 40). The Court of Justice described the latter of these as a 'general principle of good administration' in *Kuhner* (Case 33/79):

> … a general principle of good administration to the effect that an administration which has to take decisions, even legally, which cause serious detriment to the persons concerned, must allow the latter to make known their point of view, unless there is a serious reason for not doing so. [para 25]

The principle of natural justice is referred to explicitly in relation to decisions affecting an individual's free movement rights on the grounds of public policy, public security and public health (Arts 27–32, Directive 2004/38), and implicitly in other decisions affecting the exercise of those rights. It involves the right to be given full reasons for a decision in order that they may be challenged. The right to natural justice is thus closely linked to the right to an effective remedy (see *Unectef* v *Heylens and Others* (Case 222/86)).

3.3.2 Fundamental rights

> See section 4.3.2 for the Solange cases and section 4.3 on the supremacy of EU law

The Court of Justice has emphasised its commitment to human rights in general on several occasions, starting with *Stauder* (Case 29/69). In this case the Court of Justice declared that 'fundamental human rights [are] enshrined in the general principles of Community [i.e. Union] law and protected by the Court' (para 7). However, until the TEU came into force in 1993, there were no specific provisions for the protection of human rights in the Treaties.

As mentioned above, **Article 6 TEU** (as amended by the ToL) now declares that:

> 1 The Union recognises the rights, freedoms and principles set out in the Charter of Fundamental Rights of the European Union ... which shall have the same legal value as the Treaties.
>
> 2 ...
>
> 3 Fundamental rights, as guaranteed by the European Convention for the Protection of Human Rights and Fundamental Freedoms and as they result from the constitutional traditions common to the Member States, shall constitute general principles of the Union's law.

The effect of Article 6 TEU is to give formal recognition in the Treaty to that which has been part of the jurisprudence of the Court of Justice of the European Union since *Stauder* (Case 29/69). Subsequent to paragraphs 1 and 3 of Article 6 TEU, fundamental and human rights thus comprise principles with the status of primary EU law, which the Court of Justice can derive from (i) the **Charter of Fundamental Rights of the European Union** (the Charter), (ii) the **European Convention on Human Rights** (the ECHR) and (iii) the **constitutional rights** common to the Member States.

As all Member States are party to the ECHR, the legitimacy of the ECHR within EU law is partly derived from its status as common to all Member States. Additional rights and freedoms have then been drawn from the constitutions of the Member States. Rights and freedoms recognised by national constitutions as being 'fundamental' are so both in the sense that they protect and promote the most essential human values, such as the dignity, personality, intellectual and physical integrity, or the economic and social well-being of the individual, and in the sense that they are inseparably attached to the person.

Even where a right is recognised by the Court as a 'fundamental' Union right, that recognition is not conclusive. The designation by the Court of a right as fundamental does not always mean that all other rules must give way before it. In some circumstances, one fundamental right may have to give way to another which the Court regards as even more important. Much will depend on the context in which the fundamental right is called upon, and the nature of the right itself.

> **Reflection:** How the EU became a human rights system
>
> It is arguable that the Court has been reluctant to take on the protection of fundamental rights, and did so largely to protect the supremacy of its jurisdiction:
>
>> Reading an unwritten bill of rights into Community [i.e. Union] law is indeed the most striking contribution the Court made to the development of a new constitution for Europe ... [T]hat contribution was forced on the court from outside, by the German and, later, the Italian Constitutional Courts.
>>
>> (Mancini, 1989)
>
> The reference to the German Court made here by Mancini, who was a Judge of the Court of Justice, was to the 'Solange' cases. In the case known as **Solange I** (Judgment of May 29, 1974, 37 BVerfGE 271), the German Federal Constitutional Court ruled that if a case should arise where there was a conflict between Community [i.e. Union] law and a fundamental right guaranteed by the German constitution, the constitutional rights would prevail. This conflicted with an earlier ruling by the Court of Justice (**Internationale Handelsgesellschaft** (Case 11/70)), where the Court asserted that Community [i.e. Union] law was supreme over national laws, even where fundamental rights were concerned (see Chapter 4).
>
> In the face of the challenge to the supremacy of Union law that was posed by **Solange I,** the EU sought to develop its doctrine of human rights protections. Subsequently, the German Federal Constitutional Court revised its position in **Solange II** in 1983 (Judgment of Oct. 22, 1986, 73 BVerfGE 339). Here, the German Court asserted that, so long as the Union generally ensured the protection of fundamental rights, it would assume that level of protection to be substantially equivalent to that provided by German constitutional law. The challenge to the supremacy of Union law was thus resolved through the incorporation of fundamental rights protections within the Union legal system – a process which has continued ever since.

This section on fundamental rights considers the ECHR and the Charter before examining the substance of some of the rights that they enshrine.

The European Convention on Human Rights (ECHR)

To begin with, it should be noted that the ECHR is not EU legislation, but rather falls within the domain of the Council of Europe, which is an entirely separate organisation. Accordingly, the ECHR is presided over by the European Court of Human Rights (ECtHR), rather than the Court of Justice of the European Union. Although the ECHR is external to the Union, and is therefore also mentioned in the later section of this chapter on international sources of EU law, it is included here to reflect the way in which the ECHR has been incorporated as a collection of general principles of Union law.

▶ See 'Reflection: Distinguishing between the two European courts' in section 1.3.3 (page 43)

In *A* v *Commission* (Case T-10/93) the Court of First Instance (now the General Court) noted the commitment in what is now Article 6 TEU to respect the fundamental rights guaranteed by the ECHR and said, repeating the words of the Court of Justice in *ERT* (Case C-260/89), 'the Court draws inspiration from the constitutional traditions common to Member States and from the guidelines supplied by international treaties for the protection of human rights on which Member States have collaborated or of which they are signatories' (see, in particular, the judgment in *Nold* v *Commission* (Case 4/73)).

The ECHR has special significance in that respect. It follows that, as the Court of Justice held in its judgment in *Wachauf* v *Germany* (Case 5/88), the Union cannot accept measures which are incompatible with observance of human rights as they are recognised and guaranteed in the ECHR. What this means is that when there is a conflict between national law which is, for example, intended to implement Union law, but does so in such a way as to breach the ECHR, the Court will rule that the national measure is contrary to Union law. For example, in **Johnston v Chief Constable of the Royal Ulster Constabulary** (Case 222/84), national measures intended to prohibit sexual discrimination in Northern Ireland and to provide a remedy for those alleging discriminatory behaviour, were held contrary to Union law because the Court of Justice held that they did not give **complainants** an effective remedy as required by Article 13 ECHR.

It must, however, be emphasised that the Court of Justice can only rule on compatibility between the ECHR and Union law in those areas of national law affected by Union law. It could not, for example, rule on the compatibility with the ECHR's provisions on fair process of a criminal trial in a Member State that was unrelated to any rules of Union law, even if the individual involved was an EU citizen (**Kremzow v Austria** (Case C-299/95)). In the case of **Demirel v Stadt Schwbisch Gmünd** (Case 12/86), the Court of Justice held that it has 'no power to examine the compatibility with the European Convention on Human Rights of national legislation lying outside the scope of Community [i.e. Union] law' (para 28).

The application of the ECHR and the development of the jurisprudence of fundamental rights has been a somewhat erratic process, depending very much on the types of cases which have come before the Court. Some provisions of the ECHR, particularly those relating to due process under Article 6 ECHR, have been discussed frequently by the Court, while others, such as those relating to the right to life, have hardly been discussed at all.

The status of the ECHR as a source of general principles of Union law was first recognised in the Treaties in Article F(2) of the original TEU of 1993. However, the TEU as amended by the ToL not only includes this recognition in Article 6(3), but also provides for the Union to accede to the ECHR in **Article 6(2)**:

> The Union shall accede to the European Convention for the Protection of Human Rights and Fundamental Freedoms. Such accession shall not affect the Union's competences as defined in the Treaties.

Accession to the EHCR would place the same obligations and human rights scrutiny on the Union as accession to the Convention by any country would. Thus, once the Union accedes to the ECHR, EU law will have to be interpreted and applied in accordance with the ECHR, not simply as a 'general principle of the Union's law', but because: (i) the ECHR is **directly applicable** to the Union; and (ii) the Union is required (in international law) to adhere to the ECHR's provisions. Following accession to the ECHR, it will be possible for a decision of the Court of Justice to be contested by taking the case to the European Court of Human Rights in Strasbourg, claiming the Court of Justice has breached a provision of the ECHR.

Official ECHR accession talks started between the EU and the Council of Europe on 7 July 2010. A draft agreement was concluded in April 2013 and an opinion of the EU Court of Justice was then sought on the compatibility of the draft agreement with EU Treaties. Opinion 2/13 was delivered by the Court of Justice on 18 December 2014, which, because of problems identified by the Court, concluded that the draft agreement was not compatible with Union law. If the issues identified by the Court of Justice can be satisfactorily resolved through amendments to the draft agreement, the European Council will have to adopt a decision to authorise the signing of the accession agreement, acting unanimously. All Member States would then have to complete their internal procedures to ratify the agreement. The Union would then ratify the agreement and the Committee of Ministers of the Council of Europe would have to adopt it. It would then have to be ratified (i.e. approved) by all 47 contracting parties to the ECHR in accordance with their respective constitutional requirements. It is therefore safe to assume that the Union's accession to the ECHR will not take place in the foreseeable future.

> **Reflection:** The UK's Human Rights Act 1998
>
> The UK was one of the original signatories of the ECHR and ratified the Convention in 1951. All public bodies (including courts and tribunals) and even private bodies implementing public law have to abide by the principles of the ECHR. However, it was not until 1998 that the ECHR was incorporated into the law of England, Wales, Scotland and Northern Ireland by the Human Rights Act. Currently, then, ECHR rights may be applied in the UK either: (i) as a matter of Union law where they concern a measure within the competence of the Union; or (ii) under national law following the procedures set out in the Act.
>
> As the ECHR is external to and separate from the Union, Brexit will not affect the UK's national obligations under the Convention. Furthermore, while the Conservative Party pledged to repeal the Human Rights Act in their 2015 manifesto this was dropped as Brexit took centre stage in UK political discourse. The 2019 Conservative manifesto states only that they 'will update the Human Rights Act ... to ensure that there is a proper balance between the rights of individuals, our vital national security and effective government'. It is currently unclear what such updates might look like.

The Charter of Fundamental Rights of the European Union

The Charter of Fundamental Rights of the European Union was signed by the then 15 Member States in December 2000 during the meeting of the European Council held in Nice, France. The Charter combines in a single text the civil, political, economic, social and societal rights which had previously been laid down in a variety of international, European and national sources. It includes the following:

- dignity (e.g. the right to life, and respect for private and family life);
- freedoms (e.g. freedom of assembly and of association);
- equality (e.g. respect for cultural, religious and linguistic diversity);
- solidarity (e.g. right of collective bargaining and action);
- citizens' rights (e.g. freedom of movement and residence);
- justice (e.g. presumption of innocence and right of defence).

Originally, the Charter was not legally binding. A Declaration annexed to the ToN provided that an Intergovernmental Conference would be held in 2004 to consider, *inter alia*, the status of the Charter. This resulted in the adoption of the proposed Constitutional Treaty and subsequently the adoption of the ToL.

The Charter, which was amended on 12 December 2007, is given legal recognition by **Article 6(1) TEU**, as amended by the ToL, which provides as follows:

> The Union recognises the rights, freedoms and principles set out in the Charter of Fundamental Rights of the European Union of 7 December 2000, as adapted at Strasbourg, on 12 December 2007, which shall have **the same legal value as the Treaties**.
>
> The provisions of the Charter shall **not** extend in any way the competences of the Union as defined in the Treaties.

The Charter is therefore an integral part of Union law, setting out the fundamental rights every Union citizen can benefit from. However, it does not create fundamental rights which are of general application in national law; it only applies within the scope of Union law. Furthermore, the latter paragraph explicitly provides that the Charter does not introduce any new EU powers or tasks.

During the adoption of the ToL, the UK and Poland sought reassurance that the Charter would not be indirectly incorporated into their national law. **Article 1 of Protocol No. 30** (which is annexed to the TEU and TFEU) provides that:

> 1 The Charter does not extend the ability of the Court of Justice of the European Union, or any court or tribunal of Poland or of the United Kingdom, to find that the laws, regulations or administrative provisions, practices or action of Poland or of the United Kingdom are inconsistent with the fundamental rights, freedoms and principles that it [i.e. the Charter] reaffirms.
>
> 2 In particular, and for the avoidance of doubt, nothing in Title IV of the Charter creates justiciable rights applicable to Poland or the United Kingdom except in so far as Poland or the United Kingdom has provided for such rights in its national law.

As discussed in Chapter 1, in order to secure the Czech Republic President's signature to the ToL, it was agreed that at the time of the conclusion of the next Accession Treaty a new Protocol would be added to both the TEU and TFEU to provide that Protocol No. 30 (which currently only applies to the UK and Poland) would also apply to the Czech Republic. The next Accession Treaty was concluded at the end of 2011 to pave the way for Croatia's entry to the EU on 1 July 2013. However, due to the prominence of opposition parties in the Czech Senate at the time, it was not possible to gain sufficient support for opting out of the Charter during the ratification of the Croatian Accession Treaty. Following a change in leadership after presidential and parliamentary elections in 2013, the Czech Republic formally withdrew their request to add a protocol to limit the application of the Charter in 2014. Under section 5(4) of the European Union (Withdrawal) Act 2018, the Charter of Fundamental Rights will not apply to the UK after Brexit, even for the purposes of interpreting retained EU law.

> See 'Reflection: EU secondary legislation in the UK after Brexit' in section 3.4.5 (page 147)

The following case concerned a direct application by the Court of Justice of the Charter:

A, B, C v *Staatssecretaris van Veiligheid en Justitie* (Joined Cases C-148/13 to C-150/13)

Facts:

Directives 2004/83 and 2005/85 establish, respectively, the minimum requirements that third-country nationals must fulfil in order to be able to claim refugee status, and the procedures for examining applications for asylum and the rights of applicants. A, B and C were third-country nationals. They each lodged an application for asylum in the Netherlands, relying on their fear of persecution in their country of origin on account of their homosexuality. However, the competent authorities rejected their applications on the grounds that their sexual orientation had not been proven.

The three applicants appealed against those decisions. Hearing the dispute, the Raad van State (Council of State, Netherlands) was uncertain whether there were any limits imposed by Union law as regards the verification of the sexual orientation of applicants for asylum. The Raad van State took the view that the mere fact of putting questions to an applicant for asylum could infringe the rights guaranteed by the Charter of Fundamental Rights of the European Union.

The Raad van State referred the case to the Court of Justice for a preliminary ruling pursuant to Article 267 TFEU.

Ruling:

The Court of Justice stated that the declarations by an applicant for asylum as to their sexual orientation were merely the starting point in the process of assessment of the application and that confirmation could be required. However, the methods used by the competent authorities to assess the statements and the evidence submitted in support of applications for asylum **had to be consistent with Union law and, in particular, the fundamental rights guaranteed by the Charter, such as the right to respect for human dignity and the right to respect for private and family life**.

Furthermore, the assessment had to be made on an individual basis and must take account of the individual situation and personal circumstances of the applicant (including factors such as background, gender and age), in order for it to be determined whether the acts to which the applicant has been or could be exposed would amount to persecution or serious harm. Against that background, the Court gave guidance as to the methods of assessment which could be used by national authorities to ensure compliance with Union law and the Charter.

Significance:

Union law must be implemented in such a way that does not infringe upon the rights and freedoms enshrined in the Charter, which applies to EU citizens and non-EU citizens within the scope of Union law.

Where a fundamental right is recognised by both the Charter and by the European Convention on Human Rights (ECHR), the Charter provides that the right has the same meaning and scope as laid down by the ECHR. One of the rights recognised by the Charter (Art 50) and the ECHR (Art 4) is the fundamental right not to be tried or punished in *criminal* proceedings twice for the same offence. The following case is concerned with this prohibition on being punished twice:

Åklagaren v Åkerberg Fransson (Case C-617/10)

Facts:

Mr Åkerberg Fransson was self-employed. The Swedish tax authorities accused him of having provided false tax information in 2004 and 2005, which resulted in a loss of revenue from various taxes. The Swedish tax authorities imposed penalties for the 2004 and 2005 tax years.

In 2009, criminal proceedings were brought against Åkerberg Fransson in the Haparanda Tingsrät (Haparanda District Court). The Public Prosecutor's Office accused him of having committed an offence of tax evasion (in respect of 2004 and 2005) punishable, under Swedish law, by a term of imprisonment of up to six years. The acts of providing false information which gave rise to those proceedings were the same as the acts that led to the tax penalties.

The Swedish court referred the case to the Court of Justice to determine whether the criminal charges against Åkerberg Fransson had to be dismissed on the ground that he had already been punished for the acts in question.

Ruling:

The Court of Justice stated that fundamental rights guaranteed by the Charter must be complied with where national legislation implements Union law. The Court explained that tax penalties and criminal proceedings for tax evasion constituted implementation of a number of provisions of Union law which related to VAT. Therefore, the Charter applied and the prohibition on being punished twice, as set out in the Charter, was applicable to Åkerberg Fransson's situation.

> The Court stated that a national court which is called upon to apply provisions of Union law is under a duty to give full effect to those provisions. If necessary, it should refuse to apply any conflicting provision of national legislation and it is not necessary for the court to request or wait for the national provision to be set aside by legislative or other constitutional means.
>
> However, the Court observed with regard to the principle which prevents a person from being punished twice that this does not preclude a Member State from imposing, for the same acts, a combination of tax penalties and criminal penalties. In order to ensure that all VAT revenue is collected and, in so doing, that the financial interests of the Union are protected, Member States have freedom to choose the applicable penalties. These penalties may therefore take the form of administrative penalties, criminal penalties or a combination of the two. It is only if the tax penalty is criminal in nature and has become final within the meaning of the Charter that the principle preventing a person from being punished twice precludes criminal proceedings being brought against the same person for the same acts.
>
> **Significance:**
>
> The case confirms the primacy of the Charter, as primary EU legislation, over national legislation. The case also clarified the principle that a person should not be punished twice for a single offence by determining that multiple types of penalty may be applied to an offence, but new charges may not be brought after the original case has been finalised.
>
> Additionally, this case illustrates the overlap between fundamental rights and administrative procedural principles, as it concerns a principle that fits within both categories.

Examples of specific human rights

This section provides an overview of some of the most prominent and influential human rights that are general principles of EU law by virtue of being stipulated in the TEU, the Charter and/or the ECHR. In addition to the content and location of each right, reference to key cases and additional legislation and documents is included as a starting point for further research where appropriate. Rights to the protection of personal data and to intellectual property are notable for their especially recent and rapid development.

Table 3.1 in no way provides an exhaustive list of the human rights that have been incorporated into Union law, nor of the corpus of legislation and jurisprudence pertaining to those rights; it is merely intended to be indicative of the human rights protections that are afforded by Union law. The rights are listed in the order that they appear in the Charter.

Table 3.1 Human rights that have been incorporated into Union law

Right	Text of the right	Relevant secondary legislation and case law
Dignity	Art 2 TEU: The Union is founded on the values of respect for human dignity, freedom, democracy, equality, the rule of law and respect for human rights. Art 1 Charter: Human dignity is inviolable. It must be respected and protected.	Opinion of the Advocate General in ***S Coleman* v *Attridge Law and Steve Law*** (Case 303/06) Opinion of the Advocate General and judgment in ***OMEGA*** (Case C-36/02) Opinion of the Advocate General in ***The Netherlands* v *European Parliament and Council of the European Union*** (Case C-377/98) ***Oliver Brüstle* v *Greenpeace e.V*** (Case C-34/10)

3.3 GENERAL PRINCIPLES (INCLUDING FUNDAMENTAL RIGHTS)

Right	Text of the right	Relevant secondary legislation and case law
Right to life, integrity and liberty	Art 2 Charter: 1. Everyone has the right to life. 2. No one shall be condemned to the death penalty, or executed. Art 3 Charter: 1. Everyone has the right to respect for his or her physical and mental integrity. 2. … Art 1 ECHR: The death penalty shall be abolished. No one shall be condemned to such penalty or executed. Art 2 ECHR: 1. Everyone's right to life shall be protected by law. No one shall be deprived of his life intentionally save in the execution of a sentence of a court following his conviction of a crime for which this penalty is provided by law. … Art 5 ECHR: 1. Everyone has the right to liberty and security of person. No one shall be deprived of his liberty…	***Netherlands*** v ***European Parliament and Council of the European Union*** (Case C-377/98)
Prohibition of torture	Art 4 Charter: No one shall be subjected to torture or to inhuman or degrading treatment or punishment. Art 3 ECHR No one shall be subjected to torture or to inhuman or degrading treatment or punishment.	***Bundesrepublik Deutschland*** v ***Kaveh Puid*** (Case C-4/11)
Prohibition of slavery and forced labour	Art 5 Charter: 1. No one shall be held in slavery or servitude. 2. No one shall be required to perform forced or compulsory labour. 3. Trafficking in human beings is prohibited. Art 4 ECHR: 1. No one shall be held in slavery or servitude. 2. No one shall be required to perform forced or compulsory labour. 3. …	**Directive 2004/81** on the residence permit issued to third-country nationals who are victims of trafficking in human beings or who have been the subject of an action to facilitate illegal immigration

Table 3.1 (Continued)

Right	Text of the right	Relevant secondary legislation and case law
Respect for private and family life, right to marry	Art 7 Charter: Everyone has the right to respect for his or her private and family life, home and communications. Art 9 Charter: The right to marry and the right to found a family shall be guaranteed in accordance with the national laws governing the exercise of these rights. Art 33(2) Charter: 2 To reconcile family and professional life, everyone shall have the right to protection from dismissal for a reason connected with maternity and the right to paid maternity leave and to parental leave following the birth or adoption of a child. Art 8 ECHR: 1. Everyone has the right to respect for his private and family life, his home and his correspondence. 2. .... Art 12 ECHR: Men and women of marriageable age have the right to marry and to found a family, according to the national laws governing the exercise of this right.	**Directive 2003/86** on the right to family reunification ***X v Commission*** (Case C-404/92) ***Digital Rights Ireland*** and ***Seitlinger and Others*** (Joined Cases C-293/12 and C-594/12) ***Mary Carpenter v Secretary of State for the Home Department*** (Case C-60/00)
Protection of personal data	Art 8 Charter: 1. Everyone has the right to the protection of personal data concerning him or her. 2. Such data must be processed fairly for specified purposes and on the basis of the consent of the person concerned or some other legitimate basis laid down by law. Everyone has the right of access to data which has been collected concerning him or her, and the right to have it rectified. 3. ...	**Directive 2002/58** on privacy and electronic communications **Regulation 2016/679** on the protection of natural persons with regard to the processing of personal data and on the free movement of such data (the General Data Protection Regulation, GDPR) **Directive 2016/680** on the processing of personal data for the purposes of the prevention, investigation, detection or prosecution of criminal offences or the execution of criminal penalties, and on the free movement of such data ***X v Commission of the European Communities*** (Case C-404/92 P) ***Bodil Lindqvist*** (Case C-101/01) ***P Commission v Bavarian Lager*** (Case C-28/08) ***Volker und Markus Schecke and Eifert*** (Joined Cases C-92/09 and C-93/09) ***Google Spain v AEPD and Mario Costeja Gonzalez*** (Case C-131/12) ***Digital Rights Ireland*** and ***Seitlinger and Others*** (Joined Cases C-293/12 and C-594/12)

Right	Text of the right	Relevant secondary legislation and case law
Freedom of thought, conscience and religion	Art 10 Charter: 1. Everyone has the right to freedom of thought, conscience and religion. This right includes freedom to change religion or belief and freedom, either alone or in community with others and in public or in private, to manifest religion or belief, in worship, teaching, practice and observance. 2. The right to conscientious objection is recognised, in accordance with the national laws governing the exercise of this right. Art 9 ECHR: 1. Everyone has the right to freedom of thought, conscience and religion; this right includes freedom to change his religion or belief and freedom, either alone or in community with others and in public or private, to manifest his religion or belief, in worship, teaching, practice and observance. 2.	***Liga van Moskeeën en Islamitische Organisaties Provincie Antwerpen VZW and Others v Vlaams Gewest*** (C-426/16)
Freedom of expression and information	Art 15(3) TFEU Any citizen of the Union, and any natural or legal person residing or having its registered office in a Member State, shall have a right of access to documents of the Union institutions, bodies, offices and agencies, whatever their medium, subject to the principles and the conditions to be defined in accordance with this paragraph. Art 11 Charter: 1. Everyone has the right to freedom of expression. This right shall include freedom to hold opinions and to receive and impart information and ideas without interference by public authority and regardless of frontiers. 2. The freedom and pluralism of the media shall be respected. Art 42 Charter: Any citizen of the Union, and any natural or legal person residing or having its registered office in a Member State, has a right of access to European Parliament, Council and Commission documents. Art 10 ECHR: 1. Everyone has the right to freedom of expression. This right shall include freedom to hold opinions and to receive and impart information and ideas without interference by public authority and regardless of frontiers. . . .	**Regulation 1049/2001** regarding public access to European Parliament, Council and Commission documents (see section 2.8.2) ***The Society for the Protection of Unborn Children Ireland Ltd*** (Case C-159/90) (see also ECtHR case ***Open Door Counselling and Dublin Well Women and Others v Ireland*** (App Nos 14234/88 and 14235/88)) ***Elleneki Radiophonia Tileorasi (ERT)*** (Case C-260/89)

Table 3.1 (*Continued*)

Right	Text of the right	Relevant secondary legislation and case law
Freedom of assembly and association	Art 12 Charter: 1. Everyone has the right to freedom of peaceful assembly and to freedom of association at all levels, in particular in political, trade union and civic matters, which implies the right of everyone to form and to join trade unions for the protection of his or her interests. 2. . . . . Art 11 ECHR: 1. Everyone has the right to freedom of peaceful assembly and to freedom of association with others, including the right to form and to join trade unions for the protection of his interests. 2.	**Union Syndicale v Council** (Case 175/73) **Rutili** (Case 36/75) and **Association de Soutien aux Travailleurs Immigrés** (Case C-213/90) **Schmidberger** (Case C-112/00)
Right to education	Art 14 Charter: 1. Everyone has the right to education and to have access to vocational and continuing training. 2. This right includes the possibility to receive free compulsory education. 3.	
Workers' rights	Art 15 Charter: 1. Everyone has the right to engage in work and to pursue a freely chosen or accepted occupation. 2. Every citizen of the Union has the freedom to seek employment, to work, to exercise the right of establishment and to provide services in any Member State. Art 31 Charter: 1. Every worker has the right to working conditions which respect his or her health, safety and dignity. 2. Every worker has the right to limitation of maximum working hours, to daily and weekly rest periods and to an annual period of paid leave. Art 28 Charter: Workers and employers, or their respective organisations, have, in accordance with Community law and national laws and practices, the right to negotiate and conclude collective agreements at the appropriate levels and, in cases of conflicts of interest, to take collective action to defend their interests, including strike action.	Community Charter of the Fundamental Social Rights of Workers **Commission v Germany** (Case C-280/93)

Right	Text of the right	Relevant secondary legislation and case law
Right to property	Art 17 Charter 1. Everyone has the right to own, use, dispose of and bequeath his or her lawfully acquired possessions. No one may be deprived of his or her possessions, except in the public interest and in the cases and under the conditions provided for by law… 2. Intellectual property shall be protected.	**Regulations 2016/1103 and 2016/1104** on implementing enhanced cooperation in the area of jurisdiction, applicable law and the recognition and enforcement of decisions in matters of matrimonial property regimes and the property consequences of registered partnerships **Directive 2019/790** on copyright and related rights in the Digital Single Market ***Nold* v Commission** (Case 4/73) **Hauer v Land Rheinland-Pfalz** (Case 44/79) **Wachauf** (Case 5/88) **Commission v Germany** (Case C-280/93) **Zino Davidoff SA v A & G Imports Ltd** and **Levi Strauss & Co. and Others v Tesco Stores Ltd and Others** (Joined Cases C-414/99 to C-416/99)
Right to asylum	Art 18 Charter: The right to asylum shall be guaranteed with due respect for the rules of the Geneva Convention of 28 July 1951 and the Protocol of 31 January 1967 relating to the status of refugees and in accordance with the Treaty establishing the European Community.	**Directive 2003/9** laying down minimum standards for the reception of asylum seekers **Directive 2004/83** on minimum standards for the qualification and status of third country nationals or stateless persons as refugees or as persons who otherwise need international protection **Directive 2005/85** on minimum standards on procedures in Member States for granting and withdrawing refugee status **Minister voor Immigratie en Asiel** (Case C-199/12)
Equality and non-discrimination	Art 2 TEU: The Union is founded on the values of respect for human dignity, freedom, democracy, equality, the rule of law and respect for human rights, including the rights of persons belonging to minorities. These values are common to the Member States in a society in which pluralism, non-discrimination, tolerance, justice, solidarity and equality between women and men prevail. Art 3(3) TEU: The Union … shall combat social exclusion and discrimination, and shall promote social justice and protection, equality between women and men, solidarity between generations and protection of the rights of the child.	**Directive 2000/43** implementing the principle of equal treatment between persons irrespective of racial or ethnic origin **Directive 2000/78** establishing a general framework for equal treatment in employment and occupation **Directive 2004/113** implementing the principle of equal treatment between men and women in the access to and supply of goods and services **Directive 2006/54** implementing the principle of equal opportunities and equal treatment of men and women in matters of employment and occupation **Framework Decision 2008/913** on combating certain forms and expressions of racism and xenophobia by means of criminal law

Table 3.1 (Continued)

Right	Text of the right	Relevant secondary legislation and case law
	Art 9 TEU: In all its activities, the Union shall observe the principle of the equality of its citizens, who shall receive equal attention from its institutions, bodies, offices and agencies. . . . Art 8 TFEU: In all its activities, the Union shall aim to eliminate inequalities, and to promote equality, between men and women. Art 10 TFEU: In defining and implementing its policies and activities, the Union shall aim to combat discrimination based on sex, racial or ethnic origin, religion or belief, disability, age or sexual orientation. Art 18 TFEU: Within the scope of application of the Treaties, and without prejudice to any special provisions contained therein, any discrimination on grounds of nationality shall be prohibited. Art 19 TFEU: … the Council … may take appropriate action to combat discrimination based on sex, racial or ethnic origin, religion or belief, disability, age or sexual orientation. Art 157 TFEU: 1. Each Member State shall ensure that the principle of equal pay for male and female workers for equal work or work of equal value is applied. 2. . . . . Art 20 Charter: Everyone is equal before the law. Art 21 Charter: 1. Any discrimination based on any ground such as sex, race, colour, ethnic or social origin, genetic features, language, religion or belief, political or any other opinion, membership of a national minority, property, birth, disability, age or sexual orientation shall be prohibited.	Proposal for a Directive on implementing the principle of equal treatment between persons irrespective of religion or belief, disability, age or sexual orientation (COM (2008) 420) *Graff v Hauptzollamt Köln-Rheinau* (Case C-351/92) *Dekker v Stichting Vormingscentrum voor Jonge Volwassen (VJV-Centrum) Plus* (Case C-177/88) *Webb v EMO Air Cargo (UK) Ltd* (Case C-32/93) *P v S and Cornwall County Council* (Case C-13/94) *Association belge des Consommateurs Test-Achats ASBL and Others v Conseil des ministres* (Case C-236/09) *Elbal Moreno v Instituto Nacional de la Seguridad Social* (Case C-385/11) *Enderby v Frenchay Health Authority and Secretary of State for Health* (Case C-127/92) *S Coleman v Attridge Law and Steve Law* (Case 303/06) *Kücükdeveci v Swedex* (Case C-555/07) *Coman and Others v Inspectoratul General pentru Imigrări* (Case C-673/16) *Villar Láiz v Instituto Nacional de la Seguridad Social* (Case C-161/18) *Cresco Investigation v Achatzi* (Case C-193/17)

Right	Text of the right	Relevant secondary legislation and case law
	2. Within the scope of application of the Treaty establishing the European Community and of the Treaty on European Union, and without prejudice to the special provisions of those Treaties, any discrimination on grounds of nationality shall be prohibited. Art 23 Charter: Equality between men and women must be ensured in all areas, including employment, work and pay. The principle of equality shall not prevent the maintenance or adoption of measures providing for specific advantages in favour of the under-represented sex. Art 14 ECHR: The enjoyment of the rights and freedoms set forth in this Convention shall be secured without discrimination on any ground such as sex, race, colour, language, religion, political or other opinion, national or social origin, association with a national minority, property, birth or other status.	
Rights of the child	Art 3(3) TEU: The Union … shall promote … protection of the rights of the child. Art 24 Charter: 1. Children shall have the right to such protection and care as is necessary for their well-being. … 2. In all actions relating to children, whether taken by public authorities or private institutions, the child's best interests must be a primary consideration. 3. … Art 32 Charter: The employment of children is prohibited. The minimum age of admission to employment may not be lower than the minimum school-leaving age… Young people admitted to work must have working conditions appropriate to their age and be protected against economic exploitation and any work likely to harm their safety, health or physical, mental, moral or social development or to interfere with their education.	**Directive 94/33** on the protection of young people at work ***Doris Povse* v *Mauro Alpago*** (C-211/10 PPU)

Table 3.1 (Continued)

Right	Text of the right	Relevant secondary legislation and case law
Rights of elderly and disabled persons	Art 25 Charter: The Union recognises and respects the rights of the elderly to lead a life of dignity and independence and to participate in social and cultural life. Art 26 Charter: The Union recognises and respects the right of persons with disabilities to benefit from measures designed to ensure their independence, social and occupational integration and participation in the life of the community.	Proposal for a Directive on implementing the principle of equal treatment between persons irrespective of religion or belief, disability, age or sexual orientation (COM (2008) 420) **Commission v Italy** (Case C-312/11)
Social security and social assistance	Art 34 Charter: 1. The Union recognises and respects the entitlement to social security benefits and social services providing protection in cases such as maternity, illness, industrial accidents, dependency or old age, and in the case of loss of employment, in accordance with the rules laid down by Community law and national laws and practices. 2.	See Chapters 9 and 10
Health care	Art 35 Charter: Everyone has the right of access to preventive health care and the right to benefit from medical treatment under the conditions established by national laws and practices. A high level of human health protection shall be ensured in the definition and implementation of all Union policies and activities.	
Environmental protection	Art 37 Charter: A high level of environmental protection and the improvement of the quality of the environment must be integrated into the policies of the Union and ensured in accordance with the principle of sustainable development.	Many secondary acts, for example: **Directive 92/43** on the conservation of natural habitats and of wild fauna and flora; and **Directive 2011/92** on the assessment of the effects of certain public and private projects on the environment
Consumer protection	Art 38 Charter: Union policies shall ensure a high level of consumer protection.	**Directive 2011/83** on consumer rights **Regulation 2019/115** on promoting fairness and transparency for business users of online intermediation services

Right	Text of the right	Relevant secondary legislation and case law
Freedom of movement and residence	Art 21 TFEU: Every citizen of the Union shall have the right to move and reside freely within the territory of the Member States. . . . Art 45 Charter: 1. Every citizen of the Union has the right to move and reside freely within the territory of the Member States. 2. . . .	See Chapters 9 and 10
Right to an effective remedy and to a fair trial	Art 47 Charter: Everyone whose rights and freedoms guaranteed by the law of the Union are violated has the right to an effective remedy before a tribunal in compliance with the conditions laid down in this Article. Everyone is entitled to a fair and public hearing within a reasonable time by an independent and impartial tribunal previously established by law. Everyone shall have the possibility of being advised, defended and represented. Legal aid shall be made available to those who lack sufficient resources in so far as such aid is necessary to ensure effective access to justice. Art 48 Charter: 1. Everyone who has been charged shall be presumed innocent until proved guilty according to law. 2. Respect for the rights of the defence of anyone who has been charged shall be guaranteed. Art 49 Charter: 1. No one shall be held guilty of any criminal offence on account of any act or omission which did not constitute a criminal offence under national law or international law at the time when it was committed. . . . Art 50 Charter: No one shall be liable to be tried or punished again in criminal proceedings for an offence for which he or she has already been finally acquitted or convicted within the Union in accordance with the law.	**Directive 2016/343** on the strengthening of certain aspects of the presumption of innocence and of the right to be present at the trial in criminal proceedings **Directive 2016/1919** on legal aid for suspects and accused persons in criminal proceedings and for requested persons in European arrest warrant proceedings **Johnston v Chief Constable of the RUC** (Case C-222/84) **Montecatini SpA v Commission** (C-235/92 P) **Omer Nazli and Others v Stadt Nurnburg** (Case C-340/97) **Alpha Steel v Commission** (Case C-14/81) **Commission of the European Communities v Hellenic Republic** (Case C-387/97) **Hoechst v Commission** (Case 46/87) **Australia Mining & Smelting Ltd v Commission** (Case 155/79) **Alassini and Others** (joined cases C-317/08 to C-320/08) **Åklagaren v Hans Åkerberg Fransson** (Case C-617/10) **Melloni v Ministerio Fiscal** (Case C-399/11) **Taricco and others** (Case C105/14) **MAS and MB** (Case C42/17 – '**Taricco II**')

Table 3.1 (Continued)

Right	Text of the right	Relevant secondary legislation and case law
	Art 4 ECHR: 1. No one shall be liable to be tried or punished again in criminal proceedings under the jurisdiction of the same State for an offence for which he has already been finally acquitted or convicted in accordance with the law and penal procedure of that State. 2. . . . . Art 5 ECHR: 2. Everyone who is arrested shall be informed promptly, in a language which he understands, of the reasons for his arrest and of any charge against him. 3. Everyone arrested or detained in accordance with the provisions of paragraph 1 (c) of this Article shall be brought promptly before a judge or other officer authorised by law to exercise judicial power and shall be entitled to trial within a reasonable time or to release pending trial… Art 6 ECHR: 1. In the determination of his civil rights and obligations or of any criminal charge against him, everyone is entitled to a fair and public hearing within a reasonable time by an independent and impartial tribunal established by law… 2. Everyone charged with a criminal offence shall be presumed innocent until proved guilty according to law. Art 13 ECHR: Everyone whose rights and freedoms as set forth in this Convention are violated shall have an effective remedy before a national authority notwithstanding that the violation has been committed by persons acting in an official capacity.	

The European Pillar of Social Rights (ESPR)

While currently only having the status of soft law, the ESPR is worthy of consideration in so far as it indicates the potential direction of the Union's fundamental rights development. The ESPR primarily consists of a recommendation by the Commission (26 April 2017) and a draft proclamation expressing the commitment of the Commission, the Council and the

European Parliament to 20 principles (17 November 2017). These principles are divided into three main categories:

- Equal opportunities and access to the labour market;
- Fair working conditions; and
- Social protections and inclusion.

While some of the principles reiterate rights that are well-established under EU law, others look beyond the current scope of Union law. For example, the ESPR includes principles on a right to fair wages that provide a decent standard of living, assistance for the homeless and social protection for the self-employed. Therefore, if enforced, the ESPR would represent a significant expansion of the Union's fundamental rights corpus. However, the ESPR's current status as soft law means that it is not legally binding and essentially just indicates agreement between the Union institutions on social rights that they would like to be able to protect. It may therefore prove to be inconsequential. However, it is also possible that the ESPR could provide inspiration and guidance for the Court of Justice of the European Union in its rulings on relevant cases; it is possible that certain principles could subsequently become woven into the fabric of EU fundamental rights protections in this way.

> See section 3.6.1 on recommendations

3.4 Secondary legislation – regulations, directives and decisions

Objective 4

Article 288(1) TFEU sets out the different types of Union legal acts:

> To exercise the Union's competences, the institutions shall adopt regulations, directives, decisions, recommendations and opinions.

Each of these types of legal act is different in nature and produces different consequences:

- **Regulations** shall have general application. They shall be binding in their entirety and directly applicable in all Member States (Art 288(2) TFEU).
- **Directives** shall be binding, as to the result to be achieved, upon each Member State to which they are addressed, but shall leave to the national authorities the choice of form and methods (Art 288(3) TFEU).
- **Decisions** shall be binding in their entirety. A decision which specifies those to whom it is addressed shall be binding only upon them (Art 288(4) TFEU).
- **Recommendations and opinions** shall have no binding force (Art 288(5) TFEU).

Article 288 TFEU provides that regulations, directives and decisions are 'binding' and are therefore legally enforceable. In contrast, recommendations and opinions have 'no binding force' and are therefore not legally enforceable. The former three measures are considered below, whereas the latter two are considered in section 3.6 on '**Soft law**' in this chapter. After regulations, directives and decisions have been examined, information is provided on the procedures by which they are adopted and the criteria they must fulfil in order to be legally valid are briefly mentioned.

3.4.1 Regulations

Article 288 TFEU provides that a regulation shall be binding upon all Member States and is **directly applicable** within all such states. Normally, if a state enters into an agreement with another state, although that agreement may be binding in international law, it will only be effective in the legal system of that state if it is incorporated into national law in accordance with the state's constitutional requirements. For example, if the UK entered into an agreement with France, in order for the agreement to be enforceable in UK courts an Act of Parliament would have to be enacted. The Act may incorporate (e.g. copy) the agreement into the relevant Act, or it may simply refer to the agreement and provide for it to be effective in the UK.

The incorporation of EU regulations into national legislation would be very burdensome, however, because the Union adopts a vast number of regulations each year. The whole Union system would very quickly grind to a halt if a regulation had to be incorporated into the national law of each Member State before it was effective. Regulations, especially in the agricultural policy area, quite often require rapid implementation in order to have the desired effect. Such regulations would lose their effect if the Union had to wait for each Member State to incorporate them into their respective national legal systems.

> See section 3.4.5 on the Official Journal

For this reason, **Article 288 TFEU** provides that a regulation shall be **directly applicable.** This means that EU regulations shall be taken to have been incorporated into the national legal system of each of the Member States automatically, and will come into force within the Member State on the date that is specified within the regulation or on the twentieth day after publication in the **Official Journal** (Art 297 TFEU). Regulations are binding on anyone coming within their scope throughout the whole of the European Union. They require no further legislative action by Member States and can be applied by the courts of the Member States as soon as they become operative.

> The European Communities Act 1972 is discussed in section 4.4.1

In the UK, the **European Communities Act 1972** (as amended) provides for the direct applicability of EU regulations. Under the European Union (Withdrawal) Act 2018, the European Communities Act 1972 was repealed on the day that the UK exited the Union (31 January 2020) and all EU law that was in force at that time was transposed into domestic legislation.

3.4.2 Directives

A directive differs from a regulation in that it applies only to those Member States to whom it is addressed, although normally a directive will be addressed to all the Member States. A directive sets out the result to be achieved, but leaves some choice to each Member State as to the form and method that they can adopt to achieve the end result. A directive will quite often provide a Member State with a range of options it can choose from when implementing the measure.

> See Chapter 8 for further information on the implementation and enforcement of directives

A directive is not directly applicable. It requires each Member State to incorporate the directive in order for it to be given effect in the national legal system. In the UK, this requires the enactment of an Act of Parliament or delegated legislation.

As with regulations, directives will come into force on the date specified in the directive or, if no date is specified, on the twentieth day after publication in the **Official Journal** (Art 297(1) TFEU). They will also specify a deadline by which Member States must have implemented the directive.

> **Reflection:** Regulation or directive?
>
> Enabling the Union to legislate by means of either a regulation or a directive provides some flexibility. Usually the Union institution empowered to propose legislation is provided with some degree of flexibility as to the form of instrument, be it a regulation, a directive or some other

instrument. However, some Treaty articles state the mode of instrument (e.g. Art 109 TFEU, which specifies that the Council may make regulations, and Art 115 TFEU, which specifies that the Council should issue directives).

The choice of whether to issue a regulation or a directive can be important given the difference between the instruments. As discussed above, regulations are directly applicable in that they become part of the Member States' national legal systems just as they are. It is therefore necessary for a regulation to be precise and clear. Comparatively, directives can be a much looser instrument. A directive sets out the result to be achieved, while leaving some degree of discretion to the Member State as to the choice of form and method for achieving that end result. However, despite this apparent flexibility, a directive may nevertheless contain very specific provisions, which may combine with the general principles of EU law that Member States must uphold to leave limited options available to the Member State in practice.

3.4.3 Decisions

Article 288 TFEU provides that a decision is binding in its entirety. **Article 297(2) TFEU** provides that if a decision specifies those to whom it is addressed, such persons must be notified of the decision, and the decision will only take effect upon such notification. However, if a decision does not specify those to whom it is addressed, it will take effect either on the date specified in the decision or, if there is no such date specified, on the twentieth day following its publication in the **Official Journal** (Art 297(2) TFEU).

The same can be said of decisions as can be said of regulations and directives, in that the Treaty articles are generally left open to allow the relevant institutions to determine whether a decision or a different type of act would be best. However, some articles specify when the mode of the instrument shall be a decision, such as Article 105(2) TFEU concerning the infringement of Union competition rules.

3.4.4 Procedures for adopting legislative acts

Article 288 TFEU provides that regulations, directives and decisions constitute 'legal acts' of the EU. **Article 289(3) TFEU** provides that '**legal acts** adopted by **legislative procedure** shall constitute **legislative acts**'. There are two legislative procedures prescribed by the TFEU:

(i) the '**ordinary legislative procedure**' (Art 289(1) TFEU); and
(ii) the '**special legislative procedure**' (Art 289(2) TFEU).

Therefore, a regulation, directive or decision adopted by either the ordinary or special legislative procedure will constitute a legislative act. In a few cases, the EU Treaties make provision for regulations, directives and decisions to be adopted using some other procedure. Where the procedure used is neither the ordinary nor special legislative procedure, the resultant act is a 'legal act' but not a 'legislative act'. The practical impact of the differentiation between a legal act which is a legislative act and one which is not, is that the EU Treaties contain additional provisions which apply solely to legislative acts. For example, Article 290 TFEU allows a legislative act to incorporate a power of delegation, which if exercised will enable the Commission to adopt non-legislative acts of general application. This distinction is also relevant in relation to legal standing to challenge the validity of Union acts (see Chapter 6).

▶ See below on delegated acts

The ordinary legislative procedure, as suggested by its title, applies in the vast majority of cases. This procedure is practically identical to the former co-decision procedure (Art 294 TFEU (previously Art 251 EC Treaty)); see below.

The special legislative procedure refers to specific cases where the Treaties provide for the adoption of a regulation, directive or decision by the European Parliament with the Council's involvement, or by the Council with the participation of the European Parliament (Art 289(2) TFEU).

There now follows a detailed discussion of the ordinary legislative procedure, the special legislative procedure and procedures that produce non-legislative legal acts.

Ordinary legislative procedure

The ordinary legislative procedure must be applied wherever the **legal base** (sometimes also referred to as the legal basis) provides that an act shall be adopted 'in accordance with the ordinary legislative procedure' (Art 294(1) TFEU).

The ordinary legislative procedure starts with the Commission submitting a proposal to the European Parliament and the Council (Art 294(2) TFEU). The European Parliament and the Council may then amend the proposal and must agree on a final version before the Council can adopt the measure. Figure 3.4 comprises a flowchart setting out the application of the **Article 294 TFEU** ordinary legislative procedure. The bright blue boxes indicate the successful adoption of a legislative act, while the dark grey boxes indicate the termination of the procedure and the failure to adopt an act.

Each stage of the procedure is then discussed in depth.

Legislative proposals

▶ See section 4.2.2 for more detail on selecting a legal base

Under the **principle of conferral**, as stipulated in **Article 5(2) TEU**, secondary legislation can only be enacted if the relevant institution is empowered by the Treaties to adopt measures in the relevant area and/or in pursuit of a relevant objective (see Chapter 4). The provision that confers the competence to Union institutions to enact legislation for a specific purpose is referred to as the **legal base** of that measure. Whenever the institutions seek to adopt secondary legislation, the institution which makes the proposal, which is normally the **Commission**, must identify a relevant legal base within the Treaty. This facilitates the assessment of proposed legislation, as it can be questioned, for example, whether the legislation is an effective and proportionate means of pursuing the aim established by the legal base. Additionally, the relevant provision of the Treaties may specify that a particular form of secondary legislation should be used. Without a legal base, the institutions are prevented from acting.

However, if no specific power has been provided by the Treaties, **Article 352(1) TFEU** (also known as the **flexibility clause**) provides the Union with a **general legislative power**:

> If action by the Union should prove necessary, within the framework of the policies defined in the Treaties, to attain one of the objectives set out in the Treaties, and the Treaties have not provided the necessary powers, the Council, acting unanimously on a proposal from the Commission and after obtaining the consent of the European Parliament, shall adopt the appropriate measures.

▶ See section 4.2.2 on Article 352 TFEU

Compared to the former Article 308 EC Treaty, the scope of Article 352 TFEU appears wider, as the former article was confined to the internal market. However, the conditions under which Article 352 TFEU can be exercised are stricter in that, as well as requiring unanimity in the Council, the consent of the European Parliament must also be obtained. Through the Parliament, then, there has been a degree of democratic oversight over the use of the general legislative power since the ToL.

3.4 SECONDARY LEGISLATION – REGULATIONS, DIRECTIVES AND DECISIONS

Figure 3.4 The ordinary legislative procedure

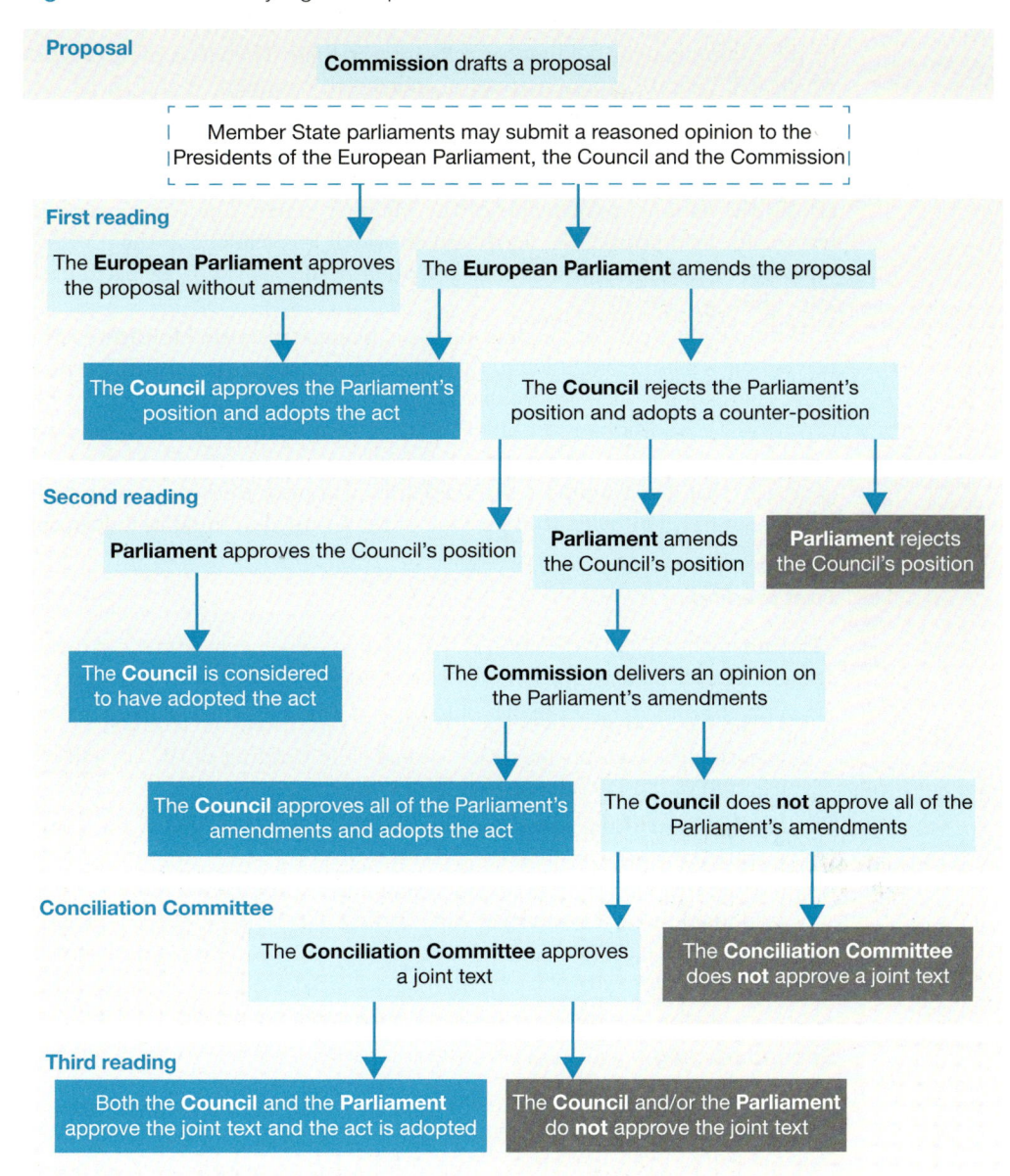

Proposal
- Commission drafts a proposal
- Member State parliaments may submit a reasoned opinion to the Presidents of the European Parliament, the Council and the Commission

First reading
- The European Parliament approves the proposal without amendments
  - The Council approves the Parliament's position and adopts the act
- The European Parliament amends the proposal
  - The Council rejects the Parliament's position and adopts a counter-position

Second reading
- Parliament approves the Council's position
  - The Council is considered to have adopted the act
- Parliament amends the Council's position
  - The Commission delivers an opinion on the Parliament's amendments
    - The Council approves all of the Parliament's amendments and adopts the act
    - The Council does **not** approve all of the Parliament's amendments
- Parliament rejects the Council's position

Conciliation Committee
- The Conciliation Committee approves a joint text
- The Conciliation Committee does **not** approve a joint text

Third reading
- Both the Council and the Parliament approve the joint text and the act is adopted
- The Council and/or the Parliament do **not** approve the joint text

If the Commission is not forthcoming with a proposal that the European Parliament feels is warranted, **Article 225 TFEU** provides that the Parliament, acting by a majority of its component members, may:

> … request the Commission to submit any appropriate proposal on matters on which it considers that a Union act is required for the purposes of implementing the Treaties. If the Commission does not submit a proposal it shall inform the European Parliament of the reasons.

> The organisational structure of the Commission is outlined in section 2.3.2

The appropriate Directorate General – assisted by one of the Commission's advisory committees – will prepare the first draft of a legislative proposal, which will initially be approved by the Commissioner holding the relevant portfolio. The views of the advisory committees, which will contain representatives of industrial, commercial and social interests from the Member States, are not in any sense binding on the Commission. The Commission, voting as a collegiate body on a simple majority basis, will then consider the proposal.

The Commission sends a draft proposal to the European Parliament, the Council and also to the national parliaments of the Member States. The Commission is bound to give reasons for its proposal, the legal base on which it is made, and the process through which it passed, including the institutions and other bodies which participated in the decision (Art 296 TFEU).

> The principle of subsidiarity is discussed in section 3.3.1

Within eight weeks of the draft proposal being transmitted to them, national parliaments may submit a reasoned opinion to the Presidents of the European Parliament, the Council and the Commission if they believe that the proposal infringes upon the principle of subsidiarity (Protocol 2). Additionally, in order to facilitate agreement between the Parliament and the Council, and therefore to smooth the legislative process, the Council may adopt a 'general approach' that it communicates to the Parliament prior to the first reading. This enables the Parliament to keep the general outlook of the Council in mind as it develops its position.

First reading

The Parliament adopts its position at first reading, which may or may not involve amendments, and communicates it to the Council (Art 294(3) TFEU). There are then two possibilities:

(i) **If the Council approves** the Parliament's position, the Council, acting by a qualified majority, shall adopt the act concerned. The wording of the act will correspond to the position of the Parliament (Art 294(4) TFEU); or

(ii) **If the Council does not approve** the Parliament's position, the Council, acting by a qualified majority, shall adopt a counter-position and communicate it to the Parliament (Art 294(5) TFEU). The Council shall inform the Parliament fully of the reasons why it adopted its own position at first reading (Art 294(6) TFEU), including reasons why the Council has rejected the Parliament's position. The Commission shall also inform the Parliament fully of its position (Art 294(6) TFEU).

Second reading

Within three months of the Council's position being communicated to the European Parliament, if the Parliament either fails to make a decision, or approves the Council's position, the Council will be deemed to have adopted the act in accordance with its position (Art 294(7)(a) TFEU). Alternatively, within this three-month period, Parliament may:

- by a majority of its component members reject the Council's position, in which case the act is deemed not to have been adopted (Art 294(7)(b) TFEU); or
- by a majority of its component members, propose amendments to the Council's position (Art 294(7)(c) TFEU).

If amendments have been proposed by the European Parliament, the amended text is forwarded to both the Council and the Commission. The Commission then delivers an opinion on the Parliament's amendments (Art 294(7)(c) TFEU).

Within three months of receiving the Parliament's amended text, the Council has two options:

- the Council approves *all* the amendments of the Parliament acting: (i) by a qualified majority if the Commission has also accepted all the amendments; (ii) by unanimity if the Commission has rejected all the amendments; or (iii) by a mixture of the two if the Commission has accepted some (qualified majority) and rejected others (unanimity). In this case the act is deemed to have been adopted (Art 294(8)(a) and 294(9) TFEU); or
- the Council does not approve all the amendments. In this case, the President of the Council, in agreement with the President of the European Parliament, shall convene a meeting of the Conciliation Committee within six weeks (Art 294(8)(b) TFEU).

Conciliation Committee

The details of the conciliation procedure are set out in **Article 296 TFEU**. The Conciliation Committee consists of an equal number of members or representatives of the Council and of the European Parliament (Art 296(10) TFEU). Their task is to agree a joint text based on the positions of the Council and the European Parliament at second reading (Art 296(10) TFEU). This joint text will be accepted by the Council representatives acting by a qualified majority and the Parliament representatives acting by a majority. The Commission takes part in the discussions and 'shall take all necessary initiatives with a view to reconciling the positions of the European Parliament and the Council' (Art 296(11) TFEU). There are two possible outcomes. If, within six weeks of being convened, the Conciliation Committee:

- **approves a joint text**, then the act will be adopted in accordance with the joint text in a third reading within six weeks of such approval, by the Parliament acting by a majority of the votes cast (i.e. simple majority), and the Council acting by a qualified majority (Art 296(13) TFEU). The act will not be adopted if approval is not obtained from either institution; or
- **does not approve a joint text**, then the act is not adopted (Art 296(12) TFEU).

There are provisions in Article 296 TFEU for the above periods of three months and six weeks to be extended by one month and two weeks, respectively, at the initiative of the European Parliament or the Council (Art 296(14) TFEU).

It should be appreciated that the ordinary legislative procedure is very complicated and cumbersome and it is necessary to understand that this is a reflection of the competing interests between the three institutions involved in the legislative process. The European Parliament demands more powers, but the Council resists such demands. However, Article 296 TFEU has shifted some power from the Council to the Parliament because now the Parliament can actually veto a proposal. The Parliament ultimately has either to accept the proposal in totality or reject it in totality. It is therefore a negative power rather than a true (positive) legislative power. Article 296 has also made an inroad into the Commission's territory, because, if a Conciliation Committee is set up, the Council and the Parliament can agree a joint text, which may amend the Commission's proposal.

While the Article 296 procedure is an important development in the evolution of the European Parliament's legislative powers, it should be noted that:

- it only grants the Parliament an ultimate power to veto;
- the Parliament must cooperate with the Council in order to agree amendments (or at least seek a qualified majority if the matter proceeds to a Conciliation Committee);

- it is limited to certain policy areas, although the policy areas have been substantially extended by amendments made by the ToA and ToN and then further extended by the ToL, such that it is now referred to as the ordinary legislative procedure.

Special legislative procedure

As stated above, although the 'ordinary legislative procedure' applies in the vast majority of cases, **Article 289 TFEU** provides that a legislative act can also be adopted by a 'special legislative procedure'.

The special legislative procedure refers to specific cases where the Treaties provide for the adoption of a regulation, directive or decision:

(i) by **consent procedure** (formerly called the assent procedure), which gives the Parliament the power to accept or reject an act drafted by the Council; or

(ii) by **consultation procedure**, which requires the Council to consult with Parliament.

In both instances, the Council will normally be acting on a proposal from the Commission. The legal base will detail the exact role of each institution, together with the voting procedure (in the case of the Council, the voting procedure is qualified majority unless otherwise stated (Art 16(3) TEU)). The difference between the two is that the former enables the Parliament to reject a draft outright, whereas the latter only requires the Council to consult with the Parliament. In practice, the Parliament will be consulted throughout a **consent procedure** so as to maximise the likelihood that consent will be achieved and a draft will be successful. While the Council is required to consider fully the opinion of the Parliament in the **consultation procedure**, neither procedure enables the Parliament to amend a draft act. An example of a legal base where the special legislative procedure provides for the adoption of a legislative act by the **consent procedure** is Article 86(1) TFEU, which provides that:

> In order to combat crimes affecting the financial interests of the Union, the Council, by means of regulations adopted in accordance with a special legislative procedure, may establish a European Public Prosecutor's Office from Eurojust. The Council shall act unanimously after obtaining the **consent** of the European Parliament.

An example of a legal base where the special legislative procedure provides for the adoption of a legislative act by the **consultation procedure** is Article 64(3) TFEU, which provides that:

> ... only the Council, acting in accordance with a special legislative procedure, may unanimously, and after **consulting** the European Parliament, adopt measures ...

Although the Council is not required to follow the opinion of Parliament in the consent procedure, the consultation must be genuine. Parliament must have a proper opportunity to respond to the proposal. This was recognised as an essential procedural requirement by the Court of Justice in the case of *Roquette Frères* **v** *Council* (Case 138/79):

> The consultation provided for in ... the Treaty is the means which allows the Parliament to play an actual part in the legislative process of the Community [i.e. Union]. Such power represents

an essential factor in the institutional balance intended by the Treaty. Although limited, it reflects at Community [i.e. Union] level the fundamental principle that the peoples should take part in the exercise of power through the intermediary of a representative assembly. Due consultation of the Parliament in the cases provided for by the Treaty therefore constitutes **an essential formality** disregard of which means that the measure concerned is void. [p. 3360]

This principle was further developed to require re-consultation when a measure on which Parliament had already given an opinion was subsequently changed. In *European Parliament* v *Council* (Case C-65/90) the Court of Justice said that further consultation was required unless the amendments essentially corresponded to the wishes already expressed by the Parliament. Although the Council should not come to a final decision without giving the Parliament an opportunity to respond, it does not have to suspend all discussion until it receives that opinion (*European Parliament* v *Council* (Case C-417/93)).

Other procedures

As stated above, in a few cases the Treaties provide for legal acts to be adopted using a procedure other than the ordinary or special legislative procedure. Because the procedure used is neither the ordinary nor the special legislative procedure, the resultant act is a 'legal act' but not a 'legislative act' pursuant to Article 289(3) TFEU (see above).

Commission acting alone

The Commission is, in very limited policy areas, empowered by the Treaties to enact legislation. One example is Article 106(3) TFEU, which provides that:

> The Commission shall ensure the application of the provisions of this Article and shall, where necessary, address appropriate directives or decisions to Member States.

This Article is concerned with the role of the state in relation to public bodies or other bodies, to which the state has granted special or exclusive rights (e.g. privatised utility companies, such as water, gas, electricity, etc.).

Additionally, the Commission can, where provided for, adopt **delegated acts** or **implementing acts**. Under **Article 290 TFEU**, legislative acts adopted since the entry into force of the ToL on 1 December 2009 'may delegate to the Commission the power to adopt non-legislative acts of general application to supplement or amend certain non-essential elements of the legislative act'. Delegated acts may therefore make minor additions or adjustments to the substance of the original legislation. **Article 291 TFEU** then grants the power to the Commission to adopt implementing acts 'where uniform conditions for implementing legally binding Union acts are needed'. Implementing acts are therefore concerned with procedural aspects of implementing legislation. Examples of such acts include the awarding of funds, market authorisations, implementing the Common Agricultural Policy and implementing Annual Action Programmes for third countries. Delegated and implementing acts represent a simplified means of adopting minor but necessary acts of Union law. Thus, the **Interinstitutional Agreement on Better Law-Making** describes these acts as 'an integral tool for Better Law-Making, contributing to simple, up-to-date legislation and its efficient, swift implementation'. Delegated and implementing acts are adopted through a process of comitology, which is discussed in section 2.3.3. However, it is not always clear which procedure should be used to adopt a given measure.

Council and Commission acting alone

The EU Treaties empower the Council to adopt a Commission proposal, without the involvement of the Parliament, in a very limited number of policy areas. For example, Article 31 TFEU provides as follows:

> Common Customs Tariff duties shall be fixed by the Council on a proposal from the Commission.

3.4.5 Legal validity and grounds for annulment of legal acts

Secondary legislation must meet certain conditions in order to be considered valid. Under Article 263 TFEU, the Court of Justice of the European Union has the power to review the legal validity of legal acts. Such acts can be annulled by the Court on one of the following grounds:

- lack of competence;
- infringement of an essential procedural requirement;
- infringement of the Treaties or of any rule of law relating to their application; or
- misuse of powers.

These grounds for the annulment of legal acts of the Union are discussed in detail in Chapter 6.

Additionally, **Article 297(1) TFEU** provides that all legislative acts must be published in the **Official Journal**. The Official Journal is a Union publication which consists of two related series and a supplement:

- **The L series (legislation)** contains all the legislative acts that the Treaties require to be published, as well as other acts.
- **The C series (information and notices)** covers the complete range of information other than legislation, including recommendations and opinions.
- **The S series** is a supplement containing invitations to tender for public works and supply contracts.

The L and C series are published daily (except Sunday) and the supplement is published every day from Tuesday to Saturday. Legislative acts and non-legislative acts (i.e. regulations, directives and decisions) will be published in the L series. The act will be cited alongside a reference, such as OJ 1990 L 257/13. In full, this reference can be decoded as: Official Journal, published in 1990, L series, issue number 257, page 13. In accordance with **Article 288(1) TFEU**, secondary legislation enters into force on the date specified in the act, or – if there is no such date specified – on the twentieth day following its publication in the Official Journal.

Issues of the *Official Journal* which have been published since 1998 can be accessed from the Eur-lex website:

> https://eur-lex.europa.eu/homepage.html

> **Reflection:** EU secondary legislation in the UK after Brexit
>
> As EU directives have been incorporated into UK law through national legislative acts, these national acts automatically remain in force after Brexit. However, as the UK is no longer bound to implement EU law, it is likely that, sooner or later, these national acts will be reviewed and may be subject to amendments or repeal where they are deemed not to be in the best interests of the UK.
>
> EU regulations, on the other hand, are directly applicable within the Member States, so there are no national legislative acts through which EU regulations will continue to be enforceable in the currently UK after Brexit. In response to this predicament, the European Union (Withdrawal) Act 2018 provides for the transposition of regulations and other relevant EU law into domestic legislation. This creates a new category of domestic legislation: 'retained EU law'. Retained EU law includes all 'direct EU legislation' – i.e. any EU legislation that is directly applicable to the UK immediately prior to Brexit – as well as EU and domestic case law that pertains to such legislation. The European Union (Withdrawal) Act 2018 sets out the procedures that can be used to amend, repeal or revoke retained EU law.
>
> The process of disentangling EU law from UK law is highly complex. For one thing, EU law permeates many different areas of UK law and is not always easy to distinguish. Additionally, simply stating that EU regulations and national measures implementing EU directives continue to be binding in UK law does not work in the many instances where these acts refer to EU institutions or bodies. Furthermore, agreeing which EU laws should be amended and how is likely to prove extremely challenging and, at times, controversial. Indeed, the provisions in the European Union (Withdrawal) Act 2018 for the modification of retained EU law have provoked concern over the scope of the powers that they grant, with some commentators referring to them critically as 'Henry VIII' provisions.

3.5 Decisions of the Court of Justice of the European Union

Objective 5

Article 19(1) TEU, as amended by the ToL, provides that 'the Court of Justice, the General Court and specialised courts' shall be collectively referred to as the Court of Justice of the European Union. The General Court is now the name given to the former Court of First Instance.

The jurisprudence (i.e. case law) of the Court of Justice of the European Union is a major source of law. It encompasses not only all the formal decisions of the Court, but also the principles enunciated in its judgments and opinions. The Treaties and the implementing legislation do not, between them, contain an exhaustive statement of the relevant law, and much of the work of the Court of Justice of the European Union has been to put flesh on the legislative bones. The creative jurisprudence of the Court in particular, and its willingness to interpret measures in such a way as to make them effective, to achieve the *effet utile*, has done much to assist in the attainment of the general objectives of the Treaties.

The role of the Court of Justice of the European Union in developing Union law is noted above in relation to the general principles of EU law and is discussed further throughout the following chapters.

3.6 Soft law

Objective 6

Instruments which are not legally enforceable but which may aid the interpretation and/or application of Union law are referred to as 'soft laws'. Such instruments may be referred to by the Court of Justice of the European Union when interpreting Union law and should be taken into consideration by the Member States where they supplement or otherwise shed light on binding provisions. In addition, soft law can provide a means of establishing a position in instances when it is not possible or practical to enact 'hard' law (Snyder, 1993). Two particular forms of 'soft law' are considered further here: recommendations and opinions.

3.6.1 Recommendations and opinions

Article 288 TFEU explicitly states that recommendations and opinions shall not have any binding force. However, the use of these two instruments may be used to clarify matters in a formal way. The former Article 211 EC Treaty empowered the Commission to formulate recommendations or deliver opinions on matters dealt with in the Treaty, not only where expressly provided for, but also whenever it considered it expedient. This provision has not been replicated in the TEU or the TFEU, as amended by the ToL. However, **Article 17(1) TEU** states that the Commission shall 'promote the general interest of the Union and take appropriate initiatives to that end'. This provision empowers the Commission to formulate recommendations or deliver opinions as appropriate, provided they 'promote the general interest of the Union'.

Although recommendations and opinions have no immediate legal force, they may achieve some legal effect as persuasive authority if they are subsequently referred to, and taken into account, in a decision of the Court of Justice of the European Union. National courts are bound to take them into account when interpreting Union measures where they elucidate the purpose of the legislation: *Grimaldi* v *Fonds des Maladies Professionnelles* (Case C-322/88).

3.7 International sources of law

Objective 7

In addition to its own internally developed law, the activities of the Union are regulated by the international treaties to which it is a party. Furthermore, the Union may refer to treaties outside of the structure of the Union to which its Member States are parties. The status of these external sources of law within EU law is examined below.

3.7.1 International treaties negotiated by the Union

Article 47 TEU provides that the Union shall have legal personality, enabling it to enter into international treaties and agreements on behalf of the Member States in areas where it has exclusive competence (see Chapter 4). The procedure for negotiating and concluding treaties with third (i.e. non-EU) countries or international organisations is set out in **Article 218 TFEU**. Paragraph 2 states that:

> The Council shall authorise the opening of negotiations, adopt negotiating directives, authorise the signing of agreements and conclude them.

Article 218(3) TFEU then provides for the involvement of the Commission or the High Representative of the Union for Foreign Affairs and Security Policy if the international agreement in question relates exclusively or principally to the common foreign and security policy.

The category of international treaties includes not only **multilateral treaties** to which the Union is a party but also **accession treaties** and **association agreements** concluded by the Union with individual states. Additionally, with the initiation of the Article 50 TEU exit process by the UK in March 2017, **withdrawal treaties** are also relevant to this category.

Multilateral treaties

One example of a multilateral treaty to which the Union is a party is the General Agreement on Tariffs and Trade (GATT). The GATT agreement was held in the case of *International Fruit* (Case 21–24/72) to be binding on the Union. The Court of Justice has also held that undertakings which complain to the Commission of illicit commercial practices in breach of the Union's commercial policy instrument may rely upon the GATT as forming part of the rules of international law to which the instrument applies (*Fediol* (Case 70/87)).

Accession treaties

▶ Accession criteria and procedures are outlined in section 1.1.3

A Treaty of Accession is necessary when the Union is enlarged through the addition of new Member States. The most recent Accession Treaty was concluded in 2011 to pave the way for Croatia's membership on 1 July 2013. Like the original Treaties themselves, the Treaties of Accession have been held to confer directly enforceable rights on individuals (*Rush Portuguesa* v *Office National d'Immigration* (Case C-113/89)).

Withdrawal agreements

▶ See section 1.1.3 for the full text of Article 50 TEU

Article 50(2) TEU authorises the Union to negotiate a withdrawal agreement with a Member State that is seeking to exit the Union. Although a withdrawal agreement is not necessary when a Member State leaves the Union, such an agreement helps to smooth the exit process as it establishes arrangements for the withdrawal and lay the foundations for the state's future relationship with the Union. Key features of the UK withdrawal agreement include:

- a transition period until the end of December 2020, during which the UK will remain a member of the customs union and the single market and EU law will continue to apply to the UK;
- the payment of a 'divorce' settlement;
- special arrangements for Northern Ireland to remain aligned with EU trade regulations, so as to prevent a 'hard' border with the Republic of Ireland;
- executive powers to deal with issues arising from withdrawal, including in relation to the border between Northern Ireland and Ireland;

The UK withdrawal agreement, which has been approved by the UK parliament and the EU, leaves many other details – especially relating to trade – to be determined during the transition period. The agreement has been criticised for failing to provide guarantees in relation to workers rights, the protection of refugees and parliamentary oversight of trade negotiations.

The process for negotiating a withdrawal agreement, and the corresponding details applying to Brexit at the time of writing, are set out in Figure 3.5 below.

If a withdrawal agreement is not reached and extensions are not agreed, the exiting state nevertheless ceases to be a member of the Union two years after they notified the European

Figure 3.5 Procedure for withdrawing from the Union

General withdrawal agreement procedure

- The Member State that wishes to exit the Union **notifies** the **European Council** of its intention.
- The **European Council** (excluding representatives from the exiting Member State) agrees **guidelines** setting out the Union's priorities for the negotiation of a withdrawal agreement.
- The **Commission** submits recommendations to the **Council**, which then authorises the opening of negotiations and nominates a negotiator.
- Once a withdrawal agreement is finalised, it is concluded by the **Council** acting by **qualified majority** and with consent from the **European Parliament**.
- The Treaties cease to apply to the exiting state.

Brexit withdrawal agreement procedure

- UK Prime Minister notified the European Council of the UK's intention to exit the Union on **29 March 2017**.
- The European Council established guidelines for Brexit negotiations on **27 April 2017**.
- The Council issued a decision on **22 May 2017** to open Article 50 negotiations with the UK and nominated the European Commission's Chief Negotiator.
- The withdrawal agreement was passed into UK law on **23 January 2020**, was consented to by the European Parliament on 29 January 2020 and was ratified by the Council on **30 January 2020**.
- The UK ceased to participate in Union institutions on **31 January 2020** and it is expected that the Treaties will cease to apply to the UK from **1 January 2021**.

Council of their intent to exit. Unlike accession treaties, withdrawal agreements do not need to be ratified by each Member State.

Association agreements

The Union is provided with the competence to conclude association agreements in **Article 217 TFEU**:

> The Union may conclude with one or more third countries or international organisations agreements establishing an association involving reciprocal rights and obligations, common action and special procedure.

Where a country is seeking accession to the Union, an association agreement provides a basis for the implementation of the accession process. The Union also concludes association agreements with third countries for a wide range of other reasons, including the development of political, trade, social, cultural and security relationships. After Brexit, it is likely that an association agreement will be negotiated to provide for a new relationship between the UK and the Union.

In *Kupferberg* (Case 104/81), the Court of Justice held that Article 21 of the EEC–Portugal Association Agreement was directly enforceable in the national courts. The principle of direct enforcement of such agreements has enabled the nationals of states which are parties to such agreements to enforce the agreement's provisions against Member States of the Union. Similarly, in *Kziber* (Case C-18/90), the Court of Justice held that parts of the EEC–Morocco Cooperation Agreement are directly enforceable (see also, *Yousfi* v *Belgium* (Case C-58/93)).

> The principle of direct enforceability (or direct effect) is considered in section 8.2

3.7.2 International treaties negotiated by EU Member States

Member States may choose to negotiate treaties outside of the EU system either because the Union does not have the competence to legislate in a particular area or because the agreement of all Member States that is required for an act of Union legislation cannot be reached. Such international treaties are subordinate to the provisions of Union law – i.e. Member States cannot make commitments under international treaties that would affect their rights and obligations under Union law. However, this relationship between international and Union law is reversed in the case of the ECHR, as is explained below.

The European Convention on Human Rights (ECHR)

The ECHR warrants a special mention here as it crosses several of the categories that the sources of EU law are divided into. It is an external source of law that is presided over by an entirely separate court – the European Court of Human Rights (ECtHR) – but the ECHR has been internalised by the Union to a significant extent: first through the recognition of the ECHR as enshrining general principles of EU law, then by establishing that the ECtHR provides an authoritative interpretation of the rights codified in the Union's own rights document, the Charter of Fundamental Freedoms of the EU. The Court of Justice, therefore, like national courts, takes account of the ECHR when interpreting and applying Union law. Moreover, if the EU successfully accedes to the ECHR, as it is mandated to by Article 6(2) TEU, it will become fully incorporated and directly enforceable within the EU legal system. While any treaty that the Union enters into must be honoured within the relevant activities of the Union, the ECHR would – and effectively already is – unique in that it must be upheld across all areas of the Union's competence.

The ECHR is considered in further detail in section 3.3.2

Intergovernmental treaties between Member States

While the ECHR is an external source of law to which all EU Member States are a party, several other international treaties have been negotiated between some of the EU Member States externally to the Union legal system. Such treaties are often the result of the failure to achieve the necessary agreement between all EU Member States in order for a new act of EU law to be created. However, they are often formally incorporated into Union law, either in whole or in part, at a later date. Such treaties include:

- The **Schengen Agreement and Convention** was initially adopted by five of the then ten Member States with the aim of gradually abolishing border controls between them. The Treaty of Amsterdam then incorporated the Schengen acquis into Union law, with opt-outs for the UK and Ireland. Norway, Iceland and Switzerland have since joined the Schengen Area through association agreements with the Union.

- The **Prüm Convention** on the stepping up of cross-border cooperation, particularly in combating terrorism, cross-border crime and illegal migration, was signed on 27 May 2005 and has been ratified by 14 EU Member States. Some aspects of the Convention were then adopted into Union law by Council Decision 2008/615/JHA on the stepping up of cross-border cooperation, particularly in combating terrorism and cross-border crime, which was implemented by Council Decision 2008/616/JHA. These 'Prüm Decisions' were included in the UK's block opt-out of police and criminal justice measures under Protocol 36 of the ToL, but the UK later decided to participate in them.

> ➤ The Schengen acquis is discussed in depth in section 9.6; the Treaty on Stability, Coordination and Governance in the Economic and Monetary Union is briefly discussed in section 1.2.12

- The **Treaty establishing the European Stability Mechanism** was concluded by all Eurozone countries and entered into force in 2012. The Commission has expressed the intention to integrate the European Stability Mechanism (ESM) within the Union legal system in order to enhance the Economic and Monetary Union.

- The **Treaty on Stability, Coordination and Governance in the Economic and Monetary Union (TSCG)**, which was adopted as an international treaty between Member States after the UK vetoed its adoption as EU law. The TSCG became operational in all 25 Member States that signed it on 1 April 2014 (along with the UK, the Czech Republic is not a party to the TSCG).

> ➤ See section 3.2.4 on the simplified revision procedure

To better accommodate the ESM, the European Council, following the simplified revision procedure, adopted **Decision 2011/119** aiming at the amendment of **Article 136(3) TFEU**. The ensuing amendment, which entered into force once on 1 May 2013, inserted the following text:

> The Member States whose currency is the euro may establish a stability mechanism to be activated if indispensable to safeguard the stability of the euro area as a whole. The granting of any required financial assistance under the mechanism will be made subject to strict conditionality.

This amendment formalises the capacity of the Eurozone countries to act without the agreement of non-Eurozone Member States that would be required for the adoption of legal acts within the Union system. This may prove advantageous in instances when action is required rapidly in order to be effective, even if such intergovernmental actions may later be integrated into the Union, as may be the case with the ESM. However, it remains unclear whether and how intergovernmental treaties such as the ESM treaty and the TSCG can be administered and enforced by Union institutions.

> **Reflection:** Brexit and international agreements
>
> International agreements that have been negotiated by the EU in areas where it has exclusive competence (see Chapter 4) will cease to apply to the UK after the end of the transition period. Where the UK wishes to continue with such agreements, which include most trade agreements, it will need to negotiate new treaties to that end. It may be possible in some instances for parties to agree to 'roll over' the provisions of the treaty to the UK; however, in the example of trade agreements, UK-specific quotas will need to be negotiated and there is no guarantee that countries won't take the opportunity to make new demands.

> Mixed agreements represent further challenges. Here, EU-only elements of the agreement will cease to apply to the UK after the end of the transition period, but elements that the UK signed and ratified in its own right will continue to apply. If it wished to withdraw from such a treaty, the UK would be subject to any withdrawal procedures specified within it and may need to negotiate transitional periods to mitigate any negative practical, economic or financial consequences. If the UK wished to remain a party of such a treaty, it might be able to do so as a third party. This would require a legal act to declare the rights and responsibilities of the UK in relation to the agreement in question, which would then need to be agreed to by the EU, its 27 Member States and any other third parties. Again, there would be no guarantee that other countries would not take this opportunity to renegotiate certain aspects of the agreement.
>
> International agreements that the UK has concluded independently from the EU, however, are not affected directly by Brexit. In particular, it should be noted that the UK's membership of the Council of Europe and the European Convention on Human Rights is not affected.

CHAPTER SUMMARY

The Treaties

- The Treaty on European Union (**TEU**) and the Treaty on the Functioning of the European Union (**TFEU**) are referred to as 'the Treaties'.
- The Treaties perform the **role of a constitution** for the Union; the Union institutions may only act in the areas, according to the procedures and to the extent to which they are permitted by the Treaties (**Art 5(2) TEU**).
- The articles of Treaties have been **renumbered** by the Treaty of Amsterdam in 1999 and by the Treaty of Lisbon in 2009.
- The Treaties were most recently revised by the **Treaty of Lisbon** in 2009, in accordance with the **ordinary revision procedure**.

General principles of EU law

- There is no comprehensive list of general principles, nor universal agreement on their exact status.
- The **Charter of Fundamental Freedoms of the EU** codifies a range of fundamental rights principles and has been legally binding since the Treaty of Lisbon entered into force in 2009 (**Art 6(1) TEU**).
- General principles may also be drawn from **constitutional rights common to the Member States** and from the **European Convention on Human Rights** (ECHR) (**Art 6(3) TEU**).
- Other general principles have been recognised as such by the Court of Justice in its interpretation of EU law.

Secondary legislation

- **Regulations, directives** and **decisions** are legally binding (**Art 288 TFEU**).
- Regulations and decisions are **directly applicable**; directives allow some discretion as to how Member States may implement them (**Art 288 TFEU**).

- **Recommendations** and **opinions** are not legally binding (**Art 288 TFEU**).
- Legislative acts must be enacted by either the **ordinary legislative procedure** or a **special legislative procedure** (Art 294 TFEU).

Case law of the Court of Justice of the EU

- The judgments of the Court of Justice of the EU are authoritative interpretations of EU law (see Chapter 4 for more detail).

International sources of law

- The Union has **legal personality** which enables it to enter into international treaties and agreements on the behalf of its Member States (**Art 47 TEU**).
- The Union can negotiate **multilateral treaties** and **association agreements** with non-Union countries, as well as **accession treaties** with countries seeking to join and **withdrawal agreements** with countries seeking to leave the Union.
- **Intergovernmental treaties** negotiated by EU Member States outside of the Union legal system are sometimes incorporated into Union law, either fully or in part, at a later date (e.g. the **ECHR**, the **Schengen acquis**, the **Prüm Convention** and potentially the **European Stability Mechanism**).

Chapter 4
Competence and supremacy of the Union

Learning objectives

At the end of this chapter you should understand:

1 The unique nature of the Union legal order.

2 The levels and types of Union competence and how the Union's powers are limited by the principles of conferral, subsidiarity and proportionality.

3 What is meant by 'the supremacy of Union law'.

4 How Union law has been incorporated into UK legislation and how this has been and will be affected by Brexit.

Key terms and concepts

Familiarity with the following terms will be helpful for understanding this chapter:

Approximation of laws – the harmonisation of the national laws of Member States

Competence – the power to take action in a particular policy area, or the general scope of an entity's authority

Conferral – the principle that the Union can only act to the extent to which the competence to do so has been bestowed upon it (conferred) by the Member States

Proportionality – the principle that the Union may only act to the extent that is necessary to achieve a legitimate aim (i.e. an aim that the Union has competence to pursue)

Subsidiarity – the principle that the Union may only act when the objectives in question cannot be better or equally well achieved by action at the national level

Supremacy – taking precedence over conflicting rules or laws, having the final say

4.1 Introduction

Objective 1

Starting in the early 1960s, the Community (now the Union) took a line of decisions that aimed to increase the effectiveness of Union law as a whole and to ensure that Member State governments abided by their Union law obligations. These decisions, which brought about the principles of **supremacy**, direct effect, indirect effect and state liability, have been described as engendering the 'constitutionalisation' of the Treaty (now the Treaties). These developments changed the nature of the Union legal order from an international organisation to something more reminiscent of the legal order of a federal state, but one that is wholly comparable to no other national or international legal system. As the commentator Alec Stone Sweet has said, these decisions of the Court of Justice transformed the EC Treaty (and therefore now the Treaties) 'from a set of horizontal legal arrangements between sovereign states, into a vertically integrated legal regime conferring judicially enforceable rights and obligations on all legal persons and entities, public and private, within the EC [i.e. Union] territory' (1998, p. 306).

This chapter focuses on the **competence** of the Union and the principle of supremacy (the principles of direct effect, indirect effect and state liability are considered in Chapter 8). These two dynamics are essential to the unique character of Union law. The competences of the Union define the scope of the Union's powers, not only by specifying when the Union institutions may act, but also by setting limits that establish when they may **not** act. Practically, such limitations on the powers of the Union promote clarity as to which policy areas are under the jurisdiction of the Union and which are the responsibility of Member States. Such limitations – within EU law and as enforced in practice – are also important for maintaining the trust of the Member States. This trust is especially important for the functioning of the principle of supremacy, which means that Union law takes precedence over any national legislation with which it conflicts. Supremacy is essential to the **effectiveness** of Union law and its **uniform application** across the Member States. In turn, the uniform application of Union law across the Member States ensures that they are all subject to the same benefits and obligations, which fosters the international relationships of equality and mutuality upon which the Union is built.

The last section of this chapter considers how Union law has been incorporated into UK law and some of the issues relating to supremacy and the division of competences that are presented by Brexit. While the supremacy of Union law will cease to apply in the UK after the transition period, this section demonstrates how domestic law has been shaped by Union law and its ongoing legacy after Brexit.

4.2 Competence of the Union

Objective 2

This section examines the factors that determine the areas in which the Union may act and the extent of the actions that it may take. The areas in which the Union has authority to act are known as **Union competences** or **areas of Union competence**. Union actions outside of or beyond these competences constitute a violation of Union law.

While the term 'competence' is often used in other contexts to mean ability or aptitude (e.g. she is a competent programmer; they were sacked for incompetence), this is not the meaning that applies in relation to EU law. Here, competence is instead synonymous with power or authority (e.g. the Union does not have the competence to act in this area).

4.2.1 The conferral of competence

The institutions of the European Union may only act in the areas in which they are granted the competence to do so by the Treaties. This is known as the principle of **conferral**. **Article 5(1) TEU** states that 'The limits of Union competences are governed by the principle of conferral'. This is then expanded upon by **Article 5(2) TEU** as follows:

> Under the principle of conferral, the Union shall act only within the limits of the competences conferred upon it by the Member States in the Treaties to attain the objectives set out therein. Competences not conferred upon the Union in the Treaties remain with the Member States.

New or expanded powers may only be conferred on the Union through the amendment of the Treaties in accordance with the **ordinary revision procedure**. For example, the Union's competence in environmental policy was added by the Single European Act in 1987. Adherence to the ordinary revision procedure ensures that there is a wide scope for the discussion of any proposed expansion of the Union's competences. The procedure also requires each Member State to ratify the final amendments, ensuring that the power to determine the scope of the Union's competence ultimately rests with the Member States.

➤ The ordinary revision procedure is set out in section 3.2.4

Competence disputes

Despite the various safeguards limiting the **competence** of the Union – including the principles of conferral, **subsidiarity** and **proportionality** (see below) – concerns and disputes still arise. Such disputes can be described as either horizontal or vertical.

Horizontal disputes occur between the Union institutions and mostly concern which legal base should be used. As explained in Chapter 3, the question of an appropriate legal base can determine which, if any, institution has the competence to act and which other institutions have to be involved. For example, cases have arisen where the Council (which predominantly represents national interests) has sought to curb the powers of the Commission (which predominantly represents Union interests), and where Parliament has challenged the competence of the Council to act without first consulting it or gaining its consent.

Vertical disputes concern the division of competences between the Union and its Member States. One particular area which remains somewhat foggy is the issue of *kompetenz-kompetenz*. This is the question of who has the competence to determine the scope of the Union's powers (who has the competence to determine competence), or, more specifically, the extent to which the Court of Justice of the EU has the competence to determine the scope of its own jurisdiction. The issue of *kompetenz-kompetenz* is examined further below in relation to the issue of the supremacy of EU law (see section 4.3.2).

4.2.2 Types of competence

Explicit competence

The European Union has three levels of explicit competence. In areas where the Union has **exclusive competence**, Member States have transferred all capacity to enact legislation to the Union. **Article 3 TFEU** lists the areas in which the Union has exclusive competence as:

- The customs Union
- The establishing of the competition rules necessary for the functioning of the internal market
- Monetary policy for the Member States whose currency is the euro
- The conservation of marine biological resources under the common fisheries policy
- Common Commercial Policy
- The conclusion of certain international agreements

In areas of **shared competence**, both the European Union and its Member States can enact legislation, but Members States may only do so where the Union has not. **Article 4 TFEU** lists the areas of shared competence as:

- The internal market
- Social policy, but only for aspects specifically defined in the Treaty
- Economic, social and territorial cohesion (regional policy)
- Agriculture and fisheries (except conservation of marine biological resources)
- The environment
- Consumer protection
- Transport
- Trans-European networks
- Energy
- The area of freedom, security and justice
- Shared safety concerns in public health matters, limited to the aspects defined in the TFEU
- Research, technological development, space
- Development cooperation and humanitarian aid

Finally, **Article 6 TFEU** sets out areas in which the Union has competence to support, coordinate or supplement the actions of Member States at a European level. These **supporting competences** are:

- Protection and improvement of human health
- Industry
- Culture
- Tourism
- Education, vocational training, youth and sport
- Civil protection
- Administrative cooperation

Particular cases which do not fit into this threefold classification are dealt with separately. This includes the following two areas, for example: coordination of economic and employment policies (Art 2(3) TFEU); and common foreign and security policy (Art 2(4) TFEU). Further information on the competences of the Union in all of the areas mentioned above can be found in the texts of the TEU and the TFEU.

Implied powers

Implied powers (also sometimes called implicit competence or derivative competence) are powers that are not explicitly conferred by the Treaties but that may be logically derived from Treaty provisions. The doctrine of implied powers has been established through the case law of the Court of Justice of the European Union, and it is therefore through the case law that it can best be understood.

In the following case, the Court of Justice was asked to determine whether the presence of an *explicit* competence to act within a particular area *internally* produced an *implicit* competence to act within that area *externally*, e.g. to conclude relevant international treaties:

Commission v Council (Case 22/70)

Facts:

The European Agreement concerning the work of crews of vehicles engaged in international road transport (known by its French acronym, AETR) was signed by the then six Member States of the EEC and other non-Member State countries in 1970. The Council had determined that the AETR should be concluded by the individual Member States and adopted a common position for the negotiations. The Commission, however, brought an action for the annulment of the Council proceedings on the grounds that it was the Community (now the Union) which had the power to negotiate international treaties in the field of transport. The Commission argued that Article 75(1) EEC Treaty (now Art 91(1) TFEU), which states that the European Parliament and the Council may take 'any other appropriate provisions' in the pursuit of a common transport policy, provided for the Union to take external actions within the field of transport. The Council, on the other hand, argued that it was not sufficient for such external powers to be implied, but rather that they must be explicitly stipulated in the Treaty.

Ruling:

The Court considered that the legality of the Council proceedings in question could not be determined without first answering the question of whether 'power to negotiate and conclude the AETR was vested in the Community [now Union] or in the Member States'.

To answer this question, the Court first referred to Article 210 EEC Treaty (now Art 47 TEU) which states that the Union has legal personality which enables it to negotiate treaties with third countries. The Court then established a link between internal measures and external relations, stating that **where the Union has the competence to establish internal rules on an issue, Member States do not then have the competence to negotiate external agreements that would affect those rules**.

The Court then considered the common transport policy in particular, noting that it encompassed transport to and from third countries and that the subject matter of the AETR was within the Union's competence. In addition, the Court noted the Union objective of establishing a common transport policy, and the Article 75(1) EEC Treaty (now Art 91(1) TFEU) permission to take 'any other appropriate provisions' in the pursuit of that objective.

The Court therefore concluded that the negotiation of international agreements in the field of transport fell within the Union's competence, regardless of the absence of a provision in the Treaties that explicitly conferred such a power to the Union.

Significance:

This judgment was innovative in its assertion that the Union has the power to conclude an international agreement in the absence of the explicit conferral of such power in the Treaties. However, this was not a broad extension of Union powers, as such competence was strongly implied within the Treaties and could only be derived in relation to areas in which the Union had internal competence.

Furthermore, the Court suggested that the Union has **exclusive competence** to negotiate international treaties in areas where it has established internal rules. This is important for ensuring that Member States cannot conclude international agreements that conflict with any rules or objectives of EU law.

Whereas the above case concerned the competence of the Union to act externally in an area where they had explicit internal competence, in the following case it was questioned whether the Commission had an implied competence to enact binding measures that it deemed to be a necessary pre-requisite for the exercise of a conferred power:

Germany v Commission (Case 287/85)

Facts:

Germany was one of several Member States that brought a case to the Court of Justice against Decision 85/381 of the Commission. The Decision required Member States to notify the Commission of draft policies concerning the migration of workers from third countries, and then to undergo a process of consultation so as to ensure that such policies were in conformity with Union policies and objectives. The applicant Member States argued that, as migration was within their exclusive competence, the Commission did not have the power to issue a binding decision in this area.

Ruling:

The Court considered the former Article 118 EEC Treaty (now Art. 153 TEU), on which Decision 85/381 was premised. The former Article mandates the Commission to promote close cooperation between the Member States in the social field, including with regard to employment and working conditions, and thereby to arrange consultations both on problems arising at national level and on those of concern to international organisations. The Court first established that information on migration policies was relevant to the Commission's tasks as established in the former Article 118 EEC Treaty. The Court then ruled that, although the competence to require notification of Member States' draft policies was not expressly conferred to the Commission by the EEC Treaty, that power was necessary in order for the Commission to exercise the power that is conferred, i.e. to arrange consultations, and was therefore implied.

Significance:

The Court established the rule that if a power is conferred by the Treaty, any auxiliary power that is required for the exercise of that first power is implicitly conferred. If this were not the case, Union institutions might often find that they are prevented from using a power that is explicitly conferred on them because the exercise of that power requires an act that they do not have the explicit competence to perform.

Subsidiary powers (flexibility and harmonisation clauses)

Where no such competence is explicitly or implicitly provided for in the Treaties, **Article 352 TFEU** (also known as the **flexibility clause**) empowers the Union to adopt measures that are necessary to attain objectives that are specified in the Treaties. This principle was first established by the Court of Justice in its Opinion 1/76. In relation to the competence of the Union to negotiate international agreements, the Court stated that:

> Whenever Community law has created for the institutions of the Community [i.e. Union] powers within its internal system **for the purpose of attaining a specific objective**, the Community [i.e. Union] has authority to enter into the international commitments necessary for the attainment of that objective even in the absence of an express provision in that connexion.

This is distinct from the implicit powers established in *Germany* v *Commission* (above), as the implicit powers there concerned the competence to take actions that are *necessary to exercise a conferred power*, whereas there are no implicit powers to take actions that are *necessary to obtain a Union objective*.

While Article 352 TFEU enables the Union to take actions that are not explicitly or implicitly provided for in the Treaties, such actions are limited in scope and are subject to heightened procedural requirements. Article 352(1) provides that:

> 1 If action by the Union should prove **necessary**, within the framework of the policies defined in the Treaties, **to attain one of the objectives set out in the Treaties**, and the Treaties have not provided the necessary powers, the Council, **acting unanimously** on a proposal from the Commission and after obtaining the consent of the European Parliament, shall adopt the appropriate measures. Where the measures in question are adopted by the Council in accordance with a special legislative procedure, it shall also act unanimously on a proposal from the Commission and after obtaining the consent of the European Parliament.

Subsidiary powers, then, are limited by the objectives of the Union that are specified in the Treaties and must be agreed to by the Commission, the Council and the Parliament. Furthermore, Article 352(3) stipulates that 'Measures based on this Article shall not entail harmonisation of Member States laws or regulations in cases where the Treaties exclude such harmonisation' and Article 352(4) excludes Article 352(1) from being used to pursue objectives pertaining to the common foreign and security policy. However, it is possible that a Union act could serve more than one objective. Therefore, the fact that a Union act serves an objective that is *beyond* the scope of the Treaties does not necessarily invalidate that act, providing that it is also necessary for the attainment of an objective that is *within* the scope of the Treaties.

The second provision in the Treaties that provides subsidiary powers is **Article 114 TFEU** (known as the **harmonisation clause**). Article 114(1) TFEU provides as follows:

> Save where otherwise provided in the Treaties, the following provisions shall apply for the achievement of the objectives set out in Article 26 [on the common market]. The European Parliament and the Council shall, acting in accordance with the **ordinary legislative procedure** and after consulting the Economic and Social Committee, adopt the **measures for the approximation of the provisions** laid down by law, regulation or administrative action in Member States **which have as their object the establishment and functioning of the internal market**.

Therefore, while Article 352 TFEU provides a general mandate to adopt measures to fulfil the objectives of the Treaties, Article 114 provides a specific power to adopt measures for the **approximation of laws** that pursue the establishment and functioning of the internal market. Article 114 TFEU thus aims to facilitate the harmonisation of laws that could otherwise result in competitive advantages and disadvantages between the different Member States. It may extend to cover harmonising measures that affect goods irrespective of their ultimate destination, including goods manufactured exclusively for export, if there is a risk that their re-import could undermine the harmonising measure.

> See Chapter 12 on the removal of barriers to the free movement of goods

Article 114(3) TFEU states that, in proposing measures under Article 114(1) concerning health, safety, environmental protection or consumer protection, the Commission 'will take as a base a high level of protection, taking account in particular of any new development based on scientific facts'. This was of particular relevance to cases challenging the use of Article 114 as a legal base for the adoption of secondary legislation concerning tobacco products, which are examined in the next section.

4.2.3 Competence to adopt secondary legislation

It is because of the limitations imposed by the principle of conferral that secondary legislation must be premised on an appropriate **legal base** (sometimes also referred to as legal basis) within the Treaties. Whenever the institutions seek to adopt secondary legislation, the institution which makes the proposal (normally the Commission) must identify a relevant legal base within the Treaty, which confers upon the institution the competence to take the action in question. Without a legal base, the institutions are prevented from acting.

It is not always clear what the correct legal base for a Union act of secondary legislation should be and there may be more than one provision in the Treaties that could be identified as providing authorisation. For example, a proposal on animal feed could be mandated by provisions in the area of agriculture or in the area of consumer protection. It may therefore be possible for the Commission or other institution to be strategic in selecting the legal base that best suits the intended aim of the legislation.

Prior to the SEA, the choice of legal base rarely gave rise to controversy. However, subsequently there were some disputes, largely either because Member States contested the competence of the Union to legislate at all or because a legal base was chosen allowing for a qualified majority vote within the Council of Ministers, when some Member States demanded a base requiring unanimity and therefore the opportunity to block the measure by exercising their national veto (see ***Commission v Council*** (Case C-300/89); ***European Parliament v Council*** (Case C-295/90)). This, however, is less likely following the entry into force of the ToL because the vast majority of legal bases are now governed by the **ordinary legislative procedure** (see Chapter 3).

Union institutions or Member States can challenge the legal validity of an act of secondary legislation under **Article 263 TFEU** on the ground that the wrong legal base has been used. If the Court of Justice of the European Union finds that the legal base of an act is incorrect, the act will be annulled (see Chapter 6). Not very many challenges on this ground have been successful but in the following case the Court of Justice annulled a directive on the ground that **Article 114 TFEU** provided an insufficient legal base:

Germany v *Parliament and Council* (Case C-376/98) – 'Tobacco advertising I'

Facts:

Directive 98/43/EC, on the approximation of the laws, regulations and administrative provisions of the Member States relating to the advertising and sponsorship of tobacco products, cited the former Article 100a EC Treaty (now Art 114 TFEU) as its legal base. The Article provides that:

> The Council shall … adopt the measures for the approximation of the provisions … which have as their object the establishing and functioning of the internal market.

Germany brought a case to the Court of Justice to request the annulment of Directive 98/43/EC on the grounds that the former Article 100a EC Treaty (now Art 114 TFEU) did not provide a legal base for the legislation. Germany argued that Directive 98/43/EC did not contribute to the improvement of the internal market, as mandated by Article 100a, but rather introduced permanent obstacles to trade in tobacco products between Member States.

Ruling:

The Court of Justice stated that:

> in considering whether Article 100a [now Art 114 TFEU] was the proper legal basis, the Court must verify whether the measure whose validity is at issue in fact pursues the objectives stated by the Community [i.e. Union] legislature.

Consequently, the Court determined that the former Article 100a EC Treaty (now Art 114 TFEU) would be an appropriate legal base if the Directive:

- contributed to the elimination of obstacles to the free movement of goods;
- ensured the free movement of goods which were in conformity with its provisions;
- contributed to eliminating appreciable distortions of competition.

> The Court concluded that the Directive did not pursue any of these objectives and therefore did not contribute to the functioning of the internal market in any way that made the former Article 100a EC Treaty an appropriate legal base.
>
> **Significance:**
>
> This case was the first instance of a directive being successfully challenged on the grounds of an incorrect legal base. The case was significant for demonstrating the commitment of the Union to ensuring that it does not exceed the competences conferred upon it by the Treaties.

Other examples where Commission acts have been annulled on the grounds of lack of competence include *France* v *Commission* (Case C-327/91) and *Laboratoires Servier* v *Commission* (Case T-147/00). *France* v *Commission* concerned the competence of the Commission to conclude an agreement with the US to promote cooperation and reduce conflict in the application of their competition laws. The Court of Justice ruled that the Commission had exceeded its competence, as while the former Article 228 EEC Treaty conferred the power to the Commission to negotiate such agreements, only the Council had the power to conclude them. In *Laboratoires Servier*, the CFI (now the General Court) annulled a Commission decision withdrawing marketing authorisation for certain medicinal products. Although the applicant had not specifically challenged the decision on the basis of a lack of competence, the CFI noted that it was required, according to well-established case law and for reasons of public policy, to raise its own motion to examine whether the decision in question exceeded the Commission's competence.

In the following case, a challenge to the validity of a later tobacco directive was unsuccessful:

> ### *Germany* v *Parliament and Council* (Case C-380/03) – 'Tobacco advertising II'
>
> **Facts:**
>
> Germany challenged the validity of Directive 2003/33, which was adopted to replace the Directive declared illegal in **Tobacco Advertising I** (see above). The new Directive prohibited the advertising of tobacco products in all printed press with the exception of publications intended for professionals (Article 3), on the radio (Article 4) and through sponsorship (Article 5). Unlike its predecessor, the Directive contained a market access provision (Article 8), which prohibited Member States from preventing the free movement of products and services that comply with the Directive.
>
> **Ruling:**
>
> The Court upheld the validity of the Directive, stating that:
>
> > ... when there are obstacles to trade, or it is likely that such obstacles will emerge in the future, because the Member States have taken, or are about to take, divergent measures with respect to a product or a class of products, which bring about different levels of protection and thereby prevent the product or products concerned from moving freely within the Community [i.e. Union], Article 95 EC [now Art 114 TFEU] authorises the Community [i.e. Union] legislature to intervene by adopting appropriate measures ... [para 41]

> See section 12.4.5 on the market access rule, which the Court of Justice established in the interim between the two tobacco advertising cases

> As the forms of advertising affected by the Directive have 'cross-border' effects, the Directive was found to have the objective of harmonising divergent national laws that could affect competition in trade between the Member States. The Court therefore concluded that the Directive is within the competence conferred by what is now Article 114 TFEU, as its objective was to facilitate the functioning of the internal market.
>
> **Significance:**
>
> This case developed a broad approach to the use of what is now Article 114 TFEU as a legal base for a directive. Although the Court stated that divergent national laws must cause or be likely to cause obstacles to trade in order to justify recourse to the subsidiary powers of the harmonisation clause (Art 114 TFEU), these criteria were applied loosely to the case at hand. The Court referred only vaguely, rather than precisely, to divergent measures that Member States had or were about to take, suggesting a more flexible approach to the invocation of the harmonisation clause than had previously been applied.

The approach set out in the above case has since been confirmed in three challenges to yet another tobacco directive, Directive 2014/40: *Poland* v *Parliament and Council* (Case C-358/14); *Pillbox 38 (UK) Limited* v *Secretary of State for Health* (Case C-477/14); *Philip Morris Brands SARL and Others* v *Secretary of State for Health* (Case C-547/14). In each of these cases, the Court upheld that the provisions of the Directive sought to facilitate the smooth functioning of the internal market of tobacco products by harmonising divergent Member State regulations.

4.2.4 The principles of subsidiarity and proportionality

Article 5(1) TEU stipulates that 'The use of Union competences is governed by the principles of subsidiarity and proportionality'. These two principles therefore limit the extent to which the Union can act, even in areas where it has been conferred the relevant competence.

The principle of subsidiarity is set out in **Article 5(3) TEU**:

> Under the principle of subsidiarity, in areas which do not fall within its exclusive competence, the Union shall act only if and in so far as the objectives of the proposed action cannot be sufficiently achieved by the Member States, either at central level or at regional and local level, but can rather, by reason of the scale or effects of the proposed action, be better achieved at Union level.

The principle of proportionality is then set out in **Article 5(4) TEU**:

> Under the principle of proportionality, the content and form of Union action shall not exceed what is necessary to achieve the objectives of the Treaties.

In other words, the Union can only act in the pursuit of an objective that cannot be sufficiently achieved by a Member State acting alone, and can only act to the extent that is necessary to achieve that objective.

Protocol No. 2 on the application of the principles of subsidiarity and proportionality, which is annexed to the TEU and TFEU, contains provisions on how subsidiarity and proportionality should be ensured in practice. **Article 5** of the Protocol requires that:

> Draft legislative acts shall be justified with regard to the principles of subsidiarity and proportionality. Any draft legislative act should contain a detailed statement making it possible to appraise compliance with the principles of subsidiarity and proportionality.

The Protocol then sets out an 'early-warning system', which involves national parliaments in monitoring adherence to the principle of subsidiarity. National parliaments must be informed of all new legislative initiatives (Art 4) and if at least one-third of them are of the view that a proposal infringes the principle of subsidiarity, the Commission will have to reconsider the proposal (Art 7). Additionally, Member States can bring actions for the annulment of a legislative act before the Court of Justice of the European Union on grounds of infringement of the principle subsidiarity (Art 8).

In policy areas where the Union has exclusive and explicit competence, adherence to the principle of subsidiarity is assumed – the Member States agreed that action would be more effective at the Union level than at the national level when they ratified the relevant Treaty provisions and thereby transferred their sovereignty to the Union in that area. Conversely, in areas where the Union has shared or supporting competence, where the Union's competence is only implied by provisions in the Treaties or where Article 352 TFEU is invoked, the test of subsidiarity is essential.

Reflection: Competence creep

The term 'competence creep' has been used to describe the incremental – or sometimes more considerable – expansion of Union competences into areas that previously remained under the control of Member States. In particular, the term does not refer to the overt expansion of competences through the revision of the Treaties, to which all Member States must consent, but rather to the implementation and interpretation of the Treaty articles in such a way that the Union is afforded wide powers. This may occur through the initiation of new secondary legislation by the Commission which is based on a wide interpretation of a Treaty article, or through creative interpretations by the Court of Justice, which are often based on the development and application of broad principles of Union law, as will be demonstrated throughout the rest of this chapter.

The principle of subsidiarity was developed as a means of limiting the expansion of Union powers. However, its effectiveness has been subjected to criticism. J H H Weiler (1997) stated on the topic that:

> Subsidiarity has not truly resolved the issue of competences. It appears so far to be a political tool which gives the Union an excuse not to act when it is expedient, but does not offer a meaningful restraint when it is not.
>
> The principle of subsidiarity has since been strengthened by the ToL, which provides national parliaments with the right to (i) object to draft legislation or (ii) challenge a legislative act on the ground that the principle has not been observed. However, the issue of competence creep remains a prominent political challenge for Member States, especially those in which Eurosceptic political parties have gained populist influence in recent years.

4.3 The supremacy of EU law

Objective 3

The issue of supremacy concerns how conflicts between EU law and the national laws of the Member States are resolved. The doctrine of the supremacy of EU law stipulates that where such conflicts arise, it is EU law that should prevail. The supremacy of EU law therefore requires Member States to amend or repeal any provisions of their national legislation that conflict with EU law (although such laws may remain in place insofar as they apply to situations beyond the scope of EU law). Equally, it means that the Court of Justice of the EU is the ultimate arbiter of EU law in all matters relating to its interpretation. As far as is possible, this ensures that EU law is interpreted and applied consistently between Member States and in a manner that is consistent with the objectives of the Union.

4.3.1 Recognition of the supremacy of EU law

Nowhere in the Treaty is there a reference to the supremacy of Union law over the national law of the Member States. However, Declaration 17 to the ToL states as follows:

> The Conference recalls that, in accordance with well settled case law of the Court of Justice of the European Union, the Treaties and the law adopted by the Union on the basis of the Treaties have primacy over the law of Member States, under the conditions laid down by the said case law.

In this instance, and in most others, the term 'primacy' is used synonymously with supremacy.

After first establishing that Union law can be directly enforceable within the national courts of the Member States in *Van Gend en Loos* (Case 26/62 – see Chapter 8), supremacy over national legislation was established as a defining feature of EU law in the following case:

Costa v *ENEL* (Case 64/4)

Facts:
Flamino Costa had owned shares in a private electricity company when it was nationalised by the Italian government. Opposing the nationalisation, he was then sued by the new company, Ente Nazionale Energia Elettrica (ENEL), for refusing to pay an electricity bill. Costa argued that the nationalisation had contravened the EEC Treaty (now the TFEU), while the government argued

that the EEC Treaty provisions were not applicable in this instance as more recently enacted national legislation should take precedence. A question on the interpretation of EEC Treaty provisions was subsequently referred to the Court of Justice.

Ruling:

The Court of Justice first considered the autonomous nature of Community (now Union) law, ruling that, through the EEC Treaty (now the TFEU), Member States had transferred some of their sovereign powers to the Union:

> By contrast with ordinary international treaties, **the EEC Treaty [now the TFEU] has created its own legal system** which, on the entry into force of the Treaty, became an integral part of the legal systems of the Member States and which their courts are bound to apply.
>
> By creating a Community of unlimited duration, having its own institutions, its own personality, its own legal capacity and capacity of representation on the international plane and, more particularly, real powers stemming from a limitation of sovereignty or a transfer of powers from the states to the community [now the Union], **the Member States have limited their sovereign rights and have thus created a body of law which binds both their nationals and themselves**.

The Court then considered the implications of this for the relationship between national law and Union law:

> The integration into the laws of each Member State of provisions which derive from the community [now the Union] and more generally the terms and the spirit of the treaty, make it **impossible for the states, as a corollary, to accord precedence to a unilateral and subsequent measure over a legal system accepted by them on a basis of reciprocity**. Such a measure cannot therefore be inconsistent with that legal system.
>
> ...
>
> **The law stemming from the Treaty, an independent source of law, could not because of its special and original nature, be overridden by domestic legal provisions**, however framed, without being deprived of its character as Community [now Union] law and without the legal basis of the Community [now the Union] itself being called into question.

Thus, the Court found that Union law could only function effectively as a multilateral legal system if Member States could not unilaterally override it, concluding that Union law must therefore be supreme.

Significance:

The Court established that the European Community (i.e. the Union) comprised an **autonomous** legal order that is capable of acting independently at an international level. Additionally, the Court established the **supremacy** of Union law over the domestic law of Member States. This means that, because Member States agreed to the EEC Treaty (now the TFEU), and because all Union law necessarily stems from the powers conferred by the Treaties, Member States are legally bound to ensure that their national legislation does not contradict Union law. This was a pivotal judgment in the history of the Union, as the alternative outcome of siding with the Italian government would have enabled Member States to disregard EU law by simply enacting contradictory national provisions.

4.3.2 Challenges to the supremacy of EU law

Now, the supremacy of EU law is generally accepted by the Member States and the Union has developed safeguards, such as those pertaining to subsidiarity and proportionality, for maintaining an acceptable balance of powers between the Union and the Member States.

For some Member State court systems, however, the supremacy of EU law as formulated in *Costa* was highly novel and conflicted with national constitutional powers. In the following case, the Court of Justice confirmed that Union law takes precedence over even the constitutional laws of Member States:

Internationale Handelsgesellschaft mbH (Case 11/70)

Facts:
Two Council regulations adopted in 1967 established a system of deposits, whereby export licences for certain agricultural products were conditional upon prior payment of a deposit, which was to be forfeited if the export was not made. This forfeiture provision was challenged by the trading company Internationale Handelsgesellschaft mbH before a German administrative court, which found that the system violated principles, including fundamental rights, of the German Basic Law (i.e. the German Constitution). The German Court therefore referred a question to the Court of Justice regarding the validity of the relevant Community (now Union) provisions.

Ruling:
The Court ruled that national law may not be used to assess the validity of Community (i.e. Union) rules:

> Recourse to the legal rules or concepts of national law in order to judge the validity of measures adopted by the institutions of the community would have an adverse effect on the uniformity and efficacy of community law. The validity of such measures can only be judged in the light of Community [now Union] law. In fact, the law stemming from the treaty, an independent source of law, cannot because of its very nature be overridden by rules of national law, however framed, without being deprived of its character as Community [now Union] law and without the legal basis of the Community [now Union] itself being called in question. Therefore **the validity of a Community [now Union] measure or its effect within a member state cannot be affected by allegations that it runs counter to either fundamental rights as formulated by the constitution of that state or the principles of a national constitutional structure**.

However, the Court then went on to consider whether there were any protections in Community (i.e. Union) law by which the system of deposits could be found to be invalid. Here, the Court recognised for the first time that fundamental rights form an integral part of the general principles of Union law, which are protected by the Court and could be used to render a Union provision invalid. After considering fundamental rights principles, though, the Court concluded that the regulations establishing the system of deposits were valid Community (now Union) law and therefore could not be challenged within a domestic legal system.

Significance:
This case reaffirmed the **autonomy** of the EU legal system, meaning that EU law can only be interpreted and reviewed by Union institutions. Therefore, EU law always takes precedence over domestic laws, even if it conflicts with provisions enshrined within a Member State's constitution. In light of the Court's earlier judgment in *Costa*, this case has little significance in countries such as the UK, where all national legislation is comprised of acts of parliament, which can always be amended or repealed by later acts of parliament. Other Member States, however, have constitutions that cannot be so easily amended to accommodate the supremacy of EU law.

This case also reinforced the status of fundamental rights as general principles of EU law that are protected by the Court of Justice (see Chapter 3).

The ruling of the Court of Justice in ***Internationale Handelsgesellschaft*** was not initially fully accepted by the German Federal Constitutional Court. In the case known as **'Solange I'** (Judgment of 29 May 1974, 37 BVerfGE 271), the German Court ruled that if a case should arise where there was a conflict between Community (i.e. Union) law and a fundamental right guaranteed by the German constitution, the constitutional rights would prevail. In response to the challenge to the supremacy of EU law that was posed by Solange I, the Union sought to develop its doctrine of human rights protections. Subsequently, the German Federal Constitutional Court revised its position in **Solange II** (Judgment of 22 Oct. 1986, 73 BVerfGE 339). Here, the German Court asserted that, so long as the Union generally ensured the protection of fundamental rights, it would assume that level of protection to be substantially equivalent to that provided by German constitutional law. The incorporation of fundamental rights protections within the Union legal system therefore enhanced the legitimacy and authority of EU law in the eyes of the German Court.

▶ See section 3.3.2 on fundamental rights in EU law

However, Germany has continued to be uneasy over the absolute supremacy of Union law. For example, Germany's ratification of the ToL was delayed while domestic legislation was passed to increase the involvement of the national parliament in Union decision-making, due to concerns that the ToL increased the Union's powers without sufficiently remedying its 'democratic deficit'. In a judgment on the compatibility of the ToL with German Basic Law (i.e. constitution), the German Constitutional Court stated:

> The European Union continues to constitute a union of rule (Herrschaftsverband) founded on international law, a union which is permanently supported by the intention of the sovereign Member States. The primary responsibility for integration is in the hands of the national constitutional bodies which act on behalf of the peoples. With increasing competences and further independence of the institutions of the Union, safeguards that keep up with this development are necessary in order to preserve the fundamental principle of conferral exercised in a restricted and controlled manner by the Member States. With progressing integration, fields of action which are essential for the development of the Member States' democratic opinion-formation must be retained. In particular, it must be guaranteed that the responsibility for integration can be exercised by the state bodies of representation of the peoples. [Press Release No. 72/2009 of 30 June 2009, on Judgment of 20 June 2009, 2 BvE 2/08]

Here, the German Constitutional Court reaffirmed the sovereignty of Member States and their power as the ultimate arbiters of Union law, i.e. that Union law is ultimately constrained by the will of the populations of the Member States, as expressed through their national democratic regimes.

This democratic aspect then came into play in ***Gauweiler*** (Case C-62/14), where the German Federal Constitutional Court (BverfG) made its first reference to the Court of Justice for a preliminary ruling. The reference did not symbolise an olive branch in the troubled relationship between the German and the Union courts, however. The BverfG effectively presented the Court of Justice with an ultimatum: either rule that the European Central Bank's Outright Monetary Transaction (OMT) programme is invalid, or it will be found incompatible with the democratic principles of German Basic Law and disregarded in Germany. The BverfG thus reserved the right to disregard the judgment of the Court if it disagreed with it, which is a position that is clearly contrary to the principle of the supremacy of Union law. The Court of Justice held its ground and ruled that the OMT programme is compatible with the Treaties. However, it softened its rejection of the BverfG's position by stipulating that certain safeguards will have to be applied in the implementation of the OMT programme in order to ensure that it remains within the competence of the European Central Bank. This seems to have been sufficient to resolve the standoff, as the BverfG has since upheld the compatibility of the OMT programme with German constitutional law (Judgment of 21 June 2016, 2 BvR 2728/13).

The confrontational approach of the German Federal Constitutional Court can be contrasted with the more amicable approach demonstrated by the Italian Constitutional Court in the recent case of **MAS and MB** (Case 42/17). This case is also referred to as **Taricco II**, as it pertained to the same issue regarding the application of the Italian statute of limitations to cases of fraud as *Taricco and Others* (Case 105/14 – **Taricco I**). In this earlier case, the Court of Justice ruled that a national rule setting limitation periods for criminal offences must be disapplied to the extent that it prevented Italy from giving full effect to Article 325 TFEU on the combat of fraud. The effect of this ruling in Italy was that criminal cases that had been time-barred could now be brought in droves. The **Taricco I** case was therefore widely criticised for (i) creating legal uncertainty through the legal vacuum created by the *ad hoc* disapplication of a national law and (ii) failing to balance the financial interests of the Union in the application of Article 325 TFEU with the fundamental rights to legal certainty and non-retroactivity.

In the **Taricco II** case, then, the Italian Constitutional Court (ICC) effectively invited the Court of Justice to reconsider its earlier judgment. The ICC tactfully pointed out the requirement under Article 49 of the EU Charter of Fundamental Rights that rules on criminal liability must be sufficiently precise and the requirement under Article 7 of the European Convention on Human Rights that the criminal nature and applicable penalties of an offence must be clearly determinable at the time that the offence is committed. The Court of Justice, claiming that the particular requirements of Italian law in this area had not previously been drawn to its attention, then reconsidered its position. In this second case, the Court stated that the contentious national law should be disapplied 'unless that disapplication entails a breach of the principle that offences and penalties must be defined by law because of the lack of precision of the applicable law or because of the retroactive application of legislation imposing conditions of criminal liability stricter than those in force at the time the infringement was committed' (para 62). In essence, therefore, the Court of Justice, on the invitation of the Italian Constitutional Court, conceded that a balance must be struck with fundamental rights.

In addition to posing a challenge to parliamentary sovereignty in general, for the UK and several other Member States the supremacy of EU law clashed with the established principle that when two statutory laws conflict, the more recently enacted legislation always takes precedence. The Court of Justice addressed this issue in the following case:

Simmenthal S.P.A. (Case 106/77)

Facts:

A local Italian magistrate, the Pretore di Susa, asked the Court of Justice whether, given that directly applicable Community (i.e. Union) provisions must have full effect in the legal systems of the Member States, any subsequent national measures that conflict with a Community (i.e. Union) provision must be immediately discarded, without waiting for the measure to be repealed or rendered unconstitutional in accordance with national procedures.

Ruling:

The Court of Justice ruled that:

> in accordance with the principle of the precedence of Community [i.e. Union] law, ... directly applicable measures ... not only by their entry into force render automatically inapplicable any conflicting

provision of current national law but – in so far as they are an integral part of, and take precedence in, the legal order applicable in the territory of each of the Member States – also **preclude the valid adoption of new national legislative measures to the extent to which they would be incompatible with community provisions**.

The Court then justified this position, stating that the recognition of national legislative measures that either encroached on the exclusive competences of the Union, or were otherwise incompatible with Union law, would amount to a denial of the effectiveness of Member States' obligations under the Treaty and would thus 'imperil the very foundations of the Community'. Therefore, the Court concluded that:

> every national court must, in a case within its jurisdiction, apply Community [i.e. Union] law in its entirety and protect rights which the latter confers on individuals and **must accordingly set aside any provision of national law which may conflict with it, whether prior or subsequent to the Community [i.e. Union] rule**.

Significance:

This case determined that Union law takes precedence over all national legislation, regardless of whether that legislation was enacted before or after the relevant provisions of Union law entered into force. Member States therefore cannot apply the principle that the most recently enacted legislation takes precedence in order to pass domestic laws that undermine the effectiveness of Union law in their jurisdiction.

While the challenge to the supremacy of Union law in the Solange cases stemmed from concerns that the Union did not offer sufficient human rights protections, in other instances concerns have been expressed about the expansion of the Union's powers into this field. For example, in *Mangold* v *Helm* (Case C-144/04), the Court of Justice ruled that 'The principle of non-discrimination on grounds of age must ... be regarded as a general principle of Community [i.e. Union] law'. The classification of this principle as a *general* principle was controversial, as, although the international instruments and traditions common to the constitutions of the Member States (from which general principles of Union law are derived) clearly enshrine a broad principle of equal treatment, only the Finnish and Portuguese constitutions at the time expressly prohibited discrimination on the ground of age. Additionally, while age is mentioned in the non-discrimination clause of the Charter of Fundamental Rights (Art 21), this was not binding at the time. The ruling in *Mangold* therefore provoked widespread criticism (see for example the Opinion of Advocate General Mázak in *Félix Palacios de la Villa* v *Cortefiel Servicios SA* (Case C-411/05)).

▶ See section 3.3 on the general principles of Union law

Discrimination on the ground of age was also at issue in the following case, where the Court of Justice reinforced the supremacy of Union law in the field of human rights:

Kücükdeveci v *Swedex GmbH & Co KG* (Case C-555/07)

Facts:

A provision in the German Civil Code allowed employment prior to the age of 25 years to be discounted in the calculation of the statutory minimum notice period for dismissal. Ms Kücükdeveci had worked for Swedex for 10 years, from the age of 18. When she was dismissed at the age of 28, she was given only one month's notice on the basis that only three years of her employment needed to be taken into account, rather than the 4 months' notice she would be due if the full 10 years of her employment were accounted for.

Ruling:

The Court of Justice ruled that the relevant provision of German law was contrary to the Employment Equality Directive (2000/78) and also to the general principle of non-discrimination on the ground of age that the Court established in ***Mangold***. While the aim of the national legislation of affording employers greater flexibility was held to be legitimate, the provision itself was found to be an inappropriate means of achieving it.

The Court then reaffirmed the duty of a national court to uphold the supremacy of Union law, including with regards to general principles:

> ... it is for the national court, hearing a dispute involving the principle of non-discrimination on grounds of age as given expression in Directive 2000/78, to provide, within the limits of its jurisdiction, the legal protection which individuals derive from European Union law and to ensure the full effectiveness of that law, *disapplying if need be any provision of national legislation contrary to that principle*.

Significance:

In referring to the ruling in ***Mangold***, this case confirmed the ability of the Court of Justice to declare certain principles to be general principles of Union law, which national courts must then uphold – including where doing so requires a court to disapply provisions of national law.

Reflection: Political negotiation or rule of law?

Much scholarly attention has been paid to the governance of the Union and what exactly has compelled its Member States to accept the supremacy of Union law over their own national regimes. Some, such as Geoffrey Garret (1995), argue that Member States accept the rule of the Court of Justice because it is a necessary and reasonable price to pay for the benefits brought by the internal market. The Court ensures that all Member States abide by the same rules, without which the fair functioning of the common market would not be possible. Member States accept this and acquiesce to the Court and the other Union institutions accordingly. However, Garret argues that this rational decision-making at the national level contains the possibility that a Member State might consider compliance with a particular ruling of the Court to be, on balance, against its national interests. The possibility of Member State defiance therefore acts as a limiting factor on the decisions of the Court – the Court will be careful not to take decisions that Member States will find unacceptable, as one Member State's rebellion against the supremacy of Union law could undermine the authority of the Court altogether.

Walter Mattli and Anne-Marie Slaughter (1995) agree that the Court, if unconstrained, would likely move towards deeper and more rapid integration than the Member States would find acceptable, and that for the Court to 'outrun' its constituents would lead to the loss of its legitimacy. However, they argue that the Court is not so much constrained by political consideration of the economic or other interests of the Member States, but rather by the constraints of the substantive legal doctrine and the principles of legal reasoning. In this framing, the subservience of Member States to the Court appears to be the result of the Court's fidelity to the Union legal framework, which has ultimately been negotiated and agreed to by the Member States.

4.4 The incorporation and extrication of Union powers in the UK

Objective 4

In the UK, the supremacy of EU law clashed first with the fundamental principle of Parliamentary sovereignty, and second with the principle that more recent legislation always takes precedence over older legislation. The UK therefore needed to establish how the requirements of Union law could be reconciled with British legal traditions. Having successfully achieved this, the challenge now is how to withdraw from the Union after EU law has become so deeply embedded in the domestic system.

4.4.1 The European Communities Act 1972

Joining the Union

The European Communities Act 1972 incorporated Union law into UK domestic legislation. The effect of s 2(1) of the 1972 Act was that all provisions of Union law which were enforceable in the UK – either through direct or indirect effect – were given the force of law in UK courts and tribunals. The text of s 2(1), as amended (see below), is as follows:

> All such rights, powers, liabilities, obligations and restrictions from time to time created or arising by or under the Treaties, and all such remedies and procedures from time to time provided for by or under the Treaties, as in accordance with the Treaties are **without further enactment** to be given legal effect or used in the United Kingdom shall be recognised and available in law, and be enforced, allowed and followed accordingly . . .

This applies to Union law made both before and *after* the entry into force of the Act. Section 2(4) provides that:

> . . . any enactment passed **or to be passed** . . . shall be construed and have effect subject to the foregoing provisions of this section.

There are three interpretations of the 1972 Act's incorporation of Union law into domestic law:

1 Union law is supreme and always takes precedence over any conflicting UK legislation, regardless of whether a statute states that the Act of Parliament was to have effect notwithstanding any Union law to the contrary. This view is clearly adopted by the Court of Justice (see e.g. *Costa* v *ENEL*, above).

2 Provisions of the European Communities Act 1972, and therefore Union law, can be impliedly repealed if a later statute conflicts with it. This is the traditional doctrine of UK parliamentary sovereignty, as affirmed in *Vauxhall Estates Ltd* v *Liverpool Corpn* [1932] 1 KB 733 and *Ellen Street Estates* v *Minister of Health* [1934] 1 KB 590, whereby in the event of a conflict between two statutes, the later statute takes precedence and the former statute is impliedly repealed to the extent of the inconsistency. This approach would undermine s 2(4), as it insists that UK legislation always, by implication, repeals an earlier legislative provision with which it is inconsistent.

3 Section 2(4) is, in effect, a rule of interpretation. It is assumed that the UK Parliament, in enacting legislation, intends to legislate consistently with Union law. Therefore if the UK Parliament wishes to act inconsistently, it should state its intention expressly in an Act of Parliament.

The third, middle-ground approach has generally been favoured by the UK courts. This approach is based on the premise that the UK Parliament partially surrendered its sovereignty by enacting the 1972 Act, thus providing for the application of Union law in the UK courts.

Section 3(1) of the 1972 Act further provides that:

> For the purposes of all legal proceedings any question as to the meaning or effect of any of the Treaties, or as to the validity, meaning or effect of any EU instrument, shall be treated as a question of law and, if not referred to the European Court, be for determination as such in accordance with the principles laid down by and any relevant decision of the European Court.

▶ See section 5.3.1 on the exclusive jurisdiction of the Court of Justice regarding the interpretation of Union law

This provision recognises the exclusive competence of the Court of Justice of the European Union to interpret Union law and therefore provided for the presence of effective Union law within the UK, which the domestic courts must apply but may not interpret. This is important for ensuring the uniform application of Union law across the Member States.

Limiting and reversing the transfer of sovereign powers

The European Communities Act 1972 was amended over 100 times. For example, the European Union (Amendment) Act 2008 gave effect to the Treaty of Lisbon and changed the terminology used throughout the 1972 Act, replacing all references to the 'Community' with 'Union'.

While the 2008 Act effectively transferred further powers to the Union, as provided for by the Treaty of Lisbon, the **European Union (Amendment) Act 2011** signalled a more cautious and restrictive attitude. Part 1 of the 2011 Act is entitled '**Restrictions on treaties and decisions related to the EU**' and stipulates that treaties amending or replacing the TEU and/or the TFEU shall only be ratified by the UK after a positive referendum result. While Brexit has rendered these provisions obsolete before they have ever been applied, the enhanced requirement for ratification would have afforded greater powers to Eurosceptics to block future amendments to the Treaties and therefore to block any further transfer of powers to the Union.

The European Union (Amendment) Act 2011 also included affirmation of the principle that Union law is only effective in the UK in so far as is provided for by domestic legislation. The text of s 18 of the 2011 Act is as follows:

> Directly applicable or directly effective EU law (that is, the rights, powers, liabilities, obligations, restrictions, remedies and procedures referred to in section 2(1) of the European Communities Act 1972) falls to be recognised and available in law in the United Kingdom **only by virtue of that Act** or where it is required to be recognised and available in law by virtue of any other Act.

> See section 1.1.3 for an overview of the withdrawal process

> See 'Reflection: EU secondary legislation in the UK after Brexit' in section 3.4.5 (page 147)

The UK's surrender of sovereign powers to the Union was limited, therefore, not only to the areas in which the Union is conferred the competence to act, but also because the UK Parliament retained the ability to repeal the 1972 Act and thus reverse the transfer of sovereign powers. However, prior to repealing the 1972 Act, the UK first invoked **Article 50 TEU**, signalling to the Union its intention to exit. As held in *R v Secretary of State for Exiting the European Union* [2017] UKSC 5, this in itself required an act of Parliament; the **European Union (Notification of Withdrawal) Act** was passed on 16 March 2017.

The repeal of the 1972 Act is then a core element of the **European Union (Withdrawal) Act 2018** (informally known as the 'Great Repeal Act'). The Act stipulates that all EU-derived domestic law continues to be operative and that all 'direct EU legislation' became domestic law ('retained EU law') on the day of the UK's exit from the Union (ss 2 and 3). Section 1 of this Act repealed the European Communities Act 1972 and formally ended the supremacy of EU law in the UK on 'exit day'. However, since amendments in 2020, Section 1A of the European Union (Withdrawal) Act 2018 states that the European Communities Act 1972 nevertheless continues to apply during the transition period. All EU law therefore continues to have effect during 2020 and the UK has effectively established an extension of EU supremacy during this time.

4.4.2 Division of competences in Brexit negotiations

Horizontal division of competences between institutions

Following the UK's formal notification to the European Council of its intention to exit the Union, the competence of the Union to negotiate and conclude an exit agreement with the UK, setting out the arrangements for the country's withdrawal, is conferred by **Article 50(2) TEU**. However, Article 50 only specifies that it shall be the Council, acting with the consent of the European Parliament, which concludes the exit agreement; it does not specify which Union institution should lead the negotiations. Additionally, **Article 218(3) TFEU**, which is to be applied to the negotiations, does not fully clarify the matter, as it merely specifies that the Council may nominate a Union negotiator. As a European Parliament briefing paper explained:

> The role of the European Commission in the withdrawal procedure is not entirely clear in the Treaties. According to Article 218(3) TFEU, the European Commission would make recommendations to the Council to open negotiations with the withdrawing state. As a general rule, the Commission negotiates agreements with third countries on behalf of the EU, but Article 218(3) leaves it open for the Council to nominate a different Union negotiator.
>
> (European Parliament 2016, p. 4)

While the Commission argued that Article 50 TEU treats a withdrawing state as though it is already a third country, suggesting that negotiations should be led by the Commission, governments concerned by the federalist tendencies of the Commission under Jean-Claude Junker's presidency argued that the UK was not a third country until the formal termination of its membership and that the Council should therefore lead the negotiations.

On 28 June 2016, the Parliament voted in favour of the Commission leading the negotiation talks. The Commission then submitted a proposed decision and negotiating directives to the Council, which would authorise the Commission to commence withdrawal negotiations with the UK. The Council adopted the decision and the negotiating directives on 22 May 2017, resolving this initial question over the horizontal division of competences between the Union institutions.

Vertical division of competences between national and Union levels

Questions relating to the vertical division of competences in the Brexit process are concerned with which aspects of the negotiations undertaken during the transition period must be ratified by the Member States and which aspects the Union has the power to conclude by itself. In the following opinion, the Court of Justice clarified the division of competences in the area of trade and thus subsequently clarified the involvement of Member States in the negotiation of a trade agreement between the UK and the EU:

Opinion 2/15

Facts:

On 20 September 2013, the EU and Singapore signed a bilateral Free Trade Agreement (FTA). This agreement was more extensive than previous FTAs concluded by the Union. In addition to the usual provisions on custom duties and non-tariff barriers in the field of trade in goods and services, the agreement with Singapore also included provisions in additional areas, including intellectual property, foreign direct investment, public procurement, competition and sustainable development.

On 10 July 2015, the Commission submitted a request to the Court of Justice for an opinion on whether the Union, acting alone, has the competence to sign and conclude the FTA with Singapore.

Opinion:

In its Opinion of 16 May 2017, the Court found that the Union does not have the full competence required to conclude the FTA with Singapore in its current form. The Court determined that the Union has exclusive competence in the majority of the areas covered by the agreement, but that there remain two areas – foreign direct investment and dispute settlement between investors and states – in which the Union's competence is shared with the Member States. The inclusion of these two areas within the FTA means that it can only be concluded with the Union and Member States acting jointly.

Significance:

In addition to stalling the conclusion of the FTA between the EU and Singapore, Opinion 2/15 has implications for the conclusion of an FTA between the EU and the UK. The Court found that the Union does have exclusive competence in a considerable range of areas relating to trade. For the most part, then, when it comes to agreeing a trade deal, the UK would only have to negotiate with the single entity of the Union, rather than with the Union as well as its 27 Member States. In response to Opinion 2/15, the Commission divided the Singapore agreement into a narrower FTA, which only the Union needed to ratify, and an 'investment protection agreement', which both the Union and its Member States will need to ratify. A similar approach could therefore be taken to smooth the passage of a UK FTA. Regardless, there are widespread concerns at the time of writing that it will be impossible to negotiate a comprehensive FTA before 31 December 2020, when the UK is set to exit the customs union and the single market.

CHAPTER SUMMARY

Competence of the Union

- Union institutions can only act to the extent that the Treaties **confer** competences upon them (**Arts 5(1) and 5(2) TEU**).
- The Union's **explicit competences** are divided into areas of **exclusive competence**, **shared competence** and **supporting competence** (**Arts 3, 4 and 6 TFEU**).
- The competence of the Union is limited by the principles of **subsidiarity** and **proportionality** (**Arts 5(3) and 5(4) TEU** and **Protocol No. 2**).

Supremacy of Union law

- Union law takes precedence over all conflicting provisions of national law (*Costa* v *ENEL*), regardless of whether it is constitutional law (*Internationale Handelsgesellschaft*) or has been more recently enacted (*Simmenthal*).

Union law in the UK

- Union law was incorporated into UK domestic law by the **European Communities Act 1972**.
- The 1972 Act was repealed on the day that the UK exited the Union by the **European Union (Withdrawal) Act 2018**. However, all EU law continues to apply during the transition period.

Chapter 5
Judicial methodology and preliminary rulings of the Court of Justice

Learning objectives

At the end of this chapter you should understand:

1. The Court of Justice's exclusive jurisdiction to interpret EU law.
2. The methodology that the Court of Justice uses to interpret EU law and reach decisions.
3. The preliminary ruling procedure, including which questions can be referred and which national courts may or must refer them.
4. The special forms of procedure that can be used to streamline preliminary rulings.

Key terms and concepts

Familiarity with the following terms will be helpful for understanding this chapter:

Acte clair – when the solution to a legal question is self-evident

Acte éclairé – when the Court of Justice has previously ruled on an identical question

Preliminary ruling – a ruling by the Court of Justice on the interpretation of a particular area of Union law, which is necessary to enable a national court to decide a case before it

Teleological interpretation – seeking to understand something by referring to its purpose, e.g. referring to the reasons why a law was enacted in order to determine how it should be applied

5.1 Introduction

Objective 1

As noted in Chapter 2, Article 13(1) TEU recognises the Court of Justice of the European Union as a Union institution. **Article 19(1) TEU** then states that:

> The Court of Justice of the European Union shall include the Court of Justice, the General Court and specialised courts. It shall ensure that in the interpretation and application of the Treaties the law is observed.

An overview of the jurisdictions and compositions of these courts is provided in Chapter 2. This chapter focuses on how the Court of Justice ensures the correct and uniform interpretation of Union law through **preliminary rulings**. To promote better understanding of the case law that is so integral for understanding the development of Union law, this chapter begins with a look at the different judicial methods that the Court of Justice of the European Union employs to reach a decision.

The chapter then considers the procedure whereby national courts can – or in some situations must – make a **reference for a preliminary ruling** from the Court of Justice under **Article 267 TFEU**. The preliminary ruling mechanism enables national courts to refer questions to the Court of Justice where a point of Union law is at issue. This provides a means for national courts to apply Union law whilst ensuring that only the Court of Justice may interpret it. Through the Court of Justice's exclusive jurisdiction to interpret Union law, in theory at least, the uniformity of such interpretation is safeguarded, along with the status of the Union as an autonomous legal order. As noted in *Costa v ENEL* (Case 64/4), such autonomy is essential for the supremacy of Union law and is therefore essential for the effective functioning of the Union legal order.

➤ *Costa v ENEL* is considered in section 4.3.1 (page 169)

5.2 Judicial methods of interpretation

Objective 2

The sources of law to which the Court has to give effect are diverse (and are considered in detail in Chapter 3). Many of the Treaty provisions, and some of the implementing legislation, are expressed in broad terms, and the Court of Justice plays a crucial role in developing the law and constitution of the Union.

The Court of Justice employs a 'European way' of interpreting EU law, which is totally different from that employed by the English judiciary. This was recognised by Lord Denning, sitting in the English Court of Appeal, in ***Bulmer* v *Bollinger*** [1974] 3 WLR 202:

> The [EC] Treaty [now the TFEU] is quite unlike any of the enactments to which we have become accustomed … It lays down general principles. It expresses its aims and purposes. All in sentences of moderate length and commendable style. But it lacks precision. It uses words and phrases without defining what they mean. An English lawyer would look for an interpretation clause, but he would look in vain. There is none. **All the way through the Treaty there are gaps and lacunae. These have to be filled by the judges, or by regulations or directives**.
>
> **It is the European way** … Seeing these differences, what are the English courts to do when they are faced with a problem of interpretation? They must follow the European pattern. No longer must they argue about the precise grammatical sense. **They must look to the purpose and intent … They must divine the spirit of the Treaty and gain inspiration from it**. If they find a gap, they must fill it as best they can … These are the principles, as I understand it, on which the European Court acts.

> See section 4.4.1 on the European Communities Act 1972

The approach of Lord Denning in the above case has its source in s 3(1) of the **European Communities Act 1972**, a UK Act of Parliament, which, prior to Brexit, provided as follows:

> For the purposes of all legal proceedings any question as to the meaning or effect of any of the Treaties, or as to the validity, meaning or effect of any Community [i.e. Union] instrument, shall be treated as a question of law (and, if not referred to the European Court, be for determination as such in accordance with the principles laid down by and any relevant decision of the European Court or any court attached thereto).

The 'principles laid down by … the European Court' is wide enough to encompass the Court of Justice's method of interpretation. The Court employs the following four methods of interpretation:

- literal;
- historical;
- contextual;
- **teleological**.

It has emerged that the last two, which were novel to the English legal system, and the last one in particular, are the most often employed by the Court of Justice. However, it may be difficult to identify a clear *ratio decidendi* (i.e. the rule of law on which a decision is based) from a judgment because of the style of the Court's single decision, which will often need to encompass the differing views of the judges.

The four methods of interpretation are considered below, after a brief examination of the extent to which the Court of Justice abides by its own precedent.

5.2.1 Precedent

The doctrine of precedent (*stare decisis*) does not apply to the Court of Justice of the European Union. However, the Court generally follows its own previous decisions. This is necessary for the sake of **legal certainty**. Nonetheless, if the Court is faced with a very persuasive

Advocate General's Opinion, it may be persuaded to develop its past case law, perhaps to introduce a new legal principle of EU law. Additionally, the Court may, of its own volition, depart from its own previous case law, for example on policy grounds (see, for example, *Keck and Mithouard* (Joined Cases C-267 and 268/91), see section 12.4.5). Such deviations, especially when concerning substantive matters of constitutional law, will tend to be incremental, with new principles established and refined over a series of cases (Lenaerts, 2015). In this way, the jurisprudence of the Court of Justice has been built gradually and great leaps or dramatic changes in position are generally avoided.

> Precedent is discussed further in section 5.3.4

It is usual for lawyers to cite previous case law when arguing a point of law before the Court. The Advocate General in their Opinion and the Court in its judgment, will also generally refer to previous cases to support their interpretations.

5.2.2 Literal interpretation

This method is commonly used by the English judiciary when interpreting national legislation. You begin with the words of the text and give them their ordinary meaning. The Court of Justice, however, may refuse to employ this method, even where the words of the measure in question appear to be perfectly clear (see, e.g., *Commission v Council* (Case 22/70)).

Literal interpretation may be more difficult for the Court of Justice to apply due to the lack of interpretation sections in the relevant legislative measure. It will therefore be left to judicial interpretation to develop the meanings of certain words and phrases. Examples of words and phrases from the TFEU which have required interpretation include:

- 'charges having equivalent effect' (Arts 28 and 30 TFEU);
- 'worker' and 'public policy' (Art 45 TFEU);
- 'abuse of a dominant position' (Art 102 TFEU).

Secondary legislation may be drafted more specifically (especially regulations which are to be directly applicable as they stand (see Chapter 3)). Nevertheless, the Court of Justice may apply one of the other methods rather than the literal method.

5.2.3 Historical interpretation

Historical interpretation requires a consideration of the subjective intention of the author of the text. This will involve an examination of the preliminary debates and may be equated with the English **mischief rule**, where the judge seeks to establish the legislative intent, i.e. to ascertain why the legislation was enacted and what its purpose was conceived to be at the time of enactment.

Historical interpretation is occasionally used by the Court of Justice, but generally the Court is not prepared to examine records of debates. With regard to regulations, directives and decisions, **Article 296 TFEU** provides that the reasons why they have been enacted must be given. These reasons will be contained in the preamble. The Court of Justice may be guided by these historical reasons in ascertaining the legislative intention of the relevant Union institutions. They are occasionally referred to in judgments of the Court of Justice (see, for example, *Markus v Hauptzollamt Hamburg-Jonas* (Case 14/69)).

5.2.4 Contextual interpretation

This method is extensively used by the Court of Justice when interpreting the EU Treaties and secondary legislation. It involves placing the provision within its context and interpreting it in relation to the other provisions. A particular paragraph of a directive or regulation, for example, must not be considered in isolation, but rather within the context of the whole instrument. When interpreting an article of the TEU or TFEU, the Court of Justice may have regard to 'the general scheme of the Treaty as a whole', as illustrated in the following case:

Commission v *Luxembourg and Belgium* (Cases 2 and 3/62)

Facts:

The Court of Justice was considering the former Article 12 EEC Treaty (now Art 30 TFEU), which provides that:

> Customs duties on imports and exports and charges having equivalent effect shall be prohibited between Member States. This prohibition shall also apply to customs duties of a fiscal nature.

Ruling:

The Court of Justice held that:

> The position of those Articles [former Arts 9 and 12 EC Treaty, now Arts 28 and 30 TFEU] towards the beginning of that Part of the Treaty dealing with the 'Foundations of the Community' [now 'Union policies and internal actions'] ... is sufficient to emphasise the essential nature of the prohibitions which they impose.

The Court, relying upon the 'general scheme' of these provisions and of the Treaty as a whole, went on to state that there was:

> ... a general intention to prohibit not only measures which obviously take the form of the classic customs duty but also all those which, presented under other names or introduced by the indirect means of other procedures, would lead to the same discriminatory or protective results as customs duties.

Significance:

In this case, the Court of Justice gave a wide interpretation to the general words 'charges having equivalent effect', whereas an English court may have applied the *ejusdem generis* rule to limit its scope: i.e. where specific categories are followed by general words, then the general words are limited to the context of the specific categories. The Court of Justice used the general expression as a catch-all provision, looking at the specific provision in context and in relation to the Treaty as a whole, the aim of which is to abolish all restrictions on the free movement of goods. This demonstrates the extent to which the Court can prioritise the aims of an instrument in general over a literal and isolated interpretation of its individual provisions.

5.2.5 Teleological interpretation

When applying this method of interpretation, the Court will interpret the provision in question in confluence with the aims and objectives of the Union as a whole. As discussed in Chapter 3, the EU Treaties set out a broad programme rather than a detailed plan. The preamble to the Treaties and some of the introductory articles (e.g. Art 3 TEU) set out the broad aims and objectives of the Union in very general terms. When interpreting the Treaties or other Union legislation, the Court of Justice may be guided by these overarching aims and objectives. Therefore, while the contextual approach considers a specific section of a legal instrument in the context of all the sections of that instrument, the teleological approach goes outside the actual instrument and considers the whole purpose, aims and objectives of the Union.

The Court has become accustomed to interpreting Union law teleologically, by reference to the broad policy objectives of the Treaties, rather than, as in an English court, by the meaning of the words before it and their immediate context. In ***Parliament* v *Council*** (Case C-70/88) it was, for example, accepted that the European Parliament had the right to bring an action for the annulment of an instrument of secondary legislation against the Council or Commission, even though the Parliament had not specifically been given such a right in the former Article 230(1) EC Treaty (now Art 263 TFEU). The Court of Justice held that not to imply such a right for the Parliament would deprive it of the legal means with which to protect its privileges against incursions by the other institutions. The former Article 230 EC Treaty was subsequently amended by the TEU to give the Parliament the right to take such action to protect its prerogatives.

Similarly, in ***Procureur du Roi* v *Royer*** (Case 48/75), the Court extended the right of free movement of workers to those looking for work, even though the former Article 39 EC Treaty (now Art 45 TFEU) appeared to confer the right only on those to whom an offer of work had actually been made. The Court of Justice considered that the object of the Treaty to secure the free movement of labour would not be achieved if only those with an offer of employment from another Member State were enabled to move freely. In these, and in many other matters, the Court has used its interpretative powers to put flesh on the bones of Treaty provisions, and to do so in such a way as to facilitate the effective development of the Union.

Underlying these decisions is what can be described as the policy of the Court. All national courts have unstated policy objectives, such as the maintenance of the rule of law or the discouragement of anti-social behaviour. The law will be interpreted as far as possible to achieve those ends. The Court of Justice's objectives are more clearly discernible. Broadly, the Court's policies could be said to consist of strengthening the Union's authority, increasing the scope and effectiveness of Union law and enhancing the powers of the Union institutions.

The Court's policy of securing greater effectiveness for Union law is achieved partly by interpreting the law in such a way that it achieves the broader objectives of the EU Treaties, even if this has to be done, in some cases, by ignoring the express words of Union legislation. It can also be seen in the doctrine of the direct effect of directives under which the measures originally intended to bind only the Member States have become means by which individuals can secure their rights in national courts (see Chapter 8). In pursuit of the same policy objectives, remedies in national courts, which were originally seen as being of purely national concern and beyond the competence of the Court, are now judged by the Court in terms of their effectiveness to secure the implementation of Union law. If they are not effective, they must be set aside and an effective remedy provided (for example, ***R* v *Secretary of State for Transport, ex parte Factortame (No. 2)*** (Case C-213/89)).

5.3 Preliminary Rulings under Article 267

Objective 3

5.3.1 The jurisdiction of the Court of Justice to interpret Union law

National courts perform a crucial role in administering and applying Union law. There is a clear danger that, given the disparate national legal traditions of the Member States, Union law could be applied differently in the national courts of different Member States. If this were to happen, individuals and businesses in the Union would be operating under different rules and many of the benefits of an open Union and a genuine internal market would be lost. The Union has, therefore, a fundamental interest in ensuring that its law has the same meaning and effect across all the Member States.

The problem of the consistent application of Union law was first dealt with through the Court of Justice's establishment of the principle of the supremacy of Union law, which is discussed in Chapter 4. Here, it was determined that Union law comprises an autonomous legal regime that the Court of Justice of the European Union has the exclusive competence to interpret. In order to enforce the exclusivity of this competence – and thus the uniformity of the interpretation of Union law – there needed to be a means of ensuring that the Court of Justice has the final word on all questions pertaining to the interpretation of Union law. The most effective way of doing this would have been to establish the Court of Justice as a final Court of Appeal on matters of Union law. However, that option was perceived as too direct a challenge to the sovereignty of national legal systems and was rejected by the founders of the Union. Instead, a system whereby national courts are to refer questions on the interpretation of Union law to the Court of Justice was established.

While the Court of Justice has developed an important body of case law on the application of Union provisions by the national courts of the Member States (see Chapter 8), **Article 267 TFEU** on the preliminary rulings procedure is the only provision of the Treaties that expressly acknowledges the enforcement role of the national courts. Indeed, it is the role of the national court to make a reference to the Court of Justice and, after receiving a judgment on the correct interpretation of the Union law in question, it is for the national court to then apply that ruling.

The text of Article 267 TFEU is as follows:

> The Court of Justice of the European Union shall have jurisdiction to give preliminary rulings concerning:
>
> (a) the interpretation of the Treaties;
>
> (b) the validity and interpretation of acts of the institutions, bodies, offices or agencies of the Union.
>
> Where such a question is raised before any court or tribunal of a Member State, that court or tribunal may, if it considers that a decision on the question is necessary to enable it to give judgment, request the Court to give a ruling thereon.

> Where any such question is raised in a case pending before a court or tribunal of a Member State against whose decisions there is no judicial remedy under national law, that court or tribunal shall bring the matter before the Court.
>
> If such a question is raised in a case pending before a court or tribunal of a Member State with regard to a person in custody, the Court of Justice of the European Union shall act with the minimum of delay.

Article 256(3) TFEU provides as follows:

> The **General Court** shall have jurisdiction to hear and determine questions referred for a preliminary ruling under Article 267, in specific **areas laid down by the Statute**.

As noted in Chapter 2, the Statute has not made provision for the General Court to have jurisdiction to hear and determine Article 267 TFEU cases. Therefore, only the Court of Justice currently has such jurisdiction.

The majority of cases which come before the Court of Justice are cases referred by national courts pursuant to Article 267 TFEU. This workload has affected the operation of the Court, but the average length of time taken for a judgment to be delivered overall has nevertheless decreased over the last 20 years, such that in 2016 the average length of time was just less than 15 months (this increased to 15.7 months in 2018). While the Court of Justice has historically been keen to assist national courts with preliminary rulings, Nils Wahl and Luca Prete (2018) argue that the Court is becoming increasingly strict in assessing the admissibility of questions referred to it by national courts.

Once the Court of Justice is satisfied that it has the jurisdiction to deal with a reference, it is, in principle, bound to give a ruling. It cannot refuse to do so on the basis that, if its ruling were to have the effect of annulling a Union or national provision, this would create a 'legal vacuum' in a Member State. In such a situation it would be for the national court to interpret national law in such a way as to fill any gap (*Gmurzynska* (Case C-231/89); *Helmig and Others* (Joined Cases C-399, 409 and 425/92 and C-34, 50 and 78/93)).

Reflection: The difference between an Article 267 reference and an appeal

Article 267 TFEU envisages a partnership between the Court of Justice and the national court, whereby the Court of Justice interprets Union law and the national courts apply it. Article 267 references therefore have a different function from an appeal. In an appeal, the initiative lies with the litigants and if the appeal is successful the appellate court can substitute its own decision for that of the lower court. In a reference, however, it is the national court itself which takes the decision to refer the case. The Court of Justice rules on the issues raised, but it is then for the lower (national) court to apply the ruling of the Court of Justice to the facts of the case before it. Ultimately, the national court will make the final decision, although the Court of Justice's judgment will sometimes leave little room for discretion in this regard. The objective of the reference procedure is to retain the independence of the national courts, while at the same

> time safeguarding against 'a body of national case law not in accord with the rules of Community [i.e. Union] law from coming into existence in any Member State' (**Hoffmann La Roche v Centrafarm** (Case 107/76)). It must, however, be emphasised that in many instances the national court will be able to apply Union law *without* making a reference to the Court of Justice. National courts do so throughout the European Union, quite properly, in many cases each day.

5.3.2 Discretion or obligation to refer

Depending on the status of the court or tribunal, some *may* and others *must* refer questions of interpretation of the Treaties or interpretation/validity of Union acts to the Court of Justice. When a court or tribunal has discretion to make a reference under Article 267 TFEU and when they have an obligation to do so is now examined and is summarised in Figure 5.1 below.

Discretion to refer

The second paragraph of Article 267 TFEU provides that:

> Where such a question is raised before any court or tribunal of a Member State, that court or tribunal **may**, if it considers that a decision on the question is necessary to enable it to give judgment, request the Court of Justice to give a ruling thereon.

Each national court and tribunal has 'the widest discretion' in deciding whether to refer a question to the Court of Justice (**Rheinmühlen** (Case 166/73)), provided that (i) the question pertains to the interpretation or validity of a measure of Union law ('such a question') and (ii) that an answer to the question is considered by the court to be 'necessary to enable it to give judgment' (these criteria are considered below). This discretion cannot be overridden by a higher court, or any national procedural rule (**Križan v Slovenská inšpekcia životného prostredia** (Case C-416/10)). However, a court has no real discretion in cases where its decision depends on the disputed *validity* of a Union act. It has itself no power to declare the Union act invalid, so it has no choice but to refer the matter to the Court of Justice for a ruling on its validity (**Foto-Frost** (Case 314/85)).

National bodies that can make a reference

While the discretion under Article 267 may be wide, it is limited to those bodies that are considered a 'court or tribunal'. At first glance, it would appear that references can only be made by courts and tribunals within the state's judicial structure. However, the essential elements to determine the status of the body in relation to Article 267 are: (i) its power to make **legally binding decisions**, (ii) its **independence** from the parties and (iii) the **recognition** of its decision-making function by the state. To be able to make references under Article 267, a body will have to satisfy all of these criteria. For example, an arbitrator, although conferred with a power by contract to make legally binding decisions on the parties, and also being independent of the parties, lacks the official state recognition to make their decisions 'judicial' in character, and they cannot, therefore, make a reference under Article 267 (**Nordsee v Reederei Mond** (Case 102/81)). However, an arbitration board or a disciplinary body which is recognised by the state as having a function in making legally binding decisions in relation to an industry or a professional body may well be a 'court or tribunal' for the purpose of Article 267, as illustrated in the following case:

Broekmeulen v *Huisarts Registratie Commissie* (Case 246/80)

Facts:

The applicant, Dr Broekmeulen, was a Dutch national who had qualified as a general medical practitioner in Belgium. The applicant was authorised to practise medicine in the Netherlands by the Netherlands Secretary of State for Health and the Environment, but the General Practitioners Registration Committee refused to register him. Dr Broekmeulen appealed to the Appeals Committee for General Medicine, which referred a question for a preliminary ruling to the Court of Justice regarding the interpretation of Directive 75/362 concerning the mutual recognition of diplomas, certificates and other evidence of formal qualifications in medicine.

Both the Appeals Committee and the Registration Committee were established by the Royal Netherlands Society for the Promotion of Medicine, which is a private association, but were recognised indirectly in some national legal provisions. The Appeals Committee was not a court or tribunal under national law. Before considering the question on interpretation, then, the Court of Justice needed to determine whether the Appeals Committee was a 'court or tribunal' within the meaning of what is now Article 267 TFEU.

Ruling:

The Court of Justice stated that:

17 In order to deal with the question of applicability in the present case of Article 177 of the Treaty [now Article 267 TFEU], it should be noted that it is incumbent upon Member States to take the necessary steps to ensure within their own territory the provisions adopted by the Community [i.e. Union] institutions are implemented in their entirety. If, under the legal system of a Member State, **the task of implementing such provisions is assigned to a professional body acting under a degree of governmental supervision**, and if that body, in conjunction with the public authorities concerned, creates **appeal procedures which may affect the exercise of rights granted by Community [i.e. Union] law**, it is imperative, in order to ensure the proper functioning of Community [i.e. Union] law, that the Court should have an opportunity of ruling on issues of interpretation and validity arising out of such proceedings.

18 As a result of all the foregoing considerations and in **the absence, in practice, of any right of appeal to the ordinary courts**, the Appeals Committee, which operates with the consent of the public authorities and with their cooperation, and which, after an adversarial procedure, delivers **decisions which are recognised as final**, must, in a matter involving the application of Community [i.e. Union] law, be considered as a court or tribunal of a Member State within the meaning of Article 177 of the Treaty [now Art 267 TFEU]. Therefore, the Court has jurisdiction to reply to the question asked.

Significance:

The judgment in this case presented several factors that combined to lead the Court to the conclusion that the Dutch Appeals Committee was a 'court or tribunal' within the meaning of what is now Article 267 TFEU. Essentially, this case established that such a body must be assigned the task of implementing Union provisions and must subsequently be able to affect the exercise of rights granted by a Union act. The case suggests a broad rather than a restrictive approach to the question of which bodies can make a reference for a preliminary ruling.

In *Walter Schmid* (Case C-516/99), the Court of Justice held that the Fifth Appeal Chamber of the regional finance authority for Vienna (Austria) was not a 'court or tribunal' within the scope of Article 267 TFEU, because it was not independent. The Chamber was established to enable taxpayers to resolve any dispute with the tax authority. However, the tax authority personnel would sit as adjudicators (together with others not employed by the tax authority). The adjudicators who were not employed by the tax authority were nevertheless selected by the authority and they did not have a sufficient period of tenure to detach themselves sufficiently from the tax authority.

The concept of 'court or tribunal' was also at issue in the following case:

De Coster v Collège des Bourgmestres et Échevins de Watermael-Boitsfort (Case C-17/00)

Facts:
A dispute arose between De Coster and the Collège, when the Collège levied a municipal charge on De Coster in respect of his satellite dish. He contended, *inter alia*, that this tax breached the former Article 49 EC Treaty (now Art 56 TFEU) because it was a restriction on the free movement of services. The Collège decided to refer the case to the Court of Justice for a preliminary ruling pursuant to what is now Article 267 TFEU.

Ruling:
The first question before the Court was whether or not the Collège was a 'court or tribunal'. The Court stated that:

> 10 It is settled case-law that in order to determine whether a body making a reference is a court or tribunal for the purposes of Article 234 EC [now Art 267 TFEU], which is a question governed by Community [i.e. Union] law alone, the Court takes account of a number of factors, such as **whether the body is established by law, whether it is permanent, whether its jurisdiction is compulsory, whether its procedure is *inter partes*, whether it applies rules of law and whether it is independent**.

To determine the extent to which these factors applied to the Collège, the Court considered the Law of 12 January 1989 concerning the Brussels institutions (Moniteur belge of 14 January 1989). The Court was subsequently satisfied that the Collège was a permanent body established by law, which gave legal rulings and had compulsory jurisdiction concerning local tax proceedings.

The Court then went on to consider whether the Collège followed an *inter partes* procedure, i.e. a procedure in which two or more parties are involved. The Court found this condition to be satisfied as, *inter alia*, preparatory inquiries were adversarial and the parties could present their oral observations at a public hearing. The Court then went on to find that the Collège was sufficiently independent and impartial and therefore that it had standing to refer to the Court for a preliminary ruling.

Significance:
The Court's careful consideration of each of the factors that it sets out in paragraph 10 of the ruling suggests that a reference pursuant to what is now Article 267 TFEU may be ruled inadmissible if any of these criteria are not met.

A national court determining an appeal against an arbitration award, not according to law but according to what is 'fair and reasonable', may be regarded as a 'court or tribunal' for the purpose of Article 267 TFEU (***Municipality of Almelo and Others* v *Energiebedvijf***

NV (Case C-394/92)). A court delivering an advisory 'opinion' may likewise be a 'court or tribunal' for the purpose of Article 267. In ***Garofalo and Others* v *Ministero della Sanità and Others*** (Joined Cases C-69–79/96) an opinion delivered by the Italian Consiglio di Stato to the Italian President, although not binding on him, was held to be a proper subject for a reference under Article 267 TFEU. In the UK, besides references from magistrates' courts, crown courts and county courts, there have also been references from VAT tribunals, employment tribunals and social security commissioners.

Obligation to refer

The third paragraph of Article 267 TFEU provides that:

> Where any such question is raised in a case pending before a court or tribunal of a Member State against whose decisions there is no judicial remedy under national law, that court or tribunal **shall** bring the matter before the Court.

> See section 8.4 on state liability

This third paragraph therefore provides an exception to the discretion that is provided in the second paragraph. Accordingly, a court or tribunal which satisfies the above criteria has no discretion; it is *required* to refer the case to the Court of Justice for a preliminary ruling. A refusal to meet this obligation can give rise to state liability against the Member State (***Ferreira da Silva and others*** (Case C-160/14)).

The criteria under which a court is obliged to make a reference are as follows:

- a question pertaining to the interpretation or validity of a provision of Union law is raised;
- a decision on that question is necessary to enable it to give judgment;
- and there is no further judicial remedy available under national law.

These three criteria, the former two of which are also required where a court or tribunal has discretion to refer, are considered in the following subsections of this chapter.

5.3.3 Questions on the interpretation or validity of Union law

Article 267 TFEU refers to two types of question which can be the subject of a reference to the Court of Justice for a preliminary ruling:

- questions pertaining to the interpretation of the Treaties;
- questions pertaining to the validity and interpretation of acts of the institutions, bodies, offices or agencies of the Union.

Interpretation of the Treaties

'Interpretation of the Treaties' covers the **TEU**, the **TFEU**, the **amending treaties** and the **Treaties of Accession**. There are some policy areas in both the TEU and TFEU where the Court of Justice has either limited jurisdiction or no jurisdiction, and therefore the power to interpret such provisions within an Article 267 referral will likewise be limited. These are the areas relating to the Common Foreign and Security Policy, Judicial Cooperation in Criminal Matters and Police Cooperation.

Figure 5.1 Discretion or obligation to refer a question for a preliminary ruling under Article 267 TFEU

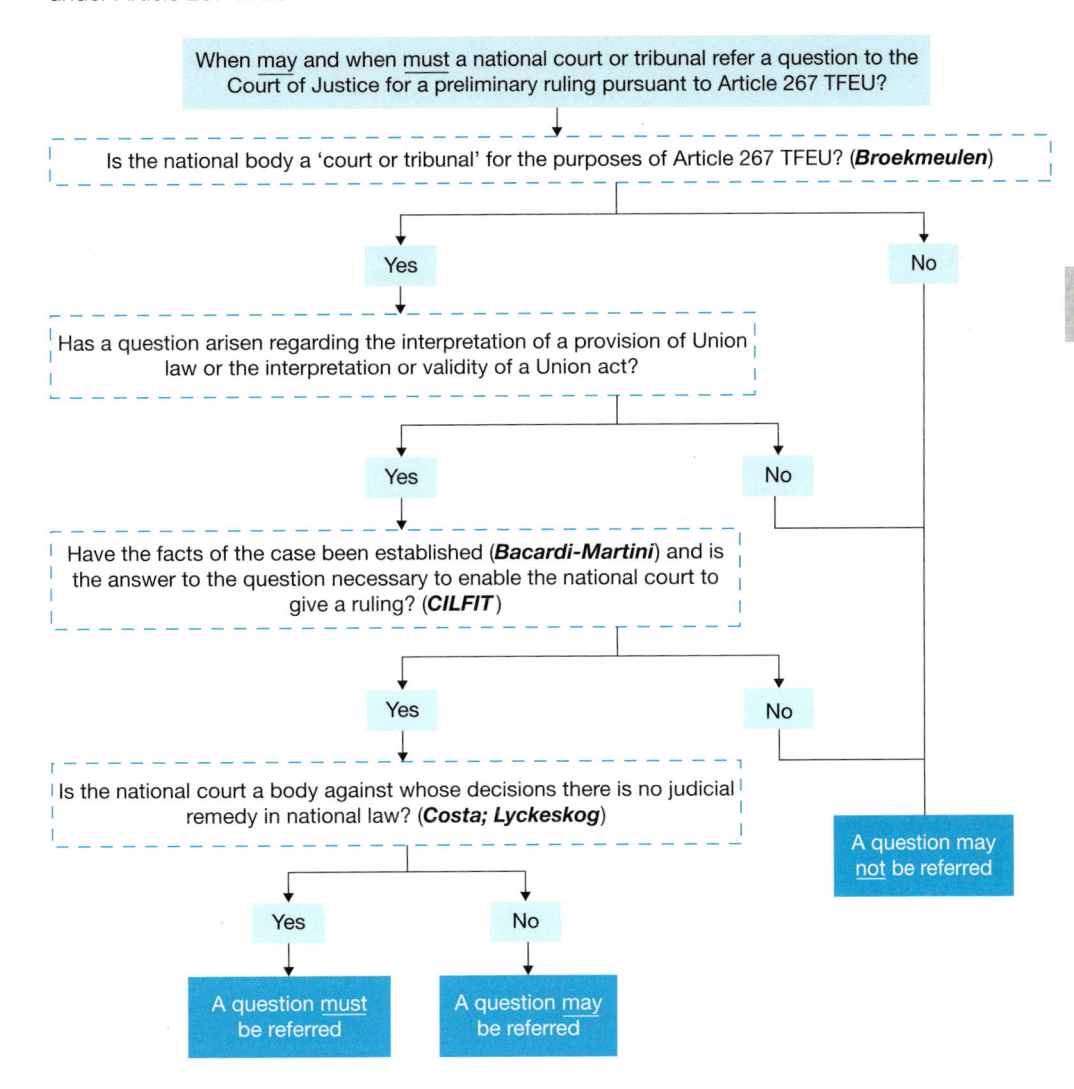

```
When may and when must a national court or tribunal refer a question to the
Court of Justice for a preliminary ruling pursuant to Article 267 TFEU?
                                │
                                ▼
    Is the national body a 'court or tribunal' for the purposes of Article 267 TFEU? (Broekmeulen)
                    │                                               │
                   Yes                                              No
                    │                                               │
    Has a question arisen regarding the interpretation of a provision of Union
    law or the interpretation or validity of a Union act?
                    │                               │
                   Yes                              No
                    │                               │
    Have the facts of the case been established (Bacardi-Martini) and is
    the answer to the question necessary to enable the national court to
    give a ruling? (CILFIT)
                    │                               │
                   Yes                              No
                    │                               │
    Is the national court a body against whose decisions there is no judicial
    remedy in national law? (Costa; Lyckeskog)
            │                       │               │
           Yes                      No              │
            │                       │               │
    A question must         A question may    A question may
    be referred             be referred       not be referred
```

Interpretation or validity of Union acts

'Acts of the institutions, bodies, offices or agencies of the Union' includes not only legally binding acts, such as regulations, directives and decisions, but also opinions and recommendations where these are relevant to the interpretation of Union law by the courts of Member States: *Frecassetti* v *Amministrazione delle finanze dello Stato* (Case 113/75); ***Grimaldi*** v ***Fonds des Maladies Professionnelles*** (Case C-322/88).

▶ See section 3.4 for a full explanation of 'Union acts'

In ***Deutsche Shell AG*** v ***Hauptzollamt Hamburg*** (Case C-188/91), the Court of Justice held that 'arrangements' made by a joint committee responsible for implementing a convention on a common transit policy between the EU and EFTA formed 'part of the Community [i.e. Union] legal order'. The Court noted that the fact that a Union legal measure lacked compulsory effect did not exclude the Court from giving a legal ruling on it, because national courts were obliged to take it into account when interpreting the Convention.

The Court also emphasised in the ***Deutsche Shell*** case that it did not have jurisdiction under what is now Article 267 TFEU to give a ruling on the compatibility of a national measure with Union law. However, it does effectively do this. Generally, the Court will describe the national measure in hypothetical terms and state that, if there was such a measure, it would or would not be compatible with Union law.

Although the Court can only give a ruling on the interpretation of *Union* law, it has been prepared to rule on the meaning of *national* provisions which are based on the wording of a Union provision: ***Gmurzynska-Bscher*** (Case C-231/89).

In addition to their interpretation, the Court has the power to give preliminary rulings on the *validity* of Union acts (excluding the Treaties). Such questions of validity give rise to an obligation, rather than discretion, to refer a question. In ***Foto-Frost v Hauptzollamt Lübeck-Ost*** (Case 314/85), the Court of Justice first stated that, to protect of the uniform application of Union law, 'the national courts have no jurisdiction themselves to declare that acts of Community institutions are invalid'. It follows from this that all national courts, even those whose decisions are subject to appeal, must refer a question to the Court when they have doubts about the validity of a Union act.

Consider the following scenario: a levy is imposed by an EU regulation; the regulation may provide for the levy to be collected by a national agency. An individual may be sued when he refuses to pay the levy. In his defence he may argue that the regulation is not valid because a procedural step in the legislative process has not been followed. The national court may refer the matter to the Court of Justice pursuant to Article 267 to ascertain if the regulation (i.e. a Union act) is valid. The Court of Justice will make the ruling and pass the case back to the national court. The national court will then apply the law as determined by the Court of Justice. If the Court of Justice rules that the regulation is invalid, the national court will be obliged to rule in favour of the defendant. As is discussed above, this indirect way of challenging the validity of a Union act may be a much more effective mechanism than the restricted power to challenge such an act directly under Article 263 TFEU (see Chapter 6).

5.3.4 Questions that are necessary to enable a national court to give a judgment

As discussed above, a court or tribunal will have **discretion** (pursuant to the second paragraph of Art 267 TFEU) to refer a case to the Court of Justice for a preliminary ruling only if it 'considers a decision on the question to be **necessary** to enable it to give judgment'. It is thus for the national court to determine whether it is 'necessary' to refer a question. There is no express reference to this criterion in the third paragraph of Article 267 TFEU, which stipulates the **obligation** to refer. However, in ***CILFIT*** (Case 283/81) the Court of Justice stated that the criterion of necessity is also applicable to the third paragraph:

> ... it follows from the relationship between the second and third paragraphs of Article 177 [now Art 267 TFEU] that the courts or tribunals referred to in paragraph 3 have the same discretion as any other national court or tribunal to ascertain whether a decision on a question of Community [i.e. Union] law is necessary to enable them to give judgment.

▶ See below for detail on the *CILFIT* case (page 200)

This element of necessity is now explored further and is followed by consideration of two reasons why a court or tribunal might consider a referral to be **un**necessary: the development of precedent and the doctrine of *acte clair*.

Information required for a referral, including reasons for necessity

A reference to the Court of Justice may be made at any stage in the proceedings (*Simmenthal* v *Amministrazione delle Finanze dello Stato* (Case 70/77); *Balocchi* v *Ministero delle Finanze dello Stato* (Case C-10/92)). The Court does, however, think it desirable that an *inter partes* hearing (i.e. a hearing where all the parties are invited to take part) takes place before the reference, if that is possible (*Eurico Italia Srl* v *Ente Nazionale Risi* (Case C-332/92)).

Additionally, the Court does expect the case to have reached a stage at which the relevant facts have been established and the issues identified on which the assistance of the Court is required (*Irish Creamery Milk Suppliers Association* v *Ireland* (Case 36/80)). Although the Court will tend to use general and hypothetical language in its judgment, it will only give a preliminary ruling where the outcome of an actual case is at issue. To this end, the Court refused to give a ruling in *Telemarsicabruzzo SpA* (Joined Cases C-320–322/90), stating that the need to give a practical interpretation of Union law requires the national court to define the factual and legal framework in which the questions arose, or at least to explain the factual assumptions on which those questions are based. Neither had been done in this case.

In the following case, the Court of Justice held inadmissible a question referred to it, as it was unclear how an answer would enable the referring court to give a judgment:

Bacardi-Martini and Cellier des Dauphins (Case C-318/00)

Facts:
The applicants were companies that had entered into a contractual agreement to advertise alcoholic beverages on displays around the touchline of a football pitch in the UK. The contracts were breached when a match was to be televised in France, where laws on the advertisement of alcoholic beverages are stricter. The UK High Court referred a question for a preliminary ruling by the Court of Justice as to the conformity of the French laws on advertising with the former Article 49 EC Treaty (now Article 56 TFEU) on freedom of services.

Ruling:
The Court of Justice stated that:

> 43 ... the Court has held that it has no jurisdiction to give a preliminary ruling on a question submitted by a national court where it is quite obvious that the interpretation or the assessment of the validity of a provision of Community law sought by that court bears no relation to the actual facts of the main action or its purpose, or where the problem is hypothetical, or where the Court does not have before it the factual or legal material necessary to give a useful answer to the questions submitted to it...
>
> 44 ...
>
> 45 Moreover, the Court must display special vigilance when, in the course of proceedings between individuals, a question is referred to it with a view to permitting the national court to decide whether the legislation of another Member State is in accordance with Community law.

The Court therefore found the question to be inadmissible, in line with its earlier ruling in *Foglia* v *Novello* **(No. 2)** (Case 244/80). However, in its explanation of this finding, the Court stated that the relevance of the French law to the English proceedings had not been demonstrated, suggesting that the breach of contract in question could not be justified with reference to French

> law. Therefore, while the Court refused to rule on the compatibility of the French law with Union law, it effectively advised how the English court should rule.
>
> **Significance:**
>
> This case demonstrated care by the Court not to exceed its jurisdiction under Article 267. Questions referred to it pursuant to Article 267 must therefore be clear as to how they fall within the scope of the Article, i.e. how they pertain to the interpretation of the Treaties or the interpretation/validity of a Union act and – as was at issue in this case – how they are necessary to enable the national Court to give judgment.

Additionally, if one of the parties to the national proceedings withdraws, the Court cannot continue to deliver a judgment on the reference, because such a judgment would then no longer be 'necessary' for the outcome of the case (*Teres Zabala Erasun and Others* v *Instituto Nacional de Empleo* (Joined Cases C-422–424/93)).

The development of precedent

It was noted in section 5.2.1 that the doctrine of precedent does not apply to the Court of Justice, but that the Court generally follows its own previous decisions for the sake of legal certainty. With regard to Article 267 TFEU, the Court of Justice ruled in **CILFIT** (Case 283/81) that it may not be necessary to make a referral to it if the question has already been answered in a previous case:

> ... the authority of an interpretation under Article 177 [now Art 267 TFEU] already given by the Court may deprive the obligation of its purpose and thus empty it of its substance. Such is the case when the question raised is materially identical with a question which has already been the subject of a preliminary ruling in a similar case.

> ➤ See below for detail on the *CILFIT* case (page 200)

This is known as the doctrine of **acte éclairé**. However, a national court **may** refer a question on interpretation or validity even if the Court of Justice has already ruled on the point. If the case does not raise any new fact or argument, the Court may simply restate the substance of the earlier case (e.g. *Da Costa* (Joined Cases 28–30/62)).

The Court's response to questions on which it has already ruled suggests that the Court is informally bound by the doctrine of precedent. The following case lends additional support to this notion:

> ### International Chemical Corporation (Case 66/80)
>
> **Facts:**
>
> The Court of Justice had previously ruled in a former Article 177 EEC Treaty referral (now Art 267 TFEU) that Regulation 563/76 was invalid. This case concerned the regulation's validity. The Italian court hearing the case referred the matter to the Court of Justice, asking whether the previous decision that the regulation was invalid applied only to that particular case, or whether it was effective in any subsequent litigation.
>
> **Ruling:**
>
> The Court of Justice held that the purpose of the former Article 177 EEC Treaty (now Art 267 TFEU) was to ensure that Union law was applied uniformly by national courts. Uniform application

did not only concern the interpretation of Union law, it also concerned the validity of a Union act. The Court said that in the previous case, the ruling that the regulation in question was void was addressed to the national court making the reference. However, as it was declared to be void, any other national court could likewise regard the act as void for the purpose of a judgment which it had to give.

Significance:

When, during a preliminary ruling, a Court of Justice rules that a Union act is void, the national courts may subsequently treat that act as void.

In the following case the Court of Justice applied this principle when it was called upon to interpret a measure (rather than decide on its validity):

Kühne & Heitz (Case C-453/00)

Facts:

The case concerned the classification of poultry meat parts. This was of significance to the applicant, who was an exporter of such meat, as different tariffs were applied according to which category a product fell into. After a case in which a national court upheld one definition, the Court of Justice gave a judgment on a separate case which presented an alternative interpretation. The applicant then brought a fresh case, seeking to apply the Court of Justice's ruling to the facts of their previous case. The national court referred a question to the Court of Justice as to whether its interpretive ruling should be applied retroactively.

Ruling:

The Court of Justice stated that, in view of the obligation on all the authorities of the Member States to ensure observance of Union law, and also of the retroactive effect inherent in interpretative judgments, **a rule of Union law which has been interpreted on the occasion of a reference for a preliminary ruling must be applied by all State bodies within the sphere of their competence, even to legal relationships which arose or were formed before the Court gave its ruling on the request for interpretation.**

With regard to compliance with that obligation, the Court stated that account must be taken of the demands of the principle of legal certainty, which is one of the general principles of Union law.

Significance:

This case established that interpretations of Union law pronounced by the Court of Justice in preliminary rulings should be applied retrospectively – i.e. to cases that national courts have already decided – provided that to do so does not compromise the principle of legal certainty.

▶ The methods of interpretation used by the Court of Justice are explained in further detail in section 5.2

The doctrine of *acte clair*

A situation where an interpretative point appears obvious is normally referred to in Union law as *acte clair*. In the following case, the Court described in detail the circumstances in which the solution to a question is sufficiently transparent to negate the obligation to make a reference under Article 267 TFEU:

CILFIT (Case 283/81)

Facts:

The Italian Court of Cassation, against whose decisions there are no judicial remedies under national law, referred a question to the Court of Justice as to whether it was obliged to refer a question pursuant to what is now Article 267 TFEU 'when the solution of a question on the interpretation of acts performed by the Community [i.e. Union] institutions is so obvious as to preclude the very possibility of their being open to another interpretation'.

Ruling:

The Court of Justice stated that:

> 16 … the correct application of Community [i.e. Union] law may be so obvious as to leave no scope for reasonable doubt as to the manner in which the question raised is to be resolved. Before it comes to the conclusion that such is the case, the national court or tribunal must be convinced that the matter is **equally obvious to the Courts of the other Member States and to the Court of Justice**. Only if those conditions are satisfied, may the national court or tribunal refrain from submitting the question to the Court of Justice and take upon itself the responsibility for resolving it.

The Court then provided some guidance as to the factors that a national court should consider in determining whether a matter is equally obvious to the courts of other Member States and to the Court of Justice:

> 18. To begin with, it must be borne in mind that Community [i.e. Union] legislation is drafted in several languages and that the different language versions are equally authentic. An interpretation of a provision of Community [i.e. Union] law thus involves a **comparison of the different language versions**.
> 19. It must also be borne in mind, even where the different language versions are entirely in accord with one another, that **Community [i.e. Union] law uses terminology which is peculiar to it**. Furthermore, it must be emphasised that **legal concepts do not necessarily have the same meaning in Community [i.e. Union] law and in the law of the various Member States**.
> 20. Finally, every provision of Community [i.e. Union] law must be placed in its **context** and interpreted in the light of the provisions of Community [i.e. Union] law as a whole, regard being had to the objectives thereof and to its state of evolution at the date on which the provision in question is to be applied.

Significance:

While this case established that the solution to a question of interpretation can be so obvious as to negate the obligation to refer the question to the Court of Justice, the Court set a very high standard for determining that obviousness. The national court must determine not only that the solution is obvious to them, but must take account of all of the peculiarities of Union law to determine that it is also obvious to the courts of other Member States and to the Court of Justice itself. As noted in section 5.1, the Court of Justice does not interpret Union law literally, but generally favours a contextual or teleological approach, which can make it difficult to predict how it will rule. The doctrine of *acte clair* can therefore only be applied in the most exceptionally straightforward and unambiguous matters.

In *X & Van Dijk* (Joined Cases C-72/14 and C-197/14) the Court of Justice established that the fact that a lower national court has referred a question pursuant to Article 267 TFEU does not preclude a supreme national court from finding a matter to be *acte clair*. However, a failure of a national supreme court to make a referral to the Court of Justice when the interpretation of a provision of Union law is **not** *acte clair* may lead to the Member State being held liable for damages incurred as a result (*Ferreira da Silva and others* (Case C-160/14); see Chapter 8 on state liability).

> **Reflection:** The UK's view on when to refer a case to the Court of Justice
>
> In *Bulmer v Bollinger* [1974] 2 WLR 202, the English Court of Appeal considered when it is necessary for a question to be referred to the Court of Justice under what is now Article 267 TFEU. Lord Denning laid down guidelines as to when such necessity arises, which may be summarised as follows:
>
> (i) A question need only be referred when it is **conclusive**, i.e. when the interpretation of the relevant provision of Union law will determine the outcome of the case.
>
> (ii) If the Court of Justice has already ruled on the same point, or substantially the same point, that **precedent** should be followed. Only if a national court thinks that a previous ruling may have been wrong, or if there are new factors to bring to the Court's attention, should they refer a question on such a point.
>
> (iii) If a point is 'reasonably clear and free from doubt', then 'there is no need to interpret the Treaty but only to apply it', i.e. there is no need to refer a question when the principle of **acte clair** applies.
>
> (iv) The relevant **facts of the case** should be decided before a question is referred, so as to ensure that a question is indeed necessary to the proceedings.
>
> Lord Denning then went on to outline several other factors that should be considered when a court has **discretion** to refer a question, including the wishes of the parties, the time and expense that such a referral would cost and the concern that the Court of Justice should not be overloaded. Additionally, Denning considered the difficulty and importance of a point of interpretation, stating that:
>
>> Unless the point is really difficult and important, it would seem better for the English Judge to decide it himself. For in so doing, much delay and expense will be saved. The UK will no longer be able to make a reference to the Court of Justice for a preliminary ruling after 'exit day' (31 January 2020).

5.3.5 Courts against whose decisions there is no judicial remedy under national law

The concept of 'no judicial remedy under national law' clearly includes the situation where there can be no further appeal. This situation may arise if the national court is, like the UK Supreme Court, the highest in the hierarchy of courts. It may also arise in specific cases where no appeal is possible from a court which is very low in the hierarchy. In some jurisdictions, for example, there may be no appeal where the amount claimed or the value of the goods concerned is below a certain figure. In the landmark case of *Costa* v *ENEL* (Case 6/64), the amount claimed was less than £2. There was no appeal from the magistrate's decision because of the smallness of the sum. The magistrate was therefore obliged to refer the question before him to the Court of Justice under what is now Article 267 TFEU. In *Parfums Christian Dior BV* v *Evora BV* (Case C-337/95), the Dutch Court of Appeal (the Hoge Raad) had the power to refer a question on trade mark law to the Benelux Court, the highest court for points of law affecting the **Benelux Agreement**. The Court of Justice held that, if the Hoge Raad decided *not* to refer the case to the Benelux Court, it was *obliged* to refer the case to the Court of Justice. If it did refer the case to the Benelux Court, the Benelux Court was itself, as the ultimate court *in that case*, obliged to refer the matter to the Court of Justice.

In the following case, the Court of Justice was required to consider the application of what is now Article 267 TFEU to the Swedish District Court:

Kenny Roland Lyckeskog (Case C-99/00)

Facts:

A Swedish District Court referred a question to the Court of Justice, asking the court whether a case came within the third paragraph of the former Article 234 EC Treaty (now Art 267 TFEU), as an appeal against its decision to the Swedish Supreme Court would only materialise if the Supreme Court declared that the appeal was admissible.

Ruling:

The Court of Justice stated that decisions of a national court which can be challenged before a supreme court are not decisions of a 'court or tribunal of a Member State against whose decisions there is no judicial remedy under national law' within the meaning of the former Article 234 EC Treaty (now Art 267 TFEU). The fact that examination of the merits of such appeals is subject to a declaration of admissibility by the Swedish Supreme Court does not have the effect of depriving the parties of a judicial remedy. Therefore, because there was the possibility of an appeal to the Supreme Court, the District Court did not come within the scope of the third paragraph of the former Article 234 EC Treaty (now Art 267 TFEU), even though the Supreme Court could refuse to hear the appeal (if it held the appeal to be inadmissible).

Significance:

This case clarified that the phrase 'no judicial remedy' within what is now Article 267 TFEU is to be understood as meaning that there is **no possibility of appeal**, rather than merely that an appeal is not guaranteed. However, it should be noted that while there was no obligation on the District Court to refer in this case, that court could still have used its discretion to do so.

Within the English legal system, the term 'judicial remedy' is wide enough to include applications for judicial review. Even when, for example, there is no appeal from the Immigration Appeal Tribunal, its decisions are subject to judicial review and may subsequently be referred to the Court of Justice in the course of those judicial review proceedings (see, for example, *R v Immigration Appeal Tribunal, ex parte Antonissen* (Case C-292/89)). In such a case, it would appear that there is no obligation on the tribunal to refer and an English tribunal has, in fact, refused to refer a case because it held that it was not obliged to do so due to the availability of judicial review of its decisions (*Re A Holiday in Italy* [1975] 1 CMLR 184 (National Insurance Commissioner)). This would seem to be compatible with the Court of Justice's decision in *Lyckeskog* (Case C-99/00).

Reflection: Mind the gap in the obligation to refer

Consider the following situation: in the English legal system a litigant whose case comes before the Court of Appeal can request leave (i.e. permission) to appeal to the UK Supreme Court if they lose their case. If the Court of Appeal refuses leave to appeal, the litigant can then request it from the Supreme Court, but the Supreme Court could also refuse leave.

> If the Court of Appeal does not grant leave to appeal and neither does the Supreme Court, then ***Parfums Christian Dior BV v Evora BV*** would seem to apply with the effect that the Court of Appeal *would* be considered to be a court 'against whose decisions there is no judicial remedy'. Here, the Court of Appeal effectively determines that there shall be no further judicial remedies under national law and the onus is therefore on it to refer a question to the Court of Justice, if a question on the interpretation or validity of Union law is necessary to enable it to give a judgment.
>
> If, alternatively, the Court of Appeal granted leave to appeal, but the Supreme Court then found the case to be inadmissible, the Court of Justice's ruling in ***Lyckeskog*** would seem to apply, with the effect that the Court of Appeal *would not* be considered to be a court 'against whose decisions there is no judicial remedy'. Here, it is not the Court of Appeal which determines that there are to be no further judicial remedies under national law, so it is under no obligation to refer a question to the Court of Justice under Article 267 TFEU. Indeed, in such a situation it would make no sense to hold that there is such an obligation on the Court of Appeal, as it cannot predict whether the Supreme Court will hear the case and is in no position to make a reference under Article 267 after the appeal has been refused.
>
> The Court of Justice has yet to clarify that its case law would necessarily be applied in this way. However, there seems to be a risk in the latter situation, where the Court of Appeal does not exercise its discretion to refer and the Supreme Court does not find the case to be admissible, that the litigant is left without the protection that is intended to be provided by the obligation to refer contained in the third paragraph of Article 267 TFEU.

5.4 Special forms of procedure

Objective 4

▶ See section 2.7.1 for the ordinary judicial procedure of the Court of Justice

From 1 July 2000, the Court's Statute and Rules of Procedure have provided a simplified procedure or an accelerated procedure for certain types of case referred to it under Article 267 TFEU. Since early 2008, the Court's Statute and Rules of Procedure have also provided an urgent preliminary ruling procedure. Each of these special forms of procedure will now be considered further.

5.4.1 Simplified procedure

The simplified procedure is provided for in **Article 99 of the Rules** of the Court of Justice. This Article states that:

> Where a question referred to the Court for a preliminary ruling is identical to a question on which the Court has already ruled, where the reply to such a question may be clearly deduced from existing case-law or where the answer to the question referred for a preliminary ruling admits of no reasonable doubt, the Court may at any time, on a proposal from the Judge-Rapporteur and after hearing the Advocate General, decide to rule by reasoned order.

Therefore, the simplified procedure may be applied when: (i) a question is referred to the Court that is identical to a question that has already been answered, (ii) the answer to the question can be clearly deduced from existing case law or (iii) the answer admits of no reasonable doubt. Under such circumstances, the Court can produce a **reasoned order** rather than a full judgment.

Use of the simplified procedure has undoubtedly had an effect on reducing the average time taken to deliver a judgment in Article 267 TFEU proceedings.

5.4.2 Accelerated (or expedited) procedure

Article 105(1) of the Rules provides for an accelerated procedure, as follows:

> At the request of the referring court or tribunal or, exceptionally, of his own motion, the President of the Court may, where the nature of the case requires that it be dealt with within a short time, after hearing the Judge-Rapporteur and the Advocate General, decide that a reference for a preliminary ruling is to be determined pursuant to an expedited procedure derogating from the provisions of these Rules.

If the accelerated procedure is applied, Article 105(2) provides that the date for the hearing shall be fixed immediately, thus enabling the Court to deliver its judgment in a shorter period of time.

The accelerated procedure will only be used if the President of the Court determines that the case is 'exceptionally urgent'. Use of the accelerated procedure is rare as few cases are found to meet this requirement.

In addition, it should be noted that Article 20 of the Statute provides that, after hearing the Advocate General assigned to a particular case, if the Court considers that the case raises no new point of law, it may decide to determine the case without a submission (i.e. Opinion) from the Advocate General. This provision will apply to cases referred to the Court of Justice for a preliminary ruling pursuant to Article 267 TFEU, in addition to other categories of case.

5.4.3 Urgent preliminary ruling procedure

The urgent preliminary ruling procedure (PPU) enables questions relating to the area of freedom, security and justice that are referred for a preliminary ruling to be dealt with expeditiously and appropriately. After establishing that existing procedures, including the accelerated procedure, are not capable of ensuring that such cases would be dealt with rapidly enough, the Court proposed the creation of this new procedure in order to be able to decide such cases within a short time and without delaying the handling of other cases pending before the Court.

The procedure is contained in **Article 23a of the Statute** of the Court of Justice and **Article 107 of the Rules**. The urgent preliminary ruling procedure is designed to be swifter than the ordinary and accelerated preliminary ruling procedures in the following ways: first, the written procedure is limited to the parties to the main proceedings, the Member State from which the reference is made, the European Commission and other Union institutions if a measure of theirs is at issue. All such interested persons will be able to participate in an oral procedure, where they can express a view on the written observations that have been lodged. Second, cases subject to the urgent preliminary ruling procedure will, as soon as they arrive at the Court, be assigned to a Chamber of five Judges specially designated for this purpose. Finally, communications for urgent preliminary cases will, for the most part, be conducted electronically.

The urgent preliminary procedure was applied for the first time in 2008 in *Inga Rinau* (Case C-195/08 PPU). In this case, the Court of Justice clarified the law relating to the return of a child wrongly retained in another Member State. During 2018, 12 cases were conducted under the urgent preliminary ruling procedure at an average duration of 3.1 months.

CHAPTER SUMMARY

Judicial methods of interpretation

- The Court of Justice of the European Union is **not bound by precedent** but will aim to rule consistently.
- The Court favours **teleological** and **contextual** methods of interpretation, but may sometimes also use literal or historical methods.

References for a preliminary ruling under Article 267 TFEU

- Questions for a preliminary ruling must either be on the **interpretation of a Treaty provision** or **the interpretation or validity of an act of a Union institution** or other Union body.
- Any court or tribunal of a Member State **may** refer such a question to the Court of Justice.
- A court against whose decisions there is no judicial remedy **must** refer such a question if it is **necessary** to enable them to decide a case.
- **Special procedures** may be used to streamline preliminary rulings.

Chapter 6
Review of the legality of Union acts

Learning objectives

At the end of this chapter you should understand:

1. The procedures of the Court of Justice of the European Union by which the legality of Union law may be reviewed.

2. The scope of judicial review of the legality of the acts of Union institutions under Article 263 TFEU.

3. Challenges to the failure of an institution to act and indirect challenges to the legality of Union acts.

4. When damages can be claimed for unlawful Union acts under Article 340 TFEU.

Key terms and concepts

Familiarity with the following terms will be helpful for understanding this chapter:

Annulment – the declaration that an act is invalid and ceases to have effect

Legislative act – an act adopted by the ordinary legislative procedure or a special legislative procedure

Locus standi – the right of a person or body to bring a case before a court

Regulatory act – a non-legislative act of a Union institution or other Union body, office or agency i.e. an act that has not been adopted by a legislative procedure

6.1 Introduction

Objective 1

This chapter considers the avenues that are available for challenges to be brought against acts of the Union institutions. The first such avenue that is considered is the **review of legality** procedure that is provided for in **Article 263 TFEU**. This procedure, which may also be referred to as judicial review or actions for **annulment**, enables individuals to bring an action for the annulment of a Union act directly before the Court of Justice of the European Union. However, such actions for the review of legality of Union acts are subject to several limitations: the applicant must fulfil strict criteria for admissibility, they must be brought on certain grounds and they must be brought within a specific time limit.

Where individuals fail to meet the admissibility criteria of the time limit to challenge a Union act under Article 263 TFEU, they may be able to raise an **indirect challenge** under **Article 277 TFEU**. Such challenges generally arise through a reference for a preliminary ruling (Article 267 TFEU). Additionally, individuals can challenge a Union institution's **failure to act** under **Article 265 TFEU**.

Where a Union act has been ruled unlawful by the Court of Justice, it may subsequently be possible for affected persons to claim **damages** against the relevant Union institution under **Article 340 TFEU**.

Along with references for a preliminary ruling (see Chapter 5), these procedures (Arts 263, 265, 267, 277 and 340 TFEU) are intended to provide 'a complete system of legal remedies and procedures designed to ensure judicial review of the legality of acts of the institutions' (*Unión de Pequeños Agricultores* v *Council* (Case C-50/00 P; see Figure 6.1)). The extent to which they do, in practice, provide such complete protection will be discussed throughout this chapter.

Figure 6.1 Procedures under Articles 267, 263 and 258 TFEU

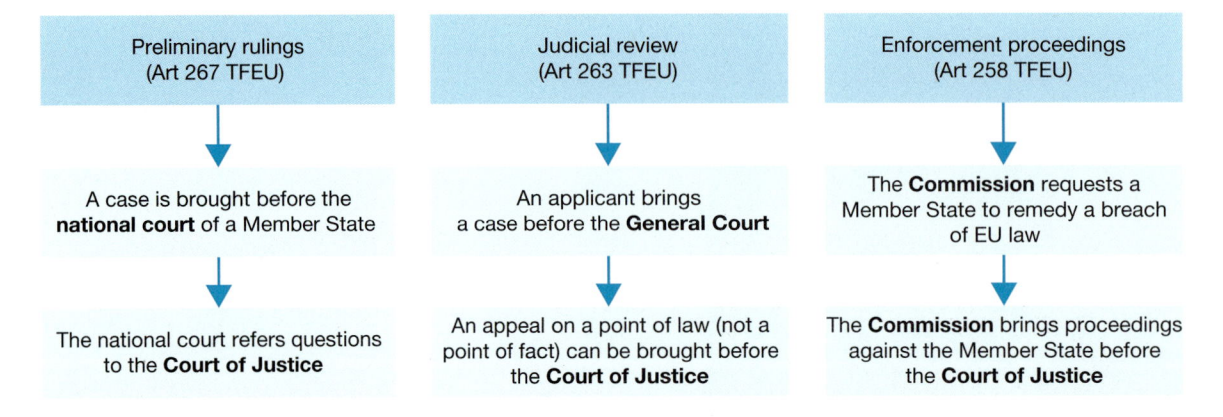

Preliminary rulings (Art 267 TFEU)	Judicial review (Art 263 TFEU)	Enforcement proceedings (Art 258 TFEU)
A case is brought before the **national court** of a Member State	An applicant brings a case before the **General Court**	The **Commission** requests a Member State to remedy a breach of EU law
The national court refers questions to the **Court of Justice**	An appeal on a point of law (not a point of fact) can be brought before the **Court of Justice**	The **Commission** brings proceedings against the Member State before the **Court of Justice**

It may be helpful to note at this stage that the division of competences between the General Court and the Court of Justice mean that review of legality cases, which are initially brought before the General Court, may be appealed to the Court of Justice, while references for preliminary rulings (see Chapter 5) and infringement proceedings against Member States (see Chapter 7) will always be brought straight to the Court of Justice – see Figure 6.1. Since 1989, when the Court of First Instance (CFI, renamed as the General Court by the ToL) was first introduced, cases before the CFI/General Court have been prefixed with a 'T' (e.g. Case T-00/00) and cases before the Court of Justice have been prefixed with a 'C' (e.g. Case C-00/00).

6.2 Review of legality of Union acts under Article 263 TFEU

Objective 2

Each of the institutions has a limited competence and must carry out its functions in the way specified in the Treaties and according to general principles of Union law (Art 13 TEU; see Chapter 4). If it is believed that an institution has exceeded its powers or used them unlawfully, its acts may be subject to review by the Court of Justice under **Article 263 TFEU**. If the Court concludes that an institution has acted in breach of Union law, the act in question will be annulled.

The full text of Article 263 TFEU is as follows:

> The Court of Justice of the European Union shall review the legality of **legislative acts**, of acts of the Council, of the Commission and of the European Central Bank, other than recommendations and opinions, and of acts of the European Parliament and of the European Council intended to produce legal effects *vis-à-vis* third parties. It shall also review the legality of acts of bodies, offices or agencies of the Union intended to produce legal effects *vis-à-vis* third parties.
>
> It shall for this purpose have jurisdiction in actions brought by a Member State, the European Parliament, the Council or the Commission on grounds of lack of competence, infringement of an essential procedural requirement, infringement of the Treaties or of any rule of law relating to their application, or misuse of powers.
>
> The Court shall have jurisdiction under the same conditions in actions brought by the Court of Auditors, by the European Central Bank and by the Committee of the Regions for the purpose of protecting their prerogatives.
>
> Any natural or legal person may, under the conditions laid down in the first and second paragraphs, institute proceedings against an act addressed to that person or which is of direct and individual concern to them, and against a **regulatory act** which is of direct concern to them and does not entail implementing measures.
>
> Acts setting up bodies, offices and agencies of the Union may lay down specific conditions and arrangements concerning actions brought by natural or legal persons against acts of these bodies, offices or agencies intended to produce legal effects in relation to them.
>
> The proceedings provided for in this Article shall be instituted within two months of the publication of the measure, or of its notification to the plaintiff, or, in the absence thereof, of the day on which it came to the knowledge of the latter, as the case may be.

Article 263 TFEU is substantially the same as the former Article 230 EC Treaty, although there are some subtle differences, which will be discussed throughout this chapter. The case law considered within this chapter is almost exclusively based on the former Article 230 EC Treaty.

The constituent parts of Article 263 TFEU (and the former Art 230 EC Treaty) raise five issues:

1. What are the grounds for challenge?
2. What type of Union act may be reviewed?
3. Who may challenge such an act, i.e. who has, in the language of English administrative law, the *locus standi* to mount a challenge?
4. When is an action barred by lapse of time?
5. What are the consequences of an annulment?

Each of these five issues will now be considered.

6.2.1 Grounds for judicial review

Article 263 TFEU (like the former Art 230 EC Treaty) provides four possible grounds upon which a reviewable Union act may be challenged. These are:

- lack of competence;
- infringement of an essential procedural requirement;
- infringement of the Treaties or any rule of law relating to their application;
- misuse of powers.

These are not mutually exclusive and two or more may be cited together in an application for judicial review (see case study on the UK's challenge to the Working Time Directive, below). Each of these four grounds will now be considered in more detail.

Lack of competence

A legal act may be annulled if it is found to have an inappropriate or inadequate legal base, i.e. if its enactment exceeds the competence conferred to the relevant Union institution by the Treaties. The equivalent to this in English law is ***substantive ultra vires***.

▶ See Chapter 4 on the competences of the Union and the principle of conferral

It is not always clear what the correct legal base for a Union act of secondary legislation should be and there may be more than one provision in the Treaties that could be identified as authorising it. For example, a proposal on animal feed could be mandated by provisions in the area of agriculture or in the area of consumer protection. It may therefore be possible for the Commission to be strategic in selecting the legal base that best suits the intended aim of the legislation.

▶ The ordinary legislative procedure is set out in section 3.4.4

Prior to the SEA, the choice of legal base rarely gave rise to controversy. However, subsequently disputes have arisen, largely either because Member States contested the competence of the Union to legislate on the matter in question at all or because a legal base allowing for a qualified majority vote within the Council was chosen, when some Member States demanded a base requiring unanimity and the opportunity to block the measure by exercising their national veto (see ***Commission* v *Council*** (Case C-300/89); ***European Parliament* v *Council*** (Case C-295/90)). Such contention, however, is less likely following the ToL's entry into force, as the vast majority of legal bases are now governed by the **ordinary legislative procedure**.

With regards to legal acts, paragraph 25 of the **Interinstitutional Agreement on Better Law-Making** of April 2016 establishes that:

> The **Commission** shall provide, in relation to each proposal, an **explanation and justification** to the European Parliament and to the Council regarding its choice of legal basis and type of legal act in the explanatory memorandum accompanying the proposal. . . .
>
> The Commission shall also explain in its explanatory memoranda how the measures proposed are justified in the light of the **principles of subsidiarity and proportionality** and how they are compatible with **fundamental rights**.

This information can inform an assessment of whether the correct legal base has been used and whether the general principles of Union law have been adhered to, and therefore whether the act is within the institution's competence.

In *Commission* v *Council* (Case 45/86), the Court of Justice clarified that:

> The choice of a legal base for a measure may not depend simply on an institution's conviction as to the objective pursued but must be based on objective factors which are amenable to judicial review. [para 11]

A number of challenges have been mounted on the grounds that the Commission has chosen the wrong legal base for the proposal of a legislative act. Some of these, including the tobacco advertisement cases, are examined in Chapter 4.

Infringement of an essential procedural requirement

In order to be legally valid, a Union act must be enacted or otherwise conducted in adherence to the correct procedure, as provided for in Union law. This is probably the most common basis for annulment procedures and is equivalent in English law to *procedural ultra vires*. It encompasses breaches of both formal procedural requirements laid down in the Treaties and in secondary legislation, and the more informal rules of fairness required by general principles of Union law (see Chapter 3). The breach of a procedural requirement may be so fundamental that the decision or other measure may be void *ab initio*, i.e. the decision will be held to have never existed.

There are numerous procedural requirements that a Union act may be in breach of. Under **Article 296 TFEU**, acts of secondary legislation 'shall state the reasons on which they are based'. A breach of this provision led the CFI to annul Commission decisions withdrawing approval or partial support of projects financed by the European Social Fund in *Eugénio Branco Ld* v *Commission* (Case T-85/94) and two similar previous cases (*Consorgan Lda* v *Commission* (Case C-181/90); *Socurte Ld and Others* v *Commission* (Cases T-432, 434/93)). In addition to the obligation imposed by what is now Article 296 TFEU, there was also a breach of the requirement imposed by Article 6(1) of Regulation 2950/83, under which the Commission, before deciding to suspend, reduce or withdraw fund aid, had to give the relevant Member State the opportunity to comment.

In another example, a measure can be ruled to be invalid if the European Parliament is not consulted as required (*Roquette Frères* v *Council* (Case 138/79)). The case of *European Parliament* v *Council* (Case C-388/92) considered a situation where the Council had consulted the Parliament on an initial legislative draft, but had not then consulted Parliament again after substantial amendments had been made. The Court of Justice held that, where consultation was a procedural requirement, an obligation to re-consult arose 'on each occasion when the text finally adopted, viewed as a whole, departs substantially from the text on which Parliament has already been consulted'. On that basis the Court annulled Regulation 2454/92 on the ground that the Council infringed procedural requirements by disregarding the prerogatives of Parliament.

Infringement of the Treaties or any rule relating to their application

Union acts must not infringe any of the provisions of the Treaties or the general principles of EU law. This includes the values and principles established in the Treaties, the rights enshrined in the Charter of Fundamental Rights, the rights established by the European Convention on Human Rights and other principles that have been recognised as general principles of EU law by the Court of Justice of the European Union (see Chapter 3). This ground therefore encompasses a wide range of legal provisions, including the principles of subsidiarity and proportionality.

Complicating the application of this infringement ground is the fact that the rights and principles of Union law are not absolute and may, in appropriate circumstances, have to give way to restrictions imposed in the interest of the common organisation of the internal market, 'provided that those restrictions in fact correspond to objectives of general interest pursued by the Community [i.e. Union], and do not constitute a disproportionate and intolerable interference, impairing the very substance of the rights guaranteed' (*Germany* v *Commission* – '**Banana Market**' (Case C-280/93)).

Misuse of powers

This is the equivalent, in English administrative law, of using a power for an improper or illegitimate purpose. As the power is itself lawful, a challenger must prove that the purpose for which it has been used is inappropriate (*Netherlands* v *High Authority* (Case 6/54)). In *Parliament* v *Commission* (Case C-156/93), the Court of Justice stated that:

> An act of a Community institution is vitiated by misuse of powers if it is adopted with the exclusive or main purpose of achieving an end other than that stated or evading a procedure specifically prescribed by the Treaty.

Most of the few successful cases that have resulted in the annulment of a measure have relied on published documents or the reasons given under what is now Article 296 TFEU to argue that the relevant institution has misunderstood the purpose for which a power has been conferred on it (*Giuffrida* v *Council* (Case 105/75)).

Case study: the UK's challenge to the Working Time Directive

The following case demonstrates the reasoning of the Court in response to arguments relying on a number of the grounds for judicial review:

UK v *Council of the European Union* (Case C-84/94)

Facts:

The **Working Time Directive 93/104** was adopted by the Council, acting by qualified majority, on 23 November 1993, with an implementation date of 23 November 1996. On 8 March 1994 the UK brought an action under what is now Article 263 TFEU for the annulment of the Directive or, alternatively, the annulment of specific parts of the Directive. In support of its action, the UK relied on four pleas which will now be examined.

Ruling:

Defective legal base (lack of competence):
The main thrust of the UK's argument centred on the first plea that the Directive was not concerned with the improvement of the health and safety of workers and therefore should not have been adopted under the former Article 118a EC Treaty (now Art 153 TFEU).

First, the UK contended that the correct legal base was either the former Article 100 EC Treaty (now Art 122 TFEU) or the former Article 235 EC Treaty (now Art 352 TFEU), which at the time both required the Council to act unanimously. With regard to the former Article 100, the Court of Justice held that the former **Article 118a was a more specific legal base and was therefore to be preferred**. With regard to the former Art 235 EC Treaty, the Court of Justice simply noted that the Article could be used as the legal base for a measure only where no other Treaty provision conferred on the Union institutions the necessary power to adopt it; this was not the case here.

Second, the UK argued that a strict interpretation of the former Article 118a EC Treaty only permitted the adoption of directives with a genuine and objective link to the health and safety of workers and which therefore related to **physical** conditions and risks at the workplace. This did not apply to measures concerning, in particular, weekly working time (Art 6 of the Directive), paid annual leave (Art 7) and rest periods (Arts 4 and 5). The UK's alternative plea was for the annulment of these specific provisions. The Court held that **a broad scope was to be given to health and safety**. This was supported by reference to the Constitution of the World Health Organization (to which all the Member States belong), in which 'health' is defined as 'a state of complete physical, mental and social well-being which does not consist only in the absence of illness or infirmity'.

Third, the UK argued that the former Article 118a did not empower the Council to adopt directives which dealt with the question of health and safety in a 'generalised, unspecific and unscientific manner'. The UK supported this argument with reference to previous directives which had been adopted under the former Article 118a, which covered specific areas of activity. The Court likewise rejected this argument, ruling that **past practices of the Council could not create a precedent binding on the Union institutions with regard to the correct legal base**.

The Court of Justice concluded that 'where the principal aim of the measure in question is the protection of the health and safety of workers, [the former] Art 118a must be used'. While the Court noted that the preamble of the Directive established the approach of viewing working time provisions in terms of the favourable impact they may have on the health and safety of workers, **the Court did not accept that specifically choosing Sunday as the weekly rest day (Art 5, second sentence) had any bearing on the health and safety of workers**. The Court therefore upheld this part of the UK's alternative claim and annulled the second sentence of Article 5.

Breach of the principle of proportionality (infringement of rules):
First, the UK argued that the reference to the adoption of 'minimum requirements' in the former Article 118a (2) only empowered the Council to adopt measures which were at a level acceptable to all Member States. This was rejected by the Court of Justice, which stated that **the concept of 'minimum requirements' does not limit Union action to the lowest level of protection provided by the various Member States**, but means a Member State can adopt provisions more stringent than those of the Directive.

Second, the UK argued that the Directive's objective of safeguarding the health and safety of workers could be attained by measures which were less restrictive than those of the Directive. The Court held that the Council, acting as legislature, must be allowed a wide discretion to make social policy choices. **The Court would only rule such a measure to be disproportionate if the exercise of the Council's discretion had been vitiated by manifest error or misuse of powers, or if it had manifestly exceeded the limits of its power**. This could not be proven and was therefore rejected by the Court.

Third, the UK argued that a measure could only be proportionate if it complied with the principle of subsidiarity. The Court held that **it had been demonstrated that Union action was necessary to adopt minimum requirements** with the objective of raising the level of the health and safety protection of workers.

Misuse of powers:

The Court referred to its definition of the misuse of powers in *Parliament* v *Commission* (Case C-156/93, see above). As the Court had already held that the former Article 118a EC Treaty was the appropriate legal base and that misuse of powers could not be proved, this plea was dismissed.

Infringement of essential procedural requirements:

The UK argued that the directive was inadequately reasoned because there was a failure to demonstrate a connection between the health and safety of workers and the provisions of the Directive, such as those concerned with improving the living and working conditions of workers or the internal market. The Court disagreed, ruling that **the various recitals in the preamble to the Directive clearly demonstrated the connection between working time and the health and safety of workers**.

Significance:

This case demonstrates how several grounds for judicial review may be combined in an action for the annulment of a measure and how these grounds often overlap. The case also illustrates the possibility of the partial annulment of a measure, as all of the UK's claims here resulted in the annulment of just one sentence of the Working Time Directive.

6.2.2 Reviewable acts

Not every act of a Union institution may be reviewed. The former Article 230 EC Treaty *prima facie* restricted the scope of review to those acts defined as legally binding by the former Article 249 EC Treaty (now Art 288 TFEU) – i.e. regulations, directives and decisions. Opinions and recommendations were not reviewable. However, other acts not specified in the former Article 249 EC Treaty (now Art 288 TFEU) have been treated by the Court of Justice as subject to review. **Article 263 TFEU** (which replaced Art 230 EC Treaty) has been rewritten to accommodate the case law of the Court of Justice, and in particular to extend the range of acts to include those of 'bodies, offices or agencies of the Union intended to produce legal effects *vis-à-vis* third parties'. The case law considered below concerned the former Article 230 EC Treaty but is directly relevant to the current Article 263 TFEU.

Acts that are intended to have legal effects

In *Commission* v *Council* (Case 22/70), the Court of Justice held that a resolution passed by the Council to participate in a European Transport Agreement was reviewable under the former Article 230 EC Treaty (now Art 263 TFEU). The Court refused to interpret the former Article 249 EC Treaty (now Art 288 TFEU) restrictively and declared that 'an action for annulment must ... be available in the case of all measures adopted by the institutions, whatever their nature and form, which are intended to have legal effects'. In *IBM* v *Commission* (Case 60/81), the Court of Justice emphasised that the determining factor is whether or not an act has legal consequences, regardless of how they are produced:

> In order to ascertain whether the measures in question are acts within the meaning of Article 173 [now Art 263 TFEU] it is necessary ... to look to their **substance**. According to the consistent case law of the Court any measure the legal effects of which are binding on, and

capable of affecting the interests of, the applicant by bringing about a distinct change in his legal position is an act or decision which may be the subject of an action under Article 173 [now Art 263 TFEU] for a declaration that it is void. However, the **form** in which such acts or decisions are cast is, in principle, immaterial as regards the question whether they are open to challenge under that article.

It is, however, often difficult to distinguish between form and substance. An act may not have any legal consequence precisely because it has not been adopted in the form required. In *Air France* v *Commission* (Case T-3/93) the Commissioner responsible for competition policy, Sir Leon Brittan, had issued a press statement about the merger between Dan Air and British Airways, declaring that it would not result in a sufficient concentration of air transport to have a Union dimension. Air France's attempt to challenge this press statement failed at the first hurdle, because the statement had not been adopted by the whole Commission and did not have the *form* of a legal act. It could, therefore, have no legal consequences (see also *Nefarma* v *Commission* (Case T-113/89)).

As it was originally written, the former Article 230 EC Treaty made no mention of measures adopted by the European Parliament. Despite this, the Court of Justice held in *Parti Ecologiste ('Les Verts')* v *European Parliament* (Case 294/83) that measures adopted by the Parliament that were intended to have legal effects *vis-à-vis* third parties were subject to annulment procedures under the former Article 230 EC Treaty (see also *Luxembourg* v *European Parliament* (Case C-213/88)). The Court of Justice has also held that a declaration made by the President of the Parliament at the conclusion of the debate by Parliament on the Union's budget has the character of a legal act and is also subject to annulment (*Council* v *Parliament* (Case 34/86); *Council* v *European Parliament* (Case C-284/90)). This situation should be contrasted with that in the following case, which likewise concerned whether a declaration of the President of the Parliament was a measure open to challenge:

Le Pen v *Parliament* (Case T-353/00)

Facts:
A declaration of the President of the Parliament stated that, in accordance with Article 12(2) of the Act concerning the election of representatives to the Parliament by direct universal suffrage, annexed to the Council Decision of 20 September 1976, 'the ... Parliament takes note of the notification of the French government declaring the disqualification of Mr Le Pen from holding office'.

Ruling:
The CFI (now the General Court) held that the declaration was not open to challenge. In its judgment, the CFI stated that the intervention of the European Parliament under the first sub-paragraph of Article 12(2) of the above mentioned Act was restricted to taking note of the declaration, already made by the national authorities, that the applicant's seat was vacant. The CFI accordingly held that the declaration of the President of the Parliament was not intended to produce legal effects of its own, distinct from those of the decree dated 31 March 2000 of the French Prime Minister stating that the applicant's ineligibility brought to an end his term of office as a representative in the European Parliament.

Le Pen's appeal to the Court of Justice was dismissed (Case C-208/03P).

Significance:
This case clarifies that the question of whether an act was intended to produce legal effects is the essential test for determining whether an act is reviewable.

Measures taken by the Parliament affecting third parties were made specifically subject to review as a result of amendments made to the former Article 230 EC Treaty; Article 263 TFEU contains a similar right of review.

A decision by the Commission to close the file on a complaint alleging a breach of the former Article 82 EC Treaty (now Art 102 TFEU) has also been held to be a 'decision' reviewable under the former Article 230 EC Treaty (***SFEI and Others v Commission*** (Case C-39/93P)). However, in ***Philip Morris International and Others v Commission*** (Joined Cases T-377/00, T-379/00, T-380/00, T-260/01 and T-272/01), the CFI (now the General Court) held that a decision to bring court proceedings is not a reviewable decision as it does not in itself alter the legal position in question, but has the effect merely of opening a procedure whose purpose is to achieve a change in that position through a judgment. While noting that the commencement of legal proceedings may give rise to certain consequences by operation of law, the CFI held that their commencement does not in itself determine definitively the obligations of the parties to the case and that this determination results only from the judgment of the court.

Although the acts of the Council are reviewable, it has been held that representatives of the Member States must be acting *as* Council members for what is now Article 263 TFEU to apply. In ***Parliament v Council*** (Cases C-181/91 and C-248/91), the Parliament attempted to challenge a decision made at a Council meeting granting special aid to Bangladesh. The Court of Justice held that acts adopted by representatives of the Member States acting not as members of the Council but as representatives of their governments amounted to the collective exercise of the competences of the Member States. They were not acts of the Council and were not, therefore, subject to review by the Court of Justice.

Union acts explicitly excluded from judicial review

Acts that are explicitly excluded from review are those under policy areas of the Treaties where the Court of Justice of the European Union has either limited jurisdiction or no jurisdiction. These are mainly the policy areas that, prior to the entry into force of the ToL and the resultant simplification of the structure of the Union, comprised the second and third pillars of the Union. Now, they are:

- Title V, Chapter 2, Sections 1 and 2 (Arts 23–46) TEU, relating to the Common Foreign and Security Policy;
- Title V, Chapter 4 (Arts 82–86) TFEU, relating to Judicial Cooperation in Criminal Matters
- Title V, Chapter 5 (Arts 87–89) TFEU, relating to Police Cooperation.

Referring to the above articles, **Article 24(1) TEU** provides that 'The Court of Justice of the European Union shall not have jurisdiction with respect to these provisions'. Similarly, **Article 276 TFEU** provides that:

> In exercising its powers regarding the provisions of Chapters 4 [judicial cooperation in criminal matters] and 5 [police cooperation] of Title V of Part Three [of the TFEU] relating to the area of freedom, security and justice, **the Court of Justice of the European Union shall have no jurisdiction to review the validity or proportionality of operations carried out by the police or other law-enforcement services of a Member State or the exercise of the responsibilities incumbent upon Member States with regard to the maintenance of law and order and the safeguarding of internal security.**

The former Article 230 EC Treaty (now Art 263 TFEU) was likewise subject to similar exclusions. In the context of the former Article 230 EC Treaty, the Court, however, decided that it does have jurisdiction to determine the *scope* of such exclusions (see, for example, ***Svenska Journalistforbundet*** v ***Council of European Union*** (Case T-174/95)).

Negative acts

The CFI (now the General Court) has held that where, in the context of an action for annulment, the contested measure is **negative** (i.e. a refusal), it is the request to which it responds that should be assessed to determine whether or not it is reviewable. In particular, the refusal by a Union institution to withdraw or amend a measure may constitute a reviewable decision under what is now Article 263 TFEU *only* if the measure which the Union institution refuses to withdraw or amend could itself have been contested under that provision (***Institouto N Avgerinopoulou and Others*** v ***Commission*** (Case T-139/02) and ***Comunidad Autónoma de Andalucía*** v ***Commission*** (Case T-29/03)).

In ***Comunidad Autónoma de Andalucía*** v ***Commission***, the European Anti-Fraud Office (OLAF) issued a final report following an external investigation. OLAF forwarded the report to the competent Spanish authorities in accordance with Article 9 of Regulation 1073/1999. The CFI (now the General Court) held that a letter from the Director-General of OLAF, informing the applicant that it was not possible to investigate its complaint directed against the final report, could not be regarded as a decision against which proceedings could be brought. This was due to the fact that the report did not constitute a measure producing binding legal effects such as to affect the applicant's interests; rather, it was commensurate to a recommendation or an opinion, which lack binding legal effects.

6.2.3 *Locus standi* (legal standing)

There are three categories of applicant who may bring a case for the judicial review of a Union act:

1. **Privileged applicants**: Member States, the European Parliament, the Council or the Commission.
2. **Semi-privileged applicants**: the Court of Auditors, the European Central Bank and the Committee of the Regions.
3. **Non-privileged applicants**: any natural or legal person.

Different rules apply depending upon whether the applicant is privileged or non-privileged. It is much more difficult to prove legal standing to bring a claim (***locus standi***) for a non-privileged applicant. An overview of the conditions required for each type of applicant to have legal standing under Article 263 TFEU is provided in Figure 6.2.

Privileged applicants

Article 263 TFEU confers specific and unlimited rights of challenge to the **Member States,** the **European Parliament,** the **Council** and the **Commission**. Under the previous iteration of this Article (Art 230 EC Treaty), the European Parliament was not included as one of the Union institutions with a specific and unlimited right of challenge (the Parliament only had a right of challenge to enable it to protect its prerogatives). In ***Regione Siciliana*** v ***Commission*** (Case C-417/04), the Court of Justice determined that the term 'Member State', within the meaning of what is now Article 263 TFEU, only includes government authorities of the

Member States. However, the Court stated that a local or regional entity may, to the extent that it has legal personality under national law, institute proceedings on the same terms as a 'non-privileged applicant' (see below).

Semi-privileged applicants

Article 263 TFEU grants rights of challenge to the Court of Auditors, the European Central Bank and the Committee of the Regions only to the extent necessary to protect their prerogatives. For example, they may bring a case where their right to participate or to be consulted in the legislative process, as laid down by the Treaties, is at issue.

Other bodies, agencies or offices that are not listed in Article 263, including the European Council, can bring actions for the annulment of Union acts, but only as non-privileged applicants, which must meet strict *locus standi* criteria.

Non-privileged applicants

Under Article 263 TFEU, a non-privileged applicant is empowered to challenge the legality of a Union act in three situations:

- where an *act* is addressed to the applicant;
- where an *act* is of *direct and individual concern* to the applicant;
- where a *regulatory act* is of *direct concern* to the applicant, and does not entail implementing measures.

Additionally, the Court has determined that an applicant must have a legal interest in bringing proceedings.

An 'act' under these provisions could be a regulation, a directive or a decision. The right to challenge an 'act' addressed to the applicant under Article 263 TFEU is therefore broader than the right only to challenge a 'decision' addressed to the applicant that was provided under the former Article 230 EC Treaty.

The first situation, where an act is addressed to the applicant, is straightforward in scope. Many decisions which were subject to challenge by individuals under the former Article 230 EC Treaty had been adopted by the Commission in relation to Union competition law, and they were challenged by individuals and companies to whom the decision was addressed.

The latter two situations are less straightforward. Questions as to the scope of the terms 'direct concern' and 'direct and individual concern' have produced a catalogue of litigation. Then, regarding the third situation, the precise scope of what constitutes a **'regulatory act'** has required clarification by the Court of Justice, as this was not included in the former Article 230 EC Treaty. Such issues pertaining to the standing of non-privileged applicants will now be considered in turn.

Non-privileged applicants' legal interest in bringing proceedings

Although a legal interest in bringing proceedings is not expressly required by Article 263 TFEU (or the former Art 230 EC Treaty), the CFI (now the General Court) has stated that proof of such an interest is an essential and fundamental prerequisite for any legal proceedings under what is now Article 263 TFEU (***Schmitz-Gotha Fahrzeugwerke* v *Commission***

6.2 REVIEW OF LEGALITY OF UNION ACTS UNDER ARTICLE 263 TFEU

Figure 6.2 Legal standing to challenge a Union act under Article 263 TFEU

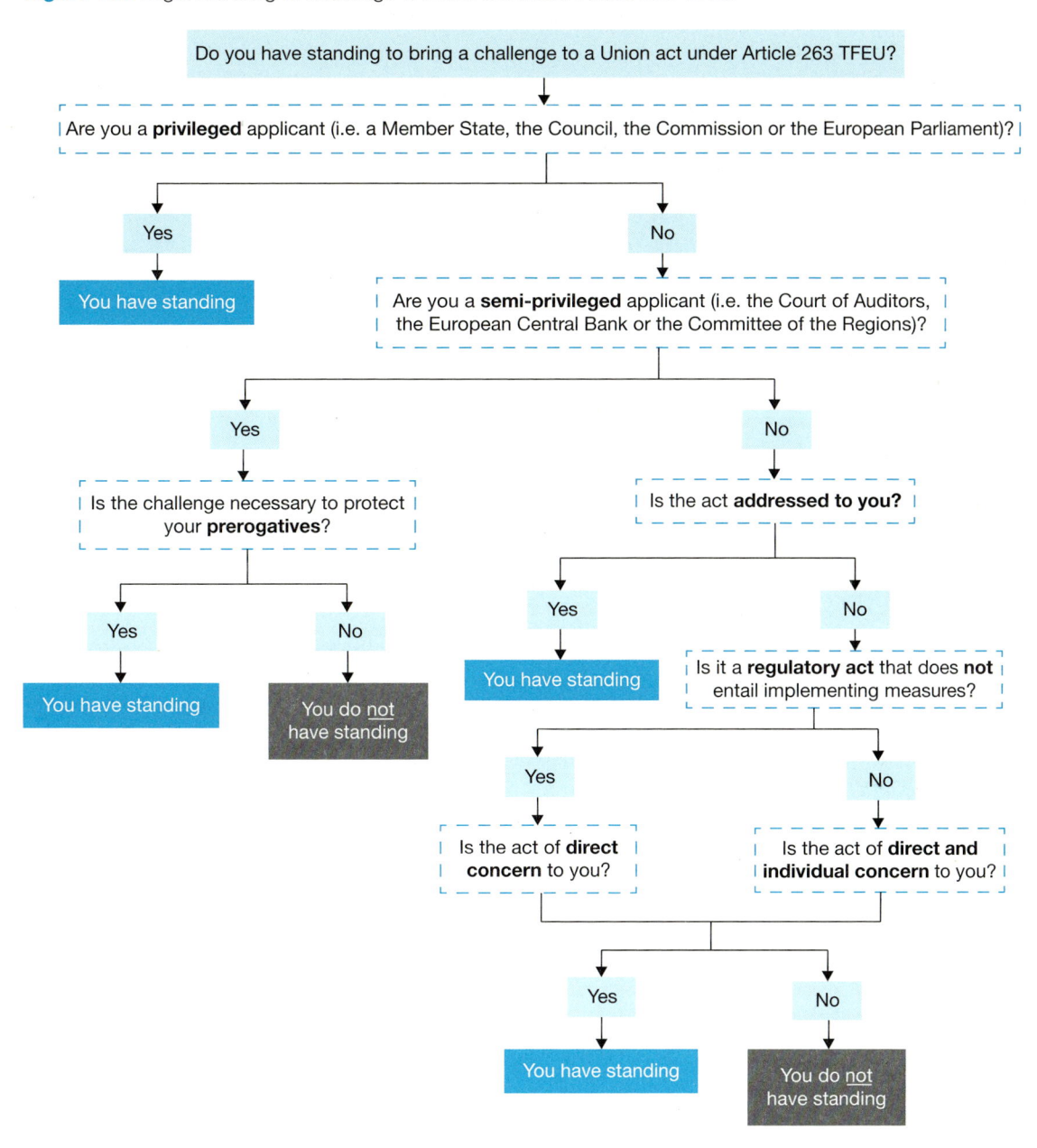

```
Do you have standing to bring a challenge to a Union act under Article 263 TFEU?
                                    ↓
Are you a privileged applicant (i.e. a Member State, the Council, the Commission or the European Parliament)?
         ↓ Yes                                          ↓ No
  You have standing          Are you a semi-privileged applicant (i.e. the Court of Auditors,
                              the European Central Bank or the Committee of the Regions)?
                    ↓ Yes                                          ↓ No
       Is the challenge necessary to protect              Is the act addressed to you?
              your prerogatives?
        ↓ Yes         ↓ No                        ↓ Yes                   ↓ No
  You have     You do not                    You have standing    Is it a regulatory act that does not
  standing     have standing                                      entail implementing measures?
                                                              ↓ Yes                   ↓ No
                                                    Is the act of direct        Is the act of direct and
                                                     concern to you?            individual concern to you?
                                                         ↓ Yes         ↓ No
                                                    You have standing   You do not have standing
```

(Case T-167/01); see also *Olivieri v Commission and European Agency for the Evaluation of Medicinal Products* (Case T-326/99)).

That interest must be a **vested and present** interest and is assessed as at the date when the action is brought. If the interest which an applicant claims concerns a future legal situation, he must demonstrate that the prejudice to that situation is already certain (***NBV*** v ***Commission*** (Case T-138/89)). The CFI (now the General Court) applied these principles in the following cases:

> ### *Gruppo Ormeggiatori del Porto di Venezia and others* v *Commission* (Joined Cases T-228, 229, 242, 243, 245 to 248/00, 250, 252, 256 to 259, 267, 268, 271, 275, 276, 281, 287 and 296/00), *Sagar* v *Commission* (Case T-269/00) and *Gardena Hotels and Comitato Venezia Vuole Vivere* v *Commission* (Case T-288/00)
>
> **Facts:**
>
> Actions were brought by Italian undertakings against a Commission decision declaring certain aid to firms incompatible with the internal market. The applicants were concerned that this would lead the Italian state to reclaim the aid in question.
>
> **Ruling:**
>
> Raising an absolute bar to proceeding of its own motion, the CFI found that the applicants had no legal interest in bringing proceedings, as the Italian state had decided **not** to proceed with the recovery of aid from the applicants. To substantiate their interest in bringing proceedings, the applicants cited only future and uncertain circumstances, namely the possibility that the Commission would make a different assessment from that made by Italy and would require it to recover the alleged aid from the applicant undertakings.
>
> Accordingly, because it was only in the uncertain event of a future Commission decision that their legal position would be affected, **the applicant undertakings had not demonstrated that there was a vested, present interest in seeking the annulment of the contested decision**. Moreover, even in that event, the applicants would have recourse to legal remedy, as they could bring actions in the national courts against any decisions of the competent national authority requiring them to return the aid.
>
> **Significance:**
>
> In this case, the CFI established that a measure could not be annulled on the basis that it *might* lead to certain further measures in the future. In such a situation, an applicant has no present legal interest. If the future measures that an applicant predicted were to materialise, they could then raise actions against these measures in the appropriate way, depending on the nature of the measures.

The Court reaffirmed the principles of the above case in ***Sniace*** v ***Commission*** (Case T-88/01), where the CFI also ruled that the applicant had not demonstrated a vested and present interest.

Although the applicant's interest in bringing proceedings must be assessed as at the time when the application is lodged, in ***First Data*** v ***Commission*** (Case T-28/02) the CFI (now the General Court) established an exception. Here, the applicants contested a decision in which the Commission opposed certain rules governing membership of a bank card scheme. Those rules were withdrawn after the action was brought so that any interest the applicants may have had in bringing the proceedings had ceased to exist. The CFI established that proceedings could be dismissed due to an event which occurred *after* that application was lodged, as in this case, provided that, as a result of that event, the applicant had **lost all personal interest** in having the contested decision annulled.

Non-privileged applicants' direct concern

The Court considers the issue of **direct concern** and **individual concern** as two separate issues, both of which have to be satisfied in the case of 'an act addressed to another person' and only the former of which has to be satisfied in the case of a 'regulatory act' that does not entail implementing measures. Individual concern is considered under the next subheading and is followed by the scope of a 'regulatory act'.

In *Dreyfus* v *Commission* (Case C-386/96 P), the Court of Justice consolidated the definition of direct concern as follows:

> ... for a person to be directly concerned by a Community [i.e. Union] measure, the latter must **directly affect the legal situation of the individual** and **leave no discretion to the addressees** of that measure who are entrusted with the task of implementing it, such implementation being purely automatic and resulting from Community [i.e. Union] rules without the application of other intermediate rules.

These two conditions for determining direct concern (that the measure directly affects the legal situation of the applicant and that it leaves no discretion regarding its implementation) are subsequently known as the **Dreyfus test**.

The question of **discretion** was considered in *NV International Fruit Company and Others* v *Commission* (Joined Cases 41-44/70), which concerned the import of apples from third countries. The contested Commission measure imposed a quota, which the Court found allowed no discretion to the national authorities with regard to the issue of import licences. The measure was therefore found to be of direct concern to the applicants.

In *Municipality of Differdange and Others* v *Commission* (Case 222/83), however, it was found that the applicants were not directly concerned by a Commission decision that permitted Luxembourg to grant aid to steel producers on the condition that production capacity would be reduced. The applicant municipalities claimed that the resultant factory closures would cause a loss of tax revenue to them, but the Court ruled that they were not directly concerned by the decision, as the national authorities had discretion in how to reduce capacity, i.e. which factories to close.

A more flexible approach to the question of direct concern was adopted in the following case (which is also examined below in relation to individual concern):

A E Piraiki-Patraiki v *Commission* (Case 11/82)

Facts:

The applicants were Greek exporters of yarn to France. They contested a Commission decision which allowed France to impose a quota system on the amount of yarn that could be imported from Greece during the period November 1981 to January 1982. The Commission argued that the importers were not directly concerned by the decision, as France had discretion as to whether or not to implement the quota system.

Ruling:

The Court of Justice ruled as follows:

> 7 It is true that without implementing measures adopted at the national level the Commission decision could not have affected the applicants. In this case, however, that fact does not in itself prevent the decision from being of direct concern to the applicants if **other factors justify the conclusion that they have a direct interest in bringing the action.**

> 8 In that respect it should be pointed out that, as the Commission itself admitted during the written procedure, even before being authorized to do so by the Commission the French Republic applied a very restrictive system of licences for imports of cotton yarn of Greek origin. It should moreover be observed that the request for protective measures not only came from the French authorities but sought to obtain the Commission's authorization for a system of import quotas more strict than that which was finally granted.
>
> 9 **In those circumstance the possibility that the French Republic might decide not to make use of the authorization granted to it by the Commission decision was entirely theoretical, since there could be no doubt as to the intention of the French authorities to apply the decision.**
>
> **Significance:**
>
> This case established that the Court is willing to consider more than just whether a decision affects the applicant directly without any implementing measures, but will also consider the extent to which it is certain, and known to the relevant Union institution, that such implementing measures will be taken. This widens the scope of direct concern and places greater emphasis on the responsibility of Union institutions.

In *Instituto N Avgerinopoulou and Others* v *Commission* (T-139/02) and *Regione Siciliana* v *Commission* (Case T-341/02), the CFI dismissed both applications for lack of direct concern because the national authorities had discretion in implementing the contested measures. In these cases, the discretion afforded to the national authorities meant that the Union act did not *directly* concern the applicants; their challenge should instead be raised against the implementing measures.

In *Comité Central d'Entreprise de la Société Générale des Grandes Sources and others* v *Commission of the European Communities* (Case T-96/92), the CFI (now the General Court) considered whether the contested measure had **direct legal effects** on the applicants. The case concerned challenges to Commission decisions approving mergers that were likely to result in redundancies, which were brought by representatives of the employees concerned. While the CFI was not satisfied that redundancies were an inevitable consequence of the mergers, it ruled that, even if they were, the effect of the redundancies on the *representatives* would 'only be of an indirect nature' and they did not, therefore, have standing to challenge the decisions. Similarly, in *PAN Europe* v *Commission* (Case T-600/15), the General Court ruled that an association of beekeepers and environmental protection organisations were not directly concerned by a Commission implementing regulation that approved the marketing of products containing a particular substance, sulfoxaflor. The Court stated that even if the use of such products would endanger the business activities of the beekeepers, this would only affect their factual situation and not their legal situation.

The direct legal effects on the applicants were also pivotal to a string of cases concerning Regulation 2004/2003, which governs political parties within the European Parliament and the rules regarding their funding. In *Bonde and Others* v *Parliament and Council* (Case T-13/04), the Court held that Members of Parliament acting in their own name (and not on behalf of the party to which they belong) were not directly concerned by the Regulation because, *inter alia*, the economic consequences of that Regulation did not affect their *legal* position but only their *factual* situation. The Court then adopted a more flexible approach in the following case:

Emma Bonino and Others v Parliament and Council (Case T-40/04)

Facts:

The Liste Emma Bonino was a political party that did not qualify as a party at the 'European level', as defined in Regulation 2004/2003. Consequently, the Regulation had the effect of excluding the party from Community (i.e. Union) funding. The applicant party argued that this was discriminatory.

Ruling:

In response to the question of whether the Regulation was of direct concern to the applicant party, the CFI (now the General Court) first ruled on whether it affected the legal situation of the applicants. The Court held that:

> 42 … As the Liste Emma Bonino did not enjoy the status of a political party at European level, and therefore funding, either before or after the adoption of the contested regulation, **its legal situation is not affected**.

However, the Court then went on to state that:

> 43 … the creation of an advantageous legal status from which some political formations may benefit while others are excluded **is capable of affecting the equality of opportunities of political parties**. Accordingly, the legal effect to take into consideration in the present case is that of the exclusion of the Liste Emma Bonino from the status of political party at European level and, accordingly, from the benefit of Community funding, in conjunction with the possibility that certain of its political competitors might benefit from such funding.

The Court also found that the Regulation did not provide any discretion to the Parliament in how to implement it. Therefore, the conditions for direct concern (effect on the applicants' legal situation and no discretion in implementation) were met. However, the Court found that the Regulation was not of *individual* concern to the Liste Emma Bonino and therefore dismissed the action as inadmissible.

Significance:

This case established that it is not always necessary for a contested measure to affect the legal situation of an applicant in order for it to directly concern them, as suggested by the *Dreyfus* test. The requirement of direct concern can also be established if the contested measure could prejudice the equal opportunities of political parties. This reference to equality suggests that direct concern may be found where a measure infringes upon the fundamental rights of the applicant, regardless of whether or not such an infringement affects their legal status. The Court has yet to confirm whether it is a rule that, where a measure is found to infringe the fundamental rights of an applicant, this finding negates the need to demonstrate that the applicant's legal status is also affected.

Non-privileged applicants' individual concern

In the following case, the Court of Justice established a test to ascertain whether a measure was of 'individual concern' to an applicant:

Plaumann & Co v Commission (Case 25/62)

Facts:

The German government requested permission from the Commission to suspend the collection of taxes on imports of clementines from non-Member States. The Commission refused the request in a letter addressed to the German government (i.e. a decision addressed to the government). An importer of clementines sought to challenge the legality of this decision.

> **Ruling:**
>
> The Court of Justice adopted the following test to ascertain if the applicant was individually concerned by the decision addressed to the German government:
>
> > Persons other than those to whom a decision is addressed may only claim to be individually concerned if **that decision affects them by reason of certain attributes which are peculiar to them or by reason of circumstances in which they are differentiated from all other persons and by virtue of these factors distinguishes them individually just as in the case of the person addressed**. In the present case the applicant is affected by the disputed Decision as an importer of clementines, that is to say, by reason of a commercial activity which may at any time be practised by any person and is not therefore such as to distinguish the applicant in relation to the contested Decision as in the case of the addressee. For these reasons the present action for annulment must be declared inadmissible.
>
> **Significance:**
>
> This case established a highly restrictive test (known as the **Plaumann test**) for discerning whether a measure is of individual concern to an applicant. The fact that other persons could be in the same position of concern as the applicant was found to render the applicant's concern insufficiently individual. Therefore, by stating that the applicant must be differentiated from all other persons, and by reason of these distinguishing features singled out in the same way that the initial addressee was singled out, the Court effectively defined *individual* concern as *exclusive* concern.

The *Plaumann* test is open to severe criticism as the application of the test may make it virtually impossible for an applicant to succeed. The Court of Justice will nearly always be able to say that the applicant does not have distinguishing features because any other person *may*, in the future, take on such features. However, the *Plaumann* test has been cited and established as authoritative in a number of cases.

Although the *Plaumann* test is very difficult to satisfy, the Court of Justice found that it had been fulfilled soon after it was established in the following case:

> ### Alfred Toepfer and Getreide-Import Gesellschaft v Commission (Cases 106 and 107/63)
>
> **Facts:**
>
> The applicants were grain importers who had applied for an import licence in Germany on 1 October 1963, when a licence levy of zero was in place. Later on that day, the Commission took a decision that fixed new levies for maize imports from France to Germany, which would be effective from 2 October. Then, on 3 October, the Commission issued a decision authorising Germany to take certain protective measures, which included suspending the issue of licences between 1 October and 4 October. This decision had the effect of retroactively excluding the applicants from acquiring licences with zero levies. The applicants sought to have this decision annulled on the ground of infringement of the Treaty or any rule relating to its application.
>
> **Ruling:**
>
> With regard to the standing of the applicants, the Court of Justice held that:
>
> > … the only persons concerned by the said measures were importers who had applied for an import licence during the course of the day of 1 October 1963. **The number and identity of these**

importers had already become fixed and ascertainable before 4 October, when the contested decision was made. The Commission was in a position to know that its decision affected the interests and the position of the said importers alone.

The factual situation thus created differentiates the said importers, including the applicants, from all other persons and distinguishes them individually just as in the case of the person addressed.

[Note: where the Court refers to **4** October as the date of the contested decision, this appears to be an error. Elsewhere in the judgment the Court refers to the decision of the Commission of **3** October.]

The Court therefore ruled that the applicants had standing and the case was admissible. The Court then went on to rule in the applicant's favour and annul the contested decision.

Significance:

This case established that the condition of individual concern can be met when the applicants occupy a distinct status by virtue of historical circumstances that preclude other persons from being in the same situation in the future. Therefore, because the applicants' concern arose from their status as importers who had applied for an import licence on 1 October 1963, they formed a **closed group** capable of being individually concerned.

Similarly, in ***International Fruit Company BV v Commission*** (Cases 41–44/70), the Court held that the regulation in question applied to a closed category of persons on the date the regulation was passed, i.e. those who had made import applications in the previous week. Accordingly, an action to challenge the regulation by a person falling within this group was admissible.

The concept of a closed group was also at issue in the following case (which is also examined above in relation to direct concern):

A E Piraiki-Patraiki v *Commission* (Case 11/82)

Facts:

As stated above, the applicants were Greek exporters of yarn to France. They contested a Commission decision which allowed France to impose a quota system on the amount of yarn that could be imported from Greece during the period November 1981 to January 1982.

Ruling:

Following its ruling in ***Plaumann***, which was factually similar in this respect, the Court of Justice stated that the exportation of yarn to France was 'clearly a commercial activity which can be carried on at any time by any undertaking whatever'. Thus, the Court determined that 'the mere fact that the applicants export goods to France is not therefore sufficient to establish that they are individually concerned by the contested decision'.

However, some of the applicants had already entered into contracts that included the period covered by the contested decision. The Court therefore ruled as follows:

> It follows that the undertakings which were party to contracts meeting that description **must be considered as individually concerned** for the purpose of the admissibility of this action, **as members of a limited class** of traders identified or identifiable by the Commission and by reason of those contracts particularly affected by the decision at issue.

On this basis, the Court upheld the admissibility of those applicants who had entered into contracts to import yarn prior to the contested decision.

Significance:

This case provides a further example of a situation in which applicants can meet the *Plaumann* test for individual concern by virtue of historical circumstances that preclude other persons from being in the same situation in the future, and therefore render the applicants a **closed group**.

In the following more recent joined cases, the CFI (now the General Court) held that the applicants belonged to a closed group of persons on the date of the decision and that the measure in question was therefore of individual concern to them:

Boyle and Others v *Commission* (Joined Cases T-218/03 to T-240/03)

Facts:

Owners of vessels belonging to the Irish fishing fleet brought an action for a review of the legality of a Commission decision, which rejected a request by Ireland to expand the objectives of the Multiannual guidance programme for the Irish fishing fleet ('MAGP IV').

Ruling:

The CFI (now the General Court) held that although the applicants were not the addressees of the decision, it nevertheless concerned them. Ireland's request to the Commission comprised all the individual requests of vessel-owners, including the applicants' requests. **Although the decision was addressed to Ireland, it applied to a series of identified vessels and had therefore to be considered to be a series of individual decisions, each affecting the legal situation of the owners of those vessels.** The number and identity of the vessel-owners in question was fixed and ascertainable even before the date of the contested decision and the Commission was in a position to know that its decision affected solely the interests and positions of those owners. **The contested decision thus concerned a closed group of identified persons at the time of its adoption, whose rights the Commission intended to regulate.** The *Plaumann* test was therefore fulfilled, as the applicants were differentiated from all other persons, and by reason of these distinguishing features were singled out in the same way that the initial addressee was singled out.

Significance:

In this case, the measure was deemed to be of individual concern to the applicants because the addressee of the measure had acted on behalf of specific applicants, who were subsequently directly affected by the Commission's response.

In general, the Court of Justice has been quite inconsistent in its application of the *Plaumann* test. In *Calpak SpA and Società Emiliana Lavorazioni Frutta SpA* v *Commission* (Joined Cases 789-790/79) the Court applied the test extremely restrictively. Then in *Codorníu SA* v *Council* (Case /c-309/89) the Court applied a more relaxed interpretation of the individual concern condition. Here, Regulation 2045/89, which limited the use of the label 'crémant' to certain French and Luxembourg wines, was contested by a Spanish wine producer. The Spanish wine producer was held to be differentiated from other concerned persons – and therefore individually concerned – as they had used the trademark 'Gran Crémant de Codorníu' since 1924. In *P Buralux SA v Council* (Case C-209/94), however, a regulation was found by the Court not to be of individual concern to the applicants on the basis that those affected by it did not count as a closed group of operators, even though they were practically the only undertaking operating in their particular field.

The CFI (now the General Court) has shown willingness to diverge from the *Plaumann* test and interpret the condition of individual concern more flexibly. In *Jégo-Quéré et Cie SA v Commission* (Case T-177/01), the CFI decided to reformulate the scope of individual concern as follows:

> A natural or legal person is to be regarded as individually concerned by a Community [i.e. Union] measure of general application that concerns him directly if the measure in question affects his legal position, in a manner which is both definite and immediate, by restricting his rights or imposing obligations on him. The number and position of other persons who are likewise affected by the measure, or who may be so, are of no relevance in that regard.

This seemed to remove the core of the distinction between individual concern and direct concern. However, this judgment received a swift rebuff from the Court of Justice less than three months later:

Unión de Pequeños Agricultores v Council of the European Union (supported by the Commission) (Case C-50/00P)

Facts:

The Unión brought an action for the partial annulment of a regulation regarding the common organisation of the market in oils and fats. The CFI (in a ruling prior to its ruling in *Jégo-Quéré*) declared the action inadmissible due to a lack of individual concern. The Unión appealed to the Court of Justice.

Ruling:

With regard to the condition of individual concern, the Court of Justice held as follows:

> ... according to the system for judicial review of legality established by the Treaty, a natural or legal person can bring an action challenging a regulation only if it is concerned both directly and individually. Although this last condition must be interpreted in the light of the principle of effective judicial protection by taking account of the various circumstances that may distinguish an applicant individually ... **such an interpretation cannot have the effect of setting aside the condition in question, expressly laid down in the Treaty, without going beyond the jurisdiction conferred by the Treaty on the Community [i.e. Union] Courts.**
>
> While it is, admittedly, possible to envisage a system of judicial review of the legality of Community [i.e. Union] measures of general application different from that established by the founding Treaty and never amended as to its principles, it is for the Member States, if necessary, in accordance with Article 48 [T]EU to reform the system currently in force.

The Court therefore held that the CFI had been correct in its finding that the action brought by the Unión was inadmissible.

> **Significance:**
>
> The Court of Justice – seemingly responding to the CFI's ruling in *Jégo-Quéré* as much as the case at hand – effectively argued that the Union Courts did not have the jurisdiction to interpret the condition of individual concern in such a way that would have the effect of setting it aside; such a departure from the Treaty provisions (i.e. what is now Art 263 TFEU) could only be brought about by the Member States enacting an amendment to the Treaty. In this case, therefore, the Court of Justice signalled its intention to continue to apply the strict interpretation individual concern, as set out in *Plaumann*, and effectively quashed the CFI's preference for greater flexibility in this regard.

When *Jégo-Quéré* came before it on appeal almost two years after the above case, the Court of Justice reversed the CFI's ruling and declared the action for annulment to be inadmissible (Case C-263/02P). The Court of Justice applied the *Plaumann* test and referred extensively to its judgment in *Unión de Pequeños Agricultores,* ruling that the CFI had erred in law as its broad interpretation had 'the effect of removing all meaning from the requirement of individual concern' as set out in what is now Article 263 TFEU. The restrictive criteria established in the *Plaumann* test therefore remain the standard for determining whether a measure is of individual concern to an applicant and therefore whether an applicant has standing in a case where the contested act is addressed to another person.

Regulatory act which does not entail implementing measures

In *Unión de Pequeños Agricultores* (see above), the Court of Justice ruled that only an amendment to the relevant Treaty provisions could enable the condition of individual concern to be set aside. When the ToL came into force on 1 December 2009, Article 263 TFEU did just this in relation to a 'regulatory act'. Initially, it was unclear what would qualify as a regulatory act. In *Inuit Tapiriit Kanatami and Others* v *Parliament and Council* (Case T-18/10) and then one month later in *Microban International Ltd and Microban (Europe) Ltd* v *Commission* (Case T-262/10), the General Court ruled that a regulatory act encompassed 'all acts of general application apart from legislative acts'. This interpretation was then confirmed conclusively by the Court of Justice when *Inuit Tapiriit Kanatami* went to appeal.

> ### *Inuit Tapiriit Kanatami and Others* v *European Parliament and Council* (Case C-583/11 P)
>
> **Facts:**
>
> The applicants brought an action to annul Regulation 1007/2009 on the trade of seal products. While the applicants claimed that the Regulation was a regulatory act for the purpose of Article 263 TFEU, the General Court disagreed and dismissed the action as inadmissible. The applicants appealed to the Court of Justice.
>
> **Ruling:**
>
> The Court of Justice held that a regulation is not a regulatory act. The Court first noted that the 'acts' stipulated in the first two limbs of the Article 263 TFEU determination of admissibility (i.e. where the applicant is the addressee and where the applicant is not the addressee but is directly

and individually concerned) encompass any Union act that produces legal effects. A regulatory act which does not entail implementing measures, as stipulated in the third limb, must therefore refer to a narrower range of measures in order for the distinction between acts and regulatory acts to be meaningful.

The Court of Justice then applied a historical method of interpretation to Article 263 TFEU. The Court concluded that a 'regulatory act' is an act that **i) is an act of general application and ii) is not a legislative act** (i.e. not an act adopted by a legislative procedure). As the measure in question in this case was a legislative act, the second limb of admissibility under Article 263 TFEU was applied. The Court consequently ruled against the applicants on the ground that the regulation was not of individual concern to them.

Significance:

This case established the definition of a regulatory act for the purpose of Article 263 TFEU as a **non-legislative act of general application**. This means that, by introducing the concept of a regulatory act in conjunction with the lesser condition of only direct concern, the Treaty of Lisbon made it easier to bring an action against non-legislative acts. However, the requirements for bringing an action for the annulment of a legislative act remain extremely stringent. In essence, this case determined that the tough condition of individual concern (see above) must be met for an Article 263 TFEU challenge to a legislative act.

> See section 3.4.4 for further information on legislative and non-legislative acts

Therefore, a regulatory act is an act of general application that has not been adopted by either the ordinary or special legislative procedures. This may include **implementing acts** or **delegated acts**, which are adopted by the Commission. Indeed, the language that the Court of Justice used to define a regulatory act in *Inuit* replicates that of Article 290 TFEU on delegated acts.

Once a measure is identified as a regulatory act, it is also necessary to determine that it does not entail further implementing measures from Member States. This is because Article 263 TFEU is only intended to provide access to judicial remedy where no such remedy is available at the national level. If a regulatory act requires further implementing measures, then it is against these actions, before the national courts, that a complainant should bring their case. However, where a regulatory act does not entail further implementing measures by Member States, the only way to challenge that act before the national court would be to infringe it and raise a challenge during ensuing proceedings (see section 6.3.2). In such situations, non-privileged applicants should instead be able to bring a challenge directly to the EU under Article 263 TFEU (*Telefónica* v *Commission* (Case C-274/12 P)).

The question of when a regulatory act does not entail implementing measures for the purposes of Article 263 TFEU was discussed in the following case:

T & L Sugars and Sidul Açúcares v Commission (Case C-456/13 P)

Facts:

T & L Sugars and Sidul Açúcares were sugar cane refiners who brought an application for the annulment of one regulation and three subsequent implementing regulations (i.e. three regulatory acts) regarding the marketing and import of sugar. The General Court dismissed the case as inadmissible on the basis that the regulatory acts in question entailed further implementing measures by Member States, and that their case should therefore be brought at the national level. The General Court argued that the level of discretion enjoyed by Member States is irrelevant in determining whether a regulatory act entails implementing measures.

The parties brought an appeal to the Court of Justice on the ground that the General Court had misinterpreted the concept of an 'act not entailing implementing measures' within Article 263 TFEU. They argued that challenging national measures before a national court would not provide effective judicial protection (as required by the Charter of Fundamental Rights) when those measures were automatic or merely ancillary to Union regulations.

Ruling:

The Court of Justice began by restating the significance of the 'implementing measures' aspect of Article 263 TFEU:

> Where a regulatory act directly affects the legal situation of a natural or legal person without requiring implementing measures, that person could be denied effective judicial protection if he did not have a direct legal remedy before the European Union judicature for the purpose of challenging the legality of the regulatory act.... Where ... implementation is a matter for the Member States, those persons may plead the invalidity of the basic act at issue before the national courts and tribunals and cause the latter to request a preliminary ruling from the Court of Justice, pursuant to Article 267 TFEU. (paras 29 and 31)

The Court of Justice then confirmed the General Court's ruling. The Court noted that the regulations in question only produced legal effects vis-à-vis the appellants through the subsequent acts taken by national authorities. Those subsequent acts must therefore be viewed as implementing measures, regardless of how 'mechanical' and non-discretionary those acts might be. The Court determined that this did not infringe the protections of the Charter of Fundamental Rights.

As the regulations in question in this case were thus held to entail implementing measures, the Court applied the other limbs of Article 263 and ruled against the appellants on the grounds that the regulations at issue were neither addressed to them nor of individual concern to them.

Significance:

The Court of Justice established that **even when national authorities have no discretion** in the measures that they are required to take pursuant to a regulatory act, they still count as implementing measures for the purposes of Article 263 TFEU. Therefore, challenges to such regulatory acts may only be brought directly before the EU courts if they are addressed to the applicant or if the applicant can show individual as well as direct concern.

The *Inuit* and *T & L Sugars* cases demonstrate that, in addition to understanding the concepts of direct and individual concern, it is necessary to be able to differentiate between the different types of legal acts that are produced by the Union in order to know when non-privileged applicants have standing to bring a case under Article 263 TFEU. These different types of legal acts are set out, for the purposes of Article 263 TFEU, in Figure 6.3.

6.2 REVIEW OF LEGALITY OF UNION ACTS UNDER ARTICLE 263 TFEU

Figure 6.3 Types of legal act relevant to Article 263 TFEU

- **Legislative act**: An act adopted by the ordinary legislative procedure or a special legislative procedure, i.e. normally an act adopted by the Council and the Parliament working together (see section 3.4.4).
- **Non-legislative act**: Any other type of act, of any Union institution or Union body, that produces legal effects vis-á-vis third parties (e.g. a decision, implementing act or delegated act).

- **Act of general application**: An act that applies to all Member States.
- **Act of specific application** (e.g. a decision that has specific addressees).

- **Regulatory act entailing implementing measures**: Acts that only produce legal effects by virtue of further actions that they allow or require Member States to take.
- **Regulatory act not entailing implementing measures**: Acts that directly affect the legal situation of natural or legal persons.

(Non-privileged applicants do not need to prove individual concern in order to challenge the validity of these acts.)

Reflection: The 'individual concern' obstacle to judicial review

The requirement for a non-privileged applicant to demonstrate that a Union act they are seeking the annulment of is of 'individual concern' to them has been widely criticised. The Court of Justice has largely maintained a highly restrictive interpretation of the term 'individual concern', upholding its judgment in **Plaumann & Co v Commission** (Case 25/62) whereby:

> Persons other than those to whom a decision is addressed may only claim to be individually concerned if that decision affects them by reason of certain attributes which are peculiar to them or by reason of circumstances in which they are differentiated from all other persons and by virtue of these factors distinguishes them individually just as in the case of the person addressed.

Advocate General Jacobs formulated a particularly comprehensive and authoritative critique of this approach in his Opinion in **Unión de Pequeños Agricultores v Council** (Case C-50/00 P). Jacobs argued that application of the current interpretation of 'individual concern' resulted in a gap in judicial protection. In particular, Jacobs pointed out two problematic consequences of the current interpretation.

First, the requirement that an applicant be differentiated from all others who are or who might be affected by the act in question creates the perverse situation where an act that affects many people is more difficult to challenge than an act that affects just a few.

Secondly, when an applicant is barred from bringing an action for the annulment of a legislative act before the Court of Justice under Article 263 TFEU due to lack of 'individual concern', and when that act does not have any implementing measures that can be challenged in their national court, the only effective means of challenging the act is to break it. Then, once infringement proceedings are brought against the individual in the national courts, they can invoke Article 277 TFEU to request that the matter be referred to the Court of Justice for a preliminary ruling under Article 267 TFEU (see below). This places the individual in a precarious position: the national court may refuse to make such a reference or the Court of Justice may find that the relevant Union act is valid, leaving the individual at risk of sanctions for their infringement of it.

Advocate General Jacobs suggested that the best solution to these problems was to define an applicant as 'individually concerned' when 'the measure has, or is liable to have, a substantial adverse effect on his interests'. He argued that this reinterpretation would resolve the complex and conflicting case law on the matter and would be more consistent with approaches to *locus standi* in the legal systems of Member States, as well as being in line with the general tendency of the case law to expand the scope of judicial protection against actions of the Union.

In **Unión de Pequeños Agricultores**, the Court declined to adopt the position put forward by the Advocate General (see above). While it may be hoped that the ruling in **Inuit Tapiriit Kanatami and Others v Parliament and Council** (Case C-583/11 P) indicates that the scope of judicial protection against Union acts is indeed expanding, where non-regulatory acts (i.e. legislative acts) are concerned the problems outlined by Advocate General Jacobs persist. Furthermore, pressure for a solution is increasing. In March 2017, the Compliance Committee for the UN Convention on Access to Information, Public Participation in Decision-making and Access to Justice in Environmental Matters (Aarhus Convention) found that the Court of Justice's restrictive interpretation of 'individual concern' was incompatible with the access to justice provisions of the Convention. This suggests that, sooner or later, the Court of Justice will be compelled to revise its position.

6.2.4 Time limits for applications

Article 263 TFEU provides that proceedings should be instituted within two months of:

- the date of publication of the measure; or
- notification of the measure to the applicant; or, in the absence thereof;
- the day on which the measure came to the knowledge of the applicant.

This is identical to the wording of the former Article 230 EC Treaty. Therefore the case law decided under this former provision is directly relevant to Article 263 TFEU.

With regards to the third criterion, it is for the party who has knowledge of a decision to request the whole text thereof within a reasonable period. Accordingly, the CFI (now the General Court) held in ***COBB* v *Commission*** (Case T-485/04) that when an applicant requests communication of a decision more than four months after becoming aware of it, a reasonable time is exceeded.

In the following case, the CFI had an opportunity to add an important condition to the application of these principles in a case concerning state aid:

Olsen v *Commission* (Case T-17/02)

Facts:

The applicant contested a Commission decision authorising state aid to be paid to a Spanish competitor. Its action was lodged just over six months after Spain, the only addressee of the contested decision, was notified of it.

> **Ruling:**
> As the applicant was not the addressee of the contested decision, the CFI (now the General Court) held in its judgment that the criterion of notification of the decision was not applicable to it. As to whether, in this case, the criterion of publication or that of the day on which a measure came to the knowledge of an applicant was applicable, the CFI cited the case law according to which, with regard to measures which are published in the Official Journal, the criterion of the day on which a measure came to the knowledge of an applicant was not applicable; **in such circumstances it was the date of publication which marked the starting point of the period prescribed for instituting proceedings** (Case C-122/95 *Germany v Council* [1998] ECR I-973, at para 39).
>
> In the area of state aid, decisions of the Commission, after a preliminary examination, that the measure is compatible with the common market are to be the subject of a summary notice published in the Official Journal (Regulation 659/99). The summary notice includes a reference to the website of the Secretariat General of the Commission and the statement that the full text of the decision in question, from which all confidential information has been removed, can be found there. **The CFI held that the fact that the Commission gives third parties full access to the text of a decision placed on its website, combined with publication of a summary notice in the Official Journal enabling interested parties to identify the decision in question and notifying them of this possibility of access via the internet, must be considered to be publication for the purposes of the former Article 230 EC Treaty (now Art 263 TFEU).** In this case, the applicant could legitimately expect that the contested decision would be published in the Official Journal.
>
> Olsen's subsequent appeal to the Court of Justice was dismissed (Case C-320/05P).
>
> **Significance:**
> This case clarifies when each of the circumstances that trigger the beginning of the time period should be applied and elucidates what amounts to 'publication'. The case suggests that the two-month time period will always commence from the date that the full text of a decision is published in the Official Journal if such publication occurs, or the date that access to the text of the decision is provided and notification of such access is published in the Official Journal.

The two-month period expires at the end of the day which bears the same number as the day of the occurrence of the event which caused time to start running (*Misset v Council* (Case 152/85)). So, for example, if the measure had been published in the Official Journal on 2 February 2017, the two-month period would expire at midnight on 2 April 2017. The CFI has held that where an applicant lets the time limit for bringing an action against a decision expire, they cannot start time running again by asking the institution to reconsider the decision and then start proceedings against the confirmation of the decision (*Cobrecaf SA v Commission* (Case T-514/93)). The expiry of the period of time allowed for bringing proceedings may be disregarded if the applicant can rely on Article 45 of the Statute of the Court, which provides:

> ... No right shall be prejudiced in consequence of the expiry of the time limit if the party concerned proves the existence of unforeseeable circumstances or of *force majeure*.

The Court of Justice has, however, shown reluctance in allowing applications outside the statutory time limits.

6.2.5 Consequences of annulment

Under **Article 264 TFEU**:

> If the action is well founded, the Court of Justice of the European Union shall declare the act concerned to be void.
>
> However, the Court shall, if it considers this necessary, state which of the effects of the act which it has declared void shall be considered as definitive.

Under **Article 266 TFEU**:

> The institution whose act has been declared void or whose failure to act has been declared contrary to the Treaties shall be required to take the necessary measures to comply with the judgment of the Court of Justice of the European Union.

If the Court finds a Union act to be invalid, the Court of Justice will declare it to be void from the moment of delivery of the judgment. It can also declare an act to be non-existent, but the Court is reluctant to do this because of the disruption this may cause to any actions which had been based on the assumption that the act was valid (see *Commission* v *BASF AG and Others* (Case C-137/92)). Article 264 enables the Court to declare part of an act void. In the case of Union legislation, it will frequently declare that, for example, the provisions of an annulled directive or regulation will remain effective until a new regulation is adopted (see, for example, *European Parliament* v *Council* (Case C-295/90), and *European Parliament* v *Council* (Case C-388/92)).

Article 266 TFEU requires the institution concerned to take the necessary remedial action to correct the error which has been established by the judgment of the Court. There is no time limit for this, but the Court of Justice has held that such steps should be taken within a 'reasonable period' from the date of the judgment (*European Parliament* v *Council* (Case 13/83)).

6.3 Other procedures

Objective 3

This section considers the possibility of raising **indirect challenges** to the legality of Union acts under **Article 277 TFEU** and challenging a Union institution's **failure to act** under **Article 265 TFEU**.

6.3.1 Challenging a failure to act under Article 265 TFEU

Institutions may act unlawfully not only by exceeding or abusing their powers, but also by failing to carry out a duty imposed on them by the Treaties or some other provision having legal effect. Where this takes the form of an explicit refusal to act, such a refusal may constitute a decision that can be challenged under Article 263 TFEU (*SFEI and Others* v *Commission* (Case C-39/93P), see above). Alternatively, where there is a failure to act, proceedings may be brought under **Article 265 TFEU**, the full text of which is as follows:

> Should the European Parliament, the European Council, the Council, the Commission or the European Central Bank, in infringement of the Treaties, fail to act, the Member States and the other institutions of the Union may bring an action before the Court of Justice of the European Union to have the infringement established. This Article shall apply, under the same conditions, to bodies, offices and agencies of the Union which fail to act.
>
> The action shall be admissible only if the institution, body, office or agency concerned has first been called upon to act. If, within two months of being so called upon, the institution, body, office or agency concerned has not defined its position, the action may be brought within a further period of two months.
>
> Any natural or legal person may, under the conditions laid down in the preceding paragraphs, complain to the Court that an institution, body, office or agency of the Union has failed to address to that person any act other than a recommendation or an opinion.

Standing to challenge a failure to act

The position of 'privileged' applicants (i.e. Member States and Union institutions) that can bring proceedings under Article 265 TFEU irrespective of any particular interest, and 'non-privileged' applicants (i.e. legal and natural persons) that need to establish a special interest, is the same under Article 265 TFEU as under Article 263 TFEU (see above). The Court has, in fact, stated that 'in the system of legal remedies provided for by the Treaty, there is a close relationship between the right of action given in [Art 263 TFEU] ... and that based on [Art 265 TFEU]' (*European Parliament* v *Council (Re Transport Policy)* (Case 13/83)).

Scope for challenge

There have not been many successful actions brought under Article 265 TFEU as, for the most part, such proceedings can be easily avoided by an institution. First, many of the duties conferred on the institutions are, in reality, 'powers', whereby the institution has discretion as to whether, and how, to exercise that 'duty'. Secondly, to satisfy Article 265, the institution generally only needs to have responded to the issue and defined its position. In the case of natural or legal persons, if the only outcome of the institution's response to an issue will be an opinion or a recommendation, a failure to produce either is not a failure which can be dealt with by Article 265 TFEU.

Where there is a clear duty to act, as imposed on the Commission by Article 105(1) TFEU in relation to breaches of Articles 101 and 102 TFEU, for example, a statement by the Commission that it is not going to respond to a complaint might give grounds for an action under Article 265 TFEU, after the appropriate warning has been given. For example, in *Ladbroke Racing (Deutschland) GmbH* v *Commission* (Case T-74/92), Ladbroke had complained to the Commission about a denial of access for the televising of horse racing, alleging a breach of the former Articles 81 and 82 EC Treaty (now Arts 101 and 102 TFEU) by German and French companies in the horse racing and communications businesses. After deciding to investigate the complaint in December 1990, the Commission had still not defined its position on the alleged breach by June 1992, when it was formally requested to do so. Following the instigation of proceedings under what is now Article 265 TFEU, the CFI (now the General Court) found that the Commission was in breach of its duties. The Commission could have either initiated the procedure for establishing a breach of the former Article 82 EC Treaty, dismissed the complaint in a formal letter to the complainant, or made a reasoned decision not to pursue the complaint on the ground of a lack of Union interest.

It had, however, done none of these things. (It should be noted that the infringement procedures, in relation to Union competition law, have changed following the entry into force of Regulation 1/2003.)

The difficulty of completing a successful action under Article 265 TFEU is illustrated by the ***Transport Policy*** case (Case 13/83). This case concerned the former Articles 70 and 71 EC Treaty (now Arts 90 and 91 TFEU), which required the Council to adopt a common transport policy for the Union. More than 20 years after the Treaty had come into force, no such policy had been adopted. After a number of requests had been made to the Council for progress in this area, the Parliament brought proceedings against the Council for failure to act under what is now Article 265 TFEU. The Court of Justice agreed that the Council had been 'called upon to act, by the Parliament, as required by [Art 265 TFEU] … and had produced equivocal replies as to what, if any, action it proposed to take'. The requirement in the former Articles 70 and 71 EC Treaty was found to be insufficiently precise, however, to amount to an enforceable obligation. Other cases have failed because the Court decided that all that was required was an opinion (***Chevally* v *Commission*** (Case 15/70)) or because the decision the applicant required was not to be addressed to them (***Lord Bethell* v *Commission*** (Case 246/81)).

6.3.2 Indirect challenges to a Union act

The legality of a Union act can occasionally become an issue in proceedings that have been brought for reasons other than the annulment of that act. Challenges to the legality of Union acts in this way are normally called indirect challenges, as they are ancillary to the main proceedings and can only be raised if they are relevant thereto (***Italy* v *Commission*** (Case 32/65)). Indirect challenges to the validity of a Union act can be raised by either an applicant or a defendant and may occur in cases before either national or Union courts.

Examples of when an indirect challenge could arise include the following:

- the validity of a Union act that is subject to an action for annulment brought under Article 263 TFEU is found to depend on the validity of another Union act which it implements;
- the answer to a question referred to the Court of Justice for a preliminary ruling under Article 267 TFEU is found to depend on the validity of a Union act;
- an infringement action brought against a Member State under Article 258 is found to depend on the validity of the Union act that the Member State is accused of having breached;
- an action regarding a contract concluded by the Union brought under Article 272 TFEU is found to depend on the validity of the contract.

Where an indirect challenge arises before a national court, the court may request, or may be obliged to request, a preliminary ruling from the Court of Justice under **Article 267 TFEU** (see section 5.3). Where an indirect challenge arises in a case before a Union court, it is subject to the rules laid down in **Article 277 TFEU**, which provides as follows:

> Notwithstanding the expiry of the period laid down in Article 263, sixth paragraph, any party may, in proceedings in which an act of general application adopted by an institution, body, office or agency of the Union is at issue, plead the grounds specified in Article 263, second paragraph, in order to invoke before the Court of Justice of the European Union the inapplicability of that act.

One point to note here is that an indirect challenge under Article 277 is only available in relation to 'an act of general application'. This is, however, broader than the pre-ToL iterations of the provision which applied only to 'regulations'. Indeed, the Court had already adopted a wide interpretation of the scope of this provision in *Simmenthal* (Case 92/78), where it stated that the application of the Article must 'include acts of the institutions which, although they are not in the form of a regulation, nevertheless produce similar effects'. Where an act is not 'of general application', it is more likely that a complainant will be able to bring a *direct* challenge under Article 263 TFEU (as the addressee of a decision, for example).

In *Salerno and Others* v *Commission and Council* (Joined Cases 87 and 130/77, 22/83, 9 and 10/84), the Court of Justice clarified the scope of what is now Article 277 TFEU as follows:

> The sole purpose of Article 184 [now Art 277] is to protect parties against the application of an unlawful regulation where the regulation itself can no longer be challenged owing to the expiry of the period laid down in Article 173 [now Art 263]. However, in allowing a party to plead the inapplicability of a regulation, **Article 184 [now Art 277] does not create an independent right of action**; such a plea may only be raised indirectly in proceedings against an implementing measure, the validity of the regulation being challenged in so far as it constitutes the legal basis of that measure.

The distinction between whether an indirect action should be brought via Article 267 TFEU or Article 277 TFEU depends on whether it is the Member States or the Union institutions that are charged with implementing the act in question. The Court of Justice explained this in its ruling in *Inuit Tapiriit Kanatami and Others* v *European Parliament and Council* (Case C-583/11 P).

> ➤ *Inuit* is considered in more detail on page 228

> Accordingly, natural or legal persons who cannot, by reason of the conditions of admissibility stated in the fourth paragraph of Article 263 TFEU, challenge directly European Union acts of general application do have protection against the application to them of those acts. **Where responsibility for the implementation of those acts lies with the European Union institutions,** those persons are entitled to bring a direct action before the Courts of the European Union against the implementing measures under the conditions stated in the fourth paragraph of Article 263 TFEU, and to plead, pursuant to **Article 277 TFEU**, in support of that action, the illegality of the general act at issue. **Where that implementation is a matter for the Member States,** such persons may plead the invalidity of the European Union act at issue before the national courts and tribunals and cause the latter to request a preliminary ruling from the Court of Justice, pursuant to **Article 267 TFEU**. (para 93)

> ➤ See section 6.2.3 on direct concern and individual concern

The benefit of an indirect challenge, either through the national courts via Article 267 TFEU or before the Court of Justice under Article 277 TFEU, is that an applicant can challenge the legality of a Union act without having to meet the stringent admissibility criteria of Article 263 TFEU. This means that an indirect challenge may result in the judicial review of the legality of a Union act long after the Article 263 TFEU time limit has passed, and Article 267 or Article 277 may be used to indirectly challenge the legality of a 'non-regulatory act' (i.e. a legislative act) without necessarily having to meet the restrictive *Plaumann* test for individual concern. Thus, where a legislative act is challenged indirectly, it may be challenged with a lower requirement for *locus standi* than would apply if it were challenged directly under Article 263.

An important restriction on indirect challenges to Union acts was also laid down by the Court in *TWD Deggendorf* (Case C-188/92). In that case, the Court of Justice held that no indirect challenge to a Commission decision could be made under what is now Article 267 TFEU where the party had been informed of the Commission decision and could 'without doubt' have challenged it directly before the Court under what is now Article 263 TFEU, but had not done so. Therefore, indirect challenges can only be brought in situations where the complainant could not have brought a direct challenge under Article 263 TFEU.

6.4 Damages for unlawful Union acts under Article 340 TFEU

Objective 4

As in English law, the fact that a public body has acted unlawfully does not, *per se*, mean that the body concerned is under a duty to compensate those adversely affected by its action. Whether or not damages are payable under Union law depends on the way in which the Court interprets the provisions of **Article 340 TFEU**. The text of Article 340 TFEU provides as follows:

> The contractual liability of the Union shall be governed by the law applicable to the contract in question.
>
> In the case of non-contractual liability, the Union shall, in accordance with the general principles common to the laws of the Member States, make good any damage caused by its institutions or by its servants in the performance of their duties.
>
> Notwithstanding the second paragraph, the European Central Bank shall, in accordance with the general principles common to the laws of the Member States, make good any damage caused by it or by its servants in the performance of their duties.
>
> The personal liability of its servants towards the Union shall be governed by the provisions laid down in their Staff Regulations or in the Conditions of Employment applicable to them.

The first paragraph of Article 340 TFEU establishes that the liability of Union institutions under contracts will generally be governed by the law of the Member State where the institution is situated. Liability in non-contractual matters (tort, in English law) is governed by the second paragraph of Article 340. This provision is substantially the same as in the former Article 288 EC Treaty, which means that the case law pertaining to the former provision, which is examined below, remains relevant to the current Article 340.

The jurisdiction of the Court of Justice of the European Union to award damages is established in **Article 268 TFEU**:

> The Court of Justice of the European Union shall have jurisdiction in disputes relating to compensation for damage provided for in the second and third paragraphs of Article 340.

The corresponding duty of the relevant Union institution is then stated in **Article 266 TFEU**:

> The institution whose act has been declared void or whose failure to act has been declared contrary to the Treaties shall be required to take the necessary measures to comply with the judgment of the Court of Justice of the European Union.
>
> This obligation shall not affect any obligation which may result from the application of the second paragraph of Article 340.

6.4.1 Scope of liability

The Court of Justice laid down some basic rules for liability in the following case:

Lütticke v Commission (Case 4/69)

Facts:

The applicant had been compelled to pay a turnover equalisation tax on milk powder, which the Commission had refused to use its powers under the former Article 97 EEC Treaty (now Art. 113 TFEU) to abolish. The applicant therefore requested the Court to order subsequent damages to be made good.

Ruling:

First, with regard to a question of admissibility, the Court of Justice determined that 'the action for damages provided for by Article 178 [now Art 266 TFEU] and the second paragraph of Article 215 [now Art 340 TFEU] was established by the Treaty as an 'independent form of action'. The possibility that an action for damages might have the effect of establishing a failure to act (which at the time was provided for specifically under Article 175 EEC Treaty and is now provided for by Article 265 TFEU was therefore no barrier to admissibility.

Considering the substance of the proceedings, the Court determined that:

> The liability of the community presupposes the existence of a set of circumstances comprising **actual damage**, a **causal link** between the damage claimed and the conduct alleged against the institution, and the **illegality** of such conduct.

The Court then went on to establish that, to be liable for damages, where there is a positive duty in Union law to do something, the relevant institution must have failed to do it and where there is discretion, it must have been exercised in an unlawful way. The Court found that the Commission had not failed in its supervisory role as defined by the former Article 97 EEC Treaty and there was therefore no unlawful conduct to be made good.

Significance:

This case established three conditions for the liability of a Union institution: (i) **actual damage** to the applicant, (ii) a **causal link** between that damage and the alleged conduct of the institution and (iii) **unlawful conduct** by the institution. This third criteria was later ruled not to be essential – see below.

The conditions for liability established in the above case were later limited by the so-called *Schöppenstedt formula* (*Zückerfabrik Schöppenstedt* **v** *Council* (Case 5/71)). Here, the Court ruled that 'the Community [i.e. Union] does not incur liability on account of a legislative measure which involves choices of economic policy unless a **sufficiently serious breach** of a superior rule of law for the protection of the individual has occurred' (see *HNL* **v** *Council and Commission* (Case 83/77), para 4; *Unifruit Hellas* **v** *Commission* (Case T-489/93)).

▶ The scope of state liability is considered in detail in section 8.4

The Court of Justice has subsequently extended the requirement of a 'sufficiently serious breach' to all cases for damages under what is now Article 340 TFEU, unless there is a particular justification for a departure from this requirement:

Bergaderm and Goupil v Commission (Case C-352/98 P)

Facts:

A para-pharmaceutical and cosmetics company sought the reparation of damages that they claimed resulted from a Commission Directive, which added annexes to Council Directive 76/768 on the approximation of the laws of the Member States relating to cosmetic products. The applicant company claimed that the Commission had committed a series of wrongful acts in the preparation of its directive and that the resulting directive had caused the company significant financial damage, leading to its liquidation.

Ruling:

The Court of Justice referred to the conditions it had established in relation to **state liability** (see Chapter 8) and thereby sought to harmonise its approach to damages, regardless of whether a Member State or a Union institution was held to be liable for a breach of Union law. The Court thus ruled as follows:

41 The Court has stated that the conditions under which the State may incur liability for damage caused to individuals by a breach of Community [i.e. Union] law cannot, in the absence of particular justification, differ from those governing the liability of the Community [i.e. Union] in like circumstances. The protection of the rights which individuals derive from Community [i.e. Union] law cannot vary depending on whether a national authority or a Community [i.e. Union] authority is responsible for the damage (*Brasserie du Pêcheur and Factortame*, paragraph 42).

42 As regards Member State liability for damage caused to individuals, the Court has held that Community [i.e. Union] law confers **a right to reparation where three conditions are met: the rule of law infringed must be intended to confer rights on individuals; the breach must be sufficiently serious; and there must be a direct causal link between the breach of the obligation resting on the State and the damage sustained by the injured parties** (*Brasserie du Pêcheur and Factortame*, paragraph 51).

43 As to the second condition, as regards both Community [i.e. Union] liability under Article 215 of the Treaty [now Art 340 TFEU] and Member State liability for breaches of Community [i.e. Union] law, **the decisive test for finding that a breach of Community [i.e. Union] law is sufficiently serious is whether the Member State or the Community [i.e. Union] institution concerned manifestly and gravely disregarded the limits on its discretion** (*Brasserie du Pêcheur and Factortame*, paragraph 55; and Joined Cases C-178/94, C-179/94, C-188/94, C-189/94, C-190/94 *Dillenkofer and Others* v *Germany* [1996] ECR I-4845, paragraph 25).

44 Where the Member State or the institution in question has only considerably reduced, or even no, discretion, the mere infringement of Community [i.e. Union] law may be sufficient to establish the existence of a sufficiently serious breach (see, to that effect, Case C-5/94 *Hedley Lomas* [1996] ECR I-2553, paragraph 28).

Significance:

In line with its previous judgments on state liability, this case established three conditions for the non-contractual liability of a Union institution for an unlawful act:

(i) the rule of law infringed must be intended to **confer rights** on individuals;

(ii) the breach of that rule of law must be **sufficiently serious**;

(iii) there must be a **direct causal link** between the breach of the obligation resting on the Union institution and the damage sustained by the injured party.

> Also in line with case law on state liability, this case defined a 'sufficiently serious' breach of Union law as one in which a Union institution has **manifestly and gravely disregarded the limits on its discretion** – i.e. exceeded its powers (see Chapter 8).

The condition that liability can only be incurred in a case concerning a 'rule of law intended to confer rights on individuals' has been analysed on several occasions by the CFI (now the General Court). For instance, it has been held that the rules determining the division of powers between the various Union institutions aim to ensure that the balance between the institutions provided for in the Treaties is maintained and therefore do not confer rights on individuals. Accordingly, any unlawful delegation of the Council's powers to the Commission cannot incur liability (*Afrikanische Frucht-Compagnie and Internationale Fruchtimport Gesellschaft Weichert Co* v *Commission* (Joined Cases T-64/01 and T-65/01)). Similarly, it has also been held that infringement of the Article 296 TFEU obligation to state reasons for the adoption of a legislative act is not such as to give rise to the liability of the Union (*Afrikanische Frucht-Compagnie*).

On the other hand, in its judgment in *Cantina Sociale di Dolianova and Others* v *Commission* (Case T-166/98), the CFI (now the General Court) held that the prohibition on unjust enrichment and the principle of non-discrimination were intended to confer rights on individuals. A breach by the Commission of those principles was held to be sufficiently serious to incur liability.

6.4.2 Liability for a lawful act

In a case of non-contractual liability under Art 340 TFEU, the Union has, in accordance with the general principles common to the laws of the Member States, to make good any damage caused by its institutions or by its servants in the performance of their duties. In a series of judgments the CFI (now the General Court), sitting as a Grand Chamber, expressly recognised that the Union could incur liability even in the absence of unlawful conduct:

> **FIAMM and FIAMM Technologies; Laboratoire du Bain; Groupe Fremaux and Palais Royal; CD Cartondruck v Council and Commission; and Fedon & Figli and Others v Council and Commission and Beamglow v Parliament and Others (Cases T-69, 151, 301, 320 and 383/00)**
>
> Facts:
>
> In 1993, the Council adopted Regulation 404/93 introducing common rules for the import of bananas. This Regulation contained preferential provisions for bananas from certain African, Caribbean and Pacific States. Following complaints, the Dispute Settlement Board (DSB) of the World Trade Organization (WTO) held that the Union regime governing the import of bananas was incompatible with WTO agreements. In 1998, the Council therefore adopted a regulation amending that regime. As the US took the view that the new regime was still not compatible with the WTO agreements, it requested, and obtained, authorisation from the DSB to impose increased customs duties on certain imports of Union products. Six companies established in

the EU brought proceedings before the CFI (now the General Court) claiming compensation from the Commission and the Council for the damage alleged to have been suffered by them because the retaliatory measures applied to their exports to the US.

Ruling:

In its judgment, the CFI first held that the Union could not incur liability in this case for unlawful conduct. However, it ruled that:

> Where, as in the present case, it has not been established that conduct attributed to the Community institutions is unlawful, that does **not** mean that undertakings which, as a category of economic operators, are required to bear a disproportionate part of the burden resulting from a restriction of access to export markets can in no circumstances obtain compensation by virtue of the Community's non-contractual liability.

Referring to what is now the Article 340 TFEU requirement to make good any damage 'in accordance with the general principles common to the laws of the Member States', the Court noted that:

> National laws on non-contractual liability allow individuals, albeit to varying degrees, in specific fields and in accordance with differing rules, to obtain compensation in legal proceedings for certain kinds of damage, even in the absence of unlawful action by the perpetrator of the damage.

The Court established the conditions necessary to incur liability in such instances:

> When damage is caused by conduct of the Community institution not shown to be unlawful, the Community can incur non-contractual liability if the conditions as to sustaining **actual damage**, to the **causal link** between that damage and the conduct of the Community institution and to the **unusual and special nature of the damage** in question are all met.

The CFI held that the conditions requiring the applicants to have sustained damage and relating to the causal link between that damage and the conduct of the institutions were satisfied in the case at hand. Conversely, the applicants had not succeeded in proving that they sustained unusual damage. The possibility of tariff concessions being suspended is among the vicissitudes inherent in the current system of international trade and, accordingly, has to be borne by every operator who decides to sell his products on the market of one of the WTO members. The CFI therefore dismissed the six actions.

Significance:

This case established that the Union can incur non-contractual liability in the absence of unlawful conduct on the part of its bodies. The conditions for incurring liability in such a case were established as (i) **actual damage** is sustained, (ii) there is a **causal link** between that damage and the conduct of the Union institution, and (iii) the damage in question is of an **unusual and special nature**.

In *Galileo* v *Commission* (Case T-279/03), the CFI reaffirmed that Union liability can arise in the absence of unlawful conduct, provided that the damage in question is unusual and special. As with the above cases, the CFI found that the damage to the applicant, caused by a lawful Union action, did not exceed the limits of the economic risks inherent in operating in the sector concerned.

6.4.3 Remedies

The Court has not developed a comprehensive set of principles concerning the type and extent of damages which may be recovered, but the case law has given rise to certain rules. Actual financial loss that results from the unlawful action by the Commission may be recovered, but it must be established that this resulted directly from the unlawful conduct (***Dumortier Frères* v *Council*** (Case 64/76)). The Court has also awarded damages for shock, disturbance and uneasiness, in Union staff cases (***Algera* v *Common Assembly*** (Case 7/56)).

Difficulties may arise where a national authority has acted on what subsequently transpires to have been an unlawful act by a Union institution. Who is liable? Should the injured party sue the institution which promulgated the unlawful act, or the national institution which implemented it, or both? Where the claimant's loss has occurred as a result of being obliged to pay money under an unlawful act and they are claiming restitution, they will be expected to claim in the national courts against the relevant national institution (***Vreugdenhil* v *Commission*** (Case C-282/90)). Where there is no remedy in the national courts, claims can be brought against the relevant Union institution in the Court of Justice (***Krohn* v *Commission*** (Case 175/84)).

CHAPTER SUMMARY

Review of Legality of Union acts under Article 263 TFEU

- The Court can review legislative acts and other Union acts intended to produce legal effects *vis-à-vis* third parties.
- There are four **grounds for review**: lack of competence, infringement of an essential procedure, infringement of the Treaties or any rule relating to their application and misuse of powers.
- **Non-privileged applicants** who are not the addressees of the act in question must show that it is of **direct concern** to them.
- A **non-regulatory act** (i.e. a legislative act) must also be of **individual concern** to a non-privileged applicant (see ***Plaumann***).
- Proceedings under Article 263 TFEU must be initiated within a **two-month time limit**.

Indirect challenges and failures to act

- Individuals can challenge a Union institution's **failure to act** under **Article 265 TFEU**.
- If an applicant has no legal standing under Article 263, they can **indirectly challenge** a Union act of general application under **Article 277 TFEU**.

Damages for unlawful acts under Article 340 TFEU

- Contractual liability is governed by the law of the Member State where the relevant institution is situated.
- Non-contractual liability arises when the rule or law infringed **confers rights** on individuals, when the breach is **sufficiently serious** and when there is a **direct causal link** between the breach and the damage sustained (***Bergaderm and Goupil***).
- The Court of Justice has jurisdiction to award damages for non-contractual liability (**Art 268 TFEU**).

Chapter 7
Infringement proceedings against Member States

Learning objectives

At the end of this chapter you should understand:

1 The obligation on the Member States to observe Union law and the actions that they may face if they fail to do so.

2 The stages of infringement actions that may be taken against a Member State for a breach of EU law under Article 258 TFEU.

3 When lump sums or penalty payments may be imposed under Article 260 TFEU.

4 When interim measures may be ordered.

5 The measures that the Council may take against Member States under Article 7 TEU.

Key terms and concepts

Familiarity with the following terms will be helpful for understanding this chapter:

Lump sum – a single, one-off payment

Pecuniary penalty – any monetary penalty

Penalty payment – a penalty that is paid in regular instalments until the breach of Union law is resolved

7.1 Introduction

Objective 1

Member States of the EU are under an obligation to comply with Union law. Article 267 TFEU on references for preliminary rulings and Article 263 TFEU on the judicial review of Union acts assist the Member States in their compliance with Union law by providing means by which they can clarify or challenge particular acts or provisions thereof (see Chapters 5 and 6). These provisions thus facilitate a degree of dialogue between the Member State and the Union judiciary. This chapter considers what can happen if Member States nevertheless fail to fully adhere to Union law, i.e. the actions that the Commission or another Member State can bring before the Court of Justice with the aim of enforcing Union law within a Member State. Thus, while the last two chapters concerned the Court of Justice of the European Union's role as an interpreter and sole arbiter of Union law, this chapter considers the Court of Justice's function as a law enforcer.

Infringement proceedings against a Member State for a breach of Union law may be brought by another Member State under **Article 259 TFEU**, but they are more commonly brought by the Commission under **Article 258 TFEU**. This introductory section examines the obligation that is placed on Member States to observe Union law and these provisions under which infringement actions can be taken if they fail to do so. The chapter then considers the different stages of the proceedings, before outlining the **pecuniary penalties** that may be imposed on Member States under **Article 260 TFEU**. Such penalties can result from the failure to implement a directive or from a failure to comply with a judgment made pursuant to Article 258 proceedings.

This chapter also includes a brief consideration of **interim measures**, which may be ordered by the Court of Justice of the European Union under **Article 279 TFEU**, or in exceptional circumstances by a national court, to minimise the harm that could be caused by an act that may be in breach of Union law prior to the date of a full hearing on the matter. It should be noted that interim procedures are not confined to cases brought under Articles 258 or 259 TFEU; they may also be ordered in review of legality cases brought under Article 263 TFEU (see Chapter 6).

Finally, **Article 7 TEU** is considered. This Article enables the Council to suspend certain rights of a Member State if the European Council has determined the existence of a 'serious and persistent breach' of Union **values**. These measures were first invoked against Poland in 2017 and Hungary in 2018.

7.1.1 The obligation on Member States

The obligation on Member States to observe Union law is set out in **Article 4(3) TEU** (also known as the **loyalty clause** or the principle of **sincere cooperation**), which includes the following:

> The Member States shall take any appropriate measure, general or particular, to ensure fulfilment of the obligations arising out of the Treaties or resulting from the acts of the institutions of the Union.
>
> The Member States shall facilitate the achievement of the Union's tasks and refrain from any measure which could jeopardise the attainment of the Union's objectives.

This obligation to observe Union law – which includes both positive obligations to take certain actions and negative obligations to refrain from others – extends beyond the Treaties and secondary legislation to agreements made by the Union with third countries and international organisations pursuant to Article 218 TFEU (*SZ Sevince* (Case 192/89); Opinion 1/94 of the Court of Justice).

The obligation to observe Union law binds not only the state, but also bodies that can be described as emanations of the state, as is discussed in relation to the direct effect of directives in Chapter 8. Such organs include government departments, state-funded and state-regulated agencies providing public services, state governments in federal systems, local authorities (*Costanzo* (Case 103/88); *Johnston* v *RUC* (Case 222/84)) and the courts. All are, potentially, the subject of infringement proceedings, although the actual defendant in each case will be the relevant Member State.

> The principle of 'direct effect' is fully explained in section 8.2

Direct actions against Member States can either be brought by the Commission under **Article 258 TFEU** or by another Member State under **Article 259 TFEU**. These two possibilities will now be considered. The Council can also take measures against a Member State under **Article 7(3) TEU** in the instance of a 'serious and persistent breach' of Union values. These measures are considered at the end of this chapter.

7.1.2 Actions by the Commission under Article 258 TFEU

Article 17(1) TEU provides that the Commission shall 'ensure the application of the Treaties, and of measures adopted by the institutions pursuant to them'. This provision thus authorises the Commission to bring actions against Member States for breaches of Union law.

In some cases where action is required, lack of Commission resources may limit or delay its response to unlawful action or inaction by Member States. Indeed, the Commission stated in 2017 that it intends to take a more strategic approach to infringement proceedings and to prioritise the most important breaches of EU law (2017/C 18/02). In 2018, the Commission launched 644 new infringement proceedings against Member States, compared to 716 in 2017 and 986 in 2016.

If an individual is legally and materially able to bring a case to their national courts, they may be able to address the breach through the direct or indirect infringement of the relevant provision of Union law (see Chapter 8). However, this may not always be possible. If an individual is unable or unwilling to commence proceedings in relation to the alleged breach, there may be no practical alternative to action by the Commission. Regardless, it should also be noted that action by individuals in the domestic courts does not preclude action by the Commission before the Court of Justice.

Where Member States fail to fully implement Union law, or fail to eliminate obstacles to its implementation, the Commission can take the necessary action under **Article 258 TFEU**:

> If the Commission considers that a Member State has failed to fulfil an obligation under the Treaties, it shall deliver a reasoned opinion on the matter after giving the State concerned the opportunity to submit its observations.
>
> If the State concerned does not comply with the opinion within the period laid down by the Commission the latter may bring the matter before the Court of Justice of the European Union.

7.1.3 Actions by another Member State under Article 259 TFEU

As an alternative to Article 258 TFEU, action can be brought against a Member State by other Member States under **Article 259 TFEU**:

> A Member State which considers that another Member State has failed to fulfil an obligation under the Treaties may bring the matter before the Court of Justice of the European Union.
>
> Before a Member State brings an action against another Member State for an alleged infringement of an obligation under the Treaties, it shall bring the matter before the Commission.
>
> The Commission shall deliver a reasoned opinion after each of the States concerned has been given the opportunity to submit its own case and its observations on that of the other party's case both orally and in writing.
>
> If the Commission has not delivered an opinion within three months of the date on which the matter was brought before it, the absence of such opinion shall not prevent the matter from being brought before the Court of Justice.

Member States have shown a marked reluctance to use Article 259 TFEU. Although Member States have quite frequently brought breaches of Union law to the attention of the Commission, it could be politically damaging to international relations for a Member State to take an action all the way to the Court of Justice. Only five cases have proceeded to judgment in the life of the Union: *France* v *UK* (Case 141/78), *Belgium* v *Spain* (Case C-388/95), *Spain* v *United Kingdom* (Case C-145/04), *Hungary* v *Slovakia* (Case C-364/10) and *Austria* v *Germany* (Case C-591/17). A further case, *Slovenia* v *Croatia* (Case C-457/18), is in progress at the time of writing. To protect goodwill between states, any complaint to the Commission about the failure of a Member State to meet its obligations is likely to be brought to the Court of Justice by the Commission under Article 258 TFEU. Article 259 TFEU can therefore be usefully employed by a Member State to prompt the Commission to take action under Article 258.

In 1999, when the Union lifted a worldwide ban on UK beef (which had originally been imposed for health reasons), France refused to allow UK beef to be imported and sold in France. The UK informed the Commission that it intended to take action against France under what is now Article 259 TFEU. The Commission, which had been involved in negotiations with France in an attempt to resolve the dispute, eventually decided to take action against France under what is now Article 258 TFEU, and thus prevented the UK from taking its own independent action. The case came before the Court of Justice and France was held to be in breach of the Treaty (*Commission* v *France* (Case C-1/00)). France eventually lifted its ban.

7.2 The stages of Article 258 TFEU proceedings

Objective 2

Proceedings against Member States under Article 258 TFEU can be divided into three main stages: an administrative stage, a reasoned opinion and the judicial stage. These are set out in Figure 7.1 and then explained in detail below.

Figure 7.1 Article 258 TFEU infringement proceedings

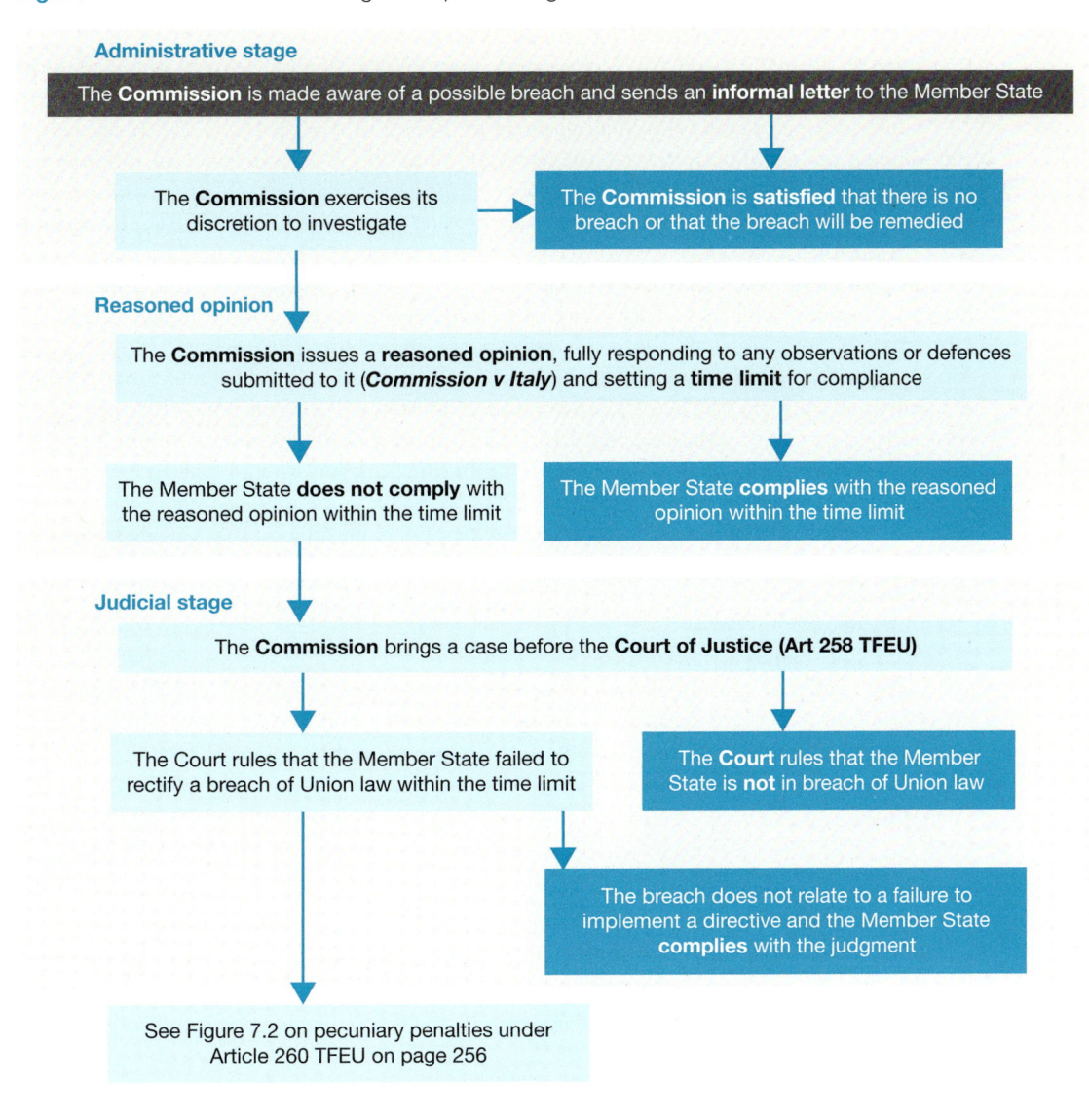

Administrative stage

The **Commission** is made aware of a possible breach and sends an **informal letter** to the Member State

↓

The **Commission** exercises its discretion to investigate → The **Commission** is **satisfied** that there is no breach or that the breach will be remedied

Reasoned opinion

The **Commission** issues a **reasoned opinion**, fully responding to any observations or defences submitted to it (*Commission v Italy*) and setting a **time limit** for compliance

↓

The Member State **does not comply** with the reasoned opinion within the time limit | The Member State **complies** with the reasoned opinion within the time limit

Judicial stage

The **Commission** brings a case before the **Court of Justice (Art 258 TFEU)**

↓

The Court rules that the Member State failed to rectify a breach of Union law within the time limit | The **Court** rules that the Member State is **not** in breach of Union law

↓

The breach does not relate to a failure to implement a directive and the Member State **complies** with the judgment

↓

See Figure 7.2 on pecuniary penalties under Article 260 TFEU on page 256

7.2.1 The administrative stage

Suspected breaches of Union law generally come to the attention of the Commission as a result of complaints from individuals or businesses affected by the breach. The first stage is usually an informal inquiry by letter to the government of the Member State concerned to ascertain the relevant facts. Member States have a legal duty to cooperate with Commission investigations into alleged breaches by them (***Commission* v *Spain*** (Case C-375/92)).

In ***Greece* v *Commission*** (Case 240/86), the Commission was investigating the possible breach by Greece of certain Treaty articles relating to the free movement of goods. The Commission requested certain information, which Greece refused to give. Accordingly, the Commission could not ascertain whether Greece was in breach of the Treaty provisions. The Commission initiated proceedings against Greece under what is now Article 258 TFEU, alleging that Greece was in breach of its duty under what is now **Article 4(3) TEU** (the principle of sincere cooperation) because of its failure to cooperate with the Commission. The Court of Justice ruled in the Commission's favour.

Therefore, if the Commission is unable to ascertain if a Member State is in breach of its Union law obligations due to a refusal to provide information, it can pursue Article 258 TFEU proceedings against the Member State for breach of Article 4(3) TEU. If successful, the Member State will have to 'take the necessary measures to comply with the judgment of the Court' (Art 260(1) TFEU) and provide the requested information. If the information discloses a breach, the Commission will have to start fresh Article 258 TFEU proceedings with regard to this breach.

The Commission does not have to carry out a formal investigation, but it does at least have to 'consider' whether or not there may have been a breach of Union law. Where the Commission does consider there has been a breach, it **must** proceed, after giving the Member State an opportunity to submit observations on the suspected breach, to the delivery of a **reasoned opinion** (see below). The reasoned opinion will often follow prolonged correspondence between the Member State and the Commission. The Commission will have to decide, at some stage in its discussions with (or, in some cases, non-cooperation by) Member States, whether or not to deliver a **formal opinion** which will stipulate a date by which the necessary remedial action should have taken place. The Commission may decide to take no further action if it considers the breach is not serious and that its resources would be better deployed elsewhere.

In ***Commission* v *France*** (Case 7/71), Advocate General Roemer opined that it might be justifiable not to start formal proceedings where: (i) there is a possibility that an amicable settlement may be achieved if formal proceedings are delayed; (ii) the effects of the violation are only minor; (iii) there is a major political crisis which could be aggravated if proceedings are commenced in relation to relatively minor matters; and (iv) there is a possibility that the Union provision at issue might be altered in the near future. The Advocate General commented that Member States resent proceedings being brought against them and the Commission is not always keen, for this reason alone, to take action. The Commission stated in 2017 that it will prioritise cases where:

- a Member State has failed to communicate measures transposing EU law into domestic law, or where those measures implement a directive incorrectly;
- infringements reveal systemic weaknesses that undermine the effective functioning of EU law within a Member State (e.g. infringements that hinder the effective application of EU law in a national judicial system);

- a Member State shows a persistent failure to apply EU law correctly;
- infringements impact the attainment of important policy objectives (e.g. the free movement of people, goods, services and capital).

Many breaches of Union law continue for years without being remedied. For example, the UK failed to implement Directive 64/221 on the movement and residence of foreign nationals for more than 20 years after it had been held to be in default in *Van Duyn* (Case 41/74). In 1996, the French government was again before the Court of Justice for failing to amend its Code du Travail Maritime, 22 years after the Court in *Commission v France (Re French Merchant Seamen)* (Case 167/73) held that the Code breached the former Articles 12 and 39 EC Treaty (*Commission v France* (Case C-334/94); see also *Commission v Belgium* (Case C-37/93) which concerned similar restrictions on Belgian ships). Some of the cases in which action has not been taken involve immigration and social issues, which tend to be more politically sensitive. Additionally, the Commission is likely to refrain from bringing infringement proceedings when a case concerns matters on which a reference for a preliminary ruling is pending or in situations where complainants could seek redress through a national judicial system.

7.2.2 The reasoned opinion

> See section 6.2.1 on essential procedural requirements

If the Commission decides that a violation of Union law has occurred, it must record the infringement in a reasoned opinion or decision delivered to the offending Member State. To arrive at that opinion, the Commission must take into account the replies to its inquiries from the State and any defences which may have been advanced. The Court of Justice has ruled that an opportunity to submit such observations before a reasoned opinion is served is an essential procedural requirement, an infringement of which may invalidate the whole process (*Commission v Italy* (Case 31/69)).

Types of infringement

A large number of infringements concern either the failure to implement directives or a failure to implement them properly. Other infringements may involve direct breaches of Treaty provisions. It will also be a breach by the Member State if, while implementing the directive, it does not provide an effective remedy or uses means which cannot be relied upon by individuals in the national courts. For example, Directive 77/187 protects employees who are employed by an undertaking which is transferred to a new owner. The Directive had been implemented in the UK by the Transfer of Undertakings (Protection of Employment) Regulations 1981, which, *inter alia*, provided for consultation with employee representatives. The UK's implementing regulations, however, provided no means for recognising employee representatives, such that an employer's refusal to recognise employee representatives would result in a failure to consult. In *Commission v UK* (Case C-382/92), the Court of Justice held that where a Union directive does not specifically provide any penalty for an infringement, what is now Article 4(3) TEU nevertheless requires the Member States to guarantee the application and effectiveness of Union law.

Contents of the opinion

The opinion must set out the Union provision and specific details of the breach, together with a response to the Member State's arguments that it has complied or its justification for not having complied, and it must detail the steps to be taken by the Member State to correct the infringement. The opinion has to be even more fully reasoned than a legislative act under

Article 296 TFEU (***Commission v Germany (Re Brennwein)*** (Case 24/62) and ***Commission v Italy*** (Case C-439/99)).

The Commission must also set a **time limit** within which the Member State must rectify its violation. The Court of Justice has held that a Member State must be given a 'reasonable period of time' within which to comply with the opinion and thus prevent the Commission from bringing proceedings before the Court of Justice (***Commission v Ireland*** (Case 74/82)). It is normal practice for a Member State to be given at least two months to respond to a reasoned opinion, but a shorter period might be permissible in certain cases.

Effect of complying with the reasoned opinion

If a Member State complies with the reasoned opinion within the time-limit laid down, the Commission does not have the power to bring the matter before the Court of Justice (***Commission v Italy*** (Case 7/61); ***Commission v Italy*** (Case C-439/99)). This in effect gives the Member State a period of grace within which it is protected from the threat of legal proceedings. If the Commission does subsequently bring proceedings, it must prove that the violation was not ended before the expiry of the time-limit (***Commission v Belgium*** (Case 298/86)).

Failure to implement a directive

> For an example of this situation, see the case study on the UK's implementation of the Working Time Directive in section 6.2.1 (page 212)

If a Member State fails to implement a directive within the time-limit stipulated in the directive, once this time-limit has expired the Commission may move swiftly against the defaulting Member State. If it has still failed to implement it by the date specified in the reasoned opinion, the Commission may take infringement action in the Court of Justice irrespective of whether the Member State subsequently implements the directive. However, if the directive has been implemented within the time period laid down within the reasoned opinion, no further action can be taken pursuant to Article 258 TFEU.

7.2.3 The judicial stage

The Commission does not have to commence proceedings immediately on the expiry of the period specified in its opinion. In one case it waited six years before commencing judicial proceedings (***Commission v Germany*** (Case C-422/92)). The Commission has discretion to give the offending state more time to take the necessary remedial action if it so wishes (***Commission v France*** (Case 7/71)).

Altering the subject matter

When a case comes before the Court of Justice pursuant to Article 258 TFEU, the Commission cannot rely on matters which have not been included in the reasoned opinion (***Commission v Belgium*** (Case 186/85).

In the following case, the Court of Justice held that this applies even if both parties consent:

Commission v Italy (Case 7/69)

Facts:

After the date for complying with a reasoned opinion which had been served on Italy had expired, the Commission started infringement proceedings in the Court of Justice. After starting these proceedings, Italy amended its law in an attempt to comply with the reasoned opinion, but the

Commission still considered Italy to be in breach of Union law. The two parties agreed that the Court of Justice should decide whether the new Italian law complied with Union obligations, rather than adjudicate on Italy's initial breach.

Ruling:
The Court of Justice refused to consider this question. The nature of the proceedings could not be altered, even by consent. The subject matter of the Commission's complaint had changed significantly since it had issued the reasoned opinion, the issuing of which is a compulsory part of the Article 258 TFEU procedure. The proceedings (as set out in the reasoned opinion) only concerned a breach existing at the time the proceedings were initiated; what transpired afterwards was irrelevant for the current proceedings. If the Commission wished to have the new law tested, the full Article 258 TFEU proceedings must be started afresh.

Significance:
Any actions taken by a Member State in response to a reasoned opinion of the Commission cannot then be the subject of Article 258 proceedings without commencing the procedure anew, i.e. with a new formal letter and reasoned opinion concerning these actions.

Member State defences

Member States have attempted to rely upon a number of defences to justify their breaches of Union law, but the Court has not, generally, been receptive. In relation to non-transposition of directives, it is frequently argued either that there has been a shortage of parliamentary time or, alternatively, that transposition is not necessary because the terms of the directive are, in fact, observed and conflicting national legislative provisions are not adhered to. The first defence was resolutely disposed of by the Court of Justice in the following case:

Commission v *Belgium* (Case 77/69)

Facts:
Belgium had imposed a discriminatory tax on wood which violated Article 95 EEC Treaty (now Art 110 TFEU). A draft law to amend the tax scheme had been laid before the Belgian Parliament, but had fallen when the Parliament was dissolved. The Belgian government argued that these were matters out of its control and it had been prevented from legislating by **force majeure**.

Ruling:
The Court of Justice was curt in its dismissal of the argument:

15 The obligations arising from Article 95 of the Treaty [now Art 110 TFEU] devolve upon States as such and the liability of a Member State under Article 169 [now Art 258 TFEU] arises whatever the agency of the State whose action or inaction is the cause of the failure to fulfil its obligations, even in the case of a constitutionally independent institution.

16 The objection raised by the defendant cannot therefore be sustained [see also ***Commission* v *Belgium*** (Case 1/86)].

Significance:
This case established that national obstacles to the adoption of measures required to give effect to Union law do not constitute a defence against a breach.

The fact that the requirements imposed by a directive are difficult to meet was also not accepted as a defence in *Commission v UK* (Case C-56/90). Here, the UK attempted to justify its failure to take all necessary measures to ensure that bathing beaches in Blackpool and Southport met the environmental and health standards set by Directive 76/160 by arguing that implementation was made more difficult by local circumstances. The Court of Justice stated that the UK had not, however, established that it was physically impossible to fulfil its obligations in this regard.

Similarly, Member States cannot qualify their obligations imposed by directives in response to the demands of particular economic or social interest groups. In *Commission v Hellenic Republic* (Case C-45/91), the Greek government attempted to justify its failure to implement a directive on the safe disposal of toxic waste because of 'opposition by the local population'. The Court commented that it had consistently held that a Member State cannot rely on an internal situation to justify disregard of its obligations (see also *Commission v Netherlands (Re Protection of Wild Birds)* (Case 339/87); *Commission v Spain* (Case C-355/90)).

In *Commission v Greece* (Case C-105/91), the Greek government defended its admittedly unlawful and discriminatory tax on foreign vehicles by arguing that the Greek vehicles concerned constituted no more than ten per cent of the internal demand and that there was no manifest discrimination. The Court of Justice rejected the defence on the ground that it had consistently held that a Member State was guilty of a failure to fulfil its obligations under the Treaty regardless of the frequency or the scale of the infringement.

The defence that a directive or regulation is observed in practice or 'administratively' where there are conflicting national provisions has also been rejected by the Court of Justice on a number of occasions (*Commission v Italy* (Case 166/82); *Commission v Germany (Re Nursing Directives)* (Case 29/84); *Commission v UK (Re Tachographs)* (Case 128/78)). However, the use of existing, legally binding provisions of national law may be acceptable if they provide an effective means of implementing the directive. Such legislation may, therefore, provide a defence to non-implementation (*Commission v Netherlands* (Case C-190/90)). Either way, individuals must be able to rely on a text of national law that accurately reflects their rights and on which they can rely in the event of a judicial challenge (*Commission v France* (Case 167/73)). For this reason, a Union obligation cannot be implemented by the government of a Member State simply by accepting assurances from the bodies affected that they will meet the terms of the Union provision.

7.3 Pecuniary penalties

Objective 3

Once judgment has been given against a Member State, failure to observe the terms of that judgment will constitute a breach of **Article 260(1) TFEU**. Article 260 TFEU provides:

> 1 If the Court of Justice of the European Union finds that a Member State has failed to fulfil an obligation under the Treaties, the State shall be required to take the necessary measures to comply with the judgment of the Court.
>
> 2 If the Commission considers that the Member State concerned has not taken the necessary measures to comply with the judgment of the Court, it may bring the case before the Court after giving that State the opportunity to submit its observations. It shall

> specify the amount of the **lump sum** or **penalty payment** to be paid by the Member State concerned which it considers appropriate in the circumstances.
>
> If the Court finds that the Member State concerned has not complied with its judgment it may impose a lump sum or penalty payment on it.
>
> This procedure shall be without prejudice to Article 259.
>
> 3 When the Commission brings a case before the Court pursuant to Article 258 on the grounds that the Member State concerned has failed to fulfil its obligation to notify measures transposing a directive adopted under a legislative procedure, it may, when it deems appropriate, specify the amount of the lump sum or penalty payment to be paid by the Member State concerned which it considers appropriate in the circumstances.
>
> If the Court finds that there is an infringement it may impose a lump sum or penalty payment on the Member State concerned not exceeding the amount specified by the Commission. The payment obligation shall take effect on the date set by the Court in its judgment.

Following a judgment of the Court of Justice pursuant to Article 258 TFEU, the Member State is obliged to take the necessary measures to give effect to the Court's judgment (Art 260(1) TFEU). This may require national legislation to be implemented, amended or repealed to resolve the Member State's breach of Union law. If the Member State fails to comply with the judgment it will be in breach of its Article 260(1) TFEU duty. The Commission is then empowered by **Article 260(2) TFEU** to initiate fresh infringement proceedings for a breach of Article 260(1). Unlike its predecessor (Art 228(2) EC Treaty), Article 260(2) TFEU does not require a new administrative stage and reasoned opinion before referral to the Court of Justice.

Alternatively, if the breach concerns a failure to implement a directive, **Article 260(3) TFEU** empowers the Commission to recommend a penalty when it brings an initial infringement action under Article 258 TFEU – this is a separate procedure which is discussed below.

Prior to the Treaty of Maastricht, the former Article 228(2) EC Treaty carried no sanction. All the Court of Justice was empowered to do was to make a declaration that a Member State was acting in breach of its Union law obligations. Under the current Article 260(2), however, the Court can impose a lump sum and/or a penalty payment. This incorporation of financial sanctions into the infringement procedure strengthened the Commission's hand in ensuring that Member States complied with their Union law obligations. However, the Commission will still seek to resolve the conflict informally; it will explore every possible avenue before initiating Court proceedings.

7.3.1 Calculation of payments

On 8 January 1997, the Commission recommended a formula to the Court of Justice for calculating penalties. It started with a basic penalty of 55 euros per day, which would be multiplied by factors to account for the gravity of the breach, the duration of the breach and the relative wealth of the state. For example, France and Germany have larger economies and therefore would face increased penalties, while Italy would be liable to a slightly lower penalty.

Figure 7.2 Pecuniary penalties

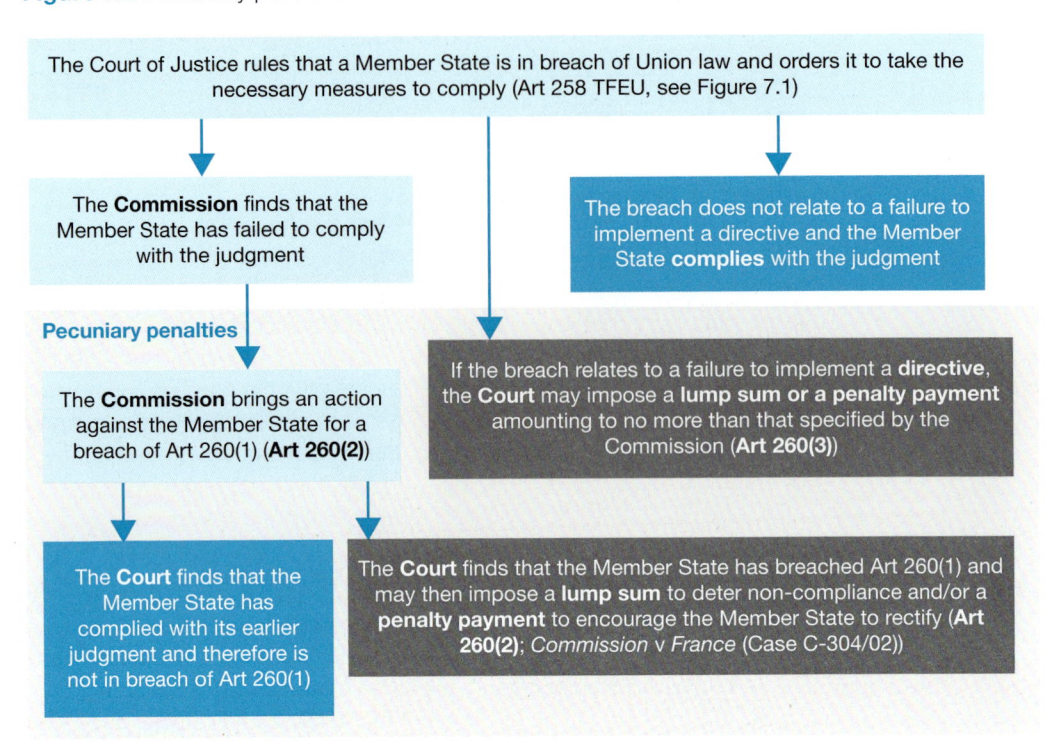

```
The Court of Justice rules that a Member State is in breach of Union law and orders it to take the
necessary measures to comply (Art 258 TFEU, see Figure 7.1)
```

- The **Commission** finds that the Member State has failed to comply with the judgment
- The breach does not relate to a failure to implement a directive and the Member State **complies** with the judgment

Pecuniary penalties

- The **Commission** brings an action against the Member State for a breach of Art 260(1) (**Art 260(2)**)
- If the breach relates to a failure to implement a **directive**, the **Court** may impose a **lump sum or a penalty payment** amounting to no more than that specified by the Commission (**Art 260(3)**)

- The **Court** finds that the Member State has complied with its earlier judgment and therefore is not in breach of Art 260(1)
- The **Court** finds that the Member State has breached Art 260(1) and may then impose a **lump sum** to deter non-compliance and/or a **penalty payment** to encourage the Member State to rectify (**Art 260(2)**; *Commission* v *France* (Case C-304/02))

In the following case, the Court of Justice imposed a financial penalty on Greece in proceedings initiated by the Commission under what is now Article 260(2) TFEU:

Commission v Greece (Case C-387/97)

Facts:

Greece had failed to fulfil its obligations under Articles 4 and 6 of Directive 75/442 and Articles 5 and 12 of Directive 78/319 on the management and disposal of toxic and dangerous waste. The Commission brought proceedings under the former Article 169 EC Treaty (now Art 258 TFEU), which culminated in a judgment in the Commission's favour in Case C-45/91, given on 7 April 1992.

After further communications between the Commission and the Greek government between 1993 and 1996, the Commission issued a reasoned opinion to the effect that, by continuing not to draw up or implement requisite waste disposal plans, Greece had failed to comply with the 1992 judgment. The Commission therefore brought an action under the former Article 171(2) EC Treaty (now Art 260(2) TFEU).

Ruling:

In its judgment, the Court of Justice concluded that it had not been proved that Greece had failed to comply with the judgment in Case C-45/91 in relation to Article 5, Directive 78/319, but that in other respects that judgment had not been complied with.

The Court of Justice stated that the former Article 171(2) EC Treaty (now Art 260(2) TFEU) did not specify the period within which a judgment had to be complied with, but the importance of immediate and uniform application of Union law meant that **the process of compliance had to be initiated at once and completed as soon as possible**.

In the absence of provisions in the Treaty at the time, the Court stated that the Commission could adopt guidelines for determining how the lump sums or penalty payments which it intended to propose to the Court should be calculated, so as in particular to ensure equal treatment between the Member States. The Court of Justice then referred to these guidelines prepared by the Commission and continued:

> The Commission's suggestion that account should be taken both of the gross domestic product of the Member State concerned, and of the number of votes in the Council, appeared appropriate in that it enabled that State's ability to pay to be reflected while keeping the variation between Member States within a reasonable range.
>
> Those suggestions could not bind the Court but were a useful point of reference.
>
> First, since the principal aim of penalty payments was that the Member State should remedy the breach of obligations as soon as possible, **a penalty payment had to be set that was appropriate to the circumstances and proportionate both to the breach which had been found and to the State's ability to pay**.
>
> Second, the degree of urgency that the Member State should fulfil its obligations could vary in accordance with the breach.
>
> In that light, and as the Commission had suggested, **the basic criteria which were to be taken into account in order to ensure that penalty payments had coercive force and Community [i.e. Union] law was applied uniformly and effectively were, in principle, the duration of the infringement, its degree of seriousness and the ability of the Member State to pay**.
>
> In applying those criteria, regard should be had in particular to the **effects of the failure to comply on private and public interests, and to the urgency of getting the Member State to fulfil its obligations**.

The Court of Justice ordered Greece to pay to the Commission, into the account of 'EC [i.e. EU] own resources', a penalty payment of 20,000 euros for each day of delay in implementing the measures necessary to comply with the judgment in Case C-45/91, from delivery of the present judgment (i.e. 4 July 2000) until the judgment in Case C-45/91 had been complied with.

Significance:

This case established three criteria for calculating a penalty payment: (i) the **duration** of the infringement, (ii) its degree of **seriousness** and (iii) the **ability** of the Member State to pay. It also demonstrated the potency of the **pecuniary penalty** system. The Court only applied the daily penalty from the date of the current judgment (i.e. 4 July 2000) and not 'a reasonable period' after its initial judgment when it had been held that Greece was in breach of its Union law obligations (i.e. 7 April 1992). This suggests that the aim of the penalty was to encourage compliance in the future rather than to punish non-compliance in the past.

In the following case, an action was brought before the Court of Justice pursuant to what is now Article 260(2) TFEU, for France's failure to fulfil its obligations under what is now Article 260(1) TFEU:

Commission v France (Case C-304/02)

Facts:
It was alleged that France had failed to comply with the judgment of 11 June 1991 in ***Commission v France*** (Case C-64/88), in which it had been found that France had failed to fulfil its obligations under regulations concerning fishing and the control of fishing activities.

Ruling:
The Court held that France had not taken all the necessary measures to comply with the judgment in ***Commission v France*** (Case C-64/88). In relation to the financial penalties which could be imposed on France and in the light of the Advocate General's Opinion, the Court raised the issue of: (i) its ability to impose a lump sum penalty, although the Commission had requested a penalty payment; and (ii) its right to impose both a lump sum penalty and a penalty payment. The Court of Justice reopened the oral procedure for discussion on these two issues.

In relation to the possibility of imposing both a penalty payment and a lump sum, the Court observed that the former Article 228(2) EC Treaty (now Art 260(2) TFEU) has the objective 'of inducing a defaulting Member State to comply with a judgment establishing a breach of obligations and thereby of ensuring that Community [i.e. Union] law is in fact applied'. The Court considered that the measures provided for by that provision (the lump sum and the penalty payment) do not pursue the same objective. The purpose of a penalty payment is to induce a Member State to put an end as soon as possible to a breach of obligations which, in the absence of the measure, would tend to persist (persuasive effect), while the lump sum 'is based more on assessment of the effects on public and private interests of the failure of the Member State concerned to comply with its obligations, in particular where the breach has persisted for a long period since the judgment which initially established it' (deterrent effect).

The Court concluded that where the breach of obligations has continued for a long period and is inclined to persist, it is possible to have recourse to both types of penalty. Therefore, the conjunction 'or' in the former Article 228(2) EC Treaty (now Art 260(2) TFEU), 'may . . . have an alternative or a cumulative sense and must therefore be read in the context in which it is used'. The Court stated that the fact that both measures were not imposed in previous cases could not constitute an obstacle, if imposing both measures appeared appropriate, regard being had to the circumstances of the case.

Finally, the Court referred to its judgment in ***Commission v Hellenic Republic*** (above) to consider its discretion as to the financial penalties that can be imposed. Here, it restated that the basic criteria which must be taken into account in order to ensure that penalty payments have coercive force and Union law is applied uniformly and effectively are, in principle, **the duration of the infringement, its degree of seriousness and the ability of the Member State concerned to pay**. In applying those criteria, regard should be had in particular to the effects of failure to comply on private and public interests and to the urgency of getting the Member State concerned to fulfil its obligations.

The Court found that France's breach of obligations had persisted over a long period and imposed a dual financial penalty:

> (i) a **penalty payment** of 57,761,250 euros for each period of six months, from delivery of the current judgment, at the end of which the judgment in ***Commission v France*** (Case C-64/88) had not yet been fully complied with;
>
> (ii) a **lump sum penalty** of 20,000,000 euros.
>
> **Significance:**
>
> This case clearly established the principle that the Court of Justice can impose both a penalty payment and a lump sum penalty. A penalty payment is imposed to **persuade** the defaulting Member State to comply with the judgment, whereas a lump sum penalty is imposed to **deter** all Member States from breaching their Union law obligations.

In a later case, ***Commission v France*** (Case C-177/04), the Court of Justice levied a penalty payment on France which was greater than that which had been recommended by the Commission. The Court agreed with the coefficients the Commission had used relating to the seriousness of the breach, France's gross domestic product and its number of votes in the Council. However, the Court disagreed with the coefficient the Commission had used relating to the duration of the infringement. The Court stated that for the purpose of calculating this coefficient, regard is to be had to the period between the Court's first judgment and the time at which it assesses the facts, not the time at which the case is brought before it.

Subsequently, in ***Greece v Commission*** (Case C-369/07), the Court of Justice imposed both a penalty payment and lump sum penalty on Greece. The Court stated that Greece's failure to fulfil its Union law obligations (to comply with the Court's previous judgment) had lasted for more than four years. The Court imposed upon Greece a periodic penalty payment of 16,000 euros per day of delay in implementing its judgment of four years previous, commencing from one month after the delivery of the present judgment, allowing Greece to demonstrate that it had ended the failure to fulfil its Union obligations. The amount of the lump sum payment had to be determined by reference to the persistence of the failure to fulfil obligations (since the *first* judgment establishing that failure) and to the public and private interests in question. The Court levied on Greece a lump sum penalty payment of 2 million euros (see also *Commission v Spain* (Case C-610/10)).

In ***Commission v Ireland*** (Case C-279/11 and C-374/11) the Court imposed both a lump sum penalty and a periodic penalty upon Ireland. However, the Court reduced the amount the Commission had recommended because Ireland's ability to pay had, to a certain degree, been diminished as a result of the economic crisis which started in Ireland during 2008. This economic crisis gripped the whole of the EU, but it affected some countries more than others.

In ***Greece v Commission*** (Case C-407/09), the Court of Justice did not impose a penalty payment on Greece following the Commission's withdrawal of its request. The Commission withdrew its request because Greece had remedied the default two months after the Commission had issued proceedings. However, the Commission did not withdraw its request for the imposition of a lump sum and the Court ordered Greece to pay a lump sum of 3 million euros. Similarly, in ***Commission v Italy*** (Case C-119/04), the Commission requested the imposition of a penalty payment on Italy for its failure to comply with an early ruling, but the Court declined to do so as the breach of obligations no longer persisted on the date of the Court's examination of the facts.

7.3.2 Collection of payments

In the following case, France brought a case before the General Court, challenging a decision by the Commission pertaining to the collection of payments that were imposed in the earlier case of *Commission* v *France* (Case C-304/02, see above):

France v Commission (T-139/06)

Facts:

In Case C-304/02, the Court of Justice imposed a dual financial penalty, reflecting France's prolonged failure to comply with its judgment in **Commission v France** (Case C-64/88). The Court had imposed:

(i) a penalty payment of 57,761,250 euros for each period of six months from delivery of the judgment in Case C-304/02 at the end of which the judgment in Case C-64/88 had not yet been fully complied with;

(ii) a lump sum penalty of 20,000,000 euros.

After conducting inspections and finding that France continued to be in breach of its obligations, the Commission sent France a decision (Decision C (2006) 659 Final) on 2 March 2006 requesting payment of the periodic penalty. France brought a case before the General Court requesting the annulment of that decision or, alternatively, a reduction to the amount of the periodic penalty.

Ruling:

The General Court confirmed that the Commission was competent to require the payment of the periodic penalty imposed by the Court.

In effect, in its second judgment, delivered in 2005, the Court of Justice clearly determined the rights and obligations of France, fixed the penalties and conditions attached to them and, therefore, authorised the Commission to fulfil those conditions, i.e. to make inspections and request payments based on their findings.

Furthermore, the General Court ruled that France had not shown that the Commission's decision was vitiated by an error of assessment or that the Commission had exceeded its powers. The Commission, when adopting its decision, did not determine that there was a new infringement but rather that there was an absence of any significant change to the infringements found by the Court in its two judgments. The periodic penalty was thus payable.

The General Court concluded that the full amount of the periodic penalty must be paid. Even on the assumption that the information provided by France could be considered to show an improvement in the situation, it nevertheless remained that as of 1 March 2006 France had not fully implemented the Court's judgment of 11 June 1991. The Commission, bound by the 2005 judgment, was not able to reduce the amount and the efforts made by France were not such as to excuse the infringements.

Significance:

This case confirmed the power of the Commission to determine that a breach of Union law had not been resolved and to request payments set by the Court of Justice accordingly. It also established that penalty payments cannot be reduced in acknowledgement of improvements; either the breach persists and the full penalty should be paid, or the breach has been rectified and no penalty is due.

This aspect was considered further by the Court of Justice in the following case:

Commission v Portugal (Case C-292/11P)

Facts:

By judgment of 14 October 2004 (*Commission v Portugal* (Case C-275/03)), the Court of Justice held that Portugal had failed to fulfil its obligations by not repealing national legislation which made the award of damages to persons injured by a breach of Union law, in the field of public procurement, conditional on proof of fault or fraud.

Taking the view that Portugal had failed to comply with that judgment, the Commission brought a fresh action seeking imposition of a penalty payment. By its judgment of 10 January 2008 (*Commission v Portugal* (Case C-70/06)), the Court of Justice held that Portugal had not complied with its first judgment of 2004, as the Portuguese legislation had not been repealed by the end of the period prescribed by the Commission. The Court accordingly ordered Portugal to pay to the Commission a penalty payment of 19,392 euros for each day of delay in implementing the measures necessary to ensure compliance with the first judgment of 2004, with effect from the date of delivery of the second judgment, 10 January 2008.

On 31 December 2007 (i.e. a few days before the 2008 judgment was delivered), Portugal adopted Law No 67/2007, which repealed the national legislation in question and put in place a new system of compensation for damage caused by the State. That law came into force on 30 January 2008. The Commission, however, took the view that this new law was not adequate to ensure compliance with the 2004 judgment. Although Portugal disagreed, it adopted Law No 31/2008 amending Law No 67/2007 in order to avoid prolonging the dispute. Law No 31/2008 came into force on 18 July 2008, at which point the Commission viewed Portugal to be in compliance with the 2004 judgment. Accordingly, in its decision of 25 November 2008, the Commission determined that the daily penalty payment was payable up to 17 July 2008, the day before Law No 31/2008 came into force.

Portugal then brought an action before the General Court against that decision of the Commission. By judgment of 29 March 2011 (*Portugal v Commission* (Case T-33/09)), the General Court annulled the decision. It held that the assessment of the content of new legislation adopted by a Member State with a view to complying with a judgment of the Court of Justice delivered pursuant to Art 260(2) TFEU comes in all cases within the exclusive jurisdiction of the Court of Justice and must, if there is a disagreement between the Commission and that Member State, be the subject of a fresh procedure.

The Commission appealed the decision of the General Court and brought the current case before the Court of Justice.

Ruling:

The Court of Justice dismissed the Commission's appeal, essentially due to the exclusive jurisdiction of the Court of Justice to rule on whether national legislation is in conformity with Union law.

The Court noted that the Commission's review of the measures adopted by a Member State for the purpose of complying with a judgment and the recovery of any sums owed had to be carried out having regard to the scope of the failure to fulfil obligations that the Court of Justice had determined. In this case, that breach of obligations amounted to a failure to repeal certain national legislation. In deciding that Law No 67/2007, repealing the national legislation at issue, did not ensure proper compliance with the 2004 judgment, the Commission formed a view on the issue of the conformity of the new Portuguese law with Union law, even though that Portuguese law introduced a system of liability distinct from that of the repealed legislation. **The Commission's power of appraisal, in the context of compliance with a judgment of the Court of Justice, cannot be exercised in such a manner which is prejudicial to the Court's exclusive jurisdiction to rule on the conformity of national legislation with EU law.**

It followed that, **in the case where there is a difference between the Commission and the Member State concerned as to whether a national practice or national legislation which the Court of Justice has not examined beforehand is appropriate for ensuring compliance with a judgment, the Commission cannot, by adopting a decision, resolve such a difference itself and draw from this the necessary inferences for the calculation of the penalty payment.**

Likewise, as the General Court acknowledged in the judgment under appeal, **the General Court also cannot rule on the conformity of national legislation with Union law, and therefore cannot confirm or refute the Commission's assessment on this matter.** However, the General Court correctly restricted its judgment to the scope of Portugal's failure to fulfil its obligations as the Court of Justice had already determined. It therefore follows that, in the judgment under appeal, the General Court did not unduly limit the powers of the Commission in the verification of compliance by Portugal with the 2008 judgment or, consequently, its own jurisdiction in relation to the review of the Commission's assessment in that regard.

Significance:

This case established the limits of the Commission's competence to determine compliance with a judgment by referring to the Court of Justice's exclusive jurisdiction to rule on whether a national measure complies with Union law. Essentially, the Commission may only find non-compliance, and request payments accordingly, with regard to measures already ruled on by the Court of Justice.

The case of *Commission* v *Italy* (Case C-119/04), see above, can be contrasted with the following case:

Commission v France (Case C-121/07)

Facts:

The Commission took action against France under what is now Article 258 TFEU in *Commission v France* (Case C-419/03) for its failure to implement Directive 2001/118. This Directive, which concerns the deliberate release into the environment of genetically modified organisms (GMOs), should have been implemented by 17 October 2002. On 15 July 2004, in Case C-419/03, the Court of Justice held that France was in breach of its Union law obligation to implement the Directive. France failed to comply with this judgment and therefore the Commission issued proceedings before the Court of Justice pursuant to what is now Article 260(2) TFEU.

The Commission proposed that France be ordered to pay both a penalty payment and a lump sum payment. However, before the Court of Justice gave judgment, France implemented the Directive. The Commission therefore informed the Court of Justice that its request to order France to pay a penalty payment was devoid of purpose (in line with the Court's judgment in *Commission* v *Italy* (Case C-119/04), see above) but that it wanted to continue with its request that France be ordered to pay a lump sum payment.

Ruling:

The Court of Justice stated that the reference date for assessing whether there had been a failure to comply with its first judgment was February 2006 (i.e. the date specified by the Commission in its reasoned opinion as the date by which France was required to comply with the Court's judgment). By this date, France had failed to take any steps to comply with the Court's judgment in Case C-419/03.

The Court considered that the imposition of a penalty payment was not necessary because by June 2008 France had fully transposed the Directive. However, the Court of Justice ordered France to pay a lump sum payment of 10 million euros.

The Court stated that **an order for the payment of a lump sum is not made automatically; it depends on the specific details of the breach and the approach adopted by the Member**

> **State concerned**. In this particular case, the Court stated that France's unlawful conduct in the GMO sector was of such a **nature** as to require the adoption of a dissuasive measure, such as a lump sum payment. The Court also noted the considerable length of **time** for which the breach persisted after its initial judgment in Case C-419/03. Furthermore, the Court deemed that this was a **serious** breach of Union law, given the objectives of the Directive, which pertained to public health and the free movement of goods.
>
> **Significance:**
>
> This case clarified that an order for a payment of a lump sum is not an automatic consequence of a finding of a failure in an Article 260 TFEU case, but rather that such an order will depend on an assessment of the extent to which such a deterrent is deemed appropriate.

The approach with regard to failures to implement directives was subsequently modified by introduction of Article 260(3) in the ToL.

7.3.3 Article 260(3) TFEU

Since the entry into force of the ToL on 1 December 2009, Article 260(3) TFEU has provided a new means of applying pecuniary penalties in cases where a Member State has 'failed to fulfil its obligation to notify measures transposing a directive adopted under a legislative procedure'. This 'failure to notify' includes instances where a Member State has either entirely or partially failed to adopt measures implementing a directive, as of course there can be no notification of measures that do not exist. Article 260(3) thus provides that if the Commission brings Article 258 TFEU proceedings against a Member State that has failed to implement a directive, the Commission may, if it considers it appropriate, specify a lump sum or penalty payment that the Member State should be required to pay. If the Court subsequently finds the Member State to be in breach of its Union law obligations, it can impose the lump sum or penalty payment on the Member State. The amount imposed by the Court must **not** exceed that specified by the Commission.

This new provision has resulted in the imposition of significant penalties in several cases, including *Commission* v *Poland* (Case C-245/12), *Commission* v *Poland* (Case C-544/12) and *Commission* v *Poland* (Case C-320/13). The penalties imposed in these cases demonstrate the effectiveness of Article 260(3) in addressing the previous deficiency, whereby Article 258 proceedings effectively enabled Member States to attain an extension to the deadline for the implementation of a directive.

7.4 Interim measures

Objective 4

Interim measures can be ordered by a court with the aim of preventing or minimising harm prior to the date of a full hearing. There are three main scenarios where interim measures may be imposed:

(i) The validity of a **Union act** is challenged; the **Court of Justice or the General Court** requires the suspension of the act until the matter is determined. This is most likely to occur during a review of legality proceedings under Article 263 TFEU.

(ii) A **national law** is alleged to be in breach of Union law; the **Court of Justice** requires the suspension of the national law until the matter is determined. This is most likely to occur during infringement proceedings brought under Article 258 or 259 TFEU.

(iii) A **national law** is alleged to be in breach of Union law; a **national court** requires the suspension of the national law until the matter is determined. This is most likely to occur while a national court is waiting for a reference for a preliminary ruling under Article 267 TFEU.

This section focuses on the latter two possibilities.

7.4.1 Interim measures ordered by the Court of Justice

Breaches of Union law may occur inadvertently or intentionally. In the former case, Member States will normally take remedial action when the breach is brought to their attention by the Commission. In the latter case, Member State governments may choose to risk action by the Commission when they are confronted by internal political pressures they cannot, or will not, resist. They will often do so in the hope that, by the time the Commission commences proceedings, a solution can be found and the unlawful action or inaction can be put right. For example, such considerations appear to have motivated the French government in the ban it imposed on the import of lamb and mutton from other Member States, principally the UK (***Commission*** v ***France (Re Sheepmeat)*** (Case 232/78)), and similar considerations seem to have been in the mind of the French government during 1999 when it refused to lift the ban on the sale of UK beef (***Commission*** v ***France*** (Case C-1/00), see above).

Given that several years may elapse between an initial complaint to the Commission and a hearing before the Court of Justice, the Commission, in circumstances where continuing damage is being caused while the case is being processed, may apply to the Court for interim relief. Interim relief may be granted by the Court under **Article 279 TFEU**, which simply states:

> The Court of Justice of the European Union may in any cases before it prescribe any necessary interim measures.

The speed of the relief available is demonstrated by ***Commission*** v ***Ireland*** (Case 61/77R). In this case, Ireland had introduced fisheries conservation measures which the Commission regarded as contrary to the Treaty. The Commission commenced proceedings under what is now Article 258 TFEU and, at the same time, made an application for an interim order requiring Ireland to suspend the operation of the legislation. The Court gave judgment only nine days later. It doubted the conformity of the Irish legislation with the Treaty and, after several adjournments to promote a settlement, ordered the Irish government to suspend the measures within five days (see also ***Commission*** v ***UK*** (Case C-246/89R)).

Article 160(3) of the Rules of Procedure of the Court of Justice sets out the requirements for an application for interim measures. It provides that such an application 'shall state the **subject-matter** of the proceedings, the circumstances giving rise to **urgency** and the pleas of fact and law establishing a ***prima facie*** case for the interim measure applied for'. These requirements were at issue in the following case:

Commission v *Germany* (Case C-195/90R)

Facts:
Germany imposed a new tax on heavy goods vehicles with the aim of encouraging greater use of water transport on the country's inland waterways. This tax was to take effect on 1 July 1990. The

Commission applied for what was, in effect, an ***ex parte*** interim order from the President of the Court of Justice, which was ordered on 28 June 1990, pending the full hearing of the application.

The Commission argued that the new German tax breached the 'standstill' provisions of the former Article 76 EEC Treaty (now Art 92 TFEU), which were intended to protect the present position until a common Union transport policy was adopted under the former Articles 74 and 75 EEC Treaty (now Art 90 TFEU). It also breached the former Article 95 EEC Treaty (the prohibition against discriminatory taxation, now Art 110 TFEU), as the charge, although payable by all vehicles of the appropriate weight, was offset for German vehicles by a reduction in German vehicle tax.

Ruling:

The Court of Justice accepted that the Commission's arguments were sufficient to establish a ***prima facie*** case and subsequently focused its attention on the question of urgency. The Court had previously determined that urgency was to be assessed according to the extent to which an interim order was **necessary to avoid serious and irreparable damage** (***Commission* v *Greece*** (Case C-170/94R)). The Commission argued that the new German tax would disrupt its attempts to create a common transport policy and would drive a number of carriers out of business before the full proceedings could be heard. The German government insisted that if the tax was suspended it would suffer irreparable damage in the loss of tax, which could not be recovered subsequently if the tax was found to be lawful in the main proceedings. The Court accepted the Commission's argument of the need to protect the *status quo* and the need to avoid irreparable damage to transport undertakings. The German government could hardly be said to be suffering a loss to its exchequer, because the tax had not existed before. The interim order to suspend the operation of the new tax was, therefore, confirmed.

Significance:

This case confirmed that the requirement of urgency for interim measures is met when such measures are necessary to avoid serious and irreparable damage. It also suggests that the Court of Justice will prioritise protection of the *status quo* and the protection of private undertakings over the income of the state from new measures.

In the following case, the Court of Justice rejected a request for interim measures on the ground that the Commission had not demonstrated a sufficiently urgent need for them:

Commission v *Belgium* (Case C-87/94 R)

Facts:

The Commission applied for interim relief in a case where Belgium had allegedly breached procedures laid down in Directive 90/531 in the award of contracts to replace old buses. The contract had been awarded (wrongly, the Commission maintained) and the delivery of the first buses was due before the full hearing could take place. The Commission argued that there was a risk of serious and irreparable damage, in that the award of the contract and the first deliveries would confront the Commission with a ***fait accompli*** and would therefore present a serious and immediate threat to the Union legal order.

Ruling:

The Court agreed that the failure to comply with a directive applicable to a public contract constituted a serious threat to the Union legal order and that a declaration at the conclusion of the proceedings under what is now Article 258 TFEU could not cancel the damage suffered. However, the Court felt that an application for interim relief should be pursued with regard to the **balance of interests**. The court thus considered Belgium's argument that a suspension of the contract to replace the buses could lead to problems, or even accidents, due to the poor condition of the existing buses, which were up to 18 years old.

Furthermore, the Commission had allowed more than three months to elapse between receiving notification of the situation and informing the Member State that it would seek authorisation to suspend the contract. The Court therefore concluded that 'the Commission has failed to display the diligence required of a party relying on the urgency of interim measures, and that the balance of interests tilts in favour of the Kingdom of Belgium'. The Commission's application for interim relief was refused.

Significance:

This case established that the Court of Justice will consider both the harm that would be caused if potentially unlawful measures are allowed to continue until a full hearing and the harm that would be caused if such measures were suspended. Additionally, it suggests that a claim by the Commission that interim measures are urgently required will be undermined if the Commission itself fails to act as though the matter is urgent.

7.4.2 Interim measures ordered by a national Court

In *Zückerfabrik Süderdithmarschen* v *HZA Itzehoe* (Case C-143/88), the Court of Justice declared that national courts must have the power to grant interim relief in order for references for preliminary rulings (now under Art 267 TFEU) to work effectively. This applies in situations where the validity of a Union act, on which a national measure is based, is called into question during national proceedings. The Court held that such relief should be granted on the same grounds as when the compatibility of a national measure with Union law is contested – i.e. they must be necessary to avoid serious and irreparable damage. However, the national court has to be careful:

> Where a national court or tribunal has serious doubts about the validity of a Community [i.e. Union] act on which a national measure is based, it may, **in exceptional circumstances**, temporarily suspend application of the latter measure or grant other interim relief with respect to it. It must then refer the question of validity to the Court of Justice, stating the reasons for which it considers that the Community [i.e. Union] act is not valid.

National courts can apply national criteria when deciding, in the particular circumstances, whether or not to grant suspensory relief, but the national measures must be effective in providing the necessary remedies to protect rights conferred by Union law (*Factortame (No. 2)* (Case C-213/89)) and to prevent 'irreparable damage' to the person seeking relief, pending the outcome of the reference (*Atlanta Fruchthandelsgesellschaft GmbH* v *Bundesamt für Ernährung und Forstwirtschaft* (Case C-465/93)). In *Factortame (No. 2)*, the Court of Justice also established that a national court is obliged to set aside any national rule that would prevent them from granting interim measures while awaiting a preliminary ruling from the Court of Justice.

7.5 Measures under Article 7 TEU

Objective 5

While the Commission can bring cases against Member States in order to enforce Union law, **Article 7 TEU** concerns respect for the Union values set out in **Article 2 TEU**.

> Article 2 TEU is cited in section 1.1.1

Articles 7(1), 7(2) and 7(3) set out three different levels of response to a situation where a Member State is failing to respect Union values. **Article 7(1) TEU** concerns a situation where the Council perceives a clear **risk** of a serious breach of Union values within a Member State. This can be referred to as a **preventative mechanism**. The text of this provision is as follows:

> On a reasoned proposal by one third of the Member States, by the European Parliament or by the European Commission, **the Council**, acting by a majority of four fifths of its members after obtaining the consent of the European Parliament, **may determine that there is a clear risk of a serious breach by a Member State of the values referred to in Article 2**. Before making such a determination, the Council shall hear the Member State in question and may address **recommendations** to it, acting in accordance with the same procedure. The Council shall regularly verify that the grounds on which such a determination was made continue to apply.

Articles 7(2) and 7(3) TEU then concern situations where a **serious and persistent breach** is found to exist within a Member State. These provisions work together to form a **sanctioning mechanism**. The texts of these provisions are as follows:

> 2. The **European Council**, acting by unanimity on a proposal by one third of the Member States or by the Commission and after obtaining the consent of the European Parliament, **may determine the existence of a serious and persistent breach by a Member State of the values referred to in Article 2**, after inviting the Member State in question to submit its observations.
>
> 3. Where a determination under paragraph 2 has been made, **the Council**, acting by a qualified majority, **may decide to suspend certain of the rights deriving from the application of the Treaties to the Member State** in question, including the voting rights of the representative of the government of that Member State in the Council. In doing so, the Council shall take into account the possible consequences of such a suspension on the rights and obligations of natural and legal persons.
>
> The obligations of the Member State in question under the Treaties shall in any case continue to be binding on that State.

Article 7 was initially introduced by the Treaty of Amsterdam (Article F.1 TEU) in preparation for the enlargement of the EU. The aim was to safeguard against new Member States 'backsliding' in their protection of fundamental values once they had joined the Union. At this time, Article F.1 TEU (now Article 7 TEU) only contained provisions regarding a serious and persistent breach of Union values. There was therefore no mechanism for Union institutions to intervene prior to this high threshold being reached. This was rectified by the Treaty of Nice, which introduced the preventative mechanism now provided in Article 7(1) TEU. However, the preventative provision is often overlooked by commentators who refer to Article 7 TEU as the EU's **'nuclear option'**. This description reflects the view that the sanctions available under Article 7(3) TEU are so severe that they function more as a rhetorical threat than a politically viable option.

At the time of writing, Article 7(1) proceedings have been initiated against Poland and Hungary; these are discussed below. Additionally, a resolution adopted by the European Parliament in December 2019 calls for the Commission to begin a dialogue with Malta in relation to the rule of law and indicates that Malta's failure to enact judicial reforms could form the basis for triggering Article 7 procedures.

7.5.1 Rule of law in Poland

The rule of law is listed as a founding value of the Union in **Article 2 TEU**. The rule of law pertains to the proper balance of powers between a legislature, judiciary and executive, and, broadly, to the ability of a state to deliver justice for its citizens. With regards to the EU, the rule of law within a Member State is essential for ensuring the proper application of Union law, including through the correct use of the preliminary reference procedure (see Chapter 5) and by ensuring that the nationals of that state can benefit from the rights bestowed on them by Union law (see Chapter 8). Additionally, rule of law within Member States ensures the legitimacy of Union decisions in which they partake. In addition to Article 2 TEU, the rule of law is protected by **Article 19(1) TEU**, which states that 'Member States shall provide remedies sufficient to ensure effective legal protection in the fields covered by Union law'.

On four occasions across 2016 and 2017, the **Commission** issued **Rule of Law Recommendations** to Poland with regard to the enactment of national legislation that undermines the independence of the national judiciary. On the last of these occasions, on 20 December 2017, the Commission also initiated **Article 7(1) TEU** procedures by submitting a **reasoned proposal** for a decision by the Council to determine a clear risk of a serious breach of the rule of law by Poland. The Commission (2017) described its concerns as follows:

> Over a period of two years, the Polish authorities have adopted more than 13 laws affecting the entire structure of the justice system in Poland, impacting the Constitutional Tribunal, Supreme Court, ordinary courts, National Council for the Judiciary, prosecution service and National School of Judiciary. The common pattern is that the executive and legislative branches have been systematically enabled to politically interfere in the composition, powers, administration and functioning of the judicial branch.

In June, November and December 2018, the Council conducted **hearings** as required under Article 7(1) TEU. However, the Council has yet to make the determination that Poland is at risk of a clear and serious breach of Union values. Indeed, it seems happy to use the Article 7(1) hearings as a means of monitoring the progress achieved by the Commission in its protracted dialogue with Poland, even though the Polish government seems to be undeterred from further compromising the independence of the judiciary.

This has left the Commission in a difficult situation and the stagnation of the procedures has left many commentators frustrated with the apparent impotence of Article 7. As Articles 7(1) and 7(2) are independent of each other, it would be possible for the Commission to overcome the Council's reluctance to take a stance under Article 7(1) by using Article 7(2) to submit a proposal to the European Council to determine the existence of a serious and persistent breach of Union values. However, even if the Commission were willing to resort to the 'nuclear option', with the possibility that Article 7(3) sanctions could then be applied, such proceedings would be extremely unlikely to progress due to the requirement of

unanimity from the European Council. The Commission has therefore continued to address the problem pragmatically by persisting in its dialogue with Poland and by continuing to initiate infringement proceedings against specific Polish laws under Article 258 TFEU (for example, ***Commission* v *Poland*** (Case C-619/18)).

7.5.2 Rule of law in Hungary

On 12 September 2018, the **European Parliament** adopted a reasoned proposal for the Council to determine a clear risk of a serious breach of Union values by Hungary. To be adopted, the proposal needed an absolute majority of MEPs (367) and two-thirds of votes cast. The proposal received 448 votes in favour, 197 votes against and 48 abstentions. The Parliament's concerns about Viktor Orbán's far right government include several rule of law issues – such as judicial independence and corruption – as well as freedom of expression and the rights of minorities, asylum seekers and refugees. At the time of writing, the Council has not yet commenced Article 7(1) hearings.

> **Reflection:** Is Article 7 TEU useful?
>
> Rhetorically at least, the activation of Article 7 TEU against Hungary sends a clearer rebuke than the use of the Article against Poland, as it was the Parliament – the direct representative of the EU's citizens – that took action. However, Sergio Carrera and Petra Bárd (2018) have described the action against Hungary as 'too late, too little, too political'. It is **too late** because Prime Minister Viktor Orbán has embarked on a systematic and sustained attack on judicial independence, media diversity, academic freedoms and civil society since entering into office in 2010. Such damage is difficult to undo. Given the scale and duration of Hungary's deviation from Union values, the Parliament's activation of the *preventative* mechanism of Article 7 seems far **too little** of a response. Finally, the absence of any independent or judicial input within the entire Article 7 procedures render them **too political**. The completion of Article 7(1) requires the Council to act by a majority of four-fifths of its members, while Article 7(2) requires unanimity from the European Council. Neither of these thresholds is likely to be reached due to loyalties between countries and risks to diplomatic relationships. Additionally, without independent or judicial oversight, there is no guarantee of rigour or equal treatment of the Member States within Article 7 proceedings.
>
> Carrera and Bárd propose two developments to make the enforcement of Union values more effective and legitimate. First, the TEU should be amended to reduce the voting threshold required of the Council under Article 7(1) and to provide judicial oversight from the Court of Justice over outputs from all Article 7 proceedings. Second, an independent periodic review of compliance with democracy, rule of law and fundamental principles should be established and applied to all Member States. In this way, problems could be flagged as they emerge in any Member State, without political prejudice.
>
> For now, however, Orbán's dismissal of the Parliament's activation of Article 7(1) against Hungary, the unlikelihood that the Council will exercise what little declaratory powers it has and the certainty that Poland and Hungary will not vote against each other should a proposal under Article 7(2) come before the European Council, all suggest that Article 7 TEU is not currently an effective means of enforcing adherence to Union values.

CHAPTER SUMMARY

Infringement actions against Member States

- Actions against a Member State for a breach of Union law may be brought by the Commission (**Art 258 TFEU**) or by another Member State (**Art 259 TFEU**).
- Infringement proceedings under Article 258 TFEU involve an **administrative stage**, a **reasoned opinion** and a **judicial stage**.

Pecuniary penalties

- If the Court of Justice finds that a Member State has failed to implement a **directive**, it can impose **pecuniary penalties** no greater than those suggested by the Commission (**Art 260(3) TFEU**).
- If a Member State fails to comply with a judgment requiring it to rectify any breach of Union law, the Court of Justice can impose **pecuniary penalties** (**Art 360(2) TFEU**).
- A **lump sum** may be imposed on a Member State to **deter** breaches of Union law and a **penalty payment** may be imposed to **persuade** the Member State to rectify the breach (*Commission v France* (Case C-304/02)).
- Penalty payments will be calculated according to the **duration** of the infringement its degree of **seriousness** and the **ability** of the Member State to pay (*Commission v Greece* (Case C-387/97)).

Interim measures

- The Court of Justice can order **interim measures**, such as the suspension of a potentially unlawful measure prior to the date of a full hearing on its validity (**Art 279 TFEU**).

Article 7 TEU

- The Council can determine that a Member State is at **risk of a serious breach** of Union values (**Art 7(1) TEU**).
- If a **serious and persistent breach** of Union values is found to exist within a Member State, the Council can suspend some of their rights (**Art 7(3) TEU**).

Chapter 8
Direct effect, indirect effect and state liability

Learning objectives

At the end of this chapter you should understand:

1 The lacunae in the enforcement of EU law that the principles of direct effect, indirect effect and state liability were developed to address.

2 The principle of **direct effect** and the tests for ascertaining whether a provision of Union law is capable of having vertical direct effect and horizontal direct effect.

3 The principle of **indirect effect** and the limits of its application.

4 The principle of state liability, as established by the Court of Justice in *Francovich*, and how this principle has developed.

5 The enforcement of Union law and the principles of direct effect and indirect effect in the UK courts.

Key terms and concepts

Familiarity with the following terms will be helpful for understanding this chapter:

Direct applicability – the capacity of a provision of Union law to be applied within a Member State without the enactment of further implementing measures

Direct effect – the capacity of a provision of Union law to be enforced by private persons within the national courts of a Member State, including when such provisions are not directly applicable

Estoppel – the legal principle that a party cannot base a claim on grounds that conflict with their previous actions

Horizontal effect – legal effects on a relationship between two or more private actors

Indirect effect – the obligation of the national courts of Member States to interpret relevant national legislation in accordance with EU law

Vertical effect – legal effects on a relationship between a Member State (including state authorities and emanations of the state) and one or more private actors

8.1 Introduction

Objective 1

Once the Court of Justice had established the supremacy of EU law as a principle, the problem remained as to how to ensure the full and effective implementation of EU law in practice. As is discussed in Chapter 5, Article 267 TFEU facilitates the uniform application of EU law in the national courts by permitting, or under certain conditions requiring, questions on the interpretation of Union law to be referred to the Court of Justice for a **preliminary ruling**. Chapter 6 then sets out the Article 253 procedure for the **judicial review** of the legality of Union law, which further facilitates dialogue on the implementation of the Treaties between the national and Union levels. Where such dialogue and cooperation is ineffective, Chapter 7 then considers the Article 258 TFEU mechanism by which the Commission can bring **infringement proceedings** against a Member State that is in breach of its Union law obligations and the Article 260 TFEU provision for the imposition of penalties to compel compliance. However, the process from first complaint to judgment may take several years and the Commission may not choose to even pursue a complaint due to the need to prioritise its resources or for political reasons. Additionally, while the enforcement provisions examined in Chapter 7 enable the Union to hold Member States to account for failures to fully implement and apply EU law, they do not offer any means of redress to *citizens* who have been adversely affected by their Member State's breaches of EU law.

The impact on individual citizens can be illustrated by considering the Working Time Directive 93/104, which the UK failed to implement by the deadline of 23 November 1996 (see the case study on the UK's challenge to the Working Time Directive in section 6.2.1). The Directive provides rights for individual workers, including paid annual leave, minimum daily and weekly rest periods and a 48-hour maximum working week, all of which are subject to certain exceptions and derogations. A relatively short breach by the UK could have had an enormous impact on an indeterminate number of workers. The UK implemented the Directive through the Working Time Regulations 1998, which entered into force on 1 October 1998 (almost two years after the date stipulated in the Directive). The Commission, which has discretion in bringing infringement proceedings before the Court of Justice under what is now Article 258 TFEU, chose not to take action against the UK. Even if it had taken action and the Court had ruled against the UK and imposed a penalty, it would not have had the power to award compensation to those workers who had been affected by the UK's failure to implement the Directive.

As Union acts, such as the Working Time Directive, often afford rights to citizens of the Member States, it follows that such citizens should be able to access remedies when those rights have been infringed. The Court of Justice has therefore developed three principles that enable citizens to enforce the rights that they are afforded by EU law within their national courts. These three principles, which are now considered in depth, are the principles of **direct effect**, **indirect effect** and **state liability**.

National courts should consider whether a provision of Union law has indirect effect *before* considering whether it has direct effect (***Dominguez* v *Centre informatique du Centre Ouest Atlantique, Préfet de la région Centre*** (Case C-282/10)). However, direct effect is examined first in this chapter as it was developed first chronologically and, as a result, an understanding of direct effect is helpful for understanding the subsequent principle of indirect effect.

8.2 Direct effect

Objective 2

8.2.1 The principle of direct effect

The Court of Justice established the principle of direct effect in the following landmark case:

> See Chapter 5 on preliminary rulings

> ### *Van Gend en Loos* v *Nederlandse Administratie der Belastingen* (Case 26/62)
>
> **Facts:**
>
> Van Gend en Loos had been charged a customs duty upon its importation of ureaformaldehyde from Germany into the Netherlands. This breached the rules on the free movement of goods between Member States and in particular the former Article 12 EEC Treaty (now Art 30 TFEU). Van Gend en Loos issued proceedings in a Netherlands court, claiming reimbursement of the customs duty from the Netherlands government. The court referred the question to the Court of Justice of whether or not the claimant could rely on the former Article 12 EEC Treaty in the national court.
>
> **Ruling:**
>
> The Court of Justice first considered the extent to which Community (i.e. Union) law addressed and concerned not only the contracting Member States, but also their citizens. With regards to the general question of whether Treaty provisions could confer directly effective rights on individuals – i.e. rights that they could claim in national courts – the Court held as follows:
>
>> The Community [i.e. Union] constitutes **a new legal order of international law** for the benefit of which the States have limited their sovereign rights, albeit within limited fields, and **the subjects of which comprise not only the Member States but also their nationals**. Independently of the legislation of Member States, **Community [i.e. Union] law therefore not only imposes obligations on individuals but is also intended to confer on them rights which become part of their legal heritage**. These rights arise not only where they are expressly granted by the Treaty, but also by reason of **obligations which the Treaty imposes in a clearly defined way** upon individuals as well as upon Member States and upon institutions of the Community [i.e. Union].

> The Court then ruled that the former Article 12 EEC Treaty was **clear** and **unconditional** and could therefore produce direct effects, as it imposed a negative obligation on Member States to refrain from increasing or introducing new customs duties on imports and exports. It was not qualified by any reservation on the part of the Member States which would make its implementation conditional upon a positive legislative measure being enacted under national law. The Court thus concluded that:
>
>> According to the spirit, the general scheme and the wording of the Treaty, Article 12 [now Art 30 TFEU] must be interpreted as producing direct effects and creating individual rights which national courts must protect.
>
> **Significance:**
>
> This case established the principle of **direct effect** by stating that the subjects of EU law are not only the Member States – i.e. the contracting parties – but also their citizens. Consequently, in instances of a failure to fully implement provisions of EU law that confer rights on individuals, Member States are accountable to both the Union *and* to their citizens. The case also determined that it is for the Court of Justice to determine when Union laws confer rights upon individuals that the national courts of Member States must protect, ensuring that direct effect is applied uniformly across the Union.
>
> The new ability for citizens to hold their governments to account for breaches of EU law greatly expanded the **effective supervision** of Member States in this regard. The profusion of subsequent litigation from individuals and companies seeking to uphold the rights conferred to them under EU law has played an important role in the effectiveness of EU law in the Member States. Additionally, such litigation has resulted in a significant number of references to the Court of Justice for preliminary rulings on the interpretation of EU law, under what is now Article 267 TFEU, which in turn has catalysed the development of EU jurisprudence.

Since ***Van Gend en Loos***, the principle of direct effect has come to be regarded as fundamentally important to the development of the Union. As a judge of the Court of Justice has declared:

> Without direct effect, we should have a very different Community [i.e. Union] today – a more obscure, more remote Community [i.e. Union] barely distinguishable from so many other international organisations whose existence passes unnoticed by ordinary citizens. (Mancini and Keeling, 1994)

An overview of the conditions required for direct effect is provided in Figure 8.1 on page 292.

8.2.2 The scope of direct effect

While ***Van Gend en Loos*** established the principle of direct effect, the scope of its application was unclear. As a general principle of international law, international treaties and agreements are not capable of conferring rights on individuals in the courts of their own state. Since the principle of direct effect diverges from this norm, the realm of international law does not provide any guidance on how to define the scope of this new legal dynamic. Therefore, as with the doctrine of supremacy, it has been through the rulings of the Court of Justice that the scope of direct effect has been defined.

The Court has had to grapple with several questions relating to the principle of direct effect, which are outlined here before being explored in greater detail below. The Court has had to determine:

- which of the sources of EU law can produce direct effect. Initially only **Treaty articles, regulations** and **decisions** were considered to produce direct effect, but then **directives** were also included;

- what exactly it means to say that provisions producing direct effect must be **sufficiently precise** and **unconditional**. The Court has applied these criteria quite flexibly, with the result that articles of the Treaty and provisions of directives have been held to be directly effective by the Court in circumstances where a national court could easily have come to the opposite conclusion;
- whether EU law can produce **horizontal direct effect** and if so under what conditions. In *Van Gend en Loos*, the Court established the possibility of **vertical direct effect**, where persons can hold the state accountable for breaches of EU law. The Court has since determined that some provisions, under particular circumstances, can also produce horizontal direct effect, where private persons can hold each other accountable for failures to adhere to provisions of EU law;
- which entities may be considered 'the state' for the purpose of enforcing vertical direct effect. The Court has expanded the scope of vertical direct effect by setting relatively broad criteria for defining an '**emanation of the state**', against which vertical direct effect can be enforced.

▶ See Figure 8.1 (section 8.2.3, page 292) for a flowchart relating to the principle of direct effect

The direct effect of Treaty articles, regulations and decisions will now be considered, before moving on to the more extensive case law pertaining to the direct effect of directives.

Direct effect of Treaty articles

▶ *Reyners* is also considered in section 11.3.1 in relation to freedom of establishment (page 444)

In *Van Gend en Loos* it was established that certain Treaty provisions were to be enforceable against Member States by their citizens, provided that the obligations imposed were 'clear' and 'unconditional'. These were necessary preconditions because many Treaty provisions are set out in the most general terms and do not appear to impose a commitment to do anything. Sometimes they express no more than a statement or an aspiration. In the following case, the Court of Justice examined the possibility that the former Article 52 EEC Treaty (now Art 49 TFEU) could have direct effect:

Reyners v *Belgian State* (Case 2/74)

Facts:

Reyners was a Dutch national who was qualified as a lawyer in Belgium, but was excluded from legal practice in the country on the grounds that he was not Belgian. Reyners argued that the former Article 52 EEC Treaty (now Art 49 TFEU) on freedom of establishment was a clear and complete provision that was capable of producing direct effect. In response to his complaint, the Belgian government argued that the former Article 52 EEC Treaty merely laid down a principle, the implementation of which was subject to further provisions at both the national and Community (i.e. Union) level.

Ruling:

The Court of Justice ruled that:

26   In laying down that freedom of establishment shall be attained at the end of the transitional period, Article 52 thus imposes an obligation to attain a precise result, the fulfilment of which had to be made easier by, but not made dependent on, the implementation of a programme of progressive measures.

27   The fact that this progression has not been adhered to leaves the obligation itself intact beyond the end of the period provided for its fulfilment.

> **Significance:**
> This case established that, provided a Treaty provision produces a clear obligation, the absence of further implementing measures at the Community level does not diminish that obligation. This was a marked development from *Van Gend en Loos*. Despite the slow pace of harmonisation of national laws, the Court determined that the Treaty could be directly invoked by individuals to challenge obvious instances of discrimination on grounds of nationality with regards to freedom of establishment.

In *Van Gend en Loos* and *Reyners*, the Court found that Treaty provisions could have **vertical direct effect** – i.e. could enable Union citizens to bring claims against Member States. It had reached this position, to some extent at least, on the basis that the state had entered into a commitment when it signed the Treaty. That commitment was owed not only to the other Member States in the spirit of reciprocity, but also to its own citizens – and the citizens of other Member States – as actual or potential beneficiaries of the Treaty. However, the decision did not resolve the status of Treaty provisions between private citizens. Could a private citizen rely on an article of the Treaty, provided that it was clear and unconditional, against another private citizen or undertaking? The Court gave a clear reply to this question of **horizontal direct effect** in the following case:

> ### *Defrenne* v *Sabena* (Case 43/75)
>
> **Facts:**
> A woman working as an 'air hostess' made a claim against her employer as she received less payment than that afforded to male 'cabin stewards' who performed the same tasks. The former Article 119 EEC Treaty (now Art 157 TFEU) provided that 'Each Member State shall during the first stage ensure and subsequently maintain the application of the principle that men and women should receive equal pay for equal work'. Belgium had not enacted legislation to bring this about. The issue was whether the claimant could rely on the former Article 119 EEC Treaty (now Art 157 TFEU) in her national court. The case was referred to the Court of Justice for a preliminary ruling under the former Article 177 EEC Treaty (now Art 267 TFEU).
>
> **Ruling:**
> The Court of Justice dismissed the suggestion that the wording of the article confined the obligation to the Member State itself, and held as follows:
>
>> 35 In its reference to 'Member States', Article 119 [now Art 157 TFEU] is alluding to those States in the exercise of all those of their functions which may usefully contribute to the implementation of the principle of equal pay ... Thus ... this provision is far from merely referring the matter to the powers of the national legislative authorities. Therefore, the reference to 'Member States' in Article 119 [now Art 157 TFEU] cannot be interpreted as excluding the intervention of the courts in the direct application of the Treaty ... **Since Article 119 [now Art 157 TFEU] is mandatory in nature, the prohibition on discrimination between men and women applies not only to the action of public authorities, but also extends to all agreements which are intended to regulate paid labour collectively, as well as to contracts between individuals.**
>
> The Court held that the principle of 'equal pay for equal work' is a sufficiently clear principle to produce direct effects.

> **Significance:**
>
> The effect of the above judgment was that what is now Article 157 TFEU could be used between individuals in relation to a contract of employment. Some articles of the Treaty could thus be vertically effective (i.e. directly enforceable by private individuals/undertakings against the state, as in *Van Gend en Loos*) or **both vertically and horizontally effective** (i.e. directly enforceable by private individuals/undertakings against the state *and* against other private individuals/undertakings), according to their wording and the context.
>
> Additionally, this case determined that a Treaty article does not have to be 100% clear in order to be directly effective. Notions of 'pay' and 'equal work' were not defined in the former Article 177 EEC Treaty and the Article was therefore perceived as containing a general rule rather than a specific obligation (Craig and De Búrca 2015, p. 192). Nevertheless, the Court of Justice applied the 'clear and unconditional' criteria established in *Van Gend en Loos* relatively loosely in order to hold that the principle of 'equal work for equal pay' was *sufficiently* clear to be directly enforceable.

The judgment in *Defrenne* v *Sabena* was consistent with an earlier ruling of the Court of Justice in *Walrave and Koch* v *Association Union Cycliste Internationale* (Case 36/74). Here, the Court stated in relation to the prohibition on discrimination on the ground of nationality (now Art 18 TFEU) that:

> ... prohibition of such discrimination does not only apply to the action of public authorities, but extends likewise to rules of any other nature aimed at regulating in a collective manner gainful employment and the provision of services.

Other Treaty provisions have also been held to be both horizontally and vertically effective, including:

- Articles 34 and 35 TFEU – prohibiting the imposition of restrictions on the export and import of goods: *Dansk Supermarked* (Case 58/80);
- Article 45 TFEU – free movement of workers: *Donà* v *Mantero* (Case 13/76);
- Articles 49 and 50 TFEU – the right of establishment of businesses and professions and the right to provide services: *Thieffry* v *Paris Bar Association* (Case 71/76);
- Articles 101 and 102 TFEU – the prohibition of restrictive agreements and the abuse of a monopoly position: *Brasseries de Haecht* (Case 48/72); *Marty* (Case 37/79).

The accumulation of case law in relation to a number of these provisions has resulted in a subtle change in the terminology of the Court of Justice. In the jurisprudence of the Court, many of these Treaty provisions, especially those relating to freedom of movement, have come to be regarded not merely as directly effective Treaty provisions at the suit of individuals in national courts, but also as **fundamental rights** of Union citizens.

Direct effect of regulations

Article 288 TFEU provides that:

> A regulation shall have general application. It shall be binding in its entirety and directly applicable in all Member States.

> See section 3.4.1 for further discussion on EU Regulations and the concept of direct applicability

The reference to **'directly applicable'** means that domestic legislation is not required in order to incorporate a regulation into national law. Union regulations are thus part of the national law of Member States from the moment of their entry into force without any further need for implementation. Indeed, any attempt at express incorporation is illegal, unless it is explicitly or implicitly required by the regulation itself (*Fratelli Variola SpA* v *Amministrazione Italiana delle Finanze* (Case 34/73)). Whether or not a directly applicable measure is directly effective (i.e. is capable of creating individual rights which a national court must recognise) will depend on whether the regulation is **sufficiently precise and unconditional** (see above). In practice, many are directly effective and are a fruitful source of individual rights (see, for example, Regulation 492/2011 on employment rights of migrant workers and Regulation 883/2004 on social security benefits for those employed and self-employed in other Member States, both of which are discussed in Chapter 10). Regulations which are 'sufficiently precise and unconditional' will be **both vertically and horizontally effective** (see, for example, *Politi SAS* v *Italian Ministry of Finance* (Case 43/71)).

Direct effect of decisions

Article 288 TFEU states that:

> A decision shall be binding in its entirety. A decision which specifies those to whom it is addressed shall be binding only on them.

While, unlike regulations, decisions are not directly applicable, the Court held in the following case that they may have **vertical direct effect**:

Grad v *Finanzamt Traunstein* (Case 9/70)

Facts:

The Finanzgericht Muenchen, a regional financial court in Germany, referred a question to the Court of Justice as to whether a provision within a decision created rights for individuals that the national courts must protect – i.e. whether a decision can have vertical direct effect. The German government argued that the former Article 189 EEC Treaty (now Art 288 TFEU) confines the capacity of secondary legal acts to produce direct effects to regulations.

Ruling:

The Court of Justice ruled that:

> Although it is true that by virtue of Article 189 [now Art 288 TFEU], regulations are directly applicable and therefore by virtue of their nature capable of producing direct effects, it does not follow from this that other categories of legal measures mentioned in that article can never produce similar effects.... **It would be incompatible with the binding effect attributed to decisions by Article 189 [now Art 288 TFEU] to exclude in principle the possibility that persons affected may invoke the obligation imposed by a decision**.... Although the effects of a decision may not be identical with those of a provision contained in a regulation, this difference does not exclude the possibility that the end result, namely the right of the individual to invoke the measure before the courts, may be the same as that of a directly applicable provision of a regulation.

> In order to determine whether this potential for direct effect was realised by a particular decision, the Court stated that:
>
>> in each particular case, it must be ascertained whether the nature, background and wording of the provision in question are capable of producing direct effects in the legal relationships between the addressee of the act and third parties.
>
> Considering the provision of the decision in question, the Court determined that it established an obligation on the Member state that was unconditional and sufficiently clear and precise to be capable of producing direct effects.
>
> **Significance:**
> This case established that decisions can have vertical direct effect, provided that they establish unconditional and sufficiently clear and precise obligations on Member States.

While regulations, by virtue of their being directly applicable, have direct effect as soon as they enter into force, a decision may, like a directive, specify a time by which its prescribed measures should be implemented. In the case of ***Hansa Fleisch Ernst Mundt*** (Case C-156/91), the Court ruled that:

> Where the decision grants the Member States a specified period in which to comply with the obligations resulting from it, the decision may not be relied on by individuals as against the Member States before the expiry of the period in question.

The direct effect of decisions, by virtue the fact that decisions are not directly applicable, is therefore contingent on the passing of any deadlines for implementation.

In the case of ***Carp Snc di L Moleri e V Corsi* v *Ecorad Srl*** (Case C-80/06), the Court confirmed that, like directives (see below), decisions addressed to Member States cannot produce obligations for non-Member State entities and therefore cannot have horizontal direct effect. However, the wording of Article 288 TFEU suggests that decisions that are addressed to individuals or private undertakings, since they are binding on such addressees, can produce horizontal direct effect.

8.2.3 Direct effect of directives

Implementation of directives

Unlike regulations, which must be adhered to by all persons within the jurisdiction of the Union, directives are addressed only to Member States. In the case of Treaty articles, this did not deter the Court from finding that individuals could also be bound by them (see *Defrenne*, above). However, unlike Treaty articles, directives are never directly applicable; they always depend, under Article 288 TFEU, on the Member States giving effect to them. Since the inception of the Union, they have provided a form of legislative subsidiarity, giving the Member States options in the ways in which they implement the directive in order to meet the Union's objectives. The problem, as became clear to both the Commission and the Court of Justice, was that sometimes Member States either simply did not implement directives by the date required, or they implemented them in such a way as to fail, in whole or in part, to achieve the directive's objectives.

Implementation does not mean that a directive must be directly transposed into national law. The Court described the Member States' obligations as follows in ***Commission* v *Germany (Re Nursing Directives)*** (Case 29/84):

> The implementation of a directive does not necessarily require legislative action in each Member State. In particular, the existence of general principles of constitutional and administrative law may render the implementation by specific legislation superfluous, provided, however, that those principles guarantee that the national authorities will, in fact, apply the directive fully, and where the directive is intended to create rights for individuals, the legal position arising from those principles is sufficiently clear and precise, and the persons concerned are made fully aware of their rights, and, where appropriate, are afforded the possibility of relying upon them before national courts. [para 23]

Although legislation may not always be necessary in relation to directives which are not intended to confer rights on individuals, the vast majority either intend that legislation should be enacted or require legislation to be enacted for effective implementation in practice. For example, the issue of circular letters within a government, urging a change of policy or a change in administrative practice, will not constitute implementation. Such practices, which may alter from time to time at the whim of the authority and be quite unknown to the ordinary citizen, completely lack the certainty and transparency that Union law demands (***Commission* v *Belgium*** (Case 239/85)).

A failure to implement a directive, either correctly or at all, often results in a complaint by interested individuals and groups to the relevant Directorate-General in the Commission. This will usually be followed by protracted correspondence between the Commission and the offending state. If this is unsuccessful, formal Article 258 TFEU proceedings may be instituted by the Commission before the Court of Justice, as outlined in Chapter 7. The process from first complaint to judgment may take several years and, given the limited resources and strategic approach of the Commission, infringement procedures can only be a partial solution to the problem. Until all Member States have implemented a directive, however, those states which fail to do so may gain an unfair competitive advantage, as many directives, such as those aimed at enhancing workers' rights, can significantly increase business costs. In addition, individuals may be deprived of rights that the Union has sought to provide them with. It is this situation to which the Court of Justice responded in its application of the doctrine of direct effect to unimplemented (or incorrectly implemented) directives.

Establishing the vertical direct effect of directives

Directives were not originally seen as being capable of creating directly effective rights. In contrast to regulations, they are not described as having **direct applicability**. **Article 288 TFEU** provides that:

> A directive shall be binding, as to the result to be achieved, upon each Member State to which it is addressed, but shall leave to the national authorities the choice of form and methods.

It is clear from the wording of Article 288 TFEU (and previous versions) that directives were not to be directly applicable in the same way as regulations. They required Member States to act to give the directives effect in their territories. However, in ***Grad*** (Case 9/70),

> *Van Duyn* is also considered in section 9.4.2 in relation to restrictions on free movement rights (page 359)

which concerned the effects of a decision, the Court suggested that a directive might have some effect in a state where it had not been implemented by the due date. In the following case, the Court of Justice took its first important step towards recognising the direct effect of a directive:

Van Duyn v *Home Office* (Case 41/74)

Facts:

The claimant in the case, Ms Van Duyn, was a Dutch national and a member of the Church of Scientology. She wished to enter the UK to work at the headquarters of the organisation. She was refused leave to enter as the UK government viewed the Church of Scientology as an undesirable organisation.

As a worker, Van Duyn had a right of entry under the former Article 48 EEC Treaty (now Art 45 TFEU, see Chapter 10). That right is subject to the right of the host state to exclude and expel individuals on public policy and public security grounds. The limits of the powers of the host state to derogate from its Treaty obligation on these grounds, and the extent of the procedural rights of those affected by such a decision, were set out in the former Directive 64/221 (which has since been repealed and replaced by Directive 2004/38). In particular, Article 3(1) of Directive 64/221 provided that a decision should be based 'exclusively on the personal conduct of the individual concerned'. Van Duyn argued that membership of an organisation could not be 'personal conduct' under Article 3(1). The UK government maintained that its power to refuse entry could not be limited in this way, because the UK had not yet implemented Directive 64/221 (it remained unimplemented for 20 years). The case was referred to the Court of Justice under the former Article 177 EEC Treaty (now Art 267 TFEU).

Ruling:

The Court refused to accept the position taken by the UK government and held as follows:

> The UK observes that, since Article 189 [now Art 288 TFEU] of the Treaty distinguishes between the effects ascribed to regulations, directives and decisions, it must therefore be presumed that the Council, in issuing a directive rather than making a regulation, must have intended that the directive should have had an effect other than that of a regulation and accordingly that the former should not be directly applicable ... However ... it does not follow from this that other categories of acts mentioned in that article can never have similar effects. It would be incompatible with the binding effect attributed to a directive by Article 189 [now Art 288 TFEU] to exclude, in principle, the possibility that the obligation which it imposes may be invoked by those concerned. In particular, **where the Community [i.e. Union] authorities have, by directive, imposed on Member States the obligation to pursue a particular course of conduct, the useful effect of such an act would be weakened if individuals were prevented from relying on it before their national courts** and if the latter were prevented from taking it into consideration as an element of Community [i.e. Union] law.

Having established the possibility for a directive to produce direct effects, the Court then determined that 'it is necessary to examine in every case, whether the nature, general scheme and wording of the provision in question are capable of having direct effects'. In considering Article 3(1) of the former Directive 64/221, which provides that 'measures taken on the grounds of *public policy* or of *public security* shall be based exclusively on the personal conduct of the individual concerned', the Court concluded that this was sufficiently precise to be capable of having direct effect, despite the fact that the scope of 'public policy' and 'public security' was not self-evident. However, Van Duyn was unsuccessful in her case: the Court held that, although membership of a particular organisation was not sufficient to amount to 'personal conduct', active participation and identification with an organisation was and could therefore warrant exclusion.

> **Significance:**
> The Court determined that the failure of a Member State to implement a directive could not prevent that directive from having effects in that Member State. If the Court had ruled otherwise, it would have undermined the extent to which directives are legally binding and enforceable.
>
> This case also followed on from ***Defrenne*** by more explicitly establishing a broad interpretation of the 'sufficiently precise' criterion as encompassing terms that the Court of Justice is required to clarify.

The guiding principle adopted by the Court of Justice in the above case is that of ensuring the *effet utile* (i.e. the useful effect) of a measure in the territories and courts of Member States. In addition to this guiding principle is another (implied) principle referred to as the equitable doctrine of **estoppel**. In general, estoppel is the principle that an actor cannot make a claim that contradicts their past claims or actions. With regards to ***Van Duyn***, the past action in question was the Member State's accession to the Union and its concurrent commitment to implement EU law. Application of the principle of estoppel therefore means that a Member State should not be able to benefit from its failure to act in accordance with its commitments (see Advocate General Van Gerven in *Barber* (Case C-262/88)). The Court of Justice affirmed the application of this principle and its relation to direct effect in ***Becker*** (Case 8/81):

> a Member State which has not adopted the implementing measures required by the directive within the prescribed period may not plead, as against individuals, its own failure to perform the obligations which the directive entails.
>
> Thus, wherever the provisions of a directive appear, as far as their subject matter is concerned, to be unconditional and sufficiently precise, those provisions may, in the absence of implementing measures adopted within the prescribed period, be relied upon as against any national provision which is incompatible with the directive or in so far as the provisions define rights which individuals are able to assert against the State.

➤ See section 8.4.1 on *Francovich* in relation to state liability (page 299)

A directive can therefore be *vertically* effective.

In the following case, the Court clarified the criteria that directly effective provisions must be sufficiently precise and unconditional in relation to a directive:

Francovich v *Republic of Italy* (Cases C-6/90 & 9/90)

Facts:
An Italian company went into liquidation, leaving Francovich and other employees with unpaid salary arrears. Directive 80/987 required Member States to set up a compensation scheme for employees in these circumstances, but Italy had not established one. Francovich therefore sought compensation from the Italian government. The case was referred to the Court of Justice. The Court was asked: (i) whether the Directive had direct effect; (ii) whether the Member State was liable for the damage arising from its failure to implement the Directive; and (iii) to what extent it was liable for damages for violation of its obligations under Union law.

Ruling:
Regarding the first question on direct effect (the others will be considered later in this chapter), the Court considered three indicators of whether the Directive was sufficiently precise and

unconditional: 'the identity of the persons entitled to the guarantee provided, the content of that guarantee and the identity of the person liable to provide the guarantee'. On the first point, the persons entitled to the rights under Directive 80/987 were employees who were claiming against an employer in a state of insolvency. The Court of Justice held that the scope of these terms was sufficiently defined within the Directive to allow a national judge to ascertain the identity of the persons entitled to the right.

The content of the right was more problematic. In implementing the Directive, the Member State was given a number of choices, which included, *inter alia*:

- a choice of date from which the payment of wages would accrue. As a result, Member States could limit the payment of wages to periods of three months or eight weeks; and
- a discretion to set a liability ceiling so that payment of wages would not exceed a certain sum.

Given these legislative choices, it would appear that the Directive was not unconditional or sufficiently precise. However, the Court of Justice held that it was possible to calculate the *minimum* guarantee provided for by the Directive. With regard to the discretion to set a liability ceiling, the Court of Justice held that this discretion was only available to a Member State that had actually implemented the Directive and taken advantage of this provision in its implementing legislation. The failure to establish a liability ceiling did not therefore compromise the ability to calculate a minimum guarantee.

Under the Directive, Member States enjoyed a wide discretion with regard to the functioning and financing of the 'guarantee institution' (i.e. the body liable to provide the benefit). The Member State had to identify the institution which would be liable to provide the benefit. The Court of Justice held this provision was not sufficiently precise or unconditional and therefore that the Directive was not capable of having direct effect.

Significance:

This case established a three-point test for determining whether a directive is sufficiently precise and unconditional to have direct effect: it must be possible from the directive to identify the **beneficiaries** of the rights it confers, the **contents** of those rights and the **entity responsible** for administering those rights.

A similar approach was adopted by the Court of Justice in ***Kampelmann v Landschaftsverband Westfalen-Lippe*** (Cases C-253–258/96). This case concerned Article 2(2)(c) of Directive 91/583, which imposed an obligation on employers to inform their employees of the conditions applicable to their contract or employment relationship. The Court held that this provision was sufficiently clear and precise to be capable of having direct effect.

In ***Ratti*** (Case 148/78), the Court of Justice established that a directive cannot have direct effect until the **deadline for its implementation** has passed. However, in ***Inter-Environnement Wallonie ASBL*** (Case C-129/96), the Court established that, during the period specified for a directive's transposition into national law, Member States 'must refrain from taking any measures liable seriously to compromise the result prescribed' by that directive. A directive for which the deadline for implementation had not yet passed could therefore be relied on in an action against the government of a Member State, where the government had introduced new measures that were contrary to that directive. Member States therefore have a duty to progress towards the implementation of a directive, and not to retreat from its objectives. This was confirmed, albeit controversially, in the case of ***Mangold*** v ***Helm*** (Case C-144/04).

Denying the horizontal direct effect of directives

As discussed above, the Court of Justice held that if a directive was 'sufficiently precise and unconditional' then it could be enforced against the state (i.e. **vertical direct effect**). In the following 1986 case, the Court explicitly stated that directives could **not** be enforced horizontally against private individuals and legal persons.

> ### *Marshall* v *Southampton Area Health Authority* (Case 152/84)
>
> **Facts:**
>
> Ms Marshall was employed by the Health Authority. She wished to retire at 65, the same age as her male colleagues. The rules of the authority required her to retire at the age of 60. She was dismissed on the grounds of her age at 62 and subsequently brought proceedings against the Authority on grounds of sex discrimination. Discrimination on grounds of sex in relation to conditions of employment was prohibited by Directive 76/207. The UK's Sex Discrimination Act 1975, which had been enacted to implement the Directive while it was still in draft form, contained an exception that permitted differential male and female retirement ages. There was no such exception in the Directive. The question to be determined was whether Ms Marshall could enforce the Directive against the Health Authority.
>
> **Ruling:**
>
> The Court of Justice declared that a directive could only be directly enforced against the state. After considering the effect of the third paragraph of the former Article 189 EEC Treaty (now Art 288 TFEU), the Court stated that:
>
>> the binding nature of a directive … exists only in relation to 'each Member State to which it is addressed'. It follows that **a directive may not of itself impose obligations on an individual** and that a provision of a directive may not be relied upon as such against such a person.
>
> The Court then considered the claimant's argument that the directive could be enforced against the Health Authority because it was an 'emanation of the State'. The Court ruled that:
>
>> Where a person involved in legal proceedings is able to rely on a directive as against the State, he may do so regardless of the capacity in which the latter is acting, whether employer or public authority. In either case it is necessary to prevent the State from taking advantage of its own failure to comply with Community [i.e. Union] law.
>
> The Court added that it was for the national courts to determine the status of a body for the purpose of determining whether or not a directive could be directly enforced against it.
>
> **Significance:**
>
> As what is now Article 288 TFEU does not provide for directives to bind individuals, this case established that directives, by themselves, cannot create obligations for individuals and therefore **cannot have horizontal direct effect**. However, this case affirmed the principle that a State should not be able to defend an action on the basis of its own wrongdoing, i.e. its failure to correctly implement a directive. Therefore, directives that are sufficiently precise and unconditional can be enforced against the institutions of a Member State, even if they are only operating in the capacity of an employer.

The following case revisited and confirmed the Court of Justice's position on whether or not a Union directive could have horizontal direct effect:

Paola Faccini Dori v Recreb SRL (Case C-91/92)

Facts:
Ms Dori had concluded a contract to buy a language course at Milan Railway Station. Under Italian law, she was not entitled to a 'cooling off' period during which she could withdraw from the contract, whereas under the former Directive 85/577 she would have had seven days to do so. The issue before the Court of Justice was whether Ms Faccini Dori could rely upon the unimplemented Directive in an Italian court against a private company (which was not an emanation of the state).

Opinion:
On 9 February 1994, the Opinion of Advocate General Lenz was delivered at a sitting of the full Court. The Advocate General recognised that the Court of Justice had consistently held that directives could not have direct effect in relations between individuals and that for reasons of legal certainty this should be maintained with regard to situations in the past. However, as regards the future, the Advocate General was of the opinion that for future cases the Union should recognise that directives may be directly effective both vertically and horizontally.

Ruling:
The Court of Justice rejected the Advocate General's Opinion. The Court stated that ever since the *Marshall* case it had been held that a directive could not of itself impose obligations on an individual. Accordingly, a directive could not be relied upon against such an individual.

Significance:
As discussed in Chapter 5, the Court of Justice is not bound by the doctrine of precedent and accordingly could have departed from its own previous decisions. However, for the sake of legal certainty the Court generally follows and builds upon its own previous case law. This case therefore confirmed the judgment in *Marshall* and thus seems to settle conclusively that directives cannot have horizontal direct effect.

Defining an emanation of the state

While the Court determined in *Marshall* that it is for the national courts of a Member State to determine whether a body constitutes an emanation of the state or not, the Court has provided guidance on this matter in subsequent judgments. In particular, the Court of Justice has given 'Member State' a broad interpretation. Initially, it referred to the state as exercising various functions and it was not deemed necessary that a body in question be engaged in activities normally carried out by (or associated with) the state. It decided in *Costanzo v Comune di Milano* (Case 103/88) that 'the state' included 'all organs of the administration, including decentralised authorities such as municipalities'. In the following case, the Court of Justice addressed the issue of just how 'decentralised' a body could be, and still be bound by an unimplemented or incorrectly implemented directive:

Foster v British Gas (Case C-188/89)

Facts:
Ms Foster was employed by the British Gas Corporation (BGC), which, at the material time, had not yet been privatised. In line with company policy, Ms Foster was made to retire at the age of

60 while male employees were required to retire at the age of 65. As noted above, the Sex Discrimination Act 1975, which was in force in the UK at the material time, prohibited discrimination against women, except for 'provisions in relation to death or retirement'. Foster therefore sought to rely upon the Equal Treatment Directive (Directive 76/207), which did not allow for discriminatory retirement ages.

Foster's application to an employment tribunal was dismissed on the ground that the BGC was not a state authority within the meaning of *Marshall* and therefore the Directive could not be relied upon against it. This decision was subsequently confirmed by both the Employment Appeal Tribunal and the Court of Appeal. The UK House of Lords (the judicial functions of which are now exercised by the Supreme Court) requested a preliminary ruling from the Court of Justice on the question of whether the BGC was, at the material time, a body of such a type that individuals could directly enforce a directive against it in the national courts and tribunals.

Ruling:

The Court of Justice first noted that it had previously held in a series of cases that:

> 18 ... unconditional and sufficiently precise provisions of a directive could be relied on against organisations or bodies which were subject to the authority or control of the State **or** had special powers beyond those which result from the normal rules applicable to relations between individuals.

The Court then developed a narrower test to ascertain if a body constituted an emanation of the state for the purpose of having a directive enforced against it:

> 20 ... a body, whatever its legal form, which has been made responsible, pursuant to a measure adopted by the State, for **providing a public service under the control of the State** and has for that purpose **special powers** beyond those which result from the normal rules applicable in relations between individuals is included in any event among the bodies against which the provisions of a directive is capable of having direct effect may be relied upon.

As in *Marshall*, the Court left it up to the national courts of the Member State to determine whether the body in question, the BGC, met this description.

Significance:

The three criteria for determining whether a body is an 'emanation of the state' established in paragraph 20 of this case have come to be known as the *Foster* test. This test stipulates that a body constitutes an emanation of the state when it 1) provides **public services,** 2) does so under **state control** and 3) has **special powers**. Through the concept of an emanation of the state, the Court broadened the scope of vertical direct effect and mitigated the potentially restrictive consequences of its ruling in *Marshall* that directives cannot be horizontally effective.

The Court of Justice returned the case to the House of Lords (the judicial functions of which are now exercised by the Supreme Court) for the test to be applied to the facts of the case. In *Foster* v *British Gas (No. 2)* ([1991] 2 AC 306), the House of Lords found that the BGC was made responsible for providing a public service by an act of the State (the Gas Act 1972), that it was not independent from State control and that it was afforded a monopoly in the supply of gas. Therefore, the House of Lords held that the BCG satisfied the three criteria established by the Court of Justice and amounted to an 'emanation of the state' against which the directive could be enforced. Soon after the Court of Justice's decision in *Foster*, three cases which concerned the concept of 'emanation of the state' and the application of the *Foster* test came before the UK courts (see section 8.5.1).

In ***Kampelmann* v *Landschaftsverband Westfalen-Lippe*** (Joined Cases C-253–258/96), the Court of Justice considered the ***Foster*** test further. Here, the Court considered only the *two* criteria that had been applied prior to ***Foster*** (being subject to the control of the state **or** having special powers (see para 18 of ***Foster****,* above)), rather than the *three* criteria set out in para 20 of ***Foster*** (public services, state control **and** special powers). In stating that any body under state control **or** with special powers could have the provisions of a directive enforced against it, ***Kampelmann*** presented a much wider bipartite test than the tripartite test set out in ***Foster***.

The Court of Justice subsequently considered the concept of an 'emanation of the state' in the following case:

Rieser Internationale Transporte GmbH v *Autobahnen- und Schnellstraßen-Finanzierungs-AG (Asfinag)* (Case C-157/02)

Facts:

Asfinag was an Austrian company that had been authorised by the Austrian government to construct and maintain public roads and to levy toll charges for their use. Reiser was a haulier company which claimed that it had been over-charged by Asfinag in breach of Directive 93/89 on certain vehicles used for the carriage of goods by road and tolls and charges for the use of certain infrastructures. Reiser argued that the relevant provisions of the Directive were sufficiently precise and unconditional to have direct effect and that they could be enforced against Asfinag since, although governed by private law, it was a body subject to State control.

Ruling:

The Court first cited ***Marshall*** and ***Foster*** to affirm that 'where a person is able to rely on a directive as against the State he may do so regardless of the capacity in which the latter is acting'. The Court then affirmed the ***Foster*** test (see above) for establishing whether a body is an emanation of the State, and proceeded to assess the case on that basis.

The Court found that the Austrian State was the sole shareholder in Asfinag, that Asfinag was required to submit financial and other reports to the State, that the State could monitor and impose objectives on Asfinag's activities and that the amount of tolls to be levied for the use of roads was set by federal law. The Court thus found that:

> 27 Those facts clearly show that Asfinag is a body to which, pursuant to an act adopted by the public authorities, the performance of a public-interest service (namely: the constructing, planning, operating, maintaining and financing of motorways and expressways in addition to the levying of tolls and user charges), has been entrusted, under the supervision of those public authorities, and which for that purpose possesses special powers beyond those resulting from the normal rules applicable in relations between individuals.

The Court therefore concluded that:

> 29 ... when contracts are concluded with road users, the provisions of a directive capable of having direct effect may be relied upon against a legal person governed by private law where the State has entrusted to that legal person the task of levying tolls for the use of public road networks and where it has direct or indirect control of that legal person.

Significance:

This case established that a private company can be found to be an emanation of the state for the purpose of directly enforcing a directive. The Court did not refer to the ***Kampelmann*** judgment in this case, but instead referred to all three criteria specified in paragraph 20 of ***Foster*** in the cumulative manner in which they were first iterated. This suggests that the Court might favour the stricter, tripartite test in cases where the defendant is a private company.

▶ Cases where the UK courts have considered the scope of a state emanation are examined in section 8.5.1

The different criteria applied in *Kampelmann* and *Rieser*, as initially set out in paragraphs 18 and 20 of *Foster* respectively, have caused considerable confusion as to when one test or the other should be applied. This matter was clarified in the following case:

Farrell v *Whitty* (Case C-413/15)

Facts:

Ms Farrell sought the enforcement of a directive that had not been fully implemented against the Motor Insurers Bureau of Ireland (MIBI). The Supreme Court of Ireland therefore needed to determine whether the MIBI constituted an emanation of the state, against which such a directive could be enforced. To this end the Supreme Court requested a preliminary ruling from the Court of Justice on the question, *inter alia*, of whether the three criteria set out in paragraph 20 of the *Foster* judgment are to be applied conjunctively (i.e. **all** three criteria must be met) or disjunctively (i.e. **any** of the criteria must be met).

Opinion:

Considering the distinction between paras 18 and 20 of the *Foster* judgment, Advocate General Sharpston stated that:

> ... the Court in *Foster* ... created an **abstract formulation** out of existing case-law (paragraph 18), which it then applied with glosses to identify a body whose characteristics meant that it was **in any event** to be included in the category of emanations of the State (paragraph 20).... Neither the derivation of the actual test from pre-existing case-law in paragraph 18 nor the application of that test in paragraph 20 purport to be exhaustive; and both logic and good sense militate against retrospectively categorising them as such.
>
> It follows that ... the test in *Foster* as to what constitutes an emanation of the State for the purposes of vertical direct effect of directives is to be found in paragraph 18, not paragraph 20, of the judgment in that case. The test there formulated is to be read neither conjunctively nor disjunctively. Rather, it contains a **non-exhaustive listing of the elements that may be relevant to such an assessment**. [paras 52 and 53]

Ruling:

The Court of Justice agreed with Advocate General Sharpston and referred extensively to her Opinion. The Court thus concluded that:

> 28 ... the conditions that the organisation concerned must, respectively, be subject to the authority or control of the State, and must possess special powers beyond those which result from the normal rules applicable to relations between individuals **cannot be conjunctive**.
>
> 29 In the light of the foregoing, the answer to the first question is that Article 288 TFEU must be interpreted as meaning that it does **not**, in itself, preclude the possibility that **provisions of a directive that are capable of having direct effect may be relied on against a body that does not display all the characteristics** listed in paragraph 20 of the judgment of 12 July 1990, Foster and Others (C-188/89, EU:C:1990:313), read together with those mentioned in paragraph 18 of that judgment.

Significance:

This case establishes clearly that the *Foster* criteria do not comprise a restrictive test, but may be applied more flexibly, as indeed they have been in cases such as *Kampelmann*. The *Foster* criteria can therefore be viewed only as guidelines to what may constitute an emanation of the state, leaving the Court of Justice and national courts with a potentially wide scope for applying vertical direct effect.

Incidental direct effect

The Court of Justice has implicitly allowed horizontal direct enforcement in situations where such enforcement has the effect of *removing* an obligation on a private party rather than imposing additional obligations. This possibility, which is known as **incidental horizontal direct effect**, was established, in *CIA Security International* v *Signalson and Securitel* (Case C-194/94). This case concerned technical regulations that had been adopted by Belgium in contravention of a requirement within Directive 83/189 to notify the Commission. CIA Security International were accused by a competitor of having breached the technical regulations, but sought to rely on the Directive in order to defend itself, arguing that the regulations should be disapplied due to their non-compliance with Union law. The matter was referred for a preliminary ruling and the Court of Justice considered that:

> ... the aim of the directive is to protect freedom of movement for goods by means of preventive control and that the obligation to notify is essential for achieving such Community control. The effectiveness of Community control will be that much greater if the directive is interpreted as meaning that breach of the obligation to notify constitutes a substantial procedural defect such as to render the technical regulations in question inapplicable to individuals. [para 48]

The Court subsequently concluded that a 'breach of the obligation to notify renders the technical regulations concerned inapplicable, so that they are unenforceable against individuals' (para 54). It was therefore established that a directive may be invoked to relieve a private party of obligations imposed in contravention of that directive. This is sometimes referred to as the ability of a private party to use an unimplemented or incorrectly implemented directive horizontally as a shield (i.e. defensively in a case brought against them), but not as a sword (i.e. not to impose obligations on a defendant).

The principle of incidental horizontal direct effect was then confirmed in *Unilever Italia SpA* v *Central Food SpA* (Case C-443/98), in which the Court of Justice referred often to its judgment in *CIA Security International*. In this case, Central Food refused to pay for a consignment of olive oil that did not to comply with Italian labelling regulations, but Unilever sought to rely on the fact that the regulations had been introduced in contravention of Directive 83/189 in order to enforce the contractual obligation on Central Food to pay for the goods received. The Court of Justice stated that:

> Whilst it is true, as observed by the Italian and Danish Governments, that a directive cannot of itself impose obligations on an individual and cannot therefore be relied on as such against an individual ... that case-law does not apply where non-compliance with Article 8 or Article 9 of Directive 83/189, which constitutes a substantial procedural defect, renders a technical regulation adopted in breach of either of those articles inapplicable.
>
> In such circumstances, and unlike the case of non-transposition of directives with which the case-law cited by those two Governments is concerned, Directive 83/189 does not in any way define the substantive scope of the legal rule on the basis of which the national court must decide the case before it. It creates neither rights nor obligations for individuals. [paras 50 and 51]

The Court therefore stated that, as in *CIA Security International*, Directive 83/189 could be invoked to disapply the national regulations that were enacted in contravention of it. Unlike in *CIA Security International*, however, this had the effect of requiring a private party to uphold their contractual obligations and thus to make a payment, rather than relieving a party of obligations. In the former paragraph cited above, the Court phrased this as an exception to the principle that directives may not have horizontal direct effect that applies specifically to the provisions of the Directive in question. However, in more general terms,

Figure 8.1 Direct effect

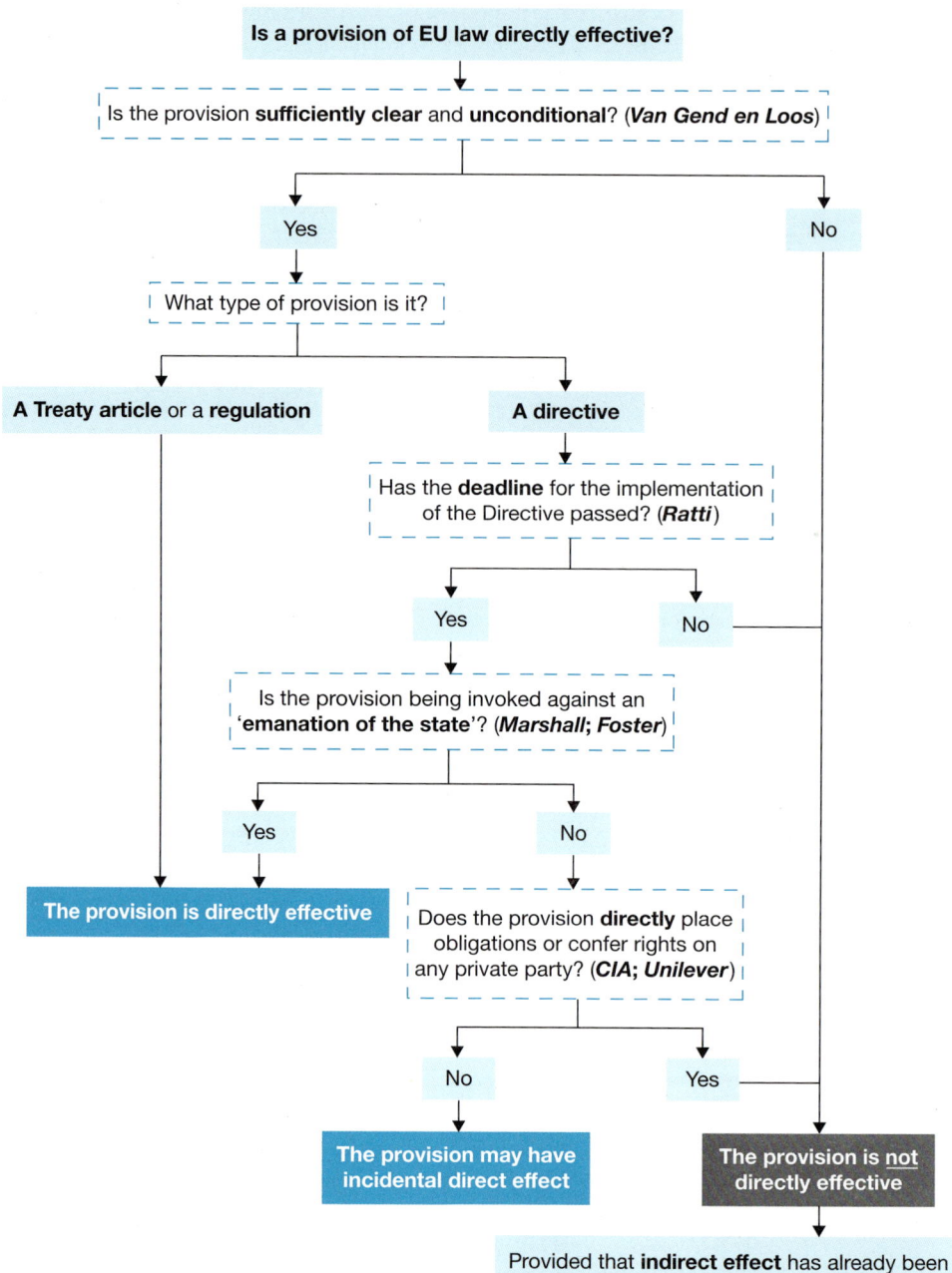

Is a provision of EU law directly effective?

Is the provision **sufficiently clear** and **unconditional**? (*Van Gend en Loos*)

- **Yes** → What type of provision is it?
  - **A Treaty article or a regulation** → **The provision is directly effective**
  - **A directive** → Has the **deadline** for the implementation of the Directive passed? (*Ratti*)
    - **Yes** → Is the provision being invoked against an **'emanation of the state'**? (*Marshall*; *Foster*)
      - **Yes** → **The provision is directly effective**
      - **No** → Does the provision **directly** place obligations or confer rights on any private party? (*CIA*; *Unilever*)
        - **No** → **The provision may have incidental direct effect**
        - **Yes** → **The provision is not directly effective**
    - **No** → **The provision is not directly effective**
- **No** → **The provision is not directly effective**

Provided that **indirect effect** has already been found not to apply, consider the principle of **state liability** (see Figure 8.2 on page 298) the Court justified this exception by distinguishing between the provisions of a directive that stipulate *procedural requirements* and those that set out *rights or obligations*. Therefore, the ***Unilever*** case suggests that directives can be given direct effect in cases between private parties where the *direct* effect concerns the validity of national provisions and any effects on private parties is only *incidental* to that (see also ***Wells* v *Secretary of State for Transport, Local Government and the Regions*** (Case C-201/02)).

> **Reflection:** Horizontal direct effect of directives
>
> The horizontal direct effect of directives remains a contentious prospect. On the one hand, it would facilitate the even and equal application of Union law across the Member States, with directives being more universally and predictably enforceable, regardless of correct implementation at the national level and regardless of the status of the defendant, i.e. whether or not they qualify as an emanation of the state (see Advocate General Jacobs in **Vaneetveld v Le Foyer** (Case C-316/93)). In particular, horizontal direct effect would eliminate the inequality that exists whereby public sector employees can seek the direct enforcement of rights construed by an unimplemented or incorrectly implemented directive, but private sector employees cannot (see Advocate General van Gerven in **Marshall v Southampton and South-West Hampshire Area Health Authority** (Case 271/91)).
>
> On the other hand, horizontal direct effect would seem counter to the distinction that is made in Article 288 TFEU between regulations and directives, whereby directives are not designed to be directly binding on individuals. As it is the state that is at fault for failing to implement a directive, in part or in whole, individuals should not be held responsible for the consequences of such failures, especially as they may not even be aware that such a failure has occurred. Furthermore, to develop a doctrine of horizontal direct effect of directives now would require an explicit contradiction of the Court of Justice's case law in this area (see **Marshall v Southampton Area Health Authority** (Case 152/84)).
>
> Where a directive is unimplemented or incorrectly implemented, the Court of Justice has yet to develop an adequate approach that protects the rights of individuals contained in the directive while also protecting individuals from being held liable for the failures of the state. Incidental direct effect and the principles of indirect effect and state liability, which are examined below, have provided some additional – and still highly contentious – recourse for individuals, but gaps remain beyond the scope of these principles.

8.3 Indirect effect

Objective 3

As discussed above, the doctrine of direct effect is subject to certain conditions that limit its scope of application. The Court of Justice subsequently developed the doctrine of indirect effect to expand the effectiveness of directives in Member States where they had not been fully and correctly implemented. An overview of the requirements for indirect effect is provided in Figure 8.2 on page 298.

8.3.1 The principle of indirect effect

The Court of Justice has derived the principle of indirect effect from its interpretation of what is now **Article 4(3) TEU**, which states that:

> The Member States shall take any appropriate measure, general or particular, to ensure fulfilment of the obligations arising out of the Treaties or resulting from the acts of the institutions of the Union.

The Court of Justice has interpreted Article 4(3) TEU as expressing a principle whereby Member States should interpret their national law in a manner that is consistent with EU law. With regard to directives, this means that national courts should uphold them, as far as is possible, regardless of whether they have been fully implemented and regardless of whether they are directly effective.

This novel approach was adopted by the Court in the following case, which concerned the enforcement of a directive against a state institution:

Von Colson and Kamann v Land Nordrhein-Westfalen (Case 14/83)

Facts:

Von Colson and Kamann were two female applicants for jobs within a male prison. After the positions were given to two male applicants who were less qualified, they brought a discrimination complaint pursuant to Directive 76/207 on the equal treatment for men and women as regards access to employment (now replaced by Directive 2006/54). Under the German legislation implementing the Directive, the only form of compensation that could be issued for the discrimination in access to employment was the reimbursement of travel expenses incurred in the pursuit of the job application. Questions referred to the Court of Justice sought to establish whether Directive 76/206 prescribed specific sanctions for the type of discrimination at issue and, if so, whether it had direct effects that could be relied upon by the complainants.

Ruling:

The Court determined that the relevant provision in Directive 76/207 regarding remedies for discrimination in access to employment was not sufficiently precise and unconditional to produce direct effects. However, the Court argued as follows:

> In applying the national law and in particular the provisions of a national law specifically introduced in order to implement Directive No 76/207, **national courts are required to interpret their national law in the light of the wording and the purpose of the Directive** in order to achieve the result referred to in the third paragraph of Article 189 [now Art 288 TFEU].

The 'result referred to in the third paragraph of Article 189' refers to the provision in what is now Article 288 TFEU that directives should be binding.

The Court continued that, although the Directive did not specify a form of sanction, any sanction that was imposed by the national court had to be such as to guarantee real and effective judicial protection of the right to equal treatment set forth in the Directive and to have a real deterrent effect on the employer. Consequently, if an award was made, that award had to be adequate in relation to the damage sustained and must therefore be more than purely nominal. The award of expenses provided for under the German legislation was not adequate, so the Court of Justice encouraged the German court to supplement the domestic legislation by reading it in conformity with the Directive's requirement to provide real and effective remedy.

Significance:

This case provided a means of giving effect to a directive that has not been wholly and correctly implemented and that does not meet the **Van Gend en Loos** criteria of being unconditional and sufficiently precise to have direct effect. However, because there is no direct effect, such a directive cannot be enforced per se. Rather, this case developed a principle of interpretation that requires national courts to interpret national legislation in line with the '**wording and purpose**' of relevant EU law.

While the case above concerned a claim brought against a state body and therefore established the principle of **vertical indirect effect**, the following case considered a similar claim brought against a private employer:

Harz v Deutsche Tradax (Case 79/83)

Facts:

As established in **von Colson**, Germany had incorrectly implemented Directive 76/207 on equal employment rights. Thus, Ms Harz, who had faced sex discrimination in the recruitment procedure of a private company, was only afforded nominal compensation under German law by way of compensation for travel expenses. The case was referred to the Court of Justice by the (West) German Labour Court.

Ruling:

As with **von Colson**, the Court established that the obligation in former Article 5 EEC Treaty (now Art 4(3) TEU), that Member States should take all appropriate measures to give effect to Union law, requires national courts 'to interpret their national law in the light of the wording and the purpose of the directive'. The national court was therefore under an obligation to 'interpret' the national law on sex discrimination in such a way that the compensation to which injured parties were entitled was not limited to the token reimbursement of the travel expenses. On this basis, the German court which had referred the case could award proper compensation to Harz.

Significance:

This case established that where a directive has not been correctly implemented by a Member State, the national courts should interpret the national law in line with the directive in as far as is possible, even when this affects a claim against a non-state entity. The case therefore established that directives could have **horizontal indirect effect**.

After these two cases concerning the incorrect implementation of Directive 76/207 in German law, which established the doctrine of indirect effect, it remained unclear whether this new interpretative obligation could also apply in cases where a directive had not been implemented at all. In the following case, the Court of Justice held that it could:

Marleasing SA v La Comercial SA (Case C-106/89)

Facts:

Spanish law laid down a number of grounds on which a company could be struck off the register, including 'lack of cause', meaning that the company had no real function. Spain had failed to implement Directive 68/71 on company law, which omitted this particular ground.

A Spanish court was subsequently confronted with a dispute between two private companies where La Comercial sought to rely on the unimplemented Directive when Marleasing attempted to have it struck off for lack of cause.

Ruling:

The Court of Justice confirmed that the Directive could not have horizontal **direct** effect (in accordance with **Marshall**), but ruled that the Spanish law, even though it predates the

> Directive, must be interpreted as far as possible in accordance with it. Thus, the Court of Justice held that:
>
>> ... in applying national law, whether the provisions concerned **pre-date or post-date** the directive, the national court asked to interpret national law is bound to do so in every way possible in the light of the text and the aims of the directive to achieve the results envisaged by it and thus comply with Article 189(3) of the Treaty [now Art 288 TFEU].
>
> Consequently, the national court found that the conflict between the Directive and the interpretation of the Spanish law had to be resolved in favour of the Directive.
>
> **Significance:**
>
> In this case, the Court applied indirect effect horizontally – i.e. between private enterprises – and to a directive that had not been implemented. This further expanded the *effet utile* (i.e. the useful effect) of directives within Member States.
>
> Additionally, this case established that the principle of indirect effect could be applied to a national law even if it preceded the directive by many years and had been enacted with quite different considerations in mind.

In ***Grimaldi* v *Fonds des Maladies Professionelles*** (Case C-322/88), the Court of Justice established that the principle of indirect effect was not confined to unimplemented or incorrectly implemented directives. In this case, the Court ruled that the interpretative obligation of indirect effect should be applied to a recommendation. Even though recommendations are not legally binding instruments of Union law, the Court stated that:

> The national courts are bound to take recommendations into consideration in order to decide disputes submitted to them, in particular where they cast light on the interpretation of national measures adopted in order to implement them or where they are designed to supplement binding Community [i.e. Union] provisions.

This suggests that the principle of indirect effect should also be applied to Treaty articles that are not sufficiently precise and unconditional to have direct effect and to opinions.

It should be noted that in ***Dominguez* v *Centre Informatique du Centre Ouest Atlantique, Préfet de la Région Centre*** (Case C-282/10), the Court of Justice stated that indirect effect (i.e. the interpretative obligation) should be applied by the national court before direct effect. If the national court can interpret national law to comply with Union law, the principle of direct effect becomes irrelevant. Indeed, in ***Pfeiffer and Others*** (Joined Cases C-397-403/01) the Court of Justice stated as follows:

> Although the principle that national law must be interpreted in conformity with Community law concerns chiefly domestic provisions enacted in order to implement the directive in question, it does not entail an interpretation merely of those provisions but **requires the national court to consider national law as a whole** in order to assess to what extent it may be applied so as not to produce a result contrary to that sought by the directive.

Therefore, it is only necessary to consider the principle of direct effect if the national court determines that it is 'not possible' to interpret the national law, considered as a whole, in accordance with the relevant Union provisions.

8.3.2 Limitations to the principle of indirect effect

The doctrine of indirect effect cannot be used to give effect to all unimplemented or incorrectly implemented directives under any conditions. Some limitations that the Court of Justice has placed on indirect effect are now examined.

Available national legislation

In order for the interpretative obligation of indirect effect to be applicable, there must be some relevant national law available to be interpreted. However, this does not place a very strict limitation on the scope of indirect effect. Since the Court of Justice ruled in *Pfeiffer* (Case 397-403/01) that a national court is required 'to do whatever lies within its jurisdiction, having regard to the whole body of rules of national law' to ensure that a directive is effective, it is unlikely that there will be no national law at all that can be interpreted in line with any given directive.

Duty to interpret 'so far as possible'

The doctrine of indirect effect, as established by the Court of Justice, only requires that Member States must interpret national law in accordance with Union law 'so far as possible'. This leaves scope for the national courts of Member States to find that it is not possible to interpret the available national law in accordance with an unimplemented or incorrectly implemented directive. While the Court was initially stricter about how Member States should interpret national legislation with regards to directives (*Marleasing*, see above), the Court relaxed its position in the following case:

Wagner Miret v *Fondo de Garantía Salarial* (Case C-334/92)

Facts:

Directive 80/987 required each Member State to establish a fund protecting employees from lost wages in the event of a company becoming insolvent. Spain had implemented the Directive but specifically excluded senior management from the ambit of the compensation fund it established. As a senior manager of an insolvent company, Mr Wagner Miret could not apply to the fund for compensation. Instead, he sought to rely directly on Directive 80/987, which neither required nor expressly allowed for the exclusion of senior management from compensation in the event of their company becoming insolvent.

Ruling:

The Court held that the Directive was not directly effective because it was too imprecise to satisfy the conditions for direct effect. As to the principle of indirect effect, the Court again referred to the national court's obligation to interpret national legislation in conformity with the wording and purpose of a directive in 'so far as possible'. The Court made it clear that whether such an interpretation is possible is for the national courts to determine and accepted that it appeared from the national court's reference that it was not possible to interpret the national law at issue in a way that was consistent with the requirements of the Directive.

Significance:

This case established that the indirect effect of a directive is dependent upon their being a national law that it is possible to interpret in conformity with it. Where such an interpretation is

> not possible, the directive cannot be enforced over the conflicting provisions of national law. This is therefore a clear limitation on the extent to which unimplemented and incorrectly implemented directives can be made effective within national legal systems.

The Court confirmed the limits to the principle of indirect effect set out in the above case in *Evobus Austria* v *Niederosterreichischer* (Case C-111/97), where it ruled that national courts are **not** required to distort the meaning of national legislation in order to meet their interpretive obligation.

Criminal liability

Where a national measure that ought to be interpreted in line with an unimplemented directive imposes criminal liability, the principle of indirect effect cannot be applied. In *Pretore di Salò* (Case 14/86), the Court of Justice first stated that:

> [a directive] cannot, of itself and independently of a national law adopted by a Member State for its implementation, have the effect of determining or aggravating the liability in criminal law of persons who act in contravention of the provisions of that directive.

Figure 8.2 Indirect effect

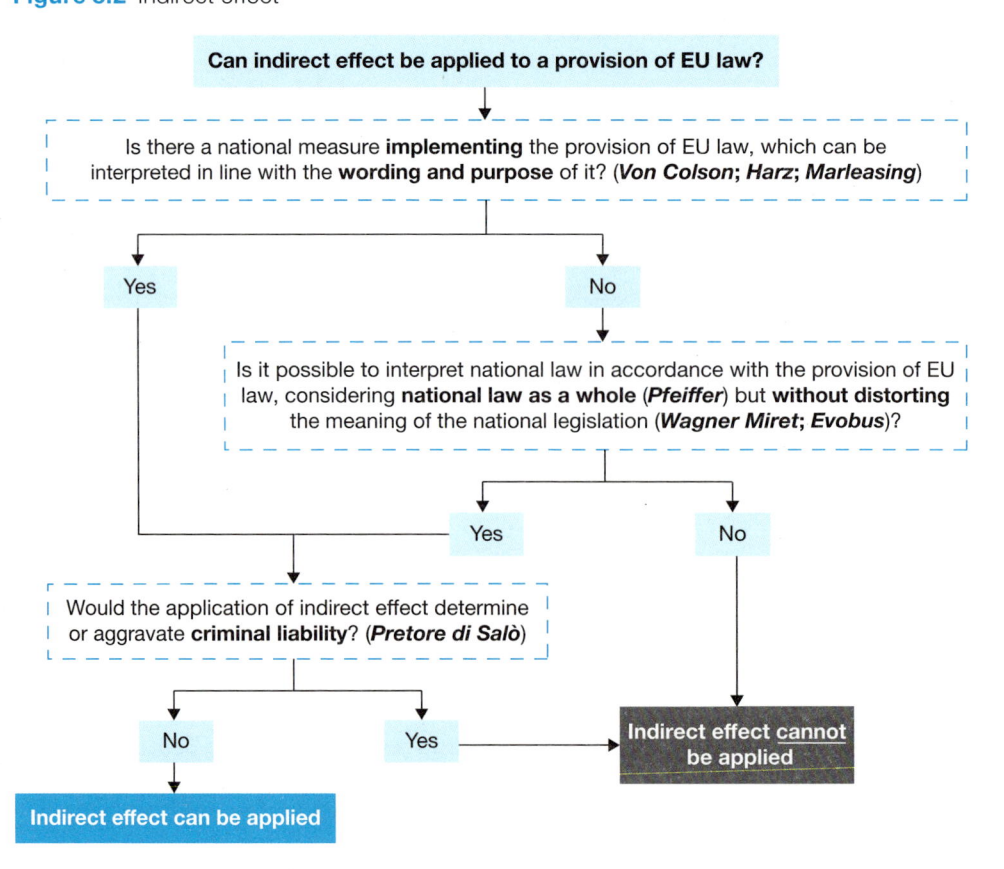

```
Can indirect effect be applied to a provision of EU law?
                          ↓
Is there a national measure implementing the provision of EU law, which can be
interpreted in line with the wording and purpose of it? (Von Colson; Harz; Marleasing)

      Yes                                         No
       ↓                                           ↓
                    Is it possible to interpret national law in accordance with the provision of EU
                    law, considering national law as a whole (Pfeiffer) but without distorting
                    the meaning of the national legislation (Wagner Miret; Evobus)?

                                        Yes              No
                                         ↓                ↓
Would the application of indirect effect determine
or aggravate criminal liability? (Pretore di Salò)

        No                    Yes         →      Indirect effect cannot
         ↓                                              be applied

Indirect effect can be applied
```

In a judgment of the same year, the Court of Justice clarified in *Kolpinghuis Nijmegen BV* (Case 80/86) that:

> [the] obligation on the national court to refer to the content of the directive when interpreting the relevant rules of its national law is limited by the general principles of law which form part of Community law and in particular the **principles of legal certainty and non-retroactivity**.

Thus, not only can unimplemented directives not, by themselves, create obligations on individuals (*Marshall*), but Member States are also **not** required to interpret national legislation in accordance with unimplemented directives where to do so would affect criminal liability (see also *Arcaro* (Case C-168/95)).

In *Lemmens* (Case C-226/97), the Court of Justice further upheld its respect for the principles of legal certainty and non-retroactivity with regards to national criminal legislation. Here, the Court held that a person can be convicted of a driving offence in a national court, even where that conviction rests upon evidence obtained under national legislation made in breach of a Union directive.

8.4 State liability

Objective 4

The principles of direct effect and indirect effect have helped to make EU law more effective in the Member States and to encourage full and proper implementation. However, while these principles can be used by citizens and companies to address their government's failures to implement EU law, it does not provide them with any remedies in cases where they have sustained losses as a result of such a failure. The principle of state liability was developed by the Court of Justice to provide remedies in such instances. An overview of the conditions for state liability is provided in Figure 8.4 on page 308.

8.4.1 State liability arising from unimplemented directives

The possibility of claiming compensation against the state for failing to implement a directive was first considered in the following case:

Francovich and Bonifaci v *Republic of Italy* (Cases C-6/90 and 9/90)

Facts:

As noted above in relation to direct effect (section 8.2.3), the case concerns an Italian company that went into liquidation, leaving Francovich and other employees with unpaid salary arrears. Directive 80/987 required Member States to set up a compensation scheme for employees in these circumstances, but Italy had not established one. Francovich therefore sought compensation from the Italian government and the case was referred to the Court of Justice. The Court was asked: (i) whether the Directive had direct effect; (ii) whether the Member State was liable for the damage arising from its failure to implement the Directive; and (iii) to what extent it was liable for damages for breaching its obligations under Union law.

Ruling:

The Court decided that the Directive was insufficiently precise to have direct effect (see above). However, it emphasised that the Treaty created a legal order which was binding upon Member

States and citizens. The **effet utile** (i.e. the useful effect) of Union law would be diminished if individuals were not able to obtain damages after suffering losses incurred because of a violation of Union law by a Member State. There was therefore an implied obligation under the former Article 5 EEC Treaty (now Art 4(3) TEU) to compensate individuals affected by such a violation. The Court held that, in cases such as this where there was a violation of the state's obligation to implement Union law under the former Article 189 EEC Treaty (now Art 288 TFEU), there was a right to compensation from the state, provided the following three conditions were satisfied:

- The result which had to be attained by the directive involved rights conferred on individuals.
- The content of those rights could be identified from the provisions of the directive.
- There was a causal link between the failure by the Member State to fulfil its obligations and the damage suffered by the person affected.

The Court did not decide how the extent of liability was to be determined, as this was to be a matter for national law. National procedures had, however, 'to ensure the full protection of rights which individuals might derive from Community [i.e. Union] law'. In this particular case, the failure of Italy to implement the directive in question had already been established by the Court.

Significance:

This case confirmed the logical consequence of the principle of direct effect: if a Member State is responsible for implementing a provision of Union law and that provision confers rights on individuals, individuals should be able to acquire meaningful remedies from the state in instances where they have incurred losses as a result of the state's failure to protect those rights.

In addition to providing remedies to individuals, the principle of state liability encourages Member States to fully implement EU law, as failures to do so may now result in swifter financial repercussions for the state (compared with the penalties that may be imposed by the Court of Justice pursuant to infringement proceedings – see Chapter 7).

▶ See Figure 8.4 (section 8.4.4, page 308) for a flowchart relating to the principle of state liability

The Court has developed the concept of state liability and entitlement to damages in a number of subsequent judgments.

Generally, a Member State cannot defend itself on the basis of simple non-implementation, as the obligation to implement Union law is strict, regardless of whatever practical difficulties there may be (***Commission* v *Belgium*** (Case 1/86)).

8.4.2 State liability arising from incorrect implementation

While ***Francovich*** established a three-point test for determining state liability in relation to unimplemented directives, i.e. where the legislature had failed to act, the following joined cases concerned state liability where directly effective Treaty articles had been actively breached by the national legislature:

Brasserie du Pêcheur v *Germany* and *R* v *Secretary of State for Transport, ex parte Factortame Ltd and Others* (Joined Cases C-46 and 48/93)

Facts:

The former case concerned a pre-existing German law which breached the former Article 30 EEC Treaty (now Art 34 TFEU); the latter case concerned a UK Act of Parliament which was enacted in breach of, *inter alia*, the former Article 52 EEC Treaty (now Art 49 TFEU). The claimants sought damages against the respective states for the legislature's breach of Union law. The national courts referred a number of questions to the Court of Justice for a preliminary ruling pursuant to the former Article 177 EEC Treaty (now Art 267 TFEU).

Ruling:

The first question in both cases concerned whether or not the *Francovich* principle of state liability would oblige Member States to remedy damage caused to individuals by an act or omission of the state legislature that contravened Community [i.e. Union] law. In assessing this question, the Court of Justice initially stated that it was irrelevant that the breach concerned a directly effective Treaty article and that it was irrelevant which organ of state was responsible for the breach.

The Court of Justice then gave consideration to the conditions under which state liability may be incurred. Reiterating its *Francovich* judgment, the Court stated that:

> 38 Although Community [i.e. Union] law imposes State liability, the conditions under which that liability gives rise to a right to reparation depend on the nature of the breach of Community [i.e. Union] law giving rise to the loss and damage.

In examining the facts of the two cases, the Court of Justice stated that the national legislatures had a wide discretion in the relevant fields of activity. Where there was such a wide discretion, three conditions had to be met in order to incur state liability:

- the rule of Community [i.e. Union] law infringed must be intended to *confer rights on individuals*;
- the breach must be *sufficiently serious*;
- there must be a *direct causal link* between the breach of the obligation resting on the state and the damage sustained by the injured parties.

The former Articles 30 and 52 EEC Treaty (now Arts 34 and 49 TFEU) are directly effective and therefore the first condition was satisfied. It is the second condition which is the most interesting. The Court of Justice stated that the decisive test for finding that a breach of Union law is sufficiently serious is whether the Member State 'manifestly and gravely disregarded the limits on its discretion' (para 55). The Court of Justice then set out a number of factors which may be taken into consideration by the national court when assessing whether or not there was such a manifest and grave disregard by the Member State of the limit on its discretion:

> 56 The factors which the competent court may take into consideration include the **clarity and precision of the rule** breached, the **measure of discretion** left by that rule to the national or Community [i.e. Union] authorities, whether the infringement and the damage caused was **intentional or involuntary**, whether any error of law was **excusable or inexcusable**, the fact that the **position taken by a Community [i.e. Union] institution may have contributed** towards the omission, and the **adoption or retention of national measures or practices contrary to Community [i.e. Union] law**.

> 57 On any view, a breach of Community [i.e. Union] law will clearly be **sufficiently serious if it has persisted despite a judgment finding the infringement in question to be established, or a preliminary ruling or settled case law** of the Court on the matter from which it is clear that the conduct in question constituted an infringement.

Significance:

These joined cases established a similar but different three-point test for identifying state liability to that established in *Francovich*, suggesting that the *Francovich* criteria may only apply in cases where a Member State has entirely failed to implement a measure of EU law. The emphasis here on whether a breach of EU law is **sufficiently serious** means that a breach need not amount to a complete failure to implement a provision in order to result in state liability. State liability may therefore arise in cases where a Member State has incorrectly implemented a measure, provided that the resulting breach stems from a **manifest and grave disregard** by a Member State of the limits that EU law imposes on its discretion.

The *Factortame* case returned to the UK court for it to apply the three conditions of state liability. The case reached the House of Lords (the judicial functions of which are now exercised by the Supreme Court), which held that the adoption of legislation which was discriminatory on the ground of nationality in respect of the registration of UK fishing vessels, in breach of clear and unambiguous rules of Union law, was **sufficiently serious** to give rise to liability for damages to individuals who suffered losses as a consequence (*R v Secretary of State for Transport, ex parte Factortame Ltd and Others (No. 5)* [1999] 3 WLR 1062). Factortame would then have to prove its losses (i.e. prove that there was a **direct causal link** between the breach and the damage they had sustained).

In the following case, although it was found that the UK had implemented a directive incorrectly, it was determined that the UK had acted in good faith and that this had not resulted in a sufficiently serious breach for the state to be held liable for damages:

R v HM Treasury, ex parte British Telecommunications plc (Case C-392/93)

Facts:

British Telecommunications (BT) sought damages from the UK government on the basis that the government's incorrect implementation of Directive 90/531 had placed BT at an operational and competitive disadvantage.

Ruling:

The Court of Justice restated the three conditions set out in *Brasserie* and *Factortame*:

> the rule of law infringed must be intended to confer rights on individuals; the breach must be sufficiently serious; and there must be a direct causal link between the breach ... and the damage sustained. [para 39]

The Court of Justice held that this approach was equally applicable to the facts of this case, where the UK had incorrectly transposed a directive. The Court reiterated that it was for the national court to determine whether or not there was a **sufficiently serious breach**. However, as the Court of Justice had all the necessary facts before it, it went on to advise the national court on the factual situation.

In the *Brasserie du Pêcheur* and *Factortame* joined cases, the Court of Justice held that one of the relevant factors was the clarity and precision of the rule breached. In this case, the Directive was imprecisely worded and was reasonably capable of bearing the interpretation given to it by the UK. Moreover, the UK had acted in good faith. The Court of Justice noted that the UK's interpretation was shared by other Member States and 'was not manifestly contrary to the wording of the directive or to the objective pursued by it'.

Additionally, as there had been no case law from the Court of Justice to guide the UK and the Commission had not questioned the UK's implementing legislation, the Court of Justice held that the breach could not be regarded as sufficiently serious to give rise to liability.

Significance:

This case provides an example where a breach of EU law stemming from the incorrect implementation of a directive was not deemed sufficiently serious to give rise to state liability.

8.4.3 Unimplemented directives revisited

The following case applied the *Brasserie* and *Factortame* criteria for state liability to a claim concerning an **unimplemented** directive:

Dillenkofer and Others v *Federal Republic of Germany* (Joined Cases C-178, 179 and 188–190/94)

Facts:
Germany had failed to implement Directive 90/314 on package holidays before the prescribed deadline. A number of claimants were subsequently unable to obtain reimbursement for financial losses following the insolvency of their tour operators. A German court referred a number of questions to the Court of Justice with the aim of establishing the extent of the state's liability.

Ruling:
The Court referred to both the *Francovich* and *Factortame* cases, and clarified that 'the condition that there should be a sufficiently serious breach, although not expressly mentioned in *Francovich*, was nevertheless evident from the circumstances of that case'.
The Court then ruled as follows:

26 So where, as in *Francovich*, a Member State fails, in breach of the third paragraph of Article 189 of the Treaty [now Art 288 TFEU], to take any of the measures necessary to achieve the result prescribed by a directive within the period it lays down, **that Member State manifestly and gravely disregards the limits on its discretion.**

27 Consequently, such a breach gives rise to a right to reparation on the part of individuals if the result prescribed by the directive entails the **grant of rights** to them, the **content of those rights is identifiable** on the basis of the provisions of the directive and a **causal link** exists between the breach of the State's obligation and the loss and damage suffered by the injured parties: no other conditions need be taken into consideration.

Significance:
This case established that a failure to implement a measure of EU law constitutes a sufficiently serious breach to give rise to state liability, provided that the other relevant criteria are also met. In applying the *Brasserie* and *Factortame* condition of a sufficiently serious breach, the Court suggested that this criterion must always be met and cannot be avoided by referring only to the *Francovich* criteria – which did not expressly include it – in instances where a measure has not been implemented at all. This suggests that the *Brasserie* and *Factortame* criteria effectively replace the *Francovich* criteria, but this has yet to be clearly confirmed by the Court.

Figure 8.3 sets out the differences between the *Francovich* and *Factortame* criteria for state liability.

Figure 8.3 Comparison of *Frankovich* and *Factortame* criteria for state liability

Francovich and Bonifaci criteria	Brasserie du Pêcheur and Factortame criteria	
The provision must confer rights on individuals	The provision must confer rights on individuals	'Sufficiently serious' will be determined according to: – the clarity and precision of the rule breached – the extent of any discretion left to the Member State – whether the breach was intentional or involuntary – whether the error of law was excusable or inexcusable – whether the position taken by a Community institution had contributed towards the Member State's action ➢ ***Dillenkofer***: failure to implement a directive = sufficiently serious
The content of those rights must be identifiable from the provision	The breach must be **sufficiently serious**	
There must be a causal link between the breach of the provision and the damages incurred	There must be a **direct** causal link between the breach of the provision and the damages incurred	

8.4.4 State liability arising from acts of the executive and the judiciary

The preceding cases have all dealt with state liability for damages resulting from breaches of EU law caused by actions or inactions of the legislature. The following case examined the question of whether state liability could arise from an act of the executive:

R v Ministry of Agriculture, Fisheries and Food, ex parte Hedley Lomas (Ireland) Ltd (Case C-5/94)

Facts:

The UK Ministry of Agriculture refused licences for the export of livestock to Spain in contravention of the former Article 34 EC Treaty (now Art 35 TFEU). The UK sought to justify this breach of EU law under Article 36 EC Treaty (now Art 36 TFEU), as it was of the view that Spain was acting contrary to Directive 74/557, which concerns the stunning of animals before slaughter.

Ruling:

The Court of Justice held that the UK had insufficient evidence to justify the refusal by the Ministry under the former Article 36 EC Treaty (now Art 36 TFEU). The UK was therefore in breach of Union law.

In reaching its judgment, the Court of Justice restated the part of its judgment in ***Brasserie du Pêcheur*** and ***Factortame*** where it held that in a field in which a Member State has a wide discretion to make legislative choices, a defaulting Member State will incur liability where three conditions are satisfied:

> 25 ... the rule of law infringed must be intended to **confer rights on individuals**; the breach must be **sufficiently serious**; and there must be a **direct causal link** between the breach of the obligation resting on the State and the damage sustained by the injured parties.

In an attempt to impose a common standard for state liability throughout the Union, the Court of Justice held that those three conditions were applicable to the case, despite the fact that the breach did not involve a legislative act and despite the fact that the Member State did not enjoy a wide discretion. However, the Court acknowledged that the concept of a 'sufficiently serious breach' will vary, depending upon the facts of the case. With regard to this particular case, the Court of Justice stated that:

> 28 ... where, at the time when it committed the infringement, the Member State in question was not called upon to make any legislative choices and **had only considerably reduced, or even no, discretion, the mere infringement of Community [i.e. Union] law may be sufficient to establish the existence of a sufficiently serious breach**.

Significance:

This case established that, where a Member State has little or no discretion in its implementation of a measure of EU law, the finding of an infringement may be sufficient to give rise to state liability, provided that the other two criteria set out in **Brasserie** and **Factortame** are also satisfied, i.e. that the measure confers rights on individuals and that there is a direct causal link between the infringement and the damages suffered. It also established that the state can be held liable for damages resulting from acts of the executive that breach Union law, as well as acts of the legislature.

➤ *Köbler* is also considered in relation to the free movement of workers in section 10.3.2 (page 399)

The following case extended the principle of state liability to 'courts of last instance':

Köbler (Case C-224/01)

Facts:

A German national had worked as an ordinary professor in an Austrian university for ten years. He applied for a special length-of-service increment, which was normally paid to professors with 15 years' experience at Austrian universities, arguing that he had completed the requisite length of service if the duration of his service in universities of other Member States was taken into consideration. The Austrian Supreme Court rejected his claim. Köbler then brought a 'Francovich' action, asserting that the Austrian court had misapplied an earlier Court of Justice ruling in its decision, that this constituted a 'sufficiently serious breach' and that he was therefore entitled to compensation.

Ruling:

In its preliminary ruling, the Court of Justice ruled that there was no reason why a 'Francovich' claim could not be brought against a court of last resort. The Court confirmed that the principle, stated in particular in **Brasserie du Pêcheur** and **Factortame**, that Member States are obliged to make good damage caused to individuals by infringements of Union law for which they are responsible, applies in cases where the alleged infringement stems from a decision of a court adjudicating at last instance. As previously ruled, a successful claim requires that the infringed measure is intended to confer rights on individuals, the breach is sufficiently serious and there is a direct causal link between that breach and the loss or damage sustained by the injured parties. With regard to the second condition, the Court of Justice made clear that for an infringement stemming from a decision of a court to be sufficiently serious it must be manifest. Finally, it added that it is for the legal system of each Member State to designate the court competent to determine disputes relating to that reparation.

Although it is generally for the national courts to consider the abovementioned criteria, the Court of Justice took the view that it had all the material facts enabling it to establish whether the conditions necessary for liability to be incurred by the Member State concerned were fulfilled. To this end, the court set forth two circumstances in which an infringement of Union law by a court adjudicating at last instance does **not** have the manifest character to be deemed sufficiently serious: (i) where Union law does not expressly cover the point of law at issue, there is no answer to be found in the Court's case law and the answer is not obvious; and (ii) where the infringement was not intentional but was the result of an incorrect reading of a judgment of the Court of Justice. On these grounds, the Court held that the Austrian court's infringement of Union law was not 'sufficiently serious'.

Significance:

In this case, the Court established that state liability can arise from the actions of a court of last instance, but that in such cases a breach of EU law is not sufficiently serious to give rise to state liability if there is **no clear answer** to the question before the court in EU legislation and case law, and where the infringement resulted from an **accidental misreading** of a ruling of the Court of Justice. The need to show that the infringement is manifest in this way places a high burden on a claimant. Therefore, even though this case establishes that a court of last instance may be liable for damages as a result of an erroneous interpretation of EU law, this decision still affords national courts a degree of protection from such claims.

Along with *Dillenkofer* (see above), the *Hedley Lomas* and *Köbler* cases suggest that the conditions relating to state liability are fixed no matter what the nature of the breach and irrespective of the organ of the state which is responsible for the breach.

The following case further develops the principles pertaining to courts of last instance that were established in *Köbler*:

Traghetti del Mediterraneo SpA v *Italy* (Case C-173/03)

Facts:

From 1981, the maritime transport company 'Traghetti del Mediterraneo' (TDM) brought a series of proceedings through the Italian courts against a competing company, Tirrenia di Navigazione. TDM sought compensation for the damage that its competitor had allegedly caused it through its policy of low fares on the maritime cabotage market, which had been made possible by public subsidies. TDM submitted in particular that the conduct in question constituted unfair competition and abuse of a dominant position, which was prohibited by the former Article 82 EC Treaty (now Art 102 TFEU).

The action for compensation was dismissed by all the Italian courts that heard the case, including the Corte Suprema di Cassazione (the Supreme Court). Taking the view that the judgment of the latter court was founded on an incorrect interpretation of the Union rules, the administrator of TDM, which had in the meantime been put into liquidation, brought proceedings against Italy before the Tribunale di Genova. That action sought compensation for the damage suffered by TDM as a result of the errors of interpretation committed by the Supreme Court and the breach of its obligation to make a reference for a preliminary ruling to the Court of Justice.

In those circumstances, the Tribunale di Genova asked the Court of Justice whether Union law and, in particular, the principles laid down by the Court in the *Köbler* judgment, preclude national legislation which: (i) excludes all liability of a Member State for damage caused to individuals by an infringement of Union law committed by a national court adjudicating at last instance, where that infringement is the result of an interpretation of provisions of law or of an assessment of the facts and evidence carried out by that court; and (ii) also limits such liability solely to cases of intentional fault and serious misconduct on the part of the court.

Ruling:

The Court began by reaffirming the principle of state liability, before examining the first part of the question. The Court stated that the interpretation of provisions of law and the assessment of facts and evidence constitute an essential part of judicial activity and may lead, in certain cases, to a manifest infringement of the applicable law. To exclude any possibility that state liability may be incurred where the infringement allegedly committed by the national court relates to its interpretation of provisions of law or its assessment of facts or evidence would amount to depriving the principle of state liability of all practical effect.

With regard to the second part of the question, the Court of Justice pointed out that state liability may be incurred where a court has 'manifestly infringed' the applicable law. **Such manifest infringement is to be assessed in the light of a number of criteria, including: (i) the degree of clarity and precision of the rule infringed; (ii) whether the error of law was excusable or inexcusable; and (iii) the non-compliance by the court in question with its obligation to make a reference for a preliminary ruling.** A manifest infringement is presumed where the decision involved is taken in clear disregard of the case law of the Court of Justice on the subject.

Accordingly, the Court of Justice held that, although it remains possible for national law to define the criteria relating to the nature or degree of the infringement which must be met before state liability can be incurred by a national court adjudicating at last instance, under no circumstances may such criteria impose requirements stricter than that of a manifest infringement of the applicable law. The Court therefore held that the limitation of state liability solely to cases of intentional fault and serious misconduct on the part of the court is contrary to Union law if such a limitation were to exclude the liability of the Member State in other cases where a manifest infringement of the applicable law was committed.

Significance:

This case clarified the scope of a 'manifest infringement' by a national court of last instance and established that national legislation may not preclude forms of state liability that are within that scope.

The principles established in *Köbler* and *Traghetti* were confirmed in *Commission* v *Italy* (Case C-379/10), where the Court of Justice ruled that Italian legislation placed undue limitations on the general principle of the liability of Member States for a breach of EU law.

Reflection: Making EU law effective in the Member States

The approach adopted by the Court of Justice to assist individuals affected by the non-implementation of directives was a pragmatic response to a perceived problem of inequality between Member States. Those states which failed to implement directives on time might actually enjoy an advantage over those states which had shouldered the burden the directive imposed, and individuals in the non-implementing state would be deprived of the benefits the directive was intended to confer upon them. Bringing defaulting Member States before the Court of Justice is slow and is only a partial solution to the problem (see Chapter 7). Even if it achieves belated implementation of a directive, it cannot provide compensation to those individuals who have been deprived of its beneficial effect. The principles of direct effect, indirect effect and state liability have therefore been developed to address this weakness in enforcement.

> Although in **Marshall** and **Faccini Dori**, the Court of Justice failed to grasp the nettle and give directives **horizontal direct effect** between individuals, this has been partly mitigated by the development of the interpretative obligation of indirect effect. However, application of the principle of indirect effect depends very much on the willingness of national courts to engage in creative interpretation of national legislation. At the present time the Court seems reluctant, as demonstrated in **Wagner Miret**, to be more specific in defining the nature of the national court's interpretative obligation.
>
> However, a claim against a Member State cannot be regarded as a wholly satisfactory substitute for the enforcement of a directive against those who were intended to be bound by it. For example, damages may not constitute a satisfactory remedy where the non-implementation of a directive results in the failure to set up an area of environmental protection. The losers may be the local community as a whole rather than an individual and it may be impossible to establish any causal link, as required by **Francovich**, between the failure to implement the directive and any specific loss suffered by an individual. These difficulties will probably persist unless and until the Court of Justice determines that unimplemented directives may have horizontal as well as vertical direct effect.

Figure 8.4 State liability

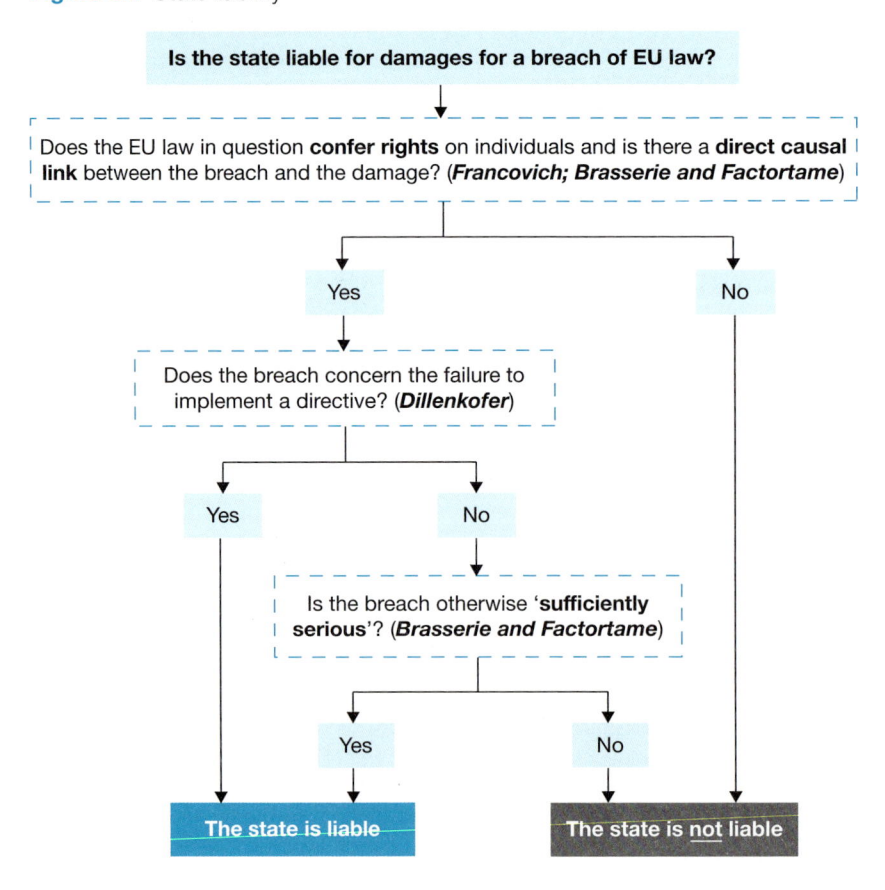

```
                Is the state liable for damages for a breach of EU law?
                                        │
    Does the EU law in question confer rights on individuals and is there a direct causal
    link between the breach and the damage? (Francovich; Brasserie and Factortame)
                            │                                │
                           Yes                              No
                            │                                │
    Does the breach concern the failure to
    implement a directive? (Dillenkofer)
                │                       │
               Yes                     No
                │                       │
                        Is the breach otherwise 'sufficiently
                        serious'? (Brasserie and Factortame)
                            │                       │
                           Yes                     No
                            │                       │
                The state is liable            The state is not liable
```

8.5 The enforcement of EU law in the UK courts

Objective 5

8.5.1 Direct effect of EU law in the UK

Direct effect of EU Treaty articles

Prior to Brexit, the EU Treaties, like any other treaty, were effective in UK law only to the extent to which they had been incorporated into the UK's legal system (*Blackburn* v *Attorney-General* [1971] 2 All ER 1380 at 1382; Lord Denning MR) and to the extent to which UK courts were prepared to interpret national law in conformity with Union obligations (*R* v *Secretary for Foreign and Commonwealth Office, ex parte Rees-Mogg* [1994] 1 CMLR 101 (QBD)).

Under s 2(1) of the European Communities Act 1972, which ceased to apply on 31 January 2020, UK courts did not have any difficulty in giving effect to Treaty provisions or regulations where the legislation of the UK Parliament could be construed in accordance with Union law. This was established in the following case:

Macarthys Ltd v *Smith* [1979] ICR 785 and [1981] QB 180

Facts:

Ms Smith was paid £50 per week for her work in a factory, while a man who had previously worked in the same job had been paid £60 per week. The company denied Ms Smith's allegation of unlawful discrimination on the basis that the Equal Pay Act 1970 did not allow for comparisons between the pay of current and former employees. Ms Smith, however, argued that the former Article 119 EEC Treaty (now Art 157 TFEU) did allow for such comparisons and should be given precedence over the domestic Act.

Ruling:

In the UK Court of Appeal, a majority held that Ms Smith had no claim under the Equal Pay Act 1970, but that the application of the former Article 119 EEC Treaty (now Art 157 TFEU) to the case was unclear. Lord Denning, in a dissenting opinion, argued that the former Article 119 EEC Treaty was reasonably clear and should be applied. He stated:

> If ... our legislation is deficient or is inconsistent with Community [i.e. Union] law by some oversight of our draftsmen then it is our bounden duty to give priority to Community [i.e. Union] law. Such is the result of ss. 2(1) and (4) of the European Communities Act 1972 ... Thus far I have assumed that our Parliament, whenever it passes legislation, intends to fulfil its obligations under the Treaty. If the time should come when our Parliament deliberately passes an Act with the intention of repudiating the Treaty or any provision in it or intentionally of acting inconsistently with it and says so in express terms then I should have thought that it would be the duty of our courts to follow the statute of our Parliament. I do not however envisage such a situation.

The UK Court of Appeal referred questions to the Court of Justice to clarify whether the former Article 119 EEC Treaty encompassed comparisons with former employees. The Court of Justice, in Case 129/79, ruled that the former Article 119 EEC Treaty (now Art 157 TFEU) encompassed situations where it was established that a woman had received less pay than a man who had previously done equal work for the same employer.

When the case returned to the Court of Appeal, Lord Denning stated as follows:

> It is important now to declare - and it must be made plain - that the provisions of article 119 of the E.E.C. Treaty take priority over anything in our English statute on equal pay which is inconsistent

> with article 119. That priority is given by our own law. It is given by the European Communities Act 1972 itself. Community law is now part of our law: and, whenever there is any inconsistency, Community law has priority. It is not supplanting English law. It is part of our law which overrides any other part which is inconsistent with it.
>
> **Significance:**
>
> By and large, this case established the supremacy of Union law over domestic legislation in the UK. However, in his initial dissent, Lord Denning left open the possibility that an Act of Parliament that expressly and intentionally contradicted an act of Union law could be binding on the UK courts, over the conflicting Union provisions. This reflects the situation where the supremacy of Union law was ultimately subject to the continued willingness of Parliament not to deliberately undermine it, which would in turn have constituted a breach of the UK's duty to implement Union law under what is now Article 4(3) TEU. Lord Denning stated that he could not envisage such a wilful derogation from Union law being passed by Parliament, as this would have had serious ramifications for the UK's relationship with the Union and could have potentially eroded the foundations of the entire Union.

While in *Macarthys*, there was scope for the national legislation to be interpreted in accordance with Union law, matters have been less straightforward where national law has been enacted in a way that clearly conflicted with a directly effective Treaty provision. The *Factortame* litigation provides an illustration of the way in which the UK courts have dealt with this situation. In *Factortame Ltd* v *Secretary of State for Transport* [1990] 2 AC 85, the question arose as to whether the Merchant Shipping Act 1988, and regulations made pursuant to it, deprived the applicants of their rights under Union law. The Divisional Court referred the substantive matter to the Court of Justice under what is now Article 267 TFEU for a preliminary ruling.

On 25 July 1991, the Court of Justice (Case C-221/89) held that the 1988 Act conflicted with the former Article 7 EEC Treaty (now Art 18 TFEU) on non-discrimination on grounds of nationality, and the former Article 43 EEC Treaty (now Art 49 TFEU) on freedom of establishment. On 2 October 1991, the Divisional Court (in an unreported decision) granted the appropriate declaration, in effect refusing to enforce the 1988 Act against the applicants. If the traditional doctrine of parliamentary sovereignty had been applied, the 1988 Act would have impliedly repealed those provisions of the earlier legislation to the extent that they were inconsistent with it (i.e. s 2(4), European Communities Act 1972). Instead, however, the Divisional Court held for the first time that an Act of Parliament could be disapplied due to its incompatibility with prior Union law.

▶ See section 8.4.2 (page 300) for an overview of *Factortame* before the Court of Justice

Direct effect of directives

The UK courts have experienced some difficulty with directly enforcing directives. As discussed above, *prima facie*, directives are not directly applicable, and so did not fall into the category of Union provisions which, without further enactment, would have had legal effect under s 2(1) of the European Communities Act 1972. However, where they had been held by the Court of Justice to create directly enforceable rights they were applied vertically against emanations of the state by UK courts, following references to the Court of Justice (e.g. *Marshall* and *Foster* v *British Gas* (see above)). However, the UK courts have had some difficulty in determining the scope of 'state emanation', as demonstrated in the following three cases.

The first case was factually similar to the *Marshall* and *Foster* cases:

Doughty v *Rolls-Royce Plc* [1992] CMLR 1045

Facts:
Ms Doughty was compulsorily retired at age 60, in accordance with company policy that women retire at 60 whereas men retire at 65. As considered above, such discrimination was, at the material time, expressly permitted under English law. Ms Doughty sought to rely upon the Equal Treatment Directive (Directive 76/207). The question before the Court of Appeal was whether or not Ms Doughty's employer, Rolls-Royce, was an emanation of the state.

Ruling:
Lord Justice Mustill gave the leading judgment with which Lady Justice Butler-Sloss and Sir John Megaw agreed. Mustill LJ quoted extensively from the employment tribunal's findings of fact as to the nature of Rolls-Royce, which at the material time had not been privatised (see p. 1048, para 8). All of Rolls-Royce's shares were held on behalf of the Crown; the ultimate power in relation to the company and its business rested with the shareholder (i.e. the Crown) by virtue of its ability to pass resolutions in General Meetings. In December 1980 a 'Memorandum of Understanding with Rolls-Royce – Relationship with Government' was issued. This provided that the government had three separate roles in its relationship with Rolls-Royce:

- that of 100 per cent shareholder;
- that of principal customer for the development and production of military engines; and
- that of its overall sponsorship of the aerospace industry.

The employment tribunal held that Rolls-Royce was an emanation of the state because, as 100 per cent shareholder, the state had the power to require the directors to alter the contracts of employment of the company's employees so as to comply with the Directive.

This decision was reversed by the Employment Appeal Tribunal ([1987] IRLR 447), which held that the crucial question was whether or not Rolls-Royce could be said to be an organ or agent of the state carrying out a state function (see paras 11–12).

The appeal to the Court of Appeal was heard after the decisions of the Court of Justice and the House of Lords in *Foster*. Mustill LJ stated that the *Foster* test was not intended to be an exhaustive statement for determining the status of the entity, but, nevertheless, it was Mustill LJ's opinion that in a case factually similar to *Foster*, the test:

> ... **must always be the starting point and will usually be the finishing point.** If all the factors identified by the Court are present it is likely to require something very unusual to produce the result that an entity is not to be identified with the State. Conversely, although the absence of a factor will not necessarily be fatal, it will need the addition of something else, not contemplated by the formula ... [para 24]

Mustill LJ went on to examine whether or not the three *Foster* criteria were satisfied, i.e. whether Rolls-Royce 1) provided public services, 2) was under state control and 3) had special powers. He accepted that the second criterion, requiring the service to be provided under the control of the state, was satisfied. He stated that with regard to this criterion, the relevant question was whether the public *service* (rather than the *body* providing the service) was under the state's control. He concluded that the other two criteria were not satisfied: Rolls-Royce could not be said to have been made responsible for providing a public service, pursuant to a measure adopted by the state, nor was there any evidence that Rolls-Royce possessed or exercised any 'special powers'.

> Accordingly, Ms Doughty could not enforce the directive against Rolls-Royce, because Rolls-Royce was deemed not to be an emanation of the state.
>
> **Significance:**
>
> This case demonstrates the narrow scope afforded to defining an 'emanation of the state', as it was found that all the elements of the *Foster* test would normally need to be proved. One element, such as state control of an organisation, was not sufficient by itself to make that organisation an emanation of the state that may have been liable to direct effect.

The second case centred on the question of whether the provisions of the Collective Redundancies Directive 92/129 could be enforced directly against a privatised company, South West Water (SWW). In *Griffin and Others* v *South West Water Services Ltd* [1995] IRLR 15, the English High Court confirmed that all three of the *Foster* criteria must be met in order for an entity to be considered an emanation of the state. Whereas in *Doughty*, the 'state control' criterion was the only one that Rolls-Royce was found to fulfil, in *Griffin* this was the only criterion that was contested. The High Court found that it was irrelevant whether or not SWW carried out any of the traditional functions of the state or was an agent of the state. In line with *Doughty*, the High Court focused on whether the public services in question were under state control (as opposed to whether the body in question was) and found that the powers of the Secretary of State and the Director General of Water Services over the public provision of water and sewerage were such that the services provided by SWW were under the control of the state. The three *Foster* criteria were therefore satisfied, meaning that SWW was an emanation of the state and a body against which the Directive was capable of being enforced. However, as discussed above, a directive could only be directly enforced if the relevant provisions are **sufficiently precise and unconditional**. In *Griffin*, the High Court decided that the relevant provisions were **not** sufficiently precise and unconditional and therefore the Directive could not be enforced against SWW.

The following is the third and final case:

> ### *National Union of Teachers and Others* v *The Governing Body of St Mary's Church of England (Aided) Junior School and Others* [1997] IRLR 242
>
> **Facts:**
>
> The school at which the applicants had worked closed down and they were not re-employed to work at a new school which was subsequently established under the control of a temporary governing body. The applicants argued that the Acquired Rights Directive 77/187 applied automatically to the transfer of their contracts of employment to the new school and that therefore their dismissals were unlawful. It was common ground that, at the material time, English law could not assist the applicants.
>
> **Ruling:**
>
> The employment tribunal applied the *Foster* test and concluded that the governing body did not satisfy the 'special powers' criterion and was not, therefore, an emanation of the state against which the Directive could be directly enforced. The appeal to the Employment Appeal Tribunal ([1995] ICR 317) was dismissed, but the Court of Appeal unanimously allowed the appeal.

Schiemann LJ, who delivered the leading opinion, recognised that the Court of Justice had not established a test which should be applied to all situations. Although each party to the case had relied on the *Foster* test, he stated that:

> It is clear from the wording of paragraph 20 [of the Court's judgment in *Foster*] and in particular the words 'is included among' that the formula there used was not intended to be an exclusive formula.

The governing body relied heavily upon the Court of Appeal's decision in *Doughty*, and in particular on Mustill LJ's observation that in a case of the same general type as *Foster*, the test formulated by the Court of Justice would always be the starting point and would usually be the finishing point. However, Schiemann LJ was of the view that this case was not of the same general type as that of *Foster*:

> That case and *Rolls-Royce* were both concerned with commercial undertakings in which the Government had a stake. The present case is not concerned with any commercial undertaking but rather with the provision of what would generally in the Community [i.e. Union] be regarded as the provision of a public service.

He said that the Employment Appeal Tribunal was wrong in applying the *Foster* test as if it was a statutory definition. Although he agreed that the 'special powers' condition was not convincingly met, Schiemann LJ held that the governing body was an emanation of the state:

> **The financial position is that the failure to transpose the Directive will, if the present appeal is dismissed, have the effect of allowing the local education authority and the State to benefit from the failure to transpose the Directive.** The *Rolls-Royce* case indicates that the mere fact that some incidental benefit may arise to the State from a failure to implement a directive does not necessarily bring the doctrine of vertical effect into play. In the present case the benefit is direct to the local education authority, as is conceded because of the provisions of s 46 of the Education Reform Act 1988, and the local education authority, as is further conceded, is an emanation of the State for the purposes of the doctrine of direct vertical effect.

Section 46 of the Education Reform Act 1988 provided that local education authorities were responsible for redundancy payments. The nature of the service being provided and the fact that the body providing the service was financially dependent upon the local education authority determined the outcome of the case. Schiemann LJ departed from a strict application of the *Foster* test, preferring to apply the principle that the state should not benefit from its own failure to implement a directive (the principle of estoppel).

Significance:

This case established a more flexible approach to identifying an emanation of the state than had been suggested by earlier UK rulings. Here, the *Foster* criteria were not held to be exhaustive or conjunctive and the principle of estoppel was prioritised over a restrictive application of the test. Thus the *Foster* test was a starting point, but not necessarily an end point, for determining whether a body was an emanation of the state. This approach was aligned with the Court of Justice's flexible interpretation of the *Foster* criteria in the subsequent case of *Farrell* v *Whitty* (see section 8.2.3, page 290).

The UK courts complied fully with the principle that directives can have vertical direct effect. Indeed, the House of Lords (the judicial functions of which are now exercised by the Supreme Court) went so far as to hold that parts of the Trade Union and Labour Relations Act 1978 were incompatible with a directly effective directive (Directive 76/207) in ***Equal Opportunities Commission*** v ***Secretary of State for Employment*** [1994] 1 All ER 910. However, it is clear that the UK courts had difficulty with defining an emanation of the state, not least because of the extent to which the teleological methodology of the Court of Justice is at odds with the British legal tradition. This was demonstrated unequivocally by Lord Templeman in *Foster v British Gas Plc* (No 2) [1991] 2AC 306:

> I decline to apply the ruling of the ECJ, couched in terms of broad principle and purposive language characteristic of Community Law in a manner which is, for better or worse, sometimes applied to enactments in the United Kingdom parliament.

8.5.2 Indirect effect of EU law in the UK

Prior to *Marleasing*

The House of Lords (of which the judicial functions as a court of last instance are now exercised by the Supreme Court), was required to determine the extent to which national legislation can be interpreted in accordance with measures of EU law on several occasions.

The House of Lords took a restrictive approach in the following case:

Duke v Reliance Systems Ltd [1988] AC 618

Facts:

The case turned on the legality of different retirement ages for men and women – the same point of law as in *Marshall* and *Foster*, above. In this case, however, the employer was a private undertaking, so vertical direct effect could not be applied. The question before the House of Lords was whether it had an obligation to interpret the Sex Discrimination Act 1975 in accordance with the Equal Treatment Directive dated 9 February 1976.

Ruling:

The House of Lords decided that it did not have such an interpretative obligation. Parliament had passed the Act in the belief that it was entitled to have discriminatory retirement ages even when the Directive (which was then in draft format) came into effect. Lord Templeman stated that:

> Of course, a UK court will always be willing and anxious to conclude that UK law is consistent with Community [i.e. Union] law. Where an Act is passed for the purpose of giving effect to an obligation imposed by a directive or other instrument a British court will seldom encounter difficulty in concluding that the language of the Act is effective for the intended purpose. But the construction of a British Act of Parliament is a matter of judgment to be determined by British courts and to be derived from the language of the legislation considered in the light of the circumstances prevailing at the date of the enactment ... It would be most unfair to the **respondent** to distort the construction of the Sex Discrimination Act 1975 in order to accommodate the Equal Treatment Directive 1976 as construed by the European Court of Justice in the 1986 *Marshall* case.

Significance:

In this case, the UK refrained from interpreting a national act in line with a Community (i.e. Union) directive, as such an interpretation would be contrary to the intentions of Parliament and would undermine legal certainty for the respondent. This case therefore demonstrated a more restrictive approach than the Court of Justice would set out in *Marleasing*.

Where legislation has clearly been enacted to implement a directive, the courts have shown themselves capable of creative interpretation, on the basis that Parliament would have intended that the legislation be interpreted in conformity with the relevant directive. The following case subsequently showed more flexibility than was presented in *Duke*:

Litster v Forth Dry Dock [1989] 2 WLR 634

Facts:

The House of Lords (the judicial functions of which are now exercised by the Supreme Court) had to consider Directive 77/187, which was intended to protect workers dismissed in connection with a business transfer. The Directive had been implemented in the UK by the Transfer of Undertakings (Protection of Employment) Regulations 1981 (SI 1981/1794). The UK regulations protected employees who had been dismissed immediately before the transfer of the undertaking. In this case, the employees had been dismissed one hour before the transfer. On a literal interpretation of the regulations the employees were not employed immediately before the transfer and therefore they could not rely on the regulations.

Ruling:

The House of Lords considered several decisions where the Court of Justice had held that workers dismissed prior to the transfer, but for a reason connected with the transfer, would (for the purposes of the Directive) be treated as having been employed by the undertaking at the time when it took place. The House of Lords decided that it was the duty of the UK court to give the UK regulations 'a construction which accords with the decisions of the European Court upon the corresponding provisions of the directive to which the regulation was intended to give effect' (Lord Keith). Accordingly, the House of Lords read into the regulations 'or would have been so employed if he had not been unfairly dismissed', and the dismissed employees were held to come within the scope of the regulations.

However, the House of Lords made clear that they were only adhering to the interpretative obligation of indirect effect in this case because the legislation in question had been enacted specifically to implement – and not to limit – the Directive.

Significance:

This case provides an example of indirect effect at work in the UK judiciary. However, the House of Lords was cautious in applying the principle of indirect effect and suggested that they would not apply it in instances where it was not apparent that Parliament would have intended the legislation to be interpreted in conformity with the measure of EU law in question. In this way, this ruling did not contradict the ruling in *Duke* and left scope for the refusal to apply indirect effect in future cases.

After *Marleasing*

The application of the principle of indirect effect by the UK post-*Marleasing* is usefully illustrated by the approach adopted by the House of Lords (the judicial functions of which are now exercised by the Supreme Court) in the following case:

Webb v EMO Cargo (UK) Ltd (No. 2) [1995] IRLR 647

Facts:

Ms Webb was employed to cover for Ms Stewart while she was on maternity leave. Ms Webb later discovered that she herself was pregnant and that she would not be able to provide the requisite cover during Stewart's maternity leave. EMO Cargo dismissed Ms Webb who subsequently made a complaint that she had been discriminated against on grounds of sex.

An employment tribunal dismissed her complaint. It held that the correct approach was to compare the treatment of Ms Webb with that which would have been accorded to a man in comparable circumstances. If a man had told his employer that he would be absent from work for a similar period, there is very little doubt that he would likewise have been dismissed. Accordingly, Ms Webb was not treated less favourably than EMO Cargo would have treated a man and her treatment did not therefore amount to unlawful discrimination under the Sex Discrimination Act 1975. The Employment Appeal Tribunal ([1990] IRLR 124) dismissed Ms Webb's appeal, as did the Court of Appeal ([1992] IRLR 116).

On Ms Webb's appeal to the House of Lords ([1993] IRLR 27), Lord Keith of Kinkel acknowledged the **Marleasing interpretative obligation**. He therefore referred the matter to the Court of Justice for a preliminary ruling to ascertain if, on the facts of the case, there was a breach of the Directive.

Ruling:

The Court of Justice (Case C-32/93) held (at para 29) that Ms Webb's dismissal contravened the Directive. The Court of Justice was influenced by the fact that Ms Webb was initially employed some months prior to Ms Stewart's expected maternity leave so that she could be trained and that EMO Cargo intended to retain her following Ms Stewart's return to work. The Court of Justice decided that the contract of employment was for an unlimited duration rather than for a specific period directly related to the length of Ms Stewart's maternity leave and that discrimination had therefore occurred.

The case was then referred back to the House of Lords ((No. 2) [1995] IRLR 647), which sought to ascertain whether it was 'possible to construe the relevant provisions of the Act of 1975 so as to accord with the ruling of the European Court' (para 2).

Lord Keith held (at para 11) that it was possible to interpret s 5(3) in such a fashion:

> in a case where a woman is engaged for an indefinite period, the fact that the reason why she will be temporarily unavailable for work at a time when to her knowledge her services will be particularly required is pregnancy is a circumstance relevant to her case, being a circumstance which could not be present in the case of a hypothetical man.

The House of Lords held that Ms Webb's dismissal constituted direct sex discrimination contrary to the 1975 Act and remitted the case back to the employment tribunal for compensation to be assessed.

Significance:

As with **Litster**, this case found that an act of UK law could be interpreted in accordance with an EU measure that afforded greater protection. The application of **Marleasing** was possible because it did not involve **distorting** the meaning of the Act, which preceded the Directive.

The above case is not in conflict with the decision in the ***Duke*** case. In that case, Parliament had expressly permitted the discriminatory retirement ages complained of. In order for the House of Lords to have applied the directive in question, they would have had to *distort* the clear wording of the Sex Discrimination Act 1975. However, it would have been possible that a case similar to ***Duke*** could have led to a state liability case, whereby a claimant could have brought a claim against the state for damages or loss caused by the state's failure to correctly implement the Equal Treatment Directive.

After Brexit

Under the European Withdrawal Act 2018, the European Communities Act 1972 was repealed on 31 January 2020, which is known as 'exit day'. However, EU law will continue to apply in the UK until the end of the transition period (31 December 2020). After the transition period, the UK may seek to remain aligned with developments to EU law in certain areas, but will have to enact domestic legislation in order to do so. All EU law that had effect in the UK prior to exit day has been transposed into domestic legislation, as described in section 4.4.1.

CHAPTER SUMMARY

Direct effect

- The national courts of Member States must protect **sufficiently precise and unconditional** rights conferred to individuals by Union law (*Van Gend en Loos*; *Reyners*).
- Treaty articles and regulations can have both **vertical direct effect** and **horizontal direct effect** (*Defrenne*); directives and decisions can have vertical direct effect (*Van Duyn*; *Grad*; *Marshall*).
- Directives can only be enforced against an **emanation of the state**, which includes bodies that provide public services, are under state control and have special powers (*Foster*).

Indirect effect

- Member States have an **interpretive obligation** to construe national legislation in line with relevant Union law (*Von Colson*).
- Indirect effect can be applied both **vertically** and **horizontally** (*Harz*; *Marleasing*).
- National courts should seek to apply indirect effect before considering direct effect (*Dominguez*).
- Indirect effect does not apply when it is not possible to interpret any national law as required (*Wagner Miret*), nor when such interpretation would affect criminal liability (*Pretore di Saló*).

State liability

- National courts are obliged to hear compensation claims brought against the state for its failure to correctly implement Union law (*Francovich*).
- A Member State is liable when: there is a breach of a Union measure that **confers rights** on private persons, the breach is **sufficiently serious** and there is a **direct causal link** between the breach and the damages claimed (*Brasserie* and *Factortame*).
- State liability applies to acts or omissions of the executive (*Hedley Lomas*) and of courts of last instance (*Köbler*), as well as the legislature.

Enforcement of Union law in the UK courts

- Prior to Brexit, UK courts applied **indirect effect** to interpret UK law as in conformity with the Treaties (e.g. *Macarthys*) and with directives, providing that the national legislation was not distorted (*Litster*; *Webb*).
- An act of Parliament that was not in conformity with Union law could be disapplied (*Factortame*).
- UK courts applied the *Foster* test strictly in *Doughty* and *Griffin*, but showed more flexibility in *NUT*.
- EU law continues to be effective in the UK until the end of the transition period.

Part 2
Substantive areas of EU law

9 European Union citizenship and free movement rights

10 Free movement of workers

11 Freedom of establishment and the free movement of services

12 Free movement of goods

Chapter 9
European Union citizenship and free movement rights

Learning objectives

At the end of this chapter you should understand:

1 The legal framework that establishes EU citizenship and the free movement of persons.

2 The scope of EU citizenship and free movement rights afforded to EU citizens.

3 The scope of 'family members' and the rights to free movement and equal treatment afforded to such persons.

4 Limitations on the rights to free movement.

5 The entitlement of EU citizens and their family members to social benefits while they are residing in a host member state.

6 The Schengen *acquis* and the UK's participation in the Schengen arrangements.

7 The free movement rights of UK citizens in the EU and EU citizens in the UK after Brexit.

Key terms and concepts

Familiarity with the following terms will be helpful for understanding this chapter:

EU citizen – a citizen of a Member State of the EU (also referred to as a Union citizen, EU national or Union national)

Home Member State – the Member State of which a person is a citizen

Host Member State – the Member State in which an EU citizen resides but of which they are not a citizen

Internal border – borders between Member States, i.e. borders within the territory of the Union

Nationality – at the national level, the terms nationality/national and citizenship/citizen are used interchangeably to refer to the legal status of national citizenship

Naturalisation – the process by which national citizenship is acquired when not obtained at birth

Non-EU national – a citizen of a country that is not a Member State of the EU (sometimes referred to as a third-country national)

9.1 Introduction to the free movement of persons

Objective 1

This chapter begins with an introduction to the main concepts (free movement, non-discrimination and EU citizenship) and the main legal provisions (Arts 18, 20 and 21 TFEU and Directive 2004/38) that are essential for understanding the free movement of persons within the Union. The scope of EU citizenship and the free movement rights afforded to citizens is then examined in more depth. The next section considers the application of these rights to the family members of **EU citizens** who have exercised, or are seeking to exercise, their free movement rights. The restrictions and limitations to free movement rights that are provided for in the relevant Union legislation are then outlined and analysed, before the rights of EU citizens and their family members to social benefits are considered. In each of these sections, discussion of the legislation and cases concerning the free movement of workers is deferred to the next chapter, which focuses specifically on the rights of workers. This chapter also includes look at the Schengen *acquis*.

Throughout this chapter, attention is paid to how the UK has implemented and interpreted Union law on the free movement of persons. The chapter also concludes with a section on the impact of Brexit on citizenship and the freedom of movement.

9.1.1 Free movement of persons and non-discrimination

The free movement of persons has been a cornerstone of the European Union since its inception. In particular, free movement rights are closely connected to the measures taken to create the **internal market**, which shall, under **Article 26(2) TFEU**, 'comprise an area without internal frontiers in which the free movement of goods, persons, services and capital is ensured in accordance with the provisions of the Treaties'. Although Article 26(2) TFEU creates a commitment for the Union to remove border restrictions, it has **not** been found to have direct effect (*Wijsenbeek* (Case C-378/97); *R v Secretary of State for the Home Department, ex parte Flynn* [1995] 3 CMLR 397). Article 26(2) TFEU has, however, been a foundation for numerous other articles of both primary and secondary legislation.

The free movement of persons was not, initially, an entitlement for citizens of Member States to move anywhere in the Union for any purpose, but was linked to a number of specific economic activities. Specific provisions confer free movement rights in relation to:

- workers – Articles 45–48 TFEU;
- establishment of businesses and self-employment activity – Articles 49–54 TFEU; and
- provision of services – Articles 56–62 TFEU.

Each of these Treaty provisions has been elaborated by detailed secondary legislation. The rights of individuals and undertakings in these three principal categories are examined in more detail in Chapter 10 (workers) and Chapter 11 (establishment and services). In line with the broader development of the Union, secondary legislation and, moreover, Union case law, has incrementally expanded free movement rights beyond the economic functions of the Union.

Non-discrimination on grounds of nationality

Free movement means not only the right of Union citizens to enter and reside in the territory of another Member State, but also the right to be treated the same as nationals of that Member State. A person exercising their free movement rights within the Union should therefore not face any discrimination or disadvantage for doing so, as such discrimination could deter free movement and would therefore be inimical to the internal market objectives of Article 26(2) TFEU. This principle of non-discrimination on grounds of **nationality** is therefore central to Union legislation and case law on the free movement of persons, and is set out in **Article 18 TFEU**:

> Within the scope of application of the Treaties, and without prejudice to any special provisions contained therein, any discrimination on grounds of nationality shall be prohibited.

It should be noted, however, that this prohibition on discrimination applies only 'within the scope of the application of the Treaties' and therefore cannot be invoked to protect against discrimination on grounds of nationality in matters beyond the scope of the Union.

Free movement rights as fundamental freedoms

All free movement rights (free movement of persons, goods, services and capital) are **directly effective** and enforceable in the courts of Member States as **fundamental freedoms**. The entry or residence of those exercising the free movement of persons is not dependent upon any consent granted by the **host Member State**, provided that an individual meets the conditions set out in Union legislation (*Pieck* (Case 157/79)). As free movement rights are fundamental rights, the Court of Justice has held that they must be transparent in national legislation. Incompatible provisions of national law which, for example, exclude the employment of foreign nationals, even if they are not applied to EU citizens in practice, must be amended to make it absolutely clear that EU citizens enjoy equal access (***Commission* v *France (Re French Merchant Seamen)*** (Case 167/73)). Those entitled to such rights must be made aware of them and, should the need arise, must be able to rely upon them before a court of law (***Commission* v *Germany (Re Nursing Directives)*** (Case 29/84)).

Free movement rights for EU citizens in the UK and for UK citizens in the EU will continue until 31 December 2020, when the Brexit transition period expires. From 2021, both types of migrants will be able to *continue* residing in their host Member State, but may face extra requirements in relation to registration and access to services.

9.1.2 EU citizenship

In 1993, when the Treaty of Maastricht entered into force, free movement rights became attached to the new status of EU citizenship. This was a significant step in moving the project beyond purely economic aims. Now, **Articles 20–25 TFEU** set out the scope of and rights attached to EU citizenship, with **Article 20(1) TFEU** stating that 'Citizenship of the Union is hereby established.' Both Article 20(1) TFEU and **Article 9 TEU** then define EU citizenship as follows:

> Every person holding the nationality of a Member State shall be a citizen of the Union. Citizenship of the Union shall be additional to and not replace national citizenship.

Article 20(2) TFEU goes on to establish the rights that are conferred on citizens as follows:

> Citizens of the Union shall enjoy the rights and be subject to the duties provided for in the Treaties. They shall have, *inter alia*:
> (a) the right to move and reside freely within the territory of the Member States;
> (b) the right to vote and to stand as candidates in elections to the European Parliament and in municipal elections in their Member State of residence, under the same conditions as nationals of that State;
> (c) the right to enjoy, in the territory of a third country in which the Member State of which they are nationals is not represented, the protection of the diplomatic and consular authorities of any Member State on the same conditions as the nationals of that State;
> (d) the right to petition the European Parliament, to apply to the European Ombudsman, and to address the institutions and advisory bodies of the Union in any of the Treaty languages and to obtain a reply in the same language.
>
> These rights shall be exercised in accordance with the conditions and limits defined by the Treaties and by the measures adopted thereunder.

While the rights pertaining to the enfranchisement of EU citizens and their right to petition to European Parliament are important, they are outlined elsewhere in this book (see section 1.3.2). This chapter focuses on the right to move and reside freely, which is further developed in **Article 21 TFEU**:

> Every citizen of the Union shall have the right to move and reside freely within the territory of the Member States, subject to the limitations and conditions laid down in the Treaties and by the measures adopted to give them effect.

Article 21(1) TFEU clarifies that EU citizenship does not produce any new free movement rights *per se*. Rather, citizenship determines who is entitled to the pre-existing rights, which retain all their qualifications and exceptions. This is because the provision makes reference to the limitations and conditions laid down in the Treaties and in secondary legislation. The primary effect of citizenship in the field of free movement, then, is that it raises a presumption of a right of entry or residence for citizens, which would have to be rebutted by the host Member State if it were to refuse or terminate those rights. However, Article 21(1) envisages the existing rights as a basis for further development, as it authorises the adoption of further measures 'to give them effect' (Art 21(1)).

9.1.3 Directive 2004/38

Directive 2004/38 on the rights of citizens of the Union and their family members to move and reside freely within the territory of the Member States, which is also known as the **Citizen's Rights Directive (CRD)** or the **Free Movement Directive (FMD)**, was enacted on 29 April 2004 to consolidate Union legislation in this area. Member States had to transpose the Directive into national law by 30 April 2006. Directive 2004/38 is divided into chapters as follows:

- I – General provisions
- II – Right of exit and entry
- III – Right of residence
- IV – Right of permanent residence
- V – Provisions common to the right of residence and the right of permanent residence
- VI – Restrictions on the right of entry and the right of residence on grounds of public policy, public security or public health
- VII – Final provisions

Detail on the rights contained in this Directive are provided throughout this chapter. However, it is worth noting at this stage that **Article 6** of Directive 2004/38 provides EU citizens and their family members with 'the right of residence on the territory of another Member State for a period of **up to three months without any conditions** or any formalities other than the requirement to hold a valid identity card or passport'. The establishment of the three-month right of residence without any kind of economic requirement was a new development in free movement rights, which contributed to the continuing expansion of Union rights beyond the common market.

9.2 Free movement and EU citizenship

9.2.1 Scope

Objective 2

Scope of EU citizenship

Citizenship is a legal status that determines the rights and duties that are conferred upon an individual within a particular jurisdiction. However, it should also be noted that, as a concept, citizenship is bound up with notions of identity and belonging which can be far more vague, ephemeral or politically sensitive. Therefore, EU citizenship should be understood as a unique innovation that serves both as a means of conferring rights and duties on individuals and as a rhetorical device for eliciting a greater sense of shared community and solidarity between nationals of the Member States.

The legal status of EU citizenship, which was first introduced by the **Treaty of Maastricht** in 1993, is now central to the free movement of persons as it determines who qualifies for free movement rights within the Union. While it is not only EU citizens who can avail themselves of free movement rights under the EU free movement provisions, others can do so only by virtue of their status as a family member of an EU citizen.

As noted above, EU citizenship is established in Article 20(1) TFEU, which then goes on to state that:

> Every person holding the nationality of a Member State shall be a citizen of the Union. Citizenship of the Union shall be additional to and not replace national citizenship.

As it is for Member States to determine who is and is not a citizen of their country, access to EU citizenship is determined at the national level. **Nationality** therefore remains a matter that is internal to the Member States. As the Court of Justice stated in *Uecker and Jacquet* (Joined Cases C-64 and 65/96), EU citizenship 'is not intended to extend the scope *ratione materiae* of the Treaty also to internal situations which have no link with Community law'. EU citizenship can be seen as a means of expressing the principle of non-discrimination between the nationals of different Member States. When an individual has not moved between Member States, nationality is an internal matter that is to be determined by the Member State; **EU citizenship provides no additional protections for persons who have not exercised their free movement rights**. However, when a national of one Member State has moved to another Member State, they should be treated primarily as an EU citizen and should therefore be treated equally to nationals of the host Member State where provided for in the Treaties and relevant secondary legislation.

The first case where the concept of EU citizenship was interpreted by the Court of Justice was *Martinez Sala* v *Freistaat Bayern* (Case C-85/96). Here, the Court determined that Union citizens should not face discrimination on the basis of their nationality in relation to welfare and other benefits, even in a situation where they do not have a right to reside under EU law but are nevertheless permitted to reside by a host Member State. This case illustrates how the introduction of EU citizenship expanded the scope of the Union beyond the strictly economic realm. The concept of EU citizenship, as currently set out in Article 20 TFEU and as interpreted by the Court, thus gave greater *effet utile* (useful effect) to the principle of non-discrimination on grounds of nationality, as currently set out in Article 18 TFEU (see section 9.1.1).

The significance of EU citizenship was expressed by the Court of Justice in *Grzelczyk* v *Centre Public d'Aide Sociale d'ottignies-Louvain-la-Neuve* (Case C-184/99), where it stated that:

> Union citizenship is destined to be the **fundamental status** of nationals of the Member States, enabling those who find themselves in the same situation to enjoy the same treatment in law irrespective of their nationality, subject to such exceptions as are expressly provided for. (para 31)

This suggests that, although EU citizenship is additional to and does not replace national citizenship, the Court anticipates that it will be of increasing importance and will perhaps one day cease to be bound to the exercise of free movement rights. Indeed, while the Court has yet to adopt this as a consistent approach, EU citizenship rights were accorded to an individual who had not exercised their free movement rights in *Ruiz Zambrano* v *Office national de l'emploi* (Case C-34/09, see section 9.3.1 below). The excerpt from *Grzelczyk* can be compared with later rulings, such as in *Minister voor Vreemdelingenzaken en Integratie* v *RNG Eind* (Case C-291/05), where the Court stated more cautiously that Union citizenship 'is **intended** to be the fundamental status of nationals of the Member States'. Thus, while qualification for EU citizenship may ultimately be determined at the national level, the significance of this citizenship status will largely be determined by the Union.

However, Member States do not have complete discretion with regard to national citizenship. For one thing, Member States may be parties to international treaties that enshrine certain principles relating to statelessness (UN Convention relating to the Status of Stateless Persons 1954 and UN Convention on the Reduction of Statelessness 1961) and the right to nationality (including the Universal Declaration of Human Rights (Art 15); International Covenant on Civil and Political Rights (Art 24(3)); UN Convention on the Nationality of Married Women 1957). Moreover, in *Micheletti and Others* (Case C-369/90) the Court of Justice established that 'it is for each Member State, **having due regard to Community [i.e. Union] law**, to lay down the conditions for the acquisition and loss of nationality'. Therefore, in situations where Union law is concerned, nationality may not only be an internal matter. Such a situation arose in the following case:

Rottmann v *Freistaat Bayern* (Case C-135/08)

Facts:
Dr Rottmann was originally an Austrian national who moved to Germany and gained German citizenship through **naturalisation**. In accordance with Austrian law, when he became a German national, he lost his Austrian citizenship. However, during his application for German citizenship Dr Rottmann had failed to disclose that proceedings had been brought against him for serious fraud in Austria, where there was a warrant for his arrest. When the German administration became aware of this, the German courts sought to withdraw his German citizenship on the ground that it had been obtained through deception. As Dr Rottmann was no longer an Austrian citizen, however, the effect of this would also be to withdraw his EU citizenship and to make him stateless. The German Federal Administrative Court referred a question to the Court of Justice for a preliminary ruling regarding whether the withdrawal of Dr Rottmann's German citizenship would be contrary to Union law.

Ruling:
The Court of Justice first referred to the principle established in *Micheletti* (Case C-369/90), adding that 'the fact that a matter falls within the competence of the Member States does not alter the fact that, in situations covered by European Union law, the national rules concerned must have due regard to the latter'. Due to the potential loss of EU citizenship and the rights attached thereto, the Court found that the situation with regard to Dr Rottmann did fall within the ambit of Union law.

The Court then clarified the relationship between national powers and Union law with regard to citizenship as follows:

> 48 The proviso that due regard must be had to European Union law does not compromise the principle of international law ... that the Member States have the power to lay down the conditions for the acquisition and loss of nationality, but rather enshrines the principle that, in respect of citizens of the Union, **the exercise of that power, in so far as it affects the rights conferred**

and protected by the legal order of the Union, as is in particular the case of a decision withdrawing naturalisation such as that at issue in the main proceedings, **is amenable to judicial review carried out in the light of European Union law**.

Provided that the loss of EU citizenship resulted from actions taken by a Member State in pursuit of a legitimate aim and which were proportionate, the Court ruled that Union law would not be infringed. The Court held that it was for the national courts to determine whether the measure was proportionate, but with regard to legitimacy, the Court stated:

> 51 A decision withdrawing naturalisation because of deception corresponds to a reason relating to the public interest. In this regard, it is legitimate for a Member State to wish to protect the special relationship of solidarity and good faith between it and its nationals and also the reciprocity of rights and duties, which form the bedrock of the bond of nationality.

The Court therefore concluded that:

> 59 ... it is not contrary to European Union law, in particular to Article 17 EC [now Art 20 TFEU], for a Member State to withdraw from a citizen of the Union the nationality of that State acquired by naturalisation when that nationality has been obtained by deception, on condition that the decision to withdraw observes the principle of proportionality.

Significance:

This case confirms that Member States have the power to withdraw an individual's EU citizenship as a result of withdrawing their national citizenship, but that such decisions are reviewable by the Court of Justice. Therefore, this power is not absolute. By virtue of the fact that such a decision affects the application of Union rights with regard to the individual concerned, the national court should ensure that such decisions adhere to the principles of Union law, i.e. that they pursue a legitimate aim, are proportionate and do not violate human rights.

The issue of withdrawing EU citizenship as a corollary of withdrawing national citizenship was also considered in the following case. While the above case considered the individual circumstances of Dr Rottmann, the below case concerned the withdrawal of citizenship through the routine application of national legislation.

Tjebbes and Others v *Minister van Buitenlandse Zaken* (Case C-221/17)

Facts:

Under national legislation in the Netherlands, a dual-national adult loses their Dutch citizenship if they live outside of the Union for an uninterrupted period of ten years. The ten-year time period is considered to be interrupted by the issuance of a Dutch passport. This case concerned four persons who had lived outside of the Union for over ten years and whose Dutch passports had expired more than ten years ago. The Minister for Foreign Affairs of the Netherlands refused to consider their applications for a new Dutch national passport on the basis of the national legislation at issue, under which they had lost their citizenship of the Netherlands. As none of them were citizens of another EU Member State, the application of the national legislation also had the effect of withdrawing their Union citizenship.

The individuals appealed the decisions of the Minister before the Raad van State (Dutch Council of State), which referred the case to the Court of Justice. The Raad van State asked whether the national legislation was compatible with EU law, especially Articles 20 and 21 TFEU and the case of **Rottmann**.

Ruling:

The Court of Justice began by establishing that the case did not concern Article 21 TFEU on the free movement of persons as none of the appellants had exercised their right to move between Member States. The Court then referred to its ruling in **Rottmann** to confirm that, although the conditions for acquiring and losing nationality fall within the competence of Member States, they must have **due regard** to EU law in situations where an individual's status under Article 20 TFEU (i.e. their Union citizenship) would be affected.

The Court described the condition for loss of citizenship of ten years of residence outside of the Union as pursuing the legitimate aim of ensuring that 'nationality is the expression of a **genuine link**' between a Member State and its nationals. The Court also argued that the legitimacy of the legislation was further supported by its application only to individuals with dual nationality – as this ensured that there was no risk of statelessness – and who, effectively, no longer possessed a Dutch passport. Furthermore, in line with the principle of proportionality, the national law required both the Minister for Foreign Affairs and the national courts to undertake an individual assessment of the person concerned and any effects on their family during the procedure governing applications for passport renewal.

The Court concluded that Article 20 TFEU does not preclude Member State legislation which provides conditions for the loss of nationality that may also entail the loss of Union citizenship, so long as the competent national authorities are in a position to examine the consequences and, where appropriate, to have the persons concerned recover their nationality. Such examination, when the loss of Union citizenship is at issue, must have due regard to the principle of proportionality and the Charter of Fundamental Rights with regard to the situation of each person concerned and, if relevant, to that of their family members.

Significance:

The Court of Justice confirmed that procedures for the loss of national citizenship, where loss of Union citizenship would occur as a corollary, must be undertaken with due regard to Union law. Provided that the principle of proportionality and the Charter were upheld, the Court did **not** find that the loss of citizenship *ex lege* (by operation of law) for dual citizens who had lived abroad for ten years was contrary to Union law. An individual's Union citizenship is therefore premised on their maintenance of a '**genuine link**' with a Member State.

Reflection: Unravelling *Tjebbes*, unravelling the fundamental status of Union citizenship?

The case of **Tjebbes** illustrates the Court of Justice's careful approach in negotiating the balance between Member State competence to establish conditions for acquiring and losing nationality on the one hand, and the Union interest in protecting the rights of EU citizens on the other. For some, the ruling shows the increasing scope of EU law into matters of nationality, as **Tjebbes** established that legislation affecting EU citizenship must conform with EU principles and the Charter of Fundamental Rights (Boekestein, 2019). Within this application of EU law, however, the Court emphasised private and professional considerations (i.e. the EU rights to build a family and do business across Member States), but neglected the public and political dimensions

> of citizenship (Coutts, 2019). The ruling can therefore be criticised for presenting a narrow, market-oriented vision of EU citizenship that neglects any consideration of the loss of voting rights and political participation stemming from a loss of citizenship.
>
> **Tjebbes** can also be criticised for undermining the fundamental status of EU citizenship by essentially allowing it to be routinely withdrawn for a failure to renew a passport (Kochenov, 2019). This can be viewed as a considerable step beyond **Rottmann**, where loss of citizenship resulted from criminal activity and deceit. Indeed, loss of citizenship is a severe penalty that is not even inflicted on known terrorists (with the notable exception of UK policy). We might question whether the timely renewal of a passport is an appropriate indicator of whether a person has a genuine link to a country or whether they deserve to be stripped of their Union citizenship and all rights attached thereto. The principle of proportionality thus seems to be under considerable strain in **Tjebbes**, as the Court contorts it to protect Member State competence in the area of nationality.
>
> **Tjebbes** can also be viewed as permitting discrimination against dual nationals, who could lose their national and Union citizenship in situations where others would not. This is particularly problematic given that one of the appellants in the **Tjebbes** case acquired dual citizenship automatically, by virtue of Swiss law, upon her marriage to a Swiss man. In this instance, gender discrimination could also be at issue, as a Dutch man marrying a Swiss woman would not automatically acquire Swiss citizenship and would not, therefore, face the same risk of losing their Dutch – and EU – citizenship (de Hart and Mantu, 2017).

▶ See section 9.3.1 for further detail on *Zhu and Chen* (page 345). See also *Ruiz Zambrano* (page 346) which further develops this area of case law in relation to family members

While Member States should have regard for Union law when regulating national citizenship, the Court of Justice held in ***Zhu and Chen*** (Case C-200/02) that one Member State may not restrict the effects of nationality granted by another Member State by imposing additional conditions on the recognition of that nationality for the purpose of limiting the exercise of free movement rights. The case concerned a Chinese national who deliberately travelled to Northern Ireland to give birth to her daughter so that she would have Irish citizenship and would then, as a result, have a right to reside in the UK under Union free movement rights. The Court determined that the EU citizenship rights of the daughter could not be denied on the grounds of either the intentions of the mother or the young age of the daughter.

Scope of free movement rights

Article 3(1) of Directive 2004/38 (the Citizens' Rights Directive) states that:

> This Directive shall apply to all Union citizens who move to or reside in a Member State other than that of which they are a national, and to their family members as defined in point 2 of Article 2 who accompany or join them.

The condition that an EU citizen must have moved to or resided in a Member State other than that of which they are a national was reinforced in ***Morson and Jhanjan v Netherlands*** (Case 35/82). Here, the Court of Justice ruled that a pair of Dutch nationals could not use EU citizenship rights to bring their non-EU parents to the Netherlands; the EU free movement rights did not apply to the Dutch nationals as they had not moved to and were not residing in a Member State of which they were not nationals. Such situations are considered to be purely internal to a Member State.

A similar situation arose in the following case:

McCarthy (Case C-434/09)

Facts:

Ms McCarthy was a British national who was born in the UK and had always lived there. In 2002, she married a Jamaican national who was not eligible for leave to remain in the UK. Subsequently, Ms McCarthy applied for and acquired Irish citizenship based on her ancestry. Her and her non-EU husband then sought leave for him to remain in the UK as the family member of an EU citizen under Directive 2004/38. Successive applications and appeals to secure Mr McCarthy's right of residence in the UK were rejected by the UK courts, until the Supreme Court referred a question to the Court of Justice for a preliminary ruling.

Ruling:

The Court of Justice examined whether Directive 2004/38 could be applied to a citizen who has never exercised their rights to free movement within the Union and who has always resided in the Member State of which they are a national, but who is also the national of another Member State. The Court ruled as follows:

39 … in circumstances such as those of the main proceedings, in so far as the Union citizen concerned has never exercised his right of free movement and has always resided in a Member State of which he is a national, that citizen is not covered by the concept of 'beneficiary' for the purposes of Article 3(1) of Directive 2004/38, so that that directive is not applicable to him.

40 That finding cannot be influenced by the fact that the citizen concerned is also a national of a Member State other than that where he resides.

41 Indeed, the fact that a Union citizen is a national of more than one Member State does not mean that he has made use of his right of freedom of movement.

Significance:

In this case, the Court of Justice clarified that Directive 2004/38 only confers rights on nationals of one Member State who have moved to another, regardless of whether they are citizens of more than one Member State. Such movement is essential for qualifying for EU citizenship rights under Directive 2004/38, but may not be essential under Articles 20 and 21 TFEU, as shown in *Tjebbes* (above) and *Zambrano* (below).

➤ *McCarthy* is considered further in section 9.3.1 in relation to the free movement rights of family members

In addition to EU citizens and their family members, the scope of which is explored in detail in section 9.3 of this chapter, free movement rights are also afforded to the nationals of other countries in the **European Economic Area (EEA)** (i.e. nationals of Iceland, Lichtenstein and Norway) and to Swiss citizens by virtue of a bilateral agreement on the free movement of persons.

➤ See section 1.1.5 on the EEA

Returning citizens (*Surinder Singh* cases)

Under international law, a country must allow their own citizens to enter and reside within their territory. However, a country ordinarily has discretion over whether to afford the same rights to any non-national family members of a citizen. The following case concerned the rights of an EU citizen, who had exercised their free movement rights and then returned to their **home Member State**, to have a non-EU family member reside with him:

> ### R v Immigration Appeal Tribunal and Surinder Singh, ex parte Secretary of State for the Home Department (Case C-370/90)
>
> #### Facts:
> A UK national married an Indian national in the UK. They then moved to Germany where they both worked for two and a half years before returning to the UK. The UK argued that the spouse's right to re-enter the UK derived from national law, not Union law (i.e. that it was an internal situation).
>
> #### Ruling:
> The Court of Justice considered the period of work in another Member State, and stated as follows:
>
> 19 A national of a Member State might be deterred from leaving his country of origin in order to pursue an activity as an employed or self-employed person as envisaged by the Treaty in the territory of another Member State if, on returning to the Member State of which he is a national in order to pursue an activity there as an employed or self-employed person, the conditions of his entry were not at least equivalent to those which he would enjoy under the Treaty or secondary law in the territory of another Member State.
>
> 20 He would in particular be deterred from so doing if his spouse and children were not also permitted to enter and reside in the territory of his Member State of origin under conditions at least equivalent to those granted them by Community [i.e. Union] law in the territory of another Member State.
>
> #### Significance:
> Union law provisions on the free movement of persons (in this case workers) can be relied upon by an individual against the Member State of which they are a national *provided* they have exercised their free movement rights. While this makes sense with regard to the removal of barriers to free movement, it presents the possibility of unequal treatment within a Member State: a Union citizen who is moving from a host Member State back to their home Member State may have rights under Union law that are not provided by domestic law for persons who have not left that Member State or who have returned from a non-EEA state. This difference in treatment against the nationals of a Member State by that Member State is known as reverse discrimination.

The above case was then confirmed in ***Minister voor Vreemdelingenzaken en Integratie* v *RNG Eind*** (Case C-291/05), where it was held that a Dutch national who had lived and worked in the UK for a year and a half, and who had been joined there by his non-EU daughter, was entitled to have his daughter reside with him when he returned to the Netherlands. Additionally, while ***Surinder Singh*** and ***RNG Eind*** established that EU citizens returning to their *home* Member State are entitled to be joined by their family members just the same as when moving to a *host* Member State, it left open the question as to what degree of movement was required to trigger EU citizenship rights. In other words, it was unclear what amounted to the exercise of free movement rights. For example, was it necessary to have been employed in another Member State? Did an individual have to have resided in another Member State for a certain period of time? Such considerations arose in the following joined cases:

> ### O and B v Minister voor Immigratie, Integratie en Asiel (Case C-456/12)
>
> #### Facts:
> O and B were both **non-EU nationals** who sought the right to reside in the Netherlands as family members of their Dutch partners. O was a Nigerian national who had lived with his partner in Spain for two months. His partner had then returned to the Netherlands as she was unable

to find work in Spain, but had regularly visited O, who remained in Spain. B was a Moroccan national who had lived for several years with his partner in the Netherlands. B then moved to Belgium, where his partner resided with him at the weekends. The Dutch court subsequently referred questions to the Court of Justice to establish whether O and B had a right to reside in the Netherlands as family members of their Dutch partners.

Ruling:

The Court reiterated that, as held in **McCarthy**, Directive 2004/38 only confers rights on EU citizens moving to or residing within a Member State of which they are not a national. The Directive therefore cannot confer a derived right of residence on non-EU nationals who are family members of a Union citizen residing in their home Member State, such as O and B. The Court therefore turned to see if such a right could be derived from Article 21(1) TFEU, reiterating the principle established in **Surinder Singh** and **Eind**, that:

> 49 ... The grant, when a Union citizen returns to the Member State of which he is a national, of a derived right of residence to a third-country national who is a family member of that Union citizen and with whom that citizen has resided, seeks to ... [guarantee] that that citizen will be able, in his Member State of origin, to continue the family life which he created or strengthened in the host Member State.

The Court then stated that, even though Directive 2004/38 does not apply to situations where an EU citizen is returning to their home Member State, the conditions for granting a derived right of residence to their family members should be no stricter in such situations than the conditions established by the Directive for situations where an EU citizen is moving to a host Member State. The Court also established that an obstacle to the free movement of persons, such as that which was considered in **Surinder Singh** and **Eind**, can only arise when a returning EU national has created or strengthened their family life in the host Member State. Therefore,

> 61 ... Article 21(1) TFEU must be interpreted as meaning that **where a Union citizen has created or strengthened a family life with a third-country national during genuine residence**... in a Member State other than that of which he is a national, the provisions of that directive [2004/38] apply by analogy where that Union citizen returns, with the family member in question, to his Member State of origin.

Referring to the distinction in Directive 2004/38 between residence for less than three months (Art 6) and residence for longer than three months (Art 7), the Court ruled that periods of residence of less than three months do not constitute 'genuine residence' within a host Member State and therefore do not amount to an exercise of free movement rights from which a right to residence for non-EU family members in the EU citizen's home Member State can be derived.

The Court left it to the national courts to decide whether the partners of O and B had genuinely resided within another Member State in conformity with the conditions set out in Article 7 of Directive 2004/38.

Significance:

While this case reaffirms that Directive 2004/38 is not strictly applicable to EU citizens residing in their home Member State, it also builds on **McCarthy** to clarify that this is so even if they have exercised their free movement rights. However, the Court determined that the Directive should be applied 'by analogy' in such cases in order to avoid obstacles to free movement. The Court thus ruled that:

(i) in order to be considered to have exercised their free movement rights for the purpose of deriving rights for their family members to reside with them in their *home* Member State, an EU citizen must have created or strengthened their life with those family members during a period of **genuine residence** in a *host* Member State; and

(ii) genuine residence is that which conforms with the conditions set out in **Article 7 of Directive 2004/38**, and must therefore include a period of residence of **over three months** in duration.

In *S and G* v *Minister voor Immigratie, Integratie en Asiel* (Case C-457/12), which was decided on the same day as the above case, the Court of Justice ruled that persons living in the Member State of which they were a national and commuting daily to another Member State did not qualify for free movement rights, which would have required their home Member State to permit the residence of their non-EU family members.

UK approach to EU citizenship and returning citizens (pre-Brexit)

After *McCarthy* (above), the UK adopted a restrictive approach to dual citizenship, whereby persons who possessed both British citizenship and the citizenship of another EU Member State could not use the latter to claim EU rights in the UK. This approach was formalized in an amendment to the **Immigration (European Economic Area) Regulations 2006** (EEA Regulations), which defined an EEA national for the purposes of exercising free movement rights, as 'a national of an EEA State who is not also a British citizen'. The UK therefore viewed EU citizenship as irrelevant to British citizens residing on British territory, even if they were also citizens of another Member State **and** had exercised their free movement rights by migrating between Member States.

This position was challenged in the following case:

Lounes (Case C-165/16)

Facts:

Ms García Ormazábal, a Spanish national, moved to the UK, acquired permanent residence and then acquired British citizenship through naturalisation. She then married an Algerian national, Mr Lounes, and they resided together in the UK. Mr Lounes sought a residence card for the UK as a family member of an EU citizen, but the UK authorities rejected this application and issued a decision to deport him on the basis that he had overstayed his visa. The rejection of Mr Lounes' application was based on the EEA Regulations, according to which Ms García Ormazábal's status as a British citizen meant that she was no longer considered to be an EEA national.

Mr Lounes subsequently brought a case before the High Court of Justice of England and Wales against the decision to refuse his application for a residence card. The High Court referred questions to the Court of Justice for a preliminary ruling as to whether Mr Lounes and Ms García Ormazábal were beneficiaries of Directive 2004/38.

Ruling:

The Court of justice followed the Opinion of Advocate General Bot and first determined that Mr Lounes and Ms García Ormazábal are not beneficiaries of Directive 2004/38, as defined by Article 3(1) thereof. The Court stated that:

> 33 ... it follows from a literal, contextual and teleological interpretation of Directive 2004/38 that the directive governs only the conditions determining whether a Union citizen can enter and reside in Member States **other than that of which he is a national** and does not confer a derived right of residence on third-country nationals who are family members of a Union citizen in the Member State of which that citizen is a national.

The Court then considered whether Mr Lounes and Ms García Ormazábal's situation was within the scope of **Article 21(1) TFEU**. The Court approached this question by first establishing the scope of the rights of family members of EU citizens as follows:

> 48 ... a derived right of residence of a third-country national who is a family member of a Union citizen exists, in principle, **only when it is necessary in order to ensure that the Union**

citizen can exercise his freedom of movement effectively. The purpose and justification of a derived right of residence are therefore based on the fact that a refusal to allow such a right would be such as to interfere, in particular, with that freedom and with the exercise and the effectiveness of the rights which Article 21(1) TFEU affords the Union citizen concerned.

The Court then determined that the acquisition of British citizenship did not render Ms García Ormazábal's rights to family life a purely internal matter. Such naturalisation did not negate the fact of her migration from one Member State to another and therefore did not override the EU citizenship rights that she was entitled to as a result of that migration. Thus, the Court held that:

> 53 A national of one Member State who has moved to and resides in another Member State cannot be denied that right [the right to family life] merely because he subsequently acquires the nationality of the second Member State in addition to his nationality of origin, otherwise the effectiveness of Article 21(1) TFEU would be undermined.

The Court pointed out that to hold otherwise would be to discourage the very integration that Article 21(1) TFEU seeks to facilitate, as EU citizens who migrate to another Member State would face the loss of their EU citizenship rights, including the right to family life, if they chose to naturalise. The Court therefore concluded as follows:

> 60 ... if the rights conferred on Union citizens by Article 21(1) TFEU are to be effective, **citizens in a situation such as Ms Ormazabal's must be able to continue to enjoy, in the host Member State, the rights arising under that provision, after they have acquired the nationality of that Member State** in addition to their nationality of origin and, in particular, must be able to build a family life with their third-country-national spouse, by means of the grant of a derived right of residence to that spouse.

Significance:

This case differed from ***McCarthy*** and ***O and B***, where it was found that the individuals had not, or had not sufficiently, exercised their free movement rights. In this case, it was established that the exercise of free movement rights could not be negated by the subsequent acquisition of citizenship of a host Member State. As a result, the definition of an EEA national that is stipulated in the EEA Regulations is not in conformity with Article 21(1) TFEU. This also effectively expands the beneficiaries of EU citizenship rights, including the right to family life, beyond the scope set out in Article 3(1) of Directive 2004/38.

This case resolved a difficult situation facing EU citizens living in the UK prior to Brexit. Such individuals were at risk of losing their EU rights to have their family reside with them if they acquired British citizenship, which they may desire in order to secure their own right to reside in the UK after Brexit. Indeed, the EEA Regulations produced a paradoxical situation whereby acquiring citizenship could mean losing rights. This case, however, determined that the acquisition of citizenship cannot result in the loss of EU free movement rights derived from Article 21 TFEU. While this will continue to apply to other Member States, in the UK context close family members will be able to join EU citizens in the UK until 29 March 2022, and potentially later depending on whether this is provided for in a deal between the UK and the EU (see section 9.7).

With regard to returning citizens, it seems that the UK sought to adopt as restrictive an approach as possible to 'Surinder Singh' cases. Regulation 9 of the **Immigration (European Economic Area) Regulations 2006**, as updated in 2016, set out several factors to be taken into consideration when determining whether a UK citizen's residence in another Member State with their family member(s) was 'genuine'. These factors included, but did not need to be limited to:

(a) whether the centre of the UK citizen's life transferred to the EEA State;

(b) the length of the UK citizen's joint residence with their family in the EEA State;

(c) the nature and quality of their accommodation in the EEA State and whether it is or was the UK citizen's principal residence;

(d) the degree of the UK citizen and their family's integration in the EEA State;

(e) whether the family member's first lawful residence in the EU with the UK citizen was in the EEA State.

These factors went beyond the conditions set out in Article 7 of Directive 2004/38, which the Court of Justice established as a means of determining 'genuine' residence in *O and B*. However, this may have been permissible under Union law as *O and B* only deals with criteria for establishing whether an EU citizen has exercised their free movement rights, not for establishing whether the EU citizen genuinely created or strengthened their family life during such a period of residence. This latter question has yet to be clarified by the Court of Justice.

Additionally, however, guidance published by the UK Home Office on the application of Regulation 9 required an assessment as to whether the purpose of the residence in another Member State was specifically to circumvent UK immigration regulations. The guidance stated that:

> If the motivation behind the joint residence in the EEA host country was for the purpose of bringing the family member to the UK under European Union (EU) law instead of [UK immigration] rules, the applicant will not be eligible to enjoy a right to reside in the UK as the family member of a British citizen under the Immigration (European Economic Area) Regulations 2016 (the 2016 regulations) and the residence card application will be refused.

If an application for the residence of a family member in a *Surinder Singh* case was refused on this ground and a challenge had subsequently been brought before the Court of Justice, it is again unclear whether this condition would have been found to be in breach of free movement rights. On the one hand, it could be argued that a person's rights are not conditional upon their motivation in exercising them. Indeed, the Court of Justice's definition of 'genuine residence' in *O and B* did not include any reference to motivations. On the other hand, it is possible that the use of free movement rights to deliberately circumvent national immigration rules could be defined as an abuse of rights akin to marriages of convenience.

9.2.2 Rights of entry and residence

The rights of EU citizens to enter and reside in any Member State are now provided in Directive 2004/38. References to articles in this section therefore refer to the provisions of this Directive.

Right of exit and entry (Articles 4 and 5)

All EU citizens have the right to leave or enter another Member State by virtue of having a valid identity card or valid passport (Arts 4(1) and 5(1)). Under no circumstances can an entry or exit visa be required (Arts 4(2) and 5(1)). Where an EU citizen does not have the necessary travel documents, the host Member State must afford them every facility to obtain the requisite documents or to have them sent (Art 5(4)).

Article 5(5) provides that the host Member State may require each person travelling to, or residing in, another Member State to register their presence in the country within a reasonable and non-discriminatory period of time. Failure to comply with this requirement may make the person liable to a proportionate and non-discriminatory sanction.

Residence for up to three months (Article 6)

Article 6(1) provides that EU citizens shall have the right to reside in another Member State for a period of up to three months without any conditions or formalities other than the requirement to hold a valid identity card or passport.

Article 14(1) provides that EU citizens and their family members shall have the right of residence under Article 6, 'as long as they do not become an **unreasonable burden** on the social assistance system of the host Member State'. Expulsion shall not be an automatic consequence if an EU citizen or their family members have recourse to the host Member State's social assistance system (Art 14(3)). Article 14(4) further provides that (other than in accordance with the provisions relating to restrictions on the right of entry and residence on grounds of public policy, public security or public health) an expulsion order cannot be issued against an EU citizen or their family members, if:

(i) the EU citizen is a worker or self-employed person in the host Member State; or

(ii) the EU citizen entered the host Member State to seek employment and provided he can supply evidence that he is continuing to seek work and has a genuine chance of being employed.

These conditions are examined in detail in Chapter 10.

Residence for more than three months (Article 7)

The right of residence for more than three months remains subject to certain conditions. Article 7(1) of Directive 2004/38 provides that EU citizens have the right to reside in another Member State, for a period exceeding three months, if they:

> (a) are **workers or self-employed persons** in the host Member State; or
>
> (b) have **sufficient resources** for themselves and their family members not to become a burden on the social assistance system of the host Member State during their period of residence and have comprehensive **sickness insurance** cover in the host Member State; or
>
> (c) —are enrolled at a private or public establishment, accredited or financed by the host Member State on the basis of its legislation or administrative practice, for the principal purpose of **following a course of study**, including vocational training; and
>
> —have comprehensive **sickness insurance** cover in the host Member State and assure the relevant national authority, by means of a declaration or by such equivalent means as they may choose, that they have **sufficient resources** for themselves and their family members not to become a burden on the social assistance system of the host Member State during their period of residence; or
>
> (d) are **family members** accompanying or joining a Union citizen who satisfies the conditions referred to in points (a), (b) or (c).

In relation to Article 7(1)(a), Article 7(3) sets out the conditions under which an EU citizen shall retain their status as a worker or self-employed person in a host Member State. These conditions and the corresponding case law are discussed in Chapter 10.

> Article 8(4) elaborates on the term 'sufficient resources' that is used in Article 7(1)(b) as follows:

> Member States **may not lay down a fixed amount** which they regard as 'sufficient resources' but they **must take into account the personal situation** of the person concerned. In all cases this amount shall not be higher than the threshold below which nationals of the host Member State become eligible for social assistance, or, where this criterion is not applicable, higher than the minimum social security pension paid by the host Member State.

▶ *Zhu and Chen* and *Kuldip Singh* are examined further in sections. 9.3.1 (page 345) and 9.3.3 (page 356) respectively. Article 7(1)(b) is considered further in section 9.3.

In *Zhu and Chen* (Case C-200/02), the Court of Justice established that the origin of the resources by which an EU citizen residing in a host Member State could support themselves was irrelevant. Therefore, it was not necessary for an EU citizen to have 'sufficient resources' of their own; it was acceptable for such resources to be provided by a non-EU family member. The Court confirmed this in *Kuldip Singh* (Case C-218/14), where it stated that to uphold such a condition on the origin of an EU citizen's access to sufficient resources would constitute a disproportionate interference with the free movement rights enshrined in Article 21 TFEU.

In the following case, the definition of comprehensive sickness insurance, which is now required under Article 7(1)(b), was at issue:

▶ See section 3.3.1 on the principle of proportionality. *Baumbast and R* is also considered in relation to the rights of family members of EU workers (page 424)

Baumbast and R v Secretary of State for the Home Department (Case C-413/99)

Facts:

Mr Baumbast was a German national who married a Colombian national in the UK. He was economically active in the UK, where he, his wife and their two daughters resided, but then was unable to find work in the UK and subsequently took up work for German companies in non-EU countries. When the family applied to renew their UK residence permits, Mr Baumbast's application was refused on the ground that he had ceased to hold the status of a worker and therefore had no right of residence in the UK.

Ruling:

As under the current Article 7(1) of Directive 2004/38, Article 1(1) of Directive 90/364 (now repealed) provided that Member States may require persons seeking to exercise their general right of residence (as specified in Art 18(1) EC Treaty at the time, now Art 21(1) TFEU) to have sufficient resources and comprehensive sickness insurance. The Court ruled that 'those limitations and conditions must be applied in compliance with the general principles of Community [i.e. Union] law and, in particular, the **principle of proportionality**' (para 94).

It was agreed that Mr Baumbast had sufficient resources to avoid himself or his family members becoming a burden on the social assistance system of the host Member State, from which he had never claimed benefits. The family also had comprehensive sickness insurance in Germany and travelled there for healthcare. However, the insurance would not have covered any emergency medical treatment that may have been required in the UK.

The Court considered that Mr Baumbast had strong ties with the UK and that neither he nor his family had ever been a burden on the public finances of the country. The Court therefore held that:

> 9 Under those circumstances, to refuse to allow Mr Baumbast to exercise the right of residence which is conferred on him by Article 18(1) EC [now Art 21(1) TFEU] by virtue of the application of the provisions of Directive 90/364 [now in Directive 2004/38] on the ground that his sickness insurance does not cover the emergency treatment given in the host Member State would amount to a disproportionate interference with the exercise of that right.
>
> **Significance:**
>
> In this case, the Court applied the principle of proportionality to allow a degree of flexibility in the application of the right to reside conditions, suggesting that the strength of a person's ties to the country and the extent of their failure to meet the conditions should be taken into account. It also made it clear that the right of residence is a fundamental right, the exercise (but not existence) of which can be limited.

The requirement for self-sufficient EU citizens and EU students to have comprehensive sickness insurance was ruled in the UK **not** to include access to the NHS, to which all EEA nationals are entitled. Therefore, in order to meet the criteria of Article 7(1)(b) or 7(1)(c), EU citizens residing in the UK needed either to have private medical insurance or to be able to demonstrate that there were reciprocal arrangements in place between the UK and their home Member State and that they fell within the scope of such arrangements (*Ahmad* v *Secretary of State for the Home Department* [2014] EWCA Civ 988). Reciprocal arrangements enable a host Member State to reclaim the cost of medical care provided to an EU citizen and their family members from the EU citizen's home Member State. On 27 March 2017, the UK Home Office clarified that self-sufficient EU citizens and students without comprehensive health insurance are not residing legally, but that the Home Office does not generally seek the removal of such persons (answer to written question HL5917). However, there have been reports of applications for permanent residence being denied as periods of study or economic inactivity without such insurance have not been counted as periods of legal residence. (This is not a problem for EU citizens applying to remain in the UK after Brexit, as comprehensive sickness insurance is not a requirement for the EU Settlement Scheme – see section 9.7.)

Although residence permits are abolished for EU citizens, Article 8(1) and 8(2) provide that Member States may require EU citizens to register with the competent authorities within a period of not more than three months from their date of arrival. A registration certificate will be issued immediately (Art 8(2)). For the registration certificate to be issued, Article 8(3) provides that Member States may only require the following documentation:

(a) for EU citizens residing under Article 7(1)(a) (i.e. a workers and self-employed persons): a valid identity card or passport and confirmation of engagement from the employer or a certificate of employment, or proof of their self-employed status;

(b) for EU citizens residing under Article 7(1)(b) (i.e. citizens with sufficient resources and comprehensive sickness insurance): a valid identity card or passport, proof of comprehensive sickness insurance and proof that they have sufficient resources for themselves and their family members not to become a burden on the social assistance system of the host Member State;

(c) for EU citizens residing under Article 7(1)(c) (i.e. a student): a valid identity card or passport, proof of enrolment at an accredited institution, proof of comprehensive sickness insurance and a declaration (or equivalent) that they have sufficient resources for themselves and their family members not to become a burden on the social assistance system of the host Member State.

Right of permanent residence (Article 16)

EU citizens acquire the right of permanent residence in the host Member State after a five-year period of continuous legal residence (Art 16(1), Directive 2004/38), provided that an expulsion decision has not been enforced against them (Art 21). This right of permanent residence is no longer subject to any conditions. The same rule applies to non-EU family members who have lived with an EU citizen in the host Member State for five years (Art 16(2)), again provided that an expulsion decision has not been enforced against them (Art 21). Although the automatic right to permanent residence was introduced by Directive 2004/38, for which the deadline for transposition into national law was April 2006, periods of continuous residence undertaken prior to that date may meet or contribute towards the five year requirement (*Lassal* (Case C-162/09)). In the UK, the right to permanent residence is provided for by the European Union Settlement Scheme – see section 9.7).

Article 16(3) provides that continuity of residence shall not be affected by:

(i) temporary absences not exceeding six months a year;

(ii) absences of a longer period for compulsory military service; or

(iii) one absence of up to 12 months for important reasons (e.g. pregnancy and childbirth, serious illness, study or vocational training, or a posting in another Member State or a non-EU country).

EU citizens entitled to permanent residence will be issued with a document certifying such residency (Art 19(1)). Article 21 provides that continuity of residence may be attested by any means of proof in use in the Member State.

The following case considered how terms of imprisonment affect the duration and continuity of residence for the purpose of acquiring the right to permanent residence:

Onuekwere v Secretary of State for the Home Department (Case C-378/12)

Facts:

By his marriage to an Irish citizen who had exercised her rights to freedom of movement and residence in the UK, Onuekwere, a Nigerian national, obtained a residence permit valid for five years in that Member State. During that time, Onuekwere was sentenced on several occasions by the UK courts for various offences and was imprisoned for a total period of three years and three months.

Onuekwere unsuccessfully requested a permanent residence card, claiming that the total duration of his residence in the UK (including periods in prison) far exceeded the duration of five years required for the grant of that right. Moreover, he pointed out that even if the periods spent in prison were not counted for that purpose, the sum of the periods not including the stays in prison was greater than five years. Onuekwere challenged the dismissal of his request before the Upper Tribunal (Immigration and Asylum Chamber), which then referred the matter to the Court of Justice.

Ruling:

The Court of Justice stated first that a non-EU national, who was a family member of a Union citizen who had exercised his right of free movement and residence, could only **count the periods he had spent with that citizen** for the purposes of the acquiring a right of permanent residence. As a consequence, the periods during which he had not resided with that citizen because of his imprisonment in the host Member State could not be taken into account for that purpose. Furthermore, the Court stated that the EU legislature made acquiring the right of permanent residence subject to the **integration** of the person concerned within the host Member State. Such integration was based not only on territorial and temporal factors but also on qualitative elements. In that regard, the Court stated that the imposition of a prison sentence by the national court demonstrated their non-compliance with the values expressed by the host Member State in its criminal law. Accordingly, taking periods of imprisonment into consideration for the purposes of the acquiring the right of permanent residence would be contrary to the aims pursued by Directive 2004/38 in establishing that right of residence.

For the same reasons, the Court held that **periods of imprisonment interrupted the continuity of residence** in a host Member State. As a consequence, the periods which preceded and followed the periods of imprisonment could not be combined to reach the minimum period of five years required for the acquisition of a permanent residence permit.

Significance:

In this case, the Court of Justice established that, for the purpose of acquiring a permanent residence card, the required five years of residence must be continuous and, where a family member is concerned, must be with the EU citizen from which their right of residence is derived. Therefore, periods of time spent in prison firstly do not count towards the five-year requirement and secondly interrupt the continuity of a period of residence.

While the above case concerned a family member, whose rights to reside were derived from their family life with an EU citizen, it was held in *Secretary of State for the Home Department* v *G* (Case C-400/12) that periods of imprisonment also do not count as periods of residence and have the effect of interrupting periods of residence for EU citizens. As family life, which imprisonment disrupts, is not a factor in the calculation of an EU citizen's right to reside, the rationale here is instead based on the question of integration. A person who has been convicted of violating the national laws of the Member State sufficiently to warrant a prison sentence cannot be said to have successfully integrated within that country. Therefore, it would be contrary to the purpose of stipulating a specific duration of residence in Directive 2004/38 if periods of imprisonment were to be included.

▶ *G* (Case C-400/12) is considered further in section 9.4.2 (page 360)

Once granted, the right of permanent residence is lost only in the event of more than two consecutive years' absence from the host Member State (Arts 16(4) and 20(3)), or if an expulsion order is made on grounds of public policy, public security or public health (see section 9.4).

Article 17 recognises the right of permanent residence for EU citizens who are workers or self-employed persons and for their family members, before the five-year period of continuous residence has expired, subject to certain conditions being met. Article 17 applies to cases where the EU citizen:

(i) has reached retirement age;
(ii) has become permanently incapable of working; or
(iii) lives in the host Member State but works in another Member State.

Common provisions on the right of residence and right of permanent residence

Article 22 of Directive 2004/38 provides that the right of residence and right of permanent residence shall cover the whole territory of the host Member State. Territorial restrictions can only be imposed if the same restrictions apply to nationals of the host Member State.

Article 25(1) provides that under no circumstances can possession of a registration certificate etc., be made a precondition for the exercise of a right or the completion of an administrative formality. Entitlement to rights may be attested by any other means of proof, where such documentation is not available. **Article 25(2)** further provides that all the documents listed in Article 25(1) shall be issued free of charge or for a charge which does not exceed that imposed on nationals for the issuing of a similar document.

Under **Article 26**, if a Member State requires their own nationals to carry an identity card, then the host Member State can require non-nationals to carry their registration certificate or residence card. The host Member State may impose the same sanction as those imposed on their own nationals if a non-national fails to comply.

9.3 Free movement rights of family members of EU citizens

Objective 3

The free movement rights of the family members of an EU citizen can be determined by:

(i)   Their relationship to the EU citizen from which their free movement rights are derived;
(ii) The status of the EU citizen from which their rights are derived;
(iii) Whether they are EU citizens or non-EU nationals.

The rights of family members are described as 'derived' rights as they exist only by virtue of the rights of an EU citizen to whom they are related. Thus an EU citizen may be described as having a 'primary' right of residence in a host Member State, upon which the rights of their family members in that Member State depend. While the rights afforded to family members are generally perceived as generous, they do not exist independently of the relationship with the EU citizen (unless they have attained the right to permanent residence). This means that if the relationship is terminated and an individual ceases to be classified as a family member of an EU citizen, they will lose all associated free movement rights. However, there are certain circumstances, which are explored below, under which the derived rights of family members can become their own individual rights.

As with EU citizens, the rights of their family members are now provided in Directive 2004/38. References to articles in this section therefore refer to the provisions of this Directive, unless otherwise stated.

9.3.1 Scope

In relation to the EU citizen, **Article 2(2)** of Directive 2004/38 defines 'family members' as:

(a) the **spouse**;
(b) the **partner** with whom the Union citizen has contracted a registered partnership, on the basis of the legislation of a Member State, if the legislation of the host Member State treats registered partnerships as equivalent to marriage and in accordance with the conditions laid down in the relevant legislation of the host Member State;
(c) the **direct descendants** who are under the age of 21 or are dependants and those of the spouse or partner as defined in point (b);
(d) the dependent **direct relatives in the ascending line** and those of the spouse or partner as defined in point (b).

This definition of 'family members' (which includes non-EU nationals) is broader than the definition formerly set out in Article 10 of Regulation 492/2011. In **Coman and Others v Inspectoratul General pentru Imigrări** (C-673/16), the Court of Justice clarified that free movement rights afforded to the spouse of an EU national must be afforded to someone who has married an EU national of the same sex in accordance with the law of a Member State, even if the EU national's home Member State does not recognise same-sex marriage. In addition to the family members listed in Article 2(2), **Article 3(2)** provides that the host Member State shall, in accordance with its national legislation, 'facilitate' entry and residence for the following persons:

> (a) any other family members, irrespective of their nationality, not falling under the definition in point 2 of Article 2 who, in the country from which they have come, are dependants or members of the household of the Union citizen having the primary right of residence, or where serious health grounds strictly require the personal care of the family member by the Union citizen;
>
> (b) the partner with whom the Union citizen has a durable relationship, duly attested.

Article 3(2) continues: 'The host Member State shall undertake an extensive examination of the personal circumstances and shall justify any denial of entry or residence to these people.' In **SM v Entry Clearance Officer** (Case C-129/18) the Court of Justice determined that a *kafala* relationship between a child and a guardian under Islamic family law does not amount to a 'family' relationship for the purposes of Article 2(2), but could amount to an 'other' family relationship for the purposes of Article 3(2)(a).

In the case of students, there is a limitation on the family members who may accompany or join them. **Article 7(4)** provides that only the spouse/registered partner and dependent children shall have the right of residence as family members of the student. Dependent direct relatives in the ascending lines, and those of his spouse/registered partner, shall have their entry and residence facilitated (in accordance with Art 3(2), see above).

Family members dependent on EU citizens

In **Centre Public d'Aide Sociale de Courcelles v Lebon** (Case 316/85), the Court of Justice held that a 'dependant' is a family member who receives support from an EU citizen; it is not necessary to consider the reasons why they have recourse to that support nor whether they might be able to find work and support themselves. A dependant may be in receipt of financial or non-financial support.

The question of how to define a situation of dependence arose in the following case, which concerned a dependent relative in the ascending line:

> #### *Jia* v *Migrationsverket* (Case C-1/05)
>
> **Facts:**
> Mr Shenzhi Li was a Chinese national who resided with his wife, a self-employed German national, in Sweden. Mr Shenzhi Li's mother, Ms Jia, was also a Chinese national. She entered Sweden on a visitor's visa and then applied for a residence permit on the basis that she was a dependent family member of an EU citizen who was exercising their free movement rights. To support her application, Ms Jia produced a certificate of relationship to Mr Shenzhi Li from the

Beijing Notary Public Office and a certificate from her former employer, China Forestry Publishing House, stating that she is financially dependent on her son and daughter-in-law. Her application was refused on the ground that there was insufficient proof that she was financially dependent on her son and daughter-in-law. Ms Jia appealed to the Utläningsnänden (Alien Appeals Board), which then referred a question to the Court of Justice as to the meaning of 'dependence' in Article 1(1)(d) of Directive 73/148 (now Art 2(2)(d), Directive 2004/38).

Ruling:

The Court ruled that, for the purposes of the former Article 1(1)(d) of Directive 73/148 (now Art 2(2), Directive 2004/38), a dependant is not merely someone who an EU citizen or their spouse undertakes to support; instead, a **real situation of dependence** should be established. Such a situation exists where family members 'need the material support of that Community [i.e. Union] national or his or her spouse in order to meet their essential needs in the State of origin of those family members or the State from which they have come at the time when they apply to join the Community [i.e. Union] national'. Proof of such need of material support may be adduced '**by any appropriate means**'.

Significance:

This case established that a dependant is a family member who relies on the material support of an EU citizen or their spouse in order to meet their essential needs in the country where they reside. Although it concerned Union legislation that has since been replaced by Directive 2004/38, this definition continues to apply.

In *Ymerga* v *Ministre du Travail, de l'Emploi et de l'Immigration* (Case C-87/12), the Court confirmed that there is no such right to have non-EU parents reside with an adult EU citizen when there is no established situation of dependence.

The following case concerned the right of residence of a dependant over the age of 21:

Reyes v *Migrationsverket* (Case C-423/12)

Facts:

Ms Reyes was a national of the Philippines who was denied permission to reside in Sweden with her mother, who had obtained German citizenship, and her Norwegian stepfather. Ms Reyes's mother and stepfather had regularly sent money to support her in the Philippines. However, the Swedish Court argued that, as Ms Reyes was young (but over the age of 21), well-educated and still had family members within the Philippines, she had not proved that she was necessarily dependent upon her mother and stepfather. The national court asked the Court of Justice to determine whether a Member State may require a person claiming to be dependent to demonstrate that they are not able to support themselves or be supported within their country of origin.

Furthermore, as Ms Reyes expressed an intention to work in Sweden, the situation of dependence upon which her residence would be based would cease to exist upon her employment. The national court asked the Court of Justice what the significance of such a situation might be with regards to the interpretation of the term 'dependent' in Article 2(2)(c) of Directive 2004/38.

Ruling:

The Court ruled that the regular transfer of money over a significant period of time, which was necessary for the descendant to sustain herself, was sufficient to establish a 'real situation of dependence'. **A descendant may not be required to demonstrate that they have tried but been unable to support themselves in their country of origin**, as such a requirement would be excessively difficult to meet in practice. Additionally, the Court ruled that:

> Article 2(2)(c) of Directive 2004/38 must be interpreted as meaning that the fact that a relative – due to personal circumstances such as age, education and health – is deemed to be well placed to obtain employment and in addition intends to start work in the Member State **does not** affect the interpretation of the requirement in that provision that he be a 'dependant'.
>
> The Court argued that it would be illogical to deny residence to a dependent on the grounds that they are likely to find work within the Member State, as this would infringe Article 23 of Directive 2004/38, which asserts the right to work of a family member who has a right of residence.
>
> **Significance:**
>
> For a person to be classified as dependent upon a Union citizen they need only demonstrate a **real situation of dependence** at the time of their application and they do not need to demonstrate that they have been unable to support themselves.

EU citizens dependent on non-EU family members

In the following case, the usual situation of dependence was reversed. The case considered whether free movement rights extended to a child who was an EU citizen in need of the care of their non-EU parent:

> ### Zhu and Chen (Case C-200/02)
>
> **Facts:**
>
> Mr and Mrs Chen were Chinese nationals and parents of a child born in China. They wanted to have a second child but came up against China's 'one child policy', which imposed financial penalties on couples who gave birth to more than one child. They therefore decided that their second child would be born in Northern Ireland. Although Northern Ireland is part of the UK, the law of Ireland (which is not part of the UK) granted Irish citizenship to persons born in Northern Ireland. The child therefore acquired Irish nationality. However, because she did not meet the requirements laid down by the relevant UK legislation, she did not acquire UK nationality. After the birth, Mrs Chen moved to Wales with her child and applied for a long-term residence permit for herself and her child, which was refused. Mrs Chen appealed and the appellate authority referred a question to the Court of Justice on the lawfulness of that refusal, pointing out that the mother and child were self-sufficient and had comprehensive health insurance.
>
> **Ruling:**
>
> The Court first stated that the enjoyment of free movement rights could not be made conditional on the attainment of a minimum age. Therefore, as a national of a Member State, and thus an EU citizen, the child could rely on the right of residence laid down by the former Article 18 EC Treaty (now Art 21 TFEU). However, this was subject to the limitations and conditions imposed, in particular, by Article 1(1) of Directive 90/364 (which has since been replaced by Directive 2004/38), which allows Member States to require that the persons concerned have sickness insurance and sufficient resources. As the child had sickness insurance and sufficient resources, the former Article 1(1) of Directive 90/364 was satisfied. The fact that the sufficient resources of the child were provided by her mother and she had none herself was immaterial; a requirement as to the origin of the resources could not be added to the requirement of sufficient resources. Similarly, conditions relating to the way in which the nationality of another Member State was acquired cannot be placed on the exercise of fundamental freedoms provided for in the Treaties.
>
> With regard to the mother's right of residence, the Court noted that the former Directive 90/364 (now Directive 2004/38) recognises a right of residence for 'dependent' relatives in the ascending line of the holder of the right of residence, which assumed that material support for

the family member was provided by the holder of the right of residence. In the present case, the Court stated the position was exactly the opposite. Mrs Chen could not thus be regarded as a 'dependent' relative of her child in the ascending line. However, **where a child was granted a right of residence by the former Article 18 EC Treaty (now Art 21 TFEU) and the former Directive 90/364 (now Directive 2004/38), the parent who was the carer of the child could not be refused the right to reside with the child in the host Member State, as otherwise the child's right of residence would be deprived of any useful effect.**

Significance:

This case established that, in addition to being accompanied or joined by family members who depend on them, EU citizens with a right to reside in a host Member State can also have the right to be accompanied by non-EU family members on whom *they* depend. This is so in the case of a child who would not be able to exercise their free movement rights without being accompanied by a parent.

The right of a non-EU parent to reside with their child who is an EU citizen, so that the child can benefit from the free movement rights conferred on them by their citizenship, was confirmed by the Court in *Secretary of State for the Home Department* v *NA* (Case C-115/15). However, the Court of Justice went one step further in the following case, where it decoupled the rights of child citizens to be accompanied by a parent from the exercise of free movement rights:

Ruiz Zambrano v *Office National de l'Emploi* (Case C-34/09)

Facts:

Mr Ruiz Zambrano, his wife and their first child were Colombian nationals who were refused asylum in Belgium but were protected from return to Colombia on **non-refoulement** grounds (i.e. to return them would have been to place them in danger). They remained in Belgium and were repeatedly refused the rights of residence and employment. They had two more children who were Belgian nationals. Questions were subsequently referred to the Court of Justice as to whether Mr and Mrs Ruiz Zambrano could derive a right of residence from their Belgian national children, even though the children had never exercised their rights to free movement.

Ruling:

The Court began by stating that Directive 2004/38 does not apply to Mr Ruiz Zambrano and his family as the EU national children had not exercised their free movement rights as required by the definition of 'beneficiaries' provided in Article 3(1). The Court then considered established case law wherein it is stated that 'citizenship of the Union is intended to be the fundamental status of nationals of the Member States' and referred to **Rottmann** (see above), where it was held that national measures should not have the effect of depriving EU citizens of the enjoyment of their citizenship rights. The Court stated that the EU national children would be deprived of the enjoyment of their citizenship rights if their parents were unable to reside with them, as the children's dependence on their parents would mean that they would have to leave the territory of the Union with them. The same would be true if Mr Zambrano was refused a work permit, as this risks the family being unable to provide for itself, leading to the same result of them all having to leave the territory of the Union. The Court therefore concluded that:

> 45 ... Article 20 TFEU is to be interpreted as meaning that it precludes a Member State from refusing a third country national upon whom his minor children, who are European Union citizens, are dependent, a right of residence in the Member State of residence and nationality of those children, and from refusing to grant a work permit to that third country national, in so far as such decisions deprive those children of the genuine enjoyment of the substance of the rights attaching to the status of European Union citizen.

> **Significance:**
>
> This case confirmed the principle established in ***Zhu and Chen*** (above) that EU citizens with a right to reside in a host Member State can also have the right to be accompanied by non-EU family members on whom they depend. However, it extended the application of this principle to dependent EU citizens who have not exercised their free movement rights. This is controversial, as the rights of the family members of citizens who have not exercised their free movement rights had previously been considered an internal matter for the Member State in question. However, this judgment establishes that **the rights of non-EU nationals to reside within a Member State can be protected by Article 20 TFEU where the refusal of that right would have the effect of forcing an EU citizen to leave the territory of the Union.** This is known as the ***Zambrano*** principle.

The limits of the ***Zambrano*** principle were articulated in the subsequent case law. The Court first considered this principle in ***McCarthy*** (Case C-434/09, see section 9.2.1), which concerned the rights of a woman with dual EU nationality to have her husband live with her in the Member State in which she had always resided. The Court decided that the refusal to grant her husband the right to reside in her home Member State did not have the effect of obliging her to leave the territory of the Union.

The case of ***Dereci and Others*** v ***Bundesministerium für Inneres*** (Case C-256/11) then concerned several non-EU persons seeking to obtain a right to reside in the Member State of which their family member was a national. Here, the Court of Justice stated that a non-EU national has **no** right to reside with an EU citizen in the Member State of which they are a national and where that EU citizen has never exercised their free movement rights, **unless** the refusal of residence would deprive the EU citizen of 'the genuine enjoyment of the substance of the rights conferred by virtue of his status as a citizen of the Union'. As in ***Zambrano***, an EU citizen is found to be unable to enjoy their rights if they have no option but to leave the territory of the Union. The Court then elucidated that:

> The mere fact that it might appear desirable to a national of a Member State, for economic reasons or in order to keep his family together in the territory of the Union, for the members of his family who do not have the nationality of a Member State to be able to reside with him in the territory of the Union, is **not** sufficient in itself to support the view that the Union citizen will be forced to leave Union territory if such a right is not granted.

Therefore, it seems that when an EU citizen has not exercised their free movement rights, their family members only have a right of residence if the EU citizen depends on them. Similarly, in ***Iida*** v ***Stadt Ulm*** (Case C-40/11), a non-EU father was not found to have a right to reside in Germany where he worked and spent time with his daughter, who had German nationality but lived in Austria. Here, there was no situation of dependence and the denial of a right of residence to the father was held not to affect the substance of the daughter's rights as an EU citizen.

In ***Alokpa, Moudoulou and Moudoulou*** v ***Ministre du Travail, de l'Emploi et de l'Immigration*** (Case C-86/12), the dependence of two infant EU citizens on their non-EU mother, Ms Alokpa, was agreed. However, as the children were French nationals, but their mother was seeking to stay with them in Luxembourg, the Court suggested that refusing the mother a right to reside in Luxembourg would not affect the substance of the rights of the children as Union citizens by compelling them to leave the territory of the Union, as they would all have a right to reside in France. This case therefore differed from ***Zambrano*** as Ms Alokpa's children did not live in the Member State of which they were nationals and from ***Zhu and***

> ▶ *Iida* is also considered in section 9.3.3 in relation to situations of divorce (page 355)

Chen, provided that the national court determined that the children did not have sufficient resources to support themselves, including through Ms Alokpa.

Then, in both *Rendón Marín* v *Administración del Estado* (Case C165-14) and *Secretary of State for the Home Department* v *CS* (Case C-304/14), the *Zambrano* **principle** was considered in relation to a non-EU parent who had been convicted of a criminal offence, but who was also the sole carer of a young child with EU citizenship. Here, the Court determined that the existence of a criminal record could not automatically entail the refusal of a residence permit or the issuance of an expulsion order where such measures would have the effect of depriving an EU citizen of the genuine enjoyment of the substance of their citizenship rights. Instead, the national court should undertake a specific assessment of all the relevant circumstances, including the interests of the child and the interests of society, in the context of the principle of **proportionality**. The fact that the children in these cases had never exercised their right to free movement was not at issue.

The Court further elaborated on the *Zambrano* principle in *Chavez-Vilchez and Others* (Case C-133/15). In this case, the Court considered a situation where a child with EU citizenship was primarily cared for by their non-EU parent, but where their other parent was an EU citizen and was willing and able to assume responsibility as a primary carer of the child. The Court ruled that willingness and ability of the EU parent to care for the child did not necessarily mean that the child would not be compelled to leave the territory of the Union with their non-EU parent if the latter were expelled. The extent to which the child had a relationship of dependency with the non-EU parent should be assessed individually and should include an assessment of the child's age, development and emotional ties with both their non-EU and their EU parent.

> ### Reflection: Just how broad is the *Zambrano* principle?
>
> The *Zambrano* **principle** establishes that a right of residence for a non-EU family member can be derived from the rights of an EU citizen, if to deny such a right would have the effect of forcing the EU citizen to leave the territory of the Union. So far, the Court of Justice has only found this principle to apply to EU citizens who are children and who are dependent on their non-EU parents. However, it is conceivable that the principle could also be applied to EU parents who are physically dependent on their non-EU children, or other EU citizens with disabilities who are dependent on a non-EU family member. In such a case, it is likely that the nature of the dependence would have to be assessed in order to determine whether alternative care arrangements might be reasonable. Not all relationships of care are analogous to the relationship of dependence between a young child and their primary carer – indeed, this issue of dependence is a likely explanation for why the *Zambrano* principle was not applied to a marital relationship in *McCarthy* (see section 9.2.1). However, in instances of dementia or autism, for example, it seems possible that the emotional ties and relationships of dependence could be sufficient to mean that the refusal of a residence permit for a non-EU carer could have the effect of forcing an EU citizen to leave the territory of the Union. Indeed, such a departure could have a more substantial effect on a person with disabilities than on non-disabled children due to the greater ability of young children to adapt to new surroundings. If the *Zambrano* principle can be extended to persons with disabilities and their carers, it might then be asked whether such a carer needs to be a family member. Indeed, in *O and S*, the Court determined that the *Zambrano* principle relies on a relationship of financial, legal or emotional dependence and not necessarily a blood relationship. The question therefore remains as to what extent the *Zambrano* principle can be extended to protect the rights of any non-EU national on whom an EU citizen genuinely depends and whom the EU citizen would, as a result of that dependence, be forced to accompany if they were to be expelled.

9.3.2 Rights of entry and residence

This section considers the rights of entry and residence of family members of EU citizens provided for in **Directive 2004/38**. References to articles in this section therefore refer to the provisions of this Directive. Further provisions pertaining specifically to the family members of workers are provided in **Regulation 492/2011** on freedom of movement for workers within the Union, which is discussed in the next chapter.

Right of entry

▶ See Figure 9.1 on page 353 for a summary of the differences between the rights afforded to EU and non-EU family members

For the most part, the rights of family members do not depend on whether they are EU citizens or not. However, some additional requirements may be placed on non-EU nationals seeking to enter a Member State. While 'No entry visa or equivalent formality may be imposed on Union citizens' (Art 5(1)), **Article 5(2) of Directive 2004/38** states that family members who do not have the nationality of a Member State (i.e. non-EU family members) may be subject to an entry visa requirement under **Regulation 539/2001**; residence cards will be deemed equivalent to visas (Art 5(2)) (see *Sean Ambrose McCarthy and Others* v *Secretary of State for the Home Department* (Case C-202/13)). Article 5(2) also requires that 'Member States shall grant such persons every facility to obtain the necessary visas. Such visas shall be issued free of charge as soon as possible and on the basis of an accelerated procedure.'

Residence for up to three months (Article 6)

While Article 6(1) of the Directive provides an unconditional right of residence for up to three months for EU citizens, Article 6(2) specifies that this right also applies to non-EU family members who accompany or join an EU citizen. Therefore, the right of family members of an EU citizen to reside within a Member State for up to three months does not depend on either the nationality of the family member or the status of the EU citizen.

Residence for over three months (Article 7)

To reside in a Member State for longer than three months, an EU citizen must meet one of the conditions set out in Article 7(1) of Directive 2004/38 (see section 9.2.2 above). When such a condition is met, the right of residence is extended to family members accompanying or joining them (Art 7(1)(d)). Article 7(2) specifies that this right of residence also applies to non-EU family members.

Under **Article 8**, host Member States may require EU citizens and their family members to register with the relevant authorities. Article 8(5) provides that registration certificates will be issued to family members who are nationals of a Member State, subject to the production of specified documentation.

Article 9 applies to family members who are **not** nationals of a Member State. Such family members must apply for a residence card not more than three months from their date of arrival (Art 9(2)). A residence card is valid for at least five years from its date of issue, or for the envisaged period of residence of the EU citizen if this is less than five years (Art 11(1)). Article 10(2) sets out the documentation required before a residence card will be issued. This provision also applies to other non-EU family members whose entry and residence to the host Member State shall be facilitated in accordance with Article 3(2). Article 11(2) provides that the validity of a residence card shall not be affected by:

(i) temporary absences of up to six months to a year;

(ii) absences of a longer period for compulsory military service; or

(iii) one absence of up to 12 months for important reasons (e.g. pregnancy and childbirth, serious illness, study or vocational training, or a posting in another Member State or a third country (i.e. non-EU country)).

In the following case, the Court of Justice considered whether Irish legislation on the residence of family members was contrary to Directive 2004/38:

Metock and Others v Minister for Justice, Equality and Law Reform (Case C-127/08)

Facts:

The Irish legislation transposing Directive 2004/38 provided that a non-EU family member of an EU citizen could only reside with or join that citizen in Ireland if they were already lawfully resident in another Member State. This requirement was laid down by the Court of Justice in *Akrich* (Case C-109/01) in 2003. The question of the compatibility of the Irish legislation with the Directive was raised in four cases pending before the High Court of Ireland. In each of those cases, a non-EU national arrived in Ireland and applied for asylum. In each case the application was refused. While resident in Ireland, those four persons married EU citizens who did not have Irish nationality but were resident in Ireland. The marriages were all genuine (i.e. not marriages of convenience).

After the marriage, each of the non-EU spouses applied for a residence card as the spouse of an EU citizen. The applications were refused by the Minister for Justice on the ground that the spouses did not satisfy the condition of prior lawful residence in another Member State. Actions were brought against those decisions in the High Court, which requested guidance from the Court of Justice on whether: (i) a condition of prior lawful residence in another Member State was compatible with the Directive; and (ii) whether the circumstances of the marriage and the way in which the non-EU spouse of the EU citizen entered the Member State had consequences for the application of the Directive.

Ruling:

The Court of Justice stated that, as regards family members of an EU citizen, the application of the Directive was not conditional on their having previously resided in a Member State. The Directive applied to all EU citizens who moved to or resided in a Member State other than that of which they were a national and to their family members who accompanied them or joined them in that Member State.

The Court emphasised that if EU citizens were not allowed to lead a normal family life in the host Member State then they would be discouraged from exercising their free movement rights and the freedoms they were guaranteed by the Treaty would be seriously obstructed. The Court also held that a non-EU spouse of an EU citizen who accompanied or joined that citizen could benefit from the Directive, irrespective of when and where their marriage took place and of how that spouse entered the host Member State.

The Court stated that the Directive did not require that the Union citizen must already have founded a family at the time when they moved to a host Member State in order for their subsequent non-EU family members to be able to enjoy the rights established by the Directive. The Court further stated that it made no difference whether non-EU family members of a Union citizen had entered the host Member State before or after becoming family members of that citizen. The host Member State was, however, entitled to impose penalties, in compliance with the Directive, for entry into and residence in its territory in breach of the national rules on immigration.

> **Significance:**
>
> The rights of family members cannot be made conditional on factors that are not explicitly provided for by Union law (i.e. Directive 2004/38). Therefore, where a family member has previously resided, the time at which they became a family member of an EU citizen and how and when a family member entered the host Member State have no bearing on the family member's right to reside, provided that there is not found to be an abuse of Union provisions or a threat to public policy, public security or public health (see section 9.4 below on these restrictions). This case has overruled the Court's earlier ruling in **Akrich** (Case C-109/01), which the Irish government had relied on.

Right of permanent residence

Article 17 of Directive 2004/38 also provides that the family members of an EU worker or self-employed person have the right of permanent residence if the EU worker or self-employed person dies before acquiring the right of permanent residence. This right, which applies to family members of whatever nationality, is subject to the following conditions:

(a) the worker or self-employed person had, at the time of death, resided continuously on the territory of that Member State for two years;

(b) the death resulted from an accident at work or an occupational disease; or

(c) the surviving spouse lost the nationality of that Member State following marriage to the worker or self-employed person.

If an EU citizen dies or departs from the host Member State, or following divorce, annulment of marriage or termination of partnership, the residence rights of EU family members are not affected (Arts 12 and 13). However, before acquiring the right of permanent residence, the persons concerned must meet the conditions set out in Article 7(1)(a), (b), (c) or (d); see above. This is the same for non-EU family members if the EU citizen dies or following divorce, annulment of marriage or termination of partnership, with the exception that Article 7(1)(c) (being a student) is not an option. The rights of family members in the situations provided for in Articles 12 and 13 of the Directive are discussed in greater depth in the next subsection (section 9.3.3).

Article 20(1) provides that non-EU family members who are entitled to permanent residence will be issued with a residence card, renewable automatically every ten years. The application for a permanent residence card has to be submitted before the residence card expires (Art 20(2)). The residence card must be issued no more than six months after the application is made (Art 20(1)). Failure to apply for a permanent residence card may render the person concerned liable to proportionate and non-discriminatory sanctions (Art 20(2)).

9.3.3 Rights of family members in the event of death, departure or divorce

Directive 2004/38 contains several provisions – which have been further developed by subsequent case law – on the rights of family members when there is a change to the family situation. References to articles in this section therefore refer to the provisions of this Directive.

Furthermore, Recital 15 suggests that the protection of family members in such situations is an important purpose of the Directive. The text of Recital 15 is as follows:

> Family members should be legally safeguarded in the event of the death of the Union citizen, divorce, annulment of marriage or termination of a registered partnership. With due regard for family life and human dignity, and in certain conditions to guard against abuse, measures should therefore be taken to ensure that in such circumstances family members already residing within the territory of the host Member State retain their right of residence exclusively on a personal basis.

In *SM* v **Entry Clearance Officer** (Case C-129/18) the Court of Justice determined that a *kafala* relationship between a child and a guardian under Islamic family law does not amount to a 'family' relationship for the purposes of Article 2(2), but could amount to an 'other' family relationship for the purposes of Article 3(2)(a).

Death or departure of an EU citizen

Article 12(1) provides that if an EU citizen dies or departs from the host Member State, their EU family members shall not have their right of residence affected. In the case of a non-EU family member, their right of residence shall not be affected if the EU citizen dies, provided that the non-EU family member has been residing in the host Member State as a family member for at least one year before the EU citizen's death (Art 12(2)). No such protections are guaranteed to a non-EU family member if the EU citizen from whom their residence rights are derived just departs the host Member State.

Article 12(3) provides that if an EU citizen dies or departs from the host Member State, if their children reside in the host Member State and are enrolled at an educational establishment, then their children and the parent who has actual custody of the children (whether or not they are EU citizens) shall have the right to reside in the host Member State until the children have completed their studies.

Divorce, annulment of marriage or termination of registered partnership

Directive 2004/38 provides, for the first time, for family members to retain their right of residence in the event of divorce, annulment of marriage or termination of registered partnership. **Article 13(1)** establishes that, in the case of family members who are a national of a Member State, divorce, annulment of marriage or termination of partnership does not affect the family member's right of residence. However, such persons will then be required to meet the conditions laid out in points (a), (b), (c) or (d) of Article 7(1) in order to obtain a right to permanent residence (see section 9.2.1).

In the case of non-EU family members, the continued right of residence is not necessarily guaranteed. However, **Article 13(2)** provides that there shall be no loss of the right of residence where:

(a) prior to the start of the divorce or annulment proceedings or termination of the registered partnership, the marriage or registered partnership had lasted at least three years, including one year in the host Member State;

(b) by agreement between the spouses or the registered partners, or by court order, the spouse or partner who is a non-EU national has custody of the EU citizen's children;

(c) this is warranted by particularly difficult circumstances, such as having been a victim of domestic violence while the marriage or registered partnership was subsisting; or

(d) by agreement between the spouses or registered partners, or by court order, the spouse or partner who is a non-EU national has the right of access to a minor child, provided that the court has ruled that such access must be in the host Member State, and for as long as is required.

Points (b) and (d) in relation to primary caregivers and access to a child are discussed below.

Figure 9.1 Differences in rights for EU and non-EU family members under Directive 2004/38

	EU family members	Non-EU family members
Entry requirements	'**No entry visa** or equivalent formality may be imposed on Union citizens' (Art 5(1))	'Family members who are not nationals of a Member State shall only be required to have an entry visa in accordance with Regulation (EC) No 539/2001 or, where appropriate, with national law' (Art 5(2))
Registration for residence longer than three months	Host Member States **may** require EU citizens and their family members to register with the relevant authorities (Art 8)	Non-EU family members **must** apply for a residence card not more than three months from their date of arrival (Art 9)
Rights following death, departure or termination of marriage/ partnership	Residence rights of EU family members are **not affected** if the EU citizen dies **or departs** the host Member State (Art 12(1))	The right of residence of non-EU family members **who have been living in the host Member State as family members for at least one year** shall **not be lost** if the EU citizen dies (Art 12(2))
	Residence rights of EU family members are **not affected** in the event of the termination of the marriage or partnership of the EU citizen (Art 13(1)).	The right of residence of non-EU family members shall **not be lost** in the event of the termination of the marriage or partnership of the EU citizen, **provided that** either (a) the marriage/partnership lasted at least three years, at least one of which was within the host Member State; (b) the spouse/partner has custody of the EU citizen's child(ren); (c) there are particularly difficult circumstances, such as domestic violence within the marriage/partnership; or (d) the spouse/ partner has a right of access to the EU citizen's child(ren) (Art 13(2)).
	In the event of an EU citizen's death **or departure** from the host Member State, or the termination of their marriage or partnership, their EU family member may attain a right to permanent residence if they satisfy the conditions set out in Article 7(1)(a) (worker), (b) (self-sufficient), **(c) (student)** or (d) (family member of another EU citizen) (Arts 12(1) and 13(1)).	In the event of an EU citizen's death or the termination of their marriage or partnership, their non-EU family member may attain a right to permanent residence if they satisfy the conditions set out in Article 7(1)(a) (worker), (b) (self-sufficient) or (d) (family member of another EU citizen) (Arts 12(2) and 13(2)).

In the following case, the Court of Justice was faced with the question of whether or not the spouse of an **EU worker** still counted as a family member for the purposes of the former Article 10(1) of Regulation 1612/68 (now Art 2(2), Directive 2004/38) if they had separated and were no longer living together:

Diatta v *Land Berlin* (Case 267/83)

Facts:
The applicant was a Senegalese (i.e. non-EU) national who had married a French national. Both were resident and working in Germany. They later separated and moved into separate accommodation and she intended to divorce him. Her application for an extension to her residence permit was refused on the ground that she was no longer a family member of an EU worker. She challenged this refusal and the national court referred the case to the Court of Justice for a preliminary ruling. The Court was asked whether an EU citizen's family had to live permanently with the EU worker in order to qualify for a right of residence.

Ruling:
The Court of Justice held as follows:

18 In providing that a member of a migrant worker's family has the right to install himself with the worker, Article 10 of the Regulation does not require that the member of the family in question must live permanently with the worker, but, as is clear from Article 10(3), only that the accommodation which the worker has available must be such as may be considered normal for the purpose of accommodating his family. A requirement that the family must live under the same roof permanently cannot be implied.

19 In addition, such an interpretation corresponds to the spirit of Article 11 of the Regulation [Art 11, Regulation 1612/68 has been repealed and replaced by Art 23, Directive 2004/38], which gives the member of the family the right to take up any activity as an employed person throughout the territory of the Member State concerned, even though that activity is exercised at a place some distance from the place where the migrant worker resides.

20 It must be added that the marital relationship cannot be regarded as dissolved so long as it has not been terminated by the competent authority. It is not dissolved merely because the spouses live separately, even where they intend to divorce at a later date.

Significance:
This case established that living separately is not sufficient to lead to any loss of rights for the spouse of an EU citizen residing under what is now Article 7 of Directive 2004/38, as a requirement that they live together permanently could inhibit the spouse's ability to exercise their right to work under what is now Article 23 of the Directive.

While the above case determined that a spouse remains a family member even if they have separated from and are no longer living with the EU citizen to whom they are married, a different conclusion was reached in the following case, which concerned a cross-border separation:

Iida v *Stadt Ulm* (Case C-40/11)

Facts:

Mr Iida was a Japanese national who had a permanent job in Germany, where he had lived with his wife and daughter. At the material time, he was separated from his wife, who was a German national and who had moved to Austria with their daughter. Mr Iida had joint responsibility for the care of their daughter, whom he saw regularly.

Mr Iida applied for a residence card on the basis that he was a family member of an EU citizen (his daughter) under Directive 2004/38. He was refused and on appeal of this decision, the Verwaltungsgerichtshof Baden-Württemberg (Higher Administrative Court, Baden-Württemberg) referred questions to the Court of Justice as to Mr Iida's rights under Union law to remain in his daughter's Member State of origin (Germany) in order to maintain regular personal relations with her, after she had moved to another Member State (Austria).

Ruling:

The Court noted that Mr Iida could be granted, if he were to apply, the status of long-term resident within the meaning of **Directive 2003/109** on the status of third-country [non-EU] nationals who are long-term residents. However, Mr Iida could **not** claim a right of residence under **Directive 2004/38** for the following reasons: first, he had no rights under this Directive as a family member of his daughter, as he did not fit the criteria of a direct relative in the ascending line who was dependent on her. Second, he had no rights under the Directive as the spouse of his wife, as he did not satisfy the condition that he had accompanied her to or joined her in a Member State of which she was not a national.

As to whether Mr Iida could derive rights from **Articles 20 and 21 TFEU**, the Court noted that the purpose of these provisions was to prevent obstacles to the free movement of Union citizens. However, Mr Iida was not seeking a right to reside in the same Member State as his wife and daughter and his residence situation had not, in fact, discouraged them from exercising their free movement rights through their move to Austria. Additionally, it was not necessary for the Treaty rights to be invoked as Mr Iida could be granted a right of residence in Germany on another legal basis, without it being necessary to rely on his daughter and his spouse's EU citizenship.

Significance:

This case entailed a strict reading of Directive 2004/38, whereby Mr Iida was found to be a 'family member' of an EU citizen (his wife), as defined by the Directive, but was also found **not** to be a beneficiary of the Directive as he had not accompanied or joined his wife when she moved to a different Member State. Mr Iida's status as the spouse of an EU citizen, even though it did not help him in this case, is nonetheless interesting as it established that such a status is retained even when a husband and wife have separated and moved to different countries. This suggests that if, at a later date, he were to move to Austria or another Member State where his wife was residing, he would then become a beneficiary of rights as a family member under Directive 2004/38. Great weight is therefore afforded to the legal act of divorce, while any *de facto* situation of separation appears to be inconsequential.

In *Diatta* the spouse *retained* their status as a family member of an EU citizen who had exercised their free movement rights, despite their later separation, but in *Iida* the spouse never had such a status as the separation occurred *before* his wife exercised her free movement rights. Therefore, Directive 2004/38 could be applied in the former, but not the latter case.

While Article 12 establishes rights *only* for EU spouses in the event of the *departure* of an EU citizen, and Article 13 establishes the rights of *both* EU and non-EU spouses in the event of a *divorce*, the following case considered the rights of non-EU spouses when there is both *departure and divorce*:

Kuldip Singh and Others v Minister for Justice and Equality (Case C-218/14)

Facts:

Three non-EU nationals married EU citizens who were exercising their free movement rights in Ireland. In all three cases, the conditions of Article 13(2)(a) were met: the marriages had been for at least three years, at least one year of which had been in Ireland. Also in all three cases, the marriages broke down, the EU citizens left Ireland and divorce proceedings were then commenced and finalised. While the appellants argued that their situation came under Article 13 of Directive 2004/38 on divorce, the referring court argued that the situation came under Article 12 on the departure of an EU citizen.

Ruling:

The Court began by emphasising that the rights of non-EU family members are not autonomous, but are derived from the free movement rights of EU citizens. The Court then proceeded to closely analyse the wording of Directive 2004/38. It referred to the fact that a 'host Member State' is defined in Article 2(3) only in relation to the free movement rights of an EU citizen, and noted the reference in Article 13(2)(a) to the '*initiation* of divorce ... proceedings'. In light of this wording, the Court stated that:

61 ... the right of residence of the Union citizen's spouse who is a third-country national can be retained on the basis of Article 13(2)(a) of Directive 2004/38 only if the Member State in which that national resides is the 'host Member State' within the meaning of Article 2(3) of Directive 2004/38 on the date of commencement of the divorce proceedings.

62 That is not the case, however, if, before the commencement of those proceedings, the Union citizen leaves the Member State in which his spouse resides for the purpose of settling in another Member State or a third country. In that event the third-country national's derived right of residence based on Article 7(2) of Directive 2004/38 has come to an end with the departure of the Union citizen and can therefore no longer be retained on the basis of Article 13(2)(a) of that directive.

Thus, once the EU citizen has left the country where they resided with their spouse, it ceases to be a 'host Member State' in relation both to the EU citizen and their non-EU family members. Any family members remaining in that Member State do not fulfil the criteria for a right to reside under Article 7(2). Therefore, a non-EU spouse can only rely on Article 13(2) if divorce proceedings are initiated prior to the EU citizen's departure and the resulting loss of their Article 7(2) rights.

Significance:

This case determines that the right of a non-EU national to continue to reside in a Member State after their divorce from an EU citizen is dependent on when divorce proceedings were initiated. If they were initiated while the EU citizen was still in the country, the non-EU national can, if they meet the relevant conditions, benefit from Article 13(2)(a). If divorce proceedings were initiated after the EU citizen had left the country, the situation is classed as a departure under Article 12, whereby non-EU nationals do not retain their right to reside.

The principle established in the above case that an independent right to reside in a host Member State under Article 13(2)(a) depends on whether the EU citizen spouse was in the country when divorce proceedings were initiated was then applied to Article 13(2)(c) in *Secretary of State for the Home Department* v *NA* (Case C-115/15). Therefore, 'a third-country national, who is divorced from a Union citizen at whose hands she has been the victim of domestic violence during the marriage, **cannot** rely on the retention of her right of residence in the host Member State ... where the commencement of divorce proceedings post-dates the departure of the Union citizen spouse from that Member State' (para 51). However, in this case a right to reside for the non-EU divorcee was available as she was the primary carer of her EU national children.

> **Reflections:** Are we satisfied with the *Kuldip Sing* judgment?
>
> The **Kuldip Singh** judgment is open to criticism for several reasons. For one thing, the timing of divorce proceedings seems to be an arbitrary factor upon which to pin an individual's right to reside, especially considering that the judgment places considerable power in the hands of the EU spouse: an EU citizen might depart suddenly and unexpectedly, denying their non-EU spouse any opportunity to benefit from Article 13(2)(a) or even Article 13(2)(c).
>
> Additionally, Francesca Strumia (2016) argues that the text of Article 13(2) does not imply that an EU citizen must reside in the territory of the host Member State at the time when divorce proceedings are initiated. Conversely, she argues that the condition that the couple had spent at least one year of their marriage in the host Member State is not accompanied by any specification of when that should have occurred. The provision does not therefore suggest that the location of the EU citizen when divorce proceedings are initiated has any bearing on the rights of the non-EU spouse. Furthermore, Strumia argues that the judgment in **Kuldip Singh** diverges from a teleological interpretation of Directive 2004/38, which, taking account of Recital 15 (see above), could have resulted in a ruling that was more cognisant of the possibility for the derived rights of non-EU nationals to become non-derived personal rights.
>
> However, if the Court had ruled otherwise, it may have had to somehow establish a means of distinguishing between the departure of a spouse, as referred to in Article 12, and the breakdown of a marriage, as provided for in Article 13. This distinction might be in the form of a time period within which divorce proceedings should be initiated after a spouse has left the country, which might at least provide a non-EU spouse with an opportunity to initiate divorce proceedings immediately following a sudden and unexpected departure. Alternatively, it could be noted that Article 12 does not *exclude* the retention of residence rights for a non-EU national in the event that their EU spouse departs the host Member State; the rights contained in Article 12 could therefore be extended to non-EU spouses. This would have the advantage of placing less emphasis on formal divorce proceedings, which couples may wish to delay for a number of reasons. The problem here, though, is that such a development would probably be politically unpopular, as it would be viewed as a further incursion of Union law into the immigration decisions of Member States. Indeed, there are no easy or obvious solutions to the question posed in **Kuldip Singh** as to the rights of non-EU spouses when the EU citizen to whom they were married departs prior to the initiation of divorce proceedings.

9.3.4 Rights to equal treatment

Article 23 of Directive 2004/38 provides that 'irrespective of nationality, the family members of a Union citizen who have the right of residence or the right of permanent residence in a Member State shall be entitled to take up employment or self-employment there'.

Thus, once installed with an EU citizen in a host Member State, the citizen's family member is entitled to access to employment as if they were an EU citizen (***Gül* v *Regierungsprsident Düsseldorf*** (Case 131/85)).

9.4 Expulsion and restrictions on free movement rights

Objective 4

As with previous sections of this chapter, references to articles in this section refer to the provisions of Directive 2004/38, unless otherwise specified.

9.4.1 General protection from expulsion

Article 14(2) provides that EU citizens and their family members shall have the right of residence under Articles 7, 12 and 13 'as long as they meet the conditions set out therein'. Expulsion shall not be an automatic consequence if an EU citizen or their family members have recourse to the host Member State's social assistance system (Art 14(3), see also ***Brey*** on page 365). Article 14(4) further provides that (other than in accordance with the provisions relating to restrictions on the right of entry and residence on grounds of public policy, public security or public health) an expulsion order cannot be issued against an EU citizen or their family members if:

(i) the EU citizen is a worker or self-employed person in the host Member State; or
(ii) the EU citizen entered the host Member State to seek employment and can provide evidence that they are continuing to seek work and have a genuine chance of being employed.

Additionally, expiry of the identity card or passport on the basis of which the persons concerned entered the host Member State and were issued with a registration certificate or residence card shall not constitute a ground for expulsion from the host Member State (Art 15(2)).

9.4.2 Expulsion on grounds of public policy, public security or public health

Under **Article 27**(1), EU citizens or members of their family may be refused entry to, or expelled from, the host Member State on grounds of **public policy**, **public security** or **public health**. Under no circumstances may these grounds be invoked to serve economic ends (Art 27(1)). Measures taken on the grounds of public policy or public security must comply with the **principle of proportionality** and must be based on the **personal conduct** of the individual concerned; previous criminal convictions do not automatically justify such measures (Art 27(2)). The personal conduct must represent a **genuine, present and sufficiently serious threat** which affects one of the fundamental interests of society (Art 27(2)).

Article 27(3) provides that in order to ascertain whether the person concerned represents a danger to public policy or public security, the host Member State, if it considers it essential, may request the Member State of origin or other Member States to provide information concerning any previous police record the person concerned may have. The request is to be made by the host Member State:

(i) when issuing the registration certificate;
(ii) if there is no registration system, no later than three months from the date of the person's arrival in the host Member State or the date the person reported their presence in the host Member State as provided for in Art 5(5); or
(iii) when issuing a residence card.

Such enquiries must not be made as a matter of routine. The Member State consulted should provide its reply within two months.

A person who is expelled from a Member State on grounds of public policy, public security or public health shall have the right to re-enter the Member State which issued him with a passport or identity card, even if the document is no longer valid, or if the nationality of the holder is in dispute (Art 27(4)).

The issue of personal conduct was raised in the case of ***Van Duyn* v *Home Office*** (Case 41/74), where the UK refused entry to an EU worker due to her membership of the Church of Scientology, which it viewed as an undesirable organisation. The Court of Justice ruled that a person could not be excluded only on the basis of their *membership* of a particular organisation, as this did not amount to personal conduct, but the UK could exclude Van Duyn as her *active participation* in the organisation did meet this criterion. However, it is not certain whether Van Duyn would have met the threshold now set by Article 27(2) of the Directive, following ***Bouchereau*** (Case 30/77), whereby personal conduct must represent a genuine, present and sufficiently serious threat for exclusion on public policy grounds to be justified.

> *Van Duyn* is considered in more depth in section 8.2.3 in relation to the vertical direct effect of directives (page 283)

Additionally, the judgment in ***Van Duyn*** allowed a discrepancy in the treatment of national and non-national participants in an undesirable organisation: while national participants in the Church of Scientology faced no consequences, a non-national could be refused entry. This aspect of the case law was effectively revised in the joined cases of ***Adoui and Cornuaille*** (Joined Cases 115 and 116/81). In these cases, which concerned the refusal to allow two prostitutes to reside in Belgium on public policy grounds, despite the fact the prostitution was not prohibited in Belgium, the Court of Justice ruled that:

> … a Member State may not … expel a national of another Member State from its territory or refuse him access to its territory by reason of conduct which, when attributable to the former State's own nationals, does not give rise to repressive measures or other genuine and effective measures intended to combat such conduct. [para 9]

This ruling was then applied by the EFTA Court in the following case:

Wahl (Case E-15/12)

Facts:
Mr Whal was an EEA national and a member of the Norwegian Hell's Angels who was refused entry into Iceland on public policy and security grounds. While he contended that the organisation of which he was a member was a lawful organisation and that his personal conduct had always been lawful, the authorities believed that his visit to Iceland was linked to the final stages of an Icelandic motorcycle group becoming a full member of the Hell's Angels. The Hell's Angels were generally viewed as a threat to public order and it was noted that everywhere this organisation had established itself, an increase in organised crime had followed.

Wahl contested the decision to refuse him entry, eventually bringing his case to the Supreme Court of Iceland, which referred questions to the EFTA Court regarding the right to refuse entry on grounds of public policy and security.

Ruling:
While the EFTA Court ultimately left it to the national court to determine whether the refusal of entry was justified, it elaborated on the conditions of personal conduct; genuine, present and sufficiently serious threat to fundamental interests of society; and proportionality that are set out in Article 27 of Directive 2004/38. The Court held that the condition of personal conduct was met, not only by Wahl's present association with the Hell's Angels, but by a danger assessment that had been carried out specifically regarding his role in the establishment of the Hell's Angels in Iceland. The likelihood that such establishment would ferment organised crime within Iceland was held to pose a genuine, present and sufficiently serious threat to a fundamental interest of society. Echoing the judgment in ***Van Duyn***, the Court held that it was not necessary for the

Hell's Angel to be a prohibited organisation in Iceland, but that 'the competent authorities of an EEA State must have clearly defined their standpoint as regards the activities of the particular organisation in question and, considering the activities to be a threat to public policy and/or public security, they must have taken administrative measures to counteract these activities'.

With regard to the principle established in ***Adoui and Cornuaille*** that States should not restrict the free movement rights of non-nationals on the basis of conduct that would not give rise to repressive measures in relation to nationals, the Court noted that the specific threat at issue could only be posed by a foreigner: as the establishment of a new Hell's Angels charter required support from an existing charter, and as there were no existing charters in Iceland, only a foreign member of the organisation could pose the threat that the Hell's Angels would become established in Iceland.

Significance:

This case provides an example of how a derogation from a free movement right must be construed narrowly, so that there is a high burden on the State to prove that the denial of the right is justified. In this instance, the EFTA Court suggests that the refusal of the right to enter is justified due to the threat of organised crime posed by the personal conduct of the individual, who was a member of an organisation that, while not prohibited by the State, has been subject to measures aimed at the repression of its activities.

Regarding expulsion from the territory of a Member State, **Article 28(1)** provides that:

Before taking an expulsion decision on grounds of public policy or public security, the host Member State shall take account of considerations such as how long the individual concerned has resided on its territory, his/her age, state of health, family and economic situation, social and cultural integration into the host Member State and the extent of his/her links with the country of origin.

If the EU citizen or their family members have acquired the right of **permanent residence** in the host Member State, an expulsion decision can only be taken against them on **serious grounds** of public policy or public security (Art 28(2)). In addition, an expulsion decision may not be taken against an EU citizen or their family members who have resided in the host country for **ten years** or if they are **minors**, unless the decision is based on **imperative grounds** of public security (Art 28(3)). In the case of a minor, they may also be expelled if such a measure is necessary for the best interests of the child (Art 28(3)).

The following case concerned the calculation of the ten-year residence period for the purpose of invoking enhanced protection against expulsion:

Secretary of State for the Home Department v G (Case C-400/12)

Facts:

Ms G, a Portuguese national, had resided in the UK since 1998 and acquired a right of permanent residence in 2003. In 2009, she was sentenced by the UK courts to 21 months of imprisonment for abusing one of her children. While she was still in prison, the UK authorities ordered her deportation on grounds of public policy and public security.

Ms G contested the expulsion order before the UK courts, contending in particular that, having resided in the UK for more than 10 years, she benefited from the highest level of protection from expulsion that EU law provides to EU citizens. The Upper Tribunal (Immigration and Asylum Chamber), before which the dispute had been brought, referred the case to the Court of Justice to ascertain whether, despite her imprisonment, Ms G could benefit from that enhanced protection against expulsion.

Ruling:

The Court of Justice first stated that, unlike the requisite period for acquiring a right of permanent residence, which begins when the person concerned commenced lawful residence in the host Member State, the 10-year period of residence necessary for the grant of the enhanced protection against expulsion should be calculated by counting back from the date of the decision ordering that person's expulsion. Furthermore, the Court stated that **this period of residence must be continuous** and that **periods of imprisonment could not be taken into consideration** for the purpose of calculating the 10-year period of residence necessary for the grant of enhanced protection from expulsion. The Court ruled that:

> 38 ... Article 28(3)(a) of Directive 2004/38 must be interpreted as meaning that a period of imprisonment is, in principle, capable both of interrupting the continuity of the period of residence for the purposes of that provision and of affecting the decision regarding the grant of the enhanced protection provided for thereunder, even where the person concerned resided in the host Member State for the 10 years prior to imprisonment...

However, the Court also stated that, in order to determine the extent to which a non-continuous period of residence prevents the person concerned from enjoying enhanced protection, **an overall assessment must be made of their situation** each time the question of expulsion arises. Thus:

> 38 ... the fact that that person resided in the host Member State for the 10 years prior to imprisonment may be taken into consideration as part of the overall assessment required in order **to determine whether the integrating links previously forged with the host Member State have been broken**.

Significance:

In line with ***Onuekwere*** (Case C-378/12, see section 9.2.2), this case affirmed that periods of imprisonment do not count towards periods of residence required by Directive 2004/38. This case then added that periods of imprisonment interrupt periods of residence for the purpose of gaining rights under the Directive, even for EU citizens (for whom disruption to family life is not at issue). However, where expulsion is at issue an overall assessment of the individual's situation must be made, which should consider all periods of residence in order to determine the extent of the individual's integration within the host Member State.

Article 29 is concerned with the restriction on the right of entry and residence on the ground of public health. The only diseases which can justify restricting the right of entry and residence are:

(i) those with epidemic potential as defined by the relevant instruments of the World Health Organization (WHO);

(ii) other infectious diseases or other contagious parasitic diseases if they are subject to protection provisions applying to nationals of the host Member State (Art 29(1)).

Article 29(2) provides that diseases occurring after a three-month period from the date of arrival shall **not** constitute grounds for expulsion from the host Member State. A Member State can require the person concerned to undergo a medical examination, which must be provided free of charge, if there are serious indications that a medical examination is necessary. Such medical examinations must not be carried out as a matter of routine (Art 29(3)).

Under **Article 30**(1), the person concerned by a decision refusing leave to enter or reside in a Member State on the ground of public policy, public security or public health must be notified in writing of that decision, in such a way that they are able to comprehend its content and the implications for them. The grounds for the decision must be given precisely and in full, unless this is contrary to the interests of state security (Art 30(2)), and the person concerned must be informed of the appeal procedures available to them (Art 30(3)). Except in cases of urgency, the subject of such decision must be allowed at least one month in which to leave the Member State (Art 30(3)).

Article 31 sets out the procedural safeguards which apply if a decision is taken against a person's right of entry and residence on the grounds of public policy, public security or public health. Article 31 provides as follows:

1. The persons concerned shall have access to judicial and, where appropriate, administrative redress procedures in the host Member State to appeal against or seek review of any decision taken against them on the grounds of public policy, public security or public health.

2. Where the application for appeal against or judicial review of the expulsion decision is accompanied by an application for an interim order to suspend enforcement of that decision, actual removal from the territory may not take place until such time as the decision on the interim order has been taken, except:
   - where the expulsion decision is based on a previous judicial decision; or
   - where the persons concerned have had previous access to judicial review; or
   - where the expulsion decision is based on imperative grounds of public security under Article 28(3).

3. The redress procedures shall allow for an examination of the legality of the decision, as well as of the facts and circumstances on which the proposed measure is based. They shall ensure that the decision is not disproportionate, particularly in view of the requirements laid down in Article 28.

4. Member States may exclude the individual concerned from their territory pending the redress procedure, but they may not prevent the individual from submitting his/her defence in person, except when his/her appearance may cause serious troubles to public policy or public security or when the appeal or judicial review concerns a denial of entry to the territory.

Persons excluded from a Member State on grounds of public policy or public security can apply for the exclusion order to be lifted after a reasonable period, and in any event after a maximum of three years, by putting forward arguments to establish that there has been a material change in the circumstances which justified the decision ordering their exclusion (Art 32(1)). The Member State concerned is required to reach a decision on such application within six months of its submission (Art 32(1)). The person applying for the lifting of the exclusion order does not have a right of entry into the Member State concerned while the application is being considered (Art 32(2)).

An expulsion order cannot be issued by a Member State as a penalty or legal consequence of a custodial penalty, unless the requirements of Articles 27–29 (see above) are complied with (Art 33(1)). Where an expulsion order is issued under this provision, and where it is enforced more than two years after it was issued, the Member State is required to check that the individual concerned is a current and genuine threat to public policy or public security, and the Member State shall assess whether there has been any material change in circumstances since the expulsion order was issued (Art 33(2)).

9.5 Social benefits

> **Objective 5**

In addition to the rights of entry and residence for EU citizens and their family members that are discussed above, free movement rights also encompass rights to equal treatment in accessing social benefits. However, entitlement to access benefits on an equal basis with nationals of a host Member State is subject to certain conditions and limitations depending on the status of the EU citizen (worker, jobseeker, economically inactive or student) and the type of benefit that they are claiming. Union legislation and case law on social benefits is complex, but four sometimes overlapping types of social benefit may be distinguished:

(i) **Social security** – benefits that insure against possible loss of income resulting from unemployment, disability, pregnancy, old age and other related circumstances that result in loss of income, and which are not based on any individual assessment.

(ii) **Social advantages** – benefits that are granted on the basis of worker or residence status, or that could facilitate the mobility of Union workers; these cannot be exported to another Member State.

(iii) **Social assistance** – non-contributory benefits that aim to enable a person to meet their basic subsistence needs.

(iv) **Special non-contributory cash benefits** – benefits that supplement social security provisions so as to guarantee that a person can meet their basic subsistence needs.

> See 'Reflection: Overview of social benefits' in section 10.4.2 (page 417)

Directive 2004/38 refers only to the rights of EU citizens to 'social assistance'. Special non-contributory cash benefits may be classified as social assistance for the purpose of the Directive if the primary function of such benefits is to meet subsistence needs.

Social security benefits and other provisions that relate to workers and work-seekers, which are primarily contained in Regulation 492/2011, are discussed in detail in the next chapter. This also includes more in-depth discussion of Regulation 883/2004 on the coordination of social security systems.

9.5.1 Equal treatment regardless of nationality

Prima facie, the principle that EU citizens exercising their free movement rights should receive equal treatment to nationals of a host Member State applies to accessing social benefits. As noted above, **Article 18 TFEU** prohibits discrimination on grounds of nationality within the scope of application of the Treaties. The proviso 'within the scope of application of the Treaties' is important here, as otherwise this Article would conflict with the establishment of EU citizenship, which essentially sets out certain rights on the basis of nationality in its distinction between EU nationals and non-EU nationals. With this proviso, however, the Article requires EU citizens and their family members who are exercising their free movement rights to be treated the same as nationals of the host Member State, but permits differential treatment of other non-EU nationals.

The case of ***Palermo*** (Case 237/78) provides an example of the principle of non-discrimination in action. In this case, an Italian woman applied for a benefit that was payable to French women of at least 65 years of age and without sufficient means, who were married and who had raised at least five children of French nationality. The French authorities refused the claim, not on the basis of the woman's nationality but because five out of her seven children were not French nationals. The Court of Justice ruled that the payment of a benefit could not be made conditional on the nationality of the claimant or her children, provided that both she and the children held the nationality of a Member State.

In the case of ***Martinez Sala* v *Freistaat Bayern*** (Case C-85/96), the Court of Justice determined that a Union citizen should not face discrimination on the basis of their nationality in relation to welfare and other benefits, even in a situation where they do not have a right to reside under EU law but are nevertheless permitted to reside by a host Member State. In a recent case, the Court also extended the principle of equal treatment in access to social assistance to non-EU nationals who have been granted refugee status, regardless of whether they possess a permanent or temporary residence permit (***Ayubi* v *Bezirkshauptmannschaft Linz-Land*** (Case C-713/17)).

The principle of equal treatment of Union citizens is set out more fully in **Article 24(1) of Directive 2004/38**, which reads as follows:

> Subject to such specific provisions as are expressly provided for in the Treaty and secondary law, all Union citizens residing on the basis of this Directive in the territory of the host Member State shall enjoy equal treatment with the nationals of that Member State within the scope of the Treaty. The benefit of this right shall be extended to family members who are not nationals of a Member State and who have the right of residence or permanent residence.

However, **Article 24(2)** then establishes that for the first three months of residence, or while the EU citizen is exercising their right to reside while seeking work under Article 14(4)(b) (see Chapter 10), the host Member State is **not** obliged to grant **social assistance** to persons other than employed or self-employed workers and the members of their family. Equally, host Member States are not required to provide maintenance aid (i.e. student grants or student loans) to persons with a right of residence who have come to the country in question to study.

In addition to these provisions of Directive 2004/38, **Article 4 of Regulation 883/2004** on the coordination of social security systems (which has been amended by Regulation 988/2009), provides that EU citizens shall enjoy the same benefits and be subject to the same obligations under the legislation of any Member State as the nationals thereof. Unlike its predecessor (Regulation 1408/71) Regulation 883/2004 applies to EU citizens who are not economically active so as to facilitate the free movement of all EU citizens, irrespective of their economic status. However, it should be noted that the Regulation aims to coordinate, not harmonise, the separate social security systems of the Member States.

➤ See section 10.3.4 for detail on Regulation 883/2004

A difference in treatment between the nationals of different Member States does not always constitute discrimination in contravention of Article 18 TFEU. Certain derogations from the principle of equal treatment are provided for in the secondary legislation, such as Article 24(2) of Directive 2004/38, for example. Additionally, a difference in treatment may be justified if it pursues a **legitimate aim** and is a **proportionate** means of achieving that aim.

The next sections examine the rights of EU citizens who are not economically active to social benefits within a host Member State and the rights of EU students.

9.5.2 Rights of economically inactive EU citizens to social benefits

As noted above, Article 7(1)(b) provides a right of residence to EU citizens who 'have sufficient resources… not to become a burden on the social assistance system of the host Member State'. The following case concerned an EU citizen who claimed to have a right of residence under Article 7(1)(b) and who was seeking to claim a social benefit:

Pensionsversicherungsanstalt v Brey (Case C-140/12)

Facts:
Mr Brey and his wife were German nationals who moved to Austria. Although Mr Brey had been issued with a certificate of lawful residence in Austria, he was refused a compensatory supplement for pensioners. Under Austrian law transposing Article 7(1)(b) of Directive 2004/38, EU citizens were entitled to reside in Austria for longer than three months if they had comprehensive sickness insurance and sufficient resources to support themselves so as not to need recourse to social assistance benefits or the compensatory supplement. There was therefore a discrepancy between Mr Brey's right to reside and his right to receive the supplement, whereby his request for the supplement was deemed to be evidence that he did not have sufficient resources to support himself and therefore did not meet the residence conditions.

Ruling:
The Court first began by defining the concept of a 'social assistance system', specifically in relation to Directive 2004/38, as 'covering all assistance introduced by the public authorities … that can be claimed by an individual who does not have resources sufficient to meet his own basic needs and the needs of his family and who, by reason of that fact, may become a burden on the public finances of the host Member State during his period of residence which could have consequences for the overall level of assistance which may be granted by that State'. The Court then confirmed that the Austrian compensatory supplement comes under such a system. While being eligible to receive the supplement may therefore indicate that a person does not have sufficient resources to support themselves, the Court ruled that 'the competent national authorities cannot draw such conclusions without first carrying out an **overall assessment of the specific burden** which granting that benefit would place on the national social assistance system as a whole, by reference to the **personal circumstances characterising the individual situation** of the person concerned'. This is consistent, the Court noted, with the requirement in Article 8(4) of Directive 2004/38 that Member States must take into account the personal situation of the individual concerned. Therefore, the Court concluded that 'the mere fact that a national of a Member State receives social assistance is not sufficient to show that he constitutes an unreasonable burden on the social assistance system of the host Member State'. The Court left it to the national court to conduct the necessary assessment to determine whether Mr Brey constituted such an unreasonable burden.

Significance:
National legislation may not determine that any recourse to social assistance automatically constitutes an *unreasonable* burden on the social assistance system with the effect that a person no longer meets the conditions for residence set out in Article 7(1)(b). To determine such an outcome, an **individual assessment** must be conducted.

The following case also concerned an application to a host Member State for social benefits by an economically inactive EU citizen:

Dano v Jobcenter Leipzig (Case C-333/13)

Facts:

Ms Dano and her son were Romanian nationals who lived in Germany with her sister. Ms Dano was supported materially by her sister and also claimed child benefits from the German state. Ms Dano was neither a worker nor a jobseeker, but had been issued with a residence certificate of unlimited duration. The case concerned the refusal of Ms Dano's application for a 'basic provision' benefit for jobseekers under the German Social Code (SGB II). The application was refused under a provision in the Social Code that excluded foreign nationals whose right of residence arose solely from their search for employment. *Inter alia*, the referring court asked the Court of Justice whether national legislation could exclude economically inactive nationals of another Member State from a benefit that would be granted to nationals of the Member State who are in the same situation.

Ruling:

The Court determined that, while **Article 18 TFEU** prohibits any discrimination on grounds of nationality within the scope of application of the Treaties, this is subject to any special provisions therein. Both **Articles 20(2)** and **21(1) TFEU** specify that the free movement rights they contain may be limited by implementing measures. The Court must therefore interpret the relevant implementing measures: **Article 24 of Directive 2004/38** and **Article 4 of Regulation 883/2004**. These measures were held to be relevant on the basis that the benefit in question was a 'special non-contributory cash benefit' for the purpose of Regulation 883/2004, which also amounts to 'social assistance' for the purpose of Directive 2004/38.

The Court first established that a benefit cannot be refused to Ms Dano on the basis of the derogation provided in **Article 24(2)** of the Directive. This provision only applies to persons who have resided for less than three months or persons seeking work, neither of which applied to Ms Dano.

The Court then turned to **Article 24(1)**, noting that **this provision only provides for equal treatment with nationals for EU citizens residing on the basis of the Directive**. Access to equal treatment under Article 24(1) is therefore dependent on compliance with the conditions set out in either Article 7(1) (which applies to periods of residence between three months and five years in duration) or Article 16(1) (which applies to periods of continuous residence of over five years).

As an economically inactive EU citizen who had resided in a host Member State for a period of between three months and five years, Ms Dano would have to meet the requirements of Article 7(1)(b), i.e. she would have to have comprehensive health insurance and sufficient resources for herself and her son to avoid becoming a burden on the social assistance system of the host Member State. The Court ruled that **it must be possible for a Member State to exclude an economically inactive foreign national who does not have sufficient resources to support themselves from recourse to social benefits that are intended to cover a person's subsistence**. If this were not the case, Article 7(1)(b) would be deprived of all effect, as a foreign national would always have sufficient resources by virtue of recourse to such social benefits. As the national court had found that Ms Dano and her son did not have sufficient resources to support themselves, the Court of Justice stated that she cannot claim a right of residence under Article 7(1)(b) and therefore cannot invoke the principle of non-discrimination provided in Article 24(1).

Similarly, the Court held that equal treatment under **Regulation 883/2004** applies only to persons residing in a Member State in accordance with national legislation. As such legislation could establish the same requirements contained in Directive 2004/38, Regulation 883/2004 does not preclude national legislation that excludes economically inactive nationals of other Member States from access to subsistence benefits that would be provided to nationals of the host Member State in the same situation.

Significance:

This case established that an EU citizen can only claim equal treatment with regard to social benefits if their residence within the host Member State complies with the conditions set out in Directive 2004/38. An economically inactive EU citizen who does not have sufficient funds to support themselves can therefore be denied access to benefits, at least for the first five years of their residence. The case was therefore reported in the media as heralding an end to 'welfare tourism', where EU citizens move to another Member State with the sole intention of accessing the benefit system.

However, although this case referenced the principle established in **Brey** that Union law does not preclude the grant of benefits being made subject to the fulfilment of residence conditions set out in Directive 2004/38, this case is not a straightforward development of that earlier judgment. The Court did not mention its finding in **Brey** that the authorities are required to undertake an individual assessment of the specific burden that granting a benefit would place on the national social assistance system.

In *Jobcenter Berlin Nuköln* v *Alimanovic and Others* (Case C-67/14), the Court of Justice continued its departure from the requirement established in **Brey** of an individual assessment of the burden placed on the national social assistance system. In this case the Court of Justice established that EU citizens may be automatically excluded from entitlement to social assistance within a host Member State once their status as a worker is lost. Nevertheless, in *Bogatu* v *Minister for Social Protection* (Case C-322/17) the Court of Justice ruled that Regulation 833/2004 did not necessarily require a person to be economically active within a host Member State in order to be eligible for equal treatment with regard to family benefits. Although this seems to contradict the Court's ruling in *Dano*, there is an important distinction between the two cases. Ms Dano was **not** residing in a host Member State on the basis of her rights as a Union citizen: she did not meet the criteria for residence set out in Article 7(1) of Directive 2004/38. Conversely, prior to becoming economically inactive, Mr Bogatu had worked in his host Member State for a continuous period of over five years: he therefore had a right of permanent residence under Article 16 of Directive 2004/38. Therefore, while Ms Dano fell under the exemption to equal treatment provided in Article 24(2) of Directive 2004/38, Mr Bogatu had to be treated equally on the basis of Article 24(1).

➤ See section 10.4.2 for detail on the *Alimanovic* case (page 415)

Reflection: Welfare tourism and 'ever greater union'

This chapter depicts the evolution of Union citizenship with regard to the expansion of the rights that are available to citizens and the situations in which they are available. As with other areas of Union law, such as the internal market, this evolution is the product of a legal system that is based not only on what it *is* at the material time, but also on what it *aims to become* in the future. This forward-looking approach is evident in the focus of the Treaties on objectives (see Art 3 TEU) and, specifically in relation to citizenship, the Court of Justice's assertion that 'Union citizenship is destined to be the fundamental status of nationals of the Member States' (*Grzelczyk*). Based on this observation, Ronan McCrea (2017) depicts the Union at present as in a transitional, partially-integrated state, within which integration in some areas has created incoherencies that require further integration in other areas in order to be resolved. However, as the project of 'ever closer union' (Art 1 TEU) has come under increasing political strain and demands for compromise in light of national concerns have increased, McCrea argues that the ability of the Union to continue towards the fulfilment of its objectives and the resolution of policy incoherencies has become destabilised. We are therefore at risk of being left with a system in limbo, a system that can neither move forward as intended nor continue in its incompleteness.

This unsatisfactory situation is perhaps most apparent in relation to social benefits and concerns over welfare tourism. 'Welfare tourism' is a term that emerged in the 1990s to express the concern that migrants deliberately abuse the welfare system of their host state. In particular, the concern is that EU free movement rights enable people to migrate with their families to the Member State with the most generous welfare programme. Limits to free movement have therefore been written into the relevant legislation to prevent such practices, such as the 'sufficient resources' stipulation in Article 7(1)(b) and the exemption of work-seekers from social assistance provided for in Article 24(2) of Directive 2004/38 (see Chapter 10).

Thus, in **Dano**, McCrea (2017) argues that the Court of Justice presented the limitations on Union citizenship as more permanent than it had previously, and in doing so, along with the supporting judgments of **Alimanovic** and **Garcia-Nieto** (see Chapter 10), reassured Member States and their citizens that the destiny of Union citizenship does not include unlimited access to welfare. Yet, these limitations on social assistance are at odds with rights of entry, for example: although Ms Dano was found to have no right to reside, if the German authorities were to expel her they would nevertheless be unable to prevent her re-entry. Additionally, Herwig Verschueren (2015) points to the tension between making the right to reside conditional on possession of 'sufficient resources' and the central policy objectives of the Union of combating poverty and social exclusion. Political resistance to the expansion of Union citizenship rights and the Court of Justice's sensitivity to such resistance, can therefore be seen to be forcing a reassessment of the 'destiny' of citizenship and the ways in which current incoherencies can be resolved (see Blauberger et al., 2018). Indeed, this reassessment is perhaps also evident in the recent **Tjebbes** judgment (see page 328).

9.5.3 Rights of EU students to social benefits

As noted above, **Article 7(1)(c)** provides a right of residence for longer than three months to persons who are enrolled on a course of study, who have comprehensive sickness insurance **and** who have sufficient resources to avoid becoming a burden on the social assistance system of the host Member State. However, **Article 24(2)** provides a derogation from the principle of equal treatment with regard to students, which states that Member States are **not** obliged to grant maintenance aid for studies, including vocational training, consisting of student grants or student loans, **unless** that person is classed as a worker, self-employed person or a member of such a person's family. Therefore, economically inactive students are not subject to equal treatment with regards to certain benefits.

Grzelczyk v Centre Public d'Aide Sociale d'Ottignies-Louvain-la-Neuve (Case C-184/99)

Facts:
Mr Grzelczyk was a student of French nationality who paid his own way throughout his first three years of full-time studies at a Belgian university by taking on minor jobs and obtaining credit. At the start of his fourth and final year he applied for a Belgian social security benefit known as minimum

subsistence allowance (minimex). His application was refused on the ground that under the relevant Belgian legislation, a non-Belgian applicant was only eligible if *inter alia* Regulation 1612/68 (which has since been repealed and replaced by Regulation 492/2011, see Chapter 10) applied to him. Belgian nationals were entitled to the benefit regardless of whether or not they came within the scope of Regulation 1612/68 (now Regulation 492/2011), which applied to workers.

The Belgian tribunal had doubts as to whether the national legislation was compatible with the former Articles 12 and 17 EC Treaty (now Arts 18 and 20 TFEU).

Ruling:

The Court of Justice first noted that Mr Grzelczyk's nationality was the only bar to his entitlement to the benefit in question. The Court then stated that:

> 31 **Union citizenship is destined to be the fundamental status of nationals of the Member States**, enabling those who find themselves in the same situation to enjoy the same treatment in law irrespective of their nationality, subject to such exceptions as are expressly provided for.

The Court then referred to the requirement that EU students have sufficient resources to avoid becoming a burden on the social assistance system of the host Member State. A Member State may consider that a student's recourse to social assistance means that they no longer fulfil the condition of self-sufficiency and may accordingly withdraw or refuse to renew their residence permit. However, such consequences should never be the automatic result of recourse to benefits as, especially where such recourse is temporary, the grant of such benefits may not amount to an *unreasonable* burden on the public finances of the host Member State. The Court therefore concluded that:

> 46 ... Articles 6 and 8 of the Treaty [now Arts 18 and 20 TFEU] preclude entitlement to a non-contributory social benefit, such as the minimex, from being made conditional, in the case of nationals of Member States other than the host State where they are legally resident, on their falling within the scope of Regulation No 1612/68 [now Regulation 492/2011] when no such condition applies to nationals of the host Member State.

Significance:

The Court established in this case that EU citizens who are nationals of other Member States may not have their access to social assistance made subject to conditions that are not imposed on nationals of the Member State. Although, in the case at hand, it would have been possible for Mr Grzelczyk to have been denied the benefit if the refusal was based on his unlawful residence, such a refusal would need to consider the burden that granting such a benefit would place on public finances on an individual basis, as suggested by **Brey**, and would need to comply with the principle of proportionality, as suggested by **Baumbast**. Whether the subsequent rulings in **Dano** and **Alimanovic** would affect such considerations for students residing under Article 7(1)(c) of Directive 2004/38 remains to be seen. This case initially raised the profile and status of EU citizenship, which seems to have since been downplayed in these two more recent judgments (see above).

The following case concerned an EU student's right to a maintenance loan at a preferential rate of interest:

Bidar (Case C-209/03)

Facts:

Mr Bidar, a French national, had been dependent on his family while he completed the last three years of his secondary education in the UK. He applied for financial assistance to cover his maintenance costs when he started a course at a UK university. A national of another Member State was eligible to receive such a loan if they were 'settled' in the UK and had been resident there throughout the three-year period preceding the start of the course. However, under English law, a national of another Member State residing in the UK as a student could not obtain the status of being 'settled' in the UK. Mr Bidar brought proceedings before the English High Court, which referred questions to the Court of Justice for a preliminary ruling.

Ruling:

The Court first held that the former Article 12 EC Treaty (now Art 18 TFEU) on non-discrimination was applicable to the case. The Article had to be read in conjunction with the provisions on EU citizenship and, in the case of students who moved to another Member State to study there, there was nothing in the text of the Treaty to suggest that they lost the rights the Treaty conferred on EU citizens. The Court added that a national of a Member State who lived in another Member State where they pursued and completed their secondary education, without it being raised that they did not have sufficient resources or sickness insurance, enjoyed a right of residence on the basis of the former Article 18 EC Treaty (now Art 21 TFEU) and Directive 90/364 (now Directive 2004/38).

The Court then considered whether, where the requirements for granting assistance were linked to the fact of being settled or to residence, and where these requirements were likely to place nationals of other Member States at a disadvantage, the difference in treatment between nationals and non-nationals of the Member State concerned could be justified. The Court stated that it was permissible for Member States to ensure that the granting of social assistance did not become an unreasonable burden. In the case of assistance covering the maintenance costs of students, **it was thus legitimate to seek to ensure a degree of integration** by checking that the student in question had resided in the host Member State for a certain length of time. However, in so far as it precluded any possibility for a student who was a national of another Member State to obtain the status of settled person, and hence to receive the assistance even if they had established a **genuine link** with the society of the host Member State, **the requirement was not a proportionate means of pursuing that aim of ensuring the existence of a degree of integration**. Therefore, the aim did not justify the difference in treatment and the legislation in question was incompatible with the former Article 12 EC Treaty (now Art 18 TFEU).

Significance:

This case established that, where access to a benefit is conditional on a person being 'settled' or otherwise integrated within a Member State, such a condition may not be defined in such a way as to exclude nationals of other Member States who have established a **genuine link** with the host Member State. Thus, in relation to accessing student maintenance loans, the exclusion of EU citizens studying in the UK from being able to attain the required 'settled' status unjustifiably excludes persons with a genuine link to the host Member State. This judgment had the effect of extending rights to maintenance to sufficiently integrated persons, despite the fact that Directive 2004/38 excludes the provision of maintenance for students.

The above case was applied by the Court of Justice in *Förster* v *Hoofddirectie van de Informatie Beheer Groep* (Case C-158/07). In the *Förster* case, the Dutch body which administered educational maintenance grants adopted a policy rule which stipulated that a student from the EU must have been lawfully resident in the Netherlands for an uninterrupted period of at least five years before claiming a maintenance grant. Resonating with the Article 16, Directive 2004/38 right to permanent residence, the Court of Justice held that this period was appropriate for the purpose of demonstrating that the applicant was integrated into the society of the host Member State.

In the following joined cases, which also concerned eligibility for a maintenance grant, the Court was not called on to consider a difference of treatment, but rather an obstacle to free movement:

Morgan v Bezirksregierung Köln and Iris Bucher v Landrat des Kreises Düren (Joined Cases C-11/06 and C-12/06)

Facts:
Ms Morgan, a German national, completed her secondary education in Germany and then moved to the UK. She worked for a year in the UK before commencing her university studies there, for which she applied to the German authorities for a grant. Her application was rejected because, under German legislation, the grant was subject to the condition that the course of study should constitute a continuation of education or training pursued for at least one year in a German establishment (the 'first-stage studies' requirement). Ms Bucher's application for the same grant for her studies in the Netherlands was also rejected on this basis. However, both applicants argued that, as professional education and training courses in their respective fields of study were not available in Germany, they were unable to meet the first-stage studies requirement. The administrative court in Aachen asked the Court of Justice whether freedom of movement for EU citizens precluded the condition that studies abroad had to be a continuation of education or training pursued for at least one year in Germany.

Ruling:
On account of the personal inconvenience, additional costs and possible delays entailed, the obligation to have attended an education or training course for at least one year in Germany and to continue only that same education or training in another Member State was **liable to discourage EU citizens from leaving Germany in order to pursue studies in another Member State**. It therefore constituted a restriction on freedom of movement for EU citizens.

The Court recognised that the objective of ensuring that students completed their courses in a short period of time could constitute a legitimate aim in the context of the organisation of the education system. However, the Court held that the requirement of continuity between the studies in Germany and those pursued abroad was **not proportionate** to the objectives, *inter alia*, of:

(i) ensuring that students completed their studies within a short period of time, as the first-stage studies requirement did not ensure this;

(ii) enabling students to determine whether they had made 'the right choice' in respect of their studies, as the first-stage studies requirement discouraged them from changing their educational path; and

(iii) ensuring that grants are only awarded to students who could demonstrate a certain degree of integration into the society of the Member State, as this could be achieved by less restrictive means.

In particular, the first-stage studies requirement seemed an excessively restrictive means of pursuing the third objective as it excluded the two applicants, who had both been raised and educated in Germany. Furthermore, where students sought to undertake education or training courses of which there were no equivalents in Germany, the students concerned were obliged to choose between giving up the course they had planned to attend or losing entirely their entitlement to the grant.

Therefore, the Court concluded that the first-stage studies requirement was contrary to the free movement rights enshrined in Articles 17 and 18 EC Treaty (now Arts 20 and 21 TFEU).

> **Significance:**
> This case found that a condition placed on eligibility for a maintenance grant which could dissuade EU citizens from exercising their free movement rights was contrary to the Treaty. It therefore established that access to social benefits should not be provided for in such a way that restricts the free movement of EU citizens. Any such restrictions must pursue a **legitimate** aim **and** be a **proportionate** means of achieving that aim.

The German legislation which was at issue in the above case was amended in 2008. The new legislation provided that students could obtain a maintenance grant for their studies in another Member State for one year. To be eligible to receive a grant for a period of more than one year, the student had to show he had resided in Germany for at least three years prior to commencing his studies. The compatibility of this new legislation with Union law was considered by the Court of Justice in *Prinz* v *Region Hannover* and *Seeberger* v *Studentenwerk Heidelberg* (Case C-523/11). The Court of Justice stated that while it may be legitimate for a Member State to grant assistance to students who have demonstrated a sufficient degree of integration into German society, the condition of three years' permanent residence was too general and exclusive and went beyond what was necessary to achieve the objective. The residence condition risked excluding students who were sufficiently connected with German society but who did not have an uninterrupted three-year period of residence.

9.6 The Schengen *acquis* and its integration into the European Union

9.6.1 Development of the Schengen area

Objective 6

During the 1980s, a debate opened up about the meaning of the concept of the 'free movement of persons'. Some Member States felt that this should apply to EU citizens only, which would involve keeping **internal border** checks in order to distinguish between EU citizens and non-EU citizens. Others argued in favour of free movement for everyone, which would mean an end to internal border checks altogether. As the Member States found it impossible to reach an agreement, France, Germany, Belgium, Luxembourg and the Netherlands decided in 1985 to create a territory without internal borders. This became known as the 'Schengen area'. Schengen is the name of the town in Luxembourg where the first agreements were signed.

The first agreement between the five original members was signed on 14 June 1985. A further Convention was drafted and signed on 19 June 1990. When this Convention came into effect in 1995 (by which time Portugal and Spain had also joined), it **abolished the internal borders** of the signatory states and created a single external border where immigration checks for the Schengen area were carried out in accordance with a single set of rules. Common rules regarding visas, asylum rights and checks at external borders were adopted to allow the free movement of persons within the signatory states, without disturbing law and order. Some internal border controls were temporarily reintroduced in 2016 and 2017 (see below).

Accordingly, in order to reconcile freedom and security, freedom of movement was accompanied by so-called 'compensatory' measures. This involved improving coordination between the police, customs and the judiciary and taking necessary measures to combat problems such as terrorism and organised crime. In order to make this possible, an information system known as the **Schengen Information System (SIS)** was set up to exchange data on people's identities and descriptions of objects which were either stolen or lost. Although the UK is was never a member of the Schengen area, it has operated the SIS in a limited capacity.

The Schengen area was expanded to include 13 countries when the Treaty of Amsterdam entered into force on 1 May 1999. The ToA incorporated into EU law: (i) the decisions taken since 1985 by Schengen group members; and (ii) the associated working structures. From this point the Schengen Agreement was no longer an independent treaty, but can now only be amended and executed according to the rules set out in the EU Treaties. When the Treaty of Lisbon came into force on 1 December 2009, the Schengen area was extended to include every Member State except for the UK and Ireland (Art 5, Protocol No. 19). Denmark has reserved the power to determine whether future decisions will apply to it (Art 4, Protocol No. 22). **Protocol No. 19** provides for the integration of the **Schengen** *acquis* into the framework of the European Union. **Article 1** of Protocol No. 19 provides as follows:

> The ... [Member States of the EU, excluding Ireland and the UK] shall be authorised to establish closer cooperation among themselves in areas covered by provisions defined by the Council which constitute the Schengen *acquis*. This cooperation shall be conducted within the institutional and legal framework of the European Union and with respect for the relevant provisions of the Treaties.

9.6.2 Participation in the Schengen *acquis*

The Member States that joined the European Union on 1 May 2004, 1 January 2007 and 1 July 2013 are bound by the entire Schengen *acquis*. Following the SIS-II becoming operational on 9 April 2013 (see below), border controls have been abolished for all Member States, apart from Bulgaria, Croatia, Cyprus and Romania (in addition to the UK and Ireland which, as discussed above, have opted out). Bulgaria and Romania are working towards joining the Schengen area. Croatia and Cyprus have a temporary derogation from joining the Schengen area.

Iceland, Liechtenstein, Norway and Switzerland are associate members of the Schengen area and operate the SIS.

The participation of Denmark

As stated above, although Denmark has signed the Schengen Agreement, it can choose whether or not to apply any new decisions. **Article 4 of Protocol No. 22** (which is annexed to the TEU and TFEU) provides:

> 1 Denmark shall decide within a period of six months after the Council has decided on a proposal or initiative to build upon the Schengen *acquis* covered by this Part, whether it will implement this measure in its national law. If it decides to do so, this measure will create an obligation under international law between Denmark and the other Member States bound by the measure.
>
> 2 If Denmark decides not to implement a measure of the Council as referred to in paragraph 1, the Member States bound by that measure and Denmark will consider appropriate measures to be taken.

The participation of Ireland and the United Kingdom

In accordance with **Article 5 of Protocol No. 19** (which is annexed to the TEU and TFEU), Ireland and the UK (prior to Brexit) can take part in all or some of the Schengen arrangements if the Schengen group Member States and the government representative of the country in question vote unanimously in favour within the Council.

In March 1999, the UK asked to take part in some aspects of Schengen, namely police and judicial cooperation in criminal matters, the fight against drugs and the Schengen Information System (SIS). A Council Decision approving the request by the UK was adopted on 29 May 2000. Ireland asked to take part in some aspects of Schengen, broadly corresponding to the aspects covered by the UK's request, in June 2000. The Council adopted a decision approving Ireland's request on 28 February 2002. The Commission had issued opinions on the two applications, stressing that the partial participation of the two Member States should not have the effect of reducing the consistency of the *acquis* as a whole.

After evaluating the conditions that must precede implementation of the provisions governing police and judicial cooperation, the Council decided on 22 December 2004 that this part of the Schengen *acquis* could be implemented by the UK.

The following joined cases concerned a refusal by the Council to allow the UK to take part in the adoption of two regulations concerning the Schengen *acquis*. Although this case concerned a previous Protocol, the principles apply equally to the current Protocol No. 19:

UK v *Council* (Case C-77/05 and Case C-137/05)

Facts:

According to the Protocol integrating the Schengen *acquis* into the framework of the European Union, Ireland and the United Kingdom may at any time request to take part in some or all of the provisions of the *acquis*. If the UK and/or Ireland do not notify their wish to take part in the adoption of a measure to build upon the Schengen *acquis*, the other Member States are free to adopt the measure without the participation of those countries. A decision of 29 May 2000 listed the provisions of the Schengen *acquis* in which the UK was to participate and provided that the UK was deemed irrevocably to have notified its wish to take part in all proposals and initiatives based on those provisions.

On 11 February 2004, the UK informed the Council of its intention to take part in the adoption of the regulation establishing the Frontex Agency (Regulation 2007/2004). On 19 May 2004, the UK informed the Council that it also intended to take part in the adoption of the regulation establishing standards for security features and biometrics in passports (Regulation 2252/2004). Despite those notifications the UK was not allowed to take part in the adoption of those two regulations, on the ground that they constituted developments of provisions of the Schengen *acquis* in which the UK did not take part. Both regulations were adopted without the UK's participation.

The UK claimed that the Council's refusal to allow it to take part in the adoption of the regulations was in breach of the Schengen Protocol. The UK considered that its right to take part in the adoption of such measures was independent of whether or not it took part in the provisions of the Schengen *acquis* on which the measure was based. Accordingly, the UK brought two actions before the Court of Justice.

Ruling:

The Court considered that the provision in the Schengen Protocol on the participation of the UK and Ireland in *existing* measures and the provision making it possible for those Member States to take part in the adoption of *new* measures had to be read together, not independently, even though they related to two different aspects of the Schengen *acquis*.

> The Court held that it followed from the use of the words 'proposals and initiatives to build upon the Schengen *acquis*' that the measures in question were based on the Schengen *acquis*, of which they constituted merely an implementation or further development. Logically, such measures had to be consistent with the provisions they implemented or developed.
>
> In those circumstances, the Court concluded that the possibility of the UK and Ireland taking part in the adoption of a new measure in connection with the Schengen *acquis* was applicable only to proposals and initiatives to build upon an area of the *acquis* in which those countries had already been authorised to take part. The Court held that in the present case, the UK had not accepted the area of the Schengen *acquis* which was the context of the regulations in question, and therefore the Council was right to refuse to allow the UK to take part in the adoption of those measures.
>
> **Significance:**
>
> The UK and Ireland can choose from the outset which areas of the Schengen *acquis* they wish to partake in, but cannot choose to participate in the development or implementation of an area that they have not previously been authorised to participate in.

The UK's partial participation in the Schengen *acquis* will continue throughout the Brexit transition period. After 31 December 2020, the extent of this participation will be subject to the provisions of any relevant agreements that have been concluded.

9.6.3 Measures adopted by Schengen group members

Among the main measures are:

- the removal of checks at common borders, replacing them with external border checks;
- a common definition of the rules for crossing external borders and uniform rules and procedures for controls there;
- separation of people travelling within the Schengen area from those arriving from countries outside the area in air terminals and ports;
- harmonisation of the rules regarding conditions of entry and visas for short stays;
- coordination between administrations on surveillance of borders (liaison officers and harmonisation of instructions and staff training);
- the definition of the role of carriers in measures to combat illegal immigration;
- requirement for all non-EU nationals moving from one country to another to lodge a declaration;
- the drawing up of rules for asylum seekers (Dublin Convention, replaced in 2003 by the Dublin II Regulation, amended in 2013 by the Dublin III Regulation);
- the introduction of cross-border rights of surveillance and hot pursuit for police forces in the Schengen states;
- the strengthening of legal cooperation through a faster extradition system and faster distribution of information about the implementation of criminal judgments;
- the creation of the **Schengen Information System (SIS)**.

The **Schengen *acquis*** comprises these measures, together with:

(i) the agreement signed on 14 June 1985;

(ii) the Convention implementing that agreement, signed on 19 June 1990;

(iii) the decisions and declarations adopted by the Executive Committee set up by the 1990 Convention;

(iv) the steps taken in order to implement the 1990 Convention by the authorities on whom the Executive Committee conferred decision-making powers;

(v) the subsequent protocols and accession agreements.

9.6.4 The Schengen Information System (SIS)

An information network was set up to allow all border posts, police stations and consular agents from Schengen group Member States to access data on specific individuals or on vehicles or objects which had been lost or stolen.

Member States supply the network through national networks (N-SIS) connected to a central system (C-SIS), and this is supplemented by a network known as SIRENE (Supplementary Information Request at the National Entry).

The second-generation Schengen Information System (SIS-II)

The Schengen Information System (SIS) was not designed, and therefore lacked the capacity, to operate in more than 15 or so countries. It was therefore necessary to develop a second-generation Schengen Information System (SIS-II) to enable new and future Member States to use the system and to take account of the latest developments in information technology. The SIS-II became operational on 9 April 2013.

> See section 1.1.3 for a list of the new Member States which joined the EU in 2004, 2007 and 2013

In March 2017, the Council adopted Regulation 2017/458 as regards the reinforcement of checks against relevant databases at external borders. This measure will increase the use of the SIS as it obliges Member States to carry out systematic checks on all persons both entering and exiting the Union.

9.6.5 Temporary reintroduction of border controls

Regulation 562/2006 establishing a Community Code on the rules governing the movement of persons across borders was adopted on 25 March 2016 and is also known as the **Schengen Borders Code**. Article 29 of the Schengen Borders Code provides that, subsequent to a proposal from the Commission which is adopted by a qualified majority of the Council, **temporary internal border controls** may be reintroduced. Such controls may apply to specific parts or all of a border and they may last for a period of up to six months. Controls may be prolonged no more than three times.

On 12 May 2016, following a proposal from the Commission, the Council recommended that five countries reintroduce internal border controls: **Austria**, **Denmark**, **Germany**, **Norway** and **Sweden**. The controls were in response to deficiencies in external border controls in the context of elevated levels of immigration during the European migrant crisis and were to last a maximum of six months. On 11 November 2016, the Council recommended that proportionate temporary measures in the affected countries be extended by three months and then recommended a further three-month extension on 7 February 2017. On 2 May 2017, the Council recommended a final extension of up to six months, during which the controls should be gradually phased out.

In addition to Article 29, Article 25 of the Schengen Borders Code enables Member States to reintroduce border controls for periods of time no longer than six months. Here, the Commission must be notified of such actions and it may issue an opinion regarding their necessity and proportionality. However, providing that the procedures established in the Borders Code are adhered to, the Commission does not have the power to prevent or terminate the reintroduction of border controls under Article 25. Seven Member States used Article 25 to reintroduce border controls in 2019. Among these, only Poland reintroduced border controls to heighten security on the days that specific high-profile events were held on its territory; others cited broader security concerns, mostly linked to migration and/or terrorism, in order to justify the reintroduction of border controls for several months at a time. Indeed, Norway, Denmark and Germany have taken to operating border controls under Article 25 for consecutive six-month periods, suggesting that the reintroduction of border controls in these countries may not, in fact, be temporary.

9.7 Free movement rights after Brexit

Objective 7

Free movement rights under EU law will continue to apply to the UK and to UK citizens until the end of the Brexit transition period (31 December 2020). At that point, EU citizens living in the UK and UK citizens living in a host Member State will continue to have a right to remain there, although application for a new residency status may be required. If no deal stating otherwise is agreed, the UK will be treated as a non-EU country after 31 December 2020 and travel between the UK and the EU may therefore be subject to the attainment of visas.

In order to retain their right to remain within the UK, EU citizens who moved there before 31 December 2020 must either acquire British citizenship (if they are eligible) or apply under the **European Union Settlement Scheme (EUSS)**. Under the EUSS, an EU citizen will be granted 'settled status' if they have been resident in the UK for at least five years or if they have a permanent residence document. If they do not meet these conditions they will be granted **'pre-settled status'**, which can then be upgraded to settled status once they have completed five years of residence in the UK. The difference between these two types of status are set out in Figure 9.2. If an EU citizen has 'indefinite leave to remain' in the UK, they can continue living in the UK without applying to the EUSS. However, a successful application to the EUSS will enable such persons to leave the UK for up to five years without losing their 'settled' status. EU citizens who continue to reside in the UK without acquiring British citizenship, settled or pre-settled status, or indefinite leave to remain may be at risk of removal after 31 December 2020, or after a later date that is stipulated in a deal.

Irish citizens will not need to apply under the EUSS and will continue to have free movement rights into the UK under the **Common Travel Area**. The Common Travel Area (CTA) is an agreement to apply reduced travel controls between the UK, Ireland, the Isle of Man and the Channel Islands. Under the national law of the UK and of Ireland, neither state considers citizens of the other to be foreigners. Citizens of both states are therefore generally free to travel to, reside within and work in the other state, and there is a long and mutually-beneficial history of Irish citizens migrating to work in the UK. The CTA will continue after Brexit.

Figure 9.2 Differences between 'settled' and 'pre-settled' status under the EU Settlement Scheme

	Settled status	**Pre-settled status**
Requirements	Five years continuous residence in the UK (i.e. resident in the UK for at least six months in any 12-month period) **or** possession of a permanent residence document **or** possession of indefinite leave to remain.	Began living in the UK before 31 December 2020.
Rights	– To work in the UK – To access the UK's National Health Service – To enrol in education or continue studying – To access public funds such as benefits and pensions, if eligible – To leave and return to the UK	
Children	Children born in the UK to a parent with settled status will be **British citizens**.	Children born in the UK to a parent with pre-settled status will be eligible for **pre-settled status**.
Other family members	If a deal is not agreed that states otherwise, close family members may join an EU citizen with settled or pre-settled status in the UK until 29 March 2022, provided that the relationship began before Brexit. They will need to apply to the EUSS.	
Loss of status	Settled status will be lost if more than **five** consecutive years are spent outside of the UK.	Pre-settled status will be lost if more than **two** consecutive years are spent outside of the UK (spending more than six months outside of the UK may also jeopardise the ability to attain full settled status).

CHAPTER SUMMARY

Concepts of free movement of persons and EU citizenship

- **Article 20(1) TFEU** and **Article 9 TEU** establish that every person who holds the nationality of a Member State is an EU citizen.
- The right of EU citizens to move and reside freely within the Union is established in **Article 21 TFEU**.
- **Article 18 TFEU** prohibits discrimination on grounds of nationality.

Free movement of EU citizens

- Free movement rights are available to EU citizens when they move to and reside within a Member State of which they are not a national (**Art 3(1), Directive 2004/38**) and when they return to their home Member State after a period of **genuine residence** in another Member State (**Surinder Singh**; **O and B**).
- EU citizens and their family members have an **unconditional** right to reside in a host Member State for **up to three months** (**Art 6, Directive 2004/38**).

- EU citizens may reside in a host Member State for **longer than three months** if they are **workers** or self-employed, have **sufficient resources** to support themselves, are a **student** with sufficient resources or are a **family member** of one of the above (**Art 7(1), Directive 2004/38**).
- EU citizens acquire a right of **permanent residence** after **five years** of continuous residence within a host Member State (**Art 16(1), Directive 2004/38**).

Free movement of family members

- The family members of an EU citizen may accompany or join that citizen in a host Member State (**Art 7(1), Directive 2004/38**).
- Family members include the **spouse or registered partner** of an EU citizen, their **direct descendants** who are under the age of 21 or are dependent on them and their **direct ascendants** who are dependent on them (**Art 2(2), Directive 2004/38**).
- A non-EU parent may derive a right of residence if their EU child is dependent on them (*Zhu and Chen*; *Zambrano*; *Chavez-Vilchez*).
- In certain circumstances, family members can retain their right of residence in the event of the **death, departure or divorce** from the EU citizen from whom their rights were derived (**Arts 12 and 13, Directive 2004/38**).

Restrictions on free movement rights

- EU citizens or their family members may be expelled from or refused entry to a Member State on grounds of **public policy, public security or public health** (**Art 27(1), Directive 2004/38**).
- Such an expulsion or refusal must be based on an assessment of the **personal conduct** of the individual, which must represent a **genuine, present and sufficiently serious threat** affecting one of the fundamental interests of society (**Art 27(2), Directive 2004/38**).

Social benefits

- In general, lawfully residing EU citizens and their family members are entitled to social benefits on the same basis as nationals of the host Member State (**Art 18 TFEU**; **Art 24(1), Directive 2004/38**).
- However, a host Member State is not obliged to provide **social assistance** during a person's first three months of residence (**Art 24(2), Directive 2004/38**).

The Schengen *acquis*

- Within the Schengen Area, internal border checks are abolished and external border checks are enhanced through the **Schengen Information System**.
- **Denmark**, the **UK** and **Ireland** have special arrangements whereby they need not take part in or apply all areas of the Schengen *acquis*.
- Several Member States have 'temporarily' **reintroduced internal border controls** in accordance with the **Schengen Borders Code**.

Free movement rights after Brexit

- Free movement between the UK and the EU will cease after the Brexit transition period.
- UK citizens residing in EU Member States and EU citizens residing in the UK will have the right to remain.

Chapter 10
Free movement of workers

Learning objectives

At the end of this chapter you should understand:

1 The legal framework that establishes and facilitates the free movement of workers.

2 The meaning and scope of the term 'Union worker'.

3 The rights afforded to workers, including rights to free movement, equal treatment in employment, equal access to social advantages and social security coordination.

4 The scope of the term 'work-seekers' and the rights to free movement and social benefits afforded to such persons.

5 The rights afforded to the family members of Union workers and work-seekers, including rights to free movement and social benefits.

Key terms and concepts

Familiarity with the following terms will be helpful for understanding this chapter:

Direct discrimination – when legislation affords less favourable treatment to a certain group of people

Frontier worker – a person who lives in one Member State but works in another Member State

Indirect discrimination – when legislation is formulated or implemented in such a way that – although no explicit distinction between groups of people is made – a certain group of people is disadvantaged in practice

Objective justification – a permissible reason for indirect discrimination on the grounds that the difference in treatment pursues a legitimate aim and goes no further than is necessary for the realisation of that aim

Social advantages – benefits that are granted on the basis of worker or residence status, or that could facilitate the mobility of Union workers

Social assistance – non-contributory benefits that aim to enable a person to meet their basic subsistence needs

Social security – benefits that insure against possible loss of income resulting from unemployment, disability, pregnancy, old age and other related circumstances that result in loss of income, and which do not involve any individual assessment

Union worker – a national of one Member State who works in another Member State

10.1 Introduction to the free movement of workers

Objective 1

The free movement of workers is of great economic and social importance to the Union. In the early days of the Union the right to move to other Member States for employment was seen as no more than an economic function, whereby a surplus of labour and skills in one part of the Union could meet a shortage in another. However, the worker was soon recognised in the Union's legislation and in the decisions of the Court of Justice as more than merely a unit of labour. The right to free movement is expounded in the preamble of **Regulation 492/2011** as 'a fundamental right' of workers which is to be 'exercised in freedom and dignity'. Furthermore, Advocate General Trabucchi in *Mr and Mrs F v Belgian State* (Case 7/75) stated that 'The migrant worker is not to be viewed as a mere source of labour, but as a human being'.

The exercise of a migrant worker's rights is to be facilitated in the workplace and in the broader social context of the host Member State. The implementing legislation and the jurisprudence of the Court of Justice is directed at facilitating the worker's departure from his state of origin and his entry, residence and integration, in the widest sense, into the economic and social fabric of the host Member State.

10.1.1 Primary legislation

Article 45 TFEU establishes the basic principles of free movement of workers and non-discrimination against Union citizens working in a host Member State. The importance of the principles of free movement and of non-discrimination have been emphasised repeatedly by the Court of Justice. However, whether a migrant worker is employed, self-employed or seeking work in another Member State, as well as the duration and type of economic activity they are or have been engaged in, can affect their rights and the rights of their family members to residence, education and **social security** in the host state.

Article 45 TFEU applies to Union citizens who are working within the territory of a Member State and is directly effective with regards to both the worker and the employer (*Clean Car Autoservice GmbH* v *Landeshauptmann von Wien* (Case C-350/96)). The text of Article 45 is as follows:

> ► See section 8.2 for an explanation of the principle of direct effect

1. Freedom of movement for workers shall be secured within the Union.
2. Such freedom of movement shall entail the abolition of any discrimination based on nationality between workers of the Member States as regards employment, remuneration and other conditions of work and employment.
3. It shall entail the right, subject to limitations justified on grounds of public policy, public security or public health:
   (a) to accept offers of employment actually made;
   (b) to move freely within the territory of Member States for this purpose;
   (c) to stay in a Member State for the purpose of employment in accordance with the provisions governing the employment of nationals of that State laid down by law, regulation or administrative action;
   (d) to remain in the territory of a Member State after having been employed in that State, subject to conditions which shall be embodied in regulations to be drawn up by the Commission.
4. The provisions of this Article shall not apply to employment in the public service.

Article 45 is supported by Articles 46–48 TFEU. **Article 46 TFEU** provides a legal base for the Parliament and the Council to enact measures using the ordinary legislative procedure to bring about freedom of movement for workers. This includes the adoption of directives and/or regulations to:

- ensure close cooperation between national employment services;
- abolish administrative procedures and practices that would form an obstacle to liberalisation of the movement of workers;
- abolish conditions regarding the free choice of employment other than those imposed on workers of the State concerned;
- set up appropriate machinery to bring offers of employment into touch with applications for employment.

Article 47 TFEU then requires Member States to encourage the exchange of young workers between them and **Article 48 TFEU** states that such measures shall be adopted in the field of social security as are necessary to facilitate freedom of movement for workers.

The most important secondary legislation adopted pursuant to Article 46 TFEU will now be briefly outlined.

10.1.2 Secondary legislation

As noted in Chapter 9, **Directive 2004/38** of 29 April 2004 on the right of citizens of the Union and their family members to move and reside freely within the territory of the Member States is also known as the **Citizen's Rights Directive (CRD)** or the **Free Movement Directive (FMD)**. Chapters within the Directive include:

- right of exit and entry;
- right of residence;
- right of permanent residence; and
- restrictions on the right of entry and the right of residence on grounds of public policy, public security or public health.

▶ See Chapter 9 on the provisions of Directive 2004/38 that concern EU citizenship

Regulation 492/2011 of 5 April 2011 on freedom of movement for workers within the Union (repealing Regulation 1612/68) includes provisions on equal access to employment and equal treatment in matters of employment, remuneration and conditions of work for **Union workers**. Chapter II on the clearance of vacancies and applications for employment has now been replaced by **Regulation 2016/589** of 13 April 2016 on a European network of employment services (EURES), workers' access to mobility services and the further integration of labour markets.

Directive 2014/54 of 16 April 2014 on measures facilitating the exercise of rights conferred on workers in the context of freedom of movement for workers, was then enacted with the aim of facilitating the uniform application and enforcement of the rights enshrined in Article 45 TFEU and in Articles 1 to 10 of Regulation 429/2011.

It is also worth mentioning **Regulation 883/2004** of 29 April 2004 on the coordination of social security systems, which seeks to implement Article 48 TFEU. Regulation 883/2004 has been amended by Regulation 465/2012 and Commission Regulation 1224/2012. Implementing provisions for Regulation 833/2004 are contained in **Regulation 987/2009**. Further amendments to Regulation 883/2004 and Regulation 987/2009 are likely to be forthcoming in a new regulation, as provisionally agreed by the Council and the Parliament in March 2019 (see section 10.3.4).

To further facilitate labour mobility and social security coordination, **Regulation 2019/1149** establishes the **European Labour Authority**. Article 2 of the Regulation sets out the objectives of the Authority as to:

(a) facilitate access to information on rights and obligations regarding labour mobility across the Union as well as to relevant services;

(b) facilitate and enhance cooperation between Member States in the enforcement of relevant Union law across the Union, including facilitating concerted and joint inspections;

(c) mediate and facilitate a solution in cases of cross-border disputes between Member States; and

(d) support cooperation between Member States in tackling undeclared work.

10.2 Scope of the term 'worker'

Objective 2

The range of rights accruing under **Article 45 TFEU** and the secondary legislation is dependent upon a person coming within the scope of the term 'worker'. However, neither the TFEU nor the secondary legislation defines a 'worker'. In *Hoekstra (née Unger)* v *Bestuur der Berijfsvereniging voor Detailhandel en Ambachten* (Case 75/63), the Court held that the activities which confer Union worker status are a matter of Union law. It is therefore for the Court to determine its meaning and scope, so as to avoid the unequal application of the rights to free movement throughout the Union that would occur if Member States each applied their own definitions. In *Levin* v *Staatssecretaris van Justitie* (Case 53/81) the Court stated that, because the concept of 'worker' determines the scope of application of a fundamental freedom of the Union, it should **not** be interpreted restrictively. Indeed, defining the term has not been a straightforward task, as the Court pointed out in *van Delft and Others* (Case C-345/09):

> On the question of the applicability of Article 45 TFEU, it should be noted at the outset that there is **no single definition of worker/employed or self-employed person in European Union law**; it varies according to the area in which the definition is to be applied. Thus the concept of 'worker' used in the context of Article 45 TFEU does not necessarily coincide with the definition applied in relation to Article 48 TFEU and Regulation No 1408/71. [para 88]

Despite this, the Court has set out several factors that determine who is and who isn't a Union worker, which will now be discussed.

10.2.1 Definition of a Union worker

First, it should be noted that rights pertaining to the free movement of workers only apply to nationals of one Member State who are or have been economically active in another Member State. This cross-border requirement was demonstrated in the following case:

Morson and Jhanjan v *Netherlands* (Cases 35 and 36/82)

Facts:

Two Dutch nationals were working in their home state, the Netherlands. They wanted to bring their parents (Surinamese: i.e. non-EU nationals) into the Netherlands to live with them. Had they been nationals of any other EU Member State working in the Netherlands, their situation would have been covered by Directive 2004/38 and their parents would have been able to join them.

Ruling:

Because the Dutch nationals were working in their own Member State and had not exercised their right of free movement within the Union, Union law did not apply. The situation was therefore ruled to be internal to the Netherlands and beyond the scope of EU law.

Significance:

Legislation and case law that has developed under Article 45 TFEU include measures to remove obstacles that could inhibit workers from exercising their right to free movement. Where Member States have not provided for commensurate rights for their national workers, migrant workers may be entitled to rights that are not available to national workers such as Morson and Jhanjan. This can be described as **reverse discrimination** and is beyond the jurisdiction of the Court of Justice.

> ### Reflection: Reverse discrimination
>
> Reverse discrimination refers to situations where a minority or generally less privileged group is treated more advantageously than a majority or generally more privileged group. Discrimination in such situations is described as 'reverse' because the usual relations of privilege are inverted.
>
> Reverse discrimination can be a very politically sensitive topic and is often portrayed in a negative light. For example, where quotas are implemented to encourage the employment of women or ethnic minorities within particular sectors, opponents of such measures might describe them as reverse discrimination on the basis that equally qualified men might consequently face disadvantages.
>
> With regard to Union citizens, reverse discrimination occurs due to the limited jurisdiction of the EU: principles and standards set by the EU can only be enforced in situations that concern movement across Member State borders and the EU has no competence in matters that are purely internal to a Member State (see section 4.2 on competences). There is therefore a risk that the rights afforded to Union citizens by virtue of their having moved between Member States might be greater than the rights afforded to those who have not moved from their home Member State. This can cause tensions where nationals feel that immigrants are being treated better than they are and can therefore be counterproductive to the aim of creating a shared sense of community among Union citizens.
>
> One solution in such situations is for Member States to improve the rights that they afford to their nationals so that they are aligned with those that they are obliged to provide to Union citizens. However, seeking to avoid reverse discrimination in this way could compromise the autonomy of Member States over internal matters, such as the immigration of non-EU nationals who are the family members of nationals, as in **Morson and Jhanjan**.

▶ See *Surinder Singh* in section 9.2.1 (page 332), in which previous work in another Member State enabled a UK citizen to rely on Union freedom of movement rights upon their return to the UK

The ruling in ***Morson and Jhanjan* v *Netherlands*** was confirmed by the Court of Justice in ***Land Nordrhein-Westfalen* v *Uecker***; and ***Jacquei* v *Land Nordrhein-Westfalen*** (Cases C-64 and 65/96).

In the case of ***Lawrie-Blum* v *Baden-Württemberg***, which is also discussed further below, the Court of Justice provided the following definition of a worker:

> Objectively defined, a 'worker' is a person who is obliged to provide services for another in return for monetary reward and who is subject to the direction and control of the other person as regards the way in which the work is to be done. [para 14]

Here, the Court defined a worker as an employee, i.e. as someone who performs work under a contract *of* service. This is distinct from a person who is self-employed, who performs work under a contract *for* services. This amounts to a **formal definition** of a worker, i.e. whether an individual is employed. In the following case, the Court established a **material definition**, i.e. a definition based on the economic nature and significance of the work performed. The question before the Court of Justice was whether the concept of 'worker' within the meaning of Article 45 TFEU includes a part-time employee who earns less than the minimum required for subsistence, as defined under national law:

Levin v Staatssecretaris van Justitie (Case 53/81)

Facts:

Ms Levin was a British national married to a South African national. She was refused a residence permit by Dutch authorities because it was claimed that she was not a 'worker' within the scope of what is now Article 45 TFEU (Art 48 EEC Treaty at the time). She challenged the refusal before the national courts, which referred the matter to the Court of Justice for a preliminary ruling. The Court was asked to explain the concept of 'worker' for Union law purposes, and in particular whether it included an individual who worked part-time and earned an income less than the minimum required for subsistence as defined under national law.

Ruling:

The Court stated that, because the concept of 'worker' determines the scope of application of a fundamental freedom of the Union, it should not be interpreted restrictively:

> 15 An interpretation which reflects the full scope of these concepts is also in conformity with the objectives of the [EEC] Treaty which include, according to Articles 2 and 3, the abolition, as between Member States, of obstacles to freedom of movement for persons, with the purpose *inter alia* of promoting throughout the Community [i.e. Union] a harmonious development of economic activities and a raising of the standard of living. Since part-time employment, although it may provide an income lower than that considered to be the minimum required for subsistence, constitutes for a large number of persons an effective means of improving their living conditions, **the effectiveness of Community [i.e. Union] law would be impaired and the achievement of the objectives of the Treaty would be jeopardised if the enjoyment of rights conferred by the principle of freedom of movement for workers were reserved solely to persons engaged in full-time employment** and earning, as a result, a wage at least equivalent to the guaranteed minimum wage in the sector under consideration.

> ...

> 17 It should however be stated that whilst part-time employment is not excluded from the field of application of the rules on freedom of movement for workers, **those rules cover only the pursuit of effective and genuine activities, to the exclusion of activities on such a small scale as to be regarded as purely marginal and ancillary**. It follows both from the statement of principle of freedom of movement for workers and from the place occupied by the rules relating to that principle in the system of the Treaty as a whole that those rules guarantee only the free movement of persons who pursue or are desirous of pursuing an economic activity.

Significance:

This case made three major contributions to the definition of a worker:

1 The Court clarified that part-time workers could be covered by the Union law provisions on free movement of workers, because part-time work is not only a valuable contribution to the economies of the Member States, but also contributes to the raising of living standards for the employees concerned.

2 The case established the test that in order to be considered a worker an individual must undertake '**effective and genuine**' economic activity which must not be on such a small scale as to be 'purely marginal and ancillary'.

3 Finally, the Court concluded that the intention of the applicant was irrelevant: it was irrelevant that the applicant had taken up an economic activity in order to obtain a residence permit.

The Court of Justice has not laid down any comprehensive criteria as to what constitutes 'effective and genuine' work and at what point work may be discounted as 'purely marginal and ancillary', although some guidance can be gained from the case law. For example, the following case determined that claiming social security benefits is not a criterion that can be used to determine that work is 'purely marginal and ancillary':

Kempf v Staatssecretaris van Justitie (Case 139/85)

Facts:

A German national was living and working in the Netherlands as a music teacher. He gave 12 lessons a week. His application for a residence permit was refused. He challenged this refusal and the national court referred the case to the Court of Justice for a preliminary ruling. It was argued by the Netherlands and Denmark that work providing an income below the minimum level of subsistence was not 'effective or genuine' if the person undertaking the work claimed social security benefits. If it was not 'effective or genuine' then the person would not come within the scope of a Union worker and therefore could not benefit from the rights under the Treaty or secondary legislation.

Ruling:

The Court of Justice held as follows:

> 14 … In that regard, it is irrelevant whether those supplementary means of subsistence are derived from property or from the employment of a member of his family, as was the case in *Levin*, or whether, as in this instance, they are obtained from financial assistance drawn from the public funds of the Member State in which he resides, provided that the effective and genuine nature of his work is established.

Significance:

This case established that even though an individual supplemented his income with social benefits, his work may still be 'effective and genuine' for the purpose of defining him as a worker. Therefore, 1) an individual does not need to be earning more than the minimum income required for subsistence in order to qualify as a worker, and 2) claiming social security benefits cannot automatically preclude an individual from qualifying as a worker.

The same was held in **Lawrie-Blum** (see above), where the Court held that a trainee teacher qualified as a Union worker, even though her remuneration was only nominal. The fact that the salary was less than a teacher's full salary was immaterial. What mattered was that she received some remuneration for services that she provided and was therefore deemed to be in an employment relationship, as defined in **Levin** (see above).

Surprisingly small amounts of work can be regarded as sufficient to come within the scope of a Union worker. In **Raulin v Netherlands Ministry for Education and Science** (Case C-357/89), the person claiming Union worker status had been 'on call' for a period of eight months. During that period she only actually worked for a total of 60 hours. Nonetheless, the Court of Justice held that the brevity of her employment period did not exclude her from the status of a Union worker. This principle was subsequently reaffirmed by the Court of Justice in **Ninni-Orasche** (Case C-413/01).

In *Steymann* v *Staatssecretaris van Justitie* (Case 196/87), the individual was engaged in maintenance and repair work for a religious community. He received his keep (i.e. accommodation, meals, etc.), but no wages. Despite the fact that his reward was 'in kind' rather than monetary, the Court of Justice held that he came within the scope of Union worker.

In contrast, in the case of *Bettray* v *Staatssecretaris van Justitie* (Case 344/87), the individual concerned was engaged in paid work as part of a form of therapy. The work was considered to be ancillary, as the economic aspect was incidental to the therapeutic objective. The distinction between 'effective and genuine' work and 'purely marginal and ancillary work' was further developed by the Court in the following case:

Trojani v CPAS (Case C-456/02)

Facts:

A destitute French national had been given accommodation in a Salvation Army hostel in Brussels (Belgium) where, in return for his board and lodging and a small amount of pocket money, he performed a variety of jobs for about 30 hours per week as part of a personal socio-occupational reintegration programme. The question arose as to whether he could claim a right of residence as a worker, a self-employed worker or a person providing or receiving services within the terms of the former Articles 39, 43 and 49 EC Treaty (now Arts 45, 49 and 56 TFEU) respectively. If not, could he claim a right to residence by direct application of the former Article 18 EC Treaty (now Art 21 TFEU) in his capacity merely as a Union citizen (see Chapter 9)? The Tribunal du Travail de Bruxelles (Labour Court, Brussels) referred the case to the Court of Justice.

Ruling:

The Court found that, in this case, **the constituent elements of any paid employment relationship, as established in *Levin*, were present**: the benefits in kind and in cash that the Salvation Army provided for Trojani constituted remuneration for the services he performed for and under the direction of the hostel. **However, it remained to be determined whether those services were effective and genuine** or whether, on the contrary, they were on such a small scale as to be regarded as purely marginal and ancillary, with the result that the person concerned could not be classified as a worker. The Court left this to the national court to determine, but also provided some guidelines: the national court had, in particular, to ascertain **whether the services performed were capable of being treated as forming part of the normal labour market**, regard being had to the status and practices of the hostel, the content of the social reintegration programme, and the nature and details of performance of the services.

However, if the national courts were to determine that Trojani was not a worker, the Court ruled that he would still be entitled to enjoy a right of residence under the former Article 18(1) EC Treaty (now Art 21 TFEU) by virtue of his Union citizenship, subject to the limitations and conditions referred to in that provision and in the corresponding secondary legislation (see Chapter 9).

Significance:

Seeming to diverge from *Bettray*, the case established that an individual may be defined as a worker even if the economic nature of their work is secondary to another objective, such as, as in this case, socio-occupational reintegration. Rather than whether the economic nature of the work was its primary purpose, what was important was whether the services performed could be considered as part of the national labour market.

In *Fenoll* v *APEI* (Case C-316/13), the Court affirmed the test established in *Trojani* that, to determine whether or not someone is a worker, national courts must consider whether the services performed by an individual form part of the normal labour market.

> **Reflection:** UK implementation of the EU case law on the definition of a worker
>
> Guidance produced by the UK Home Office in 2014 established that a person who meets a 'Primary Earnings Threshold' is automatically considered to be a worker. Those who earn less than the threshold, which is based on 24 hours of work per week at minimum wage, should be subjected to investigations to determine whether their work is marginal or ancillary. Such investigations should consider:
>
> - whether there is a genuine employer-employee relationship;
> - whether there is an employment contract;
> - whether the work is regular or intermittent;
> - how long the EU national has been employed for;
> - the number of hours worked;
> - the level of earnings.
>
> Some commentators expressed concern that such considerations could have been problematic for persons employed in low-wage and irregular 'zero hours' jobs, which are readily available on the UK labour market. Self-employed EU nationals who did not meet the Primary Earnings Threshold may also have found it difficult to be classified as a worker according to these considerations.
>
> After Brexit, being classified as an EU worker will no longer be relevant for EU citizens in the UK with settled or pre-settled status, while EU citizens seeking to move to the UK to work will be subject to domestic immigration provisions.

▶ See section 9.7 on settled and pre-settled status

▶ See the Reflection box in section 9.5.2 for discussion of welfare tourism (page 367)

In view of the broad scope that the Court of Justice has given to the definition of a Union worker, some Member States have expressed concern that EU nationals from Member States with less generous welfare benefit provisions would migrate to those with more generous provisions. However, Member States have a number of options available to them in this regard. One of them, in relation to part-time workers, is to provide that certain benefits will only be available to national and non-national workers who are 'available for full-time work'.

In terms of geographical scope, the Court of Justice has held that workers employed on gas-drilling platforms at sea, on the continental shelf adjacent to a Member State, are as a rule subject to EU law (*Salemink* v *Raad van bestuur van het Uitvoeringsinstituut Werknemersverzekeringen* (C-347/10)).

10.2.2 Retention of worker status after cessation of employment

A person retains Union worker status as long as they continue to be employed. However, that status is not necessarily lost as soon as a person ceases to work. It may be important for a person to retain their status as a worker so that they can continue to avail themselves of the associated rights and benefits.

Before Directive 2004/38

Article 45(3)(d) TFEU specifies the right 'to remain in the territory of a Member State after having been employed in that State, subject to conditions which shall be embodied in regulations to be drawn up by the Commission'. This was generally taken to mean that a person could remain within the Member State they had worked in after retirement or if they became incapable of working. Regulation 1251/70 was then adopted to enshrine this right, specifying the periods of employment necessary to qualify for the right and that it was a *permanent* right to remain. Regulation 1251/70 has since been repealed by Regulation 635/2006, as its provisions have been replaced and enhanced by Article 17 of Directive 2004/38 (see below).

For persons whose employment terminates for reasons other than retirement or incapacity, however, it was not clear for how long they could retain Union worker status. For example, the Court of Justice in *Lair* v *University of Hannover* (Case 39/86) referred to what is now **Article 45(3)(d) TFEU** in general terms, saying that 'migrant workers are granted certain rights linked to their status of worker even when they are no longer in the employment relationship'. The Court did not indicate for how long that status might continue.

Article 7(1) Directive 68/360 (which has been repealed and replaced by Directive 2004/38) stated that a residence permit could not be withdrawn from a person solely on the grounds that they were involuntarily unemployed or temporarily unable to work. As a Union worker's right of residence is not dependent on the possession of a residence permit, it was assumed that the provisions of the former Directive 68/360 would also apply to someone who had no such permit. This was the view of the UK Immigration Appeal Tribunal in *Lubbersen* v *Secretary of State for the Home Department* [1984] 3 CMLR 77.

The Court of Justice has considered the concept and implications of 'voluntary' unemployment in relation to educational **social advantages** and fixed-term employment contracts. In connection with obtaining access to educational 'social advantages', the Court has held that an individual will retain their status as a Union worker, even though they have voluntarily left that employment to take up a vocational course, provided there is a link between the course and their previous employment (*Raulin* (Case C-357/89), para 21). In *Ninni-Orasche* (Case C-413/01), the Court of Justice held that a Union worker who had been employed in the host Member State for a fixed term (which had been set at the outset) would not be considered voluntarily unemployed when that fixed term expired. In this case, the Union worker had been employed for a fixed term of two-and-a-half months and the worker had applied for a study grant from the host Member State for when that fixed term expired.

Additionally, in *Tetik* v *Land Berlin* (Case C-171/95), it was found that a worker who does become voluntarily unemployed may lose their worker status, but can benefit from the rights afforded to work-seekers (see below).

After Directive 2004/38

Directive 2004/38 now sets out the circumstances in which a Union citizen will retain the status of a worker (or self-employed person). **Article 7(3)** provides that a Union citizen shall retain the status of a worker or self-employed person in the host Member State in the following circumstances:

(a) they are temporarily unable to work as the result of an illness or accident;

(b) they are in duly recorded involuntary unemployment after having been employed for more than one year and have registered as a jobseeker with the relevant employment office in the host Member State;

(c) they are in duly recorded involuntary unemployment after completing a fixed-term employment contract of less than a year or after having become involuntarily unemployed during the first 12 months and have registered as a jobseeker with the relevant employment office in the host Member State. In this case, the status of worker shall be retained for not less than six months; or

(d) they embark on vocational training. Unless they are involuntarily unemployed, the retention of the status of worker shall require the training to be related to the previous employment.

In relation to Article 7(1)(c), the Court of Justice has determined that the status of a worker can be retained for at least six months after a period of employment of just two weeks (*Tarola v Minister for Social Protection* (Case C-483/17)).

The following case considered the retention of worker status during and after pregnancy:

Saint Prix v Secretary of State for Work and Pensions (Case C-507/12)

Facts:

Ms Saint Prix was a French national who entered the UK on 10 July 2006, where she worked, mainly as a teaching assistant, from 1 September 2006 until 1 August 2007. At the beginning of 2008, Ms Saint Prix took up agency positions in nursery schools. On 12 March 2008, at nearly six months pregnant, Ms Saint Prix stopped that work because the demands of caring for young children had become too strenuous. The claim for income support made by Ms Saint Prix was refused by the UK authorities on the ground that she had lost her status as a worker. Three months after the birth of her child, Ms Saint Prix resumed work. The Supreme Court of the United Kingdom referred the case to the Court of Justice to ascertain whether a woman who gave up work, or seeking work, because of the physical constraints of the late stages of pregnancy and the aftermath of childbirth was a 'worker' for the purposes of EU law.

Ruling:

The Court determined that pregnancy should not be classified as an illness, but observed that **Article 7(3) of Directive 2004/38** was not an exhaustive list of the circumstances in which a Union worker who was no longer in employment may continue to benefit from the status of being a worker. Furthermore, the Directive, which expressly sought to facilitate the exercise of the rights of a Union citizen to move and reside freely within the territory of the Member States, could not, by itself, limit the scope of the concept of worker within the meaning of the TFEU.

Therefore, **the fact that the physical constraints of the late stages of pregnancy and the immediate aftermath of childbirth required a woman to give up work for a period did not in principle terminate her status as a 'worker', provided she resumed work within a reasonable period after childbirth**. Otherwise, a Union citizen might be deterred from exercising their free movement rights. The Court held that, in order to determine whether the period that had elapsed between childbirth and starting work again could be regarded as reasonable, the national court should take account of all the specific circumstances of the case and the national rules on the duration of maternity leave.

Significance:

The Court's ruling means that women moving within the EU to work can retain their status as workers – and can therefore remain eligible for benefits that are dependent upon that status – if they become unable to work due to pregnancy and/or childbirth. Thus, although not classified as an illness, women who are temporarily unable to work due to pregnancy and/or childbirth should be afforded protection of their worker status that is commensurate with that which is provided under Article 7(3)(a) of Directive 2004/38.

10.3 Rights of workers

> **Objective 3**

10.3.1 Rights to free movement

Article 45 TFEU provides that a Union worker should have the right to:

- accept offers of employment actually made;
- move freely within the territory of Member States for this purpose;
- stay in a Member State for the purpose of employment;
- remain in the territory of a Member State after having been employed in that state.

▶ See section 10.1.1 for the full text of Article 45 TFEU

Implementing legislation has given detailed effect to these provisions.

- **Directive 2004/38** defines the obligations of national immigration authorities in relation to the rights of Union workers and their family members to exit, enter and reside within the territory of a Member State (see Chapter 9).
- **Regulation 492/2011** (which repealed and replaced Regulation 1612/68) deals with matters relating to equal access to employment and equality in terms of employment, housing, education and social rights (see below).
- **Regulation 883/2004** (which repealed and replaced Regulation 1408/71) ensures that workers who are entitled to contributory and related benefits continue to enjoy them in the host Member State and on return to their home state.
- **Directive 2014/54** lays down provisions which facilitate the uniform application and enforcement in practice of the rights conferred by Article 45 TFEU and by Articles 1 to 10 of Regulation 492/2011.

All of these measures create **directly effective** rights.

The primary and secondary legislation has been interpreted as placing a duty on states not only to permit the free movement of workers, but also to facilitate their mobility and to remove any obstacles to mobility as far as is reasonable.

Football players moving between teams in different Member States have been profoundly affected by the implementation of Article 45. This is therefore used as an example here to illustrate the effects of the requirement to remove obstacles to the free movement of workers. In *Donà* v *Mantero* (Case 13/76), the Court of Justice determined that sporting bodies that are not emanations of the state, such as a football association, are liable to uphold the rights contained in Article 45 TFEU in so far as they undertake economic activities (i.e. Art 45 can have horizontal direct effect, see Chapter 8). This applies to the activities of professional or semi-professional footballers, where they are in gainful employment or provide a remunerated service. The ruling in the following case then had a considerable impact on the international transfer of football players between teams:

> ### *Union Royale Belge des Sociétés de Football Association ASBL* v *Bosman* (Case C-415/93)
>
> **Facts:**
> Football transfer rules established that a football player could only transfer internationally if their current club requested their national football association to issue a transfer certificate, regardless of whether the player's contract with that club had expired. The request for a transfer certificate

was generally made once an agreement on a 'transfer fee' had been reached, whereby the player's new club effectively compensated their old club for training and development expenses.

Mr Bosman was a footballer whose contract with a Belgian team, RFC Liege, had expired. A transfer fee for his move to the French team US Dunkerque was agreed, but Liege did not request a transfer certificate as they had concerns over Dunkerque's solvency. Mr Bosman was therefore prevented from playing for a new team and subsequently argued that the transfer rules had obstructed his freedom of movement as a worker.

Additionally, rules set by the Union of European Football Associations (UEFA) permitted national associations to limit the number of foreign players fielded in a first division match to three, plus two non-nationals who had played continuously within the country for five years.

Ruling:

The Court of Justice first reaffirmed the ruling in **Donà** that the former Article 48 EC Treaty (now Art 45 TFEU) applies to rules laid down by sporting associations. On the question of whether the transfer rules breached the article, the Court stated that:

> Since they provide that a professional footballer may not pursue his activity with a new club established in another Member State unless it has paid his former club a transfer fee agreed upon between the two clubs or determined in accordance with the regulations of the sporting associations, **the said rules constitute an obstacle to freedom of movement for workers.** [para 100]

The aims put forward to justify the transfer rules, including the encouragement of clubs to recruit and train young players, were found to be legitimate. However, the Court held that **the aims could be met in ways that did not impede the free movement of workers** and therefore that they were not proportionate.

Additionally, the Court stated that restrictions on the fielding of foreign players, although not directly limiting their employment opportunities, would have this effect in practice. These restrictions therefore also violated the former Article 48 EC Treaty (now Art 45 TFEU).

Significance:

The ruling brought free movement rights to out-of-contract footballers, whose future employment does not now depend upon the satisfaction of their former club. This has been beneficial to footballers, as once they are out-of-contract their ability to transfer freely makes them more desirable to new clubs and therefore enables them to negotiate higher salaries. However, it has been argued that this has been detrimental to smaller clubs, which are unable to afford to sign players on long contracts to retain them and which now receive less income from transfer fees. The free movement of workers in football – and the ability to field as many foreign players as they like – has therefore contributed to the dominance of big clubs that can afford to offer sky-high wages to the best players.

The following case expands upon the above case law and considers the issue of **objective justification** in more depth:

Olympique Lyonnais Sasp v *Bernard and Newcastle United FC* (Case C-325/08)

Facts:

At the material time, the Professional Football Charter of the Fédération Française de Football (French Football Federation) contained rules applicable to the employment of football players in France. According to the Charter, '*joueurs espoir*' were football players between the ages of

16 and 22 who were employed as trainees by a professional club under a fixed-term contract. At the end of the period of training, the Charter obliged a *joueur espoir* to sign his first professional contract with the club that trained him, if the club required him to do so.

In 1997, Mr Bernard signed a *joueur espoir* contract with Olympique Lyonnais for three seasons. Before that contract was due to expire, Olympique Lyonnais offered him a professional contract for one year. Mr Bernard refused to sign that contract and instead signed a professional contract with Newcastle United FC, an English football club.

Olympique Lyonnais sued Bernard, seeking an award of damages against him and Newcastle United of over 50,000 euros, equivalent to the salary Bernard would have received over one year if he had signed the contract offered by Olympique Lyonnais. The Cour de cassation, before which a final appeal was brought, asked the Court of Justice whether clubs that prevented or discouraged their *joueurs espoir* from signing a professional contract with a football club in another Member State were in breach of the principle of free movement of workers.

Ruling:

The Court held that **the rules at issue, which required a *joueur espoir* to sign a professional contract with the club which trained him, or to be liable for damages, was likely to discourage that player from exercising his right of free movement**. However, the Court had already held in the ***Bosman*** case that, in view of the considerable social and educational importance of sporting activities in the European Union, **the objective of encouraging the recruitment and training of young players had to be accepted as legitimate**. The question was therefore whether the scheme sufficiently ensured that the legitimate objective would be attained and did not exceed what was necessary to attain it (i.e. that it was proportionate).

In the Court's view, the prospect of receiving training fees was likely to encourage football clubs to seek new talent and train young players. The Court stated that **liability for damages amounted to a scheme of compensation for training where a young player signs a professional contract with a club other than the one which trained them. This could, in principle, be justified by the objective of encouraging the training of young players**.

With regard to the French scheme at issue in the main proceedings, the Court noted that the payments to the club which provided the training were not compensation for the costs incurred by the training, but damages that were calculated in relation to the total loss suffered by the club. Therefore, the Court held **the French scheme went beyond what was necessary to encourage and fund the recruitment and training of young players**.

Significance:

Restrictions on the free movement of workers may be justified by a legitimate objective, provided that the restrictions in question ensure that the objective is met, but go no further than is necessary to do so, i.e. they must be proportionate to the aim. Sporting activities should be granted special considerations relating to their social and educational importance.

For the most part, the rights of Union workers pertain to their treatment within a host Member State. However, in ***R v Immigration Appeal Tribunal and Surinder Singh, ex parte Secretary of State for the Home Department*** (Case-370/90), the Court of Justice determined that Union law provisions on the free movement of workers can be relied upon by a worker against the Member State of which they are a national, provided they have resided and been employed in another Member State. Similarly to the possibility of reverse discrimination considered in section 10.2 of this chapter, this ruling presents the possibility of unequal treatment within a Member State: a Union worker who is returning to their home state may have rights that are not extended to workers who have not left that Member State or who are returning from employment in a non-EU state.

The principle that the rights of free movement for workers may affect the treatment of a Union worker upon returning to their home Member State was then confirmed by the Court of Justice in *Terhoeve* v *Inspecteur van de Belastingdienst Particulieren/Ondernemingen Buitenland* (Case C-18/95). Then, in *O and B* v *Minister voor Immigratie, Integratie en Asiel* (Cases C-456/12 and C-457/12), the Court of Justice stated that the Union citizen must have been legally resident in another Member State for longer than three months in order to be able to rely upon Union law against the Member State of which he is a national.

> The *Surinder Singh* and *O and B* cases are considered in greater depth in relation to free movement rights in section 9.2.1 (page 332)

Rights to reside under Directive 2004/38

Under **Directive 2004/38**, Union citizens acquire the right of permanent residence in the host Member State after a five-year period of continuous legal residence (Art 16(1)), provided that an expulsion decision has not been enforced against them (Art 21). However, Union citizens who are workers may not be subjected to expulsion measures (Art 14(4)). Furthermore, Article 17 of the Directive recognises the right of permanent residence for Union citizens who are or have been workers, and for their family members, before the five-year period of continuous residence has expired, subject to certain conditions being met. See Chapter 9 for further detail on the right to reside.

Directive 2004/38, in line with Article 45(3) TFEU, allows for the exercise of workers' rights to be made subject to national rules relating to public policy, public security or public health. Any such restrictions must be proportional to their objectives, may not serve economic ends and must consider the particulars of an individual's case, rather than applying a generalised restriction (see section 9.4).

Transitional arrangements for new Member States

Joining the EU does not automatically mean that nationals of a new Member State can immediately avail themselves of the rights pertaining to the free movement of workers. While pre-existing Member States may not restrict the general rights of nationals of new Member States to travel, they may restrict their rights to work for a period of up to seven years. For the first two years after accession, the national law and policy of a pre-existing Member State determines the access that workers from new Member States have to the national labour market. Provided that they notify the Commission, a Member State may choose to extend this period by three years, and may then be granted a further two-year extension if they experience serious disturbances to their labour market. After seven years, workers from new Member States may not be treated any differently to those from other Member States.

> See sections. 1.1.3 and 1.4.1 on the enlargement of the Union

The majority of pre-existing Member States applied restrictions to the free movement of workers from the ten Member States that acceded to the Union on 1 May 2004. The UK, however, opted not to restrict access to its labour market, although it did require workers from the new Member States to register with the Workers Registration Scheme within 30 days of starting work. Ireland and Sweden also allowed full free movement rights. Germany and Austria, on the other hand, applied national restrictions for the full seven years.

Transitional arrangements were also applied to workers from **Bulgaria** and **Romania**, which became Member States on 1 January 2007. The UK applied restrictions for the full seven years, applying quotas in certain sectors and requiring Bulgarian and Romanian workers to obtain a 'worker authorisation document' prior to commencing employment. As required by the accession agreements, all such restrictions ended on 31 December 2013.

Croatia became a Member State on 1 July 2013. Thirteen Member States applied restrictions to Croatian workers during the initial two-year period after Croatia's accession to the Union. Five Member States – Austria, Malta, the Netherlands, Slovenia and the UK – extended restrictions from 1 July 2015 to 30 June 2018. Only Austria then applied the final two-year extension, with all restrictions to Croatian workers to be removed on 30 June 2020.

10.3.2 Equal treatment in employment

Freedom of movement for Union workers within the Union entails the abolition of discrimination based on nationality in relation to access to employment, remuneration and other conditions of work. As such, **Article 45(2) TFEU** applies to workers the prohibition of discrimination on grounds of nationality that is established in **Article 18 TFEU** (the wording of which is practically unchanged from the former Art 12 EC Treaty).

Regulation 492/2011

Regulation 492/2011 provides a wide range of directly enforceable rights designed to enable the migrant worker to obtain employment, and to provide the means:

> … by which workers are guaranteed the possibility of improving their living and working conditions and promoting their social advancement … The right of freedom of movement, in order that it may be exercised, by objective standards, in freedom and dignity, requires that equality of treatment be ensured in fact and in law in respect of all matters relating to the actual pursuit of activities as employed persons and to eligibility for housing, and also that obstacles to the mobility of workers be eliminated, in particular as regards the conditions for the integration of the worker's family into the host country. [preamble]

Articles 1, 3 and 4 of Regulation 492/2011 require equal treatment of employment applications and prohibit national quotas and other systems that limit access to employment for foreign nationals. Where these exist, it is not sufficient for the Member State to issue instructions that they are not to be applied in relation to Union citizens. They must be repealed or amended so that Union workers can be made fully aware of their right to access that type of employment. In ***Commission* v *France (Re French Merchant Seamen)*** (Case 167/73), the Court held that a quota system excluding foreign deck officers from French ships, under the Code Maritime, was unlawful under both the former Articles 1–4, Regulation 1612/68 (now Arts 1–4, Regulation 492/2011) and what is now Article 18 TFEU. The Court refused to accept an assurance that it was not enforced against EU nationals as individuals needed to be able to see a clear statement of their rights in the national legislation. The Court came to a similar decision in relation to the reservation of seamen's jobs for Belgian nationals (***Commission* v *Belgium*** (Case C-37/93)). The same principle of transparency was again applied by the Court in relation to nursing posts in the German health service (***Commission* v *Germany (Re Nursing Directives)*** (Case 29/84)).

Under Regulation 492/2011, Union work-seekers are entitled to receive the same assistance as is offered to national worker-seekers from the state's employment offices (Art 5). Recruitment should not depend on medical, vocational and other criteria which are discriminatory on grounds of nationality (Art 6). The Court of Justice has held that refusal by a government department in one Member State to take into account the employment experience of a job applicant in the government service of another Member State amounts to unlawful discrimination (***Schöning-Kougebetopoulo* v *Hamburg*** (Case C-15/96)). Those entitled to

Union free movement rights are also entitled to equal access to any form of employment, even that requiring official authorisation (*Gül* v *Regierungsprsident Düsseldorf* (Case 131/85)). The only exception to this is in relation to 'public service' provisions under Article 45(4) TFEU (see below).

In his opinion on *Gül*, Advocate General Mancini emphasised that the equal treatment provisions of the former Regulation 1612/68 (now Regulation 492/2011) are not confined to the employment relationship, but also covers the need to eliminate obstacles to the mobility of the worker. The general prohibition on discrimination contained in **Article 45(2) TFEU** thus covers not only measures that directly affect the rights of access to employment, but also any conditions that may make the engagement of Union workers more difficult or result in their employment on less favourable terms, as illustrated in the following case:

Allué and Coonan v *Università Degli Studi di Venezia* (Case 33/88)

Facts:
The applicants challenged national legislation under which the contracts of foreign-language assistants at Italian universities were limited to one year and could only be renewed for a maximum of five years, while no such limitations applied to other university teaching contracts. As about three-quarters of foreign-language assistants were from other Member States, the applicants claimed that the limitation on their contracts was discriminatory and that they were entitled to the same pay and social security cover as teachers on permanent contracts. The national court requested a preliminary ruling on whether the limited duration of foreign-language assistants' contracts breached what is now Article 45(2) TFEU (Art 48(2) EEC Treaty at the time).

Ruling:
The Court of Justice compared the position of foreign-language assistant to the position of researcher within the university, finding that both jobs entailed largely the same duties and responsibilities. As researchers, who were mostly Italian nationals, were not subject to the contract limitation, the limitations on foreign-language assistants' contracts, which were mostly filled by non-Italian nationals, were held to be discriminatory.

Significance:
A situation where Union workers are likely to face less favourable terms of employment than national workers counts as discrimination if there is no public interest justification for the difference in treatment. This is true even in cases where no distinction is made on the grounds of nationality *per se*, but unequal treatment results from a criterion that applies to significantly more non-nationals than nationals in practice – in this case, employment as a foreign-language assistant. Such situations, where ostensibly neutral criteria result in different treatment in practice, are known as **indirect discrimination**.

▶ *Köbler* was also an important case on state liability, see section 8.4.4 (page 305)

Under **Article 7(1) and (4) of Regulation 492/2011**, Union workers are entitled to the same treatment in relation to all conditions of employment, including pay, dismissal, reinstatement and re-employment, and they should benefit equally from the terms of any collective agreement negotiated with the management. The former Article 7(1) of Regulation 1612/68 was at issue in the following case:

Köbler (Case C-224/01)

Facts:

Austria's national legislation provided a special length-of-service increment to university professors who had held that role for at least 15 years within Austrian universities. The national legislation did not allow periods completed at universities in other Member States to be taken into account.

Ruling:

The Court of Justice noted that a loyalty bonus constitutes an obstacle to the free movement of workers, as it discourages workers from exercising their free movement rights. However, provisions rewarding the loyalty of an employee to their employer, in the context of a policy concerning research or university education, could amount to a **pressing public interest** that could justify an obstacle to the free movement of workers. The Court found that this was **not** the case with regards to the Austrian legislation in question, as it did not reward loyalty to a particular university, but rather rewarded employment within any university within the territory of Austria. The Court therefore ruled that such a regime was an unjustified disincentive to the free movement of workers. Furthermore, as nationals of other Member States were more likely to have been employed in universities in other Member States than Austrian nationals, and were therefore more likely to be excluded from the bonus, the provision also constituted indirect discrimination.

Significance:

Bonuses or other benefits may not be granted to workers in such a way that they discourage the exercise of free movement rights or are indirectly discriminatory, unless they can be justified by reason of a pressing public interest. While a bonus rewarding loyalty to a specific employer may meet this condition, a bonus rewarding and incentivising long-term employment within the territory of a specific Member State does not. This illustrates that the Court will measure the coherence of a justification claimed by a Member State against the likely effects of the actions that they have taken.

The case of *Merida* (C-400/02) concerned an allowance in Germany that was calculated on the basis of tax payments into the German system. This was held to indirectly discriminate against a French national who had been stationed in Germany with the French armed forces. While Mr Merida was entitled to the allowance, the taxes he had paid into the French system were not taken into account. The Court therefore held that double taxation agreements and the subsequent effects of tax-based calculations must be taken into account in order to ensure that Union workers are not disadvantaged.

A question related to indirect discrimination against **frontier workers** was also raised in the following case, which concerned a German couple who were employed in Germany but resident in France. The issue was whether they could rely upon what is now **Article 45 TFEU** to allow them to offset losses on their French home against their income tax liability in Germany:

Ritter-Coulais (Case C-152/03)

Facts:

Mr and Mrs Ritter-Coulais worked in Germany but lived in France. German tax legislation prohibited the offsetting of losses incurred on foreign residences.

> **Ruling:**
>
> The Court of Justice held that the situation of Mr and Mrs Ritter-Coulais fell within the scope of the former Article 39 EC Treaty (now Art 45 TFEU). The Court stated that although the German tax legislation was not specifically directed at non-residents, it was apparent that non-residents were more likely to own a home outside the national territory and were also more likely to be nationals of other Member States. The Court held that this less favourable treatment was contrary to the former Article 39 EC Treaty (now Art 45 TFEU).
>
> **Significance:**
>
> This is an example of **indirect discrimination**, where legislation does not specifically single out a group for different treatment, but nevertheless disadvantages that group in practice.

Article 7(1) of Regulation 492/2011 also provides Union workers with a right to participate equally in trade unions and staff associations, and workers should not be penalised for taking part in legitimate trade union activities (*Rutili* v *Minister of the Interior* (Case 36/75); *Association de Soutien aux Travailleurs Immigrés* (Case C-213/90)).

Other equal treatment provisions

Directive 2014/54 contains provisions that aim to guarantee the effectiveness of the rights of workers established under Article 45 TFEU and Articles 1–10 of Regulation 492/2011. For example, Article 3 provides that Member States should ensure that Union workers and their family members have recourse to competent authorities and, where necessary, judicial procedures for the enforcement of these rights. Article 4 then requires Member States to establish bodies to promote equal treatment and Article 6 requires Member States to ensure that accessible and up-to-date information on the rights of Union workers is brought to the attention of such workers, their employers and any other relevant persons.

The exception to the principle of equal treatment is the right given to Member States by **Article 45(3) TFEU** to exclude EU nationals from public service positions, which is examined below. However, it is also permissible to make knowledge of the state's national language a precondition of appointment, provided that it is necessary for the type of post to be filled. This may be so, even if it is a language which the applicant will not be required to use to carry out the job. In *Groener* v *Minister of Education* (Case 379/87), the Court of Justice held that a requirement in Irish law that teachers in vocational schools in Ireland should be able to speak Irish was permissible under the former Article 3(1) of Regulation 1612/68 (now Art 3(1), Regulation 492/2011) because the national policy to maintain and promote the national language as a means of sustaining national education and culture amounted to an objective justification. However, in *Angonese* (Case C-281/98), the Court stated that, regarding proof of the required linguistic knowledge, the principle of proportionality must be respected (para 44).

In addition to the Article 18 TFEU prohibition of discrimination on the ground of nationality, **Article 19 TFEU** provides a legal base for the adoption of measures to 'combat discrimination based on sex, racial or ethnic origin, religion or belief, disability, age or sexual orientation', provided such measures do not exceed the powers of the Union as conferred upon it by the EU Treaties. In other words, measures can be adopted to combat discrimination provided they are within the existing powers of the Union. Three of the most important anti-discrimination directives adopted pursuant to **Article 19 TFEU** are: **Directive 2000/43** (the **Racial Equality Directive**), **Directive 2000/78** (the **Employment Equality**

Directive) and **Directive 2006/54** (the **Equal Treatment Directive**). These apply to all persons within the Union, regardless of whether they are Union citizens and regardless of whether they have exercised their free movement rights.

> See section 3.4.4 for an explanation of what is meant by 'legal base'

The 'public service' exception

> See section 9.4.2 on restrictions on free movement on grounds of public policy, public security and public health

As mentioned above, free movement rights may be restricted on grounds of public policy, public security and public health (Art 27, Directive 2004/38). These restrictions may only be implemented on the basis of an individual's conduct and must not consider nationality or economic factors. There is, however, one area in which Member States are permitted to restrict the free movement of workers on grounds of nationality: under **Article 45(4) TFEU**, the right of equal access to employment 'shall not apply to employment in the public service'.

The term 'public service' is not defined in the Treaty or the implementing legislation. The Commission issued a notice in 1988 which indicated that it viewed a number of occupations in public employment as **not** falling within the Article 45(4) TFEU exception. This included posts in public health care, teaching in state education, non-military research and public bodies involved in the administrative services. This was a far from exhaustive list, which also did not have the force of law. The scope of Article 45(4) TFEU has thus primarily been left to be determined by the Court of Justice. The Court has interpreted the scope of the exception narrowly, in order to give the widest employment opportunities to Union workers.

In the following Opinion on case *Sotgiu* v *Deutsche Bundespost* (Case 152/73), Advocate General Mayras offered a definition of public service, which has largely been adopted in subsequent judgments of the Court of Justice:

> It is clear … that for the interpretation of [Article 45(4) TFEU] the concept of employment in the public service cannot be defined in terms of the legal status of the holder of the post. A Community [i.e. Union] interpretation which would allow a uniform application of the exception provided for by this provision requires us therefore to have resort to factual criteria based on the duties which the post held within the administration entails and the activities actually performed by the holder of the post.
>
> The exception will only be applicable if this person possesses a **power of discretion with regard to individuals** or if his activity **involves national interests** – in particular those which are concerned with the internal or external security of the State.

In the following case, the Court of Justice elaborated on the two central criteria proposed by Advocate General Mayras:

Commission v *Belgium* (Case 149/79)

Facts:
The Commission brought a case against Belgium, challenging the numerous posts that Belgium considered to fall within the public service exception of Article 45(4) TFEU (Art 48(4) EEC Treaty at the time).

Ruling:
The Court of Justice held that the public service exception:

> … removes from the ambit of Article 48(1) to (3) [now Article 45(1)–(3) TFEU] a series of posts which involve **direct or indirect participation in the exercise of powers conferred by public law and duties designed to safeguard the general interests of the State or of other public**

> **authorities**. Such posts in fact presume on the part of those occupying them the existence of a **special relationship of allegiance to the State and reciprocity of rights and duties which form the foundation of the bond of nationality**.
>
> On this basis, the Court accepted that the posts of head technical office supervisor, principal supervisor, works supervisor, stock controller and night-watchman within the municipalities of Brussels and Auderghem fell within the exception. Other posts within these municipalities and posts with the Belgian National Railways and the National Local Railways were found by the Court to be outside of the public service exception.
>
> **Significance:**
>
> The Court of Justice adopted a somewhat broader definition than that offered by Advocate General Mayras. Instead of the limitation applying to a person with a power of discretion with regard to individuals, the Court held that it applied to posts participating in the exercise of such powers. In other words, all those who acted under the instructions of the person vested with the public powers would be included in the exception.

> *Lawrie-Blum is also considered above in section 10.2.1 (page 386), with regard to the formal definition of a worker*

It is clear that a person with specific statutory powers, such as an environmental health officer, a registrar of births and deaths and a police officer, would all occupy posts falling within the exception relating to the exercise of public powers. In relation to national security and allegiance, appointments with the defence ministry dealing with issues relating to national defence would fall within the 'allegiance' aspect of the exception. Some posts, such as a police officer at a defence establishment, would seem to fall within both.

The essential factor defining a public service is the nature of the work, not the status of the employer or of the worker, as illustrated in the following case:

> ### Lawrie-Blum v Land Baden-Württemberg (Case 66/85)
>
> **Facts:**
>
> The applicant was a trainee teacher employed by the Ministry of Education, with the status of a civil servant. The local state government argued that she came within the exception in the former Article 48 EEC Treaty (now Art 45(4) TFEU), because she performed 'powers conferred by public law', including the preparation of lessons, the awarding of marks and participation in the decision of whether or not pupils should progress to a higher class.
>
> **Ruling:**
>
> The Court of Justice rejected this argument. It held that the exception in the former Article 39(4) (now Art 45(4) TFEU) 'must be construed in such a way as to limit its scope to what is strictly necessary for safeguarding the interests which that provision allows the Member States to protect'. Therefore, trainee teachers cannot be excluded from Article 45 protections as they do not perform 'functions whose purpose is to safeguard the general interests of the State'. The Court stated that a worker's civil servant status is not sufficient to bring their position within the scope of the public service exception, as this would enable Member States to exclude non-nationals from any job by simply calling it a civil service position.
>
> **Significance:**
>
> The Court determined that neither the performance of 'powers conferred by public law' nor a worker's designated status is sufficient to invoke the Article 45(4) TFEU exception. However, the

> Court did not elaborate on the special qualities of public employment to which Article 45(4) TFEU is applicable, except to repeat, almost verbatim, its formulation in **Commission v Belgium**. The Court did not make it clear at what level the Article 45(4) TFEU exception would start to apply. For example, although it does not apply to trainee teachers, senior officers in the government's Education Service would undoubtedly take major public policy decisions affecting education.

The finding that access to positions could not be limited simply because the host Member State designated such workers as civil servants was affirmed in *Bleis* v *Ministère de l'Education Nationale* (Case C-4/91). The derogation permitted by Article 45(4) TFEU applies only to access to employment. It does not apply to the terms of employment once access has been permitted; it would not be permissible for national and Union citizens to be engaged in the same work but on different contractual terms or conditions (*Sotgiu* v *Deutsche Bundespost* (Case 152/73); *Allué and Coonan* v *Università di Venezia* (Case 33/88)).

In the following case, the Court of Justice had to interpret Article 45(4) TFEU in relation to the criterion of a 'special relationship of allegiance to the State'.

Anker and Others (Case C-47/02) and *Colegio de Oficiales de la Marina Mercante Española* (Case C-405/01)

Facts:

The complainants were seamen who had been refused positions due to provisions of German and Spanish law which excluded non-nationals from:

(i) employment as master of a vessel used in small-scale maritime shipping;

(ii) employment as master or chief mate on merchant navy ships.

The Court of Justice was asked to determine whether such exclusions were compatible with Article 39 EC Treaty (now Art 45 TFEU).

Ruling:

The Court of Justice stated that the concept of public service within the meaning of the former Article 39(4) EC Treaty (now Art 45(4) TFEU) covered posts which involved direct or indirect participation in the exercise of powers conferred by public law and duties designed to safeguard the general interests of the state or of other public authorities. This was a restatement of the formulation in **Commission v Belgium** (above). The Court then went on to consider the posts at issue in this case. It held that the rights conferred on those holding the posts (i.e. the master of the ship) were connected to the maintenance of safety and to the exercise of police powers. The master of the ship also had certain auxiliary duties in respect of the registration of births, marriages and deaths. The Court pointed out that **the fact that masters were employed by a private natural or legal person was not, as such, sufficient to exclude the application of the former Article 39(4) EC Treaty (now Art 45(4) TFEU)** because in order to perform the public functions which were delegated to them, masters acted as representatives of public authority in the service of the general interests of the flag state.

The Court pointed out that the derogation had to be limited to what was strictly necessary for safeguarding the general interests of the Member State concerned, which would not be imperilled if the public law rights were only exercised sporadically or even by nationals of other Member States. Therefore, the Court of Justice concluded that the former Article 39(4) EC Treaty (now Art

45(4) TFEU) had to be construed as allowing a Member State to reserve the posts at issue for its own nationals **only if the rights under powers conferred by public law granted to persons holding such posts were in fact exercised on a regular basis and did not represent a very minor part of their activities.**

Significance:

The Court continued its very narrow interpretation of the public services exception, this time determining that the powers conferred by public law must be exercised on a regular basis in order for a position to be justifiably reserved for nationals.

Reflection: Public services in the UK

Until May 1991, all Civil Service posts in the UK were unavailable to all EU nationals, with the exception of Irish citizens who were not classified as aliens under the Aliens Employment Act 1955. The 1955 Act provided some limited exceptions, but it was far too sweeping to comply with Article 45(4) TFEU, as interpreted by the Court of Justice in **Commission v Belgium** (above). The European Communities (Employment in the Civil Service) Order 1991 was brought into effect to enable Union citizens and their families to have access to Civil Service posts in accordance with Union law. It did not specify the posts which were to be opened up, but an internal Civil Service Circular (GC/378) listed a large number of jobs which would be open to Union citizens. At that time, about 97,000 (18 per cent) of all posts within the UK Civil Service were reserved for UK nationals only. The European Communities (Employment in the Civil Service) Order 2007 then achieved a reduction in the number of posts reserved for UK nationals throughout the Civil Service to less than five per cent of the total number of posts in the Civil Service; approximately, a further 70,000 posts were made available to non-UK nationals.

After Brexit, there is no guarantee that these jobs will remain available to non-UK citizens; the UK will be free to reintroduce restrictions.

10.3.3 Equal access to social advantages

Article 7(2) of Regulation 492/2011 provides that Union workers in a host Member State 'shall enjoy the same social and tax advantages as national workers'. The principle of **equal treatment** for Union workers that is established in Article 45(2) TFEU is thus applied to social advantages. The Court of Justice has produced significant case law to determine the scope of 'social advantages'. With the aim of facilitating the removal of obstacles to free movement and assisting the worker in the process of integrating into the social fabric of the Member State, the Court has held a very diverse range of benefits to come within the scope of 'social advantages'. (It may be helpful at this stage to review the differences between 'social security', 'social advantages' and '**social assistance**', as set out in the 'key terms and concepts' section at the start of this chapter.)

In the following case, the Court built on existing case law (***Scrivner and Cole*** v *Centre Public d'Aide Sociale de Chastre* (Case 122/84)) to establish three criteria for the classification of a benefit as a social advantage:

Ministère Public v Even and ONPTS (Case 207/78)

Facts:
Mr Even was a French national working in Belgium. He received an early retirement pension from the Belgian authorities. A percentage was deducted from the pension based on the number of years early he had received the pension. This rule was applied to all recipients, except Belgian nationals who were in receipt of a Second World War service invalidity pension granted by an Allied nation. Mr Even was in receipt of a French war service pension and pleaded the principle of equality of treatment between nationals and non-nationals to claim the benefit of an early retirement pension without any deduction. The national court referred the matter to the Court of Justice for a preliminary ruling under what is now Article 267 TFEU.

Ruling:
The Court of Justice held as follows:

22 It follows from all its provisions and from the objective pursued that the advantages which this regulation extends to workers who are nationals of other Member States are all those which, whether or not linked to a contract of employment, are generally granted to national workers primarily because of their objective status as workers or by virtue of the mere fact of their residence on the national territory and the extension of which to workers who are nationals of other Member States therefore seems suitable to facilitate their mobility within the Community [i.e. Union].

The Court ruled that the exemption from the pension deduction did **not** fulfil the essential characteristics of a 'social advantage' as referred to in the former Article 7(2) of Regulation 1612/68 (now Art 7(2), Regulation 492/2011), first because the main reason for exemption from the pension reduction was to provide an advantage to those who had suffered hardships in the service of their country, rather than stemming from worker status or residence, and secondly because the advantage was not suitable for facilitating mobility within the Union.

Significance:
The Court established that a benefit constitutes a social advantage for the purpose of what is now Article 7(2) of Regulation 492/2011 – and should therefore be applied equally to nationals of other Member States – if the benefit: 1) is granted on the basis of the claimant's status as a worker; 2) is granted on the basis of the claimant's residence within the national territory; or 3) could facilitate the mobility of workers within the Union. These three criteria are known as the '***Even* formula**'.

> See section 10.5.3 for an overview of *Cristini* (page 423) and further information on how case law pertaining to family members has broadened the scope of social advantages

The Court relied on the ***Even*** formula in the similar case of ***Baldinger*** (Case C-386/02), where it held that a benefit granted to prisoners of war did not fulfil the characteristics of social advantages. In ***Mutsch*** (Case 137/84), however, the Court used the ***Even*** formula to determine that the right of a national to have a criminal trial conducted in a language other than that which is usually used in such proceedings constituted a social advantage to which a Union worker should be entitled.

Initially, the Court of Justice determined that the former Article 7(2) of Regulation 1612/68 (now Art 7(2), Regulation 492/2011) only encompassed social advantages that were connected to employment and that benefited workers themselves (***Michel S v Fonds national de reclassement social des handicaps*** (Case 76-72)). However, the Court has since broadened its interpretation and held that Article 7(2) also encompasses social advantages that are not actually linked to an employment contract and that benefit the family members of a worker (***Cristini v SNCF*** (Case 32/75)).

> See section 10.4.2 for an outline of *Lebon* (page 412)

While the Court of Justice made it clear in *Centre Public d'Aide Sociale* v *Lebon* (Case C-316/85) that Article 7(2) can be invoked only when the advantage is actually of some direct or indirect benefit to the worker and not **only** to a family member or dependant, the rights of family members to social assistance have since been clarified by the adoption of Directive 2004/38 (see section 10.5.3).

Along with social advantages, Article 7(2) of Regulation 492/2011 requires equal treatment for tax advantages. Such tax advantages were held in *Biehl* (Case C-175/88) and *Schumacher* (Case C-279/93) to require that different rates of tax payable by residents and non-residents could not be applied to workers from other Member States.

Access to vocational training

Union workers are entitled, by virtue of **Article 7(3) of Regulation 492/2011**, to equal access to vocational schools and retraining centres. A person who loses their job and takes up an educational course is entitled to an educational grant as a social advantage (*Lair* v *University of Hannover* (Case 39/86)). This will be the case even if the worker gives up their job voluntarily, provided that there is a link between the job and the course that is undertaken (*Raulin* (Case C-357/89)).

In *Brown* v *Secretary of State for Scotland* (Case 197/86), the issue of access to higher education maintenance grants came before the Court of Justice. The Court held that, although access to education in terms of admission fees and admission criteria came within the scope of the Treaties (and thus within the prohibition against discrimination under what is now Article 18 TFEU), access to educational maintenance grants did not. Brown argued, however, that he was a Union worker and therefore had the right to an education grant as a social advantage under the former Article 7(2) of Regulation 1612/68 (now Art 7(2), Regulation 492/2011):

Brown v *Secretary of State for Scotland* (Case 197/86)

Facts:
Brown, who was a French national of Anglo-French origin, had applied for a discretionary grant from the Scottish Education Department to attend an electrical engineering course at Cambridge. Prior to the commencement of the course, he had obtained employment with an engineering company in Edinburgh for eight months. This job was described as 'pre-university industrial training'. Although he did not qualify for a grant under the Scottish regulations, he argued that he was entitled to receive one as a social advantage in his capacity as a Union worker, under the former Article 7(2) of Regulation 1612/68 (now Art 7(2), Regulation 492/2011). The case was referred to the Court of Justice pursuant to what is now Article 267 TFEU.

Ruling:
The Court of Justice first of all ruled that, although universities may provide vocational training, as held in *Blaizot*, they do not constitute vocational schools for the purposes of Article 7(3) of Regulation 1612/68 (now Art 7(3), Regulation 492/2011). Furthermore, although access to education in terms of admission fees and criteria came within the scope of the Treaties (and thus within the prohibition against discrimination under what is now Art 18 TFEU), access to educational grants did not.

However, the Court then determined that Brown did possess the status of a worker, stating:

> [a person who] enters into an employment relationship in the host State for a period of eight months with a view to subsequently undertaking university studies there in the same field of activity and who would not have been employed by his employer if he had not already been accepted for admission to university is to be regarded as a worker within the meaning of Article 7(2) of Regulation 1612/68 [now Art 7(2), Regulation 492/2011]. [para 23]

> That should have concluded the issue in Brown's favour, but the Court then added that:
>
>> it cannot be inferred from that finding that a national of a Member State will be entitled to a grant for studies in another Member State by virtue of his status as a worker where it is established that he acquired that status exclusively as a result of his being accepted for admission to university to undertake the studies in question. In such circumstances, **the employment relationship, which is the only basis for the rights deriving from Regulation No. 1612/68 [now Regulation 492/2011], is merely ancillary to the studies to be financed by the grant**.
>
> **Significance:**
>
> As discussed above, where the employment is 'ancillary' to some other purpose (e.g. 'therapy' as in the case of **Bettray** (Case 344/87), above), the individual may not be regarded as a Union worker under either Article 45 TFEU or Article 7(2) of Regulation 492/2011, for the purpose of social advantages. On that basis, the Court could well have concluded that Brown was not a Union worker at all. His entitlement to social advantages would not, therefore, have arisen, as in the case of **Lebon**, (mentioned above on page 406 and examined more fully below on page 412). However, the Court, decided to hold that he was both a Union worker and disentitled to the social advantages to which such workers would normally be entitled, because the employment that would have rendered him eligible for the study grant was, at the same time, ancillary to the study.

▶ See section 9.5.3 on Union citizenship and access to maintenance grants

The judgment in *Brown* was reconsidered in light of European citizenship in *Grzelczyk v Centre Public d'Aide Sociale d'Ottignies-Louvain-la-Neuve* (Case C-184/99). Here, the Court stated that Union citizenship was destined to be the fundamental status of nationals of the Member States, enabling those who found themselves in the same situation to enjoy the same treatment in law irrespective of their nationality, subject to some exceptions as were expressly provided for. In a reversal of *Brown*, then, it was ruled that the Belgian minimum subsistence allowance (minimex) that was granted to nationals solely on the basis of their need could not, for EU nationals, be made conditional on their falling within the scope of the former Regulation 1612/68 (now Regulation 492/2011).

10.3.4 Social security coordination

Given the variation in level and type of contributions required in each Member State, and the dissimilarity of social security schemes, the coordination of social security throughout the Union is a complex task. It must, however, be emphasised that Union law on social security is not intended to equalise the level of social security benefits throughout the Union. It is simply directed at ensuring that the migrant worker obtains, as far as possible, equal treatment within local social security schemes and does not lose out on entitlements due from his home state. The coordination of social security systems is therefore an important element in the task of minimising obstacles to the exercise of free movement rights. In 2019, a new **European Labour Authority** was established, with one of its primary objectives being the effective coordination of social security systems in the Union.

▶ The European Labour Authority is briefly considered in section 10.1.2

The coordination of social security systems within the EU is based on four principles: one country at a time, equal treatment, aggregation and exportability.

EU law governs which country's social security system a person is covered by at any point in order to avoid the complications that would arise from the overlapping application of different systems. Subsequently, a Union citizen should only ever be paying contributions and/or receiving benefits from **one social security scheme at a time**.

Article 48 TFEU deals with the difficulties arising from workers moving between the different social security systems of Member States. It requires the adoption of measures in the field of social security that are necessary to facilitate freedom of movement for workers. To this end, Article 48 TFEU requires Member States to make arrangements to secure for Union workers and their dependants:

- aggregation of all periods taken into account under the laws of the relevant Member States for the purpose of acquiring and retaining the right to social security benefits and of calculating the amount of such benefits;
- payment of social security benefits to persons resident in the territories of Member States.

Article 48 TFEU is thus aimed at enabling a migrant worker to take their accrued rights with them, and to avoid being disadvantaged by the exercise of their free movement rights, in two ways. First, the principle of **aggregation** determines that a worker's contributions and periods of contribution in their home state will be taken into account in any relevant calculations made by the host Member State and, correspondingly, that their contributions in the host Member State will be taken into account in calculating the level of benefits that they are entitled to from their home state. Secondly, the principle of **exportability** determines that a worker's contributions in their home state will entitle them to the payment of benefits by that state wherever they are in the Union.

The Court of Justice has declared that, when applying national social security law to Union workers, the host Member State should interpret its own legislation in the light of the aims of Articles 45–48 TFEU. Therefore, Member States should, as far as possible, avoid interpreting their own legislation in such a way as to discourage Union workers from exercising their rights to freedom of movement (*Van Munster* (Case C-165/91)).

On the basis of **Article 48 TFEU**, several regulations have been adopted. **Regulation 883/2004** (which repealed and replaced Regulation 1408/71 and has since been amended by Regulation 988/2009) contains the current substantive provisions. Regulation 883/2004 seeks to simplify and clarify the Union rules governing the coordination of the Member States' social security systems. It now includes persons who are not economically active within its scope, with the aim of facilitating the free movement of *all* Union citizens, irrespective of their economic status. Article 4 of Regulation 883/2004 provides for non-discrimination on the grounds of nationality with regard to social security, stating that 'persons to whom this Regulation applies shall enjoy the same benefits and be subject to the same obligations under the legislation of any Member State as the nationals thereof'. **Regulation 987/2009** (which repealed and replaced Regulation 574/72) contains the current implementing provisions.

In December 2016, the European Commission formally proposed a new regulation that would amend Regulation 883/2004 on the coordination of social security systems and Regulation 987/2009, laying down the procedure for implementing Regulation 883/2004. The Council and the Parliament reached a provisional agreement on this proposal in March 2019, prior to the commencement of the ordinary legislative procedure. The anticipated regulation will clarify rules relating to:

- the exportability of unemployment benefits;
- the aggregation of insurance periods;
- the provisions and services applicable to frontier workers;
- the status of cash benefits awarded to persons who stop working in order to care for a child;

- the coordination of benefits available to persons requiring long-term care;
- the procedures and requirements for posting workers; and
- the rights to social benefits of economically inactive EU citizens.

In the following case, the Court of Justice sought to address a former worker's entitlement to benefits following their departure from the host Member State:

Ghislain Leclere, Alina Deaconescu v *Caisse Nationale des Prestations Familiales* (Case C-43/99)

Facts:
Leclere was a Belgian national, who lived in Belgium and travelled to Luxembourg every day to work (i.e. a frontier worker). Following an accident at work he became entitled to an invalidity pension from Luxembourg. Leclere therefore gained the right to the pension by virtue of his status as a Union worker at the time. However, he was denied a benefit from the Luxembourg authorities for a child he had after his employment had ended on the ground that he was neither a worker nor a resident there.

Ruling:
The Court of Justice held that Leclere was protected against any discrimination affecting rights he had acquired during his former employment by what are now Article 45 TFEU and Regulation 492/2011. However, because he was no longer employed and was not resident in Luxembourg, he could not claim new rights which had no links with his former occupation. The Court of Justice held as follows:

> 61 A person receiving an invalidity pension who resides in a Member State other than the State providing his pension is not a worker within the meaning of Article 7 of Regulation 1612/68/EEC [now Art 7(2), Regulation 492/2011] and does not enjoy rights attaching to that status unless they derive from his previous professional activity.

Significance:
The case established that a person who is not or is no longer resident in the Member State in which they worked cannot claim new benefits from that State once they no longer have the status of a worker. This is in line with the 'one social security system at a time' principle.

Further information on social security is provided in relation to each category of person to whom it applies within this chapter, i.e. within the sub-sections on work-seekers and family members of workers.

10.4 Work-seekers

Objective 4

Not every individual wishing to go to another Member State to work will have already arranged employment. Work-seekers are entitled to entry and limited rights of residence but not necessarily the full range of benefits enjoyed by those who have full Union worker status.

10.4.1 Rights to free movement

Before Directive 2004/38

The beneficiaries of Article 45 TFEU are described as those in a position 'to accept offers of employment actually made'. If a literal interpretation had been applied to this provision, it seems that work-seekers would not have qualified for a right of free movement. However, in *Procureur du Roi* v *Royer* (Case 48/75) the Court of Justice delivered a remarkably creative judgment:

> ... the right of nationals of a Member State to enter the territory of another Member State and reside there for the purposes intended by the Treaty – **in particular to look for or pursue an occupation** or activities as employed or self-employed persons, or to re-join their spouse or family – is a right conferred directly by the Treaty, or, as the case may be, by the provisions adopted for its implementation. [para 31]

▶ See Chapter 5 on the Court's methods of interpreting EU law

Although the Court of Justice decided in *Royer* that work-seekers were entitled to enter another Member State to look for work, it did not give any indication as to how long a right to reside should continue. For a number of years it was thought that the appropriate period was three months, partly because that was the maximum duration for which a migrant job-seeker was entitled to unemployment benefits from their home Member State under the former Regulation 1408/71 (which has been repealed and replaced by Regulation 883/2004), and partly because the Council had made a declaration to that effect at the time of approval of Regulation 1612/68 (now Regulation 492/2011) and the former Directive 68/360 (see the opinion of Advocate General Lenz in *Centre Public d'Aide Sociale* v *Lebon* (Case C-316/85)). However, the Court of Justice rejected both of these bases for limiting work-seekers' rights of residence and took a different approach in the following case:

R v *Immigration Appeal Tribunal, ex parte Antonissen* (Case C-292/89)

Facts:
Antonissen was a Belgian national who came to the UK in 1984 to find work. He did not find work. In 1987 the Secretary of State decided to deport him, following his conviction and imprisonment for a drug-related offence. He sought judicial review of the decision and the case was referred to the Court of Justice. The relevant issue here concerned the length of time a person could stay in the territory of another Member State while seeking work.

Ruling:
Rejecting the claim that a period of three months had been established as the minimum duration, the Court said that there was 'no necessary link between the right to unemployment benefit in the Member State of origin and the right to stay in the host State' (para 20). The Court also stated that the Council of Ministers' declaration had 'no legal significance', as it was not part of any binding legal provision (para 18).

The Court stated that work-seekers should be afforded:

> 16 ... **reasonable time** in which to apprise themselves, in the territory of the Member State concerned, of offers of employment corresponding to their occupational qualifications and to take, where appropriate, the necessary steps in order to be engaged.

In relation to the particulars of the case, the Court then elaborated:

> 21 In the absence of a Community [i.e. Union] provision prescribing the period during which Community [i.e. Union] nationals seeking employment in a Member State may stay there, **a period of six months, such as that laid down in the national legislation at issue in the main proceedings, does not appear in principle to be insufficient** to enable the persons concerned to apprise themselves, in the host Member State, of offers of employment corresponding to their occupational qualifications and to take, where appropriate, the necessary steps in order to be engaged and, therefore, does not jeopardise the effectiveness of the principle of free movement. However, **if after the expiry of that period the person concerned provides evidence that he is continuing to seek employment and that he has genuine chances of being engaged, he cannot be required to leave the territory of the host Member State**.

Significance:

The Court did not establish the duration for which work-seekers should be permitted to reside within a Member State for the purpose of seeking work. However, two tests for determining a work-seeker's right to reside emerged from the case:

1. An EU national may reside within a Member State for **a 'reasonable' period of time** for the purpose of finding work. In the context of the UK legislation at the material time, six months was found to be reasonable. However, this did not mean that a period of less than six months would necessarily be unreasonable.

2. An EU national cannot be deported from a Member State if they can show that they are still seeking employment and that they have **'genuine chances' of finding work**.

The Court of Justice subsequently decided, in ***Commission* v *Belgium*** (Case C-344/95), that the period of **three months** provided by Belgium to EU nationals to find work was also 'reasonable', provided that it could be extended if the work-seeker was looking for employment and had 'genuine chances' of finding work.

After Directive 2004/38

The 'reasonable time' criteria established in *Antonissen* did not provide much clarity for either Member States or work-seekers, leaving the potential for differing interpretations across the Union and, subsequently, the uneven application of Union law. Directive 2004/38 therefore provides a more concrete provision upon which work-seekers, and Union citizens in general, can rely in relation to their rights of residence: **Article 6(1) of Directive 2004/38** establishes that Union citizens shall have the right of residence in another Member State for a period of up to three months without any conditions or formalities other than the requirement to hold a valid identity card or passport. **Article 14(4)(b)** then provides that a Union work-seeker may not be subjected to expulsion measures so long as they can provide evidence that they are continuing to seek employment and that they have a genuine chance of being engaged.

With regard to social assistance, **Article 24(2)** of the Directive provides that the host Member State is not obliged to grant social assistance to a Union citizen during their first three months of residence as provided for under Article 6(1), nor during a longer period of residence that is premised on the citizen's continued search for work as provided for under Article 14(4)(b).

> ➤ Directive 2004/38 is considered in relation to general rights of entry and residence in Chapter 9

10.4.2 Rights to social benefits

Before Directive 2004/38

The current situation is highly complex. While Directive 2004/38 has improved clarity in some areas, the case law has not been straightforward. The Court of Justice initially interpreted the scope of the former Regulation 1612/68 (now replaced by Directive 2004/38), as excluding non-workers. Therefore, a person who had never worked in the host Member State could not base a claim for social advantages on the equal treatment provisions of the time, even if they were looking for work. This interpretation was applied in the following case:

Centre Public d'Aide Sociale de Courcelles v *Lebon* (Case 316/85)

Facts:

The applicant, a French national living in Belgium, claimed a minimum subsistence benefit as a family member of her father, who was also French and who was a retired Union worker. She no longer satisfied the 'family member' provisions of the former Article 10 of Regulation 1612/68 (now Art 2(2)(c), Directive 2004/38) because she was over the age of 21 and was no longer dependent upon her father. She had never found employment.

Ruling:

The Court of Justice held in this case that, as she was no longer dependent, she was not entitled to a social advantage as a member of a retired Union worker's family, and could not claim such an advantage as a work-seeker in her own right:

> where a worker who is a national of one Member State was employed within the territory of another Member State and remains there after obtaining a retirement pension, his descendants do not retain the right to equal treatment with regard to a social benefit provided for by the legislation of the host Member State and guaranteeing in general terms the minimum means of subsistence where they have reached the age of 21, are no longer dependent on him and do not have the status of workers. [para 14]

Significance:

When a descendant ceases to fulfil the definition of a family member (now provided in Art 2(2), Directive 2004/38), their rights become determined by their own status. A person who has never acquired the status of a worker and who is not currently a family member of a worker as defined by EU law was found not to be entitled to social assistance, such as a subsistence benefit or a jobseekers' allowance.

However, the Court's position in *Lebon* became untenable with the adoption of Directive 2004/38 and the introduction of Union citizenship. The ruling in *Lebon* thus became outdated and the Court adopted a new approach in *Collins* (see below). Before looking at *Collins*, however, it is helpful to consider the relevant provisions of Directive 2004/38.

After Directive 2004/38

As discussed in Chapter 9, **Article 14(1) of Directive 2004/38** provides that Union citizens and their family members shall have the right of residence provided under Article 6, 'as long as they do not become an **unreasonable burden** on the social assistance system of the host

Member State'. However, expulsion shall not be an automatic consequence if a Union citizen or his family members have recourse to the host Member State's social assistance system (Art 14(3)). **Article 14(4)(b)** further provides that, unless in accordance with the provisions relating to restrictions on the right of entry and residence on grounds of public policy, public security or public health, an expulsion order cannot be issued against a Union citizen or their family members if, *inter alia*, the Union citizen entered the host Member State to seek employment and provided they can supply evidence that they are continuing to seek work and have a genuine chance of being employed.

With regard to social assistance, **Article 24(2)** provides that for the first three months of residence, or while the Union citizen is exercising their right to reside while seeking work under Article 14(4)(b), the host Member State is not obliged to grant entitlement to social assistance to persons other than employed (or self-employed) workers and the members of their family (see Chapter 9). In other words, Union citizens have the right to reside within a Member State for the purpose of seeking work, but Member States do not have to provide social assistance to such persons. In determining whether a benefit constitutes social assistance, the Court has held that the purpose and conditions under which it is granted, rather than simply how the benefit is labelled under national legislation, should be considered (***Scrivner and Cole*** v ***Centre Public d'Aide Sociale de Chastre*** (Case 122/84)).

The following case concerned a work-seeker's right to claim a social security benefit. In this case, the Court considered 'Union citizenship' and subsequently adopted a new approach:

Collins (Case C-138/02)

Facts:

In the UK, the grant of a 'jobseekers' allowance' to persons seeking employment was subject to the applicants satisfying one of the following conditions:

(i) they were habitually resident in the UK;

(ii) they were a worker for the purposes of the former Regulation 1612/68 (now Regulation 492/2011); or

(iii) they had a right to reside in the UK pursuant to the former Directive 68/360 (now Directive 2004/38).

Mr Collins was born in the United States and had dual American and Irish nationality. Having spent one semester in the UK in 1978 as part of his university studies and having worked for ten months in 1980 and 1981 on a part-time and casual basis in bars and the sales sector, he returned to the UK in 1998 for the purpose of seeking employment. He applied for a jobseeker's allowance but was refused on the grounds that he did not satisfy one of the three conditions above.

Three questions were referred to the Court of Justice for a preliminary ruling. The first two concerned the Regulation and the Directive, while the third asked whether there could be some provision or principle of Union law capable of assisting the applicant in his claim.

Ruling:

On the question of whether Collins was a worker within the terms of the former Regulation 1612/68 (now Regulation 492/2011), the Court took the view that, as no link could be established between the casual work performed by Collins 17 years previously and the work that he was now seeking, **Collins did not have a sufficiently close connection with the employment market in the UK to be considered a worker**. The Court ruled that the situation of Collins was comparable to that of a person seeking their first employment. While all Union work-seekers benefit from equal access to employment, **only those who have already entered the employment market of the Member State, and are thus considered to be Union workers, can claim the same social and tax advantages as national jobseekers**.

With regard to whether Collins had a right to reside in the UK under the former Directive 68/360 (replaced by Directive 2004/38), the Court found that the right to reside in a Member State conferred by the former Directive 68/360 was reserved for nationals who were already employed in that Member State. Although Collins was residing in the UK legally, he was not within the particular scope of Directive 68/360.

The Court of Justice concluded by examining the UK legislation in the light of the fundamental principle of equal treatment in access to employment. The Court considered that, while nationals of one Member State who were seeking employment in another Member State were entitled to equal treatment with regards to access to employment, equal treatment with regards to social and tax advantages as provided for by the former Article 7(2) of Regulation 1612/68 (now Art 7(2), Regulation 492/2011) applied only to workers. However, the Court then considered Collin's right to equal treatment as a Union citizen who was lawfully residing within the UK:

> 48 As a citizen of the Union lawfully residing in the United Kingdom, he was clearly entitled to the protection conferred by Article 6 of the Treaty against discrimination on grounds of nationality in any situation falling within the material scope of Community law. That is precisely the case with regard to **jobseeker's allowance**, which **should be considered to be a social advantage** within the meaning of Article 7(2) of Regulation No 1612/68.

Therefore, non-workers are entitled to equal treatment with regard to social advantages by virtue of their Union citizenship. So:

> 63 **In view of the establishment of Union citizenship and the interpretation in the case law of the right to equal treatment enjoyed by citizens, it is no longer possible to exclude, from the scope of Article 39(2) EC Treaty [now Art 45(2) TFEU] a benefit of a financial nature intended to facilitate access to employment in the labour market of a Member State**.

As the residence requirement was applied equally to all applicants, Collins could be said to be receiving equal treatment with nationals in his access to the benefit in question. However, the Court ruled that the requirement was indirectly discriminatory, as more non-nationals than nationals were likely to be denied the allowance on the grounds that they did not meet this condition. The question was then whether the indirect discrimination was objectively justifiable. The Court ruled that it was: **the residence requirement pursued the legitimate aim of ensuring that there was a genuine link between an applicant for the allowance and the national labour market, and that it was a proportionate measure for the achievement of this aim**, i.e. it did not go further than was necessary. The legitimacy of ensuring a 'genuine link', as referred to here, was established in ***D'Hoop*** (Case C-224/98).

Significance:

The Court established that any 'benefit of a financial nature intended to facilitate access to employment in the labour market of a Member State' should be subject to the principle of equal treatment, i.e. should be available on an equal basis to both nationals and EU nationals, with no extra criteria relating to worker status applied to EU nationals. This went back on the Court's ruling in ***Lebon*** (see above), with the effect that access to benefits was, in theory at least, extended to work-seekers, even if Collins did not actually win the right to the allowance in question. The reason for this change in approach was to bring access to benefits for work-seekers in line with the concept of Union citizenship, which was introduced by the **Maastricht Treaty** in 1992 and

> consolidated by **Directive 2004/38** a month after this judgment. Union citizenship meant that social benefits could be applied to non-workers and it would not have made sense to continue denying benefits to persons seeking work when other benefits were accessible to persons who were in no way a part of the labour market. However, Article 24(2) of Directive 2004/38 does enable Member States to exclude work-seekers from social assistance for the first three months of their residence (or longer periods where their residence remains conditioned on their search for work). The current situation, then, where **lawfully resident Union citizens are entitled to equal treatment with regard to social advantages but may be excluded from social assistance**, has drawn heightened attention to the distinction between these types of benefit.

In the case of *Ioannidis* (Case C-258/04), which was decided after the adoption of Directive 2004/38, the Court of Justice confirmed that financial benefits that are intended to facilitate access to the labour market should now be accessible to Union citizens. The Court's approach in *Collins* and *Ioannidis* has been controversial as it created a new category of social benefits: a 'benefit of a financial nature intended to facilitate access to employment in the labour market of a Member State'.

The Court further affirmed its approach to jobseekers' allowances in *Vatsouras and Koupatantze* v *Arbeitsgemeinschaft (ARGE) Nürnberg* (Cases C-22/08 and 23/08). Here, in its guidance to national courts on whether an applicant should receive a jobseekers' allowance, the Court confirmed that 'benefits of a financial nature which... are intended to facilitate access to the labour market cannot be regarded as constituting 'social assistance' within the meaning of Article 24(2)'. Furthermore, 'nationals of the Member States seeking employment in another Member State who have established real links with the labour market of that State can rely on Article 39(2) EC [now Article 45(2) TFEU] in order to receive a benefit of a financial nature intended to facilitate access to the labour market'.

In light of *Collins* and *Vatsouras*, a Union citizen who does not possess the status of a worker appears to be entitled to social advantages in a host Member State if a) the benefits in question are intended to facilitate access to the national labour market and b) a genuine link could be established between the claimant and the labour market.

The following case then complicated matters, as the benefits at issue, which included a jobseeker's allowance, were in fact classified by the Court as 'social assistance':

> ### *Jobcenter Berlin Neukölln* v *Alimanovic and Others* (Case C-67/14)
>
> **Facts:**
> Nazifa Alimanovic was a Swedish national who lived in Germany with her three children who were also Swedish nationals. Nazifa Alimanovic and her eldest daughter, Sonita, worked in temporary jobs for eleven months. They were then unemployed for over six months, leading Nazifa and Sonita to lose their status as workers. As a result, benefits they received for the two younger children and a subsistence allowance for unemployed persons were terminated, as required under national legislation.
>
> The Berlin Social Court argued that the Alimanovics were entitled to the benefits in question because they were 'special non-contributory cash benefits'. Article 70 of Regulation 883/2004 specifies that such benefits are within the scope of the regulation as a whole, including Article 4, which provides for equal treatment. The Job Centre, however, argued that, as the benefits covered subsistence costs, they constituted 'social assistance', which could be denied to non-workers who were not nationals under Article 24(2) of Directive 2004/38.

Opinion:

Advocate General Wathelet argued that Article 24(2) of Directive 2004/38 should be interpreted narrowly, as it is a derogation from the principle of equal treatment that is enshrined in Article 18 TFEU. Although the Advocate General determined that the benefits at issue constituted social assistance as their predominant function was to meet subsistence needs, rather than to facilitate access to the labour market, the Advocate General also referred to the real link test established in *Vatsouras and Koupatantze*. He therefore concluded that persons in the Alimanovics' situation should not automatically be refused the benefits in question without having the opportunity to demonstrate that they have a real link with the national labour market. If such a link were to be demonstrated, they should then be entitled to the benefits on an equal basis as nationals.

Ruling:

The Court of Justice only followed Advocate General Wathelet's Opinion in so far as it ruled that the benefits at issue constituted 'social assistance' for the purposes of Article 24(2). The Court ruled that, although Member States are obliged to consider the individual circumstances of a case when a right to reside is at issue (as ruled in *Brey*, see Chapter 9), **no such individual assessment is required with regards to the provision of social assistance to persons whose right of residence is derived from their search for employment**. This was because:

> Directive 2004/38, establishing a gradual system as regards the retention of the status of 'worker' which seeks to safeguard the right of residence and access to social assistance, itself takes into consideration various factors characterising the individual situation of each applicant for social assistance and, in particular, the duration of the exercise of any economic activity. [para 60]

> See *Brey* in section 9.5.2 (page 365). See also *Dano* in section 9.5.2 (page 366), which first curtailed the principles established in *Brey* and laid the foundations for *Alimanovic*

Additionally, the Court argued that it did not make sense to require individual assessments of whether a claim to social assistance would place an 'unreasonable burden' on the national system within the meaning of Article 14(1) of Directive 2004/38, as no one claim would amount to such a burden. Legislation that would exclude persons in certain situations from entitlement to social assistance may therefore be justifiable on the grounds that the **accumulation** of such claims would lead to an 'unreasonable burden'.

The Court also ruled that the retention of worker status for six months after the cessation of employment, as provided for in Article 7(3)(c) of Directive 2004/38, provides a proportionate duration for which social assistance should be provided. Therefore, **national legislation may make entitlement to social assistance, including jobseekers' allowance, conditional on an EU national's residence situation, without requiring further individual assessment**.

Significance:

The Court took a novel approach in its assertion that, even where special non-contributory cash benefits are part of a scheme to facilitate access to the national labour market, this is irrelevant if their predominant function is to meet subsistence needs. In such cases, they should be classified as social assistance, and Article 24(2) of Directive 2004/38 can subsequently be applied to the effect that the benefit may be denied to EU nationals whose right to reside is premised on their search for work (Art 14(4)(b), Directive 2004/38). This limits the scope of application of the *Collins* and *Vatsouras* judgments, as Member States now seem to be able to deny a jobseekers' allowance to EU jobseekers who have real links to the national labour market by combining that allowance with benefits that are primarily intended to meet subsistence needs and can thus be classified as social assistance.

Additionally, the Court diverged from the principle established in *Brey* that applicants should be considered on an individual basis. To do this, the Court distinguished between matters of residence (expulsion orders) and social provisions, ruling that while the particular circumstances of the individual must be considered with regard to the former, they need not be with regard to the latter. Therefore, as a result of the *Alimanovic* judgment, non-nationals may be automatically excluded from entitlement to social assistance once they lose the status of a worker – a situation that Advocate General Wathelet described as problematic.

It is worth noting that this case would have been moot if the Alimanovics had worked for one month longer, as they would then have completed a year of work and would have retained their worker status for as long as they were recorded as involuntarily unemployed and registered as jobseekers (Art 7(3), Directive 2004/38).

Reflection: Politics and benefits

In *Alimanovic*, as in *Dano* (see section 9.5.2), the Court of Justice passed a judgment that was unexpectedly restrictive on the rights of Union citizens to benefits in a host Member State. As legal developments do not occur in a political vacuum, it is worth considering how this change in direction, and particularly the court's departure from *Brey*, may have been influenced by political considerations.

At the time of the *Alimanovic* ruling, former UK Prime Minister David Cameron had presented his reform agenda to the European Council and had pledged to hold a referendum on the UK's membership of the Union in 2016. The social security and welfare benefits that the UK is obliged to provide to Union citizens and their family members was one of the main areas in which Cameron was seeking reform. The governments of other Member States also faced pressures in relation to immigration, partly as a result of a resurgence in right wing political influence in several countries. Indeed, the *Vatsouras*, *Dano* and *Alimanovic* cases demonstrate the keenness of the German authorities to limit benefit payments to EU nationals. The *Dano* and *Alimanovic* judgments can therefore be seen as conceding to Member States' concerns about increasing expenditure on welfare since rights were expanded by the introduction of Union citizenship and within an enlarged Union.

A similar question as in *Alimanovic* was then referred to the Court in *Garcia-Nieto and others* (Case C-299/14). While *Alimanovic* dealt with the national legislation implementing Article 24(2) of Directive 2004/38 in relation to EU jobseekers who had resided in the host Member State for longer than three months (i.e. where their right to residence was derived from Article 14(4)(b) of the Directive), *Garcia-Nieto* dealt with such implementing measures in relation to EU jobseekers who had resided in the host Member State for less than three months (i.e. where their right to residence was derived from Article 6(1) of the Directive). In *Garcia-Nieto*, the Court repeated its ruling in *Alimanovic* – and consolidated its turn away from *Brey* and *Vatsouras* – finding that the benefits in question constituted 'social assistance' and could therefore be automatically denied to non-nationals who did not have the status of a worker.

The current situation therefore remains highly complex, suggesting that further judgments will be required from the Court in order to clarify matters.

Reflection: Overview of social benefits

This box provides a consolidated overview of the different types of social benefit that are identified in EU law and expands upon the definitions provided at the beginning of this chapter and in section 9.5.

> The **Even** formula defines **social advantages** as benefits that are granted to individuals on the basis of their worker or residence status or that could facilitate the mobility of workers within the Union. Union workers are entitled to enjoy the same social advantages as nationals under Article 7(2) of Regulation 492/2011. It was established in **Collins** that all Union citizens should generally be granted social advantages on the same grounds as nationals so long as they are lawfully resident in the host state. However, conditions requiring them to demonstrate a genuine link with the national labour market may justify the exclusion of certain Union citizens, as in **Collins**.
>
> **Social assistance** comprises non-contributory benefits that aim to ensure an individual is able to meet their basic subsistence needs. Under Article 24(2) of Directive 2004/38, Member States can deny social assistance to nationals of another Member State who have been resident within the host state for less than three months (as in **Garcia-Nieto**) or whose continued residence is premised on their search for work (i.e. who fall within Art 14(4)(b), Directive 2004/38, as in **Alimanovic**). This connects with the condition stipulated in Article 7(1) of Directive 2004/38 that EU nationals who are neither workers nor family members thereof may only reside within a host Member State if they have sufficient resources to avoid becoming a burden on the social assistance system of that state.
>
> **Special non-contributory cash benefits**, as defined in Article 70 of Regulation 883/2004, are benefits that aim to guarantee minimum subsistence by supplementing social security provisions, and that can therefore be described as containing elements of both social security and social assistance. Everyone who falls within the scope of Regulation 883/2004 (EU nationals, stateless persons and refugees residing in a host Member State, as well as the members of their families) are entitled to receive special non-contributory cash benefits on equal grounds as nationals, according to Article 4 of that Regulation. However, it was ruled in **Alimanovic** that such benefits may be classified as social assistance for the purpose of Directive 2004/38, and may thus be subject to the exclusions therein, if the primary purpose of the benefit is to meet subsistence needs.

10.5 Family members of workers

Objective 5

It is not only the worker who derives benefits from Union law, but also the family of the worker. However, the rights of the family are dependent upon the worker's status as a Union worker (see *Morson and Jhanjan* above). Although the worker has to be an EU national, the family of the worker does not.

The rights of family members of Union citizens in general are covered in Chapter 9. This section examines those rights which pertain specifically to a Union citizen's status as a worker, or that otherwise involve questions related to the free movement of workers. First, however, it is useful to review the definition of a family member, as set forth in **Directive 2004/38**.

10.5.1 Definition of a family member

A Union worker may be accompanied by, or be joined by:

(i) their spouse (including a same-sex spouse where the marriage has been conducted according to the law of a Member State – ***Coman and Others*** (C 673/16)) or a registered partner (if the host Member State's legislation recognises registered partnerships as equivalent to marriage);

(ii) the Union worker's descendants who are under the age of 21 or who are dependent (this applies to the descendants of the Union worker and also those of their spouse/registered partner); and

(iii) the Union worker's dependent relatives in the ascending line and those of their spouse/registered partner (Arts 2(2), 6(2) and 7(1)(d), Directive 2004/38).

> See section 9.3.1 on the scope of 'dependence'

Therefore, dependent children and grandchildren have the right to install themselves with the worker, and the same applies to the parents and grandparents of both the Union worker and their spouse/registered partner, if they are dependent.

Other family members not coming within the ascending or descending lines, such as aunts, uncles, nephews and nieces, should have their entry 'facilitated' if: (i) they are dependent on the worker; (ii) they are members of the worker's household; or (iii) serious health grounds strictly require the worker to provide the family member with personal care. The same applies to the 'partner' of the worker provided they have a 'durable relationship' which is duly attested (Arts 3(2), 6(2) and 7(1)(d), Directive 2004/38). Where a person has the right to have their entry 'facilitated', the host Member State is required to undertake an extensive examination of the personal circumstances of such persons and shall justify any denial of entry or residence (Art 3(2), Directive 2004/38). In the case of family members who are not nationals of a Member State, it is permissible that they should obtain an entry visa before being admitted, unless they have been issued with a residence card under Directive 2004/38, in which case the residence card will suffice (Art 5(2)). In cases where a visa is required, Member States should grant such persons 'every facility to obtain the necessary visas'; the visa shall be issued free of charge (Art 5(2)).

10.5.2 Rights to free movement of family members

Directive 2004/38 establishes the rights of family members to reside with a Union worker. A family member should not need to prove the relationship at the point of entry, although Article 5(5) provides that the host Member State may require each person travelling to, or residing in, another Member State to register their presence in the country within a reasonable and non-discriminatory period of time. Failure to comply with this requirement may make the person liable to a proportionate and non-discriminatory sanction.

If the worker is resident in the host Member State for no longer than three months, the family members will have the right of entry and residence without any conditions or formalities other than the requirement to hold a valid identity card or passport (Art 6(1)); in the case of non-EU family members only a passport will suffice (Art 6(2)).

If the worker is resident in the host Member State for longer than three months, a registration certificate will be issued to family members who are nationals of a Member State (i.e. EU family members); this is subject to the production of specified documentation (Art 8(5)). This provision also applies to other EU family members whose entry to and residence in the host Member State is facilitated in accordance with Art 3(2); see above. In the case of family members who are not nationals of a Member State (i.e. non-EU family members), such family members must apply for a residence card not more than three months from their date of arrival (Art 9(2)). A residence card is valid for at least five years from its date of issue, or for the envisaged period of residence of the worker if this is less than five years (Art 11(1)). Article 10(2) sets out the documentation required before a residence card will be issued. This provision also applies to other non-EU family members whose entry and residence to the host Member State shall be facilitated in accordance with Article 3(2). Article 11(2) provides that the validity of a residence card shall not be affected by:

(i) temporary absences of up to six months a year;

(ii) absences of a longer period for compulsory military service; or

(iii) one absence of up to 12 months for important reasons (e.g. pregnancy and childbirth, serious illness, study or vocational training, or a posting in another Member State or a non-EU country).

The following case was brought before the Court of Justice before the adoption of Directive 2004/38. It concerned national legislation which required spouses of migrant workers who were nationals of other Member States to have resided in the territory of that Member State for four years before they became entitled to apply for indefinite leave to remain, but which required residence of only 12 months for the spouses of persons who were settled in that territory:

Kaba v Secretary of State for the Home Department (Case C-356/98)

Facts:

Kaba, a Yugoslav national, married a French national who found work in the UK in April 1994 and with whom he lived there. In 1996, Kaba applied for indefinite leave to remain in the UK, but was refused on the ground that paragraph 255 of the Immigration Rules 1994 was not satisfied because his wife (an EU national) had only resided in the UK as a Union worker for one year and ten months and not the required four years. However, if Kaba's wife had been a UK citizen he would have been eligible for indefinite leave to remain in the UK after just one year. Kaba therefore challenged the refusal, maintaining there was discrimination contrary to the former Article 7(2) of Regulation 1612/68 (now Art 7(2), Regulation 492/2011).

Ruling:

The Court of Justice noted that Kaba's application for indefinite leave to remain was an application for a more extensive right of residence than that which was available to his wife at the time. The Court therefore ruled that:

31 ... **Member States are entitled to rely on any objective difference there might be between their own nationals and those of other Member States**, when they lay down the conditions under which leave to remain indefinitely in their territory was to be granted to the spouses of [Union workers].

32 More particularly, **Member states are entitled to require the spouses of persons who do not themselves enjoy an unconditional right of residence to be resident for a longer period than that required for the spouses of persons who already enjoy such a right, before granting the same right to them.**

33 Once leave to remain indefinitely had been granted, no condition could be imposed on the person to whom such leave had been granted, and therefore **the authorities must be able, when the application was made, to require the applicant to have established sufficiently enduring links with the state...** .

34 Furthermore, migrant workers who are nationals of other Member States may themselves acquire the status of a person present and settled in the United Kingdom, so that their spouses will then qualify to be granted indefinite leave to remain after only 12 months' residence pursuant to paragraph 287 of the Immigration Rules.

> Therefore, the residence requirement for spouses of non-national workers was held not to infringe Article 7(2) of Regulation 1612/68 (now Art 7(2), Regulation 492/2011).
>
> **Significance:**
>
> A longer residence requirement for spouses of non-national Union workers than for spouses of national workers can be justified if it is premised on the residence status of the worker, rather than their nationality. Although this might result in indirect discrimination because a national is more likely to have a permanent residence status, Member States may place conditions on indefinite leave to remain for the legitimate purpose of ensuring that an applicant has established sufficiently enduring links with the state.

This case came back before the Court of Justice in a second ***Kaba*** case (Case C-466/00). The Court was asked to rule on whether its reply would have been different had the Court taken into consideration the fact that the situation of those two categories of person (i.e. national worker and Union worker) were comparable in all respects under UK law, except with regard to the period of prior residence which was required for the purpose of being granted indefinite leave to remain in the UK. The Court held that this made no difference to its previous decision. The Court stated that the right of residence of a Union worker is subject to the condition that the person remains a worker or is seeking employment, unless they derive that right from other provisions of Union law. A Union worker's situation is **not** comparable to that of a national who is not subject to any restriction regarding the period for which they may reside within the territory of that Member State. A national would not, during their stay, need to satisfy any condition comparable to those laid down by the provisions of Union law, which grant Union workers a right of residence in another Member State. The Court held that because the rights of residence of these two categories of persons (i.e. Union worker and national worker) are not in all respects comparable, the same holds true with regard to the situation of their spouses, particularly so far as concerns the question of the duration of the residence period on completion of which they may be given indefinite leave to remain in the UK.

Article 16 of Directive 2004/38 now sets out the right of permanent residence for a Union worker and his family members. Union citizens acquire the right of permanent residence in the host Member State after a five-year period of continuous legal residence (Art 16(1)), provided that an expulsion decision has not been enforced against them (Art 21). This right of permanent residence is not subject to any conditions. The same rule applies to non-EU family members who have lived with a Union citizen in the host Member State for five years (Art 16(2)), also provided that an expulsion decision has not been enforced against them (Art 21).

Articles 12 and 13 are also relevant to rights of residence. Article 12(1) provides that if a Union citizen dies or departs from the host Member State, their family members who are nationals of a Member State shall not have their right of residence affected. Article 13 governs a family member's right of residence following divorce, annulment of marriage or termination of partnership. Article 17 also provides that the family members of a Union worker or self-employed person have the right of permanent residence if the Union worker or self-employed person dies before acquiring the right of permanent residence.

The free movement rights of family members apply not only in relation to a Union worker's host Member State, but also in relation to their home state when they return after having worked in another Member State. In ***R v Immigration Appeal Tribunal and Surinder***

> See section 9.2.1 (page 332) for more information on *Surinder Singh*

Singh (Case C-370/90), the Court of Justice held that a national of a Member State who has gone to work in another Member State, and then returns to their home Member State, has the right to return to that state under the same conditions as are laid down by the former Regulation 1612/68 (now Regulation 492/2011) or Directive 2004/38. This meant that, after working in Germany for two and a half years, Surinder Singh was entitled to bring his non-EU wife with him to his home country on the same grounds as if he were migrating to a host Member State.

Family members have a right to work in the host Member State. Under **Article 23 of Directive 2004/38**, all family members who have the right of residence in a Member State are entitled to take up employment or self-employment there, even if they are not nationals of any Member State (i.e. non-EU family members). The fact that a family member's right to residence is based on their dependence on a Union citizen does not affect their right to work (*Reyes* v *Migrationsverket* (Case C-423/12), see section 10.3.1).

10.5.3 Rights to social benefits for family members

The Court of Justice has developed a considerable body of case law on the application of the right to equal treatment with regard to social and tax advantages that is established in **Article 7(2) of Regulation 492/2011** to family members. Some examples are outlined below.

In *Inzirillo* v *Caisse d'Allocations Familiales de l'Arrondissement de Lyon* (Case 63/76), the applicant was an Italian working in France, who had been refused a disability allowance for his adult son on the ground that French nationality was a condition of entitlement. It was argued that the former Article 7(2) of Regulation 1612/68 (now Art 7(2), Regulation 492/2011) was not applicable because the allowance was not a social advantage to the worker (as provided for in Art 7(2)) but rather to his son. The Court of Justice held that dependent offspring counted as family members under the former Article 10(1) of Regulation 1612/68 (now Art 2(2)(c), Directive 2004/38) and that an allowance for disabled adults that a Member State awarded to its own nationals constituted a social advantage to which an EU national should be equally entitled under such circumstances.

Netherlands v *Reed* (Case 59/85) provides an interesting illustration of how Article 7(2) of Regulation 1612/68 (now Art 7(2) Regulation 492/2011) may come to the aid of a worker when other provisions cannot assist. The case concerned a UK national who travelled to the Netherlands to live with her long-term partner, who was also a UK national working in the Netherlands. The Court of Justice held that 'spouse' within the former Article 10(1) of Regulation 1612/68 (now Art 2(2)(a), Directive 2004/38) only referred to a married relationship. However, the problem was resolved by applying the former Article 7(2) of Regulation 1612/68 (now Art 7(2), Regulation 492/2011) to the specific facts of the case. In Dutch law, a foreigner who had a stable relationship with a working national was treated as that person's spouse. The Court referred to the *Even* **formula** and held that the opportunity to have a partner reside with a Union worker constituted a 'social advantage' within Article 7(2), as it would further the policy of free movement of persons. This situation is now covered by Article 2(2)(b) of Directive 2004/38, which includes within the scope of family members a 'registered partner' if the legislation of the host Member State treats registered partnerships as equivalent to married partnerships.

> See section 10.3.3 on *Even* and the *Even* formula (page 405)

The Court ruled in *Lebon* that for a family member to be entitled to a social advantage it must be of some direct or indirect benefit to the worker themselves. However, as set out above, this is not necessarily the case if the worker has died or become estranged from their family members. The following case considered the extent to which a worker's surviving family members were entitled to social advantages in a host Member State:

Cristini v SNCF (Case 32/75)

Facts:
SNCF, the French railway company, offered a fare reduction to large families of French nationality. Cristini, an Italian national resident in France and the widow of an Italian national who had worked in France, was refused the reduction card on the basis of nationality. SNCF argued that the former Article 7(2) of Regulation 1612/68 (now Art 7(2), Regulation 492/2011) covered only advantages connected with the contract of employment. The national court referred a question to the Court of Justice under what is now Article 267 TFEU. It should be noted that Cristini was entitled to remain in France under what is now Article 17(4) of Directive 2004/38 (see above) as the spouse of a deceased worker.

Ruling:
The Court of Justice first held that, for Article 7(2):

> 13 ... **the substantive area of application must be delineated so as to include all social and tax advantages, whether or not attached to the contract of employment**, such as reduction in fares for large families.

The Court then considered whether a widow and the children of a Union worker are entitled to claim a new social advantage after the worker's death. The Court ruled that:

> 15 If the widow and infant children of a national of the Member State in question are entitled to such cards provided that the request has been made by the father before his death, the same must apply where the deceased father was a migrant worker and a national of another Member State.

> 16 It would be contrary to the purpose and the spirit of the Community [i.e. Union] rules on freedom of movement for workers to deprive the survivors of such a benefit following the death of the worker whilst granting the same benefit to the survivors of a national.

Significance:
The Court of Justice held that 'social advantages' under Article 7(2) do not have to be connected with the worker's contract of employment and may therefore be granted to surviving family members, even if they apply for such benefits after the death of the Union worker. This established a broad definition of social advantages.

Access to education and vocational training

> ▶ See section 10.3.3 on Article 7(3) of Regulation 492/2011

In this section, the application of **Article 7(2)** of Regulation 492/2011 to social advantages for family members of Union workers in the field of education is considered. Union workers are entitled, by virtue of Article 7(3) of Regulation 492/2011, to equal access to vocational schools and retraining centres. **Article 10** of Regulation 492/2011 also provides that Union workers' children are to be admitted to the host Member State's 'general educational, apprenticeship and vocational training courses under the same conditions as nationals of that State, if such children are residing in its territory'. The broad application of the principle of equal treatment to the field of education was established in *Casagrande* (Case 9/74). Here, the Court of Justice ruled that equal treatment in admission to educational courses that was provided for in the former Article 12 of Regulation 1612/68 extended to measures intended to facilitate educational attendance.

The former Article 12 of Regulation 1612/68 (now Art 10, Regulation 492/2011) received further attention from the Court of Justice in a number of other cases. In the following case, the Court clarified the rights of the child of a Union worker to attend school in the event that the worker and/or relationship status of their parent(s) changed.

Baumbast and R v Secretary of State for the Home Department (Case C-413/99)

Facts:

The case concerned the families of both a German national and a French national who had moved to the UK as Union workers. The EU nationals had both been married to non-EU nationals with whom they had children and then divorced. The German national, Baumbast, subsequently lost his status as a Union worker and was refused leave to remain in the UK, while his children and ex-wife were permitted to remain. With regards to the family of the French national, his children but not his ex-wife, R, were granted leave to remain in the UK. R's application was refused on the basis that their children were deemed young enough to adapt to life in her home country. With regards to R, the questions put to the Court of Justice concerned the rights of the children, one of whom was not a Union citizen, to remain in the UK in order to undergo general educational courses and the subsequent right of their primary carers to reside with them.

Ruling:

The Court of Justice stated that:

> **Children of a citizen of the European Union who have installed themselves in a Member State during the exercise by their parent of rights of residence as a migrant worker in that Member State are entitled to reside there in order to attend general educational courses there**, pursuant to Article 12 of Regulation (EEC) No 1612/68 [now Art 10, Regulation 492/2011] ... The fact that the parents of the children concerned have meanwhile divorced, the fact that only one parent is a citizen of the Union and that parent has ceased to be a migrant worker in the host Member State and the fact that the children are not themselves citizens of the Union are irrelevant in this regard. [para 63]

The Court then went further, stating that:

> Where children have the right to reside in a host Member State in order to attend general education courses pursuant to Article 12 of Regulation No 1612/68 [now Art 10, Regulation 492/2011], **that provision must be interpreted as entitling the parent who is the primary carer of those children, irrespective of his nationality, to reside with them in order to facilitate the exercise of that right** notwithstanding the fact that the parents have meanwhile divorced or that the parent who has the status of citizen of the European Union has ceased to be a migrant worker in the host Member State. [para 64]

Significance:

The Court of Justice decided that where the child was exercising the right to attend general educational courses, the parent who had primary care of the child had the right to reside with the child, even if this parent did not have Union worker status and irrespective of whether or not this parent was a Union citizen. This principle of allowing a parent to reside with a child in order to enable the child to benefit from their rights under Union law can be seen as laying the groundwork for the Court's ruling in *Zambrano* (Case C-34/09) (see page 346).

Now, **Article 12(3) of Directive 2004/38** provides that if a Union citizen dies or departs from the host Member State while their children are residing in the host Member State and are enrolled at an educational establishment, then their children and the parent who has actual custody of the children (whether or not they are Union citizens) shall have the right to reside in the host Member State until the children have completed their studies.

In the following case, the Court of Justice confirmed that *Baumbast* was still good law following the entry into force of Directive 2004/38:

London Borough of Harrow v *Ibrahim* (Case C-310/08) and *Teixeira* v *London Borough of Lambeth* (Case C-480/08)

Facts:

The Court of Appeal of England and Wales, which was hearing these two cases, asked the Court of Justice:

(i) whether the interpretation of the former Article 12, Regulation 1612/68 (now Art 10, Regulation 492/2011) adopted in the *Baumbast* judgment was applicable following the entry into force of Directive 2004/38;

(ii) whether the right of residence of the person who was the child's primary carer was now subject to the conditions laid down by the Directive for the exercise of the right of residence, especially the requirement that the parent must have sufficient resources not to become a burden on the social assistance system.

Ruling:

In its judgments, the Court pointed out that **the former Article 12 of Regulation 1612/68 (now Art 10, Regulation 492/2011) allowed the child of a migrant worker to have an independent right of residence in connection with the right of access to education in the host Member State**. The right of access to education laid down by the former Article 12 of Regulation 1612/68 (now Art 10, Regulation 492/2011) was not conditional on the child retaining, throughout the period of education, a specific right of residence under the former Article 10 of Regulation 1612/68. Once the right of access to education had been acquired, the right of residence was retained by the child and could no longer be called into question. The former Article 12 of Regulation 1612/68 (now Art 10, Regulation 492/2011) required only that the child had lived with at least one of their parents in a Member State while that parent resided there as a worker. That Article had to be applied independently of the provisions of Union law, which expressly govern the conditions on exercising the right to reside in another Member State.

That independence was not called into question by the entry into force of the new Directive 2004/38. The Court pointed out that the former Article 12 of Regulation 1612/68 (now Art 10, Regulation 492/2011) was not repealed or even amended by Directive 2004/38, unlike other articles of the regulation. Furthermore, the legislative history of the Directive showed that it was designed to be consistent with the *Baumbast* judgment.

The Court held that **the right of residence of a parent who was the primary carer for a child of a migrant worker, where that child was in education in the host Member State, was not conditional on that parent having sufficient resources not to become a burden on the social assistance system of the host Member State**. That interpretation was supported by Directive 2004/38, which provided that the departure or death of the citizen did not entail the loss of the right of residence of the children or the parent.

On a separate point, the Court held that the right of residence of such a parent ended when the child reached the age of majority, unless the child continued to need the presence and care of that parent in order to be able to pursue and complete their education in the host Member State.

Significance:

The Court reaffirmed the ruling in *Baumbast* by establishing that the entry into force of Directive 2004/38 had not affected the rights of a Union worker's child to access education.

It is worth noting, however, that the Court of Justice had earlier stated in ***Brown* v *Secretary of State for Scotland*** (Case 197/86) that a child did not have any rights under the former Article 12 of Regulation 1612/68 (now Art 10, Regulation 492/2011) if their parents had lost their Union worker status before they had been born. This remains consistent with both ***Baumbast*** and Directive 2004/38.

Neither the Treaties nor any implementing measures define 'vocational training' for the purposes of the former Article 12 of Regulation 1612/68 (now Art 10, Regulation 492/2011), but in ***Gravier* v *City of Liège*** (Case 293/83) the Court of Justice said that 'any form of education which prepares for a qualification for a particular profession, trade or employment or which provides the necessary skills for such a profession, trade or employment is vocational training whatever the age and level of the pupil or student'. The applicant's course in ***Gravier*** – strip cartoon design – clearly fell into that category. This definition was clarified further in ***Blaizot*** (Case 24/86), where the Court held that academic work at university level was not excluded, provided that the studies lead to a required qualification or provided specific training and skills for a particular trade, profession or employment.

Despite the need for a course of study to include at least some career-orientated skills, the Court in ***Lair* v *University of Hannover*** (Case 39/86) did not appear to doubt that a course in Romance and Germanic languages and literature, which had no immediate vocational orientation, was nonetheless a 'vocational training course' (see Flynn, 1988).

> ### Reflection: Overview of access to university
>
> This box combines information from this chapter and elsewhere to provide an overview of rights relating to university education for different categories of person.
>
> All EU nationals are entitled to the same university access conditions and fees as nationals of a Member State (***Gravier***). They are also entitled to the same assistance with paying fees. However, Member States may condition equal access to maintenance loans and grants on having acquired permanent residence status, i.e. having resided in the country for five years (Art 24(2), Directive 2004/38) (see Chapter 9).
>
> Under Article 7(3) of Regulation 492/2011, Union workers are entitled to equal access to vocational schools and retraining centres. In ***Brown***, the Court ruled that, although university courses may include vocational training, universities are not vocational schools for the purpose of Article 7(3). However, if a worker ceases employment in order to undertake a related vocational training course, they retain the status of a worker (Art 7(3), Directive 2004/38). Accordingly, Article 7(2) of Regulation 492/2011 can entitle a student with Union worker status to equal access to social advantages, which may include maintenance loans or grants (***Lair*** and ***Raulin***).
>
> The Court has been generous in its interpretation of the rights of family members under Article 10 of Regulation 492/2011. Article 10, which stipulates the right of family members to be admitted to general educational and vocational training courses under equal conditions as nationals, has been interpreted as a right to equal conditions of admission to universities in most instances (***Blaizot***). This is significant for family members of a Union worker who are not themselves Union citizens. Furthermore, family members are entitled to equal treatment with regard to maintenance loans or grants in so far as they amount to a social advantage for a Union worker on whom they would otherwise be dependent (***Lebon***).

> See *Bidar* and *Förster* in section 9.5.3 to see how the Court ruled differently in cases concerning access to social advantages in the field of education for students who were not workers or family members thereof

In the following two more recent cases, the Court considered objective justifications for indirectly discriminatory residence conditions for access to higher education benefits:

Commission v Netherlands (Case C-542/09)

Facts:

Funding for higher education studies in the Netherlands was available to students who were aged between 18 and 29 years old and who were either nationals of the Netherlands or any other Member State of the European Union. To receive funding for higher education pursued outside the Netherlands, students had to be eligible for funding for higher education in the Netherlands and had to additionally have resided lawfully in the Netherlands for at least three out of the six years preceding enrolment at an educational establishment abroad. This condition, known as the '3 out of 6 years' requirement, applied irrespective of the student's nationality.

The Commission brought an action before the Court of Justice against the Netherlands, claiming that the '3 out of 6 years' requirement constituted indirect discrimination against migrant workers and members of their families, as prohibited by Article 45 TFEU and contrary to the former Article 7(2) of Regulation 1612/68 (now Art 7(2), Regulation 492/2011).

Ruling:

The Court pointed out that study finance granted by a Member State to the children of workers constituted a social advantage for the purpose of Article 7(2), where the worker continued to support the child.

Considering that the principle of equal treatment prohibits indirect discrimination, the Court held that **the '3 out of 6 years' residence requirement created inequality in treatment** between Dutch workers and migrant workers residing in the Netherlands or employed there as **frontier workers**, as the latter were more likely to be disadvantaged by the requirement in practice. **Such an inequality constituted unlawful indirect discrimination, unless it was objectively justified**.

With regard to objective justification, the Court rejected the argument that the residence requirement was necessary in order to avoid an unreasonable financial burden which could have consequences for the very existence of the assistance scheme. The objective of avoiding an unreasonable financial burden could not be accepted as to do so would enable the principle of non-discrimination to be applied varyingly according to the state of public finances at any given time or place.

The Netherlands also claimed that, given that the national legislation at issue was intended to encourage students to pursue studies outside the Netherlands, the requirement ensured that the portable funding was available solely to those students who, without it, would pursue their education in the Netherlands. By contrast, students who did not reside in the Netherlands would be more likely to study in the Member State in which they were resident. For such students, therefore, the funding in question would not encourage mobility. Additionally, the Netherlands pointed to the enrichment brought by studies outside the Netherlands, not only to the students but also to Dutch society and its employment market when such students returned to the Netherlands to reside and work there.

The Court noted that **the objective of encouraging student mobility was in the public interest and constituted an overriding reason relating to the public interest, capable of justifying a restriction of the principle of non-discrimination on grounds of nationality**. However, legislation that was liable to restrict a fundamental freedom guaranteed by the Treaties, such as freedom of movement for workers, could be justified only if it was appropriate for attaining the legitimate objective pursued and did not go beyond what was necessary in order to attain that objective (i.e. if it was proportionate).

The Court acknowledged that a residence requirement was appropriate for attaining the objective of promoting student mobility. However, the Netherlands had failed to demonstrate that the '3 out of 6' rule was proportionate, as a worker's length of residence within the Netherlands will not necessarily affect where their child would attend university.

Significance:

This case provides an example of the wide interpretation that the Court has granted to the right to equal treatment and the high threshold of justification that a Member State must meet in order for national provisions that have a discriminatory effect on Union workers to be lawful.

The following case also concerned funding for higher education studies, but this time with regard to the child of a frontier worker:

Giersch and Others v Luxembourg (Case C-20/12)

Facts:

Luxembourg granted financial aid, in the form of a grant and a loan, in order to promote higher education studies by students in its territory or in the territory of any other state. That aid was granted to students holding Luxembourg nationality, or the nationality of another Member State, and who were resident in Luxembourg when they were about to embark on higher education studies. Thus, the children of frontier workers, who usually resided in a country bordering upon Luxembourg, were not entitled to the aid.

A number of children of frontier workers to whom financial aid had been denied contested the lawfulness of their exclusion from the category of beneficiaries of the aid before the Luxembourg courts. The tribunal administratif (Luxembourg), before which those disputes were brought, referred the case to the Court of Justice.

Ruling:

As in **Commission v Netherlands**, the Court of Justice stated that aid granted in order to finance the university studies of the child of a migrant worker constituted, for that worker, a social advantage which had to be granted to them under the same conditions as those applying to national workers. The Court made clear in that regard that the principle of equal treatment could not be limited to migrant workers residing in a host Member State but had to extend to frontier workers.

The Court further held that **the condition of residence required by Luxembourg legislation amounted to indirect discrimination on grounds of nationality in so far as it was liable to operate mainly to the detriment of nationals of other Member States**. In that context, the Court stated that such discrimination could not be justified by budgetary considerations, as the application and the scope of the principle of non-discrimination on grounds of nationality could not depend on the state of the public finances of the Member States.

The Court nevertheless considered that **the condition of residence was appropriate for attaining the objective pursued by Luxembourg of promoting higher education studies and of significantly increasing the proportion of Luxembourg residents who held a higher education degree**. Students who were resident in Luxembourg when they were about to embark on their higher education studies would be more likely than non-resident students to settle in Luxembourg and become integrated in the Luxembourg labour market after completing their studies, even if those studies were undertaken abroad.

> However, the Court held that the system of financial aid in question was too exclusive in nature. By imposing a prior condition of residence by the student in Luxembourg territory, the law favoured an element which was not necessarily the sole representative element of the actual degree of attachment of the person concerned to Luxembourg. Thus, it was possible that a non-resident student could also have an attachment to Luxembourg sufficient to make it reasonably probable that they would return to settle in Luxembourg and make themselves available to the labour market of that Member State. That would be the case where that student resided alone or with their parents in a Member State which bordered Luxembourg and where, for a significant period of time, their parents had worked in Luxembourg and lived near to that Member State.
>
> The Court pointed out in that regard that **less restrictive measures were available which would make it possible to attain the objective sought by the Luxembourg legislature**. For example, where the aid granted consisted of a loan, a system of financing which made the grant of that loan, or even the outstanding balance thereof, or its non-reimbursement, conditional on the student who received it returning to Luxembourg after his studies abroad in order to work and reside there, would be better adapted to the special situation of the children of frontier workers. In addition, in order to avoid 'study grant forum shopping' and to ensure that the frontier worker parent of the student had a sufficient link with Luxembourg society, the financial aid could be made conditional on that parent having worked in Luxembourg for a certain minimum period of time.
>
> Finally, the risk of duplication with equivalent financial aid paid in the Member State in which the student resides, with or without his parents, could be avoided by taking that aid into account in the grant of the aid paid by Luxembourg.
>
> In those circumstances, the Court held that the contested Luxembourg legislation went beyond what was necessary to attain the objective pursued by the legislature and was therefore contrary to the principle of proportionality and the freedom of movement for workers.
>
> **Significance:**
>
> The case demonstrates that national legislation can be found to be disproportionate to the attainment of a legitimate aim if there are less restrictive means available of attaining it. The case thus demonstrates the Court's protective approach to the principle of equal treatment.

Luxembourg policy on financial aid for higher education was again at issue in the more recent case of *Aubriet* (Case C-410/18), which also echoes the Court's ruling on the '3 out of 6' provision in *Commission* v *Netherlands* (Case C-542/09). In this case, Mr Aubriet resided in France but had worked in Luxembourg and contributed to the Luxembourg social security system for 17 years. However, because he had not worked in Luxembourg for five years out of the preceding seven, his son's application for financial aid to support his studies was refused. The Court again ruled that, although the aim of promoting higher education within the population of Luxembourg is legitimate, the '5 out of 7' criterion for establishing a genuine connection with the country was disproportionate.

Housing provisions

The entry of family members used to be conditional upon the Union worker having available for them 'housing considered as normal for national workers in the region where he is employed' (Art 10(3), Regulation 1612/68). This condition was operative only at the time of the family's entry. An attempt by the German authorities to make access to reasonable housing provisions a precondition for the renewal of a residence permit was held by the Court of Justice in *Commission* v *Germany (Re Housing of Migrant Workers)* (Case 249/86)) to be unlawful. The reference to adequate housing in Article 10(3) related only to the 'installation' of the worker's family. The Court emphasised the importance of family reunion, as guaranteed by Article 8 of the European Convention on Human Rights, and the need to facilitate 'the integration of the worker and his family into the host Member State without any difference in treatment in relation to nationals of that State'. Perhaps for this reason, Directive 2004/38 (which repealed and replaced Art 10, Regulation 1612/68) makes no reference to a need for the Union worker to have such housing available for their family members.

The need for equal treatment in the housing field is dealt with in **Article 9 of Regulation 492/2011**. Under this provision, the worker 'shall enjoy all the rights and benefits accorded to national workers in matters of housing, including ownership of the housing he needs'. If their family remained in the country from which they came, the family shall be considered for this purpose as residing in the region where the Union worker is working. On this basis, the Union worker is entitled to be treated, for the purpose of both applying for public housing and the purchase of a private house, as having their family with them. The Court of Justice held in ***Commission* v *Germany*** (above) that the acquisition of housing solely to secure a residence permit could be penalised if the family then moved into less suitable accommodation, but that any penalty should fall short of measures leading to expulsion.

CHAPTER SUMMARY

The scope of the term 'worker'

- Only workers who have migrated between Member States qualify for EU free movement rights (***Morson***).
- A worker may undertake full-time or part-time work (***Kempf***), and may be paid wages or 'in kind' (***Steymann***), but their work must be **'effective and genuine'** and not of so small a scale so as to be 'purely marginal and ancillary' (***Levin***).

The rights of Union workers

- The right to **move** between and **reside** within Member States for the purpose of employment (**Art 45(3) TFEU**).
- The right **not to be discriminated against** on the grounds of nationality, either directly or indirectly, in access to employment, in conditions of employment and in social and tax advantages (**Art 45(2) TFEU**; **Art 7, Regulation 492/2011**; **Art 4, Regulation 883/2004**).
- Access to employment may be restricted to nationals under **Article 45(4) TFEU** only if: 1) the position requires the exercise of powers conferred by public law (***Commission* v *Belgium***); 2) these powers are exercised on a regular basis (***Anker***); and 3) the restriction is necessary for the safeguarding of the interests of the Member State (***Lawrie-Blum***).

The rights of Union work-seekers

- The right to reside within a host Member State for as long as they are seeking employment and have a genuine chance of being employed (**Art 14(4)(b), Directive 2004/38**).
- The right to equal treatment in access to employment (**Arts 1, 3 and 4, Regulation 492/2011**), but not social assistance (**Art 24(2) Directive 2004/38**).
- The right to equal entitlement to social advantages, such as a benefit that is intended to facilitate access to the national labour market (*Collins*), unless: 1) the applicant fails to demonstrate a required 'real link' to the host Member State (*Collins*; *Vatsouras and Koupatantze*); or 2) this function of the benefit is secondary to the purpose of meeting subsistence needs (*Alimanovic*).

Family members of Union workers

- Family members joining a worker who is residing in the host Member State for no more than three months only need valid identification (**Art 6, Directive 2004/38**), but may be required to register for longer periods (**Art 8**) and to apply for a residence card if they are non-EU nationals (**Art 9**).
- Family members have the right to work (**Art 23, Directive 2004/38**).
- Family members have the right to equal treatment with regard to social and tax advantages (**Art 7(2), Regulation 492/2011**), so long as the advantage at least indirectly benefits the Union worker (*Lebon*).
- The children of Union workers should be admitted to a host state's education system on the same grounds as nationals (**Art 10, Directive 2004/38**).

Chapter 11
Freedom of establishment and the free movement of services

Learning objectives

At the end of this chapter you should understand:

1. The Treaty provisions and implementing directives that establish the freedom of establishment and the freedom to provide services.
2. The scope of the terms 'establishment' and 'services'.
3. The rights afforded to service providers, including their rights to establishment and the rights of their employees, and including the relevant provisions of Directive 2006/123.
4. The rights afforded to recipients of services, including the relevant provisions of Directive 2006/123.
5. Directive 2005/36 and the rules in place for the recognition of professional qualifications.

Key terms and concepts

Familiarity with the following terms will be helpful for understanding this chapter:

Collective agreement – a contract setting out the terms and conditions of employment, often in relation to a particular sector, which has been agreed by employers and trade unions.

Establishment – the pursuit of an economic activity by a service provider for an indefinite period and through a stable infrastructure (e.g. offices or consulting rooms)

Home Member State – the Member State from which a service provider originates

Host Member State – the Member State in which a non-national becomes established or in which a professional or undertaking established in another Member State provides services

Member State of establishment – the Member State in which a service provider is established

Objective justification – a permissible reason for indirect discrimination on the grounds that the difference in treatment pursues a legitimate aim in an appropriate manner and goes no further than is necessary for the realisation of that aim

Posted worker – a worker of any nationality who is employed by an undertaking that is established in one Member State, but who is sent by that employer to provide services within another Member State

Service provider – a self-employed professional or undertaking that is established in a Member State and that offers or provides a service for which they are normally remunerated

11.1 Introduction

Objective 1

The freedom to provide services concerns the rights of EU citizens to undertake activities as a self-employed person or to practise a profession or trade within a Member State of which they are not a national. Freedom of **establishment** then concerns the rights of such persons when they seek to set up a business or practice a profession or trade on a permanent or semi-permanent basis. Where a person seeks to practise a profession in another Member State in an employed capacity (i.e. as an EU worker), Union law provisions relating to workers may apply (see Chapter 10).

The Court of Justice has summarised the distinction between freedom of establishment and the freedom to provide services as follows:

> As regards the definition of the respective scopes of the principles of freedom to provide services and freedom of establishment, it should be noted that **the key element is whether or not the economic operator is established in the Member State in which it offers the services in question**. Where it is established (in a principal or secondary establishment) in the Member State in which it offers the service (Member State of destination or **host Member State**), it falls within the scope of the principle of freedom of establishment, as defined in Article 43 EC [now Art 49 TFEU]. On the other hand, where the economic operator is **not** established in that Member State of destination, it is a transfrontier **service provider** covered by the principle of freedom to provide services laid down in Article 49 EC [now Art 56 TFEU]. [*Commission v Portugal* (Case C-171/02), para 24].

While establishment requires a degree of stable and continuous operation within a host Member State, the provisions on services can cover more temporary or sporadic activities within a host Member State or any kind of activities that involve the provision of services across borders.

This chapter first provides an overview of the relevant primary and secondary **legislation** pertaining to the freedom of establishment and the freedom to provide services. This is then elaborated by a section on the **scope** of the terms 'establishment' and 'services'. The following two sections then consider in detail the **rights of service providers**, including their rights to establishment and the rights of their workers, and the **rights of recipients of services**. Finally, the **recognition of qualifications** is considered, as this is integral to the ability of individuals to provide professional services and become established within other Member States.

Freedom of establishment and the free movement of services will largely continue to apply to the UK during the Brexit transition period. After 31 December 2020, the scope of these freedoms will be determined by the provisions of a Withdrawal Agreement or by domestic legislation.

11.1.1 Primary legislation

Article 49 TFEU provides for the freedom of establishment:

> Within the framework of the provisions set out below, restrictions on the freedom of establishment of nationals of a Member State in the territory of another Member State shall be prohibited. Such prohibition shall also apply to restrictions on the setting-up of agencies, branches or subsidiaries by nationals of any Member State established in the territory of any Member State.
>
> **Freedom of establishment shall include the right to take up and pursue activities as self-employed persons and to set up and manage undertakings**, in particular companies or firms within the meaning of the second paragraph of Article 54, under the conditions laid down for its own nationals by the law of the country where such establishment is effected, subject to the provisions of the Chapter relating to capital.

Articles 56 and 57 TFEU provide for the abolition of restrictions on the provision of services in a Member State other than that in which an individual is established. **Article 56 TFEU** provides that:

> Within the framework of the provisions set out below, **restrictions on freedom to provide services within the Union shall be prohibited** in respect of nationals of Member States who are established in a Member State other than that of the person for whom the services are intended.
>
> The European Parliament and the Council, acting in accordance with the ordinary legislative procedure, may extend the provisions of the Chapter to nationals of a third country who provide services and who are established within the Union.

Extra care should be taken here to avoid confusing the former Article 49 EC Treaty on services (now Art 56 TFEU) with the current Article 49 TFEU on establishment.

Article 57 TFEU provides that:

> Services shall be considered to be 'services' within the meaning of the Treaties where they are **normally provided for remuneration**, in so far as they are not governed by the provisions relating to freedom of movement for goods, capital and persons.
>
> 'Services' shall in particular include:
>
> (a) activities of an industrial character;
>
> (b) activities of a commercial character;
>
> (c) activities of craftsmen;
>
> (d) activities of the professions.
>
> Without prejudice to the provisions of the Chapter relating to the right of establishment, the person providing a service may, in order to do so, temporarily pursue his activity in the Member State where the service is provided, under the same conditions as are imposed by that State on its own nationals.

The list of services provided in Article 57 is not an exhaustive list.

There is a close link between the freedom to provide services and the right of establishment. The right to provide the service confers a right of residence as long as the service is provided. If the service provider wishes to provide that service in the host Member State on a long-term basis then Article 49 TFEU will apply, and they may become established in that state. The crucial element that differentiates the service provider from the established business is the process of 'setting up'. This may involve anything from leasing or buying business premises, to acquiring a licence to run a company in the host Member State (see *Steinhauser* v *City of Biarritz* (Case 197/84) and *R* v *Secretary of State for Transport, ex parte Factortame* (Case C-213/89)).

With regard to services, **Article 61 TFEU** provides as follows:

> As long as restrictions on freedom to provide services have not been abolished, each Member State shall apply such restrictions without distinction on grounds of nationality or residence to all persons providing services within the meaning of the first paragraph of Article 56.

Article 18 TFEU, the Treaty's general anti-discrimination provision, has been applied by the Court of Justice when determining cases relating to the freedom of establishment and the provision and receipt of services.

11.1.2 Secondary legislation

Directive 2006/123

Directive 2006/123 on services in the internal market, which is also known as the **Services Directive**, was adopted on 12 December 2006 and had to be implemented by 28 December 2009. The Directive incorporates five main objectives for creating an internal services market:

- to facilitate freedom of establishment;
- to facilitate the free movement of services;
- to strengthen rights of recipients of services;
- to promote the quality of services; and
- to establish effective administrative cooperation among the Member States.

Directive 2006/123 is divided into chapters as follows:

    I – General provisions
    II – Administrative simplification
    III – Freedom of establishment for providers
            Section 1 – Authorisations
            Section 2 – Requirements prohibited or subject to evaluation
    IV – Free movement of services
            Section 1 – Freedom to provide services and related derogations
            Section 2 – Rights of recipients of services
    V – Quality of services
    VI – Administrative cooperation
    VII – Convergence programme
    VIII – Final provisions

In the UK, Directive 2006/123 was implemented by the **Provision of Services Regulations 2009**, which entered into force on 28 December 2009.

Directive 2005/36

Directive 2005/36 on the recognition of professional qualifications, which is also known as the **Qualifications Directive**, was adopted on 7 September 2005 and had to be transposed into national law by 20 October 2007. The Directive consolidated three general directives (Directives 89/48, 92/51 and 99/42) into a single text, along with 12 sector-specific directives (Directives 93/16, 77/452, 77/453, 78/686, 78/687, 78/1026, 78/1027, 80/154, 80/155, 85/432, 85/433 and 85/384), covering the seven professions of doctor, nurse, dental practitioner, veterinary surgeon, midwife, pharmacist and architect. The consolidation of these 15 directives resulted in their repeal on 20 October 2007 (Art 62). While the recognition of lawyers' qualifications is now covered by Directive 2005/36, the specific directives on the provision of services and establishment of lawyers (i.e. Directives 77/249 and 98/5) have not been integrated, as they concern the authorisation to practise rather than the recognition of qualifications.

Directive 2005/36 applies to all EU citizens seeking to practise a 'regulated profession' in a Member State other than that in which they obtained their professional qualifications, on either a self-employed or employed basis (Art 2(1)). The Directive has subsequently been amended by Directive 2013/55, which had to be implemented by 18 January 2016.

Directive 2005/36 is divided into the following titles:

    I – General provisions
    II – Free provision of services
    III – Freedom of establishment

Chapter I – General system for the recognition of evidence of training
Chapter II – Recognition of professional experience
Chapter III – Recognition on the basis of coordination of minimum training conditions
Chapter IV – Common provisions on establishment
IV – Detail rules for pursuing the profession
V – Administrative cooperation and responsibility for implementation
VI – Other provisions

Other relevant directives

Directive 2004/38

> The provisions of Directive 2004/38 are discussed in detail throughout Chapter 9 and are discussed in relation to workers in Chapter 10

Providers – and recipients – of services can avail themselves of the **Article 6** right for all EU citizens and their family members to reside in another Member State for up to three months without any conditions or formalities, other than the requirement to hold a valid identity card or passport (only a passport will suffice in the case of non-EU family members). Providers of services and their family members can also reside for longer than three months as a worker or self-employed person under **Article 7(1)(a)**. Recipients of services can reside for longer than three months if they are EU citizens and they fulfil any of the conditions set out in in Article 7(1), i.e. if they are a worker or self-employed, if they are self-sufficient, if they are a student or, regardless of their nationality, if they are a family member of one of the above.

Directive 96/71

This Directive concerns the posting of workers in relation to the provision of services. As such, it sets out the rights of workers of any nationality who are employed by a company established in one Member State but are sent by that company to provide services in another Member State. Directive 96/71 had to be transposed into the national legislation of Member States by 16 December 1999.

11.2 Scope of establishment and services

11.2.1 Establishment

Objective 2

It should be noted that, just like Union citizenship rights and Union workers' rights, there must be a cross-border element to establishment in order for a situation to fall within the scope of Union law.

Article 4 of Directive 2006/123 defines establishment as follows:

> 'establishment' means the actual pursuit of an economic activity, as referred to in Article 43 of the Treaty [now Art 49 TFEU], by the provider for an indefinite period and through a stable infrastructure from where the business of providing services is actually carried out.

This reflects the Court of Justice's ruling in ***R v Secretary of State for Transport, ex parte Factortame*** (Case C-221/89), where the Court referred to 'establishment' as 'the actual pursuit of an economic activity through a fixed establishment for an indefinite period' (para 20).

> *Gebhard* is considered further in section 11.3.4 (page 459) in relation to the objective justification of restrictions on freedom of establishment and the free movement of services

Then, in *Gebhard* (Case C-55/94), the Court described the concept of establishment within the Treaty as 'very broad' and determined that the provisions relating to freedom of establishment applied where there was **stable and continuous participation in the economic life** of the Member State.

Article 49 TFEU prohibits 'restrictions on the freedom of establishment of nationals of a Member State in the territory of another Member State', and provides that this prohibition:

> … shall also apply to restrictions on the setting-up of agencies, branches or subsidiaries by nationals of any Member State established in the territory of any Member State.

Article 49 then further states that freedom of establishment includes:

> … the right to take up and pursue activities as self-employed persons and to set up and manage undertakings, in particular companies or firms … under the conditions laid down for its own nationals by the law of the country where such establishment is effected.

Article 49, which is directly effective (*Reyners* (Case 2/74), covers both **primary establishment**, where an EU citizen becomes established or has control over an undertaking that is primarily established in a Member State of which they are not a national, and **secondary establishment**, which pertains to the right of an individual or an undertaking to be established in more than one Member State (see *Inasti* (Case C-53/95)). The Court of Justice has determined in its case law that an individual who ordinarily resides in one Member State and who holds the majority of shares of a company that is established in another Member State, or a proportion of shares which gives them a 'definite influence' over such a company's decision making, falls within the scope of Article 49 (*Geurts* v *Belgische Staat* (Case C-464/05); *X* (Case C-87/1)).

Article 54 TFEU clarifies that 'companies or firms' means companies and firms constituted under civil or commercial law, including cooperative societies, and other legal persons governed by public or private law, except for those which are non-profit-making. Although the inclusive term 'other legal persons' would seem to exclude the English partnership, as this has no legal personality, this is not in fact the case. The rights both to the provision of services and establishment belong to both natural and legal persons (*Commission* v *Greece* (Case C-140/03)). In practice, it does not matter whether a partnership enjoys the right to set up branches in another Member State by virtue of being a 'legal person' or a collection of 'natural persons', provided that both have their registered office, central administration or principal place of business within the EU (see *Scheunemann* (Case C-31/11)). In this way, where a company has its seat (i.e. where it is headquartered) is treated in the same way as the nationality of an individual (*ICI* (Case C-264/96); *SCA Group Holding* (Joined cases C-39/13, C-40/13 and C-41/13)).

11.2.2 Services

There is a close link between the provision of services and the establishment of businesses in another Member State: one frequently precedes the other. Thus, the TFEU provisions dealing with establishment, particularly the preliminaries to becoming established, will often overlap with the provisions on services. However, it should be noted that the provisions on services and those on establishment are mutually exclusive and that the latter take precedence, i.e. the provisions relating to services only apply in situations where the provisions relating to establishment do not (see ***Commission* v *Portugal*** (Case C-171/02)). Thus, in ***Commission* v *Italy*** (Case C-131/01), the Court distinguished between the application of the provisions on establishment and those on services, stating as follows:

> The decisive criterion for the purposes of the application of the chapter of the Treaty concerning services to an economic activity is the **absence of stable and continuous participation** by the person concerned in the economic life of the host Member State. [para 23]

Article 56 TFEU, which prohibits restrictions on the freedom to provide services, is **directly effective** (see, for example, *Van Binsbergen* (Case 33/74)). However, as with the freedom of establishment, there must be a cross-border element in order for the provision of services to fall within the scope of Union law. In the following case the Court of Justice held that what is now Article 56 TFEU does not apply to a totally internal situation:

Jägerskiöld v *Gustafsson* (Case C-97/98)

Facts:

On 29 May 1997, Mr Gustafsson fished with a spinning rod in waters belonging to Mr Jägerskiöld in the township of Kimoto in Finland. Two days earlier, on 27 May 1997, Mr Gustafsson had paid the fishing licence fee provided for in Finnish law, which allowed him to practise that type of fishing even in private waters.

Mr Jägerskiöld brought an action before the national court for a declaration that Mr Gustafsson could not, without his permission, fish with a rod in his waters, notwithstanding the fact that Mr Gustafsson had paid the fishing licence fee provided for by Finnish law. In support of his action, Mr Jägerskiöld argued that the Finnish law, on which the right to fish with a rod was based, was contrary to the Union rules concerning the free movement of goods or to those relating to the freedom to provide services.

Ruling:

The Court held that the provisions relating to the free movement of goods did not apply, but those relating to the freedom to provide services did apply. However, the Court of Justice continued:

42 As regards the provisions of the Treaty relating to the freedom to provide services, it is sufficient to observe that these provisions are not applicable to activities which are confined in all respects within a single Member State.

43 It is clear from the case-file that **the legal proceedings pending before the Tingsrtt are between two Finnish nationals, both established in Finland, concerning the right of one of them to fish in waters belonging to the other situated in Finland**.

44 Such a situation does not present any link to one of the situations envisaged by Community [i.e. Union] law in the field of the free provision of services.

Significance:

In the freedom to provide services, there must be a cross-border element in order for Union law to apply. This means that, had Gustafsson happened to have been a national of another Member State, he could potentially have benefited from rights in Finland that were not available to him as a Finnish national.

While there must be a cross-border element, it is not necessary for an EU citizen to have moved to a host Member State in order for their situation to fall within the scope of Union law; services may be provided to other Member States from within the **home Member State**.

Additionally, rights pertaining to the freedom to provide services may be claimed against a home Member State where that state has imposed restrictions or obstacles to the provision of services in other Member States (***Alpine Investments BV v Minister van Finançien*** (Case C-384/93); ***Carpenter*** (Case 60/00, see below)).

Services may be provided by sole traders, companies or partnerships. If the providers are companies, they do not need to be owned or controlled by nationals of the Member State in which they are based, nor do the employees of the company providing a service in another Member State have to be EU citizens. The service provider should be able to operate in other Member States without restriction, unless such restrictions can be objectively justified.

Article 57 TFEU defines services as within the scope of the Treaties when they (i) are normally provided for remuneration and (ii) in so far as they are not governed by the provisions relating to freedom of movement for goods, capital and persons. These two criteria are now considered.

Remuneration

In ***Belgium v Humbel*** (Case 263/86), the Court of Justice stated that:

> The essential characteristic of remuneration thus lies in the fact that it constitutes consideration [i.e. compensation] for the service in question, and is normally agreed upon between the provider and the recipient of the service. [para 17]

The Court held, on this basis, that courses of study provided in the framework of a national educational system were not provided for remuneration. The situation was not affected by the fact that students had to pay a registration fee or some other charge. By establishing and maintaining a national educational system, the State 'is not seeking to engage in gainful activity but is fulfilling its duties towards its own population in the social, cultural and educational fields'. [para 18].

Education can, however, constitute a service if it is provided by a private body on a commercial basis (see ***Luisi*** and ***Carbone v Ministero del Tesoro*** (Joined Cases 286/82 and 26/83)). Services are, therefore, either of a commercial character, or they are, at least, provided in exchange for money.

In contrast, in ***Geraets-Smits v Stichting Ziekenfonds*** and ***Peerbooms v Stichting CZ Groep Zorgverzekeringen*** (Case C-157/99), the Court of Justice held that the fact that hospital medical treatment is financed directly by sickness insurance funds on the basis of agreements and pre-set scales of fees does not remove such treatment from the sphere of services within the meaning of Article 57 TFEU. Article 57 TFEU does not require the service to be paid for by those to whom the service is provided (see also ***Bond van Adverteerders*** (Case 325/85)). The Court reiterated that the essential characteristic of remuneration lies in the fact that it constitutes compensation for the service in question.

The Court of Justice has also held that there must be an **economic link** in order for services to come within the provisions of the Treaty:

SPUC v *Grogan* (Case C-159/90)

Facts:
Ireland had a restriction on the publication of information about the provision of abortion in other Member States (prior to 20 December 2018, abortion was illegal in Ireland, unless required to save the life of the mother). A Students' Union in Dublin provided information about abortion

services which were lawfully available in London. This practice was challenged before the Irish courts by the Society for the Protection of Unborn Children (SPUC). The matter was referred by the national court to the Court of Justice pursuant to what is now Art 267 TFEU (previously Art 234 EC Treaty).

Ruling:

The Court of Justice held that the provision of abortion could constitute a service. However, the Court held that because the Students' Union was not distributing the information **on behalf of the economic operators** (i.e. the clinics providing the service), Ireland could restrain its activity. The Students' Union had no economic link with the clinics – it was not being paid.

Significance:

This case elucidated the distinction between a service and its advertisement. If the information had been distributed by the service providers, it would have been part of the economic activity of providing the service. However, where the information is provided by a third party **for no remuneration**, that third party cannot be said to be providing a service for the purpose of the Treaties. This distinction was politically expedient, as it enabled the Court to avoid becoming embroiled in the highly sensitive issue of abortion rights in Ireland.

Not covered by provisions on the movement of goods, capital or persons

The Court of Justice considered the distinction between importing goods and providing a service in the following case:

Schindler (Case C-275/92)

Facts:

The undertakings concerned were agents of four local state lotteries in Germany. They sent letters from the Netherlands to the UK enclosing application forms with invitations to participate in the German lotteries. The letters were confiscated by Customs and Excise on the grounds that they infringed national legislation on lotteries and gaming.

Ruling:

The Court of Justice held that the letters were not 'goods', so the restrictions did not fall to be considered under the former Article 30 EEC Treaty (now Art 34 TFEU). Even though the lottery operators sent materials into the UK to advertise and sell lottery tickets, the import of these materials was not their main object. The materials should instead be seen as a stage in the process of providing a service: the services provided by the lottery operators enabled purchasers of tickets to participate in a game of chance with the hope of winning, by arranging for that purpose for the stakes to be collected, the draws to be organised and the prizes for winnings to be ascertained and paid out. The services were '**normally provided for remuneration**', represented by the price of the lottery ticket. They were **cross-border**, as they were offered in a Member State other than that in which the lottery operator was established.

In this case, however, the Court determined that restrictions could be placed on the provision of lottery services for the protection of consumers and the maintenance of order in society,

> provided that such restrictions did not discriminate on grounds of nationality, i.e. they were applied equally to nationals and non-nationals.
>
> **Significance:**
>
> Services, in this case, amounted to the provision of an opportunity to play a game. The Treaty provisions on services could be applied because the advertising materials in question did not fall under the provisions on the free movement of goods. They were not goods because importing the materials was not the core of the economic activity, but merely a stage in the provision of a service.

The Court of Justice reached a similar conclusion in relation to the offer of financial services by telephone to potential recipients in another state (*Alpine Investments BV v Minister van Financiën* (Case C-384/93)) and in relation to the provision of insurance (*Safir v Skattemyndigheten i Dalarnas Lan* (Case C-118/96); *Skandia and Ramstedt* (Case C-422/01)).

11.2.3 The 'official authority' exception

Article 51 TFEU stipulates that the right of establishment 'shall not apply ... to activities ... connected, even occasionally, with the exercise of official authority'. Like the public service exception in Article 45(4) TFEU (see Chapter 10), 'the exercise of official authority' is not defined in the Treaty. However, its scope was considered by the Court of Justice in *Reyners v Belgian State* (Case 2/74), where it was questioned whether the profession of *avocat* (i.e. lawyer) was exempt from the chapter of the Treaty on rights of establishment because it sometimes involved the exercise of official authority. The Court of Justice ruled that:

> An extension of the exception allowed by Article 55 [now Article 51 TFEU] to a whole profession would be possible only in cases where such activities were linked with that profession in such a way that freedom of establishment would result in imposing on the Member State concerned the obligation to allow the exercise, even occasionally, by non-nationals of functions appertaining to official authority. This extension is on the other hand **not** possible when, within the framework of an independent profession, the activities connected with the exercise of official authority are **separable from the professional activity in question taken as a whole**. [paras 46 and 47]

> ➤ *Reyners* is also considered in section 11.3.1 relation to direct effect

The 'exercise of official authority' would therefore seem to be analogous to the exercise of 'public service' under Article 45(4) TFEU (*Commission v Belgium* (Case 149/79); see Chapter 10), and has been just as narrowly construed by the Court of Justice. For example, road traffic experts were held not to come within the scope of the Article 51 TFEU exception in *Commission v Greece* (Case C-306/89), and the provision of computer services for the state lottery was likewise held not to come within the scope of the exception in *Commission v Italy* (Case C-272/91). In *Hiebler v Schlagbauer* (Case 293/14), the Court held that chimney sweeps did not exercise official authority as, although they performed fire safety regulation tasks, these tasks were performed under the supervision of the mayor of the relevant municipality and the chimney sweeps themselves did not have any personal power of enforcement, constraint or coercion vis-à-vis their customers.

11.3 Rights of service providers and their employees

11.3.1 Rights to establishment and to provide services

Objective 3

The right of establishment and the right to provide services have been described by the Court of Justice as 'fundamental rights' and the Court has been active in asserting that businesses and the self-employed should be able to provide services in Member States, not only without discrimination, but also free from non-discriminatory obstacles that could hinder such access.

Articles 49 and **57 TFEU** provide that nationals of other Member States should be subject to the same conditions as nationals of a Member State in which they are seeking to establish themselves or provide services, respectively. In addition, service providers are protected by the general prohibition on discrimination on grounds of nationality that is provided by **Article 18 TFEU**. The issue of discrimination is discussed further below in section 11.3.4.

Prior to Directive 2006/123

The former Articles 54 and 63 EEC Treaty (now Arts 50 and 59 TFEU) provided for the drawing up of **General Programmes** for the abolition of restrictions on freedom of establishment and for the abolition of restrictions on freedom to provide services. Both general programmes were approved in December 1961 and set out a plan for the stage-by-stage removal of barriers in their respective areas. The general programmes were to be implemented through directives on each sector or professional activity. The Commission drew up a wide range of directives which were intended to facilitate access to a variety of professions, including itinerant traders, film producers, hairdressers and the providers of gas, water and electricity services. It was thought that, until an appropriate directive was in place, national measures would continue to apply and, in many cases, would have the effect of excluding EU nationals from participating in the relevant business or occupation. However, in 1974, before a complete system of directives was in place, the Court of Justice determined in two separate judgements that the provisions that are now Articles 49 and 56 TFEU are **directly effective**.

With regards to **Article 49 TFEU** on freedom of establishment (previously Art 52 EEC Treaty), the Court established direct effect in the following case:

> ### Reyners v Belgian State (Case 2/74)
>
> **Facts:**
>
> Mr Reyners was a Dutch national who qualified as a lawyer in Belgium, but was excluded from legal practice in the country on the grounds that he was not Belgian. Reyners argued that the former Article 52 EEC Treaty (now Art 49 TFEU) on freedom of establishment was a clear and complete provision that was capable of producing direct effect. In response to his complaint, the Belgian government argued that the former Article 52 EEC Treaty merely laid down a principle, the implementation of which was subject to further provisions at both the national and Community (i.e. Union) level.
>
> **Ruling:**
>
> The Court of Justice ruled that:
>
> 26 In laying down that freedom of establishment shall be attained at the end of the transitional period, Article 52 thus imposes an obligation to attain a precise result, the fulfilment of which

had to be made easier by, but not made dependent on, the implementation of a programme of progressive measures.

27 The fact that this progression has not been adhered to leaves the obligation itself intact beyond the end of the period provided for its fulfilment.

Significance:

Regardless of the slow pace of harmonisation of national laws through the adoption and implementation of Directives, the Court determined that the Treaty could be directly invoked by individuals to challenge obvious instances of nationality discrimination. Thus, the basic principle of non-discrimination was deemed to be directly effective in the area of freedom of establishment, even though the conditions for genuine freedom of establishment were far from being achieved. This placed a more immediate responsibility for the implementation of the relevant Treaty articles on the Member States.

➤ *Reyners* is also considered in section 8.2.2 in relation to the principle of direct effect (page 277)

With regards to **Article 56 TFEU** on the freedom to provide services, the Court established direct effect in the following case:

Van Binsbergen v Bestuur van de Bedrijfsvereninging voor de Metaalnijverheid (Case 33/74)

Facts:

A national of the Netherlands acted as legal adviser to the applicant in relation to legal proceedings before a Dutch court. The legal adviser moved to Belgium during the course of the proceedings and was told that he could no longer represent the applicant, because under Dutch law only persons established in the Netherlands could act as legal advisers. The national court referred the matter to the Court of Justice under what is now Article 267 TFEU to determine whether or not the Dutch rule was compatible with the former Articles 59 and 60 EEC Treaty (now Arts 56 and 57 TFEU). It was undoubtedly indirectly discriminatory because it would be more difficult for a non-national to satisfy than a national.

Ruling:

Considering the former Articles 59 and 60 EEC Treaty, the Court stated as follows:

10 The restrictions to be abolished pursuant to Articles 59 and 60 [now Arts 56 and 57 TFEU] include all requirements imposed on the person providing the service by reason in particular of his nationality or of the fact that he does not habitually reside in the state where the service is provided, which do not apply to persons established within the national territory or which may prevent or otherwise obstruct the activities of the person providing the service.

11 In particular, **a requirement that the person providing the service must be habitually resident within the territory of the state where the service is to be provided may, according to the circumstances, have the result of depriving Article 59 [now Art 56 TFEU] of all useful effect**, in view of the fact that the precise object of that article is to abolish restrictions on freedom to provide services imposed on persons who are not established in the state where the service is to be provided.

> The Court then considered whether the failure to comply with the freedom to provide services could be objectively justified. The Court did not find any such justification. The Court then considered whether these particular Treaty provisions had direct effect and concluded as follows:
>
> > 26 ... as regards at least the specific requirement of nationality or of residence, Articles 59 and 60 [now Arts 56 and 57 TFEU] impose **a well-defined obligation, the fulfilment of which by the Member States cannot be delayed or jeopardized by the absence of provisions which were to be adopted** in pursuance of powers conferred under Articles 63 and 66 [now Arts 59 and 62 TFEU].
> >
> > 27 Accordingly, the reply should be that **the first paragraph of Article 59 and the third paragraph of Article 60 [now Arts 56 and 57 TFEU] have direct effect and may therefore be relied on before national courts**, at least in so far as they seek to abolish any discrimination against a person providing a service by reason of his nationality or of the fact that he resides in a member state other than that in which the service is to be provided.
>
> **Significance:**
>
> As with **Reyners**, the Court held that the absence of specific directives should not hold back the implementation of a 'well-defined obligation' that is established by the Treaty. The obligation that is now established in Articles 56 and 57 TFEU, that a Member State may not restrict the freedom to provide services of persons established in another Member State, is therefore directly effective.

▶ *Van Binsbergen* is also considered in section 11.3.4 (page 458) in relation to the objective justification of a restriction on the freedom of services

By pronouncing that what are now Articles 49 and 56 have direct effect, the Court made the prohibition on restricting the freedom of establishment and freedom to provide services within the Union independent of the body of directives that had been adopted under the general programmes. However, these directives, and others that were to be enacted after the *Reyners* and *Van Binsbergen* judgments, continued to provide further substance and detail on what the Treaty provisions entailed in specific sectors.

More recently, the Court of Justice has also determined that Articles 49 and 56 TFEU can have **horizontal direct effect** in order to protect the freedoms of establishment and service provision from the effects of what it deemed to be disproportionate industrial action (i.e. strikes). In *International Transport Workers' Federation and Finnish Seamen's Union v Viking Line ABP* (Case C-438/05), the Court ruled that Article 43 EC (now Article 49 TFEU) is capable of producing rights that a private undertaking can rely on against a trade union. Similarly, in *Laval un Partneri Ltd v Svenska Byggnadsarbetareförbundet and Others* (Case C-341/05), the Court ruled that actions taken by trade unions can constitute barriers to the freedom to provide services that are contrary to what is now Article 56 TFEU.

▶ See Chapter 8 on horizontal direct effect.

▶ *Laval* is considered more fully in section 11.3.3 (page 456).

Where the domestic legislation of a Member State contains restrictions or obstacles to the freedom of establishment or the free movement of services, it is not sufficient to issue instructions not to apply the relevant measures to EU nationals; for the sake of clarity and transparency such measures must be repealed (*Commission v Italy (Re Freedom of Establishment)* (Case 168/85)).

Directive 2006/123: the Services Directive

Directive 2006/123, which was adopted on 12 December 2006 and had to be implemented by 28 December 2009, seeks to establish 'a general legal framework which benefits a wide variety of services while taking into account the distinctive features of each type of activity or profession and its system of regulation' (Recital 7). With regard to the directives that had already been enacted on the freedom of establishment and the freedom to provide services, Recital 30 explains that Directive 2006/123 builds on these and seeks to address any conflicts through derogations within the Directive.

Table 11.1 shows which services are and which services are not covered by Directive 2006/123. The list of services that are specified as covered by Directive 2006/123 is not exhaustive. For example, in *Visser Vastgoed Beleggingen BV* v *Raad van de gemeente Appingedam* (Case C-31/16), the Court determined that retail trade in goods was a service for the purposes of the Directive.

Table 11.1 Services included and excluded from the scope of Directive 2006/123

Services covered by the Directive:	Services not covered by the Directive:
• **distributive trades** including retail and the wholesale of goods and services; • activities of most **regulated professions** such as legal and tax advisers, architects, engineers, accountants or surveyors; • **construction services and crafts**; • **business-related services** such as office maintenance, management consultancy, event organisation, debt recovery, advertising and recruitment services; • **tourism services** such as travel agents; • **leisure services** such as sports centres and amusement parks; • **installation and maintenance of equipment**; • **information society services** such as publishing for print and web, news agencies, computer programming; • **accommodation and food services** such as hotels, restaurants and caterers; • **training and education services**; • **rentals and leasing services** including car rentals; • **real estate services**; • **household support services** such as cleaning, gardening and private nannies.	• **financial services**; • **electronic communications services** with respect to matters covered by other EU instruments; • **transport services** falling within the scope of Title VI of the Treaty on the Functioning of the European Union (TFEU); • **healthcare services** provided by health professionals to assess, maintain or restore the state of patients' health where those activities are reserved to a regulated health profession; • **temporary work agencies' services**; • **private security services**; • **audio-visual services**; • **gambling**; • **certain social services** provided by the State, by providers mandated by the State or by charities recognised by the State; • **services provided by notaries and bailiffs** appointed by an official act of government.

(Source: European Commission, https://ec.europa.eu/growth/single-market/services/services-directive/in-practice/quick-guide_en)

While, like other areas of Union law, there must be a cross-border element to the services in question in order for them to fall within the scope of Directive 2006/123, such an element need only be possible rather than actually manifest at the material time. The Court of Justice explained this in *Sokoll-Seebacher* (Case C-367/12), which concerned a restriction on the establishment of pharmacies in Austria:

> ... while national legislation such as that at issue in the main proceedings – which applies indiscriminately to Austrian nationals and to nationals of other Member States – is, generally, capable of falling within the scope of the provisions relating to the fundamental freedoms

established by the Treaty on the Functioning of the EU **only to the extent that it applies to situations connected with trade between the Member States**, it is far from inconceivable that nationals established in Member States other than the Republic of Austria have been or are interested in operating pharmacies in that Member State.

While it is admittedly clear from the case-file before the Court that the applicant in the main proceedings is an Austrian national and that all the factual aspects of the main proceedings are confined to one Member State, namely the Republic of Austria, **the legislation at issue in the main proceedings is nevertheless capable of producing effects which are not confined to that Member State**. [paras 10 and 11]

Therefore, a purely internal situation may be contested under Directive 2006/123 where a national measure that is 'capable of producing effects which are not confined to that Member State' is concerned. This was confirmed in ***Visser Vastgoed Beleggingen BV v Raad van de gemeente Appingedam*** (Case C-31/16), where the Court ruled that the provisions of Chapter III of Directive 2006/123, regarding the removal of administrative barriers to establishment, 'must be interpreted as meaning that they also apply to a situation where all the relevant elements are confined to a single Member State'. The Court's reasoning for this was as follows:

> If, however, the internal market in services is to be fully achieved, that requires, above all, **the elimination of obstacles** which are encountered by providers in becoming established in the Member States, **whether in their own Member State or in another Member State**, and which are liable to affect adversely their ability to supply services to recipients located throughout the European Union. [para 105]

The main provisions of Directive 2006/123 that aim to facilitate freedom of establishment and the freedom to provide services will now be outlined.

Provisions to facilitate freedom of establishment

Chapter II of the Directive sets out measures for the **simplification of administrative procedures**. **Article 5(1)** requires the Member States to examine and, if need be, simplify the procedures and formalities applicable to accessing and exercising a service activity. **Article 6(1)** provides that a service provider should be able to complete all procedures and formalities required to access their service activities, and any authorisation required to exercise those activities, through a single point of contact. Furthermore, **Article 7(3)** provides that all information pertaining to such procedures and formalities must be accessible online, and **Article 8** provides that it must be possible to complete all such procedures and formalities at a distance and by electronic means. This enables providers to avoid the expense and inconvenience of multiple visits to authorities in the Member State within which they intend to provide services.

Chapter III of the Directive concerns the **removal of administrative barriers** to the development of service activities. **Article 9** requires Member States to ensure that accessing and exercising service activities within their territories is not subject to authorisation schemes, unless such schemes are:

(i) **non-discriminatory**;
(ii) **necessary**, i.e. justified by an overriding reason relating to the public interest; and
(iii) **proportionate**, i.e. the objective pursued cannot be attained by less restrictive means.

Additionally, authorisation schemes must be transparent and accessible (**Art 10**). **Article 10(3)** then seeks to lessen the burden placed on service providers by authorisation schemes by providing that:

> The conditions for granting authorisation for a new establishment shall not duplicate requirements and controls which are equivalent or essentially comparable as regards their purpose to which the provider is already subject in another Member State or in the same Member State.

The duplication of requirements and controls was initially ruled to present a disproportionate restriction on the freedom to provide services in the case law; see *Webb* (Case 297/80) and *Jean-Claude Arblade, Arblade & Fils SARL* and *Bernard Leloup, Serge Leloup, Sofrage SARL* (Cases C-369 and 376/96). Generally, authorisation should not be for a limited duration (**Art 11(1)**). Where authorisations are limited in number, Member States should apply an impartial and transparent selection procedure (Art 12, see *Promoimpresa srl* and *Mario Melis and Others* (Joined Cases 458/14 and 67/15)). **Article 13** sets out further requirements related to authorisation that seek to ensure that authorisation is provided in an objective, impartial and timely manner.

Article 14 sets out eight requirements which Member States may not impose on access to or the exercise of service activities, including requirements that are directly or indirectly discriminatory on grounds of nationality. **Article 15(2)** then lists eight further requirements which Member States are obliged to evaluate. Such requirements may only be imposed on access to or the exercise of service activities if they are found to comply with the conditions set out in **Article 15(3)**. These conditions, as with authorisation schemes under Article 9, are that they must be **non-discriminatory**, **necessary** and **proportionate**.

Provisions to facilitate the free movement of services

Echoing the provisions on freedom of establishment, **Article 16(1)** stipulates that Member States shall not make access to or exercise of a service activity in their territory subject to compliance with any requirements which do not conform to the principles of **non-discrimination**, **necessity** and **proportionality**. **Article 16(2)** lists requirements that Member states may not impose with the effect of restricting the freedom to provide services in the case of a provider established in another Member State. **Article 16(3)** then provides for the following derogation:

> The Member State to which the provider moves shall not be prevented from imposing requirements with regard to the provision of a service activity, where they are justified for reasons of **public policy**, **public security**, **public health** or the **protection of the environment** and in accordance with paragraph 1. Nor shall that Member State be prevented from applying, in accordance with Community law, its **rules on employment conditions**, including those laid down in **collective agreements**.

These derogations, along with further ones that are stipulated in Article 17, are discussed further below in section 11.3.4.

Rights of lawyers

In certain areas, the freedom of establishment and the freedom to provide services continue to be governed by sector-specific directives. The Union law pertaining to the rights of lawyers is now briefly considered by way of an example.

With regard to the **establishment** of lawyers, **Directive 98/5** to facilitate practice of the profession of lawyer on a permanent basis in a Member State other than that in which the qualification was obtained was adopted at the end of 1997. The Directive, which had to be implemented by March 2000:

- permits EU lawyers to be established under their home title in another Member State;
- requires them to register with an appropriate regulatory body in the host state;
- gives them a right to representation within the host regulatory body;
- subjects them to the rules and regulatory regime of the host regulatory body;
- offers them a 'fast track' to requalification as a lawyer of the host state.

Directive 98/5 was implemented in the UK by the **European Community (Lawyer's Practice) Regulations 2000**, as amended, which came into force on 22 May 2000.

Directive 77/249 to facilitate the effective exercise by lawyers of freedom to provide **services** was enacted on 24 March 1977 and had to be transposed into national legislation by 25 March 1979. The Directive sets out that:

- a lawyer shall use the professional title that is used in their home Member State;
- a lawyer shall observe the conditions and rules of professional conduct of a host Member State;
- a host Member State may require a lawyer who is established in another Member State to work in conjunction with a lawyer who practises before the relevant judicial authority;
- a host Member State may request a person providing services as a lawyer to establish their qualifications to do so.

Directive 77/249 has been implemented in the UK by the **European Communities (Services of Lawyers) Order 1978**, as amended.

Neither Directive 98/5 nor Directive 77/249 has been affected by Directive 2005/36, which is considered below (see section 11.5.2).

11.3.2 Rights of entry and residence

Directive 2004/38

As discussed in Chapters 9 and 10, **Directive 2004/38** concerns the rights of EU citizens to move to and reside within the Member States. One of the instruments that Directive 2004/38 repealed and replaced was Directive 72/148 on the abolition of restrictions on movement and residence within the Community [i.e. Union] for nationals of Member States with regard to establishment and the provision of services. Protecting the freedom to provide services is therefore embedded within the objectives of Directive 2004/38.

Article 6(1) of the Directive provides that EU citizens shall have the right of residence in another Member State for a period of up to three months without any conditions or formalities other than the requirement to hold a valid identity card or passport (or a valid passport in the case of non-EU family members).

Article 7(1)(a) provides a right of residence for longer than three months for EU citizens who are workers or are self-employed in the territory of a host Member State. **Article 14(4)** further provides that such persons and their family members cannot be subject to an expulsion order, other than in accordance with the provisions relating to restrictions on grounds of public policy, public security or public health. This prolonged right of residence for self-employed persons provides the necessary guarantees that a person will be able to reside in a host Member State while they establish and grow their business. Without such guarantees, the risk of being expelled would likely deter individuals from establishing businesses in Member States of which they are not a national.

Under **Article 7(3)**, self-employed persons can retain their status as such under the same conditions as workers can retain their status. These conditions are:

(a) he/she is temporarily unable to work as the result of an **illness or accident**;

(b) he/she is in **duly recorded involuntary unemployment after having been employed for more than one year** and has registered as a jobseeker with the relevant employment office in the host Member State;

(c) he/she is in **duly recorded involuntary unemployment after completing a fixed-term employment contract of less than a year** or after having become involuntarily unemployed during the first 12 months *and* has registered as a jobseeker with the relevant employment office in the host Member State. In this case, the status of worker shall be retained for not less than six months; or

(d) he/she embarks on **vocational training**. Unless he is involuntarily unemployed, the retention of the status of worker shall require the training to be related to the previous employment.

Under **Article 16(1)**, EU citizens acquire the right of permanent residence in the host Member State after a five-year period of continuous legal residence, provided that an expulsion decision has not been enforced against them (Art 21). The same rule applies to non-EU family members who have lived with an EU citizen in the host Member State for five years (Art 16(2)). Once granted, the right of permanent residence is lost only in the event of more than two successive years' absence from the host Member State (Arts 16(4) and 20(3)).

Article 17 recognises the right of permanent residence for EU citizens who are self-employed persons, and for their family members, before the five-year period of continuous residence has expired, subject to certain conditions being met. The family members of self-employed EU citizens are subject to the same protections in the event of their death, departure or divorce under Articles 12, 13 and 17 as the family members of any other EU citizens who reside in a host Member State on the basis of Article 7 or Article 16 (see Chapter 9).

The Treaty provisions

In the following case, the Court of Justice considered the right of residence of a non-EU national who resided with her husband in his home Member State, but where he provided services to persons established in other Member States. The wife had to rely directly on the former EC Treaty (now TFEU) provisions because the relevant directives did not apply to this situation (arguably Directive 2004/38 would also not apply):

Carpenter v Secretary of State for the Home Department (Case C-60/00)

Facts:

Mrs Carpenter was a national of the Philippines who was initially given leave to enter the UK as a visitor for six months. She overstayed that leave and failed to apply for an extension of her stay, as she was required to under UK law. She later married a UK national, Mr Carpenter, who ran a business selling advertising space in journals and offered various services to the editors of those journals. His business was established in the UK, but a large proportion of the business was conducted with advertisers in other Member States. Mr Carpenter travelled to those other Member States for the purpose of his business. Mrs Carpenter applied for leave to remain as the spouse of a UK national but her application was refused. A deportation order was made against her.

Mrs Carpenter appealed. She argued that because her husband's business required him to travel around the EU, providing and receiving services, her presence within the UK made it easier for him to do this because she could look after his children from his first marriage. Therefore if she was deported it would restrict Mr Carpenter's enjoyment of his right to provide and receive services under the former Article 49 EC Treaty (now Art 56 TFEU). The appeal tribunal referred the case to the Court of Justice for a preliminary ruling pursuant to the former Article 234 EC Treaty (now Art 267 TFEU).

Ruling:

The Court of Justice first confirmed that Mr Carpenter's business activities came within the scope of 'services' for the purpose of Union law. The Court then stated that:

> 39 It is clear that the separation of Mr and Mrs Carpenter would be detrimental to their family life and, therefore, to the conditions under which Mr Carpenter exercises a fundamental freedom. That freedom could not be fully effective if Mr Carpenter were to be deterred from exercising it by obstacles raised in his country of origin to the entry and residence of his spouse.

The Court of Justice held as follows:

> 46 ... Article 49 EC [now Art 56 TFEU] read in the light of the fundamental right to respect for family life, is to be interpreted as precluding, in certain circumstances such as those in the main proceedings, a refusal, by the Member State of origin of a provider of services established in that Member State, who provides services to recipients established in other Member States, of the right to reside in its territory to that provider's spouse, who is a national of a third country.

Significance:

This case established that the refusal of a right of residence to the spouse of a national can, in certain circumstances, constitute an infringement of the freedom to provide services. While the likelihood that Mrs Carpenter's homemaking and childcare activities facilitated Mr Carpenter's ability to provide services to other Member States was considered by the Court, it is unclear to what extent her role as a carer for Mr Carpenter's family members is essential to the Court's ruling.

11.3.3 Rights of posted workers

Where a company that is established in one Member State seeks to provide services in another Member State, they may transfer their workers from one Member State to the other in order to do so. Such workers are referred to as **posted workers**. The right to post workers in another Member State for the purpose of providing services was at issue in the following case:

Van der Elst v OMI (Case C-43/93)

Facts:

The claimant operated a demolition company which was established in Belgium. He employed a number of foreign workers from third countries. They had work permits and were lawfully employed in Belgium. The company was engaged to carry out a demolition contract in France. Foreign employees were not permitted by the French authorities to work on the contract without French work permits. The national court referred the case to the Court of Justice under what is now Article 267 TFEU (Art 177 EEC Treaty at the time).

Ruling:

The Court of Justice held that the Belgian undertaking was providing a service under what are now Articles 56 and 57 TFEU (Arts 59 and 60 EEC Treaty at the time). The question before the Court was whether the company could post its workforce to France to service the demolition contract.

The Court of Justice held that where a service was being provided pursuant to what are now Articles 56 and 57 TFEU, the provider of the service has the right to post its workforce in a host Member State, irrespective of the workforce's nationality. Any attempt to impose further controls on its workforce would amount to an unlawful restriction on the provision of services. The imposition of further work permit requirements would, the Court said, amount to the duplication of the procedures the company had already gone through in its home Member State.

Significance:

So long as the workers are legally employed in the home Member State, a company which is established in one Member State can post its workforce in order to provide services in another Member State.

The Court of Justice considered the effects of similar domestic requirements placed on non-EU workers in *Commission* v *Germany* (Case C-244/04). This case concerned Germany's Law on Aliens, which provided that non-EU nationals who intended to reside for more than three months on German territory and to pursue paid employment there had (i) to be in possession of a specific residence visa and (ii) to have been employed by the relevant company for one year prior to their posting. The Court ruled that both requirements impeded the freedom to provide services in the context of posted workers.

Directive 96/71, which had to be transposed into the national law of Member States by 16 December 1999, concerns the posting of workers within the context of the provision of services, i.e. where an individual/undertaking provides services in another Member State and the service provider sends their own workers to the host Member State. Directive 96/71 has been amended by **Directive 2018/957**, which Member States must transpose into national legislation by 30 June 2020.

Article 3(1) of the Directive establishes that, regardless of the law that is applicable to the employment relationship, workers posted to the territory of another Member State should be afforded certain terms and conditions of employment that are applicable to workers in that host Member State. These conditions, as provided in the original version of Directive 96/71, are as follows:

(a) maximum work periods and minimum rest periods;
(b) minimum paid annual holidays;
(c) the minimum rates of pay, including overtime rates; this point does not apply to supplementary occupational retirement pension schemes;
(d) the conditions of hiring-out of workers, in particular the supply of workers by temporary employment undertakings;
(e) health, safety and hygiene at work;
(f) protective measures with regard to the terms and conditions of employment of pregnant women or women who have recently given birth, of children and of young people;
(g) equality of treatment between men and women and other provisions on non-discrimination.

Directive 2018/957 makes two additions to this list:

(h) the conditions of workers' accommodation where provided by the employer to workers away from their regular place of work;
(i) allowances or reimbursement of expenditure to cover travel, board and lodging expenses for workers away from home for professional reasons.

Additionally, in point (c), instead of requiring posted workers to receive the same 'minimum rates of pay' as nationals of a host Member State, Directive 2018/957 specifies that posted workers should receive the same 'remuneration'. Therefore, where posted workers meet national requirements for pay above the minimum rate, they will be entitled to such remuneration as of 30 June 2020, or sooner if the host Member State implements Directive 2018/957 before the deadline. **Article 3(7)** of Directive 96/71 clarifies that these provisions do not prevent the provision of more favourable terms and conditions to posted workers.

Reflection: Different perspectives on Directive 2018/957

The amendments made by Directive 2018/957 aim to reduce the extent to which employers are able to use posted workers to provide services within a host Member State at a lower cost than if they were to employ nationals of that Member State. This practice is called **social dumping** and has been responsible for considerable opposition at the local level to EU free movement rights, where it is perceived that local jobs are taken by cheap immigrant labour. While protections

> against social dumping, such as those provided by Directive 2018/957, are popular in more economically prosperous Member States, such as France and Germany, they are less popular among Member States that have more recently joined the Union. For Member States such as Poland and Romania, for example, cheap labour represents their one competitive advantage over more economically developed countries. Therefore, anti-social dumping measures can be viewed as an interference in the labour market that is akin to price-fixing in the goods market. At the level of the individual worker, however, Directive 2018/957 introduces important protections against exploitation. In particular, high deductions from wages for travel, board and lodging expenses, which must now comply with the law of the host Member State, are often a feature of modern slavery.

The following case relates to the rules which may be enacted by Member States with regard to the payment of posted workers. It is indicative of the ways in which loopholes to the fair payment of posted workers could be found, and which the new Directive aims to prevent:

Commission v *Germany* (Case C-341/02)

Facts:

The Commission brought an action against Germany for non-compliance with Article 3 of Directive 96/71. The Commission argued that, when assessing whether workers posted to Germany by employers established in another Member State were being paid the minimum rate established under German law, German law only recognised one general bonus provided to construction industry workers and did not recognise all of the other allowances and supplements paid by such employers. As employers in other Member States may be obliged to pay such allowances and supplements, the failure to take them into account resulted in higher wage costs for employers established in other Member States, who were thus disadvantaged in the provision of their services in Germany. While the Commission acknowledged that, under Directive 96/71, the host Member State was allowed to determine the minimum rate of pay, the fact nonetheless remained that the host Member State could not, in comparing that rate and the wages paid to posted workers, impose a certain payment structure.

Ruling:

The Court of Justice began by observing that the parties were in agreement that – in accordance with Directive 96/71 – account need **not** be taken, as constituent elements of the minimum wage, of the following: (i) payment for overtime; (ii) contributions to supplementary occupational retirement pension schemes; (iii) the amounts paid in respect of reimbursement of expenses actually incurred by reason of the posting; and (iv) flat-rate sums calculated on a basis other than that of the hourly rate. **It was the gross amounts of wages that must be taken into account**.

The Court then stated that, in the course of the proceedings, Germany had adopted and proposed a number of amendments to its rules, which the Court considered appropriate for removing several of the inconsistencies between German law and the Directive. These included the taking into account of allowances and supplements paid by an employer which, in the calculation of the minimum wage, did **not** alter the relationship between the service provided by the worker and the compensation received in return. The Court observed that it was entirely normal that, **if an employer required a worker to carry out additional work or to work under particular**

> conditions, **compensation had to be provided to the worker for those additional services without it being taken into account for the purpose of calculating the minimum wage**. Directive 96/71 did not require that such forms of compensation, which, if taken into account in the calculation of the minimum wage, altered the relationship between the service provided and the consideration received in return, be treated as elements of the minimum wage.
>
> However, the amendments made by Germany were made after the expiry of the period laid down in the reasoned opinion, i.e. too late to be taken into consideration by the Court. Therefore, the Court had to declare that Germany had failed to fulfil its obligations (see Chapter 7).
>
> **Significance:**
>
> This case established a distinction between allowances and supplements which do not alter the relationship between the services provided by a worker and the compensation that they receive, and those that do. Where such a relationship is not altered, the relevant allowances and supplements should, subject to certain exceptions, be considered as constituent elements of the minimum wage.

The ruling in the above case, regarding payments that may and may not be taken into account in the calculation of a minimum wage, was confirmed by the Court in *Isbir* v *DB Services GmbH* (Case C-522/12).

Directive 96/71, as amended, provides that the terms and conditions of employment guaranteed to workers posted to the host Member State are to be laid down by law, regulation or administrative provision and/or by collective agreements or arbitration awards which have been declared universally applicable. Prior to amendment by Directive 2018/957, terms and conditions of employment guaranteed by universally applicable collective agreements or arbitration awards were only applicable to posted workers in the construction sector.

Swedish law on the posting of workers sets out the terms and conditions of employment falling within the matters listed in Directive 96/71, save for minimum rates of pay. Swedish law is silent on remuneration, which in Sweden is traditionally determined through collective negotiations. Under Swedish law, trade unions are entitled to have recourse to collective action, under certain conditions, which is aimed at compelling any employer to enter into negotiations on pay and to sign a collective agreement. The following case concerned Directive 96/71 (prior to amendment by Directive 2018/957), the Swedish law relating to the Directive and the right of trade unions to take collective action (note: this case also considers the issue of **objective justification**, which is considered in detail below):

> ### *Laval un Partneri Ltd* v *Svenska Byggnadsarbetareförbundet and Others* (Case C-341/05)
>
> **Facts:**
>
> In May 2004, Laval un Partneri Ltd ('Laval'), a Latvian company, posted workers from Latvia to work on building sites in Sweden. The work was carried out by a subsidiary, L&P Baltic Bygg AB ('Baltic Bygg').
>
> In June 2004, Laval and Baltic Bygg, on the one hand, and the Swedish building and public works trade union, Svenska Byggnadsarbetareförbundet (SB), on the other, began negotiations with a view to determining the rates of pay for the posted workers and persuading Laval to sign

the collective agreement for the building sector. However, the parties were unable to reach an agreement. In September and October, Laval signed collective agreements with the Latvian building sector trade union, with which 65 per cent of the posted workers were affiliated.

On 2 November 2004, SB began collective action in the form of a blockade of all Laval's sites in Sweden. The Swedish electricians' trade union joined in with a sympathy action, the effect of which was to prevent electricians from providing services to Laval. None of the members of those trade unions were employed by Laval. After work had stopped, Baltic Bygg was declared bankrupt and the posted workers returned to Latvia.

Laval brought proceedings before the Arbetsdomstolen (Swedish Labour Court), questioning the lawfulness of the collective action and claiming compensation for the damage suffered. The Arbetsdomstolen asked the Court of Justice if Union law precluded trade unions from taking collective action in the circumstances described above.

Ruling:

The Court accepted that **the right to take collective action had to be recognised as a fundamental right** which formed an integral part of the general principles of Union law the observance of which the Court ensured, but stated that the exercise of that right could be subject to certain restrictions. The Court pointed out that Directive 96/71 expressly determined that undertakings established in other Member States *had* to guarantee to their posted workers only the *minimum* wage applicable in a host Member State. The Court pointed out that the right of trade unions of a Member State to take collective action meant that undertakings established in other Member States could be forced into pay negotiations and could be forced to sign a collective agreement with terms beyond the minimum protection guaranteed by Directive 96/71. This was likely to make it less attractive, or more difficult, for such undertakings to carry out construction work in Sweden and therefore constituted a restriction on the freedom to provide services.

The Court then considered whether this restriction could be objectively justified as a proportionate measure that pursued a legitimate objective. In that regard, the Court determined that the right to take collective action for the protection of the workers of the host State against possible **social dumping** (using cheaper labour than is ordinarily available) could constitute an overriding reason of public interest. However, collective action could **not** be justified with regard to the public interest objective of protecting workers where **the negotiations on pay formed part of a national context characterised by a lack of provisions, of any kind, which were sufficiently precise and accessible** to enable an undertaking to determine the obligations with which it was required to comply as regards minimum pay.

Finally, the Court considered rules in Sweden that prohibited trade unions from taking collective action with the aim of having a collective agreement between other parties set aside or amended. That these rules failed to take into account collective agreements negotiated between an undertaking and its posted workers in another Member State gave rise to discrimination against such undertakings, in so far as under those national rules they were treated in the same way as national undertakings that had not concluded a collective agreement. As this discrimination was not justified on grounds of public policy, public security or public health, the Court held that the rules were contrary to Articles 49 and 50 EC Treaty (now Arts 56 and 57 TFEU).

Significance:

A careful balancing act between the rights of workers and the rights of undertakings was required in this case, with the Court ultimately ruling in the favour of the free movement of services. This case established that it is contrary to the free movement of services for an undertaking that is providing services in a host Member State to be forced to guarantee its posted workers more favourable conditions than those required by Directive 96/71. After the deadline for the implementation of Directive 2018/957 has passed, it will no longer be true that an undertaking need only provide posted workers with the minimum wage applicable in a host Member State, and the conditions required by Directive 96/71 will therefore have changed. However, the Court's restrictive interpretation of a collective agreement of universal application in this case suggests that posted workers will not be able to attain equal wages to nationals of a host Member State when the conditions of remuneration are stipulated by collective agreements that are 'not sufficiently precise or accessible'.

Additionally, an instance of discrimination was found in the failure of national rules to take account of collective agreements that have been negotiated in another Member State. The possibility suggested in the case of applying collective agreements negotiated in the home Member State to posted workers may provide a means of perpetuating the payment of posted workers (to whom the *home* Member State collective agreement applies) at a lower rate than nationals (for whom a *host* Member State collective agreement may establish more favourable conditions of remuneration). This could potentially be the case even if the host Member State collective agreement had been declared 'universally applicable'.

11.3.4 Permissible restrictions on the rights of providers

> *Van Binsbergen* is also discussed in section 11.3.1 (page 445) in relation to the direct effect of what is now Article 56 TFEU

Restrictions or impediments to the freedom of establishment and the freedom to provide services, as provided for in the Treaties and the relevant secondary legislation, may be permitted if certain conditions are met. These conditions were initially developed through the case law, including the following case on the freedom to provide services:

Van Binsbergen v *Bestuur van de Bedrijfsvereninging voor de Metaalnijverheid* (Case 33/74)

Facts:

As noted above, this case concerned a Dutch legal adviser who moved to Belgium during the course of legal proceedings in the Netherlands. He was told that he could no longer represent his client, because under Dutch law only persons established in the Netherlands could act as legal advisers.

Ruling:

The Court first stated that a requirement that a service provider must be habitually resident within the Member State where the service is provided is *prima facie* contrary to what is now Article 56 TFEU. However, the Court then recognised that this could be permissible in certain circumstances:

12 However, taking into account the particular nature of the services to be provided, specific requirements imposed on the person providing the service cannot be considered incompatible with the Treaty where they have as their purpose the application of professional rules **justified by the general good** - in particular rules relating to organization, qualifications, professional ethics, supervision and liability - **which are binding upon any person established in the state in which the service is provided**, where the person providing the service would escape from the ambit of those rules being established in another member state.

Considering the specifics of the case, the Court then stated that:

14 ... the requirement that persons whose functions are to assist the administration of justice must be permanently established for professional purposes within the jurisdiction of certain courts or tribunals cannot be considered incompatible with the provisions of Articles 59 and 60 [now Arts 56 and 57 TFEU], where such requirement is **objectively justified by the need**

> to ensure observance of professional rules of conduct connected, in particular, with the administration of justice and with respect for professional ethics.
>
> 15 That cannot, however, be the case when the provision of certain services in a Member State is not subject to any sort of qualification or professional regulation and when the requirement of habitual residence is fixed by reference to the territory of the State in question.

Furthermore, the Court stated that, with regard to the administration of justice, this objective could be satisfactorily ensured through less restrictive means than a requirement of habitual residence within the Member State. Therefore, the Court concluded that:

> 17 ... the first paragraph of Article 59 and the third paragraph of Article 60 of the EEC Treaty [now Arts 56 and 57 TFEU] must be interpreted as meaning that **the national law of a member state cannot, by imposing a requirement as to habitual residence within that State, deny persons established in another Member State the right to provide services, where the provision of services is not subject to any special condition under the national law applicable**.

Significance:

This case established that a restriction on the freedom of services may be justified where it upholds professional rules '**for the general good**', such as those regarding (i) professional ethics and (ii) the administration of justice. However, with regard to professional ethics, a restriction cannot be justified on this ground when the provision of the services in question is not subject to any sort of qualification or professional regulation within the Member State. With regard to the administration of justice, the restriction was found to go beyond that which was necessary, i.e. not to comply with the principle of **proportionality**. Therefore, neither objectively justified the restriction.

➤ Directive 77/249 is outlined briefly in section 11.3.1

While the **above** case demonstrated the process of establishing whether a restriction on the freedom to *provide services* can be objectively justified, the conditions for objective justification were clearly set out in relation to the freedom of *establishment* in the following case:

Gebhard v *Consiglio dell'Ordine degli Avvocati e Procuratori di Milano* (Case C-55/94)

Facts:

Mr Gebhard was a German national who was authorised to practise as a lawyer in Germany. He lived with his wife and children in Italy, where he was initially a collaborator in a set of lawyers' chambers, then an associate member of those chambers. He later opened his own chambers. Complaints were lodged against Mr Gebhard's use of the title of **avvocato**, and he was subsequently prohibited from using this title by the Milan Bar Council, which also brought proceedings against him for having used the title in the past. Those proceedings culminated in the decision that Mr Gebhard would be suspended from pursuing his professional activities for six months. Mr Gebhard appealed against that decision to the Consiglio Nazionale Forense, alleging that it violated his right to pursue professional activities under **Directive 77/249** on the effective exercise by lawyers of freedom to provide services, and simultaneously raised the issue that his application to be entered onto the roll of members of the Bar had received no response. The Consiglio Nazionale Forense referred questions to the Court of Justice on the compatibility of national provisions with the Directive.

Ruling:

The Court of Justice first determined that Mr Gebhard's situation came under the chapter of the Treaty on establishment rather than services, as he pursued professional activities on a stable and continuous basis, rather than temporarily.

> The Court then observed that the pursuit of certain self-employed activities within a Member State may be made conditional on compliance with certain provisions that are 'justified by the general good'. Where there are **no** such rules, nationals of other Member States are entitled to establish themselves and pursue that activity. Where there are such rules, nationals of other Member States must generally comply with any such provisions relating to an activity that they wish to pursue. The Court then determined that:
>
>> 37 ... national measures liable to hinder or make less attractive the exercise of fundamental freedoms guaranteed by the Treaty must fulfil **four conditions**: they must be applied in a **non-discriminatory** manner; they must be justified by imperative requirements in the **general interest**; they must be **suitable** for securing the attainment of the objective which they pursue; and they must not go beyond what is **necessary** in order to attain it.
>
> It was for the national court to determine whether each of these criteria were satisfied by national provisions that limited freedom of establishment for nationals of other Member States seeking to pursue professional activities as a lawyer.
>
> ### Significance:
>
> This case established that measures that might interfere with fundamental freedoms, including the freedom of establishment, must meet four conditions. These conditions can be summarised as **non-discriminatory**, in the **general interest**, **suitable** and **necessary**. A restriction which meets all of these conditions is said to be **objectively justified** and will not be deemed contrary to Union law.

> ▶ The Cassis rule of reason is fully discussed in section 12.5.2

Rather than 'imperative requirements in the general interest', as it was phrased in the above case, **Directive 2006/123** refers to 'overriding reasons relating to the public interest', which can be taken to mean much the same. This is also similar to the concept of a 'legitimate objective', which is a term sometimes used by the Court of Justice (e.g. in ***Bosman*** (Case C-415/93) and ***Bernard*** (Case C-325/08) (see section 10.3.1)) and to the application of the '**Cassis rule of reason**' relating to the free movement of goods (see Chapter 12).

Article 4(8) of Directive 2006/123 sheds some light on the scope of overriding reasons relating to the public interest:

> 'overriding reasons relating to the public interest' means reasons recognised as such in the case law of the Court of Justice, including the following grounds: public policy; public security; public safety; public health; preserving the financial equilibrium of the social security system; the protection of consumers, recipients of services and workers; fairness of trade transactions; combating fraud; the protection of the environment and the urban environment; the health of animals; intellectual property; the conservation of the national historic and artistic heritage; social policy objectives and cultural policy objectives.

The word 'including' in Article 4(8) determines that this list is not exhaustive and that the Court of Justice is free to establish that other grounds also amount to 'overriding reasons relating to the public interest'. Indeed, it may be noted that **Recital 40** of the Directive lists several further grounds, including safeguarding the sound administration of justice, the need to ensure a high level of education, the maintenance of press diversity and the promotion of the national language.

Article 52 TFEU gives special weight to three of these grounds, stating as follows:

> The provisions of this Chapter and measures taken in pursuance thereof shall not prejudice the applicability of provisions laid down by law, regulation or administrative action providing for **special treatment for foreign nationals** on grounds of **public policy, public security** or **public health**.

> ➤ The grounds of public policy, public security and public health as a justification for restrictions to the right to enter and reside are discussed in section 9.4.2

This means that grounds of public policy, public security or public health can not only justify a non-discriminatory and proportionate restriction to freedom of establishment, but can also justify a restriction that directly discriminates on grounds of nationality. By virtue of **Article 62 TFEU**, Article 52 also applies to the provision of services. However, in *Rina Services and Others* (Case 593/13), the Court of Justice established that the Article 52 TFEU grounds cannot be used to justify any of the eight requirements which Member States may **not** impose on access to or the exercise of service activities set out in **Article 14 of Directive 2006/123**; the prohibition on these restrictions is absolute. Furthermore, while each Member State is entitled to determine what constitutes a risk to public policy, public security or public health, restrictions taken to allay such a risk must be necessary and proportionate to that end. As with restrictions on the right to enter and reside, restrictions based on public policy, public security or public health must represent a **genuine and sufficiently serious threat** to one of the fundamental interests of society (see *Commission v Luxembourg* (Case C-319/06)).

With regard to the provision of services, **Article 16(1) of Directive 2006/123** provides that any requirements imposed on access to or the exercise of a service activity must be **non-discriminatory**, must be **justified** by reasons of public policy, public security, public health or the protection of the environment, and must be **proportionate**. Additionally, **Article 16(3)** states as follows:

> The Member State to which the provider moves shall not be prevented from imposing requirements with regard to the provision of a service activity, where they are justified for reasons of **public policy, public security, public health** or the **protection of the environment** and in accordance with paragraph 1. Nor shall that Member State be prevented from applying, in accordance with Community law, its **rules on employment conditions**, including those laid down in collective agreements.

The proviso that a requirement must be justified by one of the four listed grounds **and** be 'in accordance with paragraph 1', suggests that such requirements must always be non-discriminatory and proportionate. However, the application of Article 52 TFEU, via Article 62 TFEU, suggests that discriminatory measures restricting the provision of services may still be justified on grounds of public policy, public security or public health. This is in line with the permissible restrictions to the freedom of establishment under Article 52 TFEU, the free movement of workers under Article 45(3) TFEU and the free movement of EU citizens and their family members under Article 27 of Directive 2004/38.

It may be noted that the ground of protecting the environment represents an additional ground which is listed only in relation to the provision of services. Additionally, Article 16(3) of Directive 2006/123 adds the ground of applying rules on employment conditions. This ensures that the freedom to provide services may in no way facilitate the exploitation of workers.

Some of the case law where the Court of Justice has considered whether restrictions on the freedom of establishment or the freedom to provide services can be objectively justified is now considered. An overview of the objective justification test is provided in Figure 11.1.

Figure 11.1 Objective justification in relation to freedom of establishment and the freedom to provide services

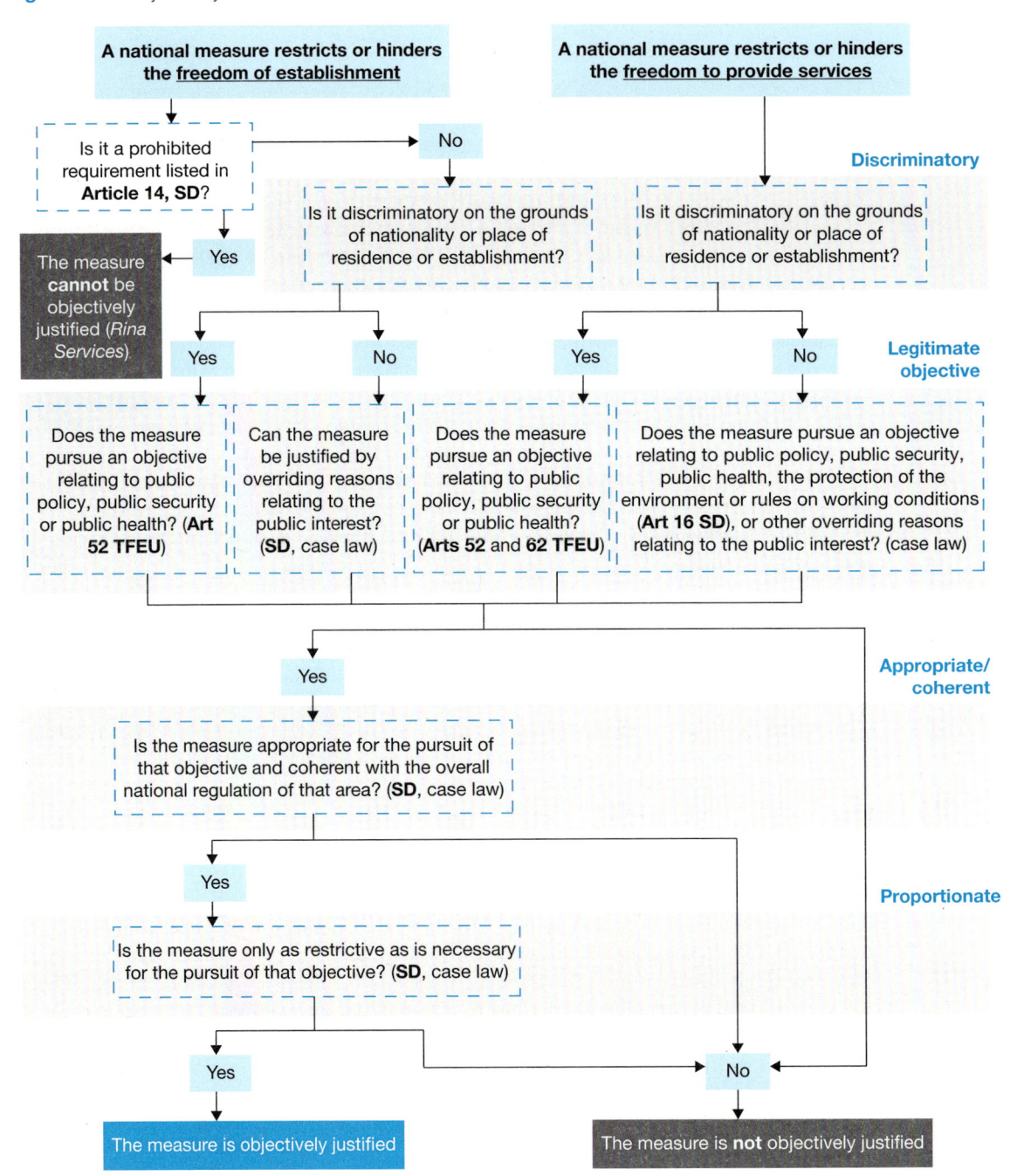

```
A national measure restricts or hinders        A national measure restricts or hinders
      the freedom of establishment                  the freedom to provide services
                    │                                            │
                    ▼                                            │
          Is it a prohibited     ──── No ────┐                   │
          requirement listed in              │                   │
          Article 14, SD?                    ▼                   ▼                                Discriminatory
                    │                 Is it discriminatory on the grounds    Is it discriminatory on the grounds
                   Yes                of nationality or place of             of nationality or place of
                    │                 residence or establishment?            residence or establishment?
                    ▼
          The measure                    Yes          No            Yes          No                Legitimate
          cannot be                       │            │             │            │                objective
          objectively                     ▼            ▼             ▼            ▼
          justified (Rina         Does the measure  Can the measure  Does the measure  Does the measure pursue an objective
          Services)               pursue an objective  be justified by  pursue an objective  relating to public policy, public security,
                                  relating to public  overriding reasons  relating to public  public health, the protection of the
                                  policy, public security  relating to the  policy, public security  environment or rules on working conditions
                                  or public health? (Art  public interest?  or public health?  (Art 16 SD), or other overriding reasons
                                  52 TFEU)            (SD, case law)   (Arts 52 and 62 TFEU)  relating to the public interest? (case law)
```

Yes

Is the measure appropriate for the pursuit of that objective and coherent with the overall national regulation of that area? (**SD**, case law)   Appropriate/coherent

Yes

Is the measure only as restrictive as is necessary for the pursuit of that objective? (**SD**, case law)   Proportionate

Yes → The measure is objectively justified

No → The measure is **not** objectively justified

Objective justification on grounds of public health

In the following cases, the Court of Justice was required to determine whether Union law precluded provisions contained in Italian and German legislation which provided that only pharmacists may own and operate a pharmacy:

Commission v Italy (Case C-351/06); Apothekerkammer des Saarlandes and Others (Joined Cases C-171 and 172/07)

Facts:
Case C-351/06 was brought by the Commission, which argued that an Italian rule that excluded non-pharmacists from holding and operating a pharmacy was contrary to the freedom of establishment. In Joined Cases C-171 and 172/07, a number of pharmacists had brought proceedings against the authorities of the German state of Saarland. They argued that the issuance of a licence to operate a pharmacy to a Dutch company breached a rule in German law, similar to that in Italy, which excluded non-pharmacists. Questions on these cases were referred to the Court of Justice by a German administrative court.

Ruling:
The Court of Justice held that legislation which provided that only pharmacists could own and operate a pharmacy constituted a restriction on, *inter alia*, the freedom of establishment. However, **this restriction could be justified by the objective of ensuring that the provision of medicinal products to the public was reliable and of good quality**.

The Court stated that where there was uncertainty as to the existence or extent of risks to human health, it was important that a Member State should be able to take protective measures without having to wait until the reality of those risks became fully apparent. Furthermore, a Member State could take measures that reduced, as far as possible, a public-health risk – this more specifically included a risk to the reliability and quality of the provision of medicinal products to the public.

In this context, the Court drew attention to the very particular nature of medicinal products, the therapeutic effects of which distinguished them substantially from other goods; if medicinal products were consumed unnecessarily or incorrectly, they could cause serious harm to health.

The Court observed that although a pharmacist, like other persons, would pursue the objective of making a profit, it was presumed that a pharmacist would operate the pharmacy not with a purely economic objective, but also from a professional viewpoint. Their private interest in making a profit was thus tempered by their training, by their professional experience and by the responsibility which they owed, given that any breach of the rules of law or professional conduct undermined not only the value of their investment but also their own professional existence. The Court then observed that non-pharmacists, by definition, lacked training, experience and responsibility equivalent to those of pharmacists, and accordingly they did not provide the same safeguards.

The Court held that **a Member State could therefore take the view, in the exercise of its discretion, that the operation of a pharmacy by a non-pharmacist could represent a risk to public health**, in particular to the reliability and quality of the supply of medicinal products at retail level.

Significance:
This case provides insight into the justification of a restriction to a fundamental freedom on the ground of public health. In particular, it clarifies that Member States have discretion in determining what constitutes a risk to public health and that measures for the protection of public health may be taken proactively.

The following case concerned a Spanish law which made the setting-up of a new pharmacy conditional upon certain demographic and geographical factors:

Blanco Pérez and Chao Gómez v Consejería de Salud y Servicios Sanitarios, Principado de Asturias (Joined Cases C-570/07 and C-571/07)

Facts:

In the Spanish region of Asturias, a decree established a licensing system that limited the number of pharmacies in an area by reference to the population of that area. Only one pharmacy could be opened per unit of 2,800 inhabitants and the system prohibited the opening of a pharmacy within 250 metres of another pharmacy. The decree also set out criteria for making a selection from among pharmacists competing for a licence, with points awarded on the basis of their professional experience and academic record.

Mr Blanco Pérez and Ms Chao Gómez, both qualified pharmacists, brought an action against a call for applications for pharmacy licences launched by Asturias and against the decree. Uncertain whether the Asturian decree was compatible with the principle of the freedom of establishment, the Tribunal Superior de Justicia de Asturias (Spain), before which the proceedings were brought, referred the case to the Court of Justice for a preliminary ruling.

Ruling:

The Court of Justice held that the conditions, established by the Asturian decree, linked to population density and the minimum distance between the pharmacies constituted a restriction on the freedom of establishment. However, the Court observed that such measures could be justified, provided that the measures were applied in a **non-discriminatory** manner; were justified by overriding reasons relating to the **general interest**; were **appropriate for attaining the objective** pursued; and did **not go beyond what was necessary** for attaining that objective (i.e. were proportionate).

The Court found that the conditions linked to population density and the minimum distance between pharmacies in the region **applied without discrimination** on grounds of nationality.

The Court then held that the objective of the demographic and geographical restrictions laid down by the Asturian decree was to ensure that the provision of medicinal products to the public was reliable and of good quality. Accordingly, **that objective constituted an overriding reason relating to the general interest** and was capable of justifying national legislation such as that at issue in the main proceedings.

The Court considered that the Asturian legislation was **appropriate to the attainment of that objective**. The Court considered that, if that field was wholly unregulated, it was not inconceivable that pharmacists would become concentrated in the areas considered to be attractive, so that certain other less attractive areas would suffer from a shortfall in the number of pharmacists needed to ensure a pharmaceutical service which was reliable and of good quality.

However, the Court also observed that the uniform application of the '2,800 inhabitants' and '250 metres' rules fixed by the Asturian decree could well be unsuccessful in ensuring adequate access to pharmaceutical services in **areas which had certain special demographic features**. First, if the '2,800 inhabitants' rule were uniformly applied in certain rural areas where the population was generally scattered and less numerous, some inhabitants would find themselves beyond reasonable reach of a pharmacy. Secondly, in densely populated areas, the strict application of the '250 metres' rule could well give rise to a situation in which more than 2,800 inhabitants lived inside the perimeter laid down for a single pharmacy. However, the Court observed that, although the Asturian decree implemented the national legislation, the national legislation provided for certain adjustment measures to address these issues.

Finally, the Court stated that the Asturian legislation **did not go beyond what was necessary** to attain the objective of ensuring that the provision of medicinal products to the public was reliable and of good quality.

The Court held, therefore, that **the conditions linked to population density and the minimum distance between pharmacies were not in breach of the freedom of establishment, provided that the basic '2,800 inhabitants' and '250 metres' rules did not, in any geographical area which had special demographic features, prevent the establishment of a sufficient number of pharmacies to ensure adequate pharmaceutical services**. This proviso was a matter for the national court to ascertain.

Regarding the selection criteria for licences for new pharmacies, the Court stated that the priority that was given by these criteria to candidates who had acquired professional qualifications and experience within Asturias could be met more easily by Spanish nationals than by nationals of other Member States. **The Court concluded, therefore, that these selection criteria were discriminatory and were precluded by the freedom of establishment**.

Significance:

This case provides an example of where the Court of Justice has sought to balance the freedom of establishment with overriding general interests. The objective of providing reliable and quality medical services was legitimate and was pursued in a proportionate manner, meaning that the restrictions relating to population density and distance were justified. Criteria that, in practice, gave nationals an advantage over non-nationals, however, were not justified.

Similar provisions were at issue in the following case:

Ottica New Line di Accardi Vincenzo v *Comune di Campobello di Mazara* (Case 539/11)

Facts:

A Regional law in Italy established conditions relating to population density and distance between establishments with regard to the opening of opticians' shops. When a licence was granted in breach of this law, an existing optician's, Ottica New Line, brought a case against the decision before a regional administrative tribunal. The tribunal declared that the law was contrary to the Union provisions of freedom of establishment. Ottica New Line appealed this decision and the appellate court referred the matter to the Court of Justice, asking whether Union law precludes such restrictions relating to population density and distance between establishments.

Ruling:

First, the Court noted that, although in force, Directive 2006/123 did not apply to this case, as healthcare services are excluded from the scope of the Directive (Art 2(2)(f)). However, due to the restrictions that the Italian law imposed on the establishment of optician's shops, the law constituted a restriction to the freedom of establishment under Article 49 TFEU.

Regarding whether the restrictions could be justified, the law was found to be **non-discriminatory**, as the restrictions applied regardless of nationality. Additionally, referring to the Court's judgment in ***Pérez and Gómez***, the objectives of protecting public health and, to that end, ensuring an even distribution of healthcare facilities are legitimate, and the restrictions relating to population density and geographic distance are an appropriate means of pursuing those objectives.

However, the Court then drew a distinction between the services provided by opticians and those provided by pharmacies, which it had previously considered, stating that 'the need for rapid access to those products is less great than is inherently the case for the provision of many medicinal products, with the result that the interest in having an optician's shop close by is not as acute as is the case with the distribution of medicinal products'. However, **the degree of protection that Member States wish to afford to public health and how such protection is to be achieved are matters that fall within the discretion of the Member State.**

Nevertheless, the Court held that it was still necessary to determine whether the restrictions were **appropriate** for ensuring the attainment of the objective. To that end, **the measures must genuinely reflect a concern to attain that objective in a consistent and systematic manner.** While this was ultimately for the national court to determine, the Court of Justice noted that the local authorities, in practice, enjoyed a wide discretion as to whether or not to license additional opticians' shops.

The Court therefore concluded that the restrictions on the establishment of opticians' shops relating to population density and geographical distance were not contrary to Article 49 TFEU, 'provided that the competent authorities use appropriately, in accordance with transparent and objective criteria, the powers made available under the legislation concerned, with a view to attaining, in a coherent and systematic manner, the objectives pursued by that legislation relating to the protection of public health throughout the given territory, which is a matter for the national court to assess'.

Significance:

In this case, the Court concerned itself not only with the text of a domestic provision, but also with the way in which it was implemented. The case therefore establishes that a restriction to a fundamental freedom can only be objectively justified if it genuinely pursues a legitimate objective in a **consistent and systematic** manner.

While the three cases above invoke the ground of public health to justify restrictions on providers of health services, this ground can also be invoked to justify restrictions on other services that may affect public health. The following case provides an example of such restrictions with regard to the advertisement of alcoholic products:

Konsumentombudsmannen (KO) v *Gourmet International Products AB (GIP)* (Case C-405/98)

Facts:

An edition of the magazine 'Gourmet', which was published by GIP, contained three pages of advertisements for alcoholic beverages. These adverts were only published within the version that was sent to subscribers. The Swedish Consumer Ombudsman brought actions against GIP for violating national legislation on the marketing of alcoholic beverages. The Stockholms Tingsrätt (district Court) referred questions to the Court of Justice, including whether national rules imposing an absolute prohibition on certain advertisements were incompatible with the freedom to provide services.

Ruling:

The Court of Justice held that the Treaty provisions on freedom to provide services precluded a prohibition on the advertising of alcoholic beverages, as this had a particular effect on the cross-border supply of advertising space, given the international nature of the advertising market in the category of products to which the prohibition related.

➤ KO v GIP is also considered in relation to the free movement of goods in section 12.4.5 (page 557)

> The Court, however, held that such a restriction may be justified by the protection of public health. The Court stated that it was for the national court to determine whether, in the circumstances of law and fact which characterise the situation, the prohibition on advertising at issue in the main proceedings met the condition of proportionality required in order for the derogation from the freedom to provide services to be justified. Therefore, the Court concluded that what is now Article 49 TFEU does not preclude prohibitions on the advertising of alcoholic beverages, unless it is apparent that the protection of public health against the harmful effects of alcohol can be ensured by measures having less effect on intra-Union trade.
>
> **Significance:**
>
> This case established that, providing such measures comply with the principle of proportionality, restrictions on the advertising of alcohol can be objectively justified on the ground of public health. It also clarified that advertising can fall under the freedom to provide services as well as the free movement of goods.

The advertisement of alcoholic beverages was also at issue in ***Commission v France*** (Case C-262/02). This case concerned a French regulation that French broadcasters could only transmit sporting events taking place in another Member State if any advertising for alcoholic beverages was removed. The French sought to justify the restriction on public health grounds. The Court of Justice held that although the French regulation was in breach of what is now Article 56 TFEU, it was objectively justified and it was proportionate.

Objective justification in the area of gambling

Gambling is an area in which the Court has repeatedly had to consider whether restrictions on the freedom of establishment and the freedom to provide services can be justified by Member State claims that such restrictions are based on overriding reasons relating to the public interest. The following case considers reasons relating to the reduction of social harm and fraud:

> ### *Questore di Verona* v *Zenatti* (Case C-67/98)
>
> **Facts:**
>
> Italian law made it a criminal offence to conduct or organise games of chance. Only certain forms of betting were permitted, but the organisation of these was exclusively reserved for two particular organisations (CONI and UNIRE) and to organisations holding a concession that had been granted by them. CONI and UNIRE were required to promote sporting activities through investments in sports facilities, especially in the poorest regions and in the peripheral areas of large cities, and to support equine sports and the breeding of horses. The restriction was intended to satisfy social policy concerns (relating to the harmful effects of gambling) and the concern to prevent fraud.
>
> Mr Zenatti had acted as an intermediary in Italy for the London company SSP Overseas Betting Ltd (SSP), a licensed bookmaker. Zenatti ran an information exchange for the Italian customers of SSP in relation to bets on foreign sporting events. He would send forms to London, by fax or internet, which had been filled in by customers, together with bank transfer forms. He would receive faxes from SSP for transmission to the same customers. Action was taken against Zenatti

because he had not been licensed to provide such a service in Italy, and he was ordered by the national court to cease the activity. The Italian court referred the case to the Court of Justice pursuant to what is now Article 267 TFEU, to consider whether the restriction was compatible with the Union law provisions on the freedom to provide services.

Ruling:

The Court of Justice first held that, as the Italian legislation applied without distinction on grounds of nationality, it was **non-discriminatory**, but that it nevertheless constituted an obstacle to the freedom to provide services. Such an obstacle may be justified by overriding reasons relating to the public interest. The objectives of the legislation were put forward as 'to avoid risks of crime and fraud and the damaging individual and social consequences of the incitement to spend which it represents and to allow it only to the extent to which it may be socially useful as being conducive to the proper conduct of competitive sports'.

The Court then considered whether the legislation was a suitable and proportionate means of obtaining these objectives. The Court stated that:

35 … the fact that the games in issue are not totally prohibited is not enough to show that the national legislation is not in reality intended to achieve the public-interest objectives at which it is purportedly aimed, which must be considered as a whole. Limited authorisation of gambling on the basis of special or exclusive rights granted or assigned to certain bodies, which has the advantage of confining the desire to gamble and the exploitation of gambling within controlled channels, of preventing the risk of fraud or crime in the context of such exploitation, and of using the resulting profits for public-interest purposes, likewise falls within the ambit of those objectives.

36 However … such a limitation is acceptable only if, from the outset, it reflects a concern to bring about a genuine diminution in gambling opportunities and if the financing of social activities through a levy on the proceeds of authorised games constitutes only an incidental beneficial consequence and not the real justification for the restrictive policy adopted.… **even if it is not irrelevant that lotteries and other types of gambling may contribute significantly to the financing of benevolent or public-interest activities, that motive cannot in itself be regarded as an objective justification for restrictions on the freedom to provide services**.

37 It is for the national court to verify whether, having regard to the specific rules governing its application, the national legislation is **genuinely directed to realising the objectives which are capable of justifying it** and whether the restrictions which it imposes do not appear disproportionate in the light of those objectives.

Significance:

This case established that it is not sufficient that a restriction *can* be justified by overriding reasons relating to the public interest, but rather that a restriction must be **genuinely directed** towards the realisation of such objectives. This requires a deeper assessment of the national circumstances to ensure that the measures are genuine, suitable and proportionate to the attainment of objectives relating to the public interest. Such objectives cannot be economic, and where a contribution is made from the profits of the authorised provider to benevolent activities, this contribution should constitute only an incidental beneficial concern.

The Court of Justice considered similar reasons in *Marcello Costa* and *Ugo Cifone* (Joined Cases C-72/10 and C-77/10). These joined cases concerned a condition on the grant of new gambling licences whereby a minimum distance had to be observed between new outlets and those for which a licence had been awarded previously. The Court stated that a national system which required minimum distances between outlets would **not** be justifiable if its true objective was the protection of the market position of the existing operators. This, and whether any other objective was legitimate and pursued proportionately, was a matter for the national court to determine.

The Court of Justice had to adjudicate on betting over the internet in ***Gambelli*** (Case C-243/01). The Court held that Italian legislation, which made it punishable as a criminal offence, without a concession or licence from the state, to collect, accept, register or transmit proposed bets, particularly on sporting events via the internet, was contrary to what are now Articles 49 and 56 TFEU. However, the Court held that the restriction could be objectively justified on moral, religious and/or cultural grounds. In deciding whether or not the restriction was objectively justified, consideration could be given to the morally and financially harmful consequences for the individual and society. Following on from this case, ***Liga Portuguesa de Futebol Profissional (CA/LPFP) and Bwin International Limited* v *Departamento de Jogos da Santa Casa da Misericórdia de Lisboa*** (Case C-42/07) concerned the grant, by Portugal, of the sole and exclusive right to operate lotteries, lotto games and sporting bets over the internet. The body to which this sole and exclusive right was granted was a non-profit-making organisation which operated under the strict control of the Portuguese authorities. Portugal claimed its objective was to prevent the operation of such activities over the internet for fraudulent and criminal purposes. This sole and exclusive right was challenged. The Court of Justice reaffirmed that because of the specific features associated with the offering of games of chance (i.e. gambling) over the internet, a prohibition may be objectively justified on the grounds of combating fraud and crime. Similar decisions were reached by the Court of Justice in the following cases, which regulated games of chance: ***Sporting Exchange* v *Minister van Justitie and Ladbrokes Betting Gaming* and *Ladbrokes International* v *Stichting de Nationale Sporttotalisator*** (Case C-203/08 and Case C-258/08); ***Criminal proceedings against Otto Sjöberg and Anders Gerdin*** (Joined Cases C-447/08 and C-448/08); and ***Zeturf Ltd* v *Premier ministre*** (Case C-212/08).

On the facts of the following cases, the Court of Justice held that a public monopoly for the organisation of sporting bets and lotteries could *not* be objectively justified, because the regulation at issue did not limit games of chance in a consistent and systematic manner:

Winner Wetten GmbH v Bürgermeisterin der Stadt Bergheim (Case C-409/06); Markus Stoss and Others v Wetteraukreis and Kulpa Automatenservice Asperg GmbH and Others v Land Baden-Württemberg (Joined Cases C-316/07, C-358/07 to C-360/07, C-409/07 and C-410/07); and Carmen Media Group Ltd v Land Schleswig-Holstein and Others (Case C-46/08)

Facts:

In Germany, there was a regional monopoly for the organisation of sporting bets and lotteries in most of the Länder (regions), while bets on horse racing and the operation of gaming machines and casinos were organised and operated by licensed private operators. Each of the cases concerned the compatibility of the German rules on games of chance with the freedom of establishment and the freedom to provide services.

Ruling:

The Court of Justice held that the German rules on sporting bets constituted a restriction on the freedom to provide services and the freedom of establishment, but that they could be justified by imperative reasons in the public interest, such as preventing incitement to squander on gambling and combating gambling addiction. To such ends, the Court determined that Member States are free to establish public monopolies, as they can be an effective means of combatting the risks connected with the gambling industry. However, the national measures in question must be suitable and proportionate for the pursuit of those objectives.

The Court stated that the fact that only sporting bets and lotteries were subject to public monopolies, while other forms of gambling were subject to a licensing system, did not necessarily mean that the German system was inconsistent, as those games had different characteristics. However, the Court found that the rules **did not limit games of chance in a consistent and systematic manner** for two reasons: (i) the holders of public monopolies sought to maximise profits from lotteries by carrying out intensive advertising campaigns; and (ii) the German authorities permitted policies designed to encourage the use of casinos and gaming machines, which carry a greater risk of addiction than the games which were subject to monopolies. In such circumstances, **the protective objectives that the rules supposedly pursued were undermined, meaning that those objectives could not justify the monopolies established under those rules**.

Significance:

This case further develops the condition established in **Zenatti** that non-discriminatory measures that restrict or hinder freedom of establishment or the freedom to provide services must be genuinely directed at the attainment of objectives relating to the public interest. Where such objectives are not pursued in a **consistent and systematic** manner, they cannot be used to justify measures that restrict a fundamental freedom, i.e. the overall national regulation of the area at issue (gambling) must be coherent with the pursuit of such objectives.

Three subsequent cases concerning games of chance, which centred around the issue of objective justification, are: *Criminal proceedings against Jochen Dickinger and Franz Ömer* (Case C-347/09); *Stanleybet International Ltd and Others* v *Ypourgos Oikonomias kai Oikonomikon and Others* (Joined Cases C-186/11 and C-209/11); and *HIT and HIT LARIX* v *Bundesminister für Finanzen* (Case C-176/11).

The central issue in the following case was whether the measure taken was disproportionate:

Engelmann (Case C-64/08)

Facts:

Austrian legislation established a **state monopoly** over games of chance, with the effect that only the state had the right to organise and operate them. The federal law in force was intended to regulate games of chance with a view to their supervision and to enable the state to derive the maximum amount of revenue from them.

The Federal Minister for Finance was permitted to grant a total of 12 concessions, entitling their holders to organise and operate gaming establishments. **The concessionaire had to be a public limited company headquartered in Austria and to be subject to supervision by the ministry**. The organisation of games of chance without authorisation could give rise to criminal proceedings.

At the time, the 12 concessions were held by a single company, Casinos Austria AG. They were granted and renewed without a public tendering procedure. Mr Engelmann, a German national, operated two gaming establishments in Austria without previously having applied for a concession from the Austrian authorities. By a judgment at first instance, he was found guilty of unlawfully organising games of chance and ordered to pay a fine of 2,000 euros. Mr Engelmann appealed to the Landesgericht Linz (Regional Court, Linz, Austria). The Austrian court referred questions to the Court of Justice for a preliminary ruling on the compatibility of the Austrian legislation with the freedom of establishment and the freedom to provide services.

Ruling:

The Court of Justice stated that the requirement that persons holding concessions to operate gaming establishments had to have headquarters in Austria constituted a restriction on the freedom of establishment. That obligation discriminated against companies which had their seat in another Member State and prevented those companies from operating gaming establishments in Austria through an agency, branch or subsidiary.

With regard to the possibility of justifying that restriction in the interest of preventing those activities from being carried out for criminal or fraudulent purposes, the Court held that **the categorical exclusion of operators who were headquartered in another Member State was disproportionate**, as it went beyond what was necessary to combat crime. There were various less restrictive measures available to monitor the activities and accounts of such operators. In addition, any undertaking established in a Member State could be supervised and could have sanctions imposed on it, regardless of the place of residence of its managers.

With regard to the grant of the concessions, the Court considered that limiting the number of concessions could be justified by the need to limit opportunities for gambling. The grant of concessions for a duration of 15 years could also be justified having regard to the concessionaire's need to have a sufficient length of time to recoup their investments. However, **the absence of a competitive procedure when the concessions were granted to Casinos Austria AG did not comply with the freedom of establishment**. The Court stated that the obligation of transparency required the concession-granting authority to ensure a degree of publicity sufficient to enable a service concession to be opened up to competition and the impartiality of the award procedures to be reviewed. The grant of a concession, in the absence of any transparency, to an operator located in the Member State of the awarding authority constituted a difference in treatment to the detriment of operators located in other Member States. Such a difference in treatment was contrary to the prohibition of discrimination on grounds of nationality and constituted indirect discrimination on grounds of nationality prohibited by Union law.

Significance:

This case established that freedom of establishment entails **transparent** and **impartial** competitive procedures for the award of concessions and that such procedures must be open to interested parties across the Union. It was also established that it is not proportionate to exclude all service providers established in other Member States from a tendering process on grounds of combatting crime.

Objective justification in the area of tax

The Court of Justice has held that until such time as national rules on company taxation are harmonised throughout the Union, it is permissible for a Member State to impose a restriction on companies, so that they cannot move their principal place of business without the consent of the national tax authorities (***R v HM Treasury, ex parte Daily Mail and General Trust plc*** (Case 81/87)). The retention of national company taxation rules should not, however, allow Member States to operate discriminatory tax rules which operate as a barrier to the establishment of branches of foreign undertakings in their territories (***R v IRC, ex parte Commerzbank AG*** (Case C-330/91)).

In the following case, a UK court referred questions to the Court of Justice for a preliminary ruling in relation to the interpretation of what are now Articles 49 and 54 TFEU:

Marks & Spencer (Case C-446/03)

Facts:

Marks & Spencer, a company resident in the UK, was the principal trading company of a retail group which had subsidiaries in the UK and in a number of other Member States. In 2001 it ceased trading in continental Europe because of losses incurred from the mid-1990s.

In 2000 and 2001, Marks & Spencer submitted claims to the UK tax authorities for group tax relief in respect of the losses incurred by the German, Belgian and French subsidiaries. United Kingdom tax legislation (the Income and Corporation Taxes Act 1988 (ICTA)) allowed the parent company of a group, under certain circumstances, to offset its profits by losses incurred by its subsidiaries. However, those claims were rejected on the ground that the rules governing group relief did not apply to subsidiaries not resident or trading in the UK. Marks & Spencer appealed against that refusal to the Special Commissioners of Income Tax, which dismissed the appeal. Marks & Spencer then brought an appeal before the English High Court, which decided to stay proceedings and to refer questions to the Court of Justice for a preliminary ruling on whether the UK provisions were compatible with the former Articles 43 and 48 EC Treaty (now Arts 49 and 54 TFEU).

Ruling:

The Court of Justice recalled that, although direct taxation came within the competence of Member States, national authorities had to exercise that competence consistently with Union law. The Court held that the UK legislation constituted a restriction on freedom of establishment, in that it applied different treatment for tax purposes to losses incurred by a resident subsidiary from that applied to losses incurred by a non-resident subsidiary. This would deter parent companies from setting up subsidiaries in other Member States.

However, the Court acknowledged that such a restriction could be permitted if it pursued a legitimate objective that was compatible with the Treaty and was justified by imperative reasons in the public interest, and if the restriction was a proportionate means of achieving that objective. The objectives put forward were:

(i) the protection of a balanced allocation of the power to impose taxation between the various Member States concerned, so that profits and losses were treated symmetrically in the same tax system;

(ii) the fact that the legislation provided for avoidance of the risk of double use of losses which would exist if the losses were taken into account in the Member State of the parent company and in the Member State of the subsidiaries;

(iii) escaping the risk of tax avoidance which would exist if the losses were not taken into account in the Member State where the subsidiary was established, because otherwise the losses which accrued to a group of companies could be transferred to the companies established in the Member States which applied the highest rates of taxation and in which the tax value of the losses was the highest.

The Court held that **these objectives were compatible with the Treaty and constituted overriding reasons in the public interest.**

> However, the Court held that **the UK legislation did not comply with the principle of proportionality** and went beyond what was necessary to attain the objectives pursued where: (i) the non-resident subsidiary had exhausted the possibilities available in the Member State where it was established of having the losses taken into account for the accounting period concerned by the claim for relief and also for previous accounting periods; and (ii) there was no possibility for the foreign subsidiary's losses to be taken into account in the Member State where it was established for future periods either by the subsidiary itself or by a third party, in particular where the subsidiary had been sold to that third party.
>
> Consequently, the Court of Justice held that where, in one Member State, the resident parent company demonstrated to the tax authorities that those conditions were fulfilled, it was contrary to the freedom of establishment to preclude the possibility for the parent company to deduct from its taxable profits in that Member State the losses incurred by its non-resident subsidiaries.
>
> **Significance:**
>
> This case demonstrates that freedom of establishment does not only pertain to the setting up of the business, but rather concerns all situations relevant to the running – and closure – of an undertaking. Thus, at no stage should an undertaking be disadvantaged by its operation in other Member States, including with regard to tax deductions, unless such disadvantage can be objectively justified.

Similarly, in *Test Claimants in the FII Group Litigation* v *Commissioners of Inland Revenue and The Commissioners for Her Majesty's Revenue and Customs* (Case C-35/11), the Court of Justice held that the differential tax treatment which was applied to share dividends received by a company, which varied depending on whether such dividend was received from a resident company or non-resident company, constituted a discriminatory restriction on the freedom of establishment.

FKP Scorpio Konzertproduktionen (Case C-290/04) concerned national legislation under which a procedure of retention of tax at source was applied to payments made to providers of services not resident in the Member State in which the services were provided, whereas payments made to resident providers of services were not subject to a retention. The Court of Justice held that the obligation on the recipient of services to make a retention if he is not to incur liability was a breach of what is now Article 56 TFEU. It constituted indirect discrimination because the non-residency rule would apply primarily to non-nationals. The Court held, however, that such legislation was justified by the need to ensure the effective collection of income tax from persons established outside the Member State of taxation and constituted a means which was proportionate to the objective pursued.

In *Duomo Gpa Srl and Others* v *Comune di Baranzate and Others* (Joined Cases C-357/10 to C-359/10), Italy awarded contracts to third parties for the collection of taxes. To be considered for a contract, a private company required a fully paid-up share capital of ten million euros. The only ground of justification put forward for this requirement was the need to protect public authorities against possible non-performance by the contractor, in the light of the high overall value of the contracts awarded. In practice, the contractors, by first collecting the tax revenue, would hold and deal with millions of euros which they were required to pay over to the public authorities. The Court of Justice did not rule out the possibility that such an objective could constitute an overriding reason in the public interest. However, according to the national court which had referred the case to the Court of Justice, other provisions were capable of providing adequate protection for public authorities (e.g. proof of the contractor's technical and financial capacity, creditworthiness and solvency and/or the application of minimum thresholds for share capital that varied depending on the value of the contracts actually awarded to the contractor). Consequently, the Court held that, as the Italian provision went beyond the objective of protecting the public authorities against non-performance by the contractor, it contained disproportionate, and therefore unjustified, restrictions on fundamental freedoms.

Other cases concerned with overriding reasons relating to the public interest

The cases of *Football Association Premier League and Others* v *QC Leisure and Others*; *Karen Murphy* v *Media Protection Services Ltd* (Joined Cases C-403/08 and C-429/08) concerned the grant of the exclusive right to broadcast live English Premier League football games. The English Football Association Premier League granted broadcasters the exclusive right on a territorial basis. In the agreement, the broadcaster was required to encrypt its signal and only to transmit the encrypted signal to subscribers, in order to prevent access to subscribers outside the territory. The agreement prohibited the broadcaster from supplying decoder cards to persons outside the territory. The Court of Justice held that the prohibition on the import, sale or use of decoder cards to persons outside the territory was contrary to the freedom to provide services and could not be justified either in light of the objective of protecting **intellectual property rights** or by the objective of encouraging the public to attend football stadiums.

The following case concerned objective justification on the grounds of **consumer protection** and **road safety**:

Grupo Itevelesa SL and Others v *OCA Inspección Técnica de Vehículos SA and Generalidad de Cataluña* (Case C-168/14)

Facts:

National legislation in Spain established an authorisation system for operators carrying out vehicle roadworthiness tests. This system was challenged on the basis that two conditions placed on authorisation were contrary to, *inter alia*, Directive 2006/123. These conditions were: (i) a requirement of a minimum geographical distance between roadworthiness testing centres belonging to one or a group of undertakings, and (ii) a prohibition on holding more than 50 per cent of the market share within the region of Catalonia. The Spanish Supreme Court referred the matter to the Court of Justice for a preliminary ruling under Article 267 TFEU.

Ruling:

The Court first referred to its judgment in *Sokoll-Seebacher* (Case C-367/12) to determine that it had jurisdiction, as although the facts of the case did not contain any cross-border element, it was conceivable that undertakings seeking to offer vehicle roadworthiness testing in Spain could be established in other Member States and that the legislation would therefore present an obstacle to their freedom to provide services.

The Court then established that vehicle roadworthiness testing does **not** come within the scope of Directive 2006/123. Such testing amounts to 'services in the field of transport', which are expressly excluded from the Directive by Article 2(2)(d) thereof. However, the Court also established that vehicle roadworthiness testing is **not** covered by the 'official authority' exemption of Article 51 TFEU, as the powers enjoyed by such operators (i.e. the power to take vehicles off the road) was subject to supervision by the authorities and did not involve any physically coercive powers. Therefore, the case would be determined by the compatibility of the national legislation with **Article 49 TFEU**.

The Court noted that the distance and market-share conditions amounted to a non-discriminatory restriction to the freedom of establishment. The regional and national governments contended that these restrictions were justified by reasons of consumer protection and road safety, as they sought to ensure the territorial coverage and competitiveness – and therefore quality – of the testing services. Both consumer protection and road safety had already been established in the case law as overriding reasons relating to the public interest which are capable of justifying restrictions to freedom of establishment.

While it was ultimately for the national court to determine whether the national legislation was proportionate to these objectives and whether it pursued them in a coherent way, the Court of Justice noted that neither the distance nor market-share conditions seemed to contribute to consumer protection or road safety, especially considering that the quality of services was already protected by the harmonisation of the content of vehicle roadworthiness testing at Union level.

Significance:

> Sokoll-Seebacher is considered above on page 447

This case emphasised the importance of determining that measures are appropriate for guaranteeing their purported objectives in a consistent and systematic manner. If they do not effectively contribute to, in this case, consumer protection or road safety, then restrictions on freedom of establishment cannot be justified by these objectives.

In the following case, Directive 2006/123 was held to apply to a restriction on the freedom of establishment that was justified by reasons relating to **public order**:

Harmsen v *Burgemeester van Amsterdam* (Case C-341/14)

Facts:

Mr Harmsen operated a window prostitution business in Amsterdam and sought authorisation to operate two further such businesses. This request for authorisation was refused on the basis of reports compiled by supervisory authorities and the police regarding Mr Harmsen's existing business. The reports indicated that the existing business was not managed in such a way as to prevent abuse, especially relating to the fact that Mr Harmsen rented rooms to foreign prostitutes who did not speak a language that he could understand. The Raad van State (Dutch administrative court), however, was unsure whether the language requirement was disproportionate to the objectives of preventing criminal offences, such as forced prostitution and human trafficking, as Mr Harmsen could communicate through the use of interpreters and provide protection through camera surveillance. The Raad van State referred a question to the Court of Justice, asking whether **Article 10(2)(c) of Directive 2006/123** precludes making the grant of an authorisation subject to the condition that the service provider must speak the same language as the service recipients.

Ruling:

The Court first claimed that the objective of the restriction in question – the prevention of criminal offences – amounts to grounds of **public order**, which falls within the 'overriding reasons relating to the public interest' listed in **Article 4(8) of Directive 2006/123**. While it was ultimately for the national court to determine whether the restriction was appropriate and proportionate, the Court stated as follows:

> 73 Such a measure **appears to be appropriate for achieving the objective pursued**, since, by allowing prostitutes to give the operator of prostitution businesses directly and in person any evidence making it possible to establish the existence of an offence related to prostitution, it

is likely to facilitate the performance by the competent national authorities of the necessary checks to ensure compliance with the provisions of national criminal law.

74 As regards, secondly, the question of whether the measure at issue goes beyond what is necessary to achieve the objective pursued, it should, first, be noted that that measure merely requires the use of any language that can be understood by the parties concerned, which is less intrusive on the freedom to provide services than a measure which imposes the exclusive use of an official language of the Member State concerned or another specific language.

75 Next, it does not appear that the measure at issue in the main proceedings requires a high degree of linguistic knowledge, merely that the parties can understand each other.

76 Finally, **there do not appear to be any less restrictive measures capable of securing the legitimate objective of general interest pursued**. In particular, as submitted by the Netherlands Government, the intervention of a third party, as suggested by Mr Harmsen, could, given the particularities of the type of activities at issue, be the source of harmful interference in the relationship between the operator and the prostitutes, which it is for the referring court to determine. As for camera checks, they do not necessarily allow for the preventive identification of criminal offences.

Significance:

In this case, the Court applied a strict interpretation to the requirements that a restriction on the freedom of establishment must be appropriate and proportionate. This strictness likely reflects the serious risks to the well-being of the service recipients that was at issue, i.e. forced prostitution and human trafficking. Confusingly, however, the Court stated that the prevention of such criminal offences comprises a reason relating to 'public order' and claimed that this falls within the 'overriding reasons relating to public interest' that are listed in Article 4(8) of Directive 2006/123; but 'public order', as such, is not mentioned in this Article. The most likely explanation is that the Court has taken public order to be synonymous with public security, which is listed in Article 4(8). Alternatively, as the list in Article 4(8) is not an exclusive list, 'public order' is added to the list of 'overriding reasons relating to the public interest'.

11.4 Recipients of services

Objective 4

While the Treaties do not mention a right to receive services, the Court of Justice has understood certain rights of recipients as a corollary to the freedom to provide services under Article 56 TFEU, and such rights have been expressly included in the relevant secondary legislation. The rights of recipients to access services without facing discrimination or unwarranted barriers due to their nationality or place of residence are important to the functioning of the internal market, as such rights ensure that service providers do not, through their denial of service to certain persons, create barriers within the internal market. The rights of service receivers also pertain to consumer protection, which ensures that certain standards and safeguards are upheld. This, in turn, facilitates trust in the internal market (see Directive 2011/83).

This section examines the rights of recipients under the Treaties, Directive 2004/38 and Directive 2006/123, and then considers the rights of service receivers to equal treatment with regard to social advantages.

11.4.1 Rights of recipients under the Treaties

In the following joined cases, the Court of Justice held that the Treaty provisions on services cover the recipients thereof:

Luisi and Carbone v *Ministero del Tesoro* (Joined Cases 286/82 and 26/83)

Facts:

The applicants were Italian nationals who were prosecuted for attempting to export more than the legal maximum of Italian currency for use abroad. They argued that they had exported it for use within the Union to pay for services as tourists and to pay for medical treatment and that the currency restrictions were contrary to Union law. The Court was asked whether the restrictions were covered by the rules on the payment for services covered by what are now Article 123 TFEU on credit facilities and Articles 56 and 57 TFEU on services (Arts 106, 67 and 68 EEC Treaty at the time).

Ruling:

The Court of Justice held as follows:

10 By virtue of Article 59 of the Treaty [now Art 56 TFEU], restrictions on freedom to provide such services are to be abolished in respect of nationals of Member States who are established in a Member State other than that of the person for whom the service is intended. **In order to enable services to be provided, the person providing the services may go to the Member State where the person for whom it is to be provided is established or else the latter may go to the State in which the person providing the service is established**. Whilst the former case is expressly mentioned in the third paragraph of Article 60 [now Article 57 TFEU], which permits the person providing the service to pursue his activity temporarily in the Member State where the service is provided, the latter case is the necessary corollary thereof, which fulfils the objective of liberalising all gainful activity not covered by the free movement of goods, persons and capital.

...

16 It follows that **the freedom to provide services includes the freedom, for the recipient of services, to go to another Member State in order to receive a service there, without being obstructed by restrictions**, even in relation to payments and that tourists, persons receiving medical treatment and persons travelling for the purposes of education or business are to be regarded as recipients of services.

Significance:

This case established that the freedom to *receive* services follows from the freedom to *provide* services, and that, therefore, restrictions should not be imposed on persons travelling to a Member State of which they are not a national for the purpose of receiving services.

In the above case, the Court of Justice held that tourism was a service which was covered by what is now Article 56 TFEU. In ***Cowan* v *Le Trésor Public*** (Case 186/87), the Court of Justice declared that tourists were entitled to full equal treatment under what is now Article 18 TFEU, and that equal treatment included access to the criminal process and to national provisions on criminal injuries compensation (see section 11.4.4). In addition, leisure activities pursued by recipients of services from other Member States must not be subject to discriminatory treatment (***Commission* v *Greece*** (Case C-62/96); ***Commission* v *Spain*** (Case C-45/93); ***Commission* v *Italy*** (Case C-388/01)).

11.4.2 Rights of recipients to residence

Initially, the former Directive 64/221 protected the position of a recipient of services who resided in or travelled to another Member State for that purpose, and the former Article 1(b) of Directive 73/148 required the abolition of restrictions on the movement and residence of nationals wishing to go to another Member State as recipients (as well as providers) of services. Recipients of services were entitled to remain in the host Member State only for as long as the service was received. However, given the breadth of the concept of 'services', it would seem that any EU citizen or national of an EEA state could have remained in another Member State for as long as they were paying for a service, such as paying rent for accommodation. As long as they were relying exclusively on their own resources, however modest, they would be providing 'remuneration' and would seem to have been entitled to remain under what are now Articles 56 and 57 TFEU (see *Belgium* v *Humbel* (Case 263/86)).

These two directives were repealed and replaced by **Directive 2004/38**, which, as discussed in Chapter 9, creates a general right of entry and residence for up to three months for all EU citizens and their family members without any conditions or formalities, other than the requirement to hold a valid identity card or passport (**Art 6**). Additionally, recipients of services can reside in a host Member State for longer than three months if they are EU citizens and they fulfil any of the conditions set out in **Article 7(1)**, i.e. if they are a worker or self-employed, if they are self-sufficient, if they are a student or, regardless of their nationality, if they are a family member of one of the above. Recipients of services are also able to attain the right to permanent residence under **Article 16** on the same basis as any other EU citizen. **Article 24(1)** of Directive 2004/38 also provides that EU citizens qualifying for the right of residence or the right of permanent residence and the members of their family benefit from equal treatment with host-country nationals in the areas covered by the Treaty.

11.4.3 Rights of recipients under Directive 2006/123

Directive 2006/123 provides specifically for the rights of service receivers, primarily through the establishment of rights pertaining to consumer protection. Thus, while the first half of Directive 2006/123 sets out the rights of service providers, the second half sets out the obligations that Member States may impose on providers in order to protect the rights of service receivers.

Provisions to strengthen the rights of recipients of services

These provisions affirm the right of recipients to use the services of other Member States and aim to enhance consumer protection. **Article 19** prohibits Member States from imposing requirements on recipients of services that restrict the use of a service supplied by a provider established in another Member State. Member States are also obliged to ensure that recipients of services are not subject to requirements set by service providers that discriminate on grounds of their nationality or place of residence (**Art 20**). While discrimination based on **place of residence** has often been held by the Court of Justice to amount to indirect discrimination on the ground of nationality (e.g. *Clean Car* (Case C-350/96); *Finanzamt Köln-Altstadt* v *Schumacker* (Case C-279/93)), it is notable that it is explicitly prohibited here in relation to the provision of services. **Article 21** obliges Member States to make certain information accessible to recipients of services. This includes information pertaining to the requirements that are placed on the exercise of service activities and the means of redress available in the case of a dispute between a provider and a recipient of a service.

Promoting the quality of services

Article 22 obliges Member States to ensure that certain information is provided by service providers to recipients and specifies further information that providers must provide on the request of the recipient. Further consumer information requirements are then stipulated in **Directive 2011/83** on consumer rights.

Article 23 of Directive 2006/123 provides that Member States may ensure that service providers have professional liability insurance, but may not require cover that has been provided in another Member State to be duplicated. **Article 24** requires Member States to remove any total prohibitions on commercial communications, such as advertising services and canvassing (see *Société fiduciaire nationale d'expertise comptable* v *Ministre du Budget, des Comptes publics et de la Fonction publique* (Case C-119/09)), by the regulated professions and to ensure that such communications adhere to professional standards. **Article 25** requires Member States to ensure that service providers are not restricted to the exclusive exercise of a specific activity, except where issues such as professional independence and impartiality are at stake. **Article 26** outlines measures that Member States may take to ensure the quality of service provision, such as by encouraging the development of and participation in certification schemes. **Article 27** then sets out the obligations on Member States to facilitate settlement disputes.

11.4.4 Rights of recipients to social advantages

Neither the self-employed nor recipients of services benefit from **Article 7(2) of Regulation 492/2011** relating to equal treatment in access to social advantages, as the regulation applies only to workers. On the face of it, this is an important distinction, as social advantages have played an important part in the jurisprudence of the Court of Justice in relation to the integration of workers and their families into the host Member State (see Chapter 10). However, the Court has considerably mitigated the exclusion of recipients of services from Regulation 492/2011 by creatively applying the general prohibition on discrimination on grounds of nationality under what is now **Article 18 TFEU**.

▶ The scope of 'social advantages' under Article 7(2), Regulation 492/2011 is considered in section 10.3.3

In *Commission* v *Italy (Re Housing Aid)* (Case 63/86), the Court of Justice held that Italian law contravened what is now Article 18 TFEU, where the law in question confined a discounted mortgage facility to Italian nationals. The following case subsequently came before the Court of Justice:

> #### *Cowan* v *Le Trésor Public* (Case 186/87)
>
> **Facts:**
>
> Mr Cowan, a British citizen, was assaulted and injured at the exit of a Metro station while he was visiting France as a tourist (i.e. as a recipient of services (see above)). As his assailants were not identified, he applied to the French Commission d'Indemnisation (Board of Compensation) for compensation. However, the national rules stipulated that such compensation should only be granted to French nationals, persons in possession of a residence permit or nationals of a State that has concluded a reciprocal agreement with France (i.e. where it has been agreed that a French national in the same situation in their country would receive such compensation).

> Mr Cowan argued that these provisions discriminated in contravention of Union law and that they hindered the free movement of tourists. The Commission d'Indemnisation referred the matter to the Court of Justice for a preliminary ruling.
>
> **Ruling:**
>
> The Court reiterated its finding in **Luisi and Carbone** that the freedom to provide services includes the freedom to travel to other Member States to receive services, including through tourism. It then ruled in Mr Cowan's favour, stating as follows:
>
>> 17 ... When Community law guarantees a natural person the freedom to go to another Member State **the protection of that person from harm in the Member State in question, on the same basis as that of nationals and persons residing there, is a corollary of that freedom of movement.** It follows that the prohibition of discrimination is applicable to recipients of services within the meaning of the Treaty as regards protection against the risk of assault and the right to obtain financial compensation provided for by national law when that risk materializes.
>
> **Significance:**
>
> This case was a precursor to the development of EU citizenship, as it implicitly established that almost anyone at any time can be considered a recipient of services and can be granted equal treatment under what is now Article 18 TFEU by virtue of being in a Member State of which they are not a national. While Mr Cowan was deemed a recipient of services on the basis that he was a tourist, he was in fact staying with a relative. It was not deemed necessary to specify exactly which services he was receiving, but rather his mere presence within the territory of another Member State seemed to be sufficient to trigger his right to equal treatment.

In *Commission* v *Spain* (Case C-45/93), the Court of Justice held that the principle of equal treatment extended to the right of visitors from other EU states to free admission to museums, where this facility was available to Spanish nationals (see also *Commission* v *Italy* (Case C-388/01)). In this case, the visitors could rely upon what is now Article 18 TFEU, because while visiting other EU states they were considered to be the recipients of services (see above) and thus came within the scope of what is now Article 56 TFEU.

In *Gravier* v *City of Liège* (Case 293/83), the Court of Justice held that Ms Gravier was exercising a Union right to receive education. In the course of exercising such a right, she was entitled to benefit from what is now Article 18 TFEU. On that basis she should receive equal treatment in relation to payment of the university admission fee, the *minerval*, so that she would only have to pay the same amount as 'home' students (see also *Commission* v *Belgium (Re University Fees)* (Case C-47/93)).

Although the Court of Justice has generally been keen to apply what is now Article 18 TFEU to enable an individual to overcome obstacles, either overt or covert, to the exercise of rights conferred by what are now Articles 49, 56 and 57 TFEU, it has been more reluctant to do so when the obstacle relates to the individual's shortage of resources. For example, the Court has held that the right to equal treatment in relation to access to vocational education does not extend to financial assistance to enable an individual to go to another Member State and receive a grant to support themselves while at a vocational school or on a vocational course. Such a right did not exist under what was then Article 12 EC Treaty, nor under what is now Article 18 TFEU (see *Lair* v *University of Hannover* (Case 39/86)). Indeed, the right to receive education as a 'service' under Article 56 TFEU depends on the individual providing 'remuneration' for it (*Humbel* (Case 263/86), paras 8–13). Now, **Article 24(2) of Directive 2004/38** expressly states that Member States are only obliged to grant maintenance aid to students who have not yet attained a permanent right of residence if they hold the status of a worker, a self-employed person or a family member thereof (see Chapter 10).

11.4.5 Permissible restrictions on the rights of recipients

As discussed above in the context of providers of services, the freedom to provide services may be restricted by non-discriminatory rules which are justified by overriding reasons relating to the public interest (Directive 2006/123), or by measures pursuing public policy, public security or public health objectives (Art 52 TFEU). Some of the relevant provisions and case law on restrictions on the receipt of services are now examined in two areas: medical services and public policy.

Restrictions on the receipt of medical services

In the area of health services, the cases of *Geraets-Smits* v *Stichting Ziekenfonds* and *Peerbooms* v *Stichting CZ Groep Zorgverzekeringen* (Case C-157/99) established that the receipt of medical services in a Member State in which the recipient does not normally reside and for which remuneration is paid, either by the recipient or by their insurance provider, counts as the provision of services for the purpose of what is now Article 56 TFEU. In this case, an insurer would only cover the costs of medical treatment in another Member State if the recipient of services first attained authorisation from them. This was deemed to amount to a restriction on the freedom to provide services under what is now Article 56 TFEU, but it was held that such a restriction could be justified by reasons relating to the maintenance of the national social security and healthcare systems, **provided** that the refusal of such treatment only occurred when the same or equally effective treatment was available in the home Member State without undue delay (see also *Commission* v *France* (Case C-512/08); *Commission* v *Portugal* (Case C-255/09)).

Article 20(1) of Regulation 833/2004 on the coordination of social security systems now provides as follows:

> Unless otherwise provided for by this Regulation, an insured person travelling to another Member State with the purpose of receiving benefits in kind during the stay shall seek authorisation from the competent institution.

Article 20(2) of that Regulation then qualifies the requirement for authorisation as follows:

> ... The authorisation shall be accorded where the treatment in question is among the benefits provided for by the legislation in the Member State where the person concerned resides and where he cannot be given such treatment within a time-limit which is medically justifiable, taking into account his current state of health and the probable course of his illness.

Therefore, where an EU citizen travels to a host Member State specifically to receive medical treatment, their health insurer from their home Member State need only cover the costs if the individual has first sought authorisation from them. However, an insurer is obliged to provide such authorisation, and therefore to cover the costs of treatment abroad, (i) where such treatment would be covered by the insurance in the home Member State; and (ii) where such treatment is not available in the home Member State within an appropriate time period. The second criteria equates to the condition established in *Smits* and *Peerbooms* (Case C-157/99) that authorisation to receive treatment in another Member State may only be refused on the ground that the '**same or equally effective treatment**' could be obtained '**without undue delay**' in the home Member State.

In *Inizan* (Case C-56/01), the Court of Justice referred to its judgments in *Smits* and *Peerbooms* and elaborated its position regarding the need for treatment to be available 'without undue delay':

> ... in order to determine whether treatment which is equally effective for the patient can be obtained without undue delay in the Member State of residence, **the competent institution is required to have regard to all the circumstances of each specific case** and to take due account not only of the patient's medical condition at the time when authorisation is sought and, where appropriate, of the degree of pain or the nature of the patient's disability which might, for example, make it impossible or extremely difficult for him to carry out a professional activity, but also of his medical history. [para 46]

This case therefore clarified how the 'undue delay' criterion should be assessed, i.e. with regard to **all** the circumstances of **each** specific case. This judgment was applied in *Watts* v *Bedford Primary Care Trust*, which concerned the E112 scheme (now the **S2 scheme**) which provides cross-border health service users with authorisation from their home Member State insurer. In this case, an applicant to the scheme was refused authorisation to receive an operation abroad as she was on a waiting list in her home Member State. The Court asserted that the authorisation for medical treatment abroad may not be refused unless the competent institution can establish that the waiting time for treatment in the home Member State 'does not exceed the period which is acceptable on the basis of an objective medical assessment of the clinical needs of the person concerned in the light of all of the factors characterising his medical condition at the time when the request for authorisation is made or renewed'.

Objective justification on grounds of public policy

The following case concerned a restriction on certain leisure activities that was justified on grounds of public policy:

Omega (Case C-36/02)

Facts:

Omega operated a sports centre in Bonn (Germany) for the practice of a 'laser sport'. This laser sport was inspired by the film *Star Wars* and it featured machine-gun-style laser targeting devices and sensory tags installed either in the firing corridors within the sports centres or on the jackets worn by players. The police authority took the view that games for entertainment featuring simulated killing were contrary to human dignity and thus constituted a danger to public order. They therefore issued a prohibition order against the company, requiring it to cease operating equipment intended for firing on human targets. Following the dismissal of its administrative complaint and of appeals brought by Omega, the company brought an appeal on a point of law before the Bundesverwaltungsgericht (Federal Administrative Court).

In support of its appeal, Omega submitted, *inter alia*, that the contested order infringed the freedom to provide services under the former Article 49 EC Treaty (now Art 56 TFEU) because the sports centre in question had to use equipment and technology supplied by a UK company, and was therefore a service receiver. The Bundesverwaltungsgericht acknowledged in this regard that, while the commercial exploitation of a 'killing game' did indeed, as the lower court had ruled, constitute an affront to human dignity contrary to the Grundgesetz (German Basic Law), its prohibition infringed the freedom to provide services guaranteed under the former Article 49 EC Treaty (now Art 56 TFEU). The national court therefore referred the matter to the Court of Justice for a preliminary ruling.

Ruling:

The Court of Justice held that, by prohibiting Omega from operating the laser sport within its sports centre in accordance with the model developed by a UK company and lawfully marketed by that company in the UK, the contested order affected the freedom to provide services which the former Article 49 EC Treaty (now Art 56 TFEU) guaranteed both to providers and to the persons receiving those services who are established in another Member State. However, the Court stated that **the protection of fundamental rights is a legitimate interest which could, in principle, justify a derogation from the obligations imposed by Union law**, even under a fundamental freedom guaranteed by the Treaty such as the freedom to provide services. Measures which restricted the freedom to provide services could be justified on public policy grounds only if they were necessary for the protection of the interests they were intended to guarantee and only in so far as those objectives could not be attained by less restrictive measures, i.e. only if they were necessary and proportionate.

The need for, and proportionality of, the provisions adopted could not be excluded merely because one Member State differed from another in the protection that it provided. In other words, **Germany could justifiably prohibit that which the UK authorised, if it could be established that the measure imposing the prohibition was both necessary and proportionate**. The Court observed that these conditions were met in this case. In the first place, the prohibition of the commercial exploitation of games involving the simulation of acts of violence against persons corresponded to the level of protection of human dignity which the national constitution sought to guarantee within Germany. Second, by prohibiting only the variant of the laser game that encouraged firing on human targets, the contested order did not go beyond what was necessary in order to attain the objective pursued. For those reasons, the Court concluded that the restriction to the freedom to provide services posed by the order was objectively justified.

Significance:

This case established that the public policy exception under what is now Article 52 TFEU can be used to justify restrictions to the freedom to provide services that aim to protect fundamental rights enshrined within a Member State's constitution. It is not necessary for such rights to be afforded a uniform level of protection across the Union in order for such a justification to be acceptable.

➤ For further information on the Article 52 TFEU derogations, see section 11.3.4

The following two cases considered the public policy exception in relation to the control of drug use:

Calfa (Case C-348/96)

Facts

Ms Calfa, an Italian national, was charged with the possession and use of prohibited drugs while staying as a tourist in Greece. She was found guilty and sentenced to three months imprisonment, after which she was to be expelled from Greece for life, in accordance with national law. The national court was under an obligation to order her expulsion for life unless there were compelling reasons, in particular family reasons, not to. That decision could only be revoked after a period of three years and at the discretion of the Minister of Justice.

Ms Calfa contested that the expulsion for life breached her Union law rights to travel to Greece as a tourist (i.e. to receive services in accordance with what is now Article 56 TFEU). The Greek authorities argued that she could be expelled in accordance with the public policy derogation under what is now Article 52 TFEU. The Greek court referred the case to the Court of Justice under what is now Article 267 TFEU, seeking guidance on whether the penalty was compatible with Union law.

Ruling:

The Court of Justice determined that the penalty of expulsion for life clearly constituted an obstacle to the freedom to provide services, but that it was necessary to consider whether such a penalty could be justified by the public policy exception provided by what is now Article 52 TFEU. The Court noted, according to its case law, that:

20 … [Article 52 TFEU] permits Member States to adopt, with respect to nationals of other Member States, and in particular on the grounds of public policy, measures which they cannot apply to their own nationals, inasmuch as they have no authority to expel the latter from the territory or to deny them access thereto …

21 Under the Court's case law, the concept of public policy may be relied upon in the event of a genuine and sufficiently serious threat to the requirements of public policy affecting one of the fundamental interests of society.

The Court held that the use of prohibited drugs met this description. However, such a derogation from a fundamental freedom of Union law needed to be interpreted restrictively. The Court referred to Article 3 of Directive 64/221 (now Art 27, Directive 2004/38), which states that (i) measures taken on the grounds of public policy or of public security that have the effect of restricting the residence of a national of another Member State must be based exclusively on the **personal conduct of the individual** concerned, and (ii) that previous criminal convictions cannot in themselves constitute grounds for the taking of such measures. The Court therefore held that:

25 … an expulsion order could be made against a Community [i.e. Union] national such as Ms Calfa only if, besides her having committed an offence under drugs laws, her **personal conduct created a genuine and sufficiently serious threat affecting one of the fundamental interests of society**.

As the national legislation in question made expulsion for life an automatic consequence of a criminal conviction, it did not allow for the personal conduct of the offender or the danger that they represented to be taken into account. Therefore, the Court concluded that the conditions for the application of the public policy exception had not been met and that the exception therefore did not objectively justify the restriction to the freedom to provide services that was imposed by the national legislation.

Significance:

In this case, the Court's case law, and especially the principles established in ***Bouchereau*** (Case 30/77) regarding the need to consider the personal conduct and threat represented by an individual, was applied to the freedom to provide services. This case also follows in the footsteps of the Court's judgment in ***Cowan*** (Case 186/87), as Ms Calfa was able to rely on her status as a tourist to invoke the Treaty rights pertaining to the freedom to provide services.

▶ *Adoui and Cornuaille* is discussed further in section 9.4.2

The following case concerned the right of EU citizens to use 'coffee shops' in the Netherlands:

Josemans v Burgemeester van Maastricht (Case C-137/09)

Facts:

In the Netherlands, the supply and use of cannabis is tolerated, subject to certain conditions. Local authorities authorise the establishment of 'coffee shops', the main activities of which are the sale and consumption of cannabis. A number of coffee-shops also sell non-alcoholic beverages and food.

In an effort to stymy drug tourism, the Municipal Council of Maastricht introduced the condition that coffee shop owners in Maastricht may not provide admission to their establishment to persons who did not reside in the Netherlands. Mr Joseman's coffee shop was subsequently shut down by the Mayor of Maastricht, following two reports attesting that persons who were not resident in the Netherlands had been admitted to it. Mr Josemans contested that decision, arguing that the measure constituted a discriminatory restriction on his freedom to provide services to EU citizens from other Member States, not only relating to the sale of cannabis, but also to the sale of non-alcoholic beverages and food in coffee shops.

It was against this background that the Raad van State (Council of State), before which the dispute was brought, made a reference for a preliminary ruling to the Court of Justice.

Ruling:

The Court of Justice noted that the harmfulness of narcotic drugs such as cannabis was generally recognised and that trade in the drug was restricted throughout the Member States. The freedoms of movement and the principle of non-discrimination did not apply, as the release of narcotic drugs into the economic and commercial operations of the Union was prohibited. However, rejecting the argument of the Mayor of Maastricht that the sale of non-alcoholic beverages and food within coffee shops was a secondary activity, the Court held that such activity constituted a catering activity, and therefore came under the freedom to provide services. Moreover, the Court stated that there was a restriction on the exercise of the freedom to provide services in so far as the proprietors of coffee shops were not entitled to market lawful goods to persons residing in other Member States and those persons were precluded from enjoying such services.

The Court then ruled that the restriction on the freedom to provide services could be justified by the objectives of combating drug tourism and the associated public nuisance, under the public policy exception in what is now Article 52 TFEU (Art 46 EC Treaty at the time). Such reasons were deemed legitimate as they were associated with the objectives in the general interest of combating crime, maintaining public order and protecting public health.

Additionally, the Court considered its judgment in **Adoui and Cornuaille** (Joined Cases 115/81 and 116/81), where it ruled that the grounds of public policy may not be relied upon to restrict the behaviour of non-nationals where such behaviour by nationals would not be subject to repressive measures. The Court determined that the case at issue was part of a different legal context: while **Adoui and Cornuaille** concerned prostitution, which is tolerated in a number of Member States, there is, under international law and European Union law, a prohibition in all the Member States on the marketing of narcotic drugs.

The Court stated that a prohibition on admitting non-residents to coffee shops constituted a **suitable** measure as it was capable of substantially limiting drug tourism and, consequently, reducing the problems it caused.

With regard to the principle of **proportionality**, the Court stated that other measures implemented to combat drug tourism and the accompanying public nuisance had proved to be insufficient and ineffective in light of the objectives pursued. As for the possibility of granting non-residents access to coffee shops but refusing to sell cannabis to them, the Court pointed out that it was not easy to control and monitor whether the product was served to or consumed by non-residents. Furthermore, there was a danger that such an approach would encourage the illegal trade in or the resale of cannabis by residents to non-residents inside coffee shops. Additionally, the Court observed that the rules in question did not preclude a non-resident from going to other catering establishments in the municipality of Maastricht in order to consume non-alcoholic beverages and food. The Court therefore concluded that the restriction on the freedom to provide services was objectively justified.

Significance:

This case represents a development of the principle established in *Adoui and Cornuaille* that Member States cannot use the public policy derogation to justify a restriction on the behaviour of non-nationals where nationals behaving in the same way are not subject to repressive measures. The Court introduced a caveat to this principle, whereby the public policy derogation can justify such a restriction on the behaviour of non-nationals when the harms of that behaviour are widely recognised and are subjected to repressive measures throughout the Union.

11.5 Recognition of professional qualifications

Objective 5

Freedom of establishment includes the right of individuals to practise a profession or trade (e.g. lawyer, doctor, vet, etc.) on a permanent or semi-permanent basis. However, entitlement to practise such a profession in any given Member State may be subject to specific qualifications, periods of training and/or periods of work experience. In order to facilitate freedom of establishment and the freedom to provide services, it has therefore been necessary to establish means by which such qualifications and entitlements that have been awarded in one Member State can be recognised and made effective in other Member States.

This section first considers the Treaty provisions on the recognition of professional qualifications, then provides a detailed overview of Directive 2005/36, which consolidated the relevant secondary legislation and now provides a general system for the recognition of qualifications across the regulated professions. Case law is used to develop the discussion of the legislation where relevant. As the 'three systems' directives have been consolidated in Directive 2005/36, discussion of cases brought under those directives are discussed in relation to what are now the relevant articles of Directive 2005/36.

11.5.1 Treaty provisions

Article 53(1) TFEU provides as follows:

In order to make it easier for persons to take up and pursue activities as self-employed persons, the European Parliament and the Council shall, acting in accordance with the ordinary legislative procedure, issue directives for the mutual recognition of diplomas, certificates and other evidence of formal qualifications and for the coordination of the provisions laid down by law, regulation or administrative action in Member States concerning the taking-up and pursuit of activities as self-employed persons.

Article 53(1) TFEU therefore provides the legal base for the harmonising directives on the recognition of professional qualifications, which then went on to form the 'three systems' that are discussed below. However, in *Reyners* (Case 2/74) (see section 11.3.1) the Court of Justice stated that:

> Since the end of the transitional period, Article 52 of the Treaty [now Art 49 TFEU] is a directly applicable provision despite the absence in a particular sphere, of the directives prescribed by Articles 54(2) [now Art 50(1)] and 57(1) [now Art 53(1) TFEU] of the Treaty.

The direct effect of Article 49 on the freedom of establishment therefore applies to the recognition of qualifications. However, in the following case the Court relied on the principle of **indirect effect** to give effect to what is now Article 49 TFEU:

> ▶ Indirect effect is covered in section 8.3

Thieffry v *Conseil de l'Ordre des Avocats à la Cour de Paris* (Case 71/76)

Facts:

Mr Thieffry was a Belgian national who had obtained a doctorate in law in Belgium, where he practised as an advocate for a number of years. His qualifications were recognised by a French university as *equivalent* to a degree in French law and he obtained a certificate stating that he was qualified for the profession of *avocat*. However, the French Bar refused him admission to the training stage solely on the ground that he did not have a degree in French law. Mr Thieffry appealed that decision and the appellate court referred the matter to the Court of Justice.

Ruling:

The Court held that the freedom of establishment was an objective of the Treaty. It then stated as follows:

16 In so far as Community law makes no special provision, these objectives [i.e. freedom of establishment] may be attained by measures enacted by the Member States, which under Article 5 of the Treaty [now Art 4(3) TEU] are **bound to take 'all appropriate measures**, whether general or particular, to ensure fulfilment of the obligations arising out of this Treaty or resulting from action taken by the institutions of the community', **and to abstain 'from any measure which could jeopardize** the attainment of the objectives of this treaty'.

17 Consequently, if the freedom of establishment provided for by Article 52 [now Art 49 TFEU] can be ensured in a member state either under the provisions of the laws and regulations in force, or by virtue of the practices of the public service or of professional bodies, **a person subject to Community [i.e. Union] law cannot be denied the practical benefit of that freedom solely by virtue of the fact that, for a particular profession, the Directives provided for by Article 57 of the Treaty [now Art 53 TFEU] have not yet been adopted**.

The Court therefore held that if the applicant had already obtained what was recognised (professionally and academically) as an **equivalent qualification** and had **satisfied the necessary training requirements** then the French Bar was not justified in excluding him from admission solely because he did not have a French law degree.

Significance:

In this case, the Court invoked the principle that Member States should interpret their national law in a manner that is consistent with Union law, i.e. the principle of indirect effect. It was thus established that Member States are obliged to facilitate freedom of establishment regardless of whether any relevant directives had been adopted under what is now Article 53 TFEU.

A month later, the **direct effect** of Article 49 in relation to the recognition of qualifications was confirmed in the following case:

Patrick v Ministre des Affaires Culturelles (Case 11/77)

Facts:
Mr Patrick had obtained an architect's certificate in the UK and sought authorisation to practise as an architect in France. His application for authorisation was rejected because, although his certificate was recognised as equivalent to the certificate required for French architects, there was no convention of reciprocity between France and the UK, as required under French legislation. Mr Patrick then made an application for the annulment of this decision to the Tribunal Adminstratif of Paris, which referred the matter to the Court of Justice.

Ruling:
The Court of Justice stated as follows:

12 It is not possible to invoke against **the direct effect of the rule on equal treatment with nationals contained in Article 52** [now Art 49 TFEU] the fact that the Council has failed to issue the directives provided for by Articles 54 and 57 [now Arts 50 and 53 TFEU] or the fact that certain of the directives actually issued have not fully attained the objectives of non-discrimination required by Article 52 [now Art 49 TFEU].

…

15 Thus a Member State cannot … make the exercise of the right to free establishment by a national of a new Member State subject to an exceptional authorisation in so far as he fulfils the conditions laid down by the legislation of the country of establishment for its own nationals.

Significance:
This case firmly established the direct effect of what is now Article 49 with regard to the equal treatment of nationals of other Member States who possess equivalent qualifications, irrespective of whether implementing directives had been adopted.

In the absence of a harmonising directive for a particular profession, and in light of the direct effect of what is now Article 49 TFEU, the following case considered how the equivalence of qualifications should be assessed:

UNECTEF v Heylens (Case 222/86)

Facts:
Mr Heylens was a Belgian national who held a Belgian football trainer's diploma. He was taken on as the trainer of a French football team and subsequently applied for recognition of his diploma as equivalent to the French football trainer's diploma. His application was refused. Mr Heylens continued to practise as a trainer and was prosecuted by the French football trainers' union (UNECTEF). The French court referred the case to the Court of Justice under what is now Article 267 TFEU for a preliminary ruling, questioning the compatibility of the French system with Union law.

Ruling:

The Court of Justice noted that:

> 10 In the absence of harmonisation of the conditions of access to a particular occupation, the Member States are entitled to lay down the knowledge and qualifications needed in order to pursue it and to require the production of a diploma certifying that the holder has the relevant knowledge and qualifications.

However, the Court also referred to its judgments in both *Thieffry* and *Patrick* with regard to the duty of Member States to take all appropriate measures to achieve the objectives of the Treaty, which includes freedom of establishment. Considering the recognition of foreign qualifications, the Court then stated as follows:

> 13 Since it has to reconcile the requirement as to the qualifications necessary in order to pursue a particular occupation with the requirements of the free movement of workers, the procedure for the recognition of equivalence must enable the national authorities to assure themselves, on an objective basis, that the foreign diploma certifies that its holder has the knowledge and qualifications which are, if not identical, at least equivalent to those certified by the national diploma. **That assessment of the equivalence of the foreign diploma must be effected exclusively in the light of the level of knowledge and qualifications which its holder can be assumed to possess in the light of that diploma**, having regard to the nature and duration of the studies and practical training which the diploma certifies that he has carried out.

The Court then went on to rule that if a competent national authority should refuse an application for a qualification issued by another Member State to be recognised as equivalent to that required by the host Member State, it must inform the applicant of the reasons for that refusal. This is so that an applicant can make an informed decision as to whether or not to contest that refusal. The Court held that:

> 14 Since free access to employment is a fundamental right which the treaty confers individually on each worker in the Community [now Union], the existence **of a remedy of a judicial nature against any decision of a national authority refusing the benefit of that right is essential** in order to secure for the individual effective protection for his right.

Significance:

This case established that an assessment of the equivalence of a foreign diploma must only consider the level of knowledge and qualifications which the holder of such a diploma can be assumed to possess. This may include consideration of the duration of the studies and the practical training undertaken. The case also confirmed that, in line with the direct effect of what is now Article 49 TFEU, it must be possible to challenge a refusal to recognise a foreign diploma as equivalent to national requirements before a national court.

This was further emphasised by the Court of Justice in the following case:

Vlassopoulou v *Ministerium für Justiz, Bundes- und Europaangelegenheiten Baden-Württemberg* (Case C-340/89)

Facts:

Ms Vlassopoulou had obtained a Greek law degree and had been admitted to the Athens Bar. Most of her professional practice had been undertaken in Germany and involved the application of German law. She applied for admission to the German Bar. Her application was rejected on the ground that she lacked the necessary qualifications. The case came before the German Federal Supreme Court, which referred the matter to the Court of Justice to determine whether it was permissible under Union law to refuse admission to the German Bar for this reason.

Ruling:

The Court of Justice held as follows:

15 It must be stated in this regard that, even if applied without any discrimination on the basis of nationality, national requirements concerning qualifications may have the effect of hindering nationals of the other Member States in the exercise of their right of establishment guaranteed to them by ... [Article 49 TFEU]. That could be the case if the national rules in question took no account of the knowledge and qualifications already acquired by the person concerned in another Member State.

16 Consequently, a Member State which receives a request to admit a person to a profession to which access, under national law, depends upon the possession of a diploma or a professional qualification **must take into consideration the diplomas, certificates and other evidence of qualifications which the person concerned has acquired** in order to exercise the same profession in another Member State **by making comparison between the specialised knowledge and abilities certified by those diplomas and the knowledge and qualifications required by the national rules**.

...

19 If that comparative examination of diplomas results in the finding that the knowledge and qualifications certified by the foreign diploma correspond to those required by the national provisions, the Member State must recognize that diploma as fulfilling the requirements laid down by its national provisions. If, on the other hand, the comparison reveals that the knowledge and qualifications certified by the foreign diploma and those required by the national provisions correspond only **partially**, the host Member State is entitled to require the person concerned to show that he has acquired the knowledge and qualifications which are lacking.

20 In this regard, the competent national authorities **must assess whether the knowledge acquired in the host Member State, either during a course of study or by way of practical experience, is sufficient in order to prove possession of the knowledge which is lacking.**

The Court then reiterated that it must be possible to challenge a decision to refuse recognition before a national court.

Significance:

This case established that national authorities are required to consider any education or training received by that person that is indicated by the qualification, and to contrast that with the knowledge and skills required by the domestic qualification. If they are equivalent then the Member State *must* recognise the qualification. Moreover, if they are not considered equivalent, then they must go on to consider the 'knowledge or training received by the applicant through study or experience'; this may be sufficient to make up for what was lacking in the formal qualification.

The approach taken in the above case was subsequently confirmed in a number of cases. In *Haim* v *Kassenzahnarztliche Vereinigung Nordrhein* (Case C-319/92), an individual did not possess a qualification that was listed in the relevant sector-specific directive, but the Court ruled that the German authority to which he applied for authorisation to practise as a dentist should recognise the eight years that he had spent working as a dentist in Belgium.

> *Haim* is also discussed in section 11.5.3 (page 500) in relation to non-EU qualifications

Then in *Fernandez de Bobadilla* v *Museo Nacional del Prado and Others* (Case C-234/97), the Court determined that it was the responsibility of a public body seeking to fill a vacancy to determine whether the foreign qualification and/or experience of a candidate were such as to afford equivalence to the qualifications specified for the post (see also *Morgenbesser* (Case C-313/01)). See also *Colegio Oficial de Agentes de la Propriedad Inmobiliara* v *Aguirre, Newman and Others* (Case C-104/91).

As in *Haim*, the Court of Justice in *Conseil National de l'Ordre des Architectes* v *Dreesen* (Case C-31/00) made it clear that, where a harmonising directive exists but does not mention the qualification in question, there is still a requirement for a comparative examination of the education and training received by the applicant. This principle was applied in following case in relation to the possibility of partial access to a profession:

Nasiopoulos v *Ipourgos Igias kai Pronoias* (Case C-575/11)

Facts:

Mr Nasiopoulos was a Greek national who trained for two-and-a-half years to qualify as a masseur-hydrotherapist in Germany. This was not a regulated profession in Greece, so he applied to practise physiotherapy. However, as the minimum training required to practise as a physiotherapist in Greece was three years, the Greek Ministry of Health rejected Mr Nasiopoulos's application. He appealed that rejection before the Simvoulio tis Epikratias (Council of State), which referred the case to the Court of Justice. In particular, the national court questioned whether the principle of freedom of establishment precluded national legislation that excluded partial access to a profession where a person was qualified to carry out some of the activities coming under that profession.

Ruling:

The Court first noted that where a qualification from another Member State is sufficiently similar to that of a host Member State to be deemed comparable, it falls within the scope of Directive 2005/36. In the case at hand, however, the matter falls outside the scope of the Directive due to the great differences between the fields of activity. The Court reiterated that Member States have the competence to define the conditions for access to professions that are not subject to harmonising provisions at the Union level, provided that due regard is afforded to the basic freedoms guaranteed by the Treaties.

The Court then determined that the exclusion within national legislation of partial access to a regulated profession would be likely to hinder freedom of establishment or make it less attractive. It may be possible, however, for such a measure to be objectively justified by overriding reasons relating to the public interest. While the protection of public health and the protection of consumers from being misled with regard to the scope of a professional's qualifications constituted such reasons, the Court held that less restrictive measures could be applied to meet that end, i.e. the exclusion was **not proportionate**. For example, specifications relating to the use of professional titles could ensure that an individual's partial qualification is communicated.

The Court ruled that the decisive factor in the case at hand was whether the activities of a masseur-hydrotherapist could be **objectively separated** from the other activities comprising the profession of physiotherapist in the host Member State. The fact that it could be separated in this way was demonstrated by the fact that the profession of masseur-hydrotherapist could be pursued independently in Germany, where the training had been undertaken. Therefore, concerns regarding potential harms to the recipients of services did not justify the restriction to the freedom of establishment caused by the preclusion of any possibility of partial recognition of that qualification in the host state.

> **Significance:**
> This case established that national legislation that precludes the possibility of partial access to a profession, where the activities concerned can be objectively separated from the profession as a whole, amounts to a restriction to freedom of establishment. It may be possible for such a restriction to be objectively justified, although in this case it was held to be disproportionate.

11.5.2 Directive 2005/36: the recognition of professional qualifications

Directive 2005/36 on the recognition of professional qualifications, which is also known as the **Qualifications Directive**, was adopted on 7 September 2005 and had to be transposed into national law by 20 October 2007. The Directive has subsequently been amended by Directive 2013/55, which had an implementation date of 18 January 2016 (see below).

The 'three systems' prior to Directive 2005/36

Pursuant to what is now Article 53(1) TFEU, freedom of establishment with regard to professional qualifications was initially implemented through three systems:

(i) directives on the mutual recognition of diplomas (Directive 89/48 and Directive 92/51);
(ii) Directive 99/41 on the recognition of various commercial and industrial sectors;
(iii) directives harmonising specific professions.

These three systems now comprise Chapters I, II and III of Title III of Directive 2005/36. As they have now been consolidated within Directive 2005/36, these earlier directives were all repealed on the day by which Directive 2005/36 had to be transposed into national legislation: 20 October 2007. **Article 62 of Directive 2005/36** clarifies that 'references to the repealed Directives shall be understood as references to this Directive and the acts adopted on the basis of those Directives shall not be affected by the repeal'.

The main provisions under each of the Titles of Directive 2005/36, and the relevant case law, will now be outlined. As the 'three systems' directives have been consolidated in Directive 2005/36, discussion of cases brought under those directives is included under what are now the relevant articles of Directive 2005/36.

Title I: General provisions

Articles 1–4 set out the purpose, scope, definitions and effects of the Directive. The purpose of the Directive is to establish rules whereby, when Member States make access to a particular profession dependent on the possession of specific qualifications, they shall recognise such qualifications obtained within another Member State. This enables EU citizens who have obtained professional qualifications in one Member State to practise the relevant profession in any Member State (**Art 1**).

The Directive applies to all EU citizens seeking to practise a **regulated profession** in a Member State other than that in which they obtained their professional qualifications, on either a self-employed or employed basis (**Art 2(1)**). The regulated professions are listed in **Annex 1** of the Directive and are defined in **Article 3(1)(a)** as:

> a professional activity or group of professional activities, access to which, the pursuit of which, or one of the modes of pursuit of which is subject ... to the possession of specific professional qualifications; in particular, the use of a professional title limited by legislative, regulatory or administrative provisions to holders of a given professional qualification shall constitute a mode of pursuit.

Additionally, **Article 3(2)** states that 'a profession practised by the members of an association or organisation listed in Annex I shall be treated as a regulated profession'.

In *Burbaud* (Case C-285/01), the Court of Justice clarified that an occupation in the public sector could count as a regulated profession. In this case, the Court ruled that a requirement to attain a French qualification irrespective of whether an equivalent qualification from another Member State had already been attained was contrary to Union law.

Title II: Free provision of services

The freedom to provide services is distinguished from the freedom of establishment on a case-by-case basis and according to criteria identified by the Court of Justice: duration, frequency, regularity and continuity of the provision of services (**Art 5(2)**). A Member State may not restrict an EU citizen from providing services within its territory provided that they are legally established in another Member State **or**, if they move and the profession is **not** regulated, provided that they have pursued their profession within the **Member State of establishment** for at least two years (**Art 5(1)**). **Article 6** stipulates requirements that service providers established in another Member State should be exempt from.

Article 5(3) states that an individual who provides professional services temporarily or occasionally within a host Member State shall be subject to the professional rules that are applicable to such professionals in that host Member State, such as rules relating to the definition of the practice, the use of titles and malpractice.

Article 7(1) provides that, when a service provider moves to a host Member State, that state may require a written declaration in advance of the provision of services, which should include details of their professional liability insurance. A Member State may require that an initial declaration must be accompanied by certain documents (**Art 7(2)**) and that it must be renewed annually (**Art 7(1)**).

Article 7(3) states that a service 'shall be provided under the professional title of the Member State of establishment ... Where no such professional title exists in the Member State of establishment, the service provider shall indicate his formal qualification in the official language or one of the official languages of that Member State.' However, the professional title of the host Member State shall be used in the professions provided for in Chapter III of Title III (see below). Service providers in the regulated professions **not** covered by Chapter III of Title III may also be subject to professional qualification checks by a host Member State if, and only if, such checks are necessary to avoid serious risks to health and safety (**Art 7(4)**).

Article 8 stipulates information about the service provider that a host Member State may request from their Member State of establishment and **Article 9** stipulates information that a host Member State may require a service provider to provide to recipients of their services, including information relating to their registration, professional title and insurance.

Title III: Freedom of establishment

Title III of the Directive comprises the three former systems for the recognition of qualifications:

1. the general system for the recognition of **professional qualifications** (all the professions not covered by specific rules of recognition);
2. the system of automatic recognition of qualifications attested by **professional experience** (industrial, craft and commercial activities); and
3. the system of automatic recognition of qualifications for **specific professions** (doctors, nurses responsible for general care, dental practitioners, specialised dental practitioners, veterinary surgeons, midwives, pharmacists and architects).

Each of these systems is set out in Chapters I–III of Title III, which are then followed by a fourth chapter containing common provisions.

Chapter I: General system for the recognition of professional qualifications

The general system laid out in Chapter I is applicable to all the professions not covered by specific rules of recognition set out in Chapters II and III, and to certain, specified situations where the migrant professional does not meet the conditions set out in those Chapters (**Art 10**).

Article 11 sets out **five levels of professional qualification**:

A. an **attestation of competence** which corresponds to general **primary or secondary** education, or an attestation of competence on the basis of a **training course** or examination not forming part of a certificate or diploma (as below), or of **three years' professional experience**;

B. a **certificate** which corresponds to training at **secondary level**, supplemented by **additional training** in the form of a professional course or period of practice;

C. a **diploma** certifying successful completion of training at **post-secondary level** of a duration of at least **one year**, or professional training which is comparable in terms of responsibilities and functions;

D. a **diploma** certifying successful completion of training at **higher or university level** of a duration of **at least three years** and less than four years;

E. a **diploma** certifying successful completion of training at **higher or university level** of a duration of **at least four years**.

Other types of qualification that are considered by the Member State within which they were awarded as being of an equivalent level and as conferring the same rights to access or practice a profession within that Member State should be treated as a qualification at that level (**Art 12**). This was at issue in the case of *Commission* v *Greece* (Case C-274/05), where the Court ruled that Greece had infringed the former Directive 89/48 by failing to recognise diplomas awarded by the competent authorities of another Member State. The situation was somewhat more complex, however, in the following case:

Consiglio degli Ingegneri v *Ministero della Giustizia, Cavallera* (Case C-311/06)

Facts:

The pursuit of the profession of engineer in both Italy and Spain was conditional on possession of a university diploma and registration with the relevant professional body. In addition, the Italian system required a candidate to pass a state examination.

Mr Cavallera was an Italian national who held a mechanical engineering diploma awarded in 1999 by the University of Turin (Italy) after three years of education and training. In 2001 he applied for, and obtained, approval in Spain of his Italian qualification, allowing him to join to the regulated profession. On that basis, Mr Cavallera enrolled on the register of one of the 'colegios de ingenieros técnicos industriales', in order to be entitled to pursue the regulated profession of industrial technical engineer in Spain.

Mr Cavallera did not work professionally outside of Italy and did not follow any course of study or take any examinations under the Spanish education system. Likewise, he did not take the state examination provided for under Italian legislation for the purpose of being entitled to pursue the profession of engineer.

In 2002, on application by Mr Cavallera, the Italian Ministero della Giustizia (Ministry of Justice) recognised the validity of the Spanish certificate for the purpose of his enrolment in the register of engineers in Italy. The Consiglio Nazionale degli Ingegneri (National Council of Engineers) challenged that decision, arguing that, under the former Directive 89/48 and the relevant national legislation, the Italian authorities could not recognise Mr Cavallera's Spanish certificate, because such recognition would have the effect of exempting him from the state examination required under Italian law.

The Consiglio di Stato (the Italian court of final instance) referred the case to the Court of Justice to determine whether the former Directive 89/48 could be relied on by Cavallera for the purpose of gaining access to the profession of engineer in Italy.

Ruling:

The Court stated that, according to the actual definition in the former Directive itself, a 'diploma' excluded a certificate issued by a Member State if that certificate: (i) did not attest to any education or training covered by the education system of that Member State; and (ii) was not based on either an examination taken or professional experience acquired in that Member State. The application of the former Directive in such circumstances would be tantamount to allowing a person who had merely obtained a qualification in the Member State in which he studied, which did not in itself provide access to that regulated profession, nonetheless to gain access to that profession, even though a certificate obtained elsewhere provided no evidence that the holder had acquired an additional qualification or professional experience. That would be contrary to the principle, enshrined in the former Directive, that Member States reserve the option of fixing the minimum level of qualification necessary to guarantee the quality of services provided within their territory.

Significance:

This case established that the system for recognising qualifications awarded in other Member States may not be used to circumnavigate requirements for entry into a regulated profession. In particular, a certificate issued by one Member State that recognises a qualification obtained in another Member State (known as a certificate of **homologation**) does not by itself provide evidence of training or education.

The above case can be compared with the later judgment in ***Koller*** (Case C-118/09), which also concerned an entitlement to practise a profession in a host Member State. However, in this case, that entitlement was based both on training completed in the individual's home Member State and on additional training that the individual had undertaken in the host Member State. The home Member State was therefore bound to recognise the qualification and entitlement to practise that had been obtained in the host Member State.

When a profession is regulated within a host Member State (i.e. subject to possession of specific professional qualifications), nationals of other Member States should be able to access and pursue that profession under the same conditions as nationals, provided that they hold a qualification issued by the competent authorities of another Member State which attests to a level of training at least equivalent to the level immediately below that required in the host Member State (**Art 13(1)**), or at least level C (**Art 13(3)**). When a profession is regulated within a host Member State but is **not** regulated within a home Member State, a migrant professional may also be required to have pursued a profession full time for two years (**Art 13(2)**). The question of what it means to pursue a profession was raised in ***Toki* v *Ipourgos Ethnikis Pedias kai Thriskevmaton*** (Case C-424/09) in relation to the former Directive 89/48. In this case the Court determined that three conditions must be met:

(i) the experience must consist of full-time work for at least **two years** out of the previous ten years (as is now specified in Art 13(2), Directive 2005/36);

(ii) the work must have consisted of the **continuous and regular** pursuit of a range of professional activities which characterise the profession in question; and

(iii) where the profession as it is pursued in the home Member State covers **equivalent activities** as in the host Member State.

Under **Article 14 (1)**, the host Member State can also make recognition of qualifications subject to the completion of a **compensation measure** (aptitude test or adaptation period of a maximum of three years) if:

(i) a migrant professional's training is **one year shorter** than that required by the host Member State; or

(ii) their training covers **substantially different matters** to those covered by the evidence of formal training required in the host Member State; or

(iii) the profession, as defined in the host Member State, comprises one or more regulated professional **activities which do not exist in the corresponding profession** in the migrant's home Member State, and that difference consists of specific training which covers substantially different matters from those completed by the migrant.

Generally, the host Member State must offer the applicant the choice between an adaptation period and an aptitude test (**Art 14(2)**). The host Member State can only derogate from this requirement in cases specified in **Article 14(3)** or for a limited period with the Commission's authorisation (see Art 61). Additionally, host Member States may not require such compensation measures where a **common platform** has been established, by Member States or by representative professional associations at both national and European level, in accordance with the procedure set out in **Article 15(2)**. A common platform is defined as 'a set of criteria of professional qualifications which are suitable for compensating for substantial differences which have been identified between the training requirements existing in the various Member States for a given profession' (**Art 15(1)**).

> **Reflection:** Example of applying compensation measures
>
> France and Germany both regulate the profession of dragon hunter. In France, an individual may practise as a dragon hunter after three years of university training, while Germany requires four years of training. Thus, under **Article 11** of Directive 2005/36, the 'Diplôme de Chasse au Dragon' that is awarded in France is a 'level D' qualification, while the 'Drachenjagddiplom' that is awarded in Germany is a 'level E' qualification. Therefore, based on **duration** of study, under **Article 13(1)** a dragon hunter that is qualified as such in Germany may practise in France without any additional requirements; a dragon hunter that is qualified as such in France may practise in Germany, but, pursuant to **Article 14(1)**, may first be required to undertake a compensation measure of either an aptitude test or an adaptation period of no more than three years. Under **Article 14(2)**, a dragon hunter who qualified in France should be allowed to choose which compensation measure to complete if they are required to do so.
>
> However, although practising as a dragon hunter in Germany requires four years of training, the relevant course only involves training on how to track different types of dragon, whereas in France the shorter period of training also covers how to slay dragons. Therefore, due to the substantially different **content** of the professional training required in Germany, France may also require dragon hunters that are qualified in Germany to undertake a compensation measure prior to practising in France.
>
> In Portugal, on the other hand, an individual may practise as a dragon hunter without any specific qualification, i.e. the profession is **unregulated**. Dragon hunters from France or Germany may therefore also practise in Portugal without any specific qualifications. For a dragon hunter who has trained in the UK to be able to practise in France or Germany, however, they (i) must hold a qualification that is at least a 'level C' diploma; (ii) may be required to have completed two years of full-time work as a dragon hunter; and (iii) may be required to undertake a compensation measure if the host Member State qualification requires a year longer of training than they have completed or covers substantially different matters.
>
> In the cases of both a Portuguese dragon hunter seeking to practise in France or Germany and a German dragon hunter seeking to practise in France, if the differences between the activities pursued under that title in the home Member State are so great that compensation measures in a host Member State would effectively amount to complete retraining, **partial access** to the profession may be granted. This was initially provided for in *Nasiopoulos v Ipourgos Igias kai Pronoias* (Case C-575/11, see section 11.5.1) but has since been incorporated into Directive 2005/36 (**Art 4f**) by Directive 2013/55 (see below).

Chapter II: Recognition of professional experience

Article 16 provides as follows:

> If, in a Member State, access to or pursuit of one of the activities listed in **Annex IV** is contingent upon possession of general, commercial or professional knowledge and aptitudes, **that Member State shall recognise previous pursuit of the activity in another Member State** as sufficient proof of such knowledge and aptitudes. The activity must have been pursued in accordance with **Articles 17, 18 and 19**.

Annex IV is divided into three lists, which cover a wide range of industrial, craft and commercial activities. **Articles 17**, **18** and **19**, respectively, specify the duration and form of professional experience that is required for the professions in each of those three lists.

Chapter III: Recognition on the basis of coordination of minimum training conditions

Article 21 sets out the principle that each Member State automatically recognises the certificates of training of other Member States, specified in **Annexes V** and **VI**, which grant access to professional activities as a doctor, nurse responsible for general care, dental practitioner, veterinary surgeon, midwife, pharmacist or architect. **Article 22** provides for part-time training and the continuance of training after qualifications have been obtained. **Article 23** provides for the recognition of qualifications issued prior to current requirements, such as those attained in former Soviet Republics, subject to certain conditions.

The minimum training conditions for automatic recognition in the seven professions are set out **Sections 2–8** of the Chapter (Arts 24–49).

Chapter IV: Common provisions on establishment

Article 50 provides that an individual application for authorisation to pursue a regulated profession in a host Member State must be submitted to the competent authority there, accompanied by certain documents and certificates as listed in **Annex VII**. The competent authorities will have one month to acknowledge receipt of an application and to draw attention to any missing documents (**Art 51(1)**). A decision then has to be taken within three months of the date on which the application was received in full (**Art 51(2)**). Reasons have to be given for any rejection and a rejection, or a failure to make a decision by the deadline, may be contested in the national courts (**Art 51(3)**).

Nationals of other Member States who are authorised to practise a regulated profession on the basis of Title III can use the corresponding professional title of the host Member State (**Art 52(1)**). If a profession is regulated in the host Member State by an association or organisation (see Annex I), nationals of other Member States must be able to become members of that association or organisation, and therefore to be able to use the title, under the same conditions as nationals (**Art 52(2)**).

Title IV: Detailed rules for pursuing the profession

Article 53 provides that:

> Persons benefiting from the recognition of professional qualifications shall have a **knowledge of languages** necessary for practising the profession in the host Member State.

Articles 54 and **55** provide further detail on the use of professional titles and health insurance requirements respectively.

Title V: Administrative cooperation and responsibility for implementation

Provisions under this Title seek to foster close collaboration between the competent authorities in the Member States in order to facilitate the implementation of the above provisions.

Article 56 requires the competent authorities to collaborate and exchange information and for such activities to be organised by a designated 'coordinator'. In addition, Member States are required to establish a single contact point for providing citizens and other Member States with information concerning the recognition of professional qualifications (**Art 57**). **Article 58** provides for a **Committee** on the recognition of professional qualifications that is composed of representatives from the Member States and **Article 59** provides for the appropriate consultation of professional groups by the Committee.

Directive 2013/55: amendments to Directive 2005/36

Directive 2013/55 has amended Directive 2005/36 with updated conditions and procedures. These amendments had to be implemented by 18 January 2016. The amendments, which are intended to make the process of professional recognition easier for migrant professionals, include the following:

- the introduction of a **European Professional Card** (**Arts 4a–4e**);
- provision for greater use of **online tools**;
- recognition of **traineeships** (**Art 55a**, *inter alia*);
- the possibility of **partial access** to a regulated profession in some cases (**Art 4f**);
- **modernised minimum training requirements** for the Chapter III, Title III professions, i.e. doctors, dentists, nurses, midwives, pharmacists, architects and veterinary surgeons;
- provision for **common training frameworks** (**Art 49a**) and **common training tests** (**Art 49b**) to facilitate greater harmonisation of qualifications;
- clarification of the controls that may be exercised with regard to **language requirements** (**Art 53**);
- an **alert mechanism** to let all relevant authorities know when professionals with patient safety implications, or those working with children, have been banned from practising (**Art 56a**).

Directive 13/55 was implemented in the UK by the **European Union (Recognition of Professional Qualifications) Regulations 2015**, which entered into force on 18 December 2016.

11.5.3 Non-EU qualifications

As with most of the Treaty provisions on the free movement of persons, Directive 2005/36 does not cover non-EU nationals or qualifications obtained in a non-EU country. In the following case, the issue was whether the Treaty provisions applied to qualifications obtained outside the EU:

Tawil-Albertini v *Ministre des Affairs Sociales* (Case C-154/93)

Facts:

Mr Tawil-Albertini was a French national who had obtained a dentistry qualification in Lebanon. This qualification was later recognised in Belgium as equivalent to the Belgian dentistry qualification. Mr Tawil-Albertini subsequently applied to the French authorities to practise in France, but his application was refused. The qualifications listed in the sector-specific directive, Directive 78/686 on the mutual recognition of dental qualifications (which has since been repealed and replaced by Directive 2005/36), did not include any qualification obtained outside the EU. However, because his qualification had been recognised as equivalent to the Belgian diploma, and the Belgian diploma was included in the Directive, Mr Tawil-Albertini argued that his qualification was also covered by the Directive.

Ruling:

The Court of Justice held that the mutual recognition of qualifications in dentistry was based on minimum specific levels of competence agreed between all the Member States. Even though one Member State accepted a qualification as equivalent to its own standards it did not follow that this would bind all the other Member States. Only the qualifications listed in the specific Directive were guaranteed to be equivalent.

Significance:

This case established that a Member State is not obliged to recognise a qualification attained in a non-EU country on the basis that it has been recognised by another Member State as equivalent to that country's requirements. This can be compared with the later judgment in *Cavallera* (Case C-311/06, see section 11.5.2) where it was held that the recognition of a qualification by a Member State does not itself provide evidence of training or education and therefore places no obligations on other Member States.

In the following case, the individual concerned had a non-EU qualification, but also had experience within a Member State:

Haim v Kassenzahnarztliche Vereinigung Nordrhein (Case C-319/92)

Facts:

Mr Haim was an Italian national who held a Turkish diploma rather than one of the qualifications specified in Directive 78/686 on the mutual recognition of dentistry qualifications (which has since been repealed and replaced by Directive 2005/36). Nevertheless, he received authorisation to practise as a dentist in Germany. His Turkish qualification had also been recognised as equivalent to the requirements for the practice of dentistry in Belgium. Mr Haim practised in Belgium for eight years, providing services for a social security scheme. He then applied to work on a social security scheme in Germany, but was told that he would have to complete a further two-year training period. His appeal against this decision was rejected, but he then appealed on a point of law to the Bundessozialgericht (Federal Social Court), which referred the matter to the Court of Justice.

Ruling:

The Court of Justice cited the *Vlassopoulou* case (see section 11.5.1) and ruled as follows:

> 28 The competent national authority, in order to verify whether the training period requirement prescribed by the national rules is met, **must take into account the professional experience of the plaintiff** in the main proceedings, including that which he has acquired during his appointment as a dental practitioner of a social security scheme in another Member State.

Significance:
This case established that, when assessing whether a person possesses sufficient qualifications, their professional experience in another Member State must be considered. This is so even when an applicant does not have an EU qualification and even though one Member State's recognition of a qualification does not oblige another Member State to also recognise it, as held in *Tawil-Albertini*.

The following case concerned the extent to which what is now Article 49 TFEU can be relied on in relation to professions that are covered by a harmonising directive:

Hocsman v Ministre de l'Emploi et de la Solidarité (Case C-238/98)

Facts:
Dr Hocsman held a diploma of doctor of medicine awarded in 1976 by a university in Argentina. He acquired Spanish nationality in 1986 and became a French citizen in 1998. During 1980 the Spanish authorities recognised Dr Hocsman's Argentinian qualification as equivalent to the Spanish university degree in medicine and surgery, which allowed him to practise medicine in Spain and train there as a specialist. Due to the fact that he was not a Spanish national at the time of his specialist training, the qualification he was subsequently awarded (specialist in urology) was an academic title. When he became a Spanish national in 1986 he obtained authorisation to practise as a specialist in urology.

In 1990 he entered France and held various urology posts. He applied to be registered to practise general medicine, but in 1997 the French authorities rejected his application on the ground that his Argentinian qualification did not entitle him to practise general medicine in France. Dr Hocsman issued proceedings in a French court to have that decision annulled.

Although there was a harmonising directive which applied to medicine (Directive 93/16, which has since been repealed and replaced by Directive 2005/36), Dr Hocsman's Argentinian qualification was not included. The French court referred the case to the Court of Justice pursuant to the former Article 234 EC Treaty (now Art 267 TFEU) and asked, *inter alia*, whether a person could rely on the former Article 43 EC Treaty (now Art 49 TFEU) where there was a directive covering the relevant profession.

Ruling:
The Court of Justice first referred to its judgments in *Vlassopoulou* (Case 340/89, see section 11.5.1), *Haim* (see above) and *Bobadilla* (Case 234/97, see section 11.5.1) to affirm that:

> 23 ... it is settled that the authorities of a Member State to whom an application has been made by a Community [i.e. Union] national for authorisation to practise a profession access to which depends, under national law, on the possession of a diploma or professional qualification, or on periods of practical experience, **must take into consideration all the diplomas, certificates and other evidence of formal qualifications of the person concerned and his relevant experience**, by comparing the specialised knowledge and abilities so certified and that experience with the knowledge and qualifications required by the national rules.

The Court then referred to its ruling in *Thieffry* (Case 71/76, see section 11.5.1) to affirm that freedom of establishment as provided for by Article 52 EC Treaty (now Art 49 TFEU) can be relied upon where a Member State's laws or practices allow for it, even when no applicable directives have been adopted under Article 57 EC Treaty (now Art 53 TFEU).

The Court highlighted the experience attained by Dr Hocsman and concluded as follows:

> 39 It is for the national court, or if appropriate the competent national authorities, to assess in the light of all the evidence in the case and the above considerations, whether Dr Hocsman's

diploma is to be accepted as equivalent to the corresponding French diploma. In particular, it will have to be considered whether recognition in Spain of Dr Hocsman's diploma from Argentina as equivalent to the Spanish university degree in medicine and surgery was given on the basis of criteria comparable to those intended, in the context of Directive 93/16 [which has since been repealed and replaced by Directive 2005/36], to ensure that Member States may rely on the quality of the diplomas in medicine awarded by the other Member States.

Significance:

In this case, the Court of Justice held that even though there was a harmonising directive covering medical training diplomas, Dr Hocsman could still rely directly on what is now Article 49 TFEU. In this instance, the principles espoused by the Court in its previous case law have to be applied to ascertain if Dr Hocsman's qualifications and experience are sufficient to warrant recognition of his professional qualifications.

Additionally, while the recognition of his Argentinian qualification in Spain does not oblige France to also recognise it, the Court nevertheless stated that the recognition by another Member State of Dr Hocsman's diploma as equivalent to one included within the harmonising directive should be considered.

The following case concerned the position of a sector-specific directive on training that had been conducted outside of the Union:

Tennah-Durez (Case C-110/01)

Facts:

Dr Tennah-Durez carried out part of her doctor's training in Algeria. This training was subsequently recognised in Belgium, where, after one more year of study, she was awarded a basic medical diploma. She then undertook a further two years of study, after which she was authorised to practise as a general medical practitioner in Belgium.

Dr Tennah-Durez sought to have her diploma recognised in France, but she was denied authorisation to practise on the basis that her medical training had not been received mainly in a Member State. She contested this decision before the Conseil d'État (Council of State, France), which referred the matter to the Court of Justice.

Ruling:

The Court of Justice began by stating that the former, sector-specific Directive 93/16 (which has since been repealed and replaced by Directive 2005/36) established automatic and unconditional recognition of certain diplomas issued by Member States, requiring Member States to acknowledge their equivalence without being able to demand that the persons concerned comply with conditions other than those expressly stipulated.

Concerning the extent to which medical training may consist of training received in a non-member country, the Court held that the Directive did **not** require all or any particular part of that training to be provided at a university of a Member State or under the supervision of such a university, and that neither did the general scheme of the Directive preclude medical training leading to a diploma, certificate or other evidence of a medical qualification eligible for automatic recognition from being received **partly** outside the EU. According to the Court, what mattered was not where the training had been provided but whether it complied with the qualitative and quantitative training requirements laid down by the former Directive 93/16. Moreover, responsibility for ensuring that the training requirements, both qualitative and quantitative, laid down by the former Directive 93/16 were fully complied with fell wholly on the competent authority of the Member State awarding the diploma. A diploma thus awarded amounted to a '**doctor's passport**', enabling the holder to work as a doctor throughout the EU without the professional qualification attested to by the diploma being open to challenge in a host Member State, except in specific circumstances laid down by Union law.

Consequently, provided the competent authority in the Member State awarding the diploma was in a position to validate medical training received in a non-EU country and to conclude on that basis that the training duly complied with the training requirements laid down by the former Directive 93/16, that training could be taken into account in deciding whether to award a doctor's diploma. In that respect, **the proportion of the training carried out in a non-EU country, and in particular the fact that the major part of the training was received in such a country, was immaterial**. Indeed, the former Directive 93/16 contained no reference or even allusion to such a criterion. Moreover, a requirement for training to have been received mainly within the EU would undermine legal certainty, since such a concept was open to varying interpretations.

As for the extent to which national authorities were bound by a certificate confirming that the diploma conformed with the requirements of the former directive, the Court held that the system of automatic and unconditional recognition would be seriously jeopardised if it was open to Member States at their discretion to question the merits of a decision taken by the competent institution of another Member State to award the diploma. However, where new evidence cast serious doubt on the authenticity of the diploma presented, or as to its conformity with the applicable legislation, it was legitimate for Member States to require from the competent institution of the Member State which awarded the diploma confirmation of its authenticity.

Significance:

This case established that, where an individual possesses a diploma awarded by the competent authority of a Member State, the place where training towards that diploma was received is immaterial. The essential difference between this case and those of **Tawil-Albertini** and **Hocsman**, then, is that those cases concerned the *recognition* of a *non-EU* diploma by another Member State, whereas this case concerned the *award* of an *EU* diploma by another Member State. While the former does not attest to any training or education by itself, the latter does, and must be afforded recognition as such in line with the relevant directive.

All of the above cases concerned EU nationals who had obtained all or part of their qualifications in non-EU countries. It should be noted, however, that non-EU nationals who are established in the EU have no rights of recognition or permission to practise under Union law. This is so even if they have obtained their professional qualification in one of the Member States and their qualification is listed in one of the sector-specific directives.

11.5.4 The internal situation

From the wording of Article 49 TFEU there would appear to be a limitation in that it cannot be relied upon by a person seeking to establish themself in the Member State of their nationality (although see ***Neri*** (Case C-153/02), below). A national may therefore be disadvantaged where they obtain a qualification in another Member State and then seek to have it recognised in their home Member State.

In ***Knoors* v *Secretary of State for Economic Affairs*** (Case 115/78), the Court of Justice held that what is now Article 49 TFEU could be relied upon in a person's home Member State in respect of a qualification they had obtained in another Member State. However, the following case suggested that there were limitations to this. The case of ***Ministère Public* v *Auer*** (Case 136/78) concerned a French citizen who obtained a veterinary qualification in Italy, but had been refused authorisation to practise in France on the basis that the Italian qualification was not equivalent. At the time, there was no harmonising directive in force. The Court of Justice held that what is now Article 49 TFEU 'concerns only – and can concern only – in each Member State the nationals of other Member States' (para 20). The Court therefore held that the existence of a directive recognising the foreign qualification was essential and that Article 49 TFEU by itself could not assist nationals established in the Member State of their nationality.

Following the Court of Justice's judgment in ***Auer***, the Council adopted Directives 78/1026 and 78/1027 (both of which have since been repealed and replaced by Directive 2005/36) which governed veterinary qualifications, thus recognising the qualification Mr Auer had obtained. Subsequently, the case came before the Court of Justice for a second time, but on this occasion Mr Auer was able to rely on the directives (***Auer* v *Ministère Public*** (Case 271/82)).

Most situations involving a **regulated** profession will now be covered by Directive 2005/36 and therefore reliance solely on Article 49 TFEU will not be necessary. Accordingly, an individual may rely upon the relevant directive in the Member State of their nationality with regard to qualifications and training obtained in another Member State. However, in ***Bobadilla*** (Case C-234/97, see section 11.5.1), the Court of Justice cast doubt on whether or not the first ***Auer*** case (Case 136/78) was correctly decided. In this case, the Court of Justice held as follows:

> . . . if a national of a Member State, owing to the fact that he has lawfully resided in the territory of another Member State and has acquired a professional qualification there, finds himself with regard to his State of origin in a situation which may be assimilated to that of a migrant worker, he must also be entitled to enjoy the rights and freedoms guaranteed by the Treaty. [para 30]

In the above case, the Court of Justice was undecided whether or not the former Directives 89/48 and 92/51 (both of which have since been repealed and replaced by Directive 2005/36) applied, and therefore it decided the case on the basis that they did not. It held that even if there was no directive applicable to the test of equivalence of the applicant's qualifications, she could rely on the general principles of Union law.

The above applies only where there is some 'Union element'. In the ***Bobadilla*** case, the Union element was the completion of an educational course and training in another Member State. If there is no Union element present then this will constitute a wholly internal situation and Union law will not provide a remedy (see ***Nino and Others*** (Cases 54 and 91/88 and 14/89)). This is broadly in line with the Court's judgment in ***Surinder Singh*** (Case C-370/90), where it ruled that a home Member State's refusal to apply EU rights to a national who had exercised their free movement rights constituted an unacceptable disincentive to exercising those rights (see section 9.2.1, page 332).

In the following case, the Court of Justice was faced with a different issue:

Neri (Case C-153/02)

Facts:

Ms Neri intended to commence a course that was arranged by a private company to be conducted in Italy, but that would entitle her to a diploma awarded by a UK university. However, she discovered that an Italian administrative practice only afforded recognition to diplomas awarded by universities in other Member States to Italian students if they had attended courses in the States in which the diploma was issued. The matter was referred to the Court of Justice by a national court, which questioned whether the administrative practice was contrary to, *inter alia*, freedom of establishment.

Ruling:

The Court of Justice held that the Italian refusal to recognise the diplomas was incompatible with the former Article 43 EC Treaty (now Art 49 TFEU). In the view of the Court, the former Article 43 EC Treaty (now Art 49 TFEU) required the elimination of restrictions on freedom of establishment, whether they prohibited the exercise of that freedom, impeded it or rendered it less attractive. The Court stated that non-recognition in Italy of degrees likely to facilitate the access of students to the employment market was likely to deter students from attending such courses and thus seriously hinder the pursuit by the educational establishment concerned of its economic activity in that Member State.

The Italian government sought to justify the restriction by the objective of ensuring high standards of university education. However, as the non-recognition of diplomas related solely to degrees awarded to Italian nationals, the measure did not appear suitable for attaining the objective of ensuring high standards of university education. Similarly, precluding any assessment and, consequently, any possibility of recognition of degrees did not comply with the requirement of proportionality and went beyond what was necessary to ensure the objective pursued. Therefore the restriction could not be justified.

Significance:

As with ***Tennah-Durez*** (Case C-110/01, **see section 11.5.3**), it was found in this case that the place where the studies were carried out was immaterial to the question of whether or not the resultant qualifications should be recognised. A Member State was therefore obliged, if not to recognise automatically, at least to assess the equivalence of qualifications obtained by their own nationals within their own territory, where the qualifications had been awarded by an institution established in another Member State.

CHAPTER SUMMARY

Concepts of freedom of establishment and freedom to provide services

- **Article 49 TFEU** prohibits restrictions on the **freedom of establishment** of EU citizens within Member States of which they are not nationals.
- An individual is 'established' in a Member State when there is **stable and continuous participation in the economic life** of that Member State (***Gebhard***).

- **Article 56 TFEU** prohibits restrictions on the **freedom to provide services** in a Member State of individuals or undertakings that are established in another Member State.
- The provision of services must be for **remuneration** (*Humbel*).

Rights of service providers

- **Directive 2006/123** requires Member States to **simplify administrative procedures** and **remove administrative barriers** to the freedom of establishment and the freedom to provide services.
- **Directive 2004/38** provides **rights of residence** for service providers, whose family members may also be able to derive rights from the Treaty provisions (*Carpenter*).
- **Directive 96/71** sets out the rights of **posted workers**.
- **Discriminatory restrictions** on freedom of establishment or the freedom to provide services may be justified on grounds of public policy, public security or public health (**Arts 52** and **56 TFEU**).
- **Non-discriminatory restrictions** may be objectively justified by **overriding reasons** relating to the public interest, provided they are **appropriate and proportionate** (*Gebhard*).

Rights of recipients of services

- **Article 56 TFEU** applies to the freedom to *receive* services (*Luisi and Carbone*).
- Almost any EU citizen in another Member State may be classified as a recipient of services (*Cowan*).
- **Directive 2006/123** stipulates requirements that Member States must enforce against service providers for the protection of service recipients.
- Service recipients are entitled to residence rights under **Directive 2004/38** and social advantages under **Directive 883/2004**.

Recognition of professional qualifications

- Under **Article 49 TFEU**, **equivalent qualifications** issued by the competent national authorities of a Member State must be recognised (*Thieffry*; *Patrick*) and professional experience acquired within another Member State must be considered (*Vlassopoulou*; *Haim*).
- **Article 53(1) TFEU** provides for the adoption of directives for the mutual recognition of qualifications, several of which have been amalgamated within **Directive 2005/36**.
- **Directive 2005/36**, as amended by Directive 2013/55, sets out the conditions for the recognition of qualifications in the **regulated professions**.

Chapter 12
Free movement of goods

Learning objectives

At the end of this chapter you should understand:

1 The Treaty provisions that provide for the free movement of goods.

2 The scope of the prohibition on customs duties and charges having equivalent effect, including the exception regarding the provision of services.

3 The prohibition on internal taxation that discriminates against imports from other Member States or that affords indirect protection to domestic products.

4 The prohibition on quantitative restrictions and measures having equivalent effect, including the difference between distinctly applicable measures, indistinctly applicable dual-burden measures and indistinctly applicable equal burden measures.

5 When quantitative restrictions and measures having equivalent effect may be permitted under Union law, including the Article 36 TFEU exemptions and the **Cassis** rule of reason.

6 How Brexit may affect the free movement of goods between the UK and the EU

Key terms and concepts

Familiarity with the following terms will be helpful for understanding this chapter:

Customs duty – a charge that is imposed on goods that cross a border; a financial barrier to the free movement of goods

Distinctly applicable measure – a measure that applies to imported or exported goods, but not to domestic goods

Domestic goods – goods that are marketed in the same country in which they were produced

Dual-burden rule – a measure that requires an exporting manufacturer to meet product requirements in the country of sale in addition to requirements in the country of manufacture; measures relating to the characteristics of a product or its packaging

Equal-burden rule – a measure that affects the sale or marketing of domestic and imported products equally; measures relating to selling arrangements or product use

Excise duty – a charge that is imposed on a manufacturer of goods

Harmonising measure – a measure that establishes a Union-wide standard or 'essential requirements' in relation to a particular type of product

Indistinctly applicable measure – a measure that, *prima facie*, applies without distinction to both imported or exported and domestic goods

Quantitative restriction – a ban or a restriction on the import or export of certain goods between Member States; a non-financial barrier to the free movement of goods

Tariff – a tax on imports or exports

12.1 Introduction to the free movement of goods

Objective 1

The free movement of goods is one of the essential elements of the internal market of the European Union, along with the free movement of persons, services and capital (Art 26(2) TFEU). The elimination of any restrictions to the free movement of goods is central to the creation of an internal market within the territory of the Union, which is one of the main objectives of the Union (Art 3 TEU). The aim is to achieve a single, unobstructed market in products, so that goods can be traded *between* Member States as easily as they are traded *within* Member States. Producers therefore benefit from the opening up of new markets, which creates the possibility of larger and thus cheaper product runs, while consumers benefit from a far wider choice in products and lower prices.

This chapter considers the prohibitions on financial barriers (customs duties and discriminatory or protectionist internal taxation) and non-financial barriers (**quantitative restrictions**) to the free movement of goods. These prohibitions form part of a larger strategy to free up trade and to prevent Member States from adopting both overtly and covertly protectionist policies.

Tariff barriers to trade between Member States have long since been removed. Customs duties and quantitative restrictions were all removed by 1 July 1968. Border controls on goods were then swept away by the Single European Act, which entered into force in 1987. Much still remains to be done, however, to achieve a truly unobstructed market in goods.

The barriers that still persist generally take the form of differing standards and a whole range of national measures aimed at consumer and environmental protection. Until these different standards are harmonised it would be very difficult for a manufacturer in one Member State to make a product which they know with confidence they will be allowed to sell to the approximately 450 million consumers living within the 27 Member States of the EU. In the long term, these problems are being addressed by the creation of EU-wide standards through the adoption of harmonising directives and technical standards for a huge range of products. Until this expansive and ever-expanding task is achieved, however, producers have to rely on the provisions of the TFEU, and the intervention of the Court of Justice, to ensure that national rules do not have the effect of excluding or disadvantaging their products.

Although it also remains one of the objectives of the TFEU to harmonise rates of indirect taxation (Art 113 TFEU), little progress has been made in this area, and obstacles to the creation of a genuine undivided market continue to be caused by different rates of tax and other charges levied on goods by the Member States. The TFEU attempts to address these problems by the provisions of Articles 28 and 30 TFEU, which prohibit customs duties on imports and exports and all charges having equivalent effect, and the prohibition of discriminatory internal taxation pursuant to Article 110 TFEU.

Articles 28 and **30 TFEU**, which relate to customs duties and charges having an equivalent effect are considered first in this chapter. This is followed by consideration of **Article 110 TFEU**, which relates to discriminatory internal taxation. Then, **Articles 34–36 TFEU**, which relate to quantitative restrictions and measures having an equivalent effect to quantitative restrictions, are examined in detail. A final section briefly considers the possible outcomes of Brexit in relation to the free movement of goods. Before these in-depth sections, however, an overview of the relevant primary legislation is provided.

12.1.1 Primary legislation

Customs duties and charges having equivalent effect

Article 28(1) TFEU (which is practically unchanged from the former Art 23(1) EC Treaty) provides as follows:

> The Union shall comprise a **customs union** which shall cover all trade in goods and which shall involve the prohibition between Member States of customs duties on imports and exports and of all charges having equivalent effect, and the adoption of a **common customs tariff** in their relations with non-EU countries.

Article 30 TFEU (which is identical to the former Art 25 EC Treaty) then provides as follows:

▶ See Figure 12.1 in section 12.2.4 (page 521) for a flowchart which illustrates the application of Article 30 TFEU

> Customs duties on imports and exports and charges having equivalent effect shall be prohibited between Member States. This prohibition shall also apply to customs duties of a fiscal nature.

Article 30 TFEU is vertically directly effective (see, for example, *Van Gend en Loos* v *Nederlandse Administratie der Belastingen* (Case 26/62)). Furthermore, in *Édouard Dubois & Fils SA and Général Cargo Services SA* v *Garonor Exploitation SA* (Case 16/94), the Court of Justice suggested that Article 30 TFEU could be horizontally directly effective, i.e. could prohibit charges having an equivalent effect to a **customs duty** that are imposed by private undertakings.

▶ The principle of direct effect is explained in section 8.2

Internal taxation

Article 110 TFEU (which is identical to the former Art 90 EC Treaty) prohibits taxation on goods within the Union that is discriminatory or protectionist in relation to domestic products. The text of Article 110 is as follows:

> No Member State shall impose, directly or indirectly, on the products of other Member States any internal taxation of any kind in excess of that imposed directly or indirectly on similar domestic products.
>
> Furthermore, no Member State shall impose on the products of other Member States any internal taxation of such a nature as to afford indirect protection to other products.

▶ See Figure 12.2 in section 12.3.2 (page 534) for a flowchart which illustrates the application of Art 110 TFEU

Article 110 TFEU is directly effective (see *Alfons Lütticke GmbH* v *Hauptzollamt Saarlouis* (Case 57/65)).

Quantitative restrictions

▶ See Figure 12.4 in section 12.5.2 (page 581) for a flowchart which illustrates the application of Article 34 TFEU

Article 34 TFEU (which is worded identically to the previous Art 28 EC Treaty) provides that:

> Quantitative **restrictions on imports** and all measures having equivalent effect shall be **prohibited** between Member States.

The prohibition of restrictions on **imports** in Article 34 TFEU is reflected by a matching prohibition on **export** restrictions in **Article 35 TFEU** (previously Art 29 EC Treaty). Both prohibitions are, however, qualified by the right of Member States to impose limited restrictions on trade, if they can justify them under the criteria laid down in **Article 36 TFEU** (previously Art 30 EC Treaty), or in some cases under the **Cassis** rule of reason (see below). Article 36 thus provides as follows:

> The provisions of Articles 34 and 35 shall not preclude prohibitions or restrictions on imports, exports or goods in transit justified on grounds of **public morality, public policy or public security**; the protection of **health and life** of humans, animals or plants; the protection of **national treasures** possessing artistic, historic or archaeological value; or the protection of **industrial and commercial property**. . . .

Articles 34–36 TFEU attempt to strike a balance between achieving a genuine free and competitive market in goods on the one hand and the recognition of the need, in some circumstances, to protect essential public interests on the other. Much of the jurisprudence of the Court of Justice has been devoted to consideration of the extent to which such national measures infringe the relevant provisions of the Treaty or fall within the permitted derogations. The process of harmonising national standards of consumer and environmental protection, through a programme of standardising directives for goods throughout the Union, is part of a programme to reduce the need for such national exceptions to the general Union right of free movement of goods.

12.2 Customs duties and charges having equivalent effect (Arts 28–30 TFEU)

12.2.1 The customs union

Objective 2

A customs duty is a charge determined on the basis of a tariff, specifying a charge to be paid by an importer of goods. Customs duties have the effect of making imported goods more expensive than rival **domestic goods** and are thus protectionist measures.

The Union bound itself, in what is now **Article 28(1) TFEU**, to the maintenance of 'a customs union which shall cover all trade in goods and which shall involve the prohibition between Member States of customs duties on imports and exports and of all charges having equivalent effect, and the adoption of a common customs tariff in their relations with third [non-EU] countries'. The object of this provision is to create not only an internal free trade area within the Union, where border charges and fiscal barriers are eliminated when goods cross an internal border, but also a common external tariff. Goods entering the Union from a non-EU country are therefore subject to the same external tariff, irrespective of where they enter the Union. Such goods are then considered to be in free circulation within the Union and come under the free movement provisions.

Article 28(2) TFEU (which is practically unchanged from the former Art 23(2) EC Treaty) provides as follows:

> The provisions of Article 30 and of Chapter 2 of this Title shall apply to products originating in Member States and to products coming from third countries [i.e. non-EU countries] which are in free circulation in Member States.

Article 29 TFEU (which is identical to the former Art 24 EC Treaty) then clarifies as follows:

> Products coming from a third [non-EU] country shall be considered to be in free circulation in a Member State if the import formalities have been complied with and any customs duties or charges having equivalent effect which are payable have been levied in that Member State, and if they have not benefited from a total or partial drawback of such duties or charges.

These provisions establish that once goods have lawfully entered the Union from a non-EU country, with all import formalities complied with and duties and charges paid, the provisions of Article 30 TFEU, along with Articles 34–36 TFEU, will apply. Thus, all goods that are legally within the territory of the Union can cross internal borders freely, regardless of where they were originally produced.

> The 'Italian art' case is also considered in section 12.2.3 (page 518) in relation to the definition of a charge having an equivalent effect to a customs duty

12.2.2 Scope of the term 'goods'

In order to understand Union law on the free movement of goods, it is necessary to understand what the term 'goods' encompasses. The scope of this term was established by the Court of Justice in the following case:

Commission v Italy (Case 7/68) – 'Italian art'

Facts:

Italy imposed a tax on the export of articles of an 'artistic, historical, archaeological or ethnographic nature'. The Commission brought infringement proceedings against Italy pursuant to what is now Article 258 TFEU (Art 169 EEC Treaty at the time) alleging this tax was in breach of what is now Article 30 TFEU (Art 16 EEC Treaty the time). Italy argued, *inter alia*, that the tax was being levied on 'cultural articles' which were being exported and such articles should not be regarded as goods.

Ruling:

The Court of Justice rejected the argument that cultural articles were not goods and held as follows:

> Under Article 9 of the Treaty [now Art 28 TFEU] the Community [i.e. Union] is based on a customs union 'which shall cover all trade in goods'. By goods, within the meaning of that provision, there must be understood **products which can be valued in money** and which are **capable, as such, of forming the subject of commercial transactions**.
>
> The articles covered by the Italian law, whatever may be the characteristics which distinguish them from other types of merchandise, nevertheless resemble the latter, inasmuch as they can be valued in money and so be the subject of commercial transactions. That view corresponds with the scheme of the Italian law itself, which fixes the tax in question in proportion to the value of the articles concerned.

Significance:

This case established that all products which **can be valued in money**, and can therefore be the **subject of commercial transactions**, are 'goods' for the purposes of what are now Articles 28 and 30 TFEU.

In the above case, the Court of Justice established a very wide scope of what constitutes 'goods'. In the following case, which is also considered in Chapter 11 in section 11.2.2, the Court was required to distinguish the trade in goods from the provision of services:

Jägerskiöld v Gustafsson (Case C-97/98)

Facts:

As already noted, Mr Gustafsson acquired a fishing licence that granted him permission to fish with a spinning rod, even in private waters. He proceeded to fish in waters belonging to Mr Jägerskiöld, who argued that he could not do so without his permission. In an action before a national court, Mr Jägerskiöld argued that the Finnish law, on which the right to fish with a rod was based, was contrary to the Union rules concerning the free movement of goods or to those relating to the freedom to provide services.

Ruling:

The Court of Justice considered whether fishing rights or permits could be considered 'goods'. It first referred to its judgment in **Commission v Italy (Re Italian art)**, where it defined goods as products which can be valued in money and which are capable of forming the subject of commercial transactions. In that case, however, the fact that the articles in question were 'products' was not disputed. The Court also noted that not all things that can be valued in money and are capable of being the subject of commercial transactions will necessarily fall within the scope of the Treaty provisions on the free movement of goods. To demonstrate this, the Court pointed to Directive 88/361, which provides that shares and bonds come under the free movement of capital rather than goods, and its judgment in **Schindler**, which held that the organisation of lotteries comes under the free movement of services.

With regard to fishing permits, the Court then held as follows:

> 36 ... The activity consisting of making fishing waters available to third parties, for consideration [i.e. payment] and upon certain conditions, so that they can fish there **constitutes a provision of services** which is covered by ... [Art 56 TFEU] if it has a cross-frontier character. The fact that those rights or those permits are set down in documents which, as such, may be the subject of trade is not sufficient to bring them within the scope of the provisions of the Treaty relating to the free movement of goods.

In this instance, as noted in Chapter 11, the Treaty provisions on the free movement of services were not held to apply either, as there was no cross-border character to the dispute.

Significance:

This case suggested that a product that can be valued in money and can therefore be the subject of commercial transactions does **not** come under the free movement of goods if it could be dealt with more appropriately under a different area of the Treaties. As an intangible right rather than a tangible product, fishing permits were found to be within the scope of the free movement of services.

The distinction between goods and services was then further considered by the Court of Justice in the following case:

Stadtgemeinde Frohnleiten and Gemeindebetriebe Frohnleiten GmbH v Bundesminister für Land- und Forstwirtschaft, Umwelt und Wasserwirtschaft (Case C-221/06)

Facts:

Under a national law in Austria, a tax (known as the Altlastenbeitrag) was applied to the disposal of waste at waste disposal sites, unless the waste in question was deposited in the course of safeguarding or rehabilitating either suspected contaminated sites or disused hazardous sites. Such sites needed to have been entered in a national register, which meant that the exemption only applied to waste removed from suspected contaminated and disused hazardous sites in Austria.

In 2001 and 2002, shipments of waste from a contaminated site in Italy were transported to and deposited at the municipal waste disposal site at Frohnleiten, Austria. This was authorised by the Austrian authorities, but the question then arose as to whether the tax should be applied or whether doing so would violate what is now Article 110 TFEU, which prohibits discriminatory internal taxation.

> **Ruling:**
>
> *Inter alia*, Austria argued that, as the tax was to be paid by the operator of the disposal site, it pertained to the provision of services rather than the free movement of goods. The Court first noted its judgment in **Commission v Belgium** (Case C-2/90), where it had determined that waste is to be regarded as 'goods' and subject to the free movement provisions. The Court of Justice then disagreed with Austria's position and ruled as follows:
>
>> 43 ... a charge which is imposed not on products as such, but on the specific activity of an undertaking in connection with products and which is calculated according, inter alia, to the weight of the products at issue, falls within the scope of Article 90 EC [now Art 110 TFEU] and, **in so far as it has an immediate effect on the cost of national and imported products**, must be applied in a manner which is not discriminatory to imported products.
>
> The Court therefore held that the Altlastenbeitrag was an internal tax on goods, firstly because the quantity and nature of the waste was taken into account in the calculation of the tax, and secondly because the operator of the disposal site, having paid the tax, could pass the cost on through their charges to the parties depositing the waste. Therefore, as the deposit of waste was a commercial transaction the cost of which was affected by the Altlastenbeitrag, the Altlastenbeitrag came under what is now Article 110 TFEU. The Court concluded that the exclusion of waste originating from other Member States from the exemption from the Altlastenbeitrag was discrimination contrary to what is now Article 110 TFEU.
>
> **Significance:**
>
> This case further developed where the line falls between the free movement of goods and the free movement of services. While in **Jägerskiöld**, the issuance of a fishing permit was a service, as the cost of the permit was unrelated to any goods (i.e. the fish that *may* be caught), in this case a tax on the disposal of waste was directly connected to the goods in question (i.e. the quantity of waste that was effectively being traded), and **had an effect on the cost of such goods**. Therefore, a tax on waste disposal was found to affect the free movement of goods.

The above case also considered the distinction between a charge having equivalent effect to a customs duty and a measure of internal taxation, finding that the charge in this case was the latter as it was applied regardless of whether the waste had crossed a national frontier. This distinction between customs charges and internal taxation is examined further below in section 12.2.5.

12.2.3 Duties and charges having equivalent effect (CEEs)

Article 30 TFEU prohibits not only customs duties but also charges having an equivalent effect to a customs duty (**CEEs**). If this phrase had been omitted, Member States could quite easily have avoided the prohibition by simply renaming the charges that they imposed. The Court of Justice considered the definition of CEEs in **Commission v Luxembourg and Belgium** (Joined Cases 2/62 and 3/62), where it held that:

> A charge having equivalent effect within the meaning of Articles 9 and 12 [now Arts 28 and 30 TFEU], whatever it is called and whatever its mode of application, may be regarded as

12.2 CUSTOMS DUTIES AND CHARGES HAVING EQUIVALENT EFFECT (ARTS 28–30 TFEU)

> The 'statistical data' case is also considered in section 12.2.4 (page 520) in relation to the provision of services exception

a duty imposed unilaterally either at the time of importation or subsequently, and which, if imposed specifically upon a product imported from a Member State to the exclusion of a similar domestic product, has, by altering its price, the same effect upon the free movement of products as a customs duty.

The scope of CEEs was then further developed by the Court of Justice in the following case:

Commission v Italy (Case 24/68) – 'statistical data'

Facts:

Italy imposed a levy on goods which were exported to other Member States to finance the collecting of statistical data relating to trade patterns. The Commission challenged the legality of such a charge pursuant to its powers under what is now Article 258 TFEU.

Ruling:

The Court of Justice held as follows:

8. The extension of the prohibition of customs duties to charges having an equivalent effect is intended to supplement the prohibition against obstacles to trade created by such duties by increasing its efficiency. The use of these two complementary concepts thus tends, in trade between Member States, to avoid the imposition of any pecuniary charge on goods circulating within the Community [i.e. Union] by virtue of the fact that they cross a national border.

9. Thus, in order to ascribe to a charge an effect equivalent to a customs duty, it is important to consider this effect in the light of the objectives of the Treaty, in the Parts, Titles and Chapters in which Articles 9, 12, 13 and 16 [now Articles 28 and 30 TFEU] are to be found, particularly in relation to the free movement of goods.

   Consequently, **any pecuniary charge, however small and whatever its designation and mode of application, which is imposed unilaterally on domestic or foreign goods by reason of the fact that they cross a frontier, and which is not a customs duty in the strict sense, constitutes a charge having equivalent effect** within the meaning of Articles 9, 12, 13 and 16 of the Treaty [Articles 28 and 30 TFEU], **even if it is not imposed for the benefit of the State, is not discriminatory or protective in effect and if the product on which the charge is imposed is not in competition with any domestic product**.

10. It follows from all the provisions referred to and from their relationship with the other provisions of the Treaty that **the prohibition of new customs duties or charges having equivalent effect, linked to the principle of the free movement of goods, constitutes a fundamental rule which, without prejudice to the other provisions of the Treaty, does not permit of any exceptions**.

Significance:

This case established a broad scope for CEEs and indicated that the Court would allow few exceptions to their prohibition. It also reiterated the principle established in ***Commission v Luxembourg and Belgium*** that the 'designation' (i.e. what it is called) and 'mode of application' of a charge are irrelevant to the question of whether or not it is a CEE.

> The 'Italian art' case is also considered above in section 12.2.3 (page 514) in relation to the definition of 'goods'

As suggested by the above case, the Court of Justice has determined that the application of Article 30 TFEU depends on the **effect** of a duty or charge. The purpose of the duty or charge – i.e. the reason it is imposed – cannot exclude it from the scope of Article 30. This can be illustrated by returning to the *Italian art* case:

Commission v Italy (Case 7/68) – 'Italian art'

Facts:

As noted above, Italy imposed a tax on the export of articles of an 'artistic, historical, archaeological or ethnographic nature'. The Commission brought infringement proceedings against Italy, alleging this tax was in breach of what is now Article 30 TFEU (Art 16 EEC Treaty at the time). Italy argued, *inter alia*, that the purpose of the tax in question was not to raise revenue, but rather to protect the artistic, historical and archaeological heritage of the country.

Ruling:

Italy's argument was rejected by the Court of Justice, which held as follows:

Article 16 of the Treaty [now Art 30 TFEU] prohibits the collection in dealings between Member States of any customs duty on exports and of any charge having an equivalent effect, that is to say, any charge which, by altering the price of an article exported, has the same restrictive effect on the free circulation of that article as a customs duty. This provision makes **no distinction based on the purpose of the duties and charges** the abolition of which it requires.

It is **not** necessary to analyse the concept of the nature of fiscal systems on which the defendant bases its argument upon this point, for the provisions of the section of the Treaty concerning the elimination of customs duties between the Member States exclude the retention of customs duties and charges having equivalent effect **without distinguishing between those which are and those which are not of a fiscal nature**.

The disputed tax falls within Article 16 [now Art 30 TFEU] by reason of the fact that export trade in the goods in question is hindered by the pecuniary burden which it imposes on the price of the exported articles.

Significance:

This demonstrates that it is the **effect** of the tax and not its purpose which is of prime importance. To have decided otherwise would have considerably weakened the effect of what are now Articles 28 and 30 TFEU and therefore compromised the genuine free movement of goods.

The principle that it was not necessary for a charge to be levied for protective purposes in order to be prohibited was reaffirmed in *Commission* v *Italy* (Case 24/68 – 'statistical data') and *Sociaal Fonds voor de Diamantarbeiders* v *Sa Ch. Brach-feld & Sons* (Joined Cases 2 and 3/69). In the latter case, the Court explained as follows:

In prohibiting the imposition of customs duties, the Treaty does not distinguish between goods according to whether or not they enter into competition with the products of the importing country. Thus, **the purpose of the abolition of customs barriers is not merely to eliminate their protective nature**, as the Treaty sought on the contrary to give general scope and effect to the rule on elimination of customs duties and charges having equivalent effect **in order to ensure the free movement of goods**. It follows from the system as a whole and from the general and absolute nature of the prohibition of any customs duty applicable to goods moving between Member States that customs duties are prohibited independently of any consideration of the purpose for which they were introduced and the destination of the revenue obtained therefrom. **The justification for this prohibition is based on the fact that** any pecuniary charge – however small – imposed on goods by reason of the fact that they cross a frontier constitutes an obstacle to the movement of such goods.

In *Steinike und Weinlig* (Case 78/76), the Court further clarified as follows:

> Where the conditions which distinguish a charge having an effect equivalent to a customs duty are fulfilled, **the fact that it is applied at the stage of marketing or processing of the product subsequent to its crossing the frontier is irrelevant** when the product is charged solely by reason of its crossing the frontier. [para 29]

The Court has thus established the almost absolute nature of the prohibition on customs duties and charges having equivalent effect. Indeed, the prohibition is only *almost* absolute due to the following exception.

12.2.4 Charges for the provision of a service

The Court of Justice has accepted that a charge should not be regarded as a CEE when it is (i) payment for a **service that is actually rendered** to an importer, (ii) levied for a service that is of **direct and individual benefit** to that importer and (iii) of an **amount that is proportionate** to the cost of providing the service. This exception is illustrated in the following case:

Commission v *Belgium* (Case 132/82) – 'customs warehouses'

Facts:

Union rules allowed imported goods to be given customs clearance at public warehouses located inside a Member State rather than at the border. Belgium levied storage charges on goods which were stored temporarily at such warehouses at the request of the trader concerned. Charges were also levied on imported goods which simply attended the warehouse for customs clearance and were not stored there. The Commission initiated infringement proceedings against Belgium, arguing that these charges were in breach of what are now Articles 28 and 30 TFEU (Arts 9, 12, 13 and 16 EEC Treaty at the time).

Ruling:

Considering whether the disputed storage charges may be classified as CEEs, the Court of Justice held as follows:

> 10 ... It should therefore be noted, in the first place, that **the placing of imported goods in temporary storage in the special stores of public warehouses clearly represents a service rendered to traders**. A decision to deposit the goods there can indeed be taken only at the request of the trader concerned and then ensures their storage without payment of duties, until the trader has decided how they are to be dealt with. Moreover the Commission does not dispute that the placing of goods in temporary storage may legally give rise to the payment of charges commensurate with the service thus rendered.
>
> 11 **However, it appears ... that the storage charges are payable equally when the goods are presented at the public warehouse solely for the completion of customs formalities**, even though they have been exempted from storage and the importer has not requested that they be put in temporary storage.

The Belgian government claimed that the charge was nevertheless for services rendered, as the use of public warehouses was optional (customs clearance could alternatively be completed at the border) and recourse to the warehouses offered certain advantages to importers. The Court rejected this position on the basis that the charge was levied solely in connection with the completion of customs formalities and thus could not be regarded as payment for an additional service actually rendered. In particular, the use of public warehouses for customs formalities and the advantages they presented were the result of a Union scheme to increase the fluidity of the movement of goods and should not therefore be subject to such a charge. However, it was acceptable for a proportionate charge to be levied in instances where storage services were actually provided to importers.

Significance:

This case emphasised that charges may only be permitted for **services actually rendered** to an importer; the fact that storage services were available to all importers did not justify the imposition of the charge upon those who chose not to use that service.

It is clear that an argument that the charge is consideration for a service actually rendered to the importer will be closely scrutinised by the Court. In its decisions, the Court has shown considerable reluctance to accept that a particular charge falls outside of Article 30 TFEU. In *Ford España* v *Spain* (Case 170/88), the Court of Justice said that even if a specific benefit to the person or body paying the charge can be identified, the state imposing the charge will still fall foul of what is now Article 30 TFEU if it cannot be shown that the sum demanded is proportionate to the cost of supplying the benefit. In this case, Ford received a demand for 0.165 per cent of the declared value of cars and other goods imported into Spain. The Spanish government maintained that the sum related to services rendered in connection with clearing the goods through customs. The Court held that, even if a specific benefit conferred on Ford could be shown, the flat-rate way in which the charge was calculated was evidently not fixed according to the cost of the alleged service and was, therefore, a breach of what is now Article 30 TFEU.

> The 'statistical data' case is also considered above in section 12.2.3 (page 517) in relation to the definition of 'goods'

The following case, which was considered above, further illustrates the narrowness with which the Court has interpreted the exception:

Commission v *Italy* (Case 24/68) – 'statistical data'

Facts:

The Italian government had argued that a charge which was imposed at the border constituted payment for the collection of statistical information. It was argued that this information would provide importers with trade patterns and therefore give them a better competitive position in the Italian market.

Ruling:

The Court of Justice noted that the statistical information in question was beneficial to the economy as a whole and to the relevant administrative authorities, as well as to importers and exporters. Therefore, the Court held that:

> Even if the competitive position of importers and exporters were to be particularly improved as a result, the statistics still constitute **an advantage so general, and so difficult to assess**, that the disputed charge cannot be regarded as the consideration [i.e. payment] for a specific benefit actually conferred. [para 16]

Significance:

This case established that the exception cannot be applied to a charge for a service that does not definitively provide an **actual** benefit **directly** to those against whom it is levied. The broad, imprecise and speculative nature of the benefit meant that it did not amount to a service for the purpose of the exception.

Inspection fees

Even where the service provided is more direct, the Court may still be reluctant to rule that the charge amounts to payment for the service rendered. ***Bresciani* v *Amministrazione Italiana delle Finanze*** (Case 87/75) concerned a charge imposed by the Italian authorities for compulsory veterinary and public health inspections carried out on imported raw cowhide. The national court put forward three arguments: (i) the charge was proportionate to the quantity of the goods and not to their value; (ii) individuals were charged no more than required to cover the cost of the service, which was necessitated through their own action of importing products of animal origin, and (iii) although there may be differences in the method and time of its application, the duty at issue is also levied on similar products of domestic origin. The Court dismissed these factors and ruled that the fact that the public health inspections were in the general interest meant that they were **not** a service rendered **directly** to the importer. The cost of such inspections should therefore be borne by the public.

Figure 12.1 Application of Article 30 TFEU

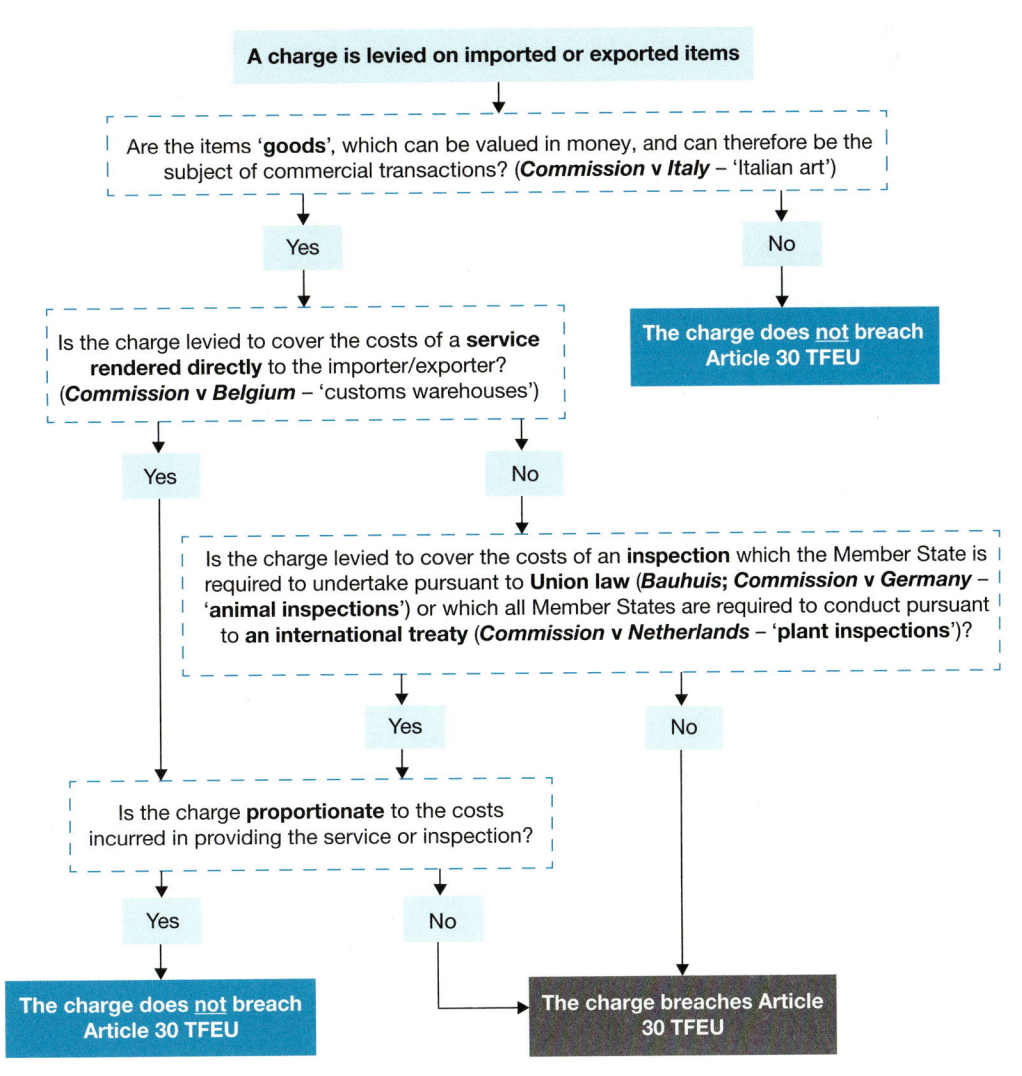

```
A charge is levied on imported or exported items
                        ↓
Are the items 'goods', which can be valued in money, and can therefore be the
subject of commercial transactions? (Commission v Italy – 'Italian art')
            ↓                                        ↓
           Yes                                       No
            ↓                                        ↓
Is the charge levied to cover the costs of a      The charge does not breach
service rendered directly to the importer/         Article 30 TFEU
exporter? (Commission v Belgium –
'customs warehouses')
       ↓            ↓
      Yes          No
                    ↓
         Is the charge levied to cover the costs of an inspection which the Member
         State is required to undertake pursuant to Union law (Bauhuis; Commission
         v Germany – 'animal inspections') or which all Member States are required
         to conduct pursuant to an international treaty (Commission v Netherlands –
         'plant inspections')?
                 ↓                          ↓
                Yes                         No
                 ↓
Is the charge proportionate to the costs
incurred in providing the service or inspection?
       ↓                ↓
      Yes              No
       ↓                ↓                           ↓
The charge does not breach     The charge breaches Article 30 TFEU
Article 30 TFEU
```

Even where Union law **permits** an inspection to be undertaken by the state, the national authorities cannot recover the cost from the importers (see *Commission* v *Belgium* (Case 314/82)). However, if Union law **requires** an inspection to be carried out, the costs of such an inspection *may* be recoverable and will not be caught by the provisions of Article 30 TFEU. This was determined in *Bauhuis* v *Netherlands* (Case 46/76), where there was a challenge to a fee imposed by the Dutch government for veterinary inspections of pigs imported into the Netherlands. Some of the checks were carried out to meet rules of national law, while others were made to meet the requirements of a Union directive. The Court held that, where such checks are mandatory under Union law and are part of the process of ensuring the free movement of goods, such fees are permitted under what is now Article 30 TFEU. The fee must, however, be proportionate to the actual cost of the inspection.

Commission v *Netherlands* (Case 89/76 – '**plant inspections**') concerned plant inspections carried out under the International Plant Protection Convention 1951. This Convention was not Union legislation, but it was binding under international law on those states which were signatories to it. The Convention was designed to liberalise trade by replacing different checks in signatory states with a single check on which all states were able to rely. The Court drew a parallel with *Bauhuis* and held that the charges imposed did not breach what is now Article 30 TFEU.

The Court of Justice clarified the conditions under which the imposition of charges for inspections is compatible with what is now Article 30 TFEU in the following case:

Commission v Germany (Case 18/87) – 'animal inspections'

Facts:

German regional authorities charged certain fees on live animals when they were imported into Germany. These charges were to cover the cost of inspections undertaken pursuant to Directive 81/389. The question before the Court of Justice was whether such charges constituted CEEs and were therefore prohibited.

Ruling:

The Court of Justice determined that the contested fee did not constitute payment for a service rendered to importers, as such importers did not obtain 'a definite specific benefit'. As found in other cases, the inspections served the public interest, rather than the interests of the importers. However, the Court then ruled that fees charged in connection with inspections carried out pursuant to a Union provision may not be classified as CEEs if the following conditions are satisfied:

(a) they **do not exceed the actual costs** of the inspections in connection with which they are charged;

(b) the inspections in question are **obligatory and uniform** for all the products concerned in the Community [i.e. Union];

(c) they are **prescribed by Community [i.e. Union] law** in the general interest of the Community [i.e. Union];

(d) they **promote the free movement of goods**, in particular by neutralising obstacles which could arise from unilateral measures of inspection adopted in accordance with Article 36 of the Treaty [now Art 36 TFEU].

The Court found that the fee at issue satisfied these conditions and was therefore not a CEE prohibited by what is now Article 30 TFEU.

> **Significance:**
>
> This case established four conditions under which inspection fees levied on imported goods are permissible under Union law. These conditions are that the inspections must be **compulsory, promote the free movement of goods** and **be prescribed by Union law**, and the fees may **only cover the costs** of the inspections.

12.2.5 Customs duty or internal taxation?

All customs duties and charges having equivalent effect (CEEs) are prohibited on goods moving within the Union (Arts 28 and 30 TFEU), but internal taxation is permitted, provided it is neither discriminatory nor protectionist (Art 110 TFEU, see below). A charge cannot be both a customs duty/CEE and a provision of internal taxation; the two sets of provisions are **mutually exclusive**. Where a charge is in the form of a tax, therefore, care must be taken to determine whether it is in fact a charge in the nature of a customs duty or CEE, or a provision of internal taxation.

Most charges which have been held to breach the prohibition in Articles 28 and 30 TFEU have been those levied directly and solely on imported or exported goods. However, a breach of Articles 28 and 30 TFEU may also occur if a charge that is applied to imported products is **not** imposed in the same way or determined according to the same criteria as a charge on a similar domestic product. In *Marimex* v *Italian Finance Administration* (Case 29/72), a veterinary inspection fee imposed on imported meat to ensure that it complied with national health standards was also imposed on domestic meat, but the inspections were conducted by different bodies applying different criteria to fix the amount of the fee. The Court therefore ruled that:

> Pecuniary charges imposed on the grounds of the sanitary inspection of products when they cross the frontier and determined in accordance with **special criteria** which are not comparable with the criteria employed in fixing the pecuniary charges imposed upon similar domestic products are to be considered as charges having an effect equivalent to customs duties' [para 8.]

Furthermore, a charge that is imposed on both imported and domestic products may be classed as a CEE when revenue from that charge is spent in such a way that domestic goods are advantaged. In *Capolongo* v *Azienda Agricola* (Case 77/72), the Court held that where a charge is levied both on imports and on domestic products, it can, nevertheless, constitute a CEE when revenue from that charge is intended exclusively to support activities which specifically benefit the taxed domestic product. In *IGAV* v *ENCC* (Case 94/74), the Court of Justice held that this was also the case where the domestic tax was remitted on the domestic product 'wholly or in part'. In such instances the tax burden is balanced by benefits for domestic products, but not for imported products, so that the charge on the imported products amounts to a barrier to the free movement of goods.

The Court of Justice later modified its position in *Fratelli Cucchi* v *Avez S.p.A* (Case 77/76). Here, the Court held that apparent internal taxation can only constitute a CEE if:

(i) it has the **sole purpose** of financing activities for the specific advantage of the taxed domestic product;

(ii) the taxed product and the domestic product benefiting from it are **the same**; and

(iii) the charges imposed on the domestic product are made good **in full**.

Now, where the charges imposed on the domestic product are only **partially** compensated, they will not be held to constitute a CEE. However, the charge will nevertheless be prohibited as discriminatory internal taxation under Article 110. For example, in *Nygård* v *Svineafgiftsfonden* (Case C-234/99), among others, the Court held that if a tax burden was fully offset by benefits afforded only to domestic products, the charge amounts to a CEE, but if the tax burden is only partially offset, it amounts to discriminatory internal taxation. This case applied this principle to discrimination between goods for domestic consumption and goods to be exported, rather than to discrimination between domestic and imported goods. Regardless, whether a discriminatory charge is deemed to fall within the scope of Article 30 or Article 110 has little consequence, as any such discriminatory or protectionist charges are prohibited either way.

In the following case, the Court of Justice held that even where a charge may be compatible with Article 30 by virtue of the provision of services exception it may still be contrary to Article 110 if it is discriminatory:

Haahr Petroleum Ltd v Abenra Havn (Case C-90/94)

Facts:

The claimant sought reimbursement for charges paid pursuant to a Danish law, under which the port of Abenra and others levied an additional import surcharge of 40 per cent on all imported goods loaded or unloaded within Danish commercial ports. The Danish government argued that the charge levied was lawful under what is now Article 30 TFEU (Arts 9–13 EEC Treaty at the time) because it constituted a charge for a service actually rendered to traders and could not therefore also fall foul of the prohibition against discriminatory taxation under what is now Article 110 TFEU (Art 95 EEC Treaty at the time).

Ruling:

The Court ruled as follows:

> ... the fact that a pecuniary charge constitutes consideration for a service actually supplied to traders and is of an amount commensurate with that service merely **enables it to escape classification as a charge having equivalent effect** within the meaning of Article 9 et seq. of the Treaty [now Art 30 TFEU], and **does not mean that it escapes the prohibition of all discriminatory internal taxation** laid down in Article 95 [now Art 110 TFEU]. [para 35]

As the charge was levied only against international traders and domestic traders were excluded from the charge, it was held to amount to discriminatory taxation regardless of whether it could be classified as a proportionate fee for services rendered.

Significance:

This case established that the exception from the Article 30 TFEU prohibition on customs duties and CEEs, on the basis that it covers the cost of services actually rendered, does not exempt a charge from the application of Article 110 TFEU. If such a charge is found to be discriminatory, it will therefore be prohibited. In this way, the Court prevented a situation where importers could be disadvantaged by being charged for services that domestic traders receive for free.

12.3 Internal taxation (Art 110 TFEU)

> Objective 3

Article 113 TFEU provides for the enactment of measures to harmonise national legislation on turnover taxes, **excise duties** and other forms of indirect taxation, but because such legislation can only be adopted by the Council acting unanimously there has been

> See Figure 12.2 in section 12.3.2 (page 534) for a flowchart which illustrates the application of Article 110 TFEU

little movement. Until a fully harmonised Union tax regime is achieved, Member States retain their national prerogative in relation to internal taxation. However, such taxation must comply with the fundamental principle of the free movement of goods. **Article 110 TFEU** (which is identical to the former Art 90 EC Treaty) provides that:

> No Member State shall impose, directly or indirectly, on the products of other Member States any internal taxation of any kind in excess of that imposed directly or indirectly on similar domestic products.
>
> Furthermore, no Member State shall impose on the products of other Member States any internal taxation of such a nature as to afford indirect protection to other products.

Protectionism, as referred to in the second paragraph of Article 110, means that a measure has the effect of protecting domestic products from competition by foreign goods. Article 110 TFEU thus prohibits taxation that discriminates against imports from other Member States or that has the effect of disadvantaging such products in the domestic market. Like Article 30, Article 110 is directly effective (see *Alfons Lütticke GmbH v Hauptzollamt Saarlouis* (Case 57/65)).

> See section 8.2 on the principle of direct effect

Along with ensuring that internal taxation does not obstruct the free movement of goods within the Union, Article 110 TFEU ensures that Articles 28–30 are effective. As discussed above, Articles 28–30 TFEU are designed to prevent financial measures from being imposed as a result of a product *crossing a frontier*. Articles 28–30 TFEU would be of little use if a Member State could impose taxes on foreign products (but not on the rival domestic product) once they were inside their territory. Article 110 TFEU seeks to prevent this. The purpose of Article 110 TFEU was set out by the Court of Justice in *Commission v Denmark* (Case 171/78) as follows:

> The ... provisions supplement, within the system of the Treaty, the provisions on the abolition of customs duties and charges having equivalent effect. Their aim is to ensure the free movement of goods between the Member States in normal conditions of competition by the **elimination of all forms of protection which result from the application of internal taxation which discriminates against products from other Member States**. As the Commission has correctly stated, Article 95 [now Article 110 TFEU] must guarantee the complete neutrality of internal taxation as regards competition between domestic products and imported products. [para 4]. (See also *Commission v France* (Case 168/78), para 4)

Article 110 TFEU is aimed at two distinct, but sometimes overlapping, national taxation practices: (i) the differential taxing of the same or similar imported and domestic products (Art 110(1) TFEU); and (ii) the taxing of different but competing imported and domestic products in such a way as to afford protection to the domestic product (Art 110(2) TFEU). The two key concepts are therefore **similarity** and **product competition** (*Commission v France* (Case 168/78)). These two concepts are discussed in depth after a note on the treatment of goods from non-EU countries under Article 110 TFEU.

Goods from non-EU countries

As **Article 110 TFEU** refers to 'products of other Member States' it might well be thought that discriminatory or protectionist taxation levied on goods coming from another Member State would be permissible provided those goods originated from outside the Union. Unlike the provisions relating to the free movement of goods in Part Three, Title II, TFEU (i.e. Arts 28–37 TFEU) which relate both to products originating in the Union and 'to products coming from third countries [i.e. non-Member States] which are in free circulation in Member States', there is no such clause in the non-discriminatory tax rules (Art 28(2) TFEU). **Initially**, therefore, the Court held that Member States were entitled to impose discriminatory or protectionist taxes on non-EU products circulating freely in the Union, provided such taxation was compatible with any concessions made to that state in any association agreement or other treaty (*Hansen* v *Hauptzollamt Flensburg* (Case 148/77)).

However, the Court modified its position in *Co-Frutta Srl* v *Amministrazione delle Finanze dello Stato* (Case 193/85). In this case, which involved Italian taxation of bananas imported through other Member States, the Court of Justice accepted that the Common Customs Tariff and the Common Commercial Policy were intended to ensure a uniform treatment of goods imported from non-EU countries and the facilitation of the free movement of such goods once they had been legitimately imported into one of the Member States. Goods from non-EU countries, once they have lawfully entered the Union, are therefore treated the same as goods originating from other Member States under Article 110 TFEU as well as under Articles 28–37.

12.3.1 Similar products (Art 110(1) TFEU)

Article 110(1) TFEU provides that Member States may not tax products from other Member States more than they tax 'similar domestic products'. Thus, Article 110(1) does not require a Member State to adopt a particular system of internal taxation, only to apply their system in such a way that products imported from other Member States are treated equally to similar domestic products, i.e. Member State tax systems may not discriminate between products imported from other Member States and domestic products. Therefore, Article 110(1) applies whenever imported and domestic products are considered to be **similar**.

In *Rewe-Zentrale des Lebensmittel-Grosshandels Gmbh* v *Hauptzollamt Emmerich* (Case 45/75), the Court of Justice stated that similar products are those which 'at the same stage of production or marketing, have similar characteristics and meet the same needs from the point of view of consumers' (para 12). The Court then further elaborated in *Commission* v *France* (Case 168/78 – '**French spirits**') that the scope of what is now Article 110(1) TFEU should be determined 'on the basis **not** of the criterion of the strictly identical nature of the products but on that of their **similar and comparable use**' (para 5). The Court has been called upon to assess the similarity of different products in several cases. For example:

> ▶ The 'French spirits' case is considered further in section 12.3.2 (page 533)

- In *Commission* v *Denmark* (Cases 106/84) the Court ruled that grape wines and other types of fruit wine were similar as they are made from the same kind of agricultural products, are made by the same process of natural fermentation, possess similar tastes and alcoholic strength and meet the same needs of consumers.
- In *John Walker & Sons Ltd* v *Ministeriet for Skatter og Afgifter* (Case 243/84), the Court decided that fruit wine liqueur and Scotch whisky were not similar for the purposes of Article 110(1) TFEU as they had different alcohol contents and different manufacturing processes.
- In *Commission* v *Italy* (Case 184/85 – '**similar fruit**'), the Court determined that bananas were not similar to other types of 'table fruit' typically produced in Italy due to the objective characteristics of the products, including their water-content and the extent to which they were viewed as especially nutritious and suitable for consumption by infants.

In each case where the Court of Justice finds that products are **not** similar for the purposes of Article 110(1), the products will then be considered under Article 110(2) (see below). Where goods **are** found to be similar, the tax will be unlawful under Article 110(1) if it is discriminatory. This discrimination can be either direct or indirect.

Direct discrimination

The application of different rates and methods of taxation to similar products is usually easy to recognise. For this reason direct discrimination of this kind is rare. However, such cases have occurred. For example, in *Lütticke GmbH* v *Hauptzollamt Saarlouis* (Case 57/65), a directly discriminatory internal tax was levied on imported dried milk but not on domestically produced dried milk. In *Bobie Getrnkvertrieb* v *Hauptzollamt Aachen-Nord* (Case 127/75), a German tax was calculated on a sliding scale on domestically produced beer, varying between DM 12 and 15 per hectolitre, according to the size of the brewery (DM (i.e. Deutsche Mark) was Germany's national currency prior to the euro). Imported beers had a flat-rate tax of DM 14.40 levied on them. The Court of Justice held that the tax was discriminatory, because small foreign breweries could not avail themselves of the low rate (DM 12) available to small domestic breweries.

Additionally, it is possible for the method by which a tax is collected to be discriminatory, even if the criteria for its payment are not. This was the situation in *Commission* v *Ireland* (Case 55/79), where an Irish tax was payable according to the same criteria irrespective of the origin of the goods. However, domestic producers were given several weeks to pay the tax, while importers had to pay immediately on importation.

Indirect discrimination

Article 110(1) TFEU also prohibits **indirectly** discriminatory taxation. An indirectly discriminatory tax will not, *prima facie*, differentiate between domestic and imported goods, but the actual effect of the tax places a greater burden on goods imported from other Member States. The following case provides an example of this:

> ### Humblot v Directeur des Services Fiscaux (Case 112/84)
>
> **Facts:**
>
> France imposed two different types of annual car tax, depending on the power rating of the car. Below 16 CV (fiscal horsepower) a differential tax was applied, which increased in proportion to the car's power rating up to a maximum of 1,100 francs (the franc was France's national currency prior to the euro). Above 16 CV, a flat-rate tax of 5,000 francs was imposed. The way in which fiscal horsepower was calculated was complex. It took into consideration: the number of cylinders; the bore in centimetres; the stroke in centimetres; and the rotation speed in revolutions per second. The result of applying this calculation was that no French car was given a fiscal horsepower rating above 16 CV. The fiscal horsepower calculation therefore had the effect that a foreign car of similar characteristics to a French car (e.g. same engine size, similar specifications, etc.) would fall within a higher rating and attract a higher level of annual tax.
>
> Mr Humblot was charged 5,000 francs on his imported car, which had been given a fiscal horsepower rating of 36 CV. He claimed the tax breached what is now Article 110 TFEU (Art 95 EEC Treaty at the time) and sought a refund. The French court referred questions to the Court of Justice under what is now Article 267 TFEU.

> **Ruling:**
>
> The Court of Justice noted that a system of internal vehicle taxation was compatible with Union law, provided that it was neither discriminatory nor protectionist in effect. Considering the French system, the Court found that:
>
>> Although the system embodies no formal distinction based on the origin of the products it **manifestly exhibits discriminatory or protective features** contrary to Article 95 [now Art 110 TFEU], since the power rating determining liability to the special tax has been fixed at a level such that only imported cars, in particular from other Member States, are subject to the special tax whereas all cars of domestic manufacture are liable to the distinctly more advantageous differential tax. [para 14]
>
> The Court held that the special tax applicable to cars with a higher fiscal horsepower disadvantaged cars imported from other Member States, as the much higher tax, which was payable on an annual basis, only applied to imports in practice. Therefore, the Court held that:
>
>> ... the special tax **reduces the amount of competition** to which cars of domestic manufacture are subject and hence is contrary to the principle of neutrality with which domestic taxation must comply. [para 16]
>
> **Significance:**
>
> This case illustrates the concept of indirect discrimination and demonstrates how seemingly neutral provisions can have the effect of protecting domestic products from competition with similar goods that have been imported from other Member States.

Following the above judgment, France amended its legislation, but the Court of Justice was required to adjudicate on the amended legislation's compatibility with what is now Article 110 TFEU on numerous occasions. See, for example:

- *Feldain* v *Services Fiscaux du Département du Haut-Rhin* (Case 433/85);
- *Deville* v *Administration des Impôts* (Case 240/87);
- *Jacquier* v *Directeur Général des Impôts* (Case C-113/94);
- *Yves Tarantik* v *Direction des Services Fiscaux de Seine-et-Marne* (Case C-421/97).

The Court considered a similar issue in the following case:

> ### Commission v Greece (Case C-132/88) – 'Greek car tax'
>
> **Facts:**
>
> The Commission brought an action against Greece on the basis that a tax levied on cars on the basis of their cylinder capacity was discriminatory. The tax, which was payable on the purchase or importation of any car, was calculated as a percentage of the price of the car. However, the progression of the tax was not constant, such that there was a significant leap in the amount of tax levied on cars that exceeded the 1,200 cc threshold and then a further leap for cars that exceeded the 1,800 cc threshold. As most cars produced in Greece had a cylinder capacity of 1,300 cc, the Commission argued that the highest rates of taxation disproportionately affected imported cars.
>
> **Ruling:**
>
> The Court noted that Article 95 EEC Treaty (now Art 110 TFEU) does not provide for any intervention in high levels of taxation. Referring first to its ruling in **Humblot** (above), the Court stated as follows:

17 ... Member States are at liberty to subject products such as cars to a system of tax which increases progressively in amount according to an **objective criterion**, such as cylinder capacity, provided that the system of taxation is free from any discriminatory or protective effect.

18 It must be made clear that a system of taxation **cannot** be regarded as discriminatory solely because only imported products, in particular those from other Member States, come within the most heavily taxed category...

19 In order to determine whether the special consumption tax and the single supplementary special tax have a discriminatory or protective effect, it is necessary to consider whether they are capable of discouraging consumers from purchasing cars of a cylinder capacity in excess of 1 800 cc, which are all manufactured abroad, in such a way as to benefit domestically produced cars.

20 If it is assumed that the particular features of the system of taxation at issue actually discourage certain consumers from purchasing cars of a cylinder capacity greater than 1 800 cc, those consumers will choose either a model in the range of cars having cylinder capacities between 1 600 and 1 800 cc or a model in the range of cars having cylinder capacities below 1 600 cc. All the models in the first mentioned range are of foreign manufacture. The second range includes cars of both foreign and Greek manufacture. Consequently, **the Commission has not shown how the system of taxation at issue might have the effect of favouring the sale of cars of Greek manufacture.**

Significance:

This case clarified that a tax rule that disproportionately affects imported products is not contrary to what is now Article 110 TFEU if the tax does not bring competitive advantages to any domestic products. Whereas in **Humblot** (Case 112/84), the French tax had been calculated in a complex manner that afforded domestic cars an advantage over similar imported cars, in this case the tax was based on an **objective criterion** (cylinder size), which meant that the highest tax rate only applied to luxury cars, which happened to only be available from other countries. When it came to less luxurious cars, Greek cars competed equally with imported cars and thus did not benefit from the system of taxation.

Objective justification of indirect discrimination

While directly discriminatory taxation can never be justified, tax rules of a Member State which tend to favour the domestic product, and are therefore indirectly discriminatory, may be held to comply with Article 110(1) TFEU if they can be objectively justified. In order for the Court of Justice to accept a measure that is indirectly discriminatory, the measure must be an appropriate and proportionate means of pursuing a legitimate objective.

The following case provides an example where the Court of Justice held that indirect discrimination was objectively justified:

Chemial Farmaceutici v *Daf Spa* (Case 140/79)

Facts:

Italian internal taxation of synthetic ethyl alcohol was higher than taxation of fermented ethyl alcohol. The products were interchangeable in use. Italy produced very little of the higher-taxed synthetic product and therefore the tax system had a harsher impact upon importers. The rationale for the tax policy was to encourage the manufacture of the fermented product (the raw material of which was agricultural products), thus preserving the petroleum ingredients used to make the synthetic product for other more economically important purposes.

> **Ruling:**
> The Court of Justice held that the objective of reserving petroleum for other uses was a legitimate economic policy choice. Additionally, it was not held to discriminate directly, as it stymied both the import and the domestic production of the synthetic product equally. As in the **Greek car tax** case (above), the taxation in question distinguished between products on the basis of an objective criterion, i.e. the raw materials used. Such a distinction complies with Union law if it pursues legitimate objectives that are themselves compatible with Union law requirements and where no direct or indirect discrimination occurs. The Court held that:
>
>> 15 Differential taxation such as that which exists in Italy for denatured synthetic alcohol on the one hand and denatured alcohol obtained by fermentation on the other satisfies these requirements. It appears in fact that the system of taxation pursues an **objective of legitimate industrial policy** in that it is such as to promote the distillation of agricultural products as against the manufacture of alcohol from petroleum derivatives. That choice does not conflict with the rules of Community [i.e. Union] law or the requirements of a policy decided within the framework of the Community [i.e. Union].
>
> **Significance:**
> In this case, as in the **Greek car tax** case, ostensibly similar products were held to be differentiated for tax purposes by an objective criterion. While in the **Greek car tax** case it was not shown that the internal taxation system resulted in any advantage to domestic products, in this case any such advantage was essentially rendered a permissible side effect of pursuing a legitimate industrial policy in a non-discriminatory manner.

If there is no actual direct or indirect discrimination then a tax is *per se* (i.e. automatically) outside of the scope of Article 110 TFEU. However, in finding that there was no actual discrimination in the above case, the Court was no doubt strongly influenced by the *reason* for the imposition of the tax (i.e. 'legitimate choice of economic policy'). This case therefore suggests that there is scope for the objective justification of an internal tax that is indirectly discriminatory.

Similarly, in **Commission v France** (Case 196/85), the Court of Justice held that a more favourable tax rate applied to natural sweet wine as compared to ordinary table wine was justified. The purpose of the tax was to assist the economy of areas that were heavily reliant on such wines, which were produced in difficult circumstances. Where such tax relief is applied, it must be operated indiscriminately (i.e. without direct discrimination), even where there is a legitimate and defensible objective. Thus, in **Hansen v Hauptzollamt Flensburg** (Case 148/77), it was held that an importer of spirits into Germany was entitled to take advantage of tax relief available in that country, *inter alia*, in respect of spirits made by small businesses and collective farms. In this case, the Court of Justice accepted that such tax concessions could meet legitimate economic and social purposes, so long as such preferential systems are applied without distinction to spirits coming from other Member States.

12.3.2 Indirect protection (Art 110(2) TFEU)

As discussed above, Article 110(1) TFEU prohibits the imposition of internal taxes on products from other Member States which are greater than those levied on *similar* domestic products. Therefore, if the imported and domestic products can be considered to be *similar*, Article 110(1) TFEU will apply and the taxes must be *equalised*.

Article 110(2) TFEU then provides that:

> Furthermore, no Member State shall impose on the products of other Member States any internal taxation of such a nature as to afford indirect protection to other products.

Article 110(2) TFEU applies to other products which are not similar, but where the effect of the tax is to afford **indirect protection** to some other domestic products: i.e. products which are not similar but which may otherwise be in competition with each other.

One of the early alcohol-related cases brought by the Commission was against the UK with regard to the discriminatory taxation of wine in comparison with beer (*Commission* v *UK* (Case 170/78 – 'wine tax')). Beer and wine were not considered to be *similar* within the meaning of what is now Article 110(1) TFEU and therefore the Court of Justice proceeded under what is now Article 110(2) TFEU. This case provides an insight into how the Court of Justice approaches the application of Article 110(2) TFEU:

Commission v *UK* (Case 170/78) – 'Wine tax'

Facts:
The UK levied a tax on certain wines, which was about five times that levied on beer in terms of 'volume'. The tax on wine represented about 38 per cent of its sale price compared to 25 per cent for beer. The UK produced vast amounts of beer, but very little wine. The Commission brought infringement proceedings against the UK pursuant to what is now Article 258 TFEU claiming the differential UK tax breached what is now Article 110(2) TFEU (Art 95(2) EEC Treaty at the time).

Ruling:
Following an adjournment while further evidence was gathered relating to the competitive relationship between beer and wine, the Court held as follows:

8   As regards the question of competition between wine and beer, the Court considered that, to a certain extent at least, the two beverages in question were **capable of meeting identical needs**, so that it had to be acknowledged that there was **a degree of substitution** for one another. It pointed out that, for the purpose of measuring the possible degree of substitution, attention should not be confined to consumer habits in a Member State or in a given region. Those habits, which were essentially variable in time and space, could not be considered immutable; **the tax policy of a Member State must not therefore crystallise given consumer habits so as to consolidate an advantage acquired by national industries** concerned to respond to them.

9   The Court nonetheless recognised that, in view of the substantial differences between wine and beer, it was difficult to compare the manufacturing processes and the natural properties of those beverages, as the Government of the UK had rightly observed. For that reason, the Court requested the parties to provide additional information with a view to dispelling the doubts which existed concerning **the nature of the competitive relationship** between the two products.

The Court then considered various means by which wine and beer could be compared in order to assess the extent to which the two categories of product were in competition in the UK market.

> The Court found that there was a competitive relationship between beer and cheaper, lighter wines. The Court then concluded as follows:
>
> 27 It is clear, therefore, following the detailed inquiry conducted by the Court – whatever criterion for comparison is used, there being no need to express a preference for one or the other – that **the UK's tax system has the effect of subjecting wine imported from other Member States to an additional burden so as to afford protection to domestic beer production**, inasmuch as beer production constitutes the most relevant reference criterion from the point of view of competition. Since such protection is most marked in the case of the most popular wines, the effect of the UK tax system is to stamp wine with the hallmarks of a luxury product which, in view of the tax burden which it bears, can scarcely constitute in the eyes of the consumer a genuine alternative to the typically produced domestic beverage.
>
> 28 It follows from the foregoing considerations that, by levying excise duty on still light wines made from fresh grapes at a higher rate, in relative terms, than on beer, the UK has failed to fulfil its obligations under the second paragraph of Article 95 EEC Treaty [now Art 110 TFEU].
>
> **Significance:**
>
> This case established a two-stage approach to determining whether what is now Article 110(2) TFEU had been breached:
>
> (i) The Court assessed the extent to which there was a **competitive relationship** between the two products. In considering this issue, the Court took account of the extent to which the goods were substitutable for each other; i.e. whether they had a high or low degree of **cross-elasticity**. In considering whether or not the goods are substitutable, the Court will ignore current consumer perceptions, as such perceptions can change over time. Indeed, such perceptions may be affected by the differential tax on the two products.
>
> (ii) Having established a competitive relationship between the two products, the Court assessed the extent to which the tax system was in fact **protective** of the domestically produced goods. In this case it was quite clear that the differential rates had a protective effect on beer.

While the difference in the tax on competing products in the above case was substantial, in other instances the difference in the level of taxation may not be that great. The Court may therefore be faced with a much more difficult task. Much will depend on the degree of cross-elasticity between the two products. If this is low then a small tax differential will probably make no difference, whereas if it is high, the level of taxation may be of critical importance to consumer decision-making. Alternatively, although the differential rate of tax between the two products may be high in percentage terms, it may only form a very low proportion of the final selling price. For example, in the UK **wine tax** case, if the tax on beer had been 2p per litre compared to 8p per litre on wine then, by volume, the tax on wine is **400 per cent greater** than that on beer. However, this amount of tax is low in absolute terms with respect to the final selling price of the products and therefore the level of taxation is unlikely to have a protective effect on domestic beer producers (i.e. the tax difference alone would be unlikely to deter a beer drinker from switching to wine).

Commission v *Italy* (Case 184/85 '**Similar fruit**') provides another example of the two-stage assessment to determine a breach of Article 110(2) TFEU, this time in relation to fruit. As noted above, the Court of Justice decided that bananas were not similar to other fruit and that what is now Article 110(1) TFEU did not apply. However, the Court decided that there was a **competitive relationship** between bananas and other fruit. It then held that the tax on bananas had a **protective effect**, because the tax levied on bananas was almost half their import price, while no tax was levied on almost all Italian-grown fruit. This was clear evidence of protectionism, contrary to what is now Article 110(2) TFEU.

Similarly, in *FG Roders BV and Others* v *Inspecteur der Invoerrechten en Accijnzen* (Joined Cases C-367 and 377/93), the Court of Justice decided that fruit wine produced in the Benelux countries (Belgium, the Netherlands and Luxembourg) was not similar to imported sherry, madeira, vermouth and champagne. However, the Court observed a competitive relationship between these imported products and domestically produced fruit wine. The essential question, then, was whether the charge imposed on the imported products had the effect of disadvantaging them in the market in question. This question was left for the national court to decide with regard to the difference between the selling prices of the products in question and the impact of that difference on the consumer's choice.

Commission v *Belgium* (Case 356/85) provides an example of a situation where there was a differential tax between domestic and imported goods, but no protective effect was established. This case concerned the taxes that Belgium levied on beer, which was produced in Belgium, and on wine, which was mostly imported. There was a six per cent difference in the tax levied, with wine being taxed more heavily. The Court of Justice held that this did not have a protective effect because the cost of the two products differed substantially before the tax and therefore a relatively minor difference in the tax rates would not serve to protect the Belgian beer producers.

The relationship between Articles 110(1) and 110(2)

The Court of Justice considered the application of what are now Articles 110(1) and (2) TFEU in the following case:

Commission v *France* (Case 168/78) – 'French spirits'

Facts:
France had higher tax rates for spirits which were based upon grain (e.g. whisky, rum, gin, vodka) than those based upon wine or other fruit products (e.g. cognac, armagnac). France produced very little of the more heavily taxed grain-based spirits, but was a major producer of the wine and fruit-based spirits. The Commission brought infringement proceedings against France pursuant to what is now Article 258 TFEU, alleging the tax breached what is now Article 110 TFEU (Art 95 EEC Treaty at the time).

Ruling:
After reviewing the purpose and scope of the first and second paragraphs of Article 95 EEC Treaty (now Art 110 TFEU), the Court of Justice held as follows:

> 7   Whilst the criterion indicated in the first paragraph of Article 95 [now Art 110(1) TFEU] consists in the **comparison of tax burdens**, whether in terms of the rate, the mode of assessment or other detailed rules for the application thereof, in view of the difficulty of making sufficiently precise comparisons between the products in question, the second paragraph of that Article is based upon a more general criterion, in other words **the protective nature** of the system on internal taxation.

This case was decided on the basis that there had been an infringement of what is now Article 110 TFEU without a detailed examination of the two paragraphs separately. The Court of Justice explained why it was not concerned whether the infringement was based on the first or second paragraph of what is now Article 110 TFEU as follows:

> 39   … the Court deems it unnecessary for the purposes of solving this dispute to give a ruling on the question whether or not the spirituous beverages concerned are wholly or partially similar

products within the meaning of the first paragraph of Article 95 [now Art 110(1) TFEU] when it is impossible reasonably to contest that without exception **they are in at least partial competition with the domestic products** to which the application refers and that it is **impossible to deny the protective nature of the French tax system** within the second paragraph of Article 95 [now Art 110(2) TFEU].

Significance:

This case established that it may not be necessary for the Court to find that imported and domestic products are not similar and thus are not covered by what is now Article 110(1) TFEU in order for Article 110(2) to be applied. Where similarity is contested but the protective nature of the tax system is apparent, the relevant tax rules will be in breach of Article 110 TFEU as a whole; as protective tax rules will be prohibited by either the first or the second paragraph, it is not necessary to determine which applies. Through this reasoning, the Court avoided making a decision on the similarity of the products.

Figure 12.2 Application of Article 110 TFEU

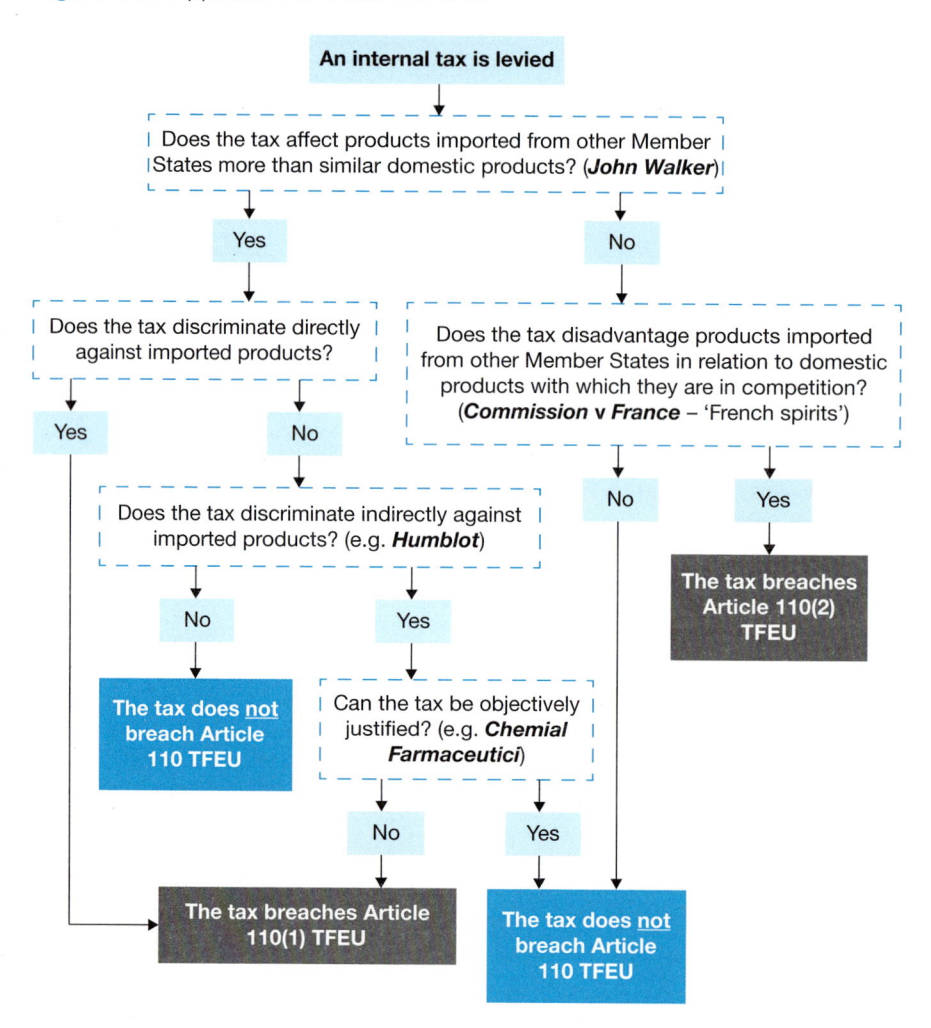

```
                        An internal tax is levied
                                  │
                                  ▼
        Does the tax affect products imported from other Member
        States more than similar domestic products? (John Walker)
                    │                               │
                   Yes                              No
                    │                               │
                    ▼                               ▼
        Does the tax discriminate      Does the tax disadvantage products imported
        directly against               from other Member States in relation to domestic
        imported products?             products with which they are in competition?
                                       (Commission v France – 'French spirits')
            │           │                       │           │
           Yes          No                      No          Yes
            │           │                       │           │
            │           ▼                       │           ▼
            │   Does the tax discriminate       │   The tax breaches
            │   indirectly against              │   Article 110(2)
            │   imported products? (e.g.        │   TFEU
            │   Humblot)
            │       │           │
            │       No          Yes
            │       │           │
            │       ▼           ▼
            │  The tax does    Can the tax be objectively
            │  not breach      justified? (e.g. Chemial
            │  Article         Farmaceutici)
            │  110 TFEU          │           │
            │                    No          Yes
            │                    │           │
            ▼                    ▼           ▼
        The tax breaches Article    The tax does not
        110(1) TFEU                 breach Article
                                    110 TFEU
```

The means of evading a decision on the similarity of products established by the Court in the above case is problematic for the defaulting Member State, which will need to take action to remedy the breach. If the tax is in breach of Article 110(1) TFEU, the tax must be equalised. However, if the tax is in breach of Article 110(2) TFEU, the protective effect must be eliminated; this does not necessarily require the tax to be equalised. In light of this problem, **the Court has distinguished between the two paragraphs more clearly in its later judgments** (e.g. *John Walker & Sons Ltd* v *Ministeriet for Skatter og Afgifter* (Case 243/84)).

Finally, it should be noted that where a tax is imposed on a product which is not produced domestically and to which there is no domestic equivalent, there will be no breach of Article 110 TFEU. In such instances, there is no similar product in relation to which discrimination can be alleged under Article 110(1), nor any product which could be afforded protection under Article 110(2), and such internal taxation therefore falls within the competence of the Member States (*Fink-Frucht* v *HZA München-Landsbergerstrasse* (Case 27/67)).

12.4 Quantitative restrictions and measures having equivalent effect (Arts 34 and 35 TFEU)

Objective 4

Articles 34 and 35 TFEU aim to eliminate non-financial barriers to the free movement of goods through the prohibition of quantitative restrictions on imports and exports, respectively, between Member States. Just as Article 30 prohibits charges having an equivalent effect to customs duties, Articles 34 and 35 also prohibit measures which have an equivalent effect to direct restrictions, even where the Member State imposing them does not intend the measures to have such an effect. Also like Article 30, the prohibition on restrictions affects all types of products and it applies not only to goods which are produced in the Member States but also to goods which come from non-EU countries and are in free circulation in a Member State. Such goods are in free circulation once they have entered the Union in compliance with all import formalities and charges required by the common external tariff (Art 29 TFEU).

12.4.1 Quantitative restrictions

Direct restrictions, such as quotas and bans on certain products of other Member States, were abolished or phased out in the early days of the Union and, for new Member States, during transitional periods after their accession. The concept of 'quantitative restrictions' (QRs) is straightforward enough: in *Geddo* v *Ente Nazionale Risi* (Case 2/73), the Court of Justice stated that:

> The prohibition on quantitative restrictions covers measures which amount to a total or partial restraint of, according to the circumstances, imports, exports, or goods in transit.

The concept of quantitative restrictions therefore applies to an outright ban on imports or exports, or the imposition of a quota.

The following case provides a rare example of a quantitative restriction which was, *prima facie*, in breach of the former Article 28 EC Treaty (now Art 34 TFEU):

Rosengren and Others v Riksåklagaren (Case C-170/04)

Facts:

Swedish law established that only the state-owned Systembolaget could retail alcoholic beverages in the country and only Systembolaget and wholesalers authorised by the state could import alcoholic beverages. Individuals were permitted to enter Sweden with alcoholic beverages for their personal consumption or the consumption of their family, but they were prohibited from having such beverages transported into Sweden on their behalf by any undertaking other than Systembolaget. However, Systembolaget was required to obtain any alcoholic beverage on request from a consumer, provided that it did not consider that there were grounds not to.

Rosengren and several other Swedish nationals ordered cases of Spanish wine to be delivered to them without going through an authorised intermediary. The wine was not declared to customs and was subsequently confiscated by customs authorities. Rosengren and the others contested the confiscation and, after a series of appeals, the matter was referred to the Court of Justice for a preliminary ruling under what is now Article 267 TFEU.

Ruling:

The Court of Justice considered the provision under national law which permitted Systembolaget to refuse a request to import alcoholic beverages. As such a refusal would result in an individual having no means of obtaining such goods from another Member State, besides personally transporting them, the Court held that this constituted a quantitative restriction on imports.

Additionally, the Court noted that individuals seeking to import alcoholic beverages through Systembolaget faced a variety of logistical and financial inconveniences which they would not encounter if they were to import the goods themselves.

The Court of Justice therefore held that the prohibition on individuals from importing alcoholic beverages amounted to a quantitative restriction on the free movement of goods, contrary to the former Article 28 EC Treaty (now Art 34 TFEU). The Court also held that the measures were not justified by the aim of protecting health and life, as they were not suitable or proportionate to that aim.

Significance:

This case demonstrates that a quantitative restriction does not need to specify a maximum amount that is to be imported or exported, but can instead be a more general limitation on the ability to import or export freely.

Some national prohibitions do survive, such as the prohibition on the importation of obscene materials into the UK under the Customs Consolidation Act 1876. It was argued by the UK government in **R v Henn and Darby** (Case 34/79) that a *ban* on the import of pornographic material under the Act was not a quantitative *restriction* under what is now Article 34 TFEU. The Court of Justice disagreed and held that what is now Article 34 TFEU 'includes such a prohibition on imports in as much as this is the most extreme form of restriction'. However, the Court held that the prohibition in this case was justified under what is now Article 36 TFEU. That aspect of the case is discussed below in section 12.5.1.

Scope of the term 'goods' for the purposes of Articles 34–36 TFEU

For the purpose of **Articles 34–36 TFEU**, the Court of Justice has held that 'goods' are **'manufactured material objects'** (*Cinéthèque* (Cases 60 and 61/84)). The term is wide enough to include not only plants, vegetables, fruit, livestock and a whole variety of animal products (*Société Civile Agricole* (Case C-323/93)), but also even covers generated electricity (*Commission* v *Netherlands* (Case C-157/94)). The context in which an item is considered may, however, result in it being regarded not as a product in itself that is subject to Articles 34–36 TFEU, but rather as ancillary to the provision of a service that is thus subject to Article 56 TFEU (*HM Customs and Excise Commissioners* v *Schindler* (Case C-275/92)). Coins, banknotes and bearer cheques are also not 'goods', as their transfer is subject to the rules on the transfer of capital under Article 63 TFEU (*Aldo Bordessa and Others* (Joined Cases C-358 and 416/93)). However, in *R* v *Thompson* (Case 7/78), the Court of Justice held that old gold coins were 'goods' as they were not a normal means of payment.

Scope of state measures

▶ See section 8.2 for an explanation of the principle of direct effect and section 8.4 for an explanation of the principle of state liability

Articles 34 and 35 TFEU have **vertical direct effect**. Any state measure breaching them can give rise to a claim in damages against the Member State concerned, provided that the criteria laid down by the Court of Justice in *Brasserie du Pêcheur* (Case C-46/93) in relation to imports and *R* v *Ministry of Agriculture Fisheries and Food, ex parte Hedley Lomas Ireland Ltd* (Case C-5/94) in relation to exports can be met (see Chapter 8).

The provisions of Article 34 TFEU have also been held by the Court of Justice to be binding on the institutions of the Union. In *Kieffer and Thill* (Case C-114/96), the Court expressed the view that it would have been prepared to strike down a Council regulation requiring Member States to gather information from importers and exporters if it had been satisfied that the regulation imposed a disproportionately heavy burden on the free movement of goods.

▶ *Fra.bo* is considered in section 12.4.4 (page 550)

In addition, in *Fra.bo SpA* v *Deutsche Vereinigung des Gas- und Wasserfaches eV (DVGW)* (Case C-171/11), the Court of Justice held that Article 34 can also have **horizontal direct effect** under certain conditions. This case **is discussed below as it** was a corollary of the rule of mutual recognition, **which is discussed later in this chapter**. In *Fra.bo*, the Court granted only a very narrow scope for when Article 34 TFEU can be horizontally directly effective. It therefore remains pertinent to consider the scope of the vertical direct effect of Article 34, as it cannot be assumed that horizontal direct effect will apply if the relevant party is found not to be a state entity. Indeed, if Article 34 were to have general horizontal direct effect this would defeat the object of a competitive market.

The Court of Justice considered the question of what constitutes a state measure for the purposes of Articles 34 and 35 TFEU in the following case:

Commission v Ireland (Case 249/81) – 'Buy Irish'

Facts:

In 1978, the Irish government introduced a three-year programme to promote Irish products. The programme included the following measures: (i) encouragement of the use of a 'Buy Irish' symbol for goods made in Ireland; and (ii) a publicity campaign organised by the Irish Goods Council that was designed to encourage consumers to buy Irish products.

The Commission brought infringement proceedings against the Irish government under what is now Article 258 TFEU, alleging that the campaign was a measure equivalent to a quantitative restriction and therefore in breach of what is now Article 34 TFEU (Art 30 EEC Treaty at the time). Ireland defended the action on the ground it had never adopted 'measures' covered by what is now Article 34 TFEU. Additionally, the campaign had been executed by the Irish Goods Council, not the government. The government argued that any financial assistance it had given to the

Council should be judged under what are now Articles 107–108 TFEU (Arts 92–93 EEC Treaty at the time), relating to aids granted by states, and not under what is now Article 34 TFEU.

Ruling:

The Court of Justice first considered whether the state could be held liable for a programme implemented by the Irish Goods Council. The Court held as follows:

15   It is thus apparent that the Irish Government appoints the members of the Management Committee of the Irish Goods Council, grants it public subsidies which cover the greater part of its expenses and, finally, defines the aims and the broad outline of the campaign conducted by that institution to promote the sale and purchase of Irish products. In the circumstances **the Irish Government cannot rely on the fact that the campaign was conducted by a private company in order to escape any liability it may have under the provisions of the Treaty**.

The Court then considered whether the campaign amounted to 'measures' having equivalent effect to quantitative restrictions for the purposes of what is now Article 34 TFEU. The Court ruled that:

21   The Irish Government maintains that the prohibition against measures having an effect equivalent to quantitative restrictions in Article 30 [now Art 34 TFEU] is concerned only with 'measures', that is to say, binding provisions emanating from a public authority. However, no such provision has been adopted by the Irish Government, which has confined itself to giving moral support and financial aid to the activities pursued by the Irish industries.

...

28   Such a practice cannot escape the prohibition laid down by Article 30 [now Art 34 TFEU] solely because it is not based on decisions which are binding upon undertakings. **Even measures adopted by the government of a Member State which do not have binding effect may be capable of influencing the conduct of traders and consumers in that state and thus of frustrating the aims of the Community** [i.e. Union].

Significance:

This case established that the prohibition on measures having an equivalent effect to quantitative restrictions does not only apply to formally binding measures. Additionally, the Irish government's involvement in the Irish Goods Council was held to be sufficient for the state to be held liable for the measures in question.

> *Apple and Pear Development Council* is considered more fully on page 543

The principle established in the above case was developed further by the Court of Justice in ***Apple and Pear Development Council* v *K.J. Lewis Ltd*** (Case 222/82). Here, the Court ruled that the fact that an obligation on fruit growers to pay a levy to the Development Council was statutory was sufficient to bring it within the scope of a state entity for the purposes of what is now Article 34 TFEU.

Similarly, in ***R v Royal Pharmaceutical Society, Ex Parte Api*** (Cases 266 and 267/87) the Court held that, although it was an independent body in the UK, the Royal Pharmaceutical Society had a sufficient measure of state support, or 'statutory underpinning', to constitute a state entity for the purposes of what is now Article 34 TFEU. Therefore, the rules of the society, which required pharmacists to supply, under a prescription, only a named branded drug, were *prima facie* in breach of what is now Article 34 TFEU.

It is, of course, not only the state and public bodies which may, either directly or indirectly, seek to exclude foreign competition. Articles 34–36 TFEU must also be considered in the light of **Articles 101 and 102 TFEU** on competition, which play an important part in preventing national cartels and national monopolies from using private economic power to keep goods from other Member States from entering national markets. Where the private body enjoys a monopoly conferred on it by the state, which enables it to restrict the import of foreign products by virtue of that monopoly, there may be an overlap between Articles 34 and 102 TFEU. In such circumstances, the state may be liable for maintaining a situation which has the effect of excluding products from other Member States in breach of Article 34 TFEU, or an unlawful state monopoly in breach of Article 37 TFEU (see *Harry Franzen* (Case C-189/95) and *Société Civile Agricole* v *Coopérative d'Elevage de la Mayenne* (Case C-323/93)).

12.4.2 Measures having equivalent effect to quantitative restrictions (MEEs)

In addition to prohibiting quantitative restrictions, Article 34 TFEU also prohibits 'measures having equivalent effect' to quantitative restrictions (**MEEs**, also known as **MEQRs**).

Directive 70/50

Directive 70/50 on the abolition of measures which have an effect equivalent to quantitative restrictions on imports was adopted in December 1969. It was intended to provide guidance on the kind of acts and activities which constituted 'measures' infringing what is now Article 34 TFEU and which were in existence when the original Treaty came into force. It was formally only of application during the Community's transitional period, but it has been very influential in its representation of the Commission's view of the scope of the relevant Treaty provisions.

Article 2 of Directive 70/50 covers measures 'other than those applicable equally to domestic or imported products, which hinder imports which could otherwise take place, including measures which make importation more difficult or costly than the disposal of domestic products'. Article 2 is thus concerned with national measures which apply specifically to, or affect only, imported goods. These are often referred to as **distinctly applicable measures**, because they explicitly distinguish between imported and domestically produced goods (see below). Article 2(3) of Directive 70/50 contains a non-exhaustive list of the sort of measures applied to imported goods which would constitute MEEs. These include:

- laying down minimum or maximum sale prices for imported products;
- fixing less favourable profit margins for imported goods;
- excluding prices for imported goods which reflect importation costs;
- making access to Member State markets dependent upon having an agent there;
- subjecting imported goods to conditions which are different from those laid down for domestic products and are more difficult to satisfy;
- requiring, for imported goods only, guarantees or payments on account;
- subjecting only imported products to conditions in respect of shape, size, weight, composition, presentation or identification;
- hindering the purchase by individuals of imported products only, or encouraging, requiring or giving preference to the purchase of domestic products only;
- totally or partially precluding the use of national facilities or equipment in respect of imported products only;
- prohibiting or limiting publicity in respect of imported products only.

The above list is indicative of the sort of national measures which will constitute MEEs, but the full range of possible measures which are intended to protect, or will have the effect of protecting, domestically produced goods can neither be anticipated nor overestimated.

Article 3 of Directive 70/50 also refers to measures which are applied indiscriminately to both domestic and imported goods but which may, nonetheless, have the effect of impeding imports. These are referred to as **indistinctly applicable measures**. Distinctly and indistinctly applicable measures are considered further below.

The *Dassonville* formula

In the following case, the Court of Justice considered the scope of what is now Article 34 TFEU in relation to MEEs and provided a useful definition:

Procureur Du Roi v *Dassonville* (Case 8/74)

Facts:

Belgian law required spirits that are marketed as of a certain origin to be accompanied by certification of their right to that designation. Dassonville was a Belgian importer of Scotch whisky who was prosecuted for selling whisky with false certificates of origin. He had imported the whisky from France, where no such certification was required for Scotch whisky, and it had been difficult to obtain the certificates of origin from the UK customs authorities. Dassonville argued that the Belgian law infringed what is now Article 34 TFEU (Art 30 EEC Treaty at the time) as it made the importation of whisky from anywhere other than the state of origin more difficult. The Belgian court referred the case to the Court of Justice under what is now Article 267 TFEU.

Ruling:

The Court of Justice held as follows:

4. It emerges from the file and from the oral proceedings that a trader, wishing to import into Belgium Scotch whisky which is already in free circulation in France, can obtain such a certificate only with great difficulty, unlike the importer who imports directly from the producer country.

5. **All trading rules enacted by Member States which are capable of hindering, directly or indirectly, actually or potentially, intra-Community [i.e. intra-Union] trade are to be considered as measures having an effect equivalent to quantitative restrictions.**

The Court therefore concluded that the requirement of a certificate of authenticity that disadvantaged importers of an authentic product that was in free circulation within the Union, compared to those who imported directly from the producing state, constituted a measure having an effect equivalent to a quantitative restriction.

Significance:

The case established that MEEs are trading rules that (i) are **enacted by Member States** and (ii) are **capable** of hindering intra-Union trade. The crucial element in determining the existence of an MEE is therefore its **potential effect**; a discriminatory intent or actual outcome is **not** required. This broad definition of an MEE, which is known as the ***Dassonville* formula**, reflects the determination of the Court to ensure that very few measures will be permitted to hinder the free movement of goods. Thus, the Court's definition of MEEs under Article 34 TFEU parallels its definition of a charge having an effect equivalent to a customs duty under Article 30 TFEU.

12.4.3 Distinctly applicable MEEs

Distinctly applicable measures, as stated above, are measures which are applied only to imported or exported goods; such measures are not applied to domestically produced goods. There are many examples where the Court of Justice has struck down national rules which apply only to imported or exported goods, including the *Dassonville* case above. Some specific categories of distinctly applicable MEEs are now considered as examples.

Import and export restrictions

In *International Fruit Company* v *Produktschap voor Groenten en Fruit (No. 2)* (Cases 51–54/71), the Court of Justice held that **import or export licences** are caught by what are now Articles 34 or 35 TFEU because, applying the *Dassonville* formula, such a measure is 'capable of hindering, directly or indirectly, actually or potentially, intra-Community [i.e. intra-Union] trade'. A requirement to apply for a licence before goods can be imported into a Member State, or exported out of a Member State, has a threefold impact:

▶ The *Dassonville* formula is set out in section 12.4.2 (page 540)

(i) goods cannot be imported or exported until the licence application has been processed (this is effectively a temporary ban);

(ii) the application could be rejected; and

(iii) applying for a licence will require additional paperwork to be completed, which will cost time and money. This additional cost will increase the cost of the goods and could subsequently decrease their competitiveness with domestically produced goods.

In *Commission* v *Italy* (Case 154/85), Italy had **procedures and data requirements** which applied only to the importation of cars, which meant that their registration was longer, more complicated and more expensive than the registration of domestic cars. The Court of Justice held that such procedures and requirements were prohibited under what is now Article 34 TFEU.

▶ The 'angry farmers' case can be contrasted with *Schmidberger* (Case C-112/00), which is considered in section 12.5.2 (page 582)

In *Rewe-Zentralfinanz* v *Landwirtschaftskammer* (Case 4/75), phyto-sanitary **inspections** on imported apples contravened what is now Article 34 TFEU because there were no similar inspections of domestically grown apples. The Court of Justice stressed the fact that border inspections made imports more difficult and costly.

In the following case, the Court of Justice held that a **failure to act** by a Member State could constitute an infringement of what is now Article 34 TFEU:

Commission v *France* (Case C-265/95) – 'angry farmers'

Facts:

Fruit and vegetables imported into France from other Member States were targeted by French farmers, who would obstruct their passage, preventing them from reaching their final destination. For more than a decade, the Commission had received complaints concerning the inactivity of the French authorities in the face of violent acts by French farmers, including the destruction of goods and means of transport. It was not denied by France that when such incidents occurred the French police were either not present at the scene, despite the fact that in some instances the competent authorities had been warned that the farmers were planning to demonstrate, or they simply failed to intervene, even where the police far outnumbered the farmers.

> The Commission took action against France, arguing that its failure to act impeded the free movement of goods imported from other Member States and constituted a breach of what is now Article 34 TFEU and Article 36 TFEU (Art 30 EC Treaty at the time).
>
> **Ruling:**
>
> The Court of Justice held as follows:
>
> > 52 ... the Court, while not discounting the difficulties faced by the competent authorities in dealing with situations of the type in question in this case, cannot but find that, having regard to the frequency and seriousness of the incidents cited by the Commission, **the measures adopted by the French Government were manifestly inadequate to ensure freedom of intra-Community [i.e. intra-Union] trade in agricultural products** on its territory by preventing and effectively dissuading the perpetrators of the offences in question from committing and repeating them.
> >
> > ...
> >
> > 65 ... it must be concluded that in the present case **the French Government has manifestly and persistently abstained from adopting appropriate and adequate measures to put an end to the acts of vandalism which jeopardise the free movement** on its territory of certain agricultural products originating in other Member States and to prevent the recurrence of such acts.
>
> The Court thus held that the failure of the French government to protect the free movement of goods within its territory amounted to a breach of its responsibilities under what is now Article 34 TFEU, in conjunction with what is now Article 4(3) TEU (which requires Member States to take any appropriate measures necessary to fulfil their Treaty obligations).
>
> **Significance:**
>
> This case established that an MEE does not necessarily need to be a positive measure, but that a failure to remove obstacles to the free movement of goods presented by non-state actors can also amount to a breach of what is now Article 34 TFEU. Through this obligation on Member States, the Court of Justice was able to safeguard the effectiveness of Article 34 TFEU while maintaining that the Article does not have horizontal direct effect.

Promotion of domestic goods

As noted in the above discussion on the scope of state measures, the promotion of a domestic product by a Member State may infringe Article 34 TFEU. This was illustrated in *Commission v Ireland* (Case 249/81 – '**Buy Irish**'), where the Court of Justice considered whether a campaign encouraging consumers to choose Irish products amounted to an MEE. The Court ruled that the campaign was a state measure that was intended to check the flow of trade between Member States by encouraging the purchase of domestic products. In particular, the Court rejected the argument that Union law should be unconcerned with the campaign because it appeared to be unsuccessful. The case therefore demonstrated that, in relation to what is now Article 34 TFEU, the Court is more interested in **substance** than **form**. Thus, as stated in *Dassonville*, it is only necessary that a measure is **capable** of hindering trade between Member States and there is no need to prove that such trade has actually been affected by the measure.

> ➤ The '**Buy Irish**' case is considered in more detail in section 12.4.1 (page 537); see section 12.4.2 for an explanation of the *Dassonville* formula

However, not all measures which promote domestic goods will be caught by Article 34 TFEU, as illustrated in the following case:

Apple and Pear Development Council v K.J. Lewis Ltd (Case 222/82)

Facts:

The Apple and Pear Development Council was set up by the UK government. Part of the Council's role was to market the fruit produced in the UK. The Council was financed by a mandatory charge imposed on UK fruit growers, which was contested on the basis that it was contrary to what is now Article 34 TFEU (Art 30 EEC Treaty at the time).

Ruling:

With regard to whether the matter fell within the scope of what is now Article 34 TFEU, the Court of Justice reiterated its decision in the '**Buy Irish**' case (see above and section 12.4.1). The Court then continued as follows:

> 18 … such a body [as the Council] is under a duty not to engage in any advertising intended to discourage the purchase of products of other Member States or to disparage those products in the eyes of consumers. Nor must it advise consumers to purchase domestic products solely by reason of their national origin.
>
> 19 On the other hand, Article 30 [now Art 34 TFEU] **does not prevent such a body from drawing attention, in its publicity, to the specific qualities of fruit grown in the Member State in question or from organising campaigns to promote the sale of certain varieties, mentioning their particular properties, even if those varieties are typical of national production.**

Significance:

This case established that it is permissible for the government of a Member State to promote, for example, specific varieties of apples and to draw attention to the particular qualities of such apples. However, such promotion may be classified as a distinctly applicable measure under Article 34 TFEU if it is intended to discourage the purchase of imported products. This is a fine line to draw in practice.

In *Commission* **v** *Germany* (Case 12/74), the Court of Justice stated that it may be possible for origin-marking (i.e. labelling a product as from a particular place) to be acceptable, where it implies a certain quality in the goods, that they were made from certain materials or by a particular form of manufacturing, or where the origin indicates a special place in the folklore or tradition of the particular region in question. However, this exception will be treated with caution by the Court, as illustrated in the following case:

Commission v Ireland (Case 113/80) – 'Irish souvenirs'

Facts:

Irish legislation required imported articles of jewellery depicting motifs or possessing characteristics which suggested they were souvenirs of Ireland to bear an indication of their country of origin or the word 'foreign'. The Commission brought an action before the Court of Justice on the basis that this measure infringed what is now Article 34 TFEU (Art 30 EEC Treaty at the time).

> **Ruling:**
>
> The Court of Justice held that the requirement indisputably constituted a discriminatory measure as no statement of origin was required for domestic products. Furthermore, it would not be enough for Ireland to require that domestic products were also marked with their origin. Rather, the Court determined that the interests of consumers and fair trading would be adequately safeguarding by allowing domestic manufacturers to mark their products with their origin if they so wished.
>
> **Significance:**
>
> This case established that a **requirement** to mark the origin of a product is contrary to what is now Article 34 TFEU when the origin bears no relevance to the qualities of the product. However, manufacturers can always **choose** to origin-mark their products.

Another way in which Member States may favour domestic products occurs in the field of public procurement (i.e. public service contracts). The following case provides an example of this:

> ### *Du Pont De Nemours Italiana Spa v Unità Sanitaria Locale No. 2 Di Cascara (Case C-21/88)*
>
> **Facts:**
>
> A national law in Italy required all public bodies and authorities to obtain at least 30 per cent of their supplies from undertakings established in Southern Italy. Du Pont De Nemours was an undertaking which subsequently challenged the fact that it only had access to the tendering of 70 per cent of a contract for the supply of radiological films and liquids. The national court referred questions to the Court of Justice, including whether the national provisions in question were compatible with what is now Article 34 TFEU (Art 30 EEC Treaty at the time).
>
> **Ruling:**
>
> The Court of Justice held as follows:
>
> 11 It must be pointed out … that such a system, which favours goods processed in a particular region of a Member State, prevents the authorities and public bodies concerned from procuring some of the supplies they need from undertakings situated in other Member States. Accordingly, it must be held that products originating in other Member States suffer discrimination in comparison with products manufactured in the Member State in question, with the result that the normal course of intra-Community [i.e. intra-Union] trade is hindered.
>
> 12 That conclusion is **not** affected by the fact that the restrictive effects of a preferential system of the kind at issue are borne in the same measure both by products manufactured by undertakings from the Member State in question which are not situated in the region covered by the preferential system and by products manufactured by undertakings established in other Member States.
>
> 13 … the fact remains that **all the products benefiting by the preferential system are domestic products**.
>
> **Significance:**
>
> This case established that what is now Article 34 TFEU prohibits measures that benefit only domestic goods produced in a certain region. Thus, measures whereby not all goods that are disadvantaged are imported, but all goods that benefit are domestic, are prohibited.

Similarly, in ***Campus Oil Ltd v Minister for Industry and Energy*** (Case 72/83), Ireland had placed an obligation on importers to buy a certain proportion of their oil supplies (35 per cent) from Ireland's only state-owned refinery, at prices fixed by the government. The Court of Justice held that this was clearly discriminatory and breached what is now Article 34 TFEU.

Price-fixing regulations

> Price-fixing is considered further in section 12.4.4 in relation to indistinctly applicable measures

Another way in which a Member State can treat imports less favourably than domestic products is by fixing prices to make it more difficult for an importer to market their goods within that Member State. If price-fixing (e.g. a minimum price for apples of £3 per kg) is applied only to the imported product, then it will clearly be caught by Article 34 TFEU as a distinctly applicable measure.

12.4.4 Indistinctly applicable MEEs: dual-burden rules

In addition to measures that explicitly distinguish between domestic and imported goods, **Article 3 of Directive 70/50** (see above) also encompasses measures which apply to both domestic and imported products, but which have a harsher impact on imported products in practice. These measures do **not** explicitly distinguish between goods according to their origin and are therefore referred to as **indistinctly applicable measures.** Specifically, Article 3 refers to measures relating to the marketing of products dealing with shape, size, weight, composition, presentation or identification 'which are equally applicable to domestic and imported products where the restrictive effect of such measures on the free movement of goods exceeds the effects intrinsic to trade rules'. This will be the case where the **proportionality test** is not met; i.e. where restrictive effects on the free movement of goods are disproportionate to their purpose and where the same objective can be attained by means which are less obstructive to trade. These criteria have been crucial in the development of the jurisprudence of the Court of Justice in relation to national measures which appear, at least, to apply indiscriminately to both imported and domestic goods.

> The Cassis case is also considered in section 12.5.2 in relation to the rule of reason defence

The Cassis rule of mutual recognition

In the following case, the Court of Justice laid down an important principle on whether such national provisions constitute MEEs:

> ***Rewe-Zentrale Ag v Bundesmonopolverwaltung Für Branntwein** (Case 120/78) – 'Cassis'*
>
> **Facts:**
>
> The applicant wished to import the liqueur 'Cassis de Dijon' into Germany from France; for this reason the case is usually referred to as the **Cassis** case. The relevant German authorities refused to allow the importation because the French liqueur was not of sufficient alcoholic strength to be marketed in Germany. Under German law, liqueurs had to have an alcoholic strength of at least 25 per cent, whereas the French liqueur was between 15 per cent and 20 per cent. The importer challenged the decision on the basis that the rule infringed what is now Article 34 TFEU (Art 30 EEC Treaty at the time).

> **Ruling:**
>
> The Court accepted that, in the absence of any common rules in the Union relating to the production and marketing of alcohol, it was up to Member States to regulate these activities in their own territories. However, the Court held as follows:
>
> > 14 ... It ... appears that the unilateral requirement imposed by the rules of a Member State of a minimum alcohol content for the purposes of the sale of alcoholic beverages constitutes an obstacle to trade which is incompatible with the provisions of Article 30 of the Treaty [now Art 34 TFEU]. **There is therefore no valid reason why, provided that they have been lawfully produced and marketed in one of the Member States, alcoholic beverages should not be introduced into any other Member State**; the sale of such products may not be subject to a legal prohibition on the marketing of beverages with an alcohol content lower than the limits set by national rules.
>
> **Significance:**
>
> In line with the **Dassonville** formula, this case confirmed that Article 34 TFEU applies to indistinctly applicable rules that inhibit trade between Member States. This case established that once goods have been lawfully marketed in one Member State, they should be free to be marketed in any other Member State without restriction. This principle is known as the **rule of mutual recognition**.

The above case demonstrates how the uniform application of rules to domestic and imported products can nevertheless hinder the free movement of goods through the imposition of unjustified product specifications. Where such rules differ from those which apply in the product's country of origin, they impose a **dual burden** on the foreign producer, as goods which are produced in one country but sold in another must meet both sets of requirements. The domestic producer (e.g. German liqueur producers) will already comply with domestic laws, whereas the foreign producer (e.g. French liqueur producers) will have to change their method of production to comply with the laws of the importing Member State, thus increasing their costs and decreasing any competitive advantage their product might have had. Furthermore, if different restrictions on alcohol content are applied by each Member State, any liqueur producer would have to navigate an extremely complex and burdensome array of rules in order to trade throughout the Union. The **rule of mutual recognition**, whereby goods that can be lawfully marketed in one Member State should not be subject to restrictions in any other Member State, therefore provided a means of realising the free movement of goods in areas where there was no specific harmonisation of standards.

> ▶ Harmonisation of standards is discussed below, in this section

Following **Cassis**, there have been a number of cases applying the rule of mutual recognition to a wide variety of different measures, some examples of which are now outlined.

Product packaging

> ### Walter Rau Lebensmittelwerke v DE Smedt PVBA (Case 261/81)
>
> **Facts:**
>
> A rule in Belgium required margarine to be marketed in cube-shaped packaging so that consumers could easily distinguish it from butter. In light of this rule, a Belgian buyer refused to accept deliveries of non-cube-shaped margarine from a German seller with whom they had a contract. The German seller challenged this breach of contract before the district court of Hamburg, which

referred a question to the Court of Justice as to whether the Belgian rule contravened what is now Article 34 TFEU (Art 30 EEC Treaty at the time).

Ruling:

The Court of Justice noted that, although the rule applied to all margarine sold in Belgium, foreign manufacturers wishing to import margarine into Belgium would have to establish a special production and packaging line for the Belgian market, which would increase their production costs. There was no consumer protection reason for the packaging requirement and the true nature of the product could just as well be conveyed to the consumer by effective labelling. The requirement that margarine be sold in cube-shaped packaging was therefore ruled to constitute a measure having an effect equivalent to a quantitative restriction.

Significance:

This case provides a clear example of the extra burden that national rules may place on manufacturers in other countries and thus how national rules relating to product specification can hinder the free movement of goods.

Origin-marking

Commission v UK (Case 207/83) – 'UK origin marking'

Facts:

UK legislation required that certain goods which were sold in retail markets had to be marked with their country of origin. French manufacturers argued that the origin-marking requirement increased production costs. The Commission brought infringement proceedings against the UK under what is now Article 258 TFEU, claiming this requirement was in breach of what is now Article 34 TFEU (Art 30 EEC Treaty at the time) as it constituted an MEE. The Commission also argued that such origin-marking encouraged consumers to exercise their prejudices in favour of national products and was likely to reduce the sale of imported goods. The UK government defended the origin-marking order on the grounds that the origin details gave important information to the consumer about the nature and quality of the product and that the requirement of origin-marking was non-discriminatory because it applied to both domestic and imported products.

Ruling:

The Court of Justice stated as follows:

> 17 ... **it has to be recognised that the purpose of indications of origin or origin-marking is to enable consumers to distinguish between domestic and imported products and this enables them to assert any prejudices which they may have against foreign products**. As the Court has had occasion to emphasise in various contexts, the Treaty, by establishing a common market [i.e. internal market] and progressively approximating the economic policies of the Member States, seeks to unite national markets in a single market, the origin-marking requirement not only makes the marketing in a Member State of goods produced in other Member States in the sectors in question more difficult; it also has the effect of slowing down economic interpenetration in the Community [i.e. Union] by handicapping the sale of goods produced as a result of a division of labour between Member States.

> See section 12.4.2 for an explanation of the *Dassonville* formula

18 It follows from those considerations that the UK provisions in question are liable to have the effect of increasing the production costs of imported goods and making it more difficult to sell them on the UK market.

Significance:

This case established that a rule that encourages the exercise of national prejudices was capable of affecting intra-Union trade. Therefore, applying the *Dassonville* formula, such a measure constitutes an MEE. As any distinctive national quality of the goods could be highlighted by individual retailers, national legislation **requiring** origin-marking was not proportionate.

National quality standard

Commission v *Ireland* (Case 45/87) – 'Water pipes'

Facts:

A water supply contract being commissioned by a local authority in Ireland (Dundalk Council) stipulated that the water pipes had to be certified as complying with Irish Standard 188. Only one manufacturer, located in Ireland, made pipes which were certified under this standard. One of the bids for the contract was based on the use of pipes not certified under the Irish standard, although they did comply with international standards. Dundalk Council refused to consider the bid for that reason. The Commission brought an action against the Irish government under what is now Article 258 TFEU, for allowing a specification relating to a water supply contract which, it alleged, breached what is now Article 34 TFEU (Art 30 EEC Treaty at the time).

Ruling:

The Court held that, although the requirement in question applied indistinctly to all products, the fact that only one undertaking had been certified to apply the Irish Standard Mark to their pipes, and that this undertaking was located in Ireland, meant that the specification had the effect of restricting the supply of pipes to a domestic manufacturer.

The Court then considered the Irish government's argument that the specification was necessary to ensure that the pipes would suit the existing network. The Court ruled that:

22 That technical argument cannot be accepted. The Commission's complaint does not relate to compliance with technical requirements but the refusal of the Irish authorities to verify whether those requirements are satisfied where the manufacturer of the materials has not been certified by the IRIS to IS 188. By incorporating in the notice in question the words 'or equivalent' after the reference to the Irish standard, as provided for by Directive 71/305 where it is applicable, **the Irish authorities could have verified compliance with the technical conditions without from the outset restricting the contract to tenderers proposing to utilise Irish materials.**

Significance:

In this case, the Court of Justice held that while it was reasonable to specify the quality of pipes to be used for the transmission of drinking water, the attainment of that objective could have been achieved in a less restrictive manner. The authorities could allow the use of pipes which had been produced to a standard which was equivalent to the Irish standard, rather than requiring certification that was not available to foreign producers.

In the two cases above, the Court of Justice considered the **effect** of the national practice, rather than its legal form. This is quite clear in the following category.

Administrative practices

Commission v France (Case 21/84)

Facts:
A French measure required approval from the authorities for both domestic and imported postal franking machines. However, administrative practices resulted in the approval of foreign machines being delayed. A UK manufacturer had failed to secure the approval of the French authorities, despite repeated applications, and even after France had repealed an earlier law which explicitly stated a preference for domestic machines. The Commission alleged that such delays violated what is now Article 34 TFEU (Art 30 EEC Treaty at the time).

Ruling:
The Court of Justice held as follows:

11 **The fact that a law or regulation such as that requiring prior approval for the marketing of postal franking machines conforms in formal terms to Article 30 of the EEC Treaty [now Art 34 TFEU] is not sufficient to discharge a Member State of its obligation under that provision.** Under the cloak of a general provision permitting the approval of machines imported from other Member States, the administration might very well adopt a systematically unfavourable attitude towards imported machines, either by allowing considerable delay in replying to applications for approval or in carrying out the examination procedure, or by refusing approval on the grounds of various alleged technical faults for which no detailed explanations are given or which prove to be inaccurate.

12 The prohibition on measures having an effect equivalent to quantitative restrictions would lose much of its useful effect if it did not cover protectionist or discriminatory practices of that type.

13 It must however be noted that **for an administrative practice to constitute a measure prohibited under Article 30 [now Art 34 TFEU] that practice must show a certain degree of consistency and generality**. That generality must be assessed differently according to whether the market concerned is one on which there are numerous traders or whether it is a market, such as that in postal franking machines, on which only a few undertakings are active. In the latter case, a national administration's treatment of a single undertaking may constitute a measure incompatible with Article 30 [now Art 34 TFEU].

14 In the light of those principles it is clear from the facts of the case that the conduct of the French postal administration constitutes an impediment to imports contrary to Article 30 of the EEC Treaty [now Art 34 TFEU].

15 It must therefore be concluded that by refusing without proper justification to approve postal franking machines from another Member State, the French Republic has failed to fulfil its obligations under Article 30 of the EEC Treaty [now Art 34 TFEU].

Significance:
This case established that a law, which on the face of it does not breach what is now Article 34 TFEU, could constitute a breach if the method of its application causes imported goods to be disadvantaged in practice.

Price-fixing regulations

Along with distinctly applicable price-fixing measures, as noted under Directive 70/50, Article 34 TFEU can also prohibit price-fixing regulations which apply to both imported and domestic goods, i.e. indistinctly applicable price-fixing measures. The Court of Justice determined this in the following case:

Openbaar Ministerie v Van Tiggele (Case 82/77)

Facts:

Dutch legislation set minimum selling prices for certain spirits. A seller sold spirits for less than this minimum and was prosecuted. In his defence, he argued that the legislation breached what is now Article 34 TFEU (Art 30 EEC Treaty at the time). The question referred to the Court of Justice pursuant to what is now Article 267 TFEU was whether this minimum price constituted an MEE.

Ruling:

The Court of Justice held as follows:

12 For the purposes of this prohibition it is sufficient that the measures in question are likely to hinder, directly or indirectly, actually or potentially, imports between Member States.

13 Whilst national price-control rules applicable without distinction to domestic products and imported products cannot in general produce such an effect they may do so in certain specific cases.

14 Thus **imports may be impeded in particular when a national authority fixes prices or profit margins at such a level that imported products are placed at a disadvantage** in relation to identical domestic products either because they cannot profitably be marketed in the conditions laid down or because the competitive advantage conferred by lower cost prices is cancelled out.

The Court thus concluded that the Dutch law contravened what is now Article 34 TFEU.

Significance:

This case established that where price-fixing places imported products at a disadvantage, what is now Article 34 is breached. This is the case both if minimum prices are fixed so high as to cancel out an imported product's competitive advantage (i.e. the imported goods cannot be sold more cheaply than domestic equivalents) or if maximum prices are fixed so low as to render the sale of the imported goods unprofitable.

Horizontal direct effect of Article 34 TFEU

> Horizontal direct effect is explained in section 8.2.2. *Farrell* v *Whitty* is considered in section 8.2.3 (page 290)

The rule of mutual recognition applies when there are no Union-wide **harmonising measures** in relation to the product in question. In order to ensure the effectiveness of this rule, the Court of Justice established the **horizontal direct effect** of Article 34 TFEU in the following case:

Fra.bo SpA v Deutsche Vereinigung des Gas- und Wasserfaches eV (DVGW) (Case C-171/11)

Facts:

The DVGW was a German non-profit body governed by private law, which produced technical standards pertaining to the gas and water sectors and certified compliance with those standards. Fra.bo was a manufacturer of copper fittings established in Italy. In June 2005, the DVWG cancelled the certification of Fra.bo's copper fittings on the basis that they had not passed a test as required by an amended technical standard. Fra.bo argued that, as the fittings were lawfully marketed in another Member State, the withdrawal of the certification constituted a breach of the free movement of goods under what is now Article 34 TFEU. The DVGW, however, argued that as it was a private body, what is now Article 34 TFEU could not be enforced against it.

Ruling:

The Court of Justice first noted that the copper fittings at issue were not covered by any Union-wide harmonising measures and that Member States were therefore permitted to make the marketing of such products in their territory subject to national provisions until the European technical specifications provide otherwise. Such national provisions must, however, be consistent with the Treaties, including the principle of the free movement of goods.

Additionally, the Court noted that the DVGW could not be held to be a state body as it received no funding from the state and the state had no decisive influence over its activities. The Court then considered whether what is now Article 34 TFEU (Art 28 EC Treaty at the material time) could be applied to the standardisation and certification activities of a private-law body. To this end, the Court observed that (i) German legislation states that all products certified by the DVGW comply with national law; (ii) compliance certificates for the copper fittings at issue could only be attained from the DVGW; and (iii) while there is no legal restriction on the marketing of non-certified copper fittings, almost all German consumers will choose to purchase certified copper fittings in practice. The Court therefore concluded as follows:

31 In such circumstances, it is clear that a body such as the DVGW, by virtue of its authority to certify the products, **in reality holds the power to regulate the entry into the German market** of products such as the copper fittings at issue in the main proceedings.

32 Accordingly ... Article 28 EC [now Art 34 TFEU] must be interpreted as meaning that it applies to standardisation and certification activities of a private-law body, where the **national legislation considers the products certified by that body to be compliant with national law** and that has the **effect of restricting the marketing of products which are not certified by that body**.

Significance:

This case established that what is now Article 34 TFEU can have **horizontal direct effect**. However, the scope for horizontal direct effect was narrowly construed by the Court of Justice, such that Article 34 TFEU may only be applied to private-law bodies whose standardisation and certification activities are **recognised under national law** and whose activities have the effect of **regulating the entry into a market**.

The Court of Justice's expansion of the application of Article 34 TFEU was then continued in *James Elliott Construction Limited* v *Irish Asphalt Limited* (Case C-613/14), which is considered below.

> **Reflection:** General horizontal direct effect of Article 34 TFEU?
>
> In his Opinion on the case of **Viking Line ABP** (Case 438/05), Advocate General Maduro argued that 'rules on freedom of movement can limit the autonomy of individuals'. To support this position, Maduro referred to **Commission v France** ('**Angry farmers**' – Case 265/95) and **Schmidberger v Austria** (Case C-112/00), which both concerned protests that had the effect of restricting the free movement of goods. However, in both of these cases the issue was the

> *Viking Line ABP* is considered in section 11.3.1 (page 446); the *Angry farmers* case is considered in section 12.4.3 (page 541); *Schmidberger v Austria* is considered in section 12.5.2 (page 582); and *Farrell v Whitty* is considered in section 8.2.3 (page 290).

> extent to which what is now Article 34 TFEU required *Member State authorities* to intervene in the actions of individuals to uphold the free movement of goods, rather than the extent to which what is now Article 34 TFEU directly imposes obligations on *individuals*. **Schmidberger** and the **Angry farmers** cases therefore do not demonstrate the horizontal direct effect of Article 34 TFEU in the same way as the Court of Justice's subsequent ruling in **Viking Line ABP** gave horizontal direct effect to Article 49 TFEU.
>
> Therefore, Article 34 TFEU only seems to have horizontal direct effect under the very narrow conditions established in **Fra.bo**, i.e. when a private undertaking's standardisation and certification activities are recognised under national law and where those activities have the effect of regulating entry into a market. Such a limited form of horizontal direct effect may even be referred to as semi-horizontal direct effect or, alternatively, may be described as merely an expansive interpretation of vertical direct effect in line with **Farrell v Whitty** (Case C-413/15).

Harmonising directives

Prior to the establishment of the rule of mutual recognition in **Cassis**, dual burdens on importers resulting from divergent standards between Member States could only be resolved through the enactment of **harmonising directives**. Such directives were enacted in order to create minimum product standards that are binding on all Member States. Through such harmonisation, producers could benefit from large product runs, without having to go to the additional expense of tailoring their products to the standards set in each Member State. Furthermore, where a common standard had been reached and the appropriate directive adopted, there was no further scope for national measures in that area and any attempts to justify such measures either as mandatory requirements or under the specific exceptions in what is now Article 36 TFEU (see below) would be rejected.

However, harmonising directives could **initially** only be enacted under what is now **Article 115 TFEU**, which empowers the Council, **acting unanimously**, to enact directives for the approximation (i.e. harmonisation) of national legislation on matters which directly affect the establishment or functioning of the internal market. (This has developed with the introduction of **Article 114 TFEU** by the Single European Act, see below.) The requirement for the Council to act unanimously meant that any Member State which felt that a harmonising directive was not in their national interest could effectively veto its adoption. The requirement for unanimity therefore meant that procedures for agreeing common standards were difficult and time-consuming. As a result, the standards adopted were, in some cases, technically obsolete by the time they came into effect and the cost, in terms of lost intra-Union trade, was high.

The **Cassis** case gave a new impetus to the harmonisation process. It led to a declaration by the Commission that it would concentrate on steps for the harmonisation of national laws which could affect intra-Union trade and which, in the absence of harmonisation, would have to be justified as mandatory requirements under the second **Cassis** principle or under one of the specific exceptions provided for in Article 36 TFEU (see below). It also led to the **Council Resolution** of 7 May 1985 on a **'new approach'** to technical harmonisation and standards. The resolution established four fundamental principles on which this approach would be based:

1 Legislative harmonisation is limited to adoption, by means of directives based on what is now Article 115 TFEU, of the **essential safety requirements** (or other requirements in the general interest) with which products put on the market must conform, and which should therefore enjoy free movement throughout the Union.

2 The task of drawing up the **technical specifications** needed for the production and placing on the market of products conforming to the essential requirements established by the directives, while taking into account the current stage of technology, is entrusted to organisations competent in the standardisation area.

3 These technical specifications are **not** mandatory and maintain their status of **voluntary standards.**

4 National authorities are obliged to recognise that products manufactured in conformity with harmonised standards (or, provisionally, with national standards) are **presumed to conform** to the 'essential requirements' established by the directive. This signifies that the producer has the choice of not manufacturing in conformity with the standards, but that in this event they have an obligation to prove that their products conform to the essential requirements of the directive. In order that this system may operate it is necessary to ensure:

- on the one hand that the standards offer a guarantee of quality with regard to the 'essential requirements' established by the directives;
- on the other hand that the public authorities retain their responsibility for the protection of safety (or other requirements envisaged) on their territory.

The new approach established a clear break with the past, and there is a clear link between the Resolution and the **Cassis** judgment. The emphasis is now on broad performance standards rather than compliance with detailed technical specifications. Now, instead of attempting to create a detailed technical specification for a 'Euro-product', which was a difficult and lengthy task, new directives only set minimum safety and other standards which can then be satisfied in a number of different ways in the Member States, including through different manufacturing methods. Once a Union directive has been adopted under this approach, and after the date for implementation has passed, performance is verified at Union level under a process monitored by the Commission.

In addition to the adoption of a broader approach to essential requirements, agreement between Union institutions was further facilitated by the amendment of what is now **Article 114 TFEU** by the Single European Act. Under Article 114, the Council can now act under **qualified majority** (rather than unanimity) to adopt 'measures for the approximation of the provisions laid down by law, regulation or administrative action in Member States which have as their object the establishment and functioning of the internal market'. Hundreds of harmonising directives were subsequently adopted in preparation for the 1992 deadline for completing the single market. Overall, the 'new approach' is widely regarded as having had considerable success in reducing national legal and technical barriers and in moving the Union towards a genuine internal market.

It should be noted, however, that the four principles of the 'new approach' are not without their challenges and are subject to the pressures of a rapidly developing field. For example, under the fourth principle noted above, where a directive has been adopted, Member States are obliged to assume that products manufactured in accordance with harmonised standards comply with the relevant essential requirements. However, in *James Elliott Construction Limited* v *Irish Asphalt Limited* (Case C-613/14), the Court held that conformity with a harmonising technical standard, as provided for under point 2 above, does not negate a contractual obligation to supply goods of merchantable quality. This case was especially significant due to the Court's ruling that, although established by non-EU bodies as provided for by the second principle noted above, harmonising technical standards are provisions of Union law.

The project of standardisation for products across the Union is a never-ending one. In July 2017, the European Parliament adopted Resolution 2016/2274, which contains no less than 85 recommendations on improving accountability and legitimacy in the Union's approach to standardisation. Both the secondary legislation and the case law in this area should therefore be expected to continue to develop rapidly.

12.4.5 Indistinctly applicable MEEs: equal-burden rules

Cassis, and many cases after it, concerned **dual-burden rules**. This term refers to rules that apply equally to domestic and imported goods, even though the importing producer would already have to comply with the relevant trade rules of their own Member State. The **Cassis** principle renders such rules incompatible with Article 34 TFEU unless they can be defended on specific grounds, which are examined below in section 12.5.

Equal-burden rules also apply to domestic and imported goods without distinction, but do not have a protectionist effect. Thus, although all goods are subjected to an identical burden, such restrictions may nevertheless be considered to pose an obstacle to the free movement of goods. While dual-burden rules have consistently been held to fall within Article 34 TFEU, the Court of Justice was initially inconsistent in its approach to equal-burden rules.

The Court of Justice held in a number of cases that indistinctly applicable rules which do **not** relate to the **characteristics** of a product and do **not** impose a dual burden on importers, but rather only concern the **conditions** under which a product is to be sold, are outside the remit of what is now Article 34 TFEU. For example, *Oebel* (Case 155/80) concerned a national rule prohibiting the delivery of bakery products to consumers and retailers during the night and *Quietlynn Ltd* v *Southend-on-Sea Borough Council* (Case C-23/89) concerned a UK law limiting the sale of lawful sex products to shops that had been licensed by the local authority.

In other cases, however, the Court of Justice held that such rules, *prima facie*, come within the scope of what is now Article 34 TFEU, but then found them to be justifiable on one of the grounds set out in Article 36 TFEU or by applying the **rule of reason** defence (see below). For example, *Cinéthèque SA* v *Fédération Nationale des Cinémas Français* (Joined Cases 60 and 61/84) concerned French legislation prohibiting the sale or rental of film videos within the first year of the film receiving its performance certificate. The objective was to encourage people to watch the film at the cinema. The effect was that neither domestic nor imported films could be sold during that period. A distributor of videos relied on what is now Article 34 TFEU before French courts to challenge the law as a trade barrier. The Court of Justice held that although 'its effect is not to favour national production as against the production of other Member States … the application of such a system may create barriers to intra-Community [i.e. intra-Union] trade in video-cassettes'. The Court thus held that there was a *prima facie* breach of what is now Article 34 TFEU, which it then found to be justified.

The difficult question of whether equal-burden cases fell within what is now Article 34 TFEU was also considered in a series of UK Sunday trading cases which came before the Court of Justice. In *Torfaen Borough Council* v *B&Q plc* (Case 145/88), B&Q was prosecuted for violating Sunday trading laws, which, at the time, restricted the **types** of goods that could be sold on Sundays. B&Q claimed that these laws constituted an MEE. The effect of the laws was to reduce turnover, but the reduction in turnover affected domestic and imported goods equally. Nevertheless, the Court of Justice held that this restriction constituted a *prima facie* breach of what is now Article 34 TFEU, which was then justified on the basis of legitimate economic and social policy (see section 12.5.2).

12.4 QUANTITATIVE RESTRICTIONS AND MEASURES HAVING EQUIVALENT EFFECT (ARTS 34 AND 35 TFEU)

The *Keck* formula

In the following case, the Court sought to address its past inconsistency in relation to equal-burden rules and adopted a general rule:

Keck and Mithouard (Joined Cases C-267 and 268/91)

Facts:

The defendants (Keck and Mithouard) were prosecuted in a French court for having resold goods at a loss, a practice which was forbidden under French law. In their defence they pleaded, *inter alia*, that this rule constituted an MEE and was unlawful under what is now Article 34 TFEU (Art 30 EEC Treaty at the time). The case was referred to the Court of Justice under what is now Article 267 TFEU.

Ruling:

The Court of Justice considered whether a prohibition on resale at a loss constituted an MEE. The Court first noted that such a prohibition is not designed to regulate trade in goods between Member States and then held as follows:

14 In view of the increasing tendency of traders to invoke Article 30 of the Treaty [now Art 34 TFEU] as a means of challenging any rules whose effect is to limit commercial freedom even where such rules are not aimed at products from other Member States, **the Court considers it necessary to re-examine and clarify its case law on this matter.**

15 It is established by the case-law beginning with '*Cassis de Dijon*' ... that, in the absence of harmonisation of legislation, obstacles to free movement of goods which are the consequence of applying, to goods coming from other Member States where they are lawfully manufactured and marketed, rules that lay down requirements to be met by such goods (such as those relating to designation, form, size, weight, composition, presentation, labelling, packaging) constitute measures of equivalent effect prohibited by Article 30 [now Art 34 TFEU]. This is so even if those rules apply without distinction to all products unless their application can be justified by a public-interest objective taking precedence over the free movement of goods.

16 By contrast, contrary to what has previously been decided, **the application to products from other Member States of national provisions restricting or prohibiting certain selling arrangements is not such as to hinder directly or indirectly, actually or potentially, trade between Member States within the meaning of the *Dassonville* judgment ... provided that those provisions apply to all affected traders operating within the national territory and provided that they affect in the same manner, in law and fact, the marketing of domestic products and of those from other Member States.**

17 Where those conditions are fulfilled, the application of such rules to the sale of products from another Member State is not by nature such as to prevent their access to the market or to impede access any more than it impedes the access of domestic products. **Such rules therefore fall outside the scope of Article 30 of the Treaty [now Art 34 TFEU].**

The Court therefore concluded that a general prohibition of resale at a loss did not come within the scope of what is now Article 34 TFEU.

Significance:

This case established a distinction between **rules that relate to goods** themselves, such as those concerning packaging, materials, size, etc., and **rules that relate to selling arrangements**. Rules relating to goods create a dual burden and are thus prohibited by what is now

> Article 34 TFEU under the **Cassis** formula. Rules relating to selling arrangements do **not** fall within the scope of what is now Article 34 TFEU, provided that they create an **equal burden** on domestic and imported products, i.e. provided that:
>
> (i) they **apply to all traders** operating within the national territory; and
> (ii) they **affect in the same manner**, in law and in fact, the marketing of domestic goods and imports.

The scope of the 'selling arrangements' referred to in the above case includes price restrictions, as in *Keck* itself, or any other national rules which govern the way products or services are sold or advertised. For example, the Court of Justice applied the *Keck* formula in *Tankstation 't Heuskse Vof* and *JBE Boermans* (Joined Cases C-401 and 402/92), which concerned rules on the maximum number of opening hours and compulsory periods of closure for petrol stations. The Court held that the rules did not fall within the scope of what is now Article 34 TFEU as 'they apply to all relevant traders without distinguishing between the origin of the products in question and do not affect the marketing of products from other Member States in a manner different from that in which they affect domestic products'. The Court has since confirmed that Article 34 does not apply to national measures indiscriminately restricting the opening hours of shops (*Punto Casa SpA* and *Promozioni Polivalenti Venete Soc coop arl* v *Sindacos del Comunes di Capena and Torri di Quartesolo* (Joined Cases C-69 and 258/93); *Pelckmans Turnhout NV* v *Walter Van Gastel Balen NV and Others* (Case C-483/12)).

Other cases in which the Court of Justice has applied the *Keck* formula and held that what is now Article 34 TFEU does not apply to the 'selling arrangements' at issue include the following:

- *Hunermund* (Case C-292/92), where the German pharmacists' association prohibited its members from advertising popular medicines outside their premises.
- *Leclerc-Siplec* (Case C-412/93), which concerned a French law preventing the advertisement of unleaded petrol sold in supermarkets (see especially the Opinion of Advocate General Jacobs on this case).
- *Morellato* (Case C-416/00), which concerned Italian legislation that prohibited the sale of bread that was the product of on-site baking of pre-cooked bread and which was not packaged prior to the point of sale. The Court held that in principle such a requirement would fall outside the scope of what is now Article 34 TFEU provided that it did not in reality constitute discrimination against imported products.

In the following two cases, the Court of Justice considered the *Keck* formula but found that it was not satisfied and that what is now Article 34 TFEU was therefore applicable:

> ### Vereinigte Familiapresse (Case C-368/95)
>
> **Facts:**
> A German newspaper publisher was selling newspapers in the German and Austrian markets in which readers were offered the opportunity to take part in games with prizes. This practice breached the Austrian Unfair Competition Act 1992. A competitor tried to stop the sale of the imported German papers and the case was referred to the Court of Justice.

12.4 QUANTITATIVE RESTRICTIONS AND MEASURES HAVING EQUIVALENT EFFECT (ARTS 34 AND 35 TFEU)

Ruling:

The Court of Justice rejected the Austrian argument that the restriction was merely a 'selling arrangement' and held as follows:

11 The Court finds that, even though the relevant national legislation is directed against a method of sales promotion, in this case **it bears on the actual content of the products**, in so far as the competitions in question form an integral part of the magazine in which they appear. As a result, the national legislation in question as applied to the facts of the case is **not** concerned with a selling arrangement within the meaning of the judgment in *Keck* ...

12 Moreover, since **it requires traders established in other Member States to alter the contents** of the periodical, the prohibition at issue impairs access of the products concerned to the market of the Member State of importation and consequently hinders free movement of goods. It therefore constitutes in principle a measure having equivalent effect within the meaning of Article 30 of the Treaty [now Art 34 TFEU].

Significance:

This case provides an example where the *Keck* formula was considered, but the rule in question was found to be concerned with the *contents* of goods rather than with their *selling arrangements*. Therefore, the rule produced a **dual burden** and came within the scope of what is now Article 34 TFEU.

Konsumentombudsmannen (KO) v *Gourmet International Products AB (GIP)* (Case C-405/98)

Facts:

A Swedish law prohibited advertisements for alcoholic beverages in periodicals. It was argued that this breached what is now Article 34 TFEU.

Ruling:

Referring to its judgment in *Keck*, the Court of Justice stated that in order for selling arrangements to avoid being caught by what is now Article 34 TFEU, they must **not** prevent access to the market by products from another Member State or impede such access any more than they impede the access of domestic products. The Court held that, in the case of products like alcoholic beverages, the consumption of which is linked to traditional social practices and to local habits and customs, a prohibition of all advertising directed at consumers in the form of advertisements in the press is liable to impede access to the market by products from other Member States more than it impedes access by domestic products. The Court therefore held that the prohibition came within the scope of what is now Article 34 TFEU.

Significance:

This case demonstrates that only '*certain* selling arrangements', as stated in paragraph 20 of *Keck*, are excluded from the scope of Article 34 TFEU. Although the rule at issue was held to be a selling arrangement, the Court held that it breached what is now Article 34. This was because, although the rule treated the marketing of domestic and imported goods equally in law, it did not affect them in the same way in practice and therefore did not satisfy the *Keck* formula.

➤ *KO* v *GIP* is also considered in relation to the free movement of services in section 11.3.4 (page 466)

The Court of Justice also determined that a rule related to selling arrangements came within the scope of what is now Article 34 TFEU on the basis that, *in practice*, it affected the marketing of imported goods differently from domestic goods in the following cases:

- ***Deutscher Apothekerverband*** (Case C-322/01), which concerned a German prohibition on the sale of medicinal products by mail order or over the internet;
- ***Ker-Optika Bt* v *Ántsz Dél-Dunántúli Regionális Intézete*** (Case C-108/09), which concerned a Hungarian prohibition on the sale of contact lenses by mail order or over the internet.

In each of the cases described above, it should be noted that the application of the ***Keck*** formula only determines whether a rule breaches Article 34 TFEU and does **not** also determine whether that breach may be justified by the rule of reason or the grounds set out in Article 36 TFEU. These defences are considered below in section 12.5.

The market access rule

In addition to measures that relate to goods, to which the rule of mutual recognition should be applied, and measures that relate to selling arrangements, to which the ***Keck*** formula should be applied, the Court of Justice has also considered rules that restrict the **use** of a product. The Court has found that such rules can be MEEs because they obstruct **market access** by virtue of the fact that potential customers will have no interest in buying a product that they know they will be unable to use (***Commission* v *Portugal*** (Case C-265/06)). In ***Commission* v *Italy*** (Case C-110/05 – '**Trailers**'), the Commission argued that a prohibition on motorcycles towing trailers was in breach of what is now Article 34 TFEU, as it effectively prevented the sale of trailers designed to be towed by motorcycles. Here, the Court first set out that MEEs include:

(i) measures which have as their object or effect the differential treatment of products imported from other Member States (i.e. distinctly applicable measures);

(ii) measures that impose requirements on goods that are lawfully manufactured and marketed in other Member States (i.e. measures that violate the rule of mutual recognition); and

(iii) 'Any other measure which hinders access of products originating in other Member States to the market of a Member State'.

The Court therefore established that indistinctly applicable measures that hinder access to a national market fall within the scope of what is now Article 34 TFEU. This can be referred to as the **market access rule**. This rule was then confirmed in ***Mickelsson and Roos*** (Case C-142/05), although in both this case and the **Trailers** case, the Court held that the restrictions at issue could be objectively justified.

In ***Scotch Whisky Association and Others* v *Advocate General for Scotland*** (Case-C 333/14), the Court of Justice then suggested that the market access rule could be applied to what appears to be a selling arrangement and, therefore, that it is not confined to restrictions on the use of a product. The case concerned the imposition of a minimum price for beverages determined by their alcohol content, known as the 'minimum price per unit' (MPU) restriction. The Court referred to the **Trailers** case to support the following statement:

> ... the fact that the legislation at issue in the main proceedings prevents the lower cost price of imported products being reflected in the selling price to the consumer means, by itself, that that legislation is **capable of hindering the access to the United Kingdom market**

of alcoholic drinks that are lawfully marketed in Member States other than the United Kingdom of Great Britain and Northern Ireland, and constitutes therefore a measure having an effect equivalent to a quantitative restriction within the meaning of Article 34 TFEU ... [para 32]

Thus, where the Court stated in *Dassonville* that 'all trading rules enacted by Member States which are capable of hindering ... intra-Community [i.e. intra-Union] trade are to be considered as measures having an effect equivalent to quantitative restrictions', in *Scotch Whisky Association*, the Court simply seemed to frame the concept of 'intra-Union trade' more precisely as market access. Once again, however, the Court held in this case that a restriction to market access could be justified, this time on the ground of protecting health and life under Article 36 TFEU (see below). Moreover, the absence of any reference to the Court's judgment in *Keck*, even though the case seemed to concern an equal burden selling arrangement, suggests that the Court may favour the application of the broad and straightforward market access rule over the more intricate and specific *Keck* formula. This conclusion is further supported by the Court's ruling in *Colruyt* (Case C-221/15), where the Court referred to its *Trailers* judgment and the market access test to determine whether a prohibition on selling tobacco products at a lower price than that indicated by the manufacturer or importer – i.e. a selling arrangement – was contrary to Article 34 TFEU.

> **Reflection:** Implications of the 'market access rule'
>
> The *Keck* formula seemed to clarify the Court's position on indistinctly applicable measures by drawing a distinction between measures relating to goods, which produce dual burdens and fall within the scope of Article 34 TFEU, and measures relating to selling arrangements, which produce equal burdens and do not fall within the scope of Article 34 TFEU. This served to constrain the *Dassonville* formula and provided Member States with relatively clear parameters within which they could enact national measures. However, these parameters have been shifted by the market access rule. This rule was first established in *Commission v Italy* ('*Trailers*') to the effect that indistinctly applicable measures restricting product *use* are prohibited under Article 34 TFEU if they hinder market access. This market access rule, as set out in *Trailers*, presented a challenge to the *Keck* formula, as restrictions on selling arrangements would surely always hinder access to a market, regardless of whether or not they produced equal burdens on importers and domestic producers. At this stage, however, the two rules could possibly have operated alongside each other: if the market access rule had been applied only to restrictions on the *use* of goods, then *Keck* could then still be applied to selling arrangements (as suggested by the Court in *LIBRO* (Case C-531/07) and *Visnapuu* (Case C-198/14)).
>
> However, in *Scotch Whisky Association* and *Colruyt*, the Court applied the market access rule to determine whether particular selling arrangements came within the scope of Article 34 TFEU. This seems to determine conclusively that the Court will choose to apply the more flexible market access rule and to disregard *Keck* going forward.
>
> The question now, then, is (i) whether *Keck* has truly been abandoned once and for all, (ii) whether the comprehensive three-part test set out in *Trailers* (see above) also replaces the *Dassonville* formula, and (iii) how broadly – and uniformly – the Court will define 'market access'. If *Keck* is no more, then the Court may find that more measures fall within the scope of Article 34 TFEU. However, if the *Dassonville* formula has also been retired, then this expansion of Article 34 TFEU is limited by the application instead of the narrower three-part test of *Trailers* (Derlén and Lindholm, 2019). Additionally, by applying the *Cassis* rule of reason, the Court can balance any expansion of Article 34 TFEU by also finding that many such measures can be justified (Barnard, 2009). However, regarding the third question, the case law is yet to provide a conclusive answer as to how broadly or narrowly the Court will interpret the market access test.

12.4.6 Quantitative restrictions and MEEs on exports (Art 35 TFEU)

Most of the cases considered so far have involved national restrictions, or measures equivalent to such restrictions, on imports. As noted above, **Article 35 TFEU** applies in much the same way as Article 34 TFEU, in that it prohibits quantitative restrictions and MEEs, but in relation to **exports** rather than imports. The principles applicable to restrictions on exports are, broadly, the same.

In *Procureur de la République de Besançon* v *Les Sieurs Bouhelier and others* (Case 53/76), the Court of Justice applied the *Dassonville* formula to exports. In this case, quality checks were imposed on watches for export, but not on those intended for the domestic market. As the requirements were imposed by the state and were capable of hindering intra-Union trade, the Court of Justice held that it was a measure equivalent to a quantitative restriction on exports in contravention of what is now Article 35 TFEU.

While MEEs that are applied indistinctly to both imports and domestic products are prohibited under Article 34, some element of discrimination, either formal or material, is required for the application of Article 35. This was emphasised in the following case:

Groenveld (Case 15/79)

Facts:
A Dutch law prohibited manufacturers of processed meats from processing horsemeat or having it in stock, even though the sale of horsemeat was permitted in the Netherlands. The purpose of this law was to ensure that Dutch processed meat products could be exported to countries where there were objections to the consumption of horsemeat or where the importation of horsemeat is prohibited. Groenveld was a manufacturer that sought to expand its operations into the production of horsemeat sausages, but which was refused an exemption from the prohibition. The question of whether the law breached what is now Article 35 TFEU (Art 34 EEC Treaty at the time) was subsequently referred to the Court of Justice.

Ruling:
The Court of Justice held that what is now Article 35 TFEU encompasses:

> national measures which have as their specific object or effect the restrictions of patterns of exports and thereby **the establishment of a difference in treatment between the domestic trade of a Member State and its export trade in such a way as to provide a particular advantage for national production of the domestic market** of the state in question at the expense of the production or of the trade of other Member States. This is not so in the case of a prohibition like that in question which is applied objectively to the production of goods of a certain kind without drawing a distinction depending on whether such goods are intended for the national market or for export. [para 7]

Significance:
This case suggested that **only distinctly applicable measures** fall within the scope of Article 35 TFEU.

However, in *Gysbrechts and Santurel Inter BVBA* (Case C-205/07), the Court of Justice ruled that a national rule prohibiting an advance payment for goods constituted an MEE. This rule was an indistinctly applicable measure, but the Court of Justice held that it would have a greater effect on traders wishing to safeguard against the risks of selling products across borders.

Whether or not there is discrimination is a matter of both national law and practice. Therefore, a national law requiring producers to deliver poultry offal to their local authority has been held to constitute a ban on exports (*Nertsvoederfabriek Nederland* (Case 118/86)). However, legislation that regulated the content and quality of all cheese produced in the Netherlands – and which therefore put Dutch producers at a disadvantage in comparison with foreign producers who did not have to produce their cheese to the same standards – was held by the Court of Justice not to be a measure equivalent to a quantitative restriction on exports (*Jongeneel Kaas BV* v *Netherlands* (Case 237/82)). In this case the Court demonstrated its willingness to tolerate indistinctly applicable measures that had an adverse effect on the competitiveness of domestic products, which it would not have tolerated in relation to imported products.

12.5 Permissible quantitative restrictions and MEEs

Objective 5

There are two ways in which quantitative restrictions or measures having an equivalent effect, which are prohibited by Article 34 or Article 35 TFEU, may be justified: by Article 36 TFEU and by mandatory requirements developed through case law. First, regardless of whether a measure is distinctly or indistinctly applicable, it will not breach Union law if it can be justified on one of the grounds set out in **Article 36 TFEU**. Secondly, if the measure is **indistinctly applicable**, it may also or alternatively be justifiable on the basis of a **mandatory requirement** under the **Cassis rule of reason**. These two types of defence, which provide Member States with a degree of flexibility in their negotiation of competing interests, are examined in detail in this section. An overview of these defences is provided in Figure 12.3 (page 574).

12.5.1 Justifications under Article 36 TFEU

Article 36 TFEU (which is worded identically to the former Art 30 EC Treaty) sets out the circumstances under which Member States may derogate from their obligation to ensure the free movement of goods. Article 36 TFEU provides that:

> The provisions of Articles 34 and 35 shall not preclude prohibitions or restrictions on imports, exports or goods in transit justified on grounds of **public morality, public policy or public security**; the **protection of health and life** of humans, animals and plants; the **protection of national treasures** possessing artistic, historic or archaeological value; or the **protection of industrial and commercial property**. Such prohibitions or restrictions shall not, however, constitute a means of arbitrary discrimination or a disguised restriction on trade between Member States.

These derogations comprise an **exhaustive** list and are interpreted strictly by the Court of Justice; national measures not falling clearly within its terms are rejected by the Court. Furthermore, the Article 36 TFEU exceptions can **only** be advanced to justify national measures in the absence of any relevant Union **harmonising directives** (*Lucien Ortscheit Gmbh* v *Eurim-Pharm Gmbh* (Case C-320/93). If there is relevant Union legislation, there will be no scope for national measures that are incompatible with it and Article 36 TFEU cannot be relied upon to justify the measure (*R* v *Ministry Of Agriculture, Fisheries and Food, Ex Parte Compassion in World Farming Ltd* (Case C-1/96)). This was established by the Court of Justice in *Tedeschi* v *Denkavit Commerciale srl* (Case 5/77), in which the Italian government sought to justify a measure on the contents of animal feed under what is now the Article 36 TFEU (Art 36 EEC Treaty at the time) ground of the protection of animal or human health. The Court stated that:

> Where, in application of Article 100 of the Treaty [now Art 115 TFEU], Community [i.e. Union] directives provide for the harmonization of the measures necessary to ensure the protection of animal and human health and establish Community [i.e. Union] procedures to check that they are observed, **recourse to Article 36 is no longer justified** and the appropriate checks must be carried out and the measures of protection adopted within the framework outlined by the harmonizing directive. [paras 34 and 35]

Article 36 TFEU is most often pleaded by Member States in defence of distinctly applicable measures (*Commission* v *Ireland* (Case 113/80 – '**Irish souvenirs**')). It is, however, equally applicable to indistinctly applicable measures (*Wurmser* (Case 25/88)). Where Article 36 TFEU can be advanced as a justification for national measures, it is for the national government relying on it to provide evidence in support of the grounds justifying its actions (*Officier Van Justitie* v *Sandoz BV* (Case 174/82)).

Where a measure may be justified under Article 36 TFEU, measures taken by Member States will still have to meet two fundamental criteria:

(i) there must be **no arbitrary discrimination** between imported and domestic products; and

(ii) any national measures **must be proportionate** to any risk and must not restrict trade any more than is necessary to protect the legitimate public interests recognised by Article 36 TFEU.

The operation of these principles is discussed further below in the context of case law of the Court of Justice relating to the specific Article 36 TFEU exceptions.

Public morality

The concept of public morality will vary widely from state to state and is not expanded upon in Article 36 TFEU or in any secondary legislation. For example, in the context of services under Article 56 TFEU, the Court did not agree that the termination of pregnancies should be excluded on the basis that it is intrinsically immoral, as it is lawfully carried out in several Member States (*Society for the Protection of the Unborn Child* v *Grogan* (Case C-159/90)). Similarly, in *HM Customs and Excise Commissioners* v *Schindler and Others* (Case C-275/92), the Court of Justice observed, with regard to gambling, that 'Even if the morality of lotteries is at least questionable, it is not for the Court to substitute its assessment for that of the legislature where that activity is practised legally' (para 32). The Court may, however, have to assess whether or not national rules are applied proportionately and without discrimination.

> ➤ *Grogan* and *Schindler* are considered in more depth in section 11.2.2

The issue of public morality first came before the Court of Justice in relation to what is now Article 36 TFEU in the following case:

R v *Henn and Darby* (Case 34/79)

Facts:

The defendants were convicted of being 'knowingly concerned in the fraudulent evasion of the prohibition of the importation of indecent or obscene articles', contrary to national law in the UK. The articles involved in the charges were six films and magazines of Danish origin, which had been brought into the UK from the Netherlands.

The House of Lords (the judicial functions of which are now exercised by the Supreme Court) referred several questions to the Court of Justice, including whether the prohibition on the importation of pornographic articles was a measure having equivalent effect to a quantitative restriction. The House of Lords also asked whether the fact that the prohibition imposed on the *importation* of pornography was different in scope from that imposed by the criminal law on the possession and publication of such material *within* the UK constituted a means of arbitrary discrimination or a disguised restriction on trade between Member States.

Ruling:

The Court was in no doubt that the ban was a quantitative restriction, as a prohibition on imports is 'the most extreme form of restriction' (para 12). However, the Court of Justice emphasised that Member States were free to take such action in appropriate circumstances:

> In principle, it is for each Member State to determine in accordance with its own scale of values and in the form selected by it the requirements of public morality in its territory. In any event, it cannot be disputed that the statutory provisions applied by the UK in regard to the importation of articles having an indecent or obscene character come within the powers reserved to the Member States by the first sentence of Article 36 [now Art 36 TFEU]. [para 15]

The Court was also satisfied that the differences between the prohibition on *imports* and the penalties applied to the possession and publication of pornographic materials *within* the UK were not significant:

> Whatever may be the differences between the laws on this subject in force in the different constituent parts of the UK, and notwithstanding the fact that they contain certain exceptions of limited scope, these laws, taken as a whole, have as their purpose the prohibition, or at least the restraining, of the manufacture and marketing of publications or articles of an indecent or obscene character. **In these circumstances it is permissible to conclude, on a comprehensive view, that there is no lawful trade in such goods in the UK.** A prohibition on imports which may in certain respects be more strict than some of the laws applied within the UK cannot, therefore, be regarded as amounting to a measure designed to give indirect protection to some national product or aimed at creating arbitrary discrimination. [para 21]

Significance:

This case established that, although there were 'certain exceptions' with regard to the trade of pornographic material in the UK, these exceptions were of such a limited scope that the Court concluded that 'there is no lawful trade in such goods in the UK'. Therefore, there was no arbitrary discrimination and the Article 36 public morality justification could be applied. This is similar to the application of the *de minimis* rule in English law.

The same area of UK law was at issue in **Conegate Ltd v HM Customs and Excise** (Case 121/85). This case concerned the seizure of inflatable sex dolls and other erotic articles by the customs authorities. The importers argued, and the Court of Justice agreed, that the situation was different to that in **Henn and Darby** because sex dolls, although not permitted to be publicly displayed, could be lawfully sold throughout the UK. The Court held that:

> A Member State may **not** rely on grounds of public morality in order to prohibit the importation of goods from other Member States when its legislation contains no prohibition on the manufacture or marketing of the same goods in its territory. [para 16]

The ruling in the above case parallels **Adoui and Cornuaille v Belgium** (Cases 115 and 116/81), which concerned the scope of the public policy exception in what is now Article 45(3) TFEU on the free movement of workers. In **Adoui**, the Court of Justice held that a Member State could not take action under the public policy exception against an EU citizen

> The *Adoui* case is discussed further in section 9.4.2

unless it took some kind of 'repressive measures' against its own nationals for engaging in the conduct on which the exclusion was based. A similar concept of equality of treatment underlies the requirement that the Member State excluding goods on the ground of public morality must in some way prohibit the manufacture or marketing of the same kind of goods within its own territory.

Public policy and public security

Very few attempts have been made by national governments to justify restrictive measures on these grounds. Public policy was, however, successfully advanced by the UK government in *R* v *Thompson and Others* (Case 7/78) to defend a prohibition on the export of silver alloy coins which had been, but were no longer, legal tender. The UK government argued that the protection of national coinage was an important aspect of public policy and the Court of Justice agreed. As the destruction of old coinage was prohibited within the UK, the Court held that the ban on exporting such coins was justified on grounds of public policy under what is now Article 36 TFEU because 'it is for the Member States to mint their own coinage and to protect it from destruction' (para 32).

In *Cullet* (Case 231/83), the French government argued before the Court of Justice that national rules fixing retail selling prices for fuel were justified on grounds of public order and public security, which would arise in relation to retailers affected by unrestrained competition. Advocate General verLoren van Themaat warned in his Opinion against the dangers of responding to public agitation:

> The acceptance of civil disturbance as a justification for encroachments upon the free movement of goods would ... have unacceptably drastic consequences. If road-blocks and other effective weapons of interest groups which feel threatened by the importation and sale at competitive prices of certain cheap products or services, or by immigrant workers or foreign businesses, were accepted as justification, the existence of the four freedoms of the Treaty could no longer be relied upon. Private interest groups would then, in the place of the Treaty and Community [i.e. Union] (and, within the limits laid down in the Treaty), determine the scope of those freedoms. In such cases, the concept of public policy requires, rather, effective action on the part of the authorities to deal with the disturbances. [para 5.3]

The Court of Justice supported the Advocate General's position and ruled that the French government had not demonstrated that it was unable to respond to the risks to public order and security in a manner that was less restrictive to the free movement of goods. Furthermore, as noted above, the Court held in *Commission* v *France* (Case C-265/95 – '**Angry farmers**') that the failure of a Member State to take action against the persistent obstruction of the free movement of goods by private groups will represent a breach of the Member State's obligation to uphold Union law and will not be justified by Article 36 TFEU.

The Irish government had more success with the public security exemption in the following case:

Campus Oil v Ministry for Industry and Energy (Case 72/83)

Facts:
Irish legislation required importers of petroleum products to purchase up to 35 per cent of their requirements from Ireland's state-owned refinery at prices fixed by the Minister. There was no doubt that the requirement breached what is now Article 34 TFEU. The government, however,

argued that the measure was necessary on the ground that the importance of oil for the maintenance of the life of the country made it essential to maintain fuel capacity in Ireland. The system it had adopted was the only means by which a fuel reserve could be built up.

Ruling:

The Court of Justice agreed that petroleum products were of fundamental importance to the country's existence, as they were needed for the country's institutions, vital services and the survival of its inhabitants. The Court therefore accepted the public security justification. It did, however, warn the Irish government that the purchasing obligation could be continued only if there was no less restrictive measure which was capable of achieving the same objective; nor should the quantities covered by the scheme exceed the minimum supply requirements without which the public security of the state would be affected. The scheme had, in other words, to be proportionate to the anticipated risk.

Significance:

This case demonstrates that the public security exemption is not interpreted so strictly as to be unusable in practice. However, the principle of proportionality must be adhered to at all times.

Protection of health and life

The principle of proportionality has been prominent in the many of decisions of the Court of Justice in which Member States have sought to rely on the exception relating to the health of humans, animals and plants. To be capable of justification as a health measure, it must form part of 'a seriously considered health policy'. This was lacking in the following case:

Commission v *UK* (Case 40/82) – 'poultry imports'

Facts:

In September 1981, the UK banned the import of turkeys from France (and some other Member States). There was evidence before the Court of Justice that, in the two years before the ban, there had been a steep rise in turkey imports for the Christmas market from France and other Member States. This had been followed by a chorus of complaints about unfair competition from UK poultry producers. The imposition of a sudden ban on the import of French turkeys was claimed to be a response to the risk of an outbreak of Newcastle Disease, a serious poultry infection. There had, however, been no recent outbreak in France and the main object of the UK government's ostensible concern was imports of turkeys into France from Eastern European countries where there was a more serious risk.

Ruling:

The Court was unconvinced by the UK's justification:

> 37 Certain established facts suggest that **the real aim of the 1981 measure was to block, for commercial and economic reasons, imports of poultry products** from other Member States, in particular from France. The UK government had been subject to pressure from UK poultry producers to block these imports. It hurriedly introduced its new policy with the result that French Christmas turkeys were excluded from the UK market for the 1981 season ... The deduction must be made that **the 1981 measures did not form part of a seriously considered health policy**.
>
> ...

> 40 Taken together, these facts are sufficient to establish **that the 1981 measures constitute a disguised restriction** on imports of poultry products from other Member States, in particular from France, unless it can be shown that, for reasons of animal health, the only possibility open to the UK was to apply the strict measures which are at issue in this case and that, therefore, the methods prescribed by the 1981 measures ... were not more restrictive than was necessary for the protection of poultry flocks in Great Britain.
>
> **Significance:**
>
> This case provides an example of where the Court found that a prohibition constituted a **disguised restriction** and could not therefore be justified under what is now Article 36 TFEU on the ground of protecting the health of animals. The Court of Justice was satisfied that, on the evidence, there were much less restrictive methods available that were appropriate to the degree of risk.

The successful action by the Commission in the above case led to a damages claim in the UK courts by an importer affected by the ban (***Bourgoin v Ministry of Agriculture, Fisheries and Food (MAFF)*** [1986] QB 716).

Many of the cases in which the health exception is raised depend on whether there is any genuine risk at all. In such cases, the Court of Justice must consider, on the best available scientific evidence: (i) whether there is a risk to health and (ii) if so, whether the Member State has responded appropriately and proportionately. In ***Commission v France*** (Case 216/84 – '**Milk substitutes**'), for example, French legislation prohibited the marketing of milk substitutes on the basis that they had a lower nutritional value and were harmful to some people. The Court of Justice rejected both arguments. The fact that milk substitutes had a lower nutritional value than milk products hardly constituted a health risk when consumers had so many other food products to choose from. While milk products themselves could pose a risk to some individuals with certain allergies or suffering from certain diseases, clear labelling would enable consumers to make a properly informed choice.

Milk was also at issue in ***Commission v UK*** (Case 124/81 – '**UHT milk**'). In this case, the Commission brought proceedings against the UK for imposing the requirement that milk processed by ultra-high temperature (UHT) should be marketed only by approved dairies or distributors. The government argued that this was necessary to ensure that milk was free from bacterial or viral infections. The effect of the restriction was that all imported milk had to be repackaged and re-treated. The Court of Justice rejected these measures as inappropriate and unnecessary. There was evidence that milk in all Member States was of similar quality and subject to equivalent controls. The restriction was, therefore, unjustified. The UK subsequently enacted the Importation of Milk Act 1983 in order to comply with this judgment.

The Court of Justice has also held that German legislation, which prohibited the import of meat products manufactured from meat that did not originate within the country of manufacture, could not be justified on health grounds as there was no reason to believe that the risk of contamination increased simply because the fresh meat crossed a Union frontier (***Commission v Germany*** (Case 153/78)).

Although the Court of Justice has held that the fact that testing has occurred in the country of origin should give rise to a presumption that the imported goods are safe to use, this is not a universal rule (***De Peijper*** (Case 104/75); ***Frans-Nederlandse*** (Case 272/80)). In particular, differences in approaches to food additives or medical products may justify additional testing by the importing Member State before authorisation to market the goods is given.

Officier Van Justitie v Sandoz BV (Case 174/82)

Facts:

Sandoz sought to retail certain food and drink products in the Netherlands, which were already available on the German or Belgian markets, but was refused authorisation to do so on the grounds that the addition of vitamins A and D to the products posed a risk to public health.

Ruling:

The Court of Justice held that the requirement to obtain authorisation for products that were lawfully marketed in other Member States on the basis that they contained certain additives was contrary to what is now Article 34 TFEU. With regard to whether the requirement could be permitted under what is now Article 36 TFEU on the basis of protecting human health, the Court noted that there was uncertainty about the point at which a large intake of vitamin additives in food could become harmful. The Court thus held that:

> ... in so far as there are uncertainties at the present state of scientific research it is for the Member States, in the absence of harmonization, to decide what degree of protection of the health and life of humans they intend to assure, having regard however for the requirements of the free movement of goods within the Community. [para 16]

The Court therefore held that the Dutch requirement that authorisation be obtained prior to the marketing of foodstuffs to which vitamins had been added could be justified under what is now Article 36 TFEU, provided that such marketing was authorised when the addition of vitamins meets a real need.

Significance:

This case established that, where there is scientific uncertainty as to health risks, discretion is left to the Member States, provided that they respond proportionately to the scientific evidence that is available.

▶ The **German Bier** case is also considered in section 12.5.2 (page 574) in relation to consumer protection

The Court then referred to the above case and elaborated on its position on additives in the following case:

Commission v Germany (Case 178/84) – 'German Bier'

Facts:

The Commission instituted proceedings against Germany, alleging a breach of what is now Article 34 TFEU (Art 30 EEC Treaty at the time) in relation to restrictions on the marketing of beer. One of the provisions at issue in this case (a second provision is considered below) was a provision under the German Foodstuffs Act 1974, which banned the marketing of beer that contained additives. It was accepted that this indistinctly applicable rule constituted a barrier to intra-Union trade, as it banned beer which was lawfully produced and marketed in other Member States. The question before the Court of Justice was whether this rule could be justified under what is now Article 36 TFEU (previously Art 36 EEC Treaty) on public health grounds.

Ruling:

The Court of Justice acknowledged that authorisation requirements for the marketing of products containing additives may be justified as meeting 'a genuine need of health policy, namely that of restricting the uncontrolled consumption of food additives' (para 42). However, the application of such requirements to imported products which have been authorised in the Member State of production is only permissible in so far as it complies with the requirements of what is now Article 36 TFEU, as it has been interpreted by the Court.

The Court then stated as follows:

44 It must be borne in mind, in the first place, that in its judgments in *Sandoz*, *Motte* and *Muller*, the Court inferred from the principle of proportionality underlying the last sentence of Article 36 of the Treaty [now Art 36 TFEU] that prohibitions on the marketing of products containing additives authorised in the Member State of production but prohibited in the Member State of importation **must be restricted to what is actually necessary to secure the protection of public health**. The Court also concluded that the use of a specific additive which is authorised in another Member State must be authorised in the case of a product imported from that Member State where, in view, on the one hand, of the findings of international scientific research, and in particular the work of the Community's [i.e. Union's] Scientific Committee for Food, the Codex Alimentarius Committee of the Food and Agriculture Organisation of the United Nations (FAO) and the World Health Organisation and, on the other, of the eating habits prevailing in the importing Member State, the additive in question does not present a risk to public health and meets a real need, especially a technical one.

45 Secondly, it should be remembered that, as the Court held in *Muller*, by virtue of the principle of proportionality, traders must also be able to apply, under a procedure which is easily accessible to them and can be concluded within a reasonable time, for the use of specific additives to be authorised by a measure of general application ...

The Court then observed that the German rule prohibited all additives, that there was no procedure whereby a trader could obtain authorisation to use a specific additive and that additives were permitted in other beverages. It was argued by the German government that if the beer was manufactured in accordance with German law (i.e. s 9 of the Biersteuergesetz) additives would not be needed. The Court continued:

51 It must be emphasised that the mere reference to the fact that beer can be manufactured without additives if it is made from only the raw materials prescribed in the Federal Republic of Germany does not suffice to preclude the possibility that some additives may meet a technological need. Such an interpretation of the concept of technological need, which results in favouring national production methods, **constitutes a disguised means of restricting trade between Member States**.

52 The concept of technological need must be assessed in the light of the raw materials utilised and bearing in mind the assessment made by the authorities of the Member States where the product was lawfully manufactured and marketed. **Account must also be taken of the findings of international scientific research** and in particular the work of the Community's [i.e. Union's] Scientific Committee for Food, the Codex Alimentarius Committee of the FAO and the World Health Organisation.

The Court therefore concluded that the general prohibition on additives in beer was contrary to the principle of proportionality and thus could not be justified by what is now Article 36 TFEU.

> **Significance:**
>
> This case established that, although individual Member States have a margin of discretion in deciding what level of protection to provide to consumers, the Court will take into account **the extent of current knowledge** in order to determine whether such national measures are proportionate. As the use of **all** additives was prohibited in the manufacturing of beer, yet additives were permitted in other products, the restriction in this case clearly did not satisfy the test of proportionality.

The Court has taken a similar position with regard to medical products. The Court of Justice has held that Member States are entitled, in the absence of a procedure for Union authorisation or the mutual recognition of national authorisation, to exclude medical products which have not been authorised by the competent national authorities (***Lucien Ortscheit GmbH* v *Eurim-Pharm GmbH*** (Case C-320/93)). Public health is also discussed in relation to the rule of reason below.

In ***Ålands Vindkraft AB* v *Energimyndigheten*** (Case C-573/12), the Court of Justice held that the Article 36 TFEU justification of the protection of the health and life of humans, animals and plants can also be applied to national measures enacted for the protection of the environment. In this case, the Court found that a Swedish requirement to purchase a licence for imports of electricity constituted a *prima facie* violation of Article 34 TFEU. However, this rule had been enacted in order to promote the national production of 'green' electricity in accordance with Directive 2009/28 on the promotion of the use of renewable energy. In its judgment, Article 36 TFEU was one of a range of provisions listed by the Court to establish that the objective of promoting the use of renewable energy sources for the production of electricity is capable of justifying distinctly applicable measures that hinder the free movement of goods. The Court confirmed this ruling a couple of months later in ***Essent Belgium NV* v *Vlaamse Reguleringsinstantie voor de Elektriciteits- en Gasmarkt*** (Joined Cases C-204-208/12).

Protection of industrial and commercial property

Industrial and commercial property rights are protected by patents, trademarks, copyrights and similar mechanisms. This ground therefore differs from the others set out in Article 36 TFEU as it essentially provides protection for private interests rather than public interests. Indeed, it is clear that a restrictive approach taken by the owners of industrial property rights could have a significant effect on the free movement of goods. Different national rules on such property rights could be used to effectively partition the internal market for affected products and thus prevent the achievement of one of the Union's primary aims.

In an attempt to strike a balance between the free movement of goods and the protection of private property, the Court of Justice has drawn a distinction between the **existence** and the **exercise** of rules affecting the ownership of such rights (***Consten and Grundig* v *Commission*** (Joined Cases 56 and 58/64); ***Parke, Davis and Co* v *Probel, Reese, Beintema-Interpharm and Centrafarm*** (Case 24/67)). The Court has therefore sought to recognise that a right may or may not be exercised in a way that falls under the prohibition that is now contained in Article 34 TFEU. In line with this, the Court has declared that the protection given to the different systems of property ownership in different Member States under what is now Article 345 TFEU does not allow national legislatures to adopt measures relating to industrial and commercial property which would adversely affect the principle of free movement of goods within the internal market (***Spain*** v ***Council*** (Case C-350/92)). It has also emphasised that this exception, as explicitly stipulated in what is now Article 36 TFEU, cannot 'constitute a means of arbitrary discrimination or a disguised restriction on trade between Member States'. National rules protecting patents and copyrights must therefore operate without discrimination.

This principle of non-discrimination was illustrated in ***Collins*** v ***Imtrat*** (Case C-92/92), which concerned proceedings brought by the performer Phil Collins against the distribution in Germany of pirated tapes and illegal recordings of his concerts. Under German law, remedies for such acts were available only to German nationals. The Court of Justice held that, although Member States were free to determine the nature and extent of protection provided by national copyright rules, such rules should be applied without discrimination.

On this basis the Court has also held that there is a breach of what is now Article 34 TFEU when national rules require that a patent be exploited only on the territory where the patent is granted and therefore prohibit or restrict its development elsewhere. Such measures mean that the patented goods may not be manufactured elsewhere and imported into the patent-granting Member State (***Commission*** v ***Italy*** (Case C-235/89); ***Commission*** v ***UK*** (Case C-30/90)).

The Court has tried to allow the property exception only in relation to the **specific subject matter** of a property right, although what this is in each case is sometimes difficult to determine. The Court provided some clarification in relation to patents in ***Centrafarm*** v ***Winthrop BV*** (Case 15/74), where it stated that:

> ... Article 36 in fact only admits of derogations from the free movement of goods where such derogations are **justified for the purpose of safeguarding rights which constitute the specific subject matter of this property**.
>
> In relation to patents, the specific subject matter of the industrial property is the guarantee that the patentee, to reward the creative effort of the inventor, has the **exclusive right to use an invention with a view to manufacturing industrial products and putting them into circulation for the first time**, either directly or by the grant of licences to third parties, as well as the right to oppose infringements. [paras 8 and 9]

This exclusive right is enjoyed in the Member State in which the goods are patented. The patentee, under the Article 36 TFEU exception, can exclude goods which breach their patent (this also applies to copyright owners; see ***Donner*** (Case C-5/11)). However, once the patented (or copyrighted) goods are circulated in another Member State, either by them or with their **consent**, their right to exclude those goods as the patentee is then said to be **exhausted**. The following case demonstrates this principle:

Centrafarm v *Winthrop BV* (Case 15/74)

Facts:
Sterling Drug Inc held patents relating to a drug called Negram in the UK and the Netherlands. In both countries the drug was marketed either by Sterling Drug itself, or by companies which it had licensed to do so. Centrafarm, an independent Dutch company, bought supplies of the drug in both the UK and Germany, where it was much cheaper, and resold it in the Netherlands.

> Sterling Drug and its subsidiaries invoked their respective patent and trademark rights before the Dutch courts to prevent Negram being marketed in the Netherlands by Centrafarm. A Dutch court referred a number of questions to the Court of Justice under what is now Article 267 TFEU.
>
> **Ruling:**
>
> The Court described the limits of national patent rights as follows:
>
> > 10 An obstacle to the free movement of goods may arise out of the existence, within national legislation concerning industrial and commercial property, of provisions laying down that a patentee's right is not exhausted when the product protected by the patent is marketed in another Member State, with the result that the patentee can prevent importation of the product into his own Member State when it has been marketed in another Member State.
> >
> > 11 Whereas an obstacle to the free movement of goods of this kind may be justified on the ground of the protection of industrial property where such protection is invoked against a product coming from a Member State where it is not patentable and has been manufactured by third parties without the consent of the patentee and in cases where there exist patents, the original proprietors of which are legally and economically independent, **a derogation from the principle of the free movement of goods is not, however, justified where the product has been put onto the market in a legal manner, by the patentee himself or with his consent, in the Member State from which it has been imported**, in particular in the case of a proprietor of parallel patents.
>
> **Significance:**
>
> This case established that an industrial and commercial property right protected by the law of one Member State cannot be invoked against the importation of products which the owner of the right has allowed to be put into circulation in another Member State. In other words, if a person holding a patent agrees that their product may be marketed in one Member State, they may not then invoke their patent to prevent it from being imported into other Member States. This is known as the **exhaustion of rights** principle, as the right-holder's actions are said to have exhausted their rights.

The exhaustion of rights principle has been applied by the Court of Justice with regard not only to patent rights, but also to trademarks, copyright and industrial design. The Court defined the proprietorial interest in relation to trademarks in ***Centrafarm* v *Winthrop BV*** (Case 16/74), which was considered alongside the above case (note the slightly different case number). Here, the Court stated that:

> In relation to trademarks, the **specific subject matter** of the industrial property is the guarantee that the owner of the trade mark has the **exclusive right to use that trade mark for the purpose of putting products protected by the trade mark into circulation** for the first time, and is therefore intended to protect him against any competitor wishing to take advantage of the status and reputation of the trade mark by selling products illegally bearing the trade mark. [para 8]

The principle of the exhaustion of rights in relation to trademarks is now set out in Article 15 of Directive 2015/2436 (see below).

Problems can occur when Member States have different intellectual property rules. For example, ***EMI Electrola* v *Patricia*** (Case 341/87) concerned the free movement of goods across national frontiers when a copyright had expired in one Member State but not in another.

To address this issue, an array of harmonising directives has since been adopted in the area of intellectual property. Such measures are now expressly provided for by **Article 118 TFEU**. The Commission has two principal aims in this field. The first is that each Member State should employ, as far as possible, the same substantive industrial property rules. The second is that intellectual property monopolies should run the length and breadth of the Union, irrespective of the country of their origin. Recent measures adopted in pursuit of these aims include:

- the **patent package**, comprising two regulations and an international Agreement establishing a Unified Patent Court (UPC), which lay the foundations for the creation of uniform patent protection across the Union (excluding Italy with regard to the UPC);
- the **trademark package**, comprising **Directive 2015/2436** (the Trade Mark Directive) and **Regulation 2015/2424**;
- **Directive 2001/29** on the harmonisation of certain aspects of copyright and related rights in the information society;
- **Directive 2019/790** on copyright and related rights in the Digital Single Market (to be implemented by Member States by 7 June 2021).

12.5.2 The Cassis rule of reason defences for indistinctly applicable measures

> Cassis is considered in section 12.4.4 in relation to the rule of mutual recognition

The **Cassis** case was considered above in so far as the Court held that what is now Article 34 TFEU can apply to indistinctly applicable measures that impose a dual burden on importers or exporters, and that once goods have been lawfully marketed in one Member State they should be free to be marketed in any other Member State without restriction. This rule of mutual recognition is known as the first **Cassis** principle. This is then subject to the second principle, which is called the **rule of reason** or the **mandatory requirements defence**:

Rewe-Zentrale AG v *Bundesmonopolverwaltung Für Branntwein* (Case 120/78) – 'Cassis'

Facts:

As noted above, the applicant wished to import the liqueur 'Cassis de Dijon' into Germany from France. The relevant German authorities refused to allow the importation because the French liqueur did not meet the German requirement for spirits of a minimum alcoholic strength of 25 per cent. The applicant argued that this rule was an MEE, since it prevented the French version of the drink being marketed in Germany.

Ruling:

The Court of Justice held as follows:

> 8 In the absence of common rules relating to the production and marketing of alcohol ... it is for the Member States to regulate all matters relating to the production and marketing of alcohol and alcoholic beverages on their own territory.
>
> **Obstacles to movement within the Community [i.e. Union] resulting from disparities between the national laws relating to the marketing of the products in question must be accepted**

> in so far as those provisions may be recognised as being necessary in order to satisfy mandatory requirements relating in particular to the effectiveness of fiscal supervision, the protection of public health, the fairness of commercial transactions and the defence of the consumer.

The Court then considered arguments that the minimum alcohol requirement was justified by reasons relating to the protection of public health and the protection of the consumer against unfair commercial practices. The Court held that the requirement could not be justified on grounds of public health, as a wide range of weaker alcoholic beverages were available on the market and those with a higher alcoholic content were often consumed in a diluted form.

The argument relating to the protection of the consumer was based on the consideration that a lower alcoholic content enables a product to be retailed at a lower price and that the fixing of minimum alcohol contents enables greater transparency in sales to the public. While the Court agreed that such standards facilitate greater transparency, it stated that:

> This line of argument cannot be taken so far as to regard the mandatory fixing of minimum alcohol contents as being an essential guarantee of the fairness of commercial transactions, since **it is a simple matter to ensure that suitable information is conveyed to the purchaser by requiring the display of an indication of origin and of the alcohol content on the packaging of products**. [para 13]

The Court therefore concluded as follows:

> 14 It is clear from the foregoing that the requirements relating to the minimum alcohol content of alcoholic beverages **do not serve a purpose which is in the general interest and such as to take precedence over the requirements of the free movement of goods**, which constitutes one of the fundamental rules of the Community [i.e. Union].... There is therefore **no valid reason** why, provided that they have been lawfully produced and marketed in one of the Member States, alcoholic beverages should not be introduced into any other Member State; the sale of such products may not be subject to a legal prohibition on the marketing of beverages with an alcohol content lower than the limits set by national rules.

Significance:

Alongside the first **Cassis** principle (the rule of mutual recognition), which is set out in paragraph 14, paragraph 8 of this case establishes that what is now Article 34 TFEU will not be breached if certain **mandatory requirements** are satisfied. These requirements may relate to **fiscal supervision, public health, fairness of commercial transactions** or **consumer protection**. This second **Cassis** principle is known as the **rule of reason**.

While Article 36 TFEU applies to both distinctly and indistinctly applicable measures (but has been interpreted very narrowly by the Court of Justice), the rule of reason can only be invoked in the defence of indistinctly applicable measures. The Court has made this clear on a number of occasions, including in *Italian State* v *Gilli and Andres* (Case 788/79). In that case, after restating the first **Cassis** principle (i.e. the rule of mutual recognition) the Court stated as follows:

> It is only where national rules, **which apply without discrimination to both domestic and imported products**, may be justified as being necessary in order to satisfy imperative requirements relating in particular to the protection of public health, the fairness of commercial transactions and the defence of the consumer that they may constitute an exception to the requirements arising under Article 30 [now Art 34 TFEU]. [para 6]

Figure 12.3 Defences for quantitative restrictions and measures having equivalent effect

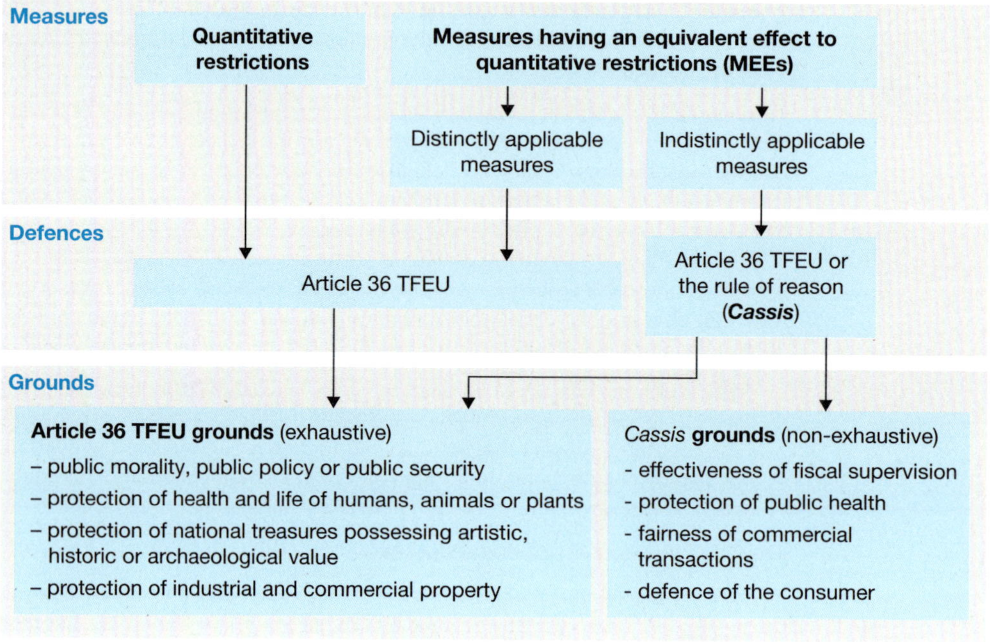

Measures
- Quantitative restrictions
- Measures having an equivalent effect to quantitative restrictions (MEEs)
  - Distinctly applicable measures
  - Indistinctly applicable measures

Defences
- Article 36 TFEU (for quantitative restrictions and distinctly applicable measures)
- Article 36 TFEU or the rule of reason (*Cassis*) (for indistinctly applicable measures)

Grounds

Article 36 TFEU grounds (exhaustive)
- public morality, public policy or public security
- protection of health and life of humans, animals or plants
- protection of national treasures possessing artistic, historic or archaeological value
- protection of industrial and commercial property

Cassis grounds (non-exhaustive)
- effectiveness of fiscal supervision
- protection of public health
- fairness of commercial transactions
- defence of the consumer

The list of mandatory requirements set out in paragraph 8 of the **Cassis** judgment is **not exhaustive** and it has been expanded by the Court of Justice in subsequent cases. Some of the mandatory requirements set out in **Cassis,** and some others that the Court has also accepted, are now considered.

Consumer protection

Commission v *Germany* (Case 178/84) – 'German Bier'

Facts:
As noted above, the Commission instituted proceedings against Germany, alleging a breach of what is now Article 34 TFEU (Art 30 EEC Treaty at the time) in relation to restrictions on the marketing of beer. One of the provisions the Commission wished to challenge (another provision is considered above) was that the name 'Bier' could only be used for products brewed using malted barley, hops, yeast and water alone. The use of other ingredients did not prohibit the product being marketed, but it could not be called 'Bier'. The German government sought to defend its law on the basis that it was necessary to protect the German consumer who associated the label 'Bier' with beverages made exclusively from the stated ingredients.

Ruling:
The Court of Justice ruled that the law was a barrier to free trade and rejected the German government's argument relating to consumer protection on two points. First, the Court noted

that consumers' perceptions vary over time as well as between Member States. Therefore, as the Court had previously held in **Commission v UK** (Case 170/78 – '**Wine tax**'), Member State legislation should not 'crystallise given consumer habits so as to consolidate an advantage acquired by national industries concerned to comply with them'. Secondly, the Court noted that designations corresponding to the German designation 'Bier' were applied more broadly in other Member States, in Union law and even in German legislation. Therefore, the Court held that the designation 'Bier' could not be restricted to beverages manufactured in accordance with the German rules.

The Court then continued as follows:

35 It is admittedly legitimate to seek to enable consumers who attribute specific qualities to beers manufactured from particular raw materials to make their choice in the light of that consideration. However, as the Court has already emphasised (Case 193/80 *Commission* v *Italy*) that possibility **may be ensured by means which do not prevent the importation of products which have been lawfully manufactured and marketed in other Member States** and, in particular, 'by the compulsory affixing of suitable labels giving the nature of the product sold'. By indicating the raw materials utilised in the manufacture of beer 'such a course would enable the consumer to make his choice in full knowledge of the facts and would guarantee transparency in trading and in offers to the public'. It must be added that such a system of mandatory consumer information must not entail negative assessments for beers not complying with the requirements of section 9 of the Biersteuergesetz.

Significance:

In this case, the Court of Justice effectively acknowledged that the measure pursued a legitimate objective, but found that the objective could be pursued in a manner that did not breach the first **Cassis** principle. In other words, the measure went beyond what was necessary and was therefore not **proportionate**.

▶ The German **Bier** case is also considered in section 12.5.1 (page 567) in relation to the protection of health

Other cases where the Court of Justice found that measures could not be justified on the ground of consumer protection due to a failure to satisfy the proportionality test include:

- *Walter Rau Lebensmittelwerke* v *DE Smedt PVBA* (Case 261/81), which concerned a Belgian requirement that margarine could only be sold in cube-shaped packaging (see section 12.4.5);
- *De Kikvorsch Groothandel-Import-Export BV* (Case 94/82), which concerned a restriction on the acidity of beers that had not been manufactured according to the stipulated procedure for 'sour beers'; and
- *Commission* v *Spain* (Case C-12/00) and *Commission* v *Italy* (Case C-14/00), which concerned prohibitions on the marketing of products designated as 'chocolate' if they contained vegetable fats other than cocoa butter.

The Court also ruled similarly in *Ministère Public* v *Deserbais* (Case 286/86), which concerned French legislation that restricted the use of the name 'Edam' to cheese with a minimum fat content of 40 per cent. The Court of Justice held that France's indistinctly applicable rule was a restriction on trade in relation to cheese with a lower fat content which had been lawfully produced and marketed in Germany. The Court then held that the breach of what is now Article 34 TFEU could not be justified under the rule of reason, as the consumer could be provided with adequate information about the fat content of the different 'Edam' cheeses through labelling.

However, although the situation did not arise in *Deserbais*, in paragraph 13 of that judgment the Court stated as follows:

> The question may arise whether the same rule must be applied where a product presented under a particular name is so different, as regards its composition or production, from the products generally known by that name in the Community [i.e. Union] that it cannot be regarded as falling within the same category.

This suggests that there may be instances where restrictions on the use of a certain designation can be justified, perhaps for example on the grounds that, even with clear labelling, a certain use is misleading or confusing for consumers.

While in each of these cases the Court held that clear labelling would be a less restrictive means of safeguarding consumer protection than the restrictions at issue, the following case demonstrates that labelling requirements themselves may breach Article 34 TFEU:

Fietje (Case 27/80)

Facts:

National legislation in the Netherlands specified that beverages containing certain ingredients must be labelled as 'likeur' (i.e. liqueur). Proceedings were brought against the defendant who had supplied beverages imported from Germany that did not include this designation.

Ruling:

The Court of Justice stated as follows:

10   Although the extension to imported products of an obligation to use a certain name on the label does not wholly preclude the importation into the Member State concerned of products originating in other Member States or in free circulation in those States it **may nonetheless make their marketing more difficult**, especially in the case of parallel imports. As the Netherlands Government itself admits in its observations, such an extension of that obligation is thus capable of impeding, at least indirectly, trade between Member States. It is therefore necessary to consider whether it may be justified on the ground of public interest in consumer protection which, according to observations of the Netherlands Government and according to 'Warenwet' [i.e. the Netherlands' Commodities Act], underlies the rules in question.

11   **If the national rules relating to a given product include the obligation to use a description that is sufficiently precise to inform the purchaser of the nature of the product and to enable it to be distinguished from products with which it may be confused, it may well be necessary, in order to give consumers effective protection, to extend this obligation to imported products also,** even in such a way as to make necessary the alteration of the original labels of some of these products. At the level of Community [i.e. Union] legislation, this possibility is recognised in several directives on the approximation of the laws of the Member States relating to certain foodstuffs as well as by Council Directive 79/112/EEC of 18 December 1978 on the approximation of the laws of the Member States relating to the labelling, presentation and advertising of foodstuffs for sale to the ultimate consumer (*Official Journal* 1979, L33, p. 1).

12   **However, there is no longer any need for such protection if the details given on the original label of the imported product have as their content information on the nature of the product and that content includes at least the same information, and is just as

> **capable of being understood by consumers in the importing State**, as the description prescribed by the rules of that State. In the context of ... [Article 267 TFEU], the making of findings of fact necessary in order to establish whether there is such equivalence is a matter for the national court.
>
> **Significance:**
>
> This case established that, although labelling may be required to ensure that consumers can distinguish a product from others with which it may be confused, a labelling requirement need not be enforced against imported products if all the necessary information is provided on the original label in a manner that consumers would be equally able to understand. The labelling requirement was therefore found to be disproportionate in this case.

The Court reinforced its ruling in the above case in *Neeltje v Houtwipper* (Case C-293/93), which concerned the hallmarking of precious metals. The Court held that:

> A Member State cannot require a fresh hallmark be affixed to products imported from another Member State in which they have been lawfully marketed and hallmarked in accordance with the legislation of that state, where the information provided by that hallmark, in whatever form, is **equivalent** to that prescribed by the Member State of importation and **intelligible** to consumers of that state. [para 48]

Therefore, labelling requirements that obstruct intra-Union trade may not be justified on the ground of consumer protection under the rule of reason where they add no significant value to consumers.

Public health

Public health is included in both Article 36 TFEU and the list of mandatory requirements. Where Member States have sought to justify a breach of Article 34 TFEU on public health grounds, the Court has repeatedly considered this defence under Article 36 TFEU rather than the **Cassis** rule of reason. The results, however, are the same.

Examples of such judgments include:

- *Commission* v *Germany* (Case 178/84 – '**German Bier**'), which concerned a prohibition on the use of additives in beer and is considered in section 12.5.1;
- *Debus* (Joined Cases C-13 and C-113/91), which concerned a restriction on the quantity of sulphur dioxide in beer which was far lower than amounts found to constitute a risk to health by the WHO;
- *Commission* v *France* (Case C-24/00) and *Greenham* v *ABEL* (Case C-95/01), which concerned requirements that the use of additives in foodstuffs to be authorised;
- *Commission* v *Germany* (Case C-387/99) and *Commission* v *Austria* (Case C-150/00), which concerned the automatic classification of products containing certain quantities of certain nutrients as medicinal products, even though they were lawfully marketed as foodstuffs in another Member State;
- *Deutscher Apothekerverband* (Case C-322/01), which concerned a prohibition on the sale of medicinal products by mail order or online.

In each of these cases, the Court assessed, in light of contemporary evidence, (i) whether the measure in question responded to a genuine risk to health and (ii) whether the measure was proportionate, i.e. whether public health could be safeguarded by alternative measures that were less restrictive to the free movement of goods.

Other mandatory requirements

As stated above, the **Cassis** list is not exhaustive. The list was left open so that the Court could respond to new defences as they arose. The Court has accepted a wide range of national measures, many of them going well beyond either those which are designed to protect consumers or the specific exceptions permitted to Member States under Article 36 TFEU. Some of the additional grounds that the Court has found to justify a breach of Article 34 TFEU are now considered.

Protection of the environment

Commission v Denmark (Case 302/86) – 'Drink containers'

Facts:

The Commission challenged a Danish law under which all containers for beer and soft drinks needed to be returnable and reusable. Such containers needed to be approved by the National Agency for the Protection of the Environment, which could refuse to authorise new types of container and was likely to do so in order to limit the number of different types of container that would need to be processed for reuse. If non-approved containers were used, a limit was placed on the quantity of beer and soft drinks that could be marketed.

Ruling:

The Court of Justice recognised that the rule constituted an obstacle to trade, as foreign manufacturers would not be set up to sell drinks in such containers and would therefore have to take special steps to supply the Danish market. However, the Court accepted that protection of the environment is one of the Union's 'essential objectives', which may justify certain limitations to the principle of the free movement of goods (see what is now Art 3(3) TEU). Those limitations must not, however, 'go beyond the inevitable restrictions which are justified by the pursuit of the objective of environmental protection'. In this regard, the Court found that 'the obligation to establish a deposit-and-return system for empty containers . . . is an indispensable element of a system intended to ensure the re-use of containers and therefore appears necessary to achieve the aims pursued by the contested rules'. However, the limitation placed on the marketing of products in containers that had not been approved by the relevant authorities, even when such containers were reusable and the manufacturer was prepared to ensure that they were reused in practice, was unnecessarily restrictive.

Significance:

This case established that, while the protection of the environment is a legitimate objective, rules enacted in pursuit of this aim may not be unduly restrictive. In this instance, where participation in a national scheme is limited due to practical considerations (i.e. the practicalities of processing a wide variety of reusable containers), manufacturers should be permitted to establish an equivalent scheme.

In ***Commission* v *Germany*** (Case C-463/01) and ***Radlberger Getrnkegesellschaft and S. Spitz*** (Case C-309/02), the Court of Justice again confirmed that indistinctly applicable measures could be justified on environmental protection grounds, provided that the measures taken are proportionate to the objective pursued. The following case demonstrates the high burden on Member States to prove that there is no less restrictive measure available for the attainment of a legitimate objective:

Commission v *Austria* (Case C-320/03) – 'Austrian lorries I'

Facts:
A 2003 Austrian regulation prohibited lorries of more than 7.5 tonnes carrying certain goods, such as waste, stone, soil, motor vehicles, timber and cereals, from being driven on a 46 km section of the A12 motorway. The aim of the contested regulation was to improve air quality so as to ensure the long-term protection of human, animal and plant health, in line with Union directives on the protection of ambient air quality. It was claimed that the specified goods could be transported more environmentally by rail. The Commission brought infringement proceedings before the Court of Justice, arguing that the restriction breached what are now Articles 34 and 35 TFEU (Arts 28 and 29 EC Treaty at the time).

Ruling:
The Court agreed that the prohibition on the transportation of specific goods in large lorries constituted an MEE, and that it could not be justified as it was disproportionate to the aim pursued. The Court stated as follows:

87 Without the need for the Court itself to give a ruling on the existence of alternative means, by rail or road, of transporting the goods covered by the contested regulation under economically acceptable conditions, or to determine whether other measures, combined or not, could have been adopted in order to attain the objective of reducing emissions of pollutants in the zone concerned, it suffices to say in this respect that, **before adopting a measure so radical as a total traffic ban on a section of motorway constituting a vital route of communication between certain Member States, the Austrian authorities were under a duty to examine carefully the possibility of using measures less restrictive** of freedom of movement, and discount them only if their inadequacy, in relation to the objective pursued, was clearly established.

88 More particularly, given the declared objective of transferring transportation of the goods concerned from road to rail, those authorities were **required to ensure that there was sufficient and appropriate rail capacity** to allow such a transfer before deciding to implement a measure such as that laid down by the contested regulation.

89 As the Advocate General has pointed out in paragraph 113 of his Opinion, it has **not** been conclusively established in this case that the Austrian authorities, in preparing the contested regulation, sufficiently studied the question whether the aim of reducing pollutant emissions could be achieved by other means less restrictive of the freedom of movement and whether there actually was a realistic alternative for the transportation of the affected goods by other means of transport or via other road routes.

Significance:
This case demonstrates that, under the rule of reason, it is **not** for the complainant to establish that less restrictive measures are available, but rather it is for the Member State to prove that the matter has been carefully considered and that less restrictive means of achieving a legitimate objective are not available.

The Court confirmed its judgment in the above case in ***Commission v Austria*** (Case C-28/09) – 'Austrian lorries II'. The Commission brought this case before the Court of Justice when the Austrian authorities re-imposed the ban on lorries of over 7.5 tonnes carrying certain goods on a longer section of the A12 motorway. This prohibition was imposed after speed limits and a prohibition on certain classes of lorry had been found to be ineffective at improving the air quality. In this case, the Court found that it **had not been proved** that an extension of the prohibition on certain types of lorries to other types of lorries and a permanent speed limit of 100km/h (as opposed to a variable speed limit) would not be effective means of reducing pollution that would be less restrictive to the free movement of goods than the sectoral ban. The Court therefore held for a second time that, by adopting a sectoral traffic prohibition without sufficiently examining the possibility of recourse to other less restrictive measures, Austria had disproportionately restricted the free movement of goods.

Protection of national, cultural and social values

The Court of Justice has shown a willingness to accept that restrictions aimed at protecting national, cultural and social values could constitute a mandatory requirement. However, the cases in which such a ground has been accepted have since been rendered outside of the scope of what is now Article 34 TFEU by the ruling in ***Keck***. For example, in ***Cinéthèque SA v Fédération Nationale des Cinémas Français*** (Joined Cases 60 and 61/84), the Court upheld a non-discriminatory French rule prohibiting the sale or hire of videos of films within a year of their first showing at a cinema. Although the rule had the effect of restricting the import of videos from other Member States, the Court held that the restriction was justified as the protection of French cinemas was a legitimate objective, presumably (although it was not stated) as a means of protecting national culture.

> See section 12.4.5 for a discussion of the *Keck* judgment

Similarly, in ***Torfaen Borough Council v B&Q Plc*** (Case 145/88), the Court held in relation to national rules governing the opening hours of retail premises that:

> Such rules reflect certain political and economic choices in so far as their purpose is to ensure that working and non-working hours are so arranged as to accord with national or regional socio-cultural characteristics, and that, in the present state of Community [i.e. Union] law, is a matter for the Member States. [para 14]

> *Torfaen Borough Council v B&Q Plc* and the issue of Sunday trading hours is also considered in section 12.4.5

Sunday trading rules were therefore held to be permissible provided that they did not present any greater restriction on intra-Union trade than that which is intrinsic to such rules.

Fundamental rights

The following case, like ***Commission v France*** (C-265/95 – '**Angry farmers**'), considered the failure of a government to take action to remedy an obstruction to the free movement of goods. However, this case concerned activities that did not distinguish on the basis of nationality, whereas the **Angry farmers** case concerned activities that did so distinguish (because only imported goods were being targeted by French farmers).

> The *Angry farmers* case is considered in section 12.4.3 (page 541)

12.5 PERMISSIBLE QUANTITATIVE RESTRICTIONS AND MEES

Figure 12.4 Application of Article 34 TFEU regarding MEEs

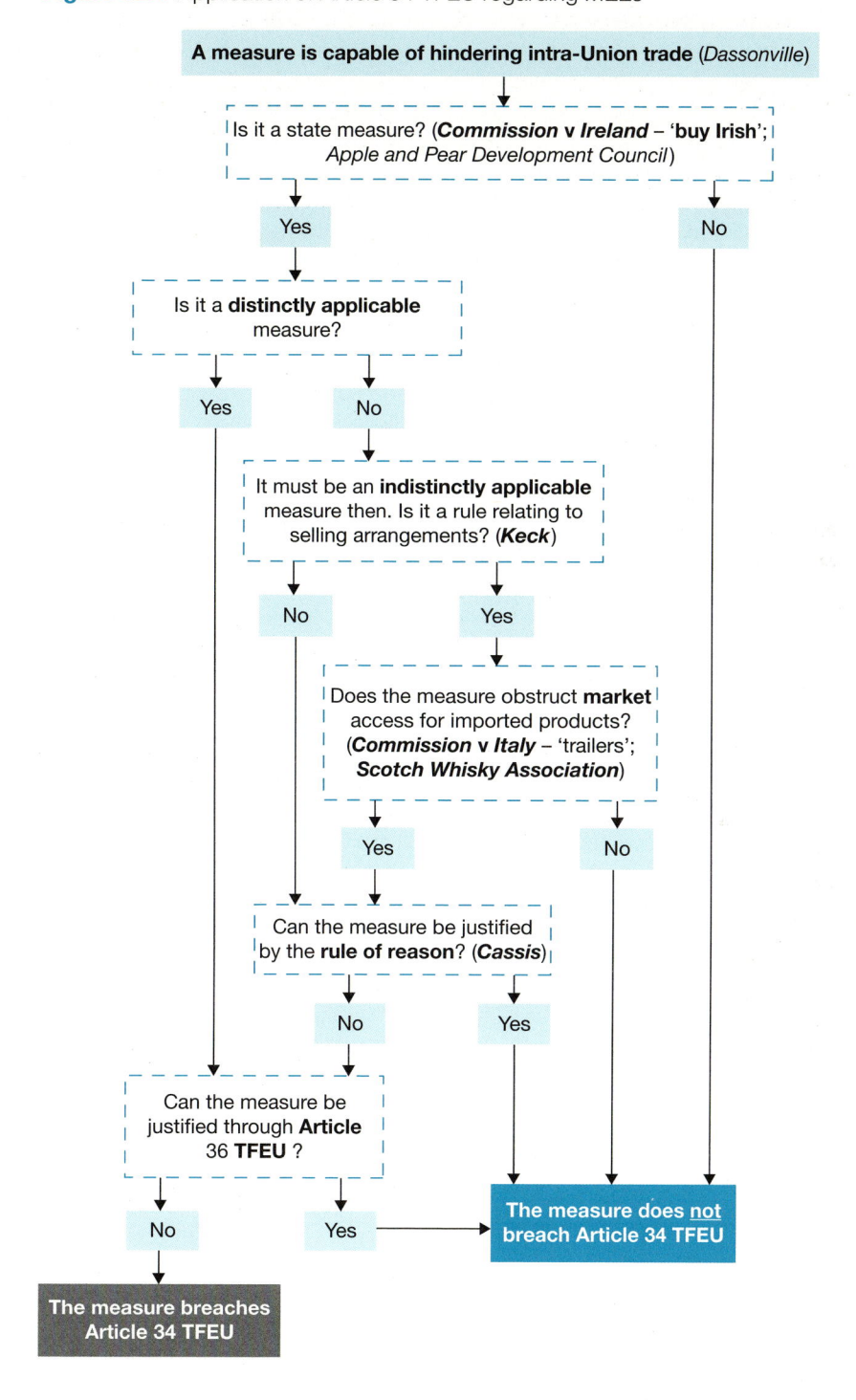

A measure is capable of hindering intra-Union trade (*Dassonville*)

Is it a state measure? (*Commission v Ireland* – 'buy Irish'; *Apple and Pear Development Council*)

- Yes → Is it a **distinctly applicable** measure?
  - Yes → Can the measure be justified through **Article 36 TFEU**?
    - No → The measure breaches Article 34 TFEU
    - Yes → The measure does not breach Article 34 TFEU
  - No → It must be an **indistinctly applicable** measure then. Is it a rule relating to selling arrangements? (*Keck*)
    - No → Can the measure be justified through Article 36 TFEU?
    - Yes → Does the measure obstruct **market** access for imported products? (*Commission v Italy* – 'trailers'; *Scotch Whisky Association*)
      - Yes → Can the measure be justified by the **rule of reason**? (*Cassis*)
        - No → (breaches)
        - Yes → The measure does not breach Article 34 TFEU
      - No → The measure does not breach Article 34 TFEU
- No → The measure does not breach Article 34 TFEU

FREE MOVEMENT OF GOODS — 12

Schmidberger v Austria (Case C-112/00)

Facts:
Austria had failed to ban a demonstration which resulted in the complete closure of a major transit route for almost 30 hours. Schmidberger, an international transport undertaking, sought damages from Austria on the basis that allowing the demonstration had restricted the free movement of goods and thereby violated the Member State's Union law duties. The national court referred the matter to the Court of Justice for a preliminary ruling.

Ruling:
The Court of Justice stated that a failure to ban such a demonstration is capable of restricting intra-Union trade in goods and must therefore be regarded as constituting a measure having equivalent effect to a quantitative restriction. In assessing whether there was any objective justification for the Austrian government's failure to take action, the Court of Justice determined that the objective pursued by the Austrian authorities in authorising the demonstration in question was to respect the freedom of expression and freedom of assembly of the demonstrators. The Court noted that these rights are guaranteed by the European Convention on Human Rights and the Austrian Constitution. **As fundamental rights form an integral part of the general principles of Union law, the Court held that their protection is a legitimate interest which can, in principle, justify a restriction to a fundamental freedom guaranteed by the Treaty**, such as the free movement of goods.

In considering whether the resulting restrictions on intra-Union trade were proportionate in the light of the objective pursued, that is the protection of fundamental rights, the Court pointed out differences between the facts of this case and those of the **angry farmers** case (***Commission v France*** (C-265/95)).

The Court of Justice found that, in the present case, unlike in the **Angry farmers** case: (i) the demonstration at issue took place following authorisation; (ii) the obstacle to the free movement of goods resulting from that demonstration was limited; (iii) the purpose of that public demonstration was not to restrict trade in goods of a particular type or from a particular source; (iv) various administrative and supporting measures were taken by the competent authorities in order to limit as far as possible the disruption to road traffic; (v) the isolated incident in question did not give rise to a general climate of insecurity such as to have a dissuasive effect on intra-Union trade flows as a whole; and (vi) taking account of the Member States' wide margin of discretion, in this case the competent national authorities were entitled to consider that an outright ban on the demonstration at issue would have constituted unacceptable interference with the fundamental rights of the demonstrators to gather and peacefully express their opinion in public.

The Court concluded that the fundamental rights of the demonstrators to freedom of expression and freedom of assembly were a legitimate interest which, in principle, justified a breach of what is now Article 34 TFEU.

Significance:
This case established that obstructions to the free movement of goods may be justified by the reason of upholding fundamental rights. Along with ***Omega*** (Case C-36/02), this was a landmark judgment with regard to the relationship between fundamental rights and the fundamental freedoms of the internal market, and as such confirmed the willingness of the Court of Justice to place the rights of individuals above Member State's obligations to the internal market.

➤ ***Omega*** is considered in relation to the freedom to provide services in section 11.4.5 (page 482)

12.5.3 Derogations from harmonising legislation (Art 114 TFEU)

As noted above, both Article 36 TFEU and the rule of reason can **only** be invoked to justify national measures when there are **no** relevant harmonising measures in place. However, where a harmonising measure has been adopted pursuant to **Article 114 TFEU**, that Article provides for Member States to **seek approval** from the Commission to maintain or introduce national provisions that derogate from that harmonising measure. The relevant sections of Article 114 TFEU provide as follows:

> 4 If, after the adoption of a harmonisation measure by the European Parliament and the Council, by the Council or by the Commission, a Member State **deems it necessary to maintain national provisions on grounds of major needs referred to in Article 36, or relating to the protection of the environment or the working environment**, it shall notify the Commission of these provisions as well as the grounds for maintaining them.
>
> 5 Moreover, without prejudice to paragraph 4, if, after the adoption of a harmonisation measure by the European Parliament and the Council, by the Council or by the Commission, a Member State **deems it necessary to introduce national provisions based on new scientific evidence relating to the protection of the environment or the working environment on grounds of a problem specific to that Member State arising after the adoption of the harmonisation measure**, it shall notify the Commission of the envisaged provisions as well as the grounds for introducing them.
>
> 6 The Commission shall, within six months of the notifications as referred to in paragraphs 4 and 5, approve or reject the national provisions involved after having verified whether or not they are a means of arbitrary discrimination or a disguised restriction on trade between Member States and whether or not they shall constitute an obstacle to the functioning of the internal market.
>
> ...
>
> 7 When, pursuant to paragraph 6, a Member State is authorised to maintain or introduce national provisions derogating from a harmonisation measure, **the Commission shall immediately examine whether to propose an adaptation to that measure**.

Since 1986, when a target of more than 300 directives was set to lay the foundations for the completion of the internal market on 1 January 1993, very few national provisions have been approved under the exception contained in what is now Article 114(4) TFEU. It remains, however, a valuable safety valve to deal with national concerns over specific products.

Regulation 764/2008

Regulation 764/2008 was adopted in July 2008 and lays down procedures relating to the application of certain national technical rules to products lawfully marketed in another Member State. As such, the Regulation stipulates requirements for permissible **exceptions to the**

rule of mutual recognition. The motivation for enacting the Regulation is set out in its preamble, which states as follows:

> Many problems still exist as regards the correct application of the principle of mutual recognition by the Member States. It is therefore necessary to establish procedures to minimise the possibility of technical rules creating unlawful obstacles to the free movement of goods between Member States.

Article 2(2) of the Regulation defines a 'technical rule' as any provision of law or other administrative provision which prohibits or restricts the marketing of a product in the territory of that Member State on the basis of the characteristics of that product. **Article 6** then establishes that, when an authority seeks to apply such a technical rule, it must set out technical or scientific evidence to the effect that:

> (a) the intended decision is **justified on one of the grounds of public interest** set out in Article 30 of the Treaty [now Art 36 TFEU] or by reference to other overriding reasons of public interest; and
>
> (b) the intended decision is **appropriate** for the purpose of achieving the objective pursued and **does not go beyond what is necessary** in order to attain that objective.

The Regulation therefore, essentially, codifies the approach that has been adopted by the Court of Justice in its case law relating to justifications based on Article 36 TFEU and the rule of reason.

12.6 Free movement of goods after Brexit

Objective 6

On 'exit day', the UK ceased to be a Member State of the EU and therefore regained the competence to set customs tariffs, quantitative restrictions and product standards, and to negotiate new terms of trade with the EU and with other countries. Boris Johnson, the current UK Prime Minister, has claimed that a trade deal between the UK and the EU can be reached during the Brexit transition period, i.e. between 1 February and 31 December 2020. Thus, the UK will remain aligned with EU trade regulations throughout the transition period and will then shift to new arrangements. However, critics argue that comprehensive trade agreements have historically taken much longer to negotiate. If a new trade agreement cannot be achieved by the end of the Brexit transition period, trading between the UK and the EU will be on the default terms established by the World Trade Organization (WTO) from 1 January 2021.

This section begins by considering the different models of trade with the EU that have been negotiated in the past and comparing these to the stated intentions of the UK government. By the time that you are reading this, the details of new trade arrangements between the UK and the EU may be available. If no trade agreement has been reached, the models considered here may still inform the approach taken to negotiating such an agreement in the future. This section also briefly outlines the difficulties that Brexit presents to the free movement of goods in relation to Northern Ireland.

12.6.1 Models of EU trade arrangements with non-EU countries

Remaining in the European Economic Area (Norway model)

This option is often referred to as the 'Norway model', although Liechtenstein and Iceland are also non-EU countries that are members of the EEA. Membership of the EEA provides access to the single market and therefore requires the free movement of goods, persons, services and capital to be upheld. As a corollary, EEA countries are required to implement EU regulatory requirements in these areas and to make considerable financial contributions, but have no input into Union decision-making.

The UK government has asserted that the UK will not remain in the single market after Brexit, and will therefore leave the EEA.

Re-joining the European Free Trade Association (Switzerland model)

The UK was a founding member of EFTA but left to join the EU. After leaving the EU, the UK could potentially re-join EFTA. As a member of EFTA, but not of the EEA, Switzerland has a looser relationship with the single market than the other EFTA members (Norway, Liechtenstein and Iceland). Switzerland's access to the single market is governed by a series of bilateral agreements, which stipulate the areas of trade that are covered (most industries, limited services), the regulatory standards that Switzerland must uphold and Switzerland's financial contributions. This approach therefore allows greater flexibility in negotiating certain aspects of the relationship. However, the requirement that Switzerland uphold the free movement of people has become politically problematic, as it would also be in the current political climate of the UK.

▶ See 'Map 1.2: EU and EFTA countries' on page 16

Remaining in the customs union (Turkey model)

Part of Turkey's Association Agreement with the EU provides for partial participation in the customs union. This means that goods (excluding agricultural goods) can move between Turkey and the EU without being subject to tariffs or quantitative restrictions. It also means that Turkey must apply the tariffs set by the EU to products that it imports from non-EU countries.

The UK government has asserted that the UK will not remain within the customs union after Brexit, although it remains to be seen at the time of writing whether participation may be agreed for certain sectors.

Free Trade Agreement (Canada model)

▶ The negotiation of the Singapore Free Trade Agreement is considered in 'Opinion 2/15' on page 179

The Comprehensive Economic Trade Agreement (CETA) is a free trade agreement that eliminates most tariffs and reduces quantitative restrictions between Canada and the EU. Under CETA, Canadian goods imported into the EU have to establish that they were made entirely in Canada and must conform with EU product standards. Unlike the EEA and EFTA models, CETA does not involve free movement of persons or hefty financial payments to the EU. CETA is one of several free trade agreements that the EU has negotiated with other countries, including Mexico, Singapore and South Korea.

A free trade agreement such as CETA may be desirable for the UK, but is unlikely to be achieved in full within the 11-month Brexit transition period – CETA took seven years to negotiate. Additionally, all of the models outlined here would place limits on access to the single market for UK services.

World Trade Organization rules

If a trade agreement between the UK and the EU cannot be reached by the 31 December 2020, and no extension of the Brexit transition period or similar interim measure is agreed, trade between the UK and the EU will be governed by WTO rules. In this scenario, the UK and the EU would have to apply to each other the same tariffs and restrictions that they apply to other countries, as WTO rules require equal treatment of its members where no other trade agreement is in place. The UK would not have to remain aligned with EU law or to make any financial contributions to the Union, but products exported to the EU would still have to meet EU standards. Trade under WTO rules would therefore be the most detrimental option in terms of the free movement of goods and services.

12.6.2 Northern Ireland and the Good Friday Agreement

The **Good Friday Agreement** (also known as the Belfast Agreement) was signed on 10 April 1998 and marked the political resolution of violent conflict between 'Unionists', who wish for Northern Ireland to be ruled directly by the UK, and 'Nationalists', who wish for the reunification of an independent island of Ireland. The Good Friday Agreement struck a compromise between the parties of Northern Ireland and the governments of the Republic of Ireland and the UK, which involved Northern Ireland remaining a part of the UK under a devolved system of governance and the removal of physical infrastructure (i.e. checkpoints and security barriers) along the border between Northern Ireland and the Republic of Ireland. The reintroduction of checkpoints along the border (referred to as a '**hard border**'), as Brexit changes it from an internal EU border to an external one, could therefore jeopardise the Good Friday Agreement and the continuance of peace. Consequently, the EU, the UK and the Republic of Ireland have all emphasised that they do not wish for the return of a hard border within the island of Ireland. However, the extent to which this will be possible, especially if no trade agreement is reached between the UK and the EU, is unclear at the time of writing.

Initially, Prime Minister Theresa May proposed a 'backstop', whereby the failure to reach a trade agreement would result in the ongoing participation of the UK in the customs union and the ongoing participation of Northern Ireland, to some extent, in the single market until an agreement could be reached. For those in the UK in favour of Brexit, this represented the possibility of indefinite participation in the customs union, from which they wished to be released. May's successor, Boris Johnson, proposed instead that, while Northern Ireland should remain aligned with EU regulatory standards, the rest of the UK may diverge. This would create a situation where Northern Ireland would legally be a part of UK customs arrangements, but would remain aligned with EU standards in practice (in so far as consented to by the Northern Ireland Assembly) so as to allow goods to move freely across the Irish border. Any discrepancy between the UK mainland and EU regulatory standards would therefore necessitate checks in the Irish Sea as goods pass from Northern Ireland to the UK mainland.

In sum, remaining aligned with EU standards is unacceptable to many who support Brexit within the UK, but diverging from EU standards will mean that either Nationalists will feel affronted by the imposition of border checks in Ireland, or Unionists will feel affronted by arrangements that further divide Northern Ireland from the rest of the UK.

CHAPTER SUMMARY

Customs duties and charges having equivalent effect

- **Article 28 TFEU** provides for a **customs union**; **Article 30 TFEU** prohibits customs duties on imports from and exports to other Member States and charges having equivalent effect (CEEs).
- **Products from non-EU countries** that have legally entered the Union are then in **free circulation** (Art 29).
- CEEs are defined by their **effect**, not by their designation (**Statistical data** case), purpose (**Italian art** case) or when they are imposed (**Steinike und Weinlig**).
- Proportionate charges for **services actually rendered** that are of **direct benefit** to the payee do not constitute CEEs (**Customs warehouses** case), nor do charges to cover the cost of **inspections required** by Union law (**German animal inspections** case) or international law (**Dutch plant inspections** case).

Internal taxation

- Member States may **not** impose any taxation on products from other Member States **in excess of that imposed on similar domestic products** or with the **effect of protecting** other products from competition (Art 110).
- Products are **similar** if they have a **comparable use** (**French spirits** case).
- Taxation is **indirectly protectionist** when it has the effect of protecting domestic goods that are in a **competitive relationship** with imported goods (**UK wine tax** case).
- **Directly discriminatory** taxation is always prohibited, but **indirectly discriminatory** taxation may be **objectively justified**.

Quantitative restrictions and measures having equivalent effect

- **Articles 34** and **35 TFEU** prohibit the imposition of quantitative restrictions and measures having equivalent effect (MEEs) on **imports** and **exports** respectively.
- MEEs are state measures that are **capable** of hindering intra-Union trade (*Dassonville*).
- Articles 34 and 35 have **vertical direct effect**, and thus apply to state measures (**Buy Irish** case and *Apple and Pear Development Council*), but may also now have limited **horizontal direct effect** in certain circumstances (*Fra.bo*).
- **Indistinctly applicable MEEs** are prohibited when they impose a **dual burden** on foreign producers.
- **Indistinctly applicable MEEs** that produce an **equal burden** on domestic and foreign importers are not prohibited by Article 34 TFEU (*Keck*), unless they **hinder market access** for imported goods (**Trailers** case; *Scotch Whisky Association*).
- The **rule of mutual recognition**: when there are **no** relevant **harmonising measures**, goods that have been lawfully marketed in one Member State should **not** face restrictions in the markets of other Member States (*Cassis* case).

Permissible quantitative restrictions and measures having equivalent effect

- **Article 36 TFEU** provides that distinctly or indistinctly applicable measures can be objectively justified on grounds of public **morality, policy or security**; the protection of **human, animal or plant life**; the protection of national **treasures**; or the protection of industrial and commercial **property**.
- The **rule of reason**: indistinctly applicable measures can be objectively justified on the basis of **mandatory requirements** in the general interest (**Cassis** case).
- **Regulation 764/2008** stipulates that derogations from the rule of mutual recognition must be **justified on grounds of public interest** and must be **proportionate**.
- **Article 114 TFEU** provides for Member States to **seek approval** from the Commission to derogate from **harmonising directives**.

Free movement of goods after Brexit

- Trade between the UK and the EU will shift to **World Trade Organization rules** if a trade agreement cannot be negotiated prior to the expiry of the Brexit transition period.
- Regulatory standards in **Northern Ireland** must remain aligned with the EU in order to uphold the **Good Friday Agreement**.

GLOSSARY

A fortiori　Latin phrase which literally means 'from the stronger', but which is more often used to mean 'even more so' or 'with even stronger reason'.

Ab initio　Latin phrase which means 'from the beginning'. In a legal context it refers to something being the situation from the start, rather than from when the court declared it so.

Accession　The process by which new Member States join the Union.

Acquis　Derived from French, *acquis* (or *acquis communautaire*) is used in Union law to refer to the total body of Union law accumulated so far. The term is also used to refer to the laws adopted under the Schengen Agreement. In this context it is referred to as the *Schengen acquis*. See also SCHENGEN AGREEMENT.

Acte clair　When the solution to a legal question is self-evident.

Acte éclairé　When the Court of Justice has previously ruled on an identical question.

Acts of the Union institutions　Article 288 TFEU (previously Art 249 EC Treaty) empowers the Union institutions to adopt regulations, directives, decisions, recommendations and opinions. These instruments are referred to as 'acts of the Union institutions'.

Advocate-General　The Court of Justice is assisted by 11 Advocates-General. The principal role of an Advocate-General is to assist the Court of Justice in reaching its judgment by delivering an Opinion in open court. The Opinion is not binding on the Court, although the Court usually follows the Opinion in its judgment.

Agencies of the EU　Independent legal entities, distinct from the main Union institutions, which are created to perform specific tasks. Examples include the European Environment Agency, the European Food Safety Authority and the European Border and Coastguard Authority (known as FRONTEX).

Aggregation of contributions　Article 48 TFEU (previously Art 42 EC Treaty) facilitates the Union's policy of free movement of workers by providing EU workers with the right to have their social security contributions and period of contribution in their home state recognised in the host Member State, and their contributions and length of service in the host Member State recognised in their home state when they return. This is referred to as 'aggregation of contributions'. *See also* EXPORTABILITY OF BENEFITS.

Annulment　The declaration that an act is invalid and ceases to have effect.

Approximation of laws　The harmonisation of the national laws of Member States.

Benelux Agreement　In 1948, Belgium, the Netherlands and Luxembourg established the Benelux customs union, which removed customs barriers between the three countries and also imposed a common customs tariff on goods entering the three countries from outside their national boundaries. In 1954, the free movement of capital was permitted between these three countries, followed by the free movement of labour in 1956. The agreement establishing these provisions is referred to as the 'Benelux Agreement'. *See also* BENELUX CUSTOMS UNION.

Benelux countries　Comprises Belgium, the Netherlands and Luxembourg. *See also* BENELUX AGREEMENT; BENELUX CUSTOMS UNION.

Benelux customs union　The Benelux customs union established the free movement of goods between the three Benelux countries (Belgium, the Netherlands and Luxembourg) from 1 January 1948. Customs barriers were removed and a common customs tariff was introduced for goods entering the customs union from outside the customs union. This developed in 1954 to include the free movement of capital, and developed further in 1956 to include the free movement of labour. *See also* BENELUX AGREEMENT.

Brexit   The withdrawal of the UK from the EU.

Brexit negotiations   The discussions between the UK and representatives of the Union from the other 27 Member States regarding the process of the UK's withdrawal from the EU and the relationship between the UK and the EU thereafter.

Brexit transition period   The time between the formal exit of the UK from the Union and the point at which the UK ceases to apply EU law. At the time of writing, this is assumed to be between 31 January 2020 and 31 December 2020. *See also* EXIT DAY.

CEE   The acronym for 'charge having an equivalent effect to a customs duty'. Articles 28 and 30 TFEU (previously Arts 23 and 25 EC Treaty) prohibit customs duties and CEEs. *See also* COMMON EXTERNAL TARIFF; CUSTOMS DUTY; CUSTOMS UNION.

Co-decision procedure   Prior to the introduction of the ordinary legislative procedure, the co-decision procedure empowered the Parliament, in certain specified policy areas, to propose amendments to and ultimately to veto a legislative proposal. The co-decision procedure, which was set out in the former Article 251 EC Treaty, no longer exists following changes made by the Treaty of Lisbon. It has been replaced by the 'ordinary legislative procedure' which applies in the vast majority of cases (Art 294 TFEU). *See also* COOPERATION PROCEDURE; ORDINARY LEGISLATIVE PROCEDURE; SPECIAL LEGISLATIVE PROCEDURE.

Collective agreement   A contract setting out the terms and conditions of employment, often in relation to a particular sector, which has been agreed by employers and trade unions.

Comitology   A process by which new legislation is drafted by the Commission which involves committees composed of civil servants of the Member States. *See also* EUROPEAN COMMISSION.

Commission   *See* EUROPEAN COMMISSION.

Committee of Permanent Representatives (COREPER)   The Committee of Permanent Representatives, known by its French acronym COREPER, comprises senior national officials from the Member States of the EU, who are based in Brussels. The role of the Committee is to provide continuity during the inevitable absences of relevant ministers from the Council. *See also* COUNCIL; EUROPEAN COUNCIL.

Committee of the Regions   The Committee of the Regions was established by the TEU as an advisory body. It is not a formal Union institution. The members of the Committee are representatives of regional and local bodies who either hold a regional or local authority electoral mandate or are politically accountable to an elected assembly (Art 300 TFEU (previously Art 263 EC Treaty)). Its main role is to deliver opinions on proposed legislation when consulted by the Council and to issue own-initiative opinions in appropriate cases. In a few policy areas (e.g. culture (Art 167(5) TFEU)), the legal base for a legislative proposal stipulates that the Committee must be consulted in relation to proposed measures. *See also* LEGAL BASE.

Common external tariff   A customs union comprises an association of countries which prohibits customs duties and charges having an equivalent effect from being levied on goods as they cross the borders of the countries within the association. A common external tariff (i.e. a fixed customs duty) is applied to goods entering the customs union from a non-member country. *See also* CEE; CUSTOMS DUTY; CUSTOMS UNION.

Common market   The common market was established by the European Economic Community (EEC) Treaty (subsequently renamed the European Community (EC) Treaty and now renamed the TFEU). The common market is a free trade area founded upon the free movement of goods, persons, services and capital. Since 1 December 2009 (when the Treaty of Lisbon came into force), it has been referred to as the 'internal market' rather than the common market. It is also sometimes referred to as the 'single market'. *See also* EUROPEAN COMMUNITIES; EUROPEAN COMMUNITY; INTERNAL MARKET.

Competence The power to take action in a particular policy area, or the general scope of an entity's authority.

Complainant Refers to a person who makes a complaint; also referred to as the applicant or plaintiff when referring to a person or entity that brings a legal case.

Conferral The principle that the Union only has the power to act where such competence has been bestowed upon it (conferred) by the Member States.

Constitutional Treaty The (proposed) Constitutional Treaty was adopted by the Member States of the EU in 2004. This Treaty would have replaced the EC Treaty and the TEU. Before it could come into force it had to be ratified (i.e. approved) by each Member State, according to each Member State's constitutional requirements. Both France and the Netherlands held electoral referendums in 2005 in which the Treaty was rejected. As a result, the (proposed) Constitutional Treaty did not come into force and was subsequently abandoned. The Treaty of Lisbon which came into force on 1 December 2009 replaced the (proposed) Constitutional Treaty. *See also* Treaty of Lisbon.

Contextual interpretation Contextual interpretation is used by courts to interpret legislation. If this method is employed, the provision being interpreted is interpreted in relation to other provisions of the legislation in question. This method of legislative interpretation, together with teleological interpretation, is extensively used by the Court of Justice of the European Union. *See also* Historical interpretation; Literal interpretation; Teleological interpretation.

Contra legem Latin phrase which means 'against the law'.

Cooperation procedure Prior to the introduction of the ordinary legislative procedure by the Treaty of Lisbon, the cooperation procedure empowered the European Parliament, in certain specified policy areas, to propose amendments to a legislative proposal. However, the Commission or the Council could vote unanimously to reject the Parliament's amendments. The cooperation procedure, set out in the former Article 252 EC Treaty, was introduced by the SEA. Following amendments to the founding treaties by subsequent treaties (e.g. the TEU, ToN, ToA), the cooperation procedure was rarely used; the co-decision procedure was more common. Following amendments by the Treaty of Lisbon, the cooperation procedure no longer exists. *See also* Co-decision procedure; Legal base; Ordinary legislative procedure; Special legislative procedure.

COREPER *See* Committee of Permanent Representatives.

Corrigendum Derived from Latin, a *corrigendum* is an error in printing. From time to time a *corrigendum* is published in the *Official Journal of the European Union* to correct errors in a previous edition of the journal.

Council The Council is one of the Union institutions. It may also be referred to as the Council of Ministers. The Council consists of a ministerial representative from each of the Member States, who is authorised to bind the government of their Member State. *See also* Committee of Permanent Representatives.

Court of Auditors The Court of Auditors is not, strictly speaking, a court. Article 13(1) TEU classifies the Court as a Union institution. It is responsible for the external audit of the general budget of the European Union.

Cross-elasticity Within the context of Article 110(2) TFEU (previously Art 90(2) EC Treaty), cross-elasticity refers to the degree to which goods are substitutable for each other (i.e. the readiness with which a consumer will switch between two competing products).

Customs duty A customs duty is a state levy charged on goods that cross a border. Articles 28 and 30 TFEU prohibit customs duties within the Union. *See also* CEE; Common external tariff; Customs union.

Customs union A customs union is an association of countries which prohibits customs duties and charges having an equivalent effect (CEEs) from being levied on goods as they cross the borders of the countries within the association. A common external tariff (i.e. a fixed customs duty) is applied to goods entering the customs union from a non-EU country. Article 28 TFEU establishes a customs union between the Member States of the EU. *See also* CEE; Customs duty; Common external tariff.

De minimis Latin phrase which, in a legal context, means matters which are not worthy of the law's attention.

Decision A decision is a legally effective Union instrument. Article 288 TFEU provides that a decision shall be binding in its entirety upon those to whom it is addressed.

Democratic deficit When the Members of the European Parliament (MEPs) were directly elected for the first time in 1979, it was argued that the Parliament's role within the legislative process should be enhanced. There was a 'democratic deficit' because the only directly elected Union institution had little or no involvement in the legislative process. Subsequent treaties (e.g. the SEA, TEU, ToN, ToA, ToL) amended the founding treaties to enhance the legislative role of the European Parliament, but ultimately the European Commission and the Council continue to dominate the legislative process. *See also* CO-DECISION PROCEDURE; COOPERATION PROCEDURE; ORDINARY LEGISLATIVE PROCEDURE; SPECIAL LEGISLATIVE PROCEDURE.

Derogation A derogation is an exception to the general rule.

Deutsche Mark The Deutsche Mark (DM) was Germany's national currency before Germany adopted the euro. *See also* EURO.

Direct discrimination When legislation affords less favourable treatment to a certain group of people.

Direct effect If a provision of Union law has direct effect, it can be enforced in national courts and tribunals, overriding any inconsistent national provisions. In order to be capable of having direct effect, a provision of Union law must be sufficiently precise and unconditional (Case 26/62 ***Van Gend en Loos***). *See also* HORIZONTAL DIRECT EFFECT; VERTICAL DIRECT EFFECT.

Directive A directive is a legally effective Union instrument. Article 288 TFEU provides that a directive shall be binding, as to the result to be achieved, upon each Member State to which it is addressed, but shall allow national authorities to choose the form and methods of implementation. This normally requires a Member State to adopt implementing legislation to incorporate the directive into the national legal system.

Directly applicable Describes an act of Union law that becomes valid law within the legal systems of Member States without them having to take any further action.

Distinctly applicable measure Within the context of Articles 34 and 35 TFEU, a distinctly applicable measure is a quantitative restriction (QR) or measure having an equivalent effect to a quantitative restriction (MEE) which is applied only to imported or exported goods; i.e. the restriction is not applied to domestically produced goods. *See also* INDISTINCTLY APPLICABLE MEASURE; MEASURE HAVING AN EQUIVALENT EFFECT TO A QUANTITATIVE RESTRICTION; QUANTITATIVE RESTRICTION.

DM *See* DEUTSCHE MARK.

Domestic goods Goods that are marketed in the same country in which they were produced.

Double-majority A type of qualified majority where two types of majority thresholds must be met in order for a measure to be adopted.

Dual-burden rule Within the context of Articles 34 and 35 TFEU, a dual-burden rule is one which imposes an additional burden on foreign producers and goods. *See also* EQUAL-BURDEN RULE.

EC *See* EUROPEAN COMMUNITY.

ECB *See* EUROPEAN CENTRAL BANK.

ECHR *See* EUROPEAN CONVENTION ON HUMAN RIGHTS.

Economic and Monetary Union (EMU) The Economic and Monetary Union was established by the EC Treaty (which has been renamed the TFEU by the Treaty of Lisbon), following amendments made to it by the TEU. A timetable for the adoption of the single currency (the euro) was set out. The euro became legal tender in 12 of the 15 pre-2004 Member States on 1 January 2002. The UK, Denmark and Sweden opted out of the single currency. The euro has now replaced the national currency in 19 of the 27 Member States. *See also* EURO; SINGLE EUROPEAN CURRENCY.

ECSC *See* EUROPEAN COAL AND STEEL COMMUNITY.

ECU *See* EUROPEAN CURRENCY UNIT.

EEA *See* EUROPEAN ECONOMIC AREA.

EEC *See* EUROPEAN ECONOMIC COMMUNITY.

EESC *See* European Economic and Social Committee.

Effet utile French phrase which means 'useful effect'.

EFTA *See* European Free Trade Association.

EIB *See* European Investment Bank.

EMU *See* Economic and Monetary Union.

Enlargement The addition of new Member States to the Union.

Equal-burden rule Within the context of Articles 34 and 35 TFEU, an equal-burden rule is a rule which applies equally to domestic and foreign producers (and goods). See also dual-burden rule.

Establishment The pursuit of an economic activity by a service provider for an indefinite period and through a stable infrastructure (e.g. offices or consulting rooms).

Estoppel The legal principle that a party cannot base a claim on grounds, or rely on assertions, that conflict with their previous actions.

EU *See* European Union.

Euratom *See* European Atomic Energy Community.

Euro Following amendments made to the EC Treaty (now the TFEU) by the TEU, a timetable for the adoption of the Single European Currency (the euro) was established. The euro became legal tender in 12 of the 15 pre-2004 Member States on 1 January 2002. The UK, Denmark and Sweden opted out of the single currency. The euro has now replaced the national currency in 19 of the 27 Member States. *See also* Economic and Monetary Union; Single European Currency.

European Atomic Energy Community (Euratom) The European Atomic Energy Community came into existence on 1 July 1958. Euratom covers the research and development of nuclear energy within the EU.

European Central Bank (ECB) Article 13(1) TEU recognises the European Central Bank as one of the Union institutions. The ECB was set up as part of the progression towards the Single European Currency (the euro). *See also* Euro.

European Coal and Steel Community (ECSC) The ECSC came into existence on 23 July 1952 and ended on 23 July 2002. It regulated the control and production of coal and steel.

European Commission The European Commission is one of the Union institutions. There are 27 Commissioners (one from each of the Member States). The Commission initiates/proposes Union legislation, acts as the watchdog of the EU to ensure Union law is being complied with and has limited direct legislative powers. *See also* Comitology.

European Communities Initially, the European Communities collectively comprised the European Coal and Steel Community (ECSC), European Economic Community (EEC) (later renamed the European Community (EC)) and European Atomic Energy Community (Euratom). The ECSC ended on 23 July 2002. Then, when the Treaty of Lisbon came into force on 1 December 2009, the EC Treaty was renamed the Treaty on the Functioning of the European Union (TFEU) and the Union replaced and succeeded the Community (Art 1 TEU). Throughout the TFEU, the word 'Community' has been replaced with the word 'Union'. The following terms are therefore no longer used: European *Community*; European *Communities*; or *Community* law. Reference is made solely to the European *Union* (or the *Union*) and European *Union* law (or *Union* law). *See also* European Atomic Energy Community; European Coal and Steel Community; European Community; European Economic Community; European Union; Treaty of Lisbon; Treaty on European Union.

European Community (EC) In 1957, the Treaty Establishing the European Economic Community (EEC Treaty) was adopted. The EEC Treaty came into force on 1 July 1958. Following subsequent amendments to the EEC Treaty, the EEC increasingly became concerned with, *inter alia*, social policy and political issues, departing from its predominantly economic roots. For this reason, the TEU renamed the EEC Treaty the 'Treaty Establishing the European Community' (EC Treaty). This change came into effect on 1 November 1993 when the TEU came into force. When the Treaty of Lisbon came into force on

1 December 2009, the EC Treaty was renamed the Treaty on the Functioning of the European Union (TFEU) and the Union replaced and succeeded the Community (Art 1 TEU). Throughout the TFEU, the word 'Community' has been replaced with the word 'Union'. The following terms are therefore no longer used: European *Community*, European *Communities*, or *Community* law. Reference is made solely to the European *Union* (or the *Union*) and European *Union* law (or *Union* law). *See also* EUROPEAN ATOMIC ENERGY COMMUNITY; EUROPEAN COAL AND STEEL COMMUNITY; EUROPEAN COMMUNITIES; EUROPEAN ECONOMIC COMMUNITY; EUROPEAN UNION; TREATY OF LISBON; TREATY ON EUROPEAN UNION.

European Convention on Human Rights (ECHR) The European Convention on Human Rights (ECHR) is a treaty to which all EU Member States are a party, along with several other European countries. The ECHR requires signatory states to protect the human rights set out in the Convention. Although the ECHR is separate and distinct from the EU, Article 6(3) TEU provides that the 'fundamental rights guaranteed by the European Convention on Human Rights and Fundamental Freedoms and as they result from the constitutional traditions common to the Member States, shall constitute general principles of the Union's law'. Since the Treaty of Lisbon came into force on 1 December 2009, Article 6(2) TEU provides that the Union will accede to the Convention, although it states that 'such accession shall not affect the Union's competences as defined in the Treaties'.

European Council Since the Treaty of Lisbon, the European Council is recognised by Article 13(1) TEU as one of the Union institutions. The European Council consists of the heads of government of the Member States. Its role is to provide the Union with the necessary impetus for its development and to define its political directions and priorities (Art 15(1) TEU). The European Council meets at least twice a year, at meetings often referred to as 'European Summits'.

European Court of Human Rights (ECtHR) The European Court of Human Rights decides cases which concern infringements of the rights provided for in the European Convention on Human Rights (ECHR). Decisions made by this court are not binding on national courts. This court is **not** a Union institution. *See also* EUROPEAN CONVENTION ON HUMAN RIGHTS.

European Economic and Social Committee (EESC) The European Economic and Social Committee, originally known by its French acronym ECOSOC but now as the EESC, was established by the TEU as an advisory body. It is not a formal Union institution. The members of the Committee consist of 'representatives of organisations of employers, of the employed, and of other parties representative of civil society, notably in socioeconomic, civic, professional and cultural areas' (Art 300(2) TFEU). Its main role is to deliver opinions on proposed legislation when consulted by the Council and to issue own-initiative opinions in appropriate cases. In a few policy areas (e.g. employment (Art 148(2) TFEU)), the legal base for a legislative proposal stipulates that the Committee must be consulted in relation to proposed legislation. *See also* LEGAL BASE.

European Economic Area (EEA) On 2 May 1992, the then seven European Free Trade Association (EFTA) states, the EU and the Member States, signed an agreement to establish the European Economic Area (EEA). The EEA, which some initially saw as an alternative to full membership of the European Union, was intended to integrate the EFTA states *economically* into the Union without giving them a role in its institutions. The EEA gave the EFTA states access for their goods, persons, services and capital to the markets of the Union. Equally, the same facilities were granted by EFTA states in their territories to Member States of the EU. Of the EFTA states, only Switzerland refused to participate in the EEA, after a hostile national referendum. In this new trading area, all the *economic* rules of the EU apply, although the Member States of EFTA are not represented in any of the EU institutions and do not participate in the EU's decision-making process. *See also* EUROPEAN FREE TRADE ASSOCIATION.

European Economic Community (EEC) The European Economic Community was created by the Treaty Establishing the European Economic Community (EEC Treaty). This Treaty (which is often referred to as the Treaty of Rome) came into force on 1 July 1958. The EEC was renamed the European Community (EC) on 1 November 1993 by the Treaty on European Union (TEU). When the Treaty of Lisbon came into force on 1 December 2009, the EC Treaty was renamed the Treaty on the Functioning of the European Union (TFEU) and the Union replaced and succeeded the Community (Art 1 TEU). Throughout the TFEU, the word 'Community' has been replaced with the word 'Union'. The following terms are therefore no longer used: European *Community*; European *Communities*; or *Community* law. Reference is made solely to the European *Union* (or the *Union*) and European *Union* law (or *Union* law). *See also* European Atomic Energy Community; European Coal and Steel Community; European Communities; European Community; European Union; Treaty on European Union.

European Free Trade Association (EFTA)   The European Free Trade Association was set up by non-Member States as an alternative to EU membership. EFTA established a free-trade area between the participating states (currently Iceland, Liechtenstein, Norway and Switzerland). *See also* European Economic Area.

European Investment Bank   The European Investment Bank (EIB) was established by Article 308 TFEU (previously Art 9 EC Treaty). It is not a Union institution within the scope of Article 13(1) TEU (previously Art 7 EC Treaty). The EIB is the European Union's long-term lending bank and the regional development bank for Europe. It makes grants and loans to projects which affect more than one Member State, where they cannot be funded sufficiently from within those Member States.

European Parliament   The European Parliament is one of the Union institutions. Members of the European Parliament (MEPs) are directly elected to the Parliament. The first direct elections took place in 1979.

European Union (EU)   The European Union was established by the Treaty on European Union (TEU). Until 1 December 2009 the EU was composed of three pillars: (i) the European Communities; (ii) Common Foreign and Security Policy; and (iii) Police and Judicial Cooperation in Criminal Matters. When the Treaty of Lisbon came into force on 1 December 2009, the Union replaced and succeeded the Community (Art 1 TEU) and the three pillars were merged. *See also* European Atomic Energy Community; European Coal and Steel Community; European Communities; European Community; European Economic Community; Treaty of Lisbon; Treaty on European Union.

European Union (EU) citizen   A citizen of a Member State of the EU (also referred to as a Union citizen, EU national or Union national).

European Union Settlement Scheme (EUSS)   The scheme to which EU citizens must apply if they wish to continue residing in the UK after Brexit. Under the scheme, they will be awarded with 'settled' status if they have already lived continuously in the UK for five years or 'pre-settled' status if they do not meet this requirement. *See also* Brexit.

European Union (EU) worker   A worker who comes within the scope of the provisions of Union law relating to the free movement of workers is referred to as an 'EU worker'. An EU worker is defined as one who is engaged in a genuine and effective economic activity which is not on such a small scale as to be marginal or ancillary (Case 53/81 *Levin*). The Union law provisions only apply to an EU citizen who is working or has worked in a Member State other than that of their nationality.

Excise duty   A charge that is imposed on a manufacturer of goods.

Exit day   The day on which the UK exited the EU (31 January 2020).

Exportability of benefits   Within the context of Article 48 TFEU and Regulation 883/2004, which establishes social security rights for EU workers, the right to receive a social security benefit, usually from the home Member State, attaches to an EU worker as they travel around the EU, irrespective of national boundaries. This is referred to as the 'exportability of benefits' and is also known as 'the portability principle'. *See also* Aggregation of contributions.

Fait accompli   French phrase which means 'an accomplished and presumably irreversible deed or fact'.

Fidelity principle   Under Article 4(3) TEU, Member States are required to act in a manner which supports, or is at least compatible with, the Union's values and objectives. This is also referred to as the principle of sincere cooperation.

Franc The franc was France's national currency before France adopted the euro. *See also* EURO.

Francovich damages Also referred to as the principle of state liability, *Francovich* damages were established by the Court of Justice in *Francovich v Republic of Italy* (Cases C-6/90 & 9/90). This principle provides that if a person suffers damage because of a Member State's breach of Union law, the Member State is liable to the aggrieved person if: (i) the rule of Union law infringed is intended to confer rights on individuals; (ii) the breach is sufficiently serious; and (iii) there is a direct causal link between the breach of the rule and the damage sustained by the person (*Brasserie du Pêcheur* and *Factortame* (Cases C-46/93 and 48/93)). See also STATE LIABILITY.

Frontier worker A person who lives in one Member State but works in another Member State.

Fundamental rights Fundamental rights are those which the Court of Justice has deemed are central to the European Union's policies. For example, the rights established by the free movement provisions of the TFEU have been classified by the Court of Justice as fundamental rights. Fundamental rights will be protected by the Court of Justice from interference, unless such interference is permitted by the Treaty.

Harmonising directive A harmonising directive is one which establishes a set of common rules which apply throughout the Member States. *See also* RULE OF MUTUAL RECOGNITION.

Historical interpretation Historical interpretation is used by courts to interpret legislation. If this method is employed, there is a consideration of the subjective intention of the author of the text of the legislation. This method may be equated with the English mischief rule of legislative interpretation, where the judge seeks to establish the legislative intent. This method of legislative interpretation is occasionally used by the Court of Justice of the European Union. *See also* CONTEXTUAL INTERPRETATION; LITERAL INTERPRETATION; TELEOLOGICAL INTERPRETATION.

Home Member State The Member State of which a person is a citizen.

Horizontal direct effect A provision of Union law which is enforceable in national courts or tribunals against natural and legal persons, overriding any inconsistent national provisions, is said to have horizontal direct effect (*Marshall* v *Southampton AHA* (Case 152/84)). Treaty articles and regulations are capable of having horizontal direct effect if the provision is sufficiently precise and unconditional (*Van Gend en Loos* (Case 26/62)). Directives cannot have horizontal direct effect (*Marshall* v *Southampton AHA* (Case 152/84)). *See also* DIRECT EFFECT; VERTICAL DIRECT EFFECT.

Host Member State The Member State in which an EU citizen resides but of which they are not a citizen.

In camera Latin phrase which means 'in the chamber' but more commonly used to mean 'in secret'.

Indirect discrimination When legislation is formulated or implemented in such a way that – although no explicit distinction between groups of people is made – a certain group of people is disadvantaged in practice.

Indirect effect National courts and tribunals are under an obligation to interpret national law in such a way that it avoids a conflict with Union law, if that is possible (*Marleasing* (Case C-106/89)). This is referred to as the principle of indirect effect or the interpretive obligation. *See also* DIRECT EFFECT; INTERPRETATIVE OBLIGATION.

Indistinctly applicable measure Within the context of Articles 34 and 35 TFEU, an indistinctly applicable measure is a quantitative restriction (QR) or a measure having equivalent effect (MEE) which is applied to all goods without distinction; i.e. the restriction is applied to both domestically produced and foreign goods. *See also* DISTINCTLY APPLICABLE MEASURE; MEASURE HAVING AN EQUIVALENT EFFECT TO A QUANTITATIVE RESTRICTION; QUANTITATIVE RESTRICTION.

Infringement proceedings Article 258 TFEU empowers the Commission to take action against a Member State which is in breach of Union law. If the Member State fails to remedy the breach, ultimately the Commission can bring proceedings against the defaulting Member State before the Court of Justice. Such proceedings are referred to as infringement proceedings.

Intellectual property rights (IP) Intellectual property rights protect the product of one person's work (by hand or brain) against unauthorised use or exploitation by another. Such rights are protected by laws relating to, *inter alia*, copyright, patents and trademarks.

Inter alia Latin phrase which means 'among other things'.

Inter partes Latin phrase which means 'between the parties'.

Intergovernmental Refers to cooperation between two or more countries.

Intergovernmental conference (IGC) An intergovernmental conference is the title given to a meeting of the European Council which is primarily concerned with drafting a treaty to amend the founding treaties (e.g. TFEU).

Interlocutory proceedings When court or tribunal proceedings have been initiated, sometimes the court will need to make an order (for example) before it finally determines the case. Such an order is referred to as an interim order. Interlocutory proceedings occur during the course of the action (i.e. before the case is finally determined), when, for example, an interim order is required.

Internal border Borders between Member States, i.e. borders within the territory of the Union.

Internal market The internal market is 'an area without internal frontiers in which the free movement of goods, persons, services and capital is ensured in accordance with the provisions of the Treaties' (Art 26(2) TFEU (previously Art 14 EC Treaty)). *See also* COMMON MARKET.

Interpretative obligation National courts and tribunals are under an obligation to interpret national law in such a way that it avoids a conflict with Union law, if that is possible (***Marleasing*** (Case C-106/89)). This is also known as the principle of indirect effect. *See also* DIRECT EFFECT; INDIRECT EFFECT.

Ioannina Declaration Under a declaration made in March 1994 at the Ioannina Summit of the European Council, it was established that where a decision is to be taken by a qualified majority, if a minority of Member States (which do not have sufficient votes to block the decision being adopted) indicate their intention to oppose the decision, the Council is required to do all in its power to reach, within a reasonable period of time, a satisfactory solution. This declaration is referred to as the Ioannina Declaration. On 1 December 2009 when the Treaty of Lisbon came into force, a revised 'Ioannina' compromise was adopted. *See also* QUALIFIED MAJORITY.

Judge-Rapporteur In Union law and politics, Rapporteur refers to a person who is appointed by a deliberative body to investigate a particular issue and to report back to that body. When a case is heard by the Court of Justice, a Judge-Rapporteur is appointed. The Court of Justice delivers a single judgment for each case (rather than each judge delivering separate judgments). It is the responsibility of the Judge-Rapporteur to draft the judgment, which will inform the discussions of all the other judges assigned to that case. A single judgment will then be agreed by the judges acting by simple majority.

Jurisdiction Normally used to refer to the power of a court or tribunal to hear a case. With regard to the Court of Justice of the European Union (i.e. the Court of Justice, the General Court and the specialised courts), its jurisdiction (i.e. power) to hear cases derives from the treaties.

Jus cogens Latin phrase which means 'fundamental rights of the human person'.

Legal act Article 288 TFEU provides that regulations, directives and decisions constitute 'legal acts' of the Union. *See also* LEGISLATIVE ACT; LEGISLATIVE PROCEDURE.

Legal autonomy The independence of a legal system such that it is not legally bound by any other system, except where it has expressly agreed to be.

Legal base The Treaty article under which a legislative instrument (e.g. regulation, directive or decision) is proposed is often referred to as the legal base (and is occasionally referred to as the legal basis). The legal base will set out the legislative procedure which must be followed for the proposed instrument to be adopted. *See also* LEGAL BASIS.

Legal basis The Treaty article under which a legislative instrument (e.g. regulation, directive or decision) is proposed is occasionally referred to as the legal basis (it is normally referred to as the legal base). The legal basis will set out the legislative procedure which must be followed for the proposed instrument to be adopted. *See also* LEGAL BASE.

Legal certainty   In ***Kloppenburg*** (Case 70/81), the Court of Justice stated that Union legislation must be unequivocal and its application must be predictable for those who are subject to it. This is referred to as the principle of legal certainty. *See also* NON-RETROACTIVITY.

Legislative act   Article 288 TFEU provides that regulations, directives and decisions constitute 'legal acts' of the Union. Article 289(3) TFEU provides that 'legal acts adopted by *legislative procedure* shall constitute *legislative acts*'. There are two legislative procedures prescribed by the TFEU: (i) the 'ordinary legislative procedure' (Art 289(1) TFEU); and (ii) the 'special legislative procedure' (Art 289(2) TFEU). *See also* LEGAL ACT; LEGISLATIVE PROCEDURE; ORDINARY LEGISLATIVE PROCEDURE; SPECIAL LEGISLATIVE PROCEDURE.

Legislative procedure   Article 289(3) TFEU provides that 'legal acts adopted by *legislative procedure* shall constitute *legislative acts*'. There are two legislative procedures prescribed by the TFEU: (i) the 'ordinary legislative procedure' (Art 289(1) TFEU); and (ii) the 'special legislative procedure' (Art 289(2) TFEU). *See also* LEGAL ACT; LEGISLATIVE ACT; ORDINARY LEGISLATIVE PROCEDURE; SPECIAL LEGISLATIVE PROCEDURE.

Legitimate expectation   The principle of legitimate expectation provides that assurances relied on in good faith should be honoured (***Compagnie Continentale* v *Council*** (Case 169/73)).

Literal interpretation   Literal interpretation is used by courts to interpret legislation. If this method is employed, words are given their natural, plain meaning. This method of legislative interpretation is widely used by courts in the English legal system, but it is rarely used by the Court of Justice of the European Union. *See also* CONTEXTUAL INTERPRETATION; HISTORICAL INTERPRETATION; TELEOLOGICAL INTERPRETATION.

Locus standi   Latin phrase which means 'a place of standing'. In a legal context it refers to an individual's right to be heard in a court or tribunal.

Lump sum   A single, one-off payment.

Luxembourg Accords   The Luxembourg Accords were the result of an impasse between France and the other Member States of the EU during 1965. France refused to attend meetings of the Council, resulting in important decision-making within the Union grinding to a halt. The Luxembourg Accords were negotiated to break the impasse. The Accords are not legally enforceable and are rarely (if ever) relied on.

Mandatory requirements defence   In the context of Articles 34 and 35 TFEU, the second ***Cassis*** principle (Case 120/78) established a rule of reason (also referred to as the 'mandatory requirements defence'), which provides that indistinctly applicable measures having an equivalent effect to a quantitative restriction (MEEs) must be accepted in so far as those provisions may be recognised as being necessary in order to satisfy mandatory requirements relating to, in particular, the effectiveness of fiscal supervision, the protection of public health, the fairness of commercial transactions and the defence of the consumer. *See also* INDISTINCTLY APPLICABLE MEASURE; MEASURE HAVING AN EQUIVALENT EFFECT TO A QUANTITATIVE RESTRICTION; PROPORTIONALITY TEST; RULE OF MUTUAL RECOGNITION; RULE OF REASON.

Marshall Plan   Following the end of the Second World War, the USA provided financial assistance to Western European states to aid economic recovery. This aid was referred to as the Marshall Plan.

Measure having an equivalent effect to a quantitative restriction (MEE or MEQR)   In the context of Articles 34 and 35 TFEU, a measure having an equivalent effect to a quantitative restriction includes 'all trading rules enacted by Member States which are capable of hindering, directly or indirectly, actually or potentially, intra-Community [i.e. intra-Union] trade' (***Procureur du Roi* v *Dassonville*** (Case 8/74)). This is also referred to as the ***Dassonville*** formula. *See also* DISTINCTLY APPLICABLE MEASURE; INDISTINCTLY APPLICABLE MEASURE; QUANTITATIVE RESTRICTION.

MEE   *See* MEASURE HAVING AN EQUIVALENT EFFECT TO A QUANTITATIVE RESTRICTION.

Member State of establishment The Member State in which a service provider is established.

MEP Member of the European Parliament. *See also* EUROPEAN PARLIAMENT.

MEQR *See* MEASURE HAVING AN EQUIVALENT EFFECT TO A QUANTITATIVE RESTRICTION.

Mischief rule The mischief rule is a method of legislative interpretation, sometimes used by courts in the English legal system. When applying this rule, the judge seeks to establish the legislative intent.

Monopoly A monopoly exists if a commodity or service is controlled solely (or primarily) by one business undertaking or the state. *See also* STATE MONOPOLY.

Mutatis mutandis Latin phrase which means 'with those things changed which need to be changed' or 'with the appropriate changes'.

Nationality At the national level, the terms nationality/national and citizenship/citizen are used interchangeably to refer to the legal status of national citizenship.

NATO *See* NORTH ATLANTIC TREATY ORGANIZATION.

Natural justice Concept in Union law derived from the English legal system and closely linked to the USA's 'due process'. The Court of Justice often refers to it as a duty to act fairly (***UNECTEF* v *Heylens*** (Case 222/86)).

Naturalisation The process by which national citizenship is acquired when not obtained at birth.

Non-EU national A citizen of a country that is not a Member State of the EU (sometimes referred to as a third-country national).

Non-retroactivity The principle that any changes to the law (through legislation or case law) should not be applied retrospectively. To do otherwise would conflict with the principle of legal certainty. In Union law this principle is applied in particular with regard to legal provisions which impose criminal sanctions. *See also* LEGAL CERTAINTY.

North Atlantic Treaty Organization (NATO) NATO was founded in 1949, following the end of the Second World War. It is a defence organisation for North America and Europe.

Obiter dictum Latin phrase which is often referred to simply as *obiter* and means 'a thing said in passing'. In a legal context it refers to an observation by a judge on a point of law which is not directly relevant to the case before the court. The point of law is neither required by the judge's decision nor does it serve as a precedent. However, it may be of persuasive authority. The plural, *obiter dicta*, may be used, for example, when reference is made to multiple *obiter* statements which are contained within a judgment.

Objective justification Objective justification is a common concept throughout much of the Union's substantive law. It is based on the premise that a restriction, which might otherwise breach Union law, will be permissible provided that: (i) the reason for the restriction is for a legitimate public interest; (ii) the restriction is suitable for the protection of that interest and (iii) the restriction is proportionate (i.e. it does not go beyond what is necessary to protect the legitimate public interest). *See also* PROPORTIONALITY TEST; RULE OF REASON.

OECD *See* ORGANISATION FOR ECONOMIC COOPERATION AND DEVELOPMENT (OECD).

Official Journal The official publication of the Union, in which the Treaties often specify that legal acts must be published.

Opinion Article 288 TFEU provides that an opinion is a non-legally enforceable Union instrument. It may have a persuasive element (i.e. it may be taken into account by the Court of Justice of the European Union when determining a case).

Ordinary legislative procedure There are two legislative procedures prescribed by the TFEU: (i) the 'ordinary legislative procedure' (Art 289(1) TFEU); and (ii) the 'special legislative procedure' (Art 289(2) TFEU). The ordinary legislative procedure applies in the vast majority of cases. The ordinary legislative procedure empowers the Parliament to propose amendments to, and ultimately to veto, a proposal. The legal base determines the legislative procedure which must be used for the adoption of a particular instrument. *See also* CO-DECISION PROCEDURE; LEGAL ACT; LEGAL BASE; LEGISLATIVE PROCEDURE; SPECIAL LEGISLATIVE PROCEDURE.

Organisation for Economic Cooperation and Development (OECD) Originally formed in 1961, the OECD is an international organisation which now has 36 member countries. The OECD produces data and research to inform social, economic and environmental policies. It is not a Union institution.

Passerelle clauses Clauses within the Treaties that allow for derogations from particular procedures, provided that certain conditions are met.

Pecuniary penalty Any monetary penalty.

Penalty payment A penalty that is paid in regular instalments until the breach of Union law is resolved.

Per Latin word which means 'by means of' or 'according to'.

Pillars The Treaty on European Union (TEU) established the European Union. The former Article A TEU provided that 'the Union shall be founded on the European Communities, supplemented by the policies and forms of cooperation established by this Treaty'. It followed from this that the EU was to be founded upon three pillars. Following amendments made to the TEU by the ToA, Article 1 TEU provided that the three pillars were: (i) the European Communities (i.e. the EC and Euratom); (ii) Common Foreign and Security Policy (CFSP); and (iii) Police and Judicial Cooperation in Criminal Matters. When the Treaty of Lisbon came into force on 1 December 2009, the pillar structure of the European Union was abolished.

Plenary meeting A meeting that all members of the institution attend.

Posted workers A business which employs workers in one Member State may send their workers to another Member State. Such workers are referred to as posted workers (i.e. a worker 'posted' from one Member State to another).

Precedent The doctrine of precedent (*stare decisis*, a Latin phrase which means 'let the decision stand'), provides that courts and tribunals are bound by points of law decided by courts higher up in the hierarchy, and sometimes they are bound by their own previous decisions. The doctrine does not apply to the Court of Justice. However, the Court of Justice normally follows its own previous decisions for the sake of legal certainty. *See also* LEGAL CERTAINTY; *Ratio decidendi*.

Preliminary ruling Pursuant to Article 267 TFEU, a national court or tribunal may (and in certain circumstances it must) refer a case to the Court of Justice if the national court or tribunal considers such a referral is necessary for it to reach its decision. The national court or tribunal asks the Court of Justice questions relating to, *inter alia*: interpretation of the Treaties or the interpretation or legal validity of regulations, directives or decisions. The Court of Justice answers those questions and sends the case back to the referring court or tribunal for it to give judgment. This procedure is referred to as the 'preliminary ruling' procedure.

Prima facie Latin phrase which means 'at first sight'. In a legal context, '*prima facie* case' refers to evidence which will suffice to support the allegation, unless there is evidence which rebuts the allegation.

Pro forma Latin phrase which means 'for form' or 'as a matter of form', i.e. prescribing a set form or procedure.

Procedural *ultra vires* When a decision maker, who is exercising a power or discretion, fails to follow an essential procedural requirement (quite often set out in the enabling legislation), this is referred to as 'procedural *ultra vires*'. The exercise of the power or discretion in such circumstances is unlawful. *See also* SUBSTANTIVE ULTRA VIRES.

Product substitution Product substitution determines which products compete with each other. *See also* CROSS-ELASTICITY.

Proportionality test The proportionality test is imported into Union law from the German legal system. The test is applied to ensure that either the acts of Union institutions or obstacles to Union free movements imposed at the national level go no further than is necessary to achieve the stated objective, which itself must be legitimate. *See also* OBJECTIVE JUSTIFICATION; RULE OF REASON.

Protectionism A rule imposed by the state or a regulatory body, the aim of which is to protect domestic traders from competition by foreign traders, is referred to as 'protectionism'.

Protocol Protocols are often annexed (i.e. attached) to EU treaties. With regard to the protocols annexed to the TEU and TFEU, Article 51 TEU states that 'The protocols and annexes to the Treaties shall form an integral part thereof'. For example, the UK's opt-out from the Single European Currency is set out in a protocol annexed to the TFEU.

QR See QUANTITATIVE RESTRICTION.

Qualified majority The legal base determines the legislative procedure which has to be used for the adoption of a particular instrument. If the legal base provides for the instrument to be adopted by the Council acting by a 'qualified majority', the votes are weighted according to the population size of the Member States. Article 16(4) TEU requires two thresholds to be achieved before a measure can be adopted: (i) the support of at least 55 per cent of the members of the Council, comprising at least 15 of them; and (ii) the support of Member States comprising at least 65 per cent of the population of the Union. In addition, the qualified majority will be considered to have been achieved if fewer than four Member States vote against a measure. See also COUNCIL; LEGAL BASE; LEGISLATIVE PROCEDURE.

Quantitative restriction (QR) In the context of Articles 34 and 35 TFEU, quantitative restrictions (QR) are measures that amount to a total or partial restraint of imports, exports or goods in transit (*Geddo* (Case 2/73)). See also DISTINCTLY APPLICABLE MEASURE; INDISTINCTLY APPLICABLE MEASURE; MEASURE HAVING AN EQUIVALENT EFFECT TO A QUANTITATIVE RESTRICTION.

Quorum A minimum threshold for persons present or votes cast in order for proceedings to be valid.

Rapporteur In Union law and politics, Rapporteur refers to a person who is appointed by a deliberative body (e.g. the European Parliament) to investigate a particular issue and to report back to that body.

Ratification The action of formally approving a treaty or agreement. Member States have different ratification procedures according to their domestic legislation.

Ratio decidendi Latin phrase which means the legal reason (or ground) for a judicial decision. It is the *ratio decidendi* (or *ratio*) of a case which will bind later courts under the system of precedent. See also PRECEDENT.

Recommendation Article 288 TFEU provides that a recommendation is a non-legally enforceable Union instrument. It may have a persuasive element (i.e. it may be taken into account by the Court of Justice of the European Union when determining a case).

Regulation A regulation is a legally effective Union instrument. Article 288 TFEU provides that a regulation shall be directly applicable. This means it is incorporated automatically into the national legal systems of the Member States.

Regulatory act A non-legislative act of a Union institution or other Union body, office or agency, i.e. an act that has not been adopted by a legislative procedure. See also LEGISLATIVE PROCEDURE.

Respondent A respondent is the person against whom a claim is made in a court or tribunal (also referred to as a defendant).

Rule of mutual recognition The first *Cassis* principle (Case 120/78), referred to as the 'rule of mutual recognition', provides that once goods have been lawfully marketed in one Member State, they should be free to be marketed in any other Member State without restriction. See also MANDATORY REQUIREMENTS DEFENCE; RULE OF REASON.

Rule of reason In the context of Articles 34 and 35 TFEU, the second *Cassis* principle (Case 120/78) established a rule of reason which provides that indistinctly applicable measures having an equivalent effect to a quantitative restriction (MEEs) must be accepted in so far as those provisions may be recognised as being necessary in order to satisfy mandatory requirements relating to, in particular, the effectiveness of fiscal supervision, the protection of public health, the fairness of commercial transactions and the defence of the consumer. See also INDISTINCTLY APPLICABLE MEASURE; MEASURE HAVING AN EQUIVALENT EFFECT TO A QUANTITATIVE RESTRICTION; MANDATORY REQUIREMENTS DEFENCE; OBJECTIVE JUSTIFICATION; PROPORTIONALITY TEST; RULE OF MUTUAL RECOGNITION.

Schengen Agreement The Schengen Agreement abolished the internal borders of the signatory states and created a single external border where immigration checks for the Schengen area are carried out in accordance with a single set of rules. Common rules regarding visas, asylum rights and checks at external borders were adopted to allow the free movement of persons within the signatory states without disturbing law and order. *See also* SCHENGEN INFORMATION SYSTEM.

Schengen Information System (SIS) The SIS is an information network which was set up to allow all border posts, police stations and consular agents from Schengen group Member States to access data on specific individuals or on vehicles or objects which have been lost or stolen. Member States supply the network through national networks (N-SIS) connected to a central system (C-SIS), and this is supplemented by a network known as SIRENE (Supplementary Information Request at the National Entry). The system was not designed to operate in more than 15 Member States. SIS-II is the second-generation SIS with greater capacity, thus enabling all Member States to use the system. *See also* SCHENGEN AGREEMENT.

SEA *See* SINGLE EUROPEAN ACT.

Secondary legislation In Union law, secondary legislation refers to Union instruments which are adopted by the Union institutions, pursuant to powers contained within the treaties. Article 288 TFEU provides that such instruments shall be in the form of regulations, directives or decisions. *See also* REGULATION; DIRECTIVE; DECISION.

Service provider A self-employed professional or undertaking that is established in a Member State and that offers or provides a service for which they are normally remunerated.

Simple majority A voting threshold of more than half of the total votes.

Single European Act (SEA) The SEA came into force on 1 July 1987 and amended the founding Treaties (in particular the EC Treaty (now renamed TFEU)).

Single European Currency Following amendments made by the TEU to the EC Treaty (renamed the TFEU by the ToL), a timetable for the adoption of the Single European Currency (the euro) was established. The euro became legal tender in 12 of the 15 pre-2004 Member States on 1 January 2002. The UK, Denmark and Sweden opted out of the single currency. The euro has now replaced the national currency in 19 of the 27 Member States. *See also* ECONOMIC AND MONETARY UNION; EURO.

SIS *See* SCHENGEN INFORMATION SYSTEM.

Social advantages Benefits that are granted on the basis of worker or residence status, or that could facilitate the mobility of Union workers.

Social assistance Non-contributory benefits that aim to enable a person to meet their basic subsistence needs.

Social Chapter The Social Chapter was annexed to the TEU as a protocol, applying to all of the then Member States except the UK. The Social Chapter covers, *inter alia*, employee protection rights. Following the election of a Labour government in the UK on 1 May 1997, the UK no longer objected to the Social Chapter and it was therefore incorporated into the EC Treaty when the Treaty was amended by the ToA on 1 May 1999.

Social security Benefits that insure against possible loss of income resulting from unemploy-ment, disability, pregnancy, old age and other related circumstances that result in loss of income, and which are not based on any individual assessment.

Soft law Non-legally enforceable instruments which may aid the interpretation and/or application of Union law are referred to as 'soft law'. Soft law, in the EU context, includes recommendations and opinions.

Special legislative procedure There are two legislative procedures prescribed by the TFEU: (i) the 'ordinary legislative procedure' (Art 289(1) TFEU); and (ii) the 'special legislative procedure' (Art 289(2) TFEU). The ordinary legislative procedure applies in the vast majority of cases. The special legislative procedure refers to specific cases where the Treaties provide for the adoption of a regulation, directive or decision: (i) by the European Parliament with the Council's involvement; or (ii) by the Council with the participation of the European Parliament (Art 289(2) TFEU). The legal base will detail the exact role of each institution, together with the voting procedure (in the case of the Council, the voting procedure is qualified majority unless otherwise stated (Art 16(3) TEU)). *See also* COOPERATION PROCEDURE; LEGAL BASE; LEGISLATIVE PROCEDURE; ORDINARY LEGISLATIVE PROCEDURE.

Stare decisis Latin phrase which means 'let the decision stand'. In a legal context it refers to the doctrine of precedent. *See also* PRECEDENT.

State aid State aid is aid (financial or non-financial) which is granted by the state to a business undertaking. The compatibility of state aid with the internal market is governed by Article 107(1) TFEU.

State liability The principle of state liability, established by the Court of Justice in *Francovich* (Cases C-6/90 and 9/90), provides that if a person suffers damage because of a Member State's breach of Union law, the Member State is liable to the aggrieved person if: (i) the rule of Union law infringed is intended to confer rights on individuals; (ii) the breach is sufficiently serious; and (iii) there is a direct causal link between the breach of the rule and the damage sustained by the person (*Brasserie du Pêcheur* and *Factortame* (Cases C-46/93 and 48/93)). *See also* FRANCOVICH DAMAGES.

State monopoly A state monopoly exists where a commodity or service is controlled solely by the state (e.g. nationalised utilities: gas, electricity, water, etc.). Article 37 TFEU regulates state monopolies. *See also* MONOPOLY.

Subsidiarity The exercise of Union competences is governed by 'the principles of subsidiarity and proportionality' (Art 5(1) TEU). In those areas which do not fall within the Union's exclusive competence, the Union shall act 'only if and so far as the objectives of the proposed action cannot be sufficiently achieved by the Member States, either at central level or at regional and local level' (Art 5(3) TEU). This is referred to as the principle of subsidiarity. Article 5(1) TEU is complemented by Protocol 2 (which is annexed to the TFEU and the TEU) on the application of the two principles of subsidiarity and proportionality, which incorporates an 'early-warning system' involving national parliaments in the monitoring of how subsidiarity is applied. National parliaments are informed of all new legislative initiatives and if at least one-third of them are of the view that a proposal infringes the principle of subsidiarity, the Commission will have to reconsider the proposal. *See also* PROPORTIONALITY; PROTOCOL.

Substantive *ultra vires* When a decision maker, who exercises a power or discretion, has no competence to exercise such power or discretion, this is referred to as 'substantive *ultra vires*'. The exercise of the power or discretion in such circumstances is unlawful. *See also* PROCEDURAL ULTRA VIRES.

Sui generis Latin phrase which means 'of its own kind' or 'in a class of its own'.

Supremacy Taking precedence over conflicting rules or laws, having the final say.

Tariff A tax on imports or exports.

Teleological interpretation Teleological interpretation is used by courts to interpret legislation. If this method is employed when interpreting Union law, the provision will be interpreted in furtherance of the aims and objectives of the Union as a whole. This method of legislative interpretation, together with contextual interpretation, is extensively used by the Court of Justice of the European Union. *See also* CONTEXTUAL INTERPRETATION; HISTORICAL INTERPRETATION; LITERAL INTERPRETATION.

TEU *See* TREATY ON EUROPEAN UNION.

TFEU *See* TREATY ON THE FUNCTIONING OF THE EUROPEAN UNION.

Third country Within Union law, the term 'third country' is used to refer to a country which is not a member of the EU (i.e. a non-EU country).

Three pillars of the European Union *See* PILLARS.

ToA *See* TREATY OF AMSTERDAM.

ToL *See* TREATY OF LISBON.

ToN *See* TREATY OF NICE.

Treaty A Treaty is an agreement between two or more countries. A treaty will not be legally enforceable unless this is provided for within the treaty. The Treaty on European Union (TEU) and the Treaty on the Functioning of the European Union (TFEU) incorporate enforcement mechanisms to ensure Member States comply with their Union law obligations. In addition, the Treaties provide for Union institutions to develop Union law through the adoption, implementation and interpretation of Union instruments.

Treaty of Accession A Treaty of Accession is adopted by the Member States to provide for enlargement of the European Union. The most recent Treaty of Accession provided for Croatia's entry to the EU on 1 July 2013.

Treaty of Amsterdam (ToA) The Treaty of Amsterdam came into force on 1 May 1999 and amended the EC Treaty (now renamed the TFEU) and the TEU.

Treaty of Lisbon (ToL) The Treaty of Lisbon came into force on 1 December 2009 and introduced substantial changes. For example, the EC Treaty was renamed the Treaty on the Functioning of the European Union (TFEU) and the articles within both the TEU and TFEU were renumbered as part of a simplification exercise. Also, the Union replaced and succeeded the Community (Art 1 TEU). Throughout the TFEU, the word 'Community' has been replaced with the word 'Union'. The following terms are therefore no longer used: European *Community*, European *Communities*, or *Community* law. Reference is made solely to the European *Union* (or the *Union*) and European *Union* law (or *Union* law).

Treaty of Maastricht *See* Treaty on European Union.

Treaty of Nice (ToN) The Treaty of Nice came into force on 1 February 2003 and amended the EC Treaty (now renamed the TFEU) and the TEU.

Treaty of Rome The EEC Treaty is often referred to as the Treaty of Rome because it was signed in Rome on 25 March 1957. However, the Euratom Treaty was also signed in Rome at the same time. The EEC Treaty's official title is 'The Treaty Establishing the European Community'. The EEC Treaty was renamed the EC Treaty by the TEU in 1993, and was then renamed the TFEU by the ToL in 2009. *See also* European Atomic Energy Community; European Economic Community.

Treaty on European Union (TEU) The Treaty on European Union (sometimes referred to as the Treaty of Maastricht) came into force on 1 November 1993. The TEU amended the founding treaties and established the European Union. The TEU renamed the EEC the EC. Following the ToL coming into force on 1 December 2009, the term 'EC' is no longer used. *See also* European Atomic Energy Community; European Coal and Steel Community; European Communities; European Community; European Economic Community; European Union.

Treaty on the Functioning of the European Union (TFEU) When the Treaty of Lisbon came into force on 1 December 2009, the EC Treaty was renamed the Treaty on the Functioning of the European Union (TFEU). The articles within the TFEU have been renumbered as part of a simplification exercise. The ToL renumbering came into effect when the ToL itself came into force (1 December 2009). The Union has replaced and succeeded the Community (Art 1 TEU). Throughout the TFEU, the word 'Community' has been replaced with the word 'Union'. The following terms are therefore no longer used: European *Community*, European *Communities*, or *Community* law. Reference is made solely to the European *Union* (or the *Union*) and European *Union* law (or *Union* law). The TEU and the TFEU now constitute the Treaties on which the Union is founded (Art 1 TEU). *See also* Treaty of Lisbon.

Ultra vires Latin phrase which means 'beyond the power' or 'without authority'. In a legal context it means an act which is in excess of that authorised by law, thus rendering the act invalid. *See also* Procedural ultra vires; Substantive ultra vires.

Undertaking An undertaking is a business. In the English legal system this could refer to a sole trader, a partnership or a company.

Vertical direct effect A provision of Union law which is enforceable in national courts or tribunals against the state or emanation of the state, overriding any inconsistent national provisions, is said to have vertical direct effect (*Foster* v *British Gas* (Case C-188/89)). Treaty articles, regulations and directives are capable of having vertical direct effect if the provision is sufficiently precise and unconditional (*Van Gend en Loos* (Case 26/62)). *See also* Direct effect; Horizontal direct effect.

Withdrawal agreement Article 50(2) authorises the Union to negotiate a withdrawal agreement with a Member State that is seeking to exit the Union. Although a withdrawal agreement is not necessary when a Member State leaves the Union, such an agreement will establish arrangements for the withdrawal and lay the foundations for the state's future relationship with the Union.

FURTHER READING

Chapter 1 An introduction to the European Union

References

De Búrca G and Weiler J, *The Worlds of European Constitutionalism* (Cambridge University Press 2011).

De Witte, B, 'An Undivided Union? Differentiated Integration in Post-Brexit Times' (2018) 55 CML Rev 227.

European Commission, 'White Paper on the Future of Europe: Reflections and Scenarios for the EU27 by 2025' (March 2017) Available at https://ec.europa.eu/commission/sites/beta-political/files/white_paper_on_the_future_of_europe_en.pdf.

Hobsbawm E, *Age of Extremes: The Short Twentieth Century* (Michael Joseph 1994).

Books and book chapters

Chalmers D, Davies G and Monti G, *European Union Law: Text and Materials* (4th edn, Cambridge University Press 2019) Chapter 1.

Craig P and De Búrca G, *EU Law: Text, Cases and Materials* (6th edn, Oxford University Press 2015) Chapter 1.

Craig P, *The Lisbon Treaty: Law, Politics and Treaty Reform* (Oxford University Press 2010).

Dougan M, 'Editor's Introduction' in M Dougan (ed) *The UK after Brexit: Legal and Policy Challenges* (Intersentia 2017) 1.

Foster N, *Foster on EU Law* (7th edn, Oxford University Press 2019) Chapter 1.

Hillion C, 'Accession and Withdrawal in the Law of the European Union' in D Chalmers and A Arnull (eds) *The Oxford Handbook of European Union Law* (Oxford University Press 2015) 126.

Schütze R, *European Constitutional Law* (Cambridge University Press 2012) Chapter 1.

Ward I, *A Critical Introduction to European Law* (3rd edn, Cambridge University Press 2009) Chapters 1 and 2.

Weatherill S, *Cases and Materials on EU Law* (12th edn, Oxford University Press 2016) Chapter 1.

Woods L, Watson P and Costa M, *Steiner Woods EU Law* (13th edn, Oxford University Press 2017) Chapter 1.

Journal articles

Avbelj M, 'Theory of European Union' (2011) 36 EL Rev 818.

Athanassiou P, 'Of Past Measures and Future Plans for Europe's Exit from the Sovereign Debt Crisis: What is Legally Possible (and What is Not)' (2011) 36 EL Rev 558.

Baker E and Harding C, 'From Past Imperfect to Future Imperfect? A longitudinal study of the third pillar' (2009) 34 EL Rev 25.

Barnard C, 'The Practicalities of Leaving the EU' (2016) 41 EL Rev 484.

Barrett G, '"The King is Dead, Long Live the King": The Recasting by the Treaty of Lisbon of the Provisions of the Constitutional Treaty Concerning National Parliaments' (2008) 33 EL Rev 66.

Boerger A and Rasmussen M, 'Transforming European law: The Establishment of the Constitutional Discourse from 1950 to 1993' (2014) 10 ECL Rev 199.

Bradley K, 'Institutional Design in the Treaty of Nice' (2001) 38 CML Rev 1095.

Craig P, 'The Treaty of Lisbon, Process, Architecture and Substance' (2008) 33 EL Rev 137.

Craig P, 'The Stability, Coordination and Governance Treaty: Principle, Politics and Pragmatism' (2012) 37 EL Rev 231.

Craig P, 'Brexit: a Drama in Six Acts' (2016) 41 EL Rev 447.

Dammann J, 'Revoking Brexit: Can Member States Rescind Their Declaration of Withdrawal from the European Union?' (2017) 23 CJEL 265.

Dashwood A, 'The United Kingdom in a Re-Formed European Union' (2013) 38 EL Rev 737.

De Witte B, 'Near-Membership, Partial Membership and the EU Constitution' (2016) 41 EL Rev 471.

Dougan M, 'The Treaty of Lisbon 2007: Winning Minds, not Hearts' (2008) 45 CML Rev 617.

Douglas-Scott S, 'Brexit, Article 50 and the Contested British Constitution' (2016) 79 MLR 1019.

Elliott M, 'Constitutional Legislation, European Union Law and the Nature of the United Kingdom's Contemporary Constitution' (2014) 10 ECL Rev 379.

Elliott M, 'The Supreme Court's Judgment in "Miller": In Search of Constitutional Principle' (2017) 76 CLJ 257.

Ehlerman C D, 'Differentiation, Flexibility, Closer Cooperation: The New Provisions of the Treaty of Amsterdam' (1998) 4 ELJ 246.

Majone G, 'Unity in Diversity: European Integration and the Enlargement Process' (2008) 33 EL Rev 457.

Majone G, 'The European Union Post-Brexit: Static or Dynamic Adaptation?' (2017) 23 ELJ 9.

Markakis M, 'Legal Issues Arising from the Brexit Referendum: A UK and EU Constitutional Analysis' (2017) 45 IJLI 14.

Martinico G, 'Dating Cinderella: On Subsidiarity as a Political Safeguard of Federalism in the European Union' (2011) 17 EPL 649.

Messina M, 'Strengthening Economic Governance of the European Union through Enhanced Cooperation: A still Possible, but Already Missed, Opportunity' (2014) 39 EL Rev 404.

Meyring B, 'Intergovernmentalism and Supranationality: Two Stereotypes for a Complex Reality' (1997) 22 EL Rev 221.

Mitsilegas V, 'The Third Wave of Third Pillar Law: Which Direction for EU Criminal Justice?' (2009) 34 EL Rev 523.

Pech L, '"A Union Founded on the Rule of Law": Meaning and Reality of the Rule of Law as a Constitutional Principle of EU Law' (2010) 6 ECL Rev 359.

Sari A, 'Reversing a Withdrawal Notification under Article 50 TEU: Can a Member State Change Its Mind?' (2017) 42 EL Rev 451.

Schutze R, 'Lisbon and the Federal Order of Competences: A Prospective Analysis' (2008) 33 EL Rev 709.

Semmelmann C, 'The European Union's Economic Constitution under the Lisbon Treaty: Soul-Searching among Lawyers Shifts the Focus to Procedure' (2010) 35 ECL Rev 516.

Snell J, '"European Constitutional Settlement", an Ever Closer Union, and the Treaty of Lisbon: Democracy or Relevance?' (2008) 33 EL Rev 619.

Tridimas T, 'Article 50: An Endgame without an End?' (2016) 27 King's LJ 297.

Usher J, 'Variable Geometry or Concentric Circles: Patterns for the European Union' (1997) 47 ICLQ 243.

Chapter 2 Institutions of the European Union

References

European Commission, *Bulletin of the European Communities* (5(15), 1982).

European Commission, 'European Governance – A White Paper', COM/2001/0428 final, [2001] OJ C287/1.

Guéguen D, 'The New Comitology Reform: Overhauling the Balance of Powers or Institutional Tinkering?' *EU Bubble* (11 April 2017) Available at http://eububble.eu/the-new-comitology-reform.

Grant C, 'The House that Jacques Built' *Independent* (29 June 1994).

Pescatore P, 'Some Critical Remarks on the Single European Act' (1987) 24 CML Rev 9.

Robert C, 'The Political Use of Expertise in EU Decision-Making: The Case of Comitology' (May 2019) Available at https://www.greens-efa.eu/files/doc/docs/9148305b9720acb26aec2f08b1b3b5b0.pdf.

Books and book chapters

Alter K, *The European Court's Political Power* (Oxford University Press 2009).

Bradley K S, 'The European Parliament and Treaty Reform: Building Blocks and Stumbling Block's in D O'Keeffe and P Twomey (eds) *Legal Issues of the Amsterdam Treaty* (Hart Publishing 1999).

Burrows N and Greaves R M, *The Advocate General and EC law* (Oxford University Press 2007).

Chalmers D, Davies G and Monti G, *European Union Law: Text and Materials* (4th edn, Cambridge University Press 2019) Chapter 2.

Craig P and De Burca G, *EU Law: Text, Cases and Materials* (6th edn, Oxford University Press 2015) Chapter 2.

Foster N, *Foster on EU Law* (7th edn, Oxford University Press 2019) Chapter 2.

Stone Sweet A, *The Judicial Construction of Europe* (Oxford University Press 2004).

Woods L, Watson P and Costa M, *Steiner Woods EU Law* (13th edn, Oxford University Press (2017) Chapter 2.

Journal articles

Alemanno A, 'Unpacking the Principle of Openness in EU Law: Transparency, Participation and Democracy' (2014) 39 EL Rev 72.

Amtenbrink F and Van Duin K, 'The European Central Bank before the European Parliament: Theory and Practice after Ten Years of Monetary Dialogue' (2009) 34 EL Rev 561.

Barents R, 'The Court of Justice after the Treaty of Lisbon' (2010) 47 CML Rev 709.

Cygan A, 'The Parliamentarisation of EU Decision-Making? The Impact of the Treaty of Lisbon on National Parliaments' (2011) 36 EL Rev 480.

De Waele H and Broeksteeg H, 'The Semi-Permanent European Council Presidency: Some Reflections on the Law and Early Practice' (2012) 49 CML Rev 1039.

Dinan D, 'Governance and Institutions: The Unrelenting Rise of the European Parliament' (2014) 52 JCMS 109.

Driessen B, 'The Council of the European Union and Access to Documents' (2005) 30 EL Rev 675.

Kaeding M and Hardacre A, 'The European Parliament and the Future of Comitology after Lisbon' (2013) 19 ELJ 382.

Laffan B, 'Becoming a "Living Institution": The Evolution of the European Court of Auditors' (1999) 37 JCMS 251.

Lang J T, 'Checks and Balances in the European Union: The Institutional Structure and the "Community Method"' (2006) 12 EPL 127.

Pech L, '"A Union founded on the rule of law": Meaning and Reality of the Rule of Law as a Constitutional Principle of EU Law' (2010) 6 ECL Rev 359.

Peers S, 'Towards a New Form of EU law?: The Use of EU Institutions outside the EU Legal Framework' (2013) 9 ECL Rev 37.

Timmermans C, 'The European Ombudsman's Remedial Powers: An Empirical Analysis in Context' (2013) 41 CML Rev 393.

Tsadiras A, 'The European Union's Judicial System' (2004) 38 EL Rev 52.

Chapter 3 Sources of EU law

References

European Parliament Policy Department C: Citizen's Rights and Constitutional Affairs, 'The General Principles of EU Administrative Procedural Law' (2015) Available at www.europarl.europa.eu/RegData/etudes/IDAN/2015/519224/IPOL_IDA%282015%29519224_EN.pdf.

Mancini G F, 'The making of a Constitution for Europe' (1989) 26 CML Rev 595.

Miller V, 'Legislating for Brexit: EU External Agreements' House of Commons Briefing Paper No. 7850 (2017) Available at http://researchbriefings.parliament.uk/ResearchBriefing/Summary/CBP-7850.

Moussis N, *Access to European Union: Law, Economics, Policies* (19th edn, Rixensart 2011).

Munro R, 'Negotiating Brexit: Briefing Paper' (Institute for Government, July 2016) Available at www.instituteforgovernment.org.uk/sites/default/files/publications/5040%20IFG%20-%20Negotiating%20Brexit%20v4.pdf.

Pescatore P, 'Fundamental Rights and Freedoms in the System of the European Communities' (1970) 18 Am J Comp L 343.

Poptcheva E, European Parliament, 'Article 50 TEU: Withdrawal of a Member State from the EU' (2016) Available at www.europarl.europa.eu/RegData/etudes/BRIE/2016/577971/EPRS_BRI(2016)577971_EN.pdf.

Snyder F, 'The Effectiveness of European Community Law: Institutions, Processes, Tools and Techniques' (1993) 56 MLR 19, 32.

Books and book chapters

Arnull A and Wincott D, *Accountability and Legitimacy in the European Union* (Oxford University Press 2002).

Chalmers D, Davies G and Monti G, *European Union Law: Text and Materials* (4th edn, Cambridge University Press 2019) Chapters 3 and 6.

Craig P and De Burca G, *EU Law: Text, Cases and Materials* (6th edn, Oxford University Press 2015) Chapters 4, 5 and 11.

Craig P, 'Integration, Democracy, and Legitimacy' in P Craig and G de Búrca (eds) *The Evolution of EU Law* (2nd edn, Oxford University Press 2011).

Foster N, *Foster on EU Law* (7th edn, Oxford University Press 2019) Chapter 4.

Gersternberg O and Sabel C, 'Directly-Deliberative Polyarchy: An Institutional Ideal for Europe?' in Joerges C and Dehousse R (eds) *Good Governance in Europe's Integrated Market* (Oxford University Press 2002).

Morano-Foadi S and Vickers L (eds), *Fundamental Rights in the EU: a Matter for Two Courts* (Hart Publishing 2015).

Morano-Foadi S. and Adreadakis S. 'Protection of Fundamental Rights in Europe' (Springer 2020).

Weatherill S, *Cases and Materials on EU Law* (12th edn, Oxford University Press 2016) Chapter 2.

Woods L, Watson P and Costa M, *Steiner Woods EU Law* (13th edn, Oxford University Press 2017) Chapters 3 and 6.

Journal articles

Anagnostaras G, 'Balancing Conflicting Fundamental Rights: the Sky Osterreich Paradigm' (2014) 39 EL Rev 111.

Bell J, 'Sources of Law' (2018) 77 CLJ 40.

Bobek M, 'Corrigenda in the Official Journal of the European Union: Community Law as Quicksand' (2009) 34 EL Rev 950.

Craig P, 'Delegated Acts, Implementing Acts and the New Comitology Regulation' (2011) 36 EL Rev 671.

Douglas-Scott S, 'The European Union and Human Rights After the Treaty of Lisbon' (2011) 11 HRL Rev 645.

Driessen B, 'Delegated Legislation after the Treaty of Lisbon: An Analysis of Article 290 TFEU' (2010) 35 EL Rev 837.

Harpaz G, 'The European Court of Justice and its Relations with the European Court of Human Rights: The Quest for Enhanced Reliance, Coherence and Legitimacy' (2009) 46 CML Rev 105.

Hancox E, 'The Meaning of "Implementing" EU Law Under Article 51(1) of the Charter: Åkerberg Fransson' (2013) 50 CML Rev 1411.

Kral R, 'National, Normative Implementation of EC Regulations: An Exceptional or Rather Common Matter?' (2008) 33 EL Rev 243.

Leczykiewicz D, '"Effective Judicial Protection" of Human Rights after Lisbon: Should National Courts be Empowered to Review EU Secondary Law?' (2010) 35 EL Rev 326.

Leczykiewicz D, 'The Horizontal Application of the Charter of Fundamental Rights' (2013) 38 EL Rev 479.

Letsas G, 'Proportionality as Fittingness: The Moral Dimension of Proportionality' (2018) 71 Current Legal Problems 53.

Lock T, 'EU Accession to the ECHR: Implications for the Judicial Review in Strasbourg' (2010) 35 ECL Rev 777.

Majone G, 'Europe's "Democracy Deficit": The Question of Standards' (1998) 4 ELJ 5.

Mancini G F, 'The Making of a Constitution for Europe' (1989) 26 CML Rev 595.

Mendes J, 'Delegated and Implementing Rule Making: Proceduralisation and Constitutional Design' (2013) 19 ELJ 22.

Sarmiento D, 'Who's Afraid of the Charter? The Court of Justice, National Courts and the New Framework of Fundamental Rights Protection in Europe' (2013) 50 CML Rev 1267.

Semmelmann C, 'The European Union's Economic Constitution under the Lisbon Treaty: Soul-Searching among Lawyers Shifts the Focus to Procedure' (2010) 35 ECL Rev 516.

Syrpis P, 'The Relationship between Primary and Secondary Law in the EU' (2015) 52 CML Rev 461.

Trstenjak V and Beysen E, 'The Growing Overlap of Fundamental Freedoms and Fundamental Rights in the Case-Law of the CJEU' (2013) 38 EL Rev 293.

Van Bockel B, 'New Wine into Old Wineskins: The Scope of the Charter of Fundamental Rights of the EU after Akerberg Fransson' (2013) 38 EL Rev 866.

Van Vooren B, 'A Case-Study of "Soft Law" in EU External Relations: The European Neighbourhood Policy' (2009) 34 EL Rev 696.

Weiss W, 'Human Rights in the EU: Rethinking the Role of the European Convention on Human Rights after Lisbon' (2011) 7 ECL Rev 64.

Chapter 4 Competences and Supremacy of the Union

References

Eeckhout P, *EU External Relations Law* (Oxford University Press 2011) Chapter 3.

Poptcheva E, European Parliament, 'Article 50 TEU: Withdrawal of a Member State from the EU' (2016) Available at www.europarl.europa.eu/RegData/etudes/BRIE/2016/577971/EPRS_BRI(2016)577971_EN.pdf.

Garret G, 'The Politics of Legal Integration in the European Union' (1995) 49(1) International Organization 171.

Mancini G F and Keeling D T, 'Democracy and the European Court of Justice' (1994) 57 MLR 175.

Mattli W and Slaughter M, 'Law and Politics in the European Union: A Reply to Garrett' (1995) 49(1) International Organization 183.

Slynn G, *Introducing a New Legal Order* (Sweet & Maxwell 1992).

Sweet Stone A, 'Constitutional Dialogues in the European Community' in A-M Slaughter, A Sweet Stone and J H H Weiler (eds) *The European Courts and National Courts: Doctrine and Jurisprudence* (Hart 1998).

Weiler J H H, 'The Division of Competences in the European Union' (1997) Available at http://www.europarl.europa.eu/workingpapers/poli/w26/default_en.htm.

Books and book chapters

Chalmers D, Davies G and Monti G, *European Union Law: Text and Materials* (4th edn, Cambridge University Press 2019) Chapters 3 and 5.

Craig P, 'Miller, EU Law and the UK' in Elliott, Williams and Young (eds) *The UK Constitution after Miller* (Hart 2018).

Kiiver P, *The Early Warning System for the Principle of Subsidiarity: Constitutional Theory and Empirical Reality* (Routledge 2014).

Foster N, *Foster on EU Law* (7th edn, Oxford University Press 2019) Chapters 3 and 5.

Konstadinides T, *Division of Powers in European Union Law: The Delimitation of Internal Competence between the EU and the Member States* (Kluwer Law International 2009).

MacCormick N, *Questioning Sovereignty* (Oxford University Press 1999).

Walker N, *Sovereignty in Transition* (Hart Publishing 2003).

Woods L, Watson P and Costa M, *Steiner Woods EU Law* (13th edn, Oxford University Press 2017) Chapters 3 and 4.

Journal articles

Avblej M, 'Theory of European Union' (2011) 36 EL Rev 818.

Avblej M, 'Supremacy or Primacy of EU Law – (Why) Does it Matter?' (2011) 17 ELJ 744.

Belling V, 'Supranational Fundamental Rights or Primacy of Sovereignty?' (2012) 18 ELJ 251.

Craig P, 'The Treaty of Lisbon, Process, Architecture and Substance' (2008) 33 EL Rev 137.

Craig P, 'The European Union Act 2011: Locks, Limits and Legality' (2011) 48 CML Rev 1915.

Craig P, 'Constitutionalising Constitutional Law' [2014] Public Law 373.

Crosby S, 'The New Tobacco Control Directive: An Illiberal and Illegal Disdain for the Law' (2002) 27 EL Rev 177.

Cooper I, 'The Watchdogs of Subsidiarity: National Parliaments and the Logic of Arguing in the EU' (2006) 44 JCMS 281.

Danielsen J, 'One of Many National Constraints on European Integration: Section 20 of the Danish Constitution' (2010) 16 EPL 181.

Dashwood A, 'The Limits of European Community Powers' (1996) 21 EL Rev 113.

Dashwood A, 'The Relationship between the Member States and the European Union/European Community' (2004) 41 CML Rev 355.

Davies G, 'Subsidiarity: The Wrong Idea, in the Wrong Place, at the Wrong Time' (2006) 43 CML Rev 63.

De Búrca G, 'The Constitutional Challenge of New Governance in the European Union' (2003) 28 EL Rev 814.

Doukas D, 'The verdict of the German Federal Constitutional Court on the Lisbon Treaty: Not Guilty, but Don't Do It Again' (2009) 34 EL Rev 866.

Elliott M, 'Sovereignty, Primacy and the Common Law Constitution: What Has EU Membership Taught Us?' in Elliott, Williams and Young (eds) *The UK Constitution after Miller* (Hart 2018).

Emilou N, 'Subsidiarity: An Effective Barrier against Enterprises of Ambition' (1992) 29 CML Review 383.

Goldoni M, 'Reconstructing the Early Warning System on Subsidiarity: The Case for Political Judgment' (2014) 39 EL Rev 647.

Gordon M and Dougan M, 'The United Kingdom's European Union Act 2011: "Who Won the Bloody War Anyway?"' (2012) 37 EL Rev 3.

Gordon M, 'The UK's Sovereignty Situation: Brexit, Bewilderment and Beyond . . . ' (2016) 27 King's LJ 333.

Hoskins M, 'Tilting the Balance: Supremacy and National Procedural Rules' (1996) 21 EL Rev 365.

Kumm M, 'Constitutionalising Subsidiarity in Integrated Markets: The Case of Tobacco Regulation in the European Union' (2006) 12 ELJ 503.

Kumm M, 'Who is the Final Arbiter of Constitutionality in Europe?' (1999) 36 CML Rev 251.

Gee G, Rubini L and Trybus M, 'Leaving the EU? The Legal Impact of "Brexit" on the United Kingdom' (2016) 22 EPL 51.

Gee G and Young A L, 'Regaining Sovereignty? Brexit, the UK Parliament and the Common Law' (2016) 22 EPL 131.

Payandeh M, 'Constitutional Review of EU Law after Honeywell: Contextualising the Relationship between the German Constitutional Court and the EU Court of Justice' (2011) 48 CML Rev 9.

Pliakos A, 'Who is the Ultimate Arbiter? The Battle over Judicial Supremacy in EU Law' (2011) 36 EL Rev 109.

Peers S, 'Taking Supremacy Seriously' (1998) 23 EL Rev 146.

Reestman J-H and Claes M, 'For History's Sake: On Costa v ENEL, Andre Donner and the External Secret of the Court of Justice's Deliberations' (2014) 10 ECL Rev 191.

Richards C, 'The Supremacy of Community Law before the French Constitutional Court' (2006) 31 EL Rev 499.

Ross M, 'Effectiveness in the European Legal Order(s): Beyond Supremacy to Constitutional Proportionality?' (2006) 31 EL Rev 474.

Schmid, C, 'All Bark and No Bite: Notes on the Federal Constitutional Court's "Banana Decision"' (2001) 7 ELJ 95.

Scott J and Trubek D, 'Mind the Gap: Law and New Approaches to Governance in the European Union' (2002) 8 ELJ 1.

Schutze R, 'Lisbon and the Federal Order of Competences: A Prospective Analysis' (2008) 33 EL Rev 709.

Swaine E T, 'Subsidiarity and Self-interest: Federalism at the European Court of Justice' (2000) 41 Harvard Intl LJ 1.

Thym D, 'In the Name of Sovereign Statehood: A Critical Introduction to the Lisbon Judgment of the German Constitutional Court' (2009) 46 CML Rev 1795.

Weatherill S, 'Better Competence Monitoring' (2005) 30 EL Rev 23.

Weatherill S, 'Competence Creep and Competence Control' (2005) 24 YEL 1.

Young A L, 'The Constitutional Implications of Brexit' (2017) 23 EPL 757.

Chapter 5 Judicial methodology and preliminary rulings of the Court of Justice

References

European Commission, 'Monitoring the Application of European Union Law: 2016 Annual Report' (2017) Available at http://eur-lex.europa.eu/legal-content/EN/TXT/PDF/?uri=COM%3A2017%3A370%3AFIN&from=EN.

Lenaerts K, 'EU Citizenship and the European Court of Justice's "Stone-by-Stone" Approach' (2015) 1(1) Intl Comparative Jurisprudence 1.

Wahl N and Prete L, 'The Gatekeepers of Article 267 TFEU: On Jurisdiction and Admissibility of References for Preliminary Rulings' 55 CML Rev 511.

Books and book chapters

Broberg M and Fenger N, *Preliminary References to the European Court of Justice* (2nd edn, Oxford University Press 2014).

Chalmers D, Davies G and Monti G, *European Union Law: Text and Materials* (4th edn, Cambridge University Press 2019) Chapters 4 and 5.

Craig P and De Burca G, *EU Law: Text, Cases and Materials* (6th edn, Oxford University Press 2015) Chapter 13.

De la Mar T and Donnelly C, 'Preliminary Rulings and EU Legal Integration: Evolution and Stasis' in G De Burca and P Craig (eds) *The Evolution of EU Law* (2nd edn, Oxford University Press 2011).

Foster N, *Foster on EU Law* (7th edn, Oxford University Press 2019) Chapter 6.

Rosas A, 'The European Court of Justice and Public International Law' in J Wouters, A Nollkaemper and E De Wet (eds) *The Europeanisation of International Law: The Status of International Law in the EU and its Member States* (Cambridge University Press 2008).

Weatherill S, *Cases and Materials on EU Law* (12th edn, Oxford University Press 2016) Chapter 7.

Woods L, Watson P and Costa M, *Steiner Woods EU Law* (13th edn, Oxford University Press 2017) Chapter 10.

Journal articles

Anagnostaras G, 'The Preliminary Problems and Jurisdiction Uncertainties: The Admissibility of Questions Referred by Bodies Performing Quasi-Judicial Functions' (2005) 30 EL Rev 878.

Arnull A, 'The Law Lords and the European Union: Swimming with the Incoming Tide' (2010) 35 EL Rev 57.

Barav A, 'Preliminary Censorship? The Judgment of the European Court in Foglia v Novello' (1980) 5 EL Rev 443.

Barnard C and Sharpston E, 'The Changing Face of Article 177 References' (1997) 34 CML Rev 1113.

Barents R, 'The Court of Justice after the Treaty of Lisbon' (2010) 47 CML Rev 709.

Barnard C, 'The PPU: Is it Worth the Candle? An Early Assessment' (2009) 34 EL Rev 281.

Bobek M, 'Landtova, Holubec, and the Problem of an Uncooperative Court: Implications for the Preliminary Rulings Procedure' (2014) 10 ECL Rev 54.

Bobek M, 'Learning to Talk: Preliminary Rulings, the Courts of the Member States and the Court of Justice' (2008) 45 CML Rev 1611.

Broberg M, 'Acte Clair Revisited: Adapting the Acte Clair Criteria to the Demands of the Times' (2008) 45 CML Rev 1383.

Broberg M and Fenger N, 'Variations in Member States' Preliminary References to the Court of Justice: Are Structural Factors (Part of) the Explanation?' (2013) 19 ELJ 488.

Broberg M and Fenger N, 'National Courts of Last Instance Failing to Make a Preliminary Reference: The (Possible) Consequences Flowing Therefrom' (2016) 22 EPL 243.

Broberg M and Fenger N, 'Preliminary References to the Court of Justice of the European Union and the Right to a Fair Trial under Article 6 ECHR' (2016) 41(4) EL Rev 599.

Craig P, 'The ECJ and Eltra Vires Action: A Conceptual Analysis' (2011) 48 CML Rev 395.

De la Serre E B and Sibony A, 'Expert Evidence before the EC Courts' (2008) 45 CML Rev 941.

Dyevre A, 'If You Can't Beat Them, Join Them: The French Constitutional Council's First Reference to the Court of Justice' (2014) 10 ECL Rev 154.

Derlén M, 'Multilingual Interpretation of CJEU Case Law: Rule and Reality' (2014) 39 EL Rev 295.

Grimmel E, 'Judicial Interpretation or Judicial Activism? The Legacy of Rationalism in the Studies of the European Court of Justice' (2012) 18 ELJ 518.

Hadroušek D and Smolek M, 'Solving the European Union's General Court' (2015) 40 EL Rev 188.

Harpaz G, 'The European Court of Justice and its Relations with the European Court of Human Rights: The Quest for Enhanced Reliance, Coherence and Legitimacy' (2009) 46 CML Rev 105.

Hinarejos A, 'Integration in Criminal Matters and the Role of the Court of Justice' (2011) 36 EL Rev 420.

Komárek J, 'In the Court(s) We Trust? On the Need for Hierarchy and Differentiation in the Preliminary Ruling Procedure' (2007) 32 CML Rev 467.

Kornezov A, 'The New Format of the Act Claire Doctrine and its Consequences' (2016) 53 CML Rev 1317.

Lacchi C, 'Multilevel Judicial Protection in the EU and Preliminary References' (2016) 53 CML Rev 679.

Lang R, 'Trigger Happy?' (2016) 7711 New Law Journal 8.

Lenaerts K, 'The Rule of Law and the Coherence of the Judicial System of the European Union' (2007) 44 CML Rev 1625.

Mance J, 'The Interface between National and European Law' (2013) 38 EL Rev 437.

Nicola F G, 'Luxembourg Judicial Style With or Without the UK' (2017) 40 Fordham Intl LJ 1505.

Póltorak N, '*Ratione Temporis* Application of the Preliminary Rulings Procedure' (2008) 45 CML Rev 1357.

Reestman J-H and Claes M, 'For History's Sake: On Costa v ENEL, Andre Donner and the External Secret of the Court of Justice's Deliberations' (2014) 10 ECL Rev 191.

Shuibhne N N, 'A Court Within a Court: Is it Time to Rebuild the Court of Justice?' (2009) 34 EL Rev 173.

Tridimas T, 'Knocking on Heaven's Door: Fragmentation, Efficiency and Defiance in the Preliminary Reference Procedure' (2003) 40 CML Rev 9.

Wallerman A, 'Towards an EU Law Doctrine on the Exercise of Discretion in National Courts? The Member States' Self-Imposed Limits on National Procedural Autonomy' (2016) 53 CML Rev 339.

Chapter 6 Review of legality of EU law

Books and book chapters

Albors-Llorens A, 'Judicial Protection before the Court of Justice of the EU' in C Barnard and S Peers (eds) *European Union Law* (Oxford University Press 2014).

Arnull A, *The European Union and its Court of Justice* (2nd edn, Oxford University Press 2006) Chapter 3.

Chalmers D, Davies G and Monti G, *European Union Law: Text and Materials* (4th edn, Cambridge University Press 2019) Chapter 9.

Craig P and De Burca G, *EU Law: Text, Cases and Materials* (6th edn, Oxford University Press 2015) Chapters 14 to 16.

Douglas-Scott A, *Constitutional Law of the European Union* (Longman 2002) Chapters 10 and 12.

Foster N, *Foster on EU Law* (7th edn, Oxford University Press 2019) Chapter 7.

Weatherill S, *Cases and Materials on EU Law* (12th edn, Oxford University Press 2016) Chapter 8.

Wards I, *Judicial Review and the Rights of Private Parties in EU Law* (2nd edn, Oxford University Press 2007).

Woods L, Watson P and Costa M, *Steiner Woods EU Law* (13th edn, Oxford University Press 2017) Chapters 12 to 14.

Journal articles

Albors-Llorens A, 'Remedies Against the EU Institutions After Lisbon: An Era of Opportunity' (2012) 71 Cambridge LJ 507.

Albors-Llorens A, 'Sealing the Fate of Private Parties in Annulment Proceedings: The General Court and the New Standing Test in Article 263(4) TFEU' (2012) 71 Cambridge LJ 52.

Arnull A, 'Private Applicants and Actions for Annulment since Cordoniu' (2001) 38 CML Rev 7.

Balthasar S, 'Locus Standi Rules for Challenges to Regulatory Acts by Private Applicants: The New Art 263(4) TFEU' (2010) 35 EL Rev 542.

Bergstrom C F, 'Defending Restricted Standing for Individuals to Bring Direct Actions against "Legislative" Measures' (2014) 10 ECL Rev 481.

Bergstrom C F, 'Shaping the New System for Delegation of Powers to the EU Agencies: United Kingdom v European Parliament and Council (Short Selling)' (2015) 52 CML Rev 219.

Bogojevic S, 'Judicial Protection of Individual Applicants Revisited: Access to Justice through the Prism of Judicial Subsidiarity' (2015) 34 YEL 5.

Buchanan C, 'Long Awaited Guidance on the Meaning of "Regulatory Act" for Locus Standi Under the Lisbon Treaty' (2012) 1 EJ of Risk Regulation 115.

Davies G, 'Legislative Control of the European Court of Justice' (2014) 51 CML Rev 1579.

Dougan M, 'Judicial Review of Member State Action under the General Principles and the Charter: Defining the "Scope of Union Law"' (2015) 52 CML Rev 1201.

Harlow C, 'Towards a Theory of Access for the European Court of Justice' (1992) 12 YEL 213.

Kornezov A, 'Shaping the New Architecture of the EU System of Judicial Remedies: Comment on Inuit' (2014) 39 EL Rev 251.

Kornezov A, '*Locus Standi* of Private Parties in Actions for Annulment: Has the Gap Been Closed?' (2014) 73 CLJ 27.

Peers S and Costa M, 'Judicial Review of EU Acts after the Treaty of Lisbon' (2010) 8 ECLR 82.

Ritleng D, 'The Dividing Line Between Delegated and Implementing Acts: The Court of Justice Sidesteps the Difficulty in Commission v Parliament and Council (Biocides)' (2015) 52 CMLRev 243.

Tridimas T and Gari G, 'Winners and Losers in Luxembourg: A Statistical Analysis of Judicial Review before the European Court of Justice and the Court of First Instance (2001–2005)' (2010) 35 EL Rev 131.

Usher J, 'Direct and Individual Concern: An Effective Remedy or a Conventional Solution?' (2003) 28 EL Rev 575.

Van Malleghem P A and Keeling D, 'Before the Law Stands a Gatekeeper – or What is a "Regulatory Act" in Article 263(4) TFEU Inuit Tapiriit Kanatami v European Parliament (C-583/11 P)' (2014) 51 CML Rev 1187.

Chapter 7 Infringement proceedings against Member States

References

Carrera S and Bárd P, 'The European Parliament Vote on Article 7 TEU against the Hungarian Government: Too Late, Too Little, Too Political?' (CEPS Policy Contribution 2018).

European Commission, 'EU Law: Better Results Through Better Application' OJ 2017 C 18/10.

Books and book chapters

Craig P and De Burca G, *EU Law: Text, Cases and Materials* (6th edn, Oxford University Press 2015) Chapter 12.

Craig P, *The Lisbon Treaty: Law, Politics and Treaty Reform* (Oxford University Press 2010) Chapter 4.

Chalmers D, Davies G and Monti G, *European Union Law: Text and Materials* (4th edn, Cambridge University Press 2019) Chapter 8.

Foster N, *Foster on EU Law* (7th edn, Oxford University Press 2019) Chapter 6.

Lenaerts K, Marelis I and Gutman K, *EU Procedural Law* (Oxford University Press 2014).

Piris J-C, *The Lisbon Treaty: A Legal and Political Analysis* (Cambridge University Press 2010) Chapter 28.

Woods L, Watson P and Costa M, *Steiner Woods EU Law* (13th edn, Oxford University Press 2017) Chapter 11.

Weatherill S, *Cases and Materials on EU Law* (12th edn, Oxford University Press 2016) Chapter 4.

Journal articles

Bieber R and Maiani F, 'Enhancing Centralized Enforcement of EU Law: Pandora's Toolbox?' (2014) 51 CML Rev 1057.

Harden I, 'What Future for the Centralised Enforcement of Community Law?' (2002) 55 Current Legal Problems 495.

Harlow C and Rawlings R, 'Accountability and Law Enforcement: The Centralised EU Infringement Procedure' (2006) 31 EL Rev 447.

Kilbey I, 'The Interpretation of Article 260 TFEU (ex Article 228 EC)' (2010) 35 EL Rev 370.

Jack B, 'Article 260(2) TFEU: An Effective Judicial Procedure for the Enforcement of Judgments?' (2013) 19 ELJ 404.

Prete L and Smulders B, 'The Coming Age of Infringement Proceedings' (2010) 47 CML Rev 9.

Smith M, 'Enforcement, Monitoring, Verification, Outsourcing: The Decline and Decline of the Infringement Process' (2008) 33 EL Rev 777.

Wenneras P, 'A New Dawn for Commission Enforcement under Articles 226 and 228 EC: General and Persistent (GAP) Infringements, Lump Sums and Penalty Payments' (2006) 43 CML Rev 31.

Wenneras P, 'Sanctions against Member States under Article 260 TFEU: Alive, but not Kicking?' (2012) 49 CML Rev 145.

Chapter 8 Direct effect, indirect effect and state liability

References

Mancini G F and Keeling D T, 'Democracy and the European Court of Justice' (1994) 57 MLR 175.

Slynn G, *Introducing a New Legal Order* (Sweet & Maxwell 1992).

Books and book chapters

Biondi A, 'In Praise of Francovich' in P Maduro and L Azoulai (eds) *The Past and the Future of EU Law* (Hart Publishing 2010).

Chalmers D, Davies G and Monti G, *European Union Law: Text and Materials* (4th edn, Cambridge University Press 2019) Chapter 5.

Craig P and De Burca G, *EU Law: Text, Cases and Materials* (6th edn, Oxford University Press 2015) Chapters 7 to 9.

Cruz J, 'Francovich and imperfect law' in P Maduro and L Azoulai (eds) *The Past and the Future of EU Law* (Hart Publishing 2010).

De Witte B, 'Direct Effect, Primacy and the Nature of the Legal Order' in P Craig and G De Búrca (eds) *The Evolution of EU Law* (2nd edn, Oxford University Press 2011).

Dougan M, 'The Vicissitudes of Life at the Coalface: Remedies and Procedures for Enforcing Union Law before the National Courts' in G De Búrca and P Craig (eds) *The Evolution of EU Law* (2nd edn, Oxford University Press 2011).

Foster N, *Foster on EU Law* (7th edn, Oxford University Press 2019) Chapter 6.

Weatherill S, *Cases and Materials on EU Law* (12th edn, Oxford University Press 2016) Chapters 3, 5 and 6.

Woods L, Watson P and Costa M, *Steiner Woods EU Law* (13th edn, Oxford University Press 2017), Chapters 5 and 9.

Journal articles

—— 'Horizontal Direct Effect: A Law of Diminishing Coherence' (2006) 43 CML Rev 1.

Albors-Llorens A, 'The Principle of State Liability in EC Law and the Supreme Courts of the Member States' (2007) 66 Cambridge LJ 270.

Albors-Llorens A, 'The Direct Effect of EU Directives: Fresh Controversy or a Storm in a Teacup? Comment on Portgas' (2014) 39 EL Rev 851.

Amstutz M, 'In-between Words: Marleasing and the Emergence if Interlegality in Legal Reasoning' (2005) 11 ELJ 766.

Anagnostaras G, 'The Quest for an Effective Remedy and the Measure of Judicial Protection Afforded to Putative Community Law Rights' (2007) 32 EL Rev 727.

Anagnostaras G, 'Erroneous Judgments and the Prospect of Damages: The Scope of the Principle of Governmental Liability for Judicial Breaches' (2006) 31 EL Rev 735.

Arnull A, 'The Law Lords and the European Union: Swimming with the Incoming Tide' (2010) 35 EL Rev 57.

Arnull A, 'The Principle of Effective Judicial Protection in EU Law: An Unruly Horse?' (2011) 36 EL Rev 51.

Beutler B, 'State Liability for Breaches of Community Law by National Courts: Is the Requirement of a Manifest Infringement of the Applicable Law and Insurmountable Obstacle?' (2009) 46 CML Rev 773.

Bettlem G, 'The Principle of Indirect Effect of Community Law' (1995) 3 E Rev Private L 1.

Craig P, 'The Legal Effect of Directives: Policy, Rules and Exceptions' (2009) 34 EL Rev 349.

Drake S, 'Twenty Years after Von Colson: the Impact of "Indirect Effect" on the Protection of the Individual's Community Rights' (2005) 30 EL Rev 329.

Dashwood A, 'From Van Duyn to Mangold via Marshall: Reducing Direct Effect to Absurdity', (2006–2007) 9 Cambridge Yearbook of European Legal Studies 81.

Davies A, 'State Liability for Judicial Decisions in European Union and International Law' (2012) 61 ICLQ 585.

De Mol M, 'The Novel Approach of the CJEU on the Horizontal Direct Effect of the EU Principle of Non-Discrimination: (Unbridled) Expansionism of EU law' (2011) 18 MJ 109.

Dougan M, 'When Worlds Collide! Competing Visions of the Relationship between Direct Effect and Supremacy' (2007) 44 CML Rev 931.

Dougan M, 'Community Directives: Explaining CIA Security' (2001) 60 CLJ 231.

Dougan M, 'The Francovich Right to Reparation: Reshaping the Contours of Community Remedial Competence' (2000) 6 EPL 103.

Doukas D, 'The Verdict of the German Federal Constitutional Court on the Lisbon Treaty: Not Guilty, But Don't Do It Again!' (2009) 34 EL Rev 866.

Elliott M, 'Constitutional Legislation, European Union Law and the Nature of the United Kingdom's Contemporary Constitution' (2014) 10 ECL Rev 379.

Fredriksen H H, 'State Liability in EU and EEA Law: The Same or Different?' (2013) 38 EL Rev 884.

Granger M-P F, 'National Applications of Francovich and the Construction of a European Administrative Ius Commune' (2007) 32 EL Rev 157.

Gutman K, 'The Evolution of the Action for Damages against the European Union and its Place in the System of Judicial Protection' (2011) 48 CML Rev 695.

Hartkamp A S, 'The Effect of the EC Treaty in Private Law: On Direct and Indirect Horizontal Effect of Primary Community Law' (2010) 18 ERPL 527.

Havu K, 'Horizontal Liability for Damages in EU Law – the Changing Relationship of EU and National Law' (2012) 18 ELJ 407.

Leczykiewicz D, '"Effective Judicial Protection" of Human Rights after Lisbon: Should National Courts be Empowered to Review EU Secondary Law?' (2010) 35 EL Rev 326.

Leczykiewicz D, 'Horizontal Application of the Charter of Fundamental Rights' (2013) 38 EL Rev 479.

Lenaerts K and Corthaut T, 'Of Birds and Hedges: The Role of Primacy in Invoking Norms of EU Law' (2006) 31 EL Rev 287.

Nassimpian D, '. . . And We Keep on Meeting: (De)Fragmenting State Liability' (2007) 32 EL Rev 819.

Pescatore P, 'The Doctrine of "Direct Effect": An Infant Disease of Community Law' (1983) 40 EL Rev 135.

Prechal S, 'Member State Liability and Direct Effect: What's the Difference After All?' (2006) 17 EBL Rev 299.

Scott H and Barber N W, 'State Liability under Francovich for Decisions of National Courts' (2004) 120 LQR 403.

Schiek D, 'The ECJ Decision in Mangold' (2006) 35 ILJ 329.

Tallberg J, 'Supranational Influence in EU Enforcement: The ECJ and the Principle of State Liability' (2000) 7 JEPP 104.

Tridimas T, 'Horizontal Effect of Directives: A Missed Opportunity?' (1994) 19 EL Rev 621.

Tridimas T, 'Liability for Breach of Community Law: Growing Up and Mellowing Down?' (2001) 38 CML Rev 301.

Vajda C, 'Liability for Breach of Community Law: A Survey of the ECJ Cases Post-Factortame' (2006) 17 EBL Rev 257.

Wakefield J, 'Retrench and Reform: The Action for Damages' (2009) 28 YEL 390.

Wattel, P. J. 'Köbler, CILFIT and Welthgrove: We can't go on meeting like this' (2004) 41 CML Rev 177.

Weatherill S, 'Breach of Directives and Breach of Contract? Direct Effect of Directives and Unilever' (2001) 26 EL Rev 177.

Chapter 9 European Union citizenship and free movement rights

References

Blauberger M et al., 'ECJ Judges Read the Morning Papers. Explaining the Turnaround of European Citizenship Jurisprudence' (2018) 25(10) Journal of European Public Policy 1422.

Boeger N, 'Minimum Harmonisation, Free movement and Proportionality' in P Syrpis (ed.) *The Judiciary, the Legislature and the Internal Market* (Cambridge University Press 2012).

Boekestein T, 'The CJEU Judgment in Tjebbes: EU Citizenship, the Advent of the Charter, and Implications for the Loss of Nationality after Criminal Conviction' (2019) Cambridge International Law Journal Available at http://cilj.co.uk/2019/06/24/the-cjeu-judgment-in-tjebbes-eu-citizenship-the-advent-of-the-charter-and-implications-for-the-loss-of-nationality-after-criminal-conviction/.

Coutts S, 'Bold and Thoughtful: The Court of Justice Intervenes in Nationality Law Case C-221/17 Tjebbes' (2019) European Law Blog Available at https://europeanlawblog.eu/2019/03/25/bold-and-thoughtful-the-court-of-justice-intervenes-in-nationality-law-case-c-221-17-tjebbes/.

Craig P and De Burca G, *EU Law: Text, Cases and Materials* (6th edn, Oxford University Press 2015) Chapters 3 and 9.

de Hart B and Mantu S, 'Loss of Dutch Nationality *ex lege*: EU Law, Gender and Multiple Nationality' (2017) GLOBALCIT Available at http://globalcit.eu/loss-of-dutch-nationality-ex-lege-eu-law-gender-and-multiple-nationality/.

European Commission, 'The EU's Position on the Rights of EU Citizens in the UK after Brexit' (2017) Available at https://publications.europa.eu/en/publication-detail/-/publication/2fa562e3-a40c-11e7-9ca9-01aa75ed71a1/language-en/format-PDF.

Kochenov D, 'The Tjebbes Fail' (2019) 4(1) European Papers 319.

McCrea R, 'Forward or Back: The Future of European Integration and the Impossibility of the Status Quo' (2017) 23(1–2) ELJ 66.

Strumia F, 'Divorce Immediately, or Leave: Rights of Third Country Nationals and Family Protection in the Context of EU Citizens' Free Movement: Kuldip Singh and Others' (2016) 53(5) CML Rev 1373.

Verschueren H, 'Free Movement for EU Citizens: Including for the Poor?' (2015) 22(1) Maastricht JECL 10.

Books and book chapters

Barnard C, 'EU Citizenship and the Principle of Solidarity' in E Spaventa and M Dougan (eds) *Social Welfare and EU Law* (Hart Publishing 2005).

Barnard C, *The Substantive Law of the EU: The Four Freedoms* (6th edn, Oxford University Press 2019) Chapters 6 and 9.

Barnard C and Peers S, *European Union Law* (2nd edn, Oxford University Press 2017) Chapters 13 and 16.

Chalmers D, Davies G and Monti G, *European Union Law: Text and Materials* (4th edn, Cambridge University Press 2019) Chapter 11.

Craig P and De Burca G, *EU Law: Text, Cases and Materials* (6th edn, Oxford University Press 2015) Chapter 23.

Dougan M and Spaventa E, '"Wish You Weren't Here. . . " New Models of Social Solidarity in the European Union' in E Spaventa and M Dougan (eds) *Social Welfare and EU Law* (Hart Publishing 2005).

Dougan M, Shuibhne N N and Spaventa E, *Empowerment and Disempowerment of the European citizenship* (Hart Publishing 2012).

Guild E, Peers S and Tomkin J, *The EU Citizenship Directive: A Commentary* (2nd edn, Oxford University Press 2019).

Kochenov D, *EU Citizenship and Federalism: The Role of Rights* (Cambridge University Press 2017).

Koutrakos P, Nic Shuibhne N and Syrpis P, *Exceptions from EU Free Movement Law: Derogation, Justification and Proportionality* (Hart Publishing 2016).

Mindus P, *European Citizenship after Brexit: Freedom of Movement and Rights of Residence* (Springer 2017).

Shaw J, 'Citizenship: Contrasting Dynamics at the Interface of Integration and Constitutionalism' in P Craig and G De Búrca (eds) *The Evolution of EU Law* (2nd edn, Oxford University Press 2011).

Tryfonidou A, *The Impact of Union Citizenship on the EU: Market Freedom* (Hart Publishing 2016).

Yong A, *The Rise and Decline of Fundamental Rights in EU Citizenship* (Hart Publishing 2019).

Weatherill S, *Cases and Materials on EU Law* (12th edn, Oxford University Press 2016) Chapter 15.

Woods L, Watson P and Costa M, *Steiner Woods EU Law* (13th edn, Oxford University Press 2017) Chapters 21 and 23.

Journal articles

Adam S and Van Elsuwege P, 'Citizenship Rights and the Federal Balance between the European Union and its Member States: Comment on Dereci' (2012) 37 EL Rev 176.

Besson S and Utzinger A, 'Introduction: Future Challenges of European Citizenship – Facing a Wide-Open Pandora's Box' (2007) 13 ELJ 584.

Cygan A, 'Citizenship of the European Union' (2013) 62 ICLQ 492.

Dougan M, 'The Constitutional Dimension to the Case Law on Union Citizenship' (2006) 31 EL Rev 613.

Faist T, 'Social Citizenship in the European Union: Nested Membership' (2001) 39 JCMS 40.

Hughes K, 'Brexit and the Right to Remain of EU Nationals' (2017) Public Law 94.

Kochenov D, 'The Right to Have What Rights? EU Citizenship in Need of Clarification' (2013) 19 ELJ 502.

Kochenov D and Plender P, 'EU Citizenship: From an Incipient Form to an Incipient Substance? The Discovery of the Treaty Text' (2012) 37 EL Rev 369.

Kostakopoulou D, 'Ideas, Norms and European Citizenship: Explaining Institutional Change' (2005) 68 MLR 233.

Kostakopoulou D, 'European Union Citizenship: Writing the Future' (2007) 12 ELJ 628.

Morano-Foadi S, 'Un-Nesting the "Matrioska" Doll: Problems and Paradoxes at the Intersection between Citizenship, Migration and Human Rights' (2014) 27 Revista de Derecho de la Unión Europea (REDUE) 301.

Nic Shuibhne N, 'The Resilience of EU Market Citizenship' (2010) 47 CML Rev 1597.

Nic Shuibhne N, 'Limits Rising, Duties Ascending: The Changing Legal Shape of Union Citizenship' (2015) 52 CML Rev 889.

Smismans S, 'EU Citizens' Rights Post-Brexit: Why Direct Effect Beyond the EU is Not Enough' (2018) 14(3) ECL Rev 443.

Somek A, 'Solidarity Decomposed: Being and Time in European Citizenship' (2007) 32 EL Rev 787.

Spaventa E, 'Seeing the Wood Despite the Trees? On the Scope of Union Citizenship and its Constitutional Effects' (2008) 45 CML Rev 40.

Tryfonidou A, 'Redefining the Outer Boundaries of EU Law: The Zambrano, McCarthy and Dereci Trilogy' (2018) 18 EPL 493.

White R, 'Free Movement, Equal Treatment and Citizenship of the Union' (2005) 54 ICLQ 885.

Chapter 10 Free movement of workers

References

Czekaj-Dancewicz A, 'Analytical Note on Social and Tax Advantages and Benefits under EU Law on Free Movement of Workers' (2013) Available at http://ec.europa.eu/social/keyDocuments.jsp?type=0&policyArea=25&subCategory=475&country=0&year=0&advSearchKey=FMWthematic&mode=advancedSubmit&langId=en.

Mantu S, 'Analytical Note on Retention of Union Worker Status – Article 7(3)(b) of Directive 2004/38' (2013) Available at http://ec.europa.eu/social/keyDocuments.jsp?type=0&policyArea=25&subCategory=475&country=0&year=0&advSearchKey=FMWthematic&mode=advancedSubmit&langId=en.

Policy Department for Citizens' Rights and Constitutional Affairs, 'Obstacles to the Right of Free Movement and Residence for Union Citizens and the Families: Country Report for the United Kingdom' (2016) Available at www.europarl.europa.eu/RegData/etudes/STUD/2016/556967/IPOL_STU(2016)556967_EN.pdf.

UK Government, 'The United Kingdom's Exit from and New Partnership with the European Union' (Command Paper No. 9417, 2017).

Books and book chapters

Barnard C, *The Substantive Law of the EU: The Four Freedoms* (6th edn, Oxford University Press 2019) Chapters 6 and 7.

Barnard C and Peers S, *European Union Law* (2nd edn, Oxford University Press 2017) Chapter 13.

Chalmers D, Davies G and Monti G, *European Union Law: Text and Materials* (4th edn, Cambridge University Press 2019) Chapter 18.

Craig P and De Burca G, *EU Law: Text, Cases and Materials* (6th edn, Oxford University Press 2015) Chapter 21.

Foster N, *Foster on EU Law* (7th edn, Oxford University Press 2019) Chapter 9.

Morano-Foadi S, 'Article 45 TFEU on Free Movement of Workers: Content and Exceptions' in P Herzog, C Campbell and G Zagel (eds) *Smit & Herzog on The Law of the European Union* (LexisNexis/Matthew Bender 2019).

Nic Shuibhne N, Koutrakos P and Syrpis P, *Exceptions from EU Free Movement Law: Derogation, Justification and Proportionality* (Hart Publishing 2016).

O'Leary S, 'The Free Movement of Persons and Services' in P Craig and G De Búrca (eds) *The Evolution of EU Law* (Oxford University Press 2011).

Spaventa E, *Free Movement of Persons in the European Union: Barriers to movement in their constitutional context* (Kluwer 2007).

Weatherill S, *Cases and Materials on EU Law* (12th edn, Oxford University Press 2016) Chapter 13.

Woods L, Watson P and Costa M, *Steiner Woods EU Law* (13th edn, Oxford University Press 2017) Chapters 22 and 25.

Journal articles

Ashiagbor D, 'Unravelling the Embedded Liberal Bargain: Labour and Social Welfare Law in the Context of EU Market Integration' (2013) 19 ELJ 303.

Barnard C and Ludlow A, 'Enforcement of Employment Rights by EU-8 Migrants Workers in Employment Tribunals' (2016) 45 ILJ 1.

Castro Oliviera A, 'Workers and Other Persons: Step by Step from Movement to Citizenship – Case Law 1995–2001' (2002) 39 CML Rev 77.

Currie S, 'Reflecting on Brexit: Migration Myths and What Comes Next for EU Migrants in the UK?' (2016) 38 JSWFL 337.

Ellis E, 'Social Advantages: A New Lease of Life' (2003) 40 CML Rev 639.

Johnson E and O'Keeffe D, 'From Discrimination to Obstacles to Free Movement: Recent Developments Concerning the Free Movement of Workers 1989–1994' (1994) 31 CML Rev 1313.

Nic Shuibhne N, 'Free Movement of Persons and the Wholly Internal Rule: Time to Move On' (2003) 39 CML Rev 731.

O'Keeffe D, 'Equal Rights for Migrants: The Concept of Social Advantages in Article 7(2) Regulation 1612/68' (1985) 5 YEL 93.

O'Leary S, 'Developing an Ever Closer Union between the Peoples of Europe?: A Reappraisal of the Case

Law of the Court of Justice on the Free Movement of Persons and EU Citizenship' (2008) 27 YEL 167.

White R, 'Free Movement, Equal Treatment and Citizenship of the Union' (2005) 54 ICLQ 885.

Chapter 11 Freedom of establishment and the free movement of services

Books and book chapters

Andenas N and Roth W H, (eds) *Services and Free Movement in EU Law* (Oxford University Press 2004).

Barnard C, *The Substantive Law of the EU: The Four Freedoms* (6th edn, Oxford University Press 2019) Chapters 7, 8 and 11.

Barnard C and Peers S, *European Union Law* (2nd edn, Oxford University Press 2017) Chapter 14.

Chalmers D, Davies G and Monti G, *European Union Law: Text and Materials* (4th edn, Cambridge University Press 2019) Chapters 17 and 18.

Craig P and De Burca G, *EU Law: Text, Cases and Materials* (6th edn, Oxford University Press 2015) Chapter 22.

Foster N, *Foster on EU Law* (7th edn, Oxford University Press 2019) Chapter 9.

Hatzopoulos V, *Regulating Services in the European Union* (Oxford University Press 2012).

Hervey T and McHave J, *European Union Health Law* (Cambridge University Press 2016).

Snell J, *Goods and Services in EC Law* (Oxford University Press 2002).

Weatherill S, *Cases and Materials on EU Law* (12th edn, Oxford University Press 2016) Chapter 14.

Woods L, Watson P and Costa M, *Steiner Woods EU Law* (13th edn, Oxford University Press 2017) Chapters 22 and 24.

Journal articles

Apps K, 'Damages Claims against Trade Unions after Viking and Lavel' (2009) 34 EL Rev 141.

Barnard C, 'Unravelling the Services Directive' (2008) 45 CML Rev 323.

Gerner-Beuerle C and Schillig M, 'The Mysteries of Freedom of Establishment after Cartesio' (2010) 5(2) ICLQ 303.

Davies G, 'The Services Directive: Extending the Country of Origin Principle, and Reforming Public Administration' (2007) 32 EL Rev 232.

Dawes A and Struckmann K, 'Rien Ne Va Plus? Mutual Recognition and the Free Movement of Services in the Gambling Sector after the Santa Casa Judgment' (2010) 35 EL Rev 236.

De la Rosa S, 'The Directive on Cross-Border Healthcare or the Art of Codifying Complex Case Law' (2012) 49 CML Rev 15.

Doukas D, 'In a Bet There is a Fool and a State Monopoly: Are the Odds Stacked against Cross-Border Gambling?' (2011) 36 EL Rev 243.

Gillies L, 'Affirming Free Movement of Services and the Scope of International Jurisdiction of a Cross-Border Consumer Credit Agreement: Case C-630/17 Milivojevic v Raiffeisenbank St Stefan-Jagerberg-Wolfsberg eGen' (2019) 8(5) Journal of European Consumer and Market Law 202.

Hatzopoulos V, 'The Court's Approach to Services (2006–2012): From Case Law to Case Load' (2013) 50 CML Rev 459.

Johnston A and Syrpis P, 'Regulatory Competition in European Company Law after Cartesio' (2009) 34 EL Rev 378.

Jørgensen S, 'The Right to Cross-Border Education in the European Union' (2009) 46 CML Rev 1567.

Kilpatrick C, 'Laval's Regulatory Conundrum: Collective Standard-Setting and the Court's New Approach to Posted Workers' (2009) 34 EL Rev 844.

Lee R, 'Liberalisation of Legal Services in Europe: Progress and Prospects' (2010) 30 Legal Studies 186.

Lombardo S, 'Some Reflections on Freedom of Establishment of Non-Profit Entities in the European Union' (2013) 14 EBL Rev 225.

Papadopoulos T, 'EU Regulatory Approaches to Cross-Border Mergers: Exercising the Right of Establishment' (2011) 36 EL Rev 71.

Pellé P, 'Companies Crossing Borders within Europe' (2008) 4 Utrecht L Rev 6.

Prechal S and De Vries S, 'Seamless Web of Judicial Protection in the Internal Market' (2009) 34 EL Rev 5.

Ross M, 'A Healthy Approach to Services of General Economic Interest? The BUPA Judgment of the Court of First Instance' (2009) 34 EL Rev 127.

Szydlo M, 'Contracts Beyond the Scope of the EC Procurement Directives – Who is Bound by the Requirement for Transparency?' (2009) 34 EL Rev 720.

Van den Gronden J and De Waele H, 'All's Well that Bends Well? The Constitutional Dimension to the Services Directive' (2010) 6 ECL Rev 397.

Van der Mei A P, 'Cross-Border Access to Healthcare and Entitlement to Complementary "Vanbraekel Reimbursement"' (2011) 36 EL Rev 431.

Van Riemsdijk M, 'Obstacles to the Free Movement of Professionals: Mutual Recognition of Professional Qualifications in the European Union' (2013) 15 EJML 47.

Chapter 12 Free movement of goods

References

Barnard C, 'Case Comment: Trailing a New Approach to Free Movement of Goods' (2009) 68(2) Cambridge LJ 288.

Derlén M and Lindholm J, 'What Happened to the Revolution? One Decade with *Trailers* and MEQRs' (2019) 41 Skrifter från Juridiska institutionen Vid Umeå Universitet 91 Available at https://ssrn.com/abstract=3405465 or http://dx.doi.org/10.2139/ssrn.3405465.

Spaventa E, 'Leaving Keck behind? The Free Movement of Goods after the Rulings in Commission v Italy and Mickelsson and Roos' (2009) 34(6) EL Rev 914.

Books and book chapters

Barnard C, *The Substantive Law of the EU: The Four Freedoms* (6th edn, Oxford University Press 2019) Chapters 2, 3, 4 and 5.

Barnard C and Peers S, *European Union Law* (2nd edn, Oxford University Press 2017) Chapter 14.

Chalmers D, Davies G and Monti G, *European Union Law: Text and Materials* (4th edn, Cambridge University Press 2019) Chapter 16.

Craig P and De Burca G, *EU Law: Text, Cases and Materials* (6th edn, Oxford University Press 2015) Chapters 17 to 19.

Foster N, *Foster on EU Law* (7th edn, Oxford University Press 2019) Chapter 8.

Gormley L, *EU Law of the Free Movement of Goods and Customs Union* (Oxford University Press 2010).

Gormley L, 'Free Movement of Goods and Pre-emption of State Power' in A Arnull and C Barnard (eds) *A Constitutional Order of States? Essays in EU Law in Honour of Alan Dashwood* (Hart Publishing 2011).

Koutrakos P, Nic Shuibhne N and Syrpis P, *Exceptions from EU Free Movement Law: Derogation, Justification and Proportionality* (Hart Publishing 2016).

Oliver P (ed) *Oliver on Free Movement of Goods in the European Union* (5th edn, Hart Publishing 2010).

Snell J, *Goods and Services in EC Law* (Oxford University Press 2002).

Spaventa E, 'The Outer Limit of the Treaty Free Movement Provisions: Some Reflections on the Significance of Keck, Remoteness and Deliège' in C Barnard and O Odudu (eds) *The outer limits of EU Law* (Hart Publishing 2008).

Weatherill S, *Cases and Materials on EU Law* (12th edn, Oxford University Press 2016) Chapters 9 to 12.

Weiss F and Kaupa C, *European Union Internal Market law* (Cambridge University Press 2014).

Woods L, Watson P and Costa M, *Steiner Woods EU Law* (13th edn, Oxford University Press (2017) Chapters 15, 17, 18 and 19.

Woods L, *Free Movement of Goods and Services within the European Community* (Ashgate 2004) Chapters 4 to 6 and 13.

Journal articles

Ankersmit L, 'What if Cassis de Dijon were Cassis de Quebec? The Assimilation of Goods of Third Country Origin in the Internal Market' (2013) 50 CML Rev 1387.

Arnull A, 'What Shall We Do on Sunday?' (1991) 16 EL Rev 195.

Barents R, 'Charges of Equivalent Effect to Customs Duties' (1978) 15 CML Rev 415.

Barnard C, 'Fitting the Remaining Pieces into the Goods and Persons Jigsaw' (2001) 26 ELR 391.

Barnard C, 'Sunday Trading: A Drama in Five Acts' (1994) 57 MLR 449.

Biondi A, 'Advertising Alcohol and the Free Movement Principle: The Gourmet Decision' (2001) 26 EL Rev 616.

Connor T, 'Accentuating the Positive: the "Selling Arrangement", the First Decade and Beyond' (2005) 54 ICLQ 127.

Davies G, 'Can Selling Arrangements be Harmonised?' (2005) 30 EL Rev 370.

Di Cicco L, 'The Visnapuu Case: the Narrow Interpretation of Article 37 TFEU and the Consequent Failure in the Application of the "Certain Selling Arrangements" Doctrine' (2016) 43 Legal Issues of Economic Integration 309.

Easson A, 'Fiscal Discrimination: New Perspectives on Article 95 of the EEC Treaty' (1981) 18 CML Rev 521.

Enchelmaier S, 'Moped Trailers, Mickelsson and Roos, Gysbrechts: The ECJs Case Law on Goods Keeps Moving' (2010) 29 YEL 190.

Gormley L, 'Inconsistencies and Misconceptions in the Free Movement of Goods' (2015) 40 EL Rev 925.

Hojnik J, 'Free Movement of Goods in a Labyrinth: Can Buy Irish Survive the Crises?' (2012) 49 CML Rev 291.

Horsley T, 'Unearthing Buried Treasure: Article 34 TFEU and the Exclusionary Rules' (2012) 37 EL Rev 734.

Jansson M and Kalimo H, 'De Minimis Meets "Market Access": Transformations in the Substance – and the Syntax – of EU Free Movement Law?' (2014) 51 CML Rev 523.

Koutrakos P, 'On Groceries, Alcohol and Olive Oil: More on Free Movement of Goods after Keck' (2001) 26 EL Rev 391.

Lianos I, 'In Memorium Keck: The Reformation of the EU Law on the Free Movement of Goods' (2015) 40 EL Rev 225.

Mortelmans K, 'The Common Market, the Internal Market and the Single Market: What's in a Market?' (1998) 35 CML Rev 101.

Oliver P and Enchelmaier S, 'Free Movement of Goods: Recent Developments in the Case Law' (2007) 44 CML Rev 649.

Reynolds S, 'Explaining the Constitutional Drivers behind a Perceived Judicial Preference for Free Movement over Fundamental Rights' (2016) 53 CML Rev 643.

Snell J, 'The Notion of Market Access: A Concept or a Slogan?' (2010) 47 CML Rev 437.

Spaventa E, 'Leaving Keck Behind? The Free Movement of Goods after the Rulings in Commission v Italy and Mickelsson and Roos' (2009) 34 EL Rev 914.

Szydło M, 'Export Restrictions within the Structure of Free Movement of Goods: Reconsideration of an Old Paradigm' (2010) 47 CML Rev 753.

Thygersen J, 'National Tax Law – Under Influence of EU Rules for Freedom of Movement of Goods' (2013) 41 Intertax 351.

Unberath H and Johnston A, 'The Double-Headed Approach of the ECJ Concerning Consumer Protection' (2007) 44 CML Rev 1237.

Van Harten H and Nauta T, 'Towards Horizontal Direct Effect for the Free Movement of Goods?' (2013) 38 EL Rev 677.

Weatherill S, 'After Keck: Some Thoughts on How to Clarify the Clarification' (1996) 33 CML Rev 885.

Weatherill S, 'Recent Developments in the Law Governing the Free Movement of Goods in the EC's Internal Market' (2006) 2 ERCL 90.

Wenneras P and Boe Moen K, 'Selling Arrangements, Keeping Keck' (2010) 35 EL Rev 387.

Woods L, 'Consistency in the Chambers of the European Court of Justice: A Case Study on the Free Movement of Goods' (2002) 31 CJQ 338.

INDEX

Page numbers to Glossary entries are in **bold**

A10 countries 33
accession to the EU
   criteria 12
   defining 6
   negotiations 12
   process 12
accountability 99
acquis, defining **590**
   see also Schengen *acquis*
acte clair doctrine 184, 196, 199–201, **590**
acte éclaire doctrine 184, 198, **590**
Acts of the Union institutions 93, 208, **590**
administrative procedural principles 116–120
   legal certainty 117–118, **599**
   legitimate expectations 118–119
   natural justice 119–120
   non-retroactivity 117–118
   proportionality 14, 117, 158, 167–168, 213, **601**
   subsidiarity 14, 26, 117, 158, 167, 169, **604**
Advocates General 10, 88–89, 92
agencies of the EU 98, **590**
Agreement on Social Policy 28
Albania, candidate country for EU membership 11, 44, 45
Amsterdam, Treaty of *see* Treaty of Amsterdam (ToA), 1999
animal inspections, customs duty 522–523
annulment
   defining 208, **590**
   and indirect challenges 236
   legality of EU acts, challenging 229, 231, 234, **590**
   registered partnership 352–357
   secondary legislation 146–147
appeal committees 67
approximation of laws 22, 240, 576, **590**
   competences of the EU 158, 164, 165
   harmonising directives 552
area of freedom, security and justice (AFSJ) 14
association agreements 150–151
Austria, membership of the EU (1995) 11, 29

Belgium, membership of the EU (1958) 10
Benelux countries 20, 22, 533
   customs union 21, **540**

Blair, Tony 29, 35
border controls, temporary reintroduction of 376–377
Bosnia and Herzegovina 11
Brexit
   Article 50, triggering of (2017) 46
   democratic accountability 99
   division of competences in negotiations 178–179
   exit agreement 46
   'exit day' 46, **596**
   free movement of goods following 584–586, 587
      models of EU trade arrangements with non-EU countries 585–586
   free movement of persons following 377–378
   and future of the EU 46–47
   indirect effect of EU law following 316–317
   and international agreements 152
   UK approach to EU citizenship/returning citizens prior to 334
   UK as a 'non-EU' country following 15
   Withdrawal Agreement (2018) 46
   see also United Kingdom
Brexit negotiations
   Article 50 guidelines 46, 57
   defining **591**
   division of competences in 178–179
   see also Brexit
Brexit transition period 46, 323, 375, 435, **591**
   end of 223, 377, 587
   free movement of goods 584, 585, 586
budget 77–78
Bulgaria, membership of the EU (2007) 33–34
Buttiglione, Rocco 78

Canada, Free Trade Agreement 585–586
CFSP *see* Common Foreign and Security Policy (CFSP)
charges having equivalent effect (CEEs) 516–519, **591**
   and customs duty 511–512
   'Italian art' case 514, 518–519
   statistical data 517
   see also customs duty
Charter of Fundamental Rights of the European Union
   adoption of 30

   fundamental rights 120, 123–126
   general principles 116
   legal recognition 123
   recognition of rights 125
   sources of EU law 108
   Treaty of Lisbon (ToL), 2009 36, 40–41
Churchill, Winston 18, 19
Citizens' Rights Directive (CRD) (Directive 2004/38)
   free movement of persons 110–111, 325
   scope of term 'worker' 391–392
   service providers and employees, rights of 450–451
   social benefits, right to 412–417
   sources of EU law 109
citizenship, EU 324–325
   death/departure of an EU citizen 352
   defining an EU citizen 322, **596**
   EEC Treaty, amendments by TEU 26
   enhanced consultative role 40
   EU citizens dependent on non-EU family members 345–348
   European Citizens' Initiative (ECI) 41
   family members dependent on EU citizens 343–345
   and free movement of persons 325–342
   fundamental status 329–330
   returning citizens (*Surinder Singh* cases) 331–334
   rights of entry and residence 336–342
   scope 325–330
   students, entitlement to social benefits 368–372
   UK approach to 331–334
   see also free movement of persons
CJEU *see* Court of Justice of the European Union (CJEU)
closed groups 225
co-decision procedure 99, 139, **591**
Cohesion Fund 60
collective agreements 398
   concept 434, **591**
   service providers and employees, rights of 449, 456, 457, 458, 461
comitology 68–69
   concept 54, 68, **591**
   legality of EU acts, challenging 145–146
   Regulation 68
   transparency 101

Commission 8, 58–69
  accession process 12
  acting alone 145–146
  allocation of EU funding 60
  comitology 68–69
  Commissioners see Commissioners
  Completing the Internal Market (White Paper) 24
  composition 9, 61–67
  Directorates 67
  enforcement of legislation 9
  functions 9, 59–61, **594**
  Green Papers 101
  as 'Guardian of the Treaties' 60
  infringement proceedings 247–248, 252
  initiation of new legislation and policies 9, 59, 67, 211
  international representation 61
  organisational structure 66–67
  President 7, 9, 65–66
  supervision by European Parliament 78
  transparency 101
  White Papers 101
  Work Programme 59, 78
  working procedures 67–69
Commissioners
  appointment 62–63
  case law 64–65
  controversial 63
  independence and integrity 63–65
  numbers 62
  termination of office 65
  see also Commission
Committee of Inquiry 77
Committee of Permanent Representatives (COREPER) 72–74
  concept 54, **591**
  the Council, and 71
  function 71, 72
Committee of the Regions 54, 97–98
common economic and monetary policy 26
common external tariff 513, 535, **591**
Common Foreign and Security Policy (CFSP) 14, 27, 194
  three pillar structure 26, 31
  Treaty of Nice (ToN), 2003 32
common market 164, 175, 233, 325
  creation by EEC Treaty 21, 24, **591**
competences of the EU 159–169
  cases 161–163
  competence creep 168–169
  conferral of 6, 14, 158, 159–160, **592**
  defining 6, 158, **592**
  disputes 159–160
  division of competences in Brexit negotiations 178–179
  exclusive 14, 162
  explicit 160–161

flexibility clauses 163
harmonisation clauses 164
horizontal division between institutions (Brexit) 178–179
implied powers 161
kompetenz-kompetenz 160
lack of, as ground for judicial review 210–211
and legislative procedures 13–14
Opinion 2/15 179
secondary legislation, adoption of 164–167
shared 14, 160
subsidiary powers 163–164
supporting 14, 161
supremacy of EU law 15, 169–175
types 160–164
and United Kingdom see United Kingdom
vertical disputes 160
vertical division between national and EU levels (Brexit) 179
Conciliation Committee 143–145
conferral principle, EU competence 6, 14, 158, 159–160, **592**
consent procedure 144
Constitutional Treaty, failed (2004) 34, 35, 37, **592**
consultation procedure 144
contextual interpretation 187, **592**
cooperation procedure 25, 74, **592**
  see also enhanced cooperation
Copenhagen criteria 12
COREPER see Committee of Permanent Representatives (COREPER)
Council of Europe (CoE) 17
Council of Ministers
  and amendments to EEC Treaty 25
  institutional reform 32
  renaming as the Council 9
  see also Council of the European Union (the Council)
Council of the European Union (the Council) 8, 9–10, 69–75
  accession process 12
  acting alone 146
  composition 9–10, 70–72
  configurations 70
  versus the European Council 8
  functions 9–10, 69
  and legislative acts 72, 99, 101
  Luxemburg Accords 74–75
  passerelle clauses 115
  President 70–71
  qualified majority voting 72–74
  simple majority voting 54, 72
  team presidencies 71
  transparency 101–102
  unanimity 74
  withdrawal process 13

working procedures 72–75
see also Council of Ministers
Court of Auditors 8, 95
Court of Justice of the European Union (CJEU) 8, 10, 86–95
  Advocate General's Opinion 92
  Chambers 89–90
  composition 10, 88–90
  contextual interpretation 187
  expedited hearing 93
  functions 10
  historical interpretation 186
  interim measures ordered by 264–266
  Judges/Advocates General 10, 88–89, 92
  judgment 92–93
  judicial interpretation and preliminary rulings see interpretation, judicial methodology (CJEU); preliminary rulings (Art 267 TFEU)
  jurisdiction 87–88
    to interpret EU law 189–191
  legislative acts 87, 168, 209
  measures of organisation and inquiry 91
  oral hearing 91–92
  preliminary report 91
  President 89
  Rules of Procedure 87, 89, 203
  sources of EU law 147
  Statute 203
  working procedures 90–91
  written proceedings 90–91
CRD see Citizens' Rights Directive (CRD) (Directive 2004/38)
criminal liability, indirect effect 298–299
Croatia
  Accession Treaty 72, 79
  membership of the EU (2013) 11, 34
cross-elasticity 532, **592**
customs duty 513–524, 587
  animal inspections 522–523
  charges for the provision of a service 519–523
  charges having equivalent effect (CEEs) 511–512
  concept 510, **592**
  'customs warehouses' 519–520
  inspection fees 521–523
  or internal taxation 523–524
  scope of term 'goods' 514–516
  statistical data 520
Customs Union 513, **592**
  remaining in (Turkish model) 585
  and WTO 17
  see also Benelux countries
Cyprus, membership of the EU (2004) 11, 33

Czech Republic
  Charter of Fundamental Rights of the European Union 42
  Constitutional Court 37
  membership of the EU (2004) 11, 33
  ratification of Treaty of Lisbon 36–37

Dassonville formula, measures having equivalent effect (MEEs) 540
de Witte, Bruno 48
death or departure of EU citizen, rights of family members 352
decentralised agencies 98
decision-making 24, 26, 47, 172
  co-decision procedure 99, 139, **591**
  consumers 532
  and European Economic Area 15, 585
  final decisions 69
  institutions of the EU 8, 10, 54, 56
    the Council 69
    and European Parliament 25, 76
  Luxembourg Accords 74, **599**
  preliminary rulings (Art 267 TFEU) 191
  rational 175
  recognition 191
  region-orientated 97
  requirements/procedures 10, 47, 58, 76, 113
  structures 31, 71
  transparency 101
decisions 191, **593**
  direct effect of 280–281
  secondary legislation 137, 139
delegated acts 229
Delors, Jacques 66
democratic deficit 25, 40, 99, 104, 172, **593**
Denmark
  and Albanian EU membership 45
  economic and monetary union 28
  euro, opting out 16, 28, 29
  membership of the EU (1973) 10, 22–23
  Schengen *acquis*, participation in 373
derogation 74, 79, 101, 108, 274, 447, 588, **593**
  harmonising directives 583–584
  passerelle clauses 108, **601**
  permitted 403, 513
  public policy 484, 486
  temporary 373
  from Treaties 74, 79, 403
  wilful 310
dialogue, accession 12
direct applicability 138, 274
direct concern 221
direct discrimination 382, 527
direct effect
  concept 274, **593**
  of decisions 280–281
  of directives 281–293
  horizontal *see* horizontal direct effect
  incidental 291–293
  principle 275–276
  of regulations 279–280
  scope 276–281
  of Treaty articles 277–279
    in the UK 309–310
  vertical *see* vertical direct effect
  see also indirect effect
directives
  Citizens' Rights Directive (CRD) *see* Citizens' Rights Directive (CRD) (Directive 2004/38)
  concept 108, **593**
  direct effect of 281–293
    in the UK 310–314
  harmonising 552–554, 583–584
  horizontal direct effect, denying 286–287
  implementation 281–282
  incidental direct effect 291–293
  measures having equivalent effect (MEEs) (Directive 70/50) 539–540
  Mutual Recognition of Qualifications Directive (*see* Mutual Recognition of Qualifications Directive (Directive 2005/36)
  Posted Workers Directive *see* Posted Workers Directive (Directive 96/71)
  regulations compared 138–139
  secondary legislation 137
  Services in the Internal Market Directive *see* Services in the Internal Market Directive (Directive 2006/123)
  state, defining an emanation of 287–290
  vertical direct effect, establishing 282–285
  Working Time Directive, UK challenge 212–214
discrimination
  direct 382, 527
  free movement of persons 322–323
  indirect 382, 527–529
    objective justification 529–530
  nationality 523
  and non-discrimination 322–323
  similar products 526–530
distinctly applicable measures 510, 541–545, **593**
domestic goods 542–545, **593**
double-majority voting 54, 73, **593**
dual-burden rules 545–554
  concept 510, **593**

EC Treaty
  origins 26, 110
  renaming/renumbering 29, 110
  see also Treaty on European Union (TEU), 1993
ECHR *see* European Convention on Human Rights and Fundamental Freedoms (ECHR)
Economic and Monetary Union (EMU) 7, 16, 27, 28, 48, 95, 152
  see also Eurozone
ECtHR *see* European Court of Human Rights (ECtHR)
EEC Treaty *see* Treaty of Rome (1957)
EESC *see* European Economic and Social Committee (EESC)
effet utile 300
EFTA *see* European Free Trade Association (EFTA)
ejusdem generis rule 187
emanation of the state, defining 287–290
employment
  equal treatment principle 397–404
  Regulation 192/2011 397–400
  see also free movement of workers; service providers and employees, rights of; workers
enhanced cooperation 25, 31, 43
  Cooperation in Justice and Home Affairs (JHA) 26, 27
  Police and Judicial Cooperation in Criminal Matters 31, 32, 374
  'two-speed' Europe, idea of 48
enlargement of the EU
  A10 countries 33
  from 1973 to 1986 22–23
  in 1995 29
  from 2004 to 2007 33–34
  in 2013 35
  defining 6
  expansion beyond economic objectives 29–30
  future enlargements 44–45
  Treaties of Accession 149
  see also membership of the EU; withdrawal from the EU
entry, rights of 336–342
  family members of EU citizens 349
  service providers and employees 450–452
  see also free movement of persons; free movement of workers; permanent residence, right of; residence
equal treatment principle
  employment 397–404
  family members of EU citizens, rights of 357
  social assistance 364, 404, 416
  social benefits 363–365
equal-burden rules 554–559
  concept 510, **594**
equality principle 40

equivalent effect *see* measures having equivalent effect (MEEs)
establishment
  concept 434, **594**
  scope 438–439
  see also freedom of establishment
Estonia, membership of the EU (2004) 11, 33
estoppel, concept 274, **594**
EU *see* European Union (EU)
EU law 13–15
  Court of Justice jurisdiction to interpret 189–191
  direct effect *see* direct effect
  general principles 42
  indirect effect *see* indirect effect
  legislative procedures and competence 13–14
  questions on the interpretation/validity of 194–196
  'special character' 14–15
  supremacy 15, 169–175
  see also European Union (EU); interpretation, judicial methodology (CJEU)
EU Treaties *see* Treaties, EU
Euratom 21, 22, 98, **594**
euro 31, 33, **594**, **602**, **603**
  opting out of 16, 28, 29
Eurojust 32
European Agricultural Guidance and Guarantee Fund 60
European Assembly 25
European Atomic Energy Community 98
European Central Bank (ECB) 8, 47, 95–96, **594**
  Outright Monetary Transaction (OMT) programme 172, 173
  Statute 17
European Citizens' Initiative (ECI) 41
European Coal and Steel Community (1952) 19–20, 22, 87, **594**
European Commission *see* Commission
European Communities Act 1972 23, 176–178
  limiting/reversing the transfer of sovereign powers 177–178
European Convention on Human Rights and Fundamental Freedoms (ECHR)
  accession talks 42–43
  contracting parties 43
  and Council of Europe 17
  functions **595**
  fundamental rights 120, 121–123, 125
  negotiated by Member States 151
  Treaty of Lisbon (ToL), 2009 42–43

European Council 8, 56–58, **595**
  Charter of Fundamental Rights of the European Union 41
  composition 8, 57–58
  versus the Council of the European Union 8
  function 56–57
  passerelle clauses 115
  President 7, 8–9, 57–58
  and SEA 24
  website 56
  working procedures 58
European Court of Human Rights (ECtHR) 17, **595**
European Court Reports (ECR) 92
European Defence Agency 14
European Economic and Social Committee (EESC) 54, 96–97, **595**
European Economic Area (EEA) 15–16, **595**
  remaining in (Norway model) 585
European Economic Community (EEC) 21–22, **595–596**
  see also Treaty of Rome (1957)
European Free Trade Association (EFTA)
  composition 22
  Court 15
  and enlargement 22
  and European Economic Area 15
  function **596**
  re-joining (Swiss model) 585
  Surveillance Authority 15
European Investment Bank (EIB) 96, **596**
European Parliament 8, 9, 76–86
  accession process 12
  budget 77–78
  case law 84–86
  committee meetings 84
  Committee of Inquiry 77
  composition 9, 78–82
    2009–2014 European Parliamentary term 79
    2014–2019 European Parliamentary term 79
    2019–2024 European Parliamentary term 80
    political groups 80–82
  enhanced cooperation 43
  functions 9, 76–78, **596**
  global superpower, as 18
  increased legislative powers 25
  Members of European Parliament (MEPs) *see* Members of European Parliament (MEPs)
  Parliamentary Ombudsman 77
  passerelle clauses 115
  plenary meetings 54, 83–84
  Protocol on the Privileges and Immunities of the European Union 84–86
  and rule of law 269

Rules of Procedure 57, 78, 79, 82
  supervision of the Commission 78
  transparency 102–103
  voting procedures 82–83
  working procedures/conduct 82–86
European Pillar of Social Rights (ESPR) 136–137
European Regional Development Fund 60
European Social Fund 60
European System of Central Banks (ESCB) 96
European Union citizen *see* citizenship, EU
European Union (EU)
  Charter of Fundamental Rights *see* Charter of Fundamental Rights of the European Union
  citizenship *see* citizenship, EU
  contemporary position 6–18
  economic aspects 15–17
  four freedoms, promoting 6
  future of 44–48
  history *see* history of the European Union
  institutions 8–10
  international Treaties negotiated by 148–151
  legal personality 17, 20
  Member States *see* Member States
  membership *see* membership of the EU
  Nobel Peace Prize awarded to (2012) 7
  observer status at the UN 18
  organisations interacting with 17–18
  three pillars *see* three pillars of the EU
  'two-speed' Europe, idea of 48
  values and objectives 6–7
  see also Commission; Council of the European Union (the Council); Court of Justice of the European Union (CJEU); EU law; European Council; European Economic Area (EEA); European Parliament; Eurozone
European Union Settlement Scheme (EUSS) 339, 340, 377, 378, **596**
Eurosystem 96
Eurozone
  economic crisis 18
  Greece, possible exit from 47
  monetary policy 17
  opting out of 16
excise duty 510, 532, **596**
exclusive competence 14, 162
executive agencies 98
exit, rights of 336
exportability of benefits 408, **596**
expulsion
  general protection from 358
  on grounds of public policy, security or health 358–363

family members, rights of
  access to education and vocational training 423–429
  defining a family member 418–419
  equal treatment 357
  EU citizens 342–357
    death, departure or divorce of 351–357
    dependence of family members on 343–345
    dependent on non-EU family members 345–348
  free movement 419–422
  housing provision 429–430
  registered partnership 352–357
  residence for over three months 349–350
  residence for up to three months 349
  right of permanent residence 351
  rights of entry 349
  scope 342–348
  social assistance 406, 425
  social benefits 422–430
  university, access to 426
  see also citizenship, EU; free movement of persons; free movement of workers
Finland, membership of the EU (1995) 11, 29
flexibility clauses 140, 163
Foreign Affairs Council 9–10, 14, 70
four freedoms, promoting 6
  see also free movement of goods; free movement of persons; free movement of services; free movement of workers
France
  European Coal and Steel Community (1952) 18, 19
  membership of the EU (1958) 10
  objections to Albanian EU membership 45
  objections to UK EU membership 23
  penalty payments 255, 260
Francovich case
  damages **597**
  state liability principle 301
  unimplemented directives 303
Frattini, Franco 78
Free Movement Directive (FMD) *see* Citizens' Rights Directive (CRD) (Directive 2004/38)
free movement of goods 510–588
  Brexit, following 587
    models of EU trade arrangements with non-EU countries 585–586
    transition period 584, 585, 586
  Canadian model (Free Trade Agreement_ 585–586
  common external tariff 513, 535, **591**

customs duty 513–524, 587
  charges having equivalent effect (CEEs) 511–512, 516–519
  import and export restrictions 541–542
  internal market 510, 552, 553, 569
  internal taxation 512
  models of EU trade arrangements with non-EU countries 585–586
  Norway model (remaining in the EEA) 585
  primary legislation 511–513
  product substitution **601**
  quantitative restrictions 535–539, 587–588
    measures having equivalent effect (MEEs) *see* measures having equivalent effect (MEEs)
    permissible 561–584, 588
    primary legislation 512–513
    scope of state measures 537–539
    scope of term 'goods' 536–537
  Swiss model (re-joining EFTA) 585
free movement of persons
  citizenship *see* citizenship, EU
  equal treatment 357, 363–365
  and EU citizenship 325–342
  expulsion/restrictions on rights 358–363
  family members of EU citizens, rights of 342–357
    death, departure or divorce 351–357
    dependence on EU citizens 343–345
    equal treatment 357
    EU citizens dependent on non-EU family members 345–348
    scope 342–348
  following Brexit 377–378
  Free Movement Directive (FMD) 325
  as fundamental freedoms 323
  Good Friday Agreement, Northern Ireland 586
  nationality, non-discrimination on grounds of 323
  and non-discrimination 322–323
  rights of entry and residence 336–342
  Schengen *acquis*
    development of the Schengen area 372–373
    integration into the EU 372–377
    participation in 373–375
  scope of rights 330–331
  social benefits 363–372
    equal treatment 363–365
    rights of economically inactive EU citizens to 365–368
    rights of EU students to 368–372
    welfare tourism and 'ever greater union' 367–368
  work-seekers *see* work-seekers
  see also citizenship, EU

free movement of services
  Mutual Recognition of Qualifications Directive (Directive 2005/36) 437–438, 493
  primary legislation 435–436
  provisions to facilitate 449–450
  see also services
free movement of workers
  defining an EU worker 385–390
  equal treatment 397–404
    public services exception 401–404
    public services in the UK 404
    Regulation 192/2011 397–400
  primary legislation 382–383
  rights of workers *see* workers
  scope of term 'worker' *see* workers
  secondary legislation 384
freedom of establishment
  Citizens' Rights Directive (CRD) (Directive 2004/38) 438
  Mutual Recognition of Qualifications Directive (Directive 2005/36) 494–498
  primary legislation 435–436
  provisions to facilitate 448–449
  see also establishment
frontier workers 382, 399, 427
  children of 428, 429
  concept 382, **597**
fundamental rights 120–137, **597**
  Charter of Fundamental Rights of the European Union 120, 123–126
  EU as a human rights system 121
  European Convention 42–43, 121–123
  European Pillar of Social Rights (ESPR) 136–137
  examples of specific human rights 126–136
  free movement of persons 323
  Germany 172
  mutual recognition rule (*Cassis* case) 580–581
  Treaty on European Union (TEU), 1993 27
  see also European Court of Human Rights (ECtHR)
funding of the EU 47, 60
future of the EU 44–48
  contractions 45–47
  enlargements 44–45
  possible directions 47–49
  Strategic Agenda (2019–2024) 48

gambling, permissible restrictions on workers' rights 467–471
Gaulle, Charles de 23
General Affairs Council 10, 70
General Court (formerly Court of First Instance)
  composition 10, 94

and Court of Justice 147
jurisdiction 93–94, 190
legality of EU acts, challenging 220, 227, 232
Rules of Procedure 87
Germany
Constitutional Court 172
European Coal and Steel Community (1952) 18, 19
fundamental rights 172
penalty payments 255
'two-speed' Europe, idea of 48
and World Wars 17–18
Good Friday Agreement 586
goods
administrative practices 549
domestic 542–545, **593**
national quality standard 548–549
origin-marking 547–548
price-fixing regulations 545, 550
product packaging 546–547
scope of term 'goods' 514–516, 536–537
see also free movement of goods; internal taxation; measures having equivalent effect (MEEs); quantitative restrictions, free movement of goods
Greece
economic and monetary union 28
Eurozone, possible exit from 47
membership of the EU (1981) 11, 23
penalty payments 259
'Guardian of the Treaties,' Commission as 60

harmonisation clauses 164
harmonising directives or measures, MEEs 510, 552–554
derogations from 583–584
hearings
expedited 93
oral 91–92
rule of law 268
Heath, Edward 23
High Representative of the Union for Foreign Affairs and Security Policy
appointment 76
enhanced cooperation 43
and European Council 8
Foreign Affairs Council, presiding over 10
legislative procedures 14
role 75–76
historical interpretation 186, **597**
history of the European Union 18–54
cooperation, enhancing 31, 32
enlargement *see* enlargement of the EU
European Coal and Steel Community (1952) 19–20, **594**

European Economic Community/Euratom 21
policies 24, 28, 33
Single European Act 24
Treaty of Amsterdam (1999) 29–31
Treaty of Nice (2003) 31–33
Treaty on European Union (TEU), 1993 25–28
World Wars, lessons from 18–19
home Member State
concept 322, 434, **597**
establishment and services 440, 441
and EU citizenship 331–334, 339, 343, 347
family members of workers 422
free movement of workers 386, 396, 410
professional qualifications, recognition 496, 497, 503, 504
recipients of services, rights of 481, 482
service providers and employees, rights of 452, 453, 458
see also host Member State; Member States
horizontal direct effect 274, 276, 278, 308, 550–552, **597**
denying 286–287
host Member State
citizenship and free movement rights 323, 325, 326, 332, 335–343
Brexit, following 378, 379
expulsion and restrictions 360–363
family members, rights of 346, 347, 350, 351, 353, 356
social benefits, right to 367–370
concept 322, 356, 534
free movement of workers 382, 391, 417–421, 431
rights of workers 393, 395, 396, 403, 404, 408, 409
work-seekers 411–413, 415
freedom of establishment/free movement of services
professional qualifications, recognition 489–491
recipients of services, rights of 479, 481
scope of establishment and services 436, 440
service providers and employees, rights of 450, 453–456, 458
social assistance 338, 339, 366, 367–369, 412–413, 425
human rights protection *see* fundamental rights
Hungary
infringement proceedings 268
membership of the EU (2004) 11, 33
rule of law in 269

implementing measures, regulatory acts 229–231
implied powers doctrine 161
index
to the TEU 111
to the TFEU 112–113
indirect challenges 234, 236–238
indirect discrimination 382, 527–529
objective justification for 529–530
indirect effect 274
available national legislation 297
criminal liability 298–299
duty to interpret 'so far as possible' 297
limitations to principle 297–299
principle 274, 293–296, **597**
sources of EU law 118
in the UK 314–317
following Brexit 316–317
following *Marleasing* 315–316
see also direct effect
indistinctly applicable measures
concept 510, **593**, **594**
dual-burden rules 510, 545–554, **593**
equal-burden rules 510, 554–559, **594**
mutual recognition rule (*Cassis* case) 545–550, 572–582
individual concern 221
infringement proceedings 274
Article 7 TEU, measures under 266–269
Commission 247–248, 252
defining **597**
direct effect 274
essential procedural requirement 211–212
as grounds for judicial review 211–212
interim measures 263–266
ordered by a national court 266
ordered by CJEU 264–266
Member States, against 244–270
Article 7 TEU 266–269
Commission actions under Article 258 TFEU 247–248
interim measures 263–266
Member State defences 253–254
by other Member States under Article 259 TFEU 248–249
pecuniary penalties 254–263
stages of Article 258 TFEU proceedings 249–254
types of infringement 251
'nuclear option' 267
pecuniary penalties, against Member States 254–263
Article 260(3) TFEU 263
calculation of payments 255–259
collection of payments 260–263
concept 246
preventative mechanism 267
sanctioning mechanism 267

infringement proceedings (*Continued*)
　serious and persistent breach 267
　stages of Article 258 TFEU proceedings 249–254
　　administrative 250–251
　　altering of subject matter 252–253
　　contents of opinion 251
　　directive, failure to implement 252
　　effect of compliance with opinion 252
　　judicial 252–254
　　Member State defences 253–254
　　reasoned opinion 251–252
　of Treaties/applicable rules 212
　types of infringement 251
inspection fees 521–523
institutions of the EU 8–10
　Acts of the Union institutions 93, 208, **590**
　agencies 98, **590**
　Committee of the Regions 54, 97–98
　composition
　　Commission 9, 61–67
　　Committee of the Regions 98
　　the Council 9–10, 70–72
　　Court of Justice of the European Union (CJEU) 10, 88–90
　　European Council 8, 57–58
　　European Economic and Social Committee (EESC) 97
　　European Parliament 9, 78–82
　　General Court (formerly Court of First Instance) 10
　Court of Auditors 8, 95
　democratic accountability 99
　European Central Bank (ECB) 8, 95–96
　European Economic and Social Committee (EESC) 54, 96–97
　European Investment Bank (EIB) 96
　functions
　　Commission 9, 59–61, **594**
　　Committee of the Regions 97–98
　　the Council 9–10, 69
　　Court of Justice of the European Union (CJEU) 10
　　European Council 56–57
　　European Economic and Social Committee (EESC) 96–97
　　European Parliament 9, 76–78, **596**
　jurisdiction
　　CJEU 87–88
　　General Court 93–94
　modelled on the ECSC 22
　recognition as 54–56
　reform 32
　roles 54
　specialised courts 94–95
　transparency 99–103
　Treaty of Lisbon (ToL), 2009 39
　Treaty on European Union (TEU), 1993 8

ultra vires acts *see ultra vires* acts (excess of powers)
working procedures
　Commission 67–69
　the Council 72–75
　Court of Justice of the European Union (CJEU) 90–91
　European Council 58
　European Parliament 82–86
see also Commission; Council of the European Union (the Council); Court of Justice of the European Union (CJEU); European Council; European Parliament; European Union (EU); General Court (formerly Court of First Instance); High Representative of the Union for Foreign Affairs and Security Policy
interim measures, infringement actions 263–266
interlocutory proceedings **598**
internal border 322
internal market 7, 15, 16, 96, 140, 175, 189, 367, **598**
　Commission 60, 67
　competences of the EU 164–167
　European Council 56, 57
　free movement of goods 510, 552, 553, 569
　free movement of persons and non-discrimination 322, 323
　freedom of establishment/free movement of services 436, 448, 476
　history of the European Union 24, 25, 39
　legality of EU acts, challenging 212, 214, 220
　see also Services in the Internal Market Directive (Directive 2006/123)
internal taxation 512, 523–524, 587
　under Art 110 TFEU 524–535
　　indirect protection, Article 110(2) 530–535
　　relationship between Articles 110(1) and (2) 533
　　similar products, Article 110(1) 526–530
　indirect protection 530–535
　similar products 526–530
　　direct discrimination 527
　　indirect discrimination 527–530
　　objective justification of indirect discrimination 529–530
　see also taxation
International Monetary Fund (IMF) 47
international treaties 148–153
　association agreements 150–151
　intergovernmental, between Member States 151–152

　multilateral 149
　negotiated by Member States 151–153
　negotiated by the EU 148–151
　Treaties of Accession 149
　withdrawal agreements 149–150
interpretation, judicial methodology (CJEU)
　acte clair doctrine 184, 196, 199–201, **590**
　contextual 187, **592**
　Court of Justice jurisdiction to interpret 189–191
　historical 186, **597**
　interpretative obligation 298, 317, **598**
　literal 186, **599**
　'no judicial remedy under national law' 201–203
　precedent 185–186
　　development of 198–199
　preliminary rulings *see* preliminary rulings (Art 267 TFEU)
　questions necessary to enable national courts to give judgments 196–201
　questions on the interpretation/validity of EU law 194–196
　special forms of procedure
　　accelerated (expedited) 204
　　simplified 203–204
　　urgent preliminary ruling 204–205
　teleological 184, 187–188, **604**
　Treaties 194–195
　see also referrals
interpretation, legal (by Court of Justice), judicial methods 184–188
Ioannina compromise 74
Ireland
　interim measures 264
　membership of the EU (1973) 10, 22–23
　Northern Ireland and Good Friday Agreement 586
　ratification of Treaty of Lisbon 36
　Schengen *acquis*, participation in 374–375
Italy 10, 19

Johnson, Boris 46
Judge-Rapporteur 88–93, 203, 204, **598**
Judicial Cooperation in Criminal Matters 194
judicial review 274
　explicit exclusion of acts from 216–217
　grounds
　　competence, lack of 210–211
　　infringement of essential procedural requirement 211–212
　　infringement of Treaties/rules applicable to interpretation 212
　　misuse of powers 212

Working Time Directive, UK
    challenge 212–214
  reviewable acts 214–217
    explicitly excluded from judicial
        review 216–217
    form and substance 214–215
    intended to have legal effects
        214–216
    negative 217
Junker, Jean Claude 45, 46, 178
jurisdiction
  Court of Justice of the European Union
      (CJEU) 87–88
    interpretation of EU law 189–191
  defining **598**
  General Court (formerly Court of First
      Instance) 93–94, 190
jus cogens **598**

Kaczyński, Lech 36
Klaus, Václav 36

Labour Party, UK 23, 28, 79
Latvia, membership of the EU (2004) 11,
    33
Law of Administrative Procedure of the
    EU 117
League of Nations 18
legal autonomy 6, **598**
legal base/basis
  appropriate 72, 159, 164, 165, 166,
      214
  Committee of Permanent
      Representatives (COREPER) 72
  competences of the EU 159, 164–166
  concept 108, **598**, **599**
  correct 164, 210, 211, 213
  defective 213
  and EESC **595**
  free movement of persons 355
  free movement of workers 383, 400
  incorrect 166
  institutional reform 32
  legality of EU acts, challenging 237
  ordinary legislative procedure 140, 142
  professional qualifications, recognition
      486–487
  special legislative procedures 144
  Treaty of Lisbon (ToL), 2009 98
  unanimity 74
legal certainty principle 117–118,
    180, **599**
legal personality 17, 20
legality of EU acts, challenging 208–243
  annulment 229, 231, 234, **590**
  comitology 145–146
  damages for unlawful acts 238–243
    liability for a lawful act 241–242
    remedies 242–243
    scope of liability 239–241

failure to act 234–236
  indirect challenges 234, 236–238
  scope for challenge 235–236
  standing to challenge 235
General Court 220, 227, 232
grounds for judicial review 210–214
indirect challenges 234, 236–238
internal market 212, 214, 220
liability for a lawful act 241–242
locus standi 208, 217–232
non-privileged applicants 217,
    218–232
privileged applicants 217–218
reviewable acts 214–217
semi-privileged applicants 217, 218
under TFEU
  Article 263 209–234
  Article 265 234–236
  Article 340 238–243
time limits for applications 232–234
legislation, EU
  Conciliation Committee 143–145
  European Parliament, powers of 25
  free movement of workers 382–384
  initiation by the Commission 59
  legislative procedures 13–14, **599**
  ordinary legislative procedure 14,
      140–144
  primary
    free movement of goods 511–513
    free movement of services 435–436
    free movement of workers 382–383
    freedom of establishment 435–436
  procedure for adopting legislative acts
      139–146
  quasi-legislative procedures 68
  special legislative procedures 14,
      144–145, **603**
  subordinate 117
  see also secondary legislation
legislative acts 14, 41, 138, 146, 147, 228,
    243
  adoption of 139–146, 241
  and Commission 59, 67, 211
  concept 208, 231, **599**
  and the Council 72, 99, 101
  and Court of Justice 87, 168, 209
  and non-legislative acts 72, 139, 146,
      208, 229, 231
  as non-regulatory acts 232, 237, 243
  reasoned opinion 251–252
  state liability 304–305
  see also regulatory acts
legitimate expectations principle 118–119,
    599
liability
  criminal, indirect effect 298–299
  damages for unlawful acts 239–241
  for lawful act 241–242
  state 299–308

Lisbon, Treaty of *see* Treaty of Lisbon
    (ToL), 2009
literal interpretation 186, **599**
Lithuania, membership of the EU (2004)
    11, 33
locus standi 208, 217–232, 237
lump sums 255–260, 262, 270
  concept 246, **599**
  see also penalty payments
Luxembourg, membership of the EU
    (1958) 10
Luxembourg Accords 74–75
  decision-making 74, **599**

Maastricht Treaty *see* Treaty on European
    Union (TEU), 1993
McAleese, Mary 36
Macron, Emmanuel 45
Malta, membership of the EU (2004)
    11, 33
mandatory requirements defence, free
    movement of goods 552, 588
mutual recognition rule (*Cassis* case)
    573, 574, 577, 578–580, **599**
permissible quantitative restrictions and
    MEEs 561, 562
Marleasing case
  indirect effect, limitations to principle
      297
  indirect effect of EU law in the UK
      before 314–315
  indirect effect of EU law in the UK
      following 315–316
Marshall Plan 19, **599**
May, Theresa 46
measures having equivalent effect (MEEs)
  Cassis case *see* mutual recognition rule
      (*Cassis* case)
  Dassonville formula 540
  defining **599**
  Directive 70/50 539–540
  distinctly applicable 510, 541–545, **593**
    domestic goods, promotion of 542–545
    exports 560–561
    harmonising directives 552–554,
        583–584
    import and export restrictions 541–542
  indistinctly applicable
    concept 510, **593**, **594**
    dual-burden rules 510, 545–554, **593**
    equal-burden rules 510, 554–559,
        594
    mutual recognition rule (*Cassis* case)
        545–550, 572–582
  justifications under Article 36 TFEU
      561–572
    'German Bier' case 567–569
    health and life, protecting 565–569
    industrial and commercial property,
        protecting 569–572

measures having equivalent effect (MEEs) (*Continued*)
   public morality 562–564
   public policy and security 564–565
   Keck formula 555–558
   market access rule 558–559
   and permissible quantitative restrictions 561–584, 588
   price-fixing regulations 545
   promotion of domestic goods 542–545
   see also free movement of goods; quantitative restrictions, free movement of goods
MEEs *see* measures having equivalent effect (MEEs)
Member States
   accession to the EU *see* accession to the EU
   constitutional rights 120
   effective supervision of 276
   home Member State *see* home Member State
   host Member State *see* home Member State
   infringement proceedings against 244–270
     Article 7 TEU, measures under 266–269
     Commission actions under Article 258 TFEU 247–248
     interim measures 263–266
     by other Member States under Article 259 TFEU 248–249
     pecuniary penalties 254–263
     stages of Article 258 TFEU proceedings 249–254
   intergovernmental Treaties between 151–152
   international Treaties negotiated by 151–153
   new, transitional arrangements for 396–397
   obligations on 246–247
   order of joining the EU 10–11
   withdrawal from the EU *see* Brexit; withdrawal from the EU
   see also membership of the EU
Members of European Parliament (MEPs)
   democratic deficit **593**
   election of 9, 79, **596**
   immunity 84
   numbers 29
   privacy rights 102
   voting procedures 83
   see also European Parliament
membership of the EU 10–13
   candidate countries 11, 44–45
   criteria for accession 12
   order of joining 10–11
   process of accession 12

Treaties of Accession 149
   see also accession to the EU; Brexit; enlargement of the EU; Member States; withdrawal from the EU
Memorandum of Understanding (MOU) 17
MEPs *see* Members of European Parliament (MEPs)
Michel, Charles 9
misuse of powers, as ground for judicial review 212
monetary policy, Eurozone 17
Monnet, Jean 18
monopolies 279, 288, **600**
   intellectual property 572
   national 539
   public 469, 470
   regional 469
   state 470, 539, **604**
Montenegro, candidate country for EU membership 11, 44, 45
multilateral Treaties 149
Mutual Recognition of Qualifications Directive (Directive 2005/36) 492–499
   administrative cooperation/implementation responsibility 498–499
   detailed rules for pursuing profession 498
   Directive 2013/55 making changes to 499
   example of qualifying measures 497
   free movement of services 437–438, 493
   freedom of establishment 494–498
   general provisions 492–493
   general system 494–497
   'three systems' prior to 492
   see also free movement of services; freedom of establishment; professional qualifications, recognition; services
mutual recognition rule (*Cassis* case) 545–550, 572–582, **602**
   'Austrian lorries' 579–581
   consumer protection 574–577
   'drink containers' 578–579
   fundamental rights 580–581
   mandatory requirements defence 573, 574, 577, 578–580, **599**
   public health 577–578

national courts
   enforcement of EU law in the UK 309–317
     direct effect 309–314
     indirect effect 314–317
   interim measures ordered by 266
   interpretation issues 196–201

nationality, non-discrimination on grounds of 323
   equal treatment 363–365
natural justice principle 119–120, **600**
naturalisation 322
Nazi Party 18
negotiations, accession 12
Netherlands
   and Albanian EU membership 45
   membership of the EU (1958) 10
Nice, Treaty of *see* Treaty of Nice (ToN), 2003
non-discrimination, and free movement of persons 322–323
non-EU national 322, **600**
   see also third countries/third-country nationals
non-retroactivity principle 117–118, **600**
North Atlantic Treaty Organization (NATO) 18, **600**
North Macedonia, candidate country for EU membership 11, 44, 45
Northern Ireland and Good Friday Agreement 586
Norway, EU trade arrangement model 585

objective justification for restrictions on rights
   concept 382, 434, **600**
   service providers and employees, rights of
     gambling 467–471
     public health grounds 463–467
     taxation 471–474
   taxation
     discrimination, similar products 529–530
     service providers and employees, rights of 471–474
Official Journal 108, 138, **600**
   structure 146
opinions, soft law 108, 137, 148, **600**
opt-outs 16, 28, 29, 30
ordinary legislative procedure 14, 140–144, **600**
   democratic accountability 99
   first reading 142
   proposals 140–142
   second reading 142–143
ordinary revision procedure 113, 114
Organisation for Economic Cooperation and Development (OECD) **601**

Paris Agreements 18
Parliament *see* European Parliament
Parliamentary Ombudsman 77
passerelle clauses 108, 115–116, **601**
pecuniary penalties, against Member States 254–263, **601**

Article 260(3) TFEU 263
calculation of payments 255–259
collection of payments 260–263
concept 246
penalty payments 255–263, 270
concept 246, **601**
periodic 259
see also lump sums
permanent residence, right of 340–341
family members of EU citizens 351
and right of residence, common provisions 341–342
see also citizenship, EU; free movement of persons; residence
persons
free movement of *see* free movement of persons
Pescatore, Pierre 75
pillars *see* three pillars of the EU
plenary meetings 54, 83–84, **601**
Poland
and Charter of Fundamental Rights of the European Union 42, 124
infringement proceedings 268
membership of the EU (2004) 11, 33
ratification of Treaty of Lisbon 36–37
rule of law in 268–269
Police and Judicial Cooperation in Criminal Matters 32, 194
policies
Court of Justice of the European Union (CJEU) 188
history of the EU 24, 28, 33
initiation by the Commission 59
monetary 17
public interest 358–363, 564–565
Portugal, membership of the EU (1986) 11, 23
Posted Workers Directive (Directive 96/71) 438
posted workers, rights of 434, 453–458, **601**
precedent 185–186, **601**
development of 198–199
see also stare decisis (let the decision stand)
preliminary rulings (Art 267 TFEU)
concept 184, **601**
concept of court or tribunal 193
Court of Justice jurisdiction to interpret EU law 189–191
discretion to refer 191–194
interpretation of Treaties 194–195
interpretation/validity of Union acts 195–196
national bodies able to make a reference 191–192
obligation to refer 194
questions on the interpretation/validity of EU law 194–196

reference versus appeal 190–191
role of CJEU 10
urgent 204–205
see also Court of Justice of the European Union (CJEU); interpretation, judicial methodology (CJEU)
procedural principles *see* administrative procedural principles
procedural *ultra vires* 211, **601**
product substitution **601**
professional qualifications, recognition 486–505, 506
detailed rules for pursuing profession 498
Directive *see* Mutual Recognition of Qualifications Directive (Directive 2005/36)
example of qualifying measures 497
general system 494–497
internal situation 503–505
levels 494
non-EU qualifications 499–503
professional experience, recognition of 497–498
qualifying measures, example of 497
Treaty provisions 486–492
property, protecting 569–572
proportionality principle 14, 117, 167–168
breach of 213
concept 158, **601**
degressive proportionality, MEPs 9
protectionism 525, 532, **601**
Protocol on the Privileges and Immunities of the European Union 84–86
public interest
health and life, protecting
expulsion on grounds of 358–363
mutual recognition rule (*Cassis* case) 577–578
permissible quantitative restrictions and MEEs 565–569
restrictions on workers' rights, permissible on grounds of 463–467
morality, permissible quantitative restrictions 562–564
policy 358–363, 564–565
public services exception 401–404
restrictions on workers' rights 474–476
public monopolies 469, 470

qualified majority voting 25
before 31 October 2014 72–73
comitology 67–68
concept 54, 108, **602**
following 1 November 2014 73–74
'no opinion scenario' 67–68
quantitative restrictions, free movement of goods 535–539, 587–588
concept 510, **602**
exports 560–561

justifications under Article 36 TFEU 561–572
'German Bier' case 567–569
health and life, protecting 565–569
industrial and commercial property, protecting 569–572
public morality 562–564
public policy and security 564–565
measures having equivalent effect (MEEs) *see* measures having equivalent effect (MEEs)
permissible 561–584, 588
Article 36 TFEU, justifications under 561–572
primary legislation 512–513
scope of state measures 537–539
scope of term 'goods' 536–537
quorum 54, **602**

ratification
concept 6, **602**
of Treaty of Lisbon 35–37
ratio decidendi 185, **602**
recommendations, soft law 108, 137, 148, **602**
referrals
discretion to refer 191–194
national bodies able to make a reference 191–192
obligation to refer 194
reasons for necessity 197–198
reference versus appeal 190–191
required information 197–198
when to refer (UK view) 201
see also Court of Justice of the European Union (CJEU); interpretation, judicial methodology (CJEU); preliminary rulings (Art 267 TFEU)
Reform Treaty *see* Treaty of Lisbon (ToL), 2009
registered partnership, divorce, annulment or termination 352–357
regulations
defining 108
derogations from harmonising legislation (Regulation 764/2006) 583–584
direct effect of 279–280
directives compared 138–139
equal treatment in employment (Regulation 192/2011) 397–400
Law of Administrative Procedure of the EU 117
legislative acts 138
secondary legislation 137
regulatory acts
concept 229, **602**
implementing measures 229–231

regulatory acts (*Continued*)
  legality of EU acts, challenging 208, 209, 229–231, 237
  and non-regulatory acts 232, 237, 243
  see also legislative acts
remedies
  judicial 202
  unlawful acts 242–243
renaming/renumbering of Treaties 29, 30, 34, 110
representative democracy principle 40
residence
  common provisions, right of residence and permanent residence 341–342
  for more than three months 337–339
  for over three months 349–350
  permanent, right of 340–341, 351
  service providers and employees, rights of 450–452
  service recipients, rights of 477–478
  for up to three months 337, 349
  workers' rights 396
returning citizens (*Surinder Singh* cases) 331–334
  UK approach to (pre-Brexit) 334
reviewable acts 214–217
  explicitly excluded from judicial review 216–217
  form and substance 214–215
  intended to have legal effects 214–216
  negative 217
  see also judicial review
Romania, membership of the EU (2007) 33–34
rule of law
  in Hungary 269
  in Poland 268–269
rule of mutual recognition *see* mutual recognition rule (*Cassis* case)
Rules of Procedure
  Court of Justice of the European Union (CJEU) 87, 89, 203
  European Parliament 57, 78, 79, 82
  General Court (formerly Court of First Instance) 87

Schengen *acquis*
  defining *acquis* 590
  Denmark, participation of 373
  development of the Schengen area 372–373
  integration into the EU 372–377
  Ireland and the UK, participation of 374–375
  measures adopted by group members 375–376
  participation in 373–375
  second-generation Schengen Information System (SIS-II) 376

  temporary reintroduction of border controls 376–377
Schengen Agreement 151, 373, **590**, **602–603**
Schengen Area 151
Schengen Information System (SIS) 376, **603**
Schumann, Robert 18
Second World War 17, 18
secondary legislation 137–147, **603**
  cases 165–167
  comparison of regulations and directives 138–139
  competence to adopt 164–167
  decisions 139
  directives 138
  free movement of services 436–438
  free movement of workers 384
  freedom of establishment 436–438
  legal validity and annulment grounds 146–147
  procedure for adopting legislative acts 139–146
  regulations 138
  types of legal acts 137
  see also decisions; directives; legislation, EU; regulations
second-generation Schengen Information System (SIS-II) 376
Security Council, UN 18
Serbia, candidate country for EU membership 11, 44, 45
service providers and employees, rights of 444–476, 506
  collective agreements 449, 456, 457, 458, 461
  concept of service provider 434, **603**
  entry and residence 450–452
  free movement of services 444–450
  freedom of establishment 444–450
  General Programmes 444
  lawyers' rights 450
  objective justification for restrictions on rights
    gambling 467–471
    public health grounds 463–467
    taxation 471–474
  permissible restrictions on workers' rights 458–476
    objective justification 463–474
    public interest reasons 474–476
  posted workers 453–458
  public interest reasons for restrictions 474–476
  Services in the Internal Market Directive *see* Services in the Internal Market Directive (Directive 2006/123)
  Treaty provisions 452
service recipients, rights of 476–486, 506
  Directive 2006/123, under 478–479

  permissible restrictions 481–486
    drug use 483–486
    medical services 481–482
    public policy grounds, objective justification for restrictions 482–486
  provisions to strengthen 478
  quality of services, promoting 479
  residence 477–478
  social advantages 479–481
  Treaties, under 476–477
services
  charges for the provision of 519–523
  Directive *see* Services in the Internal Market Directive (Directive 2006/123)
  free provision, under Mutual Recognition of Qualifications Directive 493
  not covered by other free movement provisions 442–443
  'official authority' exception 443
  public *see* public services
  quality, promoting 479
  recipients, rights of *see* service recipients, rights of
  remuneration 441–442
  scope 439–443
  service providers and employees *see* service providers and employees, rights of
Services in the Internal Market Directive (Directive 2006/123) 436–437
  free movement of services, facilitating 449–450
  freedom of establishment, facilitating 448–449
  recipients of services, rights of 478–479
  service providers and employees, rights of 446–450
  prior to Directive 444–446
simple majority 54, 72, 108, **603**
simplified revision procedure 113, 114, 115
single currency *see* euro
Single European Act (SEA), 1987 **603**
  amendments to the EEC Treaty 24–25
  internal market, completing 24
  legislative powers of the European Parliament, increasing 25
  new policy objectives 24
  Preamble 23
Single European Currency **603**
single market *see* common market
SIS *see* Schengen Information System (SIS)
Slovakia, membership of the EU (2004) 11, 33
Slovenia, membership of the EU (2004) 11, 33

social advantages
  concept 382, **603**
  service recipients, rights of 479–481
  workers' rights 404–407
social assistance 382, **603**
  concept 363, 382, 418, **603**
  denial 418
  determining what constitutes 416–418
  economically inactive EU citizens 365
  equal treatment 364, 404, 416
  family members, rights of 406, 425
  host Member State 338, 339, 366, 367–369, 412–413, 425
  loss of entitlement 417
  national systems 365, 367
  work-seekers 411–413, 415, 417
social benefits, right to 363–372
  economically inactive EU citizens to 365–368
  equal treatment, regardless of nationality 363–365
  family members 422–430
  and politics 417
  social advantages, equal access to 404–407
  social security coordination 407–409
  students, EU 368–372
  welfare tourism and 'ever greater union' 367–368
  workers 412–417
Social Chapter **603**
social policy
  Treaty of Amsterdam (ToA), 1999 31
  Treaty on European Union (TEU), 1993 28
  see also social benefits
social security
  coordination of 407–409
  exportability 408, **596**
  free movement of workers 382, 383, 409
  host Member State 383
  Luxembourg 429
  migrant workers 280
  national systems 407, 408, 481
    Belgium 368–369
  professional qualifications, recognition 500
  work-seekers 409
soft law 137, 147–148, **603**
sources of EU law 108–154
  administrative procedural principles 116–120
  background 108–109
  Charter of Fundamental Rights of the European Union 108
  CJEU decisions 147
  deductive method 109
  EU Treaties *see* Treaties, EU
  fundamental rights 120–137
  general principles 116–137
  hierarchy 109
  inductive method 109
  opinions 148
  recommendations 148
  secondary legislation 137–147
  soft law 147–148
  see also international sources of law
Soviet Union, former 18
Spain, membership of the EU (1986) 11, 23
'special character' of EU law 14–15
Special European Council 57
special legislative procedures 14, 144–145, **603**
specialised courts 94–95
stare decisis (let the decision stand) 185, **601**, **604**
  see also precedent
state liability 274, 299–308, **604**
  acts of the executive and the judiciary, arising from 304–308
  incorrect implementation, arising from 300–302
  unimplemented directives, arising from 299–300, 303
state monopolies 470, 539, **604**
Strategic Agenda (2019–2024) 48
subsidiarity principle 14, 26, 117, 167, 169
  concept 158, **604**
substantive *ultra vires* 210, **604**
supremacy of EU law 15, 158, 169–175, 180, **604**
  cases 171–175
  challenges to 170–175
  recognition 169–170
Sweden, membership of the EU (1995) 11, 29
Switzerland, EU trade arrangement model 585

tariffs
  common external tariff 513, 535, **591**
  concept 510, **604**
taxation
  internal 512, 523–535, 587
  permissible restrictions on workers' rights 471–474
teleological interpretation 184, 187–188, **604**
TEU *see* Treaty on European Union (TEU), 1993
TFEU *see* Treaty on the Functioning of the European Union (TFEU), 2009
Thatcher, Margaret 28
third countries/third-country nationals 357, **604**
  and EU citizenship 324, 333–335
  family members, rights of 346, 350, 355, 356
  free movement of goods 513, 526
  freedom of establishment/free movement of services 435, 452, 453
  see also non-EU national
three pillars of the EU **601**
  adjustments to, under ToA 30–31
  merger by ToL 38–39
  under TEU 26–27, 31
time limits, legality of EU acts, challenging 232–234
transparency 99–103
  comitology 101
  of Commission 101
  of Council 101–102
  of European Parliament 102–103
Treaties, EU
  annexes 113
  declarations 113
  evolution of 38
  interpretation 194–195
  Merger Treaty (1965) 22
  negotiating/amending 113–116
  origins 109–110
  passerelle clauses 115–116
  primary 25
  professional qualifications, recognition 486–492
  protocols 113
  renaming/renumbering 9, 29, 34, 110
  restrictions on 177
  revision procedures 113–115
  role 110–111
  scope 111–113
  service recipients, rights of 476–477
  see also EU law; international Treaties; Treaty establishing a Constitution for Europe (failed Constitutional Treaty), 2004; Treaty Establishing the European Atomic Energy Community (Euratom); Treaty of Amsterdam (ToA), 1999; Treaty of Lisbon (ToL), 2009; Treaty of Nice (ToN), 2003; Treaty of Rome (1957); Treaty on European Union (TEU), 1993; Treaty on Stability, Coordination and Governance (TSCG), 2013; Treaty on the Functioning of the European Union (TFEU), 2009
Treaties of Accession 12, 23, 33, 124, 149, 194, **604**
Treaty establishing a Constitution for Europe (failed Constitutional Treaty), 2004 34, 35, 37, **592**

Treaty Establishing the European Atomic Energy Community (Euratom) 21, 22, **594**
Treaty Establishing the European Economic Community (EEC Treaty), 1957 21–22
Treaty Establishing the European Stability Mechanism (ESM) 152
Treaty of Amsterdam (ToA), 1999 29–31, **605**
  adjustments to the three pillars 30–31
  closer cooperation 31
  entry into force 29
  expansion beyond economic objectives 29–30
  Intergovernmental Conference 48
  intergovernmental treaties 151
  Social Policy Agreement 31
Treaty of Lisbon (ToL), 2009
  changes introduced by 34, 37–43
  Charter of Fundamental Rights of the European Union 36, 40–41
  democratic principles 40–41
  entering into force 35, **605**
  and failed Constitutional Treaty 34, 35, 37, **592**
  institutional framework 39
  objectives and values 39
  ratification 35–37
  renaming/renumbering of previous treaties 9, 29, 30, 34
  structure 38
  transfer of sovereign powers, limiting/reversing 177
Treaty of Maastricht *see* Treaty on European Union (TEU), 1993
Treaty of Nice (ToN), 2003
  Charter of Fundamental Rights of the European Union 42
  enhanced cooperation 32, 43
  Eurojust 32
  institutional reform 32
  new policies 33
  security and defence 32
Treaty of Rome (1957) 21–22, **605**
  amendments to 24–25, 26
  common market established by 21, 24, **591**
  cooperation procedure, new 25
  and origins of the Treaties 109, 110
Treaty on European Union (TEU), 1993 25–28, **605**
  Article 50, triggering of (2017) 12–13, 46
  contemporary position of the EU 6
  economic and monetary union (UK and Denmark) 28
  human rights protection 27
  index to 111

infringement proceedings, Art 7
  rule of law 268–269
  usefulness of 269
institutions of the EU 8
Maastricht Treaty known as 25
objectives 7, 27
protocols 27–28
renaming/renumbering 29, 30
signature (Maastricht) 31
social policy 28
text of Article 2 6
three pillars 26–27, 31
titles 25
Treaty on Stability, Coordination and Governance (TSCG), 2013 34, 152
Treaty on the European Economic Communities (EEC Treaty), 1957 *see* Treaty of Rome (1957)
Treaty on the Functioning of the European Union (TFEU), 2009
  contemporary position of the EU 6
  free movement of goods
    exports 560–561
    horizontal direct effect (Article 34) 550–552, **597**
    internal taxation 524–535
    quantitative restrictions (Articles 34–36) 536–537, 560–572
  index to 112–113
  infringement proceedings against Member States
    Commission actions under Article 258 TFEU 247–248
    by other Member States under Article 259 TFEU 248–249
    pecuniary penalties under Article 260(3) 263
    stages of Article 258 TFEU proceedings 249–254
  internal taxation (Article 110) 524–535, 587
    indirect protection, Article 110(2) 530–535
    relationship between Articles 110(1) and (2) 533
    similar products, Article 110(1) 526–530
  legality of EU acts, challenging
    under Article 263 209–234
    under Article 265 234–236
  preliminary rulings under Art 267 *see* preliminary rulings (Art 267 TFEU)
  renaming/renumbering under 110, **605**
  and Treaty of Lisbon 34
  see also free movement of goods; infringement; legality of EU acts, challenging; taxation

Turkey
  candidate country for EU membership 11, 44–45
  EU trade arrangement model 585
Tusk, Donald 8–9, 45

Udre, Ingridia 78
ultra vires acts (excess of powers) 8, **605**
  procedural *ultra vires* 211, **601**
  substantive *ultra vires* 210, **604**
Union *see* European Union (EU)
United Kingdom
  and Charter of Fundamental Rights of the European Union 42, 124
  citizenship and returning citizens, approach to pre-Brexit 334
  direct effect of EU law in 309–314
    directives 310–314
    EU treaty articles 309–310
  economic and monetary union 28
  enforcement of EU law in national courts 309–317
    direct effect 309–314
    indirect effect 314–317
  euro, opting out 16, 28, 29
  European Communities Act 1972 176–178
  incorporation/extrication of EU powers in 176–179
  indirect effect of EU law in
    following Brexit 316–317
    following *Marleasing* 315–316
    before *Marleasing* 314–315
  membership of the EU (1973) 10, 22–23
  as a 'non-EU' country following Brexit 15
  public services in 404
  Schengen *acquis*, participation in 374–375
  withdrawal from the EU *see* Brexit; Brexit negotiations
  see also Brexit transition period
United Nations (UN) 18

Van Rompuy, Herman 57
vertical direct effect 276, 282–285
  concept 274, **605**
von der Leyen, Ursula 9
voting procedures
  the Council
    qualified majority *see* qualified majority voting
    simple majority 54, 72
  double-majority voting 54, 73, **593**
  European Parliament 82–83
  Members of European Parliament (MEPs) 83
  simple majority 54, 72, 108, **603**

Weimar Republic 17
Wilson, Harold 23
withdrawal from the EU
  agreements 149–150, **605**
  Article 50, triggering of (2017) 12–13, 46
  exit process 12–13
  future contractions 45–47
  negotiations 13
  see also Brexit
workers
  EU workers 338, 351, 354, 359, 390, **596**
  family members 418–430
  migrant 280
  objective justification for restrictions on rights
    gambling 467–471
    public health grounds 463–467
    taxation 471–474
  Posted Workers Directive (Directive 96/71) 438
  recognition of qualifications *see* professional qualifications, recognition
  rights of 393–409, 430
    free movement 393–397
    residence rights 396
    social advantages, equal access to 404–407
    social security coordination 407–409
    transitional arrangements for new Member States 396–397
  scope of term 'worker'
    defining an EU worker 385–390
    Directive 2004/38, effect of 391–392
    retention of worker status after cessation of employment 390–392
  Union worker 382
  work-seekers *see* work-seekers
  see also free movement of workers; frontier workers; service providers and employees, rights of
Working Time Directive 212–214, 274
work-seekers 409–418
  rights to free movement 410–411
  social assistance 411–413, 415, 417
  social benefits, rights to 412–418
    before Directive 2004/38 412
    following Directive 2004/38 412–417
World Trade Organization (WTO) 17, 241, 584
  Rules 586, 587